FLYING UNITS OF THE RAF

FLYING UNITS OF THE RAF

The ancestry, formation and
disbandment of all flying units
from 1912

A L A N   L A K E

Airlife

England

Copyright © 1999 Alan Lake

First Published in the UK in 1999
by Airlife Publishing Ltd

British Library Cataloguing in Publication Data
A catalogue record for this book
is available from the British Library

ISBN 1 84037 086 6

Photographs reproduced with the permission of Philip Jarrett.

Typeset by Phoenix Typesetting, Ilkley, West Yorkshire
Printed in England by Butler & Tanner Ltd, Frome and London

Airlife Publishing Ltd

101 Longden Road, Shrewsbury, SY3 9EB England
E-mail: airlife@airlifebooks.com
Website: www.airlifebooks.com

Contents

Introduction

The intention some 35 years ago was to compile a complete record of the ancestry, formation and disbandment of all the flying units of the Royal Flying Corps and the Royal Air Force and identify allocated aircraft unit identity code letters. As all researchers know only too well stating the intention is one thing, but achieving a cherished ambition is a different thing altogether. My ignorance in those early days had not prepared me to come to terms with missing or incomplete records, conflicting dates and locations, the 30 year rule or the numerous false fire alarm evacuations at the Public Record Office.

This is the work of an individual who felt there was much to warrant a totally unbiased approach to the subject, therefore the views and assumptions expressed are solely those of the author. The overwhelming majority of the information has been gathered from original documents held by the Air Historical Branch, Army Air Corps Museum, the Public Record Office, the Royal Air Force Museum Library, the Imperial War Museum Library and numerous county archives. Official press releases and Parliamentary White Papers served to gather information on units still subject to the 30-year rule.

Much of the data was extracted from Organisation Memoranda (SD.155), Location of RAF Units (SD.161) and Operations Record Books for Commands, Groups, Wings, Squadrons, Stations and Miscellaneous Units. The content of the Operations Record Book for the average unit fluctuates between detailed accounts of day to day activities of all sections of a unit, a singular British preoccupation with the weather, to the bizarre or just plain comical. For example, the ORB for the Central Flying School (Advanced) for 26th June 1954 notes "A young barn owl joined 161 Jet Conversion Course for a short while. It completed three successful sorties in a Meteor, practicing aerobatics, instrument flying and asymmetric flying from a perch behind the rear cockpit instrument panel. At the end of these trips, however, it revealed itself, and was found to be suffering from serious anoxia and air-sickness and was posted non effective sick - unfit to continue jet training".

As for missing records, the All-Weather Operational Conversion Unit, Aircraft Delivery Unit (India), Leigh Light Training Unit and the Portuguese Airman's Flight were, according to aircraft record cards, issued with aircraft and are known to have existed in one form or another. Even so, these units appear to have left little record of their activities. Then again, information of other units, including the elusive Medical Flight, was found in the most unexpected quarter.

The book spans the period from the formation of the Royal Flying Corps to April 1998 and traces the history of individual flying units of the Royal Flying Corps, Royal Air Force and Fleet Air Arm of the Royal Air Force. Also listed, together with their allocated unit identification codes, are the many Squadron numberplates that were authorised but never formed. Reference is also made to units of the Royal Australian Air Force, Burmese Volunteer Air Force, Royal Canadian Air Force, Free French Air Force, Hong Kong Auxiliary Air Force, Hong Kong Defence Force (Air Component), Indian Air Force, Indian Air Force Volunteer Reserve, Kenya Auxiliary Air Unit, Malayan Volunteer Air Force, Straits Settlements Volunteer Air Force, Southern Rhodesian Air Force and the Air Defence Unit, Tanganyika which were incorporated into the Royal Air Force during conflict, as well as joint service units and experimental and research establishments. Only those Station Flights and Maintenance Units, which were allocated unit aircraft identity codes, are included.

Units are listed in alphabetical order with a few exceptions. However, extensive cross referencing will not only guide the reader through these anomalies but will also point out the correct nomenclature of those units which, over the years, have acquired a popular though inaccurate title.

The entry for each individual unit follows a universal pattern. Firstly, the unit title and subsequent subtle changes to the title. Then, for each period the unit was operational the formation date and location together with a note of the circumstances of formation and later changes to the title, a note of each of the allocated unit identification codes and periods of use, then examples, by mark number, serial number and unit identification code, of operational aircraft allocated to the unit as well examples of communications, hack, conversion, instrument training and appropriated enemy aircraft used by the unit, then finally the disbandment date and location together with a note of the circumstances of units demise.

Location and Station place names, particularly those involving the translation of the name of a nearby Arabic town or village, are noted as having actually changed with contemporary usage. Countries, such as the Gold Coast and Tanganyika, are quoted as at the time of occupation by British forces.

Three letter aircraft unit identification codes were introduced at the time of the Munich Crisis in 1938 and displayed by the majority of operational Squadrons. The code consisted of two letters to indicate the identity of the Squadron either forward or aft of the national insignia and a single letter on the other side of the insignia to indicate the individual aircraft within the unit. By April 1939 the allocations were expanded to include the authorised nameplates of Squadrons which had yet to be formed. Air Ministry Order AMO A.298/39 dated 3rd August 1939 extended the coding system to include all units. Upon the outbreak of war the existing codes were withdrawn and re-allocated. The letters 'C' and 'I' were introduced into the unit codes during 1943 together with numerals. Codes were changed upon the move by a unit to another theatre of war and it was not uncommon that code letters were duplicated in different war theatres. Between August 1943 and July 1944 this method of coding was dropped by Coastal Command in favour of a single numeral to indicate the parent station. The three-letter coding system was gradually withdrawn during the early fifties and replaced in April 1951 by two-letter codes. A listing of aircraft identification codes, giving the identity of individual units, appears in the Appendix.

Aircraft types are attributed to the original designer or manufacturer regardless of later company mergers or takeovers. For example, Buccaneer aircraft were originally designed and built by Blackburn Aircraft who was later absorbed by Hawker Siddeley.

Aircraft role letters were introduced from February 1942 but are not reflected in the text until the full introduction of Arabic mark numbers in 1947. A listing is provided in the Appendix.

Aircraft mark numbers were originally expressed in Roman numerals. From 1942 any mark numbers above twenty were expressed in Arabic numerals and since 1947 all mark numbers have been expressed in Arabic numerals. There is, for the sake of simplicity, variation within the text. Those aircraft types spanning the milestones during their period of service are quoted throughout by their original designation. For example, reference is made at all times to an Anson XIX rather than an Anson C.19. Many prototype and pre-production military aircraft were not assigned mark numbers. The impressed civilian Tiger Moth operated alongside the pre-war military Tiger Moth I and wartime Tiger Moth II.

Diagrams showing the complex relationships between various units are included in the Appendix to compliment portions of the text. They are the product of sketches made while researching the subject to determine the correct lineage and association of seemingly related units.

I wish to express my appreciation and gratitude to the staff at the Air Historical Branch, Army Air Corps Museum, the Central Flying School Museum, the Public Record Office, the Royal Air Force Museum Library and the Imperial War Museum Library. Special acknowledgement must be paid to the many anonymous individuals who were required to keep the Operations Record Book. They possibly looked upon the task as an onerous chore and were probably never aware of their contribution to history.

As a footnote, it is worth noting the Public Record Office at Kew has recently introduced an electronic catalogue called MORIS (Means of Reference Information System). Readers are able to scan the catalogue database by entering key words to display a list and description of documents by Class, Class Number and Piece Number that correspond with the input. Readers are now able to locate relevant documents, many of which had previously lain hidden behind a nondescript reference number in the conventional catalogue, in a fraction of the time.

Alphanumeric List of Units

'A' BOAT SEAPLANE TRAINING FLIGHT
Formed 8th August 1918 at Calshot within 210 Training Depot Station.

No aircraft known.

Disbanded 1919 at Calshot.

'A' FLIGHT (1) – see 514 (Special Duty) Flight

'A' FLIGHT (2) – see 519 (Special Duty) Flight

'A' FLIGHT (3) – see 521 (Special Duty) Flight

'A' FLIGHT (4) – see 523 (Special Duty) Flight

'A' FLIGHT (5) – see 527 (Special Duty) Flight

'A' FLIGHT, CALSHOT – see Royal Air Force Base, Calshot

'A' FLIGHT, GOSPORT – see Royal Air Force Base, Gosport later Royal Air Force Station, Gosport

'A' FLIGHT, LEUCHARS – see Royal Air Force Base, Leuchars, later Royal Air Force Training Base, Leuchars

'A' SQUADRON, AEGEAN
Formed 1st April 1918 at Thásos, Aegean, by redesignating 'A' Squadron of 2 Wing, RNAS.

No aircraft known.

Disbanded 18th September 1918 at Mudros, Aegean, and merged with 'Z' Squadron to become 222 Squadron.

'A' SQUADRON, INDIA – see 3 Squadron, RAF

ABERDEEN, DUNDEE AND ST ANDREWS UNIVERSITY AIR SQUADRON
Formed 3rd October 1981 at Leuchars by redesignating Aberdeen University Air Squadron.

Bulldog T.1 XX663 B.

Disbanded 31st March 1996 at Turnhouse and absorbed by the East Lowlands University Air Squadron.

ABERDEEN UNIVERSITY AIR SQUADRON
Formed 23rd January 1941 at Aberdeen. Used Dyce for flying training.

Nil (1.41–)	*Moth AW161; Tiger Moth II provided by Edinburgh University Air Squadron and 11 Elementary Flying Training School.*
FLB	*Allocated but no evidence of use.*
RUA (4.47–4.51)	*Tiger Moth II EM907 RUA-O.*
Nil (4.51–10.81)	*Chipmunk T.10 WB724; Harvard IIB KF747; Bulldog T.1 XX561 A.*

Disbanded 3rd October 1981 at Dyce and absorbed by the newly formed Aberdeen, Dundee and St Andrews University Air Squadron.

ABERYSTWYTH UNIVERSITY AIR SQUADRON
Formed 6th January 1941 at Aberystwyth and used Towyn for flying training.

Tiger Moth BB700.

Disbanded 15th December 1945 at Aberystwyth.

ADEN BATTLE FLIGHT – see Fighter Defence Flight, Aden

ADEN COMMAND TRAINING FLIGHT
Formed September 1940 at Sheikh Othman, Aden.

Moth; Vincent; Blenheim.

Disbanded 21st April 1942 at Khormaksar, Aden, and absorbed by the Communication Flight, Aden.

ADEN COMMUNICATION SQUADRON
Formed 1st December 1951 at Khormaksar by redesignating the Headquarters British Forces Aden Communication Flight.

Dakota IV KN215; Anson; Valetta C.1 VW206 F; Pembroke; Meteor T.7 WA717; Vampire FB.9 WR135; Sycamore HR.14 XG504.

Disbanded 31st August 1955 at Khormaksar and merged with the Aden Protectorate Support Flight to become the Aden Protectorate Communication and Support Squadron.

ADEN COMMUNICATION UNIT
Formed 1st January 1944 at Khormaksar, Aden by redesignating the Headquarters British Forces Aden Communication Flight.

Hudson III AM950, IIIA FH279, VI FK492; Albacore I BF648; Ventura V JT810; Wellington X LP122; Traveler FZ428.

Disbanded by January 1946 at Khormaksar to become the Headquarters British Forces Aden Communication Flight.

ADEN CONVERSION FLIGHT
Formed March 1945 at Khormaksar, Aden.

Liberator VI KH303.

Disbanded April 1945 at Khormaksar.

ADEN DEFENCE FLIGHT (1)
Formed September 1920 at Khormaksar, Aden.

F.2B.

Disbanded 1st January 1928 at Khormaksar and absorbed by 8 Squadron.

ADEN DEFENCE FLIGHT (2) – see Fighter Defence Flight, Aden

ADEN PROTECTORATE COMMUNICATION AND SUPPORT SQUADRON
Formed 1st September 1955 at Khormaksar by merging the Aden Communication Squadron and the Aden Protectorate Support Flight.

Valetta C.1 VW837; Pembroke C.1 WV738; Meteor T.7 WA717; Sycamore HR.14 XE309.

Disbanded 31st December 1956 at Khormaksar to become 84 Squadron.

ADEN PROTECTORATE RECONNAISSANCE FLIGHT
Formed 1st August 1959 at Khormaksar, Aden, from 'C' Flight of 8 Squadron.

Meteor FR.9 VZ601 Z.

Disbanded 1st October 1959 at Khormaksar to become the Arabian Peninsular Reconnaissance Flight.

ADEN PROTECTORATE SUPPORT FLIGHT
Formed 21st September 1947 at Khormaksar, Aden, by redesignating the Anson element of the Headquarters British Forces Aden Communication Flight.

Anson XIX VL293.

Disbanded 19th September 1950 at Khormaksar and absorbed by 8 Squadron.

Reformed 4th February 1952 at Khormaksar, Aden, by redesignating 'B' Flight (the Protectorate Support Flight), 8 Squadron.

Auster VI VF548; Anson XIX VM384 U; Pembroke C.1 WV708.

Disbanded 31st August 1955 at Khormaksar and merged with the Aden Communication Squadron to become the Aden Protectorate Communication and Support Squadron.

ADVANCED AIR FIRING SCHOOL
Formed January 1917 at Lympne within 1 (Auxiliary) School Of Aerial Gunnery.

F.E.8 A4944; D.H.5; Avro 504A A8548; F.E.2b B453; F.K.8 B3326; B.E.2e B3655; Camel B5238; R.E.8.

Disbanded March 1918 at Hythe.

ADVANCED BOMBING AND GUNNERY SCHOOL (MIDDLE EAST)
Formed 1st March 1943 at El Ballah, Egypt.

Harvard II AJ781, IIA EX761, IIB FT155, III EZ102; Hurricane I Z4545, IIB BM991, IIC KX101; Spitfire VB ER702, VC ES211, IX ML419; Baltimore IIIA FA116, V FW790; Wellington X LP518.

Disbanded 20th November 1945 at El Ballah.

201 ADVANCED FLYING SCHOOL
Formed 15th March 1947 at Swinderby by redesignating 201 Crew Training Unit.

FMA (5.47–4.51)	Wellington X NA849 FMA-A; Tiger Moth II N9395 FMA-Z.
FMB (5.47–4.51)	Wellington X NB113 FMB-O.
FMC	Allocated but not used.
Nil (4.51–3.55)	Wellington X NA713; Varsity T.1 WF380 C; Valetta T.3 WJ468 Z.
Also used	Anson T.20 VS528 P; Mosquito VI TA590; Meteor F.3 EE287.

Disbanded 1st June 1954 at Swinderby to become 11 Flying Training School.

202 ADVANCED FLYING SCHOOL
Formed 15th March 1947 at Finningley by redesignating 202 Crew Training Unit.

FME (3.47–4.51)	Wellington X PG378 FME-F.
FMF	Allocated but not used.
FMG	Allocated but not used.

Disbanded 1st December 1947 at Finningley and absorbed by 201 Advanced Flying School.

Reformed 1st April 1951 at Valley.

M (4.51–3.54)	No evidence of use.
N (4.51–3.54)	Vampire FB.5 WA194 N-18, T.11 WZ558 N-30.
O (4.51–3.54)	Vampire FB.5 WA224 O-43, T.11 WZ426 53-O.
P (4.51–3.54)	Meteor T.7 WG983 P-29.
Also used	Vampire F.1 TG287; Oxford I NJ303; Tiger Moth II DE459; Chipmunk T.10 WP811.

Disbanded 1st June 1954 at Valley to become 7 Flying Training School.

203 ADVANCED FLYING SCHOOL
Formed 1st July 1947 at Keevil by redesignating 61 Operational Training Unit.

TO (7.47–8.49)	Harvard IIB FS739 TO-P; Martinet I JN297 TO-T; Tiger Moth II T5465 TO-A.
HX (7.47–8.49)	Spitfire XVI TD136 HX-F; Meteor F.4 RA372 HX-M, Meteor T.7 VW427 HX-X; Vampire FB.5 VV480 HX-C.
XY (7.47–8.49)	Anson I MH159 XY-A.
Also used	Spitfire XIX PM617; Vampire F.1 TG442; Oxford I HN832.

Disbanded 31st August 1949 at Stradishall to become 226 Operational Conversion Unit.

Reformed 1st September 1949 at Driffield by redesignating 226 Operational Conversion Unit.

FMI (9.49–4.51)	Vampire F.1 TG387 FMI-H, FB.5 VX979 FMI-K.
FMJ (9.49–4.51)	Meteor F.4 RA373 FMJ-W.
FMK (9.49–4.51)	Meteor T.7 VW416 FMK-J; Tiger Moth II DF129 FMK-W.

O (4.51–6.54)	Meteor F.4 VT303 O-27.
X (4.51–6.54)	Meteor T.7 WF881 X-55.
Also used	Oxford II X7279; Prentice T.1 VR319; Vampire FB.9 WX202 D.

Disbanded 1st June 1954 at Driffield to become 8 Flying Training School.

204 ADVANCED FLYING SCHOOL
Formed 15th March 1947 at Cottesmore by redesignating 204 Crew Training Unit.

FMO (3.47–4.51)	Mosquito III HJ898 FMO-E, VI SZ975 FMO-Z; Tiger Moth II T7025 FMO.
Nil (4.51–2.52)	Mosquito VI SZ974 S; Tiger Moth II T7025.

Disbanded 13th February 1952 at Bassingbourn to become 'D' Squadron of 231 Operational Conversion Unit.

205 ADVANCED FLYING SCHOOL
Formed 7th September 1950 at Middleton St George.

Nil (9.50–4.51)	Meteor F.3 EE283, F.4 EE529 A.
M (4.51–6.54)	Meteor T.7 WL343 M-B.
O (4.51–6.54)	Meteor T.7 WA707 O-S.
R (4.51–6.54)	Meteor F.4 VW257 R-C.
W (4.51–6.54)	Meteor T.7 WG966 W-U.
X (4.51–6.54)	Possibly allocated.
Y (4.51–6.54)	Meteor T.7 WG995 Y-J.
Z (4.51–6.54)	Meteor T.7 WH173 Z-S.
Also used	Prentice T.1 VS689; Oxford I RR331.

Disbanded 1st June 1954 at Middleton St George to become 4 Flying Training School.

206 ADVANCED FLYING SCHOOL
Formed 1st November 1951 at Oakington.

M (11.51–6.54)	Meteor F.3 EE414 M-17, F.4 VT323 M-18, T.7 WA661 M-58.
Y (11.51–6.54)	Meteor F.3 EE340 Y-30, F.4 VT182 Y-34, T.7 WG944 Y-72.
Also used	Tiger Moth II T6198; Oxford I DF220; Vampire FB.5 WA301, T.11 XD382.

Disbanded 1st June 1954 at Oakington to become 5 Flying Training School.

207 ADVANCED FLYING SCHOOL
Formed 20th November 1951 at Full Sutton by redesignating 103 Flying Refresher School.

P	Meteor F.4 VT117 P-15, T.7 WH121 P-14.
S	Meteor F.4 RA441 S-10, T.7 WH205 S-26.
Also used	Oxford I PH481; Meteor F.3 EE421; Harvard IIB FS914.

Disbanded 12th August 1954 at Full Sutton.

208 ADVANCED FLYING SCHOOL
Formed 19th November 1951 at Merryfield.

Meteor F.4 VT184, T.7 VW445; Vampire F.1 TG442 43, FB.5 WA115 75, FB.9 WX201 59, T.11 WZ566 31; Oxford I LB410.

Disbanded 1st June 1954 at Merryfield to become 10 Flying Training School.

209 ADVANCED FLYING SCHOOL
Formed 23rd June 1952 at Weston Zoyland.

Meteor F.4 RA413 82, T.7 WA608.

Disbanded 1st June 1954 at Weston Zoyland to become 12 Flying Training School.

210 ADVANCED FLYING SCHOOL
Formed 5th August 1952 at Tarrant Rushton.

Meteor F.3 EE451 R, T.7 WH129 J; Vampire FB.5 WA428 X.

Disbanded 29th April 1954 at Tarrant Rushton.

211 ADVANCED FLYING SCHOOL
Formed 11th August 1952 at Worksop.

Meteor T.7 WL461, F.8 WK851 31; Oxford II X7194; Prentice I VS330.

Disbanded 1st June 1954 at Worksop to become 211 Flying Training School.

215 ADVANCED FLYING SCHOOL
Formed 1st February 1952 at Finningley by redesignating 101 Flying Refresher School.

M	Meteor F.4 VT138 M-Z, T.7 WH186 M-C; Oxford I LX223 M-L.
N	Meteor F.4 VT286 N-L, T.7 WL371 N-B.

Disbanded 31st May 1954 at Finningley.

ADVANCED FLYING SCHOOL (INDIA)
Formed 1st April 1946 at Ambala, India, by merging 1 (Indian) Advanced Flying Unit, 1 (Indian) Service Flying Training School and 151 (Fighter) Operational Training Unit.

Spitfire VIII NH636, XIV NH759; Oxford I NM647; Harvard IIB FE380.

Disbanded 1st June 1947 at Ambala.

4 (ADVANCED) FLYING TRAINING SCHOOL – see 4 Flying Training School, later 4 Service Flying Training School, later 4 Flying Training School, later 4 (Advanced) Flying Training School

5 (ADVANCED) FLYING TRAINING SCHOOL – see 5 Flying Training School, later 5 Service Flying Training School, later 5 Flying Training School, later 5 (Advanced) Flying Training School

6 (ADVANCED) FLYING TRAINING SCHOOL – see 6 Flying Training School, later 6 Service Flying Training School, later 6 Flying Training School, later 6 (Advanced) Flying Training School

8 (ADVANCED) FLYING TRAINING SCHOOL – see 8 Flying Training School, later 8 Service Flying Training School, later 8 (Advanced) Flying Training School

9 (ADVANCED) FLYING TRAINING SCHOOL – see 9 Flying Training School, later 9 Service Flying Training School, later 9 (Advanced) Flying Training School, later 9 Flying Training School

10 (ADVANCED) FLYING TRAINING SCHOOL – see 10 Flying Training School, later 10 Service Flying Training School, later 10 (Advanced) Flying Training School, later 10 Flying Training School

14 (ADVANCED) FLYING TRAINING SCHOOL – see 14 Flying Training School, later 14 Service Flying Training School, later 14 (Advanced) Flying Training School

ADVANCED FLYING TRAINING UNIT
Formed 1st March 1943 at Amarda Road, India.

Blenheim V EH500; Vengeance TT.I AP114, IA EZ981; Hurricane IID KX247; Spitfire VC MA393, VIII MD293, XIV RM957; Harvard IIB FE423; Thunderbolt I FL751, II HD271.

Disbanded 24th May 1945 at Amarda Road and merged with the Ground Attack Training Unit to become the Tactical and Weapon Development Unit

ADVANCED FLYING UNIT, SÉTIF
Formed 19th August 1943 at Sétif, Algeria, by merging the Fighter Pilots Practice Flights, Sétif and Blida.

Spitfire VB EP905, VC EE790; Hurricane IIC KX889.

Disbanded 31st March 1944 at Sétif.

ADVANCED SHIP RECOGNITION FLIGHT
Formed 16th November 1942 at Castletown.

Anson I.

Disbanded 9th February 1943 at Skeabrae to become 1476 (Advanced Ship Recognition) Flight.

ADVANCED TRAINING SQUADRONS
The Advanced Training Squadrons of all day fighter Operational Training Units would have had 500 added to their numbers to become reserve Squadrons if plans under the code name 'Saracen', made in spring 1942 to counter a German invasion, were put into operation. Plans were revised under the code name 'Banquet' in order to accommodate additional resources. Records indicate the titles were used by several Operational Training Units and 3 Tactical Exercise Unit until at least May 1944 for standing patrols, convoy escort duties, conversion training and night flying.

Operation 'Saracen'

Squadron	Drawn From	Equipment	Advanced Base
551 Squadron	51 Operational Training Unit	Spitfire II, V	Colerne
552 Squadron	51 Operational Training Unit	Spitfire II, V	Colerne
553 Squadron	53 Operational Training Unit	Spitfire II, V	Church Fenton
554 Squadron	53 Operational Training Unit	Spitfire II, V	Church Fenton
555 Squadron	55 Operational Training Unit	Hurricane I, II	Turnhouse
556 Squadron	56 Operational Training Unit	Hurricane I, II	Peterhead
557 Squadron	57 Operational Training Unit	Spitfire II,V	Newcastle
558 Squadron	58 Operational Training Unit	Spitfire II, V	Turnhouse
559 Squadron	59 Operational Training Unit	Hurricane I, II	Newcastle
561 Squadron	61 Operational Training Unit	Spitfire II, V	Woodvale

Operation 'Banquet'

Squadron	Drawn From	Equipment	Advanced Base
550 Squadron	Air Fighting Development Unit	Spitfire II, V	
551 Squadron	51 Operational Training Unit	Spitfire II, V	Colerne
552 Squadron	51 Operational Training Unit	Spitfire II, V	Colerne
553 Squadron	53 Operational Training Unit	Spitfire II, V	Church Fenton
554 Squadron	53 Operational Training Unit	Spitfire II, V	Church Fenton
555 Squadron	55 Operational Training Unit	Hurricane I, II	Ouston
556 Squadron	56 Operational Training Unit	Hurricane I, II	Ouston
557 Squadron	57 Operational Training Unit	Spitfire II, V	Newcastle
558 Squadron	58 Operational Training Unit	Spitfire II, V	Turnhouse
559 Squadron	59 Operational Training Unit	Hurricane I, II	Newcastle
560 Squadron	56 Operational Training Unit	Hurricane I, II	Peterhead
561 Squadron	61 Operational Training Unit	Spitfire II, V	Woodvale
562 Squadron	57 Operational Training Unit	Spitfire II, V	Newcastle
563 Squadron	58 Operational Training Unit	Spitfire II, V	Turnhouse
564 Squadron	59 Operational Training Unit	Hurricane I, II	Newcastle
565 Squadron	61 Operational Training Unit	Spitfire II, V	Woodvale

AERIAL FIGHTING AND GUNNERY SCHOOL
Formed 1st April 1918 at Leysdown by redesignating the RNAS Gunnery School Flight.

1½ Strutter A5262; Avro 504K; D.H.4; D.H.9 D3117.

Ceased operations December 1918 at Leysdown and officially disbanded by February 1919.

AERIAL FIGHTING SCHOOL, HELIOPOLIS
Formed 13th November 1917 at Heliopolis, Egypt, by redesignating 196 Training Squadron. A 'Gosport Flight', using techniques developed by 1 School of Special Flying, Gosport, formed in July 1918.

B.E.2e 6293; Bristol Scout D 7045; Avro 504K E1632; F.K.3; Nieuport; S.E.5a D3518; Pup D4124.

Disbanded 4th September 1918 at Heliopolis and merged with the School of Aerial Gunnery, Aboukir, to become 5 Fighting School.

AEROPLANE AND ARMAMENT EXPERIMENTAL ESTABLISHMENT
Formed 24th March 1924 at Martlesham Heath by redesignating the Aeroplane Experimental Establishment (Home).

22 Squadron, which had reformed earlier on 24th July 1923 within the Aeroplane Experimental Establishment (Home), carried out armament testing until disbanded on 1st May 1934. 15 Squadron reformed 20th March 1924 within the Aeroplane and Armament Experimental Establishment to carry out performance and handling trials until disbanded on 1st June 1934. The units were replaced immediately by the Performance Testing Squadron (later the Performance Testing Section) and the Armament Testing Squadron (later the Armament Testing Section).

The Establishment, with one exception, moved to Boscombe Down in September 1939. 'D' Flight of the Performance Testing Section became the Royal Air Force Detachment, Perth.

'D' Flight, Performance Testing Section	Formed August 1938 at Martlesham Heath by redesignating the Experimental Co-operation Unit.
	Harrow II K7021; Anson; Battle K9207; Blenheim L1201; Magister L8168.
	Disbanded 4th September 1939 at Martlesham Heath to become the Royal Air Force Detachment, Perth.
Handling Squadron	See separate entry.
High Altitude Flight	Formed 30th December 1940 at Boscombe Down.
	Spitfire II P7661, VI BR287; Wellington V W5796, VI W5800.
	Disbanded September 1944 at Boscombe Down.

By 1944 the Flying Division was reorganised into 'A','B','C' and 'D' Squadrons. From January 1988 'A' and 'B' Squadrons merged to become the Fixed Wing Test Squadron and 'D' Squadron became the Rotary Wing Test Squadron.

Representative aircraft:

(Airspeed) Oxford I N4560, II P1070; Horsa I DP600. (ANEC) ANEC 1 J7506. (Armstrong Whitworth) Awana J6897; Wolf J6921; Starling J8027; Ajax J8802; Aries J9037; Siskin III J6981, IIIA J9308, IIIDC J9236; Atlas I J8792; A.W.XVI S1591; Scimitar G-ACCD; A.W.19 K5606; Whitley K4586, I K7183, II K7217, III K8936, V T4223, VII BD621; Albemarle P1360, GT.I P1368, ST.I P1634, ST.II V1743, IV P1406; Argosy C.1 XN814. (Auster) AOP.9 WZ662; B.4 XA177. (Avro) Avro 504K E3269, Avro 504N J8526; Aldershot J6942, III J6950; Andover J7261; Avro 560 J7322; Avian III J9182, IVM J9783; Tutor K3191; Anson I LT764, XI NK870, XII NL171, T.20 VM411; Manchester L7246, I 7277; Lancaster I R5609, I/Special PB995, II DS601, III ED825/G; York I MW112; Lincoln I RE227, II WD125; Shackleton MR.1 VP255, MR.1A WB835, MR.2 WR960, AEW.2 WL745, MR.3 WR982, T.4 WB858; Ashton 1 WB490; Avro 707A WD280; Vulcan B.1 XA892, B.1A XH499, B.2 XH533; Andover C.1 XS596. (BAC) Lightning F.3 XP696, F.3A XP693, T.5 XS418; VC.10 K.3 ZA147; One Eleven ZE432; Jet Provost T.5 XS230. (Beagle) Bassett CC.1 XS770. (Beardmore) Inflexible J7557. (Beechcraft) Traveler I FT461. (Bell) Airacobra I AH573. (Blackburn) Monoplane K4241; Shark II K5607; Roc I L3069; Skua I L2867, II L2877; Botha I L6105; Firebrand I DK365, II DK377, III DK389; YA-7 WB781; Beverley I XB260; Buccaneer S.1 XN923, S.2 XN974, S.2C XV337. (Boeing) Fortress I AN519, II FA706, IIA FK185, III KL835. (Boeing-Vertol) Chinook HC.1 ZA671, HC.2 ZA714. (Boulton Paul) Bodmin J6911; Bugle I J6985, II J7266; Partridge J8459; Sidestrand II J9186, III J9770; P.32 J9950; Defiant I N1550, TT.I DR863, II AA370, TT.III N3488; P.92/2 V3142; Balliol T.2 VR591; Sea Balliol T.21 WP333; P.111A VT935; P.120 VT951. (Brantley) B.2B XS683. (Breguet) Breguet 19 J7507. (Brewster) Buffalo I AS412. (Bristol) F.2B J6689; Bullfinch J6901; Brendon J6997; Bloodhound J7236; Berkley J7403; Bullpup J9051; Bulldog II J9567, IIA K2201, IVA K4292; Bristol 142 K7557; Bristol 148 K6551; Blenheim I L1407, IV L8662, V AD657; Beaufort I L4441; Beaufighter R2055, I R2063, IIF R2270, V R2274, VI JL871, X NV535, XI JL876; Brigand TF.1 RH742, B.1 RH773, MET.3 VS818; Buckmaster I RP122; Buckingham I KV324; Bristol 170 XF380, Sycamore 3 WA576, HR.14 XE307; Bristol 170 Mk31 WJ320; Britannia XX367. (Canadair) Sabre F.1 XB733. (Cierva) C.8L-1 J8930; C.9 J8931; C.19 Mk III K1948. (Consolidated) Liberator I AM929, II AL505, III FL927/G, V BZ714, VI KL632, VIII KL631, IX JT978. (Cunliffe Owen) Concordia G-AKBE. (Curtiss) Hawk 188; Mohawk IV AR640; Cleveland I AS468; Tomahawk I AH797, IIA AH925, IIB AK160; Kittyhawk I AK579, IIA FL220. (de Havilland) Doormouse J7005; Dingo I J7006, II J7007; Humming Bird J7268; D.H.9A J7605, D.H.9A DC J8492; Hyena J7780; Hound J9127; D.H.77 J9771; Moth J8030; Genet Moth J8817; Puss Moth X9378; Gipsy Moth BK835; Tiger Moth I K4281, II T6831; Don L2391; Flamingo R2765; Rapide R2487; D.H.89M K4772; Dominie I HG715; Mosquito W4050, I W4051, II W4052, IV DK327, VI HJ732/G, IX ML899, XII HK196, XVI ML994, XVII HK195, XVIII PZ469, B.20 KB328, B.25 KB471, FB.26 KA104, PR.32 NS586,

PR.34 RG176, PR.35 TK650, NF.38 VT654; Sea Mosquito TR.33 TW227; Hornet F.1 PX210, F.3 PX312; Vampire F.1 TG284, F.2 TX807, FB.5 VV218, NF.10 WP232, T.11 WZ414; Sea Vampire T.22 XA101; D.H.110 WG240; Devon C.1 VP954; Venom FB.1 WE260, NF.2 WL811, NF.3 WX786, FB.4 WR417; Sea Venom NF.20 WK376; Chipmunk T.10 WB550; Comet 2X XM829, 4C XS236. (Dornier) Komet J7276. (Douglas) Havoc I AE458, I (Turbinlite) BJ474; Boston II AH437, III W8269, III (Turbinlite) W8254, IIIA BZ315, IV BZ403, V BZ580; Invader I KL690; Dakota III KG402, IV KN407. (Edgar Percival) EP.9 XM797. (English Electric) Wren J6973; Canberra B.2 WD953, PR.3 WF922, T.4 WJ865, PR.7 WT507, B(I).6 WT311, B(I).8 WT328, U.10 WH876, T.18 WJ632; P.1A WG760; Lightning F.1 XM134, F.1A XM171, F.2 XN723, T.4 XM968. (Fairey) Fawn I J7187, III J7978, IV J7768, IIIF S1147; Fox I J7941, IA J9026, IIIM J9834; Long Range Monoplane J9479; Gordon K1731; Hendon K1695; Seafox K4304; TSR II K4190; Swordfish I L2829, II DK690; Battle K9223; Fantome L7045; Fulmar I N1858, II N4021; Albacore I L7075; Barracuda I P9642, II P9667, III DR318; Firefly FR.1 PP639; FD.1 VX350; FD.2 WG774. (Fieseler) Fi 156 VH751. (FMA) Pucara ZD485. (Folland) Midge G-39-1; Gnat T.1 XP519. (General Aircraft) Monospar L4671; Hotspur II BT535; Universal WF320. (Gloster) Nighthawk J6970; Grebe I J6969, II J7283, IIIDC J7519; Gamecock J7497; Gorcock I J7501, II J7503; Goral J8673; Goring J8674; Goldfinch J7940; Gamecock I J7910, II J8804; Gloster F.20/27 J9125; T.C.33 J9832; TSR.38 S1705; A.S.31 K2602; Gladiator I K7919; F.5/34 K5604; F.9/37 L8002; Meteor F.1 EE213, F.3 EE269, F.4 VW293, T.7 VW413, F.8 VZ460, FR.9 VW360, PR.10 WB164, NF.11 WA547, NF.12 WS591, NF.13 WM366, NF.14 WS724, T.20 WD767; Javelin FAW.1 XA544, FAW.2 XA770, T.3 XK577, FAW.4 XA631, FAW.5 XA641, FAW.6 XA821, FAW.7 XH704, FAW.8 XH966, FAW.9 XH759. (Grumman) Martlet II AM991, III AM956; Hellcat I FN323, II JX822; Avenger II JZ570. (Handasyde/Raynham) Light Aeroplane J7518. (Handley Page) Hyderabad J6994; Hare J8622; Hinaidi I J9299, II J9478; Clive I J9126, II J9948; H.P.43 later H.P. 51 J9833; H.P.47 K2773; Hampden I AD925; Hereford I L6003; Halifax I L9486, II R9534, III LW125, V DK145, VI NP752, VII NA366, VIII PP225; Hastings C.1 TG502, C.2 WD476, C(VIP).4 WD500; Marathon VX229; HPR.2 WE505; Victor WB775, B.1 XA917, BK.1A XA918, B.2 XH671. (Hawker) Woodcock I J6987, II J6988, IA/Heron J6989; Horsley J7721, II S1436; Hornbill J7782; Harrier J8325; Hawfinch J8776; Hawker F.20/27 J9123; Hornet J9682; Tomtit J9773; Fury K1927; Audax K1996; Hart K2466; Nimrod K2823; Demon K2905; Hind K2915; Hardy K5919; Henley III L3276; Hurricane I P3157, IIA Z2320, II Z3451, IIB Z2691, IIC LE525, IID BN965, IV KX180, X P5170; Tornado P5224; Typhoon IA R7577, IB R8762; Tempest I HM599, II PR903, V JN799; Tempest VI NV946; Hunter F.1 WT557, F.2 WN894, F.4 WT703, F.5 WN956, F.6 XE551, T.7 XL617, T.8 WT702, FGA.9 XE601, FR.10 XF429; Sea Hawk F.1 WF147; Kestrel FGA.1 XS695; Harrier T.2 XW265, GR.3 XZ136, GR.5 ZD321, GR.7 ZD318; Sea Harrier FRS.1 ZA195, FRS.2 XZ497. (Hawker Siddeley) Buccaneer S.2B XW987; Hawk T.1 XX156. (Heston) Phoenix 2 X2891; T.1/37 L7706. (Hughes) Hughes 269A XS349/XS684. (Lockheed) Hudson I T9266, III T9418, IIIA FH230, IV AE610, V AE650, VI FK406; Ventura I AE748; Lightning I AF106; Neptune MR.1 WX507; Hercules C.3 XV223; TriStar K.1 ZD953. (ML Aviation) Utility XK784. (Martin) Baltimore I AG689; Maryland I AR703; Marauder I FK111, II FB482, III HD402. (Martin-Baker) MB.2 P9594; MB.5 R2496. (McDonnell-Douglas) Phantom FG.1 XT597. (Miles) Mentor L4393; Kestrel N3300; Magister I N3939; M.15 L7714; Master I N7757, II AZ104; Hawk Major BB667; Martinet I JN303. (Morane-Saulnier) MS 500 VG919. (North American) Harvard I N7001, II BD134, IIB KF177; Mustang I AG351, IA FD438, II FR932, III FX953, IV KH648, IVA KH766, V FR409; Mitchell I FK161, II FW151, III HD347. (Northrop) Nomad I AS440; Black Widow 42-5496. (Panavia) Tornado GR.1 ZA319, F.2 ZD900, F.2T ZA267, F.3 ZE155. (Parnall) Perch N217; Pipit N232; Possum J6862; Pixie II J7323; G.4/31 K2772; Hendy Heck IIC K8853. (Percival) Prentice T.1 VR191; P.56 WG503; Provost T.1 WV421; Pembroke C.1 WV699. (Piper) Grasshopper VM286; Navajo Chieftain ZF622. (Pitcairn) PA-39 BW833. (Republic) Thunderbolt I FL844, II KJ298. (Saro) F.20/20 K1949; Cloud K2681; Skeeter 3 WF112, 6 XK773, AOP.12 XL813; SR.53 XD145. (Sayers/Handley Page) HP.22 J7233; HP.23 J7265. (SEPECAT) Jaguar GR.1A XX979. (Short) Springbok II/Chamois J7295; Valetta G-AAJY; Stirling I N3635, II N3657, III BK649, IV LJ899, V PK136; Sturgeon TT.2 VR363; SB.5 WG768; Seamew AS.1 XA213; SC.1 XG900; Belfast C.1 XR365. (Sikorsky) Hoverfly I FT833, II KN856; Sikorsky S-51 XD649.

(Supermarine) Spitfire I N3171, IIA P7661, III N3297, VA X4922, VB W3134, VC BR288, VI BR200, VII MD114, VIII JF463, IX TA822, XI PL758, XII DP845, XIII L1004, XIV JF319, XVI TB757, XVIII SM970, F.21 LA187, F.22 PK312, F.24 VN315; Seafire XV NS487, F.46 LA541; Spiteful NN667; Supermarine 508 VX133; Swift F.1 WK200, F.3 WK253, F.4 WK272, FR.5 XD900. (Taylorcraft) Auster II MZ105, III LB319, V RT540, VI TJ707. (Vickers) Vanguard J6924; Vimy IV J7442; Vernon III J7548; Virginia III J6856, VI J7558, VII J6993, VIII J6856, IX J7715, X J7717; Venture I J7277; Wibault J9029; Jockey J9122; Vickers 150 J9131; Victoria IV J9250; Vildebeest I K2819, II K2945, III S1713, IV K8087; Vellore K2133; Wellesley K7754; Wellington I L4213, IA N2865, IC P9238, II R3221, III DF627, IV Z1248, V W5796, VI DR484, X RP589, XI MP502, XIV MP714, XVII MP535; Warwick I BV301, II HG362, III HG215, V PN701; Viking C.2 VL228; Valetta C.1 VL249, Varsity T.1 WF327; Valiant WB215, B.1 WP214, B.2 WJ954. (Vought Sikorsky) Chesapeake I AL911. (Vultee) Vengeance I AN888, IV FD119; Vigilant I HL429, IA BZ103. (Waco) CG-13A KL163; Hadrian I NP664. (Westland) Weasel I F2913; Yeovil I J7508; Westbury J7765; Wapiti I J9102, IIA J9382; Westland F.20/27 J9124; Pterodactyl IV K1947, V K2770; F.7/30 K2891; P.V.6 K3488; Lysander I R2631, II L4739, III T1428, IIIA V9602; Whirlwind L6844, I P6997; Welkin I DX279; Dragonfly HR.4 XB252; Whirlwind HAR.1 XA863, HAR.2 XD164, HAS.7 XG588; Wessex HU.5 XS509; Scout AH.1 XT631; Lynx HAS.3 ZD267, HAS.8 XZ236, AH.9 ZG884; Gazelle AH.1 XZ339; Puma HC.1 XW233; Sea King HAS.1 XV373, HC.4 ZF115, HAS.6 XZ576.

Note – The codes THI, FGI, FGJ, FGK, FGL, FGM and FGN were allocated but not used.

Functional administrative control by the Royal Air Force ceased with effect from 1st November 1955. Redesignated the Aircraft and Armament Evaluation Establishment from 1st April 1992.

AEROPLANE EXPERIMENTAL ESTABLISHMENT (HOME)
Formed 16th March 1920 at Martlesham Heath by redesignating the Aeroplane Experimental Station.

(Armstrong Whitworth) Siskin III J6583; Awana J6897; Wolf J6921. (Austin) Greyhound H4319. (Avro) 504K D6382, 504N J733; Manchester II F3492; Aldershot I J6853, II J6852, III J6952. (BAT) Basilisk F2907; Bantam J6579. (Boulton Paul) Bourges I F2903; Bolton J6584; Bodmin J6910; Bugle I J6984. (Bristol) F.2B Fighter C4654; Braemar II C4297; Pullman C4298; Badger F3496, II J6492; Tramp J6912. (de Havilland) D.H.4 A7993; D.H.9 E8903, D.H.9A E753; Amiens III E5458; IIIA F8423; IIIC E5550; Gazelle J1937; Okapi J1938; Doncaster J6849; Derby J6894; Doormouse J7005. (Fairey) Fawn I J6907, II J6908, III J6907; Fairey IIIC N2246. (Gloster) Grebe J6969, II J7283; Bamel I J7234. (Handley Page) V/1500 F7135; Hyderabad J6994. (Hawker) Duiker J6918; Woodcock I J6987. (Martinsyde) Buzzard H7781. (Nieuport) Nighthawk J6295; Nightjar J6930; London H1741. (Parnall) Panther N7429. (RAF) S.E.5a. E5923. (Short) Springbok I J6974. (Sopwith) Salamander E5431; Dragon F7017; Snark I F4068; Cobham II H671. (Vickers) Ambulance J6855; Virginia I J6856; Vernon I J6879, II J6884; Vanguard J6924. (Westland) Weasel F2912, II J6577; Wagtail J6581; Limousine III J6851.

Disbanded 24th March 1924 at Martlesham Heath to become the Aeroplane and Armament Experimental Establishment.

AEROPLANE EXPERIMENTAL STATION
Formed 16th October 1917 at Martlesham Heath by redesignating the Testing Squadron.

(Avro) 504A D1631; Manchester I F3494. (Blackburn) Blackburd N114; Kangaroo B9970. (Boulton Paul) Bobolinks C8655. (Bristol) Scout D 7053; F.2B B1206. (de Havilland) D.H.4 A7993. (Fairey) IIIA N2850. (Grain) Griffin N100. (Handley Page) V/1500 F7135. (Martinsyde) Elephant A6286. (Nieuport) Triplane N532; Nighthawk F2911. (Parnall) Panther N91. (Port Victoria) PV.8 N540. (Short) Shirl N110. (Sopwith) Triplane N5430; Ship Strutter B744; Camel B2538; Cuckoo N7163; Snapper F7031, Cobham I H672. (Vickers) Vimy F9167; Bulldog X3.

Disbanded 16th March 1920 at Martlesham Heath to become the Aeroplane Experimental Establishment (Home).

AEROPLANE TESTING SQUADRON – see Testing Squadron

AI/ASV SCHOOL – see Airborne Interception/Air-to-Surface Vessel School

AI CONVERSION FLIGHT, CRANFIELD AND TWINWOOD FARM – see Airborne Interception Conversion Flight, Cranfield and Twinwood Farm

AI CONVERSION FLIGHT, ITALY – see Airborne Interception Conversion Flight, Italy

AI MK VIII CONVERSION FLIGHT – see Airborne Interception Mk VIII Conversion Flight

AI MK X CONVERSION FLIGHT – see Airborne Interception Mk X Conversion Flight

AI SCHOOL – see Airborne Interception School

AIR AMBULANCE UNIT – see 24 Squadron

1 AIR AMBULANCE UNIT, RAAF
A Royal Australian Air Force unit formed 15th February 1941 at Laverton, Australia. Departed 31st March 1941 for the Middle East, arriving at Gaza, Palestine, in August 1941.

D.H.86B A31-7; Bombay I L5838; Goose HK822; Lodestar 1371 (ex SAAF).

Disbanded February 1943 at Bari, Italy.

AIR ARMAMENT SCHOOL later 1 AIR ARMAMENT SCHOOL
Formed 1st January 1932 at Eastchurch as the Air Armament School by redesignating the Armament and Gunnery School. Redesignated 1 Air Armament School from 1st November 1937 at Manby.

Siskin IIIDC J7162; Wapiti IIA J9857; Bulldog IIA K1080; Fairey IIIF K1773; Fairey IVM S1205 Z; Avro 504N K2365; Tiger Moth I K2572; Gordon I K2716; Hart K3809; Overstrand K4552; Hind K6648; Gauntlet II K7799; Demon K8181; Wallace I K4338, II K6077; Demon K8216; Harrow I K6949; Battle K9221; Spitfire I K9803; Whitley K4587, II K7219, III K9006, V N1363; Master I N7550, II DM200; Moth AW162; Blenheim I L1180, IV T1848; Henley III L3338; Botha I L6196; Wellington I L4322, IA N2865, IC P9295, XIII MF125; Manchester I L7464; Hampden I L4141; Hereford I N9104; Defiant I L7006; Hurricane I P3769, IV KZ677; Stirling I N3669; Lysander TT.III T1442, IIIA W6939; TT.IIIA V9614; Mustang I AP221; Martinet I EM435; Beaufighter I X7683, II R2328; Moth Minor X9297.

Disbanded 28th October 1944 at Manby and absorbed by the Empire Air Armament School.

1 AIR ARMAMENT SCHOOL – see Air Armament School, later 1 Air Armament School

2 AIR ARMAMENT SCHOOL
Formed 1st November 1937 at North Coates Fitties by redesignating the Air Observers' School.

Wallis I K3908, K6027; Hart K2452; Osprey III K3631.

Disbanded 1st March 1938 at North Coates to become 1 Air Observers' School.

Reformed 1st July 1938 at Eastchurch.

No aircraft allocated.

Disbanded 20th June 1940 at Newton Down to become 3 Ground Armament School.

AIR BOMBER TRAINING FLIGHTS – see 1, 3, 4 and 5 Group Bomber Training Flights

AIR CADET CENTRAL GLIDING SCHOOL – see Central Gliding School, later Air Cadet Central Gliding School

AIR COMBAT DEVELOPMENT UNIT (MIDDLE EAST)
Formed (date and location unknown). Possibly a predecessor or

component of 1 Middle East Training School based at El Ballah, Egypt.

Hurricane I Z4572.

Disbanded (date and location unknown).

AIR COMMAND FAR EAST ALL-WEATHER FLIGHT
Formed 8th June 1948 at Changi, Singapore, as an element of the Far East Communication Squadron, by redesignating the Air Command Far East Instrument Flying Training Flight.

Harvard IIB FS923.

Disbanded 15th March 1950 at Seletar, Singapore, and merged with the Receipt, Test and Despatch Flight to become the Far East Air Force Examining Squadron.

AIR COMMAND FAR EAST AND AIR HEADQUARTERS MALAYA COMMUNICATION SQUADRON
Formed 21st August 1946 at Changi, Singapore.

No aircraft known.

Deemed inactive from 30th September 1946 but not disbanded officially until 15th January 1947 at Changi and replaced by the Far East Communication Flight.

AIR COMMAND FAR EAST INSTRUMENT FLYING TRAINING FLIGHT
Formed 1st June 1948 at Changi, Singapore, within the Far East Communication Squadron.

Harvard IIB FS923.

Disbanded 8th June 1948 at Changi to become the Air Command Far East All-Weather Flight.

AIR COMMAND SOUTHEAST ASIA COMMUNICATION UNIT
Formed 1st November 1943 at Willingdon Airport, New Delhi, India, by redesignating an element of the Air Headquarters India Communication Unit.

Argus II FS583; Dakota III FD879; Hudson VI FK504; Gull Six MA942; Anson DJ270; Vega Gull DR808; Lockheed 12A V4732.

Disbanded 31st January 1944 at Willingdon Airport, New Delhi, to become the Headquarters Air Command Southeast Asia Communication Squadron.

AIR COMMAND SOUTHEAST ASIA (INTERNAL AIR SERVICE) SQUADRON
Formed 7th June 1945 at Ratmalana, India, by redesignating elements of the Air Command Southeast Asia (Communications) Squadron and 229 Group Communication Squadron.

Dakota; Expeditor.

Disbanded 28th February 1946 at Yelahanka, India.

AIR COMPONENT FIELD FORCE COMMUNICATION SQUADRON
Formed 25th August 1939 at Andover.

Tiger Moth I K4250, II N9125; Cierva C.40 L7590; Lysander II N1243.

Disbanded 27th November 1939 at Mont Joie, France, to become 81 Squadron.

AIR COUNCIL INSPECTION SQUADRON
Formed 25th June 1918 at Waddon.

Avro 504K C4451; D.H.9 D1268; F.2B.

Disbanded 1st February 1920 at Kenley to become 24 Squadron.

AIR DEFENCE CO-OPERATION UNIT
Formed 18th June 1942 at Ismailia, Egypt, by redesignating 1 Target Towing Flight.

Gordon; Gladiator; Blenheim; Fulmar; Hurricane I W9271; Maryland.

Disbanded November 1942 at El Firdan, Egypt, to become 26 Anti-Aircraft Co-operation Unit.

AIR DEFENCE OF GREAT BRITAIN COMMUNICATION FLIGHT
Formed by January 1930 at Northolt.

Moth K1222.

Existed until at least February 1936 then probably absorbed by the Station Flight, Northolt.

Reformed 1st May 1944 at Northolt as a component Flight of the Air Defence of Great Britain Communication Squadron.

AIR DEFENCE OF GREAT BRITAIN COMMUNICATION SQUADRON
Formed 1st May 1944 at Northolt by redesignating the Station Flight, Northolt.

Petrel P5637; Falcon Six DG576; Whitney Straight DP237; Proctor I P6235; II Z7222; Spitfire IIA P7738; Oxford II V3571; Dominie I NF892; Auster V RT484.

Disbanded 16th October 1944 at Northolt to become the Fighter Command Communication Squadron.

AIR DEFENCE UNIT, TANGANYIKA
Formed September 1939 at Dar es Salaam, Tanganyika.
Disbanded 1st November 1939 at Dar es Salaam.

See: Communication Flight, Dar es Salaam (Air Defence Unit, Tanganyika)

AIR DEPOT HINAIDI TRAINING FLIGHT
Formed by December 1929 at Hinaidi, Iraq, and attached to 55 Squadron. Absorbed by 55 Squadron to become known as 55 Squadron Training Flight.

F.2B J6659; D.H.9A E775; Wapiti IIA K1382.

Disbanded 30th December 1930 at Hinaidi to become the Communication Flight Iraq and Persia.

AIR DESPATCH LETTER SERVICE SQUADRON
Formed 24th December 1944 at Northolt by redesignating 1322 (Air Despatch Letter Service) Flights.

Nil (12.44–4.46)   *Proctor III LZ688; Spitfire XI PM124; Mosquito B.25 KA933.*
OAP (12.44–4.46)   *Anson I MG569 OAPL, X NK828 OAPO.*

Disbanded 20th April 1946 at B.168 (Fuhlsbuttel, Germany).

AIR DIVISION COMMUNICATION SQUADRON
Formed 18th December 1945 at Lübeck, Germany, by redesignating 'E' Squadron, British Air Forces of Occupation Communication Wing.

Vigilant I HL432; Anson I MH181, X NK532; XI NK871, XII; Spitfire XI; Messenger; Auster V TJ592; Proctor III Z7201.

Disbanded 8th August 1946 at Detmold, Germany.

AIR ELECTRONICS AND AIR ENGINEERS SCHOOL, later AIR ELECTRONICS, ENGINEER AND LOADMASTER SCHOOL
Formed 30th January 1967 at Topcliffe by redesignating the Air Electronics School. Redesignated the Air Electronics and Air Engineer Wing of 6 Flying Training School from October 1976. Redesignated the Air Electronics, Engineer and Loadmaster School from 16th June 1983.

Varsity T.1 WF374 D; Argosy C.1 XN849.

Disbanded 1st January 1997 at Finningley to become the Navigator and Airmen Aircrew School.

AIR ELECTRONICS, ENGINEER AND LOADMASTER SCHOOL – see Air Electronics and Air Engineer School, later Air Electronics, Engineer and Loadmaster School

1 AIR ELECTRONICS SCHOOL later AIR ELECTRONICS SCHOOL
Formed 1st April 1957 at Swanton Morley by redesignating 1 Air Signallers School. Redesignated the Air Electronics School from January 1960.

Anson XIX TX218 Y, T.22 VS595 F; Valetta C.1 VX539, T.3 WJ480; Varsity T.1 WJ897 L; Chipmunk T.10 WZ846 X.

Disbanded 30th January 1967 at Topcliffe to become the Air Electronics and Air Engineers School.

1 AIR EXPERIENCE FLIGHT
Formed 8th September 1958 at Biggin Hill.

Chipmunk T.10 WK577 AL.

Disbanded November 1995 at Manston.

2 AIR EXPERIENCE FLIGHT
Formed 8th September 1958 at Hamble. Became a subordinate Flight within the Southampton University Air Squadron from November 1995.

Chipmunk T.10 WP840 9; Bulldog T.1.

Current 1st April 1998 at Boscombe Down.

3 AIR EXPERIENCE FLIGHT
Formed 8th September 1958 at Filton. Became a subordinate Flight within the Bristol University Air Squadron from November 1995.

Chipmunk T.10 WK609 L; Bulldog T.1.

Current 1st April 1998 at Colerne.

4 AIR EXPERIENCE FLIGHT
Formed 8th September 1958 at Exeter.

Chipmunk T.10 WP833.

Disbanded 27th December 1995 at Exeter.

Reformed January 1997 at Glasgow Airport, being a subordinate Flight within the Universities of Glasgow and Strathclyde Air Squadron.

Chipmunk T.10; Bulldog T.1.

Current 1st April 1997 at Glasgow Airport.

5 AIR EXPERIENCE FLIGHT
Formed 8th September 1958 at Cambridge Airport. Became a subordinate Flight within the Cambridge University Air Squadron from November 1995.

Chipmunk T.10 WP970 T; Husky XW635 B; Provost T.1 XF543; Bulldog T.1 XX529.

Current 1st April 1998 at Cambridge Airport.

6 AIR EXPERIENCE FLIGHT
Formed 8th September 1958 at White Waltham. Became a subordinate Flight within the University of London Air Squadron from November 1995.

Chipmunk T.10 WP778 Y; Bulldog T.1.

Current 1st April 1998 at Benson.

7 AIR EXPERIENCE FLIGHT
Formed 8th September 1958 at Newton. Became a subordinate Flight within the East Midlands University Air Squadron from November 1995.

Chipmunk T.10 WB562 F; Bulldog T.1.

Current 1st April 1998 at Newton.

8 AIR EXPERIENCE FLIGHT
Formed October 1958 at Cosford. Became a subordinate Flight within the University of Birmingham Air Squadron from November 1995.

Chipmunk T.10 WP859 Z; Bulldog T.1.

Current 1st April 1998 at Cosford.

9 AIR EXPERIENCE FLIGHT
Formed 8th September 1958 at Yeadon. Became a subordinate Flight within the Yorkshire Universities Air Squadron from November 1995.

Chipmunk T.10 WK638 83; Bulldog T.1 XX709.

Current 1st April 1998 at Church Fenton.

10 AIR EXPERIENCE FLIGHT
Formed 25th August 1958 at Woodvale. Became a subordinate Flight within the University of Liverpool Air Squadron from November 1995.

Chipmunk T.10 WK624 12; Bulldog T.1.

Current 1st April 1998 at Woodvale.

11 AIR EXPERIENCE FLIGHT
Formed 8th September 1958 at Ouston. Became a subordinate Flight within the Northumbrian Universities Air Squadron from November 1995.

Chipmunk T.10 WK517 84; Provost T.1 XF907; Bulldog T.1.

Current 1st April 1998 at Leeming.

12 AIR EXPERIENCE FLIGHT
Formed 8th September 1958 at Turnhouse. Became a subordinate Flight within the Aberdeen and St Andrews University Air Squadron from November 1995.

Chipmunk T.10 WB567.

Disbanded 31st March 1996 and absorbed by the Aberdeen, Dundee and St Andrews University Air Squadron.

13 AIR EXPERIENCE FLIGHT
Formed 8th September 1958 at Sydenham. Became a subordinate Flight within the Queen's University Air Squadron from November 1995.

Chipmunk T.10 WP860; Bulldog T.1 XX711 E.

Disbanded 31st July 1996 at Aldergrove.

AIR FIGHTING DEVELOPMENT ESTABLISHMENT, later AIR FIGHTING DEVELOPMENT UNIT
Formed 20th October 1934 at Northolt. Redesignated the Air Fighting Development Unit from 10th April 1940 at Northolt.

AF (.41–2.45)	*Spitfire I X4815 AF-S, IIA P8252 AF-E, VB AA937 AF-O; Defiant I V1121 AF-V; Boston III W8286 AF-Z; Hurricane IID KX227 AF-L.*
Also used	*Gladiator I K8040, II N5625; Hurricane I P2989, IIA Z2448, IV KW800; Spitfire I X4257, VA P8262, VC BR372, VI BR289, VIII JF299, IX BR140, XII EN223, XIV RB179, XIX PS853, F.21 LA201; Buffalo I AS430; Whirlwind I P6997; Kittyhawk I AK573; Tomahawk I AH770; Mohawk IV AR683; Airacobra I DS174; Mustang I AG360, IA FD442, III SR410, IVA KH704, X AM121; Martin-Baker MB.2 P9594; Typhoon IA R7595, IB DN622; Tempest V EJ529; Vigilant I HL432; Thunderbolt I HD169; Marauder I FK109; Hampden I AE373; Hudson V AM635; Ventura I AE762; Mosquito VI HJ666; Blenheim I L8850; Havoc I AX910, I (Pandora) BB903; Boston IIIA BZ363; Hotspur II BT483; Beaufighter 2056; Oxford II P6801; Anson I N9835; Mitchell II FL203; Wellington IC W5704; Lysander I K6127, IIIA V9517; Phoenix X2891; Magister L8061; Tiger Moth II R5252; Bf 109E AE479, Bf 109F-2 ES906, Bf 109G-6 TP814; Bf 110C-5 AX772; Fw 190A-4 PM679; He 111H-3 AW177; Fiat CR.42 BT474; Ju 88A-5 EE205; Welkin I DX286; Meteor F.3 EE243.*

Disbanded 1st October 1944 at Wittering to become the Air Fighting Development Squadron within the Central Fighter Establishment.

AIR FIGHTING DEVELOPMENT SQUADRON – see Central Fighter Establishment

AIR FIGHTING DEVELOPMENT UNIT – see Air Fighting Development Establishment, later Air Fighting Development Unit

AIR FIGHTING DEVELOPMENT UNIT DEMONSTRATION SQUADRON
Formed 27th November 1942 at Fowlmere from the British Aircraft Circus Flight.

Spitfire II.

Disbanded 15th February 1944 at Wittering.

AIR FIGHTING SCHOOL (MIDDLE EAST)
Formed 25th December 1941 at Edku, Egypt.

Hurricane I Z4428 S.

Disbanded 5th April 1942 at Bilbeis and absorbed by 1 Middle East Training School.

AIR FIGHTING TRAINING UNIT
Formed 23rd February 1943 at Amarda Road, India.

Blenheim IV, V AZ867; Harvard IIB FS792; Vengeance I AP114; Wellington IC HX742; Fulmar II X8532; Spitfire VC MA393; Liberator VI; Thunderbolt I FL749.

Disbanded 10th September 1945 at Amarda Road and absorbed by the Tactical and Weapon Development Unit.

AIR FORCES GULF COMMUNICATION SQUADRON
Formed 15th September 1967 at Muharraq, Bahrein, by redesignating the Middle East Command Communication Flight.

Pembroke C.1 WV744; Andover CC.2 XS611; Wessex HC.2 XR522 O.

Disbanded 8th August 1969 at Muharraq.

AIR FORCES WESTERN EUROPE COMMUNICATION FLIGHT
Formed December 1948 at Toussus-le-Noble, France.

Anson XIX TX231; Devon C.1 VP981.

Disbanded April 1951 at Melun-Villaroche, France, to become the Allied Air Forces Central Europe Communication Flight.

1 AIR GUNNERS SCHOOL
Formed 21st June 1941 at Pembrey by redesignating 1 Bombing and Gunnery School.

Tutor K3357; Audax K4859; Blenheim I L1227, IV N3536; Battle L5674; Manchester I L7484; Anson I MG404 3; Spitfire IIA P8035 22, VB BM211 7; Lysander TT.III R9114, IIIA W6944, TT.IIIA V9809; Magister T9672; Hurricane I V6803; Defiant TT.II AA470; Wellington III X3945 W, X JA346 M; Master II DL289, III DL850; Martinet I HN861 24.

Disbanded 21st June 1945 at Pembrey.

2 AIR GUNNERS SCHOOL
Formed 10th July 1941 at Dalcross.

Tutor K6102; Botha I L6110; Magister L8153; Defiant I N1759 42; Lysander I L4691, TT.III R9062 U, IIIA V9437, TT.IIIA V9812; Oxford II N4760; Tiger Moth II N5475; Battle Trainer R7378; Master III W8540; Moth AW133; Wellington III BK240, X JA466; Martinet I JN497 D1; Spitfire VII MD126 C; Anson I MG696 38.

Disbanded 24th November 1945 at Dalcross.

3 AIR GUNNERS SCHOOL
Formed 20th April 1942 at Castle Kennedy.

Tutor K3387 M7; Botha I L6373; Battle K7565, Battle Trainer P6617; Spitfire I X4253; Manchester I R5829; Defiant I N1742; Magister R1847; Lysander TT.III T1425; Moth X5127; Master III DM156; Martinet I HN968; Queen Martinet I HN909; Wellington III X3866, X LP929 T; Anson I LT304 3.

Disbanded 21st June 1945 at Castle Kennedy.

4 AIR GUNNERS SCHOOL
Formed 17th March 1942 at Morpeth.

Tutor K3256; Magister L8359; Lysander I L4693, TT.I R2578, TT.III R9070, IIIA V9544; Botha I L6122 28; Manchester I L7419; Battle Trainer P6666; Moth Minor X5133; Master II DK957 B; Martinet I JN638 19; Anson I LV300 H.

Disbanded 9th December 1944 at Morpeth.

5 AIR GUNNERS SCHOOL
Proposed formation cancelled. Was to have formed from 24th July 1941 at Castle Kennedy.

6 AIR GUNNERS SCHOOL
Formed 22nd October 1942 at Mona.

No aircraft allocated.

Disbanded 6th November 1942 at Mona in favour of relocating 3 Air Gunners School.

7 AIR GUNNERS SCHOOL
Formed 9th June 1941 at Stormy Down by redesignating 7 Bombing and Gunnery School.

Whitley I K7206 V, II K7249 K, III K8972 Z, IV K9054, V T4154 T; Battle L5637; Defiant I N1546; Lysander I R2626, TT.I R2632, TT.III P1719, IIIA W6954, TT.IIIA V9788; Anson I LT830 3; Moth Minor X9297; Dominie I R5924; Tiger Moth BB700; Master II DL407; Martinet I JN510 9; Wellington VIII LB147.

Disbanded 2nd September 1944 at Stormy Down.

8 AIR GUNNERS SCHOOL
Formed 9th June 1941 at Evanton by redesignating 8 Bombing and Gunnery School.

Tutor K3294; Whitley II K7236, III K8983, V N1428 77; Battle L5732; Botha I L6333; Manchester I L7455; Lysander I R2598, III R9026, IIIA W6958, TT.IIIA V9547; Magister R1961; Tiger Moth II T5493; Moth AW134; Master II DM237, III DM158; Martinet I HN978 W; Anson I LT304 2B.

Disbanded 26th August 1944 at Evanton.

9 AIR GUNNERS SCHOOL
Formed 7th July 1941 at Llandwrog.

Whitley II K7219, III K8941, IV K9041, V N1422; Battle K9385; Lysander TT.I L4699, II P1715, III R9121, TT.III R9104, IIIA W6956; Anson I MG495.

Disbanded 13th June 1942 at Llandwrog.

10 AIR GUNNERS SCHOOL
Formed 24th July 1941 at Castle Kennedy.

Nil (7.41–4.46)	Whitley III K8944; Henley III L3333; Botha I L6229; Manchester I L7483; Magister T9768; Defiant I N1540 33; Lysander III T1516 D, IIIA W6940; Master III W8656; Moth X5127; Gipsy Moth DG579; Spitfire IIA P7521, VB AD451 37; Anson I MG104 23; Wellington III X3600, X NC825 8; Dominie I X7368; Martinet I HP272-53.
FFA (4.46–6.46)	Wellington X HE742 FFA-L.
FFB (4.46–6.46)	Allocated but not used.
FFC (4.46–6.46)	Allocated but not used.
FFD (4.46–6.46)	Wellington X; Horsa II TL555 FFD-O.

Disbanded 30th June 1946 at Barrow.

Reformed 1st December 1946 at Valley.

No aircraft allocated – the title was used to operate the Master Diversion Airfield.

Disbanded 1st July 1947 at Valley.

11 AIR GUNNERS SCHOOL
Formed 2nd May 1943 at Andreas.

Nil (5.43–4.46)	Tutor K6113; Magister R1853; Master II AZ502; Wellington III DF572 B, X HE927 T; Martinet I JN460; Anson I LT950 A7; Spitfire VII MD112.
FFE (4.46–10.47)	Allocated but not used.
FFF (4.46–10.47)	Wellington X LP914 FFF-A.
FFG (4.46–10.47)	Master II DM325 FFG-O.
Also used	Spitfire XVI TB330; Harvard IIB KF256.

Disbanded 15th October 1947 at Jurby.

12 AIR GUNNERS SCHOOL
Formed 1st August 1943 at Bishop's Court.

Tutor K6100; Anson I LT336 J4; Wellington X LN836; Martinet I MS618 NS.

Disbanded 31st May 1945 at Bishop's Court and absorbed by 7 Air Navigation School.

13 AIR GUNNERS SCHOOL
Formed 21st November 1943 at El Ballah, Egypt.

Harvard IIA EX322, III EZ170, TT.III EZ160; Anson I LT769.

Disbanded 8th July 1945 at El Ballah.

1 AIR GUNNERY SCHOOL (INDIA)
Formed 13th May 1943 at Bairagarh, India, by redesignating 1 Armament Training Unit.

Audax K2003; Lysander II N1261; Hurricane X AG139, IIB BG675, IIC BN494, XIIA PJ739; Blenheim V EH378; Defiant TT.II AA371; Vengeance TT.I AN852, IA EZ874, II AN740, IV FD238; Liberator VI EW259 J; Harvard IIB FE610; Wellington IC HX773; Argus II FS517; Anson I LT894.

Disbanded 1st July 1945 at Bairagarh.

AIR GUNNERY TRAINING UNIT
Formed 30th April 1943 at Colombo, Ceylon.

No aircraft known.

Disbanded 4th April 1944 at Ratmalana, Ceylon, and absorbed by 20 Armament Practice Camp.

AIR HEADQUARTERS AUSTRIA COMMUNICATION FLIGHT, later AUSTRIA COMMISSION FLIGHT
Formed 5th October 1945 at Klagenfurt, Austria. Redesignated the Austria Commission Flight from 15th August 1946.

Fi 156; Bf 108; Ju 52/3; Kl 35; Dakota III KG528, IV KG528; Auster IV MT300, V RT604; Argus III KK432; Proctor III LZ642; Expeditor II HB288; Spitfire IX LZ841; Wellington X MF402; Anson XII PH665 AA.

Disbanded 1st November 1947 at Klagenfurt.

AIR HEADQUARTERS BENGAL COMMUNICATION UNIT
Formed 24th March 1943 at Barrackpore by redesignating the Bengal Communication Flight and absorbing elements of 221 and 224 Group Communication Flights.

Dominie I X7408; Dragonfly V4734; Hurricane IIB Z5687; Harvard IIB FE357; Yale Z-32; Lockheed 12A LV760; Puss Moth LV766; Zlin 212; Tourist MA926; Leopard Moth AX804; Anson I LT133; Argus II FS518; Tiger Moth T1779.

Disbanded 1st December 1943 at Comilla, India, to become the Tactical Air Force (Burma) Communication Squadron.

AIR HEADQUARTERS BURMA COMMUNICATION FLIGHT – see Headquarters Royal Air Force Burma Communication Squadron, later Air Headquarters Burma Communication Squadron, later Air Headquarters Burma Communication Flight

AIR HEADQUARTERS BURMA COMMUNICATION SQUADRON – see Headquarters Royal Air Force Burma Communication Squadron, later Air Headquarters Burma Communication Squadron, later Air Headquarters Burma Communication Flight

AIR HEADQUARTERS CEYLON COMMUNICATION FLIGHT
Formed 15th October 1945 at Ratmalana, Ceylon, by redesignating 222 Group Communication Flight.

Auster V TJ212.

Disbanded 15th January 1947 at Negombo, Ceylon.

AIR HEADQUARTERS COMMUNICATION FLIGHT IRAQ AND PERSIA
Formed 1st July 1945 at Habbaniya, Iraq, by redesignating the Communication Flight, Iraq and Persia.

Anson I DJ282, PH727; Sunderland III EK595; Wellington X LN327, XIII JA258.

Disbanded 1st March 1946 at Habbaniya to become Air Headquarters Iraq Communication Flight.

AIR HEADQUARTERS EAST AFRICA COMMUNICATION FLIGHT – see Air Headquarters East Africa Communication Squadron, later Air Headquarters East Africa Communication Flight

AIR HEADQUARTERS EAST AFRICA COMMUNICATION SQUADRON, later AIR HEADQUARTERS EAST AFRICA COMMUNICATION FLIGHT
Formed 1st November 1940 at Nairobi, Kenya, by merging 1 (Communication) Flight, Kenya Auxiliary Air Unit and the Communications Flight, Dar es Salaam of the Air Defence Unit, Tanganyika.

Dragon; Dragon Rapide; Leopard Moth; Puss Moth.

Disbanded 15th December 1941 at Nairobi to become 207 Group Communication Flight.

Reformed 16th November 1942 at Eastleigh, Kenya, as the Air Headquarters East Africa Communication Flight by redesignating 207 Group Communication Flight.

Luscombe; Vega Gull; Leopard Moth; Puss Moth; Dragon Rapide K11; Magister; Blenheim; Hudson; Anson I AX405; Dakota; Savoia-Marchetti S.73; Savoia-Marchetti S.79.

Disbanded February 1944 at Eastleigh to become the Air Transport Flight.

Reformed 1st August 1944 at Eastleigh as the Air Headquarters East Africa Communication Flight by redesignating the Air Transport Flight.

Dragon Rapide K11; Blenheim IV Z9648; Hurricane; Hudson VI EW940; Baltimore IV FA567, V FW804; Anson I NL154, XII PH708, XIX TX156; Proctor IV NP340; Dakota KP238; Valetta C.1 VW184.

Disbanded 15th September 1951 at Eastleigh to become the Eastleigh Communication Flight.

Reformed September 1954 at Eastleigh as the Air Headquarters East Africa Communication Flight.

Auster VI VF486.

Disbanded (date unknown) at Eastleigh.

AIR HEADQUARTERS EASTERN MEDITERRANEAN COMMUNICATION FLIGHT
Formed 1st February 1944 at Mariut, Egypt by redesignating 201 Group Communication Flight.

Audax K7525; Gladiator I K7931; Magister N5422; Beaufighter IC T3301; Vega Gull X1032; Blenheim IV Z7701, V BA151; Hudson VI FK397; Baltimore V FW490; Argus II FS540; Traveler I FZ433; Spitfire VC JK230; Harvard II AJ838, IIA EX814; Wellington IC HX637, XI HZ284; Proctor III HM398; Anson I AW862, XI PH611.

Disbanded 15th March 1946 at Mariut.

AIR HEADQUARTERS EGYPT COMMUNICATION FLIGHT
Formed 31st August 1944 at Heliopolis, Egypt.

No aircraft known.

Disbanded 1st April 1946 at Heliopolis, and absorbed by the Mediterranean and Middle East Communication Squadron.

AIR HEADQUARTERS GREECE COMMUNICATION FLIGHT
Formed January 1945 at Hassani, Greece.

Argus II HB589, III KK427; Storch HK987; Wellington X HZ718; Proctor III HM306; Auster VI TW635; Anson I MG117, XII PH722.

Disbanded 11th January 1947 at Hassani to become the Royal Air Force Delegation (Greece) Communication Flight.

AIR HEADQUARTERS HONG KONG COMMUNICATION SQUADRON
Formed 12th September 1945 at Kai Tak, Hong Kong.

Harvard IIB KF134; Beaufighter X RD311.

Officially disbanded 15th January 1947 at Kai Tak although deemed inactive from 21st August 1946.

AIR HEADQUARTERS INDIA COMMUNICATION FLIGHT
Formed 16th October 1928 at the Air Park, Lahore.

D.H.9; F.2B J7648; Moth; Avro 642 L9166; Envoy N9108; Leopard Moth; Lockheed 12A V4732; Blenheim IV V6079; Dominie I X7451.

Disbanded 21st January 1942 at (location unknown).

AIR HEADQUARTERS INDIA COMMUNICATION SQUADRON
Formed 1st March 1946 at Willingdon, India, by redesignating the Base Air Forces South East Asia Communication Squadron.

Dakota III KG507, IV KN682; Harvard IIB FE775; Tiger Moth I NL942; Spitfire XI PL907; York I MW102; Auster; Anson XIX VL333 R.

Disbanded 15th August 1947 at Palam, India, to become the Supreme Commanders Headquarters (Air) Communication Squadron.

AIR HEADQUARTERS INDIA COMMUNICATION UNIT
Formed 25th May 1942 at Willingdon Airport, New Delhi, India.

Lockheed 12A LV761; Lockheed 18 HX793; Dominie I X7446; Hornet Moth LR227; Gull Six MA927; Leopard Moth AX802; Puss Moth LV766; Eagle II MA945; DC-3 MA925; Hudson IIIA FH431, VI FK504; Blenheim V BA592; Dakota III FD879; Harvard IIB FH116; Argus II FZ729; Anson I LT603; Gipsy Moth MA941; Tiger Moth MA947; Expeditor I HB160; Proctor III LZ692.

Disbanded 30th September 1944 at Palam and absorbed by the Air Command Southeast Asia Communication Squadron.

AIR HEADQUARTERS IRAQ COMMAND TRAINING FLIGHT
Formed by May 1927 at Hinaidi, Iraq.

F.2B C1027.

Existed until at least September 1928 at Hinaidi.

AIR HEADQUARTERS IRAQ COMMUNICATION FLIGHT
Formed 1st March 1946 at Habbaniya, Iraq, by redesignating the Air Headquarters Communication Flight Iraq and Persia.

Argus I EV759; Baltimore IV FA551; Sunderland III EK595; Lockheed 18 AX686; Proctor III LZ573, IV NP160; Wellington XIII JA258; Ventura I FN975, V JS947; Brigand B.1 RH812; Dakota IV KJ880; Anson XII PH542, XIX VL303; Devon C.1 VP956; Valetta C.1 VW806.

Disbanded 5th August 1954 at Habbaniya to become the Iraq Communication Flight.

AIR HEADQUARTERS ITALY COMMUNICATION FLIGHT – see Air Headquarters Italy Communication Squadron, later Air Headquarters Italy Communication Flight

AIR HEADQUARTERS ITALY COMMUNICATION SQUADRON, later AIR HEADQUARTERS ITALY COMMUNICATION FLIGHT
Formed 10th November 1945 at Marcianise, Italy by redesignating the Mediterranean and Middle East Communication Squadron. Redesignated Air Headquarters Italy Communication Flight from 15th August 1946.

Hudson IIIA FK762, VI FK719; Dakota III FD892; Mitchell 43-27774; Wellington; Baltimore; Argus II, III; Auster III, IV MT224, V; Fi156; Anson I, XII PH748 V; Spitfire VB ER463, IX NH398; Auster III MT403, IV MT224, V RT604.

Disbanded 27th September 1947 at Udine, Italy.

AIR HEADQUARTERS LEVANT COMMUNICATION FLIGHT
Formed 1st April 1942 at Lydda, Palestine, by redesignating the Communications Flight Ramleh.

Audax K7515; Hart K5050; Hind L7174; Magister R1954; Lysander I R2648; Wellington IC HD952; Hawk HK863.

Disbanded 1st June 1943 at Lydda to become the Communication Flight, Lydda.

Reformed 1st October 1945 at Lydda by redesignating the Communication Flight, Lydda.

Magister L8277; Spitfire VC ES188, XI PM141; Proctor III HM458; Anson I NK219, XII PH605.

Disbanded 15th May 1948 at Amman, Jordan.

Reformed 23rd June 1955 at Habbaniya, Iraq, by redesignating the Iraq Communication Flight.

Anson XIX TX182; Vampire T.11 XE889; Sycamore HR.14 XG511; Pembroke C.1 WV700 C; Meteor T.7 WA627, F.8 WK954 G.

Disbanded 1st April 1958 at Sharjah, Oman.

AIR HEADQUARTERS MALAYA COMMUNICATION SQUADRON
Formed 1st November 1945 at Kallang, Singapore, by redesignating 224 Group Communication Flight.

Dakota III KG458, IV KJ822; Sentinel II KJ420; Expeditor II KN134; Spitfire VIII MT522; Beaufighter X RD743; Harvard IIB FE698; Auster III NJ992, V TJ431.

Disbanded 15th January 1947 at Changi, Singapore, having been deemed ineffective from 21st August 1946.

AIR HEADQUARTERS MALTA COMMUNICATION FLIGHT, later AIR HEADQUARTERS MALTA COMMUNICATION SQUADRON
Formed 1st March 1944 at Hal Far, Malta, by redesignating the Malta Communication, Ferry Unit and Air Sea Rescue Flight. Redesignated Air Headquarters, Malta Communication Squadron from 31st May 1946.

Walrus II Z1813; Spitfire IV BR665, VB EP714, VC JK777 P, IX EN199; Hurricane IIC KZ845; Wellington IC AD650, VIII LB213, X MF445; Argus II FS651; Magister L8217; Baltimore V FW811; Proctor I P6116, III LZ732, IV NP275; Dakota III KK129, IV KN279; Anson I MG683, XII PH603, XIX TX172; Beaufighter X RD809; Devon C.1 VP955; Valetta C.1 VW822, C.2 VX580; Pembroke C.1 WV736; Chipmunk T.10 WB693; Vampire FB.9 WR239.

Disbanded 1st July 1954 at Luqa to become the Malta Communication and Target Towing Squadron.

AIR HEADQUARTERS MIDDLE EAST COMMUNICATION FLIGHT
Formed by February 1942 at (unknown location), Egypt.

Gladiator I K7982; Lysander II R1993; Audax K7541; Hart K4900; Wellington IC L7794; Hudson IV AE626; VI FK486.

Disbanded (date and location unknown) having existed until at least August 1942.

AIR HEADQUARTERS NETHERLANDS EAST INDIES COMMUNICATION SQUADRON
Formed 1st November 1945 at Mingaladon, Burma, by redesignating 221 Group Communication Flight.

Dakota IV KN618; Sentinel; Sea Otter I JM766; Auster.

Disbanded 21st August 1946 at Kemajoran, Java.

AIR HEADQUARTERS WESTERN DESERT COMMUNICATION FLIGHT – see Communication Flight, Air Headquarters Western Desert

AIR LANDING SCHOOL
Formed 15th October 1941 at Willingdon Airport, New Delhi, India.

Valentia K4634; Hudson III V9164; VI EW959; Wellington IC DV549; Dakota III FD837; Argus II FS524.

Disbanded 26th February 1944 at Chaklala, India, and absorbed by 3 Parachute Training School.

AIR MINISTRY METEOROLOGICAL FLIGHT, ALDERGROVE
Formed 28th September 1936 at Aldergrove within the Station Flight, Aldergrove. Redesignated 'C' Flight, Station Flight, Aldergrove from 27th May 1939.

Bulldog IIA K2144; Gauntlet II K5283; Gladiator II N5590.

Disbanded 15th January 1941 at Aldergrove to become 402 (Meteorological) Flight.

AIR MINISTRY SERVICING DEVELOPMENT UNIT
Formed 1st January 1947 at Wattisham.

York I MW124; Tempest V SN326; Meteor F.4 RA425, T.7 VW483; Anson T.20 VS527; Vampire F.3 VT855.

Disbanded 1st June 1950 at Wittering and merged with the Servicing Demonstration Parties to become the Central Servicing Development Establishment.

AIR MOVEMENTS DEVELOPMENT FLIGHT, later AIR MOVEMENTS DEVELOPMENT UNIT
Formed March 1958 at Abingdon. Redesignated the Air Movements Development Unit from 11th March 1958.

Anson XIX.

Disbanded 31st May 1965 at Abingdon to become the Air Transport Development Unit.

AIR MOVEMENTS DEVELOPMENT UNIT – see Air Movements Development Flight, later Air Movements Development Unit

AIR NAVIGATION AND BOMBING SCHOOL
Formed 1st February 1944 at Jurby by redesignating 5 Air Observer School.

Anson I MG782 M4, X NK702; Wellington III DF603, X NA739.

Disbanded 31st May 1945 at Jurby to become 5 Air Navigation School.

AIR NAVIGATION SCHOOL
Formed 25th January 1935 at Andover by redesignating the Air Pilotage School.

Prefect K5064.

Disbanded 6th January 1936 at Manston and merged with the Navigation School to become the School of Air Navigation.

1 AIR NAVIGATION SCHOOL
Formed 9th April 1947 at Topcliffe by redesignating 5 Air Navigation School.

FFI (4.47–4.51)	*Anson I DJ625 FFI-J, XIX VM315 FFI-C, T.21 VV304 FFI-X; Oxford I DF220 FFI-C.*
FFJ (4.47–4.51)	*Tiger Moth II N9252 FFJ-Z; Anson I EF871 FFJ-C, T.21 VS569 FFJ-B; Wellington X NA781 FFJ-N.*
FFK (9.46–4.51)	*Tiger Moth II L6944 FFK-V; Wellington X NA781 FFK-Y.*
Nil (4.51–5.54)	*Anson XII PH554; Valetta T.3 VX564 P; Varsity T.1 WJ892 Q.*

Disbanded 1st May 1954 at Hullavington.

Reformed 15th March 1957 at Topcliffe.

Marathon T.11 XA258 L; Valetta T.3 WG259 K; Vampire NF.10 WM714 R, T.11 XD535 Y; Varsity T.1 WJ950; Meteor T.7 WF826 Z, NF.14 WS737 H; Dominie T.1 XS714 K; Chipmunk T.10 WG460.

Disbanded 26th August 1970 at Stradishall and absorbed by 6 Flying Training School.

2 AIR NAVIGATION SCHOOL
Formed 4th June 1947 at Bishop's Court by redesignating 7 Air Navigation School.

FFM (6.47–4.51)	*Oxford I AT680 FFM-K; Anson I LV273 FFM-L; Tiger Moth II DE378 FFM-Z.*
FFN (6.47–4.51)	*Oxford I LT521 FFN-N; Anson I NK401 FFN-E.*
FFO (6.47–4.51)	*Wellington X NC430 FFO-J.*
FFP (6.47–4.51)	*Anson T.21 VS563 FFP-P.*
Nil (4.51–6.70)	*Anson XII PH565, XIX VM394 D, T.20 VS533, T.21 WJ547 G; Spitfire F.22 PK383; Marathon T.11 XA254 L; Vampire NF.10 WP234 K; Meteor T.7 VZ644 Z, NF.14 WS737 H; Valetta T.3 WJ461 D, T.4 WG256 S; Varsity T.1 WL625 A.*

Disbanded 1st May 1970 at Gaydon and absorbed by 6 Flying Training School.

3 AIR NAVIGATION SCHOOL
Formed 5th January 1948 at Thornhill, Rhodesia, by merging elements of 4 and 5 Flying Training Schools.

W	*Tiger Moth II T7785 W-E.*
X	*Harvard IIA EX521 X-A, IIB KF541.*
Z	*Anson I NK440 Z-J, T.20 VM415 Z-T.*

Also used   Harvard III EX956 8; Anson T.21 WD408 X.

Disbanded 28th September 1951 at Thornhill and absorbed by 5 Flying Training School.

Reformed 3rd March 1952 at Bishop's Court.

Anson XIX PH845, T.21 VV302 Q; Valetta T.3 WJ471; Varsity T.1 WJ889 T.

Disbanded 14th April 1954 at Bishop's Court.

4 AIR NAVIGATION SCHOOL
Formed 22nd September 1952 at Langford Lodge.

No aircraft allocated.

Disbanded 15th November 1952 at Langford Lodge to become 5 Air Navigation School.

5 AIR NAVIGATION SCHOOL
Formed 31st May 1945 at Jurby by redesignating the Air Navigation and Bombing School.

Nil (5.45–4.46)	
FFI (4.46–4,47)	*Oxford I LX274 FFI-F; Anson I DJ625 FFI-J, T.21 VS570 FFI-D.*
FFJ (4.46–4.47)	*Wellington X NA968 FFJ-N; Anson I EG353 FFJ-B, T.21 VV242 FFJ-U; Tiger Moth II N9252 FFJ-Z.*
FFK (4.46–4.47)	*Wellington X RP567 FFK-A; Tiger Moth II L6944 FFK-V.*

Disbanded 9th April 1947 at Topcliffe to become 1 Air Navigation School.

Reformed 5th March 1951 at Lindholme.

Anson XII PH554, XIX TX256, T.20 VS508, T.21 WD407; Wellington X PG267 A; Valetta T.3 WG256.

Disbanded 15th November 1952 at Lindholme.

Reformed 15th November 1952 at Langford Lodge by redesignating 4 Navigation School.

Anson XIX TX160, T.21 WD414.

Disbanded 31st January 1953 at Langford Lodge.

6 AIR NAVIGATION SCHOOL
Formed 15th February 1952 at Lichfield by redesignating 104 Flying Refresher School.

Wellington X NA834 F; Anson XII PH558, XIX TX191, T.21 WB455 X, T.22 VV239; Valetta T.3 WG267 A; Varsity T.1 WJ950.

Disbanded 1st December 1953 at Lichfield.

7 AIR NAVIGATION SCHOOL
Formed 31st May 1945 at Bishop's Court by redesignating 7 (Observers) Advanced Flying Unit.

Nil (5.45–4.46)	*Anson I R9706; Wellington X.*
FFM (4.46–6.47)	*Anson I MG470 FFM-S.*
FFN (4.46–6.47)	*Anson I NK401 FFN-E.*
FFO (4.46–6.47)	*Wellington X HE214 FFO-L.*
FFP (4.46–6.47)	*Allocated but no evidence of use.*
Also used	*Proctor III DX200; Anson X NK355.*

Disbanded 4th June 1947 at Bishop's Court to become 2 Air Navigation School.

10 AIR NAVIGATION SCHOOL
Formed 11th June 1945 at Dumfries from an element of 10 (Observers) Advanced Flying Unit.

Nil (6.45–4.46)	*Wellington X.*
FFR	*Allocated but no evidence of use.*
FFS (4.46–3.48)	*Wellington X NC750 FFS-B.*
FFT (4.46–3.48)	*Anson I NL127 FFT-E.*
FFU	*Allocated but no evidence of use.*
Also used	*Magister T9889; Oxford I LB474.*

Disbanded 1st March 1948 at Driffield and absorbed by 1 and 2 Air Navigation Schools.

31 AIR NAVIGATION SCHOOL
Formed 11th November 1940 at Port Albert, Ontario, Canada, by redesignating 1 School of Air Navigation.

Anson I N9714, II 7210, III 6152, V 12007; Stinson 105 3476.

Disbanded 17th February 1945 at Port Albert.

32 AIR NAVIGATION SCHOOL
Formed 18th August 1941 at Charlottetown, Prince Edward Island, Canada.

Anson I L9158.

Disbanded 15th September 1942 at Charlottetown.

33 AIR NAVIGATION SCHOOL
Formed 3rd May 1941 at Mount Hope, Ontario, Canada.

Anson I N6018 34, V 6337 21.

Disbanded 6th October 1944 at Mount Hope.

AIR NAVIGATION SCHOOL, INDIA
Formed 24th July 1942 at Andheri, India, as an element of the General Reconnaissance School.

Dominie I.

Disbanded 24th October 1942 at Andheri and merged with the General Reconnaissance School to become the General Reconnaissance and Air Navigation School.

AIR OBSERVATION POST SCHOOL
Formed 1st May 1950 at Middle Wallop by redesignating 227 Operational Conversion Unit.

BD (5.50–4.51)	Tiger Moth I K4271, II N6476 BD-N; Auster V TW505 BD-E, T.7 WE558 BD-N; Chipmunk T.10 WG462 BD-L; Prentice T.1 VS629.
PF (5.50–4.51)	Oxford I PK284 PF-A.

Disbanded 3rd April 1953 at Middle Wallop to become the Light Aircraft School.

AIR OBSERVATION POST TRAINING FLIGHT/TEAM
Formed 30th September 1943 at Sétif, Algeria. Operating as an element within the Polish Air Observation Post Operational Training Unit at Eboli, Italy, by October 1944.

Auster III NJ899, V RT622.

Disbanded 11th December 1944 at Eboli and probably absorbed by 663 Squadron.

1 AIR OBSERVERS NAVIGATION SCHOOL
Formed 31st October 1939 at Prestwick by redesignating 1 Civil Air Navigation School.

Anson I N9739 7; Fokker F.XXII HM159; Fokker F.XXXVI HM161; D.H.89 V4724; D.H.89A Z7253; Magister T9889.

During October 1940, an element of the unit moved to Queenstown, South Africa, where it opened on 30th April 1941 as 47 Air School, SAAF.

Disbanded 19th July 1941 at Prestwick and absorbed by 7 Air Observers Navigation School.

2 AIR OBSERVERS NAVIGATION SCHOOL
Formed 1st November 1939 at Yatesbury by redesignating 2 Civil Air Navigation School.

Anson I L7930.

Disbanded 14th December 1940 at Yatesbury.

3 AIR OBSERVERS NAVIGATION SCHOOL
Formed 1st November 1939 at Desford by redesignating 3 Civil Air Navigation School.

Anson I L7923.

Disbanded 12th June 1940 at Weston-super-Mare and absorbed by 5 Air Observers Navigation School.

Reformed 17th February 1941 at Bobbington (later Halfpenny Green).

Botha L6138 C7; Anson I K6254; Moth Minor BK844; Magister L8230.

Disbanded 18th October 1941 at Halfpenny Green to become 3 Air Observers School.

4 AIR OBSERVERS NAVIGATION SCHOOL
Formed 1st November 1939 at Ansty by redesignating 4 Civil Air Navigation School.

Anson I N5118; Botha I W5049.

Disbanded 30th August 1941 at Watchfield.

5 AIR OBSERVERS NAVIGATION SCHOOL
Formed 1st November 1939 at Weston-super-Mare by redesignating 5 Civil Air Navigation School.

Anson I K8768; Tiger Moth II N6467.

Closed 22nd August 1940 at Weston-super-Mare.

Reopened 4th November 1940 at Oudtshoorn, South Africa.

Anson I.

Disbanded 11th November 1940 at Oudtshoorn to become 45 Air School, SAAF.

6 AIR OBSERVERS NAVIGATION SCHOOL
Formed 1st November 1939 at Staverton by redesignating 6 Civil Air Navigation School.

Anson I N9537; Demon K4522; D.H.89A Z7256; Whitney Straight DR612; Percival Q-6 X9328.

Disbanded 17th January 1942 at Staverton to become 6 Air Observers School.

7 AIR OBSERVERS NAVIGATION SCHOOL
Formed 1st November 1939 at Scone by redesignating 7 Civil Air Navigation School.

Dragon Rapide G-AFMA; Anson I R3387.

Disbanded 1st June 1940 at Scone.

8 AIR OBSERVERS NAVIGATION SCHOOL
Formed 1st November 1939 at Sywell by redesignating 8 Civil Air Navigation School.

Anson I N4935.

Disbanded 25th November 1939 at Sywell and absorbed by 9 Air Observers Navigation School.

9 AIR OBSERVERS NAVIGATION SCHOOL
Formed 1st November 1939 at Squires Gate by redesignating 9 Civil Air Navigation School.

Anson I R3347.

Disbanded 27th May 1940 at Squires Gate.

10 AIR OBSERVERS NAVIGATION SCHOOL
Formed 1st November 1939 at Grangemouth by redesignating 10 Civil Air Navigation School.

Anson I N9739.

Disbanded 2nd December 1939 at Grangemouth and absorbed by 1 Air Observers Navigation School.

11 AIR OBSERVERS NAVIGATION SCHOOL
Formed 20th November 1939 at Hamble from the Air Service Training School.

Wessex G-AAGW; Avro Five G-ABBY; Avro 652 G-ACRM; Envoy G-ADAZ; Dragonfly G-AEWZ; Anson I K6287.

Disbanded 19th July 1941 at Watchfield.

AIR OBSERVERS SCHOOL, NORTH COATES
Formed 1st January 1936 at North Coates Fitties by redesignating an element of the Air Armament School, Leuchars.

Gordon K2684; Cloud K4300; Wallace I K3907, II K6044; Hart Special K4420; Anson I K8826.

Disbanded 1st November 1937 at North Coates to become 2 Air Armament School.

1 AIR OBSERVERS SCHOOL
Formed 1st March 1938 at North Coates Fitties by redesignating 2 Air Armament School.

Gordon K1746; Wallace I K3569, II K8691; Henley III L3340; Battle L5256; Magister P2442.

Disbanded 3rd September 1939 at Penrhos to become 9 Air Observers School.

Reformed 13th September 1941 at Wigtown.

Moth AW147; Blenheim I L1163; Lysander III R9071, IIIA V9806; Anson I W2631; Tiger Moth II T6805.

Disbanded 1st February 1942 at Wigtown to become 1 (Observers) Advanced Flying Unit.

2 AIR OBSERVERS SCHOOL
Formed 15th November 1938 at Acklington by redesignating 7 Armament Training Station.

Seal K3535; Overstrand K4557; Hind K4654; Harrow II K7003.

Disbanded 3rd September 1939 at Warmwell and merged with 6 Armament Training Station to become 10 Air Observers School.

Reformed 1st June 1941 at Millom by redesignating 2 Bombing and Gunnery School.

Anson I AX539 11; Botha I W5053; Lysander III T1449, IIIA V9892; Battle L5633; Oxford I N6257; Moth X5051.

Disbanded 18th February 1942 at Millom to become 2 (Observers) Advanced Flying Unit.

3 AIR OBSERVERS SCHOOL
Formed 17th April 1939 at Aldergrove by redesignating 2 Armament Training Station.

Wallace I K3567, II K6014; Hart K3892; Heyford III K5192; Henley III L3375; Battle L4995.

Disbanded 1st December 1939 at Aldergrove to become 3 Bombing and Gunnery School.

Reformed 18th October 1941 at Bobbington by redesignating 3 Air Observers Navigation School.

Anson I K8731; Oxford I N1337; Blenheim I L1218; Botha I W5054.

Disbanded 11th April 1942 at Bobbington to become 3 (Observers) Advanced Flying Unit.

4 AIR OBSERVERS SCHOOL
Formed 17th April 1939 at West Freugh by redesignating 4 Armament Training Station.

Heyford III K5187; Wallace II K6068; Harrow II K7003; Magister P2403.

Disbanded 1st November 1939 at West Freugh to become 4 Bombing and Gunnery School.

Reformed 14th June 1941 at West Freugh by redesignating 4 Bombing and Gunnery School.

Gauntlet K7799; Battle K9233, Battle Trainer V1221; Botha I L6394 37; Manchester I L7492; Oxford I N4631; Lysander TT.I R2598, TT.III R9133; Tiger Moth II T6556; Anson I W2662 2M; Moth AW160; Dominie I X7386; Master III W8561.

Disbanded 11th June 1943 at West Freugh to become 4 (Observers) Advanced Flying Unit.

5 AIR OBSERVERS SCHOOL
Formed 18th September 1939 at Jurby by redesignating 5 Armament Training Station.

Battle K7662; Blenheim I K7141; Henley III L3393; Hampden I L4206; Magister P2442.

Disbanded 1st December 1939 at Jurby to become 5 Bombing and Gunnery School.

Reformed 19th July 1941 at Jurby by redesignating 5 Bombing and Gunnery School.

Tutor K4808; Anson I MG669 W2; Blenheim I K7118, IV N6239; Battle L5636; Master I N9069; Hampden I P1300; Hereford I N9076; Moth BD163; Lysander I R2651, II N1320, III T1444 G5; Hurricane I P3881; Martinet I MS726.

Disbanded 1st February 1944 at Jurby to become the Air Navigation and Bombing School.

6 AIR OBSERVERS SCHOOL
Formed 17th January 1942 at Staverton by redesignating 6 Air Observers Navigation School.

Tutor K3319; Tiger Moth II N9464; Moth HM582; Anson I DG974 U2; Rapide AW155; Magister T9802.

Disbanded 11th June 1943 at Staverton to become 6 (Observers) Advanced Flying Unit.

7 AIR OBSERVERS SCHOOL
Formed 1st September 1939 at Stormy Down by redesignating 9 Armament Training Station.

Wallace I K3564, II K6034; Harrow I K6964, II K6986; Battle L5001; Henley III L3360.

Disbanded 1st December 1939 at Stormy Down to become 7 Bombing and Gunnery School.

Reformed 17th May 1943 at Bishop's Court.

Tutor K6089; Gipsy Moth AV991; Anson I N9669.

Disbanded 15th February 1944 at Bishop's Court to become 7 (Observers) Advanced Flying Unit.

8 AIR OBSERVERS SCHOOL
Formed 3rd September 1939 at Evanton by redesignating 8 Armament Training Station.

Gordon K1772; Wallace II K4347; Harrow I K6942, II K6976; Battle L5026; Anson I N9590; Henley III L3317; Lysander IIIA V9802.

Disbanded 1st November 1939 at Evanton to become 8 Bombing and Gunnery School.

9 AIR OBSERVERS SCHOOL
Formed 3rd September 1939 at Penrhos by redesignating 1 Air Observers School.

Wallace I K4017, II K6028; Demon K5710; Harrow I K6939, II K7006.

Disbanded 1st November 1939 at Penrhos to become 9 Bombing and Gunnery School.

Reformed 14th June 1941 at Penrhos by redesignating 9 Bombing and Gunnery School.

Anson I K6181; Whitley II K7247, III K8987; Blenheim I K7050, IV P4858; Battle L5257; Hurricane I L1592; Defiant I N3340; Lysander I R2652, III R9012, IIIA V9890; Moth BD164.

Disbanded 1st May 1942 at Penrhos to become 9 (Observers) Advanced Flying Unit.

10 AIR OBSERVERS SCHOOL
Formed 3rd September 1939 at Warmwell by merging 2 Air Observers School and 6 Armament Training Station.

Overstrand J9187; Harrow I K6967; Henley III L3348.

Disbanded 1st January 1940 at Warmwell to become 10 Bombing and Gunnery School.

Reformed 13th September 1941 at Dumfries by redesignating 10 Bombing and Gunnery School.

Whitley II K7254, III K8978; Battle L5634, Battle Trainer P6666; Botha I L6132; Anson I AX413; Magister P2405; Dominie I X7402.

Disbanded 1st May 1942 at Dumfries to become 10 (Observers) Advanced Flying Unit.

AIR PHOTOGRAPHIC DEVELOPMENT UNIT
Formed 8th August 1947 at Benson by redesignating the Photographic Reconnaissance Development Unit.

Wellington X RP396; Spitfire XIX PM652; Mosquito PR.34 VL613, B.35 TK632; Lancaster I TW669.

Disbanded 1st March 1950 at Benson.

AIR PILOTAGE FLIGHT
Formed 5th February 1923 at Calshot.

Felixstowe F.2A N4437; Felixstowe F.5 N4193; Southampton S1040.

Disbanded December 1926 at Calshot to become the Navigation School.

Reformed by early 1933 as the Air Pilotage Flight, being an element of Royal Air Force Station, Andover.

No aircraft known.

Disbanded 5th May 1933 at Andover to become the Air Pilotage School.

AIR PILOTAGE SCHOOL
Formed 23rd December 1919 at Andover by redesignating the School of Air Pilotage.

Pup C263; F.2B E2870; D.H.9A E745; Avro 504K E3498; Snipe E6201.

Disbanded 15th January 1923 at Andover to become 11 Squadron.

Reformed 26th October 1931 at Northolt as a Flight of 24 Squadron.

Tutor K1231.

Disbanded April 1932 at Northolt.

Reformed 5th May 1933 at Andover by redesignating the Air Pilotage Flight element of RAF Andover.

Cloud K3722; Southampton II S1464; Victoria V K2797.

Disbanded 25th January 1935 at Andover to become the Air Navigation School.

AIR SEA RESCUE AND COMMUNICATION FLIGHT, MALTA – see Malta Air Sea Rescue and Communication Flight, later Malta Communication, Ferry Unit and Air Sea Rescue Flight

AIR SEA RESCUE FLIGHT, BERKA – see the Sea Rescue Flight, later Air Sea Rescue Flight

AIR SEA RESCUE FLIGHT, FAIRWOOD COMMON – see Air Sea Rescue Flight, Pembrey/Fairwood Common

AIR SEA RESCUE FLIGHT, FRISTON – see Air Sea Rescue Flight, Shoreham/Friston/Shoreham

AIR SEA RESCUE FLIGHT, HAWKINGE
Formed 4th June 1941 at Hawkinge.

Lysander IIIA V9483; Walrus I W2736.

Disbanded 22nd December 1941 at Hawkinge and merged with the Air Sea Rescue Flights Martlesham Heath and Shoreham/Friston/ Shoreham to become 'B' Flight, 277 Squadron.

AIR SEA RESCUE FLIGHT, KALAFRANA – see Seaplane Rescue Flight, Kalafrana

AIR SEA RESCUE FLIGHT, MARTLESHAM HEATH
Formed 14th May 1941 at Martlesham Heath.

Lysander IIIA V9402.

Disbanded 22nd December 1941 at Martlesham Heath and merged with the Air Sea Rescue Flights Hawkinge and Shoreham/Friston/ Shoreham to become 'A' Flight of 277 Squadron.

AIR SEA RESCUE FLIGHT, MATLASKE
Formed July 1941 at Matlaske.

Lysander IIIA V9541.

Disbanded 1st October 1941 at Matlaske to become 278 Squadron.

AIR SEA RESCUE FLIGHT, MERSTON/WESTHAMPNETT
Formed May 1941 at Merston.

Lysander IIIA V9547.

Disbanded 30th November 1941 at Westhampnett and absorbed by the Air Sea Rescue Flight, Shoreham/Friston/Shoreham.

AIR SEA RESCUE FLIGHT, NORTH AFRICA – see Sea Rescue Flight, later Air Sea Rescue Flight

AIR SEA RESCUE FLIGHT, PEMBREY/FAIRWOOD COMMON
Formed 14th May 1941 at Pembrey.

Lysander IIIA V9505.

Disbanded 21st October 1941 at Fairwood Common and merged with the Air Sea Rescue Flight Warmwell to become 'D' Flight, 276 Squadron.

AIR SEA RESCUE FLIGHT, PERRANPORTH
Formed 14th May 1941 at Perranporth.

Lysander IIIA V9735; Walrus I.

Disbanded 5th November 1941 at Perranporth and absorbed by 276 Squadron as 'C' Flight.

AIR SEA RESCUE FLIGHT, ROBOROUGH
Formed 14th May 1941 at Roborough.

Lysander IIIA V9551.

Disbanded 6th November 1941 at Roborough and absorbed by 276 Squadron.

AIR SEA RESCUE FLIGHT, SHOREHAM/FRISTON/SHOREHAM
Formed 14th May 1941 at Shoreham.

Lysander IIIA V9588; Walrus I W2735.

Disbanded 22nd December 1941 and merged with Air Sea Rescue Flights Hawkinge and Martlesham Heath to become 'C' Flight of 277 Squadron.

AIR SEA RESCUE FLIGHT, TANGMERE – see Air Sea Rescue Flight Merston/Westhampnett

AIR SEA RESCUE FLIGHT, WARMWELL
Formed 14th May 1941 at Warmwell.

Lysander III T1620; IIIA V9710.

Disbanded 21st October 1941 at Warmwell and merged with the Air Sea Rescue Flight Pembrey/Fairwood Common to become 276 Squadron.

AIR SEA RESCUE FLIGHT, WESTHAMPNETT – see Air Sea Rescue Flight, Merston/Westhampnett

1 AIR SEA RESCUE FLIGHT (FAR EAST)
Formed 1st April 1945 at Ratmalana, Ceylon, by redesignating 'C' Flight of 292 Squadron.

Warwick I HF945; Liberator VI EV972.

Disbanded 15th June 1945 at Kankesunterai to become 1346 (Air Sea Rescue) Flight.

2 AIR SEA RESCUE FLIGHT (FAR EAST)
Formed May 1945 at Agartala, India, by redesignating an element of 292 Squadron.

No aircraft known.

Disbanded 15th June 1945 at Agartala, to become 1347 (Air Sea Rescue) Flight.

3 AIR SEA RESCUE FLIGHT (FAR EAST)
Formed May 1945 at Agartala, India, by redesignating an element of 292 Squadron.

No aircraft known.

Disbanded 15th June 1945 at Agartala to become 1348 (Air Sea Rescue) Flight.

4 AIR SEA RESCUE FLIGHT (FAR EAST)
Formed May 1945 at Cox's Bazaar, India, by redesignating an element of 292 Squadron

Liberator VI EV832.

Disbanded 15th June 1945 at Agartala, India, to become 1349 (Air Sea Rescue) Flight.

5 AIR SEA RESCUE FLIGHT (FAR EAST)
Formed 1st May 1945 at Ratmalana, Ceylon, by redesignating an element of 292 Squadron.

Walrus I X9574, II HD808; Sea Otter I JM758.

Disbanded 15th June 1945 at Ratmalana to become 1350 (Air Sea Rescue) Flight.

1 AIR SEA RESCUE FLIGHT (NORTH AFRICA) – see 1 Air Sea Rescue Unit (North Africa), later 1 Air Sea Rescue Flight (North Africa)

5 AIR SEA RESCUE FLIGHT (NORTH AFRICA)
Formed by August 1943 (location unknown), having a detachment at Derna, Libya.

Walrus I P5669.

Disbanded (date and location unknown).

6 AIR SEA RESCUE FLIGHT (NORTH AFRICA)
Formed by August 1943 at El Mellaha, Libya.

Walrus I W3039.

Disbanded (date and location unknown).

1 AIR SEA RESCUE UNIT (NORTH AFRICA), later 1 AIR SEA RESCUE FLIGHT (NORTH AFRICA)
Formed 20th June 1943 at Sidi Ahmed, Tunisia. Redesignated 1 Air Sea Rescue Flight (North Africa) from 1st September 1943.

Wellington IC HE127; Hudson VI FK608.

Disbanded 1st January 1944 at Blida, Algeria, and absorbed by the Mediterranean Allied Coastal Air Force Communication Flight.

AIR SEA RESCUE TRAINING UNIT
Formed 13th October 1943 at Bircham Newton by redesignating the Warwick Training Unit.

Wellington IC L7819: Warwick I BV226; Sea Otter I JM745; Anson I LT578.

Disbanded 15th May 1944 at Thornaby and absorbed by 5 Operational Training Unit.

AIR-SEA WARFARE DEVELOPMENT UNIT
Formed 14th January 1945 at Thorney Island by redesignating the Coastal Command Development Unit.

P9 (1.45–4.51)	*Sea Otter I JM827 P9-Q; Tiger Moth II DE574 P9-T; Hudson IIIA FK745; Liberator VI KH405; VIII KN804; Wellington XIII NB917; XIV NC799; Warwick I HG186; II HG365; V LM798 P9-M; Proctor III HM480 P9-A; Hamilcar I LA728; Typhoon IB MN263; Halifax II JP298, III NA168; Beaufighter X RD389 P9-M; Catalina IVB JX604; Mosquito VI TA488 P9-V; Anson XII PH768 P9-G, XIX TX186; Hoverfly I FT834 P9-X; Sunderland V PP122 P9-S; Lancaster III RE206 P9-A; Brigand TF.1 RH748 P9-G.*
F (4.51–.56)	*Anson XII PH565 F-G; Lancaster III SW370 F-C; Shackleton GR.1 VP282 F-K; MR.1A WB833 F-B; MR.2 WG533 F-A; Sycamore HR.12 WV783 F-X.*
Nil (.56–4.70)	*Shackleton MR.1 WB833 B; MR.2 WG554 A; MR.3 WR974.*

Disbanded 1st April 1970 at Ballykelly.

AIR/SEA WARFARE DEVELOPMENT UNIT (ACSEA)
Formed 15th December 1944 at Ratmalana, Ceylon.

Catalina Y-77; Liberator GR.VI EV836; Vengeance IV; Beaufighter X NV502; Walrus II HD808; Avenger; Warwick I BV473.

Disbanded 30th November 1945 at Ratmalana.

1 AIR SIGNALLERS SCHOOL
Formed 1st May 1951 at Swanton Morley by redesignating 4 Radio School.

Anson XII PH719, XIX TX218 Y, T.21 VS599, T.22 WD419 F; Proctor IV NP224; Tiger Moth II T6581; Prentice T.1 VR235 A.

Disbanded 1st April 1957 at Swanton Morley to become 1 Air Electronics School.

2 AIR SIGNALLERS SCHOOL
Formed 5th May 1952 at Halfpenny Green.

Anson XIX PH814, T.21 VV883 C, Anson T.22 WD421; Prentice T.1 VR200.

Disbanded 13th September 1953 at Halfpenny Green.

AIR-TO-SURFACE VESSEL (ASV) TRAINING FLIGHT
Formed by January 1944 at Chivenor.

Wellington XII HF117; XIII NB868; XIV MF726.

Disbanded June 1945 at Chivenor.

AIR TRAINING CORPS FLIGHT
Formed 1st January 1943 at Halton as an element of the Station Flight, Halton.

Tutor; D.H.89; Master II; Dominie I X7395; Oxford.

Disbanded 31st May 1946 at Halton.

AIR TRAINING SQUADRON
Formed 1st May 1971 at Odiham by redesignating the Helicopter Operational Conversion Flight.

B	*Wessex HC.2 XR499 BX.*
C	*Puma HC.1 XW198 CZ.*

Disbanded 1st January 1972 at Odiham to become 240 Operational Conversion Unit.

AIR TRANSPORT AUXILIARY
Formed January 1940 at White Waltham.

Advanced Flying Training School, Air Transport Auxiliary
Formed 1st April 1942 at White Waltham by redesignating an element of the Air Transport Auxiliary School.

Harvard I N7100; Hudson; Hurricane I L1945; Wellington I L4336; Albemarle I P1658; Oxford.

Disbanded November 1945 at White Waltham.

Air Movements Flight, Air Transport Auxiliary
Formed 1st April 1942 at White Waltham.

Anson I NK821; Dominie I; Proctor III; Argus.

Disbanded August 1945 at White Waltham.

Air Transport Auxiliary School
Formed by February 1940 at Whitchurch.

Tutor K3435; Blenheim I L1158; Harvard I N7135; Magister V1008.

Disbanded 1st April 1942 at White Waltham and divided to become the Elementary Flying Training School, ATA and the Advanced Flying Training School, ATA.

Elementary Flying Training School, Air Transport Auxiliary
Formed 1st April 1942 at Luton by redesignating an element of the Air Transport Auxiliary School.

Tutor K3435 2; Hind K5468; Magister N3832.

Disbanded April 1943 at Thame to become the Initial Flying Training School, Air Transport Auxiliary.

1 Ferry Pilots Pool, later 1 Ferry Pool, Air Transport Auxiliary
Formed 5th November 1940 at White Waltham by redesignating 'A' Section, 3 Ferry Pilots Pool, ATA. Redesignated 1 Ferry Pool from 1st May 1942.

Blenheim I L1100; Oxford I N4595; Hurricane I Z7010, IV KX411; Leopard Moth AX862; Puss Moth AX872; Hawk Trainer DG665; Master II DK941; Spitfire IIA P8538, VB BP854, IX MJ413;

Tomahawk I AH805; Wellington II Z8535; Boston III (Turbinlite) W8254; Cub Coupe BV990; Mosquito II DD621; Mustang III FB348; Liberator III FK217; Hudson VI FK410; Beaufighter X LZ536; Typhoon IB JP686.

Disbanded 31st March 1946 at White Waltham.

2 Ferry Pilots Pool, later 2 Ferry Pool, Air Transport Auxiliary
Formed 5th November 1940 at Whitchurch by redesignating 'B' Section, 3 Ferry Pilots Pool. Redesignated 2 Ferry Pool from 1st May 1942.

Beaufort I AW292; Hurricane X AG610, IV KX539; Mohawk IV BK579; Monospar ST.5 DR849; Magister P2468; Dominie I R9555; Beaufighter I X7640, II T3045, X NE203; Spitfire VB AA857, VIII JG546. Anson I.

Disbanded September 1945 at Whitchurch.

3 Ferry Pilots Pool, later 3 Ferry Pool, Air Transport Auxiliary
Formed 15th February 1940 with 'A' Section at White Waltham, 'B' Section at Whitchurch, 'C' Section at Hawarden. The Women's Ferry Pilots Pool from Hatfield was absorbed to become 'D' Section.

Gauntlet II K7811; Battle L5768; Botha I L6160; Beaufort I N1177; Wellington IA N2902, IC R1156; Hudson I N7234; Master I N7761; Puss Moth AX869.

Disbanded 5th November 1940 at White Waltham with 'B', 'C' and 'D' Sections becoming 2,3 and 5 Ferry Pilots Pools respectively.

Reformed 5th November 1940 at Hawarden by redesignating 'C' Section, 3 Ferry Pilots Pool. Redesignated 3 Ferry Pool from 1st May 1942.

Anson I K8760; Harvard I N7148; Hampden I P5396; Spitfire I P9632, VB EP983; Battle Trainer P6760; Dominie I R9557; Defiant I T3927; Fox Moth X2866; Wellington III X3605; Airacobra I AH598; Tomahawk IIB AK154; Mohawk IV AR634; Hudson III AE487, V AM725; Beaufighter VI V8468, X NE228; Leopard Moth BK867; Fairchild 24C BK869; Cub Coupe BV989; Mosquito VI NT147, B.20 KB116.

Disbanded 30th November 1945 at Hawarden.

4 Ferry Pilots Pool, later 4 Ferry Pool, Air Transport Auxiliary
Formed 27th May 1940 at Prestwick. Redesignated 4 Ferry Pool from 1st May 1942.

Magister II N5434; Moth AX792; Leopard Moth AW121; Puss Moth ES918; Phoenix X9338; Hind K6838; Battle L5301; Anson I N5324; Hurricane IIA Z2486; Spitfire VB BM358; Seafire L.II NM916; Oxford I L4597; Botha I L6541; Liberator II AL562; Mohawk IV BJ440; Catalina IB FP321; Kittyhawk I AK575; Tomahawk IIA AH995; Beaufighter I X7764; Hudson IIIA FK785.

Disbanded 31st October 1945 at Prestwick.

5 Ferry Pilots Pool, later 5 Ferry Pool, later 5 (Training) Ferry Pool, Air Transport Auxiliary
Formed 5th November 1940 at Hatfield by redesignating 'D' Section, 3 Ferry Pilots Pool. Redesignated 5 Ferry Pool from 1st May 1942.

Anson I DG808; Argus I FK333; Proctor III LZ771.

Disbanded 18th May 1943 at Luton.

Reformed 15th August 1943 at Haddenham as 5 (Training) Ferry Pool by redesignating the (Training) Ferry Pool, Air Transport Auxiliary.

Spitfire IX MK999; Swordfish II LS220; Tiger Moth II T7351.

Disbanded March 1945 at Haddenham.

6 Ferry Pilots Pool, later 6 Ferry Pool, Air Transport Auxiliary
Formed November 1940 at Ratcliffe. Redesignated 6 Ferry Pool from 1st May 1942.

Hector K9733; Spitfire I K9961, IIA P7960, VB EP748; Henley III L3408; Defiant I N3337; Anson I N4872; Botha I W5103; Swordfish I V4525; Seafire LF.VIII JF844; Boston III W8266; Blenheim IV Z6080; Typhoon IB DN446; Dominie I X7322; Mohawk IV BJ445;

Auster III NJ988; Beaufort I AW379; Mitchell II FW276; Beaufighter X RD555; Mosquito VI RF847.

Disbanded October 1945 at Ratcliffe.

7 Ferry Pilots Pool, later 7 Ferry Pool, Air Transport Auxiliary
Formed November 1940 at Sherburn in Elmet. Redesignated 7 Ferry Pool from 1st May 1942.

Blenheim I K7133; Defiant I N1635; Skua I L2879; Lysander IIIA V9814; Master III W8840; Leopard Moth X9380; Dragonfly X9390; Anson I AX579; Mitchell II FR172; Warwick III HG240; Mustang III KH552; Beaufort IIA ML578; Swordfish II NE962; Beaufighter X NV195; Mosquito VI PZ461.

Disbanded October 1945 at Sherburn in Elmet.

8 Ferry Pilots Pool, later 8 Ferry Pool, Air Transport Auxiliary
Formed March 1941 at Sydenham. Redesignated 8 Ferry Pool from 1st May 1942.

Blenheim I T2327; Beaufort I N1108; Wellington II Z8424; Hudson III AE489; Hampden AD736; Mohawk IV AR651; Whitley VII LA798; Traveler I FT495.

Disbanded August 1945 at Sydenham.

9 Ferry Pilots Pool, later 9 Ferry Pool, Air Transport Auxiliary
Formed October 1941 at Aston Down. Redesignated 9 Ferry Pool from 1st May 1942.

Anson I; Spitfire IX ML294; Auster V TJ222.

Disbanded June 1945 at Aston Down.

10 Ferry Pilots Pool, later 10 Ferry Pool, Air Transport Auxiliary
Formed 11th February 1942 at Lossiemouth by redesignating a sub-Pool of 4 Ferry Pilots Pool. Redesignated 10 Ferry Pool from 1st May 1942.

Dominie I X7350; Dominie X7338; Anson I MG492; Spitfire XVI SM415.

Disbanded 10th July 1945 at Lossiemouth.

12 Ferry Pilots Pool, later 12 Ferry Pool, Air Transport Auxiliary
Formed July 1941 at Cosford by redesignating a sub-Pool of 6 Ferry Pilot Pool. Redesignated 12 Ferry Pool from 1st May 1942.

Wellington II Z8501; Spitfire IX EN248; Anson I NK861.

Disbanded June 1945 at Cosford.

14 Ferry Pilots Pool, later 14 Ferry Pool, Air Transport Auxiliary
Formed 20th January 1941 at Ringway by redesignating an element of 3 Ferry Pilots Pool. Redesignated 14 Ferry Pool from 1st May 1942.

Mustang I AG566, IVA KH838; Boston II AH463; Hurricane IIB BD722; Oxford I PH235.

Disbanded September 1945 at Ringway.

15 Ferry Pilots Pool, later 15 Ferry Pool, Air Transport Auxiliary
Formed July 1941 at Hamble by redesignating 1 Sub Ferry Pilots Pool of 1 Ferry Pilots Pool. Redesignated 15 Ferry Pool from 1st May 1942.

Albacore I L7124; Swordfish I W5902; Tomahawk I AH804; Mohawk IV BJ434; Barracuda II P9787; Spitfire VB AD555, XI EN341; Mosquito VI HP932.

Disbanded August 1945 at Hamble.

16 Ferry Pilots Pool, later 16 Ferry Pool, Air Transport Auxiliary
Formed July 1941 at Kirkbride by redesignating a sub-Pool of 4 Ferry Pilots Pool. Redesignated 16 Ferry Pool from 1st May 1942.

Spitfire VB AD395; Mustang I AG376; Airacobra I AH693; Hurricane I AG116, IIB JS346; Beaufort I DX118, IIA ML610; Beaufighter VI KW326; Anson I NK861.

Disbanded September 1945 at Kirkbride.

Initial Flying Training School, Air Transport Auxiliary
Formed April 1943 at Thame by redesignating the Elementary Flying Training School, Air Transport Auxiliary.

Tutor K6115; Hart K6522; Magister N5415; Spitfire VA P9367; Master II W9074; Harvard IIB FS832.

Disbanded April 1945 at Thame.

(Training) Ferry Pool, Air Transport Auxiliary
Formed February 1941 at White Waltham.

Tutor K3440 3; Audax K4405; Hart K4998; Anson I; Whitney Straight DJ714; Hawk Major DP848; Condor DX177.

Disbanded 15th August 1943 at White Waltham to become 5 (Training) Ferry Pilots Pool.

Women's Ferry Pilots Pool, Air Transport Auxiliary
Formed 1st January 1940 at Hatfield.

Tiger Moth II R5130; Fox Moth X2865; Puss Moth DG662.

Disbanded 15th February 1940 at Hatfield to become 'D' Section of 3 Ferry Pilots Pool.

Also used   D.H.89M K4772; Lysander I R2630, II R2003; Harvard IIB KF140; Proctor I P6130, III Z7212; Master IA T8271 6; Hudson II T9369, IV AE628; Ventura I AE730; Anson XI NK875; DH.89A R2486; Dominie II NR788; Oxford II N6421; Hurricane IIC BE574; Albemarle II V1656, VI V2029; Hampden I P1215; Spitfire VA X4908; Argus I FK313, II HB614, III HB751; Tiger Moth BB688, I NL929; Reliant X8522; Goose; Vega Gull BK872; Courier X9397; Moth Minor X5115; Hawk Major BD180; Lockheed 12A X9316; Airacobra I AH651; Stinson Junior X8522; Eagle DR609; Beech C-17R DS180; Warferry ES943; Mustang I AM138; Tipsy B.2 HM494; Cygnet II HM495.

Disbanded 30th November 1945 at White Waltham.

AIR TRANSPORT DEVELOPMENT FLIGHT
Formed 1st March 1950 at Abingdon by redesignating the Transport Command Development Unit.

Hamilcar I RR983.

Disbanded 14th October 1951 at Abingdon to become the Transport Command Development Flight.

AIR TRANSPORT DEVELOPMENT CENTRE (INDIA), later RAF ELEMENT, AIR TRANSPORT DEVELOPMENT CENTRE
Formed 6th September 1944 at Chaklala, India, by redesignating the Airborne Forces Research Centre. Redesignated RAF Element, Air Transport Development Centre.

Horsa II RZ130.

Disbanded 15th May 1947 at Chaklala and absorbed by 3 Parachute Training School.

AIR TRANSPORT DEVELOPMENT UNIT
Formed 1st June 1965 at Abingdon by redesignating the Air Movements Development Unit.

Hadrian II KK792; Hamilcar I HH967; Harvard IIB KF183; Anson XI NK790; Lincoln B.1 RE250; Beverley C.1 XB269.

Disbanded 14th November 1967 at Abingdon and merged with Army Airborne Transport Development Centre to become the Joint Air Transport Establishment.

AIR TRANSPORT FLIGHT
Formed February 1944 at Eastleigh, Kenya, by redesignating the Air Headquarters East Africa Communication Flight.

Rapide K8; Anson; Hudson VI FK568; Puss Moth; Savoia 73 K33.

Disbanded 31st July 1944 at Eastleigh to become the Air Headquarters East Africa Communication Flight.

AIR TRANSPORT TACTICAL DEVELOPMENT UNIT
Formed 14th January 1944 at Netheravon by redesignating the Airborne Forces Tactical Development Unit.

Stirling IV LK114, V PJ958; Oxford I R6018, II V3834; Oxford I R6018; Albemarle ST.II V1608; Halifax III NA137, V LK653, VIII PP217; Hadrian I 43-40593; Horsa I LJ307; Anson I NK178;

Hamilcar I NX868; Wellington X HE300; Liberator VI KG915; Dakota III FD826, IV TP187; Mustang I AG620; Mosquito XVI RF995, B.25 KB687; Buckingham I KV365; Typhoon IB JR192; Spitfire IX MJ942; York I MW168.

Disbanded 31st August 1945 at Netheravon to become the Transport Command Development Unit.

AIR WARFARE CENTRE
Formed 1st July 1993 at High Wycombe to administer elements of Strike Command including the Central Tactics and Trials Organisation (Boscombe Down), Electronic Warfare Operational Support Establishment (Wyton), Strike/Attack Operational Evaluation Unit, Tornado F.3 Operational Evaluation Unit (Coningsby) and the Support Helicopter Trials and Tactics Flight (Odiham). Current 1st April 1998 at High Wycombe.

AIRBORNE FORCES ESTABLISHMENT, later AIRBORNE FORCES EXPERIMENTAL ESTABLISHMENT
Formed 1st September 1941 at Ringway by redesignating the Central Landing Establishment. Redesignated the Airborne Forces Experimental Establishment from 15th February 1942.

Hotspur I BV139, II BT500; Horsa I DP493, II RN379; Hengist I DG573; Hamilcar I DR851; Hadrian I FR557; Waco CG-13A KL163; Baynes Carrier Wing RA809; Grunau Baby II VT762; AW.52G TS363; Rotachute I, II, III P-5, IV P-9; Rotabuggy; Fa 330A VX850; Tutor K3424; Audax K7490; Hector K9699; Leopard Moth AW165; Master II DL176; Lysander IIIA V9517; Firefly; Wildcat; Vengeance IV HB508; Hoverfly I KL105, II KN846; Mustang IVA KM482; Hurricane IV KX877; Spitfire VC AB216, IX BS434; Auster VI VF620; Tempest TT.V SN329; Martinet I MS796; Harvard II BD130, IIB KF226; Fa 223E VM479; Manchester I L7392; Oxford I EB811; II T1059; Anson I N5351, X NK530; Whitley V N1435; Blenheim IV T2323; Wellington IA P2522, IC P9237, III X3286, X HE731; Hudson III V9228, IIIA FH168, VI FK537; Albemarle GT.I/I P1361, GT.I/II P1402, ST.IV P1406; Boston IIIA BZ311; Monospar ST-25 X9372; Rapide X9450; Warwick III HG218; Dakota III FD943, IV KK127; Hamilcar X LA728; Mosquito B.35 TK634; Beaufighter X NT913; Valetta C.1 VL262; Dragonfly VW209; Sycamore VL958; Bell 47 G-AKFB; Halifax L7244, II L9612, III LL615, V EB143, VII PP350; IX RT758; Stirling I N3637, III EF432, IV LJ989, V PJ949; Lancaster I R5606, II DS819; York I MW132; Lincoln II RA664; Hastings C.1 TG503.

The codes FGT, FGU, FGV, FGW and FGX were allocated but not used.

Disbanded 14th September 1950 at Beaulieu and absorbed by the Aeroplane and Armament Experimental Establishment.

AIRBORNE FORCES EXPERIMENTAL ESTABLISHMENT – see Airborne Forces Establishment, later Airborne Forces Experimental Establishment

AIRBORNE FORCES RESEARCH CENTRE (INDIA), ROYAL AIR FORCE COMPONENT – see Air Transport Development Centre (India), Royal Air Force Component

AIRBORNE FORCES TACTICAL DEVELOPMENT UNIT
Formed 1st December 1943 at Tarrant Rushton.

Whitley LA883; Albemarle ST.II V1608; Wellington X HE300; Halifax III NA137, V LK653; Stirling III LJ465, IV LK114; Dakota; Horsa I LJ307; Hamilcar I HH967.

Disbanded 14th January 1944 at Netheravon to become the Air Transport Tactical Development Unit.

AIRBORNE INTERCEPTION/AIR-TO-SURFACE VESSEL SCHOOL
Formed 24th October 1940 at Prestwick.

Blenheim IV T2324.

Disbanded 27th December 1940 at Prestwick to become 3 Radio School.

AIRBORNE INTERCEPTION CONVERSION FLIGHT, CRANFIELD and TWINWOOD FARM
Formed 29th October 1943 at Cranfield.

Beaufighter VI.

Disbanded (date unknown) at Twinwood Farm.

AIRBORNE INTERCEPTION CONVERSION FLIGHT, ITALY
Formed 20th April 1944 at Marcianise, Italy.

Beaufighter VI KW165; Hurricane IIC KW849; IID KW696.

Disbanded 28th May 1944 at Marcianise.

AIRBORNE INTERCEPTION MK VIII CONVERSION FLIGHT
Formed 28th May 1943 in the United Kingdom. Became operational at Bône, Algeria, within 219 Squadron. Became an independent unit from 1st November 1943.

Beaufighter VI KW165; Hurricane IIC LD945; IID KW696.

Officially disbanded 28th May 1944 at Bight, India, having been absorbed on the formation of 1671 Conversion Unit.

AIRBORNE INTERCEPTION MK X CONVERSION FLIGHT
Formed 29th August 1944 at Melton Mowbray.

Wellington X ND104, XI MP563; Hurricane IIC KZ434, IID KW863.

Disbanded 20th November 1945 at Bight, India.

AIRBORNE INTERCEPTION SCHOOL
Formed 1st February 1952 at Leeming by redesignating the Brigand Squadron of 228 Operational Conversion Unit.

Brigand T.4 WA563; Buckmaster T.1 RP156.

Disbanded 15th June 1952 at Cottesmore to become 238 Operational Conversion Unit.

AIRCRAFT AND ARMAMENT EVALUATION ESTABLISHMENT
Formed 1st April 1992 at Boscombe Down by redesignating the Aeroplane and Armament Experimental Establishment. Reorganised into Fast Jet, Heavy Aircraft and Rotary Wing Test Squadrons from 1st January 1996.

Harrier T.4 ZD993, GR.7 ZD319; Tornado GR.1 ZA402, F.2T ZD900, F.3 ZE161; Navajo Chieftain ZF8822; Lynx AS.3 ZD249, AH.9 ZG884; Islander Astor ZG993.

Disbanded 1st April 1996 to become the Test and Evaluation Centre.

AIRCRAFT DELIVERY FLIGHT, COLERNE – see 2 Aircraft Delivery Flight

AIRCRAFT DELIVERY FLIGHT, GRANGEMOUTH – see 4 Aircraft Delivery Flight

AIRCRAFT DELIVERY FLIGHT, HAWARDEN – see 3 Aircraft Delivery Flight

AIRCRAFT DELIVERY FLIGHT, HENDON – see 1 Aircraft Delivery Flight

1 AIRCRAFT DELIVERY FLIGHT
Formed 3rd March 1941 at Hendon as the Aircraft Delivery Flight, Hendon. Redesignated 1 Aircraft Delivery Flight from 22nd March 1941.

Dominie I X7416; Dragon Rapide X9457; Mustang I AL999; Tomahawk I AH782; Hurricane IIC BD958; Oxford I X6744, II BM776; Master III DL556; Proctor III HM356; Typhoon IB JR127; Spitfire VC EE643; VII MD178; Auster III NJ894; Anson I NK623; Martinet I NR407.

Disbanded 9th October 1945 at Andrews Field.

2 AIRCRAFT DELIVERY FLIGHT
Formed 18th March 1941 at Colerne as the Aircraft Delivery Flight, Colerne. Redesignated 2 Aircraft Delivery Flight from 22nd March 1941.

Defiant I N3444; Proctor I P6318; Magister R1810; Master III W8841; Dominie I X7331; Hurricane IIC BD959; Mustang I AG469, III FZ132; Anson I EG539; Oxford I HN128, II T1082.

Disbanded 31st July 1944 at Cranfield.

3 AIRCRAFT DELIVERY FLIGHT
Formed 10th March 1941 at Hawarden as the Aircraft Delivery Flight, Harwarden. Redesignated 3 Aircraft Delivery Flight from 7th April 1941.

Spitfire IIA P7284; Magister R1822; Dominie I X7331; Hurricane IIA Z2349; Tiger Moth II DE464; Oxford I HM950, II T1049.

Disbanded 22nd November 1944 at Catterick.

4 AIRCRAFT DELIVERY FLIGHT
Formed 10th March 1941 at Grangemouth as the Aircraft Delivery Flight, Grangemouth. Redesignated 4 Aircraft Delivery Flight from 13th April 1941.

Oxford I X6850, II T1065; Dominie I X7333; Lysander III T1527; Beaufighter VIF V8565; Master III W8592; Mustang I AM123; Anson I EF866; Typhoon IB JR199.

Disbanded 31st October 1945 at Hutton Cranswick.

AIRCRAFT DELIVERY UNIT
Formed 15th December 1941 at Cairo, Egypt, aboard the houseboat *Medina* by redesignating 1 Delivery Unit.

Blenheim IV Z6374; Spitfire VB EP578; Kittyhawk I ET520, IIA FL338; Baltimore II AG783, IIIA FA179.

Disbanded 7th December 1942 at Cairo to become 1 Aircraft Delivery Unit.

1 AIRCRAFT DELIVERY UNIT
Formed 7th December 1942 at Cairo by redesignating the Aircraft Delivery Unit.

Blenheim V BA432; Beaufort I DW856; Kittyhawk II FS440, III FR119; Baltimore IV FA532, V FW445; Hurricane IIA BV168; IIC BP176; IV KZ374; Spitfire VC EE793; Marauder III HD432; Wellington IC N2738; XIII HZ766; Dakota III KG494; Martinet I NR474; Beaufighter VI EL346; X LX884; Ventura V JT822; Mosquito XVI NS750.

Disbanded 23rd September 1944 at Heliopolis, Egypt, to become 5 Ferry Unit.

2 AIRCRAFT DELIVERY UNIT
Formed 7th December 1942 at LG.209 (Deversoir), Egypt by redesignating 1 Section of 1 Aircraft Delivery Unit.

Blenheim V BA116; Hurricane IIC BP466, IID BP554, IV LB853; Kittyhawk I EV339, II FS481, IIA FL333, III FR316; Baltimore III AG892, V FW307; Anson I DJ207; Harvard IIA EX133; Spitfire VB ER544, VC JG892, IX MH500; Wellington VIII HF904; XI MP649; Beaufighter XI JL888.

Disbanded 23rd September 1944 at LG.237 (Gebel Hamzi), Egypt, to become 2 Ferry Unit.

3 AIRCRAFT DELIVERY UNIT
Formed 15th April 1943 at Fez, Morocco.

Blenheim V EH345; Warwick I BV360; Spitfire VB EP813, VC EF598, VIII MT653, IX MH678; Walrus II HD821; Marauder II FB515; Mustang III HK944; Proctor III HM470; Mosquito VI HX896; Beaufighter VI KV935; X NE345; Liberator VI KG941; Dakota III KG548; Anson I MG679; Wellington X HE323; XIII MF172.

Disbanded 23rd September 1944 at Oujda, Morocco, to become 3 Ferry Unit.

4 AIRCRAFT DELIVERY UNIT
Formed 25th May 1943 at Azizia, Libya.

Gladiator I K7964; Baltimore III AG915; Mustang III FB293; Kittyhawk I FS439, IV FT862; Expeditor I HB202; Spitfire VB EP693, VC EF684, VIII JF506, IX MA448; Proctor III HM465; Anson I LS995; Halifax II JN916.

Disbanded 23rd September 1944 at Catania, Italy, to become 4 Ferry Unit.

AIRCRAFT GUN MOUNTING ESTABLISHMENT
Formed 30th December 1940 at Duxford.

Hector K9714; Gladiator I K8040; Wellington I L4250, IA P9222; Spitfire IIA P8709; Whirlwind I L6844; Albacore I L7142; Beaufighter

R2055; Blenheim IV V5427; Fulmar I X8697; Puss Moth X9378; Airacobra I AH701; Tomahawk IIA AH948; Martlet I AL260; Mohawk IV AR680; Havoc I AX910; Fiat CR.42 BT474.

Disbanded 29th January 1942 at Duxford and absorbed by the Aircraft and Armament Experimental Establishment.

1 AIRCRAFT PREPARATION UNIT – see 1 Overseas Aircraft Preparation Unit, later 1 Aircraft Preparation Unit

2 AIRCRAFT PREPARATION UNIT – see 2 Overseas Aircraft Preparation Unit, later 2 Aircraft Preparation Unit

3 AIRCRAFT PREPARATION UNIT – see 3 Overseas Aircraft Preparation Unit, later 3 Aircraft Preparation Unit

4 AIRCRAFT PREPARATION UNIT – see 4 Overseas Aircraft Preparation Unit, later 4 Aircraft Preparation Unit

5 AIRCRAFT PREPARATION UNIT
Formed 5th July 1944 at Dorval, Canada, by redesignating an element of Transatlantic Aircraft Preparation and Despatch Unit, Dorval.

No aircraft known.

Disbanded 1st October 1945 at Dorval.

6 AIRCRAFT PREPARATION UNIT
Formed 5th July 1944 at Bermuda by redesignating an element of Transport Command Unit and Reception, Preparation and Despatch of Aircraft.

No aircraft known.

Disbanded 1st October 1945 at Bermuda.

7 AIRCRAFT PREPARATION UNIT
Formed 5th July at Nassau, Bahamas, by redesignating an element of the Transatlantic Aircraft Preparation and Despatch Unit, Nassau.

No aircraft known.

Disbanded 1st October 1945 at Nassau.

11 AIRCRAFT PREPARATION UNIT – see 11 (Landplane) Aircraft Preparation and Modification Unit

12 AIRCRAFT PREPARATION UNIT – see 12 (Flying Boat) Aircraft Preparation and Modification Unit

13 AIRCRAFT PREPARATION UNIT – see 13 Aircraft Modification Unit

AIRCRAFT TORPEDO DEVELOPMENT UNIT
Formed 15th September 1943 at Gosport by merging the Torpedo Development Unit and the Torpedo Experimental Establishment.

Wellesley K7736; Albacore; Lysander IIIA V9287; Beaufort I DX119 F; Hampden; Wellington XIV PG284, VIII T2977; Manchester; Lancaster I ME570, II DS606; Boston IIIA BZ315; Swordfish III NF399; Barracuda III ME230; Master III DM137; Ju 88A-6 VN874; Ju 188A-2 VN143; Buckingham I KV471; Beaufighter X KW286; Proctor III LZ708, IV NP393; Mosquito VI RF973, IX ML899, TR.33 TW227, B.35 RS707; Harvard IIB KF183; Dominie I X7396; Firebrand TF.IV EK631, V EK744; Tempest II PR857; Lincoln B.1 RE281, II RF332; Brigand TF.1 RH747; Vampire FB.5 VX985; Tiger Moth II T6702; Anson I NK940, XIX VL301; Seamew AS.1 XE171; Wyvern TF.1 VR134, TF.2 VW868, S.4 WN332; Valetta C.1 WD171; Dragonfly HR.3 WP503; Canberra B.2 WH661, B.6 XH567; Whirlwind HAR.2 XJ759, HAS.7 XG593.

Disbanded 31st August 1958 at Culdrose and control passed to the Ministry of Supply.

2 AIRCREW GRADING SCHOOL
Formed 15th August 1951 at Digby by redesignating 2 Grading School.

Tiger Moth II.

Disbanded 15th January 1952 at Digby to become 3 (Digby) Wing, 2 Initial Training School of which the Flying Wing became the Airwork Grading Unit from 30th June 1952.

AIRCREW OFFICERS TRAINING SCHOOL
Formed 1st January 1967 at South Cerney.

Chipmunk T.10 WD331.

Disbanded 15th May 1969 at Church Fenton and absorbed by the Officer Cadet Training Unit.

AIRCREW TRANSIT POOL
Formed 15th June 1943 at Poona, India, by redesignating the Surplus Aircrew Centre.

Blenheim V AZ887; Beaufighter VIF X7936; Harvard IIB FE600; Hurricane IIC KW758, IV KX876; Spitfire VIII MT838.

Disbanded 9th February 1944 at Poona to become 3 Refresher Flying Unit.

AIRCREW TESTING AND GRADING UNIT
Formed January 1945 at Melbourne.

Oxford.

Disbanded 1st November 1945 at Bramcote to become the Transport Command Aircrew Examining Unit.

AIRFIELD CONTROLLERS SCHOOL
Formed 15th November 1942 at Watchfield.

Nil (11.42–4.46)   *Anson I R9718 Z.*
FDY (4.46–5.48)   *Anson I R9718 FDY-P.*

Disbanded 1st May 1948 at Watchfield and absorbed by the School of Air Traffic Control.

AIRWORK GRADING UNIT
Formed 15th January 1952 at Digby by merging 1 and of 2 Aircrew Grading Schools.

Tiger Moth II T7120.

Disbanded 9th June 1952 at Digby to become 1 and 2 Grading Units (Airwork).

ALL-WEATHER DEVELOPMENT SQUADRON – see Central Fighter Establishment

ALL-WEATHER FIGHTER COMBAT SQUADRON – see Central Fighter Establishment

ALL WEATHER FIGHTER LEADERS SCHOOL – see Central Fighter Establishment

ALL-WEATHER FLIGHT, AIR COMMAND FAR EAST – see Air Command Far East All-Weather Flight

ALL-WEATHER OPERATIONAL CONVERSION UNIT
Formed (date and location unknown). No documented records found. Assumed to have moved from Station to Station as Squadrons re-equipped with Meteor night fighter variants.

Anson T.21 VV889; Meteor T.7 VW456; F.8 WA816; NF.12 WS615 E; NF.14 WS801 T; Vampire T.11 WZ588.

Disbanded (date and location unknown).

ALL-WEATHER WING – see Central Fighter Establishment

ALLIED AIR FORCES CENTRAL EUROPE COMMUNICATION SQUADRON
Formed April 1951 at Melun-Villaroche, France, by redesignating the Air Forces Western Europe Communication Flight.

Anson C19 TX171, T.21 VV245; Devon C.1 WB534, VP971; Pembroke C.1 WV699, C(PR).1 XF796; Vampire T.11 XE919.

Disbanded 1966 at Melun-Villaroche.

ALLIED EXPEDITIONARY AIR FORCE COMMUNICATION FLIGHT, later ALLIED EXPEDITIONARY AIR FORCE COMMUNICATION SQUADRON
Formed 13th December 1943 at Heston. Redesignated Allied Expeditionary Air Force Communication Squadron from 6th April 1944.

Spitfire I K9801, IIA P8432, VB AD381; Oxford I R6058; Anson I

L7912, X NK706, XI NK871; Oxford I R6058; Hurricane I V6982, IIC PZ766; Vega Gull X9315; Vigilant IA BZ107; Proctor III HM291; Auster V MT356; Dakota II TJ169; Messenger I RH371; Mosquito VI PZ195.

Disbanded 15th October 1944 at Heston to become Supreme Headquarters Allied Expeditionary Force (RAF) Communication Squadron.

ALLIED FLIGHT – see 1316 (Dutch) Flight, later 1316 (Transport) Flight

2ND ALLIED TACTICAL AIR FORCE COMMUNICATION SQUADRON – see 2nd Tactical Air Force Communication Flight later 2nd Tactical Air Force Communication Squadron later 2nd Tactical Air Force Communication Wing later 2nd Tactical Air Force Communication Squadron later 2nd Allied Tactical Air Force Communication Squadron

ALLIED TECHNICAL AIR INTELLIGENCE UNIT, SOUTHEAST ASIA – see Royal Air Force Element, Allied Technical Air Intelligence Unit

ANDOVER COMMUNICATION FLIGHT
Formed 28th March 1927 at Andover by merging the Wessex Bombing Area Communication Flight and the Royal Air Force Staff College Flight.

Avro 504K E3333; Woodcock II J7964; Siskin IIIA J8948; Gamecock I J8088; Hart K3961; Moth K1860; Tiger Moth I K4264; Hart K3961.

Disbanded 10th September 1938 at Andover to become the Staff College Station Flight.

ANDOVER TRAINING FLIGHT
Formed 1st July 1966 at Abingdon.

Andover C.1 XS599 S.

Disbanded 1st November 1970 at Thorney Island and absorbed by 242 Operational Conversion Unit.

ANDOVER TRAINING SQUADRON
Formed 7th January 1983 at Brize Norton by redesignating an element of 241 Operational Conversion Unit. Later incorporated into 32 Squadron.

Initially used Andover C.1 and E.3 aircraft from 115 Squadron then CC.1 from 32 Squadron.

Disbanded 1993 at Northolt.

ANTARCTIC FLIGHT – see Royal Air Force Antarctic Flight

1 ANTI-AIRCRAFT CALIBRATION FLIGHT
Formed 27th December 1940 at Gatwick.

Wallace II K6018; Lysander I L4695, III T1463.

Disbanded 17th February 1941 at Hatfield to become 116 Squadron.

2 ANTI-AIRCRAFT CALIBRATION FLIGHT
Records suggest the planned formation of unit was cancelled although Wallace II K6041 appears to have been allocated.

3 ANTI-AIRCRAFT CALIBRATION FLIGHT
Records suggest the planned formation of unit was cancelled although Wallace II K8677 appears to have been allocated.

ANTI-AIRCRAFT CO-OPERATION FLIGHT
Formed 22nd October 1931 at Biggin Hill by redesignating the Night Flying Flight.

Wallace I K3671, II K6018; Moth K1112; Gipsy Moth K1226; Tomtit K1785; Horsley I J7987, II J8002.

Disbanded 14th April 1936 at Biggin Hill to become the Anti-Aircraft Co-operation Unit.

ANTI-AIRCRAFT CO-OPERATION FLIGHT, INDIAN AIR FORCE VOLUNTEER RESERVE; later 1 ANTI-AIRCRAFT

CO-OPERATION FLIGHT, INDIAN AIR FORCE VOLUNTEER RESERVE; later 1 ANTI-AIRCRAFT CO-OPERATION UNIT, INDIAN AIR FORCE
Formed 15th July 1941 Drigh Road, India. Redesignated 1 Anti-Aircraft Co-operation Flight, IAFVR from 21st February 1942 and 1 Anti-aircraft Co-operation Unit, IAF from 13th July 1942.

Wapiti IIA J9496; Harlow PJC-5 DR424; Lysander II N1209; Hurricane I Z4871.

Disbanded 3rd December 1942 at Drigh Road to become 22 Anti-Aircraft Co-operation Unit.

2 ANTI-AIRCRAFT CO-OPERATION FLIGHT, INDIAN AIR FORCE VOLUNTEER RESERVE; later 2 ANTI-AIRCRAFT CO-OPERATION UNIT, INDIAN AIR FORCE
Formed 21st January 1942 at Juhu, India. Redesignated 2 Anti-aircraft Co-operation Unit, IAF from 13th July 1942.

Wapiti IIA J9711; Moth Minor HX796; Tiger Moth LR228.

Disbanded 17th March 1943 at Deolali and merged with 3 Anti-Aircraft Co-operation Unit, IAF and the former 22 Anti-Aircraft Co-operation Unit, RAF to become 22 Anti-Aircraft Co-operation Unit, RAF.

3 ANTI-AIRCRAFT CO-OPERATION FLIGHT, INDIAN AIR FORCE VOLUNTEER RESERVE; later 3 ANTI-AIRCRAFT CO-OPERATION UNIT, INDIAN AIR FORCE
Formed 20th March 1942 at Dum-Dum, India. Redesignated 3 Anti-Aircraft Co-operation Unit, IAF from 8th August 1942.

Lysander II DG445; Battle; Moth Minor HX796.

Disbanded 17th March 1943 at Dum-Dum and merged with 2 Anti-Aircraft Co-operation Unit, IAF and the former 22 Anti-Aircraft Co-operation Unit, RAF to become 22 Anti-Aircraft Co-operation Unit.

ANTI-AIRCRAFT CO-OPERATION UNIT
Formed 14th April 1936 at Biggin Hill by redesignating the Anti-Aircraft Co-operation Flight.

Wallace I K3571, II.

Disbanded 10th February 1937 at Biggin Hill to become 1 Anti-Aircraft Co-operation Unit.

1 ANTI-AIRCRAFT CO-OPERATION UNIT
Formed 10th February 1937 at Biggin Hill by redesignating the Anti-Aircraft Co-operation Unit.

'A' Flight	Formed 10th February 1937 at Biggin Hill by redesignating 'A' Flight, Anti-Aircraft Co-operation Unit.	
	A later A1	Wallace I K3571, II K6041; Queen Bee K5102 48; Battle K9290; Henley III L3433; Magister L8264; Magister N6749; Lysander I R2585; Defiant I DR868.
	Disbanded 1st November 1942 at Weston Zoyland to become 1600 (Anti-Aircraft Co-operation) Flight.	
'B' Flight	Formed 10th February 1937 at Bircham Newton by redesignating 'B' Flight, Anti-Aircraft Co-operation Unit.	
	B later B1	Wallace II; Henley III L3318; Battle N2050; Lysander I R2591.
	Disbanded 1st November 1942 at Carew Cheriton to become 1607 (Anti-Aircraft Co-operation) Flight.	
'C' Flight	Formed 15th March 1937 at Biggin Hill.	
	C later C1	Wallace II; Henley III L3359; Tiger Moth II N9253.
	Disbanded 1st November 1942 at Towyn to become 1605 (Anti-Aircraft Co-operation) Flight.	
'D' Flight	Formed 16th September 1937 at Biggin Hill by redesignating 1 Queen Bee Flight.	
	Queen Bee K8642 39.	
	Disbanded 11th April 1938 at Farnborough to become 'Z' Flight, 1 Anti-Aircraft Co-operation Flight.	
	Reformed 28th April 1938 at Farnborough.	

	D later D1	*Gordon K2754; Henley III L3371 G; Lysander I R2587; Tiger Moth II N9399.*

Disbanded 1st November 1942 at Cleave to become 1602 (Anti-Aircraft Co-operation) Flight.

'E' Flight Formed 11th April 1938 at Farnborough.

E later E1 *Wallace II K6041; Henley III L3254; Tutor K4823; Prefect K5066; Tiger Moth T8178; Defiant I DR877.*

Disbanded 1st October 1942 at West Freugh.

'F' Flight Formed 28th April 1939 at Farnborough.

F later F1 *Henley III L3380 FI-D; Lysander I R2588; Tiger Moth II N5450; Magister T9761.*

Disbanded 1st November 1942 at Cark to become 1614 (Anti-Aircraft Co-operation) Flight.

'G' Flight Formed 1st May 1939 at Usworth.

G later G1 *Wallace II K6050; Henley III L3434; Tiger Moth II T8180; Magister P2444; Queen Bee P4682; Lysander I R2587.*

Disbanded 1st November 1942 at Cleave to become 1603 (Anti-Aircraft Co-operation) Flight.

'H' Flight Formed 1st April 1939 at Biggin Hill.

H *Battle.*

Disbanded 1st July 1941 at Christchurch and absorbed by the Special Duties Flight, Christchurch.

Reformed 1st January 1942 at Farnborough.

H1 *Lysander III T1439; Henley III L3313 H1-B; Magister R1952; Moth X5119; Defiant I DR866.*

Disbanded 1st November 1942 at Martlesham Heath to become 1616 (Anti-Aircraft Co-operation) Flight.

'J' Flight Formed 1st December 1939 at Farnborough.

J later J1 *Henley III L3356 J1-E; Lysander III R4750; Tiger Moth II T5491.*

Disbanded 1st November 1942 at Bodorgan to become 1606 (Anti-Aircraft Co-operation) Flight.

'K' Flight Formed December 1939 at Farnborough.

K later K1 *Henley III L3320 K1-A; Magister T9750.*

Disbanded 1st November 1942 at Langham to become 1611 (Anti-Aircraft Co-operation) Flight.

'L' Flight Formed 26th March 1940 at Farnborough.

L later L1 *Wallace II K6050; Henley III L3439; Tiger Moth II R5013.*

Disbanded 1st November 1942 at Aberporth to become 1608 (Anti-Aircraft Co-operation) Flight.

'M' Flight Formed 27th September 1940 at Bircham Newton.

M later M1 *Henley III L3330 M1-A; Defiant I DR876 M1-N.*

Disbanded 1st November 1942 at Langham to become 1612 (Anti-Aircraft Co-operation) Flight.

'N' Flight Formed 13th January 1942 at Thornaby.

N1 *Henley L3342; Tiger Moth II T6809.*

Disbanded 1st November 1942 at West Hartlepool to become 1613 (Anti-Aircraft Co-operation) Flight.

'O' Flight Formed 5th November 1940 at Cleave.

O later O1 *Henley III L3355; Magister T9803; Tiger Moth II T8192; Lysander I R2589.*

Disbanded 1st November 1942 at Cleave to become 1604 (Anti-Aircraft Co-operation) Flight.

'P' Flight Formed 25th August 1941 at Weston Zoyland.

P later P1 *Henley III L3307; Lysander I R2589; Defiant I DR865.*

Disbanded 1st November 1942 at Weston Zoyland to become 1601 (Anti-Aircraft Co-operation) Flight.

'Q' Flight Formed 30th June 1941 at Aberporth.

Q later Q1 *Henley III L3421 Q1-D; Magister L8069; Lysander I R2591; Tiger Moth II T5625; Martinet I HN947.*

Disbanded 1st November 1942 at Aberporth to become 1609 (Anti-Aircraft Co-operation) Flight.

'R' Flight Formed 30th June 1941 at Farnborough.

R later R1 *Henley III L3287 R1-A; Defiant I DR914.*

Disbanded 1st October 1942 at Cark.

'S' Flight Formed 26th January 1942 at Newtownards.

S1 *Henley III L3258; Tiger Moth II DE165.*

Disbanded 1st November 1942 at Newtownards to become 1617 (Anti-Aircraft Co-operation) Flight.

'T' Flight Formed 21st January 1941 at Farnborough.

Queen Bee V4743.

Disbanded 29th April 1942 at Weybourne.

'U' Flight Formed 15th August 1940 at St Athan.

Queen Bee P4754.

Disbanded 30th October 1942 at Morfa Towyn.

'V' Flight Formed 14th May 1939 at Cleave.

Queen Bee P4711; Magister P2443; Tiger Moth II N9399.

Disbanded 1st November 1942 at Cleave to become 1618 (Anti-Aircraft Co-operation) Flight.

'W' Flight Formed 16th May 1939 at Henlow.

Queen Bee N1837.

Disbanded 18th April 1942 at Kidsdale.

'X' Flight Formed 15th May 1939 at Henlow.

Queen Bee N1844.

Disbanded 1st November 1942 at Aberporth to become 1621 (Anti-Aircraft Co-operation) Flight.

'Y' Flight Formed 11th April 1938 at Henlow.

Queen Bee P4774.

Disbanded 16th August 1942 at Manorbier and absorbed by the Pilotless Aircraft Unit.

'Z' Flight Formed 11th April 1938 at Watchet by redesignating 'D' Flight, 1 Anti-Aircraft Co-operation Unit.

Queen Bee K8651; Tutor K4823; Magister L8271.

Disbanded 1st November 1942 at Bodorgan to become 1620 (Anti-Aircraft Co-operation) Flight.

Also used *Battle K9208, Battle Trainer P6733; Swordfish I L7634; Proctor I P6230; Master I T8781; Moth X5119; Leopard Moth AX873; Oxford I EB810; Martinet I HN884.*

Disbanded 1st October 1942 at Farnborough.

2 ANTI-AIRCRAFT CO-OPERATION UNIT
Formed 15th February 1937 at Lee-on-Solent by merging 1 Gunnery Co-operation Flight and 'A' Flight, School of Naval Co-operation.

Nil (2.37– .40) *Fairey IIIF K1726; Seal K4202; Shark II K8517, III K8909; Osprey K2782; Fury K8273; Gladiator I K6149, II N2308; Battle L5666; Queen Bee N1830; Swordfish I K5927; Skua I L2980; Roc I L3162; Hampden I X3137; Moth X5119; Defiant I DR923.*

JQ (.40–2.43) *Battle L5664 JQ-O; Hector K8150 JQ-L.*

An element, known as the Co-operation Flight, Mount Batten operated Shark II K8517, III L2366 and Swordfish I K8346 in conjunction with the RN Gunnery School, Devonport.

Disbanded 14th February 1943, 'A' Flight at Gosport, 'C' Flight at Roborough and 'D' Flight at Detling becoming respectively 1622, 1623 and 1624 (Anti-Aircraft Co-operation) Flights.

3 ANTI-AIRCRAFT CO-OPERATION UNIT
Formed 1st March 1937 at Kalafrana, Malta, by redesignating 2 Gunnery Co-operation Flight.

Seal K4782; Tutor K3350; Queen Bee K4229; Swordfish I K5943; Skua L2992; Magister N5427.

Disbanded 19th September 1940 at Kalafrana, some aircraft being transferred to 830 Squadron and the personnel and the remaining aircraft transferred to form 431 (General Reconnaissance) Flight.

4 ANTI-AIRCRAFT CO-OPERATION UNIT
Formed 1st August 1938 at Seletar, Singapore.

Tutor K3462 Z; Tiger Moth I K2590; Vildebeest II K2935; Shark II K5646 P; III K8923 Q; Swordfish I P4068 F; Queen Bee N1832.

Overrun by the Japanese and officially disbanded 28th March 1942 at Mingaladon, Burma.

5 ANTI-AIRCRAFT CO-OPERATION UNIT
Formed 6th May 1940 at Ringway, moving to Perth 3rd June 1940.

No aircraft, if any, known.

Disbanded by August 1940 at Perth.

6 ANTI-AIRCRAFT CO-OPERATION UNIT
Formed 1st March 1940 at Ringway.

Blenheim I K7147, IV T2333; Battle L5034; Lysander II P1688, IIIA V9492, TT.IIIA V9356; Magister L8061; Oxford I L4544, II X7284; Master I N7455; Tiger Moth II N9190; Leopard Moth X9380; Dragon Rapide Z7253; Puss Moth AX869; Falcon Six AV973; Scion Junior AV974; Dragonfly X9327; Monospar ST-6 AV979; Monospar ST-25 X9369; Scion II X9364; Vega Gull X9371; Dragon BS816; Percival Q-6 X9407; Spartan Cruiser X9433; Hurricane IV KZ911.

Disbanded 1st December 1943 at Castle Bromwich and merged with 7 and 8 Anti-Aircraft Co-operation Units to become 577 Squadron.

7 ANTI-AIRCRAFT CO-OPERATION UNIT
Formed 26th March 1940 at Ringway.

Oxford I L4549, II V3604; Battle L5011; Magister L5982; Master I N7421; Tiger Moth II N9386; Lysander II P1671, III T1432, IIIA V9293; Blenheim IV T2351; Monospar ST-25 X9331; Dragon Rapide Z7262; Dragonfly X9337; Dragon X9379; Leopard Moth X9381; Vega Gull X9455; Spartan Cruiser X9433; Hurricane IV KW817; Martinet I HP181.

Disbanded 1st December 1943 at Castle Bromwich and merged with 6 and 8 Anti-Aircraft Co-operation Units to become 577 Squadron.

8 ANTI-AIRCRAFT CO-OPERATION UNIT
Formed 16th April 1940 at Ringway.

Tiger Moth II T7024; Master I N7497; Magister T9831; Oxford I V4079, II ED183; Blenheim IV V5467; Lysander II P9187, III T1579, IIIA V9316; Dragon AW154; Dragonfly X9327; Dragon Rapide AW155; Vega Gull X9435; Monospar ST-6 AV979; Monospar ST-12 BD150; Monospar ST-25 X9372; Leopard Moth AV975; Hurricane IV KW816.

Disbanded 1st December 1943 at Pagham Moors and merged with 6 and 7 Anti-Aircraft Co-operation Units to become 577 Squadron.

9 ANTI-AIRCRAFT CO-OPERATION UNIT
Formed 15th April 1940 at Ringway. It then appears to have moved to Woodley before being discontinued.

No aircraft, if any, known.

Disbanded (date and location unknown).

21 ANTI-AIRCRAFT CO-OPERATION UNIT
Formed December 1942 at Takoradi, Gold Coast.

Defiant I DS152.

Disbanded 31st March 1944 at Ikeja, Nigeria.

Reformed February 1945 at Robertsfield, Liberia.

Defiant I DS157.

Disbanded 10th May 1945 at Robertsfield.

22 ANTI-AIRCRAFT CO-OPERATION UNIT
Formed 3rd December 1942 at Drigh Road, India, by redesignating 1 Anti-Aircraft Co-operation Unit, Indian Air Force.

Wapiti IIA K1403; Lysander II N1204; Harlow PJC-5 DR424.

Disbanded 17th March 1943 at Drigh Road.

Reformed 17th March 1943 at Drigh Road by merging the former unit and 2 and 3 Anti-Aircraft Co-operation Units, Indian Air Force.

Hurricane I Z4229, IIC LB557, IV KX543; Blenheim IV Z6091, V BA658; Maryland I AR723; Buffalo I W8243; Defiant I DS123, II AA404; Vengeance I AN900, IA EZ899, III FB931, IV FD313; Harlow PJC-5 DR424; Harvard IIB FS949; Moth Minor HX796; Tiger Moth LR228; Martinet TT.I NR643; Beaufighter VI JL768.

Disbanded 1st April 1947 at Santa Cruz, India (HQ Flight), Drigh Road, India ('A' Flight) and Poona, India ('B' Flight). 'A' Flight became 1 Target Towing Flight, RIAF and 'B' Flight became 2 Target Towing Flight, RIAF.

23 ANTI-AIRCRAFT CO-OPERATION UNIT
Formed 1st August 1943 at Habbaniya, Iraq.

Defiant I DS131; II AA513; Hurricane IIC LD306; Vengeance II AN676; IV HB474.

Disbanded 15th March 1946 at Ciampino, Italy.

24 ANTI-AIRCRAFT CO-OPERATION UNIT
Planned opening in December 1943 at Aden cancelled.

25 ANTI-AIRCRAFT CO-OPERATION UNIT
Formed 15th January 1943 in the United Kingdom and become operational at Eastleigh, Kenya, from 10th August 1943.

Battle HK933; Puss Moth; Defiant I DS122; II AA415; Hurricane IIC KW705.

Disbanded 5th November 1945 at Eastleigh.

26 ANTI-AIRCRAFT CO-OPERATION UNIT
Formed November 1942 at El Firdan, Egypt, by redesignating the Air Defence Co-operation Unit.

Hart Trainer K6422; Gladiator I K8033; Fulmar I N3995, II N4087; Defiant II AA547; Hurricane I V7131; IIA Z4955; IIB BP282; IIC KW854; Spitfire VC MA702 26-F; Maryland I AR748, II AH295; Baltimore I AG711, II AG759, III AG938 J, IV FA631 26-O, V FW295 26-C; Argus II FS640; Vengeance IV HB412; Wellington X LN280.

Disbanded 31st March 1947 at Aqir, Palestine.

1 ANTI-AIRCRAFT CO-OPERATION UNIT, IAFVR – see Anti-Aircraft Co-operation Flight, IAFVR, later 1 Anti-Aircraft Co-operation Flight, IAFVR, later 1 Anti-Aircraft Co-operation Unit, IAF

2 ANTI-AIRCRAFT CO-OPERATION UNIT, IAFVR – see 2 Anti-Aircraft Co-operation Flight, IAFVR, later 2 Anti-Aircraft Co-operation Unit, IAF

3 ANTI-AIRCRAFT CO-OPERATION UNIT, IAFVR – see 3 Anti-Aircraft Co-operation Flight, IAFVR, later 3 Anti-Aircraft Co-operation Unit, IAF

ANTI-AIRCRAFT PRACTICE CAMPS – see Royal Air Force Regiment Anti-Aircraft Practice Camp Flights

ANTI-AIRCRAFT SPECIAL DEFENCE FLIGHT
Formed October 1918 at Gosport.

Camel.

Disbanded December 1918 at Gosport.

ANTI-LOCUST FLIGHT (PERSIA), later ANTI-LOCUST FLIGHT (MIDDLE EAST)
Formed 1st February 1943 at Ahwaz, Persia. Redesignated the Anti-Locust Flight (Middle East) from 4th March 1944.

Vincent K6349; Blenheim IV Z6436; Anson I LT843; Baltimore IV FA430; Albacore I T9171.

Disbanded 15th January 1946 at Eastleigh, Kenya.

ANTI-LOCUST FLIGHT (MIDDLE EAST) – see Anti-Locust Flight (Persia), later Anti-Locust Flight (Middle East)

ANTI-U-BOAT DEVICES SCHOOL – see Coastal Command Anti-U-Boat Devices School

ANTLER SQUADRON
Formed 1st January 1956 at Hemswell by redesignating 83 Squadron.

No aircraft allocated.

Disbanded 1st October 1957 and merged with Arrow Squadron to become 1321 Lincoln Conversion Flight.

ARABIAN PENINSULAR RECONNAISSANCE FLIGHT
Formed 1st October 1959 at Khormaksar, Aden, by redesignating the Aden Protectorate Reconnaissance Flight.

Meteor FR.9 VZ604.

Disbanded April 1960 at Khormaksar and absorbed by 8 Squadron.

ARDENNES FLIGHT – see Escadrille 'Ardennes'

ARGOSY CONVERSION UNIT
Formed 1st November 1961 at Benson.

Argosy C.1 XN855.

Disbanded 30th April 1963 at Benson to become the Argosy Flight of 242 Operational Conversion Unit.

ARGUS FLIGHT
Formed 7th October 1918 at Turnhouse before embarking aboard HMS *Argus* on 19th October 1918.

Camel N8130; Panther N7452; Fairey IIIB N2257, IIID N9456.

The following aircraft participated in deck landing and other trials while the Flight existed:

1½ Strutter; Pup; D.H.9; D.H.9A H3451; Puffin; Fairey IIIB N2259; Viking; Walrus; Seagull; Nighthawk H8535; Sparrowhawk; Cuckoo N6977; Bison; Snipe E6611; Flycatcher N163; Plover N160; Dart N9540; Blackburn N9590; Avro 504N J8539; Nightjar H8540.

Disbanded 1st April 1923 aboard HMS *Argus*.

ARMAMENT AND GUNNERY SCHOOL
Formed 1st April 1922 at Eastchurch by redesignating the School of Aerial Gunnery and Bombing.

Snipe E6310; D.H.9A F2796; Vimy F9155; F.2B J8272; Grebe II J7367, IIIDC J7530; Woodcock II J7726; Gamecock I J8033; Siskin III J7148, IIIA J8381; Avro 504N J8726; Wapiti IIA K1318; Flycatcher N9656.

Disbanded 1st January 1932 at Eastchurch to become the Air Armament School.

ARMAMENT AND INSTRUMENT EXPERIMENTAL ESTABLISHMENT – see Armament and Instrument Experimental Unit, later the Armament and Instrument Experimental Establishment

ARMAMENT AND INSTRUMENT EXPERIMENTAL UNIT, later ARMAMENT AND INSTRUMENT EXPERIMENTAL ESTABLISHMENT
Formed 1st June 1946 at Martlesham Heath. Officially absorbed the Bomb Ballistic Unit and the Blind Landing Experimental Unit from 15th November 1949, both of which retained their original identity.

Functional administrative control by the Royal Air Force ceased with effect from 1st November 1955 when the unit was redesignated the Armament and Instrument Experimental Establishment.

Dakota III KJ836; Anson XII PH622, T.21 VV319; Mosquito NF.38 VT654; Meteor F.4 VW308; Athena T.2 VR569; Lincoln B.1 RE242; Devon C.1 VP954; Short SA.4 VX161; Canberra T.4 WE189; Varsity T.1 WL664; Comet 3B XP915.

See also the Blind Landing Experimental Unit and the Bomb Ballistic Unit.

Disbanded 1st July 1957 at Martlesham Heath and absorbed by the Royal Aircraft Establishment.

ARMAMENT EXPERIMENTAL STATION
Formed 13th October 1917 at Orfordness by redesignating the Experimental Station, Orfordness.

Martinsyde S.1 710; Triplane N5430; D.H.2 A5058; R.E.8 A3432; R.E.1; B.E.2e A8636; F.E.2b B401; F.2A.

Disbanded 16th March 1920 and absorbed by the Aeroplane Experimental Establishment.

1 ARMAMENT PRACTICE CAMP
Formed 5th November 1941 at Aldergrove by redesignating 15 Group Armament Practice Camp.

Lysander II P9125, III T1446, IIIA W6957; Battle L5590; Master II DK951; Martinet I JN679; Dominie I X7406.

Disbanded 1st September 1945 at Aldergrove.

2 ARMAMENT PRACTICE CAMP
Formed 5th November 1941 at Thorney Island by redesignating 16 Group Armament Practice Camp.

Lysander III T1525, IIIA W6943; Martinet I JN668 D.

Disbanded 1st September 1945 at Bradwell Bay and absorbed by the Armament Practice Station, Spilsby.

3 ARMAMENT PRACTICE CAMP
Formed 5th November 1941 at Leuchars by redesignating 18 Group Armament Practice Camp.

Lysander II P1688, III T1741, IIIA W6943; Battle K7644; Martinet I JN541 E.

Disbanded 1st September 1945 at Leuchars.

4 ARMAMENT PRACTICE CAMP
Formed 5th November 1941 at Carew Cheriton by redesignating 19 Group Armament Practice Camp.

Lysander IIIA V9445; Battle N2118; Master II DL194; Martinet I MS689.

Disbanded 1st September 1945 at Talbenny.

11 ARMAMENT PRACTICE CAMP
Formed 18th October 1943 at Fairwood Common by merging 1487 (Fighter Gunnery) and 1498 (Target Towing) Flights.

Lysander IIIA V9745; Master I T8579, II AZ359, III W8732; Martinet I EM588; Spitfire IIA P8667; Anson I EG189.

Disbanded 30th June 1945 at Fairwood Common and merged with 18 Armament Practice Camp to become 1 Armament Practice Station.

12 ARMAMENT PRACTICE CAMP
Formed 18th October 1943 at Llanbedr by redesignating 1486 (Fighter Gunnery) Flight.

Lysander III T1555, IIIA V9799; Master II DL360, III W8861; Martinet I EM441; Hurricane IV KZ660.

Disbanded 21st February 1945 at Llanbedr.

13 ARMAMENT PRACTICE CAMP
Formed 18th October 1943 at Weston Zoyland by redesignating 1492 (Target Towing) Flight.

Master II DL130, III W8890; Martinet I HN866; Hurricane IV KX584.

Disbanded 21st February 1945 at Llanbedr.

14 ARMAMENT PRACTICE CAMP
Formed 18th October 1943 at Ayr by redesignating 1490 (Fighter Gunnery) Flight.

Henley III L3376; Lysander II R1998, III R9008, IIIA V9707; Master II AZ695, III W8736; Martinet I EM571 D; Hurricane IV KX579; Typhoon IB RB266.

Disbanded 4th October 1945 at Warmwell.

15 ARMAMENT PRACTICE CAMP
Formed 18th October 1943 at Peterhead by redesignating 1491 (Fighter Gunnery) Flight.

Lysander II N1276, III T1578, IIIA V9853; Battle L5590; Master II DK951, III DL566; Martinet I HN913.

Disbanded 21st February 1945 at Peterhead.

16 ARMAMENT PRACTICE CAMP
Formed 18th October 1943 at Hutton Cranswick by redesignating 1489 (Fighter Gunnery) Flight and absorbing 1495 (Target Towing) Flight on 14th November 1943.

Henley III L3267; Lysander II R1998, III T1697, IIIA V9824; Master III W8645; Martinet I EM476.

Disbanded 21st February 1945 at Hutton Cranswick.

17 ARMAMENT PRACTICE CAMP
Formed 18th October 1943 at Rochford by redesignating 1488 (Fighter Gunnery) Flight.

Lysander I R2638, II N1227, III T1741, IIIA V9795; Master II AZ707, III W8848; Martinet I HN972; Spitfire IX MK184.

Disbanded 4th October 1945 at Warmwell.

18 ARMAMENT PRACTICE CAMP
Formed 18th October 1943 at Gravesend by redesignating 1493 (Fighter Gunnery) Flight.

| Nil (10.43– .45) | *Lysander III T1466, IIIA V9795; Hurricane IV KX579; Typhoon IB JR434; Auster III NJ971.* |
| R4 (.45–7.45) | *Master II DL417 R4-E; Spitfire IX SM139; Martinet I JN282 R4-16.* |

Disbanded 30th June 1945 at Fairwood Common and merged with 11 Armament Practice Camp to become 1 Armament Practice Station.

20 ARMAMENT PRACTICE CAMP
Formed 30th January 1944 at Ratmalana, Ceylon, by redesignating 1571 (Ground Gunnery) Flight.

Harvard IIB FE683; Vengeance I AN981, IA EZ994; Hurricane IIB BG850.

Disbanded 19th April 1944 at Sigiriya, Ceylon.

21 ARMAMENT PRACTICE CAMP
Formed 30th January 1944 at St Thomas Mount, India, by redesignating 1572 (Ground Gunnery) Flight.

Harvard IIB FE703; Vengeance I AN893, II AN798; Wellington IC HX773.

Disbanded 18th June 1945 at Cholavarum, India.

22 ARMAMENT PRACTICE CAMP
Formed 30th January 1944 at Amarda Road, India, by redesignating 1573 (Ground Gunnery) Flight.

Harvard IIB FE371; Vengeance I AN920; Blenheim V EH508.

Disbanded November 1946 at Ranchi, India.

23 ARMAMENT PRACTICE CAMP
Formed 10th March 1944 at Salbani, India.

Harvard IIB FE607; Vengeance I AN904, IA EZ825, II AN644, III FB948.

Disbanded 31st May 1945 at Dhubalia, India.

24 ARMAMENT PRACTICE CAMP
Formed 15th July 1945 at B.170 (Westerland) later Sylt, Germany.

Master II AZ595; Martinet I MS724.

Disbanded 17th July 1946 at Sylt and merged with 25 Armament Practice Camp to become the Training Squadron, Sylt.

25 ARMAMENT PRACTICE CAMP
Formed 15th July 1945 at B.170 (Westerland) later Sylt, Germany.

Master II W9032, III DL973; Martinet I EM552 6; Tempest V EJ739; Mosquito VI RF640.

Disbanded 17th July 1946 at Sylt and merged with 24 Armament Practice Camp to become the Training Squadron, Sylt.

26 ARMAMENT PRACTICE CAMP
Formed 15th April 1948 at Nicosia, Cyprus.

Beaufighter TT.X SR917.

Disbanded 19th February 1951 at Nicosia.

27 ARMAMENT PRACTICE CAMP
Formed 1st January 1949 at Butterworth, Malaya. Operated within the Far East Training Squadron from 22nd September 1950.

Harvard IIB KF107; Beaufighter TT.X SR912; Meteor TT.8 WH410; Vampire FB.9 WL684, T.11 WZ610.

Officially disbanded 20th September 1954 at Butterworth but not absorbed by Far East Air Force Training Squadron until 4th November 1954.

ARMAMENT PRACTICE CAMP, BUTTERWORTH
Formed 31st March 1955 at Butterworth, Malaya by redesignating an element of the disbanding Far East Training Squadron. Later absorbed the Station Flight, Butterworth.

Vampire FB.9 WL564, T.11 WZ610; Meteor TT.8 WH410; Harvard IIB KF107.

Disbanded 30th April 1956 at Butterworth.

ARMAMENT PRACTICE CAMP (MIDDLE EAST AIR FORCE)
Formed 31st January 1956 at Nicosia, Cyprus.

Meteor F.8 WK953; Vampire T.11 XE889.

Disbanded 10th January 1957 at Habbaniya, Iraq.

ARMAMENT PRACTICE STATION, ACKLINGTON
Formed 1st May 1946 at Acklington by redesignating 2 Armament Practice Station, Acklington.

8I (5.46– .50)	*Master II DM128 8I-F; Harvard IIB KF342 8I-S; Mustang IV KM218 8I-K; Martinet I MS924 8I-9; Mosquito III RR319 8I-A, VI TA555 8I-B.*
WH (.50–4.51)	*Spitfire XVI TE407 WH-H; Martinet I JN543 WH-5; Oxford II R6285 WH-D; Tempest TT.V SN260 WH-17; Mosquito VI RF875 WH-E; Meteor F.4 VT195 WH-C, T.7 WF819 WH-G, F.8 WK752 WH-U; Vampire F.3 VT797 WH-P, FB.5 VZ269 WH-J, T.11 WZ615 WH-J; Balliol T.2 VR598 WH-K.*
Nil (4.51–5.56)	*Mosquito TT.35 TA633 E; Vampire F.3 VT797, FB.5 VZ269; Meteor T.7 WA599, TT.8 WL117 1; Tiger Moth II T7040; Chipmunk T.10 WD318; Anson XII PH667; Spitfire XVI TD151; Vampire T.11 XE934.*

Disbanded 27th July 1956 at Acklington.

ARMAMENT PRACTICE CAMP, SYLT
The Royal Air Force Station, Sylt, reopened during February 1949 and provided facilities for an Armament Practice Camp, operating Mosquito III and TT.35, Meteor T.7, Tempest V and VI and Vampire FB.5 aircraft, from at least June 1951. The Camp was probably disbanded in July 1955 to become the Armament Practice Station, Sylt.

ARMAMENT PRACTICE STATION, LÜBECK
Formed 1st May 1946 at Lübeck, Germany.

Mosquito III VA890, VI RS639; Meteor F.4 VT229.

Disbanded 30th September 1948 at Lübeck.

ARMAMENT PRACTICE STATION, SPILSBY
Formed 1st December 1945 at Spilsby.

Master II; Mosquito VI; Martinet I.

Disbanded 1st August 1946 at Spilsby and absorbed by the Armament Practice Station, Acklington.

ARMAMENT PRACTICE STATION, SYLT
Formed 1st August 1955 at Sylt, Germany, by redesignating the Royal Air Force Station, Sylt.

Anson XIX VP535; Mosquito III VT613 F, TT.35 TH992; Meteor T.7 WL379, F.8 WH346; F(TT).8 WL109 H; Vampire T.11 XE956; Prentice T.1 VR282; Sycamore HR.14 XG513; Hunter F.4 XF370, T.7 XL612.

Disbanded 16th October 1961 at Sylt.

1 ARMAMENT PRACTICE STATION
Formed 1st July 1945 at Fairwood Common by merging 11 and 18 Armament Practice Camps.

R4	*Master II AZ259 R4-F, III DL417 R4-E; Martinet I JN282 R4-16; Dominie I X7406; Mustang III FB382, IVA KH777; Spitfire XVI TE389; Tempest V SN236.*

Disbanded 1st May 1946 at Fairwood Common.

2 ARMAMENT PRACTICE STATION
Formed 1st July 1945 at Bradwell Bay.

8I	*Master II W9074 8I-E, III DM128; Albemarle I/III P1639; Mustang IVA KH680; Martinet I HP176 8I-14; Mosquito III VT587, VI TA490; Spitfire XVI TE342.*

Disbanded 1st May 1946 at Spilsby to become the Armament Practice Station, Acklington.

3 ARMAMENT PRACTICE STATION
Formed 10th August 1945 at Hawkinge.

QK	*Lysander III P9060; Master II DK823 QK-C, III DL857; Martinet I HP164; Spitfire IX MJ734 QK-F; Auster I LB296; Tempest V SN227.*

Disbanded 17th March 1946 at Charterhall.

Reformed 7th November 1946 at Charterhall.

Martinet I JN509.

Disbanded 26th March 1947 at Charterhall.

ARMAMENT TRAINING CAMP, KUANTAN
Formed 16th October 1941 at Kuantan, Malaya.

No aircraft known.

Abandoned December 1941 to the Japanese.

1 ARMAMENT TRAINING CAMP
Formed 1st January 1932 at Catfoss.

Moth K1215; Gordon I K1746; Audax K3071; Cloud K3722.

Disbanded 1st April 1938 at Catfoss to become 1 Armament Training Station.

2 ARMAMENT TRAINING CAMP
Formed 1st January 1932 at North Coates Fitties.

Vickers 150 J9131; Gordon I J9167; Wallace I K3562.

Disbanded 6th October 1936 at North Coates Fitties to become the Temporary Armament Training Camp, North Coates Fitties.

Reformed 6th October 1936 at Aldergrove by redesignating the Temporary Armament Training Camp, Aldergrove.

Wallace I K5072, II K8699; Hind K6681.

Disbanded 1st April 1938 at Aldergrove to become 2 Armament Training Station.

3 ARMAMENT TRAINING CAMP
Formed 1st January 1932 at Sutton Bridge.

Moth K1825; Gordon I K1747; Tutor K3468; Wallace I K3566, II K6067.

Disbanded 1st April 1938 at Sutton Bridge to become 3 Armament Training Station.

4 ARMAMENT TRAINING CAMP
Formed 1st March 1937 at West Freugh.

Wallace II K6062; Hind K6686; Tutor K3259.

Disbanded 1st April 1938 at West Freugh to become 4 Armament Training Station.

5 ARMAMENT TRAINING CAMP
Formed 1st February 1937 at Penrhos.

Wallace I K5116, II K8695: Tutor K3299.

Disbanded 1st April 1938 at Penrhos to become 5 Armament Training Station.

6 ARMAMENT TRAINING CAMP
Formed 1st May 1937 at Woodsford, later renamed Warmwell.

Wallace I K3565, II K6058; Tutor K3427.

Disbanded 1st April 1938 at Woodsford to become 6 Armament Training Station.

7 ARMAMENT TRAINING CAMP
Was to have formed 1st December 1937 at Acklington but the opening was delayed until 1st April 1938 and redesignated 7 Armament Training Station.

8 ARMAMENT TRAINING CAMP
Formed 1st September 1937 at Evanton.

Gordon I K1740; Audax K7448; Tutor K3256; Wallace K8690.

Disbanded 1st April 1938 at Evanton to become 8 Armament Training Station.

1 ARMAMENT TRAINING STATION
Formed 1st April 1938 at Catfoss by redesignating 1 Armament Training Camp.

Fairey IIIF J9787; Gordon I K2717; Henley III L3261.

Disbanded 11th September 1939 at Catfoss and absorbed by 3 Air Observers School.

1 ARMAMENT TRAINING STATION (FRANCE)
Formed 18th January 1940 at Perpignan, France.

No aircraft known.

Disbanded 31st March 1940 at Perpignan.

2 ARMAMENT TRAINING STATION
Formed 1st April 1938 at Aldergrove by redesignating 2 Armament Training Camp.

Wallace II K6083; Hind K6681.

Disbanded 17th April 1939 at Aldergrove to become 3 Air Observers School.

3 ARMAMENT TRAINING STATION
Formed 1st April 1938 at Sutton Bridge by redesignating 3 Armament Training Camp.

Gordon TT K1766; Wallace II K6067; Henley III L3258; Tutor K3467; Magister L8338.

Disbanded 5th September 1939 at Sutton Bridge and absorbed by 4 Air Observers School.

4 ARMAMENT TRAINING STATION
Formed 1st April 1938 at West Freugh by redesignating 4 Armament Training Camp.

Wallace II K6071; Hind K6686.

Disbanded 17th April 1939 at West Freugh to become 4 Air Observers School.

5 ARMAMENT TRAINING STATION
Formed 1st April 1938 at Penrhos by redesignating 5 Armament Training Camp.

Wallace II K8687; Henley III L3350; Magister P2404.

Disbanded 18th September 1939 at Jurby to become 5 Air Observers School.

6 ARMAMENT TRAINING STATION
Formed 1st April 1938 at Woodsford (later Warmwell) by redesignating 6 Armament Training Camp.

Tutor K3427; Seal K4785; Wallace II K6054; Gladiator I K7987; Henley III L3315; Magister P2405.

Disbanded 2nd September 1939 at Warmwell and merged with 2 Air Observers School to become 10 Air Observers School.

7 ARMAMENT TRAINING STATION
Formed 1st April 1938 at Acklington by redesignating 7 Armament Training Camp.

Overstrand J9187; Seal K3517; Hind K4654; Wellesley K8529.

Disbanded 15th November 1938 at Acklington to become 2 Air Observers School.

8 ARMAMENT TRAINING STATION
Formed 1st April 1938 at Evanton by redesignating 8 Armament Training Camp.

Gordon I K2723; Henley III L3301; Magister P2406.

Disbanded 3rd September 1939 at Evanton to become 8 Air Observers School.

9 ARMAMENT TRAINING STATION
Formed 24th April 1939 at Stormy Down.

Henley III L3341.

Disbanded 1st September 1939 at Stormy Down to become 7 Air Observers School.

1 ARMAMENT TRAINING UNIT
Formed 18th February 1942 at Peshawar, India.

Wapiti IIA J9716; Audax K5562; Hart K2095; Lysander II N1255.

Disbanded 12th May 1943 at Bairagarh to become 1 Air Gunners School (India).

ARMY AND NAVY CO-OPERATION FLIGHT – see Royal Air Force Base, Gosport, later Royal Air Force Station, Gosport

ARMY CO-OPERATION COMMAND COMMUNICATION FLIGHT
Formed 1st December 1940 at White Waltham by redesignating 22 Group Communication Flight.

Mentor L4413; Magister L8061; Hurricane I P2715; Vega Gull P5988; Proctor I P6173; Lysander III T1567; Dominie I X7445; Tiger Moth II T7087; Dragonfly X9327; Petrel X9406; Leopard Moth AX865.

Disbanded 31st May 1943 at White Waltham to become the 2nd Tactical Air Force Communication Flight.

ARMY CO-OPERATION DEVELOPMENT UNIT
Formed (date and location unknown). Possibly associated with the Central Landing School at Ringway.

Overstrand K8176.

Disbanded (date and location unknown).

ARMY CO-OPERATION SCHOOL – see Royal Air Force and Army Co-operation School

ARMY EXPERIMENTAL COMMUNICATION FLIGHT – see Light Communication Trial Flight

ARROW SQUADRON
Formed 1st January 1956 at Hemswell by redesignating 97 Squadron.

No aircraft allocated.

Disbanded 1st October 1957 at Hemswell and merged with Antler Squadron to become 1321 Lincoln Conversion Flight.

ARTILLERY AND INFANTRY CO-OPERATION SCHOOL
Formed 7th November 1917 at Hursley Park by redesignating the Wireless and Observers School.

R.E.8 C2472; Avro 504K B8703; B.E.2e C7003; F.2B F4292; F.K.8 C3541; F.K.8 D5055.

Disbanded 19th September 1918 at Worthy Down to become the Royal Air Force and Army Co-operation School.

ARTILLERY CO-OPERATION SQUADRON
Formed 13th January 1917 by merging the Artillery Co-operation Flight, Central Flying School and the Artillery Co-operation Flight, Lydd. Parented by 11 Training Depot Station between February and July 1919.

R.E.8 A4496; F.K.8 B3308; F.2B C9861; Avro 504K.

Disbanded 8th March 1920 at Stonehenge to become the School of Army Co-operation.

ARTILLERY FLIGHT
Formed July 1918 at Bruay, France.

No aircraft known.

Disbanded 9th July 1918 at Bruay to become 'L' Flight.

ARTILLERY OBSERVATION SCHOOL, later ARTILLERY OBSERVATION SCHOOL, EGYPT
Formed 20th November 1917 at Almaza, Egypt, by redesignating 197 Training Squadron. Redesignated the Artillery Observation School, Egypt from September 1918.

R.E.8 A3658; D.H.6.

Disbanded 22nd July 1919 at Almaza.

ARTILLERY OBSERVATION SCHOOL, EGYPT – see Artillery Observation School, later Artillery Observation School, Egypt

AUSTRALIAN FLYING CORPS TRAINING SQUADRONS

5TH (TRAINING) SQUADRON, AFC
Formed 14th January 1918 at Shawbury by redesignating 29 (Australian Flying Corps) Training Squadron, RFC.

Shorthorn A4074; Camel C106; D.H.6 C6550; S.E.5a D362; Snipe E8138; Avro 504K H1925.

Disbanded 30th April 1919 at Minchinhampton.

6TH (TRAINING) SQUADRON, AFC
Formed 14th January 1918 at Ternhill by redesignating 30 (Australian Flying Corps) Training Squadron, RFC.

1½ Strutter A5293; Avro 504K A8598; D.H.5 A9416; S.E.5a B133; Pup B1764; Camel B9162.

Disbanded June 1919 at Minchinhampton.

7TH (TRAINING) SQUADRON, AFC
Formed 14th January 1918 at Yatesbury by redesignating 32 (Australian Flying Corps) Training Squadron, Royal Flying Corps.

Avro 504; D.H.6 B2775; B.E.2e B6175; F.2B C998; R.E.8 C2476; S.E.5a E5652.

Disbanded April 1919 at Leighterton.

8TH (TRAINING) SQUADRON, AFC
Formed 14th January 1918 at Minchinhampton by redesignating 33 (Australian Flying Corps) Training Squadron, Royal Flying Corps.

Camel C127; Pup D4191; Snipe E7287; Avro 504C H1925, Avro 504K H1925.

Disbanded April 1919 at Leighterton.

AUSTRIA COMMISSION FLIGHT – see Air Headquarters Austria Communication Flight, later Austria Commission Flight

AUSTRIA COMMUNICATION FLIGHT – see Air Headquarters Austria Communication Flight, later Austria Commission Flight

ASV TRAINING FLIGHT – see Air-to-Surface Vessel (ASV) Training Flight

ATOMIC WEAPONS RESEARCH ESTABLISHMENT
The Establishment was allocated the following aircraft:

Varsity T.1 WL673; Canberra B.2 WD942; PR.3 WE147; English Electric P.1B XG310.

AUTOGIRO UNIT – see 24 Squadron

AUTOGYRO TRAINING FLIGHT
Formed 2nd April 1940 at Odiham.

Rota II L7591; Cierva C.30A V1186; C.40 T1419.

Disbanded 15th July 1940 at Odiham and absorbed by 5 Radio Maintenance Unit.

AUXILIARY FIGHTER SQUADRON (MALAYA)
Formed 1st March 1950 at Butterworth.

Tiger Moth II N9519; Spitfire; Harvard IIB.

Disbanded 1st June 1950 at Butterworth to become the Penang Fighter Squadron.

AUXILIARY FIGHTER SQUADRON (SINGAPORE), later SINGAPORE FIGHTER SQUADRON, later SINGAPORE SQUADRON
Formed 1st March 1950 at Tengah, Singapore. Redesignated Singapore Fighter Squadron from 1st October 1951 and Singapore Squadron from 20th June 1955.

Tiger Moth II; Spitfire F.24 PK681; Harvard IIB FX496; Chipmunk T.10.

Disbanded 30th September 1960 at Tengah.

1 (AUXILIARY) SCHOOL OF AERIAL GUNNERY – see School Of Aerial Gunnery, Hythe, later 1 (Auxiliary) School Of Aerial Gunnery

2 (AUXILIARY) SCHOOL OF AERIAL GUNNERY
Formed January 1917 at Turnberry.

D.H.2 5936; Shorthorn A2478; F.B.9 A8620; B.E.2e B4562; F.K.3; Camel B9222.

Disbanded 10th May 1918 at Turnberry and merged with 1 School of Aerial Fighting to become 1 School of Aerial Fighting and Gunnery.

3 (AUXILIARY) SCHOOL OF AERIAL GUNNERY
Formed 1st August 1917 at New Romney.

No aircraft known.

Disbanded 9th March 1918 and merged with 1 (Auxiliary) School Of Aerial Gunnery to become 1 (Observer) School of Aerial Gunnery.

4 (AUXILIARY) SCHOOL OF AERIAL GUNNERY
Formed 1st November 1917 at Marske.

S.E.5a; F.K.3 B9594; Dolphin; F.2B C4692 43; D.H.9 C1185, D.H.9A F952; Pup C414 103; Camel C1662 102; Bristol M.1c C4996 128.

Disbanded 6th May 1918 at Marske and merged with 2 School of Aerial Fighting to become 2 School of Aerial Fighting and Gunnery.

B-29 TRAINING SQUADRON – see Washington Conversion Unit

'B' BOAT SEAPLANE TRAINING FLIGHT
Formed 8th August 1918 at Calshot within 210 Training Depot Station.

No aircraft known.

Disbanded 1919 at Calshot.

'B' FLIGHT (1) – see 520 (Special Duty) Flight

'B' FLIGHT (2) – see 522 (Special Duty) Flight

'B' FLIGHT (3) – see 524 (Special Duty) Flight

'B' FLIGHT (4) – see 526 (Special Duty) Flight

'B' FLIGHT, CALSHOT – see Royal Air Force Base, Calshot

'B' FLIGHT, GOSPORT – see Royal Air Force Base, Gosport, later Royal Air Force Station, Gosport

'B' FLIGHT, LEUCHARS – see Royal Air Force Base, Leuchars, later Royal Air Force Training Base, Leuchars

'B' FLIGHT, PALESTINE
Formed 1917 at Aboukir, Egypt, by redesignating an element of 23 Training Squadron.

B.E.2c; B.E.12.

Disbanded December 1917, probably at Weli Sheikh Nuran, Palestine.

'B' SQUADRON – see 1 Squadron

'B' SQUADRON, AEGEAN
Formed 1st April 1918 at Mitylene, Aegean, by redesignating 'B' Squadron of 2 Wing, RNAS.

No aircraft known.

Disbanded 18th September 1918 at Stavros, Aegean, to become 223 Squadron.

BALKAN AIR FORCE COMMUNICATION FLIGHT
Formed 7th June 1944 at Bari, Italy.

Anson I MG753, XII PH537; Expeditor II HB251.

Disbanded 15th July 1945 at Bari.

BALTIMORE PHOTOGRAPHIC FLIGHT
Formed 25th June 1945 at Shandur, Egypt.

Baltimore V FW756.

Disbanded 31st October 1945 at Eastleigh, Kenya.

BANGALORE CALIBRATION FLIGHT
Formed October 1942 at Bangalore, India.

No aircraft allocated.

Disbanded 13th September 1943 at Yelahanka, India, to become 1580 (Calibration) Flight.

BASE AIR FORCES, SOUTHEAST ASIA COMMUNICATION SQUADRON
Formed 1st October 1944 at Willingdon Airport, India, to become a detached element of the Headquarters Air Command Southeast Asia Communication Squadron.

Hudson VI FK483; DC-3 MA925; Dakota III KG507, IV KN300; Expeditor I HB133, II KJ478; Harvard IIB FE775; Argus II FZ729; Anson I DG904; Proctor III LZ651; DC-3 MA925; Hurricane IIC LB666, IV LD291; Spitfire XI PL769.

Disbanded 1st March 1946 at Palam, India, to become the Air Headquarters India Communication Squadron.

BASE AND TARGET TOWING FLIGHT, ROYAL AIR FORCE MAINTENANCE BASE (FAR EAST), SELETAR
Formed 1st May 1953 at Seletar, Singapore, by redesignating the Station and Target Towing Flight, Seletar.

Beaufighter X; Pembroke C.1 WV701; Meteor F.8 WL180; Meteor TT.20 WM230.

Disbanded (date unknown) at Seletar.

1 BASIC AIR NAVIGATION SCHOOL
Formed 1st February 1951 at Hamble. Operated by Air Service Training Ltd.

Anson T.21 WD404 57.

Disbanded 30th June 1953 at Hamble.

2 BASIC AIR NAVIGATION SCHOOL
Formed 18th April 1951 at Usworth. Operated by Airwork Ltd.

N   Anson T.21 WB450 NS.

Disbanded 30th April 1953 at Usworth.

1 BASIC FLYING TRAINING SCHOOL
Formed 20th December 1950 at Booker. Operated by Air Service Training Ltd.

Chipmunk T.10 WD285 R.

Disbanded 21st July 1953 at Booker.

2 BASIC FLYING TRAINING SCHOOL (1)
Formed 21st March 1951 at Ansty. Operated by Air Service Training Ltd.

Chipmunk T.10 WD380 20.

Disbanded 31st March 1953 at Ansty.

2 (BASIC) FLYING TRAINING SCHOOL (2) – see 2 Flying Training School, later 2 Service Flying Training School, later 2 Flying Training School, later 2 (Basic) Flying Training School

3 BASIC FLYING TRAINING SCHOOL (1)
Formed 14th November 1951 at Burnaston. Operated by Air Schools Ltd.

Chipmunk T.10 WG431 38.

Disbanded 21st July 1953 at Burnaston.

3 (BASIC) FLYING TRAINING SCHOOL (2) – see 3 Flying Training School, later 3 Service Flying Training School, later 3 Flying Training School, later 3 (Basic) Flying Training School, later 3 Flying Training School

4 BASIC FLYING TRAINING SCHOOL
Formed 14th November 1951 at Sywell. Operated by Brooklands Aviation Ltd.

Chipmunk T.10 WG467 50.

Disbanded 30th June 1953 at Sywell.

5 BASIC FLYING TRAINING SCHOOL
Formed 1st February 1952 at Desford. Operated by Reid and Sigrist Ltd.

Chipmunk T.10 WG485 18.

Disbanded 30th June 1953 at Desford.

BASSETT CONVERSION FLIGHT
Formed 5th July 1965 at Topcliffe within the Northern Communication Squadron.

Bassett C.1.

Disbanded 1st January 1967 at Topcliffe.

BATTLE FLIGHT
Formed January 1940 at Ambala, India.

No aircraft known.

Last known June 1940 at Juhu, India.

BATTLE OF BRITAIN FLIGHT, later BATTLE OF BRITAIN MEMORIAL FLIGHT
Formed 11th July 1957 at Biggin Hill as the Historic Aircraft Flight. Redesignated the Battle of Britain Flight from 21st February 1958 and the Battle of Britain Memorial Flight from 1st June 1969.

Hurricane IIC PZ865; Spitfire IIA P7350; VB AB910; XVI SL574;
XIX PM631; Mosquito B.35 TA639; Lancaster I PA474; Devon C.1 VP981; Chipmunk T.10 WK518; Dakota III ZA947.

Current 1st April 1998 at Coningsby.

BATTLE OF BRITAIN MEMORIAL FLIGHT – see Battle of Britain Flight, later Battle of Britain Memorial Flight

BEAM APPROACH CALIBRATION FLIGHT – see Blind Approach Calibration Flight, later Beam Approach Calibration Flight

BEAM APPROACH DEVELOPMENT UNIT
Formed 4th October 1942 at Watchfield.

Anson I DJ581; Oxford I DF403; Master III W8458.

Disbanded 15th April 1943 at Hinton-in-the-Hedges, merged with 1551 (Beam Approach Calibration) Flight, to become 'A' Flight, Signals Development Unit.

1 BEAM APPROACH SCHOOL – see Blind Approach School, later 1 Blind Approach School, later 1 Beam Approach School

BEAM APPROACH TRAINING FLIGHT, CHURCH LAWFORD
Formed March 1942 at Church Lawford within 1 Flying Instructors School.

No aircraft known.

Disbanded 27th October 1942 at Church Lawford to become 1533 (Beam Approach Training) Flight.

BEAM APPROACH TRAINING FLIGHT, NANYUKI
Formed (date unknown) at Manyuki, Kenya.

No aircraft known.

Disbanded 26th June 1942 at Nanyuki and absorbed by 70 Operational Training Unit.

BELFAST UNIVERSITY AIR SQUADRON, later QUEEN'S UNIVERSITY AIR SQUADRON
Formed 14th January 1941 at Belfast, using Sydenham for flying from April 1941. Redesignated Queen's University Air Squadron from 1st May 1941.

Nil (5.41– .47)	*Moth X5119; Tiger Moth II X5045, Tiger Moth II provided by 11 Elementary Flying Training School.*
FLE	*Allocated but no evidence of use.*
RUQ (.47–4.51)	*Tiger Moth II N6716 RUQ.*
Nil (4.51–7.96)	*Oxford I PG987; Prentice T.1 VR264; Harvard IIB KF751 Q; Anson T.21 VS589; Chipmunk T.10; Provost T.1 XF690; Bulldog T.1 XX562 S.*

Disbanded 31st July 1996 at Aldergrove.

BELGIAN TRAINING SCHOOL – see Royal Air Force (Belgian) Training School

BELVEDERE CONVERSION UNIT
Formed August 1964 at Odiham from an element of 72 Squadron.

Belvedere HC.1 XG460 L.

Disbanded August 1966 at Odiham and absorbed by the Short-Range Conversion Unit.

BELVEDERE TRIALS UNIT
Formed 4th July 1960 at Odiham.

Belvedere HC.1 XG461.

Disbanded 15th September 1961 at Odiham to become 66 Squadron.

BENGAL/BURMA COMMUNICATION SQUADRON – see Royal Air Force Bengal/Burma Communication Squadron

BENGAL CALIBRATION FLIGHT
Formed 15th March 1943 at Amarda Road, India, by redesignating 224 Group Calibration Flight.

Blenheim V AZ997; Vengeance I AN939.

Disbanded 25th August 1943 at Alipore, India, to become 1583 (Calibration) Flight.

BENGAL COMMUNICATION FLIGHT
Formed 1st December 1942 at Dum-Dum, India, by redesignating the Communication Flight, Dum-Dum.

Hart K2095; Falcon Z-30; Yale Z-32; Hurricane IIB Z5687; Lysander II R2004; Hornet Moth V4731; Dragonfly V4734; Aeronca Chief Z2003; Leopard Moth AX802; Lockheed 12A LV700; Tiger Moth MA933; Tipsy Trainer MA930; Whitney Straight MA944.

Disbanded 24th March 1943 at Barrackpore, India, to become the Air Headquarters Bengal Communication Unit.

BENGAL COMMUNICATION UNIT – see Air Headquarters Bengal Communication Unit

BERLIN AIR COMMAND (RAF) COMMUNICATION FLIGHT
Formed 24th May 1945 at Gatow, Germany.

Dominie I NF874; Hurricane II; Auster V NJ612; Anson XI NK989.

Disbanded 1st August 1945 at Gatow to become the British Air Command, Berlin Communication Flight.

BIRMINGHAM UNIVERSITY AIR SQUADRON, later UNIVERSITY OF BIRMINGHAM AIR SQUADRON
Formed 3rd May 1941 at Birmingham. Used Castle Bromwich for flying training. Redesignated the University of Birmingham Air Squadron from 15th October 1951.

Nil (5.41–4.46)	*Tiger Moth II provided by 14 and 16 Elementary Flying Training Schools.*
FLK (4.46– .49)	*Tiger Moth II T6101 FLK-A*
RUB (.49–4.51)	*Tiger Moth I NL910, II RUB-A.*
Nil (4.51–)	*Tiger Moth II; Oxford I HN577; Anson T.21 VV311; Prentice T.1 VS358; Harvard IIB KF756; Chipmunk T.10 WD331 W; Bulldog T.1 XX669 B.*

Current 1st April 1998 at Cosford.

BLENHEIM CONVERSION FLIGHT
Formed October/November 1939 at Hendon to probably provide conversion training for the newly formed 248 Squadron and a few pupils from 12 Group Pool.

Oxford II N6365; Blenheim.

Disbanded 16th January 1940 at Hendon.

BLENHEIM FLIGHT
Believed to have formed July 1941 at Thruxton from the remaining elements of 13 and 614 Squadrons prior to their departure for North Africa.

Blenheim IV R3879, V BA737.

Believed to have been absorbed by 42 Operational Training Unit.

BLENHEIM REFRESHER UNIT
Reputed to have formed with Blenheims by July 1943 at Peshawar, India, and to have disbanded some months later at Poona, India, having been attached to the Aircrew Transit Pool.

BLIND APPROACH CALIBRATION FLIGHT, later BEAM APPROACH CALIBRATION FLIGHT
Formed 12th July 1941 at Watchfield within the Blind Approach School. Redesignated the Beam Approach Calibration Flight from October 1941.

Oxford I V4027; Anson I EF982.

Disbanded 20th November 1942 at Bicester to become 1551 (Beam Approach Calibration) Flight.

BLIND APPROACH SCHOOL, later 1 BLIND APPROACH SCHOOL, later 1 BEAM APPROACH SCHOOL
Formed 28th September 1940 at Watchfield. Redesignated 1 Blind Approach School then 1 Beam Approach School from October 1941.

Nil (9.40–4.46)	*Anson I N5351; Oxford I V4049; Dominie I X7491; Wellington I L4311.*

FDU (4.46–2.47)	*Oxford I HM479 FDU-B.*
FDV (4.46–2.47)	*Oxford I V4270 FDV-R.*
FDW (4.46–2.47)	*Oxford I MP496 FDW-B; Harvard IIB KF541 FDW-D.*
FDX (4.46–2.47)	*Allocated but no evidence of use.*

Disbanded 21st December 1946 at Watchfield.

1 BLIND APPROACH SCHOOL – see Blind Approach School, later 1 Blind Approach School, later 1 Beam Approach School

BLIND APPROACH TRAINING AND DEVELOPMENT UNIT
Formed 22nd September 1939 at Boscombe Down.

Anson I L9155.

Disbanded 6th June 1940 at Boscombe Down.

Reformed 13th June 1940 at Boscombe Down.

Anson I N9945; Whitley V P5019.

Disbanded 14th October 1940 at Boscombe Down to become the Wireless Intelligence Development Unit.

1 BLIND APPROACH TRAINING FLIGHT
Formed 12th January 1941 at Abingdon.

Whitley III K8990.

Disbanded 8th November 1941 at Abingdon to become 1501 (Beam Approach Training) Flight.

2 BLIND APPROACH TRAINING FLIGHT
Formed February 1941 at Linton-on-Ouse.

Whitley III K8941, V N1504.

Disbanded 8th November 1941 at Driffield to become 1502 (Beam Approach Training) Flight.

3 BLIND APPROACH TRAINING FLIGHT
Formed 27th January 1941 at Mildenhall.

Wellington I L4274, IA N2960, IC R1528.

Disbanded 8th November 1941 at Mildenhall to become 1503 (Beam Approach Training) Flight.

4 BLIND APPROACH TRAINING FLIGHT
Formed 17th December 1940 at Wyton.

Wellington I L4277, IA N2868, IC P9280.

Disbanded 8th November 1941 at Wyton to become 1504 (Beam Approach Training) Flight.

5 BLIND APPROACH TRAINING FLIGHT
Formed 1st January 1941 at Honington.

Wellington I L4341, IA N2960, IC L7851; Oxford I R6027.

Disbanded 8th November 1941 at Honington to become 1505 (Beam Approach Training) Flight.

6 BLIND APPROACH TRAINING FLIGHT
Formed 6th January 1941 at Waddington.

Blenheim I L1294; Hampden I AD837; Oxford I V3996; Boston I AE457.

Disbanded 8th November 1941 at Waddington to become 1506 (Beam Approach Training) Flight.

7 BLIND APPROACH TRAINING FLIGHT
Formed 18th January 1941 at Finningley.

Blenheim I K7048; Hampden I AD860; Oxford I V4017.

Disbanded 8th November 1941 at Finningley to become 1507 (Beam Approach Training) Flight.

8 BLIND APPROACH TRAINING FLIGHT
Formed January 1941 at Wattisham.

Blenheim I L1204.

Disbanded 8th November 1941 at Horsham St Faith to become 1508 (Beam Approach Training) Flight.

9 BLIND APPROACH TRAINING FLIGHT
Formed January 1941 at Thornaby.

Wellington I L4261, IC R1652; Oxford I V3991.

Disbanded 8th November 1941 at Dyce to become 1509 (Beam Approach Training) Flight.

10 BLIND APPROACH TRAINING FLIGHT
Formed January 1941 at Leuchars.

Wellington I L4284, IC R1666; Oxford I V3994.

Disbanded 8th November 1941 at Leuchars to become 1510 (Beam Approach Training) Flight.

11 BLIND APPROACH TRAINING FLIGHT
Formed 22nd September 1941 at Upwood.

Oxford I V4061.

Disbanded October 1941 at Upwood to become 1511 (Beam Approach Training) Flight.

12 BLIND APPROACH TRAINING FLIGHT
Formed 22nd September 1941 at Dishforth.

Oxford I V4083.

Disbanded October 1941 at Dishforth to become 1512 (Beam Approach Training) Flight.

13 BLIND APPROACH TRAINING FLIGHT
Formed 22nd September 1941 at Honington.

No aircraft known.

Disbanded October 1941 at Honington to become 1513 (Beam Approach Training) Flight.

14 BLIND APPROACH TRAINING FLIGHT
Formed 22nd September 1941 at Coningsby.

No aircraft known.

Disbanded October 1941 at Coningsby to become 1514 (Beam Approach Training) Flight.

15 BLIND APPROACH TRAINING FLIGHT
Formed 22nd September 1941 at Swanton Morley.

Oxford I V4061.

Disbanded October 1941 at Swanton Morley to become 1515 (Beam Approach Training) Flight.

16 BLIND APPROACH TRAINING FLIGHT
Formed 22nd September 1941 at Topcliffe.

No aircraft known.

Disbanded October 1941 at Llanbedr to become 1516 (Beam Approach Training) Flight.

17 BLIND APPROACH TRAINING FLIGHT
Formed October 1941 at Wattisham.

Oxford I V4144 F.

Disbanded October 1941 at Ipswich to become 1517 (Beam Approach Training) Flight.

20 BLIND APPROACH TRAINING FLIGHT
Formed 10th October 1941 at Breighton.

Oxford I V4142; Tiger Moth BD151.

Disbanded October 1941 at Holme-on-Spalding-Moor to become 1520 (Beam Approach Training) Flight.

21 BLIND APPROACH TRAINING FLIGHT
Formed October 1941 at Stradishall.

Oxford.

Disbanded October 1941 at Stradishall to become 1521 (Beam Approach Training) Flight.

22 BLIND APPROACH TRAINING FLIGHT
Formed October 1941 at Docking.

Oxford.

Disbanded October 1941 at Docking to become 1522 (Beam Approach Training) Flight.

23 BLIND APPROACH TRAINING FLIGHT
Formed October 1941 at Little Rissington.

No aircraft known.

Disbanded October 1941 at Little Rissington to become 1523 (Beam Approach Training) Flight.

24 BLIND APPROACH TRAINING FLIGHT
Formed October 1941 at Bottesford.

Oxford I V4172.

Disbanded October 1941 at Bottesford to become 1524 (Beam Approach Training) Flight.

25 BLIND APPROACH TRAINING FLIGHT
Formed October 1941 at Brize Norton.

No aircraft known.

Disbanded October 1941 at Brize Norton to become 1525 (Beam Approach Training) Flight.

26 BLIND APPROACH TRAINING FLIGHT
Formed 3rd October 1941 at Andover.

Oxford I V4211.

Disbanded October 1941 at Thruxton to become 1526 (Beam Approach Training) Flight.

BLIND LANDING EXPERIMENTAL UNIT
Formed 1st October 1945 at Woodbridge.

Boeing 247D DZ203; Albemarle I/III V1599; Tiger Moth II N9126; Magister P6402; Lancaster I ME861, VII NN801; Harvard IIB KF977; Proctor IV NP297; Anson I NK328, X NK707; XII NL172; Oxford I PH412; Meteor T.7 VW414; Devon C.1 VP954; Canberra VN799; Viking 1 VX141.

Disbanded 1st November 1949 at Martlesham Heath and merged with the Bomb Ballistic Unit to become the Bomb Ballistic and Blind Landing Experimental Unit.

BOMB BALLISTIC AND BLIND LANDING EXPERIMENTAL UNIT
Formed 1st November 1949 at Martlesham Heath by merging the Bomb Ballistic Unit and the Blind Landing Experimental Unit. Officially absorbed by the Armament and Instrument Experimental Establishment from 15th November 1949.

No aircraft known.

Disbanded 1st May 1950 at Martlesham Heath to become the Armament and Instrument Experimental Unit.

BOMB BALLISTIC UNIT
Formed 22nd May 1944 at Woodbridge.

OR   Halifax II HR756; Lancaster I PB137, III PB619, VI ND418; Lincoln I RA638; Mosquito XVI PF564, B.35 TA663; Anson XI NL239 H.

Disbanded 1st November 1949 at Woodbridge and merged with the Blind Landing Experimental Unit to become the Bomb Ballistic and Blind Landing Experimental Establishment.

BOMBER COMMAND BOMBING SCHOOL
Formed 15th October 1952 at Scampton.

Oxford I HM739; Lincoln II RE310; Varsity T.1 WL627 P; Hastings T.5 TG521.

Disbanded 30th April 1968 at Lindholme to become the Strike Command Bombing School.

BOMBER COMMAND COMMUNICATION FLIGHT, later BOMBER COMMAND COMMUNICATION SQUADRON
Formed 12th May 1942 at Halton by redesignating an element of the Station Flight, Halton. Redesignated the Bomber Command Communication Squadron from 1st February 1956.

Nil (5.42–7.45)	Proctor III HM480; Tiger Moth II N9211; Taylorcraft Plus D W5741; Hornet Moth W5748; Percival Q-6 X9406; Sentinel – 299015; Oxford II W6618; Anson I NK212; Messenger I RH369.
4Z (7.45– .51)	Proctor III LZ560 4Z-R; Anson I NK842 4Z-C, XI NL220 4Z-D, XII PH591 4Z-B, XIX TX183 4Z-B; Oxford I PH765 4Z-C; Dakota III KG782 4Z-A.
Nil (.51–8.63)	Anson XIX TX188, T.21 VV958 T, T.22 WD436; Devon C.1 VP952; Chipmunk T.10 WZ878; Pembroke C.1 WV740; Meteor T.7 WH205.

Disbanded 30th June 1963 at Bovingdon and merged with the Coastal and Fighter Commands Communication Squadrons to become the Bomber/Fighter/Coastal Commands Communication Squadron.

BOMBER COMMAND DEVELOPMENT UNIT, later STRIKE COMMAND DEVELOPMENT UNIT
Formed 24th August 1954 at Wittering. Redesignated Strike Command Development Unit from 30th April 1968.

O3	Allocated but no evidence of use.
Nil	Mosquito VI NT181; Canberra B.2 WH925, B.6 WH976, B(I).6 WT322, B(I).8 WT347; Valiant B.1 WP214, B(K).1 WZ400; Vulcan B.1 XA907, B.1A XA907, B(K).1 XL391.

Disbanded 31st December 1968 at Finningley.

BOMBER COMMAND EXPERIMENTAL UNIT – see Bombing Trials Unit

BOMBER COMMAND FILM UNIT
Formed 10th March 1945 at Bardney.

G7	Lancaster I PD329 G7-Y, III RF234 G7-T; Mosquito B.25 KB433 G7-Z.

Disbanded 18th December 1945 at Upwood.

BOMBER COMMAND INSTRUCTORS SCHOOL
Formed 5th December 1944 at Finningley by merging the Night Bomber Tactical School and the Bombing Analysis School.

IK (12.44–)	Halifax III MZ876 IK-X.
C2 (.45– .45)	Oxford.
ZQ (.45–6.47)	Wellington X NC652 ZQ-J; Mosquito III RR313 ZQ-W.
WB (.45–6.47)	Lancaster I HK761 WB-E, III DV200 WB-S; Lincoln I RE283 WB-D.
IP (–6.47)	Spitfire XVI SL571 IP-C.
Also used	Spitfire VB BM147; Oxford I T1401; Master II W9015; Hurricane IIC PG544.

Disbanded 15th June 1947 at Scampton to become Bomber Command Instrument Rating and Examining Flight.

BOMBER COMMAND INSTRUMENT RATING AND EXAMINING FLIGHT
Formed 15th June 1947 at Scampton by redesignating the Bomber Command Instructors School.

Lincoln B.2 RA665 WB-D.

Disbanded 10th March 1952 at Scampton.

BOMBER COMMAND JET CONVERSION FLIGHT, later BOMBER COMMAND JET CONVERSION UNIT
Formed 15th December 1950 at Binbrook.

Canberra B.2 WD951; Meteor F.4 VT179, T.7 WG942.

Disbanded 30th September 1954 at Marham.

1 BOMBER DEFENCE TRAINING FLIGHT – see 1668 Heavy Conversion Unit

BOMBER DEVELOPMENT UNIT
Formed 17th November 1940 at Boscombe Down.

Blenheim IV V5377; Wellington IC R1062; Hampden I AD751.

Disbanded 1st May 1941 at Boscombe Down.

BOMBER/FIGHTER/COASTAL COMMAND COMMUNICATION SQUADRON
Formed 1st July 1963 at Bovingdon by merging Bomber, Fighter and Coastal Commands Communication Squadrons.

Pembroke C.1 WV753.

Disbanded 1st August 1963 at Bovingdon to become the Southern Communication Squadron.

BOMBER SUPPORT DEVELOPMENT UNIT
Formed 18th April 1944 at Foulsham by redesignating the Special Duties (Radio) Development Unit.

O5	Spitfire VB EP767; Mosquito II DD619, VI NT181, XIX MM638, NF.30 MV540; Spitfire VB EP767; Oxford I HN372; Tiger Moth II N9211; Anson I NK450.

Disbanded 21st July 1945 at Swanton Morley to become the Radio Warfare Establishment.

BOMBER TRANSPORT FLIGHT
Formed 8th July 1932 at Lahore, India, by redesignating the Heavy Transport Flight.

Clive II J9948; Hinaidi I J7745; Victoria V K2807; Valentia K4634.

Disbanded 1st April 1939 at Lahore and absorbed by 31 Squadron.

1 BOMBING AND GUNNERY SCHOOL
Formed 1939 at Pembrey.

Whitley K4587.

Disbanded 21st June 1941 at Pembrey to become 1 Air Gunners School.

2 BOMBING AND GUNNERY SCHOOL
Formed 20th January 1941 at Millom.

Botha I L6431; Anson I K8731; Battle N2105, Battle Trainer P6617; Blenheim I L6736.

Disbanded 1st June 1941 at Millom to become 2 Air Observers School.

3 BOMBING AND GUNNERY SCHOOL
Formed 1st December 1939 at Aldergrove by redesignating 3 Air Observers School.

Gauntlet II K5279; Heyford III K6864; Wallace II K8696; Battle L5136 8, Battle Trainer R7384 9; Henley III L3308; Botha I L6123; Gladiator II N5592; Magister P2402.

Disbanded 11th July 1940 at Aldergrove.

4 BOMBING AND GUNNERY SCHOOL
Formed 1st November 1939 at West Freugh by redesignating 4 Air Observers School.

Heyford III K5197; Wallace I K5071, II K4348; Battle K9470; Anson I K8721; Henley III L3264; Botha I L6125; Moth AW160; Magister P2403.

Disbanded 14th June 1941 at West Freugh to become 4 Air Observers School.

5 BOMBING AND GUNNERY SCHOOL
Formed 1st December 1939 at Jurby by redesignating 5 Air Observers School.

Wallace I K3562, II K8696; Battle K9346, Battle Trainer P6753; Blenheim I K7064, IV N6218; Hampden I X3152; Hereford I L6013; Henley III L3404; Moth BD163.

Disbanded 19th July 1941 at Jurby to become 5 Air Observers School.

6 BOMBING AND GUNNERY SCHOOL
Planned opening at Pembrey cancelled in favour of forming in Canada as 31 Bombing and Gunnery School.

7 BOMBING AND GUNNERY SCHOOL
Formed 1st December 1939 at Stormy Down by redesignating 7 Air Observers School.

Wallace I K5078, II K6074; Hector K9714; Battle K9291, Battle Trainer P6764; Henley III L3337; Whitley I K7196 E, II K7237 S, III K9004 L, IV K9016, V N1475; Harrow II K6972; Magister L8210.

Disbanded 9th June 1941 at Stormy Down to become 7 Air Gunners School.

8 BOMBING AND GUNNERY SCHOOL
Formed 1st November 1939 at Evanton by redesignating 8 Air Observers School.

Wallace II K8702; Harrow I K6947, II K6972; Battle K7565; Botha I L6407; Henley III L3301; Magister P2406.

Disbanded 9th June 1941 at Evanton to become 8 Air Gunners School.

9 BOMBING AND GUNNERY SCHOOL
Formed 1st November 1939 at Penrhos by redesignating 9 Air Observers School.

Wallace I K4343, II K6058; Demon K8183; Battle K9426, Battle Trainer P6676; Whitley II K7221, III K9006, V N1491; Harrow I K6937; Henley III L3351; Magister L8341; Blenheim IV Z6361.

Disbanded 14th June 1941 at Penrhos to become 9 Air Observers School.

10 BOMBING AND GUNNERY SCHOOL
Formed 1st January 1940 at Warmwell by redesignating 10 Air Observers School.

Sidestrand II J9187; Seal K3483; Wallace I K3912, II K6054; Harrow I K6958, II K6974; Overstrand K8173; Hind K6644; Battle K9431, Battle Trainer P6666; Whitley II K7221, III K8951, V P5024; Henley III L3260; Blenheim I L1363; Hampden I L4199; D.H.89A Z7253; Magister P2405.

Disbanded 13th September 1941 at Dumfries to become 10 Air Observers School.

24 BOMBING AND GUNNERY SCHOOL – see 24 Combined Air Observers School, later 24 Combined Air Observers School

31 BOMBING AND GUNNERY SCHOOL
Opened 28th April 1941 at Picton, Canada.

Anson I K9194, II 7615; Battle L5352; Lysander III 1544; Bolingbroke 10179; Harvard II 3100; Yale 3360; Stinson 105 3476; Moth 4923.

Disbanded 17th November 1944 at Picton, Ontario.

BOMBING DEVELOPMENT UNIT
Formed 21st July 1942 at Gransden Lodge by redesignating 1418 (Gee Development) Flight.

Hampden I AD751; Wellington IC R1062, III X3403, X HE472; Beaufighter I R2258; Albemarle I P1459; Lancaster I R5668, II DS672, III ME381; Stirling I R9280, III EF403; Halifax II W1231, III LW376 S, V DG281, VI NP890; Marauder I FK109; Warwick II HG350; Spitfire VC BM585; Mosquito IV DK291, IX LR512, XVI PF388; Liberator V FL987; Lincoln I RE242; Anson I DG719; Proctor I P6311, III HM317.

Disbanded 1st December 1945 at Feltwell and absorbed by the Central Bomber Establishment.

24 BOMBING, GUNNERY AND AIR NAVIGATION SCHOOL – see 24 Combined Bombing, Gunnery and Air Navigation School

BOMBING TRIALS UNIT
Formed 1st August 1942 at West Freugh by redesignating the Bomber Command Experimental Unit.

Nil (8.42–)	*Hampden I P1255; Mitchell II HD302; Anson I MG467, XI NK790, XIX VL300 B; Halifax III MZ958, VII NA407; Mustang III HB934; Lancaster I TW923; Mosquito XVI PF611, TT.35 RS718.*
BTU (–.57)	*Lancaster I TW923 BTU-A; Mosquito TT.35 RS718 BTU-F; Sunderland V RN294; Lincoln B.2 SX930 BTU-B; Anson XII PH622 BTU-K.*

Functional administrative control by the Royal Air Force ceased with effect from 1st November 1955 at West Freugh. Disbanded 1st January 1957 at West Freugh to become the Air Armament Trials Establishment.

BRISTOL UNIVERSITY AIR SQUADRON
Formed 25th February 1941 at Bristol, using Filton for flying.

Nil (4.41–4.46)	*Moth X5124; Tiger Moth BB857, Tiger Moth II provided by 2 Elementary Flying Training School.*
FLM (4.46–7.46)	*Allocated but no evidence of use.*

Disbanded 15th July 1946 at Bristol.

Reformed 1st December 1950 at Filton.

Tiger Moth II; Harvard IIB KF709 B; Chipmunk T.10 WP872 B; Bulldog T.1 XX656 C.

Current 1st April 1998 at Colerne.

BRISTOL WIRELESS FLIGHT
14th May 1940 at Yatesbury.

Dominie I R5934; Proctor I P6246; II Z7202, III Z7237.

Disbanded July 1945 at Yatesbury.

BRITISH AIR COMMAND BERLIN COMMUNICATION FLIGHT
Formed 1st August 1945 at Gatow, Germany, by redesignating the Berlin Air Command (RAF) Communication Flight.

Anson XI NK993, XII PH535; Auster V; Spitfire XI.

Disbanded 28th February 1946 at Gatow.

BRITISH AIR FORCES OF OCCUPATION COMMUNICATION SQUADRON, later BRITISH AIR FORCES OF OCCUPATION COMMUNICATION WING, later BRITISH AIR FORCES OF OCCUPATION COMMUNICATION SQUADRON
Formed 15th July 1945 at Buckeburg, Germany, by redesignating the 2nd Tactical Air Force Communication Squadron. Redesignated the British Air Forces of Occupation Communication Wing between 10th October 1945 and 22nd September 1947.

Nil	*Magister T9812; Proctor I P6238, III HM283; Vigilant I HL429, IA BZ108; Spitfire VB BL850, VC EE745, XI PL843, XIX PS856, F.24 PK718; Auster IV MT329, V RT493; Anson I MH181, X NK532, XI NK871, XII PH529; Dakota III KG770, IV KJ994; Hurricane IIB JS369, IIC MW359; Argus II HB608, III HB739; Mosquito VI TA524, XVI NS560; Messenger RG333, I RH369; Fi 156 VM742; Si 204 VM466; Bf 108 VM495; Tempest II PR848, V SN217; Devon C.1 VP957; Valetta C.2 VX573.*
QJ	*Allocated but no evidence of use.*
9E	*Allocated but no evidence of use.*
3F	*Allocated but no evidence of use.*

Disbanded 1st September 1951 at Buckeburg to become the 2nd Tactical Air Force Communication Squadron.

BRITISH AIR FORCES OF OCCUPATION INSTRUMENT TRAINING FLIGHT
Formed 10th May 1950 at Gutersloh, Germany.

Meteor T.7 WA656; Vampire T.11 WZ498.

Disbanded 1st September 1951 at Gutersloh to become the 2nd Tactical Air Force Instrument Training Flight.

BRITISH AIR FORCES SOUTHEAST ASIA COMMUNICATION SQUADRON – see Base Air Forces, Southeast Asia Communication Squadron

BRITISH AIRCRAFT CIRCUS FLIGHT – see Air Fighting Development Unit Demonstration Squadron

BRITISH AIRWAYS REPAIR UNIT (MIDDLE EAST), later 1 BRITISH AIRWAYS REPAIR UNIT (MIDDLE EAST)
Formed 16th February 1942 at Heliopolis, Egypt. Redesignated 1 British Airways Repair Unit (Middle East) from March 1943.

Audax K3124; Lysander II L6880; Blenheim IV Z6381; Beaufort I W6504; Beaufighter I T4873; Wellington II W5430; III HF672; SM 79K AX702; Ju 52/3 HK919; Fiat G.12 HK940; Junkers 88 HK959.

Disbanded 1st March 1944 at Heliopolis to become 168 Maintenance Unit.

1 BRITISH AIRWAYS REPAIR UNIT – see British Airways Repair Unit, later 1 British Airways Repair Unit

2 BRITISH AIRWAYS REPAIR UNIT (MIDDLE EAST)
Formed March 1943 at Asmara, Sudan.

Kittyhawk; Blenheim; Harvard; Tomahawk; Hudson; Lodestar; Magister; Fiat G.12; Ju 52; Beaufort; Beaufighter; Wellington.

Disbanded 1st December 1944 at Almaza, Egypt

BRITISH AIRWAYS TRAINING UNIT – see the Transport Training Flight

BRITISH COMMONWEALTH AIR COMMUNICATION FLIGHT, later BRITISH COMMONWEALTH AIR COMMUNICATION SQUADRON
Formed 1945 at Digri, India. Later redesignated the British Commonwealth Air Communication Squadron.

Dakota IV KJ887; Harvard IIB KF111; Auster V TJ315.

Disbanded 31st March 1948 at Iwakuni, Japan.

BRITISH COMMONWEALTH AIR COMMUNICATION SQUADRON – see British Commonwealth Air Communication Flight, later British Commonwealth Air Communication Squadron.

1 BRITISH FLYING TRAINING SCHOOL
Opened 11th August 1941 at Terrell, Texas, USA.

No aircraft known.

Closed 20th August 1945 at Terrell.

2 BRITISH FLYING TRAINING SCHOOL
Opened 17th July 1941 at Lancaster, California, USA.

No aircraft known.

Closed 20th August 1945 at Lancaster.

3 BRITISH FLYING TRAINING SCHOOL
Opened 13th July 1941 at Miami, Oklahoma, USA.

No aircraft known.

Closed 20th August 1945 at Miami.

4 BRITISH FLYING TRAINING SCHOOL
Opened 24th September 1941 at Mesa, Arizona, USA.

No aircraft known.

Closed 20th August 1945 at Mesa.

5 BRITISH FLYING TRAINING SCHOOL
Opened 23rd August 1941 at Clewiston, Florida, USA.

No aircraft known.

Closed 20th August 1945 at Clewiston.

6 BRITISH FLYING TRAINING SCHOOL
Opened 23rd August 1941 at Ponca City, Oklahoma, USA.

PT-17A.

Closed 20th August 1945 at Ponca City.

BUCCANEER TRAINING FLIGHT
Formed 1st October 1991 at Lossiemouth within 208 Squadron.

Buccaneer S.2B; Hunter T.7.

Disbanded November 1992 at Lossiemouth.

BURMA COMMUNICATION FLIGHT – see Headquarters Royal Air Force Burma Communication Squadron, later Air Headquarters Burma Communication Squadron, later Air Headquarters Burma Communication Flight

BURMA COMMUNICATION SQUADRON – see Headquarters Royal Air Force Burma Communication Squadron, later Air Headquarters Burma Communication Squadron, later Air Headquarters Burma Communication Flight

BURMESE CONVERSION SQUADRON
Formed 6th November 1952 at Llandow by redesignating the Burmese Refresher Course operated by the Central Flying School. The unit trained Burmese Air Force pilots prior to the delivery of de-navalised Seafire F.15 aircraft under Class B markings G-15-212 to G-15-231.

Spitfire F.21 LA231.

Disbanded (date unknown) at Llandow.

BURMESE VOLUNTEER AIR FORCE
Formed by June 1940 in Burma. The title did not come into use until February 1941.

Tiger Moth Z-01; Gipsy Moth XY-AAA; Aeronca Chief Z-20; Rambler Z-30; Yale Z-32.

Disbanded April 1942 at Dum-Dum, India, to become the Communication Flight, Dum-Dum.

'C' BOAT SEAPLANE TRAINING FLIGHT
Formed 8th August 1918 at Felixstowe.

No aircraft known.

Disbanded 1919 at Felixstowe.

'C' FLIGHT (1) – see 510 (Special Duty) Flight

'C' FLIGHT (2) – see 528 (Special Duty) Flight

'C' FLIGHT (3) – see 530 (Special Duty) Flight

'C' FLIGHT, CALSHOT – see Royal Air Force Base, Calshot

'C' FLIGHT, GOSPORT – see Royal Air Force Base, Gosport, later Royal Air Force Station, Gosport

'C' FLIGHT, LEUCHARS – see Royal Air Force Base, Leuchars, later Royal Air Force Training Base, Leuchars

'C' SQUADRON, AEGEAN
Formed 1st April 1918 at Imbros, Aegean, by redesignating 'C' Squadron of 2 Wing, RNAS. Disbanded 18th September 1918 at Imbros to become 220 Squadron. See also 220 Squadron.

CAIRO-CAPE FLIGHT
Formed 4th November 1925 at Northolt and departed for Egypt on 22nd November, arriving at Heliopolis in January 1926. Flew to Cape Town on 1st March, returning on 19th April and arriving back at Heliopolis on 27th May. Departed Aboukir on 9th June for the United Kingdom.

Fairey IIID S1102.

Dispersed 26th June 1926 at Lee-on-Solent and officially disbanded 12th July 1926 at Henlow.

Reconstituted by March 1927 at Aboukir, Egypt.

Fairey IIIF S1143 3.

Disbanded by April 1927 at Aboukir.

CALIBRATION FLIGHT, BANGALORE – see Bangalore Calibration Flight

CALIBRATION FLIGHT, BENGAL – see Bengal Calibration Flight

CALIBRATION FLIGHT, BIGGIN HILL – see 6 Radio Maintenance Unit, later 6 Radio Servicing Section

CALIBRATION FLIGHT, CHURCH FENTON – see 4 Radio Maintenance Unit, later 4 Radio Servicing Section

CALIBRATION FLIGHT, DUXFORD – see 5 Radio Maintenance Unit 5, later Radio Servicing Section

CALIBRATION FLIGHT, DYCE – see 2 Radio Maintenance Unit, later 2 Radio Servicing Section

CALIBRATION FLIGHT, FILTON – see 7 Radio Maintenance Unit, later 7 Radio Servicing Section

CALIBRATION FLIGHT, SELETAR
Formed by 30th June 1941 at Seletar, Malaya.

Vildebeest.

Lost to Japanese forces February 1942 at Seletar.

CALIBRATION FLIGHT, SPEKE – see 8 Radio Maintenance Unit, later 8 Radio Servicing Section

CALIBRATION FLIGHT, USWORTH – see 3 Radio Maintenance Unit, later 3 Radio Servicing Section

CALIBRATION FLIGHT, WICK, later LONGMAN – see 1 Radio Maintenance Unit, later 1 Radio Servicing Section

1 CALIBRATION FLIGHT
Formed 6th November 1942 at Speke by redesignating 77 Wing Calibration Flight.

Blenheim IV; Hornet Moth.

Disbanded by May 1943 at Speke.

1 CALIBRATION FLIGHT, INDIA – see 224 Group Calibration Flight

2 CALIBRATION FLIGHT, INDIA – see 222 Group Calibration Flight

3 CALIBRATION FLIGHT, INDIA – see 225 Group Calibration Flight

4 CALIBRATION FLIGHT, INDIA – see 225 Group Calibration Flight

CAMBRIDGE UNIVERSITY AIR SQUADRON
Formed 17th February 1925 at Cambridge.

Fighter C4740, IIIDC J7689; Avro 504K E3575, 504N J9254 1; Atlas I J8798, Atlas AC K1519, Atlas Trainer K2517; Tutor K3282; Hart Trainer K4769; Audax K7414.

Disbanded 5th September 1939 at Cambridge.

Reformed 24th October 1940 at Cambridge.

Nil (9.39–4.46)	Tiger Moth BB807, Tiger Moth II provided by 22 and later 3 Elementary Flying Training Schools.
FLA (4.46– .47)	Tiger Moth II W7950 FLA-A.
FLV (4.46– .47)	Tiger Moth II T7687 FLV-A.
RUC (.47–4.51)	Tiger Moth II T5639 RUC-B; Chipmunk T.10 WB566 RUC-E.
Nil (4.51–)	Oxford I T1398; Proctor IV NP227; Anson T.21 WJ511 Z; Harvard IIB KF200; Prentice T.1 VR212; Chipmunk T.10 WD305 L; Bulldog T.1 XX659 S.

Current 1st April 1998 at Cambridge Airport.

CAMOUFLAGE FLIGHT
Formed 9th October 1939 at Baginton.

Blenheim I L6759; Dominie I R9552; Magister N3951.

Disbanded 3rd November 1939 at Baginton to become 1 Camouflage Unit.

1 CAMOUFLAGE UNIT
Formed 3rd November 1939 at Baginton by redesignating the Camouflage Flight.

Magister N3951; Dominie I R9552; Tiger Moth II T7723; Dragon Rapide V4724; Oxford II V3538; Leopard Moth X9295; Dragon X9396; Stinson X9596; Reliant W7981; Proctor III HM348.

Disbanded 1st October 1944 at Stapleford Tawney.

2 CAMOUFLAGE UNIT
Formed 3rd November 1939 at Heston by redesignating the Heston Flight.

Spitfire PR.IA N3186; Super Electra G-AFMO; Hudson I N7334; Harvard I P5830.

Disbanded 19th January 1940 at Heston to become the Photographic Development Unit.

CANADIAN EXPERIMENTAL PROVING ESTABLISHMENT
Formed 11th November 1951 at Edmonton, Canada, by redesignating the Winterisation Experimental Establishment.

Sea Hawk F.1 WF148; Javelin FAW.4 XA723.

Disbanded 15th July 1959 at Edmonton, Canada.

(CANADIAN) RESERVE SQUADRONS, later (CANADIAN) TRAINING SQUADRONS – see Reserve Aeroplane Squadrons, later Reserve Squadrons, later Training Squadrons

CANBERRA STANDARDISATION AND TRAINING FLIGHT
Formed 15th December 1990 by redesignating 231 Operational Conversion Unit.

B   Canberra T.4 WJ877 BG.

Disbanded 13th May 1991 at Wyton to become 231 Operational Conversion Unit.

CANBERRA TRIALS AND TACTICAL EVALUATION UNIT
Formed 19th January 1966 at Akrotiri, Cyprus.

Canberra.

Disbanded 31st December 1968 at Akrotiri.

CARDIFF UNIVERSITY AIR SQUADRON
Formed 19th February 1941 at Cardiff.

Moth X5049.

Existed to at least September 1944 at Cardiff.

CASUALTY AIR EVACUATION FLIGHT – see Far East Casualty Evacuation Flight

CATALINA FERRY FLIGHT
Formed June 1945 at Dar es Salaam, Tanganyika.

Catalina IB FP115.

Disbanded July 1946 at Mombasa, Kenya.

CATALINA FLIGHT, ADEN
Formed 7th September 1942 at Khormaksar, Aden, by redesignating detachments of 240 and 413 Squadrons.

Catalina I AJ160, IB FP126, IIA VA723.

Disbanded 31st January 1944 at Aden.

CATALINA SPECIAL DUTY FLIGHT – see 240 Squadron

CENTAURUS FLIGHT
Formed 22nd October 1943 at Weston-super-Mare.

Buckingham I KV307; Folland 43/37 P1781; Master I N7641, II DL222; Wellington X LN718; Warwick II HG341; Beaufighter VI ND224, X NV246.

Disbanded 30th September 1945 at Filton.

CENTRAL AIR COMMUNICATION SECTION TRAINING FLIGHT
Formed by May 1920 at Shaibah, Iraq.

D.H.9A E9915.

Disbanded 31st March 1921 at Shaibah, Iraq.

CENTRAL AIR TRAFFIC CONTROL SCHOOL
Formed 11th February 1963 at Shawbury by redesignating the Air

Traffic Control element of the Central Navigation and Control School. The flying element ceased to operate by July 1989.

Valetta C.1 VW188 X; Provost T.1 XF877 T; Vampire T.11 XE819 T; Jet Provost T.4 XP556 B.

Current 1st April 1998 at Shawbury.

CENTRAL BOMBER ESTABLISHMENT
Formed 25th September 1945 at Marham.

GN (9.45– .47)	*Lancaster I PB988 GN-X.*
DF (.47–12.49)	*Lancaster I LL780/G DF-N, III PB970 DF-J; Mosquito XVI PF556 DF-Z, B.35 VP184 DF-Y; Lincoln II RF484 DF-A.*
XE (2.46–12.49)	*Anson XI NL231 XE-D, XIX TX226 XE-A; Auster V TW442 XE-A.*
Also used	*Tiger Moth II T5838; Mosquito III LR527, XVII HK327; Oxford I HN405; Proctor III LZ578; Spitfire XVI SL563, F.22 PK658; Lincoln I RE238; Anson XI NK874; Meteor F.3 EE340, F.4 VT102.*

Disbanded 21st December 1949 at Lindholme.

CENTRAL FIGHTER ESTABLISHMENT
Authority was given on 4th September 1944 to form the unit at Wittering. The Fighter Interception Unit and the Air Fighting Development Unit were absorbed on 1st October 1944 and the Fighter Leaders School followed on 27th December 1944. The code letters quoted were certainly attributed to the Central Fighter Establishment, but doubt exists of their allocation to individual sub-units.

Air Fighting Development Squadron
Formed 1st October 1944 at Wittering by redesignating the Air Fighting Development Unit

GO (.44– .48)	*Spitfire IX PV295 GO-C, XIV MV253 GO-E, F.21 LA215 GO-C; Tempest II MN744 GO-S, V NV941; Hornet F.1 PX275 GO-F; Vampire F.1 TG332 GO-I; Reliant W7980; Tempest II MW744 GO-S.*
Nil (.48–2.56)	*Meteor F.4 EE549, T.7, F.8, NF.12; Vampire F.1, FB.5 VV590; Venom FB.1 WE382; Swift F.1 WK212; Sabre F.4 XD780; Javelin FAW.1, FAW.2, FAW.4, FAW.5, FAW.6, FAW.7, FAW.8; Hunter F.1 WT558, F.2 WN899, F.4 WT744, F.5 WN981, F.6; Pembroke C(PR).1 XF799; Lightning F.1 XM135 D, F.2 XN771 M, F.3 XP695, T.4 XM973, F.6 XR753 T.*

Disbanded 1st February 1966 at Binbrook to become the Fighter Command Trials Unit.

All-Weather Development Squadron
Formed 1st February 1956 at West Raynham by redesignating the All Weather Wing.

Meteor T.7 WF768, F.8 WA772, NF.11 WM269, NF.12 WS590; Javelin FAW.1 XA547, FAW.2 XA806 C, FAW.4 XA749 E, FAW.5 XA642 H, FAW.7 XJ758 S.

Disbanded August 1959 at West Raynham and absorbed by the Air Fighting Development Squadron.

All-Weather Fighter Combat School
Formed 15th March 1958 at West Raynham by redesignating the All-Weather Fighter Leaders School.

Meteor F.8 WK654 Y; Javelin FAW.4 XA730, FAW.5 XA653.

Disbanded 1st July 1962 at West Raynham to become the Javelin Operational Conversion Squadron.

All-Weather Fighter Leaders School
Formed July 1950 at West Raynham, as an element of the Fighter Combat School, by redesignating the Night Fighter Leaders School.

Meteor NF.11 WM191; Javelin FAW.5 XA664.

Disbanded 15th March 1958 at West Raynham to become the All-Weather Fighter Combat School.

All-Weather Wing
Formed 3rd July 1950 at West Raynham by redesignating the Night Fighter Wing.

Venom FB.3 WX808 Z; Balliol T.2 VR596; Meteor NF.11 WD585, NF.12 WS614 M; Javelin FAW.1 XA565.

Disbanded February 1956 at West Raynham to become the All-Weather Development Squadron.

Day Fighter Combat Squadron
Formed 15th March 1958 at West Raynham within the Fighter Combat School by redesignating the Day Fighter Leaders School.

Meteor F.8 WK754; Vampire T.11 WZ547; Hunter F.4 XG204, F.6 XF453, T.7 XL591 M.

Disbanded 1st November 1965 at Binbrook.

Day Fighter Development Wing
Incorporated into the Central Fighter Establishment from 27th December 1944 at Wittering. Nothing further known.

Day Fighter Leaders School
Formed 27th December 1944 at Wittering by redesignating the Fighter Leaders School.

MF (12.44–7.45)	*Typhoon IB MN208 MF-19; Tempest V SN109 MF-H.*
UX (12.44– .48)	*Proctor III LZ791 UX-X; Spitfire IX RK807 UX-Y, XIV RM704 UX-A, XVI TE353 UX-H; Meteor F.3 EE472 UX-P.*
JW (not known)	*Spitfire IX BS449 JW-L.*
Nil (.48–3.58)	*Martinet I NR499; Meteor F.4 VT234 J, T.7 VZ641, F.8 WL968 K; Vampire FB.5 WE840; Hunter F.1 WW635 L, F.2 WN945, F.4 WW664, F.6 XG209 C; Javelin FAW.1 XA568 C.*

Disbanded 15th March 1958 at West Raynham to become the Day Fighter Combat Squadron.

Enemy Aircraft Flight
Formed 17th January 1945 at Tangmere by redesignating 1426 (Enemy Aircraft) Flight.

EA	*Ju 88A-5 EE205 EA-9, Ju 88G-1 TP190, Ju 88R-1 PJ876, Ju 88S-1 TS472; Bf 109F-4 NN644, Bf 109G-2 RN228, Bf 109G-6 TP814, Bf 109G-14 VD364; Bf 110C-5 AX772; Me 410A-3 TF209; Fw 190A NF754, Fw 190A-5 PN999 EA-4; Hs 129B-1 NF756; Fiat Centauro VF204.*

Disbanded December 1945 at Tangmere.

Fighter Combat School
Formed 15th March 1958 at West Raynham. Encompassed the Day Fighter Combat Squadron and the All-Weather Fighter Combat School.

Disbanded (date and location unknown).

Fighter Command Instrument Rating Flight
Formed February 1956 at West Raynham by redesignating the Fighter Command Instrument Training Squadron.

Meteor T.7 WK340 O, WL349 Y; Vampire T.11 WZ582 B; Hunter T.7 XL567 W.

Disbanded 1st January 1960 at West Raynham to become the Fighter Command Instrument Rating Squadron.

Fighter Command Instrument Rating Squadron
Formed 1st January 1960 at West Raynham by redesignating the Fighter Command Instrument Rating Flight.

Hunter F.4 WV318, T.7 XL567 Z; Javelin T.3 XH433 A.

Disbanded 1st June 1963 at Middleton St George and merged with the Lightning Conversion Squadron to become 226 Operational Conversion Unit.

Fighter Command Instrument Training Flight
Formed 13th September 1948 at Tangmere. Became affiliated with

the Central Fighter Establishment from 20th February 1950 at West Raynham.

Oxford I LX737 J; Harvard IIB KF568; Meteor T.7 WA602 W, F.8 WF815 N.

Disbanded 1st December 1951 at West Raynham to become the Fighter Command Instrument Training Squadron.

Fighter Command Instrument Training Squadron
Formed 1st December 1951 at West Raynham by redesignating the Fighter Command Instrument Training Flight. Absorbed into the Central Fighter Establishment from 1st December 1952.

Meteor T.7 WL340; Vampire T.11 XE879 E; Hunter T.7 XL571 X.

Disbanded February 1956 at West Raynham to become the Fighter Command Instrument Rating Squadron.

Fighter Command Target Facilities Squadron
Formed 3rd August 1961 at Leeming by redesignating an element of 228 Operational Conversion Unit. Became an element of the Central Fighter Establishment at West Raynham from 10th August 1981.

Canberra B.2 WH645, T.4 WE193, T.11 WH714.

Disbanded 1st April 1963 at West Raynham to become 85 Squadron.

Fighter Experimental Flight
Formed 16th October 1944 at Wittering.

Mosquito NF.30.

Disbanded June 1946 at Wittering.

Fighter Interception Development Squadron
Formed 16th October 1944 at Ford by redesignating the Fighter Interception Development Unit.

ZQ (10.44– .46)	*Beaufighter VI MM857 ZQ-E; Mosquito III, IV TA472 ZQ-4, XII HK189, XIII, XVII, XIX MM682, NF.36; Tempest V EJ654; Wellington XVIII PG237 ZQ-IE; Meteor F.3 EE348 ZQ-J.*
Nil (–7.50)	*Oxford I PH487; Meteor F.4, T.7.*
QE (.45– .45)	*Mustang III FB172; Mosquito VI HR210 QE-T.*

Disbanded July 1950 at West Raynham to become the Radar Interception Development Squadron.

Fighter Support Development Squadron
Formed 1st March 1951 at West Raynham by redesignating the Fighter Support Development Unit.

Meteor F.4, F.8.

Disbanded (date unknown) at West Raynham.

Fighter Support Development Unit
Formed 29th January 1951 at West Raynham.

Spitfire XIX PS853.

Disbanded 1st March 1951 at West Raynham to become the Fighter Support Development Squadron.

Javelin Operational Conversion Squadron
Formed 1st July 1962 at West Raynham by redesignating the All-Weather Fighter Combat School.

Javelin FAW.5 XA652 T.

Disbanded 31st October 1962 at West Raynham.

Lightning Conversion Squadron
Formed 4th January 1960 at West Raynham. Became an independent unit from 29th June 1962 at Middleton St George.

Lightning T.4 XM969 H.

Disbanded 1st June 1963 at Middleton St George and merged with the Fighter Command Instrument Rating Squadron to become 226 Operational Conversion Unit.

Naval Air Fighting Development Squadron
Formed March 1945 at Wittering from elements of 746 Squadron, being renumbered 787 Squadron from 30th January 1946.

Firefly I DT933; Hellcat II JZ895; Reliant FK882; Sea Hornet; Sea Fury; Sea Vampire; Attacker; Wyvern; Sea Hawk.

Disbanded January 1956 at West Raynham.

Night All-Weather Wing
Formed by June 1957 at West Raynham.

No aircraft known.

Disbanded (date and location unknown).

Night Fighter Development Wing
Formed 16th October 1944 at Ford by redesignating the Fighter Interception Unit. Embraced the Fighter Experimental Flight, Fighter Interception Development Squadron, Night Fighter Training Squadron and Naval Fighter Interception Unit.

Oxford I NM354; Beaufighter VI MM850; Mosquito VI PZ191, XIII HK478, XVII HK324, NF.30 NT262.

Disbanded 1949 at West Raynham to become the Night Fighter Wing.

Night Fighter Leaders School
Formed 1st October 1945 at West Raynham by redesignating the Night Fighter Training Squadron.

ZE	*Mosquito III TV976, VI RF875 ZE-H, XVII HK327 ZE-K, NF.30 NT557 ZE-X, NF.36 RK987 ZE-R, NF.38 VT656; Oxford I PH487 ZE-A; Harvard IIB KF434.*

Disbanded July 1950 at West Raynham to become the All-Weather Fighter Leaders School.

Night Fighter Training Squadron
Formed 1945 at Ford as an element of the Night Fighter Development Wing.

No aircraft known.

Disbanded 1st October 1945 at West Raynham to become the Night Fighter Leaders School.

Night Fighter Wing
Formed 1949 at West Raynham by redesignating the Night Fighter Development Wing.

Meteor NF.11 WD585.

Disbanded 3rd July 1950 at West Raynham to become the All-Weather Wing.

Radar Interception Development Squadron
Formed July 1950 at West Raynham by redesignating the Fighter Interception Development Squadron.

Balliol T.2 WF994.

Disbanded March 1953 at West Raynham.

Also used:	
NX (10.44– .46) Nil	*Master II EM353 NX-A; Martinet I HP487 NX-M; Magister L8211; Mustang IVA KH704; Auster VI VF640; Dakota IV KN700; Spitfire IIA P7382, XIII BL378, XVIII TP434; F.21 LA201; F.22 PK614; F.24 PK624; Mosquito IX MM230, XII HK166, XVII HK327, XIX MM682, NF.38 VT656; Wellington XVII MP532; Meteor FR.9 WX964, NF.12 WS614 M, NF.14 WS751 X; Tiger Moth II T5465; Boston IIIA BZ363; Hurricane IV KZ301; Anson I NK643, XII PH667, XIX VM320, T.21 VV891; Vampire T.11 WZ582 B; Venom FB.1 WE264, NF.2 WL818, NF.3 WX807; F-86A Sabre; Swift F.2 WK216, FR.5 XD918; Devon C.1 VP975; Chipmunk T.10 WZ846; English Electric P.IA WG763.*

Disbanded 1st February 1966 at Binbrook, the Air Fighting Development Squadron becoming the Fighter Command Trials Unit.

CENTRAL FLYING SCHOOL
Formed officially 12th May 1912 at Upavon from elements of the Royal Flying Corps and the Naval Wing. Opened for flying training 19th June 1912.

B.E.1 201; Henry Farman Biplane 209; Bleriot XI 219; Duperdussin Monoplane 260; Avro 502 Type Es 285; Tabloid 326; Sopwith 80hp Biplane 319; B.E.2a 347; Shorthorn 379; Short S.43 School 402; Longhorn 403; Avro 500 Type E 406; Bristol Boxkite 407; B.E.7 408; Nieuport Monoplane 409; Deperdussin Monoplane 419; Avro 521; Short S.49 413; B.E.4 416; Flanders F.4 422; Henry Farman F.20 435; Short S.38 446; B.E.8 479; Morane Saulnier Type G 482; B.E.2b 484, B.E.2 489; Bleriot Parasol 575; Morane H 598; Martinsyde S.1 599; R.E.5 631; Bristol Scout C 1605; B.E.2c 1688; B.E.8a 2162; Curtiss JN-3 2339; D.H.1 4604; Morane BB 5167; F.K.3 5552; Gunbus 5666; D.H.2; Vickers F.B.7; Vickers F.B.12; Twin Canada 5728; F.E.2b 6337, F.E.2d 7995; B.E.12 6490; B.E.2d 6747; Elephant 7258; Vickers ES.1 7509; 1½ Strutter 7762; Bristol S.2A 7837; F.E.4 7993; F.E.8 7456; D.H.4 A2168; F.K.7 A411; Fokker A3021; Nieuport 12 A3288; F.2a A3303; Triplane N5430; Vickers FB.14 A3505; Martinsyde F.1 A3933; Bristol M.1A A5138; Bristol M.1B A5139; FK.10 A5212; Pup A7317; B.E.2e A8638; S.E.5 A8915; Avro 504A B4324, Avro 504J B3234; Dolphin D3769; Camel F9635.

Disbanded 23rd December 1919 at Upavon to become the Flying Instructors School.

Reformed 26th April 1920 at Upavon by redesignating the Flying Instructors School.

Snipe E6815, Snipe DC F2408; Avro 504K F9705, Avro 504N E3318; Buzzard IA H6541; SE.5a D7023; Humming Bird J7273; Grebe II J7383, Grebe IIDC J7585, IIIDC J7520; Genet Moth J8821; Cirrus Moth J8032; Gamecock I J8046; IDC J7900; F.2B J8453; D.H.9A J8475, D.H.9 DC J8470; Siskin IIIA J9369, IIIDC J9193; Tomtit J9780; Avro 504N K1042; Fairey IIIF K1168; Atlas Trainer K1471; Gordon DC K1168; Moth K1882; Victoria V K2344; Hart K2474; Hart Trainer K4943; Bulldog Trainer K3170, IIA K3505; Fury I K2904; Tutor K3400; Seal K3485; Hind K6453; Tiger Moth I K2585; Wallace II K8696; Gladiator I K7908; Wellesley K7714; Hurricane I L1873; Skua I L2875; Roc L3061; Henley III L3244; Hampden I L4123; Wellington I L4285; Beaufort I L4444; Bombay L5810; Magister L5916; Botha I L6106; Defiant I L6951; Blenheim I L8405, IV P6297; Oxford I N4640, II N6372; Master I N7430, II W8782; Harvard I N7181; Anson I N9597; Lysander II P1745; IV P6927; Battle Trainer R7382; Spitfire I N3293; Lysander II P1745; Typhoon IA R7579; Tiger Moth II T5371; Mustang I AG374; Boston II AH487; Tomahawk IIA AH925; Mohawk III AR632; Maryland I AR716; Dominie I X7385; Miles M.18 U-0224; Vigilant IA BZ103.

The Central Flying School Handling Flight formed 8th December 1938 at Upavon. By September 1940 was incorporated into the CFS Refresher Squadron. Became a separate entity and moved to Boscombe Down 8th November 1940 and attached to the Aeroplane and Armament Experimental Establishment. Redesignated the Handling Squadron from June 1940. Transferred August 1942 to Hullavington and absorbed by the Empire Central Flying School (later the Empire Flying School). See also Handling Flight later Handling Squadron in main text.

Disbanded 1st April 1942 at Upavon to become 7 Flying Instructors School and the Empire Central Flying School.

Reformed 7th May 1946 at Little Rissington by merging 7 (Advanced) and 10 (Elementary) Flying Instructors Schools.

FDI (5.46–4.51)	*Prentice T.1 VS251 FDI-P; Anson XIX PH844 FDI-G; Lancaster VII NX696 FDI-C.*
FDJ (5.46–4.51)	*Spitfire XVIE TB376 FDJ-O; Meteor F.3 EE419 FDJ-G, T.7 VW438 FDJ-P; Vampire F.3 VT856 FDJ-L.*
FDK (5.46–4.51)	*Magister L8262 FDK-H.*
FDL (5.46–4.51)	*Tiger Moth II N5471 FDL-F; Auster V TW440 FDL-A; Chipmunk T.10 WB551 FDL-X.*
FDM (5.46–4.51)	*Harvard IIB KF244 FDM-S; Auster V TW440 FDM-K.*
FDN (5.46–4.51)	*Harvard IIB FS742 FDN-J.*
FDO (5.46–4.51)	*Anson I NK565 FDO-N; Harvard IIB FX434 FDO-L; Mosquito III LR520 FDO-X, VI RS551 FDO-T; Buckmaster T.1 RP182 FDO-E; Balliol T.2 VR593 FDO-O.*
I (4.51–)	*Anson XII PH558 I-E, XIX TX191 I-G; Vampire FB.5 VZ876 I-R, T.11 XD393 I-S.*
K (4.51–)	*Prentice T.1.*
L (4.51–)	*Prentice T.1.*
M (4.51–)	*Harvard IIB FX419 M-P; Prentice T.1; Anson XII PH558 M-B, XIX TX225 M-K; Valetta C.1 WJ496 M-F; Varsity T.1 XD366 M-F.*
N (4.51–)	*Harvard IIB KF612 N-E; Anson XII PH784 N-C; Prentice T.1 VS319 N-I; Provost T.1 XF544 N-K.*
O (4.51–)	*Harvard IIB FX291 O-F; Meteor T.7 WH177 O-H.*
Q (4.51–)	*Provost T.1.*
R ( )	*Jet Provost T.1.*
S ( )	*Sycamore HR.12 WV781, HR.14 XL823 S-C.*
W ( )	*Whirlwind HAR.10 XP300 W-S.*
X ( )	*Anson XIX TX232 X-E; Prentice T.1; Provost T.1 XF913 X-P; Vampire T.11 XD446 X-G.*
Nil ( )	*Canberra B.2 WH712, T.4 WD944; Meteor T.7 WF791 27; Varsity T.1 WL671 20; Pembroke C.1 WV733; Chipmunk T.10 WG348 11; Hunter F.4 XF943; Skeeter 6 XK773, AOP.10 XK480, T.11 XK479, AOP.12 XM556 V; Gnat T.1 XS103 D; Bulldog T.1 XX689 D; Jet Provost T.1 XD676, T.3 XM413, T.3A XM349 H, T.4 XP571, T.5A XW421 60; Hawk T.1 XX177, T.1A XX170; Sioux AH.1 XT144 V, HT.2 XV314 M; Gazelle HT.3 XX374 L; Wessex HC.2; Tucano T.1 ZF142.*
Also Used	*Dakota III KJ994; Brigand B.1 RH759; Dragonfly HC.4 XF261; Auster VI VF611, T.7 WE568; Venom FB.1 WE264; Vampire FB.5 WA216; Meteor F.8 VZ467.*

Current at 1st April 1998 having elements within 1, 3 and 4 Flying Training Schools.

The postwar Central Flying School in greater detail:

The Central Flying School reformed 7th May 1946 at Little Rissington by merging 7 (Advanced) and 10 (Elementary) Flying Instructors Schools consisting of 1 Squadron (Lancaster, Vampire, Spitfire, Auster and Harvard), 2 Squadron (Harvard, also Prentice from July 1947), 3 Squadron (Harvard and Tiger Moth) and 4 Squadron (Mosquito). 2 Squadron was detached to Brize Norton between September 1949 and March 1950. 4 Squadron had disbanded and the Type Flight (Meteor, Prentice, Tiger Moth, Auster and Anson) formed by September 1949. The Examining Wing of the Empire Flying School, Hullavington moved to Little Rissington on 22nd April 1949 to become an integral part of the Central Flying School. The Examining Wing relocated to Brize Norton on 30th June 1949, only to return to Little Rissington in May 1950.

The Central Flying School was restructured on 1st May 1952 and split into CFS (Basic) and CFS (Advanced). The Central Flying School (Basic) formed at South Cerney, by redesignating 2 Flying Training School, comprising 1 Squadron (Prentice, Auster later Provost) and 2 Squadron (Harvard later Provost). The Central Flying School (Advanced) formed at Little Rissington consisting of 1 Squadron (including a Communication Flight with Anson, Valetta and later Provost), 2 Squadron, 3 Squadron (Meteor and Vampire, 4 Squadron (Vampire) and a Type Flight. The Provost was introduced in May 1953. The Helicopter Development Flight formed 8th March 1954 at Middle Wallop (Dragonfly 2; Skeeter 6 XK773). By June 1954 piston and jet engine training was divided between South Cerney and Little Rissington respectively. The Vampire Flight formed 1st July 1954 and operated within 1 Squadron until absorbed by 4 Squadron in November 1954. Jet Provost T.1 trials began in July 1955 at Little Rissington. The Helicopter Development Flight disbanded 1st January 1956 at South Cerney to become the Helicopter Squadron (Dragonfly HR.4 XB251, Skeeter T.11, T.12; Sycamore HC.14; Whirlwind HAR.2 XL109). The Central Flying School (Basic) at South Cerney merged with the Central Flying School (Advanced) on 1st June 1957 at Little Rissington to become the Central Flying School. The Type Squadron formed on 10th July 1957 by merging the CFS Headquarters Flight and the Type Flight having Canberra, Meteor and Communication Flights at Little Rissington and a Hunter Flight at Kemble. The Examining Wing returned to Little Rissington to disbanded in November 1957 and was divided to become the Directing Staff and the Standards Squadron. The Type Squadron disbanded in May 1961 at Little Rissington to become 3 Squadron, CFS. The Helicopter Wing formed on 10th August 1961 at Ternhill, by redesignating the Helicopter Squadron, and comprised 1 Squadron (Pilot and Instructor Courses), 2 Squadron (Operational Training Courses) and 3 Squadron (Helicopter Examining Unit). The Search and Rescue Training Squadron (later to become 3 Squadron) formed 23rd April 1962 at Valley. The Red Arrows formed 1st March 1965 at Fairford. The Standards Squadron became the Standards Wing from April 1965 and the Primary Flying Squadron formed 1st July 1965 at South Cerney with Chipmunks. The Examining Wing reformed in February 1966 at Little Rissington by redesignating the Standards Wing. Gnat Squadron moved from Fairford to Kemble in September 1966. The Training Flight formed in 1969 at Little Rissington. The Primary Flying Squadron disbanded 15th January 1970 at Church Fenton to become 2 Flying Training School. The Vintage Pair Flight formed in 1972 at Little Rissington with Meteor T.7 WF791 and Vampire T.11 XH304. In 1973 the Bulldog Squadron formed at Little Rissington, the Training Flight became the Training Squadron and the Jetstream was introduced on 26th July 1973. The Helicopter Wing disbanded 31st March 1976 at Ternhill to become 2 (Advanced) Flying Training School and the Training Squadron disbanded on 12th April 1976 at Leeming. 23 Group Advanced Flying Training School disbanded 29th September 1976 at Ternhill. The Headquarters Central Flying School, Examining Wing and Jet Provost Squadron moved from Little Rissington to Cranwell on 12th April 1976. 23 Group Advanced Flying Training School (often referred to as the CFS Squadron) formed 29th February 1974 at Ternhill by merging 2 Squadron (Ternhill) and 3 Squadron (Valley). The Hawk Squadron replaced the Gnat Squadron in November 1976 at Valley. The Headquarters Central Flying School moved from Cranwell to Leeming on 5th September 1977 and from Leeming to Scampton on 19th September 1984. The Vintage Pair Flight ceased to exist by May 1986. The Bulldog Squadron transferred from Scampton on 1st February 1989 to operate within 3 Flying Training School at Cranwell. The Tucano Squadron formed 1st September 1989 at Scampton. The Refresher Flying Flight was incorporated into the Central Flying School from late 1991 until the demise of the Jet Provost in June 1992. The Hawk Squadron became 19 (Reserve) Squadron at Valley within 4 Flying Training School. The Bulldog Squadron merged 31st March 1995 with CFS (Main) on moving to Cranwell to operate within 3 Flying Training School. Tucano Squadron moved to Topcliffe on 24th April 1995 to operate within 1 Flying Training School together with the reformed Refresher Flying Flight. The Headquarters Central Flying School moved from Scampton to Cranwell on 31st May 1995. Currently the Hawk Squadron operates as 19 (Reserve) Squadron within 4 Flying Training School at Valley, the Tucano Squadron operates alongside 1 Flying Training School at Topcliffe and the Bulldog Squadron operates within 3 Flying Training School at Cranwell.

CENTRAL FLYING SCHOOL (INDIA)
Formed 13th June 1944 at Ambala, India, by redesignating the Flying Instructors Flight, Ambala.

Tiger Moth II; Harvard IIB FE429.

Disbanded 22nd July 1945 at Ambala.

CENTRAL FLYING SCHOOL (INDIA) EXAMINING FLIGHT
Formed January 1945 at Ambala, India, within the parent unit.

No aircraft known.

Disbanded 15th October 1945 at Ambala.

CENTRAL FLYING SCHOOL (SOUTHERN RHODESIA) – see Rhodesian Central Flying School, later Central Flying School (Southern Rhodesia)

2 CENTRAL FLYING SCHOOL
Formed 14th November 1940 at Cranwell by redesignating 2 Flying Instructors School.

Tutor K3412; Oxford I N6333, II N6369; Monospar ST.12 BD150.

Disbanded 13th January 1942 at Church Lawford to become 1 Flying Instructors School.

3 CENTRAL FLYING SCHOOL
Was to have formed at Dalcross during December 1941 by redesignating 'E' and 'F' Flights of 2 Central Flying School.

CENTRAL GLIDING SCHOOL, later AIR CADET CENTRAL GLIDING SCHOOL
Formed 9th August 1971 at Spitalgate by merging 1 and 2 Gliding Centres. Redesignated the Air Cadet Central Gliding School from 1984.

Sky 1 XA876; Grasshopper TX.1 XP493; Cadet TX.3 XN253 L; Sedbergh TX.1 WB972; Swallow TX.1 XS859; Prefect TX.1 WE990; Valiant TX.1 ZD658; Vanguard TX.1 ZD649; Kestrel TX.1 ZD975; Venture T.1 XW983, T.2 ZA655 Z; Viking TX.1 ZE501; Vigilant T.1 ZH129.

Current 1st April 1998 at Syerston.

CENTRAL GUNNERY SCHOOL
Formed 6th November 1939 at Warmwell.

Nil (11.39–4.46)	*Battle L5710, Battle TT L5723; Blenheim I L1274, IV V5449; Master I N7711, II AZ595, III DL684; Hudson I N7404; Lysander I L4696, III R9009, IIIA V9813; Defiant I N1633; Spitfire I R6718, IIA P7974 RH, VB BM535, VC AR501 DK, IX MJ887; Hampden I P1315; Hereford I N9064; Albemarle I/II P1439; Wellington IA N2887 5, IC N2761, III BK199 M; Proctor I R7529; Beaufighter I V8287, X KW281, XI JL904; Warwick II HG347; Mosquito XII HK198, XIII HK428; Lancaster I HK647; Tiger Moth II T7352.*
VD (1.42–)	*(Thurleigh detachment) Hampden P1313 VD-C; Blenheim IV V5449 VD-A.*
FJR (.51–4.51)	*Tiger Moth II N9278 FJR-K.*
FJS (4.46–4.51)	*Wellington III BK354 FJS-E, X RP340 FJS-L; Lancaster VII NX645 FJS-C; Lincoln II RF386 FJS-A.*
FJT (4.46–4.51)	*Mosquito VI HP989 FJT-A; Spitfire XVI TE186 FJT-A; Meteor F.3 EE356 FJT-J.*
FJU (4.46–4.51)	*Martinet I JN670 FJU-A; Proctor IV NP326 FJU-J; Tempest V NV793 FJU-G; Harvard IIB KF282 FJU-V; Balliol T.2 VR595 FJU-B.*
FJV (4.46–4.51)	*Spitfire XVI TE259 FJV-A; Meteor F.3 EE356 FJV-N, F.4 RA365 FJV-R, T.7 VZ635 FJV-X.*
FJW (4.46–4.51)	*Spitfire XVI RW396 FJW-L; Vampire FB.5 VV559 FJW-A.*
FJX (4.46–4.51)	*Master II DK968 FJX-T; Harvard IIB FT214 FJX-A; Meteor F.8 WE917 FJX-J.*
Nil (4.51 5.55)	*Lincoln II RF514 S; Chipmunk T.10 WD309; Vampire FB.5 WA186 O, T.11 WZ424 Y; Venom FB.1 WE369 A; Sabre F.4 XB540 A.*
Also used	*Queen Martinet I EM434; Halifax III PN446.*

Disbanded 31st December 1954 at Leconfield to become the Fighter Weapons School and the Coastal Command Gunnery School.

CENTRAL GUNNERY SCHOOL (MIDDLE EAST) – see 1 (Middle East) Central Gunnery School, later Royal Air Force (Middle East) Central Gunnery School

CENTRAL LANDING ESTABLISHMENT – see Central Landing School, later the Central Landing Establishment.

CENTRAL LANDING SCHOOL, later the CENTRAL LANDING ESTABLISHMENT
Formed 31 August 1940 at Ringway by redesignating the Parachute Training Centre. Redesignated the Central Landing Establishment from 2nd October 1940 and split into Glider, Parachute and Development Sections. A Glider Flight, later to become the Glider Training Squadron, was established within the Glider Section.

Avro 504N AX874; Overstrand K8176; Hector K9755; Tiger Moth II N9150; Lysander IIIA V9517; Kite; Minimoa BGA338; Condor II BGA330; Viking BGA415; Rhonbussard BGA145; Swallow 2 BK893; Hotspur I BV134, II BT488; Whitley II K7262, V N1422; Wellington IA N2880, IC BB467.

Disbanded 1st September 1941 at Ringway to become the Airborne Forces Establishment.

CENTRAL NAVIGATION AND CONTROL SCHOOL
Formed 10th February 1950 at Shawbury by merging the Central Navigation School and the School of Air Traffic Control.

FGE (2.50–4.51)	Wellington X NA907 FGE-G.
FGF (2.50–4.51)	Anson T.21 VV989 FGF-P.
FGG (2.50–4.51)	Tiger Moth II NL694 FGG-Y; Lancaster VII NX773 FGG-C.
Nil (4.51–2.63)	Anson XII PH535 V, XIX TX159 Y, T.21 VV918 R; Lincoln II RE321 A; Vampire FB.5 WA181, NF.10 WP232 L, T.11 XH298 D; Valetta C.1 VW188 X, T.3 WJ462; Varsity WL631 F; Chipmunk T.10 WD310 P; Provost T.1 WV418-O.

Disbanded 11th February 1963 at Shawbury to become the Central Air Traffic Control School.

CENTRAL NAVIGATION SCHOOL
Formed 14th August 1942 at Cranage by redesignating 2 School of Air Navigation.

Tutor K3357; Oxford I BG663; Anson I DJ219; Master I N8066; Lysander III R9125; Magister T9895; Tiger Moth II R5012; Mohawk III AR630; Wellington VIII LB196, XIII JA383 R2; Hudson V AM581; Stirling III LK508.

Disbanded 28th October 1944 at Shawbury to become the Empire Air Navigation School.

Reformed 31st July 1949 at Shawbury by redesignating the Empire Air Navigation School.

FGE (7.49–2.50)	Wellington X NA964 FGE-A.
FGF (7.49–2.50)	Oxford I PH349 FGF-V; Anson T.21 WB448 FGF-F.
FGG	Allocated but no evidence of use.
Also used	Vampire FB.5 VV630.

Disbanded 10th February 1950 at Shawbury and merged with the School of Air Traffic Control to become the Central Navigation and Control School.

CENTRAL PHOTOGRAPHIC ESTABLISHMENT
Formed 15th August 1946 at Benson.

Proctor IV NP210; Anson XI NL234, XII PH701 M; Lancaster I TW669; Mosquito B.35 TA650; Devon C.1 VP975.

Disbanded 1st March 1950 at Benson.

CENTRAL RECONNAISSANCE ESTABLISHMENT
Formed 12th January 1957 at Brampton.

Anson XIX VP514/V.

Disbanded 1st October 1970.

CENTRAL SERVICING DEVELOPMENT ESTABLISHMENT
Formed 1st June 1950 at Wittering by merging the Air Ministry Servicing Development Unit and the Servicing Demonstration Parties.

Anson XII PH638; Varsity T.1 WF825; Shackleton MR.1 VP257; Canberra B.2 WD951, B.6 WJ775; Meteor FR.9 VW364, PR.10 VS971, NF.11 WD591; Valetta T.3 WG257; Hastings C.2 WJ338.

Current at 1st April 1997 at Wyton.

CENTRAL SIGNALS ESTABLISHMENT
Formed 1st September 1946 at Watton by merging the Radar Warfare Establishment and the Signals Flying Unit.

Nil (10.45– .46)	Dominie I X7327; Tiger Moth BB753; Master II DM406; Proctor III HM323; Hudson IIIA FK737; Lancaster I PD381, III ME535; Wellington X PG371; Mosquito VI PZ410, XVI PF459.
4S (9.46– .47)	Lancaster I PA444 4S-AU; Mosquito NF.30 NT472 4S-O, NF.36 RL266 4S-P; Oxford I PH318 4S-T; Anson XIX VM334 4S-Q2.
V7 (.47–4.51)	Anson I NK924 V7-J, XI NL205 V7-M, XII PH702 V7-L; XIX VL312 V7-U; Lancaster I PA421 V7-F; Mosquito XVI PF553 V7-V, B.25 TK629 V7-Z, PR.34 RG265 V7-X, B.35 TA708; Warwick V PN701 V7-J; Lincoln II SX956 V7-C; Proctor III DX197 V7-O, IV NP327.
Nil (4.51–7.65)	Lincoln II SS715; Anson XIX TX186 40; Hastings C.1 TG560, C.2 WJ338; Vampire NF.10 WM727; Meteor F.8 WE930, NF.11 WD646, NF.12 WS597 S, NF.13 WM363; Varsity T.1 WF376; Canberra B.2 WD935, T.4 WJ862, B.6 WH945; Chipmunk T.10 WP965; Venom NF.3 WX809; Javelin FAW.1 XA549.

Disbanded 1st July 1965 at Watton.

CENTRAL SQUADRON AND FLIGHT COMMANDERS SCHOOL
Formed 16th July 1945 at Ossington.

Oxford I NM352.

Disbanded 1st April 1946 at Bramcote.

1 CHAIN HOME LOW FLIGHT
Formed (date unknown) at Watchfield.

Oxford II W6558.

Disbanded (date and location unknown).

CHECK AND CONVERSION FLIGHT
Formed October 1943 at Mauripur, India.

Blenheim V BA611; Harvard IIB FE470; Hurricane IIC LA143, IIA PJ796; Spitfire VIII MD289; Hudson IIIA FH392; Vengeance I AP117, IA EZ824; Thunderbolt I FL732; Beaufighter VI JL762, X KW297; Liberator III BZ899, VI BZ983; Dakota III FL534.

Disbanded 1st September 1944 at Mauripur to become 1331 Conversion Unit.

1 CHECK AND CONVERSION UNIT – see 1 Middle East Check and Conversion Unit

CHINESE AIR FORCE CADET SCHOOL – see Royal Air Force Liaison Office, Chinese Elementary Flying Training School, later India Detachment, Chinese Air Force Cadet School

CHINESE ELEMENTARY FLYING TRAINING SCHOOL – see Royal Air Force Liaison Office, Chinese Elementary Flying Training School, later India Detachment, Chinese Air Force Cadet School

CHINOOK OPERATIONAL CONVERSION UNIT – see 27 Squadron, RFC, later 27 Squadron, RAF, later 27 (Reserve) Squadron

1 CIVIL AIR NAVIGATION SCHOOL
Formed 15th August 1938 at Prestwick. Operated by Scottish Aviation.

Anson I N4922.

Disbanded 31st October 1939 at Prestwick to become 1 Air Observers Navigation School.

2 CIVIL AIR NAVIGATION SCHOOL
Formed 26th September 1938 at Yatesbury. Operated by the Bristol Aeroplane Company.

Anson I L7957.

Disbanded 31st October 1939 at Yatesbury to become 2 Air Observers Navigation School.

3 CIVIL AIR NAVIGATION SCHOOL
Formed August 1938 at Desford. Operated by Reid and Sigrist.

Anson I N4923.

Disbanded 31st October 1939 at Desford to become 3 Air Observers Navigation School.

4 CIVIL AIR NAVIGATION SCHOOL
Formed September 1938 at Ansty. Operated by Air Service Training.

Anson I N4881.

Disbanded 31st October 1939 at Ansty to become 4 Air Observers Navigation School.

5 CIVIL AIR NAVIGATION SCHOOL
Formed 2nd September 1939 at Weston-super-Mare. Operated by Western Airways.

Anson I N5251.

Disbanded 31st October 1939 at Weston-super-Mare to become 5 Air Observers Navigation School.

6 CIVIL AIR NAVIGATION SCHOOL
Formed 6th August 1939 at Staverton by redesignating the Airwork Civil School of Air Navigation. Continued to be operated by Airwork Ltd.

Anson I N5246 7.

Disbanded 1st November 1939 to become 6 Air Observers Navigation School.

7 CIVIL AIR NAVIGATION SCHOOL
Formed 9th January 1939 at Scone. Operated by Airwork.

Dragon Rapide G-AFLY.

Disbanded 31st October 1939 at Scone to become 7 Air Observers Navigation School.

8 CIVIL AIR NAVIGATION SCHOOL
Formed 2nd September 1939 at Sywell. Operated by Brooklands Aviation.

Anson I N4932.

Disbanded 31st October 1939 at Sywell to become 8 Air Observers Navigation School.

9 CIVIL AIR NAVIGATION SCHOOL
Formed 25th September 1939 at Squires Gate. Operated by Brooklands Aviation.

Anson I N5384.

Disbanded 31st October 1939 at Squires Gate to become 9 Air Observers Navigation School.

10 CIVIL AIR NAVIGATION SCHOOL
Formed 1st September 1939 at Grangemouth. Operated by Scottish Aviation.

Anson I N4878.

Disbanded 31st October 1939 at Grangemouth to become 10 Air Observers Navigation School.

CIVIL AIRCRAFT FLIGHT, NATIONAL AIR COMMUNICATIONS
Formed September 1939 at Doncaster.

Ensign; Handley Page H.P.42W G-AAUC; D.H.86.

Disbanded 1st May 1940 at Doncaster to become 271 Squadron.

1 CIVILIAN ANTI-AIRCRAFT CO-OPERATION UNIT
Formed 7th December 1950 at Hornchurch.

Spitfire XVI TD344 A; Beaufighter TT.10 RD781 K; Mosquito III TV977, TT.35 TK593 5; Oxford I R6248; Anson XIX VL351 V, T.21 WB453; Chipmunk T.10 WB662.

Disbanded 31st December 1956 at Hornchurch.

2 CIVILIAN ANTI-AIRCRAFT CO-OPERATION UNIT
Formed 20th July 1951 at Little Snoring.

Spitfire XVI SL613; Beaufighter TT.10 RD811; Mosquito TT.35 TA633; Vampire FB.5 WA117, FB.9 WL573, T.11 WZ584; Oxford I NM539, II ED108; Anson T.21 WB457.

Disbanded 1st November 1958 at Langham.

3 CIVILIAN ANTI-AIRCRAFT CO-OPERATION UNIT
Formed 18th March 1951 at Exeter.

Spitfire XVI TE358 42, F.21 LA332 P; Oxford I PH318 45; Beaufighter TT.10 RD862 U; Mosquito TT.35 RS718 49, III TW117 Z; Balliol T.2 WG178 J; Meteor T.7 WLVW476 P, TT.20 WD630 Q; Chipmunk T.10 WP872; Vampire FB.5 WA430 10, FB.9 WX205, T.11 XD632 67; Hunter F.4 WV401, Hunter T.7; Jet Provost T.4 XP558.

Disbanded 1st July 1954 at Exeter and merged with 4 Civilian Anti-Aircraft Co-operation Unit to become 3/4 Civilian Anti-Aircraft Co-operation Unit.

3/4 CIVILIAN ANTI-AIRCRAFT CO-OPERATION UNIT
Formed 1st July 1954 at Exeter by merging 3 and 4 Civilian Anti-Aircraft Co-operation Units.

Oxford I PH318; Anson T.21 VV914 63; Mosquito III RR299; TT.35 TA642; Meteor T.7 VW478 P, TT.20 WM298 Z; Vampire FB.5 VZ822 111; T.11 XE921; Balliol T.2 WN509 Y; Hunter F.4 XF939, T.7 XF321.

Disbanded 31st December 1971 at Exeter.

4 CIVILIAN ANTI-AIRCRAFT CO-OPERATION UNIT
Formed 1st August 1951 at Llandow.

Spitfire XVI TE300; Beaufighter TT.10 SR919; Mosquito TT.35 TA719; Oxford I NM409; Vampire F.3 VT815.

Disbanded 1st July 1954 at Llandow and merged with 3 Civilian Anti-Aircraft Co-operation Unit to become 3/4 Civilian Anti-Aircraft Co-operation Unit.

5 CIVILIAN ANTI-AIRCRAFT CO-OPERATION UNIT
Formed 16th September 1951 at Llanbedr.

Oxford I NJ347, II W6553; Spitfire XVI SL672; Beaufighter TT.10 RD811 L; Mosquito TT.35 TJ138 Z; Meteor F.4 RA397, T.7 WF791, F.8 WH453 L, TT.20 WD646 R; Vampire F.3 VT797, FB.5 WA302; Anson T.21 VV982.

Disbanded 30th September 1971 at Woodvale.

CIVILIAN FIGHTER CONTROL CO-OPERATION UNIT
Formed 1952 at Woodvale.

Provost T.1 XF838; Oxford HN309; Meteor F.8.

Disbanded March 1957 at Woodvale.

1 CIVILIAN FIGHTER CONTROL CO-OPERATION UNIT
Formed 8th March 1957 at Scone.

Anson T.22 VV977 42.

Disbanded 31st January 1961 at Scone.

2 CIVILIAN FIGHTER CONTROL CO-OPERATION UNIT
Formed 8th March 1957 at Usworth.

Anson T.22 VV901.

Disbanded 31st January 1961 at Usworth.

3 CIVILIAN FIGHTER CONTROL CO-OPERATION UNIT
Formed 8th March 1957 at Sydenham.

Anson T.22.

Disbanded 31st January 1961 at Sydenham.

1 COAST ARTILLERY CO-OPERATION FLIGHT
Formed 14th December 1936 at Gosport by redesignating 1 Coastal Defence Development Flight, Coastal Defence Development Unit.

Hart K1426; Osprey III K3619; Seal K4788.

Disbanded 1st June 1937 at Gosport to become 1 Coast Artillery Co-operation Unit.

1 COAST ARTILLERY CO-OPERATION UNIT, later 1 COAST ARTILLERY CO-OPERATION FLIGHT, later 1 COAST ARTILLERY CO-OPERATION UNIT
Formed 1st June 1937 at Gosport by redesignating the Coast Artillery Co-operation Flight. Redesignated 1 Coast Artillery Co-operation Flight from 18th May 1945, reverting to 1 Coast Artillery Co-operation Unit from 12th January 1942.

Nil (6.37–10.43)	*Osprey III K3647; Swordfish I K5997; Spitfire IIA P8321; Blenheim IV T1951; Anson I N4911; Defiant I N1644; Tiger Moth II N6732; Master III W8537.*
SX	*Possibly allocated – no evidence of use.*

Disbanded 11th October 1943 at Detling.

COAST DEFENCE CO-OPERATION FLIGHT
Formed 1st December 1924 at Eastchurch within the Armament and Gunnery School. Became an independent entity from 16th May 1927.

D.H.9A; Vildebeest I K2821.

Disbanded 23rd May 1933 at Gosport to become the Coast Defence Training Flight.

COAST DEFENCE DEVELOPMENT UNIT – see Coastal Defence Development Unit

1 COAST DEFENCE FLIGHT, INDIAN AIR FORCE VOLUNTEER RESERVE; later 101 (COAST DEFENCE) FLIGHT, INDIAN AIR FORCE
Formed 15th December 1940 at St Thomas Mount, India, to replace 'Y' Flight. Redesignated 101 (Coast Defence) Flight, Indian Air Force from 1st April 1942.

Wapiti IIA K1260; Hart K2103; Atlantia DG450; Piper Cub Coupe MA922; Leopard Moth MA922; Moth MA931.

Disbanded 30th November 1942 at St Thomas Mount to become 101 (General Reconnaissance) Squadron, Indian Air Force.

2 COAST DEFENCE FLIGHT, INDIAN AIR FORCE VOLUNTEER RESERVE; later 102 (COAST DEFENCE) FLIGHT, INDIAN AIR FORCE
Formed 15th December 1940 at Juhu, India, to replace 'V' Flight. Redesignated 102 (Coast Defence) Flight, Indian Air Force from 1st April 1942.

Rapide AX806; Hart K2116; Wapiti IIA K2304; Atlanta DG454.

Disbanded 30th November 1942 at Juhu to become 102 (General Reconnaissance) Squadron, Indian Air Force.

3 COAST DEFENCE FLIGHT, INDIAN AIR FORCE VOLUNTEER RESERVE; later 103 (COAST DEFENCE) FLIGHT, INDIAN AIR FORCE
Formed 15th December 1940 at Dum-Dum, India, to replace 'Z' Flight. Switched identities with 4 Coast Defence Flight during February 1942. Redesignated 103 (Coast Defence) Flight, Indian Air Force from 1st April 1942.

Wapiti IIA; Blenheim IV L4832.

Disbanded 1st June 1942 at Cuttack and absorbed by 353 Squadron.

4 COAST DEFENCE FLIGHT, INDIAN AIR FORCE VOLUNTEER RESERVE; later 104 (COAST DEFENCE) FLIGHT, INDIAN AIR FORCE
Formed 15th December 1940 at Drigh Road, India, by redesignating 'Q' Flight, to partially replace 'W' Flight. Switched identities with 3 Coast Defence Flight during February 1942. Redesignated 104 (Coast Defence) Flight from 1st April 1942.

Audax, Wapiti IIA K1269; Lysander II N1224; Tiger Moth DG507.

Disbanded 30th November 1942 at Vizagapatam, India to become 104 (General Reconnaissance) Squadron, Indian Air Force

5 COAST DEFENCE FLIGHT, INDIAN AIR FORCE VOLUNTEER RESERVE; later 105 (COAST DEFENCE) FLIGHT, INDIAN AIR FORCE
Formed 15th December 1940 at Drigh Road, India, to partially replace 'W' Flight. Redesignated 105 (Coast Defence) Flight from 1st April 1942.

Wapiti IIA K1291; D.H.86 HX789; Moth K1201; Tiger Moth MA937.

Disbanded 30th November 1942 at Cochin, India, to become 105 (General Reconnaissance) Squadron, Indian Air Force.

6 COAST DEFENCE FLIGHT, INDIAN AIR FORCE VOLUNTEER RESERVE; later 106 (COAST DEFENCE) FLIGHT, INDIAN AIR FORCE
Formed 21st February 1942 at Vizagapatam, India. Redesignated 106 (Coast Defence) Flight from 1st April 1942.

Wapiti IIA K4850; Audax K1298.

Disbanded 30th November 1942 at Vizagapatam to become 106 (General Reconnaissance) Squadron, Indian Air Force.

COAST DEFENCE TORPEDO TRAINING FLIGHT
Formed 7th July 1928 at Donibristle.

Horsley S1237; Dart.

Disbanded 9th October 1928 at Donibristle to become 36 Squadron.

COAST DEFENCE TRAINING FLIGHT
Formed 23rd May 1933 at Gosport by redesignating the Coast Defence Co-operation Flight.

Fairey IIIF S1317.

Disbanded 1st August 1933 at Gosport to become 1 Coastal Defence Training Unit.

COASTAL BATTERY CO-OPERATION FLIGHT
Formed 23rd December 1919 at Gosport by redesignating the Coastal Battery Co-operation School Flight.

D.H.9A J578.

Disbanded September 1921 at Gosport.

COASTAL BATTERY CO-OPERATION SCHOOL FLIGHT
Formed September 1919 at Gosport by redesignating the School of Aerial Co-operation with Coastal Artillery.

No aircraft known.

Disbanded 23rd December 1919 at Gosport to become the Coastal Battery Co-operation Flight.

COASTAL COMMAND ANTI U-BOAT DEVICES SCHOOL
Formed 20th April 1945 at Limavady by redesignating the Loran Training Unit.

Wellington VIII.

Disbanded 25th August 1945 at Limavady.

COASTAL COMMAND COMMUNICATION FLIGHT, later COASTAL COMMAND COMMUNICATION SQUADRON, later COASTAL COMMAND COMMUNICATION FLIGHT
Formed 1st May 1944 at Northolt as the Coastal Command Communication Flight within the Air Defence of Great Britain Communication Squadron and, from 1st October 1944, the Fighter Command Communication Squadron. Redesignated as the Coastal Command Communication Squadron, becoming an independent unit, from 7th April 1945 at Leavesden.

Nil (5.44–4.45)	*Rapide R2486; Master I T8622; II X7062; Anson I DG805.*
QX (4.45–5.46)	*Dominie I NR687 QX-F; Oxford I PH420 QX-A; Hudson IIIA FK745; Proctor III HM301, IV NP250; Anson I EG223 QX-D.*

Disbanded 1st May 1946 at Leavesden.

Reformed 1st July 1951 at Bovingdon.

Anson XII PH563 F, XIX VL354 D, T.21 VV981; Dakota IV KP208 YS; Prentice T.1 VS289; Chipmunk T.10 WK567; Devon C.1 WB531; Valetta C.2 WJ504; Meteor T.7 WF840.

Disbanded 30th June 1963 at Bovingdon and merged with Bomber and Fighter Commands Communication Squadrons to become the Bomber/Fighter/Coastal Commands Communication Squadron.

COASTAL COMMAND DEVELOPMENT UNIT (1)
Records suggest the Coast Defence Development Unit was also known as the 'Coastal Command Development Unit'.

COASTAL COMMAND DEVELOPMENT UNIT (2)
Formed 30th December 1940 at Carew Cheriton by redesignating the Coastal Command Tactical Development Unit.

Anson I N5054; Hudson I N7276, IV AE610, V AM526; Beaufort I L9964 J, II AW271; Whitley V Z6626, VII BD570; Hampden I AD724; Wellington IC N2737, DW.I P9223, VIII T2982, XI MP516, XII MP626 M, XIV HF169; Albemarle I P1434; Oxford I P1926; Proctor III HM366; Liberator V BZ919, VI BZ967; Fortress I AN520; Ventura I FN988; Halifax II HR672 K; Beaufighter VI JL832 D, X KW290; Catalina IVB JX286 Z; Typhoon IB MN263; Mosquito VI PZ190 M; Hornet Moth W6422; Warwick V PN705 W.

Disbanded 1st January 1945 at Angle and transferred to Thorney Island to become the Air-Sea Warfare Development Unit from 14th January 1945.

COASTAL COMMAND FIGHTER AFFILIATION TRAINING UNIT
Formed 1st September 1945 at Langham by redesignating the Coastal Command Fighter Circus.

4Q   *Vengeance IV HB364 4Q; Martinet I HP168 4Q-M; Queen Martinet I MS515; Hurricane IIC PZ746; Spitfire XVI TE256 4Q-V.*

Disbanded 21st February 1946 at Chivenor.

COASTAL COMMAND FIGHTER CIRCUS
Formed 15th March 1944 at Gosport.

Spitfire.

Disbanded 1st September 1945 at Thorney Island to become the Coastal Command Fighter Affiliation Training Unit.

COASTAL COMMAND FLYING INSTRUCTORS SCHOOL, later COASTAL COMMAND INSTRUCTORS SCHOOL
Formed 23rd February 1945 at St Angelo by redesignating 12 Flying Instructors School. Redesignated the Coastal Command Instructors School from 29th October 1945.

EJ   *Master II AZ587 EJ-K, III DL909; Martinet I EM532; Beaufort IIA ML565 EJ-F; Mosquito III LR554; Warwick II HG452; Wellington X NC946; Liberator VIII KN738 EJ-G; Buckmaster I RP184 EJ-C; Sunderland V NJ268.*

Disbanded 1st April 1946 at Tain.

COASTAL COMMAND GUNNERY SCHOOL
Formed 1st January 1955 at Leconfield by redesignating an element of the Central Gunnery School.

Lincoln B.2 RF411 K; Vampire FB.5 WA186 O.

Disbanded 31st December 1955 at Leconfield.

COASTAL COMMAND INSTRUCTORS SCHOOL – see Coastal Command Flying Instructors School, later Coastal Command Instructors School

COASTAL COMMAND LANDPLANE PILOTS POOL
Formed 1st November 1939 at Silloth.

Anson I K8755; Hudson I N7312; Beaufort I L4480; Wellington I R2700.

Disbanded 1st April 1940 at Silloth to become 1 Operational Training Unit.

COASTAL COMMAND TACTICAL DEVELOPMENT UNIT
Formed 22nd October 1940 at Carew Cheriton.

Whitley V T4281; Hudson I N7276; Beaufort I N1174; Wellington IA P9223.

Disbanded 30th December 1940 at Carew Cheriton to become the Coastal Command Development Unit.

COASTAL DEFENCE DEVELOPMENT FLIGHTS – see Coastal Defence Development Unit

COASTAL DEFENCE DEVELOPMENT UNIT
Formed 1st April 1935 at Gosport by redesignating the Coastal Defence Training Unit. Records suggest the Unit was also known as the 'Coastal Command Development Unit'. Divided into:

1 Coastal Defence Development Flight	*Osprey III K3637.*
2 Coastal Defence Development Flight	*Vildebeest I K2822, III K4187.*
3 Coastal Defence Development Flight	*Hart K2446.*

Disbanded 14th December 1936 at Gosport, 1 Coastal Defence Development Flight becoming 1 Coast Artillery Co-operation Flight, 2 Coastal Defence Development Flight becoming 42 Squadron and 3 Coastal Defence Development Flight being absorbed by Bomber Command.

COASTAL DEFENCE TRAINING FLIGHTS – see 1 Coastal Defence Training Unit

1 COASTAL DEFENCE TRAINING UNIT
Formed 1st August 1933 at Gosport by redesignating the Coast Defence Training Flight. Divided into:

1 Coastal Defence Training Flight	*No aircraft known.*
2 Coastal Defence Training Flight	*Vildebeest I K2812, K4187.*
3 Coastal Defence Training Flight	*Hart K2998.*

Disbanded 1st April 1935 at Gosport to become the Coastal Defence Development Unit.

1 (COASTAL) ENGINE CONTROL DEMONSTRATION UNIT
Formed 19th October 1943 at Longtown within 1674 Heavy Conversion Unit by redesignating the Engine Control Demonstration Flight.

Wellington.

Disbanded 17th June 1944 at Angle to become the Engine Control Instruction Flight.

1 COASTAL PATROL FLIGHT
Formed 14th December 1939 at Dyce.

T   *Tiger Moth II N6841 TA, N6849 TK; Hornet Moth X9310.*

Disbanded 28th May 1940 at Dyce.

2 COASTAL PATROL FLIGHT
Formed 9th October 1939 at Abbotsinch.

Tiger Moth II N9202; Hornet Moth X9322.

Disbanded 29th April 1940 at Abbotsinch.

3 COASTAL PATROL FLIGHT
Formed 1st December 1939 at Hooton Park.

Tiger Moth II N6730; Hornet Moth W5784.

Disbanded 29th May 1940 at Hooton Park.

4 COASTAL PATROL FLIGHT
Formed 1st December 1939 at Aldergrove and affiliated to 502 Squadron.

Tiger Moth II N6717; Hornet Moth W9388.

Disbanded 30th May 1940 at Hooton Park.

5 COASTAL PATROL FLIGHT
Formed 1st March 1940 at Carew Cheriton and affiliated to 217 Squadron.

MW   *Tiger Moth II N9128 MW; Hornet Moth W5748.*

Disbanded 25th May 1940 at Carew Cheriton.

6 COASTAL PATROL FLIGHT
Formed 15th January 1940 at St Eval.

Tiger Moth II N9191; Hornet Moth G-ADKM.

Disbanded 31st May 1940 at St Eval.

COASTAL RECONNAISSANCE BEAUFIGHTER FLIGHT
Formed Spring 1943 at (location unknown), North Africa, with aircrew seconded from 153 Squadron.

Beaufighter

Disbanded (date and location unknown).

COLERNE COMMUNICATION SQUADRON
Formed 30th July 1952 at Colerne by redesignating 62 Group Communication Flight.

Tiger Moth II T5634; Anson XIX VM358 S, T.22 VV362; Chipmunk T.10 WG489; Varsity T.1 WJ892.

Disbanded 1st July 1957 at Colerne and absorbed by 81 Group Communication Squadron.

COLLEGE OF AIR WARFARE – see Royal Air Force College of Air Warfare

COMBAT CARGO TASK FORCE COMMUNICATION FLIGHT – see Headquarters Combat Cargo Task Force Communication Flight

1 COMBAT TRAINING WING
Formed 5th October 1943 at Tealing by redesignating 56 Operational Training Unit.

Spitfire I, V; Hurricane I, II; Master I, III; Lysander III.

Disbanded 1st January 1944 at Tealing to become 1 Tactical Exercise Unit.

2 COMBAT TRAINING WING
Formed 5th October 1943 at Grangemouth by redesignating 58 Operational Training Unit.

Spitfire I, IIA, V; Hurricane I; Master III.

Disbanded 15th October 1943 at Grangemouth to become 2 Tactical Exercise Unit.

24 COMBINED AIR OBSERVER SCHOOL, later 24 BOMBING, GUNNERY AND NAVIGATION SCHOOL
Formed 3rd August 1941 at Moffat, Southern Rhodesia. Redesignated 24 Bombing, Gunnery and Navigation School from May 1943.

Oxford I 3162; Battle V1279; Harvard I N7162; Anson I EG179.

Disbanded 13th April 1945 at Moffat.

COMMAND TRAINING FLIGHT
Formed by January 1961 at Debden.

Chipmunk T.10 WK609; Oxford I HM960.

Disbanded March 1964 at Debden.

COMMUNICATION FLIGHT, ADEN
Formed 21st April 1942 at Khormaksar, Aden, by redesignating the Station Flight, Khormaksar.

Vincent K4724; Gladiator II N5918; Argus I FK319.

Disbanded 21st March 1943 at Khormaksar to become the Headquarters British Forces Aden Communication Flight.

COMMUNICATION FLIGHT, AIR HEADQUARTERS NEW DELHI
Formed by November 1930 at Willingdon Airport, New Delhi, India.

F.2B J7648; Audax K4838; Envoy N9108; Gipsy Moth MA919; Gull Six MA927; Eagle II MA945.

Disbanded 1st April 1942 at Willingdon Airport to become 224 Group Communication Flight.

COMMUNICATION FLIGHT, AIR HEADQUARTERS WESTERN DESERT
Formed 9th October 1941 at Ma'aten Bagush, by redesignating 204 Group Communication Flight.

Hind K6826; Audax K5231; Gladiator I K7965; Lysander I L4683, II R1992, III R9022; Magister N5424; Blenheim IV Z6451; Hurricane I Z4856; Proctor I P6115.

Disbanded 27th April 1942 at Ma'aten Bagush, to become the Communication Unit, Western Desert.

COMMUNICATION FLIGHT, ALDERMASTON
Doubtful whether the Flight ever formed, although the code letters TAL were allocated.

COMMUNICATION FLIGHT, DAR ES SALAAM (AIR DEFENCE UNIT, TANGANYIKA)
Formed 6th September 1939 at Dar es Salaam, Tanganyika.

Various civilian aircraft.

Disbanded 1st November 1940 and merged with 1 (Communication) Flight, Kenya Auxiliary Air Unit to become the Air Headquarters East Africa Communication Squadron.

COMMUNICATION FLIGHT, DUM-DUM
Formed 2nd June 1942 at Dum-Dum, India, from elements of the Burmese Volunteer Air Force.

Tiger Moth Z-04; Tiger Moth I T1779; Falcon Z-30; Yale Z-32; Lysander II P9062; Hornet Moth V4731; Hurricane I Z4637; Blenheim V BA864; Lockheed 12A LV700; Zlin Tourist MA926; Tipsy Trainer MA930.

Disbanded 30th November 1942 at Dum-Dum, India, to become the Bengal Communication Flight.

COMMUNICATION FLIGHT, EASTLEIGH
Formed August 1942 at Eastleigh, Kenya.

Magister; Puss Moth; Vega Gull; Luscombe; Hudson FK568; Savoia 73 K33; Savoia 79; Rapide K8; Anson I AX405.

Disbanded 31st December 1943 at Eastleigh to become the Air Transport Flight.

COMMUNICATION FLIGHT, GHQ ROYAL FLYING CORPS, FRANCE, later COMMUNICATION SQUADRON, GHQ ROYAL FLYING CORPS, FRANCE
Formed (date unknown) at Berke-sur-Mer, France. Redesignated the Communication Squadron, GHQ Royal Flying Corps, France, by March 1918.

B.E.2; R.E.8; F.K.8.

Disbanded 1st April 1918 at Berck-sur-Mer to become the Communication Squadron, GHQ Royal Air Force, France.

COMMUNICATION FLIGHT, HELIOPOLIS, later COMMUNICATION UNIT, HELIOPOLIS
Formed 1st March 1928 at Heliopolis, Egypt.

Fairey IIIF S1143; Avro 504N J8575.

Existed until at least April 1931 at Heliopolis.

Reformed 1st June 1938 at Heliopolis by redesignating the Practice Flight, Heliopolis. Redesignated the Communication Unit, Heliopolis from 18th January 1940.

Audax K3714; Tutor K3420; Vincent K4616; Gordon K2618; Hind K5430; Gladiator I K7995; Anson I L7976; Magister N3844; Proctor I P6116.

Disbanded 19th August 1940 at Heliopolis to become 267 Squadron.

COMMUNICATION FLIGHT IRAQ
Formed 14th December 1940 at Habbaniya, Iraq, by redesignating an element of 216 Squadron.

Valentia K2792; Gladiator I K8048; II N5780; Blenheim V BA317; Lockheed 14 AX681.

Disbanded (date and location unknown).

Reformed 1st November 1942 at Habbaniya, Iraq.

Tiger Moth I K4255; Vincent K4702; Audax K7542; Blenheim I L6656, IV V5579; Rapide HK862; Percival Q-6 HK913; Puss Moth HK866; Scion Senior HK868; Bombay L5825.

Disbanded 1st January 1943 at Habbaniya to become the Communication Flight, Iraq and Persia.

COMMUNICATION FLIGHT IRAQ AND PERSIA (1)
Formed 30th December 1930 at Hinaidi, Iraq, by redesignating the Air Depot, Hinaidi Training Flight.

Moth K1200; Gordon K2737; Tiger Moth I K4252.

Disbanded 21st August 1939 at Habbaniya, Iraq, to become 'S' Squadron.

Reformed 1st January 1943 at Habbaniya, Iraq, by redesignating the Communication Flight, Iraq. Also known for a while as Communication Flight, RAF Paiforce.

Moth HK908; Tiger Moth I K4255; Wellesley L2714; Oxford I L4656; Blenheim IV Z7580; Hurricane I Z4169; Hudson VI EW935; Defiant I DR975; Ventura V JT811; Wellington III BK143.

Disbanded 1st July 1945 at Habbaniya to become Air Headquarters Communication Flight, Iraq and Persia.

COMMUNICATION FLIGHT IRAQ AND PERSIA (2) – see also Air Headquarters Communication Flight Iraq and Persia

COMMUNICATION FLIGHT, KHARTOUM
Formed 3rd November 1941 at Khartoum, Sudan.

Valentia K4630; Wellesley L2657; Proctor I P6128; Bombay L5832; Dragonfly K-13; Blenheim IV Z7594, V BA299; Savoia-Marchetti S-79K AX703; Ca 148 I-GOGG; Hudson; Lodestar; Wellington VIII HX625; X NA776; Anson I MG640, XIX VL289.

Disbanded May 1950 at Khartoum, Sudan.

COMMUNICATION FLIGHT, LYDDA
Formed by April 1941 at Lydda, Palestine.

Hart K6415; Scion Major Z7187, Scion Junior Z7189; D.H.86B AX760; Proctor I P6121.

Disbanded 1st April 1942 at Lydda to become the Air Headquarters Levant Communication Flight.

Reformed 1st June 1943 at Lydda, Palestine, by redesignating the Air Headquarters Levant Communication Flight.

Hart K6415; Audax K7515; Lysander I L4677; Blenheim IV T2385; Hudson III V9162, IV AE624; Hawk HK863; Baltimore V FW495; Traveler I FZ436; Anson I MG719, X NK427; Argus II FZ767; Auster V RT620.

Disbanded 1st October 1945 at Lydda to become the Air Headquarters Levant Communication Flight.

COMMUNICATION FLIGHT, NICOSIA
Formed June 1945 at Nicosia, Cyprus.

Anson.

Disbanded 15th September 1945 at Nicosia.

COMMUNICATION FLIGHT, RAMLEH
Formed by 1937 at Ramleh, Palestine.

Gordon K2707; Vincent.

Disbanded 1st April 1942 at Ramleh and absorbed by the Air Headquarters, Levant Communication Flight.

COMMUNICATION FLIGHT, TAKORADI
Formed January 1942 at Takoradi, Gold Coast, by redesignating the Middle East Transport Flight.

Hudson III, IV AE638; Rapide; Electra; Tiger Moth.

Disbanded November 1945 at Takoradi.

1 (COMMUNICATION) FLIGHT (KENYA AUXILIARY AIR UNIT)
Formed 6th September 1939 at Nairobi, Kenya.

Dragon Rapide K8; Dragon; Leopard Moth K12; Puss Moth K3.

Disbanded 1st November 1940 at Nairobi and merged with the Communication Flight, Dar es Salaam of the Air Defence Unit, Tanganyika to become the Air Headquarters East Africa Communication Squadron.

1 (COMMUNICATION) SQUADRON – see Communication Squadron, Hendon, later 1 (Communication) Squadron

2 (COMMUNICATION) SQUADRON
Formed 1st March 1919 at Buc, France, by redesignating an element of 1 Communication Squadron.

D.H.4 A7920, D.H.4A F5764; Buzzard D4354.

Disbanded 8th October 1919 at Kenley.

3 (COMMUNICATION) SQUADRON
Formed February 1919 at Hounslow.

No aircraft known.

Disbanded March 1919 at Hounslow and absorbed by 86 Wing Headquarters Flight.

4 (COMMUNICATION) SQUADRON
Formed 5th January 1919 at Felixstowe by renumbering 232 Squadron.

Short 184 N9140; Felixstowe F.5 N4041.

Disbanded 31st December 1919 at Felixstowe and absorbed by 230 Squadron.

5 (COMMUNICATION) SQUADRON
Formed by March 1919 at Bircham Newton.

No aircraft known.

Disbanded 15th June 1919 at Bircham Newton to become 274 Squadron.

6 (COMMUNICATION) SQUADRON
Formed by March 1919 at Bircham Newton.

No aircraft known.

Disbanded 1st October 1919 at Bircham Newton.

7 (COMMUNICATION) SQUADRON
Formed by March 1919 at Bircham Newton.

No aircraft known.

Disbanded 1st October 1919 at Bircham Newton.

8 (COMMUNICATION) SQUADRON
Formed by March 1919 at Bircham Newton.

No aircraft known.

Disbanded by September 1919 at Bircham Newton.

COMMUNICATION SQUADRON, GHQ ROYAL AIR FORCE, FRANCE, later COMMUNICATION FLIGHT, GHQ ROYAL AIR FORCE, FRANCE
Formed 1st April 1918 at Berck-sur-Mer, France, by redesignating the Communication Squadron, GHQ Royal Flying Corps, France. Redesignated Communication Flight, GHQ Royal Air Force, France from November 1918.

R.E.8 C4583; Camel F6189.

Disbanded June 1919 at Bickendorf, Germany.

COMMUNICATION SQUADRON, HENDON, later 1 (COMMUNICATION) SQUADRON
Formed 23rd July 1918 at Hendon. Redesignated 1 (Communication) Squadron from 27th July 1918.

B.E.2c 4122, B.E.2e 6233; Bristol Scout D 7053; F.2B C4885; Snipe B9963; D.H.4A F5764; D.H.9 B7582; Avro 504A D1641; Handley Page 0/400 D8326.

Disbanded 8th October 1919 at Kenley.

COMMUNICATION UNIT, DESERT AIR FORCE
Formed 1st July 1943 at Sorman, Libya, by redesignating the Communication Unit, Western Desert

Vigilant I HK928; Cub HK938; Spitfire V; Hurricane IIA Z4953, IIC KX890; Oxford L4661; Argus I EV762.

Disbanded 1st June 1944 at Orvieto, Italy, to become the Desert Air Force Communication Flight.

COMMUNICATION UNIT, HELIOPOLIS – see Communication Flight, Heliopolis, later Communication Unit Heliopolis

COMMUNICATION UNIT, WESTERN DESERT
Formed 27th April 1942 at Ma'aten Bagush, Egypt, by redesignating the Communication Flight, Air Headquarters Western Desert.

Lysander I R2644, II R1993; Blenheim IV Z7785; Boston III W8348; Maryland II AH292; Hurricane IIA Z4953; Fi 156; Me 108; Argus I EV764; Vigilant I HK928; Cub HK938; Anson XII PH539.

Disbanded 1st July 1943 at Sorman, Libya, to become the Communication Unit, Desert Air Force.

COMPOSITE CO-OPERATION FLIGHT – see Royal Air Force Base, Gosport, later Royal Air Force Station, Gosport

COMPOSITE FIGHTING SQUADRON
Formed 28th March 1917 at Hadzi Junas, Aegean, by merging 'E' Flight, 2 Wing RNAS and elements of 17 and 47 Squadrons, RFC.

B.E.12a; D.H.2; 1½ Strutter N5086.

Disbanded May 1917 at Hadzi Junas.

COMPOSITE ROYAL NAVAL AIR SERVICE/ROYAL FLYING CORPS SQUADRON
A term given to the temporary amalgamation, between 28th February and 29th June 1916, of 30 Squadron and the RNAS detachment at Ora, Iraq.

Voisin LA.S 8506; Short 827; B.E.2c; Henry Farman F.27.

CONTROL AND REPORTING SCHOOL – see Fighter Command Control and Reporting School, later School of Control and Reporting

CONVERSION AND REFRESHER SCHOOL
Formed 24th February 1942 at El Ballah, Egypt.

Kittyhawk; Hurricane; Harvard.

Disbanded 5th April 1942 at El Ballah and absorbed by 1 Middle East Training School.

CONVERSION FLIGHTS – see also Squadron Conversion Flights

26 CONVERSION FLIGHT
Formed 5th October 1941 at Waterbeach by redesignating an element of 7 Squadron.

Stirling I N3669.

Disbanded 2nd January 1942 at Waterbeach and merged with 106 Conversion Flight to become 1651 Conversion Unit.

28 CONVERSION FLIGHT
Formed 4th November 1941 at Leconfield by redesignating the Halifax Conversion Flight.

Halifax I L9534, II R9367.

Disbanded 3rd January 1942 at Marston Moor and merged with 107 Conversion Flight to become 1652 Heavy Conversion Unit.

106 CONVERSION FLIGHT – see also 106 Squadron Conversion Flight
Formed December 1941 at Waterbeach.

Stirling I N3638.

Disbanded 2nd January 1942 at Waterbeach and merged with 26 Conversion Flight to become 1651 Conversion Unit.

107 CONVERSION FLIGHT
Formed December 1941 at Leconfield.

Halifax proposed – none delivered.

Disbanded 2nd January 1942 at Leconfield and merged with 28 Conversion Flight to become 1652 Heavy Conversion Unit.

108 CONVERSION FLIGHT
Formed December 1941 at Polebrook.

Liberator proposed – none delivered.

Disbanded 9th January 1942 at Polebrook to become 1653 Conversion Unit.

1330 CONVERSION UNIT
Formed 29th June 1944 at Bilbeis, Egypt, by redesignating 1 (Middle East) Check and Conversion Unit.

Harvard IIA EX849; Baltimore IV FA573, V FW303; Vengeance IV HB441; Hudson IIIA FH308; Expeditor I HB181, II HB208; Marauder II FB419, III HD493; Ventura V JS962 61; Hellcat II JX818; Beaufighter X KW321; Spitfire VB ES244; Mustang IVA KH849; Anson I AW858; Dakota I FD779, III FD830; DC-2 HK867; Mosquito III RR275; VI HX806; Oxford I PH231.

Disbanded 1st March 1946 at Bilbeis.

1331 CONVERSION UNIT later 1331 HEAVY TRANSPORT CONVERSION UNIT
Formed 1st September 1944 at Mauripur, India, by redesignating the Check and Conversion Flight.

Vengeance IA EZ824, II AN747, IV FD324; Harvard IIB FE668; Blenheim V BA611; Thunderbolt I FL731, II KL243; Hurricane IIC PJ796; Spitfire VIII JG498; Wellington XVI DV920; Mosquito III LR558; Liberator III BZ925, VI KG889; Oxford I NM462 A; Mustang IV KM639; Beaufighter VI JL762, X NV540.

Disbanded 15th January 1946 at Risalpur, India.

Reformed 15th December 1946 at Syerston as 1331 Heavy Transport Conversion Unit by redesignating the Halifax Training Unit of 1332 (Transport) Heavy Conversion Unit.

Halifax VII NA313.

Disbanded 5th January 1948 at Syerston to become 241 Operational Conversion Unit.

1332 (TRANSPORT) HEAVY CONVERSION UNIT, later 1332 HEAVY TRANSPORT CONVERSION UNIT
Formed 5th September 1944 at Longtown. Redesignated 1332 Heavy Transport Conversion Unit from May 1947.

YY (8.44–1.48)	*Liberator VI KK222 YY-X; York C.1 MW264 YY-C.*
OG (7.47–)	*Inherited from 1665 (HT) CU but no evidence of use.*
Also used	*Liberator III FK231 N, V BZ750, VI BZ963, VII EW626, IX JT983; Stirling III LK485 C; Halifax VII PN239, IX RT793; Skymaster C.1 KL986; Oxford I NM711.*

Disbanded 5th January 1948 at Dishforth to become 241 Operational Conversion Unit.

1333 (TRANSPORT SUPPORT) CONVERSION UNIT, later 1333 TRANSPORT SUPPORT TRAINING UNIT
Formed 12 March 1945 at Leicester East by redesignating 107 Operational Training Unit. Redesignated 1333 Transport Support Training Unit from 6th July 1946.

CM	*Inherited from 107 OTU.*
ZR	*Dakota III KG422 ZR-H, IV KJ838 ZR-F.*
Also used	*Horsa I HG833, II TL185 A; Halifax VII NA350 T, IX RT848; Oxford II ED189; Magister L8359; Tiger Moth II R4783; Proctor IV NP333; Auster III NX488.*

Disbanded 5th January 1948 at North Luffenham and merged with 1382 (Transport) Conversion Unit to become 240 Operational Conversion Unit.

1334 (TRANSPORT SUPPORT) CONVERSION UNIT
Formed 11th April 1945 at Gujrat, India, by redesignating the Transport Support Training Unit.

Dakota III FD895, IV KN294.

Disbanded 31st March 1945 at Baroda, India.

1335 (METEOR) CONVERSION UNIT
Formed 8th March 1945 at Colerne.

XL	*Meteor F.1 EE228 XL-P, F.3 EE354 XL-H; Oxford II T1251 XL-Z; Martinet I HP359.*

Disbanded 15th August 1946 at Molesworth to become 226 Operational Conversion Unit.

1336 (TRANSPORT SUPPORT) CONVERSION UNIT, later 1336 TRANSPORT CONVERSION UNIT
Formed 20th June 1945 at Welford. Redesignated 1336 Transport Conversion Unit from 12th October 1945.

ZS	*Dakota III KG447 ZS-V.*

Disbanded 1st March 1946 at Welford.

1380 (TRANSPORT SUPPORT) CONVERSION UNIT, later 1380 TRANSPORT CONVERSION UNIT
Formed 10th August 1945 at Tilstock by redesignating 81 Operational Training Unit. Later redesignated 1380 Transport Conversion Unit.

EZ	*Wellington X PG251 EZ-Y.*
JB	*Anson I MG589 JB-W.*
KG	*Wellington X NC809 KG-P.*

Also used   *Proctor II Z7210; Oxford In PH120.*

Disbanded 21st January 1946 at Tilstock.

1381 (TRANSPORT) CONVERSION UNIT
Formed 10th August 1945 at Bramcote as 1381 (Transport) Conversion Unit by redesignating 105 Operational Training Unit.

8F	*Dakota IV KJ875 8F-GE.*
I5	*Wellington X MF703 I5-X.*
7Z	*Wellington X HE242 7Z-Q; Dakota III KG321 7Z-A, IV KN401 7Z-F.*
Also used	*Magister P2499; Tiger Moth II R4918; Oxford I NM605.*

Disbanded 18th February 1948 at Dishforth.

1382 (TRANSPORT) CONVERSION UNIT
Formed 10th August 1945 at Wymeswold by redesignating 108 Operational Training Unit.

NU	*Dakota III KG380 NU-L, IV KP251 NU-G.*
Also used	*Oxford I AT652; Magister L8359.*

Disbanded 5th January 1948 at North Luffenham and merged with 1333 Transport Support Training Unit to become 240 Operational Conversion Unit.

1383 (TRANSPORT) CONVERSION UNIT
Formed 1st August 1945 at Crosby-on-Eden by redesignating 109 Operational Training Unit.

GY	*Dakota III KG657 GY-N; Oxford II W6638; Halifax VII PN239.*

Disbanded 6th August 1946 at Crosby-on-Eden.

1384 (HEAVY TRANSPORT) CONVERSION UNIT
Formed 1st November 1945 at Ossington by redesignating 6 Lancaster Finishing School.

Q6	*Oxford I NM803 Q6-H.*
OYZ	*York C.1 MW108 OYZ-B.*
Also used	*Dakota I FD789.*

Disbanded 30th June 1946 at Wethersfield.

1385 (HEAVY TRANSPORT SUPPORT) CONVERSION UNIT
Formed 1st April 1946 at Wethersfield by redesignating the Operational and Refresher Training Unit.

Stirling IV LK361; Halifax VII PN294 B; Horsa II TL290; Oxford I PH119.

Disbanded 6th June 1946 at Wethersfield and absorbed by 1333 (Transport Support) Conversion Unit.

1584 (HEAVY BOMBER) CONVERSION UNIT
Formed 9th November 1943 at Kolar, India, by redesignating 1584 (Heavy Bomber Conversion) Flight.

Liberator III BZ904.

Disbanded 1st February 1944 at Salbani, India, to become 1673 Heavy Conversion Unit.

1651 CONVERSION UNIT, later 1651 HEAVY CONVERSION UNIT
Formed 2nd January 1942 at Waterbeach by merging 26 and 106 Conversion Flights. Redesignated 1651 Heavy Conversion Unit from 7th October 1942, having absorbed 15 and 214 Squadron Conversion Flights.

Nil (1.42–5.43)	*Stirling I W7442 B; Lancaster I, III.*
BS (5.43–7.45)	*Stirling I R9193 BS-P; Lancaster I HK655 BS-F, III ME325 BS-P.*
QQ (5.43–)	*Stirling III LK488 QQ-E.*
YZ (5.43–11.44)	*Stirling I EF389 YZ-T.*
Also used	*Oxford I EB800; Spitfire VB AR423; Tiger Moth II EM910; Beaufighter VI MM883; Halifax II R9493.*

Disbanded 13th July 1945 at Woolfox Lodge.

1652 CONVERSION UNIT, later 1652 HEAVY CONVERSION UNIT
Formed 2nd January 1942 at Marston Moor by merging 28 and 107 Conversion Flights. Redesignated 1652 Heavy Conversion Unit from 7th October 1942 upon absorbing 35 Squadron Conversion Flights.

GV	*Halifax I L9575 GV-H, II, V LL490 GV-O, III MZ557 GV-J.*
JA	*Halifax II HR748 JA-J, V LL237 JA-W.*
Also used	*Spitfire VB AB198; Hurricane IIC LF561, IV KZ663.*

Disbanded 25th June 1945 at Marston Moor.

1653 CONVERSION UNIT later 1653 HEAVY CONVERSION UNIT
Formed 9th January 1942 at Polebrook by redesignating 108 Conversion Flight.

MX	*Liberator II AL511.*
Also used	*Blenheim IV T1862; Ventura I AE744.*

Disbanded 31st October 1942 at Polebrook.

Reformed 21st November 1943 at Chedburgh as 1653 Heavy Conversion Unit.

A3	*Stirling I N3702 A3-J; Lancaster I HK728 A3-K, III ND877 A3-A; Mosquito XIX TA343 A3-H.*
H4	*Stirling III BK763 H4-T; Lancaster I HK549 H4-V.*
M9	*Allocated but no known use.*
Also used	*Hurricane IIC LF632; Spitfire VB AR395; Beaufighter VI ND239.*

Disbanded 15th March 1947 at Lindholme to become 230 Operational Conversion Unit.

1654 CONVERSION UNIT, later 1654 HEAVY CONVERSION UNIT
Formed 19th May 1942 at Swinderby. Redesignated 1654 Heavy Conversion Unit from 7th October 1942.

UG	*Manchester I L7288 UG-J; Lancaster I ED308 UG; Halifax V DG317UG-J; Stirling III EH923 UG-K.*
JF	*Lancaster I ME420 JF-V; Stirling III EE899 JF-B.*
Also used	*Stirling I BK615; Halifax II BB383; Oxford I R6027; Hurricane IIC LF561; Spitfire VB BL729.*

Disbanded 1st September 1945 at Woolfox Lodge.

1655 MOSQUITO CONVERSION UNIT, later 1655 MOSQUITO TRAINING UNIT
Formed 30th August 1942 at Horsham St Faith. Redesignated 1655 Mosquito Training Unit from 22nd October 1942.

Blenheim V AZ883; Mosquito IV DZ346.

Disbanded 1st May 1943 at Marham and absorbed by 13 Operational Training Unit.

Reformed 1st June 1943 at Finmere as 1655 Mosquito Training Unit.

Mosquito III LR567 L, IV DZ312 M, XVI MM115, B.20 KB123, B.25 KB456; Oxford I DF525 W, II AB644.

Disbanded 31st December 1944 at Upper Heyford and absorbed by 16 Operational Training Unit.

1656 HEAVY CONVERSION UNIT
Formed 10th October 1942 at Lindholme by merging 103 and 460 Squadron Conversion Flights.

BL	*Manchester I L7434 BL-Y; Lancaster I ME583 BL-O; Hurricane IIC PG537 BL-W; Spitfire VB AB467 BL-B.*
EK	*Lancaster I PB855 EK-J, III W4994 EK-N.*
Also used	*Halifax II BB202, V DG338; Spitfire IIA P8788, VC AB467; Tiger Moth II T6309.*

Disbanded 10th November 1945 at Lindholme.

1657 HEAVY CONVERSION UNIT
Formed 7th October 1942 at Stradishall by merging 7, 101, 149 and 218 Squadron Conversion Flights and 1427 (Training) Flight.

AK	*Stirling I R9192 AK-B, III EJ127 AK-W.*
XT	*Stirling I N3758 XT-K, III EE881 XT-T.*
Also used	*Lancaster I R5485, II DS605 V; Stirling IV EF314; Tomahawk IIB AK279; Oxford II EB996; Hurricane IIC LF542.*

Disbanded 15th December 1944 at Stradishall.

1658 HEAVY CONVERSION UNIT
Formed 7th October 1942 at Riccall by merging 10, 76 and 78 Squadron Conversion Flights.

TT	*Halifax II DT618 TT-S; Oxford II AB758 TT-L.*
ZB	*Halifax II R9454 ZB-T, III LW193 ZB-B.*
Also used	*Halifax I L9528; Spitfire VB AA728.*

Disbanded 13th April 1945 at Riccall.

1659 HEAVY CONVERSION UNIT
Formed 7th October 1942 at Leeming by merging 405 and 408 Squadron Conversion Flights.

FD	*Halifax III HX268 FD-V; Lancaster III LM753 FD-B.*
RV	*Halifax II HR801 RV-D, III MZ505 RV-J; Lancaster III PB146 RV-K.*
Also used	*Halifax I L9524 D, V EB248; Lancaster I ED971; Oxford II P8975; Spitfire VB W3834; Hurricane IIC LF400, IV KZ709; Tiger Moth AX787.*

Disbanded 10th September 1945 at Topcliffe.

1660 HEAVY CONVERSION UNIT
Formed 22nd October 1942 at Swinderby by merging 61, 97, 106 and 207 Squadron Conversion Flights.

TV	*Manchester I R5768 TV-A; Stirling III LJ624 TV-C; Lancaster I LL786 TV-Q, III PB489 TV-S.*
YW	*Lancaster I R5845 YW-T, III PB836/G YW-H; Hurricane IIC LF572 YW-B; Spitfire VC BP864 YW-E; Mosquito XIX TA356 YW-J.*
Also used	*Lancaster II DS650; Stirling I R9148, III BF574; Halifax II BB305, V DK116; Oxford I NJ282; Lysander I R2636; Puss Moth II ES921.*

Disbanded 11th November 1946 at Swinderby and absorbed by 1653 Heavy Conversion Unit.

1661 HEAVY CONVERSION UNIT
Formed 9th November 1942 at Skellingthorpe by merging 9, 44 and 49 Squadron Conversion Flights.

GP	*Halifax II L9613 GP-A; Stirling III LK616 GP-G; Lancaster I W4113 GP-J; Oxford II V3574 GP-Y.*
KB	*Lancaster I PB869 KB-L; Mosquito XIII MM617 KB-A.*
Also used	*Manchester I R5839 G; Lancaster II DS786; Halifax V DK114; Spitfire VB BM425; Hurricane IIC LF423.*

Disbanded 24th August 1945 at Winthorpe.

1662 HEAVY CONVERSION UNIT
Formed 26th January 1943 at Blyton.

KF	*Halifax V LL502 KF-G; Lancaster I W4241 KF-Q.*
PE	*Halifax II R9498 PE-F2.*
Also used	*Halifax I L9577, III NA189; Spitfire VC AB467; Hurricane IIC LF513; Tiger Moth II T6401.*

Disbanded 6th April 1945 at Blyton.

1663 HEAVY CONVERSION UNIT
Formed 2nd March 1943 at Rufforth.

OO	*Halifax II LW241 OO-A, V EB155 OO-R, III.*
SV	*Halifax V LL490 SV-J, III NA621 SV-S.*
Also used	*Halifax I L9525, III LW677; Stirling I W7623;*

Oxford II X7253; Spitfire VB BL898; Hurricane IIC LF561.

Disbanded 28th May 1945 at Rufforth.

1664 HEAVY CONVERSION UNIT, later 1664 (ROYAL CANADIAN AIR FORCE) HEAVY CONVERSION UNIT
Formed 10th May 1943 at Croft. Redesignated 1664 (RCAF) Heavy Conversion Unit from 20th November 1944.

DH	*Halifax II JN968 DH-K, III LL575 DH-N2, V LL137 DH-S.*
ZU	*Halifax III MZ587 ZU-G, V DK248 ZU-C.*
Also used	*Lancaster I R5503, III LM391, X KB720; Hurricane IIC LF564; Spitfire VB AB898; Oxford II V3533.*
Note	A Lancaster Finishing Flight operated within the Unit from 4th August 1944.

Disbanded 6th April 1945 at Dishforth.

1665 HEAVY CONVERSION UNIT, later 1665 (HEAVY TRANSPORT) CONVERSION UNIT
Formed 23rd April 1943 at Mepal. Redesignated 1665 (Heavy Transport) Conversion Unit from 10th August 1945.

NY	*Stirling III EF210 NY-P, IV LJ622 NY-X.*
OG	*Stirling I R9148 OG-T, III EF121 OG-B; Halifax III LW205 OG-P, V LL305 OG-Z, VII PP368 OG-F.*
FO	*Allocated but no evidence of use.*
Also used	*Halifax VI NP816; Mosquito VI NT127; Lancaster I PA215; Oxford II N4792; Tiger Moth II EM910; Hurricane X P5196; Spitfire IIA P8758, VB BL957.*

Disbanded 13th July 1946 at Linton-on-Ouse and absorbed by 1332 Heavy Transport Conversion Unit.

1666 HEAVY CONVERSION UNIT, later 1666 (ROYAL CANADIAN AIR FORCE) HEAVY CONVERSION UNIT
Formed 5th June 1943 at Dalton. Redesignated 1666 (RCAF) Heavy Conversion Unit from 20th November 1944.

ND	*Halifax II DT689 ND-K; Lancaster III PB578 ND-R, X KB720 ND-E.*
QY	*Halifax II JD212 QY-H, V LL519 QY-M; Lancaster I NG389 QY-Z.*
Also used	*Halifax III LW380; Lancaster II DS614; Oxford II N6418; Spitfire VB AB403; Hurricane IIC LF560.*

Disbanded 3rd August 1945 at Wombleton.

1667 HEAVY CONVERSION UNIT
Formed 1st June 1943 at Lindholme.

GG	*Halifax V EB190 GG-H; Lancaster I HK734 GG-K.*
KR	*No evidence of use.*
LR	*Lancaster III PD442 LR-J.*
Also used	*Halifax II JD307; Oxford II X7130; Spitfire VB AR390; Hurricane IIC LF423; Tiger Moth II T7967.*

Disbanded 9th November 1945 at Sandtoft.

1668 HEAVY CONVERSION UNIT
Formed 15th August 1943 at Balderton.

Halifax V DG243; Lancaster I W4103.

Disbanded 21st November 1943 at Syerston to become 5 Lancaster Finishing School.

Reformed 28th July 1944 at Bottesford.

J9	*Lancaster I R5507 J9-Y.*
2K	*Lancaster I LM170 2K-D, II LL722 2K-U, III ND749 2K-H, X FM169 2K-J; Beaufighter VI V8615 2K-T.*
Also used	*Hurricane IIC PZ745; Spitfire VB W3656; Mosquito XIX TA357.*
Note	1 Bomber Defence Training Flight, equipped with

Beaufighter and Spitfire aircraft, operated within the Unit between June 1946 and the end of the year.

Disbanded 7th March 1946 at Cottesmore.

1669 HEAVY CONVERSION UNIT
Formed 15th August 1944 at Langar.

6F	Halifax II R9418, V LK947 6F-L; Lancaster I, III.
L6	Possibly allocated.
Also used	Spitfire VB AA751; Hurricane IIC LF385.

Disbanded 16th March 1945 at Langar.

1670 (THUNDERBOLT) CONVERSION UNIT
Formed 20th June 1944 at Yelahanka, India.

Thunderbolt I FL755; II KL176; Harvard IIB FE366.

Disbanded 24th January 1945 at Yelahanka to become 8 Refresher Flying Unit.

1671 CONVERSION UNIT
Formed 1st February 1944 at Baigachi, India, by redesignating A1 Mk VIII Conversion Flight.

Beaufighter VI.

Disbanded 5th June 1944 at Baigachi.

1672 (MOSQUITO) CONVERSION UNIT
Formed 1st February 1944 at Yelahanka, India.

Blenheim V BA657; Mosquito III LR537, VI HR549 3; Oxford I NM424.

Disbanded 31st August 1945 at Yelahanka.

1673 HEAVY CONVERSION UNIT
Formed 1st February 1944 at Salbani, India, by redesignating 1584 (Heavy Bomber) Conversion Unit.

Liberator III BZ837, VI EV814 R; Anson I DJ631; Tiger Moth II EM883.

Disbanded 8th November 1944 at Kolar, India, to become 6 Refresher Flying Unit and 358 Squadron.

1674 HEAVY CONVERSION UNIT
Formed 10th October 1943 at Aldergrove.

Halifax II HX176; Liberator III LV343 12, V BZ786, VI BZ966, VIII KK297; Fortress I AN537, II FA702, IIA FK201; Wellington XIII HZ724; Martinet I JN489 19; Oxford I NM747 E, II V3822; Hurricane IIC PZ767.

Disbanded 30th November 1945 at Lossiemouth.

1675 HEAVY CONVERSION UNIT
Formed 15th October 1943 at Lydda, Palestine, by redesignating 5 Heavy Bomber Conversion Unit, Lydda.

Liberator II AL540, III BZ934; Harvard IIA EX711; Hurricane IIB BD837; Argus II FS659.

Disbanded 12th October 1945 at Abu Sueir, Egypt.

1678 HEAVY CONVERSION UNIT
Formed 16th September 1943 at Foulsham by redesignating 1678 (Heavy Conversion) Flight.

SW	Lancaster II DS623 SW-Q.

Disbanded 12th June 1944 at Foulsham.

1699 (BOMBER SUPPORT) CONVERSION UNIT, later 1699 HEAVY CONVERSION UNIT
Formed 24th October 1944 at Oulton by redesignating 1699 (Fortress Training) Flight.

4Z	Fortress II SR376 4Z-W, III HB818 4Z-A; Liberator VI TS538.

Disbanded 29th June 1945 at Oulton.

Reformed 15th January 1946 at Full Sutton as 1699 Heavy Conversion Unit by redesignating the United Kingdom-based Lancastrian Flight of 231 Squadron.

Lancastrian II VM703 R.

Disbanded 1st April 1946 at Full Sutton.

CO-OPERATION FLIGHT, MOUNT BATTEN – see 2 Anti-Aircraft Co-operation Unit

201 CREW TRAINING UNIT
Formed 28th February 1947 at Swinderby by redesignating 17 Operational Training Unit.

Wellington X PG118; Spitfire XVI TB344; Hurricane IIC MW345.

Disbanded 15th March 1947 at Swinderby to become 201 Advanced Flying School.

202 CREW TRAINING UNIT
Formed 28th February 1947 at Finningley by redesignating 21 Operational Training Unit.

Wellington X NA724; Hurricane IIC MW337; Spitfire XVI SL576.

Disbanded 15th March 1947 at Finningley to become 202 Advanced Flying School.

203 CREW TRAINING UNIT
Planned opening in February 1947 as the successor to 61 Operational Training Unit cancelled.

204 CREW TRAINING UNIT
Formed on 28th February 1947 at Cottesmore by redesignating an element of 16 Operational Training Unit.

Mosquito III RR288, XVI PF484; Oxford I PH469.

Disbanded 15th March 1947 at Cottesmore to become 204 Advanced Flying School.

CZECHOSLOVAK FLIGHT – see 1429 (Czechoslovak Operational Training) Flight

'D' BOAT SEAPLANE TRAINING FLIGHT
Formed 8th August 1918 at Felixstowe.

No aircraft known.

Disbanded 1919 at Felixstowe.

'D' FLIGHT (1) – see 509 (Special Duty) Flight

'D' FLIGHT (2) – see 513 (Special Duty) Flight

'D' FLIGHT (3)
Formed 1st February 1940 at Larkhill within 1 School of Army Co-operation.

Taylorcraft Plus D T9120; Stinson 105 X1050; Gauntlet II K5295; Piper Cub Coupe DG667.

Disbanded 20th September 1941 at Old Sarum to become 1424 (Air Observation Post) Flight.

'D' FLIGHT, PERFORMANCE TESTING SECTION, AEROPLANE AND ARMAMENT EXPERIMENTAL ESTABLISHMENT – see Aeroplane and Armament Experimental Establishment

'D' FLIGHT, GOSPORT – see Royal Air Force Base, Gosport, later Royal Air Force Station, Gosport

'D' SQUADRON, AEGEAN
Formed 1st April 1918 at Stavros, Aegean, by redesignating 'D' Squadron of 2 Wing, RNAS.

No aircraft known.

Disbanded 18th September 1918 at Stavros to become 221 Squadron.

DAY FIGHTER COMBAT SQUADRON – see Central Fighter Establishment

DAY FIGHTER DEVELOPMENT WING – see Central Fighter Establishment

DAY FIGHTER LEADERS SCHOOL – see Central Fighter Establishment

DDT SPRAY FLIGHT
Formed 10th March 1945 at Digri, India.

Liberator VI.

Disbanded 1st July 1945 at Digri to become 1354 (DDT Spraying) Flight.

DEBDEN DIVISION, ROYAL AIR FORCE TECHNICAL COLLEGE – see Royal Air Force Technical College, Debden Division

DECK LANDING FLIGHT – see Royal Air Force Base, Gosport, later Royal Air Force Station, Gosport

DEFENCE FLIGHT, ADEN – see Fighter Defence Flight, Aden

DEFENCE FLIGHT, GIBRALTAR – see Fighter Defence Flight, Gibraltar

DEFENCE FLIGHT, HELIOPOLIS
Formed 24th August 1942 at Heliopolis.

Spitfire.

Disbanded (date unknown) at Heliopolis.

DEFENCE FLIGHT, IRAQ – see Fighter Defence Flight, Iraq

DEFENCE HELICOPTER FLYING SCHOOL (ROYAL AIR FORCE ELEMENT) – see 60 (Reserve) Squadron

DEFENCE RESEARCH AGENCY – AEROSPACE DIVISION
Formed 1st April 1991 by redesignating the Royal Aerospace Establishment.

Farnborough	Hunter F.4 WV276, T.7 WV383; Canberra B.6 XH568; Wessex HAS.1 XM330; Gnat T.1 XP505; Andover C.1 XS607, C.2 XS790; Buccaneer S.2B XW987, S.2C XV344; Comet 4 XV814; Jaguar T.2 XX835; BAC 1-11 XX919; Hawk T.1 XX162; Dakota III ZA947; Lynx AH.7 ZD285; Tornado GR.1 ZD326, F.2T ZD902; Sea King ZB 4X ZB506; Gazelle HT.1 ZB646; Lynx AH.7 ZD285.
Bedford	Canberra B.6 WK163; B(I).6 WT327; BAC 1-11 XX105; Hawk T.1 XX156; Sea King 4X ZB506; Lynx AH.7 ZD559.

Disbanded 23rd and 31st March 1994 respectively.

DEFENCE TEST AND EVALUATION ORGANISATION
Formed 1st April 1995 by redesignating the Directorate General of Test and Evaluation.

Assessment and Evaluation Centre, Boscombe Down

Llanbedr	Meteor D.16 WH453; Canberra B.2 WK128; Hawk T.1 XX154; Navajo Chieftain ZF521.
West Freugh	Jetstream T.2 XX475.

Current at 1st April 1998.

DEFIANT FLIGHT, NORTHOLT – see Special Duty Flight, Northolt

1 DELIVERY UNIT
Planned formation at Cairo, Egypt, from 26th October 1941 cancelled 15th December 1941 in favour of the Aircraft Delivery Unit.

DEMON FLIGHT – see 74 Squadron

DEMONSTRATION SQUADRON
Formed March 1918 at Hounslow.

Avro 504; Fokker D.VII; Snipe.

Disbanded (date unknown) at Hounslow.

DEPOT SQUADRONS – see Reserve Aeroplane Squadrons, later Reserve Squadrons, later Training Squadrons

DERBY UNIVERSITY AIR SQUADRON
The planned opening at Burnaston in 1946 was cancelled, although the code FLT was allocated for the period April 1946 to March 1947.

DESPATCH FLIGHT, BICESTER – see Ferry Training Flight, Bicester

DESERT AIR FORCE COMMUNICATION FLIGHT
Formed 1st June 1944 at Orvieto, Italy, by redesignating the Communication Unit, Desert Air Force.

Argus I EV763, II FZ796; Auster III MT403, IV MT328, V RT458; Hurricane IIC KZ115; Spitfire VC JG869, IX ML193; Fi 156; Anson I NK171 E, XII PH539.

Disbanded 30th June 1946 at Campoformido, Italy, and absorbed by Air Headquarters Italy Communication Squadron.

DESERT AIR FORCE TRAINING FLIGHT
Formed 15th May 1944 at Canne LG, Italy.

Spitfire VC JK311, IX EN483; Kittyhawk III FR843.

Disbanded 1st July 1944 at Sinello, Italy, to become 5 Refresher Flying Unit.

DESPATCH FLIGHT – see Ferry Training Flight, Bicester

DEVELOPMENT FLIGHT – see Royal Air Force Base, Gosport, later Royal Air Force Station, Gosport

DEVELOPMENT SQUADRON, GOSPORT
Formed 17th August 1918 at Gosport.

Blackburd N115; Cuckoo I N6996; II N6926; F.2B C820; D.H.4; D.H.9 E888; Avro 504J B3155, Avro 504K E3808.

Disbanded 31st December 1918 at Gosport and merged with elements from 185 Squadron to become 186 (Development) Squadron.

DIRECTORATE GENERAL OF TEST AND EVALUATION
Formed 1st April 1992.

Llanbedr	Meteor D.16 WH453; Canberra B.2 WK128, TT.18 WH743; Devon C.2 XA880; Sea Vixen FAW.2 XN694, D.3 XP924; Hawk T.1 XX154; Navajo Chieftain ZF521.
West Freugh	

Disbanded 1st April 1995 to become the Defence Test and Evaluation Organisation.

DURHAM UNIVERSITY AIR SQUADRON
Formed 8th March 1941 at Durham using Woolsington.

Nil (4.41–4.46)	Tiger Moth BB864; Tiger Moth II then provided by 24 and 28 Elementary Flying Training Schools.
FLJ (9.46– .49)	Tiger Moth II DE953 FLJ-A.
RUD (.49–4.51)	Tiger Moth II T5616 RUD-E.
Nil (4.51–8.63)	Anson T.21 WJ516; Harvard IIB KF954; Prentice T.1 VR302; Chipmunk T.10 WZ849; Balliol T.2 WG220.

Disbanded 1st August 1963 at Ouston to become the Northumbria Universities Air Squadron.

'E' BOAT SEAPLANE TRAINING FLIGHT
Formed 8th August 1918 at Felixstowe.

No aircraft known.

Disbanded 1919 at Felixstowe.

E FLIGHT, GOSPORT – see Royal Air Force Base, Gosport, later Royal Air Force Station, Gosport

EAGLE TRIALS FLIGHT
Formed 1st April 1920 at Gosport to conduct trials aboard HMS *Eagle*.

F.2B F4453; D.H.9A H3508; Panther N7426; Camel N8134; Cuckoo; Nighthawk; Avro 504K.

Disbanded October 1920 at Gosport.

EAST AFRICA COMMUNICATION FLIGHT – see Air Headquarters East Africa Communication Squadron, later Air Headquarters East Africa Communication Flight

EAST AFRICA COMMUNICATION SQUADRON – see Air Headquarters East Africa Communication Squadron, later Air Headquarters East Africa Communication Flight

EAST AFRICAN FERRY FLIGHT
Formed (date unknown) at Mombasa, Kenya.

No aircraft known.

Disbanded 31st May 1946 at Mombasa.

EAST LOWLANDS UNIVERSITY AIR SQUADRON
Formed 1st January 1969 at Turnhouse by merging Edinburgh University Air Squadron and St Andrews and Dundee Universities Air Squadron.

Chipmunk T.10; Bulldog T.1 XX703 02.

Current at 1st April 1998 at Leuchars.

EAST MIDLANDS UNIVERSITY AIR SQUADRON
Formed 24th November 1967 at Newton by redesignating the Nottingham University Air Squadron.

Chipmunk T.10 WP784 S; Bulldog T.1 XX639.

Current 1st April 1998 at Newton.

EASTLEIGH COMMUNICATION FLIGHT
Formed 15th September 1951 at Eastleigh by redesignating the Air Headquarters East Africa Communication Flight.

Anson XIX VP530; Valetta C.1 VW860.

Disbanded June 1953 at Eastleigh.

EDINBURGH UNIVERSITY AIR SQUADRON
Formed 13th January 1941 at Edinburgh and attached to Turnhouse.

Moth X5109; Tiger Moth II (provided by 11 Elementary Flying Training School).

Disbanded January 1946 at Turnhouse.

Reformed October 1946 at Turnhouse.

FLC (10.46– .47)	Allocated but no evidence of use.
RUE (.47–4.51)	*Tiger Moth T.2 N6720 RUE-B; Chipmunk T.10 WB601 RUE-E.*
Nil (4.51–1.69)	*Harvard IIB KF244 56; Chipmunk T.10 WZ857 55.*
Also used	*Prentice T.1 VS382.*

Disbanded 1st January 1969 at Turnhouse and merged with the St Andrews and Dundee Universities Air Squadron to become the East Lowlands University Air Squadron.

ELECTRICAL AND WIRELESS SCHOOL, later 1 ELECTRICAL AND WIRELESS SCHOOL
Formed 23rd December 1919 at Flowerdown by redesignating 1 (Training) Wireless School. Redesignated 1 Electrical and Wireless School from 1st November 1938.

Avro 504K F8768, Avro 504N J9002; F.2b J6727; Moth J9110; Wapiti IIA K2299; Victoria V K2345; Atlas Trainer K1483, Atlas AC K1514; Wallace I K5073, II K6016; Tiger Moth I K4280; Valentia K8850; Hendon K5088; Hart Trainer K6448; Battle K7666; Blenheim I K7070; Don L2407; D.H.86B L8040; Harvard I N7100; Magister N3957; Envoy III P5626.

Disbanded 26th August 1940 at Cranwell to become 1 Signals School.

1 ELECTRICAL AND WIRELESS SCHOOL – see Electrical and Wireless School, later 1 Electrical and Wireless School

2 ELECTRICAL AND WIRELESS SCHOOL
Formed 1st December 1938 at Yatesbury.

D.H.89A P9589; Proctor I P6272; Botha L6477; Envoy P5778; Dominie I R5921.

Disbanded 26th August 1940 at Yatesbury to become 2 Signals School.

3 ELECTRICAL AND WIRELESS SCHOOL
Formed 10th June 1940 at Yatesbury.

Audax K2020; Hart K3869.

Disbanded 26th August 1940 at Compton Bassett to become 3 Signals School.

ELECTRONIC WARFARE AND AVIONICS UNIT
Formed 1st June 1976 at Wyton by redesignating the Electronic Warfare Engineering and Training Unit.

Varsity T.1 WJ916; Andover C.1 XS644; Canberra T.17; Nimrod R.1.

Disbanded 1st October 1993 at Wyton to become the Electronic Warfare Operational Support Establishment.

1 ELEMENTARY AND RESERVE FLYING TRAINING SCHOOL
Formed 4th August 1935 at Hatfield by redesignating the Reserve Flying School, Stag Lane. Operated by the de Havilland Aircraft Company.

Hart Special K3140, Hart Trainer K6473; Audax K8320; Hind K5382; Battle K7616; Tiger Moth BB725, I K4260, II L6924; Anson I N5308.

Disbanded 3rd September 1939 at Hatfield to become 1 Elementary Flying Training School.

2 ELEMENTARY AND RESERVE FLYING TRAINING SCHOOL
Formed 1935 at Filton by redesignating the Reserve Flying School, Filton. Operated by the Bristol Aeroplane Company.

Audax K5599; Hart Trainer K6549, Hart Special K4372; Anson I N5245; Tiger Moth G-ACBC.

Disbanded 3rd September 1939 at Filton to become 2 Elementary Flying Training School.

3 ELEMENTARY AND RESERVE FLYING TRAINING SCHOOL
Formed 1935 at Hamble by redesignating the Reserve Flying School, Coventry. Operated by Air Service Training Ltd.

Wessex G-AAGW; Tutor G-ABKS; Cadet I G-ACCN, Cadet II G-AENL; Avro 652 G-ACRN; Vega Gull G-AERL; Dragonfly G-AEWZ; Cutty Sark G-AETI; Moth K1216; Hart K3816, Hart Trainer K6532, Hart Special K4407; Audax K3697; Hind K5526, Hind Trainer L7234; Anson I N5333; Battle K7610; Tiger Moth I K4247.

Disbanded 3rd September 1939 at Hamble to become 3 Elementary Flying Training School.

4 ELEMENTARY AND RESERVE FLYING TRAINING SCHOOL
Formed 1935 at Brough by redesignating the Reserve Flying School, Brough. Operated by North Sea Aerial and General Transport Company Limited.

Blackburn B.2 G-ACBH; Swallow 2 G-AFII; Moth K1887; Hart K3849, Hart Trainer K6484, Hart Special K4418; Audax K8326; Hind L7189; Battle K7599; Anson I N5334; Magister P2150; Tiger Moth I K4282.

Disbanded 3rd September 1939 at Brough to become 4 Elementary Flying Training School.

5 ELEMENTARY AND RESERVE FLYING TRAINING SCHOOL
Formed 1st June 1935 at Hanworth. Operated by Flying Training Limited.

Blackburn B.2 G-ADFV 18; Hart K3840, Hart Trainer K6427, Hart Special K4435; Battle K7602; Anson I N5311.

Disbanded 3rd September 1939 at Hanworth to become 5 Elementary Flying Training School.

6 ELEMENTARY AND RESERVE FLYING TRAINING SCHOOL
Formed 10th June 1935 at Sywell. Operated by Brooklands Aviation.

Hart K2988, Hart Trainer K6542; Hind K5512, Hind Trainer L7235; Audax K7407; Anson I N4935.

Disbanded 3rd September 1939 at Sywell to become 6 Elementary Flying Training School.

7 ELEMENTARY AND RESERVE FLYING TRAINING SCHOOL
Formed 25th November 1935 at Desford. Operated by Reid and Sigrist Limited.

Hart K3007, Hart Trainer K6526, Hart Special K4428; Audax K7421; Hind K6692; Anson I L7951; Tiger Moth L6945.

Disbanded 3rd September 1939 to become 7 Elementary Flying Training School.

8 ELEMENTARY AND RESERVE FLYING TRAINING SCHOOL
Formed 25th November 1935 at Woodley. Operated by Phillips and Powis Limited.

Hawk Trainer G-ADZA, Hawk Trainer 2 G-AFTR, Hawk Trainer 3 G-AFWY; Hornet Moth G-ADKI; Tiger Moth G-ADJJ; Hart K2981, Hart Trainer K6472; Hind K5471; Battle K7645; Magister N2259 13; Anson I N5251.

Disbanded 3rd September 1939 at Woodley to become 8 Elementary Flying Training School.

9 ELEMENTARY AND RESRVE FLYING TRAINING SCHOOL
Formed 6th January 1936 at Ansty. Operated by Air Service Training Limited.

Moth K1851; Hart K3817, Hart Trainer K6539; Hind K5553; Cloud K4300; Audax K7409; Anson I L7962; Tiger Moth II N5450.

Disbanded 3rd September 1939 at Ansty to become 9 Elementary Flying Training School.

10 ELEMENTARY AND RESERVE FLYING TRAINING SCHOOL
Formed 1st January 1936 at Filton. Operated by the Bristol Aeroplane Company Limited.

Tiger Moth G-AESN, Tiger Moth I K4256, II N9181 56; Hart Trainer K3746; Audax K5591; Anson I L7957.

Disbanded 3rd September 1939 at Filton to become 10 Elementary Flying Training School.

11 ELEMENTARY AND RESERVE FLYING TRAINING SCHOOL
Formed 27th January 1936 at Scone. Operated by Airwork Limited.

Hart Trainer K4766; Audax K5602; Hind K6724; Battle K7606; Tiger Moth L6931; Anson I N5254.

Disbanded 3rd September 1939 at Scone to become 11 Reserve Flying School.

12 ELEMENTARY AND RESERVE FLYING TRAINING SCHOOL
Formed 17th February 1936 at Prestwick. Operated by Scottish Aviation Limited.

Hart K2459, Hind K5535; Battle K7608; Anson I L7949161; Tiger Moth L6933.

Disbanded 3rd September 1939 at Prestwick to become 12 Elementary Flying Training School.

13 ELEMENTARY AND RESERVE FLYING TRAINING SCHOOL
Formed 18th November 1935 at White Waltham. Operated by the de Havilland Aircraft Company Limited.

Hart Trainer K6499, Hart Special K3144; Audax K8322; Hind K5419; Anson I N5281.

Disbanded 3rd September 1939 at White Waltham to become 13 Elementary Flying Training School.

14 ELEMENTARY AND RESERVE FLYING TRAINING SCHOOL
Formed 1st July 1937 at Castle Bromwich. Operated by Airwork Limited.

Hart K3902; Hind L7176; Tiger Moth I K4260, II L6929; Anson I N5256.

Disbanded 3rd September 1939 at Castle Bromwich to become 14 Elementary Flying Training School.

15 ELEMENTARY AND RESERVE FLYING TRAINING SCHOOL
Formed 1st July 1937 at Redhill. Operated by British Air Transport Limited.

Moth K1858; Hart K2991, Hart Trainer K6511; Audax K7463; Hind K5480; Battle K7600; Anson I N5284; Magister N3816.

Disbanded 3rd September 1939 at Redhill to become 15 Elementary Flying Training School.

16 ELEMENTARY AND RESERVE FLYING TRAINING SCHOOL
Formed 3rd July 1937 at Shoreham. Operated by the Martin School of Air Navigation.

Hart K3871, Hart Trainer K6527; Hind K5374; Battle K7612 A; Anson I N5242: Tiger Moth I K4256.

Disbanded 3rd September 1939 at Shoreham.

17 ELEMENTARY AND RESERVE FLYING TRAINING SCHOOL
Formed 1st October 1937 at Barton. Operated by Airwork Limited.

Gipsy Moth J9925; Moth K1835 2; Tiger Moth II N5458; Anson I N5257.

Disbanded 2nd September 1939 at Barton.

18 ELEMENTARY AND RESERVE FLYING TRAINING SCHOOL
Formed 1st October 1937 at Fairoaks. Operated by Universal Flying Services.

Audax K3694; Hind K5369; Tiger Moth I K4288 3.

Disbanded 3rd September 1939 at Fairoaks to become 18 Elementary Flying Training School.

19 ELEMENTARY AND RESERVE FLYING TRAINING SCHOOL
Formed 1st October 1937 at Gatwick. Operated by Airwork Limited.

Hart K3051, Hart Trainer K5800; Audax K7373 20; Tiger Moth I K4246; Hind Trainer L7184; Anson I N5286; Magister L8351 N.

Disbanded 3rd September 1939 at Gatwick and absorbed by 18 Elementary Flying Training School.

20 ELEMENTARY AND RESERVE FLYING TRAINING SCHOOL
Formed 1st October 1937 at Gravesend. Operated by Airports Limited.

Hart K3831, Hart Trainer K6511, Hart Special K3143; Audax K7415; Tiger Moth I K4251, II N6446 S; Hind K6775; Anson I N5291.

Disbanded 3rd September 1939 at Gravesend and merged with 44 Elementary and Reserve Flying Training School to become 14 Elementary Flying Training School.

21 ELEMENTARY AND RESERVE FLYING TRAINING SCHOOL
Formed 1st January 1938 at Stapleford Abbots. Operated by Reid and Sigrist Limited.

Hart K3854, Hart Trainer K3751; Hind K5413; Audax K7454; Tiger Moth I K4250; Anson I N5294.

Disbanded 3rd September 1939 at Stapleford Abbots.

22 ELEMENTARY AND RESERVE FLYING TRAINING SCHOOL
Formed 1st February 1938 at Cambridge. Operated by Marshalls Limited.

Hart K3023, Hart Trainer K6465 31; Audax K8333; Hind K5450; Battle K7625 121; Anson I N5318; Tiger Moth I K4266.

Disbanded 3rd September 1939 at Cambridge to become 22 Elementary Flying Training School.

23 ELEMENTARY AND RESERVE FLYING TRAINING SCHOOL

Formed 1st April 1938 at Rochester. Operated by Short Brothers Limited.

Avro 504N K2419; Hart Trainer K4891; Audax K7360; Hind K5511, Hind Trainer L7236; Anson I N5323; Magister N5438.

Disbanded 3rd September 1939 at Sydenham and absorbed by 24 Elementary Flying Training School.

24 ELEMENTARY AND RESERVE FLYING TRAINING SCHOOL

Formed 1st January 1939 at Sydenham. Operated by Short Brothers Limited.

Hind K6818; Audax K3691; Demon K5698; Anson I N5261; Magister N3833.

Disbanded 3rd September 1939 at Sydenham to become 24 Elementary Flying Training School.

25 ELEMENTARY AND RESERVE FLYING TRAINING SCHOOL

Formed 24th June 1938 at Waltham. Operated by Herts and Essex Aero Club Limited.

Hart K3030; Hind L7205, Hind Trainer L7243; Magister L8204; Tiger Moth I K4251; Anson I N5263.

Disbanded 3rd September 1939 at Waltham.

26 ELEMENTARY AND RESERVE FLYING TRAINING SCHOOL

Formed 24th June 1938 at Kidlington. Operated by Marshalls Limited.

Hind L7192, Hind Trainer L7242; Audax K7552; Tipsy Trainer 1 G-AFRV; Magister N3801; Anson I N5131.

Disbanded 2nd September 1939 at Kidlington.

27 ELEMENTARY AND RESERVE FLYING TRAINING SCHOOL

Formed 24th June 1938 at Tollerton. Operated by Nottingham Airport Limited.

Hart K3837; Hind K5401, Hind Trainer L7240; Magister L8175; Anson I N5244.

Disbanded 3rd September 1939 at Tollerton.

28 ELEMENTARY AND RESERVE FLYING TRAINING SCHOOL

Formed 1st August 1938 at Meir. Operated by Reid and Sigrist Ltd.

Hart K3864, Hart Trainer K6474; Hind K6785; Magister N3785, Anson I N5327.

Disbanded 3rd September 1939 at Meir.

29 ELEMENTARY AND RESERVE FLYING TRAINING SCHOOL

Formed 1st August 1938 at Luton. Operated by Birkett Air Services Limited.

Hart K3054, Hart Trainer K6468; Hind K6765; Magister L8260; Anson I N4982.

Disbanded 3rd September 1939 at Luton.

30 ELEMENTARY AND RESERVE FLYING TRAINING SCHOOL

Formed 29th September 1938 at Burnaston. Operated by Air Schools Limited.

Audax K3707; Hind K5547; Tiger Moth II N6444; Magister N5396.

Disbanded 3rd September 1939 at Burnaston to become 30 Elementary Flying Training School.

31 ELEMENTARY AND RESERVE FLYING TRAINING SCHOOL

Formed 29th September 1938 at Cheltenham. Operated by Surrey Flying Services.

Audax K3711; Hind K5402; Hart Trainer K5797; Tiger Moth II N5452.

Disbanded 3rd September 1939 at Cheltenham.

32 ELEMENTARY AND RESERVE FLYING TRAINING SCHOOL

Formed 15th April 1939 at Greatham. Operated by Portsmouth, Southsea and Isle of Wight Aviation Limited.

Audax K3079; Hind K5440; Anson I N5330; Tiger Moth II N6535.

Disbanded 3rd September 1939 at Greatham.

33 ELEMENTARY AND RESERVE FLYING TRAINING SCHOOL

Formed 3rd December 1938 at Whitchurch. Operated by Chamier, Gilbert Lodge and Company Limited.

Hind K5439; Anson I N5307; Tiger Moth II N5472.

Disbanded 2nd September 1939 at Whitchurch.

34 ELEMENTARY AND RESERVE FLYING TRAINING SCHOOL

Formed 1st January 1939 at Rochford. Operated by Air Hire Limited.

Audax K2025; Hind K5393; Tiger Moth I K4260, II N6452.

Disbanded 3rd September 1939 at Rochford.

35 ELEMENTARY AND RESERVE FLYING TRAINING SCHOOL

Formed 1st May 1939 at Grangemouth. Operated by Scottish Aviation.

Audax K1998; Hind K5384; Anson I L7950; Tiger Moth II N6593.

Disbanded 3rd September 1939 at Grangemouth.

36 ELEMENTARY AND RESERVE FLYING TRAINING SCHOOL

Planned opening in 1939 at Sherburn in Elmet with Tiger Moths cancelled.

37 ELEMENTARY AND RESERVE FLYING TRAINING SCHOOL

Formed 3rd July 1939 at Exeter. Operated by the Straight Corporation Limited.

Anson I N5238; Tiger Moth II.

Disbanded 3rd September 1939 at Exeter.

38 ELEMENTARY AND RESERVE FLYING TRAINING SCHOOL

Formed 1st July 1939 at Kingstown. Operated by the Border Flying Club.

Audax K3060; Hind K6758; Tiger Moth II N6804.

Disbanded 3rd September 1939 at Kingstown.

39 ELEMENTARY AND RESERVE FLYING TRAINING SCHOOL

Formed 3rd July 1939 at Weston-super-Mare. Operated by the Straight Corporation Limited.

Audax K2019; Hind K5517.

Disbanded 3rd September 1939 at Weston-super-Mare.

40 ELEMENTARY AND RESERVE FLYING TRAINING SCHOOL

Formed 15th August 1939 at Mousehold. Operated by Air Contractors Ltd.

Audax K4382; Magister L8220; Hind K6837.

Disbanded 2nd September 1939 at Mousehold.

41 ELEMENTARY AND RESERVE FLYING TRAINING SCHOOL

Planned opening at Dyce, to be operated by Aberdeen Flying Services Ltd, cancelled 3rd September 1939.

42 ELEMENTARY AND RESERVE FLYING TRAINING SCHOOL

Formed 1st August 1939 at Blackpool. Operated by Reid and Sigrist Ltd.

Hind K5407; Tiger Moth II N6608.

Disbanded 2nd September 1939 at Blackpool.

43 ELEMENTARY AND RESERVE FLYING TRAINING SCHOOL

Formed 1st June 1939 at Woolsington. Operated by the Newcastle-on-Tyne Aero Club.

Audax K2018; Hind K5446; Magister N5413; Tiger Moth II N6606.

Disbanded 2nd September 1939 at Woolsington.

44 ELEMENTARY AND RESERVE FLYING TRAINING SCHOOL

Formed 1st May 1939 at Elmdon. Operated by Airwork Limited.

Audax K2024; Hind K5506; Magister N3962.

Disbanded 2nd September 1939 at Elmdon and merged with 20 Elementary and Reserve Flying Training School to become 14 Elementary Flying Training School.

45 ELEMENTARY AND RESERVE FLYING TRAINING SCHOOL
Formed 3rd July 1939 at Ipswich. Operated by the Straight Corporation Ltd.

Audax K2011; Hind K5503; Magister N5414.

Disbanded 2nd September 1939 at Ipswich.

46 ELEMENTARY AND RESERVE FLYING TRAINING SCHOOL
Formed 1st August 1939 at Roborough. Operated by Portsmouth, Southsea and Isle of Wight Aviation Limited.

Audax K4381; Hind K5396; Tiger Moth II N6947.

Disbanded 2nd September 1939 at Portsmouth

47 ELEMENTARY AND RESERVE FLYING TRAINING SCHOOL
Formed 15th July 1939 at Doncaster. Operated by Nottingham Airport Limited.

Audax K7474; Hind K4651; Tiger Moth II N6753.

Disbanded 2nd September 1939 at Doncaster.

48 ELEMENTARY AND RESERVE FLYING TRAINING SCHOOL
Planned opening in 1939 at Baginton, to be operated by Air Service Training Ltd, cancelled.

49 ELEMENTARY AND RESERVE FLYING TRAINING SCHOOL
Planned opening in 1939 at Samlesbury cancelled.

50 ELEMENTARY AND RESERVE FLYING TRAINING SCHOOL
Formed June 1939 at Booker. Operated by Whetton Aviation Ltd.

Audax K3083; Hind K6637; Tiger Moth II N6640.

Disbanded 3rd September 1939 at Booker.

51 ELEMENTARY AND RESERVE FLYING TRAINING SCHOOL
Planned opening at Abbotsinch, to be operated by Scottish Aviation Ltd, cancelled 3rd September 1939.

52 ELEMENTARY AND RESERVE FLYING TRAINING SCHOOL
Planned opening at Clifton cancelled 3rd September 1939.

53 ELEMENTARY AND RESERVE FLYING TRAINING SCHOOL
Planned opening at Yeadon cancelled 3rd September 1939.

54 ELEMENTARY AND RESERVE FLYING TRAINING SCHOOL
Planned opening at Southampton cancelled 3rd September 1939.

55 ELEMENTARY AND RESERVE FLYING TRAINING SCHOOL
Planned opening at Speke cancelled 3rd September 1939.

56 ELEMENTARY AND RESERVE FLYING TRAINING SCHOOL
Formed 24th August 1939 at Kenley. Operated by British Air Transport Ltd.

Hart Special K4426; Hind K5386; Tiger Moth II N6549.

Disbanded 2nd September 1939 at Kenley.

57 ELEMENTARY AND RESERVE FLYING TRAINING SCHOOL
Planned opening at Coventry cancelled 3rd September 1939.

58 ELEMENTARY AND RESERVE FLYING TRAINING SCHOOL
Planned opening at Braunstone Frith cancelled 3rd September 1939.

59 ELEMENTARY AND RESERVE FLYING TRAINING SCHOOL
Planned opening at Cardiff cancelled 3rd September 1939.

ELEMENTARY FLYING TRAINING SCHOOL (KENYA)
Formed 21st August 1940 at Eastleigh, Kenya, by redesignating 2 (Training) Flight, Kenya Auxiliary Air Unit.

Tiger Moth K26.

Disbanded 11th November 1940 at Eastleigh to become 30 Elementary Flying Training School.

1 ELEMENTARY FLYING TRAINING SCHOOL
Formed 3rd September 1939 at Hatfield by redesignating 1 Elementary and Reserve Flying Training School.

Nil (9.39–4.46)	*Tiger Moth BB725, I K4260, II R4750 63; Anson I N5308; Auster I LB321; Proctor I P6181, III DX199; Snargasher G-AEOD.*	
FHA (4.46–5.47)	*Tiger Moth II EM836 FHA-E.*	
FHB (4.46–5.47)	*Tiger Moth II DE836 FHB-A.*	
FHC	*Allocated but no evidence of use.*	

Disbanded 5th May 1947 at Panshanger to become 1 Reserve Flying School.

1 ELEMENTARY FLYING TRAINING SCHOOL (INDIA)
Formed 1940 at Begumpet, India.

Tiger Moth MA932, I NL960, II T6878; Cornell II.

Disbanded 10th July 1945 at Begumpet.

2 ELEMENTARY FLYING TRAINING SCHOOL
Formed 3rd September 1939 at Filton by redesignating 2 Elementary and Reserve Flying Training School.

Hart Trainer K6549; Battle L5939; Magister N3829; Tiger Moth G-ABSY; Hornet Moth W6422.

Disbanded 1st November 1941 at Staverton to become 6 (Supplementary) Flying Instructors School.

Reformed 22nd July 1942 at Worcester by redesignating 6 (Supplementary) Flying Instructors School.

Nil (7.42–4.46)	*Tiger Moth II T8250 32.*
FHE (4.46–9.47)	*Tiger Moth II N6467 FHE-B.*
FHF (4.46–9.47)	*Tiger Moth II.*
FHG (4.46–9.47)	*Anson I MG519 FHG-B.*
Also used	*Hornet Moth W5830; Tiger Moth I NL980.*

Disbanded 30th September 1947 at Yatesbury.

2 ELEMENTARY FLYING TRAINING SCHOOL (INDIA)
Formed 1940 at Jodhpur, India.

Tiger Moth MA934, I NL945, II EM867; Cornell II FX139; Oxford I NM465.

Disbanded 1st June 1947 at Jodhpur to become the Elementary Flying Training School, RIAF.

3 ELEMENTARY FLYING TRAINING SCHOOL
Formed 3rd September 1939 at Hamble by redesignating 3 Elementary and Reserve Flying Training School.

Nil (9.39–4.46)	*Tutor G-ABIR; Cadet G-ADAU; Cutty Sark G-AETI; Vega Gull G-AERL; Hart Special K4407; Magister P6367; Tiger Moth BB815, II N9311; Hotspur I BV192; Tutor HM504.*
FHI (4.46–3.48)	*Tiger Moth II T7997 FHI-S.*
FHJ (4.46–3.48)	*Tiger Moth II L6944 FHJ-S.*
FHK (4.46–3.48)	*Tiger Moth II.*

Disbanded 31st March 1948 at Shellingford.

4 ELEMENTARY FLYING TRAINING SCHOOL
Formed 3rd September 1939 at Brough by redesignating the 4 Elementary and Reserve Flying Training School.

Nil (9.39–4.46)	*Blackburn B.2 L6893; Tiger Moth BB741, I K4282, II T7029 77.*
FHM (4.46–3.47)	*Tiger Moth II R4975 FHM-I.*
FHN (4.46–3.47)	*Tiger Moth II N6580 FHN-H.*
FHO (4.46–3.47)	*Tiger Moth II R4763 FHO-D.*

Disbanded 10th March 1947 at Brough to become 4 Reserve Flying School.

5 ELEMENTARY FLYING TRAINING SCHOOL
Formed 3rd September 1939 at Hanworth by redesignating 5 Elementary and Reserve Flying Training School.

Battle L5940; Magister N3812; Swallow X5010.

Disbanded 23rd December 1941 at Meir.

6 ELEMENTARY FLYING TRAINING SCHOOL
Formed 3rd September 1939 at Sywell by redesignating 6 Elementary and Reserve Flying Training School.

Nil (9.39–4.46)	Magister L5973; Tiger Moth AX785, I K4254, II N9151 64.
FHQ (4.46–5.47)	Tiger Moth II N9116 FHQ-S.
FHR (4.46–5.47)	Tiger Moth II T7998 FHR-A.
FHS (4.46–5.47)	Tiger Moth II.
FHT	Allocated but not used.

Disbanded 12th May 1947 at Sywell to become 6 Reserve Flying School.

7 ELEMENTARY FLYING TRAINING SCHOOL
Formed 3rd September 1939 at Desford by redesignating 7 Elementary and Reserve Flying Training School.

Nil (9.39–4.46)	Magister R1963; Tiger Moth BB746, I K4260, II DF123 32.
FHV (4.46–5.47)	Tiger Moth II BB759 FHV-A.
FHW (4.46–5.47)	Tiger Moth II T6918 FHW-Z.
FHX (4.46–5.47)	Tiger Moth II T7089 FHX-A.
FHY	Allocated but not used.

Disbanded 9th May 1947 at Desford to become 7 Reserve Flying School.

8 ELEMENTARY FLYING TRAINING SCHOOL
Formed 3rd September 1939 at Woodley by redesignating 8 Elementary and Reserve Flying Training School.

Hawk Trainer G-ADZA, Hawk Trainer 2 G-AFTR, Hawk Trainer 3 G-AFWY; Hornet Moth G-ADKI; Mentor L4411; Tiger Moth II T6553; Magister N2259 13; Harvard I N7120; Petrel P5637; Vega Gull P5990; Proctor I P6227.

Disbanded 15th October 1942 at Woodley.

Reformed 7th May 1946 at Woodley as 8 Elementary Flying Training School by redesignating an element of 10 Flying Instructors School.

FDQ (5.46–3.47)	Tiger Moth II NL780 FDQ-H.
FDR (5.46–3.47)	Tiger Moth II DE678 FDR-B.
FDS (5.46–3.47)	Tiger Moth II DE719 FDS-B.
FDT (5.46–3.47)	Hawk Trainer 3 BB661 FDT-A; Anson I NK565 FDT-M.
Also used	Tiger Moth I NM140.

Disbanded 3rd March 1947 at Woodley to become 8 Reserve Flying School.

9 ELEMENTARY FLYING TRAINING SCHOOL
Formed 3rd September 1939 at Ansty by redesignating 9 Elementary and Reserve Flying Training School.

Magister L6899; Tiger Moth BB819, I K4247; Hurricane I N2555.

Disbanded 31st March 1944 at Ansty.

10 ELEMENTARY FLYING TRAINING SCHOOL
Formed 3rd September 1939 1st January 1936 at Filton by redesignating 10 Elementary and Reserve Flying Training School.

Tiger Moth II N9181 56; Leopard Moth AW121.

Disbanded 21st July 1942 at Stoke Orchard.

11 ELEMENTARY FLYING TRAINING SCHOOL
Formed 27th January 1936 at Scone. Operated by Airwork Limited. Redesignated 11 Elementary Flying Training School from 3rd September 1939.

Nil (9.39–4.46)	Magister L8153; Tiger Moth BB673, I K4262, II N9128; Hawk Trainer BB663.
FIA	Allocated but no known use.
FIB	Allocated but no known use.
FIC (4.46–3.47)	Tiger Moth II T7155 FIC-J.
FID	Allocated but no known use.

Disbanded 18th March 1947 at Scone to become 11 Reserve Flying School.

12 ELEMENTARY FLYING TRAINING SCHOOL
Formed 3rd September 1939 at Prestwick by redesignating 12 Elementary and Reserve Flying Training School.

Tiger Moth BB795; Fokker F.XXII G-AFZP; Fokker F.XXXVI G-AFZR.

Disbanded 22nd March 1941 at Prestwick.

13 ELEMENTARY FLYING TRAINING SCHOOL
Formed 3rd September 1939 at White Waltham by redesignating 13 Elementary and Reserve Flying Training School.

Tiger Moth BB741, I K4260, II N9450; Monarch W6463.

Disbanded 1st June 1941 at Peterborough to become 21 and 25 Elementary Flying Training Schools.

14 ELEMENTARY FLYING TRAINING SCHOOL
Formed 3rd September 1939 at Castle Bromwich by redesignating 14 Elementary and Reserve Flying Training School.

Tiger Moth II T8258 DB.

Disbanded 1st February 1946 at Elmdon.

15 ELEMENTARY FLYING TRAINING SCHOOL
Formed 3rd September 1939 at Redhill by redesignating 15 Elementary and Reserve Flying Training School.

Nil (9.39–4.46)	Battle Trainer P6637; Magister P2404; Tiger Moth BB755, I K4282, II T7929.
FIJ (4.46–12.47)	Tiger Moth II.
FIK (4.46–12.47)	Tiger Moth II R4904 FIK-B.
FIL	Allocated but no evidence of use.

Disbanded 31st December 1947 at Kingstown.

16 ELEMENTARY FLYING TRAINING SCHOOL
Formed 10th April 1940 at Burnaston by redesignating 30 Elementary Flying Training School.

Nil (4.40–4.46)	Magister N3774 60; Tiger Moth II T5878 33; Battle L5950.
FIN (4.46–3.47)	Tiger Moth II T7048 FIN-O.
FIO (4.46–3.47)	Tiger Moth II N9394 FIO-J.
FIP (4.46–3.47)	Tiger Moth II T5878 FIP-N.
Also used	Tiger Moth BB704; Auster I LB385.

Disbanded 27th March 1947 at Burnaston to become 16 Reserve Flying School.

17 ELEMENTARY FLYING TRAINING SCHOOL
Formed 18th January 1941 at North Luffenham.

Tiger Moth BB755, I K4251, II T7118.

Disbanded 1st June 1942 at Peterborough.

18 ELEMENTARY FLYING TRAINING SCHOOL
Formed 3rd September 1939 at Fairoaks by redesignating 18 Elementary and Reserve Flying Training School.

Nil (9.39–4.46)	Tiger Moth I K4288 3, II T6182; Proctor IV RM171; Anson I EG277.
FIR (4.46–5.47)	Tiger Moth II N6750 FIR-B.
FIS (4,46–5.47)	Tiger Moth II R4845 FIS-E.
FIT	Allocated but not used.

Disbanded 14th May 1947 at Fairoaks to become 18 Reserve Flying School.

19 ELEMENTARY FLYING TRAINING SCHOOL
Formed 21st January 1941 at Sealand.

Tiger Moth BB794, I K4259, II T8494.

Disbanded 31st December 1942 at Sealand.

20 ELEMENTARY FLYING TRAINING SCHOOL
Formed 1st March 1941 at Yeadon.

Tiger Moth BB673, II N5488.

Disbanded 9th January 1942 at Yeadon.

21 ELEMENTARY FLYING TRAINING SCHOOL
Formed 1st June 1941 at Booker by redesignating an element of 13 Elementary Flying Training School.

Nil (6.41–4.46)	Magister N3837; Proctor III HM284; Tiger Moth II DE482 64.
FIV (4.46–2.50)	Tiger Moth II DE419 FIV-C; Auster V TW471 FIV-N.

FIW (4.46–2.50)   Tiger Moth I NL993 FIW-D; Auster V RT489
                  FIW-B.
FIX (4.46–2.50)   Tiger Moth II T6802 FIX-Y.
FIY   Allocated but not used.
Also used   Tiger Moth BB704; Messenger RH372;
                  Dominie II RL950; Anson XIX TX186.

Disbanded 28th February 1950 at Booker.

22 ELEMENTARY FLYING TRAINING SCHOOL
Formed 3rd September 1939 at Cambridge by redesignating 22
Elementary and Reserve Flying Training School.

Nil (9.39–4.46)   Master I N7711, II DK890; Magister P6451;
                  Tiger Moth BB756, I K4266, II T6708 110;
                  Vega Gull III P1753; Auster I LB321 E2, III
                  MZ178; Oxford II V3523.
FJA (4.46–5.47)   Tiger Moth II R4971 FJA-D; Auster V RT489
                  FJA-Z.
FJB (4.46–5.47)   Tiger Moth II T6175 FJB-F; Auster V TW498
                  FJB-Y.
FJC (4.46–5.47)   Tiger Moth II R5216 FJC-K; Auster V TW508
                  FJC-V.
FJD (4.46–5.47)   Tiger Moth II DE241 FJD-G.

Disbanded 1st May 1947 at Cambridge to become 22 Reserve
Flying School.

24 ELEMENTARY FLYING TRAINING SCHOOL
Formed 3rd September 1939 at Sydenham by redesignating 24
Elementary and Reserve Flying Training School.

Nil (9.39–4.46)   Magister N3833; Battle L5939; Demon K3793;
                  Proctor I P6175; Tiger Moth II N9447.
FJF (4.46–5.47)   Tiger Moth II R5109 FJF-A.
FJG (4.46–5.47)   Tiger Moth II R5137 FJG-C; Magister P2493
                  FJG-W.
FJH   Allocated but not used.
Also used   Tiger Moth I NM118.

Disbanded 7th May 1947 at Rochester to become 24 Reserve
Flying School.

25 ELEMENTARY FLYING TRAINING SCHOOL
Formed 1st June 1941 at Peterborough by redesignating an
element of 13 Elementary Flying Training School.

Tiger Moth BB810, I NL995, II R5179 32; Anson I R3325 86;
Magister T9683.

Disbanded 1st November 1945 at Hucknall and absorbed by 16
Elementary Flying Training School.

25 ELEMENTARY FLYING TRAINING SCHOOL (SOUTHERN RHODESIA)
Formed 25th May 1940 at Belvedere, Southern Rhodesia.

Tiger Moth II DE162; Cornell I EW570, II 15268; Harvard IIA EX786.

Disbanded 3rd November 1944 at Belvedere.

26 ELEMENTARY FLYING TRAINING SCHOOL
Formed 14th August 1941 at Theale.

Tiger Moth BB697, II N6737 B36; Hind K5465; Mentor L4406; Puss
Moth DR607; Hornet Moth AV969.

Disbanded 9th July 1945 at Theale.

26 ELEMENTARY FLYING TRAINING SCHOOL (SOUTHERN RHODESIA)
Formed 8th August 1940 at Guinea Fowl, Southern Rhodesia.

Tiger Moth II T5554; Cornell II 15662.

Disbanded 14th August 1945 at Guinea Fowl.

27 ELEMENTARY FLYING TRAINING SCHOOL
Planned opening from August 1941 at Baginton cancelled.

27 ELEMENTARY FLYING TRAINING SCHOOL (SOUTHERN RHODESIA)
Formed 2nd February 1941 at Induna, Southern Rhodesia.

Tiger Moth II T8029; Cornell II 15319.

Disbanded 21st September 1945 at Induna.

28 ELEMENTARY FLYING TRAINING SCHOOL
Formed 15th September 1941 at Wolverhampton.

Nil (9.41–4.46)   Oxford I L4566; Tiger Moth II N6735 38.
FJJ (4.46–6.47)   Tiger Moth II T7917 FJJ-A.
FJK (4.46–6.47)   Tiger Moth L6938 FJK-G.
FJL   Allocated but no evidence of use.
Also used   Tiger Moth I NM118.

Disbanded 26th June 1947 at Wolverhampton to become 25
Reserve Flying School.

28 ELEMENTARY FLYING TRAINING SCHOOL (SOUTHERN RHODESIA)
Formed 1st April 1941 at Mount Hampden, Southern Rhodesia.

Tiger Moth II T8108 25; Cornell II 15088; Harvard IIA EX403 7.

Disbanded 30th October 1945 at Mount Hampden.

29 ELEMENTARY FLYING TRAINING SCHOOL
Formed 13th September 1941 at Clyffe Pypard.

Nil (9.41–4.46)   Battle L5978; Magister N5396; Anson I MG519;
                  Tiger Moth BB742 77.
FJN (4.46–10.47) Tiger Moth II T6861 FJN-A.
FJO (4.46–10.47) Tiger Moth II T5838 FJO-D.
FJP (4.46–10.47) Tiger Moth II T5963 FJP-L.
FJQ   Allocated but not used.

Disbanded 5th November 1947 at Clyffe Pypard and absorbed by
21 Elementary Flying Training School.

30 ELEMENTARY FLYING TRAINING SCHOOL
Formed 3rd September 1939 at Burnaston by redesignating 30
Elementary and Reserve Flying Training School.

Magister L8349.

Disbanded 10th April 1940 at Burnaston to become 16 Elementary
Flying Training School.

30 ELEMENTARY FLYING TRAINING SCHOOL (KENYA)
Formed 11th November 1940 at Eastleigh, Kenya, by redesignating
the Elementary Flying Training School, Kenya.

No aircraft known.

Disbanded 13th March 1941 at Eastleigh, having provided an
element to form 3 Elementary Flying Training School, SAAF at
Wonderboom, South Africa.

31 ELEMENTARY FLYING TRAINING SCHOOL
Opened 10th May 1941 at Calgary, Canada.

Kaydet I FJ805; Cornell I FJ669, II; Tiger Moth 4310.

Disbanded 25th September 1944 at De Winton, Canada.

32 ELEMENTARY FLYING TRAINING SCHOOL
Opened 2nd June 1941 at Swift Current, Canada.

Oxford I AR765; Harvard IIB FE407; Kaydet I FJ917; Tiger Moth II
5974; Crane 7889; Cornell II 14488 N.

Disbanded 8th September 1944 at Bowden, Canada.

33 ELEMENTARY FLYING TRAINING SCHOOL
Formed 7th December 1941 at Caron, Canada.

Tiger Moth II 8999; Cornell I, II FH679.

Disbanded 14th January 1944 at Caron.

34 ELEMENTARY FLYING TRAINING SCHOOL (CANADA)
Formed 2nd February 1942 at Assiniboia, Canada.

Tiger Moth II 5841; Cornell I, II 10600.

Disbanded 30th January 1944 at Assiniboia to become 25
Elementary Flying Training School, RCAF.

35 ELEMENTARY FLYING TRAINING SCHOOL (CANADA)
Formed 24th February 1942 at Nespawa, Canada.

Tiger Moth II 3886 60; Cornell.

Disbanded 30th January 1944 at Nespawa to become 26 Elementary Flying Training School, RCAF.

36 ELEMENTARY FLYING TRAINING SCHOOL (CANADA)
Formed 17th March 1942 at Pearce, Canada.

Tiger Moth II 5861; Kaydet I FJ808; Harvard II 2732; Anson.

Disbanded 14th August 1942 at Pearce.

ELEMENTARY FLYING TRAINING SQUADRON
Formed 1st June 1987 at Swinderby by redesignating the Flying Selection Squadron.

Chipmunk T.10 WK550 K.

Disbanded 1st April at Swinderby and merged with the Royal Navy Elementary Flying Training Squadron to become the Joint Elementary Flying Training School.

1 ELEMENTARY GLIDING TRAINING SCHOOL – see 41 Gliding School

2 ELEMENTARY GLIDING TRAINING SCHOOL – see 122 Gliding School

3 ELEMENTARY GLIDING TRAINING SCHOOL – see 123 Gliding School

29 ELEMENTARY NAVIGATION AND AIR GUNNERY SCHOOL (SOUTHERN RHODESIA)
Formed 3rd August 1941 at Moffat, Southern Rhodesia.

No aircraft allocated.

Disbanded 13th April 1945 at Moffat.

EMERGENCY FLYING TRAINING FLIGHT
Formed 26th August 1939 at Seletar, Singapore, by redesignating the Headquarters Far East Communication Flight.

Tiger Moth I K2588.

Disbanded April 1940 at Seletar to become the Headquarters Far East Communications Flight.

EMPIRE AIR ARMAMENT SCHOOL
Formed 18th April 1944 at Manby.

Nil (4.44–4.46)	*Master II W9036, III DL856; Moth Minor AW112; Proctor III Z7213, IV RM171; Wellington X ME995 18, XIII JA388 2, XIV HF226; Warwick II HG347; Anson I NK646 A; Lancaster III LM451; Halifax III MZ410; Martinet I MS832 3; Spitfire IX BS393, XII MB838.*
FGA (4.46–7.49)	*Martinet I MS820 FGA-E; Wellington X NC948 FGA-H, XIII JA423 FGA-C; Lancaster VII NX632 FGA-A; Spitfire XVI TB295 FGA-T; Lincoln II RE367 FGA-W; Lancastrian C.2 VM730 FGA-K; Anson XIX VP522 FGA-S.*
FGB (4.46–7.49)	*Wellington X LP907 FGB-F, XIII NC197 FGB-N.*
FGC (4.47–7.49)	*Wellington X LP911 FGC-D; Magister N3882 FGC-N; Master II EM392 FGC-F; Martinet I EM696 FGC-A; Mosquito VI RF853 FGC-R; Harvard IIB FT352 FGC-P; Anson I NK707 FGC-B, XIX PH843 FGC-F; Lancaster I PB873 FGC-T; Spitfire XVI TD130 FGC-R.*

Disbanded 31st July 1949 at Manby and absorbed, together with the Empire Air Armament School, by the Royal Air Force Flying College.

EMPIRE AIR NAVIGATION SCHOOL
Formed 28th October 1944 at Shawbury by redesignating the Central Navigation School.

Nil (10.44–4.46)	*Anson I DJ219; Mustang I AM133, III FB218; Master III DL982; Mosquito IV DZ630; Warwick II HG347; Stirling III LK508; Lancaster VII RT681, X FM204; Halifax III NA279 C; York I MW306.*
FGE (4.46–7.49)	*Wellington XIII NC606 FGE-A.*
FGF (4.46–7.49)	*Anson I NK398 FGF-L; Halifax VI ST814 FGF-B; Lancaster I PD328 FGF-A; Mosquito XVI RV318 FGF-H; Spitfire XVI SL733 FGF-G; Lancastrian C.2 VL975 FGF-E.*
FGG (4.46–4.51)	*Tiger Moth II NL694 FGG-Y; Halifax III PN441 FGG-K; Lancaster VII RT684 FGG-Q; Mosquito B.35 TA656 FGG-J; Lancastrian C.2 VL968 FGG-J; Anson T.21 VV318 FGG-L; Meteor F.3 EE413 FGG-I.*

Disbanded 31st July 1949 at Shawbury to become the Central Navigation School.

EMPIRE CENTRAL FLYING SCHOOL
Formed 1st April 1942 at Hullavington by redesignating elements of the Central Flying School having Instructional, Research and Examining Flights. The Handling Squadron (see separate entry) was transferred from within the Central Flying School.

Nil (4.42–4.46)	*Magister N3838 3; Tiger Moth II DE634; Gladiator I K8044; Anson I DG939; Oxford I DF231 15, II X7134; Blenheim I L8437, V AZ999; Lancaster I L7579; Spitfire IIA P7926 3, VB W3829; Hurricane I Z4791 H33, IIC PG571; Kittyhawk I AK579, IIA FL220; Hudson I T9298; Proctor III HM284; Reliant I FL141; Bermuda I FF477; Stirling I N3657; Harvard IIA BD130, IIB FX297 S, III EZ430 T; Master II W9087, III W8962 11; Mustang III FZ142; Hellcat I JV110, II JV287; Whitley IV K9050; Beaufighter I R2078, II T3444 B, X RD806; Ventura I AE748 H, II AJ193 A; Baltimore I AG690; Boston II AH487, II (Turbinlite) AH434; Mitchell II FR209 F; Wellington III DF547, X NC806 C; Martinet Trainer JN275; Halifax V LL234 D; Horsa I HG929; Mosquito III LR532, VI NT199 A; Auster IV MT161; Warwick V PN702; Lancastrian C.2 VM728; Rhonbussard VD216; Hornet F.1 PX225; Brigand TF.1 RH742; Meteor F.3 EE236 B.*
FCT (4.46–5.46)	
FCU (4.46–5.46)	*Oxford I EB863 FCU-J.*
FCV (4.46–5.46)	*Tiger Moth II R5133 FCV-C; Magister P6410 FCV-A; Hotspur II HH130 FCV-P; Master II DL459 FCV-N; Buckmaster T.1 RP186 FCV-G.*
FCW (4.46–5.46)	*Spitfire VB W3829 FCW-E, IX MA709 FCW-C.*
FCX (4.46–5.46)	*Lancaster III JA962 FCX-R; Mosquito III RR274 FCX-K.*
Also used	*Spitfire XIV NH872, XVI TD266, XVIII TP265, F.24 VN316.*

Disbanded 7th May 1946 at Hullavington to become the Empire Flying School.

EMPIRE FLYING SCHOOL
Formed 7th May 1946 at Hullavington by redesignating the Empire Central Flying School.

FCT (5.46–7.49)	*Harvard IIB FX297 FCT-I.*
FCU (5.46–7.49)	*Allocated but no evidence of use.*
FCV (5.46–7.49)	*Tiger Moth II T7809 FCV-B; Hotspur II HH130 FCV-P; Buckmaster I RP177 FCV-J; Anson XII PH769 FCV-A, XIX PH843 FCV-J.*
FCW (5.46–7.49)	*Meteor F.3 EE359 FCW-J, F.4 VT145 FCW-K.*
FCX (5.46–7.49)	*Lancaster III JA962 FCX-R, VII NX687 FCX-R; Lancastrian C.2 VM731 FCX-Z.*
Also used	*Mitchell II FR209; Spitfire IX BS348, Dakota IV KN282; Buckmaster I RP177; Hastings C.1 TG508; Prentice T.1 VN687.*

Disbanded 31st July 1949 at Hullavington to become the Royal Air Force Flying College.

EMPIRE RADIO SCHOOL
Formed 7th March 1946 at Debden by merging 12 and 14 Radio Schools.

TDE (3.46–10.49)	*Tiger Moth II T7997 TDE-H; Proctor IV NP173 TDE-E; Anson I LT154 TDE-E, T.22 VS601 TDE-A; Oxford I NM356 TDE-G; Master III DL837; Dominie II RL948; Lincoln II RE414.*

Disbanded 20th October 1949 at Debden to become the Royal Air Force Technical College, Signals Division.

EMPIRE TEST PILOTS SCHOOL
Formed 18th July 1944 at Boscombe Down by redesignating the Test Pilots School. Functional control by Royal Air Force ceased from 15th January 1959.

Many aircraft were on loan from the Aeroplane and Armament Experimental Establishment and the Royal Aircraft Establishment.

(Airspeed) Oxford I RR345 12, II AB658. (Armstrong Whitworth) Albemarle GT.II V1743; Apollo VX224 15; Argosy C.1 XR105 10. (Avro) Lancaster I R5842, III EE108; Anson XIX VP509, T.21 VV319; Athena T.2 VW893; Avro 707B VX790 17; Lincoln I RE284, II RF538 17; Shackleton MR.2 WG557; Andover C.1 XS606. (BAC) One Eleven ZE433; Jet Provost T.5 XS230; Lightning T.5 XS457. (Beagle) Basset CC.1 XS743. (Beechcraft) Traveler I FT461. (Blackburn) Beverley C.1 XB259 17. (Boulton Paul) P.108 VL892 8; Balliol T.2 VR597 6. (Bristol) Beaufort II AW343; Bristol 171 Mk 3 XH682; Britannia C.1 XX367. (de Havilland) Tiger Moth II T6859; Dominie I HG715 5; Mosquito II W4090, III HJ888 22, IV DZ590, VI RF648, B.25 KB552, B.35 RS719; Devon C.1 VP979 4; Chipmunk T.10 WB549 7; Beaver; Vampire F.1 TG345, F.3 VT818, FB.5 VZ350 30, T.11 WZ475 17; Venom FB.1 WE282; Sea Venom FAW.21 WM574 18. (DFS) Grunau Baby VN148. (Douglas) Boston IIIA BZ346; Dakota III TS431. (Elliott) Olympia 1 VV400 60. (English Electric) Canberra B.2 WJ730 18, WJ867 10; Lightning T.4 XL629 23. (Fairey) Swordfish II HS642; Firefly I PP639, T.I Z1953 9; Gannet AS.1 WN429 24, T.2 XG837 27. (Fieseler) Fi 156 VP545. (General Aircraft) Hamilcar I RR935. (Gloster) Meteor F.1 EE213, F.3 EE491, F.4 VT338, T.7 WL488 11, F.8 WK660 9, NF.11 WD797 9, NF.14 WS793 5. (Handley Page) Halifax III LV904, V LL272; Hastings C.1 TG501 17; Marathon T.2 VX231. (Hawker) Hurricane IIA Z2399, IIC LD264; Tempest II PR919, V JN739, VI NX121; Sea Fury F.10 TF895 29, Sea Fury FB.11 WE728, T.20 VX818; Sea Hawk F.1 WF146 27, FB.3 WF284 8, FGA.4 WV910 20; Hunter F.1 WT628 26, F.4 XF940 25, F.6 WW592 26, T.7 XJ615 23, FGA.9 XE601. (Hawker Siddeley) Hawk T.1 XX342 2. (Hillier) HTE-2 XB521. (Hunting Percival) Provost T.1 XF685 20; Pembroke C.1 WV710 25. (Lockheed) Hudson III V9222; Ventura I AE748. (Miles) Master III W8573; IV T8886; Mentor L4393. (North American) Mitchell II FL215; Harvard IIB FX365 1. (Panavia) Tornado F.2 ZD935. (Percival) Proctor. (Saro) Skeeter AOP.12 XL807. (Schempp-Hirth) Cirrus XZ405. (Schleicher) Rhonsegler Ka.6 XW640. (Scottish Aviation) Twin Pioneer 3 XT610 22. (SEPECAT) Jaguar GR.1 XX119, T.2 XX915. (Short) SB.5 WG768 28. (Siebel) Si 204. (Sikorsky) S-61 SH-3D XV370. (Slingsby) Sedbergh TX.1 WB920; Sky XA876 59. (Supermarine) Spitfire VA W3112, VII AB450, VIII LV674, IX SL663, XII MB878, XIII W3112, F.21 LA192, F.22 PK495; Seafire F.XVII SX135, F.46 LA546, F.47 PS945; Swift F.7 XF113 19; Scimitar F.1 XD216 22. (Taylorcraft) Auster AOP.V TJ524, AOP.VI VF627 3. (Vickers) Wellington III BK450; Viking C.2 VL231 22; Valetta C.1 WD171 24, T.3 WJ463 21; Varsity T.1 WF381 14; Viscount 744 XR801, Viscount 745 XR802. (Westland) Dragonfly HR.1 VX595 25, HAR.3 WG662 28; Scout AH.1 XP165 5; Whirlwind HAR.2 XJ759 4, HAR.5 XJ398, HAS.7 XK907 9, Wessex HU.5 XS509; Gazelle HT.3 XZ936; Sea King HAS.1 XV370, HAS.3 ZG529; 4X ZB507; Lynx AH.1 XZ179, HAS.2 XX510, HAS.3 ZD560, AH.7 ZD560; Puma HC.1 ZA934.

FGP	Allocated but not used.
FGQ	Allocated but not used.
FGR	Allocated but not used.

Current 1st April 1993 at Boscombe Down under the administration of the Defence Test and Evaluation Organisation.

ENEMY AIRCRAFT FLIGHT – see Central Fighter Establishment

ENEMY AIRCRAFT STORAGE AND SERVICING UNIT
Formed 27th September 1945 at Fuhlsbuttel, Germany.

Ju 52/3m VM982; Si 204D VM886.

Disbanded 4th August 1946 at Fuhlsbuttel.

ENGINE CONSUMPTION UNIT, later 1 ENGINE CONSUMPTION UNIT
Control transferred 6th March 1942 from Vickers Aircraft at

Weybridge to the Royal Air Force at Mildenhall. Redesignated 1 Engine Consumption Unit from 24th April 1942.

Wellington III X3277.

Disbanded 14th September 1942 at Bassingbourn to become 1 Engine Control Demonstration Unit.

ENGINE CONTROL DEMONSTRATION FLIGHT
Formed 29th September 1943 at Aldergrove within 1674 (Heavy) Conversion Unit.

Wellington.

Disbanded 19th October 1943 at Longtown to become 1 (Coastal) Engine Control Demonstration Unit.

1 ENGINE CONTROL DEMONSTRATION UNIT (1)
Formed 10th September 1942 at Mildenhall by redesignating 1 Engine Consumption Unit. Moved to Bassingbourn the following day. The Bomber Command Instructors School became parent unit from November 1944.

Wellington II Z8587, III X3277, X LN407; Lancaster III LM591; Oxford I T1401; Beaufighter II.

Disbanded December 1945 at Worksop.

1 ENGINE CONTROL DEMONSTRATION UNIT (2) – see 1 (Coastal) Engine Control Demonstration Unit

ENGINE CONTROL INSTRUCTION FLIGHT
Formed 17th June 1944 at Angle by redesignating 1 (Coastal) Engine Control Demonstration Unit.

Wellington.

Disbanded 31st December 1945 at Harwell to become the School of Flight Efficiency.

ESCADRILLE 'ARDENNES'
Formed 22nd January 1944 at St Jean d'Acre, Palestine, as the Free French Flight of 127 Squadron. Redesignated Escadrille 'Ardennes' from 1st April 1944.

Hurricane IIC HV311; Simoun 635.

Disbanded 31st July 1944 at Reghaia, Algeria.

ESCADRILLE DE CHASSE No 1
Formed January 1941 at Ismailia, Egypt. Also referred to as 1 Free French Fighter Flight. Attached to 73 Squadron from April 1941 and 274 Squadron from May 1941.

Hurricane I.

Ceased operations16th August 1942 and moved to Rayak, Syria, to be incorpoated into Groupe 'Alsace'.

ESCADRILLE DE CHASSE No 2
Formed 1st July 1940 at Heliopolis, Egypt. Became 'A' Flight of 80 Squadron from August 1940 and 'C' Flight of 274 Squadron from 15th January 1941.

Potez 29 AX678; Potez 63 699; Morane-Saulnier 406 AX684; Bloch 81 AX677; Loire 130 AX694.

Disbanded 18th June 1941 at Gerawala, Egypt

ESCADRILLE 'METZ' – see Groupe 'Lorraine'

ESCADRILLE 'NANCY' – see Groupe 'Lorraine'

EXAMINING FLIGHT – see Central Flying School

EXAMINING WING – see Central Flying School

EXETER UNIVERSITY AIR SQUADRON
Formed 21st August 1941 at Exeter.

No aircraft known.

Disbanded August 1943 at Exeter.

EXPERIMENTAL AIR AMBULANCE SERVICE
Formed 1st June 1925 at Halton.

Andover J7261.

Disbanded 16th December 1926 at Halton.

EXPERIMENTAL ARMAMENT SQUADRON
Formed 20th May 1916 within the Armament Experimental Station, Orfordness, by merging the Experimental Flight, Upavon, and 37 Squadron.

Elephant 7463; R.E.8 A66; F.K.8 B224; F.2A A3303; D.H.5 A9186; D.H.9 A7559; 1½ Strutter B762.

Disbanded 16th March 1920 at Orfordness and absorbed by the Aeroplane Experimental Establishment.

EXPERIMENTAL CO-OPERATION UNIT
Formed April 1938 at Martlesham Heath by redesignating the Wireless Direction Finding Flight.

Harrow II K7021; Battle K9207; Singapore III K8565; Moth K1876.

Disbanded August 1938 at Martlesham Heath to become 'D' Flight, Performance Testing Section, Aeroplane and Armament Experimental Establishment.

EXPERIMENTAL FLIGHT, GOSPORT (1)
Formed 31st May 1918 at Gosport to carry out W/T trials with the RN Signal School, Portsmouth.

B.E.2e B4535; D.H.4 D1764; F.2b D2607; F.K.8 D5082.

Disbanded April 1919 at Gosport.

EXPERIMENTAL FLIGHT, GOSPORT (2) – see Royal Air Force Base, Gosport, later Royal Air Force Station, Gosport

EXPERIMENTAL FLIGHT, UPAVON
Formed May 1916 at Upavon.

No aircraft known.

Disbanded 20th May 1916 at Orfordness and merged with 37 Squadron to become the Experimental Armament Squadron within the Experimental Station, Orfordness.

EXPERIMENTAL STATION, ORFORDNESS
Formed 20th May 1916 at Orfordness incorporating the Experimental Armament Squadron. Disbanded 13th October 1917 to become the Armament Experimental Station, Orfordness.

EXTENDED RECONNAISSANCE FLIGHT
Formed within 224 Squadron at Leuchars shortly after the outbreak of war in 1939.

'F' BOAT SEAPLANE TRAINING FLIGHT
Formed 15th August 1918 at Houton Bay.

Felixstowe F.3 N4412; Curtiss H.16 N4897.

Disbanded 25th November 1918 at Houton Bay.

FAMINE RELIEF FLIGHT
Formed 22nd April 1944 at Riyan, Aden.

Wellington X.

Disbanded 30th June 1944 at Riyan.

FAR EAST AIR FORCE EXAMINING SQUADRON
Formed 15th March 1950 at Seletar, Malaysia, by merging the Air Command Far East All Weather Flight (an element of the Far East Communications Squadron) and the Receipt, Test and Dispatch Flight.

Harvard IIB FT374; Dakota IV KN341; Spitfire XVIII SM972; Meteor T.7 WA681; Auster T.7 WE543.

Disbanded 1st June 1961 at Seletar and merged with the Towed Target Flight, Seletar, to become the Far East Air Force Training Squadron.

FAR EAST AIR FORCE TRAINING SQUADRON
Formed 1st June 1951 at Seletar, Malaysia, by merging the Far East Air Force Examining Squadron and the Towed Target Flight, Seletar. The Squadron included an Examining Flight (ex Far East Examining Squadron), a Training Flight and a Towed Target Flight

that had formed earlier on 15th April 1951 as an independent flight. The Towed Target Flight was transferred to the Station Flight, Seletar, from 1st July 1951. Absorbed 27 Armament Practice Camp 4th November 1954.

Mosquito III VA882; Beaufighter TT.X RD763; Buckmaster I RP235; Hornet F.3 WF960; Vampire FB.9 WL564, T.11 WZ587; Meteor T.7 WA681 M-58, TT.8 WH410.

Disbanded 31st March 1955 at Butterworth, Malaya, an element becoming the Armament Practice Camp, Butterworth.

FAR EAST CASUALTY EVACUATION FLIGHT
Formed 1st May 1950 at Kuala Lumpur, Singapore, as the Casualty Air Evacuation Flight. Redesignated Far East Casualty Evacuation Flight from 22nd May 1950 upon moving to Changi.

Dragonfly WZ749, HC.2 WF308, HC.4 WT846.

Disbanded 2nd February 1953 at Sembawang, Singapore, to become 194 Squadron.

FAR EAST COMMUNICATION FLIGHT
Formed 15th January 1947 at Changi, Singapore, to replace the Air Command Far East Communication Flight, then reduced to unmanned basis 1st April 1947. Reinstated 21st July 1947 at Changi, Singapore, by redesignating 'C' Flight, 48 Squadron as 'C' (Far East Communication) Flight of 48 Squadron.

Dakota III KG624; Anson XIX VL297; Auster VI; Harvard IIB; York I.

Disbanded 15th October 1947 at Changi to become the Far East Communication Squadron.

Reformed 31st December 1969 at Changi, as an attachment to 48 Squadron, by redesignating the Andover element of 52 Squadron.

Andover C.2.

Disbanded 1st November 1971 at Changi.

FAR EAST COMMUNICATION SQUADRON
Formed 16th October 1947 at Changi, Singapore, by redesignating 'C' Flight, 48 Squadron which, from 21st July 1947, had been known as the Far East Communication Flight.

Harvard IIB FT374; Dakota IV KN620; York I MW325, VIP.I MW102; Auster V TW363, T.7 VX926; Anson XIX VL334; Devon C.1 WB530; Valetta C.1 VX522, C.2 VX579, T.3 WJ479; Hastings C.1 TG507, C.2 WJ336, C(VIP).4 WJ325; Vampire FB.9 WG872, T.11 XD615; Meteor T.7 WF848, F.8 WA899; Pembroke C.1 WV709; Canberra B.2 WH651, T.4 WH706.

Disbanded January 1960 at Changi, Singapore, to become the VIP Flight of 52 Squadron.

FAR EAST FLIGHT
Formed 17th May 1927 at Felixstowe.

Southampton I N9900, II S1127.

Disbanded 8th January 1929 at Seletar, Singapore, to become 205 Squadron.

FAR EAST TACTICAL DEVELOPMENT UNIT
Formed by July 1943 at Ratmalana, India.

Beaufort I EK988; Tiger Moth MA939; Anson I LT479 B.

Disbanded 25th May 1945 at Ranchi and absorbed by the Tactical and Weapon Development Unit (India).

FAR EAST TRAINING SQUADRON – see Far East Air Force Training Squadron

FERRY CONVOY FLIGHT
Formed 21st June 1944 at Allahabad, India.

Hudson IIIA FH297, VI EW934; Cornell II FW959; Vengeance III FB973.

Disbanded 25th December 1944 at Mauripur, India.

FERRY CREW POOL UNIT
Formed 7th March 1943 at Filton.

Wellington II W5587.

Disbanded 3rd August 1943 Lyneham to become 1 Ferry Crew Pool.

1 FERRY CREW POOL
Formed 3rd August 1943 at Lyneham by redesignating the Ferry Crew Pool Unit, Filton.

Wellington II W5587; Mosquito III; Warwick I.

Disbanded 16th March 1944 at Lyneham and merged with 301 Ferry Training Unit to become 1 Ferry Unit.

2 FERRY CREW POOL
Formed 3rd August 1943 at Dorval, Canada, by redesignating an element of the Service Aircrew Pool, Dorval.

Hudson.

Disbanded 5th July 1944 at Dorval and merged with the Civilian Aircrew Pool, Allied Aircrew Pool and Ferry Training Flight, Dorval to become 6 Ferry Unit.

3 FERRY CREW POOL
Formed 3rd August 1943 at Nassau by merging an element of the Service Aircrew Pool, Dorval and the Ferry Training Flight, Nassau.

No aircraft known.

Disbanded 5th July 1944 at Nassau, Bahamas, to become 7 Ferry Unit.

FERRY FLIGHT, CARDINGTON
Formed by January 1939 at Cardington.

Anson I K6301.

Disbanded 16th January 1939 at Cardington to become 1 and 2 Ferry Pilot Pools.

FERRY FLIGHT, SANTA CRUZ
Formed 7th May 1944 at Santa Cruz, India.

Spitfire VIII MV402, XIV RM977; Hurricane IIC LE633, IV LE272; Cornell; Tiger Moth; Harvard; Thunderbolt II KL346; Argus II HB584.

Disbanded 29th June 1945 at Santa Cruz.

FERRY FLIGHT, TRICHINOPOLY
Formed 27th April 1944 at Trichinopoly, India.

Hurricane IIC LB562, IV KX824; Thunderbolt I FL818; Spitfire VIII JG674; Anson I DJ631; Harvard IIB FE953.

Disbanded 28th February 1946 at Trichinopoly.

FERRY PILOTS POOLS (CIVILIAN) – see Air Transport Auxiliary

FERRY PILOTS POOLS (MILITARY) – see Headquarters Service Ferry Pools, 1 Ferry Pilots Pool, 2 Ferry Pilots Pool, 4 Ferry Pilots Pool, 7 (Service) Ferry Pilots Pool, 8 (Service) Ferry Pilots Pool, 9 (Service) Ferry Pilots Pool, 10 (Polish) Ferry Flight, 11 (Service) Ferry Flight

1 FERRY PILOTS POOL
Formed 16th January 1939 at Hucknall by redesignating an element of the Ferry Flight, Cardington. Air Transport Auxiliary staff joined the unit from October 1939.

Heyford III K5185; Audax K3697; Hart K4439; Hind K6655; Anson I K6295; Skua I L2972; Harvard I N7044; Moth X5111; Scion II X9364; Percival Q-6 X9406.

Disbanded 10th May 1940 at Hucknall.

2 FERRY PILOTS POOL
Formed 16th January 1939 at Filton by redesignating an element of the Ferry Flight, Cardington. Air Transport Auxiliary staff joined the unit from October 1939.

Heyford III K5185; Demon K5685; Anson I K6296; Blenheim I L4890; Lysander II N1317; Harvard I N7062; Hudson I N7301.

Disbanded April 1940 at Cardiff to become 4 Ferry Pilots Pool.

4 FERRY PILOTS POOL, later 4 (CONTINENTAL) FERRY PILOTS POOL, later 4 FERRY PILOTS POOL
Formed April 1940 at Cardiff by redesignating 2 Ferry Pilots Pool, RAF. Redesignated 4 (Continental) Ferry Pilots Pool from 28th April 1940. Reverted to 4 Ferry Pilots Pool from September 1940.

Hector K8149; Anson I R9660; Beaufort I L9885; Hurricane I P2644; Hampden I P2086; Battle Trainer P6756; Oxford II R6374; Whitley V T4225; Blenheim IV Z5975; Phoenix II X9393; Leopard Moth AX962.

Disbanded 7th November 1940 at Kemble to become Headquarters Service Ferry Pools.

1 FERRY POOL, ROYAL AIR FORCE
Formed 3rd December 1945 at White Waltham.

Anson I N9546; Magister P2447; Master II DM279; Oxford; Mustang I AG384; Wellington II Z8375, III HF815, XIII JA627; Warwick I BV226; Argus II HB595; Liberator III FL966, V FL935; Hudson VI FK394; Auster; Typhoon IB RB313; Tempest II MW827, VI NX129; Mosquito VI NT192; Spitfire IX EN533, XIV NH695, XVI TB329.

Disbanded 31st March 1946 at White Waltham.

2 FERRY POOL, ROYAL AIR FORCE
Formed 1st December 1945 at Aston Down.

9X   *Oxford I EB739; Tiger Moth II DE834; Wellington X HE986; Anson XII PH808 9X-A, XIX VM323 9X-Q; Proctor III DX190; Mosquito VI RS567; Spitfire XVIII TP227, F.21 LA192; Dakota IV KN352; Meteor F.4 RA418.*

Disbanded 7th February 1952 at Aston Down to become 2 (Home) Ferry Unit.

3 FERRY POOL, ROYAL AIR FORCE
Formed 30th November 1945 at Lichfield.

U5   *Proctor I P6273, III HM409; Mustang IV KM535; Anson I NK957 U5-S, XIX VM310; Spitfire VII MB912, F.22 PK675; Tempest II MW813, V NV666; Beaufighter X NE228; Mosquito VI RF839, XVI RV352, T.29 KA141, B.35 RS701; Auster V RT577, VI VF563.*

Disbanded 10th September 1947 at Henlow.

4 FERRY POOL, ROYAL AIR FORCE
Formed 30th November 1945 at Hawarden.

3D (12.45 – .51)   *Proctor III LZ659 3D-L; Anson I N9546, XIX TX207 3D; Hurricane I V6563; Blenheim IV Z7491; Mosquito III VA925, B.25 KB506, B.35 TK601; Beaufort I LR983; Spitfire XVIII TP327; Halifax VI NP884.*

Nil (.51–6.52)   *Canberra B.2 WD985.*

Disbanded 7th February 1952 at Hawarden to become 4 (Home) Ferry Unit.

5 FERRY POOL, ROYAL AIR FORCE
Formed 15th October 1945 at Silloth.

D8   *Anson I N9667, XIX VL354; Wellington III Z1690, XVI R3237; Hurricane I Z4176; Mosquito XVI PF571; Spitfire XVI TB357.*

Disbanded 25th May 1950 at Silloth.

FERRY SQUADRON – see Ferry Support Squadron, later the Ferry Squadron

FERRY SUPPORT SQUADRON, later the FERRY SQUADRON
Formed 16th April 1956 at Benson replacing the Ferry Transport Flight. Redesignated the Ferry Squadron from 1st January 1958 prior to absorbing 147 and 167 Squadrons on 15th September 1958.

Unit aircraft   *Anson XIX TX219; Valetta C.1 VW806, C.2 VX572; Chipmunk T.10 WB550.*

Those ferried   *Meteor F.8 WK822, NF.11 WM152; Vampire FB.9 WL560, T.11 XE869; Varsity T.1 WF330; Balliol T.2 WN522; Venom FB.4 WR532;*

Provost T.1 WV444; Auster AOP.9 WZ698; Javelin FAW.4 XA735, FAW.9 XH791; Swift FR.5 XD925, F.7 XF123; Hunter T.7 XL600; Pioneer CC.1 XL703; Canberra B(I).8 XM262.

Disbanded 1st December 1958 at Benson.

FERRY TRAINING AND DESPATCH UNIT – see Ferry Training Unit, later Ferry Training and Despatch Unit, later Ferry Training Unit

FERRY TRAINING FLIGHT, BICESTER
Formed 24th October 1941 at Bicester, within 13 Operational Training Unit as the Despatch Flight. Redesignated the Ferry Training Flight, Bicester from 27th October 1941.

Blenheim.

Disbanded 21st January 1942 at Bicester to become 1442 (Ferry Training) Flight.

FERRY TRAINING FLIGHT, DOCKING
Formed August 1943 at Docking within the Warwick Training Unit.

FERRY TRAINING FLIGHT, DORVAL
Formed 5th November 1941 at Dorval, Canada.

Hudson IIIA FH317.

Disbanded 5th July 1944 at Dorval and merged with 2 Ferry Crew Pool, the Civilian Aircrew Pool and the Allied Aircrew Pool to become 6 Ferry Unit.

FERRY TRAINING FLIGHT, HARWELL
Formed November 1941 at Harwell alongside 15 Operational Training Unit.

Wellington.

Disbanded 21st January 1942 at Harwell to become 1443 (Ferry Training) Flight.

FERRY TRAINING FLIGHT, HORSHAM ST FAITH
Formed December 1941 at Horsham St Faith within 1428 (Hudson) Conversion Flight.

Hudson.

Disbanded 21st January 1942 at Horsham St Faith to become 1444 (Ferry Training) Flight.

FERRY TRAINING FLIGHT, NASSAU
Formed (date unknown) at Nassau.

No aircraft known.

Disbanded 3rd August 1943 at Nassau and merged with an element of Service Aircrew Pool, Dorval, to become 3 Ferry Crew Pool.

1 FERRY TRAINING FLIGHT, LYNEHAM – see Ferry Training Unit, later Ferry Training and Despatch Unit, later Ferry Training Unit

2 FERRY TRAINING FLIGHT, LYNEHAM AND FILTON – see Ferry Training Unit, later Ferry Training and Despatch Unit, later Ferry Training Unit

3 FERRY TRAINING FLIGHT, LYNEHAM – see Ferry Training Unit, later Ferry Training and Despatch Unit, later Ferry Training Unit

FERRY TRAINING UNIT, later FERRY TRAINING AND DESPATCH UNIT, later FERRY TRAINING UNIT
Formed 11th November 1941 at Honeybourne by redesignating the Service Ferry Training Squadron. Redesignated the Ferry Training and Despatch Unit from 28th March 1942 incorporating:

1 Ferry Training Flight	Formed March 1942 at Lyneham. Disbanded 3rd November 1942 at Lyneham.
2 Ferry Training Flight	Formed March 1942 at Lyneham. Disbanded 17th July 1942 at Filton.
3 Ferry Training Flight	Formed March 1942 at Lyneham.

Disbanded 20th May 1942 at Lyneham.

Oxford I L4566, II AB722; Bombay I L5836; Dominie I R9553; Phoenix II X9393; Monarch X9306; Blenheim I L1139, IV Z5973, V AZ892; Hurricane I N2338, X AF987; Wellington IA N2879, IC T2562, XIII HZ586; Beaufighter I T4717; Tomahawk IIB AK153; Master II AZ375, III W8841; Maryland I AR703; Beaufort I AW201; Mosquito II DD743; Hudson III AE555, IIIA FH264; Ventura I FN990.

Disbanded 3rd November 1942 at Lyneham and merged with 1444 and 1445 Ferry Training Flights to become 301 Ferry Training Unit.

Reformed 5th August 1952 at Abingdon as the Ferry Training Unit.

Harvard IIB KF604; Oxford I RR333; Spitfire XVI TB713; Mosquito III TV983; Lincoln II RE341; Vampire FB.5 VZ314, T.11 WZ618; Meteor T.7 VW424; Chipmunk T.10 WB580; Canberra B.2 WH651; Balliol T.2 WG207; Valetta C.1 VL281; Javelin FAW.4 XA766, FAW.6 XA831; Swift FR.5 XD919; Hunter F.4 XF295, F.6 XG192.

Disbanded 1st December 1958 at Benson.

301 FERRY TRAINING UNIT
Formed 3rd November 1942 at Lyneham by merging 1 Ferry Training and Despatch Unit and 1444 and 1445 Ferry Training Flights.

Blenheim I L1202, IV N3600, V BA793; Whitley V Z9132; Anson I AW974; Hudson I P5125, IIIA FK732, IV AE636, V AE643, VI FK396; Beaufort I L9837, II DD903; Wellington II Z8375, III BJ839, VIII LA969, X ME878, XI HZ283, XII MP690, XIII HZ596; Albemarle I P1407; Baltimore III AG837; Marauder I FK111; Beaufighter I X7802, II R2477, VI V8645, X JM291, XI JL894; Mosquito II DD743, III LR521, VI LR249, XIII HK418; Halifax II W7847, V EB154; Oxford II P8923; Liberator II AL520, III FK227, V BZ805.

Disbanded 16th March 1944 at Lyneham and merged with 1 Ferry Crew Pool to become 1 Ferry Unit.

302 FERRY TRAINING UNIT
Formed 30th September 1942 at Loch Erne.

Catalina I AH544, IB FP301 E, IIA VA728, IIIA FP531, IVA JX205, IVB JX300; Sunderland II W3989, III DDV956, V SZ567; Wellington XIII ME889; Proctor III LZ572.

Disbanded 1st April 1946 at Alness.

303 FERRY TRAINING UNIT
Formed 15th December 1942 at Stornoway.

Anson I MG865; Ventura II AJ216, V FP668; Tiger Moth II DE408; Whitley V BD208; Wellington DW.I P2521, IA N2877, IC R1531, III BK182, VIII LB147, X HE907, XI HZ275, XIII ME884, XIV NB769, XV L7776, XVI P9289; Warwick I HF941; Stirling IV LK211; Oxford II V3727.

Disbanded 8th September 1944 at Talbenny to become 11 Ferry Unit.

304 FERRY TRAINING UNIT
Formed 31st December 1942 at Port Ellen.

Beaufort I DW918 J; Mosquito III HJ967, VI HR300, XIII MM506; Wellington X LN740, XI MP518, XIII HZ762; Oxford I R5948; Anson I MG557; Stirling III LJ512; Marauder I FK109; Beaufighter VI JL542, X LX798, XI JM244; Hurricane IIC PZ834.

Disbanded 9th October 1944 at Melton Mowbray and merged with 4 Aircraft Preparation Unit to become 12 Ferry Unit.

305 FERRY TRAINING UNIT
Formed 14th December 1942 at Errol.

Albemarle GT.I P1403, ST.I P1503, GT.I/II P1448; Blenheim V EH404; Mosquito III HJ863, IV DK296.

Disbanded 30th April 1944 at Errol.

306 FERRY TRAINING UNIT
Formed 31st December 1942 at Templeton.

Beaufort I DW919, IIA ML430; Beaufighter X NE292.

Disbanded 15th January 1944 at Melton Mowbray and absorbed by 304 Ferry Training Unit.

307 FERRY TRAINING UNIT
Formed 24th December 1942 at Bicester.

Blenheim V BA789; Boston I AE460, III AL750, III (Turbinlite) W8346, IIIA BZ216; Beaufighter X LX906; Wellington XIII JA379.

Disbanded 15th January 1944 at Melton Mowbray and absorbed by 304 Ferry Training Unit.

308 FERRY TRAINING AND TEST FLYING UNIT, later 308 FERRY TRAINING UNIT
Formed 22nd March 1943 at Pembroke Dock as 308 Ferry Training and Test Flying Unit. Redesignated 308 Ferry Training Unit from 7th May 1943.

Sunderland III DP187.

Disbanded 12th January 1944 at Oban and absorbed by 302 Ferry Training Unit.

309 FERRY TRAINING AND AIRCRAFT DESPATCH UNIT
Formed 21st April 1943 at Benson by redesignating 'B' Flight of 543 Squadron.

Spitfire IV BP879, XI PL996, XIX PM505; Mosquito IX LR409.

Disbanded 17th September 1945 at Benson.

310 FERRY TRAINING UNIT
Formed 30th April 1943 at Harwell by redesignating 1443 (Ferry Training) Flight.

Wellington II R3221, III HF649, X HZ437, XI HF804, XIII HZ973; Beaufighter VI V8453.

Disbanded 17th December 1943 at Harwell and absorbed by 311 Ferry Training Unit.

311 FERRY TRAINING UNIT
Formed 1st May 1943 at Moreton-in-Marsh by redesignating 1446 (Ferry Training) Flight.

Anson I N5167; Wellington III DF727, X HF539, XIII HZ961; Blenheim V EH504.

Disbanded 1st May 1944 at Moreton-in-Marsh.

312 FERRY TRAINING UNIT
Formed 24th April 1943 at Wellesbourne Mountford.

Anson and Wellington proposed, but none allocated.

Reduced to 'number only' basis from 26th July 1943 and finally disbanded 17th December 1943 at Wellesbourne Mountford.

313 FERRY TRAINING AND CONVERSION UNIT, later 313 FERRY TRAINING UNIT
Formed 1st March 1944 at North Bay, Boucherville, Canada. Redesignated 313 Ferry Training Unit from 5th July 1944.

Hudson IIIA FH315, VI FK403; Baltimore; Mitchell II FV987; Lancaster X FM172; Mosquito T.27 KA897.

Disbanded 18th October 1945 at North Bay.

FERRY TRANSPORT FLIGHT
Formed 30th December 1954 at Benson by redesignating the Valetta element of the Ferry Training Unit.

Anson XIX TX223; Valetta C.1 VL278; Prentice T.1 VS646.

Disbanded 16th April 1956 at Benson to be replaced by the Ferry Support Squadron.

1 FERRY UNIT
Formed 16th March 1944 at Pershore by merging 301 Ferry Training Unit and 1 Ferry Crew Pool.

Beaufort I N1074, IIA ML451; Hudson I P5125; Dominie I X7347; Ventura II AJ216; Master II DL121, III DL865; Boston IIIA BZ229, IV BZ478; Mitchell III KJ686; Warwick I BV350, V LM818; Oxford I V4023, II P8925; Beaufighter I T4895, VI X8254, X RD210, XI JL906; Proctor III LZ655, IV NP168; Dakota III KG353, IV KN360; Halifax II JP134, III NA125, V EB138, VI RG788, VII NA377, IX

RT769; Wellington X LP295, XIII HZ651, XIV MP825; Mosquito III RR299, VI TA575, XIII MM527, XVI NS563, XIX TA449, FB.26 KA134, NF.30 MV564, PR.34 PF630; Lancaster III LM734; Martinet I MS856; Tempest VI NX255; Harvard IIB KF177; Spitfire VB W3931, IX MH486, F.22 PK666; Anson I LT186, X NK772, XI NL182 E, XII PH672, XIX VL285; Hornet F.1 PX227; Buckmaster I RP210: Brigand B.1 VS812; Meteor T.7 WA609.

Disbanded 17th May 1948 at Manston to become 1 (Overseas) Ferry Unit.

2 FERRY UNIT
Formed 23rd September 1944 at LG.237 (Jebel Hamzi), Egypt, by redesignating 2 Aircraft Delivery Unit.

Baltimore IV FA406; Harvard TT.IIB KF916; Anson I LT496; Wellington XIII MF301.

Disbanded 1st December 1945 at Cairo West, Egypt, and absorbed by 5 Ferry Unit.

3 FERRY UNIT
Formed 23rd September 1944 at Oujda, Morocco, by redesignating 3 Aircraft Delivery Unit.

Walrus II X9591; Boston IV BZ478; Argus II FS643, III HB739; Marauder III HD671; Hudson IIIA FH381; Baltimore III AG979, V FW872; Mustang III KH613, IVA KH801; Hurricane IIC LB723; Spitfire VC LZ940, VIII MT712; Beaufighter VI ND171, X KW333; Argus III HB739; Anson I NL173, XII PH569; Wellington XIII MF689; Warwick I BV364; Mosquito XIII MM581, XIX TA171.

Disbanded 14th January 1946 at Blida.

4 FERRY UNIT
Formed 23rd September 1944 at Catania, Sicily, by redesignating 4 Aircraft Delivery Unit.

Stirling I EF360; Baltimore V FW862; Beaufighter VI ND162; Expeditor II HB250; Kittyhawk IV FX668; Mosquito XIII HK434; Mustang IVA KH827; Hurricane IV KZ572; Liberator VI KH206; Argus II FZ821; Spitfire VC LZ807, IX EN365; Auster IV MT309, V RT571; Anson XII PH541, XIX TX184.

Disbanded 14th January 1946 at Capodichino, Italy.

5 FERRY UNIT
Formed 23rd September 1944 at Heliopolis, Egypt, by redesignating 1 Aircraft Delivery Unit.

Anson I DJ571, X NK428; Baltimore IV FA615, V FW408; Vengeance IV HB392; Wellington XIII MP757; Beaufort I LR945; Beaufighter X NV188; Warwick I BV349; Mosquito VI RF580.

Disbanded 15th March 1946 at Cairo West, Egypt.

6 FERRY UNIT
Formed 5th July 1944 at Dorval, Canada, by merging the Ferry Training Flight, Dorval, with 2 Ferry Crew Pool, the Civilian Aircrew Pool, and the Allied Aircrew Pool and Ferry Training Unit.

Hudson V AM887; Anson I AX581; Mosquito III LR579; Liberator VIII KN791.

Disbanded 30th November 1945 at Dorval.

7 FERRY UNIT
Formed 5th July 1944 at Nassau, Bahamas, by redesignating 3 Ferry Crew Pool.

No aircraft known.

Disbanded 1st October 1945 at Nassau.

8 FERRY UNIT
Formed 1st September 1944 at Mauripur, India, by redesignating 21 Ferry Control.

Wellington IA N2871; Vengeance IV FD249; Thunderbolt I FL838; Harvard IIB FT198; Mosquito VI HR142; Hurricane IIC,KW858; IV LD792; Auster III NK132; Beaufighter X NE366.

Disbanded 18th June 1945 at Drigh Road, India.

9 FERRY UNIT
Formed 1st September 1944 at Bamhrauli, India, by redesignating 22 Ferry Control.

Hurricane IIB BN265, IIC BN483, IID BN969; Blenheim V EH409; Warwick I BV348, III HG245; Hudson VI FK574; Thunderbolt I HD175; Beaufighter X KW392; Dakota III KG554, IV KJ996; Mosquito VI HR543, IX LR443; Auster III NJ995; Spitfire VIII MV429; Oxford I NM474; Tiger Moth II NL820.

Disbanded 20th June 1945 at Bamhrauli, India.

10 FERRY UNIT
Formed 1st September 1944 at Nagpur, India, by redesignating 23 Ferry Control.

Hurricane IIC KZ507, IV KZ579, XIIA PJ796; Proctor III LZ752; Mosquito III LR524, VI NS914; Spitfire VIII MT617, XIV RM993; Auster III NJ813; Tiger Moth II NL716; Harvard IIB FE613.

Disbanded 16th June 1945 at Trichinopoly, India.

11 FERRY UNIT
Formed 8th September 1944 at Talbenny by redesignating 303 Ferry Training Unit.

Oxford I R5949, II V3727; Lysander IIIA V9654; Spitfire IIA P8718, VB BL714, IX PL333; Wellington X LP408, XIII ME926, XIV PF837; Warwick I BV251, III HG274, V PN725; Anson I DJ143, XII PH720; Ventura I FN956, V FP568; Halifax III MZ971.

Disbanded 15th August 1945 at Dunkeswell and merged with 3 Aircraft Preparation Unit to become 16 Ferry Unit.

12 FERRY UNIT
Formed 9th October 1944 at Melton Mowbray by merging 4 Aircraft Preparation Unit and 304 Ferry Training Unit.

Oxford I R6025; Dominie I R5922; Lysander III R9019; Stirling I BK615, V PJ897; Master II DL121; Wellington X LP512, XIV NC849; Warwick III HG241; Mustang III FX862, IVA KH733; Lancaster X FM106; Spitfire IX PT360; Beaufighter VI ND221, X RD725; Dragon Rapide V4725; Vengeance IV FD277; Liberator VI KH213; Harvard IIB KF302; Mosquito VI RF947, XIX TA282, NF.30 MV569; Halifax III PN384.

Disbanded 7th November 1945 at Melton Mowbray.

14 FERRY UNIT
Formed 20th March 1945 at Agartala, India, by merging the Ferry Flights Kanchrapara and Bishnupur.

Dakota III FD843; Thunderbolt II HD256; Expeditor II KJ542; Hurricane IIC LD299; Spitfire VIII LV645; Tiger Moth II NL817.

Disbanded 13th July 1945 at Hathazari, India and absorbed by 209 Staging Post.

15 FERRY UNIT
Formed 1st July 1945 at Filton by redesignating 2 Aircraft Preparation Unit.

Vengeance IV FD160; Ventura I FN989, V FP580; Mustang IVA KM353; Beaufighter X NV304; Mosquito VI; XIII; NF.30; Tempest II MW825; Anson XII PH776.

Disbanded 10th October 1945 at Filton.

16 FERRY UNIT
Formed 15th August 1945 at Dunkeswell by merging 11 Ferry Unit and 3 Aircraft Preparation Unit.

Dominie I R5921; Oxford I R5949; Master II DL121, III DL865; Tiger Moth II EM743; Ventura I FN956, V FP588; Harvard IIB KF177; Vengeance IV KG818; Liberator VIII KN827; Dakota I FD772, IV KN279; Warwick I BV296, II HG399, V LM853; Spitfire IX ML428; Wellington XIII NC414, XIV NC828; Stirling V PK149; Proctor IV RM164; Beaufighter X NV304; Mosquito III HJ993, VI TA507; Anson I NK168 4, X NK446 20, XI NL220, XII PH814; Lancaster I PB915, III SW320, VII RT672; Tempest II MW770, VI NX199.

Disbanded 15th November 1946 at St Mawgan.

FIGHTER AFFILIATION TRAINING UNIT – see Coastal Command Fighter Affiliation Training Unit

FIGHTER ARMAMENT TRIALS UNIT
Formed November 1946 at Acklington by redesignating an element of the Armament Practice Station, Acklington.

No aircraft known.

Disbanded July 1956 at Acklington.

FIGHTER COMBAT SCHOOL – see Central Fighter Establishment

FIGHTER COMMAND COMMUNICATION SQUADRON
Formed 16th October 1944 at Northolt by redesignating the Air Defence of Great Britain Communication Squadron.

Nil	Tiger Moth II N6668; Oxford I R5972, II N4783; Spitfire IIA P7961, VB BL941, VII MB767, IX JL359, XI EN654, XII MB851, XVI SL721, XIX PM614; Dominie I NR714, II NR748; Whitney Straight DP237; Mitchell III KJ590; Mosquito III RR299, VI HR343 AAC, XVI NS561, PR.34 VL625; Proctor I P6254, II Z7215, III HM291, IV RM186; Hudson IIIA FK737; Hurricane IIC LF363; Meteor F.3 EE249, F.4 EE549, T.7 WL347, F.8 WH273; Harvard IIB KF333; Hornet F.1 PX286; Anson XII PH626 LG, XIX TX221 53, T.21 VV882; Auster VI TW579; Chipmunk T.10 WG430; Valetta C.1 VW856; Devon C.1 VP953; Varsity T.1 WL680.
NB	Allocated post war but no known use.

Disbanded 30th June 1963 at Bovingdon and merged with Bomber and Coastal Commands Communication Squadrons to become the Bomber/Fighter/Coastal Commands Communication Squadron.

FIGHTER COMMAND CONTROL AND REPORTING SCHOOL, later SCHOOL OF CONTROL AND REPORTING
Formed 19th December 1945 at Rudloe Manor, Wiltshire, and using Middle Wallop for flying. The School moved to Middle Wallop on 12th January 1948. Redesignated the School of Control and Reporting from 16th March 1953 and the flying element withdrawn and replaced by aircraft assigned from 288 Squadron.

3L (12.45–4.51)	Spitfire IXC EN172 3L-A, XVI TD343 3L-N, XVIII TP316 3L-E; Hoverfly II KN839; Oxford I AT480 3L-B; Anson XI NK995 3L-V.
Nil (4.51–3.53)	Balliol T.2 WN158 K.

Disbanded 30th September 1957 at Middle Wallop to become the School of Fighter Plotting.

FIGHTER COMMAND INSTRUMENT RATING FLIGHT – see Central Fighter Establishment

FIGHTER COMMAND INSTRUMENT RATING SQUADRON – see Central Fighter Establishment

FIGHTER COMMAND INSTRUMENT TRAINING FLIGHT – see Central Fighter Establishment

FIGHTER COMMAND INSTRUMENT TRAINING SQUADRON – see Central Fighter Establishment

FIGHTER COMMAND MISSILE PRACTICE CAMP
Formed 1st June 1962 at Valley by redesignating 1 Guided Weapons Trials Squadron.

Javelin FAW.7 XH902; Chipmunk T.10 WB586.

Disbanded 30th April 1968 at Valley to become the Strike Command Air to Air Missile Establishment.

FIGHTER COMMAND SCHOOL OF TACTICS – see Fighter Leaders School

FIGHTER COMMAND TARGET FACILITIES SQUADRON – see Central Fighter Establishment

FIGHTER COMMAND TRIALS UNIT
Formed 1st February 1966 at Binbrook by redesignating the Air Fighting Development Squadron, Central Fighter Establishment.

Lightning F.1 XM164 Z, F.6 XR752.

Disbanded 30th June 1967 at Binbrook.

FIGHTER COMMAND VANGUARD FLIGHT
Formed 1st November 1952 at Kinloss.

Neptune MR.1 WX499 2.

Disbanded 5th June 1953 at Topcliffe to become 1453 (Early Warning) Flight.

FIGHTER DEFENCE FLIGHT, ADEN
Formed 16th April 1942 at Sheikh Othman as the Aden Battle Flight by redesignating an element of 73 Operational Training Unit. Redesignated the Fighter Defence Flight, Aden, from 1st June 1942.

Hurricane I Z4845, X AG115; Harvard II AJ769.

Disbanded 1st February 1943 at Khormaksar.

FIGHTER DEFENCE FLIGHT, GIBRALTAR
Formed 11th September 1943 at Gibraltar by redesignating 1676 (Gibraltar Defence) Flight.

Spitfire VB EP444, VC JG864.

Disbanded 7th May 1944 at Gibraltar to become 'C' Flight of 256 Squadron.

FIGHTER DEFENCE FLIGHT, IRAQ
Formed 15th June 1943 at Shaibah, Iraq, by redesignating an element of 208 Squadron.

Hurricane IIA.

Disbanded 30th September 1943 at Abadan, Iraq.

FIGHTER DEFENCE FLIGHT, SHEIKH OTHMAN – see Fighter Defence Flight, Aden

FIGHTER DEFENCE FLIGHT, TAKORADI
Formed 1st July 1941 at Takoradi, Gold Coast.

Hurricane I.

Disbanded March 1943 at Takoradi.

FIGHTER EXPERIMENTAL ESTABLISHMENT
Formed 23rd April 1941 at Middle Wallop. Absorbed the Wellington Flight of 93 Squadron on 2nd June 1941.

Tiger Moth II R4947; Defiant I T4055; Blenheim IV V5756; Wellington II W5451; Havoc I (Turbinlite) AX930; Boston I (Pandora) BD122.

Disbanded 1st August 1941 at Middle Wallop and merged with the Blind Landing Detachment of the Royal Aircraft Establishment and the Special Duty Flight, Christchurch, to become the Telecommunications Flying Unit.

FIGHTER EXPERIMENTAL FLIGHT – see Central Fighter Establishment

FIGHTER FLIGHT, HAL FAR
Formed 19th April 1940 at Hal Far, Malta.

Sea Gladiator proposed.

Disbanded 29th April 1940 at Hal Far.

Reformed 2nd May 1940 at Hal Far.

Sea Gladiator N5519 R; Hurricane I P2623.

Disbanded 2nd August 1940 at Luqa and merged with 418 Fighter Flight to become 261 Squadron.

FIGHTER FLIGHT, SHETLANDS
Formed 18th December 1939 at Sumburgh by redesignating an element of 152 Squadron. Redesignated Fighter Flight, Sumburgh from 5th January 1940.

Gladiator II N2266.

Disbanded 1st August 1940 at Roborough to become 247 Squadron.

FIGHTER FLIGHT, SUMBURGH – see Fighter Flight, Shetlands

FIGHTER INTERCEPTION DEVELOPMENT SQUADRON – see Central Fighter Establishment

FIGHTER INTERCEPTION DEVELOPMENT UNIT – see Fighter Interception Unit, later Fighter Interception Development Unit

FIGHTER INTERCEPTION UNIT, later FIGHTER INTERCEPTION DEVELOPMENT UNIT
Formed 18th April 1940 at Tangmere. Redesignated the Fighter Interception Development Unit from 31st August 1944.

ZQ	*Blenheim I K7160, IV Z5722; Boston I AE461 ZQ-A, II AH437; Hurricane I L1592 ZQ-U, IIB Z3887 ZQ-M, IIC BN288; Beaufighter R2055, I V8329 ZQ-G, II R2335, V R2274, VI MM869; Mosquito II HJ705, IV DZ366, VI HR176, IX MM230, XII HK166, XIII HK478 ZQ-G, XV DZ385; Welkin I DX286 ZQ-X; Defiant I AA301, II AA372; Fulmar II DR715; Firefly I MB414; Spitfire IIA P8340; Mentor I L4407; Magister R1896; Havoc I BD125; Mustang I AG360, III FB172; Typhoon IB R7651; Tempest V EJ524 ZQ-A2; Wellington II W5480; Hornet Moth X9447; Me 410A-3 TF209.*

Disbanded 16th October 1944 at Wittering and absorbed, as the Fighter Interception Development Squadron of the Night Fighter Development Wing, within the Central Fighter Establishment.

FIGHTER LEADERS SCHOOL
Formed 15th January 1943 at Chedworth, albeit on a temporary basis, within 52 Operational Training Unit. The parent unit then became 52 Operational Training Unit (Fighter Leaders School) from 16th August 1943 and 52 Operational Training Unit (Fighter Command School of Tactics) from October 1943. Reconstituted as an individual entity 26th January 1944 at Milfield by merging 52 Operational Training Unit and the Specialised Low Attack Instructors School.

HK	*Spitfire VB AR399 HK-G, IX BS227 HK-J.*
OQ	*Spitfire IX BS347 OQ-Q.*
MF	*Typhoon IB EK182 MF-W.*
Also used	*Spitfire IIA P7382, VA R7298, VB AA965, XII EN227, F.21 LA217; Hurricane IIA Z2457, IV KZ245; Magister N3838; Rapide R2487; Master II DM406, III DL695; Oxford II AB710; Typhoon IB R8967; Auster I LB342.*

Disbanded 27th December 1944 at Milfield and absorbed by the Central Fighter Establishment.

FIGHTER PILOTS PRACTICE FLIGHT, BLIDA
Formed 1943 at Blida, Algeria.

Spitfire VB ER338, VC ES314; Hurricane IIC KW731.

Disbanded 19th August 1943 at Blida and merged with the Fighter Pilots Practice Flight, Sétif to become the Advanced Flying Unit, Sétif.

FIGHTER PILOTS PRACTICE FLIGHT, SÉTIF
Formed 4th March 1943 at Sétif, Algeria.

Spitfire VC BR299; Hurricane IIC BE372.

Disbanded 19th August 1943 at Sétif and merged with the Fighter Pilots Practice Flight, Blida to become the Advanced Flying Unit, Sétif.

FIGHTER SUPPORT DEVELOPMENT SQUADRON – see Central Fighter Establishment

FIGHTER SUPPORT DEVELOPMENT UNIT – see Central Fighter Establishment

1 FIGHTER SUPPORT TRAINING UNIT – see 3 Fighter Support Training Unit

3 FIGHTER SUPPORT TRAINING UNIT (possibly later 1 FIGHTER SUPPORT TRAINING UNIT)
Formed 15th December 1945 at Bairagarh, India, by redesignating 3 Refresher Flying Unit. Possibly redesignated 1 Fighter Support Training Unit from February 1946.

Harvard IIB FE901; Spitfire VIII MV439, XIV RM984; Thunderbolt II KL287.

Disbanded 15th June 1946 at Bhopal.

FIGHTER WEAPONS SCHOOL
Formed 1st January 1955 at Leconfield by redesignating an element of the Central Gunnery School.

Anson XII PH667; Meteor T.7 WL410 Y, F.8 WH395 M, NF.12 WS620 P; Vampire FB.5 WA186 F, T.11 XD433; Venom FB.1 WE289; Chipmunk T.10 WG321; Sabre F.2 XB540; Hunter F.1 WT614 B, F.4 WV320 H.

Disbanded 15th March 1958 at Driffield and absorbed by the Central Fighter Establishment.

(FIGHTER) TRAINING FLIGHT – see Royal Air Force Base, Leuchars, later Royal Air Force Training Base, Leuchars

1 FIGHTING SCHOOL
Formed 29th May 1918 at Turnberry and Ayr by redesignating 1 School of Aerial Fighting and Gunnery.

D.H.2 A5058; D.H.5; D.H.9 C1230; Bristol M.1C C5013; Handley Page 0/400; Avro 504J C5845, Avro 504K; Pup C289; Camel B6398; Snipe; F.2B C4695; Dolphin E4437; S.E.5a F5586.

Disbanded 25th January 1919 at Turnberry and Ayr.

2 FIGHTING SCHOOL
Formed 29th May 1918 at Marske by redesignating 2 School of Aerial Fighting and Gunnery.

Spad S.7 A8802; F.K.8 B252; D.H.4 B5524; R.E.8 B6619; D.H.9 C1184, D.H.9A F952; Bristol M.1C C5000; F.2B C1009; Camel D1933 59; S.E.5a; Dolphin D3765; Avro 504K D6279; Snipe E8077; Triplane N5912 94.

Disbanded November 1919 at Marske.

3 FIGHTING SCHOOL
Formed 29th May 1918 at Bircham Newton by redesignating 3 School of Aerial Fighting and Gunnery.

B.E.2e 6786; Bristol M.1C C5022; D.H.4 B2100; D.H.5; D.H.9 D7332 6, D.H.9A E9667; S.E.5a; F.2b; Pup; Avro 504A C750, Avro 504J B3202, Avro 504K E3450; Dolphin; Camel H2724; Handley Page 0/400;

Disbanded 14th March 1919 at Sedgeford to become 7 Training Squadron.

4 FIGHTING SCHOOL
Formed 29th May 1918 at Freiston by redesignating 4 School of Aerial Fighting and Gunnery.

Camel B7240; Avro 504K E2997; Snipe E6189 120.

Disbanded March 1920 at Freiston.

5 FIGHTING SCHOOL
Formed 5th September 1918 at Heliopolis, Egypt, by merging the School of Aerial Gunnery, Aboukir and the main element of the Aerial Fighting School, Heliopolis.

F.K.3 A1477; Elephant A1593; Avro 504A A8531, Avro 504K E1651; B.E.2e B4515; R.E.8 B5010; F.2B C4651; Bristol M.1C

C4905; Handley Page 0/400 C9681; Nieuport 12 9223; Nieuport 17 B1508; D.H.9 D2927; Pup D4123; S.E.5a B8535.

Disbanded 22nd July 1919 at Heliopolis.

FILM PRODUCTION UNIT – see Royal Air Force Film Production Unit, later 1 Royal Air Force Film Production Unit

FLEET AIR ARM SQUADRON – see Royal Naval Fighter Squadron

FLEET AND TORPEDO PILOT FINISHING SCHOOL – see 208 (Temporary) Training Depot Station

FLEET FIGHTER SQUADRON – see Royal Naval Fighter Squadron

FLEET REQUIREMENTS UNIT
Formed 11th August 1938 at Lee-on-Solent.

Swordfish I L2825

Disbanded 24th May 1939 at Lee-on-Solent and transferred to the Royal Navy to become 771 Squadron.

FLEET SCHOOL OF AERIAL FIGHTING AND GUNNERY – see Grand Fleet School of Aerial Fighting and Gunnery

ROYAL AIR FORCE COASTAL BASED NUMBERED FLIGHTS 1918 – 1929

300 (FLYING BOAT) FLIGHT
Formed 15th June 1918 at Catfirth.

Felixstowe F.3 N4407.

Disbanded March 1919 at Catfirth.

301 (FLYING BOAT) FLIGHT
Planned formation at Catfirth with Felixstowe F.3 cancelled.

302 (FLYING BOAT) FLIGHT
Planned formation at Catfirth with Felixstowe F.3 cancelled.

303 (FLYING BOAT) FLIGHT
Planned formation at Catfirth with Felixstowe F.3 cancelled.

304 (FLYING BOAT) FLIGHT
Planned formation at Catfirth with Felixstowe F.3 cancelled.

305 (FLYING BOAT) FLIGHT
Planned formation at Catfirth with Felixstowe F.3 cancelled.

306 (FLYING BOAT) FLIGHT
Formed 31st July 1918 at Houton Bay.

Curtiss H.16 N4065; Felixstowe F.3 N4407; Short 184 N1220.

Disbanded March 1919 at Houton Bay.

307 (FLYING BOAT) FLIGHT
Planned formation on 15th August 1918 at Houton Bay cancelled.

308 (FLYING BOAT) FLIGHT
Planned formation on 31st August 1918 at Houton Bay cancelled.

309 (FLYING BOAT) FLIGHT
Formed May 1918 at Stenness.

Felixstowe F.3 N4245.

Disbanded 1919 at Stenness.

310 (FLYING BOAT) FLIGHT
Formed 31st May 1918 at Stenness.

Felixstowe F.3 N4245.

Disbanded 1919 at Stenness.

311 (FLYING BOAT) FLIGHT
Formed 15th July 1918 at Stenness.

Felixstowe F.3.

Disbanded 1919 at Stenness.

312 (FLYING BOAT) FLIGHT
Planned formation between 15th July and 15th October 1918 at Strathbeg cancelled.

313 (FLYING BOAT) FLIGHT
Planned formation between 15th July and 15th October 1918 at Strathbeg cancelled.

314 (FLYING BOAT) FLIGHT
Planned formation between 15th July and 15th October 1918 at Strathbeg cancelled.

315 (FLYING BOAT) FLIGHT
Planned formation between 15th July and 15th October 1918 at Strathbeg cancelled.

316 (FLYING BOAT) FLIGHT
Planned formation between 15th July and 15th October 1918 at Strathbeg cancelled.

317 (FLYING BOAT) FLIGHT
Planned formation between 15th July and 15th October 1918 at Strathbeg cancelled.

318 (FLYING BOAT) FLIGHT
Formed 30th May 1918 at Dundee and absorbed by 257 Squadron when it formed on 18th August 1918.

Curtiss H.16 N4069; Felixstowe F.2A N4285.

Disbanded 30th June 1919 at Dundee together with the parent unit.

319 (FLYING BOAT) FLIGHT
Formed 30th May 1918 at Dundee and absorbed by 257 Squadron when it formed on 18th August 1918.

Curtiss H.16 N4061; Felixstowe F.2A N4285.

Disbanded 30th June 1919 at Dundee together with the parent unit.

320 (FLYING BOAT) FLIGHT
Formed May 1918 at East Halton, Killingholme.

Felixstowe F.2A; Curtiss H.12, Curtiss H.12A; Curtiss H.16.

Disbanded 20th July 1918 at East Halton, Killingholme.

321 (FLYING BOAT) FLIGHT
Formed May 1918 at East Halton, Killingholme.

Felixstowe F.2A; Curtiss H.12, Curtiss H.12A; Curtiss H.16.

Disbanded 20th July 1918 at East Halton, Killingholme.

322 (FLYING BOAT) FLIGHT
Formed May 1918 at East Halton, Killingholme.

Felixstowe F.2A; Curtiss H.12, Curtiss H.12A; Curtiss H.16.

Disbanded 20th July 1918 at East Halton, Killingholme.

323 (FLYING BOAT) FLIGHT
Planned formation on 31st October 1918 at East Halton, Killingholme, cancelled.

324 (FLYING BOAT) FLIGHT
Formed 25th May 1918 at Yarmouth and absorbed by 228 Squadron when it formed on 20th August 1918.

Felixstowe F.2A N4518.

Disbanded 30th June 1919 at Killingholme together with the parent unit.

325 (FLYING BOAT) FLIGHT
Formed 25th May 1918 at Yarmouth and absorbed by 228 Squadron when it formed on 20th August 1918.

Felixstowe F.2A N4282.

Disbanded 30th June 1919 at Killingholme together with the parent unit.

326 (FLYING BOAT) FLIGHT
Formed 15th July 1918 at Yarmouth and absorbed by 228 Squadron when it formed on 20th August 1918.

Felixstowe F.2A N4289.

Disbanded 30th June 1919 at Killingholme together with the parent unit.

327 (FLYING BOAT) FLIGHT
Formed May 1918 at Felixstowe and absorbed by 230 Squadron when it formed on 20th August 1918.

Felixstowe F.2A N4545.

Disbanded February 1919 at Felixstowe within 230 Squadron.

328 (FLYING BOAT) FLIGHT
Formed May 1918 at Felixstowe and absorbed by 230 Squadron when it formed on 20th August 1918.

Felixstowe F.2A N4298.

Disbanded February 1919 at Felixstowe within 230 Squadron.

329 (FLYING BOAT) FLIGHT
Formed 30th May 1918 at Felixstowe and absorbed by 231 Squadron when it formed on 20th August 1918.

Felixstowe F.2A.

Disbanded 7th July 1919 at Felixstowe together with the parent unit.

330 (FLYING BOAT) FLIGHT
Formed 30th May 1918 at Felixstowe and absorbed by 231 Squadron when it formed on 20th August 1918.

Felixstowe F.2A.

Disbanded 7th July 1919 at Felixstowe together with the parent unit.

331 (FLYING BOAT) FLIGHT
Planned formation on 30th September 1918 at Felixstowe cancelled.

332 (FLYING BOAT) FLIGHT
Planned formation on 15th October 1918 at Felixstowe cancelled.

333 (FLYING BOAT) FLIGHT
Formed 31st May 1918 at Felixstowe and absorbed by 232 Squadron when it formed on 20th August 1918. The Flight appears to have continued to operate as an independent entity after 5th January 1919 when 232 Squadron became 4 Communication Squadron.

Felixstowe F.2A N4541.

Disbanded March 1919 at Felixstowe.

334 (FLYING BOAT) FLIGHT
Formed 31st May 1918 at Felixstowe and absorbed by 232 Squadron when it formed on 20th August 1918. The Flight appears to have continued to operate as an independent entity after 5th January 1919 when 232 Squadron became 4 Communications Squadron.

Felixstowe F.2A.

Disbanded March 1919 at Felixstowe.

335 (FLYING BOAT) FLIGHT
Formed 15th June 1918 at Felixstowe and absorbed into 232 Squadron when it formed on 20th August 1918.

Felixstowe F.2A.

Disbanded 5th January 1919 at Felixstowe when 232 Squadron became 4 Communications Squadron.

336 (FLYING BOAT) FLIGHT
Formed 31st July 1918 at Felixstowe and absorbed by 247 Squadron when it formed on 20th August 1918.

Felixstowe F.2A.

Disbanded 22nd January 1918 at Felixstowe together with the parent unit.

337 (FLYING BOAT) FLIGHT
Formed 15th September 1918 at Felixstowe within 247 Squadron.

Felixstowe F.2A.

Disbanded 22nd January 1918 at Felixstowe together with the parent unit.

338 (FLYING BOAT) FLIGHT
Planned formation on 15th September 1918 at Felixstowe within 247 Squadron cancelled.

339 (FLYING BOAT) FLIGHT
Formed January 1919 at Felixstowe within 261 Squadron.

Felixstowe F.2A.

Disbanded 13th September 1919 at Felixstowe together with the parent unit.

340 (FLYING BOAT) FLIGHT
Planned formation on 15th October 1918 at Felixstowe within 261 Squadron cancelled.

341 (FLYING BOAT) FLIGHT
Formed January 1919 at Felixstowe within 261 Squadron.

Felixstowe F.2A.

Disbanded 13th September 1919 at Felixstowe together with the parent unit.

342 (FLYING BOAT) FLIGHT
Planned formation on 31st October 1918 at Felixstowe within 259 Squadron cancelled.

343 (FLYING BOAT) FLIGHT
Planned formation on 31st October 1918 at Felixstowe within 259 Squadron cancelled.

344 (FLYING BOAT) FLIGHT
Planned formation on 15th November 1918 at Felixstowe within 259 Squadron cancelled.

345 (FLYING BOAT) FLIGHT
Formed May 1918 at Calshot and absorbed by 240 Squadron when it formed on 20th August 1918.

Curtiss H.12B N4334; Felixstowe F.2A N4286.

Disbanded 15th May 1919 at Calshot together with the parent unit.

346 (FLYING BOAT) FLIGHT
Formed May 1918 at Calshot and absorbed by 240 Squadron when it formed on 20th August 1918.

Curtiss H.12B N3449; Felixstowe F.2A N4285.

Disbanded 15th May 1919 at Calshot together with the parent unit.

347 (FLYING BOAT) FLIGHT
Formed 15th June 1918 at Cattewater and absorbed by 238 Squadron when it formed on 20th August 1918.

Curtiss H.16; Felixstowe F.3 N4419.

Disbanded 15th May 1919 at Cattewater together with the parent unit.

348 (FLYING BOAT) FLIGHT
Formed 15th July 1918 at Cattewater and absorbed by 238 Squadron when it formed on 20th August 1918.

Curtiss H.16; Felixstowe F.3.

Disbanded 15th May 1919 at Cattewater together with the parent unit.

349 (FLYING BOAT) FLIGHT
Formed 15th October 1918 at Cattewater within 238 Squadron.

Curtiss H.16; Felixstowe F.3.

Disbanded 15th May 1919 at Cattewater together with the parent unit.

350 (FLYING BOAT) FLIGHT
Formed 31st May 1918 at Tresco and absorbed by 234 Squadron when it formed on 20th August 1918.

Felixstowe F.3 N4241; Curtiss H.12B N4341; F.B.A; Short 184 N2955.

Disbanded 15th May 1919 at Tresco together with the parent unit.

351 (FLYING BOAT) FLIGHT
Formed 30th June 1918 at Tresco and absorbed by 234 Squadron when it formed on 20th August 1918.

Felixstowe F.3; Curtiss H.12; Curtiss H.12A; F.B.A; Short 184.

Disbanded 15th May 1919 at Tresco together with the parent unit.

352 (FLYING BOAT) FLIGHT
Formed 15th September 1918 at Tresco within 234 Squadron.

Felixstowe F.3; Curtiss H.12; Curtiss H.12A; F.B.A; Short 184.

Disbanded 15th May 1919 at Tresco together with the parent unit.

353 (FLYING BOAT) FLIGHT
Formed 30th September 1918 at Tresco within 234 Squadron.

Felixstowe F.3; Curtiss H.12; Curtiss H.12A; F.B.A; Short 184.

Disbanded 15th May 1919 at Tresco together with the parent unit.

354 (FLYING BOAT) FLIGHT
Planned formation on 6th October 1918 at Alexandria, Egypt, within 270 Squadron cancelled.

Note: Records also refer to a Seaplane Squadron, Alexandria as being a term given to the merging of 354, 355 and 356 Coastal Patrol Flights prior to becoming 270 Squadron.

355 (FLYING BOAT) FLIGHT
Planned formation on 6th October 1918 at Alexandria, Egypt, within 270 Squadron cancelled.

Note: Records also refer to a Seaplane Squadron, Alexandria as being a term given to the merging of 354, 355 and 356 Coastal Patrol Flights prior to becoming 270 Squadron.

356 (FLYING BOAT) FLIGHT
Planned formation on 6th October 1918 at Alexandria, Egypt, within 270 Squadron cancelled.

Note: Records also refer to a Seaplane Squadron, Alexandria as being a term given to the merging of 354, 355 and 356 Coastal Patrol Flights prior to becoming 270 Squadron.

357 (FLYING BOAT) FLIGHT
Formed 27th September 1918 at Taranto, Italy, within 271 Squadron.

Felixstowe F.3.

Disbanded 9th December 1918 at Taranto together with the parent unit.

358 (FLYING BOAT) FLIGHT
Formed 27th September 1918 at Taranto, Italy, within 271 Squadron.

Felixstowe F.3.

Disbanded 9th December 1918 at Taranto together with the parent unit.

359 (FLYING BOAT) FLIGHT
Formed 27th September 1918 at Otranto, Italy, within 263 Squadron.

Baby N1981; Felixstowe F.3 N4320.

Disbanded 16th May 1919 at Otranto together with the parent unit.

360 (FLYING BOAT) FLIGHT
Formed 27th September 1918 at Kalafrana, Malta, within 267 Squadron.

Felixstowe F.3 N4313.

Disbanded March 1919 at Kalafrana and absorbed into the parent unit.

361 (FLYING BOAT) FLIGHT
Formed 27th September 1918 at Kalafrana, Malta, within 267 Squadron.

Felixstowe F.3.

Disbanded March 1919 at Kalafrana and absorbed into the parent unit.

362 (FLYING BOAT) FLIGHT
Formed 27th September 1918 at Kalafrana, Malta, within 267 Squadron.

Felixstowe F.3.

Disbanded March 1919 at Kalafrana and absorbed into the parent unit.

363 (FLYING BOAT) FLIGHT
Formed 27th September 1918 at Kalafrana, Malta, within 267 Squadron.

Felixstowe F.3.

Disbanded March 1919 at Kalafrana and absorbed into the parent unit.

364 (FLYING BOAT) FLIGHT
Planned formation at Gibraltar within 265 Squadron cancelled.

365 (FLYING BOAT) FLIGHT
Planned formation at Gibraltar within 265 Squadron cancelled.

366 (FLYING BOAT) FLIGHT
Planned formation at Gibraltar within 265 Squadron cancelled.

367 (FLYING BOAT) FLIGHT
Formed 27th September 1918 at Taranto, Italy, within 271 Squadron.

Felixstowe F.3.

Disbanded 9th December 1918 at Taranto together with the parent unit.

400 (SEAPLANE) FLIGHT
Formed 30th May 1918 at Dundee. Absorbed by 248 Squadron when formed on 18th August 1918.

Short 184 N2641.

Disbanded March 1919 at Killingholme within 248 Squadron.

401 (SEAPLANE) FLIGHT
Formed 30th May 1918 at Dundee. Absorbed by 248 Squadron when formed on 18th August 1918.

Short 184 N9089.

Disbanded March 1919 at Dundee within 248 Squadron.

402 (SEAPLANE) FLIGHT
Formed 30th June 1918 at Seaton Carew. Absorbed by 246 Squadron when formed on 15th August 1918.

Short 184 N2640.

Disbanded 24th March 1919 at Seaton Carew within 246 Squadron.

403 (SEAPLANE) FLIGHT
Formed May 1918 at East Halton, Killingholme. Absorbed by 246 Squadron when formed on 18th August 1918.

Short 184 N2638; Short 320 N1703; Hamble Baby N1468.

Disbanded 31st May 1919 at Seaton Carew together with the parent unit.

404 (SEAPLANE) FLIGHT
Formed May 1918 at East Halton, Killingholme. Absorbed by 248 Squadron when formed on 20th August 1918.

Short 184 N2922.

Disbanded 6th March 1919 at North Coates Fitties together with the parent unit.

405 (SEAPLANE) FLIGHT
Formed 15th June 1918 at Hornsea Mere. Absorbed by 248 Squadron when formed on 20th August 1918.

Short 184 N1226.

Disbanded 6th March 1919 at Hornsea Mere together with the parent unit.

406 (SEAPLANE) FLIGHT
Formed 25th May 1918 at Westgate. Absorbed by 219 Squadron when formed on 27th July 1918.

Short 184 N1782 5; Hamble Baby N1962.

Disbanded 7th February 1920 at Westgate together with the parent unit.

407 (SEAPLANE) FLIGHT
Formed 20th May 1918 at Dover. Absorbed by 233 Squadron when formed on 31st August 1918.

Short 184 N2939; Baby.

Disbanded 31st March 1919 at Dover within 233 Squadron.

408 (SEAPLANE) FLIGHT
Formed May 1918 at Newhaven. Absorbed by 242 Squadron when formed on 15th August 1918.

Short 184 N9061; Campania N2380.

Disbanded 15th May 1919 at Newhaven together with the parent unit.

409 (SEAPLANE) FLIGHT
Formed 15th August 1918 at Newhaven within 242 Squadron.

Short 184 N9061.

Disbanded October 1918 at Newhaven within 242 Squadron.

410 (SEAPLANE) FLIGHT
Formed 31st May 1918 at Calshot. Absorbed by 240 Squadron when formed on 20th August 1920.

Short 184; Short 320 N1707; Campania N2377.

Disbanded 15th May 1919 at Calshot together with the parent unit.

411 (SEAPLANE) FLIGHT
Planned formation at Calshot within 240 Squadron cancelled.

412 (SEAPLANE) FLIGHT
Formed 20th May 1918 at Bembridge. Absorbed by 253 Squadron when formed on 7th June 1918.

Baby N1333; Short 184 N2646; Campania N2378.

Disbanded 5th May 1919 at Bembridge together with the parent unit.

413 (SEAPLANE) FLIGHT
Formed 15th September 1918 at Bembridge within 253 Squadron.

Short 184 N9060.

Disbanded November 1918 at Bembridge.

414 (SEAPLANE) FLIGHT
Formed May 1918 at Cherbourg, France. Absorbed by 243 Squadron when formed on 20th August 1918.

Short 184 N9170; Wight Seaplane 9854.

Disbanded 15th March 1919 at Cherbourg together with the parent unit.

415 (SEAPLANE) FLIGHT
Formed May 1918 at Cherbourg, France. Absorbed by 243 Squadron when formed on 20th August 1918.

Short 184 N9170; Wight Seaplane 9858.

Disbanded 15th March 1919 at Cherbourg together with the parent unit.

416 (SEAPLANE) FLIGHT
Formed May 1918 at Portland. Absorbed by 241 Squadron when formed on 20th August 1918.

Short 184 N9062; Wight Seaplane 9841; Campania N2363.

Disbanded 18th June 1919 at Portland together with the parent unit.

417 (SEAPLANE) FLIGHT
Formed 31st May 1918 at Portland. Absorbed by 241 Squadron when formed on 20th August 1918.

Short 184 N9062; Wight Seaplane 9850; Campania.

Disbanded 18th June 1919 at Portland together with the parent unit.

418 (SEAPLANE) FLIGHT
Formed 15th June 1918 at Torquay. Absorbed by 239 Squadron when formed on 20th August 1918.

Short 184 N1622.

Disbanded 15th May 1919 at Torquay together with the parent unit.

419 (SEAPLANE) FLIGHT
Formed 15th November 1918 at Torquay within 239 Squadron. Transferred to 249 Squadron.

Short 184 N9102.

Disbanded March 1919 at Dundee within 249 Squadron.

420 (SEAPLANE) FLIGHT
Formed May 1918 at Cattewater. Absorbed by 237 Squadron when formed on 20th August 1918.

Short 184 N2953.

Disbanded 15th May 1919 at Cattewater together with the parent unit.

421 (SEAPLANE) FLIGHT
Formed May 1918 at Cattewater. Absorbed by 237 Squadron when formed on 20th August 1918.

Short 184 N2913.

Disbanded 15th May 1919 at Cattewater together with the parent unit.

422 (SEAPLANE) FLIGHT
Planned formation at Cattewater cancelled.

423 (SEAPLANE) FLIGHT
Planned formation at Cattewater cancelled.

424 (SEAPLANE) FLIGHT
Formed 20th May 1918 at Newlyn. Absorbed by 235 Squadron when formed on 20th August 1918.

Short 184 N2690.

Disbanded 22nd February 1919 at Newlyn together with the parent unit.

425 (SEAPLANE) FLIGHT
Formed 20th May 1918 at Newlyn. Absorbed by 235 Squadron when formed on 20th August 1918.

Short 184 N1601.

Disbanded 22nd February 1919 at Newlyn together with the parent unit.

426 (SEAPLANE) FLIGHT
Formed 20th May 1918 at Fishguard. Absorbed by 245 Squadron when formed on 20th August 1918.

Short 184 N2790.

Disbanded November 1918 within 245 Squadron.

427 (SEAPLANE) FLIGHT
Formed 20th May 1918 at Fishguard. Absorbed by 245 Squadron when formed on 20th August 1918.

Short 184 N9015.

Disbanded November 1918 within 245 Squadron.

428 (SEAPLANE) FLIGHT
Formed May 1918 at Great Yarmouth. Absorbed by 229 Squadron when formed on 20th August 1918.

Short 184 N2901; Short 320.

Disbanded January 1919 at Great Yarmouth within 229 Squadron.

429 (SEAPLANE) FLIGHT
Formed May 1918 at Great Yarmouth. Absorbed by 229 Squadron when formed on 20th August 1918.

Short 184; Short 320.

Disbanded January 1919 at Great Yarmouth within 229 Squadron.

430 (SEAPLANE) FLIGHT
Formed May 1918 at Houton Bay.

Short 184 N1220.

Disbanded March 1919 at Houton Bay.

431 (SEAPLANE) FLIGHT
Formed 22nd July 1918 at Port Said, Egypt. Absorbed by 269 Squadron when formed on 6th October 1919.

Short 184 N2653.

Disbanded March 1919 within 269 Squadron.

Note: Records also refer to a Seaplane Squadron, Port Said as being a term given to the merging of 431 and 432 Coastal Patrol Flights prior to becoming 269 Squadron.

432 (SEAPLANE) FLIGHT
Note: Records refer to the Seaplane Squadron, Port Said as being a term given to the merging of 431 and 432 (Seaplane) Flights prior to becoming 269 Squadron. It seems probable the Flight existed only as an administrative entity.

433 (SEAPLANE) FLIGHT
Formed October 1919 at Kalafrana, Malta, within 268 Squadron.

Short 320 N1302.

Disbanded March 1919 at Kalafrana within 268 Squadron.

434 (SEAPLANE) FLIGHT
Formed October 1919 at Kalafrana, Malta, within 268 Squadron.

Short 320.

Disbanded March 1919 at Kalafrana within 268 Squadron.

435 (SEAPLANE) FLIGHT
Formed October 1918 at Otranto, Italy, within 263 Squadron.

Short 184 N1783; Short 320 N1313; Baby N2090.

Disbanded 16th May 1919 at Otranto together with the parent unit.

436 (SEAPLANE) FLIGHT
Formed October 1918 at Otranto, Italy, within 263 Squadron.

Short 184; Short 320 N1308; Baby.

Disbanded 16th May 1919 at Otranto together with the parent unit.

437 (SEAPLANE) FLIGHT
Formed October 1918 at Mudros, Aegean, within 266 Squadron.

Short 184 N1783.

Disbanded 1st September at Petrovsk Port, Russia, together with the parent unit.

438 (SEAPLANE) FLIGHT
Formed October 1918 at Skyros, Aegean, within 266 Squadron.

Short 184.

Disbanded February 1919 at Skyros within 266 Squadron.

439 (SEAPLANE) FLIGHT
Formed October 1918 at Suda Bay, Crete, within 264 Squadron.

Short 184.

Disbanded 1st March 1919 at Suda Bay together with the parent unit.

440 (SEAPLANE) FLIGHT
Formed October 1918 at Syra, Aegean, within 264 Squadron.

Short 184.

Disbanded 1st March 1919 at Syra together with the parent unit.

441 (SEAPLANE) FLIGHT
Formed 1st October 1918 at St Maria di Leuca, Italy, within 263 Squadron.

Short 184 N1791; Short 320 N1500; Baby N1982.

Disbanded 16th May 1919 at Taranto, Italy, together with the parent unit.

442 (SEAPLANE) COASTAL FLIGHT
Formed 15th October 1918 at Felixstowe within 219 Squadron.

Fairey IIIB N2230.

Disbanded 7th February 1920 at Westgate together with the parent unit.

450 (SEAPLANE) FLIGHT
Formed 30th May 1918 at Dundee and absorbed by 249 Squadron when it formed on 18th August 1918.

Baby N1432.

Disbanded 30th September 1918 at Dundee within 249 Squadron.

451 (SEAPLANE) FLIGHT
Formed 25th May 1918 at Seaton Carew within 252 Squadron. Transferred to 246 Squadron.

Baby N2064.

Disbanded 10th October 1918 at Seaton Carew within 246 Squadron.

452 (SEAPLANE) FLIGHT
Formed 25th May 1918 at Seaton Carew within 252 Squadron. Transferred to 246 Squadron.

Baby N2064.

Disbanded 31st October 1918 at Seaton Carew within 246 Squadron.

453 (SEAPLANE) FLIGHT
Formed 30th May 1918 at Hornsea Mere and absorbed by 248 Squadron when it formed on 20th August 1918.

Baby N2078.

Disbanded 30th November 1918 at Hornsea Mere within 248 Squadron.

454 (SEAPLANE) FLIGHT
Formed 25th May 1918 at Great Yarmouth and absorbed by 229 Squadron when it formed on 20th August 1918.

Baby N2116.

Disbanded 30th September 1918 within 229 Squadron.

455 (SEAPLANE) FLIGHT
Formed 15th June 1918 at Great Yarmouth and absorbed by 229 Squadron when it formed on 20th August 1918.

Baby N2114.

Disbanded 31st October 1918 within 229 Squadron.

470 (FIGHTER) FLIGHT
Formed 27th May 1918 at Manston, also being known as the Tongue Defence or Manston Naval Flight, and absorbed by 219 Squadron when it formed on 27th July 1918. Transferred to 273 Squadron from 13th November 1918.

Camel F3918 D.

Disbanded January 1919 at Manston within 273 Squadron.

471 (FIGHTER) FLIGHT
Formed 14th June 1918 at Walmer and absorbed by 233 Squadron when it formed on 31st August 1918.

Camel F3956; Avro 504K D1631.

Disbanded 17th March 1919 at Dover within 233 Squadron.

472 (FIGHTER) FLIGHT
Formed September 1918 at Pizzone, Italy, within 226 Squadron.

Camel; D.H.9; D.H.9A.

Disbanded 18th December 1918 at Pizzone together with the parent unit.

473 (FIGHTER) FLIGHT
Formed September 1918 at Pizzone, Italy, within 226 Squadron.

Camel; D.H.9; D.H.9A.

Disbanded 18th December 1918 at Pizzone together with the parent unit.

474 (FIGHTER) FLIGHT
Formed September 1918 at Pizzone, Italy, within 226 Squadron.

Camel; D.H.9; D.H.9A.

Disbanded 18th December 1918 at Pizzone together with the parent unit.

475 (FIGHTER) FLIGHT
Formed September 1918 at Mudros, Aegean, within 220 Squadron.

Camel.

Disbanded January 1919 at Mudros within 220 Squadron.

476 (FIGHTER) FLIGHT
Formed September 1918 at Mudros, Aegean, within 220 Squadron.

Camel.

Disbanded January 1919 at Mudros within 220 Squadron.

477 (FIGHTER) FLIGHT
Formed September 1918 at Mudros, Aegean, within 220 Squadron.

Camel.

Disbanded January 1919 at Mudros within 220 Squadron.

478 (FIGHTER) FLIGHT
Formed September 1918 at Mudros, Aegean, within 222 Squadron.

Camel.

Disbanded 27th February 1919 at Mudros together with the parent unit.

479 (FIGHTER) FLIGHT
Formed September 1918 at Mudros, Aegean, within 222 Squadron.

Camel.

Disbanded 27th February 1919 at Mudros together with the parent unit.

480 (FIGHTER) FLIGHT, later 480 (COASTAL RECONNAISSANCE) FLIGHT
Formed September 1918 at Mudros, Aegean, within 222 Squadron.

Camel.

Disbanded 27th February 1919 at Mudros together with the parent unit.

Reformed 1st April 1923 at Calshot as 480 (Coastal Reconnaissance) Flight by redesignating 230 Squadron.

Felixstowe F.2A N4570, F.5 N4636; Southampton I S1037, II S1125.

Disbanded 1st January 1929 at Calshot to become 201 Squadron.

481 (FIGHTER) FLIGHT, later 481 (COASTAL RECONNAISSANCE) FLIGHT
Formed September 1918 at Andrano, Italy, within 225 Squadron.

Camel; 1½ Strutter, Hamble Baby.

Disbanded 19th December 1918 at Pizzone, Italy, together with the parent unit.

Reformed 1st August 1923 aboard HMS *Ark Royal* at Kilya Bay, Dardanelles, as 481 (Coastal Reconnaissance) Flight by redesignating 267 Squadron.

Fairey IIID S1105.

Disbanded 1st January 1929 at Kalafrana, Malta, to become 202 Squadron.

482 (FIGHTER) FLIGHT, later 482 (COASTAL RECONNAISSANCE) FLIGHT
Formed September 1918 at Andrano, Italy, within 225 Squadron.

Camel; 1½ Strutter, Hamble Baby.

Disbanded 19th December 1918 at Pizzone, Italy, together with the parent unit.

Reformed 15th September 1928 at Cattewater (later Mount Batten) as 482 (Coastal Reconnaissance) Flight.

Southampton I S1121, II S1162.

Disbanded 1st January 1929 at Cattewater to become 203 Squadron.

483 (FIGHTER) FLIGHT
Formed September 1918 at Andrano, Italy, within 225 Squadron.

Camel; 1½ Strutter, Hamble Baby.

Disbanded 19th December 1918 at Pizzone, Italy, together with the parent unit.

485 (FIGHTER) FLIGHT
Formed 7th August 1918 at Burgh Castle, also being known as Temporary 'A' Flight. Absorbed by 273 Squadron when the unit formed on 20th August 1918.

Camel.

Disbanded March 1919 at Burgh Castle within 273 Squadron.

486 (FIGHTER) FLIGHT
Formed 7th August 1918 at Burgh Castle, also being known as Temporary 'C' Flight. Absorbed by 273 Squadron when the unit formed on 20th August 1918.

Camel F3128.

Disbanded March 1919 at Burgh Castle within 273 Squadron.

487 (FIGHTER) FLIGHT
Formed 3rd September 1918 at Butley within 230 Squadron from the Supernumerary Flight, Butley that formed two days earlier.

Camel F3128.

Disbanded January 1919 at Butley within 230 Squadron.

490 (LIGHT BOMBER) FLIGHT
Formed 8th August 1918 at Great Yarmouth, by redesignating Temporary 'D' Flight, which formed on 25th May 1918. Absorbed by 212 Squadron when the unit formed on 20th August 1918.

B.E.2c 8411; Pup 9904; Camel B5707; Baby N1992; D.H.4 N6395; D.H.9 D1653.

Disbanded 9th February 1920 at Dover, together with the parent unit.

491 (LIGHT BOMBER) FLIGHT
Formed 25th May 1918 at Guston Road, Dover, and absorbed by 233 Squadron when the unit formed on 31st August 1918.

1½ Strutter 9378; Camel B7269; D.H.4 A7762; D.H.9 D1006; Dolphin C3785.

Disbanded 1st March 1919 at Guston Road, Dover, together with the parent unit.

492 (LIGHT BOMBER) FLIGHT
Formed 30th May 1918 at Prawle Point. Absorbed by 254 Squadron from 15th August 1918.

D.H.9 D1681.

Disbanded 22nd February at Prawle Point together with the parent unit.

493 (LIGHT BOMBER) FLIGHT
Formed 30th May 1918 at Mullion and absorbed by 236 Squadron when the unit formed on 20th August 1918.

D.H.6 C7832; D.H.9 D1711; 1½ Strutter N5619.

Disbanded 15th May 1919 at Mullion together with the parent unit.

494 (LIGHT BOMBER) FLIGHT
Formed 30th May 1918 at Padstow within 250 Squadron.

D.H.6 C5497; D.H.9 D1714.

Disbanded 15th May 1919 at Padstow together with the parent unit.

495 (LIGHT BOMBER) FLIGHT
Formed 30th May 1918 at Seaton Carew within 252 Squadron by redesignating the Kangaroo Flight. Transferred to 246 Squadron when the unit formed on 15th August 1918.

Kangaroo B9971.

Disbanded 30th June 1919 at Seaton Carew together with the parent unit,

496 (LIGHT BOMBER) FLIGHT
Formed September 1918 at Alimini, Italy, within 224 Squadron.

D.H.4.

Disbanded 3rd January 1919 at Pizzone, Italy, together with the parent unit.

497 (LIGHT BOMBER) FLIGHT
Formed September 1918 at Alimini, Italy, within 224 Squadron.

D.H.4.

Disbanded 3rd January 1919 at Pizzone, Italy, together with the parent unit.

498 (LIGHT BOMBER) FLIGHT
Formed September 1918 at Alimini, Italy, within 224 Squadron.

D.H.4.

Disbanded 3rd January 1919 at Pizzone, Italy, together with the parent unit.

499 (LIGHT BOMBER) FLIGHT
Planned formation by September 1918 at Pizzone, Italy, within 227 Squadron cancelled.

500 (SPECIAL DUTY) FLIGHT
Formed 31st May 1918 at Padstow within 250 Squadron.

D.H.6 C7413.

Disbanded 15th May 1919 at Padstow together with the parent unit.

501 (SPECIAL DUTY) FLIGHT
Formed 31st May 1918 at Padstow within 250 Squadron.

D.H.6 C6678.

Disbanded 15th May 1919 at Padstow together with the parent unit.

502 (SPECIAL DUTY) FLIGHT
Formed 6th June 1918 at Westward Ho! within 260 Squadron. Transferred to 250 Squadron from 15th August 1918.

D.H.6 C7417.

Disbanded 15th May 1919 at Westward Ho! together with the parent unit.

503 (SPECIAL DUTY) FLIGHT
Formed 6th June 1918 at Westward Ho! within 260 Squadron. Transferred to 250 Squadron from 15th August 1918.

D.H.6 C7422.

Disbanded 15th May 1919 at Westward Ho! together with the parent unit.

504 (SPECIAL DUTY) FLIGHT
Formed 31st May 1918 at Atwick within 251 Squadron.

D.H.6 B3061.

Disbanded 30th May 1919 together with the parent unit.

505 (SPECIAL DUTY) FLIGHT
Formed 31st May 1918 at Greenland Top within 251 Squadron.

D.H.6 B2784.

Disbanded 30th June 1919 at North Killingholme together with the parent unit.

506 (SPECIAL DUTY) FLIGHT
Formed 7th June 1918 at Owthorne within 251 Squadron.

Pup B2218; D.H.6 B3096.

Disbanded 30th June 1919 at North Killingholme together with the parent unit.

507 (SPECIAL DUTY) FLIGHT
Formed 24th May 1918 at Cramlington within 252 Squadron.

D.H.6 C2079 H.

Disbanded 30th June 1919 at North Killingholme together with the parent unit.

508 (SPECIAL DUTY) FLIGHT
Formed 24th May 1918 at Cramlington within 252 Squadron.

D.H.6 B2843.

Disbanded 30th June 1919 at North Killingholme together with the parent unit.

509 (SPECIAL DUTY) FLIGHT
Formed 7th June 1918 at Cramlington, also being known as 'D' Flight, within 252 Squadron.

D.H.6 B3018.

Disbanded 25th October 1919 at Cramlington together with the parent unit.

510 (SPECIAL DUTY) FLIGHT
Formed 7th June 1918 at Redcar, also being known as 'C' Flight, within 252 Squadron. Transferred to 251 Squadron from November 1918.

D.H.6 B2856.

Disbanded 30th June 1919 at Killingholme together with the parent unit.

511 (SPECIAL DUTY) FLIGHT
Formed 7th June 1918 at Brading within 253 Squadron.

D.H.6 C6897.

Disbanded 21st January 1919 at Bembridge within 253 Squadron.

512 (SPECIAL DUTY) FLIGHT
Formed 7th June 1918 at Brading within 253 Squadron.

D.H.6 C6897.

Disbanded 21st January 1919 at Bembridge within 253 Squadron.

513 (SPECIAL DUTY) FLIGHT
Formed 7th June 1918 at Chickerell, also being known as 'D' Flight, within 253 Squadron. Transferred to within 241 Squadron from 20th August 1918.

D.H.6 C6892.

Disbanded 23rd January 1919 at Chickerell and absorbed by the parent unit.

514 (SPECIAL DUTY) FLIGHT
Formed 7th June 1918 at Telscombe Cliffs, also being known as 'A' Flight, within 253 Squadron. Transferred to within 242 Squadron from 15th August 1918.

D.H.6 C6891.

Disbanded 20th January 1919 at Telscombe Cliffs and absorbed by the parent unit.

515 (SPECIAL DUTY) FLIGHT
Formed 6th June 1918 at Mullion within 254 Squadron. Transferred to within 236 Squadron from 20th August 1918.

D.H.6 C5740.

Disbanded 15th May 1919 at Mullion and absorbed by the parent unit.

516 (SPECIAL DUTY) FLIGHT
Formed 6th June 1918 at Mullion within 254 Squadron. Transferred to within 236 Squadron from 20th August 1918.

D.H.6 C6519.

Disbanded 15th May 1919 at Mullion and absorbed by the parent unit.

517 (SPECIAL DUTY) FLIGHT
Formed 6th June 1918 at Prawle Point within 254 Squadron.

D.H.6 B2856.

Disbanded 22nd February 1919 at Prawle Point together with the parent unit.

518 (SPECIAL DUTY) FLIGHT
Formed 6th June 1918 at Prawle Point within 254 Squadron.

D.H.6 C6514.

Disbanded 22nd February 1919 at Prawle Point together with the parent unit.

519 (SPECIAL DUTY) FLIGHT
Formed 6th June 1918 at Pembroke, also being known as 'A' Flight, within 255 Squadron.

D.H.6 B2903.

Disbanded 14th January 1919 at Pembroke together with the parent unit.

520 (SPECIAL DUTY) FLIGHT
Formed 6th June 1918 at Pembroke, also being known as 'B' Flight, within 255 Squadron.

D.H.6 B2771.

Disbanded 14th January 1919 at Pembroke together with the parent unit.

521 (SPECIAL DUTY) FLIGHT
Formed 6th June 1918 at Anglesey, also being known as 'A' Flight, within 255 Squadron. Transferred to 244 Squadron 25th July 1918.

D.H.6 B2791.

Disbanded 22nd January 1919 at Bangor together with the parent unit.

522 (SPECIAL DUTY) FLIGHT
Formed 6th June 1918 at Anglesey, also being known as 'B' Flight, within 255 Squadron. Transferred to 244 Squadron 25th July 1918.

D.H.6 B2937.

Disbanded 22nd January 1919 at Bangor together with the parent unit.

523 (SPECIAL DUTY) FLIGHT
Formed 6th June 1918 at Luce Bay, also being known as 'A' Flight, within 255 Squadron. Transferred to 258 Squadron from 15th August 1918.

Fairey IIIA N2850; D.H.6 B2960.

Disbanded 5th March 1919 at Luce Bay together with the parent unit.

524 (SPECIAL DUTY) FLIGHT
Formed 6th June 1918 at Luce Bay, also being known as 'B' Flight, within 255 Squadron. Transferred to 258 Squadron from 15th August 1918.

D.H.6 B2967.

Disbanded 5th March 1919 at Luce Bay together with the parent unit.

525 (SPECIAL DUTY) FLIGHT
Formed 6th June 1918 at Prawle Point within 254 Squadron.

D.H.6 B2972.

Disbanded 22nd February 1919 at Prawle Point together with the parent unit.

526 (SPECIAL DUTY) FLIGHT
Formed 30th May 1918 at New Haggerston, also being known as 'B' Flight, within 256 Squadron.

D.H.6 B3035.

Disbanded March 1919 at New Haggerston and absorbed by the parent unit.

527 (SPECIAL DUTY) FLIGHT
Formed 6th June 1918 at Seahouses, also being known as 'A' Flight, within 256 Squadron.

D.H.6 B2842.

Disbanded March 1919 at Killingholme and absorbed by the parent unit.

528 (SPECIAL DUTY) FLIGHT
Formed 6th June 1918 at Seahouses, also being known as 'C' Flight, within 256 Squadron.

D.H.6 B2819.

Disbanded March 1919 at Killingholme and absorbed by the parent unit.

529 (SPECIAL DUTY) FLIGHT
Formed 15th August 1918 at Luce Bay within 258 Squadron.

D.H.6 B2965.

Disbanded 5th March 1919 at Luce Bay together with the parent unit.

530 (SPECIAL DUTY) FLIGHT
Formed 15th August 1918 at Bangor, also being known as 'C' Flight, within 244 Squadron.

D.H.6 C7786.

Disbanded 22nd January 1919 at Bangor together with the parent unit.

531 (SPECIAL DUTY) FLIGHT
Formed 15th August 1918 at Machrihanish within 272 Squadron.

D.H.6 B2960.

Disbanded 5th March 1919 at Machrihanish together with the parent unit.

532 (SPECIAL DUTY) FLIGHT
Formed 15th August 1918 at Machrihanish within 272 Squadron.

D.H.6 B2964.

Disbanded 5th March 1919 at Machrihanish together with the parent unit.

533 (SPECIAL DUTY) FLIGHT
Formed 15th August 1918 at Machrihanish within 272 Squadron.

D.H.6 B2960.

Disbanded 5th March 1919 at Machrihanish together with the parent unit.

534 (LIGHT BOMBER) FLIGHT
Formed August 1918 at Covehithe, also being known as Temporary 'D' Flight, within 273 Squadron.

D.H.4 A8033; D.H.9 D1053.

Disbanded 14th March 1919 at Covehithe and absorbed by the parent unit.

550 (LIGHT BOMBER) FLIGHT
Formed September 1918 at Pizzone, Italy, within 227 Squadron.

Caproni Ca 4 proposed.

Disbanded 9th December 1918 at Pizzone together with the parent unit.

551 (LIGHT BOMBER) FLIGHT
Formed September 1918 at Pizzone, Italy, within 227 Squadron.

Caproni Ca 4 proposed.

Disbanded 9th December 1918 at Pizzone together with the parent unit.

552 (LIGHT BOMBER) FLIGHT
Formed September 1918 at Mudros, Greece, within 221 Squadron.

D.H.9A F1094 G.

Disbanded February 1919 at Petrovsk Zaskar, Russia, and absorbed by the parent unit.

553 (LIGHT BOMBER) FLIGHT
Formed September 1918 at Mudros, Greece, within 221 Squadron.

D.H.9 D2803 1.

Disbanded February 1919 at Petrovsk Zaskar, Russia, and absorbed by the parent unit.

554 (LIGHT BOMBER) FLIGHT
Formed September 1918 at Mudros, Greece, within 221 Squadron.

D.H.9.

Disbanded December 1918 at Mudros and absorbed by the parent unit.

555 (LIGHT BOMBER) FLIGHT
Formed 26th June 1918 at Manston and absorbed by 219 Squadron when it formed on 22nd July 1918.

D.H.9, D.H.9A.

Disbanded 17th July 1919 at Manston and absorbed by the parent unit.

556 (LIGHT BOMBER) FLIGHT
Formed 26th June 1918 at Manston and absorbed by 219 Squadron when it formed on 22nd July 1918.

D.H.9, D.H.9A.

Disbanded 17th July 1919 at Manston and absorbed by the parent unit.

557 (LIGHT BOMBER) FLIGHT
Formed 26th June 1918 at Yarmouth and absorbed by 212 Squadron on 20th August 1918.

D.H.9 D5709, D.H.9A F955.

Disbanded 9th February 1919 at Dover together with the parent unit.

558 (LIGHT BOMBER) FLIGHT
Formed 26th June 1918 at Yarmouth and absorbed by 212 Squadron on 20th August 1918.

D.H.9 D5793, D.H.9A F955.

Disbanded 9th February 1919 at Dover together with the parent unit.

559 (LIGHT BOMBER) FLIGHT
Formed September 1918 at Mudros within 223 Squadron.

D.H.9.

Disbanded 16th May 1919 at Mudros together with the parent unit.

560 (LIGHT BOMBER) FLIGHT
Formed September 1918 at Mudros within 223 Squadron.

D.H.9.

Disbanded 16th May 1919 at Mudros together with the parent unit.

561 (LIGHT BOMBER) FLIGHT
Formed September 1918 at Mudros within 223 Squadron.

D.H.9.

Disbanded 16th May 1919 at Mudros together with the parent unit.

562 (ANTI-SUBMARINE) FLIGHT
Formed August 1918 at Marsa Racecourse, Malta, within 17 (Malta) Wing.

D.H.9.

Disbanded 1st January 1919 at Marsa Racecourse.

ROYAL AIR FORCE NUMBERED FLIGHTS later FLEET AIR ARM OF THE ROYAL AIR FORCE NUMBERED FLIGHTS 1923 – 1936

From 1st April 1923 Royal Air Force aircraft carrier units were numbered in a new '400' series. From 1st April 1924 these Flights as well as naval Squadrons were known collectively as the Fleet Air Arm of the Royal Air Force.

401 (FLEET FIGHTER) FLIGHT, RAF, later 401 (FLEET FIGHTER) FLIGHT, FAA
Formed 1st April 1923 at Leuchars from an element of 203 Squadron. Redesignated 401 (Fleet Fighter) Flight, FAA from 1st April 1924.

Nightjar J6937; Flycatcher N9883 7; Nimrod I K2825 520.

Disbanded 3rd April 1933 at Netheravon to become 801 Squadron, FAA.

402 (FLEET FIGHTER) FLIGHT, RAF, later 402 (FLEET FIGHTER) FLIGHT, FAA
Formed 1st April 1923 at Leuchars from an element of 203 Squadron. Redesignated 402 (Fleet Fighter) Flight, FAA from 1st April 1924.

Flycatcher N9662 507; Nimrod I S1625 502; Armstrong Whitworth A.W.XVI S1591.

Disbanded 3rd April 1933 at Netheravon and merged with 404 (Fleet Fighter) Flight, FAA to become 800 Squadron, FAA.

403 (FLEET FIGHTER) FLIGHT, RAF, later 403 (FLEET FIGHTER) FLIGHT, FAA
Formed 1st June 1923 at Leuchars. Redesignated 403 (Fleet Fighter) Flight, FAA from 1st April 1924.

Nightjar H8537; Flycatcher N9961 9; Osprey III K3644 590; Walrus I K5780.

Disbanded 15th July 1936 at Kai Tak, Hong Kong, to become 715 (Catapult) Flight, FAA.

404 (FLEET FIGHTER) FLIGHT, RAF, later 404 (FLEET FIGHTER) FLIGHT, FAA
Formed 1st July 1923 at Leuchars. Redesignated 404 (Fleet Fighter) Flight, FAA from 1st April 1924.

Plover N9608; Nightjar J6933; Flycatcher N9905 6; Osprey I S1684 210, III K4333; Nimrod I S1623.

Disbanded 3rd April 1933 at Netheravon and merged with 402 (Fleet Fighter) Flight, FAA to become 800 Squadron, FAA.

405 (FLEET FIGHTER) FLIGHT, FAA
Formed 31st May 1924 at Leuchars.

Panther N7477; Plover N9704; Flycatcher N9909 19; Osprey I K2780 287.

Also used as trials aircraft – Nautilus N234 18; Fleetwing N235; Starling II J8028; Naval Hart J9052; Hornet J9682.

Disbanded 3rd April 1933 at Netheravon to become 803 Squadron, FAA.

406 (FLEET FIGHTER) FLIGHT, FAA
Formed 31st May 1924 at Leuchars.

Panther N7510; Flycatcher S1277 1; Osprey III K3630 304, IV K5750; Fairey IIIF S1548.

Disbanded 15th July 1936 at Seletar, Malaya, to become 714 (Catapult) Flight, FAA.

407 (FLEET FIGHTER) FLIGHT, FAA
Formed 1st September 1927 at Donibristle.

Flycatcher S1067; Osprey III K3918 201, IV K2775 201; Walrus I K5774.

Disbanded 15th July 1936 at Mount Batten to become 712 (Catapult) Flight, FAA.

408 (FLEET FIGHTER) FLIGHT, FAA
Formed 30th March 1929 at Donibristle.

Flycatcher S1293 19; Nimrod S1585 576.

Disbanded 3rd April 1933 aboard HMS *Glorious* and merged with 409 (Fleet Fighter) Flight, FAA to become 802 Squadron, FAA.

409 (FLEET FIGHTER) FLIGHT, FAA
Formed 7th October 1932 at Gosport.

Nimrod I S1632 562; Osprey S1687 549.

Disbanded 3rd April 1933 aboard HMS *Glorious* and merged with 408 (Fleet Fighter) Flight, FAA to become 802 Squadron, FAA.

420 (FLEET SPOTTER) FLIGHT, RAF, later 420 (FLEET SPOTTER) FLIGHT, FAA
Formed 1st April 1923 at Gosport from an element of 3 Squadron, RAF. Redesignated 420 (Fleet Spotter) Flight, FAA from 1st April 1924.

D.H.9A J6959; Walrus N9505; Blackburn I N9829, II S1048 23.

Disbanded 26th April 1929 aboard HMS *Furious* to become 449 (Fleet Spotter Reconnaissance) Flight, FAA.

421 (FLEET SPOTTER) FLIGHT, RAF, later 421 (FLEET SPOTTER) FLIGHT, FAA
Formed 1st April 1923 at Gosport from an element of 3 Squadron, RAF. Redesignated 421 (Fleet Spotter) Flight, FAA from 1st April 1924.

D.H.9A J6959; Walrus N9526; Bison I N9598, II N9849 36; Panther N7409; Fairey IIID N9770, Fairey IIIF S1189 36.

Disbanded 26th April 1929 aboard HMS *Furious* to become 447 (Fleet Spotter Reconnaissance) Flight, FAA.

422 (FLEET SPOTTER) FLIGHT, RAF, later 422 (FLEET SPOTTER) FLIGHT, FAA
Formed 1st April 1923 at Gosport from an element of 3 Squadron, RAF. Redesignated 422 (Fleet Spotter) Flight, FAA from 1st April 1924.

Walrus N9507; Fairey IIID S1008; Blackburn I N9682, II N9826 27.

Disbanded 26th April 1929 aboard HMS *Argus* to become 450 (Fleet Spotter Reconnaissance) Flight, FAA.

423 (FLEET SPOTTER) FLIGHT, RAF, later 423 (FLEET SPOTTER) FLIGHT, FAA
Formed 21st November 1923 at Gosport. Redesignated 423 (Fleet Spotter) Flight, FAA from 1st April 1924.

Walrus N9502; Bison I N9602 1, II N9848 21.

Disbanded 26th April 1929 aboard HMS *Eagle* to become 448 (Fleet Spotter Reconnaissance) Flight, FAA.

440 (FLEET RECONNAISSANCE) FLIGHT, RAF, later 440 (FLEET RECONNAISSANCE) FLIGHT, FAA
Formed 1st May 1923 at Leuchars from an element of 205 Squadron, RAF. Redesignated 440 (Fleet Reconnaissance) Flight, FAA from 1st April 1924.

Seagull III N9647 41; Fairey IIID S1002 43, Fairey IIIF S1253 43.

Disbanded 11th June 1933 at Kai Tak, Hong Kong, and absorbed by 824 Squadron, FAA.

441 (FLEET RECONNAISSANCE) FLIGHT, RAF, later 441 (FLEET RECONNAISSANCE) FLIGHT, FAA

Formed 1st April 1923 at Leuchars from an element of 205 Squadron, RAF. Redesignated 441 (Fleet Reconnaissance) Flight, FAA from 1st April 1924.

Panther N9497; Fairey IIID N9774 47, Fairey IIIF S1332 31.

Disbanded 3rd April 1933 aboard HMS *Glorious* and merged with 448 (Fleet Spotter Reconnaissance) Flight to become 823 Squadron, FAA.

442 (FLEET RECONNAISSANCE) FLIGHT, RAF, later 442 (FLEET RECONNAISSANCE) FLIGHT, FAA

Formed 1st April 1923 at Leuchars from an element of 205 Squadron, RAF. Redesignated 442 (Fleet Reconnaissance) Flight, FAA from 1st April 1924.

Panther N7527; Flycatcher N9922 5; Fairey IIID S1018 52, Fairey IIIF S1342 35.

Disbanded 3rd April 1933 at Netheravon and merged with 449 (Fleet Spotter Reconnaissance) Flight to become 822 Squadron, FAA.

443 (FLEET RECONNAISSANCE) FLIGHT, RAF, later 443 (FLEET RECONNAISSANCE) FLIGHT, FAA.

Formed 21st May 1923 at Leuchars. Redesignated 443 (Fleet Reconnaissance) Flight, FAA from 1st April 1924.

Fairey IIID S1075 51, Fairey IIIF S1189 36; Osprey III K5755, IV K5745.

Disbanded 15th July 1936 at Mount Batten and divided to become 716 and 718 (Catapult) Flights, FAA.

444 (FLEET RECONNAISSANCE) FLIGHT, FAA

Formed 15th January 1925 at Lee-on-Solent.

Fairey IIID S1084, Fairey IIIF S1509 719; Seal K3479 719; Seagull V N-2; Osprey III K3634; Walrus I K5778; Shark II K5624 091; Swordfish I K5931 092.

Disbanded 15th July 1936 at Kalafrana, Malta, and divided to become 701 and 705 (Catapult) Flights, FAA.

445 (FLEET RECONNAISSANCE) FLIGHT, FAA, later 445 (FLEET SPOTTER RECONNAISSANCE) FLIGHT, FAA

Formed 1st September 1927 at Leuchars.

Fairey IIID S1108 40, IIIF S1225 56.

Disbanded 3rd April 1933 at Gosport, with half of the unit merging with 450 (Fleet Spotter Reconnaissance) Flight to form 820 Squadron, FAA and the other half of the unit merging with 446 (Fleet Reconnaissance) Flight to become 821 Squadron, FAA.

Reformed 30th August 1935 as 445 (Fleet Spotter Reconnaissance) Flight, FAA.

Osprey III K4322 079.

Disbanded 15th July 1936 at Mount Batten to become 713 (Catapult) Flight, FAA.

446 (FLEET RECONNAISSANCE) FLIGHT, FAA

Formed 1st September 1927 at Leuchars.

Fairey IIIF S1261 41.

Disbanded 3rd April 1933 at Gosport and merged with half of 445 (Fleet Reconnaissance) Flight, FAA to become 821 Squadron, FAA.

447 (FLEET SPOTTER RECONNAISSANCE) FLIGHT, FAA

Formed 26th April 1929 aboard HMS *Furious* by redesignating 421 (Fleet Spotter) Flight, FAA.

Fairey IIIF S1403 42; Osprey III K3642 067; Swordfish I K5926.

Disbanded 15th July 1936 at Kalafrana, Malta, and divided to form the basis of 701 and 711 (Catapult) Flights, FAA.

448 (FLEET SPOTTER RECONNAISSANCE) FLIGHT, FAA

Formed 26th April 1929 aboard HMS *Eagle* by redesignating 423 (Fleet Spotter) Flight, FAA.

Fairey IIIF S1343 57.

Disbanded 3rd April 1933 aboard HMS *Glorious* and merged with 441 (Fleet Reconnaissance) Flight, FAA to become 823 Squadron, FAA.

449 (FLEET SPOTTER RECONNAISSANCE) FLIGHT, FAA

Formed 26th April 1929 aboard HMS *Furious* by redesignating 420 (Fleet Spotter) Flight, FAA.

Blackburn II S1157 28; Fairey IIIF S1515 740.

Disbanded 3rd April 1933 at Netheravon and merged with 442 (Fleet Reconnaissance) Flight, FAA to become 822 Squadron, FAA.

450 (FLEET SPOTTER RECONNAISSANCE) FLIGHT, FAA

Formed 26th April 1929 by redesignating 422 (Fleet Spotter) Flight, FAA.

Blackburn II N9825 53; Fairey IIIF S1259 745.

Disbanded 3rd April 1933 at Gosport and merged with half of 445 (Fleet Reconnaissance) Flight, FAA to become 820 Squadron, FAA.

460 (FLEET TORPEDO) FLIGHT, RAF, later 460 (FLEET TORPEDO) FLIGHT, FAA

Formed 1st April 1923 at Gosport from an element of 210 Squadron. Redesignated 460 (Fleet Torpedo) Flight, FAA from 1st April 1924.

Dart N9811 61; Ripon S1430 83; Fairey IIIF S1820 82.

Disbanded 3rd April 1933 at Gosport to become 824 Squadron, FAA.

461 (FLEET TORPEDO) FLIGHT, RAF, later 461 (FLEET TORPEDO) FLIGHT, FAA

Formed 1st April 1923 at Gosport from an element of 210 Squadron. Redesignated 461 (Fleet Torpedo) Flight, FAA from 1st April 1924.

Dart N9823 60; Ripon S1364 61.

Disbanded 3rd April 1933 aboard HMS *Glorious* and merged with 462 (Fleet Torpedo) Flight, FAA to become 812 Squadron, FAA.

462 (FLEET TORPEDO) FLIGHT, FAA

Formed 31st May 1924 at Gosport.

Dart N9803 73; Ripon S1267 73; Baffin S1662 72.

Disbanded 3rd April 1933 at Gosport and merged with 461 (Fleet Torpedo) Flight, FAA to become 812 Squadron, FAA.

463 (FLEET TORPEDO) FLIGHT, FAA

Formed 1st September 1927 at Gosport

Dart N9803 08.

Disbanded 3rd April 1933 at Gosport and merged with 464 (Fleet Torpedo) Flight, FAA to become 810 Squadron, FAA.

464 (FLEET TORPEDO) FLIGHT, FAA

Formed 1st September 1927 at Gosport.

Dart N9815 72.

Disbanded 3rd April 1933 at Gosport and merged with 463 (Fleet Torpedo) Flight, FAA to become 810 Squadron, FAA.

465 (FLEET TORPEDO) FLIGHT, FAA

Formed 20th March 1931 at Gosport.

Ripon S1569 9.

Disbanded 3rd April 1933 at Gosport and merged with 466 (Fleet Torpedo) Flight, FAA to become 811 Squadron, FAA.

466 (FLEET TORPEDO) FLIGHT, FAA

Formed 31st March 1931 at Gosport.

Ripon S1560 14; Osprey K3635.

Disbanded 3rd April 1933 at Gosport and merged with 465 (Fleet Torpedo) Flight, FAA to become 811 Squadron, FAA.

FLEET AIR ARM OF THE ROYAL AIR FORCE NUMBERED FLIGHTS 1936 – 1939

From 15th July 1936 catapult units, originating from some units within the earlier '400' series, were renumbered in a new '700' series. These Flights, as well as naval Squadrons, were known collectively as the Fleet Air Arm of the Royal Air Force until 24th May 1939 when the Royal Navy assumed responsibility for personnel, aircraft and establishments of the Fleet Air Arm.

701 (CATAPULT) FLIGHT, FAA
Formed 15th July 1936 at Kalafrana, Malta, by redesignating part of 444 (Fleet Reconnaissance) Flight, FAA.

Osprey K3640 073; Fairey IIIF S1809 072; Shark K4362; Seal II; Swordfish I Seaplane K8446 075.

Disbanded 24th May 1939 at Kalafrana to become 701 Squadron, FAA.

702 (CATAPULT) FLIGHT, FAA
Formed 15th July 1936 at Mount Batten.

Seal; Walrus I K5778.

Disbanded 24th May 1939 at Lee-on-Solent to become 701 Squadron, FAA.

705 (CATAPULT) FLIGHT, FAA
Formed 15th July 1936 at Kalafrana, Malta, by redesignating part of 444 (Fleet Reconnaissance) Flight, FAA.

Shark II Seaplane K8506; Walrus I; Swordfish I K5931 092.

Disbanded 24th May 1939 at Kalafrana to become 705 Squadron, FAA.

711 (CATAPULT) FLIGHT, FAA
Formed 15th July 1936 at Kalafrana, Malta, by redesignating part of 447 (Fleet Reconnaissance) Flight, FAA.

Osprey III Seaplane K3641 071; Walrus I L2221 068.

Disbanded 24th May 1939 at Kalafrana to become 711 Squadron, FAA.

712 (CATAPULT) FLIGHT, FAA
Formed 15th July 1936 at Mount Batten by redesignating 407 (Fleet Fighter) Flight, FAA.

Osprey III Seaplane K3918 034; Walrus L2180 038.

Disbanded 24th May 1939 at Lee-on-Solent to become 712 Squadron, FAA.

713 (CATAPULT) FLIGHT, FAA
Formed 15th July 1936 at Kalafrana, Malta, by redesignating 445 (Fleet Reconnaissance) Flight, FAA.

Osprey III Seaplane K5758; Seafox I K8580.

Disbanded 24th May 1939 at Kalafrana to become 713 Squadron, FAA.

714 (CATAPULT) FLIGHT, FAA
Formed 15th July 1936 at Seletar, Malaya, by redesignating 406 (Fleet Fighter) Flight, FAA.

Fairey IIIF S1548; Osprey III Seaplane K4330; Seafox I K8572; Walrus I.

Disbanded 24th May 1939 at Seletar to become 714 Squadron, FAA.

715 (CATAPULT) FLIGHT, FAA
Formed 15th July 1936 at Kai Tak, Hong Kong, by redesignating 403 (Fleet Fighter) Flight, FAA.

Osprey III Seaplane K3645; Walrus I L2213 WR.

Disbanded 24th May 1939 at Kai Tak to become 715 Squadron, FAA.

716 (CATAPULT) FLIGHT, FAA
Formed 15th July 1936 at Mount Batten by redesignating part of 443 (Fleet Reconnaissance) Flight, FAA.

Osprey IV Seaplane K5748; Seafox I K8590.

Disbanded 24th May 1939 at Lee-on-Solent to become 716 Squadron, FAA.

718 (CATAPULT) FLIGHT, FAA
Formed 15th July 1936 at Bermuda by redesignating part of 443 (Fleet Reconnaissance) Flight, FAA.

Fairey IIIF S1859 780; Osprey III Seaplane K5746; Walrus I K8341 780; Seafox I K8571.

Disbanded 24th May 1939 at Bermuda to become 718 Squadron, FAA.

720 (CATAPULT) FLIGHT, FAA
Formed 15th July 1936 at Mount Batten.

Walrus I K5774 Z-2.

Disbanded 24th May 1939 at Auckland, New Zealand, to become 720 Squadron, FAA.

ROYAL AIR FORCE NUMBERED FLIGHTS FROM 1940

160 SPECIAL FLIGHT – see 159 Squadron

401 (METEOROLOGICAL) FLIGHT
Formed 4th February 1941 at Mildenhall by redesignating the Royal Air Force Meteorological Flight, Mildenhall.

Gladiator II N5621.

Disbanded 1st March 1941 at Mildenhall to become 1401 (Meteorological) Flight.

402 (METEOROLOGICAL) FLIGHT
Formed 15th January 1941 at Aldergrove by redesignating 'C' Flight, Aldergrove Station Flight, previously the Air Ministry Meteorological Flight, Aldergrove.

Gladiator II N5591.

Disbanded 1st March 1941 at Aldergrove to become 1402 (Meteorological) Flight.

403 (METEOROLOGICAL) FLIGHT
Formed November 1940 at Bircham Newton.

Blenheim IV V5569.

Disbanded 1st March 1941 at Bircham Newton to become 1403 (Meteorological) Flight.

404 (METEOROLOGICAL) FLIGHT
Formed 24th December 1940 at St Eval.

Blenheim IV Z5961.

Disbanded 1st March 1941 at St Eval to become 1404 (Meteorological) Flight.

405 (METEOROLOGICAL) FLIGHT
Formed February 1941 at Aldergrove.

Blenheim IV V5691.

Disbanded 1st March 1941 at Aldergrove to become 1405 (Meteorological) Flight.

416 (ARMY CO-OPERATION) FLIGHT
Formed 1st March 1940 at Hawkinge.

Lysander II L4788.

Disbanded 31st March 1940 at Hawkinge.

Reformed 17th April 1940 at Hawkinge.

Lysander II N1264.

Disbanded 1st July 1940 at Aldergrove to become 231 Squadron.

417 (GENERAL RECONNAISSANCE) FLIGHT
Formed 15th July 1940 at St Athan.

Anson I.

Disbanded 1st March 1941 at St Athan to become 1417 (General Reconnaissance) Flight.

418 (FIGHTER) FLIGHT
Formed 18th July 1940 at Abbotsinch.

Hurricane I N2622; Skua I L2969.

Disbanded 5th August 1940 at Luqa, Malta, and merged with the Fighter Flight, Malta to become 261 Squadron.

419 (SPECIAL DUTIES) FLIGHT
Formed 21st August 1940 at North Weald.

Lysander III R9027; Whitley V P5025.

Disbanded 1st March 1941 at Stradishall to become 1419 (Special Duties) Flight.

420 ('PANDORA') FLIGHT
Formed 25th September 1940 at Christchurch.

Harrow I K6963, II K7020; Battle P5248; Wellington IC W5668; Boston III (Turbinlite) Z2160; Mentor L4404.

Disbanded 7th December 1940 at Middle Wallop to become 93 Squadron.

421 (RECONNAISSANCE) FLIGHT
Formed 8th October 1940 at Gravesend by redesignating an element of 66 Squadron.

LZ (10.40-1.41)   Hurricane IIA Z2312 LZ-H; Spitfire IIA P7735 LZ-M. DL (1.41)   Spitfire IIA P7382 DL-K.

Disbanded 11th January 1941 at Hawkinge to become 91 Squadron.

422 (FIGHTER INTERCEPTION) FLIGHT
Formed 14th October 1940 at Shoreham.

Hurricane I P8813; Hornet Moth X9447.

Disbanded 18th December 1940 at Cranage to become 96 Squadron.

430 (ARMY CO-OPERATION) FLIGHT
Formed 3rd August 1940 at Khartoum, Sudan, by redesignating 'D' Flight of 47 Squadron.

Vincent K4657; Gauntlet II K5265.

Disbanded 1st March 1941 at Sufeiya, Sudan, to become 1430 (Army Co-operation) Flight.

431 (GENERAL RECONNAISSANCE) FLIGHT
Formed August 1940 at North Coates by redesignating an element of 'C' Flight, 22 Squadron. Absorbed 3 Anti-Aircraft Co-operation Unit on arrival at Luqa, Malta, on 19th September 1940.

Maryland I AR712; Blenheim IV T2115; Skua L2882.

Disbanded 10th January 1941 at Luqa to become 69 Squadron.

1300 (METEOROLOGICAL) FLIGHT, later 1300 (METEOROLOGICAL THUM) FLIGHT, later 1300 (METEOROLOGICAL RECONNAISSANCE) FLIGHT
Formed 31st July 1943 at Alipore, India, by redesignating 1 Meteorological Flight. Later redesignated 1300 (Meteorological Thum) Flight.

Blenheim IV Z9811; Hurricane IIC LF201, IID KW879, IV KZ248; Spitfire XI PL920.

Disbanded 30th May 1946 at Kallang, Malaya.

Reformed 1st June 1946 at Mingaladon, Burma as 1300 (Meteorological Reconnaissance) Flight.

Mosquito VI TE595; Harvard IIB FS923.

Disbanded 15th March 1947 at Butterworth, Malaya, to become 18 Squadron.

1301 (METEOROLOGICAL) FLIGHT
Formed 31st July 1943 at Delhi, India, by redesignating 2 Meteorological Flight.

Blenheim IV Z7350; Hurricane IID HW720, IIC HW477.

Disbanded 1st June 1946 at Nagpur, India.

Reformed 14th June 1949 at Negombo, Ceylon, by redesignating the Brigand Flight of 45 Squadron.

Brigand MET.3 VS817; Harvard IIB FT186.

Disbanded 30th November 1951 at Negombo.

1302 (METEOROLOGICAL) FLIGHT
Formed 31st July 1943 at Yelahanka, India, by redesignating 3 Meteorological Flight.

Blenheim IV Z7611; Wellington IC HX773; Hurricane IIC LD402, IID KX243.

Disbanded 28th May 1946 at Bangalore, India.

1303 (METEOROLOGICAL) FLIGHT
Formed 31st July 1943 at Ratmalana, Ceylon, by redesignating 4 Meteorological Flight.

Blenheim IV Z9706; Hurricane IIC LD242 S, IID HW796 K.

Disbanded 30th April 1946 at Negombo, Ceylon.

1310 (TRANSPORT) FLIGHT, later 1310 FLIGHT, later 1310 (TACTICAL SUPPORT) FLIGHT
Formed 10th April 1944 at Llandow as 1310 (Transport) Flight.

| Nil | Anson I NK451. |
| WK | Allocated but no evidence of use. |

Disbanded 21st July 1944 at Bognor and absorbed by 83 Group Support Unit.

Reformed 31st March 1953 at Lyneham as 1310 (Transport) Flight.

York I MW253.

Disbanded 7th December 1953 at Mellala, Australia.

Reformed 23rd July 1964 at Odiham as 1310 Flight.

Whirlwind HAR.10 XJ757; Twin Pioneer CC.2 XP295.

Disbanded 14th October 1966 at Atkinson Field, British Guyana.

Reformed 20th August 1983 at Kelly's Garden, Falkland Islands, as 1310 (Tactical Support) Flight by redesignating elements of 7 and 18 Squadrons.

Chinook HC.1 ZA707 A.

Disbanded 1st May 1986 at Mount Pleasant, Falklands, and merged with 1564 (Tactical Support) Flight to become 78 Squadron.

Reformed December 1995 at Split, Croatia.

Chinook HC.1 drawn from 7 and 18 Squadrons.

Current 1st April 1998 at Split.

1311 (TRANSPORT) FLIGHT
Formed 19th April 1944 at Llandow as 1311 (Transport) Flight.

Anson I MG471, X NK658.

Disbanded 21st July 1944 at Thruxton and absorbed by 84 Group Support Unit.

Reformed 1st September 1953 at Seletar, Singapore.

Auster VI TW535; Pioneer CC.1 XE512.

Disbanded 15th February 1954 at Noble Field, Malaya, to become the Supply Flight of 267 Squadron.

1312 (TRANSPORT) FLIGHT, later 1312 (TRANSPORT SUPPORT) FLIGHT, later 1312 (IN-FLIGHT REFUELLING) FLIGHT
Formed 19th April 1944 at Llandow as 1312 (Transport) Flight.

Anson I NK692, X NK696.

Disbanded 21st July 1944 at Llandow.

Reformed 14th September 1954 at Abingdon as 1312 (Transport Support) Flight by redesignating the Transport Command Air Support Flight.

Hastings C.1 TG615 L, C.2 WD485; Valetta C.1 VL274.

Disbanded 1st April 1957 at Abingdon.

Reformed 20th August 1983 at Stanley, Falklands Islands, as 1312 (In-Flight Refuelling) Flight.

Hercules C.1K XV192; VC10 K.4 ZD242.

Current 1st April 1998 at Mount Pleasant.

1314 (TRANSPORT) FLIGHT
Formed 4th August 1944 at Accra, Gold Coast, from the Dakota Flight of 55 Staging Post.

Hudson VI FK536; Dakota I FD782, III KG675, IV KN646; Anson I LT597, XII PH674.

Disbanded 1st November 1945 at Accra, Gold Coast, and merged with the West Africa Command Communication Squadron to become the West Africa Transport and Communication Squadron.

1315 (TRANSPORT) FLIGHT
Formed 1st January 1945 at Merryfield by redesignating an element of 232 Squadron.

Dakota III FD870, IV KN344; Auster V TJ307; Harvard IIB KF131; Anson XIX VL336; Liberator VII EW631.

Disbanded 21st August 1946 at Iwakuni, Japan, and absorbed by the Air Component British Commonwealth Forces.

1316 (DUTCH) FLIGHT, later 1316 (TRANSPORT) FLIGHT
Formed 7th July 1944 at Hendon by redesignating 'B' Flight (Allied Flight) of the Metropolitan Communication Squadron. Later redesignated 1316 (Transport) Flight.

WK – Allocated but no evidence of use.
DC-2 NL203 (call sign); DC-3 NL202 (call sign); Dakota III NL208 (call sign), IV NL205 (call sign); Beech D-17S PB1 (call sign), C-17S PB2 (call sign); Lockheed 12A NF753; Auster III NX537.

Disbanded 4th March 1946 at Hendon.

1317 (TRAINING) FLIGHT
Formed 13th June 1945 at Woodhall Spa.

Lancaster III ND823; Mosquito IX ML914, XVI PF499.

Disbanded 27th June 1945 at Woodhall Spa.

1318 (COMMUNICATION) FLIGHT
Formed 1944 at Nassau, Bahamas.

No aircraft known.

Disbanded May 1946 at Nassau.

1320 ('ABDULLAH') FLIGHT
Formed 8th May 1944 at Holmsley South by redesignating an element of the Fighter Interception Unit.

Typhoon IB MN296.

Disbanded 14th June 1944 at Holmsley South.

1321 BOMBER (DEFENCE) TRAINING FLIGHT, later 1321 (VALIANT/BLUE DANUBE TRIALS) FLIGHT, later 1321 FLIGHT
Formed 1st September 1944 at Bottesford as 1321 Bomber (Defence) Training Flight.

Hurricane IIC PZ735.

Disbanded 1st November 1944 at Bottesford and absorbed by 1668 and 1669 Heavy Conversion Units.

Reformed 3rd August 1954 at Wittering as 1321 (Valiant/Blue Danube Trials) Flight.

Valiant B.1 WP201.

Disbanded 15th March 1956 at Wittering to become 'C' Flight of 138 Squadron.

Reformed 1st October 1957 at Hemswell as 1321 Flight by merging Antler and Arrow Squadrons.

Lincoln B.2 SX951; Canberra B.2 WJ616.

Disbanded 31st March 1958 at Hemswell and absorbed by the Bomber Command Bombing School.

1322 (AIR DESPATCH LETTER SERVICE) FLIGHT
Formed 23rd October 1944 at Northolt by redesignating the Anson element of 1697 (Air Despatch Letter Service) Flight.

Anson I NK566, X NK490.

Disbanded 24th December 1944 at Northolt to become the Air Despatch Letter Service Squadron.

1323 (AUTOMATIC GUN LAYING TRAINING) FLIGHT, later 1323 (CANBERRA) FLIGHT
Formed 29th November 1944 at Bourn as 1323 (Automatic Gun Laying Training) Flight.

QF   Lancaster III NE142 QF-H.

Disbanded 30th September 1945 at Warboys.

Reformed 20th October 1953 at Wyton as 1323 (Canberra) Flight by redesignating the 2nd Tactical Air Force Development Unit.

Canberra B.2 WH695.

Disbanded 1st November 1955 at Wyton to become 542 Squadron.

1325 (TRANSPORT) FLIGHT
Formed 1st August 1956 at Dishforth.

Dakota IV KJ945.

Disbanded 1st May 1960 at Changi, Singapore.

1340 (SPECIAL DUTIES) FLIGHT, later 1340 (ANTI-MAU MAU) FLIGHT
Formed 25th September 1944 at Sulur, India, as 1340 (Special Duties) Flight.

Vengeance III FB986; IV FD275; Thunderbolt II HD195 F; Mosquito XVI RG140; Harvard IIB FS715.

Disbanded 31st March 1946 at Cannanore, India.

Reformed 23rd March 1953 at Eastleigh, Kenya, as 1340 (Anti-Mau Mau) Flight from an element of the Rhodesian Air Training Group, Thornhill.

H   Harvard IIB FX265 H-83; Auster VI VF579.

Disbanded 30th September 1955 at Eastleigh.

1341 (SPECIAL DUTIES) FLIGHT, later 1341 (RADIO COUNTERMEASURES) FLIGHT
Formed 1st June 1944 at Abingdon. Redesignated 1341 (Radio Countermeasures) Flight from 15th May 1945.

Halifax III PN369 A, VII NA397; Liberator VI.

Disbanded 30th October 1945 at Raipur, India, and absorbed by 52 Squadron.

1342 (ROCKET PROJECTILE TRAINING) FLIGHT
Formed February 1945 at Shallufa, Egypt.

Hurricane IIC LB928, IV LD216; Harvard IIA EX102.

Disbanded 20th November 1945 at El Ballah, Egypt.

1343 (CONVERSION) FLIGHT
Formed February 1945 at Shallufa, Egypt.

Baltimore V FW817; Wellington X LP778.

Disbanded 1st October 1945 at Ballah, Egypt.

1344 (SPECIAL SIGNALS) FLIGHT
Formed 20th January 1945 at Gujrat, India.

Hurricane IIC LB734, IID KX120, IV KZ710.

Disbanded 6th December 1945 at Sambre, India.

1345 (ANTI-MALARIAL) FLIGHT
Formed 1st May 1945 at Port Reitz, Kenya, by redesignating the Baltimore element of the East Africa Communication Flight.

Baltimore IV FA518; V FW804.

Disbanded 20th September 1946 at Port Reitz.

1346 (AIR SEA RESCUE) FLIGHT
Formed 15th June 1945 at Kankesanturai, Ceylon, by redesignating
1 Air Sea Rescue Flight (Far East).

Warwick I HF975; Liberator VI EV967.

Disbanded 20th April 1946 at Kankesanturai.

1347 (AIR SEA RESCUE) FLIGHT
Formed 15th June 1945 at Agartala, India, by redesignating 2 Air
Sea Rescue Flight (Far East).

*Warwick I BV477; Liberator VI EV831 M; Lancaster ASR.III RF320
B.*

Disbanded 30th May 1946 at Chittagong, India.

1348 (AIR SEA RESCUE) FLIGHT
Formed 15th June 1945 at Agartala, India, by redesignating 3 Air
Sea Rescue Flight (Far East).

*Warwick I; Liberator B.VI KH269 K; Beaufighter X LZ276; Lancaster
ASR.III RF310.*

Disbanded 15th May 1946 at Pegu, Burma.

1349 (AIR SEA RESCUE) FLIGHT
Formed 15th June 1945 at Agartala, India, by redesignating 4 Air
Sea Rescue Flight (Far East).

Warwick I BV479; Liberator V BZ829, VI BZ983.

Disbanded 15th May 1946 at Mauripur, India.

1350 (AIR SEA RESCUE) FLIGHT
Formed 15th June 1945 at Ratmalana, Ceylon, by redesignating 5
Air Sea Rescue Flight (Far East).

*Walrus I W3038, II HD808; Sea Otter I JM758; Hurricane IIC
LD242; IID KW696.*

Disbanded 7th November 1945 at Ratmalana, Ceylon.

1351 (AIR SEA RESCUE) FLIGHT
Formed 15th June 1945 at Cox's Bazaar, India, by redesignating 'E'
Flight, 292 Squadron.

Sea Otter I JM768.

Disbanded 25th January 1946 at Patenga, India

1352 (AIR SEA RESCUE) FLIGHT
Formed 10th September 1945 at China Bay, Ceylon.

Sea Otter I JM914; Spitfire XVI TB998.

Disbanded officially 20th November 1945 at Kallang, Singapore, but
remained operational until 18th June 1946.

1353 (ANTI-AIRCRAFT CO-OPERATION) FLIGHT
Formed 26th June 1945 at West Freugh by redesignating an
element of the disbanding 289 Squadron.

*Vengeance TT.IV FD335; Spitfire VB BL530, VC AB524, XVI
TB904; Hurricane IIC LF682; Oxford I HN169.*

Disbanded 15th June 1946 at Turnhouse.

**1354 (DDT SPRAYING) FLIGHT, later 1354 (SPECIAL DUTIES)
FLIGHT, later 1354 SPRAY (INSECTICIDE) FLIGHT**
Formed 1st July 1945 at Digri, India, by redesignating the DDT
Spray Flight. Redesignated 1354 (Special Duties) Flight from
September 1945 then 1354 Spray (Insecticide) Flight from
November 1945.

Liberator VI KH355; Auster.

Disbanded 15th February 1946 Pegu, Burma.

1355 (COMMUNICATIONS) FLIGHT
Formed 18th May 1945 at Baigachi, India.

Sentinel proposed but no evidence of aircraft being allocated.

Disbanded September 1945 at Baigachi.

1356 (COMMUNICATIONS) FLIGHT
Formed 18th May 1945 at Baigachi, India.

Sentinel proposed but no evidence of aircraft being allocated.

Disbanded September 1945 at Baigachi.

1357 (PAMPA) FLIGHT
Formed 25th January 1946 at Luqa, Malta.

Mosquito XVI proposed but no aircraft allocated.

Disbanded 10th April 1946 at Luqa.

1358 (PAMPA) FLIGHT
Formed 25th January 1946 at Shaibah, Iraq.

Mosquito XVI proposed but no aircraft allocated.

Disbanded 10th April 1946 at Shaibah.

1359 (VIP TRANSPORT) FLIGHT
Formed 1st December 1945 at Lyneham.

ZW   *York VVIP.I MW100, VIP I MW101, I MW128;
Lancastrian C.2 VL970.*

Disbanded 30th June 1946 at Bassingbourn and absorbed by 24
Squadron.

**1360 (METEOROLOGICAL) FLIGHT, later 1360 (HELICOPTER)
FLIGHT**
Planned formation from January 1946 with Mosquito XVI at
Mauripur, India, cancelled.

Formed 1st August 1957 at St. Mawgan as 1360 (Helicopter) Flight
by redesignating 'X' Flight, 22 Squadron.

Whirlwind HAR.10 XD164.

Disbanded 1st February 1958 at St Mawgan to become 217
Squadron.

1361 (METEOROLOGICAL) FLIGHT
Formed 16th January 1946 at Aldergrove.

Halifax VI RG778, VIII PP282.

Disbanded 11th February 1946 at Aldergrove and absorbed by 521
Squadron.

1362 (METEOROLOGICAL) FLIGHT
Formed 16th January 1946 at Aldergrove.

Halifax VII proposed but none allocated.

Disbanded 11th February 1946 at Aldergrove.

Reformed October 1955 at Weston Zoyland.

Whirlwind HAR.2 XJ726.

Disbanded January 1958 at Maralinga, Australia.

1363 (METEOROLOGICAL) FLIGHT
Formed 16th January 1946 at Aldergrove.

Halifax VII proposed but none allocated.

Disbanded 11th February 1946 at Aldergrove.

1364 (METEOROLOGICAL) FLIGHT
Formed 16th January 1946 at Aldergrove.

Halifax VII proposed but none allocated.

Disbanded 11th February 1946 at Aldergrove.

1401 (METEOROLOGICAL) FLIGHT
Formed 1st March 1941 at Mildenhall by redesignating 401
(Meteorological) Flight.

*Gladiator II N5621 D; Spitfire I P9550, IIA P7546, IV BP931, V
X4503, VA P9550, VI R6905; Hurricane I V7225; Hampden I
P1353; Blenheim IV V5570; Hudson III T9438; Mosquito IV DZ406;
Tiger Moth II N6751; Master I T8617, II W9086 Y.*

Disbanded 22nd July 1942 at Bircham Newton to become 521
Squadron.

Reformed 1st April 1943 at Manston by redesignating an element of
521 Squadron.

TE ( )   *Hurricane IV KZ675 TE.*

BN (.43- .45)   Spitfire IX TA825 BN-S, XI PL913.
Also used   Spitfire VI BR287 G; Auster IV MT165.

Disbanded 28th June 1946 at Celle, Germany.

1402 (METEOROLOGICAL) FLIGHT
Formed 1st March 1941 at Aldergrove by redesignating 402 (Meteorological) Flight.

Gladiator I K7927, II N5620; Blenheim IV Z7345; Hampden I P1196; Hudson III V9156, IIIA FH404; Spitfire VA P8036, VI BR298, VII MD181; Hurricane IIC PG469.

Disbanded 18th September 1945 at Aldergrove and absorbed by 518 Squadron at Ballykelly.

Reformed 4th December 1945 at Langham by redesignating the Hurricane Flight of 521 Squadron.

DQ   Hurricane IIC PZ819; Master II DL414 DQ-R.

Disbanded 10th May 1946 at Langham.

1403 (METEOROLOGICAL) FLIGHT
Formed 1st March 1941 at Bircham Newton by redesignating 403 (Meteorological) Flight.

Blenheim IV Z7355; Hudson III V9161, IIIA FH384.

Disbanded 7th February 1942 at Bircham Newton and absorbed by 1401 (Meteorological) Flight.

Reformed May 1943 at North Front, Gibraltar.

Gladiator II N5630; Hudson IIIA FH384; Hampden I L4165; Hereford L6085.

Disbanded 20th September 1943 at North Front to become 520 Squadron.

1404 (METEOROLOGICAL) FLIGHT
Formed 1st March 1941 at St Eval by redesignating 404 (Meteorological) Flight.

Blenheim IV Z5959; Hudson III V8986, IV AE632; Hampden I P1204; Albemarle I P1436; Ventura II AJ444; Mosquito IV DZ363.

Disbanded 11th August 1943 at St Eval to become 517 Squadron.

1405 (METEOROLOGICAL) FLIGHT
Formed 1st March 1941 at Aldergrove by redesignating 405 (Meteorological) Flight.

Blenheim IV Z7345; Hudson III V9156, IIIA FH407; Hampden I AD724.

Disbanded 7th February 1942 at Aldergrove and absorbed by 1402 (Meteorological) Flight.

1406 (METEOROLOGICAL) FLIGHT
Formed 9th May 1941 at Wick.

Spitfire I N3059, IIA P8514, VA P8529, VI BR171; Hampden I P2118; Albemarle I P1408; Hudson III V9185, V AM531; Master I T8616.

Disbanded 7th August 1943 at Wick to become 519 Squadron.

1407 (METEOROLOGICAL) FLIGHT
Formed 2nd October 1941 at Reykjavik, Iceland.

Hudson III T9422 T, IIIA FK752; Hampden I P2130; Ventura I AE720, II AE856, V JS974; Spitfire IX MK503.

Disbanded 1st August 1944 at Reykjavik, Iceland, to become 251 Squadron.

1408 (METEOROLOGICAL) FLIGHT
Formed 3rd December 1941 at Wick.

Hudson III AE534.

Disbanded 7th February 1942 at Wick and absorbed by 1406 (Meteorological) Flight.

1409 (METEOROLOGICAL) FLIGHT, later 1409 (LONG RANGE METEOROLOGICAL RECONNAISSANCE) FLIGHT
Formed 1st April 1943 at Oakington by redesignating an element of

521 Squadron. Redesignated 1409 (Long Range Meteorological Reconnaissance) Flight from October 1945.

Nil (4.43–10.45)   Mosquito IV DZ479 R, VI NT127, IX LR502, XVI NS734 B.
AE (10.45–5.46)   Mosquito IX ML897 AE-D, XVI; Liberator VI KN702 AE-Z.VI KL486 .

Disbanded 13th May 1946 at Lyneham.

1411 (METEOROLOGICAL) FLIGHT
Formed 1st January 1942 at Heliopolis, Egypt, by redesignating the Meteorological Flight, Heliopolis.

Gladiator I K7893, II N5830; Hurricane.

Disbanded 15th August 1943 at Heliopolis and equipment passed to Royal Egyptian Air Force.

1412 (METEOROLOGICAL) FLIGHT
Formed 1st January 1942 at Khartoum, Sudan, by redesignating the Meteorological Flight, Khartoum.

Gladiator I K6140, II N5828; Hurricane IIB HL790; Spitfire VC EE664.

Disbanded 30th April 1946 at Khartoum, Sudan.

1413 (METEOROLOGICAL) FLIGHT
Formed 1st January 1942 at Ramleh, Palestine, by redesignating the Meteorological Flight, Ramleh.

Gladiator I K7949; Hurricane I Z7003, IIB HV711, IIC HL628; Spitfire VB ES209, VC JG738; Harvard IIA EX105.

Disbanded 31st January 1946 at Lydda, Palestine, equipment being absorbed by the Communication Flight, Lydda.

1414 (METEOROLOGICAL) FLIGHT
Formed December 1941 at Eastleigh, Kenya.

Gladiator I K8037, Gladiator II N5821; Defiant TT.I DS122; Hurricane IIB HV780, IIC BN347; Spitfire VB EP714, VC JK277; Proctor III HM461.

Disbanded 31st May 1946 at Eastleigh.

1415 (METEOROLOGICAL) FLIGHT
Formed 18th July 1942 at Habbaniya, Iraq.

Gladiator I K6147; Hurricane IIB BP763, IIC LD109; Spitfire VC JK259.

Disbanded 15th May 1946 at Habbaniya.

1416 (RECONNAISSANCE) FLIGHT
Formed 10th March 1941 at Hendon.

DP   Spitfire I K9969, IG L1000, IV R7143, PR.V X4784, VA X4931, VII X4907; Blenheim I L6759, IV L9244; Lysander III R9105; Tiger Moth II N9375.

Disbanded 17th September 1941 at Benson to become 140 Squadron.

1417 (GENERAL RECONNAISSANCE) FLIGHT, later 1417 (LEIGH LIGHT TRIALS) FLIGHT, later 1417 (COMMUNICATION) FLIGHT, later 1417 (FIGHTER RECONNAISSANCE) FLIGHT, later 1417 (TACTICAL GROUND ATTACK) FLIGHT
Formed 1st March 1941 at St Athan by redesignating 417 (General Reconnaissance) Flight.

Anson I.

Disbanded 18th March 1941 at St Athan.

Reformed 18th January 1942 at Chivenor as 1417 (Leigh Light Trials) Flight.

Wellington I L4319, IA P9223, IC R1231, VIII Z8721, XII MP636, XIII MF636.

Disbanded 4th April 1942 at Chivenor to become 172 Squadron.

Reformed 1st November 1953 at Muharraq, Bahrain, as 1417 (Communication) Flight.

Anson XIX TX207; Pembroke C.1 WV706.

Disbanded 29th September 1958 at Muharraq to become 152 Squadron.

Reformed 1st March 1963 at Khormaksar, Aden, as 1417 (Fighter Reconnaissance) Flight by redesignating the Reconnaissance Flight of 8 Squadron.

T   Hunter T.7 XF321 TZ, FR.10 XF460 TG.

Disbanded 8th September 1967 at Muharraq, Bahrain, and absorbed by 8 Squadron.

Reformed 18th April 1980 at Belize as 1417 (Tactical Ground Attack) Flight by redesignating a detachment of 1 Squadron.

Harrier GR.3 XW769 C.

Disbanded 6th July 1993 at Belize.

1418 (SPECIAL DUTIES) FLIGHT
Formed 6th January 1942 at Marham by redesignating the GEE (TR 1335) Development Unit.

Wellington III X3454, X Z8830; Halifax.

Disbanded 20th July 1942 at Gransden Lodge to become the Bombing Development Unit.

1419 (SPECIAL DUTIES) FLIGHT
Formed 1st March 1941 at Stradishall by redesignating 419 (Special Duties) Flight.

Lysander 1 R2626, III T1508; Whitley V T4166; Maryland I AR718.

Disbanded 25th August 1941 at Newmarket to become 138 Squadron.

1420 FLIGHT
Formed 5th May 1941 at Thornaby from 'B' Flight of 114 Squadron.

Blenheim IV.

Disbanded 15th November 1941 at West Raynham.

1422 (NIGHT FIGHTER) FLIGHT
Formed 12th May 1941 at Heston.

Boston III AL458, III (Turbinlite) W8276; Havoc I AW406, I (Turbinlite) BJ497, II AH470 (Turbinlite); Mosquito II (Turbinlite) W4087, XII HK109; Defiant I N3392; Wellington II W5480, VIII T2977; Hurricane I L1664, IIC HL859; Tiger Moth II T7190; Anson I NK494; Dominie I NF887.

Disbanded 3rd June 1944 at Heston to become the Special Projectile Flight, Royal Aircraft Establishment.

1423 (FIGHTER) FLIGHT
Formed 10th June 1941 at Kaldadarnes, Iceland, by redesignating a Flight of 98 Squadron.

Battle L5628; Hurricane I Z4048 O.

Officially disbanded October 1943 at Ouston.

1424 (AIR OBSERVATION POST) FLIGHT
Formed 20th September 1941 at Larkhill by redesignating 'D' Flight.

Cub Coupe BT440; Taylorcraft Plus D T9120; Voyager X5324; Tiger Moth II N6944; Vigilant IA BZ100; Tutor K6100; Lysander III R9011; Leopard Moth AX873; Hampden I AE264; Havoc I AX930.

Disbanded 1st October 1942 at Larkhill to become 43 Operational Training Unit.

1425 (COMMUNICATION) FLIGHT
Formed 30th October 1941 at Prestwick.

Liberator I AM913, Liberator II AL516; Ventura II AJ446.

Disbanded 10th October 1942 at Lyneham to become 511 Squadron.

1426 (ENEMY AIRCRAFT CIRCUS) FLIGHT, later 1426 (PHOTOGRAPHIC RECONNAISSANCE) FLIGHT
Formed 21st November 1941 at Duxford as 1426 (Enemy Aircraft Circus) Flight.

Bf 109E-3 AE479, Bf 109F-4 NN644, Bf 109G-2 RN228, Bf 109G-6 VX101, Bf 109G-14 VD364; Bf 110C-5 AX772; Fw 109A-4 PN999;

He 111H-3 AW177; Hs 129B-1 NF756; Ju 88A-5 EE205, Ju 88A-6 HM509, Ju 88R-1 PJ876; Ju 88S-1 TS472; Monospar ST.25 K8308; Anson I N9882; Oxford II V3781.

Disbanded 17th January 1945 at Collyweston and absorbed by the Central Fighter Establishment as the Enemy Aircraft Flight.

Reformed 1st January 1956 at Khormaksar, Aden, as 1426 (Photographic Reconnaissance) Flight.

Lincoln B.2 SX982.

Disbanded 31st December 1956 at Khormaksar.

1427 (FERRY TRAINING) FLIGHT
Formed 13th December 1941 at Thruxton.

Sterling I N6004; Halifax II R9419; Liberator II AL518.

Disbanded officially 1st April 1943 at Stradishall having been absorbed by 1657 Heavy Conversion Unit from 7th October 1942.

1428 (FERRY TRAINING) FLIGHT
Formed 29th December 1941 at Horsham St Faith and Oulton.

Hudson III AE531, V AM531.

Disbanded 6th June 1942 at Oulton, the Ferry Training Section being absorbed by 1444 (Ferry Training) Flight.

1429 (CZECHOSLOVAK OPERATIONAL TRAINING) FLIGHT
Formed 1st January 1942 at Thornaby.

Wellington IC Z8854 V; Lysander II P9077.

Disbanded 27th February 1943 at Thornaby to become the Czechoslovak Flight within 6 Operational Training Unit.

1430 (ARMY CO-OPERATION) FLIGHT, later 1430 (FLYING BOAT TRANSPORT) FLIGHT
Formed 1st March 1941 at Sufeiya, Sudan, by redesignating 430 (Army Co-operation) Flight.

Gauntlet II K5295.

Disbanded 7th October 1941 at Sufeiya and merged with elements of 261 Squadron to become 185 Squadron.

Reformed 5th August 1946 at Kai Tak, Hong Kong, as 1430 (Flying Boat Transport) Flight.

Sunderland V.

Disbanded 1st September 1946 at Kai Tak, Hong Kong, to become 88 Squadron.

1432 (PHOTOGRAPHIC RECONNAISSANCE) FLIGHT
Formed 5th September 1942 at Kaduna, West Africa.

Hurricane X AG177.

Disbanded 15th April 1943 at Kano, Nigeria.

1433 (METEOROLOGICAL/PHOTOGRAPHIC RECONNAISSANCE) FLIGHT
Formed February 1942 in the United Kingdom. Operational by May 1942 at Diego Suarez, Madagascar.

Lysander IIIA V9499; Hurricane IIC KZ710.

Disbanded 15th April 1943 at Maratsipoy, Madagascar.

1434 (PHOTOGRAPHIC SURVEY) FLIGHT, later 1434 (TARGET TOWING) FLIGHT
Formed 23rd March 1942 at Habbaniya, Iraq, as 1434 (Photographic Survey) Flight by redesignating the 60 (Photographic Survey) Squadron, South African Air Force – Royal Air Force Flight.

Blenheim IV Z7633, V BA332.

Disbanded 1st July 1943 at Beit Daras, Palestine.

Reformed March 1945 at (location unknown – possibly Bentwaters) as 1434 (Target Towing) Flight.

Master II AZ856; Martinet I EM639.

Disbanded May 1945 at (location unknown) – possibly absorbed by 1494 (Target Towing) Flight at North Weald.

1435 (NIGHT FIGHTER) FLIGHT, later 1435 (FIGHTER) FLIGHT, later 1435 FLIGHT
Formed 4th December 1941 at Takali, Malta, as 1435 (Night Fighter) Flight by redesignating the Malta Night Fighter Unit.

Hurricane IIB Z3462, IIC Z3505; Beaufighter I X7756.

Disbanded June 1942 at Luqa.

Reformed 15th July 1942 at Luqa as 1435 (Fighter) Flight.

V   Spitfire VB EN978.

Disbanded 2nd August 1942 at Luqa, Malta, to become 1435 Squadron.

Reformed 1983 at Stanley, Falkland Islands.

Harrier GR.3 XZ997.

Disbanded May 1983 at Stanley.

Reformed 1st November 1988 at Mount Pleasant, Falkland Islands, from 23 Squadron.

Phantom FGR.2 XV419 A; Tornado F.3 ZE209 H.

Current 1st April 1998 at Mount Pleasant.

1436 (BALLOON) FLIGHT
Formed 14th December 1941 at Hook by redesignating 'D' Flight, 974 Squadron.

Mk VI Balloon.

Disbanded 25th September 1944 at Aden.

1437 (STRATEGIC RECONNAISSANCE) FLIGHT
Formed 9th November 1941 at Fuka, Egypt.

Baltimore I AG704, II AG825 M, III AG863; Spitfire VB ER323, VC JG938; Mustang III HK955.

Disbanded 17th October 1943 at Gioia del Colle, Italy.

1438 (STRATEGIC RECONNAISSANCE) FLIGHT
Formed 9th August 1942 at Hadera, Palestine.

Blenheim IV Z9548, V EH338.

Disbanded 1st May 1943 at Helwan, Egypt.

1439 (STRATEGIC RECONNAISSANCE) FLIGHT, later 1439 (COMMUNICATION SUPPORT) FLIGHT
Believed to have existed by June 1942 in North Africa with Blenheims – no trace found.

Reformed 8th May 1957 at Hemswell as 1439 (Communication Support) Flight.

Varsity T.1 WL676 C; Anson XIX TX196: Whirlwind HAR.2 XD164.

Disbanded 20th November 1957 at Hemswell.

1441 (COMBINED OPERATIONS DEVELOPMENT) FLIGHT
Formed 20th January 1942 at Abbotsinch.

Lysander II P1697; Hurricane I W9187, X AF979; Mustang I AM250; Anson I DG902; Tiger Moth II N6789.

Disbanded 28th April 1943 at Dundonald to become 516 Squadron.

1442 (FERRY TRAINING) FLIGHT
Formed 21st January 1942 at Bicester by redesignating the Ferry Training Flight, Bicester.

Blenheim I L1289, IV T2136, V BA377; Wellington IC HX382, X Z8870.

Disbanded 1st August 1942 at Bicester.

1443 (FERRY TRAINING) FLIGHT
Formed 21st January 1942 at Harwell by redesignating the Ferry Training and Despatch Flight, Harwell.

Wellington IC R1774, II W5359, III BJ836, VIII HX538, X HE538, XI MP579; Anson I N9944; Beaufort I AW295.

Disbanded 30th April 1943 at Harwell to become 310 Ferry Training Unit.

1444 (FERRY TRAINING) FLIGHT
Formed 21st January 1942 at Horsham St Faith by redesignating the Ferry Training Flight, Horsham St Faith.

Hudson I P5137, III AE538, IIIA FH231, V AE643, VI EW902; Oxford II W6590; Beaufort I DW917, II DD906; Beaufighter VI V8518; Wellington III DF683.

Disbanded 3rd November 1942 at Lyneham and merged with 1445 (Ferry Training) Flight and the Ferry Training Unit to become 'B' Flight of 301 Ferry Training Unit.

1445 (FERRY TRAINING) FLIGHT
Formed 27th February 1942 at Lyneham.

Halifax II W7849; Liberator II AL510, V FL969; Hurricane IIC BP734; Fortress IIA FK199.

Disbanded 3rd November 1942 at Lyneham and merged with 1444 (Ferry Training) Flight and the Ferry Training Unit to become 'C' Flight of 301 Ferry Training Unit.

1446 (FERRY TRAINING) FLIGHT
Formed 23rd March 1942 at Bassingbourn.

Wellington IA L7779, IC DV944, II W5368, III DF573, VIII HX574, X HF739, XI MP566.

Disbanded 1st May 1943 at Moreton-in-Marsh to become 311 Ferry Training Unit.

1447 (RADAR CALIBRATION) FLIGHT
Formed 19th March 1942 at Hooton Park.

Battle L5691; Lysander III R9017; Oxford I N4566, II P1861; Cierva C.40A P9639; Pitcairn PA-39 BW833.

Disbanded 15th December 1942 at Carew Cheriton and absorbed by No.4 Radio Direction Finding School.

1448 (RADAR CALIBRATION) FLIGHT
Formed 17th February 1942 at Duxford by redesignating an element of 74 Wing Calibration Flight.

KX   Hornet Moth W6422; Rota II L7594; Cierva C.30 BV999, Cierva C.30A AP507 KX-H; Tiger Moth II T6864; Wellington II W5498.

Disbanded 15th June 1943 at Halton to become 529 Squadron.

1449 (FIGHTER) FLIGHT
Formed 10th April 1942 at St Mary's by redesignating an element of 87 Squadron

Tutor K4808; Tiger Moth II DE808; Hurricane I P3317, X AF997, IIB Z3658 VD-K.

Disbanded 17th September 1944 at St Mary's.

1451 (FIGHTER) FLIGHT
Formed 22nd May 1941 at Hunsdon.

Boston III AL469, III (Turbinlite) Z2280; Havoc I AE470, I (Turbinlite) AW405; Cygnet II HL539; Tiger Moth II T7150.

Disbanded 8th September 1942 at Hunsdon to become 530 Squadron.

1452 (FIGHTER) FLIGHT
Formed 7th July 1941 at West Malling.

Havoc I AW409, I (Turbinlite) AW412; Boston III (Turbinlite) W8265; Hurricane IIC HL604 U; Tiger Moth II T7466.

Disbanded 8th September 1942 at West Malling to become 531 Squadron.

1453 (FIGHTER) FLIGHT, later 1453 (AIRBORNE EARLY WARNING) FLIGHT, later 1453 (TACTICAL GROUND ATTACK) FLIGHT
Formed 10th July 1941 at Wittering as 1453 (Fighter) Flight.

Boston II AH461, Boston III (Turbinlite) Z2184; Havoc I AE470, I (Turbinlite) AX927; Tiger Moth II T6046.

Disbanded 8th September 1942 at Wittering to become 532 Squadron.

Reformed 5th June 1953 at Kinloss as 1453 (Airborne Early Warning) Flight by redesignating the Fighter Command Vanguard Flight.

Neptune MR.1 WX500 3.

Disbanded 30th June 1956 at Topcliffe.

Reformed 20th August 1983 at Stanley, Falkland Islands, as 1453 (Tactical Ground Attack) Flight from elements of 1 and 4 Squadrons and 233 Operational Conversion Unit.

Harrier GR.3 XZ993 L.

Disbanded June 1985 at Stanley.

1454 (FIGHTER) FLIGHT
Formed 27th June 1941 at Colerne.

Boston III (Turbinlite) W8312; Havoc I (Turbinlite) AW400; Hurricane I P3863; Tiger Moth II T6110.

Disbanded 8th September 1942 at Colerne to become 533 Squadron.

1455 (FIGHTER) FLIGHT
Formed 7th July 1941 at Tangmere.

Boston III (Turbinlite) W8327; Havoc I AX923, I (Turbinlite) AW401; Hurricane; Tiger Moth II T7458.

Disbanded 2nd September 1942 at Tangmere to become 534 Squadron.

1456 (FIGHTER) FLIGHT
Formed 24th November 1941 at Honiley.

Havoc I AX923, I (Turbinlite) AW401; Boston III (Turbinlite) Z2214; Tiger Moth II N6944; Magister L8059.

Disbanded 2nd September 1942 at Honiley to become 535 Squadron.

1457 (FIGHTER) FLIGHT
Formed 15th September 1941 at Colerne.

Boston III (Turbinlite) W8294, III AL458; Havoc I AW406, I (Turbinlite) AW407; Tiger Moth II T7601.

Disbanded 8th September 1942 at Colerne to become 536 Squadron.

1458 (FIGHTER) FLIGHT
Formed 6th December 1941 at Middle Wallop from elements of 93 Squadron.

Boston III (Turbinlite) W8277; Havoc I AW406, I (Turbinlite) AX930; Tiger Moth II R5028.

Disbanded 8th September 1942 at Middle Wallop to become 537 Squadron.

1459 (FIGHTER) FLIGHT
Formed 20th September 1941 at Hunsdon.

Boston II (Turbinlite) AH470 F, III AL760, III (Turbinlite) W8352; Havoc I AE470, Havoc I (Turbinlite) AW400; Tiger Moth II N6749.

Disbanded 2nd September 1942 at Hibaldstow to become 538 Squadron.

1460 (FIGHTER) FLIGHT
Formed 15th December 1941 at Acklington.

Boston I AE471, II (Turbinlite) AH477, III (Turbinlite) Z2246; Havoc I AW406; I (Turbinlite) AX924; Tiger Moth II DE138.

Disbanded 2nd September 1942 at Acklington to become 539 Squadron.

1471 (ANTI-AIRCRAFT CO-OPERATION) FLIGHT
Formed 1st April 1942 at Old Sarum.

Mustang I AG561; Tomahawk I AH835, IIA AH944, IIB AK135; Proctor III DX227.

Disbanded 10th October 1942 at Old Sarum.

1472 (ARMY CO-OPERATION) FLIGHT
Formed 15th June 1942 at Dishforth.

RG	*Battle P5288; Tomahawk I AH756, IIA AH918, IIB AK190; Hurricane IIB HW207; Master III W8890.*

Disbanded 15th November 1943 at Catterick.

1473 (RADIO COUNTERMEASURES) FLIGHT
Formed 10th July 1942 at Upper Heyford from 'A' (Radio Countermeasures) Flight of 109 Squadron.

ZP	*Anson I W1904 ZP-B; Whitley V BD286; Wellington IC Z1071, III HZ130 ZP-X; Mosquito IV DZ377; Halifax II DT737; Leopard Moth AX858.*

Disbanded 1st February 1944 at Foulsham to become 'C' Flight of 192 Squadron.

1474 (SPECIAL DUTIES) FLIGHT
Formed 10th July 1942 at Stradishall by redesignating 'B' and 'C' Flights of 109 Squadron.

Wellington IC AD590, X HE227; Mosquito IV DZ375; Halifax II DT737; Tiger Moth II T6862.

Disbanded 4th January 1943 at Gransden Lodge to become 192 Squadron.

1475 (TRAINING) FLIGHT
Formed 21st November 1942 at Pocklington.

Halifax II DT735.

Disbanded 15th May 1943 at Marston Moor and absorbed by 1652 Heavy Conversion Unit.

1476 (ADVANCED SHIP RECOGNITION) FLIGHT
Formed 9th February 1943 at Skeabrae by redesignating the Advanced Ship Recognition Flight.

UX	*Anson I K6184 UX-P.*

Disbanded 1st January 1944 at Skeabrae.

1477 (NORWEGIAN) FLIGHT
Formed 17th February 1943 at Woodhaven by redesignating the Royal Norwegian Navy Flight, which had operated as a detachment of 210 Squadron.

Catalina I W8424, IB FP121 C; Mosquito II DZ711.

Disbanded 10th May 1943 at Woodhaven to become 333 Squadron.

1478 FLIGHT, later 1478 (MEDITERRANEAN AIR COMMAND COMMUNICATION) FLIGHT
Formed 15th April 1943 at Hinton-in-the-Hedges and attached to the Signals Development Unit. Redesignated 1478 (Mediterranean Air Command Communication) Flight from 1st July 1943.

Whitley V Z6977.

Disbanded 2nd August 1943 at Maison Blanche, Algeria, to become the Mediterranean Air Command Communication Unit.

1479 (ANTI-AIRCRAFT CO-OPERATION) FLIGHT
Formed 1st May 1942 at Peterhead.

Defiant I AA304; Oxford I BG565.

Disbanded 1st December 1943 at Peterhead and merged with 1632 (Anti-Aircraft Co-operation) Flight and an element of 289 Squadron to become 598 Squadron.

1480 (ANTI-AIRCRAFT CO-OPERATION) FLIGHT
Formed 28th November 1941 at Ballyhalbert.

Defiant I AA306; Hurricane I L1864; Lysander II P9079, III T1652, IIIA V9401; Oxford I BG233; Martinet I MS582.

Disbanded 1st December 1943 at Newtownards and merged with 1617 (Target Towing) Flight and an element of 289 Squadron to become 290 Squadron.

1481 (TARGET TOWING) FLIGHT, later 1481 (TARGET TOWING AND GUNNERY) FLIGHT, later 1481 (BOMBER) GUNNERY FLIGHT

Formed 30th October at Binbrook by redesignating 1 Group Target Towing Flight. Redesignated 1481 (Target Towing and Gunnery) Flight from January 1942 and 1481 (Bomber) Gunnery Flight from 18th December 1942.

Whitley V Z6469 M; Lysander III R9115, IIIA V9792; Defiant I AA357; Skua I L2935; Tiger Moth II T5813; Wellington IA L7789, IC X9815 Y, III BK138 Z, X HE742; Martinet I HP323; Oxford I AS152; II ED127.

Disbanded 4th December 1944 at Ingham and absorbed by 1687 Bomber (Defence) Training Flight.

1482 (TARGET TOWING AND GUNNERY) FLIGHT, later 1482 (BOMBER) GUNNERY FLIGHT

Formed 30th October 1941 at West Raynham by redesignating 2 Group Target Towing Flight. Redesignated 1482 (Bomber) Gunnery Flight from 18th December 1942.

Lysander II R2010, III T1616, IIIA V9781; Defiant I N3434, III T4103; Blenheim I L6811, IV T2122, V BA245; Tomahawk IIA AH900, IIB AK147; Tiger Moth II N5448; Boston III W8354; Mitchell II FL178; Ventura I AE811; Hurricane IV KZ326; Martinet I HP358.

Disbanded 1st April 1944 at Swanton Morley to become 2 Group Support Unit.

1483 (TARGET TOWING AND GUNNERY) FLIGHT, later 1483 (BOMBER) GUNNERY FLIGHT

Formed 30th October 1941 at Newmarket by redesignating 3 Group Target Towing Flight. Redesignated 1483 (Bomber) Gunnery Flight from 18th December 1942.

Defiant I AA307; Lysander I R2620, III P1743, IIIA V9775 E; Blenheim IV T2071; Oxford I R6023, II N4726; Wellington IA N3011, III BJ656 M, X HE263 R; Hurricane IV KW792; Ventura I AE683; Mustang I AG618; Tiger Moth II N5468; Martinet I HN984 M.

Disbanded 11th March 1944 at Newmarket to become 1688 Bomber (Defence) Training Flight.

1484 (TARGET TOWING) FLIGHT, later 1484 (TARGET TOWING AND GUNNERY) FLIGHT, later 1484 (BOMBER) GUNNERY FLIGHT

Formed 30th October 1941 at Driffield by redesignating 4 Group Target Towing Flight. Redesignated 1484 (Target Towing and Gunnery) Flight from January 1942 and 1464 (Bomber) Gunnery Flight from 18th December 1942.

Battle K9200; Defiant I N1685; Lysander I R2620, II N1264, III T1424, IIIA V9777; Tiger Moth II T7261; Anson I N9669; Oxford I V3878, II R6374; Whitley V Z6640 Y; Martinet I MS748 B; Hurricane IIC LF764.

Disbanded 15th February 1944 at Leconfield to become 1689 Bomber (Defence) Training Flight.

1485 (TARGET TOWING) FLIGHT, later 1485 (TARGET TOWING AND GUNNERY) FLIGHT, later 1485 (BOMBER) GUNNERY FLIGHT

Formed 30th October 1941 at Coningsby. Redesignated 1485 (Target Towing and Gunnery) Flight from 7th January 1942 and 1485 (Bomber) Gunnery Flight from 18th December 1942.

Tiger Moth II R5245; Manchester I L7401; Lysander III T1579, IIIA V9867; Defiant I T4066; Whitley V Z6494; Wellington III X3659, X HE350; Oxford II P8976; Martinet I MS522.

Disbanded 26th February 1944 at Syerston to become 1690 Bomber (Defence) Training Flight.

1486 (TARGET TOWING) FLIGHT, later 1486 (FIGHTER) GUNNERY FLIGHT

Formed 30th October 1941 at Valley by redesignating 9 Group Target Towing Flight. Redesignated 1486 (Fighter) Gunnery Flight from May 1942.

Lysander III T1426, IIIA V9854; Master II DM214; Martinet I MS692.

Disbanded 18th October 1943 at Llanbedr to become 12 Armament Practice Camp.

1487 (TARGET TOWING) FLIGHT, later 1487 (FIGHTER) GUNNERY FLIGHT

Formed 30th October 1941 at Warmwell by redesignating 10 Group Target Towing Flight. Redesignated 1487 (Fighter) Gunnery Flight from May 1942.

Lysander I R2630, II R1990, III T1462, IIIA V9752; Master III W8860; Martinet I JN681.

Disbanded 18th October 1943 at Fairwood Common and merged with 1498 (Target Towing) Flight to be become 11 Armament Practice Camp.

1488 (TARGET TOWING) FLIGHT, later 1488 (FIGHTER) GUNNERY FLIGHT

Formed 30th October 1941 at Shoreham by redesignating 11 Group Target Towing Flight. Redesignated 1488 (Fighter) Gunnery Flight from May 1942.

Lysander I R2638, II L6858, III R9001, IIIA V9798; Master III W8848; Martinet I MS774.

Disbanded 18th October 1943 at Rochford to become 17 Armament Practice Camp.

1489 (TARGET TOWING) FLIGHT, later 1489 (FIGHTER) GUNNERY FLIGHT

Formed 30th October 1941 at Coltishall by redesignating 12 Group Target Towing Flight. Redesignated 1489 (Fighter) Gunnery Flight from May 1942.

Henley III L3267; Lysander II P1730, III T1564, IIIA V9860; Oxford II W6568; Master III W8839; Martinet I HP169.

Disbanded 18th October 1943 at Hutton Cranswick to become 16 Armament Practice Camp.

1490 (TARGET TOWING) FLIGHT, later 1490 (FIGHTER GUNNERY) FLIGHT

Formed 8th December 1941 at Acklington by redesignating 13 Group Target Towing Flight. Redesignated 1490 (Fighter Gunnery) Flight from May 1942.

Henley III L3376; Lysander II R1990, III T1589, IIIA V9852; Master III W8736; Martinet I HP147.

Disbanded 18th October 1943 at Ayr to become 14 Armament Practice Camp.

1491 (TARGET TOWING) FLIGHT, later 1491 (FIGHTER GUNNERY) FLIGHT

Formed 8th December 1941 at Inverness by redesignating 14 Group Target Towing Flight. Redesignated 1491 (Fighter Gunnery) Flight from May 1942.

Lysander II N1276, III T1549, IIIA V9853, Master I T8854, II DL417, III DL580; Martinet I JN443.

Disbanded 18th October 1943 at Peterhead to become 15 Armament Practice Camp.

1492 (TARGET TOWING) FLIGHT

Formed 18th October 1941 at Weston Zoyland.

Lysander II P1671, III R9068, IIIA V9506; Master III W8629; Mosquito II DD722; Martinet I HP429 C.

Disbanded 18th October 1943 at Weston Zoyland to become 13 Armament Practice Camp.

1493 (TARGET TOWING) FLIGHT, later 1493 (FIGHTER) GUNNERY FLIGHT

Formed 31st October 1941 at Ballyhalbert by redesignating 82 Group Target Towing Flight. Redesignated 1493 (Fighter Gunnery) Flight from May 1942.

Lysander II L4781, III T1447, IIIA V9744; Master III DL581; Martinet I HP257.

Disbanded 18th October 1943 at Detling to become 18 Armament Practice Camp.

1494 (TARGET TOWING) FLIGHT

Formed 18th December 1941 at Long Kesh.

Lysander II R2001, III R9115, IIIA R9112, Master II AZ856; Martinet I JN286.

Disbanded 30th June 1945 at North Weald.

1495 (TARGET TOWING) FLIGHT
Formed 8th August 1942 at Sawbridgeworth.

Lysander II N1222, III T1434; Martinet I JN305.

Disbanded 14th November 1943 at Hutton Cranswick and absorbed by 16 Armament Practice Camp.

1496 (TARGET TOWING) FLIGHT
Planned formation from 11th November 1942 at Hawarden cancelled.

1497 (TARGET TOWING) FLIGHT
Formed December 1942 at Macmerry.

Lysander III R9064, IIIA V9898.

Disbanded 18th October 1943 at Shoreham.

1498 (TARGET TOWING) FLIGHT
Formed December 1942 at Hurn.

Lysander I R2590, II R1990, III T1522, IIIA V9745; Martinet I MS752.

Disbanded 18th October 1943 at Fairwood Common and merged with 1487 (Target Towing) Flight to become 11 Armament Practice Camp.

1499 (BOMBER) GUNNERY FLIGHT
Formed 31st March 1943 at Wyton.

Martinet I JN490.

Disbanded 15th February 1944 at Ipswich and absorbed by 1696 Bomber (Defence) Training Flight.

1500 (TARGET TOWING) FLIGHT
Formed 4th May 1943 at North Front, Gibraltar.

Lysander TT.IIIA V9904; Martinet TT.I NR315.

Disbanded 25th January 1946 at Gibraltar and absorbed by 520 Squadron.

1501 (BEAM APPROACH TRAINING) FLIGHT
Formed 8th November 1941 at Abingdon by redesignating 1 Blind Approach Training Flight.

Whitley III K8979; Oxford I DF360.

Disbanded 15th November 1943 at Stanton Harcourt.

1502 (BEAM APPROACH TRAINING) FLIGHT
Formed 8th November 1941 at Driffield by redesignating 2 Blind Approach Training Flight.

Whitley III K8966, V N1469; Wellington I L4229; Oxford I AT767.

Disbanded 15th August 1943 at Leconfield.

1503 (BEAM APPROACH TRAINING) FLIGHT
Formed 8th November 1941 at Mildenhall by redesignating 3 Blind Approach Training Flight.

Wellington IA N2960, IC R1253; Oxford I DF414.

Disbanded 6th August 1943 at Lindholme.

1504 (BEAM APPROACH TRAINING) FLIGHT
Formed 8th November 1941 at Wyton by redesignating 4 Blind Approach Training Flight.

Wellington I L4277, IC L7889; Oxford I DF351.

Disbanded 21st August 1943 at Newmarket.

1505 (BEAM APPROACH TRAINING) FLIGHT
Formed 8th November 1941 at Honington by redesignating 5 Blind Approach Training Flight.

Wellington I L4293, IC L7817; Oxford I DF295 V.

Disbanded 3rd February 1943 at Upper Heyford.

1506 (BEAM APPROACH TRAINING) FLIGHT
Formed 8th November 1941 at Waddington by redesignating 6 Blind Approach Training Flight.

Wellington IC Z1093; Oxford I DF424 S.

Disbanded 21st October 1943 at Skellingthorpe.

1507 (BEAM APPROACH TRAINING) FLIGHT
Formed 8th November 1941 at Finningley by redesignating 7 Blind Approach Training Flight.

Oxford I AT652 Z, II ED182.

Disbanded 27th November 1943 at Gransden Lodge.

1508 (BEAM APPROACH TRAINING) FLIGHT, later 1508 (GEE TRAINING) FLIGHT, later 1508 (RADIO AIDS TRAINING) FLIGHT, later 1508 (ACCLIMATISATION) FLIGHT
Formed 8th November 1941 at Horsham St Faith by redesignating 8 Blind Approach Training Flight. Redesignated 1508 (Gee Training) Flight from 1st March 1944.

Blenheim I L6646; Wellington IC R1529; Oxford I DF348, II P6810; Mitchell II FV928.

Disbanded 8th August 1944 at Ouston to become 'C' Flight of 62 Operational Training Unit.

Reformed 20th September 1945 at Snaith as 1508 (Radio Aids Training) Flight. Redesignated 1508 (Acclimatisation) Flight from 20th November 1945.

Nil	*Oxford I AT777, II R6353.*
UQ	*Allocated but no evidence of use.*
8B	*Oxford I R6323, II P8921.*

Disbanded 1st April 1946 at Snaith.

1509 (BEAM APPROACH TRAINING) FLIGHT
Formed 8th November 1941 at Thornaby by redesignating 9 Blind Approach Training Flight.

Oxford I V4045.

Disbanded 14th August 1944 at Dyce and absorbed by 1510 (Beam Approach Training) Flight.

1510 (BEAM APPROACH TRAINING) FLIGHT, later 1510 (BABS) FLIGHT, later 1510 RADIO AIDS TRAINING FLIGHT
Formed 8th November 1941 at Leuchars by redesignating 10 Blind Approach Training Flight. Redesignated 1510 (BABS) Flight from March 1943 and 1510 (Radio Aids Training) from 9th August 1947.

Nil (11.41–9.45)	*Anson I N9641 F.*
RF (9.45–9.48)	*Anson I NK291 RF-A.*

Disbanded 15th September 1948 at Bircham Newton and absorbed by 240 Operational Conversion Unit.

1511 (BEAM APPROACH TRAINING) FLIGHT, later 1511 (RADIO AIDS TRAINING) FLIGHT
Formed October 1941 at Upwood by redesignating 11 Blind Approach Training Flight. Redesignated 1511 (Radio Aids Training) Flight from 15th September 1945.

Nil (11.41–4.46)	*Oxford I V4129 G.*
FKA (4.46–7.46)	*Oxford I.*
FKB (4.46–7.46)	*Oxford I.*

Disbanded 1st August 1946 at Wheaton Aston.

1512 (BEAM APPROACH TRAINING) FLIGHT
Formed October 1941 at Dishforth by redesignating 12 Blind Approach Training Flight.

Oxford I V4080.

Disbanded 30th August 1944 at Banff.

1513 (BEAM APPROACH TRAINING) FLIGHT, later 1513 (RADIO AIDS TRAINING) FLIGHT
Formed October 1941 at Honington by redesignating 13 Blind Approach Training Flight. Redesignated 1513 (Radio Aids Training) Flight from 15th September 1945.

Nil (11.41–9.45)   Oxford I V4134 H; Anson I N9989.

LL (9.45–12.46)   Oxford I NM250 LL-B, II T1198; Anson I
                    NK147.
Also used   Tiger Moth II DF207.

Disbanded 1st December 1946 at Bramcote.

1514 (BEAM APPROACH TRAINING) FLIGHT
Formed October 1941 at Coningsby by redesignating 14 Blind
Approach Training Flight.

Oxford I V4092.

Disbanded 9th January 1945 at Fiskerton.

1515 (BEAM APPROACH TRAINING) FLIGHT
Formed October 1941 at Swanton Morley by redesignating 15 Blind
Approach Training Flight.

Oxford I AT777 F.

Disbanded 1st June 1945 at Colby Grange.

1516 (BEAM APPROACH TRAINING) FLIGHT, later 1516 (RADIO AIDS TRAINING) FLIGHT
Formed October 1941 at Llanbedr by redesignating 16 Blind
Approach Training Flight. Redesignated 1516 (Radio Aids Training)
Flight from 15th September 1945.

Nil (11.41–9.45)   Oxford I AT652; II W6626 L.
QW (9.45–4.46)   Oxford I NJ356; Oxford II.

Disbanded 11th April 1946 at Snaith.

1517 (BEAM APPROACH TRAINING) FLIGHT
Formed October 1941 at Wattisham by redesignating 17 Blind
Approach Training Flight.

Oxford I V4145 G.

Disbanded 17th December 1945 at Wheaton Aston.

1518 (BEAM APPROACH TRAINING) FLIGHT
Formed 3rd November 1941 at Scampton.

Oxford I V4043.

Disbanded 30th August 1944 at Edzell.

1519 (BEAM APPROACH TRAINING) FLIGHT
Formed November 1941 at South Cerney.

Oxford I DF428 M; Anson I EG306.

Disbanded 3rd July 1945 at Feltwell.

1520 (BEAM APPROACH TRAINING) FLIGHT
Formed October 1941 at Holme-on-Spalding-Moor by redesignating
20 Blind Approach Training Flight.

Oxford I V4142.

Disbanded 29th May 1945 at Sturgate.

1521 (BEAM APPROACH TRAINING) FLIGHT, later 1521 (RADIO AIDS TRAINING) FLIGHT
Formed October 1941 at Stradishall by redesignating 21 Blind
Approach Training Flight. Redesignated 1521 (Radio Aids Training)
Flight from 15th September 1945.

Nil (11.41–9.45)   Oxford I HN426 D; Stirling I R9322.
J6 (9.45–4.46)   Oxford I PH130.

Disbanded 1st April 1946 at Longtown.

1522 (BEAM APPROACH TRAINING) FLIGHT
Formed October 1941 at Docking by redesignating 22 Blind
Approach Training Flight.

Oxford I DF301.

Disbanded April 1942 at Watchfield and absorbed by the Beam
Approach School.

1523 (BEAM APPROACH TRAINING) FLIGHT
Formed October 1941 at Little Rissington by redesignating 23 Blind
Approach Training Flight.

Oxford I MP395.

Disbanded 17th December 1945 at Little Rissington.

1524 (BEAM APPROACH TRAINING) FLIGHT
Formed October 1941 at Bottesford by redesignating 24 Blind
Approach Training Flight.

Oxford I DF349 J.

Disbanded 9th January 1945 at Tollerton.

1525 (BEAM APPROACH TRAINING) FLIGHT
Formed October 1941 at Brize Norton by redesignating 25 Blind
Approach Training Flight.

Oxford I AT729.

Disbanded 26th June 1945 at Docking.

1526 (BEAM APPROACH TRAINING) FLIGHT
Formed October 1941 at Thruxton by redesignating 26 Blind
Approach Training Flight.

Oxford I V4213; Anson I N9781; Magister P2458.

Disbanded 9th November 1944 at Hampstead Norris.

1527 (BEAM APPROACH TRAINING) FLIGHT later 1527 (RADIO AIDS TRAINING) FLIGHT
Formed 29th October 1941 at Prestwick. Redesignated 1527 (Radio
Aids Training) Flight from 15th September 1945.

Nil (10.41–9.45)   Hudson III V9112; Oxford I DF354.
PY (9.45–2.46)   Oxford I DF396 PY.

Disbanded 28th February 1946 at Prestwick.

1528 (BEAM APPROACH TRAINING) FLIGHT, later 1528 (RADIO AIDS TRAINING) FLIGHT
Formed 22nd November 1941 at West Malling.

Master II AZ540, III DL693.

Disbanded 7th December 1942 at West Malling.

Reformed 1st November 1944 at Valley. Redesignated 1528 (Radio
Aids Training) Flight from 15th September 1945.

YM   Oxford I HM865.

Disbanded 4th March 1946 at Fairford to become 1555 (Radio Aids
Training) Flight.

1529 (BEAM APPROACH TRAINING) FLIGHT
Formed 22nd November 1941 at Wittering.

Master II AZ360, III DL854.

Disbanded 7th December 1942 at Collyweston.

Reformed 1st December 1944 at St Mawgan.

Nil (1.44–9.45)   Oxford I PH357.
GL (9.45–2.46)   Oxford.
YM (9.45–2.46)   Oxford.

Disbanded 16th February 1946 at Fairford.

1530 (BEAM APPROACH TRAINING) FLIGHT
Formed 14th August 1942 at Hunsdon.

Oxford I LX639, II P8920; Tiger Moth II T7416.

Disbanded 1st August 1944 at Wittering.

1531 (BEAM APPROACH TRAINING) FLIGHT
Formed 20th July 1942 at Cranage.

Oxford I DF479 M.

Disbanded 29th May 1945 at Cranage.

1532 (BEAM APPROACH TRAINING) FLIGHT
Formed 15th October 1942 at Hullavington.

Oxford I DF406 E.

Disbanded 15th June 1945 at Babdown Farm.

1533 (BEAM APPROACH TRAINING) FLIGHT
Formed 27th October 1942 at Church Lawford by redesignating the
Beam Approach Training Flight, Church Lawford.

Oxford I DF313.

Disbanded 3rd April 1945 at Church Lawford.

1534 (BEAM APPROACH TRAINING) FLIGHT
Formed 7th December 1942 at Shawbury.

Oxford II DF512.

Disbanded 29th May 1945 at Shawbury.

1535 (RCAF BEAM APPROACH TRAINING) FLIGHT
Formed 15th December 1942 at Middleton St George.

Oxford I DF422.

Disbanded 30th August 1943 at Topcliffe.

1536 (BEAM APPROACH TRAINING) FLIGHT
Formed 8th March 1943 at Grantham (later Spitalgate).

Oxford I MP424 D.

Disbanded 8th May 1945 at Spitalgate.

1537 (BEAM APPROACH TRAINING) FLIGHT
Formed 4th May 1943 at Upavon.

Nil (5.43– .45)   Oxford I ED294.
FKD (.45–4.47)   Allocated but no evidence of use.

Disbanded 4th April 1947 at Little Rissington.

1538 (BEAM APPROACH TRAINING) FLIGHT
Formed 15th April 1943 at Croughton.

Oxford I MP473.

Disbanded 18th October 1944 at Croughton.

1539 (BEAM APPROACH TRAINING) FLIGHT
Formed 15th April 1943 at South Cerney.

Oxford I MP373 B.

Disbanded 1st June 1945 at South Cerney.

1540 (BEAM APPROACH TRAINING) FLIGHT
Formed 15th April 1943 at Lulsgate Bottom.

Oxford I DF259 S.

Disbanded 17th December 1945 at Weston Zoyland.

1541 (BEAM APPROACH TRAINING) FLIGHT
Formed 17th May 1943 at Stracathro.

Oxford I LB475.

Disbanded 11th July 1945 at Stracathro.

1542 (BEAM APPROACH TRAINING) FLIGHT
Formed July 1943 at Dallachy.

Oxford I V4206.

Disbanded 30th August 1944 at Dallachy.

1543 (BEAM APPROACH TRAINING) FLIGHT
Planned to open June 1943 at Edzell, but not formed.

1544 (BEAM APPROACH TRAINING) FLIGHT
Formed 24th January 1944 at Errol.

Oxford I V4080.

Disbanded 30th August 1944 at Errol.

1545 (BEAM APPROACH TRAINING) FLIGHT
Formed March 1944 at Wheaton Aston.

Oxford I LB515.

Disbanded 17th December 1945 at Halfpenny Green.

1546 (BEAM APPROACH TRAINING) FLIGHT
Formed 8th May 1944 at Faldingworth.

Oxford I NJ399.

Disbanded 9th January 1945 at Faldingworth.

1547 (BEAM APPROACH TRAINING) FLIGHT
Formed 1st June 1945 at Watchfield.

Nil (6.45–4.46)   Oxford I LX132 D.
FKF (4.46– .46)   Oxford I DF426 FKF-X.

Disbanded 1st January 1947 at Watchfield.

1551 (BEAM APPROACH CALIBRATION) FLIGHT
Formed 20th November 1942 at Bicester by redesignating the Beam Approach Calibration Flight.

Oxford I V4027; Anson I EF982; Beaufighter I T4642.

Disbanded 15th April 1943 at Bicester and merged with the Beam Approach Development Unit and the Operation Development Party to become 'B' (Calibration) Flight of the Signals Development Unit.

1552 (RADIO AIDS TRAINING) FLIGHT
Formed 15th September 1945 at Melbourne.

ER (9.45–10.46)   Oxford I NJ285 ER-D.
PN (9.45–10.46)   Oxford I DF276 PN-A.
SS (9.45–10.46)   Oxford I EB798 SS-J.
Also used   Anson I MH152.

Disbanded 26th October 1946 at Full Sutton.

1553 (RADIO AIDS TRAINING) FLIGHT
Formed 15th September 1945 at Melbourne.

Oxford I HN577.

Disbanded 1st October 1945 at Melbourne.

1554 (RADIO AIDS TRAINING) FLIGHT
Formed 15th September 1945 at Melbourne.

No aircraft allocated.

Disbanded 1st October 1945 at Melbourne.

1555 (RADIO AIDS TRAINING) FLIGHT
Formed 15th September 1945 at Fairford by redesignating an element of 1528 (Beam Approach) Training Flight.

DR   Oxford I NJ285 DR-D.

Disbanded 31st August 1947 at Bircham Newton.

1556 (RADIO AIDS TRAINING REFRESHER) FLIGHT
Formed 15th September 1945 at Stradishall.

VT   Oxford I T1256, II BG593.

Disbanded 1st April 1946 at Fairford.

1557 (RADIO AIDS TRAINING) FLIGHT
Planned formation from 20th September 1945 at Fairford cancelled. Allocated the code AB.

1558 (RADIO AIDS TRAINING) FLIGHT
Planned formation from 20th September 1945 at (location unknown) cancelled.

1559 (RADIO AIDS TRAINING) FLIGHT
Formed 1st October 1946 at Oakington.

Oxford I LX719.

Disbanded 9th August 1947 at Bircham Newton.

1560 (METEOROLOGICAL) FLIGHT
Formed 6th December 1942 at Maiduguri, Nigeria.

Gladiator II N5622; Hurricane IIC LF317.

Disbanded 1st November 1945 at Maiduguri.

1561 (METEOROLOGICAL) FLIGHT
Formed 1st May 1943 at Ikeja, Nigeria.

Gladiator II N5648; Hurricane IIC LF326; Argus II FS584.

Disbanded 17th December 1945 at Ikeja.

Reformed 17th December 1945 at Langham.

VM   *Spitfire XI proposed.*

Disbanded 11th February 1946 at Langham.

1562 (METEOROLOGICAL) FLIGHT
Formed 3rd February 1943 at Waterloo, Sierra Leone.

Gladiator II N5631.

Disbanded 17th December 1945 at Waterloo.

Reformed 17th December 1945 at Langham.

B9   *Spitfire XI proposed.*

Disbanded 11th February 1946 at Langham.

1563 (METEOROLOGICAL) FLIGHT, later 1563 (HELICOPTER) FLIGHT, later 1563 (TACTICAL SUPPORT) FLIGHT
Formed 22nd December 1942 at Helwan, Egypt, as 1563 (Meteorological) Flight by redesignating a detachment of 1411 (Meteorological) Flight.

Gladiator I K8003; Hurricane IIB HL927, IIC LD179; Spitfire VC JG880 B.

Disbanded 30th May 1946 at Benina, Libya.

Reformed 1st August 1963 at Nicosia, Cyprus, as 1563 (Helicopter) Flight from an element of 103 Squadron.

Sycamore HR.14 XG547 D; Whirlwind HAR.10 XP399 D.

Disbanded 17th January 1972 at Akrotiri, Cyprus, to become 84 Squadron.

Reformed 1st November 1983 at Belize as 1563 (Tactical Support) Flight from a detachment of 33 Squadron.

C   *Puma HC.1 ZA938 CW.*

Disbanded 31st July 1994 at Belize.

1564 (METEOROLOGICAL) FLIGHT, later 1564 (HELICOPTER) FLIGHT, later 1564 (TACTICAL SUPPORT) FLIGHT
Formed 1st February 1943 at Mellaha, Libya, as 1564 (Meteorological) Flight.

Hurricane I Z4855, IIB KZ134, IIC LD209, IID HV590; Spitfire VC EF683, IX MA518.

Disbanded 15th June 1946 at Istres, France.

Reformed 14th August 1963 at El Adem, Libya, as 1564 (Helicopter) Flight from an element of 103 Squadron.

Sycamore HR.14 XL824; Whirlwind HAR.10 XP354.

Disbanded 31st December 1966 at El Adem.

Reformed 1st May 1969 at El Adem, Libya, as 1564 (Helicopter) Flight from 'D' Flight, 22 Squadron.

Whirlwind HAR.10 XP300.

Disbanded 31st March 1970 in Cyprus.

Reformed 20th August 1983 at Stanley, Falkland Islands, as 1564 (Tactical Support) Flight.

S   *Sea King HAR.3 XZ597 SC.*

Disbanded 22nd May 1986 at Mount Pleasant, Falklands, and merged with 1310 (Tactical Support) Flight to become 78 Squadron.

1565 (METEOROLOGICAL) FLIGHT
Formed 1st February 1943 at Nicosia, Cyprus, by redesignating a detachment of 1413 (Meteorological) Flight.

Gladiator I K7914; Hurricane IIB Z5341, IIC BE685; Spitfire VC JK927.

Disbanded 30th April 1946 at Nicosia.

1566 (METEOROLOGICAL) FLIGHT
1st February1943 at Khormaksar, Aden.

Hurricane IIB BE701, IIC KZ896; Defiant I DR990; Spitfire VC JK135; Vengeance IA EZ895.

Disbanded 30th April 1946 at Khormaksar, Aden.

1567 (METEOROLOGICAL) FLIGHT
Formed 15th June 1943 at Khartoum, Sudan.

Hurricane IIB BG707, IIC BP114; Spitfire VB ER817, VC JK111.

Disbanded 30th April 1946 at El Geneina, Sudan.

1568 (METEOROLOGICAL) FLIGHT
Formed 1st February 1944 at Diego Suarez, Madagascar.

Lysander IIIA V9491; Hurricane IIB HV583, IIC HV905.

Disbanded 15th January 1946 at Diego Suarez, Madagascar.

1569 (METEOROLOGICAL) FLIGHT
Formed 10th March 1944 at Eastleigh, Mauritius.

Hurricane IIB HW319, IIC HV284.

Disbanded 20th July 1945 at Plaisance.

1571 (GROUND GUNNERY) FLIGHT
Formed 18th July 1943 at Ratmalana, Ceylon.

Vengeance I EZ802; Harvard IIB FE547; Hurricane IIB BH128.

Disbanded 30th January 1944 at Ratmalana, Ceylon, to become 20 Armament Practice Camp.

1572 (GROUND GUNNERY) FLIGHT
Formed 10th July 1943 at St Thomas Mount, India.

Harvard IIB FE705; Vengeance I EZ890, II AN657; Blenheim IV Z7508; Hurricane IIC HW867; Wellington IC HX773.

Disbanded 30th January 1944 at St Thomas Mount to become 21 Armament Practice Camp.

1573 (GROUND GUNNERY) FLIGHT
Formed 7th October 1943 at Amarda Road, India.

Blenheim V EH462; Baltimore IV FA481.

Disbanded 30th January 1944 at Amarda Road, India, to become 22 Armament Practice Camp.

1574 (TARGET FACILITIES) FLIGHT, later 1574 (TARGET TOWING) FLIGHT
Formed 1st May 1964 at Changi, Singapore, as 1574 (Target Facilities) Flight. Later redesignated 1574 (Target Towing) Flight.

Meteor T.7 VW487, F(TT).8 WE876, TT.20 WD591.

Disbanded 29th December 1970 at Changi.

1575 (SPECIAL DUTIES) FLIGHT
Formed 28th May 1943 at Tempsford from an element of 138 Squadron.

Ventura II AE948; Halifax II BB429 N, V EB188 M.

Disbanded 22nd September 1943 at Blida, Algeria, one element becoming 624 Squadron and the other element being absorbed by 148 Squadron.

1576 (SPECIAL DUTIES) FLIGHT
Formed 1st September 1943 at Chaklala, India, from elements of the Air Landing School.

Anson I DJ440; Hudson IIIA FH232; Spitfire VC JK142; Liberator III BZ954.

Disbanded 1st February 1944 at Chaklala to become 'A' Flight of 357 Squadron.

1577 FLIGHT, later 1577 HEAVY BOMBER FLIGHT (SPECIAL DUTIES), later 1577 (GLIDER DEVELOPMENT) FLIGHT, later 1577 (AIRBORNE EXPERIMENTAL) FLIGHT
Formed 9th August 1943 at Llandow. Redesignated 1577 Heavy Bomber Flight (Special Duties) Flight from 12th October 1943 upon arrival in India, 1577 (Glider Development) Flight from 25th April 1944 and 1577 (Airborne Experimental) Flight from 2nd August 1945.

Wellington X HF576; Halifax III NA642, V DK263; Lancaster III JA903; Horsa I LH237; Hamilcar I HH974; Dakota III KG463 X; Hadrian II FR767; Waco CG13A KK719; Commando 42-101196.

Disbanded 1st June 1945 at Dhamial, India.

1578 (CALIBRATION) FLIGHT

Formed 25th September 1943 at Blida, Algeria, by redesignating the RDF Calibration Flight, Blida.

Blenheim V EH495; Baltimore IIIA FA326, IV FA473; Beaufighter VI KV911.

Disbanded 15th June 1944 at Reghaia, Algeria, to become the Mediterranean Allied Coastal Air Forces Communication Flight.

1579 (CALIBRATION) FLIGHT

Formed July 1943 at Ratmalana, Ceylon, by redesignating 222 Group Calibration Flight.

Blenheim V EH415; Vengeance I AN908, IA EZ994, II AN690.

Disbanded 10th October 1945 at Ratmalana.

1580 (CALIBRATION) FLIGHT

Formed 13th September 1943 at Yelahanka, India, by redesignating the Bangalore Calibration Flight.

Blenheim V BA880; Vengeance I AN919, II AN832, III FB947.

Disbanded 10th October 1945 at Cholavaram, India.

1581 (CALIBRATION) FLIGHT

Formed 25th August 1943 at Alipore, India.

Blenheim V BA680; Vengeance II AN785, III FD115.

Disbanded 15th November 1945 at Dalbhumgarh, India.

1582 (CALIBRATION) FLIGHT

Formed 25th August 1943 at Kumbhirgram, India.

Blenheim V EH399 D; Vengeance I AN998, II AN728, III FD112.

Disbanded 15th November 1945 at Dalbhumgarh, India.

1583 (CALIBRATION) FLIGHT

Formed 28th August 1943 at Chittagong, India, by redesignating the Bengal Calibration Flight.

Blenheim V BA851; Vengeance I AN939, II AN808, III FB918, IV FD410.

Disbanded 15th November 1945 at Trichinopoly, India.

1584 (HEAVY BOMBER CONVERSION) FLIGHT

Formed 23rd July 1943 at Salbani, India, by redesignating the Heavy Bomber Conversion Unit, Salbani.

Liberator III BZ902 A, VI BZ989.

Disbanded 9th November 1943 at Kolar, India, to become 1584 (Heavy Bomber) Conversion Unit.

1586 (POLISH SPECIAL DUTIES) FLIGHT

Formed 4th November 1943 at Derna, Libya, by redesignating 301 Squadron Special Duties Flight.

GR	Halifax II JP166, V LL467; Liberator III BZ800 GR-D, VI KG834 GR-U; Hurricane IID HW604.

Disbanded 7th November 1944 at Brindisi, Italy, to become 301 Squadron.

1587 (AOP REFRESHER) FLIGHT

Formed 20th August 1944 at Deolali, India.

Auster III NJ905.

Disbanded 31st December 1945 at Deolali to become 'C' Flight of 659 Squadron.

1588 (HEAVY FREIGHT) FLIGHT

Formed 10th October 1945 at Santa Cruz, India, by redesignating 'K' Flight.

Stirling V PJ888.

Disbanded 20th May 1946 at Santa Cruz, India.

1589 (HEAVY FREIGHT) FLIGHT

Formed 10th October 1945 at Cairo West by redesignating 'J' Flight.

Stirling V PK143 A.

Disbanded 30th April 1946 at Cairo West, Egypt.

1600 (ANTI-AIRCRAFT CO-OPERATION) FLIGHT

Formed 1st November 1942 at Weston Zoyland by redesignating 'A' Flight of 1 Anti-Aircraft Co-operation Unit.

Henley III L3262; Battle Trainer P6682; Defiant TT.I DR879; Martinet I EM446; Tiger Moth BB863.

Disbanded 1st December 1943 at Weston Zoyland and merged with 1601 and 1625 (Anti-Aircraft Co-operation) Flights to become 587 Squadron.

1601 (ANTI-AIRCRAFT CO-OPERATION) FLIGHT

Formed 1st November 1942 at Weston Zoyland by redesignating 'P' Flight of 1 Anti-Aircraft Co-operation Unit.

Henley III L3247; Martinet I HN959; Tiger Moth II T8781.

Disbanded 1st December 1943 at Weston Zoyland and merged with 1600 and 1625 (Anti-Aircraft Co-operation) Flights to become 587 Squadron.

1602 (ANTI-AIRCRAFT CO-OPERATION) FLIGHT

Formed 1st November 1942 at Cleave by redesignating 'D' Flight of 1 Anti-Aircraft Co-operation Unit.

Henley III L3270.

Disbanded 1st December 1943 at Cleave and merged with 1603 and 1604 (Anti-Aircraft Co-operation) Flights to become 639 Squadron.

1603 (ANTI-AIRCRAFT CO-OPERATION) FLIGHT

Formed 1st November 1942 at Cleave by redesignating 'G' Flight of 1 Anti-Aircraft Co-operation Unit.

Henley III L3255; Battle Trainer P6733.

Disbanded 1st December 1943 at Cleave and merged with 1602 and 1604 (Anti-Aircraft Co-operation) Flights to become 639 Squadron.

1604 (ANTI-AIRCRAFT CO-OPERATION) FLIGHT

Formed 1st November 1942 at Cleave by redesignating 'O' Flight of 1 Anti-Aircraft Co-operation Unit.

Henley III L3260; Tiger Moth II T8192.

Disbanded 1st December 1943 at Cleave and merged with 1602 and 1603 (Anti-Aircraft Co-operation) Flights to become 639 Squadron.

1605 (ANTI-AIRCRAFT CO-OPERATION) FLIGHT

Formed 1st November 1942 at Towyn by redesignating 'C' Flight of 1 Anti-Aircraft Co-operation Unit.

Henley III L3334; Martinet I HN887; Tiger Moth II N9253.

Disbanded 1st December 1943 at Towyn and merged with 1628 (Anti-Aircraft Co-operation) Flight to become 631 Squadron.

1606 (ANTI-AIRCRAFT CO-OPERATION) FLIGHT

Formed 1st November 1942 at Bodorgan by redesignating 'J' Flight of 1 Anti-Aircraft Co-operation Unit.

D2	Henley III L3394; Battle P6727; Queen Bee N9161; Tiger Moth II T7612; Hurricane IIC LE757, IV KX829; Martinet I HN954 D2-F.

Disbanded 30th April 1945 at Bodorgan.

1607 (ANTI-AIRCRAFT CO-OPERATION) FLIGHT

Formed 1st November 1942 at Carew Cheriton by redesignating 'B' Flight of 1 Anti-Aircraft Co-operation Unit.

Henley III L3252; Martinet I HN958; Tiger Moth II R4750.

Disbanded 1st December 1943 at Aberporth and merged with 1608 and 1609 (Anti-Aircraft Co-operation) Flights to become 595 Squadron.

1608 (ANTI-AIRCRAFT CO-OPERATION) FLIGHT

Formed 1st November 1942 at Aberporth by redesignating 'L' Flight of 1 Anti-Aircraft Co-operation Unit.

Wallace I K4344; Henley III L3403; Hurricane I P3827; Oxford II W6634; Martinet I HN888; Tiger Moth II R5013.

Disbanded 1st December 1943 at Aberporth and merged with 1607 and 1609 (Anti-Aircraft Co-operation) Flights to become 595 Squadron.

1609 (ANTI-AIRCRAFT CO-OPERATION) FLIGHT
Formed 1st November 1942 at Aberporth by redesignating 'Q' Flight of 1 Anti-Aircraft Co-operation Unit.

Henley III L3287; Battle P6727, Battle Trainer P6643; Martinet I HN947; Tiger Moth II T5625.

Disbanded 1st December 1943 at Aberporth and merged with 1607 and 1608 (Anti-Aircraft Co-operation) Flights to become 595 Squadron.

1611 (ANTI-AIRCRAFT CO-OPERATION) FLIGHT
Formed 1st November 1942 at Langham by redesignating 'K' Flight of 1 Anti-Aircraft Co-operation Unit.

Henley III L3260; Tiger Moth W7954; II DE624.

Disbanded 1st December 1943 at Bircham Newton and merged with 1612 and 1626 (Anti-Aircraft Co-operation) Flights to become 695 Squadron.

1612 (ANTI-AIRCRAFT CO-OPERATION) FLIGHT
Formed 1st November 1942 at Langham by redesignating 'M' Flight of 1 Anti-Aircraft Co-operation Unit.

Henley III L3420; Tiger Moth II N6540.

Disbanded 1st December 1943 at Bircham Newton and merged with 1611 and 1626 (Anti-Aircraft Co-operation) Flights to become 695 Squadron.

1613 (ANTI-AIRCRAFT CO-OPERATION) FLIGHT
Formed 1st November 1942 at West Hartlepool by redesignating 'N' Flight of 1 Anti-Aircraft Co-operation Unit.

Henley III L3259; Tiger Moth II T6809.

Disbanded 1st December 1943 at Hutton Cranswick and merged with 1629, 1630 and 1634 (Anti-Aircraft Co-operation) Flights to become 291 Squadron.

1614 (ANTI-AIRCRAFT CO-OPERATION) FLIGHT
Formed 1st November 1942 at Cark by redesignating 'F' Flight of 1 Anti-Aircraft Co-operation Unit.

Henley III L3287; Martinet I HN883; Tiger Moth II N6728.

Disbanded 1st December 1943 at Cark and merged with 'D' Flight, 289 Squadron to become 650 Squadron.

1616 (ANTI-AIRCRAFT CO-OPERATION) FLIGHT
Formed 1st November 1942 at Martlesham Heath by redesignating 'H' Flight of 1 Anti-Aircraft Co-operation Unit.

Henley III L3249; Defiant TT.I DR895; Hurricane I P3827; Martinet I EM502; Tiger Moth II DE164.

Disbanded 1st December 1943 at Ipswich and merged with 1627 (Anti-Aircraft Co-operation) Flight to become 679 Squadron.

1617 (ANTI-AIRCRAFT CO-OPERATION) FLIGHT
Formed 1st November 1942 at Newtownards by redesignating 'S' Flight of 1 Anti-Aircraft Co-operation Unit.

Henley III L3268; Martinet I EM467; Tiger Moth II DE165.

Disbanded 1st December 1943 at Newtownards and merged with 1480 (Anti-Aircraft Co-operation) Flight and an element of 289 Squadron to become 290 Squadron.

1618 (ANTI-AIRCRAFT CO-OPERATION) FLIGHT
Formed 1st November 1942 at Cleave by redesignating 'V' Flight of 1 Anti-Aircraft Co-operation Unit.

Queen Bee P4761; Tiger Moth II N9399.

Disbanded 1st December 1943 at Cleave.

1620 (ANTI-AIRCRAFT CO-OPERATION) FLIGHT
Formed 1st November 1942 at Bodorgan by redesignating 'Z' Flight of 1 Anti-Aircraft Co-operation Unit.

Queen Bee P4774; Tiger Moth II T7449; Oxford I HN128.

Disbanded 1st December 1943 at Bodorgan.

1621 (ANTI-AIRCRAFT CO-OPERATION) FLIGHT
Formed 1st November 1942 at Aberporth by redesignating 'X' Flight of 1 Anti-Aircraft Co-operation Unit.

Queen Bee P4761; Tiger Moth II R5238.

Disbanded 1st December 1943 at Aberporth.

1622 (ANTI-AIRCRAFT CO-OPERATION) FLIGHT
Formed 14th February 1943 at Gosport by redesignating 'A' Flight of 2 Anti-Aircraft Co-operation Unit.

Gladiator I K6149; Hurricane I N2344; Defiant I DR919; Roc L3082; Oxford I V3985; Martinet I HN961.

Disbanded 1st December 1943 at Gosport and merged with 1631 (Target Towing) Flight to become 667 Squadron.

1623 (ANTI-AIRCRAFT CO-OPERATION) FLIGHT
Formed 14th February 1943 at Roborough by redesignating 'C' Flight of 2 Anti-Aircraft Co-operation Unit.

Roc L3072; Henley III L3442; Defiant I DR921; Hurricane I P2865, X AF995; Tiger Moth II N6274; Oxford I N6274.

Disbanded 1st December 1943 at Roborough to become 691 Squadron.

1624 (ANTI-AIRCRAFT CO-OPERATION) FLIGHT
Formed 14th February 1943 at Detling by redesignating 'D' Flight of 2 Anti-Aircraft Co-operation Unit.

Gladiator I K7894, II L8031; Hurricane I V7075, X P5194; Oxford I N6250; Defiant I DR881; Martinet I EM473.

Disbanded 1st December 1943 at Detling to become 567 Squadron.

1625 (ANTI-AIRCRAFT CO-OPERATION) FLIGHT
Formed 17th June 1943 at Weston Zoyland by redesignating 1 RAF Regiment Anti-Aircraft Practice Camp Target Towing Flight.

Lysander II L6856, IIIA V9782; Martinet I HP215.

Disbanded 1st December 1943 at Weston Zoyland and merged with 1600 and 1601 (Target Towing) Flights to become 587 Squadron.

1626 (ANTI-AIRCRAFT CO-OPERATION) FLIGHT
Formed 17th June 1943 at Langham by redesignating 2 RAF Regiment Anti-Aircraft Practice Camp Target Towing Flight.

Lysander I P1671, II P1725.

Disbanded 1st December 1943 at Bircham Newton and merged with 1611 and 1612 (Target Towing) Flights to become 695 Squadron.

1627 (ANTI-AIRCRAFT CO-OPERATION) FLIGHT
Formed 17th June 1943 at Ipswich by redesignating 3 RAF Regiment Anti-Aircraft Practice Camp Target Towing Flight.

Lysander III R9068; Hurricane I Z4853; Martinet I HN958.

Disbanded 1st December 1943 at Ipswich and merged with 1616 (Target Towing) Flight to become 679 Squadron.

1628 (ANTI-AIRCRAFT CO-OPERATION) FLIGHT
Formed 17th June 1943 at Morfa Towyn by redesignating 4 RAF Regiment Anti-Aircraft Practice Camp Target Towing Flight.

Henley III L3323; Lysander III P1743.

Disbanded 1st December 1943 at Morfa Towyn and merged with 1605 (Target Towing) Flight to become 631 Squadron.

1629 (ANTI-AIRCRAFT CO-OPERATION) FLIGHT
Formed 27th June 1943 at Hutton Cranswick by redesignating 5 RAF Regiment Anti-Aircraft Practice Camp Target Towing Flight.

Martinet I EM480.

Disbanded 1st December 1943 at Hutton Cranswick and merged

with 1613, 1630 and 1634 (Target Towing) Flights to become 291 Squadron.

1630 (ANTI-AIRCRAFT CO-OPERATION) FLIGHT
Formed 17th June 1943 at Acklington by redesignating 6 RAF Regiment Anti-Aircraft Practice Camp Target Towing Target Towing Flight.

Lysander III T1747; Martinet I EM510.

Disbanded 1st December 1943 at Acklington and merged with 1613, 1629 and 1634 (Anti-Aircraft Co-operation) Flights to become 291 Squadron.

1631 (ANTI-AIRCRAFT CO-OPERATION) FLIGHT
Formed 17th June 1943 at Shoreham by redesignating 7 RAF Regiment Anti-Aircraft Practice Camp Target Towing Flight.

Defiant I DR881; Lysander III P1743.

Disbanded 1st December 1943 and merged with 1622 (Anti-Aircraft Co-operation) Flight to become 667 Squadron.

1632 (ANTI-AIRCRAFT CO-OPERATION) FLIGHT
Formed 17th June 1943 at Montrose by redesignating 8 RAF Regiment Anti-Aircraft Practice Camp Target Towing Flight.

Lysander IIIA V9818; Martinet I EM513.

Disbanded 1st December 1943 at Montrose and merged with 1479 (Anti-Aircraft Co-operation) Flight and an element of 289 Squadron to become 598 Squadron.

1633 (ANTI-AIRCRAFT CO-OPERATION) FLIGHT
Proposed formation cancelled. Was to have formed from 17th June 1943 at Leysdown by redesignating 9 RAF Regiment Anti-Aircraft Practice Camp Target Towing Flight.

1634 (ANTI-AIRCRAFT CO-OPERATION) FLIGHT
Formed 17th June 1943 at Hutton Cranswick by merging 1 and 3 Royal Air Force Regiment School Target Towing Flights.

Lysander II N1210; Martinet I MS562.

Disbanded 1st December 1943 at Hutton Cranswick and merged with 1613, 1629 and 1630 (Anti-Aircraft Co-operation) Flights to become 291 Squadron.

1676 (TARGET TOWING) FLIGHT
Formed 12th April 1943 at Gibraltar.

Martinet I JN490; Spitfire VB ES186, VC MA882, IX EN446.

Disbanded 11th September 1943 at Gibraltar to become the Fighter Defence Flight, Gibraltar.

1677 (TARGET TOWING) FLIGHT, RAF
Formed 1st March 1944 at Netheravon.

HM	*Martinet I NR385; Oxford I RR331.*

Disbanded 21st May 1946 at Wethersfield.

1678 (HEAVY CONVERSION) FLIGHT, RAF
Formed 18th May 1943 at East Wretham by redesignating the Lancaster Conversion Flight of 1657 Heavy Conversion Unit.

SW	*Lancaster II DS623 SW-T.*

Disbanded 16th September 1943 at Foulsham to become 1678 Heavy Conversion Unit.

1679 (HEAVY CONVERSION) FLIGHT
Formed 18th May 1943 at East Moor.

Lancaster II DS615 R.

Disbanded 27th January 1944 at Wombleton and absorbed by 1666 Heavy Conversion Unit.

1680 (WESTERN ISLES COMMUNICATION) FLIGHT, later 1680 (TRANSPORT) FLIGHT
Formed 24th May 1943 at Abbotsinch. Redesignated 1680 (Transport) Flight from 8th April 1944.

MJ	*Dragon Rapide Z7258; Dominie I HG723 MJ-N, II NR748; Fokker XII HM159; Walrus K5775;*

Harrow II K7032; Wellington I L4263; Anson I NK675, X NK705; Oxford I NM341; Dakota I FD772; III FZ670 MJ-O; IV KJ977; Anson X NK702.

Disbanded 7th February 1946 at Prestwick.

1681 BOMBER (DEFENCE) TRAINING FLIGHT
Formed 1st July 1943 at Pershore.

Tomahawk I AH746, IIA AH920, IIB AK156; Hurricane IIC LF118.

Disbanded 21st August 1944 at Long Marston.

1682 BOMBER (DEFENCE) TRAINING FLIGHT, RAF
Formed 1st July 1943 at Abingdon.

UH	*Tomahawk I AH822, IIA AH896, IIB AK147; Hurricane IIC LF720 UH-P.*

Disbanded 1st August 1944 at Enstone.

1683 BOMBER (DEFENCE) TRAINING FLIGHT, RAF
Formed 5th June 1943 at Bruntingthorpe.

FP	*Allocated but no evidence of use.*
Nil	*Tomahawk I AH753, IIA AH929, IIB AK116; Hurricane IIC LF755.*

Disbanded 1st August 1944 at Market Harborough.

1684 BOMBER (DEFENCE) TRAINING FLIGHT, RAF
Formed 29th June 1943 at Little Horwood.

PB	*Tomahawk I AH848, IIA AH918, IIB AK162; Hurricane IIC LF757.*

Disbanded 1st August 1944 at Wing.

1685 BOMBER (DEFENCE) TRAINING FLIGHT, RAF
Formed 1st July 1943 at Ossington.

KA	*Tomahawk I AH777, IIA AH949, IIB AH999; Hurricane IIC MW368 KA-H.*

Disbanded 21st August 1944 at Ossington.

1686 BOMBER (DEFENCE) TRAINING FLIGHT, RAF
Formed 1st July 1943 at Hixon.

FI	*Tomahawk I AH769, IIA AH908, IIB AK122; Hurricane IIC LF380 FI-D.*

Disbanded 21st August 1944 at Hixon.

1687 BOMBER (DEFENCE) TRAINING FLIGHT, RAF
Formed 15th February 1944 at Ingham.

4E	*Spitfire IIA P7690, VB AB194 4E-W; Hurricane IIC PG537 4E-A; Oxford II P1089; Martinet I HP325 F.*

Disbanded 30th October 1946 at Hemswell.

1688 BOMBER DEFENCE TRAINING FLIGHT, RAF
Formed 11th March 1944 at Newmarket by redesignating 1483 (Bomber) Gunnery Flight.

6H	*Spitfire VB EP509 6H-G; Hurricane IIC LF754 6H-T, IV LD977; Tiger Moth II T7351 6H-K; Wellington X JA131.*

Disbanded 1st October 1946 at Wyton.

1689 BOMBER (DEFENCE) TRAINING FLIGHT, later 1689 (FERRY POOL PILOT TRAINING) FLIGHT
Formed 15th February 1944 at Leconfield by redesignating 1484 (Bomber) Gunnery Flight.

Hurricane IIC LF403 A, IID HW684 G, IV KZ663 H; Anson I EG646 Z; Spitfire VB BL848; Martinet I MS748 B; Beaufighter VIF MM920, X ND199; Tiger Moth II T7261.

Disbanded 7th May 1945 at Holme-on-Spalding-Moor.

Reformed 6th March 1946 at Aston Down as 1689 (Ferry Pilot Training) Flight, attached to 20 Maintenance Unit, by redesignating 41 Group Training Flight.

9X	Wellington X RP506 9X-S; Lancaster VII NX612 9X; Hornet F.3 PX348; Lincoln II RE341; Tempest V SN276, VI NX127; Mosquito III VP346 9X-T; Spitfire XVI TB713; Anson XII PH805 9X; Oxford I RR332 9X-P; Harvard IIB KF712 9X-C; Vampire F.1 VF278, FB.5 VV567; Meteor T.7 WF826.

Disbanded 9th April 1953 at Aston Down, moved to Benson and absorbed by the Ferry Training Unit.

1690 BOMBER (DEFENCE) TRAINING FLIGHT, RAF
Formed 26th February 1944 at Syerston by redesignating 1485 (Bomber) Gunnery Flight.

9M	Spitfire IIA P8177, IIB P8476; Hurricane IIC PZ740, IV LE395; Oxford II P6809; Tiger Moth II R5245; Wellington X LN457; Martinet I MS691.

Disbanded 12th October 1945 at Syerston.

1691 (BOMBER) GUNNERY FLIGHT, RAF
Formed 1st August 1943 at Dalton.

Martinet I MS554 S; Oxford II P1820.

Disbanded 15th February 1944 at Dalton to become 1695 (Bomber) Defence Flight.

1692 (SPECIAL DUTIES) FLIGHT, later 1692 (BOMBER SUPPORT TRAINING) FLIGHT
Formed 1st June 1943 at Drem as 1692 (Special Duties) Flight by redesignating the Radio Development Flight. Redesignated 1692 (Bomber Support Training) Flight 10th December 1943.

4X	Defiant II AA659; Beaufighter I X7567, VI EL170; Mosquito II HJ922, III HJ870, Mosquito VI LR301 4X-5, XII HK189, XIX TA393; Wellington XVIII ND116; Anson I DG718 4X-27.

Disbanded 16th June 1945 at Great Massingham.

1693 (GENERAL RECONNAISSANCE) FLIGHT
Formed 8th September 1943 at Skitten.

Anson I MH166 K.

Disbanded 11th August 1945 at Bircham Newton.

1694 (TARGET TOWING) FLIGHT, later 1694 BOMBER (DEFENCE) TRAINING FLIGHT
Formed 24th January 1944 at West Raynham. Redesignated 1694 Bomber (Defence) Training Flight from 1st November 1944.

Martinet I HP207; Tiger Moth I NL995.

Disbanded 30th July 1945 at Great Massingham.

1695 BOMBER (DEFENCE) TRAINING FLIGHT
Formed 15th February 1944 at Dalton by redesignating 1691 (Bomber) Gunnery Flight.

3K	Spitfire IIA P8035, Spitfire VB AR278 3K-H; Hurricane IIC LF588 3K-S, IV KZ709 3K-B; Martinet I MS869; Oxford I R6036, II N4739.

Disbanded 28th July 1945 at Dishforth.

1696 BOMBER (DEFENCE) TRAINING FLIGHT
Formed 15th February 1944 at Gransden Lodge.

Spitfire IIA P7775, VB AB183; Tomahawk IIA AH986; Hurricane IIC LF532; Martinet I HP528; Oxford I PH509, II N4739.

Disbanded 28th September 1945 at Warboys.

1697 (AIR DESPATCH LETTER SERVICE) FLIGHT
Formed 27th March 1944 at Northolt.

DR (3.44–12.44)	Hurricane IIC MW336 DR-E.
U7 (3.44–12.44)	Anson I MG865 U7-H, X NK449.
Also used	Beaufighter VI EL216; Auster I LB283.

Although disbanded officially with effect from 11th November 1944, the Flight finally ceased to exist on 7th March 1945 at Northolt,

being absorbed by the 2nd Tactical Air Force Communications Squadron.

1698 FLIGHT
Was to have formed by 15th April 1944 at Farnborough with Meteor F.1 but formation of the Flight was abandoned.

1699 (FORTRESS TRAINING) FLIGHT
Formed 24th April 1944 at Sculthorpe. Redesignated 1699 (Training) Flight from 24th October 1944.

4Z	Fortress I AN537, II SR376 4Z-W, Fortress III HB818 4Z-A; Anson X NK842 4Z-C; Oxford; Liberator IV TS538 4Z-B.

Disbanded 24th October 1944 at Oulton to become 1699 (Bomber Support) Conversion Unit.

1900 INDEPENDENT AIR OBSERVATION POST FLIGHT
Formed 1st January 1947 at Beaulieu within 657 Squadron by redesignating the Squadron's 'A' and 'B' Flights.

TS (1.47–4.51)	Tiger Moth II T5880; Auster AOP.6 TW524.
Nil (4.51–9.57)	Auster VI WJ363, T.7 WE608, AOP.9 WZ720.

Disbanded 1st September 1957 at Sha Tin, Hong Kong, to become 20 Independent Reconnaissance Flight, Army Air Corps.

1901 AIR OBSERVATION POST FLIGHT
Formed 1st January 1947 at Beaulieu within 657 Squadron by redesignating the Squadron's 'C' Flight.

TS (1.47–4.51)	Auster V TJ672 TS-D2, VI VF606 TS-N; Hoverfly II KN840 TS-L.
Nil (4.51–9.57)	Auster VI VF570.

Disbanded 1st September 1957 at Detmold, Germany, to become 1 Reconnaissance Flight, Army Air Corps.

1902 AIR OBSERVATION POST FLIGHT
Formed 1st January 1947 at Celle, Germany, within 652 Squadron by redesignating the Squadron's 'A' Flight.

XM	Auster VI TW627

Disbanded 15th February 1948 at Lüneburg, Germany.

Reformed 15th July 1948 at Taiping, Malaya.

Auster V, VI VX130, AOP.9

Disbanded 1st September 1957 at Ipoh, Malaya, to become 2 Reconnaissance Flight, Army Air Corps.

1903 AIR OBSERVATION POST FLIGHT
Formed 1st January 1947 at Celle, Germany, within 652 Squadron by redesignating the Squadron's 'B' Flight.

XM	Auster VI TW625 XM-H.

Disbanded 15th February 1948 at Lüneburg, Germany, to become 1905 Air Observation Post Flight.

Reformed 15th July 1948 at Seremban, Malaya.

Auster V TJ647, VI TW626, T.7 WE616.

Disbanded 1st September 1957 at Feltwell to become 3 Reconnaissance Flight, Army Air Corps.

1904 AIR OBSERVATION POST FLIGHT
Formed 1st January 1947 at Celle, Germany, within 652 Squadron by redesignating the Squadron's 'C' Flight.

XM (1.47–4.51)	Auster V NJ650, VI VF492 XM-G.
Nil (4.51– 9.57)	Auster VI VF579.

Disbanded 1st September 1957 at Detmold, Germany, to become 4 Reconnaissance Flight, Army Air Corps.

1905 AIR OBSERVATION POST FLIGHT
Formed 15th February 1948 at Lüneburg, Germany, within 652 Squadron.

XM (2.48–4.51)	Auster VI VF486 XM-P.
Nil (4.51–9.47)	Auster VI VF485.

Disbanded 1st September 1957 at Detmold, Germany, to become 5 Reconnaissance Flight, Army Air Corps.

1906 AIR OBSERVATION POST FLIGHT, later 1906 (HELICOPTER) FLIGHT

Formed 1st January 1947 at Ronchi, Italy, within 654 Squadron from elements of the Squadron's 'A' and 'B' Flights.

Auster IV, Auster V.

Disbanded 24th July 1947 at Qastina, Italy, to become 1910 Independent Air Observation Post Flight.

Reformed 1st May 1950 at Middle Wallop as 1906 (Helicopter) Flight.

Auster VI VF511; Sycamore HC.11 WT924; Skeeter 6 XK773, AOP.10 XK481; Hiller HT.1 XB515.

Disbanded 1st September 1957 at Middle Wallop to become 6 Independent/Liaison Flight, Army Air Corps.

1907 AIR OBSERVATION POST FLIGHT, later 1907 LIGHT LIAISON FLIGHT

Formed 1st January 1947 at Ronchi, Italy, within 654 Squadron by redesignating elements of the Squadron's 'A' and 'C' Flights.

Auster V.

Disbanded 9th September 1947 at Qastina, Italy.

Reformed 15th July 1948 at Sembawang, Singapore. Redesignated 1907 Light Liaison Flight from 1953.

Auster V TJ311, VI WJ399, T.7 WE610, AOP.9 WZ664.

Disbanded 1st September 1957 at Taiping to become 7 Reconnaissance Flight, Army Air Corps.

1908 INDEPENDENT AIR OBSERVATION POST FLIGHT

Formed 23rd December 1946 Petah Tiqva, Palestine, within 651 Squadron by redesignating 'A' Flight of 651 Squadron.

Nil (12.46– .47)	*Auster V, VI VF502.*
XM (.47–4.51)	*Auster VI VF615 XM-P.*
Nil (4.51–10.55)	*Auster VI.*

Disbanded 7th October 1955 at Idris, Libya.

Reformed 16th October 1955 at Ismailia, Egypt, from an element of 1910 Flight.

Auster VI WJ375; T.7 WE611.

Disbanded 1st September 1957 at Ismailia to become 8 Independent Reconnaissance Flight, Army Air Corps.

1909 AIR OBSERVATION POST FLIGHT

Formed 31st December 1946 at Ramat David, Palestine, within 651 Squadron by redesignating the Squadron's 'B' Flight.

Auster V, VI TW619.

Disbanded 20th July 1948 at Amman, Jordan.

Reformed 1st March 1951 at Detmold, Germany, within 652 Squadron.

XM (3.51–4.51)	*Auster VI VF505 XM-V.*
Nil (4.51–9.57)	*Auster VI VW987, T.7 WE597.*

Disbanded 1st September 1957 at Detmold to become 9 Reconnaissance Flight, Army Air Corps.

1910 AIR OBSERVATION POST FLIGHT

Formed 24th July 1947 at Qastina, Palestine, by redesignating 1906 Flight.

Auster VI VF503, T.7 WE595.

Disbanded 1st September 1957 at Kermia, Cyprus, to become 10 Independent Reconnaissance Flight, Army Air Corps.

1911 LIGHT LIAISON FLIGHT

Formed June 1950 at Changi, Singapore.

Auster VI VF528, T.7 WE540, AOP.9 WZ674.

Disbanded 1st September 1957 at Sembawang, Singapore, to become 11 Reconnaissance/Liaison Flight, Army Air Corps.

1912 (GLIDER TRAINING) FLIGHT, later 1912 LIGHT LIAISON FLIGHT

Formed 15th August 1951 at Middle Wallop. Redesignated 1912 Light Liaison Flight from 21st May 1952.

Auster VI VW999; T.7 WE535; Chipmunk T.10 WZ854.

Disbanded 1st September 1957 at Wildenrath to become 12 Independent Liaison Flight, Army Air Corps.

1913 (AIR OBSERVATION POST) FLIGHT, later 1913 LIGHT LIASION FLIGHT

Formed 12th June 1951 at Middle Wallop. Redesignated 1913 Light Liaison Flight from 1st May 1952.

Auster VI VF661 D, T.7 WE616; Cessna L-19 51-4754.

Disbanded 1st September 1957 at Feltwell to become 13 Liaison Flight, Army Air Corps.

1914 AIR OBSERVATION POST FLIGHT

Formed 1st January 1947 at Kuala Lumpur, Malaya, by redesignating an element of 656 Squadron.

Auster V TJ251, VI VF612, T.7, AOP.9.

Disbanded 1st September 1957 at Port Dickson, Malaya, to become 14 Reconnaissance Flight, Army Air Corps.

1915 LIGHT LIAISON FLIGHT

Proposed formation in 1954 in Kenya with helicopters cancelled.

Formed 6th March 1956 at Middle Wallop.

Auster VI VF486.

Disbanded 1st September 1957 at Kermia, Cyprus, to become 15 Independent Liaison Flight, Army Air Corps.

1951 AIR OBSERVATION POST FLIGHT

Formed 1st July 1949 at Ringway within 663 Squadron.

ROC (7.49–4.51)	*Auster IV MS980, V TJ340 ROC-C, VI VW993 ROC-B, T.7 WE571 ROC-O; Tiger Moth II N6616 ROC-Z.*
Nil (4.51–3.57)	*Auster VI; Chipmunk T.10 WP859 Y.*

Disbanded 10th March 1957 at Ringway.

1952 AIR OBSERVATION POST FLIGHT

Formed 1st July 1949 at Llandow within 663 Squadron.

ROC (7.49–4.51)	*Auster V TJ339, VI VX942.*
Nil (4.51–3.57)	*Auster VI VX942.*

Disbanded 10th March 1957 at Llandow.

1953 AIR OBSERVATION POST FLIGHT

Formed 20th July 1949 at Hooton Park within 663 Squadron.

ROC (7.49–4.51)	*Auster IV MS980, V, VI VF487 ROC-M.*
Nil (4.51–3.57)	*Auster VI.*

Disbanded 10th March 1957 at Hooton Park.

1954 AIR OBSERVATION POST FLIGHT

Formed 20th July 1949 at Wolverhampton within 663 Squadron.

ROC (9.49–4.51)	*Auster V TW385, VI.*
Nil (4.51–3.57)	*Auster VI VF490, T.7; Chipmunk T.10 WP859.*

Disbanded 10th March 1957 at Castle Bromwich.

1955 AIR OBSERVATION POST FLIGHT

Formed 1st July 1949 at Hooton Park within 663 Squadron.

ROC (7.49–4.51)	*Auster IV MT218, VI, Tiger Moth II N9160.*
Nil (4.51–3.57)	*Auster VI.*

Disbanded 10th March 1957 at Hooton Park.

1956 AIR OBSERVATION POST FLIGHT

Formed 1st February 1949 at Colerne within 662 Squadron.

ROB (2.49–4.51)	*Auster V TJ380 ROB-C, VI.*
Nil (4.51–3.57)	*Auster VI VX121 A.*

Disbanded 10th March 1957 at Colerne.

1957 AIR OBSERVATION POST FLIGHT
Formed 1st May 1949 at Kenley within 661 Squadron.

ROA (5.49–4.51)   Auster V TW449 ROA-A, VI.
Nil (4.51–3.57)   Auster VI.

Disbanded 10th March 1957 at Kenley.

1958 AIR OBSERVATION POST FLIGHT
Formed 1st July 1949 at Hendon within 661 Squadron.

ROA (7.49–4.51)   Auster IV MT349, Auster V TJ394 ROA-F, VI
        TW583 ROA-J.
Nil (4.51–3.57)   Auster V TJ394 F, VI VF603 G.

Disbanded 10th March 1957 at Hendon.

1959 AIR OBSERVATION POST FLIGHT
Formed 1st May 1949 at Henlow within 661 Squadron.

ROA (5.49–4.51)   Auster IV MT133, V TW392, VI TW577 ROA-M.
Nil (4.51–3.57)   Auster V TJ394 M, VI.

Disbanded 10th March 1957 at Hornchurch.

1960 AIR OBSERVATION POST FLIGHT
Formed 1st May 1949 at Kenley within 661 Squadron.

ROA (5.49–4.51)   Auster V TW384 ROA-Q, VI VX112 ROA-S.
Nil (4.51–3.57)   Auster VI.

Disbanded 10th March 1957 at Kenley.

1961 AIR OBSERVATION POST FLIGHT
Formed 1st May 1949 at Henlow within 661 Squadron.

ROA (5.49–4.51)   Auster V TW519 ROA-V, VI TW574 ROA-X.
Nil (4.51–3.57)   Auster VI VF641 W.

Disbanded 10th March 1957 at Henlow.

1962 AIR OBSERVATION POST FLIGHT
Formed 1st September 1949 at Middle Wallop within 662 Squadron.

ROB (9.49–4.51)   Auster IV MT137, V, VI VF511 ROB-X.
Nil (4.51–3.57)   Auster V, VI.

Disbanded 10th March 1957 at Middle Wallop.

1963 AIR OBSERVATION POST FLIGHT
Formed 1st February 1949 at Colerne within 662 Squadron.

ROB (2.49–4.51)   Auster IV, V, VI VF511 ROB-X; Tiger Moth II
        T7399 ROB-T.
Nil (4.51–3.57)   Auster V, VI VF575 R.

Disbanded 10th March 1957 at Colerne.

1964 AIR OBSERVATION POST FLIGHT
Formed 1st September 1949 at Yeadon within 664 Squadron.

ROD (9.49–4.51)   Auster V TW458, VI VW998 ROD-A.
Nil (4.51–3.57)   Auster VI VW998 A, T.7 WE542 E; Tiger Moth
        II PG701 E.

Disbanded 10th March 1957 at Yeadon.

1965 AIR OBSERVATION POST FLIGHT
Formed 1st September 1949 at Ouston within 664 Squadron.

ROD (9.49–4.51)   Auster V TW456, VI.
Nil (4.51–3.57)   Auster VI VX110 F.

Disbanded 10th March 1957 at Usworth.

1966 AIR OBSERVATION POST FLIGHT
Formed 1st May 1949 at Scone within 666 Squadron.

ROG (5.49–4.51)   Auster V MT363, VI; Tiger Moth II T9709
        ROG-7.
Nil (4.51–3.57)   Auster V TW575 C.

Disbanded 10th March 1957 at Scone.

1967 AIR OBSERVATION POST FLIGHT
Formed 1st December 1951 at Renfrew within 666 Squadron.

Auster V MT361, VI VW986 M.

Disbanded 10th March 1957 at Abbotsinch.

1968 AIR OBSERVATION POST FLIGHT
Formed 1st May 1949 at Turnhouse within 666 Squadron.

ROG (5.49–4.51)   Auster V TW454 ROG-K, VI VX124 ROG-G.
Nil (4.51–3.57)   Auster VI VF492 F.

Disbanded 10th March 1957 at Turnhouse.

1969 AIR OBSERVATION POST FLIGHT
Formed 1st September 1949 at Desford within 664 Squadron.

ROD (9.49–4.51)   Auster V TJ320, VI VW999 ROD-L; Tiger Moth
        II EM915 ROD-P.
Nil (4.51–3.57)   Auster VI VW995 O.

Disbanded 10th March 1957 at Wymeswold.

1970 AIR OBSERVATION POST FLIGHT
Formed 1st September 1949 at Hucknall within 664 Squadron.

ROD (7.49–4.51)   Auster V TW387, VI VX122 ROD-Q.
Nil (4.51–3.57)   Auster VI VF520 S; Tiger Moth II PG701 E.

Disbanded 10th March 1957 at Hucknall.

FLOATPLANE FLIGHT
Formed November 1943 at Kasfareet, Egypt, within 107 Maintenance Unit with later assistance from the (Middle East) Central Gunnery School, El Ballah.

Spitfire VB Floatplane EP754.

Disbanded November 1943 at the Great Bitter Lakes, Egypt.

FLOATPLANE TRAINING FLIGHT (1) – see Seaplane Training Squadron

FLOATPLANE TRAINING FLIGHT (2)
Formed April 1938 at Lee-on-Solent by redesignating the Floatplane Training Flight of the Seaplane Training Squadron.

Shark II K8513; Swordfish I K8346 46; Walrus I K8549; Seafox K8595.

Disbanded 24th May 1939 at Lee-on-Solent to become 765 Squadron, Fleet Air Arm.

FLOATPLANE TRAINING SQUADRON – see Floatplane Training Unit, later Floatplane Training Squadron

FLOATPLANE TRAINING UNIT, later FLOATPLANE TRAINING SQUADRON
Formed by 23rd June 1939 at Calshot. There is evidence to suggest the Unit became the Floatplane Training Squadron from December 1939.

Swordfish I Floatplane L2780.

Existed to at least May 1940. Possibly moved to Stranraer before disbanding.

FLOTILLE 1E – see 344 (Free French) Squadron

FLOTILLE 7E – see 343 (Free French) Squadron

FLYING BOAT CONVERSION UNIT
A loose term given to the activities of 209 Squadron between the end of 1943 and the early part of 1944.

FLYING BOAT DEVELOPMENT FLIGHT
Formed 1st October 1921 at Grain.

Cork III N87; Felixstowe F.5 N4038 E.

Disbanded 21st September 1922 at Grain.

Reformed 1st January 1924 at Cattewater.

Felixstowe F.5 N4121; Southampton I S1058, II S1231.

Disbanded 1932 at Felixstowe and absorbed by the Marine Aircraft Experimental Establishment.

FLYING BOAT PRACTICE CAMP
Formed April 1932 at Calshot.

Southampton I N9896, II S1249.

Disbanded November 1932 at Calshot.

12 (FLYING BOAT) PREPARATION AND MODIFICATION UNIT
Formed 1st September 1945 at Calshot.

No aircraft known.

Disbanded 25th April 1946 at Calshot.

FLYING BOAT TRAINING SQUADRON
Formed 2nd January 1939 at Calshot.

Stranraer I K7299; Scapa I K7304; Singapore III K4578.

Disbanded 16th March 1941 at Stranraer and merged with the Seaplane Training Squadron to become 4 Operational Training Unit.

Reformed 17th October 1953 at Pembroke Dock by redesignating 235 Operational Conversion Unit.

Sunderland V SZ560 L.

Disbanded 5th October 1956 at Pembroke Dock.

FLYING INSTRUCTORS SCHOOL, EL KHANKA
Formed 7th September 1918 at El Khanka, Egypt, by redesignating a Flight of the Aerial Fighting School, Heliopolis, upon its merger with the School of Aerial Gunnery to become 5 Fighting School.

Avro 504J D5460, Avro 504K E1631.

Disbanded 27th July 1919 at El Khanka.

FLYING INSTRUCTORS SCHOOL, THE CURRAGH
Formed 22nd October 1918 at The Curragh, Ireland.

Avro 504J; D.H.9A E8762.

Disbanded 13th June 1919 at The Curragh.

FLYING INSTRUCTORS SCHOOL (INDIA)
Formed 1944 at Ambala, India, within 1 Service Flying Training School (India).

No aircraft known.

Disbanded 13th June 1944 at Ambala to become the Central Flying School (India)

FLYING INSTRUCTORS SCHOOL, UPAVON
Formed 23rd December 1919 at Upavon by redesignating the Central Flying School.

F.2B.

Disbanded 26th April 1920 to become the Central Flying School.

1 FLYING INSTRUCTORS SCHOOL, later 1 FLYING INSTRUCTORS SCHOOL (ADVANCED)
Formed 13th January 1942 at Church Lawford by redesignating 2 Central Flying School. Redesignated 1 Flying Instructors School (Advanced) from 7th April 1942.

Oxford I N4582, II N6341; Anson I DG840; Tutor K3231.

Disbanded 27th October 1942 at Church Lawford to become 18 (Pilots) Advance Flying Unit.

2 FLYING INSTRUCTORS SCHOOL, later 2 FLYING INSTRUCTORS SCHOOL (ADVANCED)
Formed 10th September 1940 at Cranwell.

Oxford I L4621; Tutor K3219.

Disbanded 14th November 1940 at Cranwell to become 2 Central Flying School.

Reformed 5th January 1942 at Montrose. Redesignated 2 Flying Instructors School (Advanced) from 7th April 1942.

Tiger Moth II EM903; Master I N7447, II DL474, III DL575; Oxford I BF941 D, II P1089 NN; Hurricane I N2594; Magister P2499; Tutor K3256; Hudson V AM526, VI EW917; Harvard IIB KF156; Beaufort IIA ML627.

Disbanded 11th July 1945 at Montrose.

3 FLYING INSTRUCTORS SCHOOL (ADVANCED)
Formed 1st August 1942 at Hullavington.

Master I N7478, III DL683; Oxford I PH409 32, II V3792 73; Magister P1969; Harvard IIB FX283 7.

Disbanded 5th July 1945 at Lulsgate Bottom and absorbed by 7 Flying Instructors School.

4 FLYING INSTRUCTORS SCHOOL (SUPPLIMENTARY), later 4 FLYING INSTRUCTORS SCHOOL, later 4 FLYING INSTRUCTORS SCHOOL (ELEMENTARY)
Formed 3rd July 1940 at Cambridge. Redesignated 4 Flying Instructors School from 13th January 1942 and 4 Flying Instructors School (Elementary) from 7th April 1942.

Master I N7512; Tiger Moth BB807, I K4258, II DE174; Magister P6366.

Disbanded 30th April 1943 at Cambridge.

5 FLYING INSTRUCTORS SCHOOL (SUPPLIMENTARY), later 5 FLYING INSTRUCTORS SCHOOL, later 5 FLYING INSTRUCTORS SCHOOL (ELEMENTARY)
Formed September 1941 at Scone from 'E' Flight of 11 Elementary Flying Training School. Redesignated 5 Flying Instructors School from 13th January 1942 and 5 Flying Instructors School (Elementary) from 7th April 1942.

Master I N7582; Tiger Moth BB806, II N9504; Magister L8153.

Disbanded 23rd November 1942 at Scone.

6 FLYING INSTRUCTORS SCHOOL (SUPPLIMENTARY), later 6 FLYING INSTRUCTORS SCHOOL, later 6 FLYING INSTRUCTORS SCHOOL (ELEMENTARY)
Formed 1st November 1941 at Staverton by redesignating 2 Elementary Flying Training School. Redesignated 6 Flying Instructors School from 13th January 1942 and 6 Flying Instructors School (Elementary) from 7th April 1942.

Master I N7439; Tiger Moth II N9312; Magister N3821.

Disbanded 22nd July 1942 at Worcester to become 2 Elementary Flying Training School.

7 FLYING INSTRUCTORS SCHOOL, later 7 FLYING INSTRUCTORS SCHOOL (ADVANCED)
Formed 1st April 1942 at Upavon by redesignating the Central Flying School. Redesignated 7 Flying Instructors School (Advanced) from 7th April 1942.

Nil (4.42–4.46)	*Audax K7340; Magister L5976; Master II DL183, III W8694; Tiger Moth II N6725; Anson I K6308; Hudson VI EW917; Oxford I L9653, II N4734; Vigilant IA BZ103; Harvard IIB FX301 Z.*
FDI (4.46–5.46)	*Oxford I BG244 FDI-L.*
FDJ (4.46–5.46)	*Oxford I X6872 FDJ-G.*
FDK (4.46–5.46)	*Oxford I HN667 FDK-Z.*
FDL (4.46–5.46)	*Oxford I V3880 FDL-C.*

Disbanded 7th May 1946 at Upavon and merged with 10 Flying Instructors School (Elementary) to become the Central Flying School.

10 FLYING INSTRUCTORS SCHOOL (ELEMENTARY)
Formed 22nd July 1942 at Woodley.

Nil (7.42–4.46)	*Magister N3800; Hawk Trainer 3 BB662; Master I N7439, II DL350, III DL969; Tiger Moth II N9177.*
FDQ (4.46–5.46)	*Tiger Moth II T6570 FDQ-J.*
FDR (4.46–5.46)	*Tiger Moth II DE678 FDR-B.*
FDS (4.46–5.46)	*Tiger Moth II DE718 FDS-B.*
FDT (4.46–5.46)	*Hawk Trainer 3 BB661 FDT-A; Magister L8353 FDT-E; Anson I NK565 FDT-M.*

Disbanded 7th May 1946 at Woodley and merged with 7 Flying Instructors School (Advanced) to become the Central Flying School.

11 FLYING INSTRUCTORS SCHOOL
Formed 1st January 1944 at Shallufa, Egypt, by redesignating the Flying Instructors Training School.

Harvard III EZ354; Oxford I PH238; Anson I NL143; Wellington X LP778.

Disbanded 7th January 1947 at Nicosia, Cyprus.

12 FLYING INSTRUCTORS SCHOOL (OPERATIONAL)
Formed 1st May 1944 at St Angelo.

Beaufort IIA ML564 E; Mosquito III LR554; Wellington X HE262; Master II AZ587, III DL909.

Disbanded 23rd February 1945 at St Angelo to become the Coastal Command Flying Instructors School.

33 FLYING INSTRUCTORS SCHOOL, SOUTHERN RHODESIA
Formed 20th May 1942 at Belvedere, Southern Rhodesia, by redesignating the Rhodesian Central Flying School.

Oxford I AR846, II T1113; Tiger Moth II N9344; Cornell 15073; Harvard I P5829, II AJ743; Cornell II 15121.

Disbanded 9th May 1944 at Norton to become the Central Flying School, Southern Rhodesia.

FLYING INSTRUCTORS TRAINING SCHOOL
Formed 1st December 1943 at Shallufa, Egypt.

Beaufort; Harvard.

Disbanded 1st January 1944 at Shallufa to become 11 Flying Instructors School.

FLYING REFRESHER SCHOOL
Formed 1st June 1949 at Finningley by redesignating 1 (Pilot) Refresher Flying Unit.

N	*Wellington X RP325 N-B.*
O	*No evidence of use.*
Also used	*Oxford I PH113; Harvard IIB KF186; Spitfire XVI TE455.*

Disbanded 1st April 1951 at Finningley to become 101 Flying Refresher School.

101 FLYING REFRESHER SCHOOL
Formed 1st April 1951 at Finningley by redesignating the Flying Refresher School.

N	*Wellington X RP325 N-B.*
O	*Wellington X NC918 O-H.*
Also used	*Tiger Moth II T6903; Spitfire XVI SL616; Oxford I PH521; Harvard IIB FS757; Meteor F.4 VT324, T.7 VW445.*

Disbanded 1st February 1952 at Finningley to become 215 Advanced Flying School.

102 FLYING REFRESHER SCHOOL
Formed 1st May 1951 at North Luffenham.

M	*Harvard IIB FX226 M-10; Mosquito VI HX803; Spitfire XVI TE257, F.22 PK340 M-43; Vampire FB.5 WA413 M-28; Meteor T.7 VW419.*

Disbanded 15th November 1951 at North Luffenham to become 207 Advanced Flying School.

103 FLYING REFRESHER SCHOOL
Formed 16th May 1951 at Full Sutton.

Spitfire XVI TE358, F.22 PK596; Vampire F.1 TG385, FB.5 WA101; Meteor T.7 WF831.

Disbanded 20th November 1951 at Full Sutton to become 207 Advanced Flying School.

104 FLYING REFRESHER SCHOOL
Formed 23rd July 1951 at Lichfield,

Wellington X RP387 G; Oxford I X6852 N.

Disbanded 15th February 1952 at Lichfield to become 6 Air Navigation School.

FLYING SELECTION SQUADRON
Formed 9th July 1979 at Swinderby.

Chipmunk T.10 WB550 F.

Disbanded 1st June 1987 at Swinderby to become the Elementary Flying Training Squadron.

FLYING TRAINING COMMAND COMMUNICATION FLIGHT, later FLYING TRAINING COMMAND COMMUNICATION SQUADRON
Formed 27th May 1940 at White Waltham by redesignating an element of the Training Command Communication Flight.

Nil (5.40–4.46)	*Gauntlet II K7799; Tiger Moth II N6774; Vega Gull P5990; Proctor I P6316, III Z7237; Magister T9883; Lysander IIIA V9517; Monarch W6461; Gull Six AX866; Hornet Moth AV969; Master I, II AZ704, III W8792; Martinet I MS668; Auster II MZ255, III MZ255; Messenger I RH369.*
FKN (4.46–4.51)	*Magister P6407 FKN-K; Proctor III R7535 FKN-B, IV NP287; Oxford I DF220 FKN-B; Harvard IIB FS752 FKN-C; Anson I MG755 FKN-A, X AW871, XII PH558, XIX TX159 FKN-I.*
Nil (4.51–3.53)	*Anson XIX TX157, T.20 VS492 B, T.22 VV994; Harvard IIB KF266; Dakota IV KK209; Devon C.1 VP953; Balliol T.2 WN144; Provost T.1 XF914.*

Disbanded 31st March 1953 at White Waltham and absorbed by the Home Command Communications Squadron.

Reformed 1st April 1959 at White Waltham as the Flying Training Command Communication Squadron by redesignating the Home Command Communication Squadron.

Anson XIX TX157; Chipmunk T.10 WB746; Pembroke C.1 WV735.

Disbanded 1st April 1964 at White Waltham.

1 FLYING TRAINING SCHOOL, later 1 SERVICE FLYING TRAINING SCHOOL, later 1 FLYING TRAINING SCHOOL
Formed 23rd December 1919 at Netheravon as 1 Flying Training School by redesignating the Netheravon Flying School.

F.2B J6727; Snipe E6311, Snipe DC F2408; Panther N7428; D.H.9A J7315, D.H.9A DC J8462; Fawn II J7204; Dart N9542; Avro 504K F8771, 504N J8496; Blackburn II DC N9989; Vimy IV J7442; Atlas J9472; Siskin IIIDC J7158.

Disbanded 1st February 1931 at Netheravon.

Reformed 1st April 1935 at Leuchars as 1 Flying Training School by redesignating the Royal Air Force Base, Leuchars. Redesignated 1 Service Flying Training School from 3rd September 1939.

Fairey IIIF K1760; Gordon J9062; Tutor K3437; Avro 504N K2413; Bulldog TM K3175; Hart K3010, Hart Trainer K5806, Hart Special K4375; Seal K3485; Osprey I S1680, III K3620; Nimrod I S1631; Hind K6633, Hind Trainer L7233; Tiger Moth I K4249 5; Moth K1847; Harvard I N7043; Audax K3064; Battle K9559, Battle Trainer R7365 12; Master I N9005, III W8486 A12; Vega Gull X9436; Percival Q-6 X9454.

Disbanded 7th March 1942 at Netheravon.

Reformed 18th June 1947 at Spitalgate as 1 Flying Training School by redesignating 17 Service Flying Training School.

FCA (6.47–12.48)	*Harvard IIB KF959 FCA-N.*
FCB (6.47–12.48)	*Harvard IIB FX394 FCB-L.*
FCC (6.47–12.48)	*Allocated but no evidence of use.*
FCD (6.47–12.48)	*Harvard IIB KF265 FCD-A.*
FCE (6.47–12.48)	*Tiger Moth II T7870 FCE-F; Harvard IIB KF160 FCE-V.*
FCF	*Allocated but no evidence of use.*
FCG	*Allocated but no evidence of use.*

Disbanded 25th February 1948 at Spitalgate.

Reformed 1st December 1950 at Oakington as 1 Flying Training School.

FCA (12.50–4.51)	*Harvard IIB KF725 FCA-M.*
FCB	*Allocated but no evidence of use.*
K (4.51–4.55)	*Prentice T.1; Harvard IIB FX284 K-A.*
M (4.51–4.55)	*Prentice T.1 VS684 M-S.*
N (4.51–4.55)	*Harvard IIB KF487 N-T.*
P (4.51–4.55)	*Harvard IIB FX220 P-Z.*

Disbanded 20th April 1955 at Moreton-in-Marsh.

Reformed 1st May 1955 at Syerston as 1 Flying Training School by redesignating 22 Flying Training School.

M (5.55– .69)	Provost T.1 WV513 M-F.
N (5.55– .69)	Provost T.1 WV574 N-G.
P (5.55– .69)	Provost T.1 WV617 P-K.
Y (5.55– .69)	Provost T.1 WV512 Y-F.
Nil (.69–)	Vampire FB.5 WA288 18, T.11 XD403 54; Chipmunk T.10 WG308 C; Jet Provost T.3 XN504 34, T.3A XM372 55, T.4 XR668 45, T.5 XW310 70, T.5A XW320 71; Bulldog T.1 XX516 C; Tucano T.1 ZF145.

Current 1st April 1998 at Linton-on-Ouse and Topcliffe.

2 FLYING TRAINING SCHOOL, later 2 SERVICE FLYING TRAINING SCHOOL, later 2 FLYING TRAINING SCHOOL, later 2 (BASIC) FLYING TRAINING SCHOOL

Formed 26th April 1920 at Duxford by redesignating 31 Training School.

D.H.9A J7059 6, D.H.9A DC J8490 3; F.2B F4420; Snipe E8276; Avro 504K H3071, 504N J8528 R; Vimy IV J7244; Grebe II J7382; Gamecock I J8076; Siskin IIIA J8898, Siskin IIIDC J9236; Moth J8031; Atlas I K1027, Atlas Trainer K1466, Atlas AC K1541; Fairey IIIF K1774; Tomtit K1780.

Officially disbanded 15th December 1933 at Digby having ceased operations on 29th July 1933.

Reformed 1st October 1934 at Digby. Redesignated 2 Service Flying Training School from 3rd September 1939.

Tutor K3399; Hart K3816, Hart Trainer K4754, Hart Special K3144; Fury K3741; Audax K7343 4; Don L2415; Harvard I N7038; Oxford I L4552 F, II V3505; Spitfire VB W3262.

Disbanded 14th March 1942 at Brize Norton to become 2 (Pilots) Advanced Flying Unit.

Reformed 23rd July 1947 at Church Lawford as 2 Flying Training School by redesignating 20 Flying Training School.

FAI (7.47–4.51)	Harvard IIB FS891 FAI-A; Prentice T.1 VS373 FAI-D.
FAJ (7.47–4.51)	Harvard IIB KF372 FAJ-P; Prentice T.1 VR293 FAJ-Q.
FAK (7.47–4.51)	Harvard IIB KF240 FAK-B; Prentice T.1 VS396 FAK-S; Tiger Moth II N5463 FAK-A.
FAL (7.47–4.51)	Tiger Moth II; Anson I NK400 FAL-A; Prentice T.1 VS630 FAL-X.
FAM (7.47–4.51)	Tiger Moth II L6944 FAM-S.
Nil (4.51–5.52)	Harvard IIB; Prentice T.1; Balliol T.2 VR596; Auster T.7 WE570.
Also used	Wellington X NA714.

Disbanded 1st May 1952 at South Cerney to become the Central Flying School (Basic).

Reformed 1st February 1953 at Cluntoe as 2 Flying Training School. Redesignated 2 (Basic) Flying Training School from December 1966.

N (2.53– .54)	Harvard IIB KF977 N-N; Prentice T.1 VS373 N-D.
O (2.53– .59)	Harvard IIB; Provost T.1 WV679 O-J.
P (2.53– .59)	Harvard IIB FS920 P-W; Provost T.1 WV665 P-B; Anson T.21 WJ517 P-U.
Q (.54– .59)	Provost T.1 WV685 Q-A; Jet Provost T.1 XD693 Q-Z.
R (2.53– .59)	Provost T.1 WV680 R-B.
X (.53– .54)	Prentice T.1 VS724 X-B
G (.55– .57)	Jet Provost T.1.
Nil (2.53–12.70)	Jet Provost T.1 XD677, T.3 XM384 26, T.4 XP623 44.

Disbanded 16th January 1970 Syerston.

Reformed 16th January 1970 at Church Fenton as 2 Flying Training School by redesignating the Primary Flying Squadron of the Central Flying School.

Chipmunk T.10 WD310 8; Bulldog T.1 XX530 12.

Disbanded 2nd December 1974 at Church Fenton allowing the RN Elementary Flying Training School to operate as an independent entity.

Reformed 31st March 1976 at Ternhill as 2 (Advanced) Flying Training School by redesignating the Helicopter Wing of the Central Flying School.

Whirlwind HAR.10 XR453 A; Wessex HC.2 XS677 WK, HU.5 XS485 WA; Gazelle HT.2 XZ941 B, HT.3 ZA803 X.

Disbanded 30th March 1997 at Shawbury in favour of the civilian operated Defence Helicopter Flying School.

3 FLYING TRAINING SCHOOL, later 3 SERVICE FLYING TRAINING SCHOOL, later 3 FLYING TRAINING SCHOOL, later 3 (BASIC) FLYING TRAINING SCHOOL, later 3 FLYING TRAINING SCHOOL

Formed 26th April 1920 at Scopwick by redesignating 59 Training Squadron.

F.2B F4681.

Disbanded 1st April 1922 at Scopwick.

Reformed 2nd April 1928 at Spitalgate. Redesignated 3 Service Flying Training School from 3rd September 1939.

Avro 504K E3327; Siskin III J7149, IIIA J9336 2; Tomtit J9782 9; Gamecock I J8089; Grebe II J7383; Atlas J9470; Bulldog IIA K2953, Bulldog TM K3936; Avro 504N K1059 N; Tutor K2502 9; Hart K3843, Hart Special K3140, Hart Trainer K5046; Audax K7399; Fury K5680; Demon K5735; Hind K5501; Wallace I K3565; Tiger Moth I K2575; Don L2414; Anson I N9855; Oxford I L4578 27, II P1073; Battle L4993; Hurricane I N2520; Botha I L6484; Magister N3848; Proctor I P6172; Hornet Moth W9387; Puss Moth EM995.

Disbanded 1st March 1942 at South Cerney to become 3 (Pilots) Advanced Flying Unit.

Reformed 17th December 1945 at South Cerney as 3 Service Flying Training School by redesignating 3 (Pilots) Advance Flying Unit. Redesignated 3 Flying Training School from 9th April 1947.

Nil (12.45–4.46)	Tiger Moth II; Magister L5937; Harvard IIB KF153.
FBP (4.46–4.51)	Tiger Moth II DE737 FBP-D; Harvard IIB FT318 FBP-D; Prentice T.1 VR228 FBP-A.
FBQ (4.46–4.51)	Tiger Moth II; Magister I L5925 FBQ-K.
FBR (4.46–4.51)	Harvard IIB FT386 FBR-J; Prentice T.1 VR230 FBR-J.
FBS (4.46–4.51)	Harvard IIB FX265 FBS-F.
FBT (4.46–4.51)	Harvard IIB FS828 FBT-B.
FBU (4.46–4.51)	Harvard IIB FX291 FBU-S.
FBV (4.46–4.51)	Tiger Moth II T7995 FBV-A.
FBW	Allocated but no evidence of use.
FBX	Allocated but no evidence of use.
M (4.51– .54)	Prentice T.1; Provost T.1 WW382 M-A.
N (4.51– .54)	Prentice T.1; Provost T.1 WV607 N-B.
O (4.51– .54)	Harvard IIB KF237 O-P.
P (4.51– .54)	Harvard IIB FX292 P-J; Provost T.1 WW447 P-C.
Q (–.54)	Provost T.1 WW421 Q-H.
R (4.51– .54)	Harvard IIB FX379 R-E; Provost T.1 WV419 R-F.
S (–.54)	Provost T.1 XF552 S-B.
T (–.54)	Provost T.1 WV673 T-C.
Nil (.54– .58)	Provost T.1.

Disbanded 31st May 1958 at Feltwell.

Reformed 15th September 1961 at Leeming as 3 Flying Training School. Redesignated 3 (Basic) Flying Training School from December 1966.

Vampire T.11 WZ512 60; Jet Provost T.3 XM368 15, T.3A XM453 G, T.4 XR659 67; Wessex HC.2 XR519 WC; Bulldog T.1 XX709 33; Jetstream T.1 XX498 75.

Disbanded 26th April 1984 at Leeming.

Reformed 1st February 1989 at Cranwell as 3 Flying Training School by redesignating the Royal Air Force College Basic Flying School.

Jet Provost T.5 XW316 64, T.5A XW436 62; Tucano T.1 ZF489; Dominie T.1 XS727, T.2; Jetstream T.1 XX491.

Current 1st April 1998 at Cranwell.

An Avro 504N of No 4 Flying Training School, based at Abu Sueir, Egypt,
photographed in 1930.

4 FLYING TRAINING SCHOOL, later 4 SERVICE FLYING TRAINING SCHOOL, later 4 FLYING TRAINING SCHOOL, later 4 (ADVANCED) FLYING TRAINING SCHOOL

Formed 1st April 1921 at Abu Sueir, Egypt. Redesignated 4 Service Flying Training School from September 1939. 'C' Flight became the Habbaniyah Striking Force between 30th April and 6th June 1941.

Avro 504J D5454 C, Avro 504K ER1772 D6, Avro 504N FR2286 7; Camel F6302; Vimy F9170 6; F.2B H1642; D.H.9 H5551, D.H.9A J7081 D8; Grebe II J7593; Siskin IIIA JR8659; Vimy IV J7242; Fairey IIIF JR9140; Atlas I K1011, Atlas Trainer K1181; Gordon I K2744; Tutor K3313; Tiger Moth I K4255; Hart Trainer K4900 4; Audax K7502; Gladiator I K7907; Anson I L7974; Oxford I L4648.

Disbanded 1st July 1941 at Habbaniyah, Iraq.

Reformed 23rd April 1947 at Heany, Southern Rhodesia, as 4 Flying Training School.

A (4.47–)	*Tiger Moth II DE370 A-A.*
B (4.47–1.54)	*Harvard IIA EX419 B-R.*
D (4.47–1.54)	*Harvard IIA EX707 D-E; Anson I MG358 D-B.*
F (4.47–1.54)	*Harvard IIA EX529 F-J.*
G (4.47–1.54)	*Harvard IIA EX437 G-F.*
H (53–1.54)	*Harvard IIA EX784 H-62; Chipmunk T.10 WG392 H-31.*
W (4.47–)	*Tiger Moth II.*
X (4.47–1.54)	*Harvard IIB.*
Also used	*Cornell; Anson I EG388, T.20 VS524.*

Disbanded 26th January 1954 at Heany, Southern Rhodesia.

Reformed 1st June 1954 at Middleton St George as 4 Flying Training School by redesignating 205 Advanced Flying School.

Meteor F.4 RA456 43, T.7 WF771 3, F.8 WA763 18; Vampire FB.5 WA441 25, FB.9 WR158, T.11 XE853 44; Prentice T.1 VR238.

Disbanded 9th June 1958 at Worksop.

Reformed 15th August 1960 at Valley as 4 Flying Training School by redesignating 7 Flying Training School. Redesignated 4 (Advanced) Flying Training School from December 1966.

Vampire T.11 XE885 47; Varsity T.1 WJ917 B; Gnat T.1 XP534 62; Jet Provost T.4 XR660; Hunter F.6 XF384 72, T.7 XL621 81; Hawk T.1/1A XX233 233.

Current 1st April 1998 at Valley.

5 FLYING TRAINING SCHOOL, later 5 SERVICE FLYING TRAINING SCHOOL, later 5 FLYING TRAINING SCHOOL, later 5 (ADVANCED) FLYING TRAINING SCHOOL

Formed 26th April 1920 at Shotwick by redesignating 4 Training Squadron. Redesignated 5 Service Flying Training School from 3rd September 1939.

D.H.9A H3552, D.H.9A DC J8470; Avro 504K D8855 8, Avro 504N J9007 9; Snipe F2479; F.2B F4519 5; Humming Bird J7325; Moth J9928 8; Siskin III J7173 5, IIIA J8051 8; IIIDC J9207; Atlas TM J9436 2, Atlas AC K1563, Atlas Trainer K2523; Wapiti IIA J9497; Tutor K3267 9; Bulldog Trainer K3931; Hart Trainer K4941 6; Fury K3736 H; Gauntlet II K5291; Wallace II K6070; Audax K5161 E; Hind K6758; Battle L5054; Don L2419; Hurricane I L2075, X P5170; Harvard I N7042; Master I T8665 11, II DK823, III N7408; Oxford I P1960, II P1073; Magister T9684; Tiger Moth I K4280.

Disbanded 11th April 1942 at Ternhill to become 5 (Pilots) Advanced Flying Unit.

Reformed 23rd April 1947 at Thornhill, Southern Rhodesia, as 5 Flying Training School.

W	*Tiger Moth I NM190, II DX569 W-J.*
X	*Harvard IIA EX753 X-J, III EZ255.*
Z	*Anson I EG195 Z-G.*

Disbanded 4th January 1948 at Thornhill and absorbed by 4 Flying Training School and 3 Air Navigation School.

Reformed 22nd January 1951 at Thornhill as 5 Flying Training School.

G	*Harvard IIB KF401 G-45; Chipmunk T.10 WG332 G-34; Anson XIX VM329, T.20 VS520 G-98.*

Disbanded 30th December 1953 at Thornhill.

Reformed 1st June 1954 at Oakington as 5 Flying Training School by redesignating 206 Advanced Flying School. Redesignated 5 (Advanced) Flying Training School from December 1966.

Vampire FB.5 WA129 F, FB.9 WP994, T.11 XD427 23; Meteor T.7 WH186 72; Varsity T.1 WF422 B; Jetstream T.1 XX481 81.

Disbanded 31st December 1974 at Oakington.

6 FLYING TRAINING SCHOOL, later 6 SERVICE FLYING TRAINING SCHOOL, later 6 FLYING TRAINING SCHOOL, later 6 (ADVANCED) FLYING TRAINING SCHOOL

Formed 26th April 1920 at Spitalgate by redesignating 39 Training School.

Avro 504K; D.H.9A; F.2B C761; Amiens III E5497.

Disbanded 1st April 1922 at Manston.

Reformed 1st April 1935 at Netheravon. Redesignated 6 Service Flying Training School from 3rd September 1939.

Tutor K3428; Hart K3970; Hind K6695; Audax K7361; Fury II K8225; Anson I K8709; Don L2418; Harvard I N7132; Hurricane I L1846; Blenheim IV L9194; Gipsy Moth X5025; Oxford I BF942, II P1094.

Disbanded 1st April 1942 at Little Rissington to become 6 (Pilots) Advance Flying Unit.

Reformed 17th December 1945 at Little Rissington as 6 Service Flying Training School by redesignating 6 (Pilot) Advance Flying Unit. Redesignated 6 Flying Training School from 14th May 1947. Redesignated 6 (Advanced) Flying Training School from December 1966.

Nil (12.45–4.46)	*Harvard IIB KF197; Magister P6374; Oxford I ED254.*
FBG (4.46–4.51)	*Harvard IIB FT445 FBG-A; Prentice T.1 VS367 FBG-S.*
FBH (4.46–4.51)	*Harvard IIB KF358 FBH-I; Prentice T.1 VR221 FBH-N.*
FBI (4.46–4.51)	*Tiger Moth II R4785 FBI-F; Harvard IIB FS738 FBI-G; Prentice T.1 VN687 FBI-M; Balliol T.2 VR595 FBI-B.*
FBJ (4.46–4.51)	*Magister P6374 FBJ-Z; Anson I NK456 FBJ-X; Harvard IIB KF361 FBJ-F; Prentice T.1 VS334 FBJ-W.*
FBK (4.46–4.51)	*Allocated but not used.*
FBL (4.46–4.51)	*Allocated but not used.*
FBM (4.46–4.51)	*Allocated but not used.*
FBN (4.46–4.51)	*Allocated but not used.*
F (4.51– .53)	*Prentice T.1.*
G (4.51– .53)	*Harvard IIB.*
M (4.51– .62)	*Prentice T.1 VS263 M-J; Provost T.1 XF888 M-K.*
N (4.51– .62)	*Prentice T.1; Harvard IIB; Provost T.1 WV427 N-J.*
O (4.51– .62)	*Harvard IIB KF165 O-E; Provost T.1 WW390 O-U.*
P (4.51– .62)	*Harvard IIB KF472 P-L; Provost T.1 WV610 P-S.*
X (4.51– .53)	*Prentice T.1.*
Nil (.62–6.68)	*Provost T.1; Varsity T.1 WF410 F; Chipmunk T.10 WP967; Jet Provost T.3 XM468 10.*

Disbanded 30th June 1968 at Acklington.

Reformed 1st May 1970 at Finningley as 6 Flying Training School.

Varsity T.1 WJ898 D; Jet Provost T.3 XN605 9, T.4 XP635 41, T.5 XW296 Q, T.5A XW287 P; Dominie T.1 XS712 A; Bulldog T.1 XX706 06; Argosy T.2 XP411 Y; Hawk T.1 XX168, T.1A; Dominie T.1 XS737 K; Jetstream T.1 XX493 L; Tucano T.1 ZF446.

Disbanded 31st March 1996 at Finningley.

7 FLYING TRAINING SCHOOL, later 7 SERVICE FLYING TRAINING SCHOOL, later 7 FLYING TRAINING SCHOOL, later 7 (BASIC) FLYING TRAINING SCHOOL, later 7 FLYING TRAINING SCHOOL

Formed 2nd December 1935 at Peterborough. Redesignated 7 Service Flying Training School from 3rd September 1939.

Fairey IIIF S1781; Tutor K3444; Hart Special K4369 24, Hart

Trainer K5861 25; Fury K5669 9; Audax K4388 30; Wallace II K8698; Battle Trainer R7367; Master I N7478, III DL865.

Disbanded August 1940 and transferred to Canada to become 31 Service Flying Training School.

Reformed 21st December 1944 at Peterborough as 7 Service Flying Training School by redesignating 7 (Pilots) Advanced Flying Unit. Redesignated 7 Flying Training School from 1st January 1948.

Nil (12.44–4.46)	Hurricane I P2919; Master II DK918, III DM112; Anson I MG674; Oxford I PH414; Tiger Moth BB704; Harvard IIB FT218 10.
FBA (4.46–4.51)	Harvard IIB KF481 FBA-C; Oxford I MP427 FBA-Q.
FBB (4.46–4.51)	Harvard IIB FS906 FBB-J; Oxford I NM796 FBB-O.
FBC (4.46–4.51)	Tiger Moth II T5672 FBC-Z; Harvard IIB FT435 FBC-J.
FBD (4.46–4.51)	Harvard IIB KF206 FBD-N; Prentice T.1 VR234 FBD-B.
FBE (4.46–4.51)	Anson I MG834 FBE-H; Prentice T.1 VR321 FBE-F; Spitfire XVI TE240 FBE-D.
D (4.51–4.54)	Prentice T.1; Balliol T.2 WG131 D-A.
M (4.51–4.54)	Prentice T.1.
N (4.51–4.54)	Harvard IIB KF142 N-J.
O (4.51–4.54)	Harvard IIB KF288 O-E.
P (4.51–4.54)	Harvard IIB KF153 P-A; Prentice T.1.
Q (4.51–4.54)	Balliol T.2 WG116 Q-W.

Disbanded 14th April 1954 at Cottesmore.

Reformed 1st June 1954 at Valley as 7 Flying Training School by redesignating 202 Advanced Flying School.

Vampire FB.5 WA413 28, FB.9 WR194 19, T.11 XE887; Anson XIX TX209 KS; Chipmunk T.10 WP811.

Disbanded 15th August 1960 at Valley to become 4 Flying Training School.

Reformed 13th March 1962 at Church Fenton as 7 (Basic) Flying Training School.

Jet Provost T.3 XN495 31, T.4 XP684 J.

Disbanded 30th November 1966 at Church Fenton.

Reformed 2nd April 1979 at Church Fenton as 7 Flying Training School.

Jet Provost T.3A XM425 88, T.5A XW326 120; Tucano T.1 ZF242 242.

Disbanded 31st March 1992 at Church Fenton.

Reformed 1st April 1992 at Chivenor as 7 Flying Training School by redesignating 2 Tactical Weapons Unit.

Hawk T.1 XX225, T.1A XX202 P.

Disbanded 30th September 1994 at Chivenor, its advanced flying training role passing to 4 Flying Training School at Valley.

8 FLYING TRAINING SCHOOL, later 8 SERVICE FLYING TRAINING SCHOOL, later 8 (ADVANCED) FLYING TRAINING SCHOOL
Formed 1st January 1936 at Montrose as 8 Flying Training School. Redesignated 8 Service Flying Training School from 3rd September 1939.

Hart Trainer K5002, Hart Special K4410; Gordon K2726; Fury K2050; Tutor K3407; Gauntlet I K5284; Hind K6783; Audax K8313; Shark II K8909; Don L2420; Master I N8018, II AZ539; Hurricane I L1958; Anson I N9601; Moth Major AW162; Oxford I P1886, II P1824; Battle V1239.

Disbanded 25th March 1942 at Montrose and absorbed by 2 Flying Instructors School.

Reformed 1st May 1951 at Dalcross as 8 Flying Training School. Redesignated 8 (Advanced) Flying Training School from 1st June 1951.

S (5.51–12.53)	
U (5.51–12.53)	
W (5.51–12.53)	Oxford I RR339 W-W.
X (5.51–12.53)	
Also used	Tiger Moth II DE459.

Disbanded 1st December 1953 at Dalcross.

Reformed 1st June 1954 at Driffield as 8 Flying Training School by redesignating 203 Advanced Flying School.

O (6.54–)	Meteor F.4 VT308 O-16; Provost T.1 WV635 O-H.
X (6.54–)	Meteor T.7 WG999 X-66.
Nil (–3.64)	Vampire FB.5 VZ109 73, T.11 XD616 54; Varsity T.1 WF413 C; Chipmunk T.10 WG305; Prentice T.1 VS335; Marathon T.1 XA272 E.

Disbanded 19th March 1964 at Swinderby.

9 FLYING TRAINING SCHOOL, later 9 SERVICE FLYING TRAINING SCHOOL, later 9 (ADVANCED) FLYING TRAINING SCHOOL, later 9 FLYING TRAINING SCHOOL
Formed 2nd March 1936 at Thornaby. Redesignated 9 Service Flying Training School from 3rd September 1939.

Hart Special K4423, Hart Trainer K5019; Hind K5449; Gauntlet I K4090, II K5316; Fury II K8220 3; Audax K2006; Tutor K3407; Don L2416; Moth X5127; Hurricane I L1951; Anson I L7050; Oxford I L4571, II N4769; Master I N8064, III W8579.

Disbanded 14th February 1942 at Montrose to become 9 (Pilots) Advanced Flying Unit.

Reformed 1st December 1951 at Wellesbourne Mountford as 9 (Advanced) Flying Training School. Redesignated 9 Flying Training School from 1st August 1953.

M (12.51– .53)	Oxford I LX349 M-C; Harvard IIB KF290 M-E; Chipmunk T.10 WP974 M-P.
O (12.51– .53)	Oxford I.
P (12.51– .53)	Oxford I NJ382 P-D.
Nil (.53–5.54)	Oxford I.

Disbanded 1st May 1954 at Wellesbourne Mountford.

Reformed 1st July 1954 at Merryfield as 9 Flying Training School by redesignating 10 Flying Training School.

Vampire FB.5 WA247, T.11 WZ501.

Disbanded 16th February 1955 at Merryfield.

10 FLYING TRAINING SCHOOL, later 10 SERVICE FLYING TRAINING SCHOOL, later 10 (ADVANCED) FLYING TRAINING SCHOOL, later 10 FLYING TRAINING SCHOOL
Formed 1st January 1936 at Ternhill. Redesignated 10 Service Flying Training School from 3rd September 1939.

Tutor K3296; Hart K3043, Hart Trainer K3154, Hart Special K4411; Gauntlet II K5314; Hind K5530; Audax K7325; Fury K8284 3; Anson I K8720; Wallace II K8699; Harvard I N7027; Proctor I P6171; Envoy III P5626; Hornet Moth W5830;

Disbanded 1st November 1940 at Ternhill and transferred to Canada to become 32 Service Flying Training School

Reformed 15th January 1952 at Pershore as 10 (Advanced) Flying Training School.

M (1.52–4.54)	Oxford I DF418 M-X.
P (1.52–4.54)	Oxford I DF447 P-N; Chipmunk T.10 WP853 P-H.
Also used	Oxford II AB703; Vampire FB.5 WA115; T.11 WZ453.

Disbanded 14th April 1954 at Pershore.

Reformed 1st June 1954 at Merryfield as 10 Flying Training School by redesignating 208 Advanced Flying School.

Vampire FB.5 VZ224, T.11 XD530; Prentice T.1 VR281.

Disbanded 1st July 1954 at Merryfield to become 9 Flying Training School.

11 FLYING TRAINING SCHOOL, later 11 SERVICE FLYING TRAINING SCHOOL, later 11 FLYING TRAINING SCHOOL
Formed 1st October 1935 at Wittering. Redesignated 11 Service Flying Training School from 3rd September 1939.

Tutor K3248; Audax I K4405 2; Hart Trainer K4964 7; Fury K5679 3; Anson I K8703; Wallace II K8697; Gauntlet II K5329; Don L2421; Hind L7221, Hind Trainer L7225; Battle Trainer P6666; Harvard I

N7007; Magister N3821; Blenheim Oxford I L4553, II P1811; Moth X5017.

Disbanded 14th March 1942 at Shawbury to become 11 (Pilots) Advance Flying Unit.

Reformed 1st June 1954 at Swinderby as 11 Flying Training School by redesignating 201 Advanced Flying School.

Varsity T.1 WF378 A; Vampire T.11 XD612; Anson T.20 VS528.

Disbanded 7th June 1955 at Swinderby and absorbed by 2 Air Navigation School.

12 FLYING TRAINING SCHOOL, later 12 SERVICE FLYING TRAINING SCHOOL, later 12 FLYING TRAINING SCHOOL
Formed 1st December 1938 at Spitalgate. Redesignated 12 Service Flying Training School from 3rd September 1939.

Tutor K3267; Hart Trainer K6469; Hind K6725, Hind Trainer L7243; Audax K5134; Hector K9767; Harvard I N7004 10; Anson I L7063; Battle P2362, Battle Trainer P6635; Mentor L4419; Lysander I R2636; Oxford I L9637, II N6403; Gipsy Moth DG657; Hornet Moth W5776; Whitney Straight BS818; Proctor I P6186.

Disbanded 1st April 1942 at Spitalgate to become 12 (Pilots) Advanced Flying Unit.

Reformed 1st June 1954 at Weston Zoyland as 12 Flying Training School by redesignating 209 Advanced Flying School.

Meteor F.4 RA413 82, T.7 WL460 53; Prentice T.1 VR305.

Disbanded 24th June 1955 at Weston Zoyland.

13 FLYING TRAINING SCHOOL, later 13 SERVICE FLYING TRAINING SCHOOL
Formed 17th March 1939 at Drem. Redesignated 13 Service Flying Training School from 4th September 1939.

Hart K5864, Hart Trainer K3147; Audax K7479; Anson I N9600; Oxford I N4592, II N6381; Don L2428.

Disbanded 27th October 1939 at Drem and absorbed by 8, 14 and 15 Service Flying Training Schools.

14 FLYING TRAINING SCHOOL, later 14 SERVICE FLYING TRAINING SCHOOL, later 14 (ADVANCED) FLYING TRAINING SCHOOL
Formed 1st April 1939 at Kinloss. Redesignated 14 Service Flying Training School from 3rd September 1939.

Audax K5157; Demon K5706; Hind K6642; Hart K5811, Hart Trainer K4974; Harvard I P5823 K; Master I N7695; Anson I N9598; Oxford I P8823 24, II N6370; Gipsy Moth BK842.

Disbanded 26th January 1942 at Ossington to become 14 (Pilots) Advanced Flying Unit.

Reformed 3rd March 1952 at Holme-on-Spalding-Moor as 14 (Advanced) Flying Training School.

A (4.51–1.53)	Oxford I NM351 A-P.
D (4.51–1.53)	Oxford I LX285 D-W.
N (4.51–1.53)	Oxford I ED283 N-P.
Q (4.51–1.53)	Oxford I V4166 Q-P.
T (4.51–1.53)	Oxford I NJ369 T-Z.

Disbanded 31st January 1953 at Holme-on-Spalding-Moor.

15 FLYING TRAINING SCHOOL, later 15 SERVICE FLYING TRAINING SCHOOL, later 15 FLYING TRAINING SCHOOL
Formed 1st May 1939 at Lossiemouth. Redesignated 15 Service Flying Training School from 3rd September 1939.

Audax K3060; Hart Trainer K3146; Hind K5531; Battle L5026; Master I N7574; Harvard I P5849 S; Oxford I N6323 N, II N6384; Magister V1023; Gipsy Moth BK843.

Disbanded 1st March 1942 at Kidlington to become 15 (Pilots) Advanced Flying Unit.

Reformed 23rd February 1952 at Wethersfield as 15 Flying Training School.

No aircraft allocated.

Disbanded 12th May 1952 at Wethersfield.

16 FLYING TRAINING SCHOOL – see 16 Service Flying Training School, later 16 (Polish) Flying Training School

17 FLYING TRAINING SCHOOL – see 17 Service Flying Training School

19 FLYING TRAINING SCHOOL
Formed 1st May 1945 at Cranwell.

Nil (5.45–4.46)	Anson I MG916; Tiger Moth I NM126, II T6370 MD; Harvard IIB KF186.
A (5.45–4.46)	Harvard IIB KF497 A-F.
B (5.45–4.46)	Harvard IIB KF266 B-A.
C (5.45–4.46)	Harvard IIB KF572 C-J.
D (5.45–4.46)	Harvard IIB KF182 D-C.
E (5.45–4.46)	Harvard IIB KF197 E-F.
F (5.45–4.46)	Harvard IIB KF459 F-G.
G (5.45–4.46)	Harvard IIB KF259 G-E.
H (5.45–4.46)	Harvard IIB KF160 H-F.
FAA (4.46–4.47)	Harvard IIB KF170 FAA-J.
FAB (4.46–4.47)	Harvard IIB KF191 FAB-H.
FAC (4.46–4.47)	Harvard IIB KF301 FAC-C.
FAD (4.46–4.47)	Harvard IIB KF207 FAD-A.
FAE (4.46–4.47)	Tiger Moth II T7148 FAE-K.
FAF (4.46–4.47)	Allocated but no evidence of use.
FAG (4.46–4.47)	Anson I NK563 FAG-A.

Disbanded 17th April 1947 at Cranwell and absorbed by the Royal Air Force College.

20 FLYING TRAINING SCHOOL – see 20 Service Flying Training School, later 20 Flying Training School, later 20 Service Flying Training School

21 FLYING TRAINING SCHOOL – see 21 Service Flying Training School, later 21 Flying Training School

22 FLYING TRAINING SCHOOL – see 22 Service Flying Training School, later 22 Flying Training School

23 FLYING TRAINING SCHOOL – see 23 Service Flying Training School

30 FLYING TRAINING SCHOOL
Planned opening during 1940 at Souge, France, cancelled.

31 FLYING TRAINING SCHOOL
Planned opening during 1940 at Herbouville, France, cancelled.

32 FLYING TRAINING SCHOOL
Planned opening during 1940 at Luble, France, cancelled.

33 FLYING TRAINING SCHOOL
Planned opening during 1940 at Houssey, France, cancelled.

34 FLYING TRAINING SCHOOL
Planned opening during 1940 in France (location to have been decided) cancelled.

207 FLYING TRAINING SCHOOL
Formed 1st June 1954 at Full Sutton by redesignating an element of 207 Advanced Flying School.

P	Meteor F.4, T.7 WH121 P-14.

Disbanded 21st July 1954 at Full Sutton.

211 FLYING TRAINING SCHOOL
Formed 1st June 1954 at Worksop by redesignating 211 Advanced Flying School.

Prentice T.1 VS641; Meteor T.7 WN319 77; F.8 WK860 32.

Disbanded 9th June 1956 at Worksop and absorbed by 4 Flying Training School.

FORTRESS FLIGHT
Formed 1942 at Colerne.

Fortress I.

Disbanded 13th October 1942 at Colerne.

FRENCH HUDSON FLIGHT – see Hudson Flight, West Africa

FRANCO-BELGIUM AIR TRAINING SCHOOL
Formed 28th October 1940 at Odiham.

Magister L5590; Master II AZ610; Simoun; Morane 230.

Disbanded 9th June 1941 at Odiham.

1 FREE FRENCH (BOMBER) FLIGHT
Formed 28th October 1940 at Khormaksar, Aden.

Martin 167F 82/AX671; Potez 29 6.

Disbanded 30th April 1941 at Khormaksar.

FREE FRENCH COMMUNICATION FLIGHT
Formed 2nd June 1941 at Heliopolis, Egypt, under the operational control of 267 Squadron.

Simoun AX676; Bloche 81 AX677; Potez 63 AX672.

Disbanded June 1942 at Heliopolis.

1 FREE FRENCH FIGHTER FLIGHT – see Escadrille de Chasse No 1

2 FREE FRENCH FIGHTER FLIGHT – see Escadrille de Chasse No 2

FREE FRENCH FLIGHT, 127 SQUADRON – see Escadrille 'Ardennes'

FREE FRENCH FLIGHT, KHARTOUM
Formed 24th March 1941 at Gordon's Tree, Khartoum, Sudan.

Blenheim IV T1822.

Disbanded 26th July 1941 at Gordon's Tree to be incorporated in Groupe 'Lorraine'.

FREE FRENCH FLIGHT, SUDAN
Formed 10th March 1941 at El Fasher, Sudan, by redesignating a Flight of 1 Group Reserve de Bombardement.

Blenheim IV Z5728.

Disbanded 13th August 1941 at El Fasher to become an element of Groupe 'Lorraine'.

'G' BOAT SEAPLANE TRAINING FLIGHT
Formed 15th August 1918 at Dundee.

No aircraft known.

Disbanded 25th November 1918 at Dundee.

'G' FLIGHT
Formed 21st September 1940 at Helensburgh.

Short S.23 AX659; Short S.26 X8274.

Disbanded 13th March 1941 at Bowmore to become 119 Squadron.

'G' SQUADRON
Formed (date unknown) at Ratmalana, Ceylon.

Hurricane I.

Disbanded 1st March 1942 at Ratmalana to become 258 Squadron.

GCA CALIBRATION FLIGHTS – see Signals Flying Unit

GCA FLIGHT – see Signals Development Unit

GCA SQUADRON – see Signals Flying Unit

GEE-H TRAINING FLIGHT
Formed 29th December 1944 at Feltwell.

Lancaster III LM473.

Disbanded 5th June 1946 at Feltwell to become the Bomber Command Radar School.

GEE (TR1335) TRAINING UNIT
Formed 14th December 1941 at Boscombe Down.

No aircraft known.

Disbanded 6th January 1942 at Marham to become 1418 GEE (TR1335) Trials Flight.

GENERAL PURPOSE FLIGHT, SHEIKH OTHMAN
Formed 24th November 1940 at Khormaksar, Aden, by redesignating the Vincent element of 8 Squadron.

Vincent K4664.

Disbanded 30th April 1941 at Khormaksar and absorbed by 8 Squadron.

GENERAL RECONNAISSANCE AND AIR NAVIGATION SCHOOL (INDIA)
Formed 24th October 1942 at Andheri, India, by merging the Air Navigation School and the General Reconnaissance School.

Dominie I X7409; Anson I DJ585.

Disbanded 5th August 1944 at Koggala, India.

GENERAL RECONNAISSANCE SCHOOL
Formed 27th June 1942 at Andheri, India using Juhu for flying training.

Dominie I.

Disbanded 24th October 1942 at Andheri and merged with the Air Navigation School, India to become the General Reconnaissance and Air Navigation School.

31 GENERAL RECONNAISSANCE SCHOOL
Formed 20th January 1941 at Charlottetown, Canada, by merging elements of 1 and 2 Schools of General Reconnaissance.

| NK (1.41–10.42) | Anson I, V. |
| Nil (10.42–2.44) | Anson I AX137, V. |

Disbanded 21st February 1944 at Charlottetown.

1 GENERAL RECONNAISSANCE UNIT
Formed 19th December 1939 at Manston.

Wellington DW.I P2518, IC HX682; Magister R1885; Vega Gull X1034.

Disbanded 10th March 1944 at Ismailia, Egypt.

2 GENERAL RECONNAISSANCE UNIT
Formed 4th March 1940 at Bircham Newton by redesignating an element of 1 General Reconnaissance Unit.

Wellington DW.II L4374.

Disbanded 26th April 1940 at Bircham Newton.

3 GENERAL RECONNAISSANCE UNIT
Formed 22nd April 1940 at Manston.

Wellington DW.I L4356; Magister N3937.

Disbanded 26th July 1940 at Thorney Island.

GLADIATOR FLIGHT
Formed 23rd May 1940 at Manston, as a detachment of 615 Squadron, to cover the Dunkirk evacuation.

Gladiator.

Disbanded 30th May 1940 at Manston.

GLASGOW UNIVERSITY AIR SQUADRON, later UNIVERSITIES OF GLASGOW AND STRATHCLYDE AIR SQUADRON
Formed 14th April 1941 at Glasgow. Redesignated the Universities of Glasgow and Strathclyde Air Squadron from 1st January 1965 at Perth.

Nil (4.41–4.46)	Moth AW128; Moth Major BK833; Tiger Moth II provided by 11 Elementary Flying Training School.
FLD (10.46–4.47)	Allocated but no evidence of use.
RUG (4.47–4.51)	Tiger Moth II N9205 RUG-D.
Nil (4.51–)	Harvard IIB KF732; Chipmunk T.10 WP967 F; Provost T.1 XF913; Bulldog T.1 XX611 04.

Also used   *Tiger Moth BD171; Oxford I NJ347; Anson T.21 WJ559 44.*

Current 1st April 1998 at Glasgow Airport.

GLIDER EXERCISE UNIT, later GLIDER EXERCISE SQUADRON
Formed 18th July 1941 at Ringway within the Central Landing Establishment. Redesignated the Glider Exercise Squadron by December 1941.

Hotspur; Hector.

Disbanded 25th January 1942 at Ringway to become 296 Squadron.

GLIDER EXERCISE SQUADRON – see Glider Exercise Unit, later Glider Exercise Squadron

GLIDER FLIGHT, CRANWELL
Formed (date unknown) at Cranwell.

Cadet TX.1 RA915, TX.2 VW533; Prefect TX.1 WE979; Sedbergh TX.1 WB921; Kranich II VD224; Viking TX.1 ZE635.

Current 1st April 1993 at Cranwell.

GLIDER FLIGHT, HALTON
Formed 17th March 1945 at Halton as an element of the Station Flight, Halton.

Primary BGA1126; Dagling; Cadet TX.1, TX.2; Kranich; Sedbergh TX.1 WG496; Venture T.2; Viking TX.1 ZE636.

Existed to at least 1st April 1993 at Halton.

GLIDER INSTRUCTORS FLIGHT
Formed 1st February 1943 at Shobdon within 5 Glider Training School to replace the Glider Instructors School.

Master II; Hotspur; Albemarle VI.

Disbanded 31st January 1945 at Hockley Heath and absorbed by 3 Glider Training School as the Glider Instructors School.

GLIDER INSTRUCTORS SCHOOL
Formed 25th August 1942 at Thame by redesignating an element of 1 Glider Training School.

Hind K5421; Hector K8142; Master II DL472; Hotspur II BT542; Oxford I N9347.

Disbanded 31st January 1943 at Thame to be replaced by the Glider Instructors Flight within 5 Glider Training School.

Reformed 31st January 1945 at Culmhead within 3 Glider Training School by redesignating the Glider Instructors Flight.

Master; Hotspur.

Disbanded 1945 at Culmhead.

GLIDER PICK-UP TRAINING FLIGHT
Formed 8th January 1945 at Zeals by redesignating an element of 107 Operational Training Unit.

IB	*Allocated but no evidence of use.*
W4	*Allocated but no evidence of use.*
Nil	*Dakota III TS433, IV TP187; Hadrian 42-77516.*

Disbanded 15th November 1945 at Ramsbury.

GLIDER PILOT EXERCISE UNIT
Formed 12th August 1942 at Netheravon by redesignating 296B Squadron.

Hart K5819; Hind K6827; Hector K8112; Tiger Moth I K4267, II T6034; Master II DK993, III DL835; Hotspur II BT490; Hengist I DG675; Horsa I DP373, II RX928.

Disbanded 1st December 1943 at Thruxton to become the Operational and Refresher Training Unit.

GLIDER TEST AND FERRY FLIGHT, COSFORD
Formed 14th October 1942 at Cosford.

Whitley V.

Disbanded August 1945 at Cosford.

GLIDER TEST AND FERRY FLIGHT, KEMBLE
Formed by 1943 at Kemble.

Whitley V.

Disbanded 15th April 1944 at Kemble.

GLIDER TEST AND FERRY FLIGHT, WROUGHTON
Formed March 1943 at Wroughton.

Whitley V; Albemarle; Hudson.

Disbanded August 1945 at Wroughton.

1 GLIDER TRAINING SCHOOL
Formed 1st December 1941 at Thame by redesignating an element of the Glider Training Squadron.

Viking BGA425; Minimoa BGA338; Kirby Kite BGA316; Avro 504N AX874; Hind K5511; Hector K9765; Tiger Moth I K4254, II N9150; Hotspur I BV198, II BT990 S, III BT632; Master II DL493, III DL972; Oxford I BF974.

Disbanded 23rd March 1943 at Croughton and merged with 2 and 4 Glider Training Schools to become 20 (Pilots) Advanced Flying Unit.

Reformed 1st November 1944 at Croughton from an element of 20 (Pilots) Advanced Flying Unit.

Nil (11.44–4.46)	*Master II EM283; Hotspur II BT542 N; Tiger Moth II N9197; Oxford I P9041, II N4839.*
FEA (4.46–8.46)	*Master II DM323 FEA-B.*
FEB (4.46–8.46)	*Master II DL538 FEB-C.*
FEC (4.46–8.46)	*Anson I NK371 FEC-V.*
FED	*Allocated but no evidence of use.*
FEE (4.46–8.46)	*Tiger Moth II NM129 FEE-A*

Disbanded 19th June 1946 at Croughton.

2 GLIDER TRAINING SCHOOL
Formed 1st December 1941 at Weston-on-the-Green by redesignating an element of the Glider Training Squadron.

Hind K5450; Hector K8134; Audax K7328; Tiger Moth II N9347; Hotspur II BT551 L, III BT735; Master II EM261; Oxford II N6421.

Disbanded 23rd March 1943 at Weston-on-the-Green and merged with 1 and 4 Glider Training Schools to become 20 (Pilots) Advanced Flying Unit.

3 GLIDER TRAINING SCHOOL
Formed 21st July 1942 at Stoke Orchard by redesignating elements of 10 Elementary Flying Training School.

Nil (7.42–4.46)	*Master II DL369 74; Hotspur I BV138 60, II HH448 22, III BT540; Tiger Moth II NM131 7; Magister N3793; Oxford I P1895; Spitfire VII MB769; Albemarle IV LV621; Horsa I DP777.*
FEG (4.46–12.47)	*Master II DL464 FEG-A.*
FEH (4.46–12.47)	*Master II DL395 FEH-E.*
FEI (4.46–12.47)	*Tiger Moth I NL971 FEI-D.*
FEJ (4.46–7.12)	*Hotspur II BT598 FEJ-D.*
FEK (4.46–12.47)	*Master II EM380 FEK-Y.*
FEL	*Allocated but no evidence of use.*
FEM	*Allocated but no evidence of use.*
FEN	*Allocated but no evidence of use.*

Disbanded 3rd December 1947 at Wellesbourne Mountford.

4 GLIDER TRAINING SCHOOL
Formed 13th July 1942 at Kidlington by redesignating 101 (Glider) Operational Training Unit.

Audax K7328; Hind K5450; Hector K8135; Hotspur II HH255 90, III BT784; Master II DM237, III DL972; Oxford I R6276; Tiger Moth II T5379; Gull Six AX866.

Disbanded 23rd March 1943 at Kidlington and merged with 1 and 2 Glider Training Schools to become 20 (Pilots) Advanced Flying Unit.

5 GLIDER TRAINING SCHOOL
Formed 30th June 1942 at Kidlington by redesignating 102 (Glider) Operational Training Unit.

Hector K8166; Hotspur II BT722 44, III BT777; Lysander IIIA V9447; Master II EM342, III DL834; Battle L5997; Spitfire VB

AB487; Magister N5409; Oxford I ED169; Moth Minor W6458; Tiger Moth I NM122, II DF159.

Disbanded 15th November 1945 at Shobdon.

GLIDER TRAINING SQUADRON
Formed 22nd September 1940 at Ringway by redesignating the Glider Flight, Central Landing Establishment.

Hector K8145; Tiger Moth II T5604; Swallow II Glider BK895; Rhonbussard BGA145; Falcon 3 BGA244; Kite I BGA316; Viking 1 BGA425.

Disbanded 1st December 1940 at Thame (Haddenham) to become 1 and 2 Glider Training Schools.

GLIDER TRAINING UNIT
Formed 1st June 1942 at Abu Sueir, Egypt.

No aircraft known.

Disbanded 9th December 1942 at Abu Sueir.

1 GLIDING CENTRE
Formed 31st March 1959 at Hawkinge by redesignating 1 Home Command Gliding Centre.

Cadet TX.3 XA282; Sedbergh TX.1 WB987; Prefect TX.1 WE993; Grasshopper TX.1 WZ763; Swallow XT653.

Disbanded 9th August 1971 at Swanton Morley and merged with 2 Gliding Centre to become the Central Gliding School.

2 GLIDING CENTRE
Formed 31st March 1959 at Newton by redesignating 2 Home Command Gliding Centre.

Prefect TX.1 WE991; Cadet TX.3 XA293; Sedbergh TX.1 XN147; Slingsby T-53B XV951; Venture T.1 XW983.

Disbanded 9th August 1971 at Spitalgate and merged with 1 Gliding Centre to become the Central Gliding School.

GLIDING INSTRUCTORS SCHOOL (1) – see Reserve Command Gliding Instructors School

GLIDING INSTRUCTORS SCHOOL (2) – see Home Command Gliding Instructors School

GLIDING SCHOOLS, later VOLUNTEER GLIDING SCHOOLS

Air Training Corps Gliding Schools were originally numbered within blocks allocated to eleven administrative Areas. Scottish Area were allocated from 1 to 20, North East Area from 21 to 40, Midlands Area from 41 to 60, Welsh Area from 61 to 80, South West Area from 81 to 100, Eastern Area from 101 to 120, Central Area from 121 to 140, London Area from 141 to 160, South East Area from 161 to 180, North West Area from 181 to 200 and the Northern Ireland Area from 201. Many Gliding Schools within the designated blocks were not formed. By September 1949 only 49 of the Schools were still operating. Those still remaining by 1st September 1955 were renumbered and then administered by 61, 62, 63, 64, 66 and 67 Groups.

1 GLIDING SCHOOL
Formed December 1942 at Strathaven.

Slingsby Primary; Grunau Baby IIB VT924; Cadet TX.1 RA895, TX.2 VM663, TX.3 XA305; Prefect TX.1 WE984; Sedbergh TX.1.

Disbanded 1st September 1955 at Dumfries to become 661 Gliding School.

2 GLIDING SCHOOL
Formed 25th October 1942 at East Fortune.

No aircraft known.

Disbanded (date unknown) at Dumfies.

Reformed 1st November 1947 at Grangemouth.

Falcon IV VD219; Grunau Baby VT918; Cadet TX.1 RA898, TX.2 VM643, TX.3 WT894; Sedbergh TX.1 WB948.

Disbanded 1st September 1955 at Grangemouth.

3 GLIDING SCHOOL
Formed by March 1944 at Macmerry.

Cadet TX.1 RA878, TX.2 VM653.

Disbanded 1st September 1947 at Drem.

4 GLIDING SCHOOL
Formed by December 1943 at Paisley.

Cadet TX.1 RA883, TX.2 VM686; Sedbergh TX.1 WB948.

Disbanded by 1952 at Grangemouth and absorbed by 2 Gliding School.

5 GLIDING SCHOOL
Formed by October 1944 at Fordoun.

Cadet TX.1 RA907, TX.2 VM642, TX.3 XA296; Prefect TX.1 WE984; Sedbergh TX.1 WB930.

Disbanded 1st September 1955 at Edzell to become 662 Gliding School.

6 GLIDING SCHOOL
Formed by January 1945 at Grangemouth.

Cadet TX.1 RA895, TX.2 VM643; Grunau Baby IIB VT918; Sedbergh TX.1 WB930.

Disbanded late 1955 at Grangemouth and absorbed by 2 Gliding School.

7 GLIDING SCHOOL
Formed by March 1946 at Dalcross.

Cadet TX.1 RB133, TX.2 VM642, TX.3 XA297; Sedbergh TX.1 WB982.

Disbanded 1st September 1955 at Dalcross.

8 GLIDING SCHOOL
Formed May 1944 at Ayr.

Cadet TX.1 RA908, TX.2.

Disbanded 1947 at Creetown.

9 GLIDING SCHOOL
Formed by June 1945 at Errol.

Kite VD176; Cadet TX.1 RB140.

Disbanded December 1946 at Scone.

10 GLIDING SCHOOL
Formed 25th May 1945 at Turnberry.

Cadet TX.1 RA998.

Disbanded (date and location unknown).

21 GLIDING SCHOOL
Formed by July 1943 at Chester-le-Street.

Cadet TX.1 TS332.

Disbanded 1946 at Chester-le-Street.

22 GLIDING SCHOOL
Formed June 1942 at Kirbymoorside. Operations suspended during 1951.

Kirby Tutor; Grunau Baby VD168; Dagling Primary; Cadet TX.1 RA961, Cadet TX.2 VM637, TX.3 WT877; Sedbergh TX.1 WB983.

Disbanded 1st September 1955 at Kirton-in-Lindsey to become 643 Gliding School.

23 GLIDING SCHOOL
Formed May 1943 at Yeadon.

Kirby Tutor VD167; Grunau Baby VD168; Falcon III VD202; King Kite VD207; Cadet TX.1 RA929, TX.2 VM650, TX.3 WT905; Sedbergh TX.1 WB973.

Disbanded 1st September 1955 at Rufforth to become 642 Gliding School.

24 GLIDING SCHOOL
Formed August 1943 at Netherthorpe.

Kite VD165; Cadet TX.1 RB120, TX.3 WT876; Sedbergh TX.1 WB974.

Disbanded 1st September 1955 at Lindholme.

25 GLIDING SCHOOL
Formed by October 1943 at Hull.

Cadet TX.1 RA894; Kirby Tutor VD167.

Disbanded late 1947 at Leconfield.

26 GLIDING SCHOOL
Formed by November 1943 at Greatham. Operations suspended between 1946 and 1948.

Falcon III VD202; King Kite VD207; Kirby Tutor VD208; Grunau Baby IIB VT762; Cadet TX.1 RB134, TX.2 VM640, TX.3 WT895; Sedbergh TX.1 WB965.

Disbanded 1st September 1955 at Middleton St George.

27 GLIDING SCHOOL
Formed November 1943 at Woolsington.

Cadet TX.1 TS295, TX.2 VM651, TX.3 WT914; Sedbergh TX.1 WB964.

Disbanded 1st September 1955 at Ouston and merged with 31 Gliding School to become 641 Gliding School.

28 GLIDING SCHOOL
Formed by January 1945 at Firbeck.

Falcon III VD202; King Kite VD207; Grunau Baby; Cadet TX.1 RB134, TX.2 VM640.

Disbanded 1950 at Linton-on-Ouse.

29 GLIDING SCHOOL
Formed May 1944 at Sheffield.

Kite VD165; Cadet TX.1 VF179; Gull VD203.

Disbanded 1st September 1955 at Spitalgate and merged with 44 Gliding School to become 644 Gliding School.

30 GLIDING SCHOOL
Formed May 1944 at Sherburn in Elmet.

Cadet TX.1 RA923.

Disbanded by January 1946 at Sherburn in Elmet.

31 GLIDING SCHOOL
Formed by April 1944 at Usworth.

Falcon III VD202; Hols NE41 Primary; Cadet TX.1 VF191, TX.2 VM654, TX.3 XA291; Sedbergh TX.1 WB957; Gull I VW912.

Disbanded 1st September 1955 at Usworth and merged with 27 Gliding School to become 641 Gliding School.

41 GLIDING SCHOOL
Formed July 1942 at Knowle.

Slingsby Primary; Cadet TX.1 RA946, TX.2 VM662, TX.3 WT900; Sedbergh TX.1 WB928; Kirby Tutor VD218.

Disbanded April 1953 at Honiley.

Reformed May 1954 at Pembrey.

No aircraft known.

Disbanded 1st September 1955 at Pembrey.

42 GLIDING SCHOOL
Formed by October 1943 at Loughborough.

King Kite VD207; Grunau Baby IIB VT925; Gull II VD203; Cadet TX.1 RA920, TX.2, TX.3; Prefect TX.1 WE991; Sedbergh TX.1 WB984.

Disbanded 1st September 1955 at Cosford to become 633 Gliding School.

43 GLIDING SCHOOL
Formed by October 1943 at Walsall Airport. Suspended between December 1946 and May 1947.

Dagling Primary; Kirby Cadet PD685; Cadet TX.2 VM682, TX.3 XE788; Sedbergh TX.1 WB963.

Disbanded 1st September 1955 at Lichfield.

44 GLIDING SCHOOL
Formed October 1943 at Rearsby.

Falcon I VD175; Rhonbussard VD216; Kirby Tutor VD167; Cadet TX.1 RB124, TX.2 VW535, TX.3 WT874; Sedbergh TX.1; Dagling Primary.

Disbanded 1st September 1955 at Spitalgate and merged with 29 Gliding School to become 644 Gliding School.

45 GLIDING SCHOOL
Formed August 1942 at Meir.

Falcon III VD161; Kite VD213; Rhonbussard VD216; Kirby Cadet PD691; Cadet TX.2 VW537, TX.3 WT872; Prefect TX.1 WE991; Slingsby T.24 VM109; Dagling Primary.

Disbanded 1st September 1955 at Meir to become 632 Gliding School.

47 GLIDING SCHOOL
Formed by April 1945 at Camphill.

Cadet TX.1 RB121, TX.2 VM685.

Disbanded 1st April 1948 at Hucknall.

48 GLIDING SCHOOL
Formed October 1943 at Bretford.

Kirby Cadet PD651; Cadet TX.2 VM689, TX.3; Dagling; Sedbergh TX.1 WB975.

Disbanded by November 1955 at Lichfield.

49 GLIDING SCHOOL
Formed by June 1945 at Burnaston.

Slingsby Primary; Cadet TX.1 VW502; TX.2 VM684; TX.3 XE784; Sedbergh TX.1 WB977.

Disbanded 1st September 1955 at Newton.

50 GLIDING SCHOOL
Formed April 1944 at Hereford.

Grunau Baby II; Cadet TX.1, TX.2.

Disbanded 1st June 1948 at Pershore.

51 GLIDING SCHOOL
No records exist.

52 GLIDING SCHOOL
Planned opening at Hucknall cancelled.

61 GLIDING SCHOOL
Formed October 1943 at Abergavenny.

Cadet TX.1 RA953.

Disbanded by March 1946 at Abergavenny.

62 GLIDING SCHOOL
Formed by October 1943 at Cardiff.

Cadet TX.1 PD679.

Disbanded 4th August 1948 at Pengam Moors.

63 GLIDING SCHOOL
Formed by October 1943 at Tal-y-cafn.

Dagling PD654; Cadet TX.1 RA864, TX.2 VM688.

Disbanded 31st March 1948 at Valley.

64 GLIDING SCHOOL
Formed May 1944 at Merthyr.

Cadet TX.1 RA963.

Disbanded 1945 at (location unknown).

65 GLIDING SCHOOL
Formed May 1944 at Rhoose.

Kirby Cadet PD669.

Disbanded March 1947 at Cardiff.

66 GLIDING SCHOOL
No records exist.

67 GLIDING SCHOOL
No records exist.

68 GLIDING SCHOOL
Formed by December 1944 at Bridgend.

Falcon III VD161; Kirby Cadet VD171; Kirby Tutor VD218; Cadet TX.1 RB136, TX.2 VM639, TX.3 WT901; Sedbergh TX.1 WB928.

Disbanded 1st September 1955 at St Athan to become 634 Gliding School.

69 GLIDING SCHOOL
Formed (date and location unknown).

Cadet TX.1 RA985.

Disbanded (date and location unknown).

70 GLIDING SCHOOL
Formed August 1944 at Pennard.

Zogling Primary; Cadet PD662, Kirby Tutor VD212.

Disbanded (date unknown) at Fairwood Common.

72 GLIDING SCHOOL
Formed by August 1944 at Newport.

Cadet TX.1 RA944.

Disbanded 1947 (location unknown).

74 GLIDING SCHOOL
Formed by October 1944 at Templeton.

Cadet TX.1 RA957.

Disbanded December 1946 at Carew Cheriton and absorbed by 68 Gliding School.

80 GLIDING SCHOOL
Formed 1st August 1951 at Halesland by redesignating an element of 87 Gliding School.

Cadet TX.3 WT874; Prefect TX.1 WE981.

Disbanded 1st September 1955 at Halesland.

81 GLIDING SCHOOL
Formed October 1943 at Yeovil.

Dagling Primary; Zander and Scott Primary BGA358; Totternhoe VD199; Cadet TX.1 RB136, TX.2 II VM654.

Disbanded July 1948 at Yeovilton.

82 GLIDING SCHOOL
Formed late 1944 at Roborough.

Kirby Cadet PD629; Cadet TX.2, TX.3 XA294; Prefect TX.1 WE980; Sedbergh TX.1 WB967; Dagling Primary.

Disbanded 1st September 1955 at St Merryn.

83 GLIDING SCHOOL
Formed by May 1944 at Moreton Valence.

Kirby Cadet PD629; Cadet TX.2 VM635, TX.3 XA306; Sedbergh TX.1; Dagling Primary.

Disbanded by September 1955 at Aston Down.

84 GLIDING SCHOOL
Formed by September 1944 at Haldon Moor.

Dagling PD658; Cadet TX.1 TS305, TX.2 VM648, TX.3 XA300; Sedbergh TX.1 WB942.

Disbanded 1955 at Exeter to become 624 Gliding School.

86 GLIDING SCHOOL
Formed by June 1944 (location unknown).

No aircraft known.

Disbanded (date and location unknown).

87 GLIDING SCHOOL
Formed June 1944 at Locking.

Tutor VD178; Cadet PD637, TX.2 VM667, TX.3 WT874; Sedbergh TX.1 WB484; Totternhoe VD199; Gull I VW912; Prefect TX.1 WE980.

Disbanded 1st September 1955 at Locking to become 621 Gliding School.

88 GLIDING SCHOOL
Formed July 1944 at Wroughton.

Cadet TX.1 RA853.

Disbanded May 1948 at Hullavington.

89 GLIDING SCHOOL
Formed March 1944 at Christchurch.

Grunau Baby IIB VT917; Cadet TX.1 RB136, TX.2 VW538, TX.3 WT897; Sedbergh TX.1 WB990.

Disbanded 1st September 1955 at Christchurch to become 622 Gliding School.

92 GLIDING SCHOOL
Formed by January 1944 at Yate.

Totternhoe VD199; Viking I; Falcon III VD201; Tutor VD178; Cadet PD646, TX.2 VW536, TX.3 XA306; Sedbergh TX.1 WB966.

Disbanded 1st September 1955 at Colerne.

94 GLIDING SCHOOL
Formed July 1945 at Yate.

Grunau Baby IIB VT917; Cadet TX.1 RA906.

Disbanded 20th February 1948 at Yate.

95 GLIDING SCHOOL
Formed March 1945 at Perranporth.

Grunau Baby IIB VT917; Cadet TX.1 RA866.

Disbanded 31st January 1950 at St Eval.

101 GLIDING SCHOOL
No records exist. Rumoured to have operated at Great Yarmouth.

102 GLIDING SCHOOL
Formed June 1943 at Hethersett.

Dagling PD655; Grunau Baby IIB VT921; Cadet PD665, TX.1 VM591, TX.3 XA309; Sedbergh TX.1.

Disbanded 1st September 1955 at Swanton Morley to become 611 Gliding School.

103 GLIDING SCHOOL
Formed August 1943 at Westley.

Grunau Baby IIB VT921; Cadet VD181, Cadet TX.1, TX.2 VM665.

Disbanded 25th April 1948 at Honington.

104 GLIDING SCHOOL
Formed October 1944 at Ipswich.

Grunau Baby IIB VT921; Cadet TX.1 RA817, TX.2 VW529; Sedbergh TX.1.

Disbanded 1st September at Martlesham Heath to become 612 Gliding School.

105 GLIDING SCHOOL
Formed 6th May 1945 at Teversham.

Grunau Baby IIB VT923; Cadet TX.1 RB116, TX.2 VM636; TX.3 XA283; Sedbergh TX.1 WB985.

Disbanded 1st September 1955 at Teversham.

106 GLIDING SCHOOL
Formed by July 1944 at Henlow.

Grunau Baby IIB VT916; Cadet TX.1 RA931, TX.2 VM658, TX.3 XA298; Sedbergh WB961.

Disbanded 1st September 1955 at Henlow.

107 GLIDING SCHOOL
Formed September 1942 at Lincoln.

Cadet TX.1 RA880, TX.2 VM663.

Disbanded October 1949 at Digby.

108 GLIDING SCHOOL
Formed May 1945 at Corby.

Cadet TX.1 RA895, TX.2 VM692.

Existed to at least May 1949 at Desborough.

121 GLIDING SCHOOL
Formed by August 1942 at Wembley as an Elementary Gliding Training School. Later redesignated 121 Gliding School.

Cadet TX.1 RA922.

Disbanded 1945 at Halton.

122 GLIDING SCHOOL
Formed 25th October 1942 at Northwick Park as an Elementary Gliding Training School. Later redesignated 121 Gliding School.

Cadet TX.1 RA922, TX.2 VW528; TX.3 WT909; Sedbergh TX.1 WB945; Prefect TX.1 WE989.

Disbanded 1st September 1955 at Halton to become 613 Gliding School.

123 GLIDING SCHOOL
Formed by October 1942 at White Waltham as an Elementary Gliding Training School. Later redesignated 121 Gliding School.

Dagling PD664; Grunau Baby IIB VD204; Cadet TX.1 RA824, TX.2 VM645, TX.3 WT868; King Kite VD207; Prefect TX.1 WE981; Eton TX.1 WP266.

Disbanded 1st September 1955 at White Waltham to become 623 Gliding School.

124 GLIDING SCHOOL
Formed July 1943 at Aldenham.

Kirby Cadet PD645; Cadet TX.2 VM686.

Existed to at least October 1947 at Aldenham.

125 GLIDING SCHOOL
Formed by October 1943 at Denham.

Dagling PD659; Falcon III VD206; Grunau Baby VD215; Cadet TX.1 VW507, TX.2 VM659, TX.3 WT903; Prefect TX.1 WE989; Sedbergh TX.1 WB935.

Disbanded 1st September 1955 at Langley.

126 GLIDING SCHOOL
Formed August 1943 at Booker.

Grunau Baby VD215; Dagling; Cadet TX.1 RB115, TX.2 VM641, TX.3 XA292; Sedbergh TX.1.

Disbanded 1st September 1955 at Booker.

127 GLIDING SCHOOL
Formed by September 1943 at Panshanger.

Grunau Baby IIB VT916; Cadet TX.1 RA813, TX.2 VM644.

Disbanded 30th May 1948 at Panshanger.

128 GLIDING SCHOOL
Formed August 1943 at Theale.

Cadet TX.1 RA876.

Disbanded 1948 at Theale.

129 GLIDING SCHOOL
Formed September 1943 on Romney Marsh.

Cadet TX.1 RB126, TX.2 VM644.

Disbanded 30th May 1948 at North Weald.

130 GLIDING SCHOOL
Formed October 1944 at Cowley.

Dagling HM513; Grunau Baby IIB VT920; Cadet TX.1 RA882, TX.2 VM666, TX.3 WT899; Sedbergh TX.1.

Disbanded 1st September 1955 at Weston-on-the-Green.

141 GLIDING SCHOOL
Formed October 1942 at Kidbrooke.

Grunau Baby VD222; Falcon III VD160; Cadet TX.1 RA828, TX.2 VM635; Sedbergh TX.1 WB978; Prefect TX.1 WE992.

Disbanded 1st September 1955 at Detling.

142 GLIDING SCHOOL
Formed by February 1944 at Stapleford Tawney.

Dagling Cadet TX.1 RA835, TX.2 VM644; Sedbergh TX.1.

Disbanded 1st September 1955 at Hornchurch and merged with 146 Gliding School to become 614 Gliding School.

143 GLIDING SCHOOL
Formed January 1943 at Hamsey Green.

Falcon III; Grunau Baby IIB VT916; Cadet TX.1 TS350, TX.2 VM646; Sedbergh TX.1 WB925; Prefect TX.1 WE982.

Disbanded 1st September 1955 at Kenley to become 615 Gliding School.

144 GLIDING SCHOOL
Formed by August 1943 at Hounslow Heath.

Kirby Cadet PD652; Cadet TX.2 VM664.

Disbanded March 1948 at Heston.

145 GLIDING SCHOOL
Formed by September 1944 at Birch.

Cadet TX.1 RA911, TX.2 VW529.

Disbanded 25th April 1948 at Boxted.

146 GLIDING SCHOOL
Formed May 1944 at Shenfield.

Dagling PD680; Falcon III VD205; Rhonbussard VD216; Grunau Baby IIB VT925; Cadet TX.1 RA853, TX.2 VM660; TX.3 WT896; Sedbergh TX.1 WB919; Prefect TX.1 WT866.

Disbanded 1st September 1955 at Hornchurch and merged with 142 Gliding School to become 614 Gliding School.

147 GLIDING SCHOOL
Formed January 1945 at Laindon.

Cadet TX.1 RA872.

Disbanded January 1946 at Fairlop and absorbed by 146 Gliding School.

148 GLIDING SCHOOL
Formed July 1944 at Rochford.

Grunau Baby VD222; Cadet TX.1 RA988; TX.2; Gull II VD203.

Disbanded 16th June 1949 at Rochford and absorbed by 141 Gliding School.

149 GLIDING SCHOOL
Formed November 1942 at (location unknown).

Cadet TX.1 RA820.

Disbanded 1st December 1945 at Gravesend and absorbed by 141 Gliding School.

161 GLIDING SCHOOL
Formed by October 1942 at Burgess Hill.

Kirby Tutor VD212; Grunau Baby IIB VW908; Cadet TX.1, TX.2 VW539; Sedbergh TX.1 WB940.

Disbanded 1st September 1955 at Tangmere.

162 GLIDING SCHOOL
Formed by November 1943 at Hamsey Green.

BAC Primary NF746; Grunau Baby IIB VT923; Cadet PD666, TX.2; Sedbergh TX.1 WB987.

Disbanded 31st August 1950 at Biggin Hill.

163 GLIDING SCHOOL
Formed by October 1943 at (location unknown).

Grunau Baby IIB VT920; Cadet TX.1 RA959, TX.2 VW538.

Disbanded May 1948 at Gosport.

166 GLIDING SCHOOL
Formed by November 1943 at Westwell.

BAC III; Kirby Kite VD200; Cadet TX.1 RA814, TX.2 VW528, TX.3; Sedbergh TX.1 WB484.

Disbanded 5th September 1955 at Hawkinge.

167 GLIDING SCHOOL
Formed late 1943 (location unknown).

Grunau Baby IIB VT921; Dagling Primary; Cadet TX.1 RA817.

Disbanded by February 1948 at Fairoaks.

168 GLIDING SCHOOL
Formed January 1945 at Rochester.

Grunau Baby IIB VT916; BAC VII VW915; Cadet TX.1 RA882, TX.2 VM647; TX.3 WT900; Sedbergh TX.1 WB955; Slingsby T.24 VM109.

Disbanded 1st September 1955 at Detling.

180 GLIDING SCHOOL
Formed by November 1951 at Warton.

Cadet TX.1 RA895, TX.2.

Disbanded 1st September 1955 at Warton.

181 GLIDING SCHOOL
Formed by August 1943 at Blackpool.

Dagling Primary; Cadet TX.1 RA945, TX.2 VM637.

Disbanded 1st June 1948 at Warton.

182 GLIDING SCHOOL
Formed 28th May 1945 at Samlesbury.

Dagling Primary; Grunau Baby IIB VD172; Cadet PD650, TX.2 VM634; Sedbergh TX.1.

Existed to at least December 1949 at Samlesbury.

183 GLIDING SCHOOL
Formed by March 1944 at Wilmslow.

Falcon III VD161; Dagling Primary; Grunau Baby VD172; Cadet TX.1 RB139, TX.2 VM649, TX.3 WT912; Sedbergh TX.1 WB936.

Disbanded 1st September 1955 at Woodford.

184 GLIDING SCHOOL
Formed by March 1944 at Wilmslow.

Cadet TX.1 RA882.

Disbanded June 1946 at Wilmslow and absorbed by 183 Gliding School.

185 GLIDING SCHOOL
Formed March 1944 at Barton.

Kirby Cadet VD171; Condor II VW918; Cadet TX.1 RA890; Dagling Primary.

Disbanded December 1947 at Barton.

186 GLIDING SCHOOL
Formed June 1944 at Speke.

Grunau Baby IIB VT919; Cadet TX.1 RB126, TX.2 VM681; Sedbergh TX.1 WB928; Dagling Primary.

Disbanded 1st November 1955 at Hawarden to become 631 Gliding School.

187 GLIDING SCHOOL
Formed by April 1944 at Manchester.

Cadet TX.1 RB132.

Disbanded November 1947 at Stretton.

188 GLIDING SCHOOL
Formed January 1944 at Cark.

Cadet TX.1 RB139, TX.2 VW530, TX.3 XE792; Sedbergh TX.1 WB921.

Disbanded 1st September 1955 at Barrow.

189 GLIDING SCHOOL
Formed May 1945 at Kingstown.

Cadet TX.1 TS293, TX.2 VM638.

Disbanded October 1947 at Kingstown.

190 GLIDING SCHOOL
Formed by May 1945 at Cranage.

Cadet TX.1 RA889.

Disbanded 1st March 1948 at Woodvale to become 192 Gliding School.

192 GLIDING SCHOOL
Formed by July 1944 at Little Sutton.

Falcon III VD161; Cadet TX.1 RA922, TX.2; Grunau Baby IIB VT919.

Disbanded December 1947 at Woodvale.

Reformed 1st March 1948 at Sealand by redesignating 190 Gliding School.

Cadet TX.1 XA295; Sedbergh TX.1 WB944.

Disbanded 1952 at Harwarden.

201 GLIDING SCHOOL
Formed by June 1943 at Lisburn.

Grunau Baby VD209; Cadet I TS310; II VM690.

Existed to at least August 1946 at Long Kesh.

202 GLIDING SCHOOL
No record found.

203 GLIDING SCHOOL
Formed late 1943 at (location unknown).

Cadet TX.1 VM541, TX.2 VM663, TX.3 XE805; Sedbergh TX.1.

Disbanded 1st September 1955 at Long Kesh to become 671 Gliding School.

611 GLIDING SCHOOL, later 611 VOLUNTEER GLIDING SCHOOL
Formed 1st September 1955 at Swanton Morley by redesignating 102 Gliding School.

Sedbergh TX.1 WB987; Prefect TX.1 WE987; Cadet TX.3 WT907; Regal TX.1 XV951; Swallow TX.1 XS650; Venture T.1 XW983; Venture T.2 ZA653 3; Viking TX.1 ZE560.

Current 1st April 1998 at Watton.

612 GLIDING SCHOOL, later 612 VOLUNTEER GLIDING SCHOOL

Formed 1st September 1955 at Martlesham Heath by redesignating 104 Gliding School.

Sedbergh TX.1 XN149; Prefect TX.1 WE993; Cadet TX.3 XE786.

Disbanded 6th May 1963 at Martlesham Heath.

Reformed by October 1980 at Benson by redesignating an element of 613 Volunteer Gliding School.

Sedbergh TX.1 WG499; Cadet TX.3 XA288; Venture T.2 ZA654 3; Vigilant TX.1 ZH128.

Current 1st April 1998 at Abingdon.

613 GLIDING SCHOOL, later 613 VOLUNTEER GLIDING SCHOOL

Formed 1st September 1955 at Halton by redesignating 122 Gliding School.

Sedbergh TX.1 XN155; Prefect TX.1 WE989; Cadet TX.3 WT910; Swallow TX.1 XS650; Venture T.2 ZA632 2; Vigilant TX.1 ZH208.

Current 1st April 1998 at Halton.

614 GLIDING SCHOOL, later 614 VOLUNTEER GLIDING SCHOOL

Formed 1st September 1955 at Hornchurch by merging 142 and 146 Gliding Schools.

Grunau Baby IIB VT925; Grasshopper TX.1 WZ784; Sedbergh TX.1 WG498; Prefect TX.1 WE980; Cadet TX.3 XE812.

Disbanded 8th October 1978 at Debden.

Reformed January 1979 at Debden.

Sedbergh TX.1 WB988; Cadet TX.3 WT908; Viking TX.1 ZE585.

Current 1st April 1998 at Wethersfield.

615 GLIDING SCHOOL, later 615 VOLUNTEER GLIDING SCHOOL

Formed 1st September 1955 at Kenley by redesignating 143 Gliding School.

Sedbergh TX.1 WB932; Prefect TX.1 WE989; Cadet TX.3 XA292; Viking TX.1 ZE677.

Current 1st April 1998 at Kenley.

616 GLIDING SCHOOL, later 616 VOLUNTEER GLIDING SCHOOL

Formed 1st June 1958 at Henlow.

Sedbergh TX.1 WB980; Cadet TX.3 XN196; Prefect TX.1 WE993; Venture T.2 XZ559 3; Vigilant TX.1 ZH248.

Current 1st April 1998 at Henlow.

617 GLIDING SCHOOL, later 617 VOLUNTEER GLIDING SCHOOL

Formed by November 1958 at Hendon.

Sedbergh TX.1 WB986; Cadet TX.3 XN246 A; Prefect TX.1 WE982; Viking T.1 ZE656.

Current 1st April 1998 at Manston. Scheduled to operate at Odiham from 1st April 1999.

618 GLIDING SCHOOL, later 618 VOLUNTEER GLIDING SCHOOL

Formed 1st March 1963 at Manston.

Sedbergh TX.1 XN186 B; Cadet TX.3 WT914 C; Prefect TX.1 WE982; Grasshopper TX.1 XP488; Vanguard TX.1 ZD648; Valiant TX.1 ZD659; Viking TX.1 ZE658.

Existed until at least 1st April 1997 at Challock.

621 GLIDING SCHOOL, later 621 VOLUNTEER GLIDING SCHOOL

Formed 1st September 1955 at Locking by redesignating 87 Gliding School.

Sedbergh TX.1 WE990; Cadet TX.3 XA310; Grasshopper TX.1 WZ782; Prefect TX.1 WE993; Viking TX.1 ZE678.

Current 1st April 1998 at Hullavington.

622 GLIDING SCHOOL, later 622 VOLUNTEER GLIDING SCHOOL

Formed 1st September 1955 at Christchurch by redesignating 89 Gliding School.

Sedbergh TX.1 XN149; Cadet TX.3 XE806; Prefect TX.1 WE992; Swallow; Viking TX.1 ZE550.

Current 1st April 1998 at Upavon.

623 GLIDING SCHOOL

Formed 1st September 1955 at White Waltham by redesignating 123 Gliding School.

Sedbergh TX.1 WB919; Cadet TX.3; Prefect TX.1 WE992.

Disbanded 1st May 1963 at White Waltham.

Reformed 1st July 1963 at Tangmere.

Sedbergh TX.1 XN148; Cadet TX.3 XN248.

Disbanded November 1974 at Tangmere.

624 GLIDING SCHOOL, later 624 VOLUNTEER GLIDING SCHOOL

Formed 1st September 1955 at Exeter by redesignating 84 Gliding School.

Sedbergh TX.1 WB973; Cadet TX.3 XE802; Prefect TX.1 WE981; Venture T.2 ZA664 4; Vigilant T.1 ZE603.

Current 1st April 1998 at Chivenor.

625 GLIDING SCHOOL, later 625 VOLUNTEER GLIDING SCHOOL

Formed June 1958 at South Cerney.

Sedbergh TX.1 WB981; Cadet TX.3 XE793; Prefect TX.1 WE990; Grasshopper TX.1 XA241; Venture T.2 ZA627 7; Viking TX.1 ZE503.

Current 1st April 1998 at Hullavington.

626 GLIDING SCHOOL, later 626 VOLUNTEER GLIDING SCHOOL

Formed 1st June 1958 at St Eval.

Sedbergh TX.1 WB978; Cadet TX.3 WT910; Prefect TX.1 WE990; Grasshopper TX.1 XA231; Viking TX.1 ZE555.

Current 1st April 1998 at Predannack.

631 GLIDING SCHOOL, later 631 VOLUNTEER GLIDING SCHOOL

Formed 1st September 1955 at Hawarden by redesignating 186 Gliding School.

Sedbergh TX.1 XN157; Cadet TX.3 WT871; Prefect TX.1 WE991; Viking TX.1 ZE604.

Current 1st April 1998 at Sealand.

632 GLIDING SCHOOL, later 632 VOLUNTEER GLIDING SCHOOL

Formed 1st September 1955 at Meir by redesignating 45 Gliding School.

Sedbergh TX.1 WB992; Cadet TX.3 XN242; Prefect TX.1 WE991; Grasshopper TX.1 XP492; Venture T.2 XZ552 A; Vigilant T.1 ZH117.

Current 1st April 1998 Ternhill.

633 GLIDING SCHOOL, later 633 VOLUNTEER GLIDING SCHOOL

Formed 1st September 1955 at Cosford by redesignating 42 Gliding School.

Sedbergh TX.1 WB992; Cadet TX.3 XN239; Prefect TX.1 WE991; Grasshopper TX.1 XP492; Venture T.2 XZ556 B; Vigilant T.1 ZH125.

Current 1st April 1998 at Cosford.

634 GLIDING SCHOOL, later 634 VOLUNTEER GLIDING SCHOOL
Formed 1st September 1955 at St Athan by redesignating 68 Gliding School.

Sedbergh TX.1 WB926; Cadet TX.3 XA295; Prefect TX.1 WE981; Viking TX.1 ZE558.

Current 1st April 1998 at St Athan.

635 GLIDING SCHOOL, later 635 VOLUNTEER GLIDING SCHOOL
Formed October 1959 at Burtonwood.

Sedbergh TX.1 XN185; Cadet TX.3 XE801; Venture T.2 XZ564 4; Vigilant T.1 ZH247.

Current 1st April 1998 at Samlesbury.

636 GLIDING SCHOOL, later 636 VOLUNTEER GLIDING SCHOOL
Formed 1st October 1964 at Fairwood Common.

Sedbergh TX.1 WB941; Cadet TX.3 WT903; Viking TX.1 ZE682.

Current 1st April 1998 at Aberporth.

637 GLIDING SCHOOL, later 637 VOLUNTEER GLIDING SCHOOL
Formed 1st April 1966 at Gaydon.

Sedbergh TX.1 WB978; Cadet TX.3 XN241; Grasshopper TX.1 WZ796; Venture T.2 ZA661 3; Vigilant T.1 ZH144.

Current 1st April 1998 at Little Rissington.

641 GLIDING SCHOOL
Formed 1st September 1955 at Usworth by merging 27 and 31 Gliding Schools.

Sedbergh TX.1 XN187; Cadet TX.2, TX.3 XA288.

Disbanded (date unknown) at Dishforth.

642 GLIDING SCHOOL, later 642 VOLUNTEER GLIDING SCHOOL
Formed 1st September 1955 at Rufforth by redesignating 23 Gliding School.

Sedbergh TX.1 WB939 X; Cadet TX.3 WT918 H; Prefect TX.1 WE989; Venture T.2 XZ550; Vigilant T.1 ZH264.

Current 1st April 1998 at Linton-on-Ouse.

643 GLIDING SCHOOL, later 643 VOLUNTEER GLIDING SCHOOL
Formed 1st September 1955 at Kirton-in-Lindsey by redesignating 22 Gliding School.

Sedbergh TX.1 WB967; Cadet TX.3 WT889; Viking TX.1 ZE553.

Disbanded 1993 at Syerston and absorbed by the Air Cadet Central Gliding School.

644 GLIDING SCHOOL, later 644 VOLUNTEER GLIDING SCHOOL
Formed 1st September 1955 at Spitalgate by merging 29 and 44 Gliding Schools.

Sedbergh TX.1 WB977; Cadet TX.3 WT916; Prefect TX.1 WE990; T.53b XV951; Venture T.1 XW983; T.2 XZ551 H.

Disbanded 1993 at Syerston and absorbed by the Air Cadet Central Gliding School.

645 GLIDING SCHOOL, later 645 VOLUNTEER GLIDING SCHOOL
Formed 1st September 1955 at Middleton St George by merging 26 and 31 Gliding Schools.

Sedbergh TX.1 WB985; Cadet TX.3 XN198; Prefect TX.1 WE989; Vanguard TX.1 ZD644; Valiant TX.1 ZD660; Viking TX.1 ZE604.

Current 1st April 1998 at Syerston.

661 GLIDING SCHOOL, later 661 VOLUNTEER GLIDING SCHOOL
Formed 1st September 1955 at Dumfries by redesignating 1 Gliding School.

Sedbergh TX.1 WB939; Cadet TX.3 XA294; Grasshopper TX.1 WZ794; Prefect TX.1 WE984.

Disbanded January 1964 at Turnhouse.

Reformed April 1967 at Kirknewton.

Sedbergh TX.1 WB976; Cadet TX.3 XN253 L; Prefect TX.1 WE985; Swallow TX.1 XS652; Viking TX.1 ZE556.

Current 1st April 1998 at Kirknewton.

662 GLIDING SCHOOL, later 662 VOLUNTEER GLIDING SCHOOL
Formed 1st September 1955 at Edzell by redesignating 5 Gliding School.

Sedbergh TX.1 WB922 4; Cadet TX.3 XN199; Prefect TX.1 WE984; Swallow TX.1 XS652; Grasshopper TX.1 XA233; Viking TX.1 ZE650.

Current 1st April 1998 at Arbroath.

663 GLIDING SCHOOL, later 663 VOLUNTEER GLIDING SCHOOL
Formed November 1959 at Abbotsinch.

No aircraft known.

Disbanded by September 1962 at Abbotsinch.

Reformed by October 1968 at Leuchars.

Sedbergh TX.1 XN186; Cadet TX.3 WT900 S; Prefect TX.1 WE985; Swallow TX.1 XS650; Vigilant T.1 ZH211.

Current 1st April 1998 at Kinloss.

664 VOLUNTEER GLIDING SCHOOL
Formed by February 1987 at Bishop's Court.

Venture T.2 ZA629.

Disbanded October 1990 at Bishop's Court.

Reformed 1st November 1995 at Belfast City Airport and Newtownards.

Vigilant TX.1.

Current 1st April 1998 at Belfast City Airport/Newtownards.

671 GLIDING SCHOOL
Formed 1st September 1955 at Long Kesh by redesignating 203 Gliding School.

Sedbergh TX.1 XN154; Cadet TX.3 XN194.

Disbanded October 1962 at Bishops Court.

GOSPORT FLIGHT – see Aerial Fighting School, Heliopolis

GOVERNOR-GENERAL'S FLIGHT, AUSTRALIA
Formed 4th April 1945 at Canberra, Australia.

Anson XII NL153; York I MW140; Proctor NP336.

Disbanded 4th June 1947 at Canberra.

1 GRADING SCHOOL
Formed 3rd January 1951 at Digby.

Tiger Moth II N6837.

Disbanded 15th January 1952 at Digby and merged with 2 Grading School to become the Airwork Grading Unit.

2 GRADING SCHOOL
Formed 3rd January 1951 at Digby.

Tiger Moth BB735, II N6908 19.

Disbanded 15th January 1952 at Digby and merged with 1 Grading School to become the Airwork Grading Unit.

1 GRADING UNIT (AIRWORK)
Formed 9th June 1952 at Digby by redesignating an element of the Airwork Grading Unit.

Tiger Moth II T7793 68.

Disbanded 31st March 1953 at Digby.

2 GRADING UNIT (AIRWORK)
Formed 9th June 1952 at Kirton-in-Lindsey by redesignating an element of the Airwork Grading Unit.

Tiger Moth BB800, I K4259, II T5429.

Disbanded 31st March 1953 at Kirton-in-Lindsey.

GRAND FLEET SCHOOL OF AERIAL FIGHTING AND GUNNERY, later FLEET SCHOOL OF AERIAL FIGHTING AND GUNNERY
Formed 19th July 1918 at East Fortune by redesignating an element of 208 (Temporary) Training Depot Station.

Bristol Scout D N5400; Avro 504A D1616, Avro 504K E3001; Camel E4415; D.H.4; D.H.5; D.H.9A E8491; S.E.5a; Pup B2211; 1½ Strutter B2597; Snipe E6864; F.2B F4322.

Disbanded 18th March 1920 at Leuchars to become RAF Base, Leuchars.

GRANSDEN LODGE NAVIGATION TRAINING UNIT – see Navigation Training Unit

GREEK TRAINING FLIGHT
Formed September 1941 at Gaza, Egypt.

Gauntlet II K5286. Also inherited aircraft from the Lorraine Squadron.

Disbanded November 1942 at Aqir, Palestine, and absorbed by the Royal Hellenic Air Force.

GREMLIN TASK FORCE
Formed September 1945 at Tan San Nhut, French Indo-China, under the control of the RAF Element, Saigon Control Commission. Japanese aircraft were flown by Japanese crews on repatriation and food supply flights.

Kawasaki Ki-48 Lily; Kawasaki Ki-61 Tony; Mitsubishi Ki-21 Sally; Mitsubishi Ki-46 Dinah; Mitsubishi Ki-57 Topsy; Nakajima L2D Tabby; Tachikawa Ki-36 Ida; Tachikawa Ki-54 Hickory; Mitsubishi Ki-67 Peggy.

Disbanded February 1946 at Tan San Nhut.

GROUND ATTACK TRAINING UNIT
Formed April 1945 at Ranchi, India, by redesignating the Specialised Low Attack Instructors School.

Harvard IIB FE596; Hurricane IIB HV897, IIC LE798, IV LE273, XIIA PJ721; Oxford I NM448; Auster III MZ106; Mosquito VI HR628; Spitfire VIII NH620; Beaufighter X NV477.

Disbanded 24th May 1945 at Ranchi and merged with the Advance Flying Training Unit to become the Tactical and Weapon Development Unit.

GROUND CONTROLLED APPROACH FLIGHT, later GROUND CONTROLLED APPROACH SQUADRON
Formed by September 1943 at Hinton-in-the-Hedges within the Signals Development Unit. Redesignated the Ground Controlled Approach Squadron from 29th July 1944 at Honiley, having been absorbed by the Signals Flying Unit.

Oxford II X7233.

Disbanded 1st September 1946 at Honiley and absorbed by the Radio Warfare Establishment.

GROUND DEFENCE GUNNERS SCHOOL, later 1 GROUND DEFENCE GUNNERS SCHOOL
Formed 20th November 1939 at North Coates. Redesignated 1 Ground Defence Gunners School from 1st December 1939.

Wallace I K3562, II K8696; Hart K3861; Gauntlet II K5279; Lysander.

Disbanded 15th February 1942 at Ronaldsway to become 3 Royal Air Force Regiment School.

1 GROUP AIR BOMBER TRAINING FLIGHT
Formed June 1942 at Binbrook alongside 1481 (Bomber) Gunnery Flight.

Oxford.

Disbanded 15th March 1943 at Lindholme.

1 GROUP COMMUNICATION FLIGHT
The Station Flight, Hucknall, provided communication aircraft for 1 Group by December 1940. This arrangement continued until July 1941.

Formed 20th July 1941 at Bircotes.

Nil (7.41–)	*Lysander I R2619; Piper Cub Coupe BV181; Leopard Moth X9295, Tiger Moth II T5813; Whitney Straight DR612; Proctor I R7496, II Z7220.*
3V (– .47)	*Oxford I R6811, II N6345; Proctor III LZ602 3V-A, IV NP193 3V-D; Anson XII PH558, XIX TX205 3V-B.*
Nil (.47–10.64)	*Anson XIX VN387, T.21 VV967; Balliol T.2 WN311; Chipmunk T.10 WZ880; Meteor F.4 VT102; T.7 WL405; Canberra T.4 WJ876.*

Disbanded 1st October 1964 at Finningley.

1 GROUP MARKING FLIGHT
Records begin March 1944 at Binbrook.

No aircraft known.

Records cease July 1944 at Binbrook.

1 GROUP POOL
Formed 14th September 1939 by merging 52 and 63 Squadrons at Benson and 35 and 207 Squadrons at Cranfield. 35 and 207 Squadrons were withdrawn from the Group pool on 1st February 1940 and 9th December 1939 respectively.

Battle; Anson.

Disbanded 8th April 1940 at Abingdon to become 12 Operational Training Unit.

1 GROUP PRACTICE FLIGHT
Formed 6th July 1937 at Usworth.

Tutor K6109.

Probably disbanded June 1938 at Usworth.

1 GROUP SPECIAL DUTIES FLIGHT
Formed 18th April 1944 at Binbrook.

Lancaster III ND860.

Disbanded 11th August 1944 at Binbrook.

1 GROUP TARGET TOWING FLIGHT
Formed 18th September 1941 at Goxhill.

Lysander III T1465, IIIA V9794.

Disbanded 30th October 1941 at Binbrook to become 1481 (Target Towing) Flight.

2 GROUP COMMUNICATION FLIGHT, later 2 GROUP COMMUNICATION SQUADRON, later 2 GROUP COMMUNICATION FLIGHT
Formed by January 1940.

Nil (–5.47)	*Tutor K6095; Oxford I T1347, II P1829; Spitfire VB BL990, XI PL836, F.24 PK718; Proctor I P6308; Master I AZ253; Taylorcraft Plus C2 HH982; Martinet I HN975; Mitchell III KJ692; Anson I N9533; Magister R1961; Messenger I RH375; Auster III NJ975, IV MT101; V RT514; Bu 181 VM143; Fi 156 VN267; Bf 108B VH762.*
K2 (.45–5.47)	*Anson I N9533, X NK532, XI NK993; XII PH529.*
4A	*Allocated but no evidence of use.*
XR	*Allocated but no evidence of use*

Disbanded 31st May 1947 at B.58 (Melsbroek), Belgium.

Reformed 1st December 1948 at Gutersloh, Germany

Tiger Moth II T8258; Proctor IV RM223; Anson XII PH700, XIX TX213, Anson T.21 VS570; Vampire FB.5 WA308; Meteor T.7 WF836, FR.9 WB115, PR.10 WH570; Chipmunk T.10 WP898.

Disbanded 4th October 1956 at Gutersloh.

2 GROUP POOL
Formed 14th September 1939 by merging 104 and 108 Squadrons at Bicester and 90 Squadron at West Raynham. 90 Squadron was withdrawn from the Group Pool on 19th September 1939.

Anson I; Blenheim I, IV.

Disbanded 8th April 1940 at Bicester and merged with 104 and 108 Squadrons to form 13 Operational Training Unit.

2 GROUP SUPPORT UNIT
Formed 1st April 1944 at Swanton Morley by redesignating 1482 (Bomber) Gunnery Flight.

Anson I DJ105 C; Boston III W8283; Mitchell II FL183, III KJ605; Martinet I HP280; Mosquito III LR535, VI LR372.

Disbanded 1st August 1945 at Fersfield to become 2 Group Disbandment Centre.

2 GROUP TARGET TOWING FLIGHT
Formed 22nd February 1940 at West Raynham.

Gladiator II N5717; Tutor K3396; Battle K9253; Lysander III T1616, IIIA V9781; Blenheim IV N3545.

Disbanded 30th October 1941 at West Raynham to become 1482 (Target Towing) Flight.

2 GROUP TRAINING FLIGHT
Formed by March 1940 at Fersfield.

Tutor K6087; Blenheim I L1310, IV L9257; Mitchell III KJ599.

Disbanded 31st December 1945 at Fersfield.

3 GROUP AIR BOMBER TRAINING FLIGHT
Formed 15th June 1942 at Newmarket alongside 1483 (Bomber) Gunnery Flight.

Oxford.

Disbanded 15th March 1943 at Marham.

3 GROUP COMMUNICATION FLIGHT
Formed by December 1936 at Andover as 3 Group Headquarters Flight.

Nil (–4.46)	*Wallis II K8675; Mentor L4392; Lysander II L6872; Magister N6839; Oxford II N6422; Tiger Moth BB814, II N9322; Moth X5018; Hornet Moth X9319; Master II AZ702; Dominie I X7377; Whitney Straight AV970; Piper Cub Coupe BV985; Martinet I HP352; Hurricane IIC LF579.*
3S (4.46–4.51)	*Proctor III LZ567 3S-A, IV RM187; Oxford I PG929; Anson XII PH788 3S-R, XIX TX211 3S-T.*
Nil (4.51–10.64)	*Anson T.20 VS509, T.21 VV953; Meteor T.7 WF772; Chipmunk T.10 WG317.*

Disbanded 1st October 1964 at Mildenhall.

3 GROUP POOL
Formed 14th September 1939 at Harwell by merging 75 and 148 Squadrons.

Anson I; Wellington I.

Disbanded 8th April 1940 at Harwell to become 15 Operational Training Unit.

3 GROUP PRACTICE FLIGHT
Formed June 1937 with Sections at Honington and Waddington.

Tutor K6090 (Honington), K6113 (Waddington).

Probably disbanded October 1937 at Honington and Waddington.

3 GROUP TARGET TOWING FLIGHT
Formed 8th April 1940 at Marham.

Battle K9277; Lysander III R9078.

Disbanded 30th October 1941 at Newmarket to become 1483 (Target Towing) Flight.

3 GROUP TRAINING FLIGHT
Formed 1st February 1941 at Stradishall.

Wellington IA P2517, IC N2778; Battle P2260; Tiger Moth BD142.

Disbanded 7th February 1942 at Newmarket and absorbed by 1483 (Target Towing) Flight.

4 GROUP AIR BOMBER TRAINING FLIGHT
Formed 17th June 1942 at Driffield alongside 1484 (Bomber) Gunnery Flight.

Oxford.

Disbanded 15th March 1943 at Driffield.

4 GROUP COMMUNICATION FLIGHT
Formed 6th October 1940 at Yeadon.

Nil	*Magister T9824; Lysander I R2627; Leopard Moth AX862; Tiger Moth II DE405; Cub Coupe HM565; Proctor III HM477; Oxford I PG978; Anson XIX TX221.*
M8	*Allocated but no evidence of use.*

Disbanded 2nd February 1948 at Abingdon and absorbed by 38 Group Communication Flight.

4 GROUP EXPERIMENTAL FLIGHT
Formed by September 1937 at Porton Down.

Battle K7574; Hind L7217.

Existed to at least July 1938.

4 GROUP POOL
Formed 14th September 1939 at Benson by merging 97 and 166 Squadrons.

Whitley III; Anson I.

Disbanded 8th April 1940 at Abingdon to become 10 Operational Training Unit.

4 GROUP PRACTICE FLIGHT
Formed July 1937 at Dishforth.

Tutor K8169.

Probably disbanded September 1937.

4 GROUP SPECIAL DUTIES FLIGHT
Formed pre-war with Audax K1999 held on charge.

4 GROUP TARGET TOWING FLIGHT
Formed February 1940 at Driffield.

Battle K9200; Lysander.

Disbanded 30th October 1941 at Driffield to become 1484 Target Towing Flight.

5 GROUP AIR BOMBER TRAINING FLIGHT
Formed 15th June 1942 at Coningsby alongside 1485 (Bomber) Gunnery Flight.

Oxford.

Disbanded 15th March 1943 at Fulbeck.

5 GROUP COMMUNICATION FLIGHT
Formed by September 1937 at Mildenhall as 5 Group Headquarters Flight.

Nil (9.37– .45)	*Tomtit K1786; Lysander I R2636; Oxford I V4179; Hornet Moth X9326; Piper Cub Coupe BV990; Puss Moth ES921.*
4B (.45–12.45)	*Proctor III R7559; Oxford I V4197; Auster.*

Disbanded 15th December 1945 at Swinderby.

5 GROUP POOL
Formed 14th September 1939 at Finningley, the Group Pool being 7 and 76 Squadrons.

Anson I; Hampden I.

Disbanded 8th April 1940 at Upper Heyford to become 16 Operational Training Unit.

5 GROUP PRACTICE FLIGHT
Formed by August 1937 at Mildenhall.

Tutor K3271.

Probably disbanded January 1938 at Mildenhall.

5 GROUP TARGET TOWING FLIGHT
Formed February 1940 at Driffield.

Battle P2157; Lysander III R9131, IIIA V9865; Hampden I AD972.

Disbanded 7th January 1942 at Scampton and absorbed by 1485 (Target Towing) Flight.

5 GROUP TRAINING FLIGHT
Formed February 1941 at Finningley.

Lysander IIIA V9865; Wellington IA P9228; Hampden I AD792.

Disbanded 30th October 1941 at Coningsby and absorbed by 1485 (Target Towing) Flight.

6 GROUP COMMUNICATION FLIGHT
Formed 3rd April 1939 at Mousehold.

Puss Moth X9403; Hornet Moth X9446; Magister P2446;

Disbanded 11th May 1942 at Abingdon to become 91 Group Communication Flight.

Reformed 1st December 1942 at Dishforth.

Nil (12.42–.45)	Eagle DP847; Tiger Moth II N9494; Oxford II P1820; Proctor I P6187, III Z7218; Phoenix 2 X9338; Anson I DG816; Auster V MT361.
X8 (.45–7.45)	Anson I NK756 X8-S.

Disbanded 17th July 1945 at Dishforth

6 GROUP TARGET TOWING FLIGHT
Formed December 1938 at Abingdon as an element of the Station Flight, Abingdon. Role passed to within the Station Flight, Bicester, from March 1940.

Lysander II P1731.

Disbanded by March 1941 at Squires Gate.

7 GROUP COMMUNICATION FLIGHT
Formed 15th July 1940 at Wyton.

Proctor I P6128.

Disbanded 11th May 1942 at Bicester to become 92 Group Communication Flight.

Reformed 11th November 1944 at Bottesford.

Dominie X7392; Proctor III HM323; Martinet I HP427.

Disbanded 21st December 1945 at Spitalgate.

8 GROUP COMMUNICATION FLIGHT
Formed 15th August 1942 at Wyton.

Nil	Proctor II Z7220, III HM431; Hawk Trainer 3 AV978; Whitney Straight DR611; Tiger Moth II T7124; Beaufighter II V8214.
8H	Allocated but no evidence of use.

Disbanded 31st October 1945 at Wyton.

9 GROUP ANTI-AIRCRAFT CO-OPERATION FLIGHT
Formed 5th May 1941 at Speke.

Lysander II L4792, IIIA V9658; Blenheim IV T2352; Hurricane I V7192.

Disbanded 1st December 1941 at Wrexham to become 285 Squadron.

9 GROUP COMMUNICATION FLIGHT
Formed November 1940 at Samlesbury.

Magister R1977; Hornet Moth W5774; Hurricane I P2822, X AG281, IIB JS359; Spitfire VB BM523, IX MJ679; Mentor L4410; Master I N8052, III DL670; Cleveland I AS471; Oxford I V3149, II P6818; Dominie I X7492; Tiger Moth II DE310; Leopard Moth AV989.

Disbanded 17th September 1944 at Samlesbury.

9 GROUP TARGET TOWING FLIGHT
Formed 16th July 1941 at Valley.

Nil (7.41–10.41)	Lysander II N1214, III T1552.
O9 (10.41–12.41)	Lysander.

Disbanded 30th October 1941 at Valley to become 1486 (Target Towing) Flight.

10 GROUP ANTI-AIRCRAFT CO-OPERATION FLIGHT
Formed 5th May 1941 at Filton.

Lysander II R2042, IIIA V9821; Blenheim IV V6237; Hurricane I V7540.

Disbanded 17th November 1941 at Filton to become 286 Squadron.

10 GROUP COMMUNICATION FLIGHT
Formed 1st June 1940 at Hullavington.

Monospar X9335; Tiger Moth II T6194; Proctor I P6269, III HM281; Oxford II X7231; Hurricane I V6915, IIB BW924, X AF990; Spitfire VB BM532, VC AR570; Monarch W6461; Master III W8465; Dominie I X7454; D.H.89A Z7254; Cub Coupe DG667.

Disbanded 17th April 1945 at Colerne.

10 GROUP TARGET TOWING FLIGHT
Formed 16th July 1941 at Warmwell.

Nil (7.41–10.41)	Lysander II N1249, TT.III T1450.
10 (10.41–12.41)	Lysander.

Disbanded 30th October 1941 at Warmwell to become 1487 (Target Towing) Flight.

11 GROUP ANTI-AIRCRAFT CO-OPERATION FLIGHT
Formed 5th May 1941 at Croydon.

Lysander II R2027, IIIA V9799; Blenheim IV V5467; Hurricane I P2754.

Disbanded 19th November 1941 at Croydon to become 287 Squadron.

11 GROUP COMMUNICATION FLIGHT
The Station Flight, Northolt, provided communication aircraft for 11 and 26 Groups from 1st May 1936. The Station Flight became the Air Defence of Great Britain Communication Squadron from 1st May 1944 and with a designated Flight to cater for the activities of 11 and 26 Groups. This arrangement continued until October 1944 when the parent unit became the Fighter Command Communication Squadron.

Formed January 1945 at Northolt.

JC	Oxford II V3571 JC-H; Spitfire IX MK128, XVI SL574; Proctor III HM405; Mosquito VI PZ193.

Disbanded 9th July 1947 at Northolt and absorbed by the Fighter Command Communication Squadron.

Reformed 15th April 1958 at Martlesham Heath.

Anson XIX TX193, T.21 WB453; Devon C.1 VP974; Meteor T.7 WL378; Chipmunk T.10 WG465.

Disbanded 31st December 1960 at Martlesham Heath.

Reformed 1st January 1961 at Ouston by redesignating 13 Group Communication Flight.

Anson XIX VM334; Devon C.1 VP974.

Disbanded 31st March 1963 at Leconfield.

11 GROUP POOL
Formed 14th January 1939 at Andover.

Hurricane I L2006 Y; Mentor L4399; Oxford I N1190; Harvard I N7176.

Disbanded 6th March 1940 at Sutton Bridge to become 6 Operational Training Unit.

11 GROUP TARGET TOWING FLIGHT
Formed 20th May 1941 at Shoreham.

Nil (8.41–10.41)	Lysander II N1222.
11 (10.41)	Lysander II.

Disbanded 30th October 1941 at Shoreham to become 1488 (Target Towing) Flight.

12 GROUP ANTI-AIRCRAFT CO-OPERATION FLIGHT
Formed 5th May 1941 at Digby.

Lysander II P1714, IIIA V9860; Blenheim IV T2400; Hurricane I V7136.

Disbanded 18th November 1941 at Digby to become 288 Squadron.

12 GROUP COMMUNICATION FLIGHT
The Station Flight, Hucknall, provided communication aircraft for 12 Group by December 1940. This arrangement continued until July 1941.

Formed July 1941 at Hucknall.

Nil (7.41– .45)	Mentor L4431; Magister L8146; Master I T8614, III DL602; Proctor I P6268, III Z7220; Spitfire I R6632; IIA P8179; VA R7350, VB EN800; IX PL249; Oxford I T1397; II V3731; Hurricane I V6787, IIB HV915, XIIB JS359; Mustang III KH535, X AM203; Mitchell III KJ611; Martinet I HP218; Auster I LB373, V TW388.
WQ (.45– .46)	Proctor IV LZ562 WQ; Oxford I NM335 WQ, II BG149 WQ; Anson XII PH643 WQ-G.
Nil (.46–4.63)	Harvard IIB FX224; Hornet F.1 PX237, F.3 PX313; Anson XIX TX174, T.20 VM414, T.21 WJ557; Vampire F.1 VF300, FB.5 VV673; Meteor F.4 RA448, T.7 VW457; F.8 WF707, NF.14 WS777; Chipmunk T.10 WZ872.

Disbanded 31st March 1963 at Horsham St Faith.

12 GROUP POOL
Formed 15th September 1939 at Aston Down.

Gladiator I K7943; Tutor K3435; Battle K7692; Harvard I P5862; Blenheim I L1177; Hurricane I L1895.

Disbanded 6th March 1940 at Aston Down to become 5 Operational Training Unit.

12 GROUP TARGET TOWING FLIGHT
Formed August 1941 at Coltishall.

Nil (8.41–10.41)	Lysander II P9100, III R9129.
12 (10.41–12.41)	Lysander.

Disbanded 30th October 1941 at Coltishall to become 1489 (Target Towing) Flight.

13 GROUP ANTI-AIRCRAFT CO-OPERATION FLIGHT
Formed 7th June 1941 at Turnhouse by redesignating an element of 7 Anti-Aircraft Co-operation Unit.

Blenheim IV T1864; Hurricane I N2558; Lysander II P1725, IIIA V9852.

Disbanded 17th November 1941 at Kirknewton to become 289 Squadron.

13 GROUP COMMUNICATION FLIGHT
Formed 1st August 1939 at Woolsington.

Nil	Gladiator I K8026; Mentor L4426; Blenheim I L8549, IV N6141; Hurricane I P3929, IIA DG642; Proctor I P6267, III Z7103; Magister I P6402; Dominie I R9552; Spitfire VB EP515, IX TE306; Oxford I R6054; Hornet Moth W5754; Vega Gull X9332; Petrel X9454; Whitney

Straight AV970; Martinet I MS928; Whitney Straight G-AEWK; Anson XII PH625.

LG (.45–5.46)	No evidence of use.

Disbanded 20th May 1946 at Dalcross.

Reformed 1st June 1955 at Newton.

Anson XIX TX224, T.21 WB451, T.22 WB451; Devon C.1 VP974; Meteor T.7 VW488, F.8 WE876, NF.14 WS775 V; Chipmunk T.10 WG465.

Disbanded 1st January 1961 at Ouston to become 11 Group Communication Flight.

13 GROUP TARGET TOWING FLIGHT
Formed August 1941 at Acklington.

Nil (8.41–10.41)	Lysander II N1226, III T1637.
13 (10.41–12.41)	Lysander.

Disbanded 8th December 1941 at Acklington to become 1490 (Target Towing) Flight.

14 GROUP COMMUNICATION FLIGHT
Formed 20th July 1940 at Inverness.

Oxford I L4617; Lysander I R2614; Spitfire VA R7302; Tiger Moth II T7327; Defiant I V1132; Hornet Moth AV951; Harrow I; Petrel X9454.

Disbanded 15th July 1943 at Inverness and absorbed by 13 Group Communication Flight.

14 GROUP TARGET TOWING FLIGHT
Formed October 1941 at Inverness.

Lysander III T1549, IIIA V9853.

Disbanded 8th December 1941 at Inverness to become 1491 (Target Towing) Flight.

15 GROUP ARMAMENT PRACTICE CAMP
Formed October 1941 at Aldergrove.

Lysander III T1548.

Disbanded 5th November 1941 at Aldergrove to become 1 Armament Practice Camp.

15 GROUP COMMUNICATION FLIGHT
Formed 13th June 1939 at Roborough.

Mentor I L4425; Magister L5954; Anson I R3308; Envoy 3 P5625; Petrel X9336; Proctor I P6190; D.H.89A P9589; Vega Gull; Anson I R3308; Dominie I R5932; Oxford I T1378, II X7060; Tiger Moth II T5847; Monospar X9453; Hurricane IIC LF540; Dragonfly AW164.

Disbanded 1st August 1945 at Speke.

16 GROUP ARMAMENT PRACTICE CAMP
Formed October 1941 at Thorney Island.

Lysander II P9129; Battle L5681; Martinet I HP407.

Disbanded 5th November 1941 at Thorney Island to become 2 Armament Practice Camp.

16 GROUP COMMUNICATION FLIGHT
Formed 3rd September 1939 at Rochester.

Nil (9.39– .45)	Mentor L4425; Envoy 3 P5627; Proctor I P6190; Oxford I T1378; Monospar X9453; Hornet Moth AV969; Tiger Moth BB696, II T6319; Anson I AX639; Proctor III HM409; Dominie I NF896.
S9 (.45–3.46)	Proctor III LZ565 S9-C.

Disbanded 8th March 1946 at Rochester.

16 GROUP PRACTICE FLIGHT
Formed August 1937 at Donibristle.

Tutor K6122.

Disbanded mid-1938 at Donibristle.

17 GROUP COMMUNICATION FLIGHT
Formed by August 1938 at Gosport.

Tutor K4821; Magister L8053; Mentor L4427; Envoy 3 P5625; Hendy Heck NF749; Proctor III HM452; Anson I LT186 B.

Disbanded 18th September 1945 at Turnhouse

18 GROUP ARMAMENT PRACTICE CAMP
Formed October 1941 at Leuchars.

Battle K9184; Lysander II.

Disbanded 5th November 1941 at Leuchars to become 3 Armament Practice Camp.

18 GROUP COMMUNICATION FLIGHT
Formed 11th March 1940 at Turnhouse.

Nil (3.40– .45)	*Moth W7976; Mentor L4429; Proctor I P6173; Lysander III T1741; D.H.89 V4725; Oxford II V3832; Eagle 2 ES944; Walrus L2207; Hornet Moth AV952; Anson I LS998.*
2V (.45– .48)	*Oxford T1194 2V-Z; Proctor III LZ684 2V-B; Dominie I X7417 2V-D; Anson I LS998 2V-H.*
Nil (.48–10.64)	*Proctor III LZ796, IV RM171; Dakota IV KN649; Anson XII PH624, XIX TX218 A, T.21 WB450 Z; Devon C.1 VP974; Pembroke C.1 WV737, C(PR).1 XF797.*

Disbanded 1st October 1964 at Turnhouse.

19 GROUP ARMAMENT PRACTICE CAMP
Formed October 1941 at Carew Cheriton.

Lysander II P9129.

Disbanded November 1941 at Carew Cheriton to become 4 Armament Practice Camp.

19 GROUP COMMUNICATION FLIGHT
Formed 5th February 1941 at Roborough.

Nil (2.41– .45)	*Monospar Jubilee K8308; Mentor L4429; Magister L8163; Oxford I T1400; Lysander III T1440; Dragon Rapide V4725; Tiger Moth II T6138; Hornet Moth W5781; Martinet I EM439.*
G2 (.45–4.51)	*Oxford V3190 G2-D; Proctor III LZ740 G2-H; Dominie I X7338 G2-A; Sea Otter I JM905 G2-D; Anson I NK332 G2-C, XIX TX191 G2-A; Auster V RT489.*
Nil (4.51–4.60)	*Anson XII PH554 F, XIX TX222 C, T.21 VV261; Prentice T.1 VS377; Meteor T.7 VW488; Devon C.1 VP975; Chipmunk T.10 WD329; Pembroke C(PR).1 XF798.*

Disbanded 1st April 1960 at Roborough.

21 GROUP COMMUNICATION FLIGHT
Formed by November 1940 at Cranwell.

Nil (.40–4.46)	*Oxford I HM813, II N6373; Tiger Moth II R5174; Proctor III Z7213; Hornet Moth W5754; Vega Gull W6464; Master II DM292.*
FKO (4.46–4.51)	*Harvard IIB FX219 FKO-C; Proctor III R7573 FKO-B, IV RM181 FKO-L; Oxford I AS709 FKO-H; Dominie I NR697 FKO-A; Anson I MG519 FKO-B, XIX TX229 FKO-D; Spitfire XVI TE199.*
Nil (4.51–3.55)	*Anson XIX TX230 D, T.20 VS528, T.21 VS589; Prentice T.1 VS276; Chipmunk T.10 WK573.*

Disbanded 1st March 1955 at Swinderby.

22 GROUP COMMUNICATION FLIGHT
Formed 6th October 1939 at Farnborough.

No aircraft known.

Disbanded 1st December 1940 at Farnborough to become the Army Co-operation Command Communication Flight.

Reformed 1st August 1943 at Ternhill.

Nil (8.43–4.46)	*Tiger Moth II T5542; Oxford I T1341, II ED183; Dominie I X7443.*
TTE (4.46–4.51)	*Vega Gull X9340 TTE-C; Proctor IV NP346 TTE-C; Anson XI NL247 TTE-B, XII PH639, XIX TX195 TTE-B.*

Nil (4.51–4.64)	*Anson XIX TX192, T.21 WJ560, T.22 VV994; Prentice T.1 VS275; Vampire T.11 WZ447; Chipmunk T.10 WB586.*

Disbanded 1st April 1964 at Ternhill.

23 GROUP COMMUNICATION FLIGHT
Formed by September 1939 at Spitalgate.

Nil (.39–4.46)	*Magister; Proctor I P6233, III Z7238; Moth Minor X5116; Dominie I X7369; Oxford I NM583, II V3670; Puss Moth DG662.*
FKP (4.46–9.47)	*Proctor II BV651 FKP-F, IV NP273; Harvard IIB FX420 FKP-P; Oxford I PH513; Anson XII PH551, XIX VM314 FKP-T.*

Disbanded 15th September 1947 at Halton.

Reformed 29th March 1950 at Cranfield.

Prentice T.1 VR222; Provost T.1 XF888; Vampire T.11 WZ447.

Disbanded 1st October 1964 at Dishforth.

24 GROUP COMMUNICATION FLIGHT
Formed by February 1940 at Halton.

Nil (.40–4.46)	*Magister; Hornet Moth X9326; Whitney Straight V4739; Proctor III LZ680; Auster I LB330.*
THL (4.46–7.46)	*Proctor I P6242 THL-BIV NP159; Anson XII PH711, XIX TX154 THL-H; Proctor I P6242 THL-B.*
Also used	*Tiger Moth II DE603; Proctor III HM343.*

Disbanded 2nd July 1946 at Halton.

Reformed 1st January 1960 at Colerne.

Anson XIX VM391; Chipmunk T.10 WG463.

Disbanded 1st April 1964 at Colerne.

25 GROUP COMMUNICATION FLIGHT
Formed by March 1938 at Eastchurch.

Nil (.40–4.46)	*Gauntlet II K5335; Mentor L4413; Proctor I P6130, III R7559; Master II AZ520; Anson I DJ513; Dominie I NR679, II RL967.*
FKQ (4.46–4.48)	*Magister T9957 FKQ-D; Proctor III LZ710 FKQ-C, IV NP328; Anson I MG616 FKQ-A; XIX VM313 FKQ-A.*

Disbanded 15th April 1948 at Spitalgate.

Reformed 20th March 1951 at Manby.

Anson XIX VM369, T.21 VS513; Meteor T.7 WH175; Chipmunk T.10 WB724.

Disbanded 28th January 1961 at Manby and absorbed by the Flying Training Command Communication Squadron.

26 GROUP COMMUNICATION FLIGHT
The Station Flight, Northolt, provided communication aircraft for 11 and 26 Groups from 1st May 1936. The Station Flight became the Air Defence of Great Britain Communication Squadron from 1st May 1944 with a designated Flight to cater for the activities of 11 and 26 Groups. This arrangement continued until October 1944 when the parent unit became the Fighter Command Communication Squadron.

27 GROUP COMMUNICATION FLIGHT
Formed 1941 at South Cerney.

Nil (–4.46)	*Envoy III P5628; Warferry HM499; Tiger Moth II N6638.*
TSO (4.46–9.47)	*Proctor III R7565, IV NP161 TSO-B; Dominie I X7412 TSO-A; II RL948; Master II DL856 TSO-B; Anson I MG740, XII PH589 TSO; XIX VM358 TSO-A.*

Disbanded 19th September 1947 at Debden.

29 GROUP COMMUNICATION FLIGHT
Formed 7th July 1942 at Dumfries.

Gladiator I K8049; Proctor I P6305, III HM291, IV NP335; Anson I DJ513; X MG228 G; Oxford II ED189.

Disbanded 14th July 1945 at Dumfries.

38 GROUP COMMUNICATION FLIGHT
Formed 26th November 1943 at Netheravon by redesignating the Station Flight, Netheravon.

Nil (11.43– .45)	Proctor I P6183; III; Oxford I P1959; II P1804; Hurricane I R4231; Vega Gull X9436; Spitfire VC EE658; Auster III MZ160, IV MS951, V RT472; Martinet I NR388.
5N (.45–2.51)	Wellington X PG361; Spitfire XI PA886; Tiger Moth T6311; Oxford I PH299 5N-D; Proctor III LZ792 5N-S, IV NP292; Anson XII PH638, TX230.

Disbanded 1st February 1951 at Upavon.

Reformed 1st January 1960 at Upavon.

Anson XIX VL337, T.21 VV963; Devon C.1 VP957; Chipmunk T.10 WP844.

Disbanded 31st March 1976 at Benson.

40/41 GROUP COMMUNICATION FLIGHT
The Station Flight, Andover provided communication aircraft for 40 and 41 Groups from January 1939 until May 1944 when the duty was transferred to the Maintenance Command Communication Squadron. Aircraft specifically assigned to 40/41 Group included:

M7 ( )	Possibly allocated.
S6 (.45– .46)	Aldon AW167 S6-K; Miles M.28/1 HM583 S6-M; Hurricane IIC LF363; Proctor IV NP163 S6-E; Anson XIX VM371 S6-C.

41 GROUP TRAINING FLIGHT
Formed by November 1945 at Aston Down.

Harvard IIB KF712; Mosquito III VP346.

Disbanded 6th March 1946 at Aston Down to become 1689 (Ferry Pilot Training) Flight.

42 GROUP COMMUNICATION FLIGHT
Formed by 1942 at Theale.

Nil (.42– .45)	No aircraft known.
CM (.45–5.45)	Allocated but no evidence of use.

Disbanded 1st May 1955 at Theale.

43 GROUP COMMUNICATION FLIGHT
Formed 1941 at Abingdon.

Nil (.41– .45)	Proctor III HM348, IV NP159; Reliant HM593; Hawk Major NF752.
IB (.45–4.51)	Anson I EG296, XI NL234; XII PH661 IB; Dakota IV TS433 IB-F.
Nil (4.51–1.56)	Anson XIX VL312 A; Vampire FB.5 VZ122; Chipmunk T.10 WZ873.

Disbanded 2nd January 1956 at Hucknall and absorbed by 41 Group Communications Flight.

44 GROUP COMMUNICATION FLIGHT
Formed 16th August 1944 at Staverton.

HZ	Proctor III R7539; Tiger Moth II T7845; Boston II AH510; Dominie I X7393; Anson XIX TX227.

Disbanded 29th July 1946 at Staverton.

45 GROUP COMMUNICATION FLIGHT
Formed 1st April 1943 at Dorval, Canada.

Liberator II AL504; Marauder I FK115; Dakota III KG740; IV KK194.

Disbanded 5th September 1944 at Dorval.

46 GROUP COMMUNICATION FLIGHT
Formed 1st November 1949 at Abingdon by redesignating 47 Group Communication Flight.

Dakota IV KP220; Proctor III LZ681, IV RM189; Anson T.21 VS526.

Disbanded 31st March 1950 at Abingdon.

47 GROUP COMMUNICATION FLIGHT
Formed 15th May 1946 at Little Staughton by redesignating 48 Group Communication Flight.

Proctor III Z7238; IV NP333; Oxford I NM312; Messenger I RG327; Auster V TW439; Anson XI NL197, XII PH719; XIX PH845.

Disbanded 1st November 1949 at Abingdon to become 46 Group Communication Flight.

48 GROUP COMMUNICATION FLIGHT
Formed 1st November 1945 at Tempsford.

Nil ( )	Auster I LB323; Messenger RG327; Anson XI NL200.
3M ( )	Proctor III DX196 3M-M; Auster I LB323.
YV ( )	Allocated but no evidence of use.

Disbanded 15th May 1946 at Little Staughton to become 47 Group Communication Flight.

50 GROUP COMMUNICATION FLIGHT
Formed 1st February 1939 at Hendon.

Anson I EG277; Magister N3890; Tiger Moth II; Whitney Straight NF747.

Disbanded 31st May 1947 at White Waltham.

51 GROUP COMMUNICATION FLIGHT
Formed by January 1940 at Yeadon.

Tiger Moth II; Proctor I P6233, III; Magister P2455; Reliant W5791; Whitney Straight AV970.

Disbanded 14th July 1947 at Yeadon and absorbed by 50 Group Communication Flight.

54 GROUP COMMUNICATION FLIGHT
Formed by May 1943 at White Waltham.

Nil (–4.46)	Tiger Moth II; Proctor I, II, III; Anson I EG277.
FKR (4.46–6.46)	Proctor III LZ636 FKR-C, IV; Anson I.

Disbanded 17th June 1946 at White Waltham.

Reformed 1st April 1951 at Benson.

Proctor IV RM168; Anson XII PH645, XIX VL357, T.21 VS500.

Disbanded 10th July 1953 at Benson.

60 GROUP COMMUNICATION FLIGHT
Formed 23rd March 1940 at Halton.

Tiger Moth I K4254; Fairchild 24C BK869.

Disbanded 25th April 1946 at Wing.

60 GROUP RADAR NAVIGATION AIDS TEST FLIGHT
Formed 11th February 1945 at Wing.

Wellington X LP922.

Disbanded 31st October 1945 at Wing.

61 GROUP COMMUNICATION FLIGHT
Formed 10th September 1946 at Kenley.

RCE (9.46–4.51)	Anson I W1731 RCE-F, XII PH545 RCE-E, XIX VM366 RCE-B; Proctor III HM362 RCE-G, IV NP218; Dominie I NR744 RCE-A; Tiger Moth II T6917; Oxford I BG560, II V3781; Auster V TW451 RCE-D, VI VF611.
Nil (4.51–10.58)	Anson XII PH545 S, XIX TX180 F, T.20 VS514, T.21 WD412; Balliol T.2 WN158; Chipmunk T.10 WD285.

Disbanded 15th January 1959 at Biggin Hill.

62 GROUP COMMUNICATION FLIGHT
Formed 12th September 1946 at Middle Wallop.

RCF	Tiger Moth BB750, II EM723; Harvard IIB KF256; Oxford I HM650; Proctor III DX232

RCF-D, IV NP173; Dominie I NF857; Auster VI TW531; Anson I N4948, XII PH707 FCF-B, XIX VM358, T.20 VS523 14.

Disbanded 30th July 1952 at Colerne to become the Colerne Communication Squadron.

63 GROUP COMMUNICATION FLIGHT
Formed 10th September 1946 at Hawarden.

RCG (9.46–4.51)	*Spitfire XVI RW352; Anson I AX501 RCG-C, XII PH531, XIX TX235, T.21 VS566 RCG-D; Oxford II V3817; Dominie I NF870; Auster V TW453 RCG-G; Proctor III LZ596, IV NP191; Harvard IIB KF498.*
Nil (4.51–12.55)	*Oxford I HM784; Anson XII PH693 F, XIX TX235; T.21 VV323; Auster V TW453; Vampire FB.5 WA142; Prentice T.1 VR294; Chipmunk T.10 WB747.*

Disbanded January 1957 at Hawarden.

64 GROUP COMMUNICATION FLIGHT
Formed 10th September 1946 at Finningley.

RCH (9.46–4.51)	*Anson I MG969 RCH-D, XII PH644 RCH-C; Proctor III LZ597, IV NP234 RCH-B; Auster V TW460 RCH-A; Tiger Moth II R5023; Oxford I LX634.*
Nil (4.51–10.58)	*Proctor IV NP234; Anson XII NL248 G, XIX VL352 V; T.20 VS560 K, T.21 WD404; Meteor T.7 WL429; Chipmunk T.10 WB684; Provost T.1 XF690.*

Disbanded 16th February 1958 at Rufforth.

66 GROUP COMMUNICATION FLIGHT
Formed 10th September 1946 at Turnhouse.

RCI (9.46–4.51)	*Anson I MG237 RCI-B, XII PH809 RCI-B, XIX VM364 RCI-E; Dominie I HG728 RCI-K; Proctor III Z7212 RCI-G; Sea Otter I JM834; Auster V TJ348 RCI-J; Harvard IIB KF487; Oxford I PH311.*
Nil (4.51–10.52)	*Anson XII PH722 C, T.20 VS514 59.*

Disbanded 1st October 1952 at Turnhouse to become the Turnhouse Communication Squadron.

67 GROUP COMMUNICATION FLIGHT
Formed 1st April 1950 at Aldergrove by redesignating the Headquarters Royal Air Force Northern Ireland Communication Flight.

Anson XII PH601 14, T.20 VS523 15.

Disbanded January 1957 at Aldergrove.

70 GROUP COMMUNICATION FLIGHT
Formed 1st December 1940 at Farnborough.

Vega Gull X9340; Voyager X1050; Leopard Moth AX873; Oxford I X6850, II X7287; Auster I LB286, III NJ975; Proctor III LZ707; Hurricane IIC LF676.

Disbanded 17th July 1945 at Farnborough.

71 GROUP COMMUNICATION FLIGHT
Formed 15th February 1941 at Hanworth.

Mentor L4413; Leopard Moth BD167; Magister N5396.

Disbanded 22nd August 1941 at Farnborough.

80 GROUP COMMUNICATION FLIGHT
Formed (date and location unknown).

Puss Moth ES954; Anson XII PH626.

Disbanded (date and location unknown).

81 GROUP COMMUNICATION SQUADRON
Formed 28th December 1940 at Sealand.

Magister T9828; Falcon X9300; Tiger Moth II DE712; Leopard Moth AV989; Oxford I V3989; Cleveland I AS471; Dominie I X7492;

Master I T8575, III DL670; Blenheim IV V5883; Hurricane I L1877; Spitfire VA W3130, IX; Defiant I T3922; Proctor III LZ759, IV.

Disbanded 15th April 1943 at Aston Down.

Reformed 1st January 1952 at Colerne.

Anson XII PH528, XIX VM341, T.22 VV365; Auster VI TW531; Brigand T.5 WA565; Vampire FB.5 WA112; Meteor T.7 WL468, NF.11 WD757; Chipmunk T.10 WG489.

Disbanded 15th April 1958 at Colerne.

82 GROUP COMMUNICATION FLIGHT
Formed September 1941 at Ballyhalbert.

Mentor L4411; Master I N7943; Lysander III T1447; Tiger Moth II T6567.

Disbanded June 1943 at Newtownards and absorbed by the Headquarters RAF Northern Ireland Communication Flight.

82 GROUP TARGET TOWING FLIGHT
Formed August 1941 at Ballyhalbert.

Lysander III T1447.

Disbanded 31st October 1941 at Ballyhalbert to become 1493 (Target Towing) Flight.

83 GROUP COMMUNICATION FLIGHT, later 83 GROUP COMMUNICATION SQUADRON, later 83 GROUP COMMUNICATION FLIGHT
Formed 8th April 1943 at Redhill. Redesignated 83 Group Communication Squadron from 1st March 1944.

Nil	*Master II DK937; Hudson I N7251; Hurricane I V7509; Spitfire I X4488; VB AA918; IX MA450; XIV RM785; XVI TD237; Dominie I R5932; Vigilant IA BZ104; Proctor III HM290, V VN896; Taylorcraft Plus D W5740; Cub Coupe DP852; Auster I LB277; II MZ138; III MZ138; IV MT101, V MT356; Bu 181 VM199; Fi156 VM291; Ju52/3 VN712; Bf108 VM850; Messenger I RG369; Anson I DJ632; X NK667; XI NK992, XII PH536; XIX PH840.*
LN	*No evidence of use.*
M6	*No evidence of use.*

Disbanded 30th April 1946 at Schleswigland, Germany.

Reformed 7th September 1952 at Wahn, Germany, as 83 Group Communication Flight.

Anson XIX VM371; Vampire FB.5 WA123; Meteor T.7 WH204; NF.11 WD793; Prentice T.1 VS264; Chipmunk T.10 WB736.

Disbanded 27th June 1958 at Wahn.

83 GROUP SUPPORT UNIT
Formed 1st March 1944 at Redhill.

Nil (3.44–6.44)	*Mustang I AM102, III FB133; Typhoon IB JR332 S.*
7S (6.44–8.45)	*Oxford II AB650; Typhoon IB RB509 7S-X; Tempest V EJ763 7S-J; Auster IV MT130; Spitfire IX NH175 7S-O, XVI SM468; Tiger Moth II T7471; Anson I N5289, X NK667, XI NK992, XII PH536.*

Disbanded 1st August 1945 at Dunsfold to become 83 Group Disbandment Centre.

84 GROUP COMMUNICATION FLIGHT, later 84 GROUP COMMUNICATION SQUADRON (AIR 29/2354)
Formed 15th July 1943 at Cowley. Redesignated 84 Group Communication Squadron from 1st March 1944.

Nil (7.43– .45)	*Proctor I P6242; Tiger Moth II DE209; Auster I LB286, III MZ126; Ventura I FN964.*
EP (.45–11.47)	*Proctor III DX228 EP; Vigilant IA BZ107; Auster III NX534, IV MS938, V TJ568 EP; Spitfire VB EP552, XI PL836 EP; Typhoon IB EK580; Tempest II PR862; Savoia-Marchetti SM.82 VN158 EP; Tiger Moth II NL929; Mosquito VI TA489; Messenger I RH375 EP; Anson I NK546 EP, X NK727, XI NK996, XII PH765 EP,*

XIX TX185 EP; Bu181 VM252; Bf108 VM856;
Harvard IIB KF651.

| 7H | Allocated but no evidence of use. |
| 2O | Allocated but no evidence of use. |

Disbanded 30th November 1947 at Celle, Germany.

84 GROUP SUPPORT UNIT
Formed 14th February 1944 at Aston Down.

Mustang II FR904, III FX981; Hurricane IV KX696; Typhoon IB MN488; Tempest V NV658; Spitfire VB AB862, IX NH238, XVI; Anson I EG335, X NK531, XI NL132, XII PH545; Vigilant IA BZ100; Messenger I RH373.

Disbanded 1st August 1945 at Lasham to become 84 Group Disbandment Centre.

85 GROUP COMMUNICATION SQUADRON, later 85 WING COMMUNICATION SQUADRON, later 85 WING COMMUNICATION FLIGHT, later 85 GROUP COMMUNICATION FLIGHT
Formed 1st May 1944 at Castle Camps. Redesignated 85 Wing Communication Squadron from 1st July 1946, 85 Wing Communication Flight by 10th May 1947 and 85 Group Communication Flight from November 1948.

| VK | Allocated but no evidence of use. |
| Nil | Proctor III HM339; Oxford I HM832; II EB979; Spitfire I K9936; VB BM124; XI PL963; Mosquito XIII HK365; Hurricane IIC LF530, XIIB JS369; Anson I MG276; XII PH530, XIX TX182; Dominie I NF851; Auster I LB349, III MZ133, IV MS938, V TJ219; Typhoon IB SW518. |

Disbanded 1st March 1950 at Utersen, Germany.

87 GROUP COMMUNICATION FLIGHT, later 87 WING COMMUNICATION FLIGHT
Formed 15th May 1945 at Buc, France. Redesignated 87 Wing Communication Flight from 1st July 1946.

| P8 | Spitfire VB BM491; Argus II FZ782; Proctor III HM295; Anson I MG299; XII PH669; Dominie I NR787. |

Disbanded 26th August 1946 at Buc, France, to become the Royal Air Force Delegation (France) Communication Flight.

88 GROUP COMMUNICATION SQUADRON
Formed 10th May 1945 at Turnhouse by redesignating an element of 116 Squadron.

| 2Q | Anson XII PH645 2Q-J. |

Disbanded 30th September 1945 at Gardermoen, Norway.

88 GROUP SUPPORT UNIT
Formed August 1945 at Dyce.

Anson; Spitfire.

Disbanded 1st December 1945 at Dunsfold.

91 GROUP COMMUNICATION FLIGHT
Formed 11th May 1942 at Abingdon by redesignating 6 Group Communication Flight.

Monarch W6464; Proctor III HM345; Anson XIX TX229.

Disbanded 1st May 1947 at Swinderby and absorbed by 21 Group Communication Flight.

92 GROUP COMMUNICATION FLIGHT
Formed 11th May 1942 at Bicester by redesignating 7 Group Communication Flight.

Tutor K3405; Magister L8250; Tiger Moth II DE841; Proctor III LZ587; Oxford I NM805, II X7237; Anson I DJ358.

Disbanded 15th July 1945 at Little Horwood.

92 GROUP INSTRUCTORS FLIGHT
Formed March 1943 at Upper Heyford.

Wellington X JA113; Oxford II AB644.

Disbanded 15th July 1945 at Silverstone.

93 GROUP COMMUNICATION FLIGHT
Formed 17th July 1942 at Lichfield.

Warferry HM497; Proctor I P6231; III LZ578; D.H.94; Oxford I NM807.

Disbanded 14th February 1945 at Lichfield.

93 GROUP SCREENED PILOTS SCHOOL
Formed May 1943 at Church Broughton.

Wellington III, X HZ469.

Disbanded October 1944 at Leicester East.

100 GROUP COMMUNICATION FLIGHT
Formed 28th December 1943 at West Raynham.

| Nil | Oxford I R6161; Moth Minor W7972; Proctor III Z7193; Tiger Moth I NM112. |
| 3E | Allocated but no evidence of use. |

Disbanded 17th December 1945 at Swanton Morley.

106 GROUP COMMUNICATION FLIGHT
Formed 14th April 1944 at Benson.

Oxford II EB993; Anson XI NL230, XII PH654; Spitfire XI PL972.

Disbanded 15th August 1946 at Benson.

201 GROUP COMMUNICATION FLIGHT
Formed 1st June 1943 at Mariut, Egypt.

Audax K7525; Gladiator I K7936; Lysander I L4720; Hurricane I W9113, X AG156; Wellington IC HF833; Magister N5422; Wellington IC HX637; Blenheim IV Z7701, V BA498; Vega Gull X1032; Argus II FS540; Traveller I FZ433; Beaufighter IC T3301, VI V8822.

Disbanded 31st January 1944 at Mariut to become Air Headquarters Eastern Mediterranean Communication Flight.

202 GROUP COMMUNICATION FLIGHT
Formed (date and location in Egypt unknown).

Hind L7174; Magister I P2449.

Disbanded (date and location unknown).

203 GROUP COMMUNICATION FLIGHT
Formed by August 1940 at Wadi Seidna, Sudan.

Proctor I P6126.

Disbanded 10th May 1943 at Khartoum, Sudan.

Reformed 10th May 1943 at Heliopolis, Egypt.

Proctor III HM484; Hurricane, Magister; Harvard III EX930.

Disbanded 1st March 1945 at Heliopolis and absorbed by the Air Headquarters Eastern Mediterranean Communication Flight.

204 GROUP COMMUNICATION FLIGHT
Formed 14th April 1941 at Heliopolis, Egypt.

Valentia; Vincent; Lysander II P9198; Magister P2397; Proctor I P6117.

Disbanded 9th October 1941 at Ma'aten Bagush, Egypt, to become the Communication Flight, Air Headquarters Western Desert.

205 GROUP COMMUNICATION FLIGHT
Formed January 1942 at LG.20 (Qotafiya), Egypt.

Lysander I L4729; Maryland I AR732; Traveller I FL654; Petrel HK838; Expeditor II KJ493; Proctor III HM484; Wellington X NA738; Anson XII PH733, XIX TX182.

Disbanded May 1949 at Fayid, Egypt.

Officially reformed 7th June 1952 at Fayid, Egypt, but did not become operational until 1st October 1952.

Proctor IV MX454; Prentice T.1 VR269; Meteor T.7 WA613; Pembroke C.1 WV704.

Disbanded 31st January 1956 at Abu Sueir, Egypt, to become the Station Flight, Abu Sueir.

206 GROUP COMMUNICATION FLIGHT
Formed 17th June 1941 at Heliopolis, Egypt.

Tutor HK853; Puss Moth HK861; Rapide HK862.

Disbanded 1st April 1946 at Heliopolis and absorbed by the Mediterranean and Middle East Communication Squadron.

207 GROUP COMMUNICATION FLIGHT
Formed 15th December 1941 at Nairobi, Kenya, by redesignating the Air Headquarters East Africa Communication Flight.

No aircraft known.

Disbanded 16th November 1942 at Eastleigh, Kenya, to become the Air Headquarters East Africa Communication Flight.

210 GROUP COMMUNICATION FLIGHT
Formed by September 1944 at Reghaia, Algeria.

Hurricane IIC KZ454.

Disbanded 26th November 1944 at Reghaia.

211 GROUP COMMUNICATION FLIGHT
Formed 20th April 1942 at El Adem, Libya.

Lysander II P9062; Hurricane I Z4707.

Disbanded 17th September 1943 at El Adem.

212 GROUP COMMUNICATION FLIGHT
Formed 14th March 1944 at Benina, Libya.

Proctor III LZ580; Baltimore V FW350.

Disbanded (date unknown) at Benina.

216 GROUP COMMUNICATION FLIGHT
Formed 27th June 1944 at Heliopolis, Egypt.

Beaufort I DW934; Argus II FZ765; Proctor III HM468; Spitfire XI PA907; Wellington X NA738; Mosquito VI RF939; Hurricane IIC LD180; Expeditor II HB241; Dakota IV KN661; Anson I LT203; XII PH534.

Disbanded 1st April 1946 at Heliopolis and absorbed by the Mediterranean and Middle East Communication Squadron.

218 GROUP COMMUNICATION FLIGHT
Formed 1st January 1944 at Hussein Dey, Algeria.

Baltimore III AG924; Wellington X; Anson XII PH567.

Disbanded 30th June 1946 at Hussein Day, Algeria.

219 GROUP COMMUNICATION FLIGHT
Formed 1st March 1946 at Mariut, Egypt.

Hind K5422; Proctor III HM416; Anson XII PH611.

Disbanded 1st December 1946 at Mariut.

221 GROUP COMMUNICATION SQUADRON
Officially formed 1st January 1945 at Kalemyo, Burma, having operated at Imphal, India, from 1st December 1944.

Harvard IIB FX489; Tipsy Trainer MA930; Zlin 212 Tourist MA926; Expeditor I HB150; II KJ482; Argus II, III; Sentinel I KJ369; II KJ414; Dakota IV KJ951; Warwick III HG247; Lockheed 12A LV760; Tiger Moth II NL721; Auster V RT613.

Disbanded 1st November 1945 at Mingaladon, Burma, to become the Air Headquarters Netherlands East Indies Communication Squadron.

222 GROUP CALIBRATION FLIGHT
Formed 29th September 1942 at Ratmalana, Ceylon, by redesignating 2 Calibration Flight.

Vengeance I, II.

Disbanded July 1943 at Ratmalana to become 1579 (Calibration) Flight.

222 GROUP COMMUNICATION FLIGHT
Formed 25th March 1944 at Ratmalana, Ceylon, by redesignating the Ratmalana Station Flight.

Puss Moth LV765; Reliant I FB771; Harvard IIB FS806; Argus II FZ807; Tiger Moth MA940; Hurricane IIC LB875; Oxford I PH227.

Disbanded 15th October 1945 at Ratmalana to become the Air Headquarters Ceylon Communication Flight.

222 GROUP PHOTOGRAPHIC FLIGHT
Formed (date and location unknown) although evidence suggests the unit operated alongside 222 Group Communication Flight which was based at Ratmalana, Ceylon.

Electra AX700; Hurricane IIC LB875; Reliant I FB606; Puss Moth LV765; Beaufort I JM510 D, IIA ML435; Oxford I NM402.

Disbanded (date and location unknown)

223 GROUP COMMUNICATION FLIGHT
Formed 1st July 1942 at Peshawar, India.

Anson I DG904; Argus II HB558; Expeditor II KJ483; Hawk Major LV768; Proctor III LZ647.

Disbanded 15th August 1945 at Chaklala to become 1 (Indian) Group Communication Flight.

224 GROUP CALIBRATION FLIGHT
Formed 29th September 1942 at Dum-Dum, India, by redesignating 1 Calibration Flight.

Sentinel I KJ384; II KJ411; Tiger Moth II NL812; Auster III NX522; Dakota IV KN585; Warwick III HG253.

Disbanded 15th March 1943 at Armada Road, India, to become the Bengal Calibration Flight.

224 GROUP COMMUNICATION FLIGHT
Formed 1st April 1942 at Willingdon Airport, India, by redesignating the Communication Flight, Air Headquarters New Delhi.

Leopard Moth AX801; Tiger Moth II AX798; Harvard IIB FE415; Expeditor I HB155; Wellington III HZ173; Auster III NJ794; Dakota IV KN585; Walrus I W3038; Warwick III HG256.

Disbanded 31st October 1945 at Kallang, Singapore, to become Air Headquarters Malaya Communication Squadron.

Reformed 31st August 1957 at Kuala Lumpur.

Pembroke C.1 WV701.

Disbanded 1st October 1968 at Seletar, Singapore.

225 GROUP CALIBRATION FLIGHT
Formed 29th September 1942 in India by merging 3 Calibration Flight at Juhu and 4 Calibration Flight at Jakkur. The Juhu element was disbanded by April 1943.

No aircraft known.

Disbanded 13th September 1943 at Jakkur to become 1580 (Calibration) Flight.

225 GROUP COMMUNICATION FLIGHT
Formed 2nd May 1942 at Jakkur, India.

Audax K3706; Anson I DJ603; Harlow PC-5A DR426; Expeditor I HB177; II KJ535; Harvard IIB KF124; Tiger Moth II NL725; Proctor III LZ638; Hurricane IIC LD215.

Disbanded 1st May 1946 at Yelahanka to become 2 (Indian) Group Communication Flight.

226 GROUP COMMUNICATION FLIGHT
Formed 6th September 1943 at Palam, India.

Vengeance I AN884; Anson I DJ266; Harvard IIB FT182; Argus II HB552; Proctor III LZ641; Puss Moth MA946; Oxford I PH227.

Disbanded 31st July 1946 at Chakeri, India.

227 GROUP COMMUNICATION FLIGHT
Formed 1st April 1943 at Juhu, India.

Hurricane IIB LE737; Anson I DJ286; Argus II FZ821; Expeditor I HB170, II KJ490; Harvard IIB FE422; Proctor III LZ678.

Disbanded 1st May 1946 at Juhu to become 4 (Indian) Group Communication Flight.

228 GROUP COMMUNICATION FLIGHT
Formed 27th February 1945 at Alipore, India.

Lockheed 10A AX700; Vengeance II AN621; Expeditor II KJ560; Harvard IIB FE355; Argus II FZ634; Dakota IV KJ819; Spitfire VIII MD371.

Disbanded 1st May 1946 at Barrackpore, India, to become 3 (Indian) Group Communication Flight.

229 GROUP COMMUNICATION FLIGHT
Formed 16th December 1943 at Palam, India.

Expeditor II KJ507; Proctor III LZ656.

Disbanded 1st August 1946 at Palam and absorbed by the Air Headquarters India Communication Squadron.

230 GROUP COMMUNICATION FLIGHT
Formed by April 1944 at Alipore, India.

Argus II FZ732; Proctor III LZ640; Anson I LT291; Tiger Moth II NL712.

Disbanded 16th May 1945 at Barrackpore, India.

231 GROUP COMMUNICATION FLIGHT
Formed 10th January 1944 at Red Road, India.

Electra AX700; Argus II FS635; Sentinel I KJ403; Harvard IIB FS982; Tiger Moth II NL727; Anson I LT642; Proctor III LZ661; Hurricane IIB HV424; IIC HV722: Expeditor II HB275.

Disbanded 30th September 1945 at Alipore and absorbed by the Air Headquarters Burma Communication Squadron.

232 GROUP COMMUNICATION SQUADRON
Formed 27th February 1945 at Comilla, India, by redesignating the Headquarters Combat Cargo Task Force Communication Flight.

Harvard IIB FX462; Argus II FZ731, III HB648; Expeditor II KJ477.

Disbanded 31st March 1946 at Rangoon, Burma.

238 GROUP COMMUNICATION SQUADRON
Formed 20th April 1945 at Bilaspur, India.

Expeditor II KN115; Harvard IIB.

Disbanded 15th October 1945 at Bilaspur.

242 GROUP COMMUNICATION FLIGHT
Formed by 25th July 1943 at Sidi Ahmed, Tunisia.

Spitfire VB ES193, VC JK741; Hurricane IIC LB842; Anson I MG750.

Disbanded 14th September 1944 at San Vito, Italy.

GROUPE 'ALSACE'
Formed 27th August 1941 at Rayak, Syria.

Morane-Saulnier MS 406; Potez 25; Hurricane II.

Disbanded October 1942 at Damascus, Syria, and despatched to the United Kingdom to become 341 (Alsace) Squadron.

GROUPE 'ILE DE FRANCE'
Formed 23rd October 1941 at Turnhouse by redesignating an element of 615 Squadron. The Squadron consisted of 'Pares' and 'Versailles' Flights.

Spitfire IIA.

Disbanded 7th November 1941 at Turnhouse to become 340 (Ile de France) Squadron

GROUPE 'LORRAINE'
Formed 24th September 1941 at Damascus, Syria, by merging the Free French Flight, Khartoum and 1 Groupe Reserve du Bombardement. Composed of Escadrilles 'Metz' and 'Nancy'.

Blenheim IV Z7508, V BA326; Tomahawk IIB AN389.

Ceased operational duties 6th September 1942 at Shandur, Egypt. The aircrew was despatched to the United Kingdom to form 342

(Lorraine) Squadron with the aircraft being absorbed by the Free French 'Chad' unit and the Greek Training Flight.

GUIDED WEAPONS DEVELOPMENT SQUADRON
Formed 1st June 1957 at Valley by redesignating 6 Joint Services Trials Unit.

Swift F.7 XF118; Meteor T.7 WA694; Javelin FAW.7 XH782.

Disbanded 1st January 1959 at Valley to become the Guided Weapons Trials Squadron.

1 GUIDED WEAPONS TRIALS SQUADRON
Formed 1st January 1959 at Valley.

Javelin FAW.7 XH901; Meteor T.7 WA694.

Disbanded 1st June 1962 at Valley to become the Fighter Command Missile Practice Camp.

GULF COMMUNICATION SQUADRON – see Air Forces Gulf Communication Squadron

1 GUNNERY CO-OPERATION FLIGHT
Formed 1st April 1934 at Farnborough.

Queen Bee K5101.

Disbanded 14th February 1937 at Lee-on-Solent and merged with 'A' Flight, School of Naval Co-operation to become 2 Anti-Aircraft Co-operation Unit.

2 GUNNERY CO-OPERATION FLIGHT
Formed April 1936 at Alexandria, Egypt, by redesignating an element of 1 Gunnery Co-operation Flight.

Queen Bee K5107 26.

Disbanded 28th February 1937 at Kalafrana, Malta, to become 3 Anti-Aircraft Co-operation Unit.

GUNNERY RESEARCH UNIT
Formed 3rd June 1940 at Exeter by redesignating an element of 'A' Flight, Armament Testing Squadron, Aeroplane and Armament Experimental Establishment.

HP	*Wallace I K4344 HP-K; Demon K3764; Battle TT L5776 HP-J; Gloster F.9/37 L7999; Hurricane I L1695, IIA Z2320/G, Henley III L3247; Monospar L4672; Defiant I N1549 HP-M, II DR870; Mentor L4392; Spitfire I R6718, VB EN906, VC AR506 HP-A, IX BS408, XIV RM674; Wellington I L4285, II L4250/G, III X3406, X LN151 HP-O; Tiger Moth II N9495; Blenheim I L1290; Hudson I N7220; Boston I BD125; Beaufighter R2060, II T3031; Martlet IV FN224; Tempest V EJ529 HP-D; Puss Moth ES917 HP-L; Oxford II X7282; Mustang III FX899 HP-O; B-24D 123721 (USAAF); Seafire III NN349.*

Disbanded 12th March 1945 at Collyweston.

'H' FLIGHT
Formed 25th August 1939 at Ambala, India, by redesignating an element of 60 Squadron.

Blenheim I.

Disbanded 9th February 1940 at Drigh Road, India, to become 'W' Flight.

Reformed January 1940 at Ambala, by redesignating an element of the Battle Flight.

No aircraft known.

Last known October 1940 at Lahore.

'H' UNIT
Formed January 1920 in Sudan.

No aircraft known.

Disbanded late 1920 in Sudan.

HABBANIYA AIR STRIKING FORCE
Formed 30th April 1940 at Habbaniya, Iraq, by redesignating 4 Flying Training School.

Gordon K3988; Audax K7530; Gladiator I K7899; II N5857; Oxford I L4648.

Disbanded 6th June 1940 at Habbaniya to become 4 Flying Training School.

HALIFAX CONVERSION FLIGHT
Formed 29th August 1941 at Linton-on-Ouse.

Halifax II R9367.

Disbanded 4th November 1941 at Linton-on-Ouse to become 28 Conversion Flight.

HALIFAX DEVELOPMENT FLIGHT – see also 187 Squadron
Formed 15th November 1944 at Holmesly South within 246 Squadron.

Halifax III LW119.

Disbanded 3rd April 1945 at Merryfield.

HALIFAX TRAINING UNIT – see 1331 Conversion Unit, later 1331 Heavy Transport Conversion Unit

HANDLING FLIGHT, later HANDLING SQUADRON
Formed 8th December 1938 at Upavon within the Central Flying School. Separately established 8th November 1940 at Boscombe Down and redesignated the Handling Squadron from 11th June 1941. The unit then moved to become part of or supported by the Empire Central Flying School, Hullavington from 28th February 1942 and the Empire Flying School from 7th May 1946, the Royal Air Force Flying College, Manby as 3 (Handling) Squadron from 31st July 1949 and the Aeroplane and Armament Experimental Establishment at Boscombe from 12th April 1954 and the Aircraft and Armament Evaluation Establishment from 1st April 1992.

(Airspeed) Oxford I HM632. (Auster) AOP.6 TW523, T.7 WE571, AOP.9 WZ662. (Avro) Lancastrian C.2 VM729; Anson XIX TX214, T.20 VM412, T.21 WJ558; Athena T.2 VR566; Shackleton MR.2 WL752. (Blackburn) Shark III K8897; Firebrand TF.5 EK848; Beverley C.1 XB263. (Boulton Paul) Balliol T.2 VR595. (Brewster) Bermuda I FF477. (Bristol) Beaufighter X JM341, TT.X SR919; Buckingham I KV302; Brigand B.1 TH755, MET.3 VS818, T.4 WA561; Buckmaster T.1 RP123; Sycamore HR.14 XJ380. (Curtiss) Kittyhawk IIA FL220; Helldiver I JW119. (de Havilland) Dominie II RL950; Mosquito II DD636, IX LR505, B.35 TK604, TT.35 TK604, NF.38 VT653, TT.39 PF576; Sea Mosquito TR.33 TW291; Hornet F.3 PX387; Sea Hornet F.20 TT189, NF.21 VV434; Vampire F.3 VT806, FB.5 WG845, FB.9 WX203, T.11 XD507; Sea Vampire F.20 VV136; Venom FB.1 WE257, NF.2 WL846, NF.3 WX792; Sea Venom NF.20 WM523; Chipmunk T.10 WD292; Sea Hawk F.1 WF150; Devon C.1 VP962, C.2 VP971. (Douglas) Boston IV BZ413. (English Electric) Canberra B.2 WD930, PR.3 WE139, T.4 WH839, B.6 WH975, B(I).6 WT309, PR.7 WH778, B(I).8 WT328, U.10 WD951, T.11 WJ610, E.15 WH959, T.19 WH975. (Fairey) Firefly FR.1 MB750, FR.4 TW697; (Gloster) Meteor F.3 EE251, F.4 VT103, T.7 VW428, F.8 VZ464, PR.10 VS971, NF.11 WD629, NF.12 WS690; Javelin FAW.5 XA649. (Grumman) Avenger AS.5 XB357. (Handley Page) Hastings C.1 TG516, C.2 WD477; Marathon T.11 XA274. (Hawker) Hurricane IIC KX858, X AG374, IIC KX858; Typhoon IB JR192; Tempest F.2 PR533, V JN744, TT.5 NV965, F.6 NX149; Sea Fury F.10 TF902, FB.11 VR934; Hunter F.1 WR575, F.4 WV318, F.6 XF376, T.7A WV318, FGA.9 XG254. (Lockheed) Hudson VI FK415. (Miles) Monitor II NP412. (North American) Harvard IIB FS778, III EZ430; Mitchell II FL183; Mustang III FZ142, IVA KM414; Sabre F.4 XB936. (Percival) Proctor III LZ751; Prentice T.1 VN684; Pembroke C.1 WV700; Provost T.1 WV419; Jet Provost T.1 XD677. (Saro) Skeeter T.11 XK479, AOP.12 XK482. (Stinson) Reliant I FB538. (Supermarine) Seafire F.17 SX298, F.45 LA437, F.46 LA555, F.47 PS954; Spitfire VC AA874, VII EN192, VIII MT858, IX BS390, XII EN225, XIV MT858, XVI TE311, XVIII SM941, F.21 LA192, F.24 VN315; Swift FR.5 XD975, F.7 XF113. (Vickers) Wellington X NA928; Warwick II HG410; Varsity T.1 WF324. (Westland) Dragonfly HC.4 XB251; Whirlwind HAS.7 XG593.

Current at 1st April 1998 at Boscombe Down, being supported by the Assessment and Evaluation Centre.

HARRIER CONVERSION TEAM, later HARRIER CONVERSION UNIT, later HARRIER CONVERSION TEAM
Formed 1st January 1969 at Wittering. Redesignated the Harrier Conversion Unit from 1st April 1970.

Harrier GR.1 XV747, T.2 XW265; Hunter T.7 XL601 2, FGA.9 XF430 N.

Disbanded 1st October 1970 at Wittering to become 233 Operational Conversion Unit.

Reformed 1st March 1987 at Wittering as the Harrier Conversion Team within 233 Operational Conversion Unit.

Harrier GR.5.

Disbanded February 1990 at Wittering.

HARRIER CONVERSION UNIT – see Harrier Conversion Team, later Harrier Conversion Unit, later Harrier Conversion Team

HARRIER OPERATIONAL CONVERSION UNIT – see 20 Squadron, RFC, later 20 Squadron, RAF, later 20 (Reserve) Squadron

HAVOC FLIGHT – see 44 Squadron Havoc Flight

HEADQUARTERS AIR COMMAND SOUTHEAST ASIA (COMMUNICATION) SQUADRON
Formed 31st January 1944 at Willingdon Airport, New Delhi, India, by redesignating the Air Command Southeast Asia Communication Unit.

Blenheim V BB144; Anson I DJ266; Vega Gull DR808; Harvard IIB FE355; Hudson VI FK504; Argus II FZ729; Dakota I FD800; III KG518; IV KK205; Mosquito VI HR522; Expeditor I HB133; II KJ479; Lockheed 12A LV762; Proctor III LZ663; DC-3 MA925; York I MW102; Beaufighter X RD742.

Disbanded 30th September 1946 at Changi, Singapore, to become the Air Command Far East and Air Headquarters Malaya Communication Squadron.

HEADQUARTERS BRITISH FORCES ADEN COMMUNICATION FLIGHT
Formed 21st March 1943 at Khormaksar, Aden, by redesignating the Communication Flight, Aden.

Vincent K4727; Wellesley K7726; Anson I EF886.

Disbanded 1st January 1944 at Khormaksar to become the Aden Communication Unit.

Reformed by January 1946 at Khormaksar by redesignating the Aden Communication Unit

Albacore I N4388; Anson XIX VL295; Valetta C.1 VW148.

Disbanded 1st December 1951 at Khormaksar to become the Aden Communication Squadron.

HEADQUARTERS COMBAT CARGO TASK FORCE COMMUNICATION FLIGHT
Formed 5th February 1945 at Comilla, India.

Expeditor II KJ477.

Disbanded 27th February 1945 at Comilla to become 232 Group Communication Flight.

HEADQUARTERS COMMUNICATION SQUADRON, ROYAL AIR FORCE – see Communication Squadron GHQ Royal Air Force, France, later Communication Flight, GHQ Royal Air Force, France

HEADQUARTERS COMMUNICATION SQUADRON, ROYAL FLYING CORPS – see Communication Flight GHQ Royal Flying Corps, France, later Communication Squadron, GHQ Royal Flying Corps, France

HEADQUARTERS FAR EAST COMMUNICATION FLIGHT
Formed 1939 at Seletar, Singapore.

Tiger Moth I K2590.

Disbanded 26th August 1939 at Seletar to become the Emergency Flying Training Flight.

Reformed by April 1940 at Seletar by redesignating the Emergency Training Flight.

Walrus I L2319.

Disbanded June 1940 at Seletar.

HEADQUARTERS MIDDLE EAST AIR FORCE COMMUNICATION FLIGHT, later HEADQUARTERS MIDDLE EAST AIR FORCE FLIGHT

Formed 1st December 1949 at Ismailia by redesignating the Anson element of the Headquarters Middle East Communication Squadron. Redesignated Headquarters Middle East Air Force Flight from 15th March 1950.

Anson XIX VM309; Proctor IV MX450; Auster VI TW640; Harvard IIB KF391; Vampire FB.5 VZ316, FB.9 WR128.

Disbanded 1st December 1954 at Nicosia, Cyprus, and merged with the Middle East Air Force Special Communication Flight and the C-in-Cs Flight to become the Headquarters Middle East Air Force Communication Squadron.

HEADQUARTERS MIDDLE EAST AIR FORCE FLIGHT – see Headquarters Middle East Air Force Communication Flight, later Headquarters Middle East Air Force Flight

HEADQUARTERS MIDDLE EAST AIR FORCE COMMUNICATION SQUADRON

Formed 1st December 1954 at Nicosia, Cyprus, by merging the Middle East Air Force Special Communication Flight, the Headquarters Middle East Air Force Flight and the C-in-Cs Flight.

Valetta C.1, C.2 VX572, T.3 WJ476; Devon C.1 VP953; Pembroke C.1 WV730; Prentice T.1 VR264; Meteor T.7 WA613.

Disbanded 1st February 1956 at Nicosia to become the Middle East Command Communication Squadron.

HEADQUARTERS MIDDLE EAST COMMUNICATION SQUADRON

Formed 1st June 1949 at Kabrit, Egypt, by redesignating the Mediterranean and Middle East Communication Squadron.

Anson XIX VP524.

Disbanded 30th November 1949 at Kabrit.

HEADQUARTERS RHODESIAN AIR TRAINING WING COMMUNICATION FLIGHT, later HEADQUARTERS RHODESIAN AIR TRAINING GROUP COMMUNICATION FLIGHT

Formed October 1947 at Kumalo, Southern Rhodesia. Redesignated Headquarters Rhodesian Air Training Group Communication Flight from 7th May 1948.

Anson XIX VP526 L1, T.20 VS524; Harvard IIA EX818; Chipmunk T.10 WG285.

Disbanded 29th April 1954 at Kumalo.

HEADQUARTERS ROYAL AIR FORCE BURMA COMMUNICATION SQUADRON, later AIR HEADQUARTERS BURMA COMMUNICATION SQUADRON, later AIR HEADQUARTERS BURMA COMMUNICATION FLIGHT

Formed 21st April 1945 at Baigachi, India, by redesignating the Bengal/Burma Communication Squadron. Became the Air Headquarters Burma Communication Squadron from 20th September 1945 and the Air Headquarters Burma Communication Flight from 14th November 1945.

Vengeance III FB918, IV FD410; Whitney Straight MA944; Expeditor I HB203, II KN100; Sentinel I KJ369, II KJ454; Harvard III FX242; Argus II FZ750; Spitfire VIII MT906, XIV NH908; Dakota III FD882, IV KK202.

Disbanded 24th March 1947 at Mingaladon.

Reformed 21st July 1947 at Mingaladon as the Air Headquarters Burma Communication Flight.

Anson XIX VL338; Auster V TW372.

Disbanded 1st December 1947 at Mingaladon, Burma.

HEADQUARTERS ROYAL AIR FORCE NORTHERN IRELAND COMMUNICATION FLIGHT

Formed 19th November 1942 at Sydenham from the Station Flight, Sydenham.

Nil (11.42– 45)	Master I N7877; Oxford II EB992; Proctor III Z7238; Anson I MH172.
QU (.45–3.50)	Dominie I R2486; Proctor III DX187 QU-B; Sea Otter I JM827; Oxford II X7060 QU-P; Anson XII PH624 QU-D, XIX TX209 QU-F.

Disbanded 31st March 1950 at Aldergrove to become 67 Group Communication Flight.

HEADQUARTERS SERVICE FERRY POOLS/SQUADRON

Formed 7th November 1940 at Kemble by redesignating 4 Ferry Pilots Pool..

See also Service Ferry Training Squadron.

Disbanded 11th November 1941 at Kemble.

HEAVY BOMBER CONVERSION UNIT, LYDDA

Formed (date unknown) at Lydda, Palestine.

Liberator.

Disbanded 15th October 1943 at Lydda to become 1675 Heavy Conversion Unit.

HEAVY BOMBER CONVERSION UNIT, SALBANI

Formed 1st September 1942 at Salbani, India.

Liberator III BZ839.

Disbanded 23rd July 1943 at Salbani to become 1584 (Heavy Conversion) Flight.

HEAVY GLIDER CONVERSION UNIT

Formed 1st July 1942 at Shrewton by merging elements of 2, 3 and 6 (Pilots) Advanced Flying Units.

Whitley V BD663; Albemarle I P1382, GT.I P1444, ST.II V1642, ST.V 1783; Horsa I DP747 10, II LF887; Oxford I BG667, II W6579; Tiger Moth II N9440; Magister P2406.

Disbanded 20th October 1944 at Brize Norton to become 21, 22 and 23 Heavy Glider Conversion Units.

21 HEAVY GLIDER CONVERSION UNIT

Formed 20th October 1944 at Brize Norton by redesignating an element of the Heavy Glider Conversion Unit.

Nil (10.44–4.46)	Whitley V EB290, VII EB332; Albemarle GT.VI LV615 28; Hotspur I BT596, III BT731; Horsa I RN817 22, II TL146; Hadrian I FR572; Stirling IV LJ837; Halifax III LW651, VII PP378; Master II 258; Oxford I PG974; Tiger Moth I NL971.
FEP (4.46–12.47)	Halifax VII NA422 FEP-K.
FEQ	Allocated but no evidence of use.
FER	Allocated but no evidence of use.
FES	Allocated but no evidence of use.
FET	Allocated but no evidence of use.

Disbanded 3rd December 1947 at North Luffenham.

22 HEAVY GLIDER CONVERSION UNIT

Formed 20th October 1944 at Keevil by redesignating an element of the Heavy Glider Conversion Unit.

Albemarle GT.I P1383, ST.I P1651, ST.II V1627, ST.V V1825 23, GT.VI LV597 16; Hadrian I 42-78811; Horsa I DP282, II RN348; Oxford I LX761.

Disbanded 15th November 1945 at Blakehill Farm.

23 HEAVY GLIDER CONVERSION UNIT

Formed 28th October 1944 at Peplow by merging elements of the disbanding 83 Operational Training Unit and the Heavy Glider Conversion Unit.

Albemarle GT.I P1391, ST.V V1765 BQ, ST.VI V1988; Horsa I HG880, II RN371; Hadrian 43-19829; Proctor III HM282; Oxford I NM804.

Disbanded 17th January 1945 at Peplow.

HEAVY TRANSPORT FLIGHT
Formed 1st March 1929 at Lahore, India.

Hinaidi I J7745; Clive II J9949.

Disbanded 8th July 1932 at Lahore to become the Bomber Transport Flight.

HELICOPTER COMMUNICATION FLIGHT
Formed 1st January 1961 at Gutersloh, Germany.

Sycamore HC.4 XB252.

Disbanded 31st October 1961 at Gutersloh.

HELICOPTER DEVELOPMENT FLIGHT – see Central Flying School

HELICOPTER DEVELOPMENT UNIT – see Royal Air Force Element, Helicopter Development Unit

HELICOPTER FLIGHT, NICOSIA
Formed May 1955 at Nicosia, Cyprus, being known also as the Nicosia Station Flight. Became part of the Levant Communication Flight from January 1956.

Sycamore HC.14 XF268.

Disbanded 15th October 1956 at Nicosia to become 284 Squadron.

HELICOPTER OPERATIONAL CONVERSION FLIGHT
Formed 1st July 1967 at Odiham by redesignating the Short Range Conversion Unit.

Wessex HC.2 XR522 BW; Puma HC.1 XW200.

Disbanded 1st May 1971 at Odiham to become the Air Training Squadron.

HELICOPTER SQUADRON – see Central Flying School

HELICOPTER TRAINING FLIGHT
Formed 5th February 1945 at Andover within 43 Operational Training Unit. Became a separate entity from 9th April 1945.

Hoverfly I KK994 K.

Disbanded 16th January 1946 at Andover.

HELICOPTER WING – see Central Flying School

HERCULES OPERATIONAL CONVERSION UNIT – see 57 Squadron, RFC, later 57 Squadron, RAF, later 57 (Reserve) Squadron

HESTON FLIGHT
Formed 23rd September 1939 at Heston by redesignating the Secret Intelligence Service Flight.

Spitfire IA N3071; Blenheim IV.

Disbanded 3rd November 1939 at Heston to become 2 Camouflage Unit.

HIGH ALTITUDE FLIGHT, NORTHOLT
Formed August 1942 at Northolt.

Spitfire VII BS142; Mosquito XV MP469.

Disbanded 5th September 1942 at Northolt to become the Special Service Flight, Northolt.

HIGH ALTITUDE FLIGHT, 244 WING
Formed 5th September 1943 at Bari, Italy.

Spitfire IX MA527.

Records cease 27th November 1943 at Bari.

HIGH COMMISSIONER'S FLIGHT
Formed 1st November 1949 at Wahn, Germany, by redesignating the Military Governor's Flight of the British Air Forces of Occupation Communication Squadron.

Anson XII, XIX; Dakota IV; Devon C.1 VP962; Valetta C.2 (VIP) VX573.

Disbanded June 1955 at Wahn, Germany.

HIGH SPEED FLIGHT
Formed 1st October 1926 at Felixstowe. The Flight lay dormant for extended periods between the Schneider Trophy Races.

Bamel J7234; Gloster III/IIIA N194, IIIB N195, IV/IVA N222, IVB N223; VI N249; Crusader N226; Flycatcher S1288; Firefly III S1592; Vendace I N208; Avocet N209; Fleetwing N235; Atlas Floatplane J9998; Supermarine S.5 N220, Supermarine S.6/S.6A N247.

Disbanded October 1931 at Felixstowe.

Reformed 14th June 1946 at Tangmere.

Meteor IV EE454; Oxford I PH424.

Disbanded 26th September 1946 at Tangmere.

HISTORIC AIRCRAFT FLIGHT – see Battle of Britain Flight, later Battle of Britain Memorial Flight

HOME AIRCRAFT DEPOT PRACTICE FLIGHT – see Practice Flight, Home Aircraft Depot, Henlow

HOME COMMAND COMMUNICATION SQUADRON
Formed 1st August 1950 at White Waltham by redesignating the Reserve Command Communication Flight.

Tiger Moth II R4765; Harvard IIB KF392; Oxford I NM244; Proctor IV RM190; Spitfire XVI SL548, F.21 LA232; Anson XII PH531 13, XIX TX193 21, T.22 VV363 19; Auster T.7 WE598; Buckmaster T.1 RP231; Devon C.1 VP953; Prentice T.1 VR285; Chipmunk T.10 WD384; Balliol T.2 WG144 34; Provost T.1 XF679.

Disbanded 1st April 1959 at White Waltham to become the Flying Training Command Communication Squadron.

HOME COMMAND EXAMINING UNIT
Formed 1st December 1951 at White Waltham by redesignating elements of the Home Command Communication Squadron.

Tiger Moth II R4765; Oxford I V4204; Harvard IIB FT208 J-R; Mosquito III TV959; Anson XII PH535; XIX VL349; Auster T.7 WE551; Balliol T.2 WG223; Chipmunk T.10 WB571; Provost T.1 XF610; Vampire T.11.

Disbanded 15th January 1959 at White Waltham.

HOME COMMAND GLIDING CENTRE, later 1 HOME COMMAND GLIDING CENTRE
Formed 1st September 1955 at Detling by redesignating the Home Command Gliding Instructors School. Redesignated 1 Home Command Gliding Centre from 27th June 1958 and 1 Gliding Centre from 23rd March 1959.

Cadet TX.3.

Disbanded 23rd March 1959 at Hawkinge to become 1 Gliding Centre.

1 HOME COMMAND GLIDING CENTRE – see Home Command Gliding Centre, later 1 Home Command Gliding Centre

2 HOME COMMAND GLIDING CENTRE
Formed 1st July 1958 at Newton.

Cadet TX.3.

Disbanded 23rd March 1959 at Newton to become 2 Gliding Centre.

HOME COMMAND GLIDING INSTRUCTORS SCHOOL
Formed 1st August 1950 at Detling by redesignating the Reserve Command Gliding Instructors School.

Rhonbussard VD216; Grunau Baby VT920; Cadet TX.3 XA312; Sedbergh TX.1 XN146; Prefect TX.1 WE980, Gull VW912.

Disbanded 1st September 1955 at Detling to become the Home Command Gliding Centre.

HOME COMMAND INSTRUMENT TRAINING FLIGHT
Formed 1st August 1950 at Honiley by redesignating the Reserve Command Instrument Training Flight.

Harvard IIB; Chipmunk T.10 WG304.

Disbanded 22nd June 1952 at Honiley.

HOME COMMUNICATION FLIGHT
Formed 1st February 1927 at Northolt by redesignating the Inland Area Communication Flight.

F.2B E2630; Fairey IIID N9747; Flycatcher N9930; Humming Bird J7273; Woodcock II J7733; Gamecock J8036; Avro 504K H3105; Avro 504N J8763; Siskin IIIA J9902, IIIDC J9227; Moth K1221; Audax K2008; Puss Moth K1824.

Disbanded 10th July 1933 at Hendon and absorbed by 24 Squadron.

HOME DEFENCE FLIGHT, CRAMLINGTON – see 36 Squadron, RFC, later 36 Squadron, RAF

HOME DEFENCE SQUADRON
Formed 1st May 1916 at Woodford by merging 18 Wing detachments at Chingford, Croydon, Farningham, Hainault Farm, Hendon, Hounslow, Joyce Green, Northolt, Suttons Farm and Wimbledon. These detachments were originally controlled by 19 Reserve Squadron from 1st February 1916 and 18 Wing from 25th March 1916.

B.E.2c.

Disbanded 25th June 1916 at Woodford and merged with similar detachments operated by 6, 9, 12, 13, 15 Reserve Squadrons to become 16 (Home Defence) Wing.

2 (HOME) FERRY UNIT
Formed 7th February 1952 at Aston Down by redesignating 2 Ferry Pool, Royal Air Force.

Oxford I V4281; Anson XIX VM387; Canberra B.2 WH696.

Disbanded 1st February 1953 at Aston Down to become 187 Squadron.

4 (HOME) FERRY UNIT
Formed 7th February 1952 at Hawarden by redesignating 4 Ferry Pool, Royal Air Force.

Oxford I NM663; Anson XIX VM370.

Disbanded 1st February 1953 at Hawarden to become 173 Squadron.

HONG KONG AUXILIARY FLIGHT, later HONG KONG AUXILIARY SQUADRON, later HONG KONG FIGHTER SQUADRON
Formed October 1949 at Kai Tak, Hong Kong. Redesignated Hong Kong Auxiliary Squadron from 1st October 1950 and the Hong Kong Fighter Squadron from 24th November 1953.

Spitfire F.24 VN485; Harvard IIB FS952; Auster VI VF643, T.7 WE537.

Disbanded 24th November 1953 at Kai Tak.

HONG KONG AUXILIARY AIR FORCE
Formed 1st May 1949 at Hong Kong. Redesignated the Royal Hong Kong Auxiliary Air Force from 1951. Disbanded 1st April 1993 to become the Hong Kong Government Flying Services.

See below:

HONG KONG AUXILIARY FLIGHT, later HONG KONG AUXILIARY SQUADRON, later HONG KONG FIGHTER SQUADRON
Formed October 1949 at Kai Tak, Hong Kong. Redesignated Hong Kong Auxiliary Squadron from 1st October 1950 and the Hong Kong Fighter Squadron from 24th November 1953.

Spitfire F.24 VN485; Harvard IIB FS952; Auster VI VF643, T.7 WE537.

Disbanded 24th November 1953 at Kai Tak to become the Hong Kong (Auxiliary Air Force) Wing.

HONG KONG VOLUNTEER DEFENCE FORCE (AIR COMPONENT)
Formed 1939 at Hong Kong.

Moth VR-HCU; Hornet Moth VR-HCX; Cadet; Tutor.

Overrun by the Japanese 25th December 1941.

HORNET CONVERSION FLIGHT
Formed April 1949 at Linton-on-Ouse being operated within the Station Flight, Linton-on-Ouse from May 1949.

MS   Hornet F.3 PX362 MS-H; Mosquito III TW117 MS-A.

Disbanded July 1950 at Linton-on-Ouse.

HUDSON FLIGHT, WEST AFRICA
Formed December 1942 at Pointe Noire, French Congo, being a detachment of 200 Squadron.

Hudson IIIA FH272, IV AE636, VI FK639; Anson I.

Disbanded February 1944 at Accra, Gold Coast.

HULL UNIVERSITY AIR SQUADRON
Formed 5th February 1941 at Hull.

No aircraft known.

Disbanded 1943 at Hull.

Reformed 1st December 1950 at Hull using Brough for flying.

Tiger Moth II T5854; Harvard IIB KF448; Chipmunk T.10 WB754 21.

Disbanded 15th March 1969 at Brough and merged with the Leeds University Air Squadron to become the Yorkshire Universities Air Squadron.

HUNTER FLIGHT – see Central Flying School

'I' FLIGHT
Formed 9th July 1918 at Fauquembergues, France, by redesignating the Special Duty Flight, RFC.

B.E.12 6511; F.E.2b B1874.

Disbanded 14th January 1919 at Serny, France.

INDIA COMMUNICATION FLIGHT – see Air Headquarters India Communication Flight

INDIA COMMUNICATION SQUADRON – see Air Headquarters India Communication Squadron

INDIA COMMUNICATION UNIT – see Air Headquarters India Communication Unit

INDIA DETACHMENT, CHINESE AIR FORCE CADET SCHOOL – see Royal Air Force Liaison Office, Chinese Elementary Flying Training School, later India Detachment, Chinese Air Force Cadet School

1 (INDIAN) ADVANCED FLYING UNIT
Formed 13th December 1943 at Ambala, India, within 1 Service Flying Training School (India).

Harvard IIB FE361 1.

Disbanded 1st April 1946 at Ambala and merged with 151 (Fighter) Operational Training Unit and 1 (Indian) Service Flying Training School to become the Advanced Flying School (India).

1 (INDIAN) FLYING TRAINING SCHOOL, later 1 (INDIAN) SERVICE FLYING TRAINING SCHOOL
Formed 1st November 1940 at Ambala, India. Redesignated 1 Service Flying Training School (India) from 21st July 1941. Earlier, between 1st October 1939 and 21st October 1940, 27 Squadron had acted as a Flying Training School at Risalpur. The unit code letters carried by Wapiti J9393 and Hart K2101 indicate earlier ownership by 27 Squadron.

Wapiti IIA J9383 PT-B; Hart K2101 PT-O; Audax K3077; Tiger Moth AX798, II T6253; D.H.86 AX800; Leopard Moth DD818; D.H.86 AX800; Harvard IIB FE361; Hurricane IIB BH230, IIC HV301, IID KW873, IV KZ320; Spitfire VIII MD345, XIV NH786; Anson I LT674.

Disbanded 1st April 1946 at Ambala, India, and merged with 151 Operational Training Unit and 1 (Indian) Advanced Flying Unit to become the Advanced Flying School (India).

1 (INDIAN) GROUP COMMUNICATION FLIGHT
Formed 15th August 1945 at Peshawar, India, by redesignating 223 Group Communication Flight.

Expeditor II HB204; Harvard IIB FE879; Oxford; Vengeance; Tiger Moth MA936.

Disbanded 15th August 1947 at Peshawar to become the Air Headquarters Pakistan Communication Flight.

2 (INDIAN) GROUP COMMUNICATION FLIGHT
Formed 1st May 1946 at Yelahanka, India, by redesignating 225 Group Communication Flight.

Anson I LT603, XIX VL333 R; Dakota IV KN300; Harvard IIB FT123 F; Tiger Moth II NL725; Expeditor II HB177; Anson XIX VL291 T.

Disbanded 15th August 1947 at Yelahanka to become 2 Group Communication Flight, Indian Air Force.

3 (INDIAN) GROUP COMMUNICATION FLIGHT
Formed 1st May 1946 at Barrackpore, India, by redesignating 228 Group Communication Flight.

Lockheed 10A AX700; Harvard IIB FE371; Expeditor II KN102; Spitfire VIII MD371, XIV RN193; Dakota IV KJ819; Anson XIX VL341.

Disbanded 31st May 1947 at Barrackpore.

4 (INDIAN) GROUP COMMUNICATION FLIGHT
Plans to form the unit from 1st May 1946 by redesignating 227 Group Communication Flight were probably cancelled.

1 (INDIAN) SERVICE FLYING TRAINING SCHOOL – see 1 (Indian) Flying Training School, later 1 (Indian) Service Flying Training School

1 INITIAL TRAINING SCHOOL
Formed 21st May at North Coates by redesignating 50 Initial Training School.

No aircraft allocated.

Disbanded 15th October 1947 at North Coates.

Reformed 23rd January 1948 at Wittering. Reorganised 16th November 1949 with 1 Wing at Wittering and 2 Wing at Digby until both Wings transferred to Jurby from 17th April 1950.

Harvard IIB; Tiger Moth II T6256.

Disbanded 10th September 1953 at Jurby.

Reformed 1st October 1953 at Kirton-in-Lindsey by redesignating 2 Initial Training School.

Anson XIX VM329; T.20 VM418 A; Oxford I HN425; Prentice T.1 VS696; Sedbergh TX.1 WB971; Cadet TX.1 RA825; TX.2 VM637; Chipmunk T.10 WP844.

Disbanded 12th December 1966 at South Cerney to become Aircrew Officers Training School.

INLAND AREA COMMUNICATION FLIGHT
Formed 1st April 1920 at Northolt by redesignating the Southeastern Area Communication Flight.

Avro 504K E3617; Snipe E6154; Humming Bird J7273; F.2B J6597; Fawn II J7190; Vimy IV J7441; Moth K1847.

Disbanded 1st February 1927 at Northolt to become the Home Communication Flight.

INSTANT READINESS RESERVE UNIT
Formed mid-1979 at Binbrook.

Lightning F.3. F.6.

Disbanded late 1981 at Binbrook to become the Lightning Augmentation Flight.

INSTITUTE OF AVIATION MEDICINE – see School of Aviation Medicine, later Royal Air Force Institute of Aviation Medicine

INSTRUCTORS SCHOOL – see School of Special Flying, Redcar (Instructors School), later 2 School of Special Flying

INSTRUMENT DESIGN ESTABLISHMENT, later INSTRUMENT DESIGN ESTABLISHMENT (HOME)
Formed 1st November 1919 at Biggin Hill by merging the Wireless Experimental Establishment and three other experimental units. Redesignated the Instrument Design Establishment (Home) from March 1920.

F.E.2b D9108; Snipe E8393; F.2B F4875; Handley Page O/100 B9450; Handley Page 0/400 F5416; D.H.9A H3588.

Disbanded April 1922 at Biggin Hill and absorbed by the Royal Aircraft Establishment.

INSTRUMENT FLYING TRAINING FLIGHT, AIR COMMAND FAR EAST – see Air Command Far East Instrument Flying Training Flight

INSTRUMENT TRAINING FLIGHT, BRITISH AIR FORCES OF OCCUPATION – see British Air Forces of Occupation Instrument Training Flight

INSTRUMENT TRAINING FLIGHT, FIGHTER COMMAND – see Central Fighter Establishment

INSTRUMENT TRAINING FLIGHT, MIDDLE EAST AIR FORCE – see Middle East Air Force Instrument Training Flight

INSTRUMENT TRAINING FLIGHT, RESERVE COMMAND – see Reserve Command Instrument Training Flight

INSTRUMENT TRAINING FLIGHT, 2ND TACTICAL AIR FORCE – see 2nd Tactical Air Force Instrument Training Flight

INSTRUMENT TRAINING FLIGHT, TANGMERE – see Fighter Command Instrument Training Flight

INTELLIGENCE PHOTOGRAPHIC FLIGHT
Formed June 1940 at Heliopolis, Egypt.

Hudson I G-AGAR; Hurricane.

Disbanded 3rd March 1941 at Heliopolis to become 2 Photographic Reconnaissance Unit.

INTERNAL SECURITY FLIGHT, NICOSIA
Formed December 1955 at Nicosia, Cyprus, within the Station Flight, Nicosia. Became part of the Levant Communication Flight from 15th January 1956

Anson XIX VL346; Sycamore HR.14 XG542.

Disbanded 15th October 1956 at Nicosia and duties assigned to 284 Squadron.

IRAQ COMMUNICATION FLIGHT (1)
Formed 5th August 1954 at Habbaniya, Iraq, by redesignating the Air Headquarters Iraq Communication Flight.

Vampire FB.9 WR196; Devon C.1 VP956; Valetta C.1 VW822; Pembroke C.1 WV699.

Disbanded 23rd June 1955 at Habbaniya to become the Air Headquarters Levant Communication Flight.

IRAQ COMMUNICATION FLIGHT (2) – see Communication Flight Iraq

IRAQ COMMUNICATION FLIGHT (3) – see Air Headquarters Iraq Communication Flight

IRAQ AND PERSIA COMMUNICATION FLIGHT – see Communication Flight Iraq and Persia

IRISH FLIGHT
Formed by August 1922 at Collinstown.

D.H.9A F1611; F.2B F4934.

Disbanded 31st October 1922 at Collinstown.

'J' FLIGHT
Formed 28th September 1945 at Melton Mowbray.

Stirling V PJ975.

Disbanded 10th October 1945 at Cairo West, Egypt, to become 1589 (Heavy Freight) Flight.

JAGUAR CONVERSION TEAM, later JAGUAR OPERATIONAL CONVERSION UNIT (1)
Formed 1st July 1973 at Lossiemouth. Redesignated the Jaguar Operational Conversion Unit from June 1974.

Jaguar GR.1 XX111 01; T.2 XX143 F.

Disbanded 30th September 1974 at Lossiemouth to become 226 Operational Conversion Unit.

JAGUAR OPERATIONAL CONVERSION UNIT (1) – see Jaguar Conversion Team, later Jaguar Operational Conversion Unit (1)

JAGUAR OPERATIONAL CONVERSION UNIT (2) – see 16 Squadron, RFC, later 16 Squadron, RAF, later 16 (Reserve) Squadron

JAVELIN INSTRUMENT RATING SQUADRON
Formed February 1957 at Middleton St George by redesignating an element of Fighter Command Instrument Rating Squadron.

Javelin T.3 XH445 C.

Disbanded 31st December 1966 at Middleton St George.

JAVELIN OPERATIONAL CONVERSION SQUADRON – see Central Fighter Establishment

JET TRAINING FLIGHT
Formed (date unknown) at Wroughton alongside 15 Maintenance Unit.

Meteor T.7 WF879; Anson XIX TX184.

Disbanded 1st May 1963 at Lyneham and absorbed by the Handling Squadron.

JOINT AIR TRANSPORT DEVELOPMENT ESTABLISHMENT – see Air Transport Development Unit

JOINT ANTI-SUBMARINE SCHOOL FLIGHT
Formed 19th November 1945 at Ballykelly.

Nil (11.45–4.51)	Proctor III LZ572; Warwick V PN705; Lancaster GR.3 RF290.
G (4.51–.54)	Shackleton MR.1A WB850 G-X; MR.2 WR967 G-B; Anson XIX VM311 Z.
Nil (.54–6.70)	Shackleton MR.2 WR967.

Disbanded June 1970 at Ballykelly.

JOINT CONCEALMENT CENTRE (ROYAL AIR FORCE COMPONENT)
Formed 15th January 1952 at Netheravon.

Anson XII PH615; Auster T.7 WE592.

Disbanded 31st October 1958 at Netheravon.

JOINT EXPERIMENTAL HELICOPTER UNIT
Formed 1st April 1955 at Middle Wallop.

Sycamore HR.12 WV781, HR.14 XG500; Whirlwind HAR.2 XK969.

Disbanded 1st January 1960 at Andover to become 225 Squadron.

JOINT ELEMENTARY FLYING TRAINING SCHOOL
Formed 1st April 1993 at Topcliffe by merging the Elementary Flying Training Squadron and the Royal Navy Elementary Flying Training School to become the Joint Elementary Flying Training School.

Firefly G-ABONT.

Current 1st April 1998 at Barkston Heath.

JET PROVOST TRIALS UNIT
Formed September 1965 at Tengah, Singapore.

Jet Provost T.4 XS223.

Disbanded March 1966 at Tengah.

JOINT SERVICES STAFF COLLEGE FLIGHT
Formed 15th January 1947 at Booker.

TBR (1.47–4.51)	Magister L6907 TBR-K; Auster I LB334 TBR-M;

	Proctor II Z7214, III HM293 TBR-E; Oxford I V3742 TBR-A; Dominie I HG719 TBR-D; Spitfire VIII JF275 TBR-L; Auster V TJ200.
Nil (4.51–11.52)	Oxford I RR382; Proctor IIIHM293.

Disbanded November 1952 at Booker.

JOINT TRIALS AND TRAINING SQUADRON
Formed 1st April 1966 at Watton by redesignating 'B' Flight of 97 Squadron. An element from 831 Naval Air Squadron was assigned to the unit from 16th May 1966.

Canberra B.2 WJ616, T.4 WH839.

Disbanded 23rd September 1966 at Watton to become 360 Squadron.

JOINT WARFARE ESTABLISHMENT – see School of Land/Air Warfare

JUNGLE TARGET RESEARCH UNIT
Formed 5th December 1944 at Sorbhog, India.

Vengeance III FB957, IV FD368; Harvard IIB FT112; Hurricane IIC KZ393; Auster III NJ842.

Disbanded 15th July 1945 at Sorbhog and absorbed by the Tactical and Weapon Development Unit.

'K' FLIGHT
Formed 9th July 1918 at Auxi-le-Château, France, as a detached Flight of 6 Squadron.

R.E.8.

Disbanded (date and location unknown)

Reformed 1st September 1940 at Summit, Sudan, by redesignating 'B' Flight of 112 Squadron.

Gladiator I K6134, II N5815.

Disbanded 1st April 1941 at Aqir, Palestine, to become 250 Squadron.

Reformed 16th September 1945 at Melton Mowbray.

Stirling V PJ888.

Disbanded 10th October 1945 at Santa Cruz, India, to become 1588 (Heavy Freight) Flight.

'K' FLIGHT, 1 PHOTOGRAPHIC RECONNAISSANCE UNIT – see 8 Operational Training Unit

'K' SQUADRON
Formed (date unknown) at Colombo, Ceylon.

Hurricane I Z4783.

Disbanded 23rd March 1942 at Colombo and absorbed by 258 Squadron.

KALAFRANA RESCUE FLIGHT – see Seaplane Rescue Flight, Kalafrana

KANGAROO FLIGHT
Formed 9th May 1918 at Seaton Carew.

Kangaroo B9973.

Disbanded 30th May 1918 at Seaton Carew to become 495 (Light Bomber) Flight.

KENYA AUXILIARY AIR UNIT
The Air Unit of the Kenya Defence Force formed on 30th June 1933 and later became known as the Air Wing of the Kenya Regiment. It was absorbed by the Royal Air Force Unit, Kenya and became the Kenya Auxiliary Air Unit from 6th September 1939.

See: Elementary Flying Training School (Kenya)
1 (Communication) Flight, Kenya Auxiliary Air Unit
2 (Training) Flight, Kenya Auxiliary Air Unit
3 (Reconnaissance) Flight, Kenya Auxiliary Air Unit

KENYA POOL
Formed 4th September 1941 at Gilgil, Southern Rhodesia.

Waco K2; Swallow K21; Gipsy Moth K23; Tutor K3420; Hart (SAAF) 103; Audax K7531.

Disbanded 1st December 1941 at Gilgil to become the Pilot and Aircrew Pool.

KESTREL (P.1127) EVALUATION SQUADRON
Formed 15th October 1964 at West Raynham within the Central Fighter Establishment.

Kestrel FGA.1 XS694 4.

Disbanded 28th February 1965 at West Raynham.

KING'S FLIGHT
Formed 21st July 1936 at Hendon.

Dragon Rapide G-ADDD; Envoy 3 G-AEXX; Tutor K6120; Hudson I N7364; Flamingo G-AGCC; Petrel P5634.

Disbanded 15th February 1942 at Newmarket and merged with an element of 138 Squadron to become 161 Squadron.

Reformed 1st May 1946 at Benson.

Dakota IV KN386; Dominie II RL951; Viking C.1A VL227, C.2 VL248, VIP.2 VL247; Hoverfly I KL104.

Disbanded 16th November 1953 to become the Queen's Flight.

KUALA LUMPUR COMMUNICATION FLIGHT
Formed 1953 at Kuala Lumpur, Malaya.

Auster V TJ629; Anson XIX VM355.

Disbanded 15th February 1954 at Kuala Lumpur and absorbed by 267 Squadron.

KUALA LUMPUR FIGHTER SQUADRON, later KUALA LUMPUR SQUADRON
Formed 1st June 1950 at Kuala Lumpur by redesignating the Auxiliary Fighter Squadron. Redesignated Kuala Lumpur Squadron from 1st July 1952.

Tiger Moth II T7368; Harvard IIB KF380; Chipmunk T.10 WP866.

Disbanded (date unknown) at Kuala Lumpur.

'L' FLIGHT
Formed 9th July 1918 at Bruay, France, by redesignating the Artillery Flight.

F.2B C1034.

Disbanded 6th February 1919 at Aulnoy, France.

LANCASTER CONVERSION FLIGHT – see 1678 (Heavy Conversion) Flight

LANCASTER FINISHING FLIGHT – see 1664 (Heavy) Conversion Unit, later 1664 (Royal Canadian Air Force) Heavy Conversion Unit

1 LANCASTER FINISHING SCHOOL
Formed 21st November 1943 at Lindholme by merging the Lancaster flights of 1656, 1662 and 1667 Heavy Conversion Units.

3C	Lancaster I W4965 3C-Z, III W4994.

Disbanded 25th November 1944 at Hemswell.

3 LANCASTER FINISHING SCHOOL
Formed 21st November 1943 at Feltwell.

A5	Lancaster I L7532 A5-P, III ND958.

Disbanded 31st January 1945 at Feltwell.

5 LANCASTER FINISHING SCHOOL
Formed 21st November 1943 at Syerston by redesignating 1668 Heavy Conversion Unit.

CE	Manchester I L7307 CE; Lancaster I W4103 CE-E, III EE134 CE-Y.
RC	Lancaster III ED593 RC-C.
Also used	Tiger Moth II T6309.

Disbanded 1st April 1945 at Syerston.

6 LANCASTER FINISHING SCHOOL
Formed 1st January 1945 at Ossington.

Lancaster I R5855, II DS619; Dakota III; Oxford I V4192.

Disbanded 1st November 1945 at Ossington to become 1384 (Heavy Transport) Conversion Unit.

11 (LANDPLANE) PREPARATION AND MODIFICATION UNIT
Formed 1st September 1945 at Thornaby.

No aircraft known.

Disbanded 25th May 1946 at Thornaby.

LEEDS UNIVERSITY AIR SQUADRON
Formed 14th January 1941 at Leeds, using Sherburn in Elmet and Yeadon initially for flying training.

Nil (4.41–4.46)	Tiger Moth II, then aircraft provided by 24 and 28 Elementary Flying Training Schools.
FLI (4.46– .49)	Tiger Moth II T5616 FLI-A.
RUY (.49–4.51)	Tiger Moth II NM118 RUY-A; Chipmunk T.10 WB661 RUY-C.
Nil (4.51–3.69)	Tiger Moth II; Harvard IIB KF733; Chipmunk T.10 WB703.

Disbanded 15th March 1969 at Church Fenton and merged with the Hull University Air Squadron to become the Yorkshire Universities Air Squadron.

LIBERATOR CONVERSION FLIGHT – see Aden Conversion Flight

LIGHT AIRCRAFT SCHOOL
Formed 3rd April 1953 at Middle Wallop by redesignating the Air Observation Post School.

BD (4.52– .53)	Chipmunk T.10 WP972 BD-A.
Nil (.53–9.57)	Tiger Moth I NL989, II R4954; Oxford I NJ369; Auster T.7 WE546, AOP.9 WZ666; Anson T.21 VV304; Chipmunk T.10 WD296.

Disbanded 1st September 1957 at Middle Wallop and control passed to the Army Air Corps.

LIGHT COMMUNICATION TRIAL FLIGHT
Formed 15th April 1948 at Ismailia, Egypt, as a section of the Station Flight. The Flight replaced the Army Experimental Communication Flight which was to have formed from 15th November 1947 at Aqir, Palestine.

Auster VI TW639.

Disbanded 1st July 1949 at Ismailia.

LIGHTNING AUGMENTATION FLIGHT
Formed late 1981 at Binbrook by redesignating the Instant Readiness Reserve Unit.

Lightning F.3 XP702; F.6 XR760 Z.

Disbanded 1st August 1987 at Binbrook.

LIGHTNING CONVERSION SQUADRON – see Central Fighter Establishment

LIGHTNING TRAINING FLIGHT
Formed 1st October 1975 at Binbrook by redesignating 'C' Flight of 11 Squadron.

D	Lightning F.3 XR726 DF; T.5 XS419 DW; F.6 XS938 DF.

Disbanded 30th April 1987 at Binbrook.

LINCOLN CONVERSION FLIGHT
Formed 1953 at Waddington by redesignating an element of the Station Flight, Waddington.

Lincoln B.2 RF444.

Disbanded 1st August 1953 at Waddington to become 230 Operational Conversion Unit.

Reformed 1st February 1955 at Upwood by redesignating 230 Operational Conversion Unit.

Lincoln B.2 SX926.

Disbanded 18th February 1957 at Hemswell.

LIVERPOOL UNIVERSITY AIR SQUADRON, later UNIVERSITY OF LIVERPOOL AIR SQUADRON, later LIVERPOOL UNIVERSITY AIR SQUADRON
Formed 12th January 1941 at Liverpool, using Speke initially for flying training.

Nil	*Tiger Moth II provided by 24 Elementary Flying Training School.*
FLG	*Allocated, but no evidence of use.*

Disbanded 30th June 1946 at Liverpool.

Reformed 1st December 1950 at Liverpool, using Hooton Park for flying. Redesignated the University of Liverpool Air Squadron from 1st January 1952.

Chipmunk T.10 WK631 C; Harvard IIB KF755; Prentice T.1 VR247; Bulldog T.1 XX688 S.

Current 1st April 1998 using Woodvale for flying.

LONDON UNIVERSITY AIR SQUADRON – see University of London Air Squadron, later London University Air Squadron, later University of London Air Squadron

LONG-RANGE DESERT GROUP
The following aircraft, flown by British Army personnel, were held on charge by the Group:

Waco ZGC-7 AX695; Waco YKC AX697.

LONG-RANGE DEVELOPMENT FLIGHT – see Long-Range Development Unit

LONG-RANGE DEVELOPMENT UNIT
Formed 1st January 1938 at Upper Heyford.

Wellesley L2639; Tutor K3394.

Disbanded 31st December 1938 at Upper Heyford.

1 (LONG-RANGE) FERRY UNIT
Formed 17th November 1952 at Abingdon by redesignating an element of Overseas Ferry Unit.

No aircraft known.

Disbanded 1st February 1953 at Benson to become 147 Squadron.

3 (LONG-RANGE) FERRY UNIT
Formed 17th November 1952 at Abingdon by redesignating an element of the Overseas Ferry Unit.

Sabre F.4.

Disbanded 1st February 1953 at Abingdon to become 167 Squadron.

LONG-RANGE FLIGHT
Formed 1927 at Cranwell for a series of challenges on the World long-distance record.

Horsley II J8607; Fairey Long-range Monoplane I J9479, Fairey Long-Range Monoplane II K1991.

Disbanded May 1933 at Cranwell.

LONG-RANGE WEAPONS ESTABLISHMENT
The Establishment held the following aircraft on charge:

Lincoln B.1 RA638; Anson XIX VM374; Viking C.2 VL231; Freighter 21E WW378; Canberra B.2 A84-307.

LORAN TRAINING UNIT
Formed 5th October 1944 at Mullaghmore by redesignating 4 Refresher Flying Unit.

Wellington XIII NC507.

Disbanded 20th April 1945 at Limavady to become the Coastal Command Anti-U-Boat Devices School.

LORRAINE SQUADRON (1) – see Groupe 'Lorraine'

LORRAINE SQUADRON (2) – see 342 (Lorraine) Squadron

LYSANDER FLIGHT
Formed 20th November 1939 at Boscombe Down within the Special Duty Flight.

Lysander.

Disbanded (date and location unknown).

'M' FLIGHT
Formed 6th October 1918 at Longuenesse, St Omer, France.

F.2B E2162; D.H.9 D3081; Fokker DVII '2857'; S.E.5a C6424.

Disbanded August 1919 at Hangelar, Germany.

MACHINE GUN SCHOOL
Formed 3rd October 1915 at Swingate Down.

B.E.2c 5424; R.E.7 2351; F.B.5 5652.

Disbanded 13th September 1916 at Hythe to become the School of Aerial Gunnery.

MAINTENANCE COMMAND COMMUNICATION SQUADRON, later MAINTENANCE COMMAND COMMUNICATION FLIGHT, later MAINTENANCE COMMAND COMMUNICATION SQUADRON, later MAINTENANCE COMMAND COMMUNICATION AND FERRY SQUADRON
Formed 1st May 1944 at Andover. Later redesignated Maintenance Command Communication Flight. Reverted to Maintenance Command Communication Squadron from 1st August 1949 by absorbing the Royal Air Force Staff College Communication Flight. Redesignated the Maintenance Command Communication and Ferry Squadron from 1st November 1960.

S6 (5.44–4.51)	*Magister N3805; Cygnet II ES915; Proctor I P6241, II Z7209, III R7537, IV NP183 S6-D; Hornet Moth AV969; Aldon AW167 S6-K; Oxford I PH230; II V3580; Reliant X9596; Hornet Moth AV969; Cygnet II ES915; Mohawk HM503; Hudson III V9220; Miles M.28 III PW937; Spitfire F.22 PK597; Anson X NK705, XII NL247, XIX VM316 S6-A; Devon C.1 VP969.*
Nil (4.51–3.64)	*Anson XIX VM316; Chipmunk T.10 WG308; Devon C.1 VP967; Varsity T.1 WL680; Pembroke C.1 WV740.*

Disbanded 1st April 1964 at Andover and merged with the Training Command Communication Squadron to become the Western Communication Squadron.

MAINTENANCE UNITS
Code letters were allocated to Maintenance Units in September 1945. Only a few of the codes were ever taken up and displayed.

5 Maintenance Unit	*4J*	*Whitley II K7242; Tiger Moth II.*
6 Maintenance Unit	*V4*	*Oxford II ED116; Dominie NR721 V4.*
8 Maintenance Unit	*J7*	*Oxford II ED117.*
9 Maintenance Unit	*2L*	*Whitley III K8945; Tiger Moth II.*
10 Maintenance Unit	*Z4*	*Oxford II ED119; Anson I MG764 Z4.*
12 Maintenance Unit	*8C*	*Hampden I P2127; Proctor; Oxford II ED111.*
13 Maintenance Unit	*3J*	*Magister P2458; Oxford I EB969 3J-B; Tiger Moth II T5702 3J; Halifax VI RG872 3J-E; Spitfire V; Mosquito B.20; Dakota III KG311 3J.*
15 Maintenance Unit	*8Y*	*Anson I.*
18 Maintenance Unit	*W6*	*Oxford ED110.*
19 Maintenance Unit	*6Z*	*Magister I P2376.*
20 Maintenance Unit	*9Y*	*Anson I LT676 9Y, XI NL247 9Y-E.*
22 Maintenance Unit	*D8*	*Oxford II ED109.*
23 Maintenance Unit	*3B*	*Oxford II ED108.*
24 Maintenance Unit	*J8*	
27 Maintenance Unit	*L4*	*Whitley III K8945.*
29 Maintenance Unit	*Q7*	
30 Maintenance Unit	*4U*	
32 Maintenance Unit	*I6*	*Magister R1888.*
33 Maintenance Unit	*M2*	*Blenheim IV T1614; Oxford II ED118.*

38 Maintenance Unit	3X	Tiger Moth II.
39 Maintenance Unit	5K	Tiger Moth II T7870 5K-S; Anson.
44 Maintenance Unit	9O	
45 Maintenance Unit	Z8	Anson I MH225.
46 Maintenance Unit	T2	Wellington IA N2995.
48 Maintenance Unit	3D	Proctor III DX190 3D-H; Oxford I NM663 3D-N; Anson I LS998 3D, XIX VM371 3D.
51 Maintenance Unit	U5	Oxford II ED112; Anson I NK957 U5-S; Tiger Moth II.
57 Maintenance Unit	7D	Tiger Moth II.
272 Maintenance Unit	2B	
273 Maintenance Unit	DA	
274 Maintenance Unit	R8	Auster IV, V.

MAJUNGA DETACHMENT SUPPORT UNIT – see 204 Squadron, RFC, later 204 Squadron, RAF

MALAYA COMMUNICATION SQUADRON – see Air Headquarters Malaya Communication Squadron

MALAYAN VOLUNTEER AIR FORCE
Formed August 1940 at Singapore by redesignating the Straits Settlements Volunteer Air Force.

1 SQUADRON

'A' Flight (Singapore)	Moth; Cadet; Tiger Moth 41; Moth Minor VR-SBE; Whitney Straight VR-SBB; Hornet Moth VR-SAN.
'B' Flight (Singapore)	Dragon Rapide VR-SAW; Dragonfly VR-SAX.
'C' Flight (Kuala Lumpur)	Tiger Moth; Leopard Moth; Hawk Major; Falcon VR-RAP.
'D' Flight (Ipoh)	Cadet VR-RAL; Gipsy Moth; Avro 640 VR-RAJ.
'E' Flight (Penang)	Moth Major; Eagle VR-SAP; Tutor 42; Tiger Moth.

Withdrawn from Malaya during February 1942. Personnel arrived in Colombo, Ceylon, on 6th March 1942.

MALAYAN AUXILIARY AIR FORCE, later ROYAL MALAYAN AIR FORCE
Formed 1950. Redesignated Royal Malayan Air Force from 1st June 1958. Disbanded 16th September 1963 to become the Royal Malaysian Air Force.

See: Auxiliary Fighter Squadron (Malaya)
           Kuala Lumpur Fighter Squadron
           Penang Squadron

MALTA AIR SEA RESCUE AND COMMUNICATION FLIGHT, later MALTA COMMUNICATION, FERRY UNIT AND AIR SEA RESCUE FLIGHT
Formed 4th March 1943 at Hal Far, Malta, by redesignating the Communication Flight, Malta. Redesignated Communication, Ferry Unit and Air Sea Rescue Flight from 1st November 1943.

Magister L8217; Proctor I P6116; Swordfish II W5896; Walrus I X9498, II Z1813 H; Blenheim IV Z7926; Beaufort I DW836 K; Argus II FS613; Wellington IC HX639, VIII HX721, X HE539; Caproni Ca100 OK-?; Harvard IIA EX127; Spitfire IV BR665, V EP714, IX JL137; Magister L8217.

Disbanded 1st March 1944 at Hal Far, Malta, to become the Air Headquarters Malta Communication Flight.

MALTA COMMUNICATION AND TARGET TOWING SQUADRON
Formed 1st July 1954 at Luqa, Malta, by redesignating the Air Headquarters Malta Communication Squadron.

Dakota IV KN452; Beaufighter TT.10 RD850; Valetta C.1 VW144, C.2 VX574, T.3 WJ479; Pembroke C.1 WV734; Devon C.1 VP953; Meteor T.7 WG964, F.8 WH256.

Disbanded 1st August 1963 at Takali, Malta, to become the Malta Communication Flight.

MALTA COMMUNICATION, FERRY UNIT AND AIR SEA RESCUE FLIGHT – see Malta Air Sea Rescue and Communication Flight, later Malta Communication, Ferry Unit and Air Sea Rescue Flight

MALTA COMMUNICATION FLIGHT
Formed 1st August 1963 at Takali, Malta, by redesignating the Malta Communication and Target Towing Squadron.

Dakota IV KN647; Anson XIX VL343; Chipmunk T.10 WB693.

Disbanded 30th June 1968 at Luqa, Malta.

MALTA NIGHT FIGHTER UNIT
Formed 1st August 1941 at Takali, Malta.

Hurricane IIA Z2827 M, IIB Z2961, X AG156.

Disbanded 4th December 1941 at Takali to become 1435 (Night Fighter) Flight.

MANCHESTER AND SALFORD UNIVERSITIES AIR SQUADRON – see Manchester University Air Squadron, later Manchester and Salford Universities Air Squadron

MANCHESTER UNIVERSITY AIR SQUADRON, later MANCHESTER AND SALFORD UNIVERSITIES AIR SQUADRON
Formed 14th January 1941 at Manchester, using Ringway for flying training. Redesignated Manchester and Salford Universities Air Squadron from 25th May 1974.

Nil (3.41–.46)	Tiger Moth II, aircraft from 24 EFTS.
FLH (–.47)	Tiger Moth II.
RUM (.47–4.51)	Tiger Moth II N6851 RUM-A; Chipmunk T.10 WD326 RUM-A; Dominie; I X7542 RUM-A.
Nil (4.51–)	Oxford I NJ303; Tiger Moth II; Harvard KF160; Anson T.21 W~J550; Chipmunk T.10 WD322 K; Provost T.1 XF684; Bulldog T.1 XX615 2.

Current 1st April 1998 at Woodvale.

MANSTON FLIGHT
Formed November 1941 at Manston by redesignating an element of 3 Squadron.

Hurricane IIB, IIC.

Disbanded February 1942 at Manston.

MANSTON NAVAL FLIGHT – see 470 (Fighter) Flight

MARINE AIRCRAFT EXPERIMENTAL ESTABLISHMENT
Formed 1st April 1924 at Felixstowe by redesignating the Marine Aircraft Experimental Unit.

(Airspeed) Queen Wasp K8888. (Arado) Ar 196 VM748. (Armstrong Whitworth) Awana J6897; Atlas I Floatplane J9998. (Avro) Sea Tutor K2893; Rota Floatplane K4296. (Blackburn) Iris III N238, V S1263; Shark II Floatplane K5638; Roc Floatplane L3059; Blackburn B.20 V8914. (Blomm und Voss) Bv 138B VK895, Bv 138C-1 Air Min 70; Bv 222C VP501; Bv 236. (Consolidated) 28-5 P9630; Catalina I AH564, IB FP107, II AM264, IIA VA725, IVA JX202, IVB JX392, VI JX632; Coronado JX471. (Curtiss) H.16 N4892. (de Havilland) Amiens IIIC E5550; D.H.9A E8444; Moth Floatplane K2235; Hornet Moth Floatplane P6785; Mosquito IV DZ579, TR.33 TW290. (Dornier) Do 18; Do 24T-3 VM484. (Douglas) Boston IIIA BZ332. (Fairey) Atlantia I N119; Fairey IIIC N2246; IIID N9462; IIIF J9141; Gordon Floatplane K1740; Seafox K4304; Swordfish I Floatplane K5662, III NF408; Albacore Floatplane L7076. (Felixstowe) F.5 N4040. (Fokker) T.8W AV958. (Gloster) Bamel J7234; Gloster II J7504; Goring Floatplane J8674. (Handley Page) V/1500 F7135. (Hawker) Horsley II Floatplane J8612; Hawfinch Floatplane J8776; Osprey I K2777; III K3615; Hurricane IIC KX858. (Heinkel) He 115A-2 BV185. (Junkers) Ju 52/3 Floatplane. (Lockheed) Hudson I P5145. (Martin) Mariner I JX103. (North American) Mitchell II FV965. (Nieuport) London H1741; Nightjar H8553. (Parnell) Prawn S1576; Panther N93; Plover N161; Peto N182; Pike N202; Perch N217. (Phoenix) Cork I N86. (Royal Aircraft Factory) S.E.5a D7016. (Saro) Cloud K2681; Shrimp TK580 J; Saro SR/A1 TG263. (Short) Rangoon S1433; Calcutta G-EBVG; Valetta G-AAJY; Sarafand S1589; S.20 'Mercury' G-ADHJ; S.21 'Maia' G-ADHK; Singapore III K3592; Short R.24/31 K3574; Short S.23M AX660; Lerwick I L7254; Scion Senior

Floatplane L9786; Sunderland I L2159, II W3976, III JM681, V TX293; Shrimp G-AFZS; Shetland I DX166; Seaford I MZ269; Solent WM759; Sealand G-AKLN. (Sopwith) Camel N7352; Cuckoo II N8005. (Supermarine) Southampton I N9896; Scarpa S1648; Walrus I K5773; Sea Otter K8854, I JM821; Spitfire VB Floatplane EP754, VC BR351, IX Floatplane MJ892; Seagull I PA143. (Taylorcraft) Auster V Floatplane TJ207; VI Floatplane VF517. (Vickers) Valentia I N124; Vimy IV J7451; Vildebeest II Floatplane K2916; Wellington I L4250, IA P9214, III X3446, X NA929.

Disbanded 31st July 1958 at Felixstowe.

MARINE AIRCRAFT EXPERIMENTAL SECTION
Formed June 1918 at Grain by redesignating the Test Department, Grain.

Curtiss H.16 N4060; Felixstowe F.2A N4283; F.3 N4409; Camel E7274; Avro 504K E3797; Cork I N86; Cuckoo III N7990.

Disbanded March 1920 at Grain to become the Marine Aircraft Experimental Unit.

MARINE AIRCRAFT EXPERIMENTAL UNIT
Formed March 1920 at Grain by redesignating the Marine Aircraft Experimental Section.

Cork N86; Felixstowe F.5 N4038; Curtiss H.16 N4892; Cuckoo II N8005; D.H.4 E8444.

Disbanded 1st April 1924 at Felixstowe to become the Marine Aircraft Experimental Establishment.

MARINE OBSERVERS SCHOOL, ALDEBURGH
Formed October 1918 at Aldeburgh by redesignating the School for Anti-Submarine Inshore Patrol Observers.

Kangaroo B9986; D.H.6 F3389; D.H.9 D1096.

Disbanded 1st January 1919 at Aldeburgh to become 1 Marine Observers School.

MARINE OBSERVERS SCHOOL, LEYSDOWN
Formed by August at Leysdown.

1½ Strutter N5153; Pup C269; D.H.9 D5638; D.H.9A H3414.

Disbanded September 1918 at Leysdown.

1 MARINE OBSERVERS SCHOOL
Formed 1st January 1919 at Aldeburgh by redesignating the Marine Observers School, Aldeburgh.

Kangaroo B9986; D.H.6 F3389; D.H.9 D1098.

Disbanded September 1919 at Aldeburgh.

2 MARINE OBSERVERS SCHOOL
Formed 28th December 1918 at Eastchurch by redesignating 1 Observers School.

B.E.2c 9978; F.2B C903; D.H.6 C7767; Avro 504K D8253; D.H.9A E9673.

Disbanded June 1919 at Eastchurch.

MARITIME OPERATIONAL TRAINING UNIT
Formed 1st October 1956 at Kinloss by merging 236 Operational Conversion Unit and 1 Maritime Reconnaissance School.

MOTU	Shackleton MR.1 VP268 MOTU-Y, MR.1A WB824 MOTU-R, T.2 WG554 MOTU-V, T.4 WB831 MOTU-S; Nimrod MR.1 XV230.

Disbanded 1st July 1970 at St Mawgan to become 236 Operational Conversion Unit.

1 MARITIME RECONNAISSANCE SCHOOL – see School of Maritime Reconnaissance

MEDICAL FLIGHT, HENDON
Formed July 1917 at Stanmore.

D.H.4 A7993; Camel B3851; Pup B6074; F.2B C4889; D.H.6 C5178; Avro 504A D1631; Avro 504K D7651.

Existed until at least 31st May 1918 at Hendon.

MEDITERRANEAN AIR COMMAND COMMUNICATION UNIT
Formed 2nd August 1943 at Maison Blanche, Algeria, by redesignating 1478 (Mediterranean Air Command Communication) Flight.

Whitley V LA889; Blenheim V BB156; Hudson IIIA FH454, V AM629, VI EW926; Hurricane IIC KW980; Beaufighter VI EL386.

Disbanded 1st February 1944 at Maison Blanche.

MEDITERRANEAN ALLIED COASTAL AIR FORCE CALIBRATION FLIGHT
Was to have formed 1st June 1945 at Pomigliano, Italy, by redesignating the Calibration Flight, Mediterranean Allied Coastal Air Forces Communication Flight.

MEDITERRANEAN ALLIED COASTAL AIR FORCES COMMUNICATION FLIGHT
Formed 1st January 1944 at Blida, Algeria, by redesignating the Northwest Africa Coastal Air Force Communication Flight and absorbing 1 Air Sea Rescue Flight (North Africa).

Hurricane IIB BP286, IIC KX838; Spitfire VB EP973; Baltimore IV FA501, V FW327; Hudson IIIA FK772, VI FK608; Expeditor II HB252; Argus II HB563; Wellington XIII JA145; Anson I MH107.

Disbanded 1st June 1945 at Marcianese, Italy, and absorbed by the Mediterranean and Middle East Communication Squadron.

MEDITERRANEAN ALLIED TACTICAL AIR FORCES COMMUNICATION FLIGHT
Formed 1st January 1944 at Bari, Italy, by redesignating the Northwest African Tactical Air Force Communication Flight.

Argus II FZ794; Hudson VI FK608; Baltimore V FW504; Storch; Expeditor II HB254; Spitfire VIII MT800.

Disbanded 6th July 1945 at Peretola, Italy.

MEDITERRANEAN AND MIDDLE EAST COMMUNICATION SQUADRON
Formed 1st February 1944 at Maison Blanche, Algeria, by redesignating the Northwest African Air Forces Communication Flight.

Blenheim V EH443; Hudson III V9220, IIIA FH400, V AM582, VI FK454; Baltimore V FW327; Expeditor I HB205, II HB271; Argus I, II FZ742, III KK438; Wellington X LN924; Boston III W8307; Mosquito VI HP920; Hurricane IIC LB840; Proctor III HM373, Anson I MG752.

Disbanded 10th November 1945 at Marcianise, Italy, to become the Air Headquarters Italy Communication Squadron.

Reformed 10th November 1945 at Heliopolis, Egypt, by redesignating the Middle East Communication Squadron.

Hudson V, VI FK500; Ventura IIA FD592, V JT817; Lodestar I EW993; Anson XII PH559, XIX TX155; Spitfire IX MA471, XI PL915; Expeditor I HB202, II HB259; Warwick V; Buckingham C.1 KV404; Dakota IV KN377; Oxford I PG952; Proctor III HM474.

Disbanded 1st June 1949 at Kabrit, Egypt, to become the Headquarters Middle East Communication Squadron.

MEDITERRANEAN TACTICAL AIR FORCES COMMUNICATION FLIGHT
Formed January 1944 at Bari, Italy.

No aircraft known.

Disbanded October 1944 at Pomigliano, Italy.

MERCHANT SHIP FIGHTER UNIT
Formed 5th May 1941 at Speke.

KE (5.41-6.43)	Sea Hurricane IA L1889 KE-E, Hurricane I Z4936 KE-M.
LU (5.41-6.43)	Hurricane I W9313 LU-S.
NJ (5.41-6.43)	Hurricane I V6756.
XS	Possibly allocated.
Also used	Spitfire I N3051, VB AD371, VC JK514; Hurricane X P5188, IIB BW841; Tiger Moth II R5077; Master III DM195.

Disbanded 7th September 1943 at Speke.

METEOR FLIGHT
Formed February 1919 at Berck-sur-Mer, France, for weather research flights.

D.H.9 E9005; F.2B F4442; F.K.8 E8834.

Disbanded August 1919, probably at Cologne, Germany.

METEOROLOGICAL CONVERSION UNIT
Formed 28th October 1943 at Tiree.

Halifax V DG349.

Disbanded 14th February 1944 at Tiree and absorbed by 517 Squadron.

METEOROLOGICAL FLIGHT, ALDERGROVE – see 404 (Meteorological) Flight

METEOROLOGICAL FLIGHT, DUXFORD – see Royal Air Force Meteorological Flight, Eastchurch, Duxford and Mildenhall

METEOROLOGICAL FLIGHT, EASTCHURCH – see Royal Air Force Meteorological Flight, Eastchurch, Duxford and Mildenhall

METEOROLOGICAL FLIGHT, HELIOPOLIS
Formed 14th April 1941 at Heliopolis, Egypt.

Gladiator.

Disbanded 1st January 1942 at Heliopolis to become 1411 (Meteorological) Flight.

METEOROLOGICAL FLIGHT, KHARTOUM
Formed 21st September 1941 at Khartoum, Sudan.

Gladiator I K6140, II N5831.

Disbanded 1st January 1942 at Khartoum to become 1412 (Meteorological) Flight.

METEOROLOGICAL FLIGHT, MILDENHALL – see Royal Air Force Meteorological Flight Eastchurch, Duxford and Mildenhall

METEOROLOGICAL FLIGHT, RAMLEH
Formed 21st September 1941 at Ramleh, Palestine.

Gladiator I K7999.

Disbanded 1st January 1942 at Ramleh to become 1413 (Meteorological) Flight.

1 METEOROLOGICAL FLIGHT
Formed 1st July 1943 at Alipore, India.

No aircraft allocated.

Disbanded 31st July 1943 at Alipore to become 1300 (Meteorological) Flight.

2 METEOROLOGICAL FLIGHT
Formed 1st July 1943 at Delhi, India.

No aircraft allocated.

Disbanded 31st July 1943 at Delhi to become 1301 (Meteorological) Flight.

3 METEOROLOGICAL FLIGHT
Formed 1st July 1943 at Yelahanka, India.

No aircraft allocated.

Disbanded 31st July 1943 at Yelahanka to become 1302 (Meteorological) Flight.

4 METEOROLOGICAL FLIGHT
Formed 1st July 1943 at Ratmalana, Ceylon.

No aircraft allocated.

Disbanded 31st July 1943 at Ratmalana to become 1303 (Meteorological) Flight.

METEOROLOGICAL RESEARCH FLIGHT, later METEOROLOGICAL RESEARCH UNIT
Formed 1st September 1946 at Farnborough.

Mitchell II FR209; Halifax VI ST796; Liberator VI KL632; Mosquito PR.34 RG205; Hastings MET.1 TG619; Varsity T.1 WF425; Canberra B.2 WJ582, PR.3 WE146, B.6 WH952; Hercules W.2 XV208.

Current 1st April 1997 at Boscombe Down.

METROPOLITAN COMMUNICATION SQUADRON
Formed 8th April 1944 at Hendon by redesignating 510 Squadron.

Nil (4.44– .45)	*Anson I N4913; Flamingo AE444; Percival Q-6 X9407; Hudson III AE588, IIIA FH167, V AM850, VI FK482; Lockheed 12A X9316; Mohawk III AR630; Oxford I AS737; Tiger Moth II N6946; Vega Gull P5989; Proctor I P6248, III LZ576; Spitfire I X4319, VB BL385, XI PL902; Hurricane IIC LF345; Stampe S.V.4B MX457; Auster III MZ179; Monarch TP819; Dominie I X7324; Dakota III KG738; York VVIP I MW100, VIP I MW101; Messenger RG327.*
CB (.44–7.48)	*Dominie I NF865 CB-Z; Anson XII PH716 CB-S.*
VS (.44–7.48)	*Anson XII PH694 VS-AZ; Proctor III HM352 VS-U, IV NP290 VS-Z.*
ZA (.44–.46)	*Proctor III LZ803 ZA-G; Dominie I NF874 ZA-W; Oxford I NM753 ZA-K; Wellington X PG253 ZA-J.*
Also used	*Anson X NK446, XI NK994; Oxford II BM823; Meteor F.3 EE309.*

Disbanded 19th July 1948 at Hendon to become 31 Squadron.

Reformed 1st March 1955 at Hendon by redesignating 31 Squadron.

CB (3.55–6.58)	*Anson XIX VM351 CB-N, C.21 VV253 CB-A; Devon C.1 VP952 CB-A; Chipmunk T.10 WZ853 CB-H.*
Nil (6.58–2.69)	*Anson C.21 VS572; Devon C.1 VP953; Pembroke C.1 WV704, C(PR).1 XF796; Vampire T.11 WZ417; Balliol T.2 WG222; Valetta C.1 VW826, C.2 WJ504; Chipmunk T.10 WB573; Sycamore HC.11 WT923, HC.14 XL829.*

Disbanded 3rd February 1969 at Northolt to become 32 Squadron.

'METZ' FLIGHT (1) – see Groupe 'Lorraine'

'METZ' FLIGHT (2) – see 342 (Lorraine) Squadron

MIDDLE EAST ADVANCED CREW TRAINING UNIT
Formed 29th October 1942 at Gordon's Tree, Sudan, by redesignating 1 (Middle East) Pilots and Aircrew Pool.

No aircraft known.

Disbanded (date unknown) at Gordon's Tree.

MIDDLE EAST AIR FORCE ARMAMENT PRACTICE CAMP – see Armament Practice Camp (Middle East Air Force)

MIDDLE EAST AIR FORCE COMMUNICATION FLIGHT, later MIDDLE EAST AIR FORCE FLIGHT – see Headquarters Middle East Air Force Communication Flight, later Headquarters Middle East Air Force Flight

MIDDLE EAST AIR FORCE INSTRUMENT TRAINING FLIGHT
Formed 5th June 1950 at Shallufa, Egypt.

Harvard IIB KF287 F; Meteor T.7 WF849 B, F.8 WK976, TT.8 WK946.

Disbanded 10th May 1956 at Nicosia, Cyprus.

MIDDLE EAST AIR FORCE SPECIAL COMMUNICATION FLIGHT
Formed 1st September 1952 at Fayid, Egypt, by redesignating the Special Communication Squadron.

Valetta C.2 VX571; Devon C.1 VP953; Pembroke C.1 VW903;
Prentice T.1 VR280.

Disbanded 1st December 1954 at Fayid and merged with the
Headquarters Middle East Air Force Communication Flight and the
C-in-Cs Flight to become the Headquarters Middle East Air Force
Communication Squadron.

MIDDLE EAST AIR FORCE TARGET TOWING FLIGHT – see
Middle East Air Force Target Towing Unit, later Middle East Air
Force Target Towing Flight

MIDDLE EAST AIR FORCE TARGET TOWING UNIT, later
MIDDLE EAST AIR FORCE TARGET TOWING FLIGHT
Formed 1st January 1950 at Shallufa, Egypt, by merging the Target
Towing Flights Nicosia and Shallufa. Redesignated Middle East Air
Force Target Towing Flight from 15th January 1952.

Beaufighter X RD850; Meteor T.7 WF853, F.8 WK945.

Disbanded April 1956 at Nicosia, Cyprus.

1 (MIDDLE EAST) CENTRAL GUNNERY SCHOOL, later ROYAL
AIR FORCE (MIDDLE EAST) CENTRAL GUNNERY SCHOOL
Formed 1st March 1943 at El Ballah, Egypt, by redesignating 1
Middle East Training School. Redesignated Royal Air Force (Middle
East) Central Gunnery School from 25th April 1943.

Harvard II AJ840; Hurricane IIB Z3323; Spitfire VC BP983; Anson I
LV254; Wellington X HE538.

Disbanded December 1945 at El Ballah.

1 MIDDLE EAST CHECK AND CONVERSION UNIT
Formed 1st June 1943 at Bilbeis, Egypt, by merging the Check and
Conversion Flights of 2 and 3 Aircraft Delivery Units and the
Refresher Flight of 75 Operational Training Unit.

Hurricane I V6926, IIA Z4948, IIB BP340; Spitfire VB BP852, VC
BP985; Blenheim IV Z9540, V BA297; Kittyhawk I AK692; Hudson
IIIA FH308, V AM870, VI EW881; Beaufort I L9958 37; Baltimore I
AG695, II AG744, III AG955, IIIA FA154, IV FA470; Mosquito VI
HX806; Marauder II FB492, III HD444; Dakota I FD805, III FD830,
IV FJ711; DC-3 HK867; Ventura I FN960, V JS910; Beaufighter IF
V8309, X NE302; Lockheed 18 AX722; Harvard II AJ803, IIA
EX120, III EX856; Liberator VI EW249.

Disbanded 29th June 1944 at Bilbeis to become 1330 Conversion
Unit.

2 MIDDLE EAST CHECK AND CONVERSION UNIT
Formed (date and location unknown) in the Middle East.

Hurricane I Z4780; Spitfire I X4489; Blenheim IV Z9830;
Beaufighter I X7836.

Disbanded (date and location unknown). Possibly renumbered as or
absorbed by 1 Middle East Check and Conversion Unit.

MIDDLE EAST COMMAND COMMUNICATION FLIGHT – see
Middle East Command Communication Squadron, later Middle
East Command Communication Flight

MIDDLE EAST COMMAND COMMUNICATION SQUADRON,
later MIDDLE EAST COMMAND COMMUNICATION FLIGHT
Formed 1st February 1956 at Nicosia, Cyprus, by redesignating the
Headquarters Middle East Air Force Communication Squadron.

Valetta C.2 VX572, T.3 WJ476; Devon C.1 VP956; Prentice T.1
VR264; Meteor T.7 WF795; Varsity T.1 WF429; Pembroke C.1
WV700; Chipmunk T.10 WG486.

Disbanded 13th February 1961 at Akrotiri, Cyprus, and absorbed by
70 Squadron.

Reformed 1st October 1961 at Khormaksar, Aden. Redesignated
the Middle East Command Communication Flight from 15th June
1965 at Khormaksar.

Dakota IV KJ955; Hastings C.4 WJ326, Canberra WJ580; Valetta
C.2 VX571; Pembroke.

Disbanded 15th September 1967 at Khormaksar to become the Air
Forces Gulf Communication Squadron.

MIDDLE EAST COMMUNICATION FLIGHT – see Air
Headquarters Middle East Communication Flight

MIDDLE EAST COMMUNICATION SQUADRON
Formed 29th February 1944 at Heliopolis, Egypt, by redesignating
173 Squadron.

Proctor I P6122; Anson I; Lodestar I EW981, II EW988; Wellington
III HF699; DC-3 HK983; Argus II FS539, III KK506; Ju 52/3M
HK919; Cub HK939; Expeditor II KJ473.

Disbanded (date and location unknown).

Reformed 31st May 1945 at Heliopolis by redesignating the Station
Flight, Heliopolis.

Lodestar II EW993; Harvard IIA EX703; Proctor III HM474; Dakota
IV KN377; Anson I LT666; Wellington X LP803; Spitfire XI PM130.

Disbanded 10th November 1945 at Heliopolis to become the
Mediterranean and Middle East Communication Squadron.

1 (MIDDLE EAST) PILOTS AND AIRCREW POOL
Formed 6th July 1942 at Gordon's Tree, Sudan, by redesignating
the Pilots and Aircrew Pool.

Tutor; Audax K7531; Hart.

Disbanded 29th October 1942 at Gordon's Tree to become the
(Middle East) Advanced Crew Training Unit.

2 (MIDDLE EAST) PILOTS AND AIRCREW POOL
Formed 12th July 1942 at Gordon's Tree, Sudan.

No aircraft, if any, known.

Disbanded 25th September 1942 at Gordon's Tree.

1 MIDDLE EAST TRAINING SCHOOL
Formed 5th April 1942 at El Ballah, Egypt.

Blenheim I L1387, IV Z6376, V BA479; Harvard II AJ776; Hurricane
I N2629 A, X P5173, IIC BP391; Spitfire I HK856 A, VB AB253;
Beaufort I N1011, II DD931; Baltimore I AG714, II AG768 B;
Kittyhawk I AK650; Tomahawk IIA AH913, IIB AK419 P; Wellington
IC DV677, VIII LA977.

Disbanded 1st March 1943 at El Ballah to become 1 (Middle East)
Central Gunnery School.

2 MIDDLE EAST TRAINING SCHOOL
Formed 15th April 1942 at Shallufa, Egypt.

Wellington IC P9294, II Z8515; Hudson IIIA FH296; Marauder IA
FK376; Halifax II W7716 B.

Absorbed 31st October 1942 at Aqir, Palestine, by 4 Middle East
Training School, reduced to cadre by January 1943 and officially
disbanded 16th June 1943,

3 MIDDLE EAST TRAINING SCHOOL
Formed 23rd March 1942 at Amman, Jordan.

Audax K7526; Blenheim V EH319; Baltimore I AG718, III AG861;
Vega Gull X1032.

Disbanded 15th November 1944 at Amman.

4 MIDDLE EAST TRAINING SCHOOL
Formed 1st May 1942 at Kabrit, Egypt.

Blenheim IV R3883; Beaufort I N1047; Hudson III V8992, IIIA
FH244, VI EW879; Wellington IC DV569.

Disbanded 30th April 1944 at Ramat David, Palestine.

5 MIDDLE EAST TRAINING SCHOOL
Formed 15th August 1942 at Shallufa, Egypt, by redesignating the
Torpedo Bombing School.

| 5 | Blenheim IV Z9730, V BA382; Beaufort I
N1033, II DE126 5-N; Wellington IC DV550
5-G, III HZ118, VIII HX864 5-B, XI MP569, XIII
ME907; Walrus I W2710; Hurricane IIC LB902
5-W, IV LD216 5-V; Maryland II AH375; |

Marauder I FK118; Baltimore IIIA FA336, V FW748; Beaufighter VI JL721, XI JM401 5-N.

Disbanded 1st December 1944 at Shallufa.

MIDDLE EAST TRANSPORT FLIGHT
Formed November 1941 at Takoradi, Gold Coast.

Hudson III V9093.

Disbanded January 1942 at Takoradi to become the Communication Flight, Takoradi.

MIDLAND AREA FLYING INSTRUCTORS SCHOOL
Formed 1st July 1918 at Lilbourne by redesignating the Midland Area School of Special Flying.

Avro 504J/K E1700; D.H.9 D2823; Snipe F7454.

Disbanded 1919 at Feltwell.

MIDLAND AREA SCHOOL OF SPECIAL FLYING
Formed 1918 at Lilbourne.

Avro 504J/K.

Disbanded 1st July 1918 at Lilbourne to become the Midland Area Flying Instructors School.

MILITARY GOVERNOR'S FLIGHT
Formed (date and location unknown) within the British Air Forces of Occupation Communication Squadron.

Anson XII, XIX; Dakota; Messenger.

Disbanded 30th October 1949 at Celle, Germany, to become the High Commissioner's Flight.

MISCELLANEOUS FLIGHT, MALTA – see Royal Air Force Base, Malta

MOSQUITO CONVERSION FLIGHT
Formed 22nd August 1943 at Sculthorpe to convert Ventura crews of 464 and 487 Squadrons to Mosquito VI.

Mosquito VI.

Disbanded October 1943 at Sculthorpe.

MOSQUITO CONVERSION UNIT
Formed 30th August 1942 at Horsham St Faith.

Mosquito III HJ858; Blenheim V.

Disbanded 18th October 1942 at Marham to become 1655 Mosquito Conversion Unit.

MULTI-ENGINE TRAINING SQUADRON
Formed 4th May 1977 at Leeming.

Jetstream T.1 XX497 E.

Disbanded 1st July 1992 at Finningley to become 45 (Reserve) Squadron.

'N' FLIGHT
Records begin 18th September 1919 at Vert Galand, France.

F.2B D7872.

Disbanded (date and location unknown), France.

'NANCY' FLIGHT (1) – see Groupe 'Lorraine'

'NANCY' FLIGHT (2) – see 342 (Lorraine) Squadron

NAVAL AIR FIGHTING DEVELOPMENT SQUADRON – see Central Fighter Establishment

NAVIGATION FLIGHT
Formed by March 1920 at Biggin Hill.

No aircraft known.

Disbanded June 1921 at Biggin Hill.

NAVIGATION SCHOOL
Formed December 1926 at Calshot by redesignating the Air Pilotage Flight.

Southampton I S1041; II S1301; Fairey IIID S1038.

Disbanded 6th January 1936 at Calshot and merged with the Air Navigation School to become the School of Air Navigation.

NAVIGATION TRAINING SCHOOL
Formed by November 1939 at Abu Sueir, Egypt.

Anson I.

Disbanded 22nd June 1940 at Abu Sueir.

NAVIGATION TRAINING UNIT
Formed 10th April 1943 at Gransden Lodge as the Gransden Lodge Navigation Training Unit. Became the Navigation Training Unit from 18th March 1943.

QF	*Stirling I R9269/G; III EF404 QF-M; Halifax II W7874; Oxford II P6798 QF-C3; Lancaster I ED317 QF-T, III EE201; Mosquito IV DZ426; VI NT127, XX B351 QF-A2.*

Disbanded 18th June 1946 at Warboys.

NETHERAVON FLYING SCHOOL
Formed 29th July 1919 at Netheravon by redesignating 8 Training School.

No aircraft known.

Disbanded 23rd December 1919 at Netheravon to become 1 Flying Training School.

NETHERLANDS EAST INDIES COMMUNICATION FLIGHT – see Air Headquarters Netherlands East Indies Communication Flight

NEW ZEALAND FLIGHT
Formed 1st June 1939 at Marham.

Wellington I NZ300, IA P9209.

Disbanded 4th April 1940 at Feltwell to become 75 Squadron.

NIGHT ALL-WEATHER WING – see Central Fighter Establishment

NIGHT FIGHTER DEVELOPMENT WING – see Central Fighter Establishment

NIGHT FIGHTER LEADERS SCHOOL – see Central Fighter Establishment

NIGHT FIGHTER TRAINING SQUADRON – see Central Fighter Establishment

NIGHT FIGHTER UNIT, MALTA – see Malta Night Fighter Unit

NIGHT FIGHTER WING – see Central Fighter Establishment

NIGHT FLYING FLIGHT
Formed 1st July 1923 at Biggin Hill.

F.2B C798; Virginia II J6857; Bugle I J6984; Hyderabad J6994; Vimy IV J7446; Horsley I J7987; II J7999; Bison.

Disbanded 22nd October 1931 at Biggin Hill to become the Anti-Aircraft Co-operation Flight.

NIGHT GROUND ATTACK TRIALS UNIT
Formed 18th August 1952 at West Raynham and allocated to 2nd Tactical Air Force from 1st September 1952.

Balliol T.2.

Disbanded (date and location unknown) when trials were completed.

(NIGHT) TRAINING SQUADRONS – see Reserve Aeroplane Squadrons, later Reserve Squadrons, later Training Squadrons

NIMROD OPERATIONAL CONVERSION UNIT – see 42 Squadron, RFC, later 42 Squadron, later, 42 (Reserve) Squadron

NORTHEASTERN AREA FLYING INSTRUCTORS SCHOOL
Formed 1st July 1918 at Redcar by redesignating 2 School of Special Flying.

Bristol Scout D 8993; Nieuport 12 9250; Avro 504A B4314, Avro 504J D7596; Pup B6049; D.H.9 C1129; Camel B7243.

Disbanded May 1919 at Redcar and absorbed by Northwestern Area Flying Instructors School.

NORTHWEST AFRICAN AIR FORCES COMMUNICATION FLIGHT
Formed by August 1943 at Bone, Algeria.

Hurricane IIC KZ438; Argus II FS591.

Disbanded 1st January 1944 at El Aouina, Tunisia, to become the Mediterranean and Middle East Communication Squadron.

NORTHWEST AFRICAN COASTAL AIR FORCE COMMUNICATION FLIGHT
Formed March 1943 at Maison Blanche, Algeria.

Argus I; Hurricane IIC HV360.

Disbanded 1st January 1944 at Maison Blanche to become the Mediterranean Allied Coastal Air Forces Communication Flight.

NORTHWEST AFRICAN TACTICAL AIR FORCE COMMUNICATION FLIGHT
Formed November 1943 at Bari, Italy.

No aircraft known.

Disbanded 1st January 1944 at Bari to become the Mediterranean Allied Tactical Air Forces Communication Flight.

NORTHWESTERN AREA FLYING INSTRUCTORS SCHOOL
Formed 1st July 1918 at Ayr Racecourse.

Avro 504K; F.2B.

Disbanded 1st June 1919 at Redcar.

NORTHERN AREA FLYING INSTRUCTORS SCHOOL
Formed 1st June 1919 at Feltwell.

Avro 504K.

Disbanded March 1920 at Feltwell.

NORTHERN COMMUNICATION SQUADRON
Formed 1st October 1964 at Topcliffe.

Anson XIX TX176; Devon C.1 VP960; Devon C.2 VP968; Pembroke C.1 WV739, C(PR).1 XF796; Basset C.1 XS772.

Disbanded 1st January 1967 at Topcliffe to become the Training Commands Communication Squadron.

NORTHERN IRELAND COMMUNICATION FLIGHT – see Headquarters Royal Air Force Northern Ireland Communication Flight

NORTHUMBRIAN UNIVERSITIES AIR SQUADRON
Formed 1st August 1963 at Ouston by redesignating the Durham University Air Squadron.

Chipmunk T.10 WP975; Bulldog T.1 XX636 Y.

Current 1st April 1998 at Leeming.

NORWEGIAN TRAINING BASE
Formed January 1945 at Winkleigh.

Harvard IIB FS911; Oxford I NM333; Cornell.

Disbanded 10th November 1945 at Winkleigh.

NOTTINGHAM UNIVERSITY AIR SQUADRON
Formed 2nd May 1941 at Nottingham.

Nil (5.41–1.46)   Moth X5056; Tiger Moth II provided by 14 and 16 Elementary Flying Training Schools.
FLL (6.46–4.47)   Tiger Moth II DE978 FLL-B.
RUN (4.47–4.51)   Tiger Moth II DE978 RUN-B.
Nil (4.51–11.67)   Harvard IIB KF739; Chipmunk T.10 WP781.

Disbanded 24th November 1967 at Newton to become the East Midlands Universities Air Squadron.

'O' FLIGHT
Formed by 23rd October 1918 at Premont Farm, France.

F.2B C917.

Disbanded (date and location unknown).

OBSERVER TRAINING FLIGHT – see Royal Air Force Base, Gosport

1 (OBSERVERS) ADVANCED FLYING UNIT
Formed 1st February 1942 at Wigtown by redesignating 1 Air Observers School.

Anson I DJ472; Botha L6230; Blenheim I L6736, IV P4858; Dominie I X7393; Lysander III R9116; Tutor K4817; Magister N3798; Wellington II W5425, X LP148; Master II AZ695, III W8592; Halifax V EB138; Proctor III LZ636; Martinet I MS730; Mosquito III RR297.

Disbanded 12th November 1945 at Wigtown.

2 (OBSERVERS) ADVANCED FLYING UNIT
Formed 18th February 1942 at Millom by redesignating 2 Air Observers School.

Anson I AX539 11, X NK355 46; Defiant I N3313 G1; Battle R7401; Oxford I N6327; Lysander III T1502; Martinet I MS845; Moth AW147; Dominie I X7368; Magister I L8213.

Disbanded 9th January 1945 at Millom.

3 (OBSERVERS) ADVANCED FLYING UNIT
Formed 11th April 1942 at Bobbington (later Halfpenny Green) by redesignating 3 Air Observers School.

Anson I EF927 Q4; Mentor L4403; Whitley V BD394; Oxford I NM482; Dominie I X7392; Tiger Moth II DE254.

Disbanded 1st December 1945 at Halfpenny Green.

4 (OBSERVERS) ADVANCED FLYING UNIT
Formed 11th June 1943 at West Freugh by redesignating 4 Air Observers School.

Anson I W2662 2M; Botha L6333; Lysander III T1425; Tutor K6115; Martinet I MS833.

Disbanded 21st June 1945 at West Freugh.

6 (OBSERVERS) ADVANCED FLYING UNIT
Formed 11th June 1943 at Staverton by redesignating 6 Air Observers School.

Anson I EG542 V2; Oxford I PG937; Dominie I X7393; Botha I L6153; Tutor K3319; Tiger Moth II T7453; Magister T9834.

Disbanded 12th December 1944 at Staverton.

7 (OBSERVERS) ADVANCED FLYING UNIT
Formed 15th February 1944 at Bishops Court by redesignating 7 Air Observers School.

Anson I MG902 12, X NK355; Tutor K6100; Hurricane I N2599; Magister I P2403; Proctor III HM298.

Disbanded 31st May 1945 at Bishops Court to become 7 Air Navigation School.

8 (OBSERVERS) ADVANCE FLYING UNIT
Formed 15th November 1943 at Mona.

Anson I MG633 15.

Disbanded 14th June 1945 at Mona.

9 (OBSERVERS) ADVANCED FLYING UNIT
Formed 1st May 1942 at Penrhos by redesignating 9 Air Observers School.

Anson I EG472 CW; Whitley II K7219, III K8978, IV K9016; Blenheim I L1311, IV N3613; Lysander I L4699, II P1715, III T1529; Dominie I X7398; Moth BD164; Defiant I N1542; Master II DK859; Martinet I HP482 2; Magister T9957.

Disbanded 14th June 1945 at Penrhos.

10 (OBSERVERS) ADVANCED FLYING UNIT
Formed 1st May 1942 at Dumfries by redesignating 10 Air Observers School.

Anson I DG712 H2; Botha I W5023; Gladiator K8046; Henley III L3411; Lysander III T1437; Master II DK972; Tutor K3286; Rapide Z7253; Martinet I MS849; Moth Minor X5117; Tiger Moth II T7780; Magister I T9889.

Disbanded 11th June 1945 at Dumfries to become 10 Air Navigation School.

1 OBSERVERS SCHOOL
Formed July 1918 at Eastchurch.

F.2b; F.K.8; F.E.2b; D.H.4; B.E.2c 9978, B.E.2d; D.H.9 D473; R.E.8 B3424.

Disbanded 28th December 1918 at Eastchurch to become 2 Marine Observers School.

2 OBSERVERS SCHOOL
Formed 14th September 1918 at Manston.

F.K.8; B.E.2c, B.E.2d, B.E.2e; R.E.8 B2256; D.H.4 A2134; D.H.9 D3028; Camel; Avro 504K H1922; F.2B.

Disbanded 14th September 1919 at Manston to become 1 (Observers) School of Aerial Gunnery.

1 (OBSERVERS) SCHOOL OF AERIAL GUNNERY
Formed 9th March 1918 at Hythe by merging 1 and 3 (Auxiliary) Schools of Aerial Gunnery.

F.2B B1104; Pup B1815; 1½ Strutter B2594; D.H.4 B5454; Avro 504J B8769; Handley Page O/400 B8808; F.K.3 B9528.

Disbanded 14th February 1919 at Hythe.

Reformed 14th September 1919 at New Romney by redesignating 2 Observers School.

No aircraft known.

Disbanded December 1919 at Manston.

OBSERVERS SCHOOL OF RECONNAISSANCE AND AERIAL PHOTOGRAPHY
Formed 19th October 1918 at Shrewsbury.

B.E.2; R.E.8 B3424; D.H.9; Handley Page.

Disbanded May 1919 at Shrewsbury.

OFFICERS ADVANCED TRAINING SCHOOL, later 1 OFFICERS ADVANCED TRAINING SCHOOL, later THE OFFICERS ADVANCED TRAINING SCHOOL
Formed 14th February 1944 at Cranwell. Redesignated 1 Officers Advanced Training School from 1st November 1944 and the Officers Advanced Training School from 1st December 1946.

Nil (2.44–4.46) Magister N5413; Mustang IVA KM226; Proctor I, III.
TOC (4.46–7.47) Proctor IV RM225 TOC-C; Spitfire XI PL993 TOC-D.

Disbanded 18th December 1962 at Ternhill to become the Junior Command and Staff School.

1 OFFICERS ADVANCED TRAINING SCHOOL – see above

2 OFFICERS ADVANCED TRAINING SCHOOL
Formed 1st November at Kalafrana, Malta.

Anson I NL170, XII PH603 R; Wellington X.

Disbanded February 1946 at Kalafrana.

OGADEN FLIGHT
Formed 1st May 1944 at Cairo West, Egypt.

Baltimore IV FA484, V FW341.

Disbanded 22nd December 1944 at Khormaksar.

OPERATIONAL AND REFRESHER TRAINING UNIT
Formed 1st December 1943 at Thruxton by redesignating the Glider Pilot Exercise Unit.

Albemarle GT.I P1392, ST.I P1506 T, ST.II V1717 S; Whitley V BD504, V EB399; Hotspur II BT746; Oxford I DF286, II V3590; Master II DL489; Spitfire VB EP380; Tiger Moth I NL981, II R4858; Horsa I DP513, II RX867; Stirling IV LK301; Halifax III NA702, VII PN294; Hadrian 42-77341.

Disbanded 1st April 1946 at Wethersfield to become the nucleus of 1385 (Heavy Transport Support) Conversion Unit.

226 OPERATIONAL CONVERSION UNIT
Formed 15th August 1946 at Molesworth by redesignating 1335 Conversion Unit.

BB (8.46–8.49) Vampire F.1 VF312 BB-A.
HX (8.46–8.49) Meteor F.4 RA492 HX-W, T.7 VW416 HX-V, F.8 WK662 HX-N.
KR (8.46–8.49) Spitfire XVI TE281 KR-L; Meteor F.4 RA489 KR-C, T.7 VW416 KR-F, F.8 WK855 KR-L; Vampire FB.5 WA112 KR-F.
TO (8.46–8.49) Martinet I JN297 TO-T;
UU (8.46–8.49) Spitfire XIV SM896 UU-B, XVI SM245 UU-A, XVIII TP318 UU-Z, XIX PM637 UU-H, F.22 PK402 UU-H; Meteor T.7 WG943 UU-F, FR.9 WB137 UU-C; Vampire T.11 XE923 UU-T.
XL (8.46–8.49) Spitfire XVIII TP434 XL-V; Tempest II PR811 XL-L; Hornet F.1 PX281 XL-E; Meteor F.3 EE367 XL-B, F.4 RA442 XL-T; Oxford I HM759 XL-F.
Also used Tiger Moth II R4974; Martinet I NR303; Beaufighter X RD566; Mosquito III VA872, TT.35 TA711; Vampire FB.5 VV724.

Disbanded 31st August 1949 at Driffield to become 203 Advanced Flying School.

Reformed 1st September 1949 at Stradishall by redesignating 203 Advanced Flying School.

HX (9.49–4.51) Meteor F.4 RA374 HX-L, T.7 WA602 HX-W; Vampire FB.5 VZ126 HX-A.
UU (9.49–4.51) Spitfire XIX PM579 UU-D, F.22 PK402 UU-H; Meteor T.7 WG943 UU-F, FR.9 WB137 UU-C; Vampire T.11 XE923 UU-T.
KD (9.49–4.51) Meteor T.7 VW416.
KR (9.49–4.51) Meteor F.8 WH352 KR-E.
TO (9.49–4.51) Harvard IIB FX443 TO-J; Tiger Moth II T5465 TO-A.
Also used Oxford I HN410; Mosquito III HJ970, TT.35 RV365 7; Beaufighter X RD566; Tempest V NV923; Spitfire XVIII TP228.

Disbanded 3rd June 1955 at Stradishall.

Reformed 1st June 1963 at Middleton St George by merging the Lightning Conversion Squadron and the Fighter Command Instrument Rating Squadron. The Lightning element became known as 65 (Shadow) Squadron from 4th May 1971.

Javelin T.3 XM336 B; Lightning F.1 XM147 147, F.1A XM216 216, F.3 XP707 707, T.4 XM988 988, T.5 XS419 419.

Disbanded 30th September 1974 at Coltishall.

Reformed 1st October 1974 at Lossiemouth by redesignating the Jaguar Conversion Unit.

Jaguar GR.1 XX753 05, T.2 XX837 Z; Phantom FGR.2 XT892.

Disbanded 11th September 1991 at Lossiemouth to become 16 (Reserve) Squadron.

227 OPERATIONAL CONVERSION UNIT, later 227 (AIR OBSERVATION POST) CONVERSION UNIT
Formed 7th May 1947 at Andover by redesignating 43 Operational Training Unit. Redesignated 227 (Air Observation Post) Conversion Unit from 1st December 1947.

BD	Tiger Moth II W6419 BD-Z; Oxford I V3889 BD-A; Auster V TJ324 BD-R, VI VF621 BD-U.
PF	Auster V TW461 PF-D, VI TW523 PF-U, T.7 WE549 PF-G.
Also used	Auster A.2/45 VL522; Harvard IIB FX355.

Disbanded 1st May 1950 at Middle Wallop to become the Air Observation Post School.

228 OPERATIONAL CONVERSION UNIT

Formed 1st May 1947 at Leeming by merging 13 and 54 Operational Training Units.

ST (5.47–8.47)	Martinet I EM444 ST-I.
TO (5.47–8.47)	Martinet I JN647 TO-O.
Nil (8.47–11.61)	Master II AZ780; Oxford I HN205; Tiger Moth II T6562; Brigand B.1 RH761, T.4 RH758, T.5 RH757; Tempest V EJ669; Buckmaster I RP156 Y; Wellington XVIII ND120 D; Mosquito III LR571 X, VI TA504 O, NF.30 NT310, TT.35 TH977, NF.36 RL149 C; Balliol T.2 WN146 V; Valetta C.1 VX539 A, T.3 WJ462, T.4 WJ471 T; Prentice T.1 VR262; Vampire T.11 WZ467; Meteor F.4 RA474, T.7 WA609 S, NF.11 WD739 E, NF.12 WS592, NF.14 WS844 P; Anson XIX TX184; Chipmunk T.10 WP802; Javelin T.3 XH391 05.

Disbanded 15th September 1961 at Leeming.

Reformed 1st May 1965 at Leuchars.

Javelin T.3 XH435 D, FAW.5 XH692 K, FAW.7 XH837 T, FAW.9 XH883 K; Canberra T.4 WJ617, T.11 WJ610 T.

Disbanded 23rd December 1966 at Leuchars.

Reformed 1st August 1968 at Coningsby.

Nil ( )	Phantom FGR.2 XV486 X; Jet Provost T.4 XR656.
C ( )	Phantom FGR.2 XT897 CC.

Disbanded 1st July 1992 at Coningsby to become 56 (Reserve) Squadron.

229 OPERATIONAL CONVERSION UNIT

Formed 15th December 1950 at Leuchars by redesignating 'B' and 'D' Flights of 226 Operational Conversion Unit.

ES (12.50– .60)	Vampire FB.5 WE831 ES-P, T.11 WZ472 ES-30; Meteor T.7 WL345 ES-29, F.8 VZ467; Hunter F.1 WW634 ES-F, F.4 WV396 ES-68, T.7 XL579 ES-92.
RS (12.50– .60)	Tempest V EJ660 RS-30; Beaufighter X RD859 RS-W; Oxford I MP450 RS-U; Vampire FB.5 VV546 RS-K, T.11 WZ467 RS-25; Hunter F.1 WW644 RS-Y, F.4 WT801 RS-14, T.7 XL575 RS-81.
Nil (12.50–7.74)	Mosquito III VT588, TT.35 RS716 A; Martinet I NR465; Oxford II NM408; Anson T.21 WD415, T.22 VV362; Sabre F.2 XB531, F.4 XB801 Z; Hunter F.6 XF433 53, T.7 XL575 80, FGA.9 XG207 C, FR.10 WW594 11; Meteor TT.8 WH286 A; Chipmunk T.10 WP831 20; Jet Provost T.3A XM475 F.

Disbanded 2nd September 1974 at Brawdy to become the Tactical Weapons Unit.

Reformed 1st November 1984 at Coningsby. Designated 65 'Shadow' Squadron from 31st December 1986.

A	Tornado F.2(T) ZD904 AE, F.3 ZE158 AK.
Z	Tornado F.3 ZE199 ZE.

Disbanded 1st July 1992 at Coningsby to become 56 (Reserve) Squadron.

230 OPERATIONAL CONVERSION UNIT

Formed 15th March 1947 at Lindholme by redesignating 1653 Heavy Conversion Unit.

A3	Lancaster I TW667 A3-B; Mosquito XIX TA343 A3-H; Lincoln II RE338 A3-A.
YW	Mosquito XIX TA356 YW-J, B.35 TK648 YW-B.

SN	Lincoln II RE396 SN-A.
Also used	Lancaster III ME315; Mosquito NF.36 RK987; Tiger Moth BB790; Anson XIX VM326 O.

Disbanded 15th October 1952 at Scampton to become the Reserve Training Squadron.

Reformed 1st August 1953 at Upwood by redesignating the Lincoln Conversion Flight.

Lincoln B.2 RF360.

Disbanded 1st February 1955 at Upwood to become the Lincoln Conversion Flight.

Reformed 31st May 1956 at Waddington.

Vulcan B.1 XA895, B.2 XH556; Hastings T.5 TG517; Canberra T.4 WJ875.

Disbanded 31st August 1981 at Scampton.

231 OPERATIONAL CONVERSION UNIT

Formed 15th March 1947 at Coningsby by redesignating 16 Operational Training Unit.

Lancaster I R5855; Anson XII PH812, XIX TX188; Mosquito III HJ990 M, XVI PF488 T, B.35 VP179.

Disbanded 4th December 1949 at Coningsby.

Reformed 1st December 1951 at Bassingbourn by redesignating 237 Operational Conversion Unit.

Mosquito VI RS675 X, PR.34 PF669, PR.34A RG202; Anson T.22 WD426; Chipmunk T.10 WP839; Meteor T.7 WA697, PR.10 WB153; Canberra B.2 WJ677 X, PR.3 WE144, T.4 WE195 K.

Disbanded 15th December 1990 at Wyton to become the Canberra Standardisation and Training Flight.

Reformed 13th May 1991 at Wyton by redesignating the Canberra Standardisation and Training Flight.

B	Canberra B.2 WE113 BJ, B.2(T) WJ731 BK, T.4 WJ879 BH.

Disbanded 23rd April 1993 at Wyton.

232 OPERATIONAL CONVERSION UNIT

Formed 21st February 1955 at Gaydon.

Canberra T.4 WJ864; Valiant B.1 WZ362; Victor B.1 XH615, B.2 XL165.

Disbanded 30th June 1965 at Gaydon, the Victor element becoming the Tanker Training Flight.

Reformed 6th February 1970 at Marham by merging the Victor (B.2) Training Flight and the Victor Training Unit.

Victor B.1 XA923 A, B(PR).1 XA935, B.1A XH594, BK.2 XL232.

Disbanded 4th April 1986 at Marham.

233 OPERATIONAL CONVERSION UNIT

Formed 1st September 1952 at Pembrey.

Vampire FB.5 WA362 15, FB.9 WI518, T.11 WZ430; Balliol T.2 WN137; Meteor T.7 WA602, F.8 WE942; Oxford I PH146; Tiger Moth II DE840; Mosquito III HJ970, TT.35 RV365 6; Tempest V EJ598; Chipmunk T.10 WP920; Hunter F.1 WW604 F.

Disbanded 1st September 1957 at Pembrey.

Reformed 1st October 1970 at Wittering by redesignating the Harrier Conversion Unit

Harrier GR.1 XV747 29, GR.1A, T.2 XW266 51, T.2A, GR.3 XV759 E, T.4 XZ147 Z, T.4A ZB601 Z, GR.5 ZD324.

Disbanded 1st September 1992 at Wittering to become 20 (Reserve) Squadron, being the Harrier Operational Conversion Unit.

235 OPERATIONAL CONVERSION UNIT

Formed 31st July 1947 at Calshot by redesignating 4 Operational Training Unit.

TA (8.47–4.51)	Sunderland V VB888 TA-K; Seaford NJ205 TA-F.
D (4.51–10.53)	Sunderland V RN304 D-M.

Disbanded 17th October 1953 at Calshot to become the Flying Boat Training Squadron.

236 OPERATIONAL CONVERSION UNIT
Formed 31st July 1947 at Kinloss by redesignating 6 Operational Training Unit.

K7 (7.47–4.51)	Lancaster III SW338 K7-R; Oxford II N4737 K7-D; Beaufighter X RD709 K7-FG.
C (4.51–9.56)	Lancaster III SW286 C-L; Shackleton GR.1 VP292 C-S, MR.1A WB826 C-P; Neptune MR.1 WX495 C-K.
Also used	Oxford I NJ397; Martinet I NR434; Tiger Moth II NL883; Spitfire XVI SL720 V; Vampire FB.5 VZ313 T; Anson XI PH724 R, XIX TX167 U; Mosquito TT.35 RS709; Brigand T.5 VS813; Buckmaster T.1 VA360.

Disbanded 30th September 1956 at Kinloss and merged with 1 Marine Reconnaissance School to become the Maritime Operational Training Unit.

Reformed 1st July 1970 at St Mawgan by redesignating the Maritime Operational Training Unit.

Nimrod MR.1 XV231, MR.2, MR.2P (drawn from 42 Squadron).

Disbanded 30th September 1992 at Kinloss to become 42 (Reserve) Squadron, the Nimrod Operational Conversion Unit.

237 OPERATIONAL CONVERSION UNIT
Formed 31st July 1947 at Benson by redesignating 8 Operational Training Unit.

LP	Oxford I EB813 LP-73; Mosquito III HJ973 LP-73, PR.34 RG189 LP-99, PR.34A RG181; Spitfire XVI RW395, XIX PM621 LP-84; Harvard IIB FX206; Meteor T.7 WA660 LP-66, PR.10 VZ620.

Disbanded 1st December 1951 at Bassingbourn to become 231 Operational Conversion Unit.

Reformed 23rd October 1956 at Wyton by redesignating 'C' Squadron of 231 Operational Conversion Unit.

Canberra PR.3 WE137, T.4 WE194.

Disbanded 21st January 1958 at Wyton and absorbed by 231 Operational Conversion Unit.

Reformed 1st March 1971 at Honington.

C	Hunter F.6 XG152, T.7 XL591 CV, T.7A WV318, T.7B XL614 CY, T.8C XF967 CX; Buccaneer S.2A XV154 CA, S.2B XX893 CD.

Disbanded 1st October 1991 at Lossiemouth.

238 OPERATIONAL CONVERSION UNIT
Formed 15th June 1952 at Colerne by redesignating the Airborne Interception School.

Buckmaster T.1 RP156; Brigand T.4 VS837 N, T.5 RH832 F; Mosquito TT.35 TJ121; Balliol T.2 WN170 M; Meteor NF.12 WS625 F, NF.14 WS731 Q; Valetta C.1 VX542, T.3 WJ480 D.

Disbanded 13th March 1958 at North Luffenham.

240 OPERATIONAL CONVERSION UNIT
Formed 5th January 1948 at North Luffenham by merging 1333 Transport Support Training Unit and 1382 (Transport) Conversion Units.

NU	Anson I LT602 NU-D, X NK531 NU-L, XII PH756, XIX PH845; Dakota IV KN268 NU-Y; Hastings MET.1 TG565; Valetta C.1 VW142 NU-Z; Devon C.1 VP974 NU-A.

Disbanded 16th April 1951 at North Luffenham and merged with 241 Operational Conversion Unit to become 242 Operational Conversion Unit.

Reformed 29th December 1971 at Odiham by redesignating the Air Training Squadron.

B ( )	Wessex HC.2 XT674 BU.
C ( )	Puma HC.1 XW200 CX.
F ( )	Puma HC.1 XW212 FD; Chinook HC.1 ZD575 FF.

Disbanded 1st October 1993 at Odiham to become 27 (Reserve) Squadron.

241 OPERATIONAL CONVERSION UNIT
Formed 5th January 1948 at Dishforth by redesignating 1332 Heavy Transport Conversion Unit.

YY (1.48–. 50)	York C.1 MW290 YY-Q.
Nil (1.48–4.51)	Halifax IX RT767; Hastings C.1 TG582 S; Valetta C.1 VW825; Tiger Moth II T7808; Anson XI NL133, XII PH723; Tiger Moth II DF191.

Disbanded 16th April 1951 at Dishforth and merged with 240 Operational Conversion Unit to become 242 Operational Conversion Unit.

Reformed 1st July 1970 at Brize Norton.

Britannia C.1, C.2; Andover; Belfast; VC.10 C.1 XV102; TriStar C.1 ZD953; BAe 146 ZD695.

Disbanded 1st October 1993 at Marham to become 55 (Reserve) Squadron.

242 OPERATIONAL CONVERSION UNIT
Formed 16th April 1951 at Dishforth by merging 240 and 241 Operational Conversion Units.

NU (4.51)	Valetta C.1 VW859 NU-O.
Nil (4.51–7.92)	Valetta C.1 VW820; Hastings C.1 TG570, MET.1 TG572, C.1A TG610 L; Beverley C.1 XL149 X; Argosy C.1 XN818 H; Andover C.1 XS599; Hercules C.1 XV176; C.1K, C.1P, C.3.
Also used	Tiger Moth II T7808; Anson XII PH723; Chipmunk T.10 WB560.

Disbanded 1st July 1992 at Lyneham to become 57 (Reserve) Squadron, the Hercules Operational Conversion Unit.

OPERATIONAL RESERVE FLIGHT – see 81 Squadron

1 (COASTAL) OPERATIONAL TRAINING UNIT
Formed 1st April 1940 at Silloth by redesignating the Coastal Command Landplane Pilots Pool.

Tutor K3319; Anson I K6241; Shark II L2386; Swordfish I L2823; Roc I L3132; Beaufort I L4498; Battle L5633; Botha I L6123; Wellington I L4342, IA N2909, IC L7899, VIII Z8708; Whitley V P5049; Hudson I N7274 A26, II T9384, V AM608 B77, VI FK510; Blenheim I K7091, IV N3596; Lysander III T1470, IIIA W6953; Oxford I V3472; Spitfire I P9395; Halifax II R9486; Magister T9756; Fortress I AN519, IIA FK199; Liberator III FK219, V FL981; Martinet I JN503.

Disbanded 19th October 1943 at Thornaby.

1 OPERATIONAL TRAINING UNIT (INDIA)
Formed 1st June 1942 at Risalpur, India.

Harvard II AJ786; Mohawk IV LA157.

Disbanded 28th July 1942 at Risalpur to become 151 Operational Training Unit.

2 (COASTAL) OPERATIONAL TRAINING UNIT
Formed 1st October 1940 at Catfoss.

Nil (10.40–2.44)	Anson I N4890 A; Battle L5680; Blenheim I L6609 C2, IV Z6087 11, V AZ870; Beaufort I X8936, II JM575 Z3; Oxford I T1188, II T1048 S; Tiger Moth II T7024; Moth Minor BK831; Lysander III R9058, IIIA W6953; Hampden I AE125; Beaufighter IC T3270 M2, VI JL548 Y3; Master II DL469; Martinet I HP248 T5.
ZR ( )	Blenheim IV Z5723 ZR-Q6

Disbanded 15th February 1944 at Catfoss.

3 (COASTAL) OPERATIONAL TRAINING UNIT
Formed 27th November 1940 at Chivenor.

Blenheim I L1299, IV N6205; Lysander I L4687, III R9002, III

R9017, IIIA V9903; Anson I DG879; Battle L5771; Oxford II N4835; Whitley V P5049, VII Z9123; Beaufort I X8932 L2; Tiger Moth II T7731; Magister L8052; Hampden I AE368; Beaufighter I R2198; Wellington I L4219, IA N2871, IC DV925, III X3278, VIII HX388, X HF470, XI HZ409; XII MP511, XIII HZ639, XIV MP710; Martinet I MS580.

Disbanded 4th January 1944 at Haverfordwest and absorbed by 6 Operational Training Unit.

4 (COASTAL) OPERATIONAL TRAINING UNIT
Formed 16th March 1941 at Stranraer by redesignating the Flying Boat Training Squadron.

TA (3.41–)	Stranraer I K7300 TA-Y; London I K6932, II L7043 TA-K; Singapore III K8565; Lerwick I L7250 IA-U; Lysander IIIA V9858 TA-B; Catalina I AH568 TA-H; Sunderland I P9606 TA-E, II W3980 TA-S, III W4027 TA-M.
Nil ( )	Sunderland I T9049 A, III DD838 DD; Catalina I Z2147, IB FP195 N, II AM264, IIA VA728; IIIA FP526, IVA JX218; Martinet I MS866 AE.
TA (–7.47)	Sunderland V SZ568 TA-C.
QZ	Allocated but no evidence of use.
Also used	Tiger Moth II N9207; Lysander III R9002; Oxford I T1010; Hurricane IIC BE371; Spitfire XVI SL724.

Disbanded 31st July 1947 at Pembroke Dock to become 235 Operational Conversion Unit.

5 OPERATIONAL TRAINING UNIT
Formed 6th March 1940 at Aston Down by redesignating 12 Group Pool.

Gladiator I K7951; Blenheim I L1121; Defiant K8620, I L7032; Spitfire I L1015; Battle L5133; Magister L8052; Hurricane I P2548, X P5187; Tutor K3435; Master I N7479; Harvard I P5864.

Disbanded 1st November 1940 at Aston Down to become 55 Operational Training Unit.

Reformed 1st August 1941 at Chivenor.

Anson I N9606; Battle V1202; Blenheim IV R2798; Lysander II

P1680 Z, TT.IIIA V9902; Hampden I L4076; Hereford I L6049; Hudson I T9288 P, V AM522 T; Mentor L4406; Moth Minor X5122; Tiger Moth II N9213; Beaufort I DX156 40, II AW281 62; Oxford I PH526, II N4732; Ventura I AE686, II AJ181 B, V FP630 H; Beaufighter VI JL835; Warwick I BV511 J; Hurricane I L2100, IIC BE371; Martinet I HN945 Q; Wellington XIII MF576.

Disbanded 1st August 1945 at Turnberry.

6 OPERATIONAL TRAINING UNIT
Formed 10th March 1940 at Sutton Bridge by redesignating 11 Group Pool.

Hurricane I N2329; Gladiator I K8015; Mentor L4400; Master I N8011; Harvard I N7175; Battle L5707; Battle Trainer R7378.

Disbanded 1st November 1940 at Sutton Bridge to become 56 Operational Training Unit.

Reformed 1st June 1941 at Andover by redesignating 2 School of Army Co-operation.

Blenheim I K7171.

Disbanded 18th July 1941 at Andover to become 42 Operational Training Unit.

Reformed 19th July 1941 at Thornaby.

OD (7.41–10.42)	Hudson I N7336 OD-N, II T9372, III V9029 OD-J, V AM523.
Nil (10.42–7.45)	Lysander III R9058, IIIA V9847; Oxford I NM697, II N4737; Tutor K3319; Tiger Moth II T7605; Wellington IC DV801, III X3881 37, VIII Z8707 32, X HE784 46, XI HZ208 59, XII MP587 15, XIII JA638 26, XIV NB861 BS; Warwick I HF938, V PN705 W; Martinet I JN501453.
K7 (7.45–7.47)	Oxford I N4737 K7-DC; Hurricane IIC PZ775; Mosquito III TV956 K7-MC, VI RF908 K7-MB; Beaufighter X RD864 K7-FD; Spitfire XVI TE246 K7-SA; Wellington X NA903 K7-AZ; Warwick I HG115 K7-AH, II HG402; Lancaster III PB179 K7-LG; Buckmaster I RP149.
8V	Allocated but no evidence of use.

Sunderland V, SZ568 of No 4 Operational Training Unit. The aircraft survived until struck off charge on 19 October 1956.

Disbanded 31st July 1947 at Kinloss to become 236 Operational Conversion Unit.

7 OPERATIONAL TRAINING UNIT
Formed 15th June 1940 at Hawarden.

Spitfire I K9967; Master I N7831; Battle L5705; Hurricane I N2478.

Disbanded 1st November 1940 at Hawarden to become 57 Operational Training Unit.

Reformed 1st April 1942 at Limavady.

Wellington IA N3009, IC N2750, VIII HX401 35, XI HZ190, XIII HZ649; XIV MP750; Anson I L7904; Lysander III R9125, IIIA V9742; Magister T9762; Tiger Moth II T6318; Martinet I HN871.

Disbanded 16th May 1944 at Haverfordwest to become 4 Refresher Flying Unit.

8 OPERATIONAL TRAINING UNIT
Formed 18th May 1942 at Fraserburgh by merging the Photographic Reconnaissance Conversion Flight of 3 School of General Reconnaissance, Squires Gate and 'K' (Photographic Reconnaissance Advanced Training) Flight of 1 Photographic Reconnaissance Unit, Detling.

Nil (5.42–7.47)	*Gladiator I K8041; Spitfire I X4498, PR.I X4944, PR.IG X4162, PR.III X4383, PR.IV R7030, VB EP636, PR.VI P9310, VII MD142 U, PR.VII AR261, PR.X SR399, PR.XI MB906; Maryland PR.I AR740; Mosquito PR.I W4059 90, II DD659, III HJ890, IV DK319 86, VI HP906 96, PR.VIII DZ404 73, IX LR423, PR.XVI NS803, PR.34 RG115 12; Hurricane IIC PZ863 F; Moth Minor HM544; Master II DM375 X, III W8956; Tiger Moth II DE212; Battle K9272; Lysander III R9002; Anson I N5282; Oxford II AS705; D.H.89A W6455; Beaufighter II R2384; Martinet I HP250 103; Harvard IIB FX206.*
BE (.46–7.47)	*Spitfire XVI RW395 BE-80, XIX PS908 BE-82.*

Disbanded 31st July 1947 at Benson to become 237 Operational Conversion Unit.

9 OPERATIONAL TRAINING UNIT
Formed 7th June 1942 at Aldergrove.

Beaufort I N1014, II JM574; Beaufighter IC T4655 4S, VI EL357 4L, X JM220, XI JM117 4T; Martinet I HN863 3C; Tiger Moth II L6921; Magister N3957; Oxford I NM748, II P8919; Lysander III V9906.

Disbanded 11th August 1944 at Crosby-on-Eden and absorbed by 109 Operational Training Unit.

10 OPERATIONAL TRAINING UNIT
Formed 8th April 1940 at Abingdon by redesignating 4 Group Pool.

UY (4.40–9.46)	*Whitley V LA817 UY-S; Anson I AX297 UY-J; Tomahawk IIA AH882; Martinet I JN283 UY-X; Oxford I NM787 UY-U; Wellington X LP438 UY-R; Spitfire XVI TB344 UY-U.*
ZG (4.40–9.46)	*Whitley III K9013 ZG-X, V Z6952 ZG-R; Wellington X HE580 ZG-V.*
JL (8.42–)	*Whitley V BD282 JL-L, VII Z9368 JL-S.*
RK (.42–9.46)	*Whitley V T4175 RK-H, VII BD432 RK-M; Wellington X NC601 RK-L.*
EL	*Possibly allocated from 1945.*
Also used	*Whitley IV K9047; Leopard Moth X9380; Whitney Straight DJ714; Tiger Moth BB704, II N6485; Moth Minor W6458; Hornet Moth X9445; Taylorcraft Plus C ES959; Magister L5958; Lysander I R2630, III T1684, IIIA V9542; Defiant I AA327; Master II DK894; Proctor I P6230, III LZ564; Hurricane IIC PG493.*

Disbanded 10th September 1946 at Abingdon.

11 OPERATIONAL TRAINING UNIT
Formed 8th April 1940 at Bassingbourn by redesignating 215 Squadron.

KJ (4.40–9.45)	*Wellington I L4381 KJ-A, IC Z8808 KJ-E, X LP430 KJ-H; Master II AZ382 KJ-E; Defiant I*

L7011 KJ-A; Oxford I NM791 KJ-J; Martinet I JN587 KJ-B; Hurricane IIC LF757 KJ-L.

OP (4.40–9.45)	*Wellington I L4224 OP-R, IC N2750 OP-J, X JA129 OP-F.*
TX (4.40–9.45)	*Anson I N5173 TX-F; Wellington IC R1661 TX-E, Wellington X LP766 TX-A.*
KH (.43–9.45)	*Hurricane IIC PG450 KH-X.*
Also used	*Wellington IA P2528, III Z1598; Oxford II T1401; Lysander III R9025; Beaufighter II R2272; Tutor K3277; Tiger Moth II T6311; Magister L8081.*

Disbanded 18th September 1945 at Westcott.

12 OPERATIONAL TRAINING UNIT
Formed 8th April 1940 at Benson by redesignating 1 Group Pool.

Nil (4.40–12.40)	*Battle K9214; Battle Trainer P6755; Anson I EG600 F.*
FQ (12.40–6.45)	*Wellington III Z1732 FQ-S, X NC681 FQ-W.*
JP (12.40–6.45)	*Wellington III X3338 JP-P, X LN550 JP-O.*
ML (–6.45)	*Wellington III BK136 ML-R.*
Also used	*Tutor K6120; Magister L5973; Wellington IA N2938 F1, IC N2755; Lysander III; Blenheim IV Z5806; Master II DK980; Defiant I AA322; Tiger Moth II T7909; Spitfire I X4834; Proctor I P6180; Hudson I N7263; Martinet I JN291 O; Hurricane IIC PG430.*

Disbanded 22nd June 1945 at Chipping Norton.

13 OPERATIONAL TRAINING UNIT
Formed 6th April 1940 at Bicester by redesignating 2 Group Pool.

FV (4.40–5.47)	*Blenheim IV R3607 FV-E; Mitchell II FW114 FV-D; Mosquito II DD625 FV-R, VI TA538 FV-K; Tempest II MW750 FV-A.*
KQ (.42–5.47)	*Blenheim IV V6083 KQ-S; Mitchell II FW119 KQ-A; Mosquito III HJ973 KQ-A.*
OY (.44–5.47)	*Mosquito VI HJ741 OY-G.*
SL (.43–5.47)	*Anson I AX498 SL-N; Tempest II MW759 SL-X; Mosquito VI TA476 SL-A.*
UR (.43– .44)	*Mitchell III KJ602 UR-U.*
AT (4.45–)	*Inherited from 60 OTU but no evidence of use.*
XD (.43– .44)	*Boston IIIA BZ346 XD-P.*
XJ (4.40–5.47)	*Blenheim I L1269 XJ-R, IV V5810 XJ-K; Boston IIIA BZ397 XJ-O; Mosquito VI HJ776 XJ-M.*
Also used	*Blenheim V AZ884; Anson I K6165; Master II DM201; Oxford II V3819; Tutor K4811; Defiant I T4055; Albemarle GT.I P1460; Battle L4951; Lysander IIIA V9901; Spitfire IIA P8139, VB AB786; Hurricane IIA Z2321; Boston II (Turbinlite) AH447, III (Turbinlite) Z2185, IV BZ430; Ventura I AE705, II AJ231; Mosquito IV DK288, B.35 RS712; D.H.89A Z7260; Martinet I JN417; Dakota III KG489; Cadet TX.1 RA879; Tiger Moth II N9494; Dominie I NF851; Proctor III HM294; Wellington XIII HZ757.*

Disbanded 1st May 1947 at Middleton St George and merged with 54 Operational Training Unit to become 228 Operational Conversion Unit.

14 OPERATIONAL TRAINING UNIT
Formed 8th April 1940 at Cottesmore by redesignating 185 Squadron.

GL (4.40–)	*Hampden I P1316 GL-P; Hereford I L6070 GL-A2; Wellington IC AD594 GL-U.*
AM (4.40–6.45)	*Hampden I P1276 AM-M1; Wellington IC Z8963 AM-G, X LP598 AM-S; Hurricane IIC MW341 AM-A; Martinet I HP522 AM-B.*
VB (4.40–6.45)	*Wellington IC L7850 VB-Y; Anson I R9607 VB-02.*
Also used	*Wellington I L4219, IA N2981, II W5352, III DF625; Lysander III T1504, IIIA V9845; Oxford I AS903 K2, II BM835; Tomahawk IIA AH929, IIB AK136; Master II AZ657, III DL840; Harvard I P5818; Tiger Moth II T5983; Horsa I DP603.*

Disbanded 24th June 1945 at Market Harborough.

15 OPERATIONAL TRAINING UNIT
Formed 8th April 1940 at Harwell by redesignating 3 Group Pool.

EO (4.40– .43)	Wellington IC X9683 EO-F.
FH (4.40–3.44)	Wellington IC L7853 FH-W; Martinet I JN297 FH-Y.
KK (4.40–3.44)	Wellington IC T2745 KK-L.
Also used	Defiant I N1538; Wellington I L4215, IA N2869, II Z8330, III BJ582, VIII Z8712, X LN694; Bombay I L5854; Fokker F.XXII HM160; Anson I K6170; Magister L6905; Tiger Moth II T6312; Lysander IIIA V9286; Blenheim I L1130.

Disbanded 15th March 1944 at Harwell.

16 OPERATIONAL TRAINING UNIT
Formed 8th April 1940 at Upper Heyford by redesignating 5 Group Pool.

GA (.40–12.44)	Anson I N9668 GA-S; Oxford I AS146 GA-V; Lysander III T1435 GA-Y.
JS (4.40–12.44)	Hampden I P1174 JS-G; Wellington IC T2701 JS-B, III DF623 JS-T, X HE431 JS-P.
XG (4.40–12.44)	Hampden I X2980 XG-A; Wellington IC DV509 XG-12.
Also used	Hereford I L6055; Wellington I L4263, IA N2877; Defiant I AA325; Tiger Moth II N6467; Martinet I JN508; Hurricane I Z4051, IIC PG538; Magister L5944.

Disbanded 31st December 1944 at Upper Heyford.

Reformed 1st January 1945 at Upper Heyford by redesignating 1655 Mosquito Training Unit.

GA (1.45–4.47)	Mosquito III HJ976 GA-G, XVI PF488 GA-T, B.20 KB355, B.25 KB501 GA-C; Anson I R3462 GA-N; Oxford I V3995 GA-T, II AP480.
JS (1.45–4.47)	Mosquito IV DZ615 JS-K, XVI PF512 JS-E.

Disbanded 15th March 1947 at Cottesmore to become 231 Operational Conversion Unit.

17 OPERATIONAL TRAINING UNIT
Formed 8th April 1940 at Upwood by merging 35 and 90 Squadrons.

AY (4.40–11.46)	Lysander III R9075 AY; Anson I AW911 AY-F; Hurricane IIC PG442 AY-W; Spitfire IX TB674 AY-A; Wellington X LP847 AY-G; Martinet I JN422 AY-N; Tempest V JN867 AY-E.
JG (4.40–11.46)	Wellington X PF965 JG-L.
WJ (4.40–11.46)	Anson I AW909 WJ-Z; Wellington III BK212 WJ-X, X NC449 WJ-T.
Also used	Battle K9290; Wellington I L4255, XIII NC503; Blenheim IV L4844, V BA305; Oxford I NM510 P1; Master II DL304; Defiant I V1128; Magister L5951; Tiger Moth W7956.

Disbanded 28th February 1947 at Swinderby to become 201 Crew Training Unit.

18 (POLISH) OPERATIONAL TRAINING UNIT
Formed 15th June 1940 at Hucknall by redesignating the Polish Training Unit.

XW (6.40–)	Anson I N5029 XW-B; Martinet I HP526 XW-U.
VQ ( )	Lysander III T1586 VQ-Z.
Also used	Battle P2312; Wellington I L4270, IA P9221, IC X3217, III BK207 Y, IV Z1334; X MF652 J; Master II EM270; Defiant I V1112; Lysander IIIA V9900; Oxford II P6798; Martinet I HP526; Hurricane IIC PG492; Hornet Moth W5748; Magister L5996; Tiger Moth II T6313.

Disbanded 30th January 1945 at Finningley and absorbed by 10 Operational Training Unit.

19 OPERATIONAL TRAINING UNIT
Formed 27th May 1940 at Kinloss.

UO (5.40–6.45)	('A' and 'B' Flights) Whitley V P4938 UO-CA; Wellington X NC740 UO-D.
ZV (5.40– .43)	('C' and 'D' Flights) Whitley IV K9049 ZV-T, V N1419 NV-M.
XF (5.40–6.45)	('F' Flight) Whitley IV K9019 XF-K; Defiant I N1652 XF; Lysander III P9123 XF-Y; Anson I AX500 XF-K.
Also used	Magister T9814; Whitley VII Z9378; Master II DM286; Hurricane IIC PG449; Martinet I HP469.

Disbanded 26th June 1945 at Kinloss.

20 OPERATIONAL TRAINING UNIT
Formed 27th May 1940 at Lossiemouth by redesignating an element of 15 Operational Training Unit.

JM (5.40–7.45)	Wellington IC L7867 JM-J, X HE488 JM-S.
XL (5.40–7.45)	Wellington IC Z8977 XL-C, III HE490 XL-A.
YR (5.40–7.45)	Wellington IC R1089 YR-B; Hurricane IIC LF763 YR-M; Martinet I MS873 YR-L.
ZT (.40– .43)	Wellington IC R3232 ZT-H.
MK (7.44–3.45)	Anson I LT959 MK-F.
AI (–3.45)	Wellington X NA933 AI-A.
Also used	Wellington I L4270, IA N2873; Hurricane I P2859; Defiant I T3930; Lysander III R9115; Tiger Moth II T7294; Magister T9757; Master II DL351.

Disbanded 17th July 1945 at Lossiemouth.

21 OPERATIONAL TRAINING UNIT
Formed 21st January 1941 at Moreton-in-Marsh by redesignating an element of 15 Operational Training Unit.

ED (1.41–3.47)	Wellington IC R1090 ED-K, X LP716 ED-K.
SJ (1.41– .43)	Wellington IC, X LN618 SJ-N.
UH (1.41–3.47)	Oxford I PH177 UH-J; Martinet I JN301 UH-X; Hurricane IIC LF763 UH-S; Spitfire XVI TE347 UH-G; Wellington X LP156 UH-Z.
Also used	Wellington I L4338, II Z8439, III DF735; Lysander III R9018, IIIA V9800; Defiant I V1118; Master II AZ499; Magister L5957; Anson I DG718; Tempest V SN187.

Disbanded 28th February 1947 at Finningley to become 202 Crew Training Unit.

22 OPERATIONAL TRAINING UNIT
Formed 14th April 1941 at Wellesbourne Mountford.

DD (4.41–7.45)	Wellington IC T2714 DD-C, X LN546 DD-S.
LT (4.41–7.45)	Wellington III DF578 LT-C; Martinet I HP447 LT-R.
XN (.41–7.45)	Wellington III DF549 XN-R, X; Anson I AX256 XN-N.
OX (.43–)	Wellington III.
Also used	Wellington I L4247, IA P9228, XIV MP718; Master II DM401, III DL829; Defiant I AA295; Lysander III T1670; Hurricane IIC PG517; Moth Minor AW113; Oxford I NM790.

Disbanded 24th July 1945 at Wellesbourne Mountford.

23 OPERATIONAL TRAINING UNIT
Formed 1st April 1941 at Pershore.

BY (4.41–4.43)	Wellington III X3366 BY-Q.
FZ (4.41–3.44)	Wellington III BJ818 FZ.
WE (4.43–3.44)	Wellington III Z1736 WE-S.
Also used	Wellington I L4254, IC AD592 F; Lysander I L4698, III R9030, IIIA V9846; Defiant I AA317; Anson I AX500; Tomahawk I AH797; Martinet I HN950; Tiger Moth BD151, II DE253; Hornet Moth X9326.

Disbanded 7th March 1944 at Pershore and absorbed by 22 Operational Training Unit.

24 OPERATIONAL TRAINING UNIT
Formed 15th March 1942 at Honeybourne.

FB (3.42–7.45)	('A' Flight) Whitley V AD674 FB-D; Wellington X LN225 FB-Y; Hurricane IID LF751 FB-B.
TY (3.42–7.45)	('B' Flight) Whitley V AD697 TY-J; Wellington III X3939 TY-L, X LN161 TY-F; Anson I DG718 TY-E.
UF (.44–7.45)	(Fighter Affiliation Flight) Wellington X NC651

UF-H; Hurricane IIC PG548 UF-X; Martinet I
JN297 UF-C.

Also used Battle K9384; Whitley III K8959, VII Z9124;
Lysander II R2010, III R9109; Oxford II T1073;
Defiant I N3315; Master II AZ667; Tomahawk
IIA AH939; Lancaster I NG435; Tiger Moth II
N9322.

Disbanded 24th July 1945 at Honeybourne.

25 OPERATIONAL TRAINING UNIT
Formed 1st March 1941 at Finningley.

PP (3.41–2.43) Courier X9342 PP-R; Wellington IC T2715
PP-E.
ZP (.42–2.43) Wellington III BK179 ZP-Y; Anson I W1904
ZP-B.
Also used Wellington I L4263, IA N3013, II W5352 J2;
Manchester I L7276; Defiant I N3395;
Hampden I AE221; Hereford I L6073; Lysander
IIIA V9899; Tiger Moth II R5192; Proctor I
R7496.

Disbanded 1st February 1943 at Finningley.

26 OPERATIONAL TRAINING UNIT
Formed 15th January 1942 at Wing.

EU (1.42– .44) Wellington IC DV885 EU-A; Martinet I HP436
EU-W.
PB (12.41–3.46) Wellington III X3224 PB-K, X LP282 PB-D.
WG (1.42–3.46) Wellington III BK130 WG-H, X PG324 WG-D.
Also used Wellington I L4324, IA N2877, IC L7888, II
W5352; Anson I N5152 A; Oxford I LX540, II
X7237; Master II DL463; Defiant I N3509, III
AA282; Lysander III T1424, IIIA V9718;
Tomahawk I AH855, IIA AH895, IIB AK166;
Tiger Moth II T6906; Proctor III LZ587; Hawk
Trainer III NF750; Warwick II HG349; Spitfire
XVI TE396.

Disbanded 4th March 1946 at Wing.

27 OPERATIONAL TRAINING UNIT
Formed 23rd April 1941 at Lichfield.

BB (4.41–6.45) Wellington III BJ605 BB-P, X NA909 BB-H.
EN (4.41–6.45) Wellington III BJ672 EN-R.
UJ (–6.45) Wellington X JA342 UJ-P.
YL (.43–6.45) Oxford I NM800 YL-S; Martinet I JN295 YL-P.
Also used Wellington I L4218, IA N2985, IC X9610 C;
Anson I R9648; Lysander III T1650; Master II
DM427; Defiant I N3395; Albemarle I P1461;
Ventura IIC MW337; Hurricane IIC MW337;
Proctor I P6231; Moth Minor BK838; Magister
T9911; Oxford II ED121; Tiger Moth II EM972;
Mosquito VI NT178.

Disbanded 22nd June 1945 at Lichfield.

28 OPERATIONAL TRAINING UNIT
Formed 16th May 1942 at Wymeswold.

LB (5.42–10.44) Wellington IC DV864 LB-X, III BK153 LB-B, X
MF637 LB-B.
QN (5.42–10.44) Wellington X LP613 QN-O; Spitfire IX TB275
QN-F.
WY (5.42–10.44) Wellington X LN952 WY-C; Master II DM427
WY-Z.
Also used Anson I DG830; Defiant I N1685; Oxford II
X7290; Lysander III R9123, IIIA V9861; Moth
Minor AW151; Hurricane IIC LF313; Martinet I
HP439.

Disbanded 15th October 1944 at Wymeswold.

29 OPERATIONAL TRAINING UNIT
Formed 21st April 1942 at North Luffenham.

NT (4.42–5.45) Wellington III X3812 NT-K, X LP434 NT-B.
TF (12.42–5.45) Wellington X LP647 TF-Y.
Also used Wellington IA N2938, IC L7854; Martinet I
MS871; Whitley V T4210; Master II EM328;
Defiant I N1768; Hurricane IIC BW973;

Tomahawk I AH864; Lysander IIIA V9800;
Tiger Moth II T6307; Spitfire VB EP244.

Disbanded 27th May 1945 at Bruntingthorpe.

30 OPERATIONAL TRAINING UNIT
Formed 28th June 1942 at Hixon.

BT (6.42–6.45) Wellington III BK347 BT-Z, X MF503 BT-N.
KD (6.42–6.45) Wellington III BK297 KD-K, X LN180 KD-X;
Moth Minor W7975 KD-Z.
TN (12.42–6.45) Wellington X LN171 TN-U.
Also used Wellington IC N2779, VIII HX684; Lysander II
N1308, III R9105; Battle L5186; Defiant I
V1133; Master II DK888; Tomahawk I AH783,
IIA AH925; Hurricane IIC LF170; Oxford I
NM807.

Disbanded 12th June 1945 at Gamston.

31 OPERATIONAL TRAINING UNIT
Formed 23rd May 1941 at Debert, Canada.

LR (5.42–10.42) Anson I AX640; Goblin; Lysander IIA 2397;
Hudson V AM887; Bolingbroke 9170.
Nil (10.42–7.44) Hudson V AM748; Bolingbroke; Oxford V;
Mosquito III HJ998, B.20 KB275, B.25.

Disbanded 1st July 1944 at Debert to become 7 Operational
Training Unit, RCAF.

32 OPERATIONAL TRAINING UNIT
Formed 20th July 1941 at West Kirby and dispatched to Canada.
Became operational 10th December 1941 at Patricia Bay, Canada.

DK (9.41–10.42) Beaufort I N1005 DK-R; Hampden.
OP (9.41–10.44) Beaufort I N1021 OP-D; Hampden.
RO (9.41–10.44)
Nil (10.42–5.44) Anson V 6990; Lysander IIIA 2410; Oxford II
AS922; Dakota III FL618 DM; Expeditor I
HB100.

Disbanded 1st June 1944 at Comox, Canada, to become 6
Operational Training Unit, RCAF.

34 OPERATIONAL TRAINING UNIT
Formed 17th April 1942 at Yarmouth, Canada. Became operational
1st June 1942 at Pennfield Ridge, Canada.

FY (6.42–10.42) Shark III 545 FY-C; Anson I, II.
Nil (10.42–5.44) Anson I 6496, II 7082; Lysander IIIA 2403;
Ventura I FN967, II; Hudson III BW644.

Disbanded 19th May 1944 at Pennfield Ridge.

35 OPERATIONAL TRAINING UNIT
Nameplate set to one side for a proposed bomber training unit in
Canada.

36 OPERATIONAL TRAINING UNIT
Formed 11th May 1942 at Greenwood, Canada.

EF (5.42–10.42) Anson I AX612; Lysander IIIA 2395;
Bolingbroke 10096; Hudson III BW450.
Nil (10.42–7.44) Bolingbroke IV 10096; Hudson III BW770;
Mosquito III, B.20 KB336, B.25; Harvard IIB
FE622; Oxford II EB508;

Disbanded 1st July 1944 at Greenwood to become 8 Operational
Training Unit, RCAF

38 OPERATIONAL TRAINING UNIT
Nameplate set to one side for a proposed bomber training unit in
Canada.

41 OPERATIONAL TRAINING UNIT
Formed 20th September 1941 at Old Sarum by redesignating the
Training Squadron of 1 School of Army Co-operation.

Nil (9.41–6.45) Tomahawk I AH771, IIA AH972, IIB AK190;
Master I N7486, III DL828; Tutor K6114; Hector
K9707; Harvard I N7015; Lysander II P1691, III
R9029, IIIA V9284; Gladiator II N5636;
Magister T9704; Proctor I P6189, II Z7221, III

DX227; Dominie I X7410; Mustang I AP201, IA
FD505; Oxford II N4828; Hurricane I AG199,
IIC LF289, IV KZ662, X P5209; Spitfire VB
BM636; Harvard IIB KF201; Martinet I HP241;
Dragon Rapide X9387.

6R   Allocated but no evidence of use.

Disbanded 26th April 1945 at Chilbolton.

42 OPERATIONAL TRAINING UNIT
Formed 18th July 1941 at Andover by redesignating 6 Operational
Training Unit.

Tutor K4804; Harrow I K6964; Anson I EG423 U; Whitley V T4339;
Piper Cub Coupe BV990; Blenheim I K7124, IV N6143, V AZ876;
Oxford I T1021; Proctor I P6170; Hurricane 1 V7338; Spitfire I
K9940, VB W3207; Lysander II N1250, III R9107, IIIA V9848;
Magister N5433; Albemarle I/I P1378 W, I/III P1502, II/I V1644 V;
Horsa I DP557; Martinet I HN959.

Disbanded 20th March 1945 at Ashbourne.

43 OPERATIONAL TRAINING UNIT
Formed 1st October 1942 at Larkhill by redesignating 1424 (Air
Observation Post) Flight.

Nil (10.42– .43)	Stinson 105 X5324; Tiger Moth II N9451; Lysander III R9011.
BD (.43–5.47)	Auster III TJ373 BD-C; Reliant I FK913 BD-S.
PF (.44–5.47)	Auster IV MT162 PF-J, VI TW575 PF-B.
Also used	Taylorcraft Plus C HH986, Taylorcraft Plus D W5740; Vigilant I HL429, IA BZ103; Piper Cub Coupe BT440; Tiger Moth I K4256; Oxford I V3146; Beaufort I L9887; Hoverfly I KK995 E; Auster I LB330; Proctor III LZ634.

Disbanded 7th May 1947 at Andover to become 227 Operational
Conversion Unit.

51 OPERATIONAL TRAINING UNIT
Formed 26th July 1941 at Debden.

PF (7.41– .42)	Blenheim IV BA138 PF-B.
Also used	Blenheim I K7159, IV V5742, V AZ886; Beaufighter IF X7685, II V8139, VI KW106; Battle L5963; Beaufort I N1019, IIA ML613; Master II DM388; Anson I EG506; Oxford II AS898; Boston II AH524; Havoc I AX911; Owlet DP240; Dominie I X7373; Cygnet II ES915; Martinet I MS563; Commodore HH979; Magister R1978; Mosquito II DZ746, III RR302, VI PZ191, XII HK141, XIII HK416, XVII HK286/G, XIX TA238; Lysander II L6858, IIIA V9779; Spitfire I X4012, VB W3373; Hurricane I L1568, IIC PG437; Oxford I BG549; Wellington X NC869 35, XI MP525/G, XVIII ND105.

Disbanded 14th June 1946 at Cranfield.

52 OPERATIONAL TRAINING UNIT, later 52 OPERATIONAL TRAINING UNIT (FIGHTER LEADERS SCHOOL), later 52 OPERATIONAL TRAINING UNIT (FIGHTER COMMAND SCHOOL OF TACTICS)
Formed 25th March 1941 at Debden. Redesignated 52 Operational
Training Unit (Fighter Leaders School) from 16th August 1943 and
52 Operational Training Unit (Fighter Command School of Tactics)
from October 1943.

NS (–8.43)	Spitfire IIA P8348 NS-Y.
GK	Possibly allocated.
TJ	Possibly allocated.
OQ (–8.43)	Spitfire VB BM376 OQ-S.
Also used	Spitfire I N3121, IA AR240, PR.III R7146, VA P7920; Hurricane I N2343, IIA Z4969, X P5208; Blenheim I K7170; Tomahawk IIA AH917; Harvard I N7180; Master I N7504, II AZ281, III DL556; Magister T9675; Lysander I R2582; Dominie I X7351; Oxford II N4756; Hornet Moth W6421; Cygnet II ES915.

Disbanded 26th January 1944 at Aston Down to become the
Fighter Leaders School.

53 OPERATIONAL TRAINING UNIT
Formed 18th February 1941 at Heston.

KU (2.41–)	Spitfire IA AR255 KU-F, IIA P8071 KU-N.
MV (2.41–5.45)	Spitfire I N3199 MV-O, VB BM572 MV-E.
OB	No evidence of use.
QG (.43–5.45)	Spitfire VB AA738 QG-K.
Also used	Harvard I N7178, IIB KF269; Master I T8766 X, II AZ282, III DL559 D; Battle L5713; Lysander II P1698, III T1610, IIIA V9752; Dragon Rapide W6425; Hornet Moth AX857; Hurricane I N2488; Spitfire VA P7920, VC AR552; Tiger Moth II T5364; Oxford I BG234; Martinet I EM554; Wellington III BK439.

Disbanded 15th May 1945 at Kirton-in-Lindsey and absorbed by 61
Operational Training Unit.

54 OPERATIONAL TRAINING UNIT
Formed 25th November 1940 at Church Fenton.

BF (12.40– .43)	Blenheim I L6734 BF-H, IV R2778 BF-X; Beaufighter II T3158 BF-Z.
LX (.44– .45)	Lysander II L6858 LX-L; Beaufighter VI V8706 LX-L; Mosquito III TW119 LX-F, VI SZ974 LX-B.
ST (5.42–5.45)	Anson I MG899 ST-K; Beaufort I LR977 ST-B; Beaufighter II T3224 ST-H, VI KW101 ST-C; Hurricane IIC PG547 ST-S; Spitfire IX MA659 ST-U; Martinet I MS779 ST-3; Wellington XVIII ND114 ST-B.
YX (.42–5.47)	Blenheim I K7159 YX-N; Beaufighter VI ND200 YX-P; Mosquito II DZ655 YX-G, VI PZ311 YX-M, NF.30 MM817 YX-A.
Also used	Blenheim V AZ881; Defiant I N1548; Master I T8550, II AZ780; Battle L5625; Magister N3908; Tiger Moth II T5491; Oxford I V3150, II V3623; Hurricane I L1771; Typhoon IB R8882; Lysander II P9187, IIIA V9751; Dominie I X7342; Mosquito XIII HK521, XVII HK347, XIX TA249; Wellington XVII MP530, XVIII NC926.

Disbanded 1st May 1947 at Leeming and merged with 13
Operational Training Unit to become 228 Operational Conversion
Unit.

55 OPERATIONAL TRAINING UNIT
Formed 1st November 1940 at Aston Down by redesignating 5
Operational Training Unit.

UW	Hurricane I V6622 UW-U, X AG162 UW-X.
EH	Hurricane I W9135 EH-R, X AG248 EH-M.
PA	Hurricane I V7165 PA-27, IIA Z2696 PA-A, X AF998 PA-29; Master III W8647 PA-M.
ZX	Master I T8566 ZX, DL781 ZX-D; Dragon Rapide W6425 ZX.
Also used	Blenheim I K7090; Lysander II L4768, IIIA V9906; Battle L5713; Defiant I N1577; Magister L5931; Harvard I P5872; Tiger Moth II T7723;

Disbanded 26th January 1944 at Annan to become 4 Tactical
Exercise Unit.

Reformed 18th December 1944 at Aston Down by redesignating 3
Tactical Exercise Unit.

EH	Typhoon IB EK413 EH-V.
PA	Typhoon IB SR185 PA-H.
UW	Typhoon IB SW628 UW-M.
ZX	Typhoon IB MN513 ZX-4.
Also used	Mustang III FZ154; Dominie I X7378.

Disbanded 14th June 1945 at Aston Down.

56 OPERATIONAL TRAINING UNIT
Formed 1st November 1940 at Sutton Bridge by redesignating 6
Operational Training Unit.

FE	Hurricane I Z4180 FE-A.
GF	No aircraft known.
Also used	Hurricane I W9180 X AF976, IIA DG631, IIB BE405, IIE BE492; Henley III L3375; Master I T8752, II DL273 FF, III W8633; Blenheim IV L9294; Lysander II P9061, III R9129, IIIA

V9860; Battle L5707; Tiger Moth II T7732; Mentor L4403;

Disbanded 5th October 1943 at Tealing to become 1 Combat Training Wing.

Reformed 15th December 1944 at Milfield.

FE (12.44–2.46)	Typhoon IB MN240 FE-J.
GF (12.44–2.46)	Tempest V EJ861 GF-M.
HQ (12.44–2.46)	Tempest V NV662 HQ-S.
OD (12.44–2.46)	Typhoon IB JP790 OD-F; Tempest V EJ863 OD-10.
Also used	Spitfire VB BL940, VC EE681; Tiger Moth II T5534; Leopard Moth AV989; Magister L8148; Dominie I X7401; Martinet I EM511; Proctor III HM429.

Disbanded 14th February 1946 at Milfield.

57 OPERATIONAL TRAINING UNIT
Formed 1st November 1940 at Harwarden by redesignating 7 Operational Training Unit.

JZ (12.40–6.45)	Spitfire IIA P7296 JZ-22.
LV (12.40–6.45)	Spitfire IA AR212 LV-N, VB BL426 LV-N, VC EF541 LV-R.
PW (–6.45)	Spitfire VB AR424 PW-R.
XO (12.40–6.45)	Spitfire VC EE627 XO-H.
Also used	Battle L5625; Master I N7486, II AZ379 A, III W8465; Lysander I R2630; Magister T9762; Defiant I L7000; Dominie I R9552; Tiger Moth II T5968; Spitfire I K9800, PR.I R7020, Proctor III DX234; Martinet I JN279 4.

Disbanded 6th June 1945 at Eshott.

58 OPERATIONAL TRAINING UNIT
Formed 2nd December 1940 at Grangemouth.

PQ	Spitfire I X4020, IIA P7739 PQ-N, V.
Also used	Master I N7420, III DL615; Battle L5625; Whitley VII EB397; Hurricane I V6552; Lysander I R2632, II P9187, III R9018; Dominie I X7341; Tiger Moth II T8254; Magister T9874.

Disbanded 5th October 1943 at Grangemouth to become 2 Combat Training Wing.

Reformed 12th March 1945 at Poulton by redesignating an element of 41 Operational Training Unit.

P9	Spitfire VB BL365 P9-23, IX ML211 P9-57.
Also used	Master II DK804; Martinet I EM465; Proctor III DX234; Dominie I NR734.

Disbanded 20th July 1945 at Harwarden.

59 OPERATIONAL TRAINING UNIT
Formed 16th December 1940 at Turnhouse.

MF (12.40– .43)	('Z' Flight) Hurricane I V7099 MF-14, X AG162 MF-8; Master III W8650 MF-X.
Nil (12.40–1.44)	Hurricane I V6552, IIA Z2577, X AG123, IIB JS330; Magister T9828; Battle L5707, Battle Trainer P6685; Master I T8369, II AZ696 10, III W8592; Rapide R2487; Dominie I X7347; Lysander IIIA V9906; Tiger Moth II T7724; Oxford I DF302; Typhoon IB R8661.

Disbanded 26th January 1944 at Milfield and merged with the Specialised Low Attack Instructors School to become the Fighter Leaders School.

Reformed 26th February 1945 at Acklington.

II (2.45–6.45)	(2 Squadron) Typhoon IB SW572 II-S.
7L (2.45–6.45)	(3 Squadron) Typhoon IB SW635 7L-P.
4Q (2.45–6.45)	(1 Squadron) Typhoon IB SW531 4Q-AQ-C.
Also used	Master II AZ696; Proctor III LZ695; Martinet I EM519 15.

Disbanded 6th June 1945 at Acklington.

60 OPERATIONAL TRAINING UNIT
Formed 28th April 1940 at Leconfield.

Defiant I N1539; Master I T8549, III W8597; Battle L5626; Magister R1846; Blenheim I K7147, V AZ879; Master I T8551; Lysander I P1688; Oxford II V3604; Cleveland I AS471; Beaufighter I R2191, II T3036.

Disbanded 24th November 1942 at East Fortune to become 132 Operational Training Unit.

Reformed 17th May 1943 at High Ercall by redesignating 2 Squadron of 51 Operational Training Unit.

AT	Blenheim IV Z5806, V AZ897 AT-18; Oxford I EB812; Mosquito II DZ722 AT-14, III HJ881, VI HX967, XVI NS510; Lysander II P1688; Martinet I EM584; Gladiator I K8045; Dominie I R5930; Tiger Moth II T6121; Anson I AX411; Beaufort I N1020; Ventura I AE705, II AJ178; Auster I LB344.
8V	Allotted but no evidence of use.

Disbanded 11th April 1945 at Finmere and absorbed by 13 Operational Training Unit.

61 OPERATIONAL TRAINING UNIT
Formed 9th June 1941 at Heston by redesignating an element of 53 Operational Training Unit.

HX (6.41–7.47)	Spitfire VB EN917 HX-R, XVI TD136 HX-F; Master III W8526 HX-5.
UU (.43–7.47)	Mustang III FX923 UU-J; Spitfire XVI TE479 UU-F.
DE (.44–)	Spitfire XVI SL552 DE-N.
KR (–7.47)	Mustang III FX933 KR-C.
TO (.45–7.47)	Master I DK881 TO-N; Harvard IIB FX360 TO-P; Martinet I JN297 TO-T.
Also used	Gladiator I K8046; Battle L5707; Magister L5963; Master I N7418, II DL349, III DL553; Spitfire I N3026, IIA P8665, VA P7308; Harvard I N7178; Lysander II L4789, III T1655, IIIA V9549; Petrel P5639; Oxford I X7293; Dominie I X7375; Monospar X9369; Mohawk III AR634; Hornet Moth AX857; Tiger Moth II T7166; Proctor III DX185; Wellington I L4385, XVII MP522; Dominie I X7375; Auster V RT483; Hurricane IIC LF293.

Disbanded 1st July 1947 at Keevil to become 203 Advanced Flying School.

62 OPERATIONAL TRAINING UNIT
Formed 1st June 1942 at Usworth by redesignating the Airborne Interception Flight of 3 Radio School.

Hudson VI FK542; Anson I LT197 18; Wellington X ND110, XI MP546, XIV PG246 34, XVIII PG249 29; Oxford I HN840, II AB654; Hurricane IIC LF363; Master I T8365; Magister T9838; Tiger Moth II T5535; Beaufighter I R2252.

Disbanded 6th June 1945 at Ouston.

63 OPERATIONAL TRAINING UNIT
Formed 7th September 1943 at Honiley.

HI	Beaufighter II T3146 HI-U.
Nil	Blenheim V BA156; Beaufort I N1020; Beaufighter II R2453 Q; Hurricane I Z4939, IIC PG530, X P5187; Anson I AX231; Master I T8333; Wellington XI MP546, XVII MP520; Martinet I JN644; Magister N3943; Dominie I X7353; Spitfire VB BL940.

Disbanded 21st March 1944 at Honiley.

70 OPERATIONAL TRAINING UNIT
Formed 10th December 1940 at Ismailia, Egypt, by redesignating the Training Unit and Reserve Pool.

Wellesley I K8523; Hardy K4050; Hind K6797; Gauntlet I K5292; Hurricane I N2623, IIC LD239; Blenheim I K7099, IV Z6152 47, V BA240; Magister I P2398; Oxford I L4658; Anson I AW852; Baltimore I AG720, II AG792, III AH101, IIIA FA260, IV FA397, V FW730, VC FW875; Marauder II FB428 23, III HD408 30; Lodestar I EW981; Argus II FZ761.

Disbanded 16th July 1945 at Shandur, Egypt.

71 OPERATIONAL TRAINING UNIT
Formed 1st June 1941 at Ismailia, Egypt, by redesignating 'B' Flight of 70 Operational Training Unit.

Hart Trainer K6420; Wellesley I K7770; Magister I P2391; Gladiator 1341 (SAAF); Lysander I L4684, II P9051; Harvard I N7033, II AJ808, IIA EX101 18, III EX860; Blenheim IV Z7769; Anson I DJ209; Mohawk IV AR693; Tomahawk IIA AH955, IIB AN404; Mustang IVA KH837; Hurricane I P3978, IIA Z4964, IIC BN541, IID HV663, X AF988; Spitfire VB EN931, VC ER889, IX EN349; Baltimore II AG785, IIIA FA203; Vega Gull X1032; Argus II FZ766; Saiman C202 HK860.

Disbanded 11th June 1945 at Ismailia.

72 OPERATIONAL TRAINING UNIT
Formed 10th November 1941 at Cathargo, Sudan, by redesignating an element of 211 Squadron.

Blenheim I L8391 14, IV R3762, V BA152; Gladiator I K8037; Boston III Z2177; Baltimore III AH128, IIIA FA176; Tomahawk IIB AM382; Anson I AX404.

Disbanded 14th May 1943 at Nanyuki, Kenya.

73 OPERATIONAL TRAINING UNIT
Formed 1st January 1942 at Sheikh Othman, Aden.

Mohawk IV 2542; Tomahawk I AH752, IIA AH954, IIB AK195; Hurricane I R4103, IIC LB893, IID BP183; Kittyhawk I AK578, III FR841, IV FT852; Spitfire I R6840 42, VB ER570, VC JL306 33, IX ML418; Thunderbolt I FL756 15, II HD176 36; Harvard II AJ814 J, IIA EX121 Z, IIB FS846 J, III EX971 N; Defiant TT.II AA485; Hart Trainer K6423; Argus II FS655; Saimon C202 HK860.

Disbanded 25th September 1945 at Fayid, Egypt.

74 OPERATIONAL TRAINING UNIT
Formed 18th October 1941 at Aqir, Palestine, by redesignating 'C' Flight of 71 Operational Training Unit.

Hurricane I Z4071, PR.I P3725, IIA DG625, IIB HL683, IIC KX940, IID BN973, X P5173; Spitfire I P9432, PR.IV BR416 X, VB EP638, VC LZ983; Proctor III HM372; Harvard II AJ816, IIA EX131, III EZ340; Magister P6379.

Disbanded 16th July 1943 at Petah Tiqva, Palestine.

75 OPERATIONAL TRAINING UNIT
Formed 8th December 1942 at Gianaclis, Egypt.

Blenheim I L1499, V EH371; Hudson III V9101, IIIA FH314, VI FK526; Baltimore I AG720, II AG786, III AG923, IIIA FA316, IV FA421, V FW812; Ventura I FN980, V FP538; Beaufort I DW943; Hurricane IIA Z4947, IIC LB928; Anson I AW853; Wellington IC Z8720, X HE792; Magister I R1954; Harvard IIA EX761, III EX860; Argus II FS542, III HB698; Oxford I PG952.

Disbanded 25th June 1945 at Shallufa, Egypt.

76 OPERATIONAL TRAINING UNIT
Formed 1st October 1943 at Aqir, Palestine.

Wellington III HF798, X HZ817; Anson I NK592.

Disbanded 30th July 1945 at Aqir.

77 OPERATIONAL TRAINING UNIT
Formed 1st April 1944 at El Question, Palestine.

Wellington X JA505, XIII MF149; Hurricane IIC LB544; Anson I MG145.

Disbanded 9th July 1945 at El Qastina.

78 OPERATIONAL TRAINING UNIT
Formed 1st February 1944 at Ein Shemer, Palestine, by redesignating an element of 3 Operational Training Unit.

Wellington X LP262, XIII MF185; Hurricane IID HV664; Anson I MG167.

Disbanded 23rd July 1945 at Ein Shemer.

79 OPERATIONAL TRAINING UNIT
Formed 1st February 1944 at Nicosia, Cyprus.

Blenheim V BA307; Defiant TT.I AA475; Argus II FZ725; Anson I MG639; Beaufighter I X7800, VI EL169, X NV527 S, XI JL906; Baltimore IIIA FA355; Hurricane IIC KW822.

Disbanded 30th July 1945 at Nicosia.

80 OPERATIONAL TRAINING UNIT
Formed 23rd April 1945 at Morpeth.

3H	*Spitfire IX MH353 3H-J; Master II AZ282, III DL862; Anson I EF866; Wellington X HZ272; Martinet I MS905; Oxford I PH124.*

Disbanded 8th March 1946 at Ouston.

81 OPERATIONAL TRAINING UNIT
Formed 10th July 1942 at Ashbourne.

EZ	*Whitley V Z6670 EZ-S; Wellington X NA962 EZ-H.*
KG	*Whitley V T4177 KG-W.*
JB	*Whitley V N1480 JB-V; Spitfire VB EP411 JB-A; Anson I MG589 JB-W.*
Also used	*Wellington IC R1498; Hurricane I L1877, IIC PZ730; Lysander III T1450, IIIA V9844; Defiant I T4047; Oxford II N4792; Horsa I LH149; Warferry I HM497; Desoutter I HM508; Tiger Moth II R5192; Martinet I JN289; Anson I AW928; Proctor II Z7210.*

Disbanded 10th August 1945 at Tilstock to become 1380 (Transport Support) Conversion Unit.

82 OPERATIONAL TRAINING UNIT
Formed 1st June 1943 at Ossington.

BZ	*Wellington III BJ890 BZ-T, X LN282 BZ-J.*
TD	*Wellington III, X.*
KA	*Martinet I MS928 KA-E.*
9C	*Possibly allocated.*
Also used	*Oxford I NM803, II ED121; Tomahawk I AH861, IIA AH903; Master II AZ793; Hurricane IIC MW368.*

Disbanded 9th January 1945 at Ossington.

83 OPERATIONAL TRAINING UNIT
Formed 1st August 1943 at Child's Ercall (later Peplow) by redesignating an element of 30 Operational Training Unit.

GS	*Wellington III BK151 GS-A, X LN542 GS-O; Martinet I MS571 GS-Z.*
FI	*Hurricane IIC LF380 FI-D.*
MZ	*Wellington III X3793 MZ-G.*
Also used	*Whitley III K8994; Master II DL431; Oxford II R6227; Wellington IC L7797.*

Disbanded 28th October 1944 at Peplow to become 23 Heavy Glider Conversion Unit.

84 OPERATIONAL TRAINING UNIT
Formed 1st September 1943 at Desborough.

IF	*Wellington X LN247 IF-Q.*
CZ	*Martinet I HP354 CZ-P.*
CO	*Wellington X ME974 CO-W.*
Also used	*Wellington IC N2751, III X3645; Oxford I NM605; Hurricane IIC PG569.*

Disbanded 16th June 1945 at Desborough.

85 OPERATIONAL TRAINING UNIT
Formed 15th June 1944 at Husbands Bosworth by redesignating an element of 14 Operational Training Unit.

9P	*Wellington X LN758 9P-P.*
2X	*Master II DK927 2X-Y; Martinet I JN596 2X-V.*
Also used	*Wellington III X3821; Hurricane IIC PZ733.*

Disbanded 14th June 1945 at Husbands Bosworth.

86 OPERATIONAL TRAINING UNIT
Formed 15th June 1944 at Gamston by redesignating 'C' Flight of 82 Operational Training Unit.

Wellington III X3281, X LN162; Martinet I JN425; Hurricane IIC PG453.

Disbanded 15th October 1944 at Gamston.

101 (GLIDER) OPERATIONAL TRAINING UNIT
Formed 1st January 1942 at Kidlington.

Audax K2006; Hind L7207; Hector K8093; Tiger Moth I K4254, II N6611; Mentor L4413; Hotspur II HH242, III BT731; Master II DL303; Oxford II ED173.

Disbanded 13th July 1942 at Kidlington to become 4 Glider Training School.

102 (GLIDER) OPERATIONAL TRAINING UNIT
Formed 10th February 1942 at Kidlington.

Audax K7331; Hind L7223; Hector K8166; Tiger Moth II T6858; Oxford II ED169; Lysander IIIA V9720; Hotspur II BT595, III BT632.

Disbanded 30th June 1942 at Kidlington to become 5 Glider Training School.

104 (TRANSPORT) OPERATIONAL TRAINING UNIT
Formed 12th March 1943 at Nutts Corner.

Wellington IC R1077, IV Z1206; Battle P2362.

Disbanded 5th February 1944 at Nutts Corner.

105 (TRANSPORT) OPERATIONAL TRAINING UNIT
Formed 15th April 1943 at Bramcote.

8F	*Wellington X MF521 8F-R; Dakota IV KJ875 8F-GE.*
I5	*Wellington III MF703 I5-X.*
Also used	*Wellington IC DV696 J; Dakota I FD789, III FL547; Oxford I V4085, II W6609; Magister P2499; Tiger Moth II R4918; Hurricane IIC PZ832.*

Disbanded 10th August 1945 at Bramcote to become 1381 (Transport) Conversion Unit.

107 (TRANSPORT) OPERATIONAL TRAINING UNIT
Formed 3rd May 1944 at Leicester East.

CM	*Dakota III TS434 CM-O.*
ZR	*Dakota III KG595 ZR-C.*
Also used	*Oxford I V4204, II N4723; Dakota I FD782; Hadrian I 43-41053; Horsa I HG833, II PW845; Auster III NX488.*

Disbanded 12th March 1945 at Leicester East to become 1333 (Transport Support) Conversion Unit.

108 (TRANSPORT) OPERATIONAL TRAINING UNIT
Formed 10th October 1944 at Wymeswold.

Dakota I FD789, III FL596, IV KJ875 M1; Magister I L8359.

Disbanded 10th August 1945 at Wymeswold to become 1382 (Transport) Conversion Unit.

109 (TRANSPORT) OPERATIONAL TRAINING UNIT
Formed 1st August 1944 at Crosby-on-Eden by redesignating elements of 9 Operational Training Unit.

GY (8.44– .45)	*Dakota III KG657 GY-N.*
Nil (.45–8.45)	*Dakota III KG666 T.*

Disbanded 1st August 1945 at Crosby-on-Eden to become 1383 (Transport) Conversion Unit.

110 OPERATIONAL TRAINING UNIT
Nameplate set to one side for a proposed heavy bomber training unit at Alamogordo, USA.

111 (COASTAL) OPERATIONAL TRAINING UNIT
Formed 20th August 1942 at Oaks Field and Windsor Field, Bahamas.

A (8.42–7.45)	*Mitchell I FK179 AR.*
C (8.42–7.45	*Mitchell II FR378 CL.*
F (8.42–7.45)	*Mitchell II FW150 FP.*
J (8.42–7.45)	*Mitchell III KJ671 JX.*

L (8.42–7.45)	*Liberator III FL993 L, V BZ806 LU.*
M (8.42–7.45)	*Liberator V BZ810 MA.*
N (8.42–7.45)	*Liberator VI EV896 NA, VIII KH262 NH.*
X3 (.44–7.45)	*Liberator VIII KK333 X3-C; Wellington XIV PG183 X3-CC.*
3G (8.45–8.46)	*Halifax III NA253.*
H3	*Allocated but no evidence of use.*
Also used	*Bermuda I FF753; Gosling I JS996; Goose I FP742; Oxford I PK284 B; Mosquito PR.35 RG255; Spitfire XVI SL611.*

Disbanded 21st May 1946 at Lossiemouth.

112 OPERATIONAL TRAINING UNIT
Nameplate set to one side for a proposed medium bomber training unit at La Junta, Colorado, USA.

113 OPERATIONAL TRAINING UNIT
Nameplate set to one side for a proposed medium bomber training unit at La Cruces, New Mexico, USA.

114 OPERATIONAL TRAINING UNIT
Nameplate set to one side for a proposed heavy bomber training unit at Lourdsbourg, New Mexico, USA.

115 OPERATIONAL TRAINING UNIT
Nameplate set to one side for a proposed medium bomber training unit at Pratt, Kansas, USA.

116 OPERATIONAL TRAINING UNIT
Nameplate set to one side for a proposed heavy bomber training unit at Liberal, Kansas, USA.

117 OPERATIONAL TRAINING UNIT
Nameplate set to one side for a proposed medium bomber training unit at Garden City, Kansas, USA.

118 OPERATIONAL TRAINING UNIT
Nameplate set to one side for a proposed heavy bomber training unit at Dodge City, Kansas, USA.

119 OPERATIONAL TRAINING UNIT
Nameplate set to one side for a proposed medium bomber training unit at Wink, Kansas, USA.

120 OPERATIONAL TRAINING UNIT
Nameplate set to one side for a proposed heavy bomber training unit at San Antonio, Cuba.

131 (COASTAL) OPERATIONAL TRAINING UNIT
Formed 20th July 1942 at Killadeas.

Catalina I AH538 V, IB FP135 Q, II AM270, IIA VA722, IIIA FP527, IVA JX218 32, IVB JX305; Sunderland III JM666, V DP191; Anson I DG757; Oxford I PG968, II ED128; Martinet I HN979.

Disbanded 28th June 1945 at Killadeas.

132 (COASTAL) OPERATIONAL TRAINING UNIT
Formed 24th November 1942 at East Fortune by redesignating 60 Operational Training Unit.

Nil (11.42– .45)	*Blenheim I K7176, IV T2326, V AZ879 30; Beaufort I JM652, IIA ML564 102; Beaufighter I T4634, II R2459, VI JL549, X NE768, XI JM219; Lysander II P9060; Tiger Moth II L6921; Magister R1859; Spitfire VB EP785; Mosquito II DD682; Martinet I HP250 103.*
9Y (.45–5.46)	*Oxford II P6801 9Y-A; Beaufort II ML658 9Y-N; Mosquito III LR517 9Y-BG; VI NT206 9Y-AX; Beaufighter X RD525 9Y-Z; Buckmaster I RP191.*

Disbanded 15th May 1946 at East Fortune.

151 (FIGHTER) OPERATIONAL TRAINING UNIT
Formed 28th July 1942 at Risalpur, India, by redesignating 1 Operational Training Unit (India).

Hart K2100; Hurricane I V6812, IIB BE232, IIC BN135, IID KW865, IV LD449, X AF999, XIIA PJ685; Buffalo I W8233; Hawk AX799;

Lysander II N1295; Harvard II AJ783, IIB FE354; Buffalo I W8245; Mohawk IV LA157; Spitfire VIII MD323; Vengeance I AN906; Oxford I NM514.

Disbanded 1st April 1946 at Ambala, India, and merged with 1 (Indian) Service Flying Training School and 1 (Indian) Advanced Flying Unit to become the Advanced Flying School (India).

152 (BOMBER) OPERATIONAL TRAINING UNIT
Formed 22nd October 1942 at Peshawar, India.

Blenheim I L8401, IV R3919, V BA453; Vengeance I AP111 8, II AN629; Harvard II AJ785; Anson I DJ285.

Disbanded 12th March 1944 at Peshawar and absorbed by 151 Operational Training Unit.

OVERSEAS AIR DELIVERY FLIGHT – see Overseas Aircraft Despatch Flight

OVERSEAS AIRCRAFT DESPATCH FLIGHT
Formed 9th September 1940 at Kemble. Early records refer to the unit as the 'Overseas Air Delivery Flight'.

Bombay I L5834; Wellington DW.I P2518, IC W5618, II W5388; Beaufort I W6504; Beaufighter I T4651; Maryland I AR737.

Disbanded 15th August 1941 at Kemble to become the Overseas Aircraft Despatch Unit.

OVERSEAS AIRCRAFT DESPATCH UNIT, KEMBLE AND PORTREATH
Formed 15th August 1941 at Kemble by redesignating the Overseas Aircraft Despatch Flight. A detachment was set up from 28th June 1941 at Portreath. The element at Kemble disbanded on 5th November 1941 to become the Overseas Aircraft Preparation Flight.

Bombay I L5844; Beaufort I N1033; Liberator II AL577; Maryland I AR731; Blenheim IV V5528, V AZ929; Whitley V BD382; Wellington IC BB469, II Z8354, VIII BB461, X HE105; Hurricane IIC BE642; Halifax II DT493, V EB188; Mosquito II DD743; Hudson III V9025, IIIA FH334, V AM582, VI FK621; Spitfire VB EP152; Catalina IB FP116; Beaufighter I X7639, VI EL163.

Disbanded 26th January 1942 at Portreath to become 1 Overseas Aircraft Despatch Unit.

1 OVERSEAS AIRCRAFT DESPATCH UNIT
Formed 26th February 1942 at Portreath by redesignating the Overseas Aircraft Despatch Unit.

Boston III Z2166; Blenheim IV V5883, V BA793; Horsa I DP388; Hudson IIIA FH230, VI FK386; Wellington DW.I P2521, IA N2871, IC HE123, II Z8356, III HZ119, VIII HX507, X HX446, XI HZ275, XIII HZ594, XVI Z1071; Warwick I HF949; Halifax II DT486, III NA642, V DG354; Spitfire IV BP905, IX PV142, XI MB901; Beaufort I EK984, II DD904, IIA ML430; Beaufighter I X7802, VI V8437, X NE380; Mosquito II DD800, IV DZ382, VI HJ730, XVI NS789; XIX TA226; B.25 KB531, NF.30 NT243.

Disbanded 10th October 1945 at Portreath.

2 OVERSEAS AIRCRAFT DESPATCH UNIT
Formed 26th November 1942 at Treblezue (later St Mawgan).

Beaufort I N1000; Beaufighter I T4897; Wellington X LP408, XIII HZ585, XIV HF242, XVIII ND104; Warwick III HG222; Halifax III NA644, V LK742.

Disbanded 15th November 1946 at St Mawgan.

3 OVERSEAS AIRCRAFT DESPATCH UNIT
Formed 15th January 1943 at Hurn.

Albemarle I P1389; Liberator V BZ805; Halifax II LW276, V EB154; Wellington IA N2955, II Z8343, III HZ124, VIII LB139; X HE707, XI HZ299, XII HF119, XIII HZ583, XIV HF294; Warwick I HF970; Tiger Moth II T7845.

Ceased to operate 9th November 1944 at Talbenny and administratively disbanded 17th May 1945.

4 OVERSEAS AIRCRAFT DESPATCH UNIT
Formed 22nd May 1944 at Redhill.

Anson I LS986.

Ceased to operate 31st July 1944 at Bognor Regis and administratively disbanded 31st January 1945.

5 OVERSEAS AIRCRAFT DESPATCH UNIT
Formed 5th June 1944 at Aston Down.

Anson I.

Ceased to operate 31st July 1944 at Aston Down and administratively disbanded 31st January 1945.

OVERSEAS AIRCRAFT PREPARATION FLIGHT
Formed 5th November 1941 at Kemble by redesignating the Kemble element of the Overseas Aircraft Despatch Unit.

Blenheim IV, V; Wellington; Hurricane; Beaufort; Beaufighter.

Disbanded 1st January 1942 at Kemble to become the Overseas Aircraft Preparation Unit.

OVERSEAS AIRCRAFT PREPARATION UNIT
Formed 1st January 1942 at Kemble by redesignating the Overseas Aircraft Preparation Flight with 1 and 2 Flights at Kemble and 3 and 4 Flights, which had formed prematurely on 20th December 1941, at Filton.

Beaufort I N1003; Bombay I; Albemarle ST.I P1374; Hurricane; Blenheim IV Z7653, V; Wellington II W5363, X HE236; Hudson III AE550; Oxford; Halifax; Beaufighter; Mosquito.

Disbanded 1st December 1942 with 1 and 2 Flights at Kemble becoming 1 Overseas Aircraft Preparation Unit and 3 and 4 Flights at Filton becoming 2 Overseas Aircraft Preparation Unit.

1 OVERSEAS AIRCRAFT PREPARATION UNIT, later 1 AIRCRAFT PREPARATION UNIT
Formed 1st December 1942 at Kemble by redesignating 1 and 2 Flights of the Overseas Aircraft Preparation Unit, Kemble. Redesignated 1 Aircraft Preparation Unit from 5th July 1944.

Wellington IA N2877; Hudson VI EW890; Mosquito; Halifax.

Disbanded 10th October 1944 at Kemble and absorbed by 1 Ferry Unit.

2 OVERSEAS AIRCRAFT PREPARATION UNIT, later 2 AIRCRAFT PREPARATION UNIT
Formed 1st December 1942 at Filton by redesignating 3 and 4 Flights of the Overseas Air Preparation Unit, Filton. Redesignated 2 Aircraft Preparation Unit from 5th July 1944.

Beaufort I N1039; Blenheim; Albemarle I P1370; Anson X MG471; Beaufighter VI ND161; Mosquito; Tempest II MW792.

Disbanded 1st July 1945 at Filton to become 15 Ferry Unit.

3 OVERSEAS AIRCRAFT PREPARATION UNIT, later 3 AIRCRAFT PREPARATION UNIT
Formed 1st July 1943 at Llandow. Redesignated 3 Aircraft Preparation Unit from 5th July 1944.

Hudson; Hampden; Wellington; Halifax; Anson; Beaufighter; Ventura V; Lancaster; Dakota; Warwick.

Disbanded 15th August 1945 at Kirton-in-Lindsey and merged with 11 Ferry Unit to become 16 Ferry Unit.

4 OVERSEAS AIRCRAFT PREPARATION UNIT, later 4 AIRCRAFT PREPARATION UNIT
Formed August 1943 at Melton Mowbray. Redesignated 4 Aircraft Preparation Unit from 5th July 1944.

Anson I N5255; Spitfire; Boston; Stirling; Mosquito; Dakota; Beaufighter; Corsair; Vengeance; Hellcat; Halifax.

Disbanded 9th October 1944 at Melton Mowbray and merged with 304 Ferry Training Unit to become 12 Ferry Unit.

OVERSEAS EXPERIMENTAL UNIT
Formed 1st January 1960 at Idris, Libya, by redesignating the Tropical Experimental Unit.

Wessex HC.2 XR498.

Disbanded 1966 at Idris.

OVERSEAS FERRY UNIT – see 1 (Overseas) Ferry Unit, later Overseas Ferry Unit

1 (OVERSEAS) FERRY UNIT, later OVERSEAS FERRY UNIT
Formed 17th May 1948 at Pershore by redesignating 1 Ferry Unit. Redesignated the Overseas Ferry Unit from September 1950.

Harvard IIB KF604; Dakota IV KK134; Wellington X MF626; Tempest V NX128; Mosquito III VT621, VI PZ353, XVI MM412, PR.34 PF630; Buckmaster I RP232; Vampire F.3 VT794; FB.5 WA183; Meteor T.7 WA609; F.8 VZ525; Valetta C.1 WD167; Hornet F.3 WF955.

Disbanded 17th November 1952 at Abingdon to become 1 and 3 (Long Range) Ferry Units.

OVERSEAS STAFF COLLEGE COMMUNICATION FLIGHT
Formed September 1945 at Larnaca, Cyprus.

Anson X NK432.

Disbanded July 1946 at Larnaca to become the Royal Air Force Staff College (Overseas) Communication Flight.

OXFORD TEST FLIGHT
Formed 20th December 1945 at Bramcote.

Oxford I HM865.

Disbanded 12th July 1946 at Bramcote.

OXFORD UNIVERSITY AIR SQUADRON
Formed 11th October 1925 at Oxford. Used Upper Heyford and Abingdon for flying training.

Avro 504N K1812 F; D.H.9A J7836; F.2B J7838 Y; Atlas I K2519, Atlas DC K1175; Tutor K3442 P; Hart Trainer K3756.

Disbanded 3rd September 1939 at Abingdon.

Reformed 8th October 1940 at Oxford. Used Abingdon for flying training.

Nil (10.40–4.46)	Tiger Moth II (aircraft provided by 3 Elementary Flying Training School).
FLQ (4.46– .47)	Tiger Moth II.
RUO (.47–4.51)	Tiger Moth II T7793 RUO-B; Chipmunk T.10 WB624 RUO-D.
Nil (4.51–)	Tiger Moth II; Harvard IIB KF718; Prentice T.1 VS397; Chipmunk T.10 WP785 D; Bulldog XX660 A.
Also used	Tiger Moth I NM138.

Current 1st April 1998 at Benson.

OXFORD UNIVERSITY FLIGHT
Formed 25th October 1927 at Upper Heyford to provide flying training before the Oxford University Air Squadron were allocated their own aircraft.

No aircraft known.

Disbanded 4th November 1927 at Upper Heyford to become the Station Flight, Upper Heyford.

'P' FLIGHT (1)
Formed 29th August 1918 at Serny, France.

F.2B C9941.

Disbanded February 1919 at (location unknown), France.

'P' FLIGHT (2)
Formed 9th June 1919 at Ismailia, Egypt, as a detached flight of 113 Squadron.

R.E.8.

Withdrawn 25th May 1919 at Jedda, Arabia.

PALESTINE TRUCE OBSERVANCE FLIGHT
Formed 26th August 1948 at Amman, Jordan, by redesignating an element of 1909 (Air Observation Post) Flight.

Auster VI TW619.

Disbanded early 1949 at Amman and aircraft passed to United Nations control.

1 PARACHUTE AND GLIDER TRAINING SCHOOL
Formed 3rd December 1947 at Upper Heyford by redesignating 1 Parachute Training School.

Dakota IV KN394; Anson I DG719; Dominie I NF886; Oxford I RR330; Harvard IIB FX269; Horsa II TL480; Valetta C.1 VW163.

Disbanded 10th June 1950 at Upper Heyford to become 1 Parachute School.

PARACHUTE EXERCISE SQUADRON
Formed 15th December 1941 at Ringway.

Whitley V proposed.

Disbanded 22nd January 1942 at Netheravon to become 297 Squadron.

1 PARACHUTE SCHOOL
Formed 10th June 1950 at Abingdon by redesignating 1 Parachute and Glider Training School.

Dakota IV; Horsa; Oxford; Valetta C.1.

Disbanded 1st November 1953 at Abingdon to become 1 Parachute Training School.

PARACHUTE SECTION, AEROPLANE AND ARMAMENT EXPERIMENTAL ESTABLISHMENT
Formed 1st April 1924 at Martlesham Heath.

F.2B H1436.

Disbanded September 1925 at Martlesham Heath to become the Parachute Test Section, Inland Area Aircraft Depot.

PARACUTE SECTION, HOME AIRCRAFT DEPOT, later PARACHUTE SECTION, 13 MAINTENANCE UNIT, later SPECIAL DUTIES PARACHUTE SECTION, 13 MAINTENANCE UNIT
Formed 20th October 1926 at Henlow by merging the Parachute Test Section, Home Aircraft Depot and the Parachute Training Section, Northolt. Redesignated the Parachute Section, 13 Maintenance Unit from 1st November 1939 and the Special Duties Parachute Section, 13 Maintenance Unit from April 1944.

Nil (10.26–4.46)	F.2B H1436; Fawn II J7184; Vimy IV J7441; Grebe II J7568; Witch J8596; Fairey IIIF K1755; Virginia X K2327; Hind K5546; Whitley I K7250; Dakota III.
THE (4.46–9.50)	Dakota III KG311 THE; Halifax VI RG871 THE, IX RT868; Anson; Tiger Moth II.

Disbanded 1st September 1950 at Henlow to become the Parachute Test Unit.

PARACHUTE SECTION, 13 MAINTENANCE UNIT – see Parachute Section, Home Aircraft Depot, later Parachute Section, 13 Maintenance Unit, later Special Duties Parachute Section, 13 Maintenance Unit

PARACHUTE TEST SECTION, HOME AIRCRAFT DEPOT – see Parachute Test Section, Inland Area Aircraft Depot, later Parachute Test Section, Home Aircraft Depot

PARACHUTE TEST SECTION, INLAND AREA AIRCRAFT DEPOT, later PARACHUTE TEST SECTION, HOME AIRCRAFT DEPOT
Formed 2nd September 1925 at Henlow by redesignating the Parachute Test Section, Aeroplane and Armament Experimental Establishment. Redesignated Parachute Test Section, Home Aircraft Depot from 12th April 1926.

F.2B H1436; Fawn II J7184; Vimy IV J7441; Witch J8596.

Disbanded 20th October 1926 at Henlow and merged with the Parachute Training Section, Northolt, to become the Parachute Section, Home Aircraft Depot.

PARACHUTE TEST UNIT
Formed 1st September 1950 at Henlow within the Royal Air Force Technical College by redesignating an element of the Safety Equipment, Development and Test Section, Henlow.

Oxford I HM809; Lancaster I PB932; Dakota IV KJ852; Halifax A.9 RT868; Hastings C.1 TG506; Viking C.2 VL231; Prentice T.1 VR189.

Functional administrative control by the Royal Air Force ceased with effect from 1st November 1955 and the unit disbanded 1st January 1960 at Henlow.

PARACHUTE TRAINING CENTRE
Formed 21st June 1940 at Ringway.

No aircraft known.

Disbanded 31st August 1940 to become the Central Landing School.

PARACHUTE TRAINING SCHOOL, later 1 PARACHUTE TRAINING SCHOOL
Formed 15th February 1942 at Ringway by redesignating the Parachute Training Section of the Airborne Forces Establishment. Redesignated 1 Parachute Training School from 18th July 1944.

Nil	Mentor L4413; Harrow I K6964; Whitley II K7218, III K8953, V Z6797, VII BD573; Anson I AX119; Master II DM292, III W8480; Tiger Moth W7952; Hudson IV AE635, Wellington IA N2880, X NA861; Albemarle I P1452; Dakota III KG419 T, IV KK138 S; Proctor I P6173, III HM341; Dominie I NF886; Halifax IX RT845; Spitfire VB AD426.
7M	Allocated, but no evidence of use.

Disbanded 3rd December 1947 at Upper Heyford to become 1 Parachute and Glider Training School.

Reformed 1st November 1953 at Abingdon by redesignating 1 Parachute School.

Hastings C.1 TG601, C.2 WD487; then Beverley C.1; Argosy C.1; Hercules C.1, C3 from Lyneham Wing as required; Skyvan under contract.

Current at 1st April 1998 at Brize Norton.

3 PARACHUTE TRAINING SCHOOL
Formed 28th February 1944 at Chaklala, India, by redesignating the Air Landing School.

Dakota I, III FZ559; IV KN236.

Incorporated within 1 (Indian) Group 1st March 1947 to at least May 1947 and then assumed to have passed to Royal Indian Air Force control.

4 PARACHUTE TRAINING SCHOOL
Formed 2nd May 1944 at Gioia delle Colle, Italy, by redesignating an element of 4 Middle East Training School.

Wellington X; Hudson V AM817.

Disbanded 30th April 1945 at Gioia Del Colle.

PARACHUTE TRAINING SCHOOL (INDIA)
Formed 22nd September 1941 at Willingdon Airport, India.

Hudson III.

Disbanded 8th January 1942 at Willingdon Airport and absorbed by the Air Landing School.

PARACHUTE TRAINING SECTION
Formed November 1925 at Northolt within the Inland Area Communication Flight.

Vimy J7441.

Disbanded 15th October 1926 at Northolt and merged with the

Parachute Test Section, Home Aircraft Depot to become the Parachute Section, Home Aircraft Depot.

'PARES' FLIGHT – see Groupe 'Ile de France'

PATHFINDER NAVIGATION TRAINING UNIT – see Navigation Training Unit

PENANG SQUADRON, later PENANG FIGHTER SQUADRON, later PENANG SQUADRON
Formed 15th May 1950 at Penang. Redesignated Penang Fighter Squadron from 1st October 1951 and Penang Squadron from 20th June 1955.

Tiger Moth II T7368; Harvard IIB FX483; Chipmunk T.10 WD287.

Disbanded 31st December 1958 at Penang.

PERTH UNIVERSITY AIR SQUADRON
Plans to open the unit in 1946 at Perth were cancelled, although the code FLR was allocated.

PHANTOM CONVERSION FLIGHT
Formed 1st July 1969 at Leuchars.

Phantom FG.1 XV572.

Disbanded 1st September 1969 at Leuchars to become 43 Squadron.

PHANTOM POST OPERATIONAL CONVERSION UNIT – see Royal Air Force Post Operational Conversion Unit

PHANTOM TRAINING FLIGHT (1) – see Royal Air Force Post Operational Conversion Unit

PHANTOM TRAINING FLIGHT (2) – see 74 Squadron

PHOTOGRAPHIC DEVELOPMENT UNIT
Formed 19th January 1940 at Heston by redesignating 2 Camouflage Unit.

Spitfire PR.III P9308, PR.IV R6905; Blenheim I L1222, IV R3600; Lockheed 12A X9316; Hudson I N7215; Petrel P5636; Hornet Moth AX857; Tiger Moth II N9196; Eagle 1 DR609.

Disbanded 18th June 1940 at Heston to become the Photographic Reconnaissance Unit.

PHOTOGRAPHIC RECONNAISSANCE ADVANCED TRAINING FLIGHT – see 8 Operational Training Unit

PHOTOGRAPHIC RECONNAISSANCE CONVERSION FLIGHT – see 8 Operational Training Unit

PHOTOGRAPHIC RECONNAISSANCE DEVELOPMENT UNIT
Formed 28th December 1943 at Benson.

Nil (12.43– .45)	Hudson I N7399; Auster IV MT279; Mustang IVA KM236; Tempest V EJ701; Mosquito IV DZ613, IX LR422; Spitfire XIV SM882.
6C (.45–8.47)	Spitfire XIX PS925 6C-X; Wellington X RP396; Anson XI NL203; Mosquito XVI MM314, PR.34 PF632, B.35 TK632; Hornet PR.I PX216 6C-R, PR.2 VA962; Meteor PR.5 EE338 6C-Z; Oxford I DF241; Auster IV MT279.

Disbanded 8th August 1947 at Benson to become the Air Photographic Development Unit.

PHOTOGRAPHIC RECONNAISSANCE UNIT, later 1 PHOTOGRAPHIC RECONNAISSANCE UNIT
Formed 18th June 1940 at Heston by redesignating the Photographic Development Unit. Redesignated 1 Photographic Reconnaissance Unit from 14th November 1940.

LY	Spitfire I X4715, PR.III P9307 LY, PR.IVD AA784; PR.V X4491, PR.VI P9310, PR.VII R7197, IX EN261, XI EN385; Blenheim I V5808, IV P4899 LY-P; Magister P6347; Tomahawk IIA AH886; Hudson I P5116, II T9379; Wellington I R2700 LY-P, IC T2707, IV Z1418; Anson I W2633; Battle Trainer R7380;

Mentor I L4417; Master II DL402, III W8786; Beaufort I L9947; Beaufighter I X7645; Tiger Moth II N9196; Maryland I AR730; Spartan 7W-19 AX666; Mosquito PR.I W4059 LY-T, PR.II DD620, IV DK310 LY-G; Martinet I EM648; Liberator III FL936; Hornet Moth AX857.

Disbanded 19th October 1942 at Benson. 'H' and 'L' Flights (Mosquitoes) became 540 Squadron, 'B' and 'F' Flights (Spitfires) became 541 Squadron, 'A' and 'E' Flights (Spitfires) became 542 Squadron and the remaining Flights became 543 and 544 Squadrons.

Reformed 1st June 1982 at Wyton as 1 Photographic Reconnaissance Unit by redesignating 39 Squadron.

Nil (10.82–   )   Canberra PR.9 XH169, T.4 WJ861.
A (–7.92)   Canberra PR.9 XH135 AG.

Disbanded 1st July 1992 at Wyton to become 39 (1 PRU) Squadron.

1 PHOTOGRAPHIC RECONNAISSANCE UNIT – see Photographic Reconnaissance Unit, later 1 Photographic Reconnaissance Unit

2 PHOTOGRAPHIC RECONNAISSANCE UNIT
Formed 3rd March 1941 at Heliopolis, Egypt, by redesignating the Intelligence Photographic Flight.

Hind K5552; Spitfire PR.IV BP911, VC BR312; Hurricane I W9116 A, IIA Z5132; Beaufighter I T4705; SM.79K AX705; Lockheed 10A AX701; Hudson N7364.

Disbanded 1st February 1943 at Agedabia, Libya, to become 680 Squadron.

3 PHOTOGRAPHIC RECONNAISSANCE UNIT, later 3 PHOTOGRAPHIC RECONNAISSANCE UNIT (INDIA)
Formed 16th November 1940 at Oakington.

Spitfire PR.III X4383, PR.IV X4494, PR.V X4384; Audax K8320; Wellington IC T2707; Tiger Moth AX786.

Disbanded 15th August 1941 at Benson and absorbed by 1 Photographic Reconnaissance Unit.

Reformed by November 1941 in Malaya.

Buffalo.

Overrun by the Japanese February 1942.

Reformed 13th May 1942 at Pandaveswar, India, as 3 Reconnaissance Unit (India) by redesignating 5 Photographic Reconnaissance Unit.

Hurricane IIB BM922; B-25C N5-144; Spitfire PR.IV BP911.

Disbanded 25th January 1943 at Dum-Dum to become 681 Squadron.

4 PHOTOGRAPHIC RECONNAISSANCE UNIT
Formed by November 1941 in Malaya.

Buffalo.

Overrun by the Japanese February 1942.

Reformed October 1942 in the UK. Began operations from 6th November 1942 at Gibraltar.

Spitfire PR.IV, IX EN337; Hurricane IIC KW750.

Disbanded 1st February 1943 at Maison Blanche, Algeria, to become 682 Squadron.

5 PHOTOGRAPHIC RECONNAISSANCE UNIT
Formed 10th April 1942 at Asansol, India.

Hurricane II; B-25C (ex Dutch).

Disbanded 13th May 1942 at Pandaveswar, India, to become 3 Photographic Reconnaissance Unit (India).

60 (PHOTOGRAPHIC SURVEY) SQUADRON, SOUTH AFRICAN AIR FORCE – ROYAL AIR FORCE FLIGHT
Formed 1st September 1941 at Heliopolis, Egypt.

Maryland I AR738, II AH362.

Disbanded 1st March 1942 at Habbaniya, Iraq, to become 1434 (Photographic Survey) Flight.

1 (PILOTS) REFRESHER FLYING UNIT
Formed 6th August 1947 at Moreton-in-Marsh by merging 1 Refresher School and an element of 21 (Pilots) Advanced Flying Unit.

FDA	*Spitfire XVI TE203 FDA-A; Harvard IIB KF139 FDA-O.*
FDB	*Wellington X RP505 FDB-E.*
FDC	*Oxford I PH517 FDC-H.*
FDD	*Oxford I PH355 FDD-J; Harvard IIB KF334 FDD-K.*
FDE	*Allocated but no evidence of use.*
FDF	*Allocated but no evidence of use.*
FDG	*Anson I N9571 FDG-P.*

Disbanded 1st June 1949 at Finningley to become the Flying Refresher School.

2 (PILOTS) REFRESHER FLYING UNIT
Formed 6th August 1947 at Valley from an element of 21 (Pilots) Advanced Flying Unit.

Oxford I R6083; Harvard IIB KF186.

Disbanded 1st April 1948 at Valley and absorbed by 1 (Pilots) Refresher Unit.

PILOT REFRESHER TRAINING UNIT
Formed 1942 at Moreton Valence.

Master II.

Disbanded 1st May 1942 at Moreton Valence to become the Refresher Flying Training School.

PILOT TRAINING UNIT AND REINFORCEMENT POOL
Formed 6th September 1939 at Abu Sueir, Egypt.

Gordon K2719; Tutor K3317; Hardy K4320; Audax K7512; Lysander I L4686; Anson I L7975; Blenheim I L8445.

Disbanded 24th June 1940 at Abu Sueir.

PILOTLESS AIRCRAFT SECTION, later PILOTLESS AIRCRAFT UNIT
Formed 31st January 1937 at Henlow by redesignating the Base and Training Unit for Co-operation Flights. Probably redesignated the Pilotless Aircraft Unit by December 1940.

R2	*Moth K1851; Tutor K3423; Wallace II K6019; Tiger Moth II L6936; Anson I N9743; Magister I L5994; Botha I L6238; Queen Bee LF801 R2-M; Queen Wasp K8888; Lysander III T1573; Proctor IV RM170 R2-V; Queen Martinet PW979.*

Disbanded 15th March 1946 at Manorbier.

PILOTLESS AIRCRAFT UNIT – see Pilotless Aircraft Section, later Pilotless Aircraft Unit

2 (PILOTS) ADVANCED FLYING UNIT
Formed 14th March 1942 at Brize Norton by redesignating 2 Service Flying Training School.

Anson I N5014; Oxford I N6262, II N6421.

Disbanded 13th July 1942 at Brize Norton.

3 (PILOTS) ADVANCED FLYING UNIT
Formed 1st March 1942 at South Cerney by redesignating 3 Service Flying Training School.

Tutor K3214; Botha I L6198; Oxford I ED280 102, II N6345; Tiger Moth II N6926; Magister I L5937; Proctor I P6313; Hornet Moth W9387; Moth Minor X5116; Puss Moth EM995; Anson I NK288 E.

Disbanded 17th December 1945 at South Cerney to become 3 Service Flying Training School.

5 (PILOTS) ADVANCED FLYING UNIT
Formed 1st April 1942 at Ternhill by redesignating 5 Service Flying Training School.

Gladiator I K8042; Hurricane I N2325, X AG245; Master I T8452 57, II DL273 FF, III W8823 45; Magister I N3955; Spitfire I R6684, IIA P8257, VB W3817; Tomahawk I AH850; Harvard I IIB KF187 11; Anson I K6273 A; Hornet Moth W5830; Walrus I W3037, II HD920.

Disbanded 21st June 1945 at Ternhill.

Reformed 21st June 1945 at Ternhill by redesignating 9 (Pilots) Advanced Flying Unit.

B	*Harvard IIB FX227 B-X.*
E	*Harvard IIB KF221 E-P.*
H	*Harvard IIB FX406 H-L.*
Also used	*Spitfire XVI SM350.*

Disbanded 15th April 1946 at Ternhill and absorbed by 7 Service Flying Training School.

6 (PILOTS) ADVANCED FLYING UNIT
Formed 1st April 1942 at Little Rissington by redesignating 6 Service Flying Training School.

Botha I L6340; Anson I W1904; Oxford I HN649 J4, II AB645; Magister N3940; Tiger Moth BB800; Harvard IIB KF148.

Disbanded 17th December 1945 at Little Rissington to become 6 Service Flying Training School.

7 (PILOTS) ADVANCED FLYING UNIT
Formed 1st June 1942 at Peterborough.

Hind K5399; Prefect K5065; Master I T8454 61, II W9038 42, III DL826; Magister I L5967; Anson I R3587; Oxford I HM736, II X6978; Tiger Moth II T6265; Hurricane I L2087 A, IIB Z2695; Harvard IIB KF183.

Disbanded 21st December 1944 at Peterborough to become 7 Service Flying Training School.

9 (PILOTS) ADVANCED FLYING UNIT
Formed 14th February 1942 at Hullavington by redesignating 9 Service Flying Training School.

Master I N7938, II EM409 F48, III W8485; Tutor K3219; Roc I L3173; Hurricane I P5196, IIA Z2752, IIB Z3596 13; Walrus I W3037; II HD920; Oxford II X7186; Tiger Moth II DE558; Anson I DG939; Swordfish I K8354 19, II DK759 4; Albacore I N4247; Battle I L5993; Magister I N3857; Harvard IIB KF173; Horsa I HG744.

Disbanded 21st June 1945 at Errol and absorbed by 5 (Pilots) Advanced Flying Unit.

11 (PILOTS) ADVANCED FLYING UNIT
Formed 14th March 1942 at Shawbury by redesignating 11 Service Flying Training School.

Tutor K3405; Moth X5017; Magister I L5991; Master III DL947; Anson I NK645 13; Oxford I MP305 A22; Hurricane IIC LF649 R40; Harvard IIB KF174.

Disbanded 1st June 1945 at Calveley.

12 (PILOTS) ADVANCED FLYING UNIT
Formed 1st April 1942 at Grantham (later Spitalgate) by redesignating 12 Service Flying Training School.

Anson I AW940; Oxford I AS502, II N4792; Blenheim I L1139 115, IV N3611, V AZ959 48; Tiger Moth II R5133; Whitney Straight BS818; Gipsy Moth DG657; Proctor III HM312; Beaufort IIA ML686 J.

Disbanded 21st June 1945 at Hixon.

14 (PILOTS) ADVANCED FLYING UNIT
Formed 26th January 1942 at Ossington by redesignating 14 Service Flying Training School.

Anson I N5109; Oxford I BG209 DC, II V3529; Master II AZ318; Wellington IC R1490; Horsa I HG933; Gipsy Moth BK842.

Disbanded 1st September 1944 at Banff.

15 (PILOTS) ADVANCED FLYING UNIT
Formed 1st March 1942 at Leconfield by redesignating 15 Service Flying Training School.

Tutor K3384; Anson I N5262 ZA, X NK355; Oxford I EB728 DX, II N6282; Gipsy Moth BK843; Tiger Moth II R5135; Tipsy BC HM494; Wellington IV Z1382.

Disbanded 19th June 1945 at Babdown Farm.

17 (PILOTS) ADVANCED FLYING UNIT
Formed 29th January 1942 at Watton.

Master I T8541 83, II DK915 49, III DL799; Anson I K8755; Hurricane I P3715; Magister I N3920.

Disbanded 1st February 1944 at Calveley.

18 (PILOTS) ADVANCED FLYING UNIT
Formed 27th October 1942 at Church Lawford by redesignating 1 Flying Instructors School.

Tutor K3219; Prefect K5067; Oxford I R6181 84, II R6234; Anson I NK459 Z; Defiant I N3309; Magister I L8091.

Disbanded 29th May 1945 at Church Lawford.

19 (PILOTS) ADVANCED FLYING UNIT
Formed 20th October 1942 at Dalcross from an element of 2 Flying Instructors School.

Tutor K3466; Oxford I X6848, II N6400; Anson I N4989; Magister I N3904.

Disbanded 25th February 1944 at Dalcross and absorbed by 21 (Pilots) Advanced Flying Unit.

20 (PILOTS) ADVANCED FLYING UNIT
Formed 23rd March 1943 at Kidlington by merging 1, 2 and 4 Glider Training Schools.

Audax K7328; Hind K5511; Oxford I BG557 GW, II N6405; Anson I DJ657 LU; Proctor III HM284; Gull Six AX866; Hotspur II BT507, III BT823; Master II DL306; Wellington IV Z1280.

Disbanded 21st June 1945 at Kidlington.

21 (PILOTS) ADVANCED FLYING UNIT
Formed 1st August 1943 at Wheaton Aston by redesignating an element of 11 (Pilots) Advanced Flying Unit.

Nil (8.43–4.47)	*Oxford I LW954, II P1951; Anson I K6184; Battle I L5967; Harvard IIB KF211.*
FDA (4.46–8.47)	*Oxford I V3910 FDA-H; Harvard IIB FX356 FDA-T; Spitfire XVI TE247 FDA-G.*
FDB (4.46–8.47)	*Oxford I DF346 FDB-W.*
FDC (4.46–8.47)	*Oxford I PH349 FDC-Q; Harvard IIB FT401 FDC-P; Tiger Moth II NL764 FDC-O; Wellington X RP322.*
FDD (4.46–8.47)	*Oxford I DF241 FDD-I; Harvard IIB KF986 FDD-B.*
FDE (4.46–8.47)	*Oxford I EB702 FDE-W.*
FDF (4.46–8.47)	*Oxford I R5952 FDF-U.*
FDG (4.46–8.47)	*Anson I N9571 FDG-P.*

Disbanded 6th August 1947 at Moreton-in-Marsh and merged with 1 Refresher School to become 1 and 2 (Pilots) Refresher Flying Units.

PILOTS AND AIRCREW POOL
Formed 1st December 1941 at Gilgil, Southern Rhodesia, by redesignating the Kenya Pool.

Hart; Audax K7531; Tutor.

Disbanded 6th July 1942 at Gilgil to become 1 (Middle East) Pilots and Aircrew Pool.

PILOTS AND OBSERVERS AERIAL GUNNERY AND AERIAL FIGHTING SCHOOL – see Aerial Fighting and Gunnery School

PILOTS REINFORCEMENT AND RESERVE POOL, later REINFORCEMENT AND RESERVE POOL
Formed 24th June 1940 at Ismailia, Egypt. Redesignated the Reinforcement and Reserve Pool from 1st August 1940.

Gauntlet II K7891; Wellesley K7789; Blenheim I L1499.

Disbanded 21st September 1940 at Ismailia to become the Training Unit and Reserve Pool.

10 (POLISH) FERRY FLIGHT
Formed 27th March 1941 at Kington Langley by redesignating 8 Service Ferry Pool.

Dominie I R9553; Spitfire VA R7220; Hurricane I V6953, IIB Z3059.

Disbanded 27th July 1941 at Kington Langley and absorbed by the Headquarters, Service Ferry Training Squadron.

POLISH FIGHTING TEAM
Formed 16th March 1943 at Bu Grara, Tunisia, as an independent unit attached to 145 Squadron.

ZX   *Spitfire VB; IX EN268 ZX-5.*

Disbanded 12th May 1943 at Hergla, Tunisia.

1 (POLISH) FLYING TRAINING SCHOOL
Formed 28th November 1940 at Hucknall by redesignating the Polish Training and Grading Flight.

Battle N2031; Oxford I R5975, II V3558; Magister P6370; Tiger Moth II T7185.

Disbanded 9th June 1941 at Hucknall to become 16 (Polish) Service Flying Training School and 25 (Polish) Elementary Flying Training School.

16 (POLISH) FLYING TRAINING SCHOOL – see 16 Service Flying Training School, later 16 (Polish) Flying Training School

POLISH TRAINING AND GRADING FLIGHT
Formed 15th February 1940 at Redhill.

Battle L5093 4; Magister P6370.

Disbanded 28th November 1940 at Hucknall to become 1 (Polish) Flying Training School.

POLISH TRAINING UNIT
Formed 14th March 1940 at Hucknall.

Battle L5292, Battle Trainer P6718; Anson I.

Disbanded 15th June 1940 at Hucknall to become 18 (Polish) Operational Training Unit.

POOL OF PILOTS, JOYCE GREEN – see below

POOL OF PILOTS, MANSTON, later POOL OF PILOTS, JOYCE GREEN
Formed 1st April 1918 at Manston by redesignating the RNAS War School, Manston.

Avro 504A D1646, Avro 504B N6678; D.H.4 A7992; Spad B1622; Camel B5733; Pup C229; F.2B C902; D.H.9 D474; S.E.5a D3486; Snipe E7991.

Disbanded December 1919 at Joyce Green.

PRACTICE FLIGHT, BLIDA – see Fighter Pilots Practice Flight, Blida

PRACTICE FLIGHT, HELIOPOLIS
Formed 1st March 1928 at Heliopolis, Egypt, within the Station Flight, Heliopolis.

Fairey IIIF J9680; Hart K2460.

Disbanded 1st June 1938 at Heliopolis to become the Communications Flight, Heliopolis.

PRACTICE FLIGHT, HOME AIRCRAFT DEPOT, HENLOW
Formed by September 1927 at Henlow.

Moth J8817.

Existed to at least 1934 at Henlow.

Reformed by January 1937 at Henlow.

Prefect K5064; Tiger Moth I K4246; Magister P2458.

Existed to at least January 1939 at Henlow.

PRACTICE FLIGHT, MANSTON – see Training Command Practice Flight

PRACTICE FLIGHT, SÉTIF – see Fighter Pilots Practice Flight, Sétif

1 PRACTICE FLYING UNIT
Formed 4th March 1940 at Meir.

Hector K9699; Hind K4650.

Disbanded 16th June 1940 at Meir.

PRIMARY FLYING SCHOOL – see Central Flying School

PSYCHOLOGICAL WARFARE FLIGHT – see Voice Flight

PUPIL PILOTS POOL
Formed 8th March 1943 at Wolverhampton by redesignating 3 Pupil Pilots Pool.

Aircraft provided by 28 Elementary Flying Training School.

Disbanded by April 1947 at Wolverhampton and probably absorbed by 28 Elementary Flying Training School.

1 PUPIL PILOTS POOL
Formed 3rd November 1941 at Peterborough.

Aircraft provided by 17 Elementary Flying Training School.

Disbanded 8th August 1943 at Peterborough.

2 PUPIL PILOTS POOL
Formed 3rd November 1941 at Clyffe Pypard.

Aircraft provided by 29 Elementary Flying Training School.

Disbanded 8th March 1943 at Clyffe Pypard.

3 PUPIL PILOTS POOL
Formed 3rd November 1941 at Wolverhampton.

Aircraft provided by 28 Elementary Flying Training School.

Disbanded 8th March 1943 at Wolverhampton to become the Pupil Pilots Pool.

'Q' FLIGHT
Formed 25th August 1939 at Ambala, India, by redesignating an element of 60 Squadron.

Blenheim I.

Disbanded 15th December 1940 at Ambala to become 4 Coast Defence Flight, Indian Air Force Volunteer Reserve.

Reformed October 1943 at Rednal within 61 Operational Training Unit.

Gladiator I K7898; Wellington.

Disbanded by January 1944 at Rednal.

'Q' UNIT
Formed by April 1920 at Eil, Germany.

No aircraft, if any, known.

Existed to at least July 1920 at Eil.

1 QUEEN BEE FLIGHT
Formed 10th May 1937 at Henlow.

Queen Bee.

Disbanded 16th September 1937 at Biggin Hill to become 'D' Flight, 1 Anti-Aircraft Co-operation Unit.

QUEEN'S FLIGHT
Formed 16th November 1953 at Benson by redesignating the King's Flight.

Viking C.2 VL233, VVIP.2 VL246; Devon C.1 VP961; Dragonfly HC.4 XF261; Heron C.3 XH375, C.4 XM295; Dakota IV KN452; Whirlwind HAR.4 XL111, HCC.4 XV733, HCC.8 XN127, HAR.10 XP299; HCC.12 XR486; Andover CC.2 XS790; Wessex HC.2 XV726; HCC.4 XV733; Basset CC.1 XS770; Chipmunk T.10 WP903; BAe 146 CC.2 ZE700.

Disbanded 31st March 1995 at Benson and merged with 32 Squadron to become 32 (The Royal) Squadron.

QUEENS UNIVERSITY AIR SQUADRON – see Belfast University Air Squadron, later Queens University Air Squadron

RADAR INTERCEPTION DEVELOPMENT SQUADRON – see Central Fighter Establishment

RADAR METEORLOGICAL FLIGHT
Formed (date and location unknown). Reported to have operated from Brawdy between January and July 1946. Possibly a detachment of the Telecommunications Research Establishment.

Oxford I PH480.

Disbanded (date and location unknown).

RADAR NAVIGATION AIDS FLIGHT – see 60 Group Radar Navigation Aids Test Flight

RADAR RECONNAISSANCE FLIGHT
Formed 1st October 1951 at Benson by redesignating an element of 58 Squadron.

Lincoln B.2 RE319 A; Hastings C.1 TG503; Canberra PR.3 WE143, B.6 WJ770; Victor B(PR).1 XA935.

Disbanded 1st November 1963 at Gaydon.

RADAR RESEARCH FLYING UNIT, later RADAR RESEARCH SQUADRON
Formed 1st November 1955 at Defford by redesignating the Telecommunications Flying Unit. The unit thereafter provided flying duties for the Radar Research Establishment and, from 26th March 1976, the Royal Signals and Radar Establishment. Redesignated the Radar Research Squadron from 1977 on moving to Royal Aircraft Establishment, Bedford.

Lincoln B.2 RE346; Hastings C.1 TG503, C.2 WD482; Hermes II VX234; Devon C.1 VP972; Hoverfly; Ashton B.3 WB492; Valetta C.1 WJ338, T.3 WG262; Varsity T.1 WF379; Vampire FB.5 VV217, T.11 XD267; Canberra VN813, B.2 WH702, PR.3 WE147, T.4 WH854, B.6 WH953, B.6(BS) WT305, PR.7 WH776, B(I).8 WT327, B.16 XM570; Venom NF.2 WR783, NF.3 WX797; Valiant B.1 WZ370; Meteor F.8 WH284, NF.11 WM373, NF.13 WM366, NF.14 WS832; Hunter F.1 WT557, F.4 WV325; Whirlwind HAR.1 XA865, HAR.2 XJ759, HAR.3 XG588, HAS.7 XG589; Wessex HAS.1 XM926, HU.5 XT762; Buccaneer S.2 XN975, S.2B XW526; Viscount 837 XT575; Viscount 838 XT661.

Existed to at least 1988 at Bedford.

RADAR RESEARCH SQUADRON – see Radar Research Flying Unit, later Radar Research Squadron

RADAR TRAINING FLIGHT
Formed 1st September 1972 at Scampton by redesignating the Hastings element of the Strike Command Bombing School to operate in association with 230 Operational Conversion Unit.

Hastings T.5 TG505.

Disbanded 30th June 1977 at Scampton.

RADIO DEVELOPMENT FLIGHT
Formed December 1942 at Drem.

Defiant II AA661; Beaufighter VI EL170.

Disbanded 1st June 1943 at Drem to become 1692 (Radio Development) Flight.

3 RADIO DIRECTION FINDING SCHOOL
Formed 19th August 1942 at Prestwick by redesignating 3 Radio School.

Hart K5847; Botha I L6221; Tiger Moth II T6969.

Disbanded 13th December 1942 at Hooton Park to become 11 Radio School.

RADIO ENGINEERING UNIT – see Signals Development Unit

1 RADIO MAINTENANCE UNIT CALIBRATION FLIGHT, later 1 RADIO SERVICING SECTION CALIBRATION FLIGHT
Formed 1st July 1940 at Wick. Redesignated 1 Radio Servicing Section Calibration Flight from 16th October 1940.

Hornet Moth W5771; Blenheim IV T2335.

Disbanded 16th February 1941 at Longman to become 70 Wing Calibration Flight.

2 RADIO MAINTENANCE UNIT CALIBRATION FLIGHT, later 2 RADIO SERVICING SECTION CALIBRATION FLIGHT
Formed 1st July 1940 at Dyce. Redesignated 2 Radio Servicing Section Calibration Flight from 16th October 1940.

Hornet Moth W9388; Blenheim IV V5766.

Disbanded 16th February 1941 at Dyce to become 71 Wing Calibration Flight.

3 RADIO MAINTENANCE UNIT CALIBRATION FLIGHT, later 3 RADIO SERVICING SECTION CALIBRATION FLIGHT
Formed 1st July 1940 at Usworth. Redesignated 3 Radio Servicing Section Calibration Flight from 16th October 1940.

Hornet Moth W9382; Blenheim IV V5695.

Disbanded 16th February 1941 at Usworth to become 72 Wing Calibration Flight.

4 RADIO MAINTENANCE UNIT CALIBRATION FLIGHT, later 4 RADIO SERVICING SECTION CALIBRATION FLIGHT
Formed 1st July 1940 at Church Fenton. Redesignated 4 Radio Servicing Section Calibration Flight from 16th October 1940.

Hornet Moth W5778; Blenheim IV V5698.

Disbanded 16th February 1941 at Church Fenton to become 73 Wing Calibration Flight.

5 RADIO MAINTENANCE UNIT CALIBRATION FLIGHT, later 5 RADIO SERVICING SECTION CALIBRATION FLIGHT
Formed 1st July 1940 at Duxford. Redesignated 5 Radio Servicing Section Calibration Flight from 16th October 1940.

Hornet Moth W5752; Blenheim IV V5731; Cierva C.30A AP506.

Disbanded 16th February 1941 at Duxford to become 74 Wing Calibration Flight.

6 RADIO MAINTENANCE UNIT CALIBRATION FLIGHT, later 6 RADIO SERVICING SECTION CALIBRATION FLIGHT
Formed 1st July 1940 at Biggin Hill. Redesignated 6 Radio Servicing Section Calibration Flight from 16th October 1940.

Hornet Moth W5773; Blenheim IV V5739.

Disbanded 16th February 1941 at Biggin Hill to become 75 Wing Calibration Flight.

7 RADIO MAINTENANCE UNIT CALIBRATION FLIGHT, later 7 RADIO SERVICING SECTION CALIBRATION FLIGHT
Formed 15th July 1940 at Filton. Redesignated 7 Radio Servicing Section Calibration Flight from 16th October 1940.

Hornet Moth W5747.

Disbanded 16th February 1941 at Filton to become 76 Wing Calibration Flight.

8 RADIO MAINTENANCE UNIT CALIBRATION FLIGHT, later 8 RADIO SERVICING SECTION CALIBRATION FLIGHT
Formed 1st July 1940 at Speke. Redesignated 8 Radio Servicing Section Calibration Flight from 16th October 1940.

Hornet Moth W5753; Blenheim IV V5794.

Disbanded 16th February 1941 at Speke to become 77 Wing Calibration Flight.

1 RADIO SCHOOL
Formed 10th March 1941 at Cranwell.

Botha I L6218; Proctor I P6234.

Disbanded 1st January 1943 at Cranwell to become 8 Radio School.

Reformed 1st January 1943 at Cranwell by redesignating 1 Signals School.

1 (1.43–4.46)	Proctor I P6312 1-12, II Z7205, III LZ639 1-37; Dominie I X7345; Magister I N5413; Tiger Moth II R5215; Hudson I N7267; Mosquito II DD670; Hurricane IIB HV366; Halifax VI RG875 1-01.
TCA (4.46–4.51)	Proctor IV NP286 TCA-V; Halifax VI RG875 TCA-B.
TCR (4.46–4.51)	Proctor IV MX452 TCR-G; Dominie I HG692 TCR-O; Tiger Moth II DE975 TCR-K; Oxford I HN473 TCR-H; Anson T.22 VV365 TCR-A.
Nil (4.51–)	Chipmunk T.10; Varsity T.1 WL641 A; Vampire T.11 XE894.

Current at 1st April 1997 at Cosford.

2 RADIO SCHOOL
Formed 18th January 1940 at Yatesbury.

No aircraft allocated.

Disbanded 21st May 1942 at Yatesbury to become 2 Radio Direction Finding School.

Reformed 1st January 1943 at Yatesbury by redesignating 2 Signals School.

2	Tiger Moth II EM754; Botha I L6467; Proctor III Z7237, IV NP397 2-74; Blenheim IV Z6090; Dominie I HG691 2-19; Anson T.22 VV362.

Disbanded 31st October 1965 at Yatesbury.

3 RADIO SCHOOL
Formed 27th December 1940 at Prestwick by redesignating the Air Interception/Air to Surface Vessel School.

Audax K5133; Blenheim I L1115, IV T2325; Botha I L6207; Anson I N9598.

Disbanded 19th August 1942 at Prestwick to become 3 Radio Direction Finding School.

Reformed 1st January 1943 at Compton Basset by redesignating 3 Signals School.

No aircraft allocated.

Disbanded 30th November 1964 at Compton Basset.

4 RADIO SCHOOL
Formed 1st January 1943 at Madley by redesignating 4 Signals School.

4 (1.43–4.46)	Dominie I X7449 4-92, II NR739; Proctor I P6180 4-99, III R7537, IV NP365 4-32; Oxford II ED126 4-109; Magister N5413; Tiger Moth I L6934.
TMA (4.46–3.49)	Proctor IV NP365 TMA-R; Anson T.22 VS592 TMA-W.
TMD (4.46–3.49)	Proctor IV NP369 TMD-N.
TME (4.46–3.49)	Tiger Moth II T6167 TME-D.
TML (4.46–3.49)	Dominie I.
TSM (3.49–5.51)	Dominie I NR769 TSM-S; Proctor IV NP309 TSM-C; Anson T.22 VS595 TSM-P.
Also used	Master III DL856; Spitfire F.22 PK429; Anson XII PH771, XIX TX160.

Disbanded 1st May 1951 at Swanton Morley to become 1 Air Signallers School.

6 RADIO SCHOOL
Formed 1st January 1943 at Bolton by redesignating 6 Signals School.

Blenheim IV V5739; Tiger Moth II DE975.

Disbanded 21st May 1945 at Bolton.

Reformed 9th October 1950 at Cranwell by redesignating an element of 1 Radio School.

Oxford I NM356; Anson T.22 VV365 A.

Disbanded 1st December 1952 at Cranwell and absorbed by 1 Radio School.

10 RADIO SCHOOL
Formed 1st January 1943 at Carew Cheriton by redesignating 4 Radio Direction Finding School.

5	Anson I N5176 5-26, XI NK872; Oxford I LX732 5-78; Proctor III HM481 5-94; Hudson I N7259; Tiger Moth II N6655; Moth Minor W6460; Master III DL837; Spitfire VB BL450.

Disbanded 24th November 1945 at Carew Cheriton.

11 RADIO SCHOOL
Formed 11th December 1942 at Hooton Park by redesignating 3 Radio Direction Finding School.

6	Botha I L6393 6-15; Anson I EG306 6-34; Tiger Moth II T6979; Oxford II N6349.

Disbanded 31st August 1944 at Hooton Park.

12 RADIO SCHOOL
Formed 17th July 1943 at St Athan.

7	Proctor II Z7207, III HM358 7-01; Anson I NK595 7-44; Oxford I LX730 7-34, II ED126; Tiger Moth II N6749.

Disbanded 7th March 1946 at St Athan and merged with 14 Radio School to become the Empire Radio School.

14 RADIO SCHOOL
Formed 1st June 1944 at St Athan by redesignating an element of 12 Radio School.

Proctor and Anson aircraft drawn from the establishment of 12 Radio School.

Disbanded 7th March 1946 at Debden and merged with 12 Radio School to become the Empire Radio School.

1 RADIO SERVICING SECTION CALIBRATION FLIGHT – see 1 Radio Maintenance Unit Calibration Flight, later 1 Radio Servicing Section Calibration Flight

2 RADIO SERVICING SECTION CALIBRATION FLIGHT – see 2 Radio Maintenance Unit Calibration Flight, later 2 Radio Servicing Section Calibration Flight

3 RADIO SERVICING SECTION CALIBRATOIN FLIGHT – see 3 Radio Maintenance Unit Calibration Flight, later 3 Radio Servicing Section Calibration Flight

4 RADIO SERVICING SECTION CALIBRATION FLIGHT – see 4 Radio Maintenance Unit Calibration Flight, later 4 Radio Servicing Section Calibration Flight

5 RADIO SERVICING SECTION CALIBRATION FLIGHT – see 5 Radio Maintenance Unit Calibration Flight, later 5 Radio Servicing Section Calibration Flight

6 RADIO SERVICING SECTION CALIBRATION FLIGHT – see 6 Radio Maintenance Unit Calibration Flight, later 6 Radio Servicing Section Calibration Flight

7 RADIO SERVICING SECTION CALIBRATION FLIGHT – see 7 Radio Maintenance Unit Calibration Flight, later 7 Radio Servicing Section Calibration Flight

8 RADIO SERVICING SECTION CALIBRATION FLIGHT – see 8 Radio Maintenance Unit Calibration Flight, later 8 Radio Servicing Section Calibration Flight

RADIO WARFARE ESTABLISHMENT
Formed 21st July 1945 at Swanton Morley by redesignating the Bomber Support Development Unit.

U3	Fortress III KJ117 U3-E; Halifax III MZ491 U3-V.
V6	Allocated but not used.
Also used	Lancaster I ME383, III ME535; Dominie I

X7327; Oxford I LX122, II W6641; Spitfire VB AA982; Anson I DJ584; Tiger Moth II N9211; Ju 88G-6 AIR MIN 2; Proctor III HM422; Wellington X NA841; Beaufighter VI EL181, X NV542; Mosquito VI PZ227, XVI NS784; Lincoln I RE258.

Disbanded 1st September 1946 at Watton and merged with the Signals Flying Unit to become the Central Signals Establishment.

RAPID LANDING FLIGHT
Formed August 1950 at Martlesham Heath, within the Instrument Flight of the Armament and Instrument Experimental Establishment, to carry out trials involving the rapid recovery of fighter aircraft. A preliminary trial was carried out from September 1950 using Meteor T.7 VW411 and intensive trials began the following month using Mosquito NF.38s VX861, VX865, VX866 and VX888. It is interesting to note the Central Flying School concluded rapid landing trials by June 1949.

RDF CALIBRATION FLIGHT, BLIDA – see RDF Calibration Flight, Sebala II, later RDF Flight, Blida

RDF CALIBRATION FLIGHT, SEBALA II, later RDF CALIBRATION FLIGHT, BLIDA
Formed by June 1942 at Sebala II, Tunisia. Redesignated the RDF Calibration Flight, Blida from 7th August 1943.

Blenheim V EH325; Beaufighter II V8192.

Disbanded 25th September 1943 at Blida to become 1578 (Calibration) Flight.

3 (RECONNAISSANCE) FLIGHT, KENYA AUXILIARY AIR UNIT
Formed 4th September 1939 at Mombasa, Kenya.

No aircraft known.

Disbanded (date and location unknown).

RECONNAISSANCE FLIGHT, MOMBASA – see 3 (Reconnaissance) Flight, Kenya Auxiliary Air Unit

(RECONNAISSANCE) TRAINING FLIGHT – see Royal Air Force Base, Leuchars, later Royal Air Force Training Base, Leuchars

'RED ARROWS' – see Royal Air Force Aerobatic Team – the 'Red Arrows'

REFRESHER FLIGHT, 17 SERVICE FLYING TRAINING SCHOOL
A term given to an element of 17 Service Flying Training School, Coleby Grange that became 1 Refresher School.

REFRESHER FLYING SQUADRON – see School of Refresher Flying, later Refresher Flying Squadron

REFRESHER FLYING TRAINING SCHOOL, later 1 REFRESHER FLYING TRAINING SCHOOL
Formed 1st May 1942 at Moreton Valence by redesignating the Pilot Refresher Training Unit. Redesignated 1 Refresher Flying Training School from 17th May 1942.

Tutor K3414; Master II W8790, III W8960; Oxford I DF341.

Disbanded 31st October at Kirknewtown.

1 REFRESHER FLYING TRAINING SCHOOL – see Refresher Flying Training School, later 1 Refresher Flying Training School

1 REFRESHER FLYING UNIT
Planned formation from 22nd December 1943, within the North West African Coastal Air Force with Harvard IIB aircraft, cancelled 6th July 1944.

2 REFRESHER FLYING UNIT
Planned formation from 22nd December 1943, within the North West African Tactical Air Force with Harvard IIB aircraft, cancelled 6th July 1944.

3 REFRESHER FLYING UNIT
Formed 9th February 1944 at Poona, India, by redesignating the Aircrew Transit Pool.

Blenheim V BA334; Anson I DJ211; Oxford I NM463; Harvard IIB FE415; Hurricane IIB BD881, IIC KW758, IV KW910; Spitfire VC MA393, VIII MT562 T, XIV RN134; Beaufighter I X7776, VI KV899, X NE531; Beaufort I JM431; Thunderbolt II KJ174; Wellington IC HX564, III HZ180, X HE667.

Disbanded 15th December 1945 at Bairagarh, India, to become 3 Fighter Support Training Unit.

4 REFRESHER FLYING UNIT
Formed 16th May 1944 at Haverfordwest by redesignating 7 Operational Training Unit.

Wellington III X3278, X HE223, XI HZ430, XIII MF302, XIV HF224.

Disbanded 5th October 1944 at Mullaghmore to become the Loran Training Unit.

5 REFRESHER FLYING UNIT
Formed 1st July 1944 at Sinello, Italy, by redesignating the Desert Air Force Training Flight.

Boston III W8303; Spitfire VB ER486, VC JG778, IX BS559; Kittyhawk III FR828, IV FT851; Harvard IIA EX720; Mustang III FB265, IVA KH856.

Disbanded 24th August 1945 at Gaudo, Italy.

6 REFRESHER FLYING UNIT
Formed 8th November 1944 at Kolar, India, by redesignating an element of 1673 Conversion Unit.

Liberator III BZ845, VI EW220; Hurricane IIC LB895.

Disbanded 31st December 1945 at Kolar.

7 REFRESHER FLYING UNIT
Formed February 1945 at Shallufa, Egypt.

Anson I MG339.

Disbanded 17th September 1945 at Shallufa.

8 REFRESHER FLYING UNIT
Formed 25th January 1945 at Yelahanka, India, by redesignating 1670 Conversion Unit.

Thunderbolt I HD107, II KJ286; Spitfire VIII MV459; Harvard IIB FE366.

Disbanded 10th September 1945 at Bairagarh and absorbed by 3 Refresher Flying Unit.

9 REFRESHER FLYING UNIT
Formed 31st August 1945 at Ranchi, India, by redesignating an element of 1672 Conversion Unit.

Mosquito VI HR543.

Disbanded 30th November 1945 at Ranchi, India.

1 REFRESHER SCHOOL
Formed 11th November 1946 at Enstone by redesignating the Refresher Flight of 17 Service Flying Training School.

Magister; Harvard IIB; Oxford I.

Disbanded 6th August 1947 at Moreton-in-Marsh and merged with an element of 21 (Pilots) Advanced Flying Unit to become 1 (Pilots) Refresher Flying Unit.

REINFORCEMENT AND RESERVE POOL – see Pilots Reinforcement and Reserve Pool, later Reinforcement and Reserve Pool

RESEARCH AND DEVELOPMENT UNIT
Formed 14th September 1943 at Chakeri, India, within 322 Maintenance Unit.

Tiger Moth DG456; Anson I LT678 (on loan).

Disbanded 31st July 1946 at Chakeri.

RESERVE AEROPLANE SQUADRONS, later RESERVE SQUADRONS, later TRAINING SQUADRONS

The following formations were originally designated as Reserve Aeroplane Squadrons, becoming Reserve Squadrons from 13th January 1916 and Training Squadrons from 31st May 1917.

RESERVE AEROPLANE SQUADRON, later 1 RESERVE AEROPLANE SQUADRON, later 1 RESERVE SQUADRON, later 1 TRAINING SQUADRON

Formed August 1914 at Farnborough by redesignating an element of 6 Squadron, RFC. Redesignated 1 Reserve Aeroplane Squadron from 12th November 1915, 1 Reserve Squadron from 13th January 1916 and 1 Training Squadron from 31st May 1917.

Longhorn 214; Shorthorn 379; Bristol Boxkite 718; Voisin LA 1898; Avro Es 285; Bleriot XI 323; Henry Farman F.20 294; Blériot Parasol 582; B.E.2a 347, B.E.2b 709, B.E.2c 1807; Avro 504A 4753, Avro 504D 796; Morane-Saulnier G 482; Morane H 5709; Morane LA 5123; Morane N A127; Caudron G.3 1886; Martinsyde S.1 696; Bristol Scout C 4698; Pup; Curtiss JN-3 7310.

Detached elements became 10 Squadron on 1st January 1915, 15 Squadron on 1st March 1915, 'A' Flight, 31 Squadron on 11th October 1915, 60 Squadron on 15th May 1916, 81 Squadron on 7th January 1917 and 88 Squadron on 24th July 1917.

Disbanded 2nd August 1917 at Gosport and merged with 27 and 55 Training Squadrons to become the School Of Special Flying, Gosport.

Reformed 1st October 1917 at Narborough as 1 Training Squadron.

Camel B6287; Pup B7517; Dolphin; Avro 504J, Avro 504K F8713.

Disbanded 27th July 1918 at Beaulieu and merged with 73 Training Squadron to become 29 Training Depot Station.

2 RESERVE AEROPLANE SQUADRON, later 2 RESERVE SQUADRON, later 2 TRAINING SQUADRON

Formed 12th November 1914 at Brooklands. Redesignated 2 Reserve Squadron from 13th January 1916 and 2 Training Squadron from 31st May 1917.

Boxkite 718; B.E.8 740; Avro 504 784; Longhorn 4010; Shorthorn A728; B.E.2c 4721; Henry Farman F.20 719; Blériot XI 4652; Morane H 594; Vickers FB.5 32; Vickers FB.6 649; Martinsyde S.1 2452; Bristol Scout C 1607; Camel B5200; S.E.5a C5365; F.2B C4805.

Elements detached and became 46 Squadron on 19th April 1916 and 74 Squadron on 1st July 1917.

Disbanded 15th July 1918 at Northolt and merged with 4 Training Squadron to become 30 Training Depot Station.

3 RESERVE AEROPLANE SQUADRON, later 3 RESERVE SQUADRON, later 3 TRAINING SQUADRON

Formed 21st January 1915 at Netheravon. Redesignated 3 Reserve Squadron from 13th January 1916 and 3 Training Squadron from 31st May 1917.

Longhorn 549; Henry Farman F.20 699; Martinsyde S.1 717; Shorthorn A2495; Avro 504A A8518, Avro 504B B390, 504J C4415; Blériot XI 4650; Caudron G.3 5037; B.E.2e A1265; Pup B2152; F.K.8 C8468; S.E.5a D3533.

Elements detached and became 14 Squadron on 3rd February 1915 and 86 Squadron on 1st September 1917.

Disbanded 15th July 1918 at Shoreham and merged with 27 Training Squadron to become 21 Training Depot Station.

Reformed 15th May 1919 at Lopcombe Corner by redesignating 3 Training Depot Station.

No aircraft known.

Disbanded 20th June 1919 at Lopcombe Corner.

4 RESERVE AEROPLANE SQUADRON, later 4 RESERVE SQUADRON, later 4 TRAINING SQUADRON

Formed 29th January 1915 at Farnborough. Redesignated 4 Reserve Squadron from 13th January 1916 and 4 Training Squadron from 31st May 1917.

Henry Farman F.20 563; Morane H 591; Avro 500 491; Avro 504 4255, Avro 504 792, Avro 504A 2892; Shorthorn B3988; Longhorn 2966; B.E.2b 2177, B.E.2c 2117; Blériot Parasol 2861; Blériot Monoplane 4296; Martinsyde S.1 4232; F.K.2 5329; Caudron G.3 5040; Curtiss JN-3 7310; D.H.6 C5724.

Elements detached and became 18 Squadron on 11th May 1915, 'A' Flight, 1 Training Depot Station on 20th July 1917 and 18 Squadron on 11th May 1915.

Disbanded 15th July 1918 and merged with 2 Training Squadron to become 30 Training Depot Station.

Reformed 14th March 1919 at Hooton Park by redesignating 4 Training Depot Station.

No aircraft known.

Disbanded 31st May 1919 at Hooton Park.

Reformed 31st May 1919 at North Shotwick by redesignating 51 Training Squadron.

F.2B C1033.

Disbanded 26th April 1920 at North Shotwick to become 5 Flying Training School.

5 RESERVE AEROPLANE SQUADRON, later 5 RESERVE SQUADRON, later 5 TRAINING SQUADRON

Formed 11th May 1915 at Castle Bromwich. Redesignated 5 Reserve Squadron from 13th January 1916 and 5 Training Squadron from 31st May 1917.

B.E.12 6155; Longhorn B3982; Shorthorn B3981; Martinsyde S.1; B.E.2c 2736; D.H.6 A9736; Pup; Camel C127.

Elements detached and became 19 Squadron on 1st September 1915, 54 Squadron on 15th May 1916 and, together with an element of 34 Squadron, 55 Squadron on 8th June 1916.

Disbanded 1st September 1918 at Fowlmere to become 31 Training Depot Station.

Reformed 14th March 1919 at Easton-on-the-Hill by redesignating 5 Training Depot Station.

No aircraft known.

Disbanded December 1919 at Easton-on-the-Hill.

6 RESERVE AEROPLANE SQUADRON, later 6 RESERVE SQUADRON, later 6 TRAINING SQUADRON

Formed 17th July 1915 at Montrose. Redesignated 6 Reserve Squadron from 13th January 1916 and 6 Training Squadron from 31st May 1917.

Longhorn 2974; D.H.1 4624; Caudron G.3 5049; F.B.9 5275; Martinsyde S.1 5444; Shorthorn 5900; Grahame-White XV A1662; Henry Farman F.20 A1717; Avro 504A 7956, Avro 504J D7751, Avro 504K D6287; D.H.2 A2581; Bristol Scout C 4688; Curtiss JN-3 7310; Curtiss JN-4 A1260; F.K.3; F.E.8 6405; B.E.2d 6248; Pup D4030; Camel C15; 1½ Strutter A6046.

Elements detached and became 25 Squadron on 25th September 1915, 44 Squadron on 15th April 1916 and 89 Squadron on 24th July 1917.

Disbanded 17th July 1918 at Montrose and merged with 18 Training Squadron to become 32 Training Depot Station.

7 RESERVE AEROPLANE SQUADRON, later 7 RESERVE SQUADRON, later 7 TRAINING SQUADRON

Formed 28th July 1915 at Netheravon. Redesignated 7 Reserve Squadron from 13th January 1916 and 7 Training Squadron from 31st May 1917.

Longhorn 549; Shorthorn 7371; Martinsyde S.1 5452; F.K.2 5334; Curtiss JN-3 7310; Avro 504 784, Avro 504A 4745; B.E.8a 2150; R.E.5 2457; F.E.2b A857; B.E.2e B6176; R.E.8 A4504; Camel C108; D.H.6 A9688.

Elements detached and became 20 Squadron on 1st September 1915, 48 Squadron on 15th April 1916 and, together with an element of 42 Squadron, 62 Squadron on 28th July 1916.

Disbanded 15th August 1918 at Whitney and merged with 8 Training Squadron to become 33 Training Depot Station.

Reformed 14th March 1919 at Sedgeford by redesignating 3 Fighting School.

No aircraft known.

Disbanded October 1919 at Sedgeford.

8 RESERVE AEROPLANE SQUADRON, later 8 RESERVE SQUADRON, later 8 TRAINING SQUADRON

Formed 28th July 1915 at Netheravon. Redesignated 8 Reserve Squadron from 13th January 1916 and 8 Training Squadron from 31st May 1917.

Avro 504 762; Longhorn 6678; Shorthorn A325; B.E.2a 449, B.E.2b 2178, B.E.2c 1681; Voisin LA 4787; F.B.5 5658; B.E.8a 2160; R.E.8; Avro 504A 4745, Avro 504K; D.H.1 4603.

An element detached to become 21 Squadron on 23rd July 1915.

Disbanded 15th August 1918 at Whitney and merged with 7 Training Squadron to become 33 Training Depot Station.

Reformed 15th May 1919 at Netheravon by redesignating 8 Training Depot Station.

F.2B B8918; Pup D4191; Camel F1345; Snipe.

Disbanded 29th July 1919 at Netheravon to become the Netheravon Flying School.

9 RESERVE AEROPLANE SQUADRON, later 9 RESERVE SQUADRON, later 9 TRAINING SQUADRON

Formed 27th July 1915 at Mousehold. Redesignated 9 Reserve Squadron from 13th January 1916 and 9 Training Squadron from 31st May 1917.

Avro 504D 799; Longhorn 2976; Shorthorn 2468; Henry Farman F.20 565; Martinsyde S.1 2449; D.H.1a 4604; Caudron G.3 5043; F.E.2b 6963, F.E.2d A6361; B.E.2c 1720, B.E.2e A3111; F.B.5 5665; R.E.8 A3891; D.H.4 B9951; F.K.3 A8126; D.H.9 D5556.

Elements detached and became 35 Squadron on 1st February 1916, 37 Squadron on 15th April 1916, 51 Squadron on 15th May 1916 and 'C' Flight, 2 Training Depot Station on 15th August 1917.

Disbanded 1st September 1918 at Tallaght to become 25 Training Depot Station.

10 RESERVE AEROPLANE SQUADRON, later 10 RESERVE SQUADRON, later 10 TRAINING SQUADRON

Formed 1st September 1915 at Joyce Green by redesignating an element of 2 Reserve Aeroplane Squadron. Redesignated 10 Reserve Squadron from 13th January 1916 and 10 Training Squadron from 31st May 1917.

Longhorn 4008; Shorthorn 5885; B.E.2c 4700; Avro 504 779, Avro 504A A8507, Avro 504J B3108, Avro 504K D7051 S; Morane H 594; Vickers F.B.5 2883; F.B.9 A1412; JN-3 5723; 1½ Strutter; Bristol Scout C 1607; Bristol Scout D 5575; S.E.4a 5610; S.E.5a D401; D.H.1 4629; F.B.14 A3505; D.H.2 A4798; D.H.4 A7659; D.H.5 A9437; F.E.8 6406; Elephant A3996; F.E.2b B401; Pup B1849 B; R.E.8 A3185; Camel B6416.

An element detached to become 90 Squadron on 8th October 1917.

Disbanded 24th February 1919 at Gosport.

Reformed 14th March 1919 at Harling Road by redesignating 10 Training Depot Station.

F.2B E2005.

Disbanded November 1919 at Harling Road.

11 RESERVE AEROPLANE SQUADRON, later 11 RESERVE SQUADRON, later 11 TRAINING SQUADRON

Formed 12th October 1915 at Northolt by redesignating an element of 4 Reserve Aeroplane Squadron. Redesignated 11 Reserve Squadron from 13th January 1916.

Avro 500 491; Henry Farman F.20 563; Avro 504 775, Avro 504A 2903, Avro 504D 796; Longhorn 4007; Shorthorn 2466; B.E.2c 2117, B.E.2e A1822; JN-3 7310; B.E.12 6669, B.E.12a A591; Blériot Parasol 2861; Martinsyde S.1 4246; R.E.7; 1½ Strutter; Grahame-White XIV; Morane G 597; Bristol Scout D 5589.

Disbanded 8th February 1917 at Rochford to become 98 (Depot) Squadron.

Reformed 7th April 1917 at Montrose as 11 Reserve Squadron by redesignating an element of 18 Reserve Squadron. Redesignated 11 Training Squadron from 31st May 1917.

B.E.2e; B.E.12 6669; Shorthorn A4067; Avro 504J, Avro 504K; Bristol Scout D A1768; Pup B1743; Elephant A3964; D.H.4 A7827; JN-4 B1901; Camel B6425.

An element detached to become 91 Squadron on 1st September 1917.

Disbanded 15th July 1918 at Scampton and merged with 81 Squadron and 60 Training Squadron to become 34 Training Depot Station.

Reformed July 1919 at Old Sarum by redesignating 11 Training Depot Station.

No aircraft known.

Disbanded March 1920 at Old Sarum.

12 RESERVE AEROPLANE SQUADRON, later 12 RESERVE SQUADRON, later 12 TRAINING SQUADRON

Formed 15th November 1915 at Dover by redesignating an element of 9 Squadron. Redesignated 12 Reserve Squadron from 13th January 1916 and 12 Training Squadron from 31st May 1917.

Avro 504 769; Blériot Parasol 585; Blériot XI 4652; Longhorn 2996; R.E.8 B787; Shorthorn C4278; B.E.2d C7116.

An element detached to become 38 Squadron on 1st April 1916.

Disbanded 15th July 1918 at Thetford and merged with 25 Training Squadron to become 35 Training Depot Station.

13 RESERVE AEROPLANE SQUADRON, later 13 RESERVE SQUADRON, later 13 TRAINING SQUADRON

Formed 27th November 1915 at Dover. Redesignated 13 Reserve Squadron from 13th January 1916 and 13 Training Squadron from 31st May 1917.

Avro 504 769, Avro 504A A5921; Blériot Parasol 585; R.E.8 A3180; B.E.2c 4108, B.E.2d 6730, B.E.2e B4423; Curtiss JN-4 B1921; B.E.12 6589; Blériot XI 4652; D.H.2 A4991; D.H.6 A9576.

Elements detached and became 49 Squadron on 15th April 1916 and 99 Squadron on 15th August 1917.

Disbanded 15th July 1918 at Yatesbury and merged with 66 Training Squadron to become 36 Training Depot Station.

Reformed 14th March 1919 at Ternhill as 13 Training Squadron by redesignating 13 Training Depot Station.

No aircraft known.

Disbanded March 1920 at Ternhill.

14 RESERVE AEROPLANE SQUADRON, later 14 RESERVE SQUADRON, later 14 TRAINING SQUADRON

Formed 1st February 1915 at Catterick. Redesignated 14 Reserve Squadron from 13th January 1916 and 14 Training Squadron from 31st May 1917.

Longhorn 6682; Shorthorn A329; B.E.2c 2574; Avro 504A 2911; Martinsyde S.1 5448; F.B.5.

An element detached and became 53 Squadron on 15th May 1916.

Disbanded 15th July 1918 at Bramham and merged with 68 Training Squadron to become 38 Training Depot Station.

Reformed June 1919 at Lake Down by redesignating 14 Training Depot Station.

No aircraft known.

Disbanded September 1919 at Lake Down.

15 RESERVE AEROPLANE SQUADRON, later 15 RESERVE SQUADRON, later 15 TRAINING SQUADRON

Formed 15th December 1915 at Thetford. Redesignated 15 Reserve Squadron from 13th January 1916 and 15 Training Squadron from 31st May 1917.

Avro 504 784, Avro 504A 4045; Longhorn 2964; Shorthorn 5882; R.E.8 A3419; F.K.3 5509; Henry Farman F.20 7341; F.K.8 A9997; Bristol Scout C 5293; B.E.2c 4557, B.E.2e 6273; B.E.12 A6316; JN-4A B1926; D.H.6 B4013; Camel B7433; F.2B C855.

An element detached and became 82 Squadron on 7th January 1917.

Disbanded 15th August 1918 at Spitalgate and merged with 37 Training Squadron to become 39 Training Depot Station.

Reformed 14th March 1919 at Hucknall by redesignating 15 Training Depot Station.

No aircraft known.

Disbanded 4th November 1919 at Hucknall.

16 RESERVE AEROPLANE SQUADRON, later 16 RESERVE SQUADRON, later 16 TRAINING SQUADRON

Formed 15th December 1915 at Beaulieu. Redesignated 16 Reserve Squadron from 13th January 1916 and 16 Training Squadron from 31st May 1917.

Avro 504 780, Avro 504A A464; Martinsyde S.1; B.E.2b 2778, B.E.2c 2653, B.E.2e A3054; B.E.12 6666; R.E.8 A3181; JN-3 7310; JN-4A B1926; Bristol Scout D 5558; D.H.6 A9633.

Elements detached and became 84 Squadron on 7th January 1917 and 103 Squadron on 1st September 1917.

Disbanded 15th July 1918 at Yatesbury and merged with 17 Training Squadron to become 37 Training Depot Station.

17 RESERVE AEROPLANE SQUADRON, later 17 RESERVE SQUADRON, later 17 TRAINING SQUADRON

Formed 15th December 1915 at Croydon. Redesignated 17 Reserve Squadron from 13th January 1916 and 17 Training Squadron from 31st May 1917.

B.E.2c 2574, B.E.2d 5732, B.E.2e A1339; Bristol Scout C 5554; Avro 504A A486; Shorthorn 5885; 1½ Strutter A6945; R.E.8 A3706; D.H.1a A7317; Pup A7317; S.E.5a B8527; D.H.6 C7226; JN-4A B1926.

Disbanded 15th July 1918 at Yatesbury and merged with 16 Training Squadron to become 37 Training Depot Station.

18 RESERVE AEROPLANE SQUADRON, later 18 RESERVE SQUADRON, later 18 TRAINING SQUADRON

Formed 1st January 1916 at Montrose. Redesignated 18 Reserve Squadron from 13th January 1916 and 18 Training Squadron from 31st May 1917.

Martinsyde S.1 4247; B.E.2b 2771, B.E.2c A8948, B.E.2e A3144; F.E.2b; B.E.12 6663, B.E.12a A4041; Pup C287; F.K.3 A8106; JN-3 7310; Elephant; D.H.4; Camel C6; Bristol Scout C 4699, Bristol Scout D A5209; Avro 504J/K E1608.

Elements detached and became 43 Squadron on 15th April 1916, 83 Squadron on 7th January 1917 and 'A' Flight, 7 Training Depot Station on 1st November 1917.

Disbanded 15th July 1918 at Montrose and merged with 6 Training Squadron to become 32 Training Depot Station.

19 RESERVE SQUADRON, later 19 TRAINING SQUADRON

Formed 29th January 1916 at Hounslow by redesignating an element of 24 Squadron. Redesignated 19 Training Squadron from 31st May 1917.

Longhorn; Shorthorn; Henry Farman F.20 7417; Bristol Scout; B.E.12 6507; D.H.1 B3969; D.H.2 A5211; D.H.4 B9471; F.B.5 2346; B.E.2b 2776, B.E.2c 2028, B.E.2e B9469; F.E.2b 4887; Avro 504J C4312; Elephant A6297; R.E.8 A3618.

Elements detached and became 39 Squadron on 15th April 1916 and 'B' Flight, 2 Training Depot Station on 15th August 1917.

Disbanded 13th June 1919 at The Curragh.

20 RESERVE SQUADRON, later 20 TRAINING SQUADRON

Formed 1st February 1916 at Dover. Redesignated 20 Training Squadron from 31st May 1917.

B.E.2c 4094; Avro 504A 4741; R.E.8 A4429; Bristol Scout; D.H.2 5921; B.E.12 6168, B.E.12a A611; F.K.3 A8092; JN-4 B1943; D.H.6 C9434.

Elements detached and became 50 Squadron on 15th May 1916 and 104 Squadron on 1st September 1917.

Disbanded 15th July 1918 at Harlaxton and merged with 53 Training Squadron to become 40 Training Depot Station.

21 RESERVE SQUADRON, later 21 TRAINING SQUADRON

Formed 22nd May 1916 at Shoreham, embarked 18th June 1916 arriving at Abbassia, Egypt, 12th July 1916. Redesignated 21 Training Squadron from 31st May 1917.

Shorthorn; Longhorn A4093; B.E.2c 4554, B.E.2e 6780; Bristol Scout D 5600; D.H.6.

Disbanded 21st July 1918 at Ismailia to become 18 Training Depot Station.

Reformed July 1918 at Driffield by redesignating 21 Training Depot Station.

No aircraft known.

Disbanded February 1920 at Driffield.

22 RESERVE SQUADRON, later 22 TRAINING SQUADRON

Formed 24th August 1916 at Aboukir, Egypt, by redesignating a nucleus assembled earlier in the United Kingdom. Redesignated 20 Training Squadron from 31st May 1917.

Avro 504A A547, Avro 504J D5456, Avro 504K E1759; Shorthorn A4122; B.E.2c 4122; Elephant A1600; Caudron G.3; JN-3 7310; Nieuport 24 B3591; Pup D4114; Bristol Scout C 5324; Bristol Scout D 5602; D.H.2 A4778; D.H.9 D9856.

Disbanded 1st December 1918 at Aboukir and merged with 23 Training Squadron to become 60 Training Depot Station.

Reformed 14th April 1919 at Gormanston.

No aircraft known.

Disbanded September 1919 at Gormanston.

23 RESERVE SQUADRON, later 23 TRAINING SQUADRON

Formed 24th August 1916 at Aboukir, Egypt, by redesignating a nucleus assembled earlier in the United Kingdom. Redesignated 23 Training Squadron from 31st May 1917.

Bristol Scout D 5600; B.E.2c 4554, B.E.2e 6780; Pup D4117; R.E.8 B6557; D.H.6 A9644; Elephant; B.E.12; Avro 504A 4785; D.H.6 A9644.

Disbanded 1st December 1918 at Aboukir and merged with 22 Training Squadron to become 60 Training Depot Station.

24 RESERVE SQUADRON, later 24 TRAINING SQUADRON

Formed 25th May 1916 at Netheravon by redesignating an element of 32 Squadron. Redesignated 24 Training Squadron from 31st May 1917.

Longhorn; Shorthorn A362; Henry Farman F.20 2838; Vickers F.B.5; B.E.2e; F.K.8 C3527; F.2B C4702; D.H.6 C5469.

Disbanded 15th August 1918 at Whitney and merged with 59 Training Squadron to become 24 Training Depot Station.

Reformed 14th April 1919 at Collinstown.

No aircraft known.

Disbanded August 1919 at Collinstown.

25 RESERVE SQUADRON, later 25 TRAINING SQUADRON

Formed 22nd May 1916 at Thetford by redesignating 38 Squadron. Redesignated 25 Training Squadron from 31st May 1917.

F.E.2b 7668; Longhorn A4077; Camel B2505; Shorthorn B9441; D.H.6 C7253; B.E.2e B8816; R.E.8 C2576; D.H.4 B5504; D.H.9 F1793; Avro 504A B4366.

An element detached and became 39 Squadron on 15th April 1916.

Disbanded 15th July 1918 at Thetford and merged with 12 Training Squadron to become 35 Training Depot Station.

26 RESERVE SQUADRON, later 26 TRAINING SQUADRON

Formed 22nd May 1916 at Turnhouse by redesignating 44 Squadron. Redesignated 26 Training Squadron from 31st May 1917.

Longhorn 6694; Shorthorn A330; Henry Farman F.20 A1717;

B.E.2c, B.E.2e A1861; D.H.4 B2645; D.H.9 C6082; F.K.3 F4219; R.E.8 A3923; D.H.6 B2645; D.H.9 C6082

An element detached and became 'B' Flight, 1 Training Depot Station on 20th July 1917.

Disbanded 1st August 1918 at Narborough and merged with 69 Training Squadron to become 22 Training Depot Station.

27 RESERVE SQUADRON, later 27 TRAINING SQUADRON
Formed 22nd May 1916 at Fort Rowner, Gosport, by redesignating 41 Squadron. Redesignated 27 Training Squadron from 31st May 1917.

Longhorn; Shorthorn A2433; Henry Farman F.20.

Elements detached and became 41 Squadron on 14th July 1916 and 79 Squadron on 1st August 1917.

Disbanded 2nd August 1917 at Gosport and merged with 1 and 55 Training Squadrons to become the School Of Special Flying, Gosport.

Reformed 22nd March 1918 at London Colney as 27 Training Squadron.

Dolphin; Avro 504; Pup; Spad; S.E.5a E1253.

Disbanded 15th July 1918 at Driffield and merged with 3 Training Squadron to become 21 Training Depot Station.

28 RESERVE SQUADRON, later 28 TRAINING SQUADRON
Formed 1st June 1916 at Castle Bromwich. Redesignated 28 Training Squadron from 31st May 1917.

Henry Farman F.20 7426; Avro 504A B4329, Avro 504J B3127; Bristol Scout C; F.E.2d A6387; R.E.7 2212; R.E.8 A3484; 1½ Strutter A8243; Pup B7533; S.E.5a B77.

Elements detached and became 'B' Flight, 3 Training Depot Station on 22nd August 1917 and became 'C' Flight, 7 Training Depot Station on 1st November 1917.

Disbanded 15th July 1918 at Hounslow and merged with 62 Training Squadron to become 42 Training Depot Station.

29 (AUSTRALIAN FLYING CORPS) TRAINING SQUADRON, later 29 TRAINING SQUADRON
Formed 15th June 1917 at Shawbury.

Shorthorn B4789.

Disbanded 14th January 1918 at Shawbury to become 5 (Training) Squadron, Australian Flying Corps. See also Australian Flying Corps Training Squadrons.

Reformed 1st August 1918 at Hendon as 29 Training Squadron.

R.E.8 A4663; Camel B3851; F.2b; Snipe C8110; D.H.6 C7212; D.H.9 B8854; Avro 504K H3214.

Disbanded 14th July 1919 at Netheravon and absorbed by 8 Training Squadron.

30 (AUSTRALIAN FLYING CORPS) TRAINING SQUADRON, later 30 TRAINING SQUADRON
Formed 15th June 1917 at Shawbury.

Avro 504J B942; Bristol Scout D B813; 1½ Strutter A6903; Pup A6249; Camel B2315; Curtiss JN-4A; D.H.5 B4905; S.E.5a D251.

Disbanded 14th January 1918 at Ternhill to become 6 (Training) Squadron, Australian Flying Corps. See also Australian Flying Corps Training Squadrons.

Reformed May 1919 at Northolt as 30 Training Squadron by redesignating 30 Training Depot Station.

F.2B F4824.

Disbanded 15th March 1920 at Northolt.

31 RESERVE SQUADRON, later 31 TRAINING SQUADRON
Formed 1st October 1916 at Wyton. Redesignated 31 Training Squadron from 31st May 1917.

Avro 504A A426; Grahame-White XV A1685; B.E.2e A2855; F.K.3; F.K.8; D.H.4; D.H.6 B2714; D.H.9 C6203; Avro 504J C4436; R.E.8 A4537; Camel; Elephant; F.2B A7199; Shorthorn A7051; B.E.12a A4029; B.E.2c 2577; 1½ Strutter A2855; Henry Farman F.20

A1154; R.E.8 A4537; Spad S.7 A8797; Nieuport 12 A5196; R.T.1 B6625.

An element detached to become 'B' Flight, 4 Training Depot Station on 19th September 1917.

Disbanded 1st September 1918 at Wyton and merged with 51 Training Squadron to become 23 Training Depot Station.

Reformed 14th March 1919 at Fowlmere by redesignating 31 Training Depot Station.

Avro 504J C4436, 504K.

Disbanded 26th April 1920 at Fowlmere to become 2 Flying Training School.

32 (AUSTRALIAN FLYING CORPS) RESERVE SQUADRON, later 32 (AUSTRALIAN FLYING CORPS) TRAINING SQUADRON
Formed 1917 at Yatesbury. Redesignated 32 (Australian Flying Corps) Training Squadron from 31st May 1917.

B.E.12a A587; Avro 504K; R.E.8; Pup B6105.

Disbanded 14th January 1918 at Yatesbury to become 7 (Training) Squadron, Australian Flying Corps. See also Australian Flying Corps Training Squadrons.

33 (AUSTRALIAN FLYING CORPS) RESERVE SQUADRON, later 33 (AUSTRALIAN FLYING CORPS) TRAINING SQUADRON
Formed December 1916 at Ternhill. Redesignated 33 (Australian Flying Corps) Training Squadron from 31st May 1917.

B.E.12 6616.

Disbanded 14th January 1918 at Cirencester to become 8 (Training) Squadron, Australian Flying Corps. See also Australian Flying Corps Training Squadrons.

Reformed September 1919 at Witney by redesignating 33 Training Depot Station.

Avro 504K H1925.

Disbanded October 1919 at Whitney.

34 RESERVE SQUADRON, later 34 TRAINING SQUADRON
Formed 1st November 1916 at Castle Bromwich. Redesignated 34 Training Squadron from 31st May 1917.

1½ Strutter 7942; Bristol Scout C 5534; Bristol Scout D A1766; Avro 504A, Avro 504J B977; Pup B5283; Camel B6219.

An element detached and became 'A' Flight, 4 Training Depot Station on 19th September 1917.

Disbanded 15th July 1918 at Chattis Hill and merged with 43 Training Squadron to become 43 Training Depot Station.

35 RESERVE SQUADRON, later 35 TRAINING SQUADRON
Formed 1st February 1917 at Filton. Redesignated 35 Training Squadron from 31st May 1917.

D.H.1; Grahame-White XV; B.E.2c 4442, B.E.2e A3060; F.E.2b 7212; Avro 504A A8505; R.E.7 2194; R.E.8 A4653; F.K.3 A1484; D.H.6 B2817; Shorthorn B4759; F.2A A3325; F.2B A7135; F.E.2b; R.E.9 A4600.

An element detached and became 'A' Flight, 2 Training Depot Station on 15th August 1917.

Disbanded 15th August 1918 at Oxford and merged with 71 Training Squadron to become 44 Training Depot Station.

36 RESERVE SQUADRON, later 36 TRAINING SQUADRON
Formed 5th July 1916 at Beverley. Redesignated 36 Training Squadron from 31st May 1917.

Longhorn; Shorthorn; F.K.3 5553; B.E.2c 2715; F.K.3 6191; B.E.12a A4011; 1½ Strutter A6984 B; Pup C285; Camel C16; Curtiss JN-3 7310; JN-4 B1942; R.E.8 B5029; Avro 504J B4204, 504K D8295.

An element detached and became 80 Squadron on 1st August 1917.

Disbanded 115th July 1918 at Montrose and merged with 74 Training Squadron to become 26 Training Depot Station.

Reformed 15th May 1919 at Yatesbury by redesignating 37 Training Depot Station.

No aircraft known.

Disbanded 25th October 1919 at Yatesbury.

37 RESERVE SQUADRON, later 37 TRAINING SQUADRON
Formed 2nd November 1916 at Catterick by redesignating an element of 53 Squadron. Redesignated 37 Training Squadron from 31st May 1917.

Avro 504A A488; F.K.3 B9632; F.K.8 B294; B.E.2c, B.E.2d, B.E.2e A3117; R.E.8 A4575; D.H.6 B2635; D.H.9 C6209.

Disbanded 15th August 1918 at Spitalgate and merged with 15 Training Squadron to become 39 Training Depot Station.

38 RESERVE SQUADRON, later 38 TRAINING SQUADRON
Formed 1st August 1916 at Rendcomb by redesignating an element of 48 Squadron. Redesignated 38 Training Squadron from 31st May 1917.

R.E.7 2195; B.E.2e A1870; R.E.8 A3177; F.2A A3319, F.2B A7274; R.E.8 A4738; Avro 504J A2004.

An element detached and became 110 Squadron on 1st November 1917.

Disbanded 15th August 1918 at Rendcomb to become 45 Training Depot Station.

Reformed August 1919 at Tadcaster by redesignating 38 Training Depot Station.

No aircraft known.

Disbanded December 1919 at Tadcaster.

39 RESERVE SQUADRON, later 39 TRAINING SQUADRON
Formed 26th August 1916 at Montrose. Redesignated 39 Training Squadron from 31st May 1917.

B.E.2c 2583; Longhorn 4018; Shorthorn A2480; Avro 504A A518, 504J C4323; Caudron G.3 A2994; R.E.8 A3475; D.H.6; JN-4 A5161; F.K.8; Pup B6127; Camel B7301.

An element detached and became 'C' Flight, 1 Training Depot Station on 20th July 1917.

Disbanded 27th July 1918 at South Carlton and merged with 45 Training Squadron to become 46 Training Depot Station.

Reformed 14th March 1919 at Spitalgate by redesignating 39 Training Depot Station.

No aircraft known.

Disbanded 24th November 1919 at Spitalgate.

40 RESERVE SQUADRON, later 40 TRAINING SQUADRON
Formed 5th July 1916 at Northolt. Redesignated 40 Training Squadron from 31st May 1917.

Bristol Scout C 3051; Bristol Scout D A1753; D.H.5 A9377; 1½ Strutter A2394; Pup A6228; Avro 504A A5909, Avro 504J B3185, Avro 504K; Camel C152.

An element detached and became 93 Squadron on 23rd September 1917.

Disbanded 15th December 1918 at Tangmere to become 61 Training Depot Station.

41 RESERVE SQUADRON, later 41 TRAINING SQUADRON
Formed 5th July 1916 at Bramham Moor. Redesignated 41 Training Squadron from 31st May 1917.

Longhorn; Shorthorn A4074; Caudron G.3 A1899; Pup A7311; Bristol M.1C C5025; JN-4 B1934.

An element detached became 'A' Flight, 5 Training Depot Station on 24th September 1917.

Disbanded 15th July 1918 at Doncaster and merged with 49 Training Squadron to become 47 Training Depot Station.

Reformed October 1919 at London Colney by redesignating 41 Training Depot Station.

No aircraft known.

Disbanded November 1919 at London Colney.

42 RESERVE SQUADRON, later 42 TRAINING SQUADRON
Formed 2nd November 1916 at Hounslow by redesignating an element of 19 Reserve Squadron. Redesignated 42 Training Squadron from 31st May 1917.

B.E.2e A3144; R.E.7 A5156; D.H.6 B2677; B.E.12; F.K.3 A1461; R.E.8 B6478; Avro 504A A2006, Avro 504J A9787, Avro 504K H8257; Pup A7311; Camel F9637; Curtiss JN-4A B1934; Bristol M1C C5025.

Disbanded 1st February 1919 at Wye.

43 RESERVE SQUADRON, later 43 TRAINING SQUADRON
Formed 2nd November 1916 at Castle Bromwich by redesignating an element of 54 Squadron. Redesignated 43 Training Squadron from 31st May 1917.

Avro 504A A2018, Avro 504J B3105, Avro 504K; Bristol Scout C; Bristol Scout D A1766; Pup A651; 1½ Strutter A1058; D.H.5 A9413; Camel B9274.

An element detached and became 95 Squadron on 8th October 1917.

Disbanded 15th July 1918 at Chattis Hill and merged with 34 Training Squadron to become 43 Training Depot Station.

44 RESERVE SQUADRON, later 44 TRAINING SQUADRON
Formed 2nd November 1916 at Lilbourne by redesignating an element of 55 Squadron. Redesignated 44 Training Squadron from 31st May 1917.

B.E.2c/d A1350; B.E.2e A1350; R.E.7; Nieuport 20 A6741; Avro 504; D.H.4 A7783; D.H.9 D1169; Camel D6649.

An element detached and became 98 Squadron on 15th August 1917.

Disbanded 14th March 1919 at Waddington and merged with 48 Training Depot Station to become 48 Training Squadron.

Reformed August 1919 at Bicester by redesignating 44 Training Depot Station.

No aircraft known.

Disbanded December 1919 at Bicester.

45 RESERVE SQUADRON, later 45 TRAINING SQUADRON
Formed 2nd November 1916 at London Colney. Redesignated 45 Training Squadron from 31st May 1917.

F.E.8 4909; Bristol Scout D 5574; Henry Farman F.20 A1240; 1½ Strutter; D.H.2 A2588; Nieuport 12 A5196; F.B.5; D.H.5 A9402; Pup B5359; Camel B9151; Avro 504K D7601.

An element detached and became 96 Squadron on 8th October 1917.

Disbanded 27th July 1918 at South Carlton and merged with 39 Training Squadron to become 46 Training Depot Station.

Reformed June 1919 at Rendcomb by redesignating 45 Training Depot Station.

No aircraft known.

Disbanded 8th July 1919 at Rendcomb.

46 RESERVE SQUADRON, later 46 TRAINING SQUADRON
Formed 23rd October 1916 at Doncaster by redesignating an element of 15 Reserve Squadron. Redesignated 46 Training Squadron from 31st May 1917.

F.E.2b 4988, F.E.2d A6351; B.E.12 6168; B.E.2c B4412, B.E.2e A2894; R.E.8 A4482; F.E.2b; D.H.1 A1624; Camel B6668; Pup B6127; D.H.4 A7576; D.H.6 B3054; D.H.9 C1164; Avro 504A A3399, Avro 504K D2059.

An element detached and became 107 Squadron on 8th October 1917.

Disbanded 15th July 1918 at Catterick and merged with 52 Training Squadron to become 49 Training Depot Station.

Reformed July 1919 at South Carlton by redesignating 46 Training Depot Station.

No aircraft known.

Disbanded 26th April 1920 at South Carlton.

47 RESERVE SQUADRON, later 47 TRAINING SQUADRON
Formed 2nd November 1916 at Cramlington by redesignating an element of 58 Squadron. Redesignated 47 Training Squadron from 31st May 1917.

Shorthorn B8793; F.K.3 B9601; R.E.8 A4579; D.H.6 C7363; D.H.9 C1256; Avro 504J/K D109.

Disbanded 1918 at Waddington and merged with 48 Training Squadron to become 48 Training Depot Station.

48 RESERVE SQUADRON, later 48 TRAINING SQUADRON
Formed 2nd November 1916 at Narborough. Redesignated 48 Training Squadron from 31st May 1917.

Grahame-White XV A1700; Shorthorn A2218; Pup B1736; R.E.8 B4045; D.H.6 C2018.

An element detached and became 'B' Flight, 5 Training Depot Station on 24th September 1917.

Disbanded 4th July 1918 at Waddington and merged with 47 Training Squadron to become 48 Training Depot Station.

Reformed 14th March 1919 at Waddington by merging 44 Training Squadron and 48 Training Depot Station.

No aircraft known.

Disbanded 4th November 1919 at Waddington.

49 RESERVE SQUADRON, later 49 TRAINING SQUADRON
Formed 23rd September 1916 at Norwich. Redesignated 49 Training Squadron from 31st May 1917.

Longhorn 4063; Shorthorn A2192; B.E.2e 6812; F.K.3 A1507; R.E.8 A4579; Elephant; D.H.4 A7693; Avro 504A C745.

An element detached and became 106 Squadron on 23rd September 1917.

Disbanded 15th July 1918 at Doncaster and merged with 41 Training Squadron to become 47 Training Depot Station.

50 RESERVE SQUADRON, later 50 TRAINING SQUADRON
Formed 7th December 1916 at Wye. Redesignated 50 Training Squadron from 31st May 1917.

F.K.3 5542; Curtiss JN-4A B1926; F.K.8 B264; D.H.6 A9590; F.2B B1329; Avro 504J B3208.

Disbanded 15th August 1918 at Spitalgate and merged with 64 Training Squadron to become 27 Training Depot Station.

Reformed July 1919 at Ford Junction.

No aircraft known.

Disbanded 6th December 1919 at Ford Junction.

51 RESERVE SQUADRON, later 51 TRAINING SQUADRON
Formed 30th December 1916 at Filton by redesignating an element of 62 Squadron. Redesignated 51 Training Squadron from 31st May 1917.

B.E.2c A1263; D.H.4 A7546; F.E.2b; B.E.2e A8677; R.E.8 A3182; Elephant A6278; D.H.6 C7864.

Elements detached and became 97 Squadron on 1st December 1917 and 105 Squadron on 23rd September 1917.

Disbanded 1st September 1918 at Baldonnel and merged with 31 Training Squadron to become 23 Training Depot Station.

Reformed 14th March 1919 at North Shotwick by redesignating 51 Training Depot Station.

No aircraft known.

Disbanded 31st May 1919 at South Shotwick to become 4 Training Squadron.

52 RESERVE SQUADRON, later 52 TRAINING SQUADRON
Formed 14th January 1917 at Cramlington by redesignating an element of 63 Squadron. Redesignated 52 Training Squadron from 31st May 1917.

B.E.2b 2783, B.E.2c 2113, B.E.2e A2891; Elephant A1603; Avro 504A A1998; R.E.8 E95; D.H.4 A7435; D.H.6 B2701; Handley Page O/100 3118.

An element detached and became 108 Squadron on 1st November 1917.

Disbanded 15th July 1918 at Catterick and merged with 46 Training Squadron to become 49 Training Depot Station.

Reformed September 1919 at Cramlington by redesignating 52 Training Depot Station.

No aircraft known.

Disbanded 2nd October 1919 at Cramlington.

53 RESERVE SQUADRON, later 53 TRAINING SQUADRON
Formed 1st February 1917 at Sedgeford by redesignating an element of 64 Squadron. Redesignated 53 Training Squadron from 31st May 1917.

R.E.8 B7728; B.E.2c B9998; Avro 504J B957; D.H.6 B2667.

Disbanded 15th August 1918 at Harlaxton and merged with 20 Training Squadron to become 40 Training Depot Station.

54 RESERVE SQUADRON, later 54 TRAINING SQUADRON
Formed 15th February 1917 at Wyton. Redesignated 54 Training Squadron from 31st May 1917.

Avro 504A A3391; Spad S.7 A8797; Pup C215; S.E.5a D6158; Avro 504J D7553, Avro 504K D9288; D.H.6 C5813; Dolphin B2481; Camel B5215; 1½ Strutter A8203.

An element detached and became 'A' Flight, 3 Training Depot Station on 5th September 1917.

Disbanded 15th July 1918 at Eastbourne and merged with 206 Training Depot Station to become 50 Training Depot Station.

55 RESERVE SQUADRON, later 55 TRAINING SQUADRON
Formed 15th November 1916 at Filton by redesignating an element of 66 Squadron. Redesignated 55 Training Squadron from 31st May 1917.

Bristol Scout D A1753; Nieuport 12 A5192; D.H.5 B364; Pup A6193; Avro 504A A5921.

An element detached and became 94 Squadron on 30th July 1917.

Disbanded 2nd August 1917 at Gosport and merged with 1 and 27 Training Squadrons to become the School Of Special Flying, Gosport.

Reformed 15th January 1918 at Castle Bromwich by redesignating an element of 28 Training Squadron.

Avro 504J D4361; Camel D8130; S.E.5a D390.

Disbanded 15th July 1918 at Shotwick and merged with 67 Training Squadron to become 51 Training Depot Station.

Reformed 14th March 1919 at Narborough by redesignating 55 Training Depot Station

No aircraft known.

Disbanded November 1919 at Narborough.

56 RESERVE SQUADRON, later 56 TRAINING SQUADRON
Formed 7th February 1917 at London Colney by redesignating an element of 56 Squadron. Redesignated 56 Training Squadron from 31st May 1917.

Avro 504A A8505; B.E.2e 7069; B.E.12 4042; S.E.5a; Spad S.7 A253; Pup B9931; Bristol Scout D A1742; Camel B5196.

Disbanded 15th July 1918 at London Colney to become 41 Training Depot Station.

57 RESERVE SQUADRON, later 57 TRAINING SQUADRON
Formed 10th December 1916 at Ismailia, Egypt. Redesignated 57 Training Squadron from 31st May 1917.

Longhorn; Shorthorn 7369; B.E.2c 4480, B.E.2e A8696; Avro 504A; R.E.8 A4433.

Disbanded 21st July 1918 at Abu Sueir, Egypt, to become 17 Training Depot Station.

58 RESERVE SQUADRON, later 58 TRAINING SQUADRON
Formed February 1917 at Suez, Egypt. Redesignated 58 Training Squadron from 31st May 1917.

Avro 504A A2659, Avro 504J, Avro 504K; Pup B2233; S.E.5a E3918; Vickers F.B.19; Martinsyde 4250.

Disbanded 22nd July 1919 at El Rimal, Egypt.

59 RESERVE SQUADRON, later 59 TRAINING SQUADRON
Formed 1st February 1917 at Gosport by redesignating an element of 28 Squadron. Redesignated 59 Training Squadron from 31st May 1917.

D.H.1 A1646; F.E.2b, F.E.2d; B.E.2c; B.E.2e 6315; B.E.12a A4010; R.E.8 A4574; F.2B B1106; D.H.6 B2811.

An element detached and became 'C' Flight, 6 Training Depot Station on 12th October 1917.

Disbanded 15th August 1918 at Rendcomb and merged with 24 Training Squadron to become 24 Training Depot Station.

Reformed 14th March 1919 at Scopwick by redesignating 59 Training Depot Station.

No aircraft known.

Disbanded 26th April 1920 to become 3 Flying Training School.

60 RESERVE SQUADRON, later 60 TRAINING SQUADRON
Formed 7th April 1917 at Beverley by redesignating an element of 36 Reserve Squadron. Redesignated 60 Training Squadron from 31st May 1917.

B.E.12 6142; Avro 504A A5930, Avro 504J/K D175; B.E.2e A3064; R.E.8 A3498; Dolphin; Spad 7 A8825; Pup B7525; 1½ Strutter; Camel B5598; S.E.5a.

Disbanded 15th July 1918 at Scampton and merged with 61 Squadron and 11 Training Squadron to become 34 Training Depot Station.

61 RESERVE SQUADRON, later 61 TRAINING SQUADRON
Formed 1st May 1917 at Cramlington. Redesignated 61 Training Squadron from 31st May 1917.

D.H.4 A21467; D.H.6; B.E.2e A1876; R.E.8 A3914; Elephant A6269; F.K.8 B265; Camel B7476; Pup B7505.

An element detached and became 109 Squadron on 1st November 1917.

Disbanded 27th July 1918 at South Carlton and merged with 70 Training Squadron to become 28 Training Depot Station.

Reformed 20th June 1919 at Tangmere as 61 Training Squadron by redesignating 61 Training Depot Station.

No aircraft known.

Disbanded December 1919 at Tangmere.

62 RESERVE SQUADRON, later 62 TRAINING SQUADRON
Formed 1st May 1917 at Gosport by redesignating an element of 1 Reserve Squadron. Redesignated 62 Training Squadron from 31st May 1917.

B.E.2e A2918; Elephant A6252; D.H.5 A9377; 1½ Strutter A5953; Pup B6067; Camel D6510; Avro 504J B915; F.2B C4610.

An element detached and became 'C' Flight, 3 Training Depot Station on 5th September 1917.

Disbanded 15th July 1918 at Hounslow and merged with 28 Training Squadron to become 42 Training Depot Station.

63 RESERVE SQUADRON, later 63 TRAINING SQUADRON
Formed 28th March 1917 at Ternhill by redesignating an element of 34 Reserve Squadron. Redesignated 63 Training Squadron from 31st May 1917.

Pup B9440; Camel B7464; Avro 504A A8593, Avro 504K D2116; D.H.5 A9206.

An element detached and became 'B' Flight, 7 Training Depot Station on 1st November 1917.

Disbanded September 1919 at Redcar.

64 RESERVE SQUADRON, later 64 TRAINING SQUADRON
Formed 7th April 1917 at Dover by redesignating an element of 13 Reserve Squadron. Redesignated 64 Training Squadron from 31st May 1917.

Shorthorn A2238; R.E.8 A4504; Avro 504A A5923; Nieuport BB A242; D.H.6 A9760; B.E.2c 2504, B.E.2e B3668.

Disbanded 15th August 1918 at Harlaxton and merged with 50 Training Squadron to become 27 Training Depot Station.

65 RESERVE SQUADRON, later 65 TRAINING SQUADRON
Formed 1st May 1917 at Croydon by redesignating an element of 17 Reserve Squadron. Redesignated 65 Training Squadron from 31st May 1917.

Avro 504A B956; B.E.2e A2969; Elephant A3995; F.K.3 A1494; F.K.8 B297; Bristol Scout D A1779; R.E.8 A3458; Camel B6315; Pup C3502.

Disbanded 15th July 1918 at Dover (St Margaret's) to become 53 Training Depot Station.

66 RESERVE SQUADRON, later 66 TRAINING SQUADRON
Formed 1st May 1917 at Wye by redesignating an element of 20 Reserve Squadron. Redesignated 66 Training Squadron from 31st May 1917.

Pup; R.E.8 A3429; B.E.2c 4420; B.E.2e A8660; D.H.6 A9619.

Disbanded 15th July 1918 at Yatesbury and merged with 13 Training Squadron to become 36 Training Depot Station.

67 TRAINING SQUADRON
Formed 3rd June 1917 at Castle Bromwich by redesignating an element of 28 Training Squadron.

1½ Strutter A2387; Nieuport 12 A5184; Camel C10; Pup C216; Avro 504A C595, Avro 504J B3110, Avro 504K B8672.

Disbanded 15th July 1918 at Shotwick and merged with 55 Training Squadron to become 51 Training Depot Station.

68 RESERVE SQUADRON, later 68 TRAINING SQUADRON
Formed 7th April 1917 at Catterick by redesignating an element of 14 Reserve Squadron. Redesignated 68 Training Squadron from 31st May 1917.

F.E.2d 5214; D.H.1 A1627; Shorthorn A6845; D.H.6 A9564; JN-4 B1932; Camel C158; Avro 504J D6315.

An element detached and became 'C' Flight, 5 Training Depot Station on 24th September 1917.

Disbanded 15th July 1918 at Bramham Moor and merged with 14 Training Squadron to become 38 Training Depot Station.

69 TRAINING SQUADRON
Formed 1st October 1917 at Catterick by redesignating an element of 14 Training Squadron.

D.H.4; D.H.6 A9724.

Disbanded 1st August 1918 at Narborough and merged with 26 Training Squadron to become 22 Training Depot Station.

70 TRAINING SQUADRON
Formed 20th December 1917 at Netheravon by redesignating an element of 24 Training Squadron.

Shorthorn; R.E.8 B5131; Pup B5310; Camel B7142; B.E.12 C3213; Avro 504J D7554; Dolphin C3797.

Disbanded 27th July 1918 at Weston-on-the-Green and merged with 61 Training Squadron to become 28 Training Depot Station.

71 TRAINING SQUADRON
Formed 28th November 1917 at Netheravon from an element of 7 Training Squadron.

Camel B2464.

Disbanded 15th August 1918 at Port Meadow, Oxford, and merged with 35 Training Squadron to become 44 Training Depot Station.

72 TRAINING SQUADRON
Formed 10th January 1918 at Wyton by redesignating an element of 5 Training Squadron.

Avro 504A A2634; S.E.5a; Camel B9186.

Disbanded 1st March 1919 at Beverley.

73 TRAINING SQUADRON
Formed 7th July 1917 at Thetford by redesignating an element of 25 Training Squadron.

Pup B2247; Camel B6266; 1½ Strutter A6027; Avro 504J B4297.

Disbanded 27th July 1918 at Beaulieu and merged with 1 Training Squadron to become 29 Training Depot Station.

74 TRAINING SQUADRON
Formed 21st October 1917 at Netheravon by redesignating an element of 8 Training Squadron.

Pup; Camel B2518; Avro 504J, Avro 504K D6300; S.E.5a E5891.

Disbanded 15th July 1918 at Tadcaster and merged with 36 Training Squadron to become 26 Training Depot Station.

75 TRAINING SQUADRON
Formed 14th November 1917 at Waddington by redesignating an element of 47 Training Squadron.

Elephant A3969; D.H.4 A7814; B.E.2e B8832; D.H.6 C7220; D.H.9 C1203; R.E.8 E128.

Disbanded 15th July 1918 at Cramlington to become 52 Training Depot Station.

CANADIAN RESERVE/TRAINING SQUADRONS

The Royal Flying Corps carried out flying training from Camp Borden, North Toronto (Leaside and Armour Heights) and Deseronto (Rathbun, Mohawk, Beamsville and Long Branch). 42 and 43 Wings moved to Talliaferro, Texas (Everman, Hicks, and Benbrook) between November 1917 and April 1918 in order to escape the Canadian winter.

78 (CANADIAN) RESERVE SQUADRON, later 78 (CANADIAN) TRAINING SQUADRON
Formed January 1917 at Beverley. Dispatched to Canada on 15th February 1917, opening at Camp Borden in the following April. Redesignated 78 (Canadian) Training Squadron from October 1917.

Curtiss JN-4 C122.

Disbanded November 1918 at Leaside, Canada.

79 (CANADIAN) RESERVE SQUADRON, later 79 (CANADIAN) TRAINING SQUADRON
Formed January 1917 at Beverley by redesignating an element of 36 Reserve Squadron. Dispatched to Canada on 15th February 1917, opening at Camp Borden the following April. Redesignated 79 (Canadian) Training Squadron from October 1917.

Curtiss JN-4 C712.

Disbanded November 1918 at Rathbun, Canada.

80 (CANADIAN) RESERVE SQUADRON, later 80 (CANADIAN) TRAINING SQUADRON
Formed January 1917 at Doncaster by redesignating an element of 15 Reserve Squadron. Dispatched to Canada on 27th February 1917, opening at Camp Borden on 19th March. Redesignated 80 (Canadian) Training Squadron from October 1917.

Curtiss JN-4 C454.

Disbanded November 1918 at Camp Borden.

81 (CANADIAN) RESERVE SQUADRON, later 81 (CANADIAN) TRAINING SQUADRON
Formed January 1917 at Beaulieu by redesignating an element of 16 Reserve Squadron. Dispatched to Canada 15th February 1917. Opened by March 1917 at Camp Borden. Redesignated 81 (Canadian) Training Squadron from October 1917. Wintered at Everman, returning to Rathbun.

Pup; Curtiss JN-4 C300.

Disbanded November 1918 at Rathbun, Canada.

82 (CANADIAN) RESER

VE SQUADRON, later 82 (CANADIAN) TRAINING SQUADRON
Formed 20th February 1917 at Montrose by redesignating an element of 18 Reserve Squadron. Dispatched to Canada from Beverley 27th February 1917. Opened 19th March 1917 at Camp Borden. Redesignated 82 (Canadian) Training Squadron from October 1917. Wintered at Everman, returning to Mohawk.

Curtiss JN-4.

Disbanded November 1918 at Mohawk, Canada.

83 (CANADIAN) RESERVE SQUADRON, later 83 (CANADIAN) TRAINING SQUADRON
Formed January 1917 at Catterick by redesignating an element of 14 Reserve Squadron. Dispatched to Canada from Beverley during March 1917. Opened by May 1917 at Mohawk. Redesignated 83 (Canadian) Training Squadron from October 1917. Wintered at Benbrook, returning to Leaside.

Curtiss JN-4 C476.

Disbanded November 1918 at Leaside, Canada.

84 (CANADIAN) RESERVE SQUADRON, later 84 (CANADIAN) TRAINING SQUADRON
Formed January 1917 at Turnhouse by redesignating an element of 26 Reserve Squadron. Dispatched to Canada during March 1917. Opened by May 1917 at Mohawk. Redesignated 84 (Canadian) Training Squadron from October 1917. Wintered at Benbrook, returning to Mohawk.

Curtiss JN-4 C663.

Disbanded November 1918 at Mohawk, Canada.

85 (CANADIAN) RESERVE SQUADRON, later 85 (CANADIAN) TRAINING SQUADRON
Formed January 1917 at Montrose by redesignating an element of 39 Reserve Squadron. Dispatched to Canada during March 1917. Opened by May 1917 at Rathbun. Redesignated 85 (Canadian) Training Squadron from October 1917. Wintered at Benbrook, returning to Mohawk.

Curtiss JN-4A C435.

Disbanded November 1918 at Mohawk, Canada.

86 (CANADIAN) RESERVE SQUADRON, later 86 (CANADIAN) TRAINING SQUADRON
Formed January 1917 at Spitalgate by redesignating an element of 49 Reserve Squadron. Dispatched to Canada in March 1917. Opened by May 1917 at Rathbun. Redesignated 86 (Canadian) Training Squadron from October 1917. Wintered at Benbrook, returning to Camp Borden.

Curtiss JN-4 C743.

Disbanded November 1918 at Camp Borden, Canada.

87 (CANADIAN) RESERVE SQUADRON, later 87 (CANADIAN) TRAINING SQUADRON
Formed January 1917 at Gosport by redesignating an element of 28 Reserve Squadron. Dispatched to Canada from Beaulieu in March 1917. Opened by May 1917 at Mohawk. Redesignated 87 (Canadian) Training Squadron from October 1917. Wintered at Benbrook, returning to Camp Borden.

Curtiss JN-4 C1317.

Disbanded November 1918 at Camp Borden.

88 (CANADIAN) RESERVE SQUADRON, later 88 (CANADIAN) TRAINING SQUADRON

Formed 15th March 1917 at Catterick by redesignating an element of 14 Reserve Squadron. Dispatched to Canada in April 1917. Opened by May 1917 at Rathbun, then moved to Armour Heights. Redesignated 88 (Canadian) Training Squadron from October 1917.

Curtiss JN-4 C302.

Disbanded November 1818 at Camp Borden, Canada.

89 (CANADIAN) RESERVE SQUADRON, later (CANADIAN) TRAINING SQUADRON

Formed 15th March 1917 at Turnhouse by redesignating an element of 26 Reserve Squadron. Dispatched from Beverley to Canada in May 1917. Opened July 1917 at Rathbun, then moved to Leaside. Redesignated 89 (Canadian) Training Squadron from October 1917.

B.E.12; Pup; Camel; Curtiss JN-4 C274.

Disbanded November 1918 at Mohawk, Canada.

90 (CANADIAN) RESERVE SQUADRON, later 90 (CANADIAN) TRAINING SQUADRON

Formed 15th March 1917 at Doncaster by redesignating an element of 36 Reserve Squadron. Dispatched from Beverley to Canada in June 1917. Opened July 1917 at Rathbun, then moved to Leaside. Redesignated 90 (Canadian) Training Squadron from October 1917.

Curtiss JN-4 C373.

Disbanded November 1918 at Rathbun, Canada.

91 (CANADIAN) RESERVE SQUADRON, later 91 (CANADIAN) TRAINING SQUADRON

Formed 15th March 1917 at Gosport by redesignating an element of 27 Reserve Squadron. Dispatched to Canada in May 1917. Opened 15th June 1917 at Armour Heights, Canada. Redesignated 91 (Canadian) Training Squadron from October 1917.

Curtiss JN-4 C526.

Disbanded November 1918 at Leaside, Canada.

92 (CANADIAN) RESERVE SQUADRON, later 92 (CANADIAN) TRAINING SQUADRON

Formed 15th March 1917 at Netheravon by redesignating an element of 7 Reserve Squadron. Dispatched to Canada, opening at Long Branch, then moved to Armour Heights. Redesignated 92 (Canadian) Training Squadron from October 1917.

Curtiss JN-4 C184.

Disbanded November 1918 at Camp Borden, Canada.

93 (CANADIAN) RESERVE SQUADRON, later 93 (CANADIAN) TRAINING SQUADRON

Formed by July 1917 at Armour Heights, Canada.

Curtiss JN-4.

Disbanded November 1917 at Armour Heights.

94 (CANADIAN) RESERVE SQUADRON

Nameplate set aside but not formed.

95 (CANADIAN) RESERVE SQUADRON

Nameplate set aside but not formed.

96 (CANADIAN) RESERVE SQUADRON

Nameplate set aside but not formed.

97 (CANADIAN) RESERVE SQUADRON

Nameplate set aside but not formed.

98 (DEPOT) SQUADRON

Formed 8th February 1917 at Rochford by redesignating an element of 11 Reserve Squadron.

D.H.9.

Disbanded 27th June 1917 at Rochford to become 198 (Depot) Squadron.

99 (DEPOT) SQUADRON

Formed 1st June 1917 at Rochford.

No aircraft known.

Disbanded 27th June 1917 at East Retford to become 199 (Depot) Squadron.

186 (NIGHT) TRAINING SQUADRON

Formed 1st April 1918 at Throwley by redesignating an element of 112 Squadron.

Avro 504J C4451, Avro 504K E1830; F.2B C820; D.H.9 E8888.

Disbanded 1st May 1919 at East Retford.

187 (NIGHT) TRAINING SQUADRON

Formed 1st April 1918 at East Retford by redesignating an element of 199 (Night) Training Squadron.

D.H.6; B.E.2c, B.E.2e B4545; Avro 504A; Elephant B872; Avro 504K B8742; Pup; Camel.

Disbanded 1st May 1919 at East Retford.

188 (NIGHT) TRAINING SQUADRON

Formed 20th December 1917 at East Retford.

Pup B1769; Camel F2107; Avro 504K E3615; B.E.2e; F.E.2b; F.B.9.

Disbanded 1st March 1919 at Throwley.

189 (NIGHT) TRAINING SQUADRON

Formed 20th December 1917 at Ripon.

B.E.2c, B.E.2e; B.E.12, B.E.12b; Pup C306; F.2B C4777; R.E.8 E58; D.H.6; S.E.5a; Avro 504K E4339; Camel F2111.

Disbanded 1st March 1919 at Suttons Farm.

190 (DEPOT) SQUADRON, later 190 (NIGHT) TRAINING SQUADRON

Formed 24th October 1917 at Rochford by redesignating an element of 51 Squadron. Redesignated 190 (Night) Training Squadron from 21st December 1917.

B.E.2c, B.E.2e A8702; Avro 504K; D.H.6.

Disbanded April 1919 at Upwood.

191 (DEPOT) SQUADRON, later 191 (NIGHT) TRAINING SQUADRON

Formed 6th November 1917 at Marham by redesignating an element of 51 Squadron. Redesignated 191 (Night) Training Squadron from 21st December 1917.

D.H.6 C9401; B.E.2d, B.E.2e C7151; F.E.2b D9125.

Disbanded 26th June at Upwood.

192 (DEPOT) SQUADRON, later 192 (NIGHT) TRAINING SQUADRON

Formed 5th September 1917 at Gainsborough by redesignating an element of 33 Squadron. Redesignated 192 (Night) Training Squadron from 21st December 1917.

F.E.2b B404, F.E.2d; B.E.2c/d B3656.

Disbanded 31st May 1919 at Newmarket.

193 TRAINING SQUADRON

Formed 9th August 1917 at Amriya, Egypt.

D.H.6 C2033.

Disbanded 21st July 1918 at Amriya to become 20 Training Depot Station.

194 TRAINING SQUADRON

Formed 9th August 1917 at Amriya, Egypt.

D.H.6 C2033; F.E.2b 4941; B.E.2c 4487, B.E.2e; Avro 504A A2652.

Disbanded 21st July 1918 at Amriya to become 16 Training Depot Station.

195 TRAINING SQUADRON

Formed 9th August 1917 at Abu Sueir, Egypt.

Avro 504J C4441; Shorthorn; Pup; Nieuport; B.E.2c, B.E.2e; Camel D6531

Disbanded 21st July 1918 at El Rimal to become 19 Training Depot Station.

196 TRAINING SQUADRON
Formed 9th August 1917 at Heliopolis, Egypt.

Nieuport; Avro 504A A3384, Avro 504J; Bristol Scout D.

Disbanded 13th November 1917 at Heliopolis to become the Aerial Fighting School, Heliopolis.

197 TRAINING SQUADRON
Formed 9th August 1917 at Almaza, Egypt.

B.E.2c; Avro 504J D153; R.E.8.

Disbanded 20th November 1917 at Almaza to become the Artillery Observation School.

198 (DEPOT) SQUADRON, later 198 (NIGHT) TRAINING SQUADRON
Formed 27th June 1917 at Rochford by redesignating 98 (Depot) Squadron. Redesignated 198 (Night) Training Squadron from 21st December 1917.

Avro 504A A5940, Avro 504K H2200; Pup B1803; Camel F1885; F.B.12c; R.E.7 2411; B.E.2c, B.E.2e B3656; 1½ Strutter B2587; F.E.2b.

Disbanded May 1919 at Rochford.

199 (DEPOT) SQUADRON, later 199 (NIGHT) TRAINING SQUADRON
Formed 27th June 1917 at East Retford by redesignating 99 (Depot) Squadron. Redesignated 199 (Night) Training Squadron from 21st December 1917.

F.E.2b B704; 1½ Strutter; Henry Farman F.20 A1189; D.H.1.

Disbanded June 1919 at Harpswell (Hemswell).

200 TRAINING SQUADRON, later 200 (NIGHT) TRAINING SQUADRON
Formed 17th June 1917 at East Retford. Redesignated 200 (Night) Training Squadron from 21st December 1917.

Avro 504; Henry Farman F.20 A1160; F.E.2b; D.H.1 A1647; D.H.6.

Disbanded 13th June 1919 at Harpswell (later Hemswell).

201 TRAINING SQUADRON
Formed 14th August 1918 at East Fortune by merging the Torpedo Aeroplane School and 1 Torpedo Training Squadron.

Cuckoo.

Disbanded 30th April 1919 at East Fortune to become the Torpedo Training School.

RESERVE COMMAND COMMUNICATION FLIGHT, later RESERVE COMMAND COMMUNICATION SQUADRON
Formed 1st February 1939 at Hendon.

No aircraft known.

Disbanded 27th May 1940 at White Waltham.

Reformed 10th September 1946 at White Waltham. Redesignated Reserve Command Communication Squadron from February 1950.

Nil (–4.47)	Magister N3882; Dominie I R9559; Hudson IIIA FK787.
RCA (4.47–4.51)	Harvard IIB FS921 RCA-L; Proctor III HM294 RCA-E, IV NP342 RCA-K; Auster VI VX128; Anson XII PH643 RCA-P, XIX VM357 RCA-M; Spitfire XVIE TE335 RCA-N.
Nil	Martinet I EM648; Harvard IIB KF343; Devon C.1 VP967.

Disbanded 1st August 1950 at White Waltham to become the Home Command Communication Squadron.

RESERVE COMMAND COMMUNICATION SQUADRON – see Reserve Command Communication Flight, later Reserve Command Communication Squadron

RESERVE COMMAND GLIDING INSTRUCTORS SCHOOL
Formed 1st July 1949 at Detling.

Cadet TX.1, TX.2; Rhonbussard VD216; Grunau Baby VT920; Gull VW912; Sedbergh TX.1 WB925; Prefect TX.1 WE980.

Disbanded 1st August 1950 at Detling to become the Home Command Gliding Instructors School.

RESERVE COMMAND INSTRUMENT TRAINING FLIGHT
Formed 1st August 1948 at White Waltham.

Harvard IIB FX411; Chipmunk T.10 WB727.

Disbanded 1st August 1950 at Honiley to become the Home Command Instrument Training Flight.

RESERVE FLYING SCHOOL, BROUGH
Formed 21st May 1924 at Brough. Operated by North Sea Aerial and General Transport Ltd. Floatplane training was introduced from 31st March 1933.

Avro 504K; Kangaroo G-EBMD; Dart Seaplane G-EBKF; Blackburn B-2 G-ACAH.

Disbanded 1935 at Brough to become 4 Elementary and Reserve Flying Training School.

RESERVE FLYING SCHOOL, COVENTRY, later HAMBLE
Formed 31st July 1923 at Coventry. Initially operated by Armstrong Whitworth Aircraft Ltd and then by Air Service Training Ltd, a subsidiary of Armstrong Whitworth, at Hamble from 1st April 1931.

Avro 504K G-EBHE; D.H.9J G-AARS; Tiger Moth.

Disbanded 1935 at Hamble to become 3 Elementary and Reserve Flying Training School.

RESERVE FLYING SCHOOL, FILTON
Formed 28th May 1923 at Filton. Operated by the Bristol Aeroplane Company Ltd.

F.2b G-EBFS; Tiger Moth.

Disbanded 1935 at Filton to become 2 Elementary and Reserve Flying Training School.

RESERVE FLYING SCHOOL, HAMBLE – see Reserve Flying School, Coventry, later Hamble

RESERVE FLYING SCHOOL, RENFREW
Formed 24th July 1924 at Renfrew. Operated by William Beardmore and Company Ltd.

Avro; D.H.9J G-EBHP.

Disbanded 3rd November 1928 at Renfrew.

RESERVE FLYING SCHOOL, STAG LANE
Formed 1st May 1923 at Stag Lane. Operated by the de Havilland Aircraft Company Ltd.

Avro 504K; D.H.9J G-EBPG; Tiger Moth.

Disbanded 4th August 1935 at Hatfield to become 1 Elementary and Reserve Flying Training School.

1 RESERVE FLYING SCHOOL
Formed 5th May 1947 at Panshanger by redesignating 1 Elementary Flying Training School. Operated by the de Havilland Aircraft Co Ltd.

RCM (5.47–4.51)	Tiger Moth II DE352 RCM-A; Anson T.21 WB462 RCM-Z; Chipmunk T.10 WB652 RCM-L.
Nil (4.51–3.53)	Chipmunk T.10 WB653 10; Anson T.21 VV251 51.

Disbanded 31st March 1953 at Panshanger.

2 RESERVE FLYING SCHOOL
Formed 1st October 1948 at Barton. Initially operated by Reid and

Sigrist Ltd then by Short Brothers and Harland from 1st October 1952.

RCX (10.48–4.51)	Tiger Moth II T7404 RCX-B.
Nil (4.51–3.53)	Tiger Moth II DE610 15; Chipmunk T.10 WD324 H; Anson I R9809, T.21 VV327.

Disbanded 31st March 1953 at Barton.

3 RESERVE FLYING SCHOOL
Formed 15th August 1948 at Cardiff. Initially operated by British Aviation Services and then by Cambrian Air Services from 15th February 1952.

RCK (8.48–4.51)	Tiger Moth I NL929, II DE670 RCK-A; Anson T.21 VV259 RCK-1.
Nil (4.51–3.53)	Oxford I NM296 14; Anson I NK461; Chipmunk T.10 WP831.

Disbanded 31st July 1953 at Cardiff.

4 RESERVE FLYING SCHOOL
Formed 10th March 1947 at Brough by redesignating 4 Elementary Flying Training School. Operated by Blackburn Aircraft Ltd.

RCN	Tiger Moth I NM144, II T7272 RCN-L.

Disbanded 31st March 1948 at Brough.

5 RESERVE FLYING SCHOOL
Formed 1st November 1947 at Castle Bromwich. Operated by Birketts Air Services Ltd.

RCY (11.47–4.51)	Tiger Moth BB796, II N9255 RCY-B; Anson T.21 WB454 RCY-W; Chipmunk T.10 WB676 RCY-L.
Nil (4.51–5.54)	Chipmunk T.10 WP809 R-27; Anson I MG689, T.21 VV310 R-42; Prentice T.1 VS638; Oxford I X6655.
Also used	Tiger Moth BB796, I NL910.

Disbanded 20th June 1954 at Castle Bromwich.

6 RESERVE FLYING SCHOOL
Formed 12th May 1947 at Sywell by redesignating 6 Elementary Flying Training School. Operated by Brooklands Aviation Ltd.

RCO (5.47–4.51)	Tiger Moth II N6808 RCO-F; Anson I EG335, T.21 VV326 RCO-Z.
Nil (4.51–3.53)	Tiger Moth I NM142, II T6163; Oxford I HN324 37, II T1398; Anson T.21 VV325 35; Prentice T.1 VR295 10; Chipmunk T.10 WP786.

Disbanded 31st March 1953 at Sywell.

7 RESERVE FLYING SCHOOL
Formed 9th May 1947 at Desford. Operated by Reid and Sigrist Ltd.

RCP (5.47–4.51)	Tiger Moth BB800 RCP-G.
Nil (4.51–7.53)	Tiger Moth II; Anson I MG237, T.21 VV314 71; Prentice T.1 VS647 57.

Disbanded 31st July 1953 at Desford.

8 RESERVE FLYING SCHOOL
Formed 3rd March 1947 at Woodley by redesignating 8 Elementary Flying Training School. Operated by Handley Page (Reading) Ltd.

RCQ (3.47–4.51)	Tiger Moth II R5120 RCQ-F; Anson I MG290, T.21 VV293 RCQ-H.
Nil (4.51–3.53)	Tiger Moth II; Anson T.21 VV294 36; Chipmunk T.10 WB677 28.
Also used	Tiger Moth I NL914.

Disbanded 31st March 1953 at Woodley.

9 RESERVE FLYING SCHOOL
Formed 1st November 1947 at Doncaster. Operated by C L Air Surveys Ltd.

RCZ (10.47–4.51)	Tiger Moth BB701, II T6194 RCZ-E; Anson I MG629, T.21 WB453 RCZ-AF
Nil (4.51–5.54)	Tiger Moth I NM145; Anson T.21 VV903 42; Chipmunk T.10 WG487 16; Prentice T.1 VS386 18.

Disbanded 20th June 1954 at Doncaster.

10 RESERVE FLYING SCHOOL
Formed 16th May 1949 at Exeter. Operated by Exeter Airport Ltd.

RSB (5.49–4.51)	Tiger Moth II T7467 RSB-B.
Nil (4.51–5.54)	Tiger Moth II R5243 10; Oxford I T1256 24; Anson T.21 VV907 22; Chipmunk T.10 WP811 18.

Disbanded 20th June 1954 at Exeter.

11 RESERVE FLYING SCHOOL
Formed 18th March 1947 at Scone by redesignating 11 Elementary Flying Training School. Operated by Airwork Ltd.

RCR (3.47–4.51)	Tiger Moth II N6925 RCR-M; Anson I N9785 RCR-C; Hawk Trainer 3 BB666; Anson T.21 VV250 RCR-W; Chipmunk T.10 WB696 RCR-C.
Nil (4.51–6.54)	Oxford I HN433 43; Anson T.21 WD417 39; Chipmunk T.10 WB699 32; Prentice T.1 VS372.
Also used	Tiger Moth I NM154.

Disbanded 20th June 1954 at Perth.

12 RESERVE FLYING SCHOOL
Formed 1st April 1948 at Filton. Operated by the Bristol Aeroplane Co Ltd.

RCD (3.48– .49)	Tiger Moth II DE715 RCD-F; Anson T.21 VV323 RCD-3.
RCB (.49–4.51)	Tiger Moth II DE715 RCB-F; Anson T.21 VV323 RCB-1.
Nil (4.51–2.53)	Proctor III LZ570; Anson T.21 VV323 36; Oxford I NM539; Chipmunk T.10 WB687 18.
Also used	Tiger Moth BB796, I NM144.

Disbanded 31st March 1953 at Filton.

13 RESERVE FLYING SCHOOL
Formed 1st April 1948 at Grangemouth by redesignating 13 Elementary Flying Training School. Operated by Airwork Ltd.

Nil	Tiger Moth II N6925; Anson I AX115, T.21 VV261.
RCC	Possibly allocated.

Disbanded 19th April 1949 at Grangemouth and absorbed by 11 Reserve Flying School.

14 RESERVE FLYING SCHOOL
Formed 15th August 1947 at Hamble. Operated by Air Service Training Ltd.

RCL (8.47–4.51)	Tiger Moth II T7680 RCL-K; Anson I EF874 RCL-2, T.21 VV893 RCL-3; Chipmunk T.10 WB749 RCL-J.
Nil (4.51–8.53)	Harvard IIB KF709; Chipmunk T.10 WB754 21; Anson T.21 VV260 38.
Also used	Tiger Moth I NM140.

Disbanded 15th August 1953 at Hamble.

15 RESERVE FLYING SCHOOL
Formed 1st April 1948 at Redhill. Operated by British Air Transport Ltd.

RCD (4.48–4.51)	Tiger Moth II N5492 RCD-A; Anson I AX259 RCD-Z, T.21 VV302 RCD-3.
Nil (4.51–4.54)	Chipmunk T.10 WP830 27; Oxford I HN309 22; Anson T.21 VV258 10.

Disbanded 20th June 1954 at Redhill.

16 RESERVE FLYING SCHOOL
Formed 27th March 1947 at Burnaston by redesignating 16 Elementary Flying Training School. Operated by Air Schools Ltd.

RCS (3.47–4.51)	Tiger Moth II DE268 RCS-A NM126; Anson T.21 VV898 RSC-C; Harvard IIB KF371.
Nil (4.51–8,53)	Tiger Moth II; Anson I MG859, T.21 VV296 11; Oxford I LX672; Prentice T.1 VR198 14; Chipmunk T.10 WP780.
Also used	Tiger Moth I NM203.

Disbanded 30th June 1953 at Burnaston.

17 RESERVE FLYING SCHOOL
Formed 1st July 1948 at Hornchurch. Operated by Short Brothers and Harland Ltd.

RCJ (7.48–4.51)   Tiger Moth II N9402 RCJ-A; Anson I MG670, T.21 VS567 RCJ-Y.

Nil (4.51–7.53)   Tiger Moth II; Anson T.21 VV887 45; Chipmunk T.10 WB645 34.

Also used   Tiger Moth BB748, I NM204.

Disbanded 31st July 1953 at Hornchurch.

18 RESERVE FLYING SCHOOL
Formed 14th May 1947 at Fairoaks by redesignating 18 Elementary Flying Training School. Operated by Universal Flying Services Ltd.

RCT (5.47–4.51)   Tiger Moth II R4765 RCT-B; Harvard IIB FX351; Anson I LT488 RCT-1, T.21 VV254 RCT-2; Chipmunk T.10 WB631 RCT-D.

Nil (4.51–7.53)   Anson T.21 VV253 43; Chipmunk T.10 WB629 22.

Also used   Tiger Moth BB750, I NL914.

Disbanded 31st July 1953 at Fairoaks.

19 RESERVE FLYING SCHOOL
Formed 10th July 1950 at Hooton Park. Operated by Short Brothers and Harland.

Tiger Moth I NL929, II T6399; Oxford I HM973; Anson T.21 VV305 36; Prentice T.1 VS682; Chipmunk T.10 WD320.

Disbanded 20th June 1954 at Woodvale.

22 RESERVE FLYING SCHOOL
Formed 1st May 1947 at Cambridge by redesignating 22 Elementary Flying Training School. Operated by Marshalls Flying School Ltd.

RCU (5.47–4.51)   Tiger Moth II DE873 RCU-L; Anson I MG446 RCU-B; Chipmunk T.10 WB573 RCU-J.

Nil (4.51–4.54)   Tiger Moth I NL984; Chipmunk T.10 WK617 AK; Oxford II T1398 56; Anson T.21 WB458 42; Prentice T.1 VR198; Harvard IIB KF200.

Disbanded 20th June 1954 at Cambridge.

23 RESERVE FLYING SCHOOL
Formed 1st February 1949 at Usworth. Operated by Airwork Ltd.

RSA (2.49–4.51)   Tiger Moth II NM213 RSA-B; Harvard IIB KF155; Anson I NK371, T.21 VV996 RSA-W.

Nil (4.51–6.53)   Tiger Moth NM213; Anson T.21 VV328 R-12; Oxford I RR338 R-18; Prentice T.1 VS634; Chipmunk T.10 WD344 R-26.

Disbanded 31st July 1953 at Usworth.

24 RESERVE FLYING SCHOOL
Formed 7th May 1947 at Rochester by redesignating 24 Elementary Flying Training School. Operated by Short Brothers and Harland Ltd.

RCV (5.47–4.51)   Tiger Moth II R5251 RCV-L; Anson I LV327 RCV-2, T.21 VS564 RCV-A.

Nil (4.51–3.53)   Tiger Moth II; Oxford I R6248; Anson T.21 VS564 10; Chipmunk T.10 WP831 24; Prentice T.1 VR289.

Disbanded 31st March 1953 at Rochester.

25 RESERVE FLYING SCHOOL
Formed 26th June 1947 at Wolverhampton by redesignating 28 Elementary Flying Training School. Operated by Air Schools Ltd.

RCW (6.47–4.51)   Tiger Moth II DF155 RCW-L; Harvard IIB KF998; Anson I LT578, T.21 WB459 RCW-C; Chipmunk T.10 WB661.

Nil (4.51–3.53)   Tiger Moth II; Anson T.21 VV297 B; Oxford I X6655; Chipmunk T.10 WP780; Prentice T.1 VS745.

Also used   Tiger Moth BB819, I NM185.

Disbanded 31st March 1953 at Wolverhampton.

RESERVE TRAINING SQUADRON
Formed 15th October 1952 at Scampton by redesignating an element of 230 Operational Conversion Unit.

Lincoln B.2 RF344.

Disbanded 1st May 1953 at Scampton.

RHODESIAN AIR TRAINING GROUP COMMUNICATION FLIGHT – see Headquarters Rhodesian Air Training Wing Communication Flight, later Headquarters Rhodesian Air Training Group Communication Flight

RHODESIAN AIR TRAINING WING COMMUNICATION FLIGHT – see Headquarters Rhodesian Air Training Wing Communication Flight, later Headquarters Rhodesian Air Training Group Communication Flight

RHODESIAN AIR UNIT OF THE TERRITORIAL FORCES, later RHODESIAN AIR UNIT, later SOUTHERN RHODESIAN AIR FORCE
As the Rhodesian Air Unit of the Territorial Forces began training from November 1935 with civilian Tiger Moths provided by the de Havilland Aircraft Company (Rhodesia) Ltd. Separated 1st April 1939 from the parent territorial organisation to become the Rhodesian Air Unit. Redesignated the Southern Rhodesian Air Force from 19th September 1939. Disbanded 28th June 1940 to become the Rhodesian Air Training Group, RAF.

See also: Southern Rhodesia Communication Flight
1 Squadron, Southern Rhodesian Air Force

RHODESIAN CENTRAL FLYING SCHOOL, later CENTRAL FLYING SCHOOL (SOUTHERN RHODESIA)
Formed 3rd September 1941 at Belvedere, Southern Rhodesia.

Tiger Moth II.

Disbanded 20th May 1942 at Belvedere to become 33 Flying Instructors School.

Reformed 9th May 1944 at Norton, Southern Rhodesia, as the Central Flying School, Southern Rhodesia by redesignating 33 Flying Instructors School.

Harvard IIA EX699, III EZ239; Oxford I AS507; Cornell I EW540, II 15090; Hurricane I T9531; Anson I LT647.

Disbanded 9th October 1945 at Norton.

ROC FLIGHT
Formed 23rd August 1940 at Odiham, being attached to 110 Squadron, RCAF.

Roc I L3069.

Disbanded 2nd December 1940 at Odiham.

ROTA EXPERIMENT FLIGHT
Formed 20th April 1939 at Eastleigh.

Rota.

Disbanded (date and location unknown).

ROYAL AEROSPACE ESTABLISHMENT – see Royal Aircraft Establishment, later Royal Aerospace Establishment

ROYAL AIR FORCE AEROBATIC TEAM – 'THE RED ARROWS'
Formed 1st March 1965 at Fairford by redesignating the 'Yellow Jacks' of 4 Flying Training School.

Gnat T.1 XR996; Hawk T.1 XX251, T.1A XX237; Bulldog T.1 XX698.

Current 1st April 1998 at Cranwell.

ROYAL AIR FORCE AND ARMY CO-OPERATION SCHOOL
Formed 19th September 1918 at Worthy Down by redesignating the Artillery and Infantry Co-operation School.

B.E.2c; R.E.8.

Disbanded 23rd December 1919 at Worthy Down to become the School of Army Co-operation.

ROYAL AIR FORCE AND NAVY CO-OPERATION SCHOOL
Formed 16th June 1919 at Lee-on-Solent by merging 209 (Seaplane) and 210 Training Depot Stations.

Short 184 N2987.

Disbanded 14th July 1919 at Lee-on-Solent to become the Royal Air Force Seaplane Establishment.

ROYAL AIR FORCE ANTARCTIC FLIGHT
Formed 25th April 1949 at Hendon.

Auster VI VX127, T.7 WE563.

Disbanded January 1951 at (location unknown).

ROYAL AIR FORCE BASE, CALSHOT
Formed 5th February 1922 at Calshot.

'A' Flight	*Cloud K4301; Osprey III K3914.*
'B' Flight	*Cloud K2894; Sea Tutor K3375; Shark II K8452; Walrus I K5777; Swordfish I K5992.*
'C' Flight	*Southampton II S1121.*

Disbanded 1st April 1935 at Calshot to become Royal Air Force Station, Calshot.

ROYAL AIR FORCE BASE GOSPORT, later ROYAL AIR FORCE STATION, GOSPORT
Formed 1st October 1921 at Gosport having Composite Co-operation, Development, Observer Training and Torpedo Training Flights. The Observer Training and Composite Co-operation Flights ceased to exist from 1st May 1922. The Base was reorganised from 15th July 1925 into 'A' (Fighter), 'B' (Spotter), 'C' (Reconnaissance) and 'D' (Torpedo Training) Flights. These Flights then, from 1st April 1930, became the basis for the Base Training Squadron. Redesignated Royal Air Force Station, Gosport Training Squadron from 1st April 1935.

'A' Flight   Formed 1st April 1930 as 'A' (Army and Navy Co-operation) Flight.

                Fairey IIIF; Moth.

                Disbanded 26th October 1934 and absorbed by 'A' Flight, School of Naval Co-operation.

                Reformed 26th October 1934 as 'A' (Torpedo Training) Flight by redesignating 'D' (Torpedo Training) Flight.

                Vildebeest I S1709; Baffin K2886; Shark I K4357, II K8481; Swordfish I K5963.

                Disbanded February 1937 to become the Torpedo Training Unit.

'B' Flight   Formed January 1931 as 'B' (Telegraphist and Air Gunner) Flight.

                Fairey IIIF; Seal; Ripon; Vildebeest I K2814; Avro 504N K1974.

                Disbanded 26th October 1934 to become 'C' Flight, School of Naval Co-operation.

                Reformed 26th October 1934 as 'B' (Torpedo Experimental) Flight by redesignating 'E' (Experimental) Flight.

                Vildebeest I S1710, III K4163; Avro 504N K1813; Shark II K4882; Swordfish I K5998.

                Disbanded November 1938 and probably absorbed by the Torpedo Development Section.

'C' Flight   Formed January 1931 as 'C' (Deck Landing) Flight.

                Tutor K3221; Tomtit K1783; Avro 504N K1974; Osprey I K2782, II K3622, IV K5743; Nimrod II K3654; Shark I K4359; Seal K4779; Swordfish I K5995.

                Existed to at least November 1936.

'D' Flight   Formed 15th July 1925 as 'D' (Torpedo Training) Flight.

                Dart N9820 26; Ripon S1649 D7; Avro 504N J9701.

                Disbanded 26th October 1934 to become 'A' (Torpedo Training) Flight.

'E' Flight   Formed by March 1933 as 'E' (Experimental) Flight.

                Vildebeest I S1710.

                Disbanded 26th October 1934 to become 'B' (Torpedo Experimental) Flight.

ROYAL AIR FORCE BASE, LEUCHARS, later ROYAL AIR FORCE TRAINING BASE, LEUCHARS
Formed 18th March 1920 at Leuchars by redesignating the Fleet School of Aerial Fighting and Gunnery. Redesignated Royal Air Force Training Base, Leuchars from 15th July 1925.

'A' (Fighter) Training Flight	*Avro 504K H3069, Avro 504N J9428; Flycatcher N9614; Grebe IIIDC J7521; Siskin.*
'B' (Spotter) Training Flight	*Blackburn N9686 O, Blackburn DC N9589 J; Bison N9599; Fairey IIIF J9672; Siskin IIIDC J9199.*
'C' (Reconnaissance) Training Flight	*Fairey IIID N9755, IIIF S1527 7; Osprey I S1680; Avro 504N J9290.*
Base Training Flight	*Moth K1105.*
Also used	*Snipe E6952; Fairey IIID S1012; Fairey IIIF S1788 5; Ripon S1425 5; Tutor K3354; Hart K3744.*

Disbanded 1st April 1935 at Leuchars to become 1 Flying Training School.

ROYAL AIR FORCE (BELGIAN) TRAINING SCHOOL
Formed 13th October 1944 at Snailwell.

Nil	*Tiger Moth I NL916, II DF198; Master II EM405, III DL946; Martinet I EM640; Dominie I NR777.*
TSI	*Allocated but no evidence of use.*
TSN	*Allocated but no evidence of use.*

Disbanded 18th April 1946 at Snailwell and transferred to the Belgium Air Force.

ROYAL AIR FORCE BENGAL/BURMA COMMUNICATION SQUADRON
Formed 4th December 1944 at Baigachi, India, by redesignating the 3rd Tactical Air Force Communication Squadron.

Dakota IV; Blenheim BB156; Expeditor I HB163; Argus III KK385; Warwick III HG243; Lockheed 12A LV760; Tiger Moth II NL817; Harvard IIB FE770.

Disbanded 21st April 1945 at Baigachi to become the Headquarters Royal Air Force Burma Communication Squadron.

ROYAL AIR FORCE (CADET) COLLEGE
Formed 23rd December 1919 at Cranwell by redesignating the Cadet College.

D.H.9A J7317 B11; D.H.9A DC J8483; F.2B C4740 D1; Snipe E6184; Avro 504K D4432 C4; Bugle I J6985; Horsley II J8011; Avro 504N J8533; Atlas I J8789 H; Fairey IIIF J9057; Siskin IIIDC J9195, IIIA J9317.

Disbanded 5th February 1920 at Cranwell to become the Royal Air Force College.

ROYAL AIR FORCE COLLEGE, later ROYAL AIR FORCE COLLEGE SERVICE FLYING TRAINING SCHOOL, later ROYAL AIR FORCE COLLEGE
Formed 5th February 1920 at Cranwell by redesignating the Royal Air Force (Cadet) College. Redesignated the Royal Air Force College Flying Training School from September 1939.

D.H.9A DC J8466; Siskin IIIA J9216 10; Fox J7953; Horsley II J8011; Fairey IIIF J9057; Avro 504K F2269, Avro 504N J8504 9; Atlas I J8789, Atlas Trainer K1172, Atlas AC K1558; Tutor K3205 7; Bulldog IIA K2196, Bulldog Trainer K3175; Hart K3029; Wallace I K5082; Audax K5592; Fury K5682 6; Hind L2192; Hector K8115; Whitley II K7249, III K8949; Blenheim I L6651; Moth DG660; Master I T8275, II DL122 50, III DL948; Anson I EG699; Oxford I V4152 67, II N6376; Wellington IA N2909, IC N2737; Hurricane I N2344; Tiger Moth II R5038.

Disbanded 20th March 1944 at Cranwell to become 17 Service Flying Training School.

The College re-opened on 16th October 1946 but the flying element did not reform until 17th April 1947 at Cranwell by redesignating 19 Flying Training School.

FAA (4.47–4.51)	Harvard IIB KF448 FAA-Y.
FAB (4.47–4.51)	Harvard IIB KF191 FAB-O.
FAC (4.47–4.51)	Harvard IIB FX299 FAC-K.
FAD (4.47–4.51)	Harvard IIB FX441 FAD-Z.
FAE (4.47–4.51)	Tiger Moth II T5672 FAE-A; Prentice T.1 VR239 FAE-B.
FAF (4.46–4.51)	Tiger Moth II T7783 FAF-F; Prentice T.1 VS266 FAF-H.
FAG (4.47–4.51)	Tiger Moth II EM742 FAG-C; Anson I NK595 FAG-F, T.21 VV257 FAG-C; Vampire F.1 TG295 FAG-G; Meteor T.7 WA619 FAG-A.
A (4.51– .56)	Harvard IIB KF148 A-X; Balliol T.2 WN530 A-W.
B (4.51– .56)	Harvard IIB KF214 B-R; Balliol T.2 WG111 B-H.
C (4.51– .56)	Harvard IIB FT378 C-E; Balliol T.2 WG112 C-A.
D (.52– .60)	Chipmunk T.10 WK559 D-J; Provost T.1 WW393 D-J.
E (4.51–)	Anson XIX TX229 E-K.
J (.52– .60)	Anson XIX VM315 J-A; Provost T.1 XF836 J-G; Chipmunk T.10 WZ865 J-V.
N (.56– .70)	Valetta T.3 WG266 N-E; Varsity T.1 WJ893 N-X.
Nil (.70–2.89)	Chipmunk T.10 WZ853 8; Vampire FB.9 WP991, T.11 XD382 38; Jet Provost T.3 XM455 16, T.3A XN555 59, T.4 XP555 70, T.5A XW351 30; Dominie T.1 XS714.

Flying element disbanded 1st February 1989 at Cranwell to become 3 Flying Training School.

ROYAL AIR FORCE COLLEGE AIR SQUADRON
Formed 1st April 1992 at Cranwell.

Bulldog XX515 A2.

Current at 1st April 1995 at Cranwell.

ROYAL AIR FORCE COLLEGE OF AIR WARFARE
Formed 1st July 1962 at Manby by redesignating the Royal Air Force Flying College.

Meteor T.7 WA718 Y, F.8 WK914 H; Valetta C.1 VW825; Varsity T.1 WF325; Provost T.1 WV503; Canberra B.2 WD966, T.4 WH848; Hunter F.4 WV407; Jet Provost T.3 XM463, T.4 XP580 34; Dominie T.1 XS733.

Disbanded 1st April 1974 at Manby.

ROYAL AIR FORCE COLLEGE SERVICE FLYING TRAINING SCHOOL – Royal Air Force College, later Royal Air Force College Service Flying Training School, later Royal Air Force College

ROYAL AIR FORCE COMMUNICATION FLIGHT
Formed 17th December 1947 at Palam, India, by redesignating the Supreme Commander's Headquarters (Air) Communication Squadron. Detachments at Palam and Peshawar were withdrawn 31st March 1948.

Dakota IV KK163; York MW102.

Disbanded 30th June 1948 at Mauripur, India.

ROYAL AIR FORCE DELEGATION (BELGIUM) COMMUNICATION FLIGHT
Formed 17th July 1946 (location unknown).

Proctor III HM425, IV NP228.

Disbanded 31st December 1949 (location unknown).

ROYAL AIR FORCE DELEGATION (DENMARK) COMMUNICATION FLIGHT
Formed 17th July 1945 (location unknown).

Proctor III HM425; Anson XI PH764; Dominie I NF856; Fi 156 VH754.

Disbanded 31st August 1947 (location unknown).

ROYAL AIR FORCE DELEGATION (FRANCE) COMMUNICATION FLIGHT
Formed 26th August 1946 at Buc by redesignating 87 Wing Communication Flight.

Tiger Moth II DE810; Proctor III HM295; Anson XII PH669 D, XIX TX212; Spitfire IX MA683; Oxford I LX540.

Disbanded 15th November 1947 at Toussus le Noble, France.

ROYAL AIR FORCE DELEGATION (GREECE) COMMUNICATION FLIGHT
Formed 11th January 1947 at Hassani, Greece, by redesignating the Air Headquarters Greece Communication Flight.

Proctor III HM306; Auster VI VF494; Anson XIX VL296.

Disbanded 14th April 1952 at Ellenikon, Greece.

ROYAL AIR FORCE DELEGATION (WASHINGTON) COMMUNICATION FLIGHT
Formed (date and location unknown).

No aircraft known.

Disbanded 15th October 1946 (location unknown).

ROYAL AIR FORCE DETACHMENT, PERTH
Formed 4th September at Perth by redesignating 'D' Flight, Performance Testing Section, Aeroplane and Armament Experimental Establishment.

Blenheim.

Disbanded 19th September 1939 at Perth to become the Wireless Development Unit.

ROYAL AIR FORCE ELEMENT, ALLIED TECHNICAL AIR INTELLIGENCE UNIT, SOUTHEAST ASIA
Formed 1943 at Maidan, India.

Mitsubishi A6M Zeke 'BI-06'; Mitsubishi Ki-46 Dinah; Mitsubishi G4M Betty 'FI-11'; Mitsubishi J2M Jack BI-01; Mitsubishi J2M3 Raiden 'B1-01'; Kawanishi H6K Mavis; Kyushu K9W1 Cypress 'B2-20'; Nakajima A6M2-N Rufe; Tachikawa Ki-54.

Disbanded 15th May 1946 at Seletar, Singapore.

ROYAL AIR FORCE ELEMENT, HELICOPTER DEVELOPMENT UNIT
Formed 1st June 1961 at Old Sarum as the Royal Air Force Element, Helicopter Development Unit. Absorbed into the Joint Warfare Establishment from 1st April 1963.

Sycamore HR.12 WV781, HR.14 XG503; Whirlwind HAR.10 XP338.

Disbanded 1st February 1965 at Old Sarum to become the Short-Range Transport Development Unit.

ROYAL AIR FORCE ELEMENT, YUGOSLAV TRAINING FLIGHT – see Yugoslav Training Flight, Royal Air Force Element

ROYAL AIR FORCE FILM PRODUCTION UNIT, later 1 ROYAL AIR FORCE FILM PRODUCTION UNIT
Formed 30th August 1941 at Pinewood Studios by redesignating the Air Ministry Film Production Unit. The flying element lodged at Benson from 20th September 1941 and at Langley from September 1944. Redesignated 1 Film Production Unit from February 1944.

Nil	Beaufort I L9947; Anson MG861; Hudson; Havoc I BD118; Auster V RT643.
TIH	Allocated but no evidence of use.

Disbanded 1st March 1947 at Stanmore Park to become the Film Production Unit Library.

ROYAL AIR FORCE FILM UNIT
Formed (date and location unknown). Known to have operated from Catterick by October 1944.

Blenheim IV Z6176; Auster V RT488.

Disbanded (date and location unknown).

ROYAL AIR FORCE FLYING COLLEGE
Formed 1st June 1949 at Manby.

FCT (6.49–4.51)	*Allocated but no evidence of use.*
FCU (6.49–4.51)	*Athena T.1 VR573 FCU-G.*
FCV (6.49–4.51)	*Allocated but no evidence of use.*
FCW (6.49–4.51)	*Allocated but no evidence of use.*
FCX (6.49–4.51)	*Lancastrian C.2 VM731 FCX-Z; Lancaster VII NX687 FCX-R.*
FGA (6.49–4.51)	*Martinet I MS820 FGA-E; Lincoln II RF362 FGA-F; Anson XIX VP522 FGA-S; Valetta C.1 VW144 FGA-K; Hastings C.1 TG617 FGA-J.*
FGB (6.49–4.51)	*Allocated but no evidence of use.*
FGC (6.49–4.51)	*Martinet I MS820 FGC-L; Anson XIX VP522 FGC-V; Harvard IIB FX297 FGC-S; Meteor T.7 WA654 FGC-J; Vampire B.5 VZ181 FGC-Q; Athena T.2 VR567 FGC-Y.*
Nil (4.51–7.62)	*Anson T.21 WJ547, T.22 VV367; Prentice T.1 VS359; Provost T.1 XF874 L; Athena T.2 VR580; Balliol T.2 WG128; Meteor F.4 VT215, F.8 WH462, NF.11 WD590, NF.13 WM318, NF.14 WS724; Hastings C.2 WJ327; Lincoln B.2 SX934; Valetta C.1 WD157, C.2 VX580; Varsity T.1 WF326; Canberra B.2 WH699, PR.7 WT528; Hunter F.4 XF369.*

Disbanded 1st July 1962 at Manby to become the Royal Air Force College of Air Warfare.

ROYAL AIR FORCE GERMANY COMMUNICATION SQUADRON
Formed 1st January 1959 at Wildenrath by redesignating the 2nd Allied Tactical Air Force Communication Squadron.

Valetta C.2 VX573; Spitfire XIX PS889; Devon C.1 VP967; Pembroke C.1 WV743, C(PR).1 XF796.

Disbanded 3rd February 1969 at Wildenrath, Germany, to become 60 Squadron.

ROYAL AIR FORCE GERMANY INSTRUMENT TRAINING FLIGHT
Formed 10th May 1960 at Gutersloh, Germany.

Meteor T.7 WA656; Vampire T.11 WZ498.

Disbanded 1963 at Gutersloh.

ROYAL AIR FORCE INSTITUTE OF AVIATION MEDICINE – see School of Aviation Medicine, later Royal Air Force Institute of Aviation Medicine

ROYAL AIR FORCE INSTRUCTIONAL MISSION, SOUTH RUSSIA – see Royal Air Force Training Mission, South Russia

ROYAL AIR FORCE LIAISON OFFICE, CHINESE ELEMENTARY FLYING TRAINING SCHOOL, later INDIA DETACHMENT, CHINESE AIR FORCE CADET SCHOOL
Formed 1st September 1943 at Walton, Lahore, India.
Redesignated India Detachment, Chinese Air Force Cadet School.

PT-17; PT-22; Vengeance IV.

Disbanded 30th June 1946 at Walton, Lahore.

ROYAL AIR FORCE METEOROLOGICAL FLIGHT, EASTCHURCH, DUXFORD AND MILDENHALL
Formed 1st November 1924 at Eastchurch, moved to Duxford 9th January 1925 and then to Mildenhall 1st September 1936.

Snipe E6525; Grebe II J7371; Siskin IIIA J8048; Bulldog IIA K2213; Gauntlet II K7801; Gladiator II N5583.

Disbanded 4th February 1941 at Mildenhall to become 401 (Meteorological) Flight.

ROYAL AIR FORCE (MIDDLE EAST) CENTRAL GUNNERY SCHOOL – see 1 (Middle East) Central Gunnery School later Royal Air Force (Middle East) Central Gunnery School

ROYAL AIR FORCE NORTHERN IRELAND COMMUNICATION FLIGHT – see Headquarters Royal Air Force Northern Ireland Communication Flight

ROYAL AIR FORCE POST OPERATIONAL CONVERSION UNIT
Formed 1st September 1972 at Leuchars by redesignating an element of 767 Squadron.

Phantom FG.1 XT861 V.

Disbanded 31st May 1978 at Leuchars.

1 ROYAL AIR FORCE REGIMENT ANTI-AIRCRAFT PRACTICE CAMP TARGET TOWING FLIGHT
Formed by 20th January 1943 at Weston Zoyland.

Lysander III T1672, IIIA V9655.

Disbanded 17th June 1943 at Weston Zoyland to become 1625 (Anti-Aircraft Co-operation) Flight.

2 ROYAL AIR FORCE REGIMENT ANTI-AIRCRAFT PRACTICE CAMP TARGET TOWING FLIGHT
Formed by 16th February 1943 at Langham.

Lysander II N1213, III T1671.

Disbanded 17th June 1943 at Langham to become 1626 (Anti-Aircraft Co-operation) Flight.

3 ROYAL AIR FORCE REGIMENT ANTI-AIRCRAFT PRACTICE CAMP TARGET TOWING FLIGHT
Formed by 5th May 1943 at Ipswich.

Lysander III T1434.

Disbanded 17th June 1943 at Ipswich to become 1627 (Anti-Aircraft Co-operation) Flight.

4 ROYAL AIR FORCE REGIMENT ANTI-AIRCRAFT PRACTICE CAMP TARGET TOWING FLIGHT
Formed by 4th April 1943 at Morfa Towyn.

Lysander II P1743, III T1697.

Disbanded 17th June 1943 at Morfa Towyn to become 1628 (Anti-Aircraft Co-operation) Flight.

5 ROYAL AIR FORCE REGIMENT ANTI-AIRCRAFT PRACTICE CAMP TARGET TOWING FLIGHT
Formed by April 1943 at Hutton Cranswick.

No aircraft known.

Disbanded 17th June 1943 at Hutton Cranswick to become 1629 (Anti-Aircraft Co-operation) Flight.

6 ROYAL AIR FORCE REGIMENT ANTI-AIRCRAFT PRACTICE CAMP TARGET TOWING FLIGHT
Formed by 5th May 1943 at Acklington.

Lysander III T1504.

Disbanded 17th June 1943 at Acklington to become 1630 (Anti-Aircraft Co-operation) Flight.

7 ROYAL AIR FORCE REGIMENT ANTI-AIRCRAFT PRACTICE CAMP TARGET TOWING FLIGHT
Records begin 21st April 1943 at Shoreham.

Lysander III T1460.

Disbanded 17th June 1943 at Shoreham to become 1631 (Anti-Aircraft Co-operation) Flight.

8 ROYAL AIR FORCE REGIMENT ANTI-AIRCRAFT PRACTICE CAMP TARGET TOWING FLIGHT
Formed 1st May 1943 at Montrose.

Lysander III T1579.

Disbanded 17th June 1943 at Montrose to become 1632 (Anti-Aircraft Co-operation) Flight.

9 ROYAL AIR FORCE REGIMENT ANTI-AIRCRAFT PRACTICE CAMP TARGET TOWING FLIGHT

Planned formation by May 1943 at Leysdown cancelled.

1 ROYAL AIR FORCE REGIMENT SCHOOL TARGET TOWING FLIGHT

Formed February 1942 at Hutton Cranswick.

Lysander I R2639, II R2001, III R9068; Martinet I HN960.

Disbanded 17th June 1943 at Hutton Cranswick and merged with 3 Royal Air Force Regiment School Target Towing Flight to become 1634 (Anti-Aircraft Co-operation) Flight.

3 ROYAL AIR FORCE REGIMENT SCHOOL TARGET TOWING FLIGHT

Formed 15th February 1942 at Ronaldsway by redesignating the flying element of 1 Ground Defence Gunners School.

Gauntlet II K5279; Wallace II K8688; Master I T8544; Lysander I P1671, II R2001, III R9068.

Disbanded 17th June 1943 at Ronaldsway and merged with 1 Royal Air Force Regiment School Target Towing Flight to become 1634 (Anti-Aircraft Co-operation) Flight.

ROYAL AIR FORCE SCHOOL, INDIA

Formed November 1921 at Bangalore, India.

F.2B F4636; Avro 504K H2548.

Disbanded 1st November 1922 at Quetta, India.

ROYAL AIR FORCE SEAPLANE ESTABLISHMENT

Formed 14th July 1919 at Lee-on-Solent by redesignating the Royal Air Force and Naval Co-operation School.

Short 184 N2987.

Disbanded 23rd December 1919 at Lee-on-Solent to become the School of Naval Co-operation.

ROYAL AIR FORCE STAFF COLLEGE COMMUNICATION FLIGHT

Formed 24th June 1946 at White Waltham.

Hudson IIIA FK787; Dominie II RL960; Spitfire XVI TE199; Anson XIX TX214.

Absorbed 10th September 1946 into the Reserve Command Communication Squadron as the Royal Air Force Staff College Flight. Transferred 1st August 1949 and merged with the Maintenance Command Communication Flight to become the Maintenance Command Communication Squadron.

ROYAL AIR FORCE STAFF COLLEGE FLIGHT

Formed 3rd April 1922 at Andover.

F.2B J6743; D.H.9A; Avro 504K E3401.

Disbanded 28th March 1927 at Andover and merged with the Wessex Area Communication Flight to become the Andover Communication Flight.

ROYAL AIR FORCE STAFF COLLEGE (OVERSEAS) COMMUNICATION FLIGHT

Formed Administratively 16th July 1946 at Ramat David, Palestine, by redesignating the Overseas Staff College Communication Flight.

Argus II FZ770.

Disbanded 15th October 1946 at Lydda, Palestine.

ROYAL AIR FORCE TECHNICAL COLLEGE

Formed 15th August 1947 at Henlow by redesignating the School of Aeronautical Engineering (Officers). Reconstituted from 24th February 1951 to have Headquarters, Henlow and Debden Divisions.

Armament Division	Formed 16th December 1949 at Lindholme.
	Spitfire XVI TE189; Lincoln B.2 RF443 F.
	Disbanded 15th November 1950 at Lindholme to become the Engineering and Armament Division.

Engineering and Armament Division	Formed early February 1951. Became Henlow Division, Royal Air Force Technical College from 24th February 1951.
Henlow Division	Formed 24th February 1951 by redesignating the Engineering and Armament Division.
Signals Division	Formed 20th October 1949 at Debden by redesignating the Empire Radio School. Redesignated the Debden Division, Royal Air Force Technical College from 24th February 1951. Disbanded 8th April 1960.

	TDE (10.49–4.51)	*Anson T.22 VS603 TDE-C; Tiger Moth II T7997 TDE-M.*
	S (4.51–)	*Tiger Moth II T7997 S-M; Oxford I RR328 S-L; Anson I LT357 S-C, T.22 VV361 S-H; Spitfire XVI TE189 S-A; Lincoln II RF425 S-F; Chipmunk T.10 WB706 S-M.*
	Nil (–4.60)	*Varsity T.1 WL669.*

Disbanded 31st December 1965 at Henlow and absorbed by the RAF College, Cranwell.

ROYAL AIR FORCE TRAINING BASE, LEUCHARS – see Royal Air Force Base, Leuchars, later Royal Air Force Training Base, Leuchars

ROYAL AIR FORCE TRAINING MISSION, SOUTH RUSSIA

Formed 20th October 1919 at Beketovka, Russia. The flying element, known as 'A' Detachment, Royal Air Force Training Mission, South Russia, was formed by redesignating 'B' Flight, 47 Squadron. Often referred to as the Royal Air Force Instructional Mission, South Russia.

Camel B7181; Short 184 N9012; D.H.9 D2842; D.H.9A E715 – later donated to the Russian forces.

Disbanded May 1920 at Peschance, Russia.

ROYAL AIRCRAFT ESTABLISHMENT, later ROYAL AEROSPACE ESTABLISHMENT

Formed 1st April 1918 at Farnborough by redesignating the Royal Aircraft Factory. Redesignated the Royal Aerospace Establishment from 1st April 1988.

The Experimental Section formed from 3rd September 1939 being divided into the Aerodynamic, Wireless and Electrical, Engine Research and Instrument and Armament Development Flights. From 11th February 1941 the Section was reorganised into Headquarters, Aerodynamic, Engine, Wireless and Electrical, Test, Armament Defence and Research Department Flights. Other Flights formed included:

Aero Airbourne Flight	Formed 1st August 1942 at Farnborough. Moved to Hartford Bridge from 13th August 1942. Became the Glider Experimental Flight from October 1942 until disbanding on 23rd March 1943.
Glider Experimental Flight	See above.
Research Department Flight	Formed (date unknown) at Farnborough. Moved to Exeter September 1939. Disbanded 12th March 1944 at Churchstanton.
Technical Practice Flight	Formed August 1943. Disbanded (date unknown).
Special Projectile Flight	See 'S' Flight, Royal Aircraft Establishment.

The Experimental Section and RAF Station Farnborough were merged into one establishment under the Ministry of Aircraft Production from 22nd January 1945 and became the Experimental Flying Department of the RAE. A Rocket Propulsion Department was formed in 1947 by redesignating the Guided Projectile

Establishment only to be redesignated in August 1958 to become the Rocket Propulsion Establishment.

The Royal Aircraft Establishment also possessed satellite facilities at:

Bedford/Thurleigh Opened 27th June 1957. Closed 1st April 1991 to become the Defence Research Agency – Aerospace Division.

Llanbedr Opened 1954. Transferred 1st April 1992, together with RAE West Freugh, to become an element of the Test and Evaluation Establishment.

West Freugh Opened 1st May 1956. Transferred 1st April 1992, together with RAE Llanbedr, to become an element of the Test and Evaluation Establishment.

Representative Aircraft:

(Airspeed) Courier K4047; Queen Wasp P5441; A.S.45 T2449; Oxford I AS504, II N6410; Horsa I DG597. (Arado) Ar 232B AIR MIN 17; Ar 234B VH530 AIR MIN 54, Ar 234B-1 VK877. (Armstrong Whitworth) Tadpole J6585; Sinaia I J6858; Awana J6897; Wolf J6923; Ape J7754; Starling J8027; Atlas J8777; Ajax II J9128; Siskin III J6982, IIIA J9312, IIIDC J7001; AW.23 K3585; Whitley K4586, II K7217, V Z6626, VII BD674; Albemarle I P1363, GT.II V1600; AW 52G TS363; AW52 TS368; Argosy C.1 XN815. (Austin) Greyhound H4318. (Avro) Bison N155; Ava II N172; Pike N523; 504A B3292, 504K D2007, 504N AX871; Aldershot I J6853, II J6852, III J6952; Andover J7262; Antelope J9183; Avro 10 K2682; Avro C.30A AP507; Rota II L7589; Anson I EG309, X NK832, XI NK790, XII PH654, XIX TX210, T.22 VV362; Manchester I R5773; Lancaster I R5612, I/Spec PD119, II DS708, III LM517, VI ND418, VII RT690, X FM201; York I MW272; Lancastrian III VH742; Lincoln I RA637, II SS716; Athena T.2 VR568; Tudor 1 G-AGRD/TS867, 2 G-AGRZ/VZ366; Avro 707C WZ744; Ashton B.2 WB491, B.3 WB493, B.4 WB494; Shackleton GR.1 VP263, MR.2 WG557, MR.3 WR974, T.4 VP293; Vulcan B.1 XA890. (BAC) One Eleven XX105; Andover C.1 XS646. (BAT) Bantam F1653. (Bell) Airacobra I AH574; Kingcobra I FR408. (Blackburn) Monoplane K4241; Blackburn N9579; Dart N9719; Cubaroo N166; Ripon S1271; Shark I K4350, II K4880; Skua I L3006; Roc L3060; Botha I L6185; Firebrand I DK364, III DK373, IV EK740; YA-7 WB781, Y.A.8 WB788; Beverley C.1 XB259; Buccaneer S.1 XK532, S.2C XV344. (Boeing) Fortress I AN531, IIA FK190; III HB779/G. (Boulton Paul) Partridge J8459; Sidestrand III J9770; P.32 J9950; Overstrand K8175; Defiant I AA354, II AA407, TT.I DS139; Balliol T.2 VR596; P.111A VT935. (Bristol) F.2B B1201; Braemar II C4297; Badger II J6492; Bullfinch J6903; Seely II J7004; Bloodhound J7237; Berkley J7404; Bulldog IIA K2188; Type 109 G-EBZK; Type 138A K4879; Type 148A K6552; Blenheim I L1146, IV R3679; Beaufort I N1156; Beaufighter I R2125, VIF V8830, X KW292; Buckingham I KV321; Buckmaster TJ714; Brigand B.1 VS815, TF.1 RH744; Bristol 171 VL963. (British Aircraft) Swallow BK897. (Bucker) Bu 180 AIR MIN 53. (Brunswick) Zaunkonig II VX190. (Cierva) C.6C J8068; C.19 Mk III K1948; C.30A AP507; Rota II L7589. (Consolidated) Liberator II AL625, III FL927, VI BZ970, VIII KP146. (Curtiss) Hawk 188 (ex French Air Force); Mohawk IV BJ542; Tomahawk I AH764, IIB AK184; Kittyhawk I AK580; Helldiver I JW115; Seamew I JW597. (de Havilland) D.H.6 B2963; D.H.9 C1393; D.H.9A E748; Amiens III E6042; Okapi J1938; Doncaster J6849; Derby J6894; D.H.18A J6899; Doormouse J7005; Dingo J7007; Humming Bird J7325; D.H.54 G-EBKI; Hyena J7781; Canberra J9184; D.H.77 J9771; Moth J8030; Tiger Moth I K2579, II N6917; Queen Bee K5100; Rapide R2486; D.H.89M K4772; Dominie I X7382; Mosquito II DD619, III HJ898, IV DK286, VI PZ358, IX LR418, XIII HK366, XVI NS566, XVII HK298, XX KB115, B.25 KB557, NF.30 NT358, TR.33 TS444, PR.34 VL623, NF.36 RL254, NF.38 VT654; Sea Mosquito TR.37 VT724; Hornet F.1 PX211, PR.2 VA964; Vampire F.1 TG299, FB.5 VV638; Venom FB.1 WE308, NF.3 WX865; Sea Venom NF.20 WM504; Devon C.1 VP975 M, C.2 XA880; Comet 1 XM823, 2E XV144, 3 XP915, 4 XX944, 4C XS235; D.H.108 TG283; Sea Vixen FAW.1 XN649, D.3 XS587. (DFS) Olympia Meise BGA449; Kranich II BGA494; Reiher; Schulgleiter VP559. (Dornier) Komet J7276; Do 217M-1 AIR MIN 106. (Douglas) Boston II AH484, III Z2256, IIIA BZ196, IV BZ402; Havoc I BJ496; Dauntless I JS997; Dakota III ZA947, IV KJ836. (English Electric) Wren J6973; Canberra B.2 WD931, PR.3 WE146, B.6 XH568; B.6(BS) WT305, PR.7 WH776; P.1A WG763; P.1B XG327; Lightning F.2 XN725.

(Fairchild) Argus III HB720. (Fairey) IIID N9456, IIIF J9165; Fawn II J7187, III J6907, IV J7215; IIIF J9165; Fox I J7941, Fox IIM J9834; Fairey V J9154; Long Range Monoplane K1991; Gordon I K2701; P.4/34 K7555; Swordfish I L2717, II NE954; Battle I K9370; Fulmar II X8798; Albacore I L7075; Barracuda I P9642, II DR126, III MD830; Firefly I MB718; FR.IV TW735; Gannet AEW.3 XL471; FD.2 WG777. (Fiat) Fiat CR.42 BT474. (Fieseler) Fi 156C VP546; Fi 156C-7 AIR MIN 99. (Focke-Wulf) Fw 190A-3 MP499, Fw 190A-4 PE882, Fw 19A-5 PN999. (Fokker) F.VIIA/3M J7986. (Folland) Gnat T.1 XP532. (General Aircraft) Jubilee K8307; Monospar L4672; Hotspur I BV136; II BT535; Hamilcar I NX815; GAL.56 TS507. (Gloster) Nighthawk J6925; Grebe I J6969, II J7400; Gamecock J7497, I J8047, II J8804; Gorcock I J7501; Gloster II J7505; Guan J7722; Goldfinch J7940; Goral J8673; SS.19 J9125; Gauntlet I K4086, II K5279; TC.33 J9832; TSR.38 S1705; Gloster A.S.31 K2602; Gloster F.5/34 K8089; Gladiator I K7946; E.28/39 W4041/G; E.1/44 TX148; Meteor F.1 EE216, F.3 EE246, F.4 VT150, T.7 VW412, F.8 VZ439, FR.9 WB134, PR.10 WB163, NF.11 WD589, U.15 RA415, U.16 WK744; Javelin FAW.1 XA544, FAW.5 XA711, FAW.6 XA831, FAW.9 XH965. (Gotha) Go 145B BV207. (Grumman) Tigercat TT349; Avenger I JZ298; III KE442. (Grunau) Baby VT762. (Hafner) AR.III/II GD670. (Handley Page) 0/400 C9773; Hyderabad J7745; Hinaidi II J9478; H.P.51 J9833; H.P.47 K2773; Harrow I K6963, II K7021; Hampden I AD982; Hereford I N9075; Halifax I L9505, II BB319, III HX246, VI RG642, VII NP748, IX RT814; Hastings C.1 TG502; C.2 WD480; Marathon 1C XJ830; HPR.2 WE496; H.P.88 VX330; H.P.115 XP841; Victor WB775, B.1 XA917, BK.1A XA938, BK.2 XL232. (Hawker) Dieker J6918; Woodcock I J6987, II J7966; Hornbill J7782; Horsley I J7987, II J7999; Harrier J8325; Hawfinch J8776; F.20/27 J9123; Hornet J9682; Audax K2000; Demon K2856; Fury K2875; Hart K2969; Hector K8090; Henley K7554; Hotspur K8309; Hurricane I V7301, IIA Z2326, IIB BE145, IIC BN288, IV KZ706, X P5170; Tornado P5224; Typhoon IA R7576, IB R8635/G; Tempest II MW767, V SN263, VI NX121; Sea Fury SR666; Hunter F.1 WT572, F.4 WT798, F.5 WN960, F.6 XE534; T.7 WV372; T.12 XE531; P1127 XP831. (Hawker Siddeley) HS.748 XW750; Buccaneer S.2 XV344, S.2B XX897; Nimrod MR.1 XV147; Harrier GR.1 XV278, T.4 XW175; HS.125 XW930; Hawk T.1 XX154. (Heath) Parasol K1228. (Heinkel) He 111H-3 AW177; He 161A-2 AIR MIN 66; He 162A-2 VH523 AIR MIN 59; He 177A-5 TS439; He 219A-5 AIR MIN 22. (Heston) T.1/37 L7706. (Hillson) 'Slip Wing' Hurricane 321 (RCAF serial ex L1884). (Horten) Ho IV VP543. (Hover-Air) Hoverhawk III XW660. (Hunting) H.126 XN714. (Issacs) Heliogyro K1171. (Junkers) F.13 J7232; Ju 52/3m VN718; Ju 88A-1 AX919, Ju 88A-5 EE205, Ju 88G-1 TP190, Ju 88R-1 PJ876; Ju 188A-1 AIR MIN 108; Ju 290A-2 AIR MIN 57; Ju 352A AIR MIN 18. (Kay) Gyroplane G-ACVA. (Lockheed) 12A R8987; Hudson I T9327, II T9381, III T9433, IIIA FH460, IV AE610, V AM526, VI EW893; Ventura I AE692, II AE855; Lightning I AF107; Hercules W.2 XV208. (Marshalls) MA.4 VF665. (Martin) Baltimore I AG689; Maryland I AR707; Marauder I FK109. (Martinsyde) Buzzard IA H6541. (Messerschmitt) Bf 108B-1 DK280; Bf 109E-3 AE479, Bf 109F-2 ES906, Bf 109G-6 TP814; Bf 110C-5 AX772, Bf 110G-4 AIR MIN 30; Me 163B-1A VF241; Me 262-2A VH509, Me 262B-1A VH519; Me 410A-3 TF209, Me 410B-6 AIR MIN 74. (Miles) Falcon SN524, Falcon Six L9705; Mentor L4422; Kestrel N3300; Magister T9758; Sparrowhawk U-5; Master I N7413, II EM258, III W8437; Martinet I EM500; Libellula SR392; Queen Martinet PW979; Messenger I RH368. (Nieuport) Nighthawk H8535. (North American) Harvard I N7108, IIB FT375; Mustang I AG393, IA FD556, III KH505; Mitchell II FV903, III HD370; Sabre F.4 XB620. (Northrop) 2E K5053. (Panavia) Tornado GR.1 ZA326, GR.1T ZA326. (Parnall) Possum J6862; Pixie I J7324; Parasol K1228; G.4/31 K2772; Hendy Heck IIC K8853. (Percivil) Proctor IA P6062; Prentice T.1 TV163; P.46 VT789. (Peyret) Glider J7128. (Piper) Cub Coupe BT440 (Republic) Thunderbolt II KJ298. (Rolls-Royce) Thrust Measuring Rig XJ314. (Royal Aircraft Factory) S.E 5b A8947; B.E.2c 4122, B.E.2e C6980 F.E.2b D9108. (Savoia-Marchetti) SM.95 AIR MIN224. (Schleicher) Rhonbussard VT710. (Scott) Viking 2. (SEPECAT) Jaguar GR.1 XX734, T.2 XX835 V. (Short) Silver Streak G6854; Springbok I J6974; Short S.31 M-4; Stirling L7605, I N3639; Sturgeon RK787; Sperrin VX158; SB.5 WG768; SC.1 XG905. (Siebel) Si 204D-1 AIR MIN 4. (Sikorsky) Hoverfly I KL107; II KN863. (Sopwith) Triplane N5430; Pup B7565; Camel D1965; Snipe J2405, DC E6487; Salamander F6608; Snapper F7032. (Stearman-Hammond) Model Y R2676; (Supermarine) F.7/30 K2890; Walrus I K5772, II V9580; Spitfire K5054; I N3108, IA AR213; PR.IC R6903, IIA P7844; PR.IV R7030, VA X4258; VB EN948, VC BR372, VI BR205, VII EN297,

VIII LV674, XI PL827, XIII X4660, XIV RB176, XVI SM282, XVIII SM970, XIX PM501, F.21 LA188; Queen Seafire IIC MB307; Seafire XV PK245, XVII SX311, F.46 LA542; Seafang F.31 VG471; Sea Otter I JM821; Attacker TS413; Supermarine 508 VX133; Scimitar F.1 XD229. (Taylorcraft) Auster III MT407, IV MS935. (Vickers) Vimy F3151, IV J7238; Vanguard J6924; Virginia III J6992, VI J7558, VII J7432, IX J7130, X K2679; Venture I J7277; Wibault J9029; Victoria V K1314; Vildebeest I K2813, III S1713; Wellesley K7772; Wellington I L4269, DW.I P2518, IA N2878, IC L7812, II Z8407, III BK546, VIA W5802, VIII Z8707, X LN622, XI HZ202, XIII HZ657, XIV HF352; Warwick I BV292, II HG362, III HG216, V LM855; Viking G-AGOM, C.1A VL227, C.2 VL228; Valetta C.1 VW197; Varsity T.1 WL679; Wild Goose XA952; Viscount XT575; VC10 XX914. (Vultee) Vengeance II AN609, IV FD121; Vigilant IA BZ103. (Waco) Model ZVN P6330; Hadrian I FR565. (Westland) Weasel I F2913; Wagtail J6581; Yeovil I J7509, II J7510; Wapiti I J9101, IIA J9380; F.20/27 J9124; Pterodactyl IA J9251; Lysander K6128, I L4673, II N1217, III T1501, TT.III R9133, IIIA V9722; Whirlwind L6844, I P6967; Welkin I DX328; Wyvern TF.1 TS378; Whirlwind HAR.1 XA864, HAR.4 XD163, HAS.7 XK906; Wessex HAS.1 XL728, HC.2 XR503, HU.5 XS241; Scout AH.1 XP189; Wasp HAS.1 XS565; Sea King HAS.1 XV371, Mk.4X ZB507; Lynx AH.1/5 ZD285; Puma HC.1 ZA941; Gazelle HT.2 ZB648.

Disbanded 1st April 1991 at Farnborough to become the Defence Research Agency – Aerospace Division.

ROYAL FLYING CORPS DETACHED FLIGHT, MOASCAR
Formed (date unknown) at Moascar, Egypt.

Longhorn; Shorthorn, B.E.2c.

Disbanded 24th March 1915 at Moascar to become 30 Squadron.

ROYAL FLYING CORPS FLIGHT, BASRA
Formed April 1915 at Basra, Iraq, as a detached Flight of 30 Squadron.

Longhorn; Shorthorn; Caudron G.3; Martinsyde S.1.

Disbanded 4th November 1915 at Basra and absorbed by the parent unit.

ROYAL FLYING CORPS, FORCE 'D'
Formed by August 1915 at Basra, Iraq.

Henry Farman F.27 3900; Sopwith 807 920; Short 827 822; Voisin III LA.S 8506.

Existed to at least June 1916 at (location unknown).

ROYAL HELLENIC AIR FORCE COMMUNICATION FLIGHT
Formed 1st March 1945 at Hassani, Greece.

Anson I NK886, XII PH724.

Disbanded 1st March 1946 at Hassani.

ROYAL NAVAL FIGHTER SQUADRON
Formed 17th August 1941 at Sidi Heneish South, Egypt, as a temporary amalgamation of 803, 805 and 806 Squadrons.

Martlet I AX731; Hurricane I V7858; Fulmar II.

Disbanded February 1942 at LG.02 (Sidi Barrani), Egypt.

ROYAL NAVY ELEMENTARY FLYING TRAINING SCHOOL
Formed April 1973 at Church Fenton within 2 Flying Training School. Subsequently operated within 3 Flying Training School at Leeming from 29th November 1974, and 1 Flying Training School at Topcliffe from 26th April 1984.

Bulldog T.1 XX522 E.

Disbanded 8th July 1993 at Topcliffe and merged with the Elementary Flying Training Squadron to become the Joint Elementary Flying Training School.

ROYAL NORWEGIAN NAVY FLIGHT
Formed August 1942 at Woodhaven as a detachment of 210 Squadron.

He 115A-2 BV186.

Disbanded 17th February 1943 at Woodhaven to become 1477 (Norwegian) Flight.

'S' FLIGHT, ROYAL AIRCRAFT ESTABLISHMENT
Formed 3rd June 1944 at Heston as the Special Projectile Flight, RAE by redesignating 1422 (Special Project) Flight. Became known as 'S' or Special Flight, RAE from 1st November 1944.

Havoc I BB907; Mosquito II W4087; Anson I NK494/G; Tiger Moth DE712; Messenger RH368.

Disbanded 31st December 1944 at Laleham.

'S' SQUADRON
Formed 17th March 1919 at Heliopolis, Egypt, by redesignating an element of 5 Fighting School.

Avro 504K.

Disbanded June 1919 at Almaza, Egypt, and absorbed by 'Z' Squadron, Egypt.

Reformed 21st August 1939 at Habbaniya, Iraq, by redesignating the Communication Flight Iraq and Persia.

Vincent K4741.

Disbanded 1st November 1940 at Shaibah, Iraq, to become 244 Squadron.

SABRE CONVERSION FLIGHT – see 2nd Tactical Air Force Sabre Conversion Unit

ST ANDREWS AND DUNDEE UNIVERSITIES AIR SQUADRON – see St Andrews University Air Squadron, later St Andrews and Dundee Universities Air Squadron

ST ANDREWS UNIVERSITY AIR SQUADRON, later ST ANDREWS AND DUNDEE UNIVERSITIES AIR SQUADRON
Formed April 1941 at St Andrews and using Leuchars for flying training. Redesignated St Andrews and Dundee Universities Air Squadron from 1st August 1967.

Nil (4.41– 4.47)	Moth AW148; Moth Minor; Tiger Moth II provided by 11 Elementary Flying Training School.
FLF	Allocated but no evidence of use.
RUS (4.47–4.51)	Tiger Moth II N9205 RUS-C.
Nil 4 .51–1.69)	Harvard IIB FT282; Chipmunk T.10 WD363 D.

Disbanded 1st January 1969 at Leuchars and merged with the Edinburgh University Air Squadron to become the East Lowlands University Air Squadron.

SCHOOL FOR ANTI-SUBMARINE INSHORE PATROL OBSERVERS
Formed August 1918 at Aldeburgh.

Kangaroo B9984; D.H.9 D1096.

Disbanded October 1918 at Aldeburgh to become the Marine Observers School.

SCHOOL FOR MARINE OPERATIONAL PILOTS
Formed 15th October 1918 at Swingate by redesignating 53 Training Depot Station.

D.H.6 A9633; D.H.9 D576; S.E.5a D3487.

Disbanded February 1919 at Swingate.

SCHOOL FOR WIRELESS OPERATORS
Formed 24th August 1916 at Farnborough by redesignating the Wireless School, South Farnborough.

F.K.3, F.K.8.

Disbanded 18th October 1917 to become the Wireless School.

SCHOOL OF AERIAL CO-OPERATION WITH COASTAL ARTILLERY
Formed 31st January 1918 at Gosport by redesignating 'E' Flight, 39 Squadron.

B.E.2c; B.E.12 C3106.

Disbanded September 1919 at Gosport to become the Coastal Battery Co-operation School.

1 SCHOOL OF AERIAL FIGHTING
Formed 17th September 1917 at Ayr Racecourse.

Camel B9207; D.H.2 B8824; Bristol M.1C C5007; F.2B B1195; Avro 504J A9798; Spad S.7; S.E.5a D3436; F.2B B1195.

Disbanded 10th May 1918 at Ayr Racecourse and merged with 2 (Auxiliary) School of Aerial Gunnery to become 1 School of Aerial Fighting and Gunnery.

2 SCHOOL OF AERIAL FIGHTING
Formed 11th October 1917 at Eastburn.

F.K.8 B252; D.H.4 B5524; D.H.9 C1184; Camel B5582; Avro 504J B8817; F.K.3 B9594; Dolphin C3854; Bristol M.1C C4995.

Disbanded 6th May 1918 at Eastburn and merged with 4 (Auxiliary) School of Aerial Gunnery to become 2 School of Aerial Fighting and Gunnery.

SCHOOL OF AERIAL FIGHTING (CANADA) – see School of Aerial Gunnery (Canada), later School of Aerial Fighting (Canada)

SCHOOL OF AERIAL FIGHTING, HELIOPOLIS – see Aerial Fighting School, Heliopolis

SCHOOL OF AERIAL FIGHTING AND BOMB DROPPING
Formed 1st April 1918 at Freiston by redesignating the Royal Naval Air Service Gunnery School, Freiston.

Pup N6160.

Disbanded 6th May 1918 at Freiston to become 4 School of Aerial Fighting and Gunnery.

1 SCHOOL OF AERIAL FIGHTING AND GUNNERY
Formed 10th May 1918 at Turnberry by merging 1 School of Aerial Fighting and 2 (Auxiliary) School of Air Gunnery.

D.H.9 C1215; S.E.5a D411.

Disbanded 29th May 1918 at Turnberry to become 1 Fighting School.

2 SCHOOL OF AERIAL FIGHTING AND GUNNERY
Formed 6th May 1918 at Marske by merging 2 School of Aerial Fighting and 4 (Auxiliary) School of Aerial Gunnery.

F.K.8 B252; D.H.4 B5524; Bristol M.1C C4995; Avro 504A C694; F.K.8 B9594; Dolphin C3854; Camel B5582; D.H.9 D7309.

Disbanded 29th May 1918 at Marske to become 2 Fighting School.

3 SCHOOL OF AERIAL FIGHTING AND GUNNERY
Formed 6th May 1918 at Driffield by redesignating an element of 2 School of Aerial Fighting and Gunnery.

Pup.

Disbanded 29th May 1918 at Bircham Newton to become 3 Fighting School.

4 SCHOOL OF AERIAL FIGHTING AND GUNNERY
Formed 6th May 1918 at Freiston by redesignating the School of Aerial Fighting and Bomb Dropping.

B.E.2c 9473; Pup N6160; Dolphin; Camel B7263; D.H.5; S.E.5; Snipe; Avro 504J D6276.

Disbanded 29th May 1918 at Freiston to become 4 Fighting School.

SCHOOL OF AERIAL GUNNERY, ABOUKIR
Formed April 1917 at Aboukir, Egypt.

B.E.2c, B.E.2e; Longhorn; B.E.12; D.H.6 C2047.

Disbanded 5th September 1918 at Aboukir and merged with the Aerial Fighting School, Heliopolis, to become 5 Fighting School.

SCHOOL OF AERIAL GUNNERY (CANADA), later SCHOOL OF AERIAL FIGHTING (CANADA)
Formed 1st May 1917 at Camp Borden, Canada, as an element of 80 (Canadian) Training Squadron. Became an independent entity

from June 1917. Redesignated School of Aerial Fighting (Canada) from 1918.

Curtiss JN-4 C576; Camel B3772.

Disbanded November 1918 at Beamsville, Canada.

SCHOOL OF AERIAL GUNNERY, HYTHE, later 1 (AUXILIARY) SCHOOL OF AERIAL GUNNERY
Formed 13th September 1916 at Hythe, Kent, by redesignating the Machine Gun School. The School flew from Dymchurch (Redoubt). Redesignated 1 (Auxiliary) School of Aerial Gunnery from 1st January 1917. See also the Advanced Air Firing School.

F.E.2b; F.E.8; F.K.3 A8110; F.K.8 B3326; D.H.2; B.E.2c; R.E.7 2304; R.E.8; F.B.5; Camel; Handley Page O/400 B8808; Bristol Scout D.

Disbanded 9th March 1918 at Dymchurch and merged with 3 (Auxiliary) School Of Aerial Gunnery to become 1 (Observer) School of Aerial Gunnery.

SCHOOL OF AERIAL GUNNERY, LOCH DOON
Formed January 1917 at Loch Doon.

B.E.2c Floatplane 4721; D.H.2 A2610; F.K.3 A1505; Shorthorn Seaplane A3297; FBA Type B 9615 (B3984); Short 827 A9920.

Disbanded January 1918.

SCHOOL OF AERIAL GUNNERY, MARSKE – see 4 (Auxiliary) School of Aerial Gunnery

SCHOOL OF AERIAL GUNNERY, NEW ROMNEY – see 3 (Auxiliary) School of Aerial Gunnery

SCHOOL OF AERIAL GUNNERY, TURNBERRY – see 2 (Auxiliary) School of Aerial Gunnery

SCHOOL OF AERIAL GUNNERY AND BOMBING
Formed by January 1921 at Eastchurch.

D.H.9A E8692; Snipe F2411; F.2B Fighter H1572.

Disbanded 1st April 1922 at Eastchurch to become the Armament and Gunnery School.

SCHOOL OF AERIAL NAVIGATION
Formed 13th February 1920 at Calshot.

Short 184; Fairey IIID.

Disbanded 1st April 1920 at Calshot and merged with the School of Naval Co-operation to become the School of Naval Co-operation and Aerial Navigation.

1 SCHOOL OF AERIAL NAVIGATION AND BOMB DROPPING, later 1 SCHOOL OF NAVIGATION AND BOMB DROPPING
Formed 5th January 1918 at Stonehenge by redesignating 2 Training Depot Station. Later redesignated 1 School of Navigation and Bomb Dropping. Absorbed the Handley Page Squadron on 1st April 1918.

Handley Page O/100 3118 2; Handley Page O/400 D4563; D.H.4 A7871; D.H.9 C6128, D.H.9A F973; F.E.2b A5794; Pup C284; Bristol M.1C C5013; B.E.2e C7103; D.H.10; F.E.2b, F.E.2d A6589.

Disbanded 23rd September 1919 at Old Sarum and merged with 2 School of Navigation and Bomb Dropping to become the School of Air Pilotage.

2 SCHOOL OF AERIAL NAVIGATION AND BOMB DROPPING, later 2 SCHOOL OF NAVIGATION AND BOMB DROPPING
Formed 23rd June 1918 at Andover. Later redesignated 2 School of Navigation and Bomb Dropping.

Handley Page O/400 C9649; Avro 504K; D.H.4; Pup; D.H.6; D.H.9 D3049; F.E.2d; Bristol Scout D F9626; D.H.9A F1635; Bristol M.1C C5006 50; Shorthorn; B.E.2e; F.2B.

Disbanded 23rd September 1919 at Andover and merged with 1 School of Navigation and Bomb Dropping to become the School of Air Pilotage.

3 SCHOOL OF AERIAL NAVIGATION AND BOMB DROPPING, later 3 SCHOOL OF NAVIGATION AND BOMB DROPPING

Formed 17th May 1918 at Almaza, Egypt, as a detached Flight of the Artillery Observation School. Moved to Helwan in August 1918 and became an independent unit. Later redesignated 3 School Of Navigation and Bomb Dropping.

D.H.6 A9713; D.H.9 D2929; F.K.8 D5034; B.E.2e A1343; B.E.12 A6673.

Disbanded 22nd July 1919 at Helwan, Egypt.

4 SCHOOL OF AERIAL NAVIGATION AND BOMB DROPPING, later 4 SCHOOL OF NAVIGATION AND BOMB DROPPING

Formed September 1918 at Thetford. Later redesignated 4 School of Navigation and Bomb Dropping

F.E.2b; D.H.4; D.H.6; D.H.9 H7180, D.H.9A.

Disbanded 26th April 1919 at Thetford.

SCHOOL OF AIR NAVIGATION, later 1 SCHOOL OF AIR NAVIGATION

Formed 6th January 1936 at Manston by merging Air Navigation School, Andover and the Navigation School, Calshot. Redesignated 1 School of Air Navigation from June 1940.

Cloud K2898; Anson I N9838 X; Master I N7418; Tiger Moth II T5370.

Disbanded 11th November 1940 at Port Albert, Canada, to become 31 Air Navigation School.

1 SCHOOL OF AIR NAVIGATION – see School of Air Navigation, later 1 School of Air Navigation

2 SCHOOL OF AIR NAVIGATION

Formed 21st October 1940 at Cranage by redesignating an element of 1 School of Air Navigation.

Anson I N5242 F1; Master I N8017; Hudson IV AE617, V AM746; Gipsy Moth DG579.

Disbanded 14th August 1942 at Cranage to become the Central Navigation School.

SCHOOL OF AIR PILOTAGE

Formed 23rd September 1919 at Andover by merging 1 and 2 Schools of Navigation and Bomb Dropping.

No aircraft known.

Disbanded 23rd December 1919 at Andover to become the Air Pilotage School.

SCHOOL OF AIR SEA RESCUE

Formed 3rd May 1943 at Squires Gate.

5 (5.43–)	Anson I NK476 5-02.
Nil (–7.45)	Anson I LT249 63; Sea Otter I JM770.

Disbanded 23rd July 1945 at Calshot to become the Survival and Rescue Training Unit.

SCHOOL OF AIR SUPPORT

Formed 5th November 1944 at Old Sarum by redesignating 1 School of Army Co-operation.

Spitfire IX BS340, XVI SM305; Hurricane IIC LF600; Dominie I NR733; Anson XIX TX184 A.

Disbanded 1st May 1947 at Old Sarum to become the School of Land/Air Warfare.

SCHOOL OF AIR TRAFFIC CONTROL

Formed 1st November 1946 at Watchfield by redesignating the School of Flying Control.

FDY	Anson I NK273 FDY-L; Hawk Major HL538 FDY-Z.

Disbanded 10th February 1950 at Watchfield and merged with the Central Navigation School to become the Central Navigation and Control School.

SCHOOL OF AIR TRANSPORT

Formed 1st November 1944 at Netheravon.

Oxford II W6634; Dominie I X7393.

Disbanded 5th March 1946 at Netheravon.

SCHOOL OF ARMY CO-OPERATION, later 1 SCHOOL OF ARMY CO-OPERATION, later ROYAL AIR FORCE SCHOOL OF ARMY CO-OPERATION

Formed 23rd December 1919 at Worthy Down by redesignating the Royal Air Force and Army Co-operation School.

B.E.2c; R.E.8; F.2B; D.H.4; F.K.8.

Disbanded 8th March 1920 at Worthy Down.

Reformed 8th March 1920 at Stonehenge by redesignating the Artillery Co-operation Squadron. Redesignated 1 School of Army Co-operation from 20th December 1939.

F.2B C1037; Dart N9542; Snipe F2413; Atlas I J8784; Tutor K6126; Audax K3888; Rota K4230 15; Tiger Moth I K4273; Hart Trainer K4938; Hector K8122; Magister L8166; Gladiator II N5636; Battle L5190; Defiant I N1761; Harvard I N7173; Master I T8848; Lysander II P1671, IIIA V9284; Tiger Moth II N9392; Anson I N9611; Blenheim I L1273, IV P6899; Oxford II N6417; Hurricane I P2715; Tomahawk I AH811, IIA AH972, IIB AK101; Taylorcraft Plus D W5741; Stinson Voyager X1050; Cagnet W7646.

Disbanded 20th September 1941 at Old Sarum, the Training Squadron becoming 41 Operational Training Unit.

Reformed June 1943 at Old Sarum. Redesignated the Royal Air Force School of Army Co-operation from August 1943.

No aircraft, if any, known.

Disbanded 5th November 1944 at Old Sarum to become the School of Air Support.

2 SCHOOL OF ARMY CO-OPERATION

Formed 21st October 1939 at Andover by redesignating an element of the School of Army Co-operation.

Harvard I N7130; Magister N5433; Blenheim I L1501, IV N3565; Anson I N9780.

Disbanded 31st May 1941 at Andover to become 6 Operational Training unit.

SCHOOL OF ARTILLERY CO-OPERATION (CANADA)

Formed 1918 at Camp Leaside, Canada.

Curtiss JN-4.

Disbanded November 1918 at Camp Leaside.

SCHOOL OF AVIATION MEDICINE, later ROYAL AIR FORCE INSTITUTE OF AVIATION MEDICINE

Formed 30th April 1945 at Farnborough by redesignating the RAE Physiological Laboratory. Redesignated the Royal Air Force Institute of Aviation Medicine from 11th September 1950.

Spitfire F.22 PK495; Harvard IIB FX238; Mosquito III TV974; Vampire FB.5 VV463; Meteor T.7 WA619; Prone Meteor WK935; Bobsleigh VZ728; Balliol T.2 WG148; Canberra B.2 WH663, PR.3 WE145, B.6 WT2112; Javelin FAW.1 XA549, FAW.5 XA692, FAW.6 XA831; Hunter T.7 XL563; Jaguar T.2A ZB615; Hawk T.1 XX327.

Current 1st April 1998.

SCHOOL OF CONTROL AND REPORTING – see Fighter Command Control and Reporting School, later School of Control and Reporting

SCHOOL OF FIGHTER CONTROL

Formed 9th September 1957 at Hope Cove by redesignating an element of the School of Control and Reporting. The flying element operated from Hurn until April 1960.

Hunter F.4 XG152, F.6 XF418; Vampire T.11 XD588.

Disbanded 1961 at Sopley Park.

SCHOOL OF FLYING CONTROL

Formed 15th December 1941 at Watchfield by redesignating the Regional Control School, Bomber Command.

Nil (12.41–4.46)   *Blenheim IV V5639; Anson I NK564 R; Oxford I RR335; Dominie X7492.*
FDY (4.46–11.46)   *Anson I NK564 FDY-J; Hawk Major HL538 FDY-Z.*

Disbanded 1st November 1946 at Watchfield to become the School of Air Traffic Control.

SCHOOL OF GENERAL RECONNAISSANCE, later 1 SCHOOL OF GENERAL RECONNAISSANCE, later SCHOOL OF GENERAL RECONNAISSANCE
Formed 4th April 1938 at Thorney Island. Redesignated 1 School of General Reconnaissance from 19th June 1940 at Hooton Park.

Anson I K8762 G; Blenheim I L1531; Battle P6560.

Disbanded 30th September 1940 at Squires Gate whereupon an element moved to Grange, South Africa, to become 61 Air School from 11th November 1940.

Reformed 1st March 1946 at Leuchars as the School of General Reconnaissance by redesignating 3 School of General Reconnaissance.

OK   *Anson I EG428 OK-O.*

Disbanded 5th September 1947 at Leuchars.

2 SCHOOL OF GENERAL RECONNAISSANCE
Formed 28th May 1940 at Squires Gate.

Anson I K8760; Botha I L6299; Wellington I L7771.

Disbanded 16th December 1940 at Squires Gate whereupon the unit moved to Debert, Canada, where it become 31 General Reconnaissance School

3 SCHOOL OF GENERAL RECONNAISSANCE
Formed December 1940 at Squires Gate by redesignating an element of 2 School of General Reconnaissance.

1 (12.40–8.45)   *Botha I L6250 1-F; Anson I DJ356 1-F.*
2 (12.40–8.45)   *Botha I W5077 2-W; Anson I AX232 2-05.*
3 (12.40–8.45)   *Botha I L6328 3-L; Anson I EG134 3-01.*
4 (12.40–8.45)   *Botha I L6497 4-H; Anson I N5368 4-03.*
5 (12.40–8.45)   *Botha I L6297 5-B.*
OK (8.45–3.46)   *Anson I EG428 OK-O.*
2W (8.45–3.46)   *Anson I EG413 2W-H.*
Also used   *Dragon HM569; D.H.86B L8040; Eagle II ES948; Blenheim I L1125, IV V5527; Battle P6491; Spitfire I L1001, PR.I R7020, IIA P8543, PR.III R7146, PR.IV X4501, PR.V X4839; Lysander I R2616; Master III W8844; Tiger Moth L6921.*

Disbanded 1st March 1946 at Leuchars to become the School of General Reconnaissance.

SCHOOL OF LAND/AIR WARFARE
Formed 1st May 1947 at Old Sarum by redesignating the School of Air Support.

Spitfire XVI TB301; Oxford I HN324; Dominie I NF880; Firefly FR.I Z2022; Anson XI NL248, XIX TX184 A, T.21 WJ509; Tiger Moth II N6550; Vampire FB.5 WA439; Hiller HT.1.

Disbanded 31st March 1963 at Old Sarum and merged with the Amphibious Warfare School to become the Joint Warfare Establishment.

SCHOOL OF MARITIME RECONNAISSANCE, later 1 MARITIME RECONNAISSANCE SCHOOL
Formed 1st June 1951 at St Mawgan. Later redesignated 1 Maritime Reconnaissance School.

H   *Oxford I HM970; Lancaster GR.3 TX268 H-X; Anson XII PH838 M; Chipmunk T.10 WD293 L.*

Disbanded 30th September 1956 at St Mawgan and merged with 236 Operational Conversion Unit to become the Maritime Operational Training Unit.

1 SCHOOL OF MARITIME RECONNAISSANCE – see School of Maritime Reconnaissance, later 1 School of Maritime Reconnaissance

SCHOOL OF NAVAL CO-OPERATION
Formed 23rd December 1919 at Lee-on-Solent by redesignating the Royal Air Force Seaplane Establishment.

Short 184; Fairey IIID.

Disbanded 1st April 1920 at Lee-on-Solent and merged with the School of Aerial Navigation to become the School of Naval Co-operation and Aerial Navigation.

Reformed 19th April 1923 at Lee-on-Solent, by redesignating the Seaplane Training School.

Felixstowe F.5 N4636; Fairey IIID S1001 B, IIIF S1519 X; Seagull II N9563, III N9650; Flycatcher N9954; Moth K1107; Tutor K6119; Hart K3033; Wapiti Seaplane J9497; Osprey I K2777, III K4326, IV K5754; Nimrod I S1616; Seal K4201; Shark I K4363, II K8479, III K8916; Queen Bee K4227; Seafox K8573; Swordfish I K5990; Walrus I L2182 E.

Disbanded 24th May 1939 at Ford, elements becoming 753 and 754 Squadrons, FAA.

SCHOOL OF NAVAL CO-OPERATION AND AERIAL NAVIGATION
Formed 1st April 1920 at Calshot by merging the School of Aerial Navigation and the School Of Naval Co-operation.

Short 184 N9261; Felixstowe F.5 N4637; Fairey IIID.

Disbanded 5th February 1928 at Calshot.

1 SCHOOL OF NAVIGATION AND BOMB DROPPING – see 1 School of Aerial Navigation and Bomb Dropping

2 SCHOOL OF NAVIGATION AND BOMB DROPPING – see 2 School of Aerial Navigation and Bomb Dropping

3 SCHOOL OF NAVIGATION AND BOMB DROPPING – see 3 School of Aerial Navigation and Bomb Dropping

4 SCHOOL OF NAVIGATION AND BOMB DROPPING – see 4 School of Aerial Navigation and Bomb Dropping

SCHOOL OF PHOTOGRAPHY, later 1 SCHOOL OF PHOTOGRAPHY, later SCHOOL OF PHOTOGRAPHY
Formed 23rd December 1919 Farnborough by redesignating the Photographic Park. Redesignated 1 School of Photography from April 1941, reverting to the School of Photography post-war.

Nil (10.19–4.46)   *B.E.2c, B.E.2d, B.E.2e; B.E.12 B701; F.K.8 B3312; Curtiss JN-3 A3277; R.E.8; D.H.4; D.H.9; F.2B J8270; Atlas I J8788; Hart J9938; Wapiti IIA K1142; Moth K1877; Audax K2003; Avro 652 DG655; Hornet Moth W6421; Puss Moth X9402; Anson I N9833; Magister L8227; Proctor I P6230.*
TFA (4.46–1.48)   *Anson I NK340 TFA-A.*
TWM (1.48–4.51)   *Anson I NK340 TWM-A, XIX TX211 TWM-A.*
Nil (4.51–4.72)   *Anson XIX TX164 B.*

Disbanded 1st April 1972 at Wellesbourne Mountford and absorbed by the Joint School of Photography.

1 SCHOOL OF PHOTOGRAPHY – see School of Photography, later 1 School of Photography, later School of Photography

SCHOOL OF PHOTOGRAPHY, MAPS AND RECONNAISSANCE
Formed 1st October 1917 at Langham Place, London.

F.K.8; B.E.2c, B.e.2d, B.E.2c; F.2B; B.E.12 B701; D.H.4.

Disbanded 1st October 1919 to become the Photographic Park, Farnborough.

SCHOOL OF REFRESHER FLYING, later REFRESHER FLYING SQUADRON
Formed 1st July 1962 at Manby within the College of Air Warfare. Transferred to Leeming to become part of 1 Squadron within 3 Flying Training School from December 1973. Redesignated the

Refresher Flying Squadron from 1977. Transferred to within 1 Flying Training School from April 1974.

Varsity T.1; Jet Provost T.3A XM374 L, T.4, T.5A.

Disbanded April 1984 at Church Fenton to become the Refresher Flying Flight.

SCHOOL OF SPECIAL FLYING (CANADA)
Formed April 1918 at Armour Heights, Canada.

Curtiss JN-4 C1289; Camel B3772.

Disbanded November 1918 at Armour Heights.

SCHOOL OF SPECIAL FLYING, GOSPORT, later 1 SCHOOL OF SPECIAL FLYING
Formed 2nd August 1917 at Gosport as the School of Special Flying by merging 1, 27 and 55 Training Squadrons. Redesignated 1 School of Special Flying from 18th May 1918.

1½ Strutter B8912; Pup B2192; Camel B5157; Avro 504J B3168, Avro 504K D7604; Dolphin C4172; F.2B C4687.

Disbanded 1st July 1918 at Gosport to become the Southwestern Area Flying Instructors School.

SCHOOL OF SPECIAL FLYING, REDCAR (INSTRUCTORS SCHOOL), later 2 SCHOOL OF SPECIAL FLYING
Formed 1st April 1918 at Redcar by redesignating the Naval Flying School, Redcar. Redesignated 2 School of Special Flying from 18th May 1918.

Bristol Scout D 8993; Avro 504A B3286, Avro 504J D7526, Avro 504K D7643; Camel E1447.

Disbanded 1st July 1918 at Redcar to become the Northeastern Area Flying Instructors School.

1 SCHOOL OF SPECIAL FLYING – see School of Special Flying, Gosport later 1 School of Special Flying

2 SCHOOL OF SPECIAL FLYING – see School of Special Flying, Redcar, later 2 School of Special Flying

SCOUT SCHOOL, CANDAS
Formed by September 1917 at Candas, France, within 2 Aeroplane Supply Depot.

Bristol Scout C 5592; Bristol Scout D A1759; Pup B1724; Nieuport 24 B3602; Camel B5227.

Disbanded 1918 at Candas.

SCOUT SCHOOL, POOL OF PILOTS
Formed 1st April 1818 at Manston by redesignating the RNAS War School, Manston.

Spad S.7 A8834; D.H.4 A7992; Camel B3922; F.2B C902; Avro 504A D1646; S.E.5a D3486; D.H.9 D5672.

Disbanded December 1919 at Joyce Green.

SCOUT SCHOOL, ST OMER
Formed December 1917 at St Omer, France, within 1 Aircraft Supply Depot.

Bristol Scout C 4671; Bristol Scout D 5557.

Disbanded 1918 at St Omer.

SCR 584 TRAINING UNIT
Formed 25th January 1945 at Drem.

Spitfire IX BS461.

Disbanded 19th December 1945 at Manston and absorbed by the Fighter Command School of Control and Reporting.

SEA KING OPERATIONAL CONVERSION UNIT
Formed 1st April 1996 at St Mawgan by redesignating the Sea King Training Unit.

Sea King HAR.3, HAR.3A ZH543.

Disbanded 16th October 1996 at St Mawgan to become 203 (Reserve) Squadron.

SEA KING TRAINING FLIGHT – see Sea King Training Unit, later Sea King Training Flight, later Sea King Training Unit

SEA KING TRAINING UNIT, later SEA KING TRAINING FLIGHT, later SEA KING TRAINING UNIT
Formed 1st December 1977 at Culdrose, being officially commissioned on 17th February 1978, as a Royal Navy unit. Absorbed into 706 Squadron, FAA as the Sea King Flight Training Flight from 26th October 1979. Passed to RAF control as the Sea King Training Unit from 2nd April 1993.

Sea King HAR.3 XZ588, HAR.3A ZH543.

Disbanded 1st April 1996 at St Mawgan to become the Sea King Operational Conversion Unit.

SEA RESCUE FLIGHT, later AIR SEA RESCUE FLIGHT
Formed 13th August 1941 at Kabrit, Egypt. Redesignated the Air Sea Rescue Flight from 1st August 1942.

Blenheim IV Z7591, V EH330; Wellington IC HD978; Walrus II X9584 C; Goose HK822 N; Fairchild 91 HK832 M.

Disbanded 24th September 1943 at Berka, Libya, to become 294 Squadron.

SEAPLANE FLIGHT, BASRA
Formed May 1928 at Basra, Iraq.

Fairey IIIF J9064.

Disbanded 8th March 1929 at Basra.

SEAPLANE RESCUE FLIGHT, KALAFRANA
Formed by May 1941 at Kalafrana, Malta.

Walrus I L2182; Swordfish I K5949; Fulmar.

Existed to at least November 1941 at Kalafrana.

SEAPLANE SQUADRON, ALEXANDRIA
A term given to the merging of 354, 355, and 356 Coastal Patrol Flights prior to becoming 270 Squadron.

SEAPLANE SQUADRON, PORT SAID
A term given to the merging of 431 and 432 Coastal Patrol Flights prior to becoming 269 Squadron.

SEAPLANE TRAINING FLIGHT
Formed 5th February 1923 at Calshot by redesignating an element of the disbanding Seaplane Training School.

Fairey IIID N9452, Fairey IIIF DC S1454; Southampton I S1037, II N9901.

Disbanded 1st October 1931 at Calshot to become the Seaplane Training Squadron.

SEAPLANE TRAINING SCHOOL
Formed 21st April 1921 at Lee-on-Solent by redesignating the Lee-on-Solent detachment of the School of Naval Co-operation and Aerial Navigation.

Short 184 N9143; Fairey IIID N9459.

Disbanded 19th April 1923 at Lee-on-Solent to become the School of Naval Co-operation.

SEAPLANE TRAINING SQUADRON
Formed 1st October 1931 at Calshot by redesignating the Seaplane Training Flight. The Squadron's Floatplane Training Flight became an independent entity at Lee-on-Solent from April 1938.

Fairey IIID N9462, IIIF S1830; Southampton I S1059, II S1160; Osprey I S1679; Moth K1885; Cloud K2897; Scapa K4199; Swordfish I K5990.

Disbanded 16th March 1941 at Wig Bay and merged with the Flying Boat Training Squadron to become 4 Operational Training Unit.

SEARCH AND RESCUE FLIGHT, KHORMAKSAR
Formed 13th June 1958 at Khormaksar, Aden, by redesignating an element of the Station Flight, Khormaksar.

Sycamore HR.14 XE309; Whirlwind HAR.2 XJ724.

Disbanded June 1967 at Khormaksar.

SEARCH AND RESCUE FLIGHT, MUHARRAQ
Formed May 1959 at Muharraq, Bahrain.

Wessex HC.2 XT601.

Disbanded 31st May 1971 at Muharraq.

SEARCH AND RESCUE TRAINING FLIGHT – see Central Flying School

SEARCH AND RESCUE TRAINING SQUADRON – see Central Flying School

SEARCH AND RESCUE TRAINING UNIT – see Central Flying School

SECRET INTELLIGENCE SERVICE FLIGHT – see the Heston Flight

SECURITY FLIGHT, ISMAILIA
Formed mid-1945 at Ismailia, Egypt.

Spitfire VC JK250.

Disbanded (date unknown) at Ismailia.

SENTRY OPERATIONAL CONVERSION UNIT – see 23 Squadron, RFC, later 23 Squadron RAF

SENTRY TRAINING SQUADRON
Formed 1st June 1990 at Waddington.

Sentry AEW.1 (from 8 Squadron).

Disbanded 1st April 1996 at Waddington to become 23 Squadron, incorporating the Sentry Operational Conversion Unit.

11 (SERVICE) FERRY FLIGHT
Formed 4th April 1941 at Dumfries.

Rapide X9448; Blenheim I K7048, IV V6094; Battle L5219; Anson I R3344; Hurricane IIA Z2420; Spitfire I R6596, IIA P8026; Tomahawk IIB AK130.

Disbanded June 1941 at Dumfries and absorbed by Headquarters, Service Ferry Pools.

SERVICE FERRY PILOTS POOL
An element of the Headquarters, Service Ferry Pools Squadron.

Blenheim I L6720; Hurricane I L1594; Anson I L9156; Master I T8373; Magister I L8208; Tomahawk IIA AH918; Harvard I N7004; Dominie X7350; Monarch X9306; Oxford I T1010; Tiger Moth T5978; Envoy III DG663.

7 (SERVICE) FERRY PILOTS POOL
Formed 5th November 1940 at Kemble.

Anson I N9946; Dominie I R9555; Rapide X9448; Cub Coupe BV984.

Disbanded 20th February 1941 at Kemble and absorbed by Headquarters, Service Ferry Pools.

8 (SERVICE) FERRY POOL
Formed 1st November 1940 at Kington Langley (but flying from Hullavington).

Beaufort N1108; Mohawk IV AR651; Hurricane I V6541; Spitfire I X4841: Blenheim IV T2327; Anson I R3336.

Disbanded 27th March 1941 at Kington Langley to become 10 (Polish) Ferry Flight

9 (SERVICE) FERRY PILOTS POOL
Formed 1st November 1940 at Harwarden by redesignating 'B' Flight of 4 Ferry Pilots Pool, RAF.

Anson I; Spitfire I L1045; Wellington IC N2810; Moth AW135; Eagle II ES948; Typhoon IB DN269.

Disbanded 20th February 1941 at Hawarden and absorbed by Headquarters Service Ferry Pools.

SERVICE FERRY POOLS – see Headquarters, Service Ferry Pools, later Headquarters, Service Ferry Squadron

SERVICE FERRY SQUADRON – see Headquarters, Service Ferry Pools, later Headquarters, Service Ferry Squadron

SERVICE FERRY TRAINING SQUADRON
Formed 1st April 1941 at Kemble within the Headquarters, Service Ferry Pool.

Blenheim; Hurricane; Tomahawk; Maryland.

Disbanded 11th November 1941 at Kemble to become the Ferry Training Unit.

1 SERVICE FLYING TRAINING SCHOOL – see 1 Flying Training School, later 1 Service Flying Training School, later 1 Flying Training School, later 6 (Naval) Flying Training School

2 SERVICE FLYING TRAINING SCHOOL – see 2 Flying Training School, later 2 Service Flying Training School, later 2 Flying Training School, later 2 (Basic) Flying Training School

3 SERVICE FLYING TRAINING SCHOOL – see 3 Flying Training School, later 3 Service Flying Training School, later 3 Flying Training School, later 3 (Basic) Flying Training School

4 SERVICE FLYING TRAINING SCHOOL – see 4 Flying Training School, later 4 Service Flying Training School, later 4 Flying Training School, later 4 (Advanced) Flying Training School

5 SERVICE FLYING TRAINING SCHOOL – see 5 Flying Training School, later 5 Service Flying Training School, later 5 Flying Training School, later 5 (Advanced) Flying Training School

6 SERVICE FLYING TRAINING SCHOOL – see 6 Flying Training School, later 6 Service Flying Training School, later 6 Flying Training School, later 6 (Advanced) Flying Training School

9 SERVICE FLYING TRAINING SCHOOL – see 9 Flying Training School, later 9 Service Flying Training School, later 9 (Advanced) Flying Training School, later 9 Flying Training School

11 SERVICE FLYING TRAINING SCHOOL – see 11 Flying Training School, later 11 Service Flying Training School, later 11 Flying Training School

12 SERVICE FLYING TRAINING SCHOOL – see 12 Flying Training School, later 12 Service Flying Training School, later 12 Flying Training School

13 SERVICE FLYING TRAINING SCHOOL – see 13 Flying Training School, later 13 Service Flying Training School

14 SERVICE FLYING TRAINING SCHOOL – see 14 Flying Training School, later 14 Service Flying Training School, later 14 (Advanced) Flying Training School

15 SERVICE FLYING TRAINING SCHOOL – see 15 Flying Training School, later 15 Service Flying Training School, later 15 Flying Training School

16 SERVICE FLYING TRAINING SCHOOL later 16 (POLISH) FLYING TRAINING SCHOOL
Formed 9th June 1941 at Hucknall by redesignating 1 (Polish) Flying Training School. Redesignated 16 (Polish) Flying Training School from 1st November 1945.

Nil (6.41–4.46)	*Hind K6650; Battle K9221, Battle Trainer P6626; Moth Minor X9298; Master I N7447, II DL304, III W8902 43; Gipsy Moth DG588; Blenheim I K7683; Oxford I L4535; Anson I NK238 B; Magister N3774 60; Harvard IIB FX249 72.*
FAS (4.46–12.46)	*Anson I NK340 FAS-S; Oxford I PG999 FAS-M; Magister R1983 FAS-S.*
FAT (4.46–12.46)	*Magister R1918 FAT-S; Tiger Moth II DE920 FAT-E.*
FAU	*Allocated but no evidence of use.*

FAV	Allocated but no evidence of use.
FAW	Allocated but no evidence of use.
FAX	Allocated but no evidence of use.
FAY	Allocated but no evidence of use.

Disbanded 18th December 1946 at Newton.

17 SERVICE FLYING TRAINING SCHOOL
Formed 20th March 1944 at Cranwell as 17 Service Flying Training School by redesignating the Royal Air Force College Service Flying Training School.

Nil (3.44–4.46)	Blenheim I L1363 5, V AZ892; Spitfire I N3293, IIA P7283, VB BL748 17, VC JK940, XVI RK849; Proctor III Z7213; Oxford II V3578; Master II DK978, III DL884; Anson I DJ406; Harvard IIB KF174; Beaufort IIA ML458.
FCA (4.46–6.47)	Oxford I DF401 FCA-Z.
FCB (4.46–6.47)	Harvard IIB KF251 FCB-B.
FCC (4.46–6.47)	Magister L8262 FCC-Z.
FCD (4.46–6.47)	Harvard IIB FX347 FCD-Y.
FCE (4.46–6.47)	Harvard IIB KF300 FCE-L; Anson I NK371 FCE-V.
FCF (4.46–6.47)	Harvard IIB KF481 FCF-J.
FCG	Allocated but no evidence of use.

Disbanded 18th June 1947 at Spitalgate to become 1 Flying Training School.

20 SERVICE FLYING TRAINING SCHOOL, later 20 FLYING TRAINING SCHOOL, later 20 SERVICE FLYING TRAINING SCHOOL
Formed 10th July 1940 at Cranborne, Southern Rhodesia, as 20 Service Flying Training School.

Tiger Moth II DE514; Harvard I N7013 AR, II AJ717 AD, IIA EX405; III EX961 76; Oxford I NZ1281; Anson I MG327; Cornell II 15097; Hart; Audax; Hurricane I Z4086; Dragon Rapide; Gauntlet; Taylorcraft BL-2 VP-YCE.

Disbanded April 1946 at Cranborne, Southern Rhodesia.

Reformed 3rd April 1945 at Church Lawford as 20 Flying Training School. Redesignated 20 Service Flying Training School from 4th September 1946.

Nil (4.45–4.46)	Harvard IIB KF191; Anson I LT126.
FAI (4.46–7.47)	Harvard IIB FX237 FAI-C.
FAJ (4.46–7.47)	Harvard IIB KF704 FAJ-C.
FAK (4.46–7.47)	Harvard IIB FS837 FAK-S.
FAL (4.46–7.47)	Anson I NK900 FAL-B.
FAM (4.46–7.47)	Tiger Moth II L6944 FAM-S.

Disbanded 23rd July 1947 at Church Lawford to become 2 Flying Training School.

21 SERVICE FLYING TRAINING SCHOOL, later 21 FLYING TRAINING SCHOOL
Formed 8th October 1940 at Kumalo, Southern Rhodesia, as 21 Service Flying Training School.

Harvard II AJ678; Oxford I R4067, V HN340; Taylorcraft BL-2 VP-YCF; Tiger Moth II DX640; Gauntlet SRAF152; Anson I MG327.

Disbanded 18th May 1945 at Kumalo.

Reformed 3rd April 1945 at Snitterfield as 21 Flying Training School by redesignating an element of 20 Flying Training School.

Nil (4.45–4.46)	Anson I EG180; Harvard IIB KF300.
FAN (4.46–9.46)	Harvard IIB KF455 FAN-S.
FAO (4.46–9.46)	Allocated but no evidence of use.
FAP (4.46–9.46)	Harvard IIB FX440 FAP-J.
FAQ	Allocated but no evidence of use.

Disbanded 18th September 1946 at Snitterfield.

22 SERVICE FLYING TRAINING SCHOOL, later 22 FLYING TRAINING SCHOOL
Formed 25th March 1941 at Thornhill, Rhodesia.

Harvard I P5827 69, II AJ673 40, IIA BD133 A8; Hurricane I Z4119; Anson I EG433.

Disbanded 30th September 1945 at Thornhill.

Reformed 22 October 1945 at Calveley as 22 Service Flying

Training School. Redesignated 22 Flying Training School from 2nd February 1948.

Nil (10.45–4.46)	Harvard IIB; Tiger Moth.
FCI (4.46–4.51)	Harvard IIB KF209 FCI-Z.
FCJ (4.46–4.51)	Harvard IIB KF319 FCJ-H; Anson I NK956 FCJ-F.
FCK (4.46–4.51)	Tiger Moth II DE175 FCK-X; Harvard IIB KF411 FCK-A.
FCL (4.46–4.51)	Allocated but no evidence of use.
FCM (4.46–4.51)	Allocated but no evidence of use.
M (4.51–5.55)	Prentice T.1; Provost T.1 WV534 M-M.
N (4.51–5.55)	Provost T.1 WV602 N-L.
O (4.51–5.55)	Prentice T.1 VS727 O-H.
P (4.51–5.55)	Prentice T.1; Provost T.1 WV617 P-K.
R (4.51–5.55)	Harvard IIB KF264 R-J.
U (4.51–5.55)	Harvard IIB KF337 U-P.
Y (4.51–5.55)	Harvard IIB KF300 Y-H; Prentice T.1.
Also used	Tiger Moth I NL911.

Disbanded 1st May 1955 at Syerston to become 1 Flying Training School.

23 SERVICE FLYING TRAINING SCHOOL
Formed 8th July 1941 at Heany, Southern Rhodesia.

Oxford I HN239; Anson I AX226.

Disbanded 30th September 1945 at Heany.

31 SERVICE FLYING TRAINING SCHOOL
Formed 15th September at Kingston, Canada, by redesignating an element of 7 Service Flying Training School.

Battle R7421; Walrus I L2330; Harvard II AJ574 37, IIB FE837 26; Cornell I FJ674; Fawn 216; Nomad; Lysander IIIA 2343; Yale 3422; Menasco Moth 4888; Crane 8005.

Disbanded 14th August 1944 at Kingston.

32 SERVICE FLYING TRAINING SCHOOL
Formed 9th December 1940 at Moose Jaw, Canada, by redesignating 10 Service Flying Training School.

Oxford T1317; Harvard II AJ723, IIB FE407; Anson I AX239; Battle 2107.

Disbanded 17 October 1944 at Moose Jaw.

33 SERVICE FLYING TRAINING SCHOOL
Formed 26th December 1940 at Carberry, Canada.

Anson I N4861 9, II 11279 C; Crane; Harvard II AJ613, IIB; Oxford I.

Disbanded 1st December 1944 at Carberry.

34 SERVICE FLYING TRAINING SCHOOL
Opened 11th March 1941 at Medicine Hat, Canada.

Harvard II AJ930 39, IIB FE813 32; Oxford I AS505; Norseman 680; Menasco Moth 4940; Anson II 7408; Bolingbroke IV 9019.

Disbanded 17th November 1944 at Medicine Hat.

35 SERVICE FLYING TRAINING SCHOOL
Opened 19th August 1941 at North Battlesford, Canada.

Oxford I T1312 83; Harvard IIB FH140; Anson I N9907 2; Menasco Moth 4845.

Disbanded 25th February 1944 at North Battleford.

36 SERVICE FLYING TRAINING SCHOOL
Formed 28th September 1941 at Penhold, Canada.

Oxford; Anson II FP842; Harvard IIB FE447; Tiger Moth 1204.

Disbanded 3rd November 1944 at Penhold.

37 SERVICE FLYING TRAINING SCHOOL, RAF
Formed 22nd October 1941 at Calgary, Canada.

Oxford I X6557; Anson II 11300; Menasco Moth 4849; Harvard II AJ962 47, IIB FE406.

Disbanded 10th March 1944 at Calgary, Alberta.

38 SERVICE FLYING TRAINING SCHOOL
Opened 27th April 1942 at Estevan, Canada.

Anson I 6493, II JS120; Menasco Moth 4879.

Disbanded 11th February 1944 at Estevan.

39 SERVICE FLYING TRAINING SCHOOL
Formed 15th December 1941 at Swift Current, Canada.

Harvard II AJ582, IIB FE404; Oxford I X6563; Menasco Moth 4851; Cornell I FH877.

Disbanded 24th March 1944 at Swift Current, Sasketchewan.

41 SERVICE FLYING TRAINING SCHOOL
Formed 5th January 1942 at Weyburn, Canada.

Anson I 6645; Harvard II AJ922 15, IIB FE343 84; Fawn 206; Finch 1014; Menasco Moth 4936; Crane 8182.

Disbanded 22nd January 1944 at Weyburn.

SHIPPING INTERCEPTION FLIGHT
The term given the 217 Squadron detachment at Manston between October 1941 and March 1942.

SHORT RANGE CONVERSION UNIT
Formed 5th August 1964 at Odiham.

Twin Pioneer XM940 S; Wessex HC.2 XR505 N; Auster AOP.9.

Disbanded 1st July 1967 at Odiham to become the Helicopter Operational Conversion Flight.

SIGNALS COMMAND DEVELOPMENT SQUADRON
Formed (date unknown) at Watton within the Central Signals Establishment.

Lincoln II RA685; Hastings C.2 WJ338; Varsity T.1 WL686; Canberra B.2 WD935.

Disbanded 1st January 1962 at Watton to become 151 Squadron.

SIGNALS CO-OPERATION FLIGHT
Formed 1st April 1921 at Biggin Hill.

F.2B J6612.

Disbanded 1st April 1924 at Kenley to become 13 Squadron.

SIGNALS DEVELOPMENT UNIT
Formed 15th April 1943 at Hinton-in-the-Hedges by merging the Beam Approach Development Unit, 1551 (Beam Approach Calibration) Flight and the Operation Development Party, West Drayton. 1478 (Signals Communication) Flight was also attached but not incorporated into the Unit. 'A' Flight (previously the Beam Approach Development Unit) remained at Hinton-in-the-Hedges, 'B' (Calibration) Flight (previously 1551 Flight) and 'C' (Operation Development Party) Flights remained at Bicester and West Drayton respectively.

See also: Ground Controlled Approach Flight, later Ground Controlled Approach Squadron.

Whitley V BD203; Wellington XIII JA637; Anson I N9839; Oxford I V4027; Master III W8458; Beaufighter I X7747, VI ND232; Fulmar; Swordfish; Hudson IIIA FK737; Ventura I AE751, II AE884; Proctor III LZ556; Hurricane IIC PG594; Mosquito VI RF878.

The flying element disbanded on 29th July 1944 at Hinton-in-the-Hedges and was absorbed by the Signals Flying Unit. The remainder moved to Henlow on 19th October 1947 and became the Radio Engineering Unit from 1st January 1950.

SIGNALS FLYING UNIT
Formed 20th July 1944 at Honiley. The unit was divided into Headquarters, Development and Ground Controlled Approach Squadrons, the latter being formed by redesignating the Ground Controlled Approach Flight of the Signals Development Unit. The Signals Squadron later became the Signals Development Squadron and the Ground Controlled Approach Squadron was further sub-divided into Test Section, Radar Section and Calibration Flights. Further reorganisation created the Signals Development and GCA Wings.

See also: Ground Controlled Approach Flight, later Ground Controlled Approach Squadron.

9T (circa 45–46)	*Oxford I PH345 9T-S; Wellington X NC885 9T-Z.*
7N (circa 45–46)	*Anson I MG695 7N-L; Beaufighter X KW347 7N-6; Wellington XIV NC887 7N-O.*
Also used	*Beaufighter I X7747; X RD462; Spitfire XI PL758; Hudson IIIA FK737; Ventura I AE730; II AJ177; Stirling III LK443, V PJ956, XIII; Halifax III MZ390; Dakota IV KK202; Whitley V LA887; Mosquito XVI PF396; Wellington XIII NB986, XIV NC870; Hurricane IIC PG594.*

Disbanded 1st September 1946 at Honiley and merged with the Radio Warfare Establishment to become the Central Signals Establishment.

1 SIGNALS SCHOOL
Formed 26th August 1940 at Cranwell by redesignating 1 Electrical and Wireless School.

Valentia K8850; Wallace II K8701; D.H.86B AX795; D.H.89A P9589; Whitley II K7219, III K9009; Anson I K8716; Harvard I N7100; Dominie I R5930; Proctor I P6304, III R7530, IV NP186; Oxford II N4850; Warferry I HM499.

Disbanded 1st January 1943 at Cranwell to become 1 Radio School.

2 SIGNALS SCHOOL
Formed 26th August 1940 at Yatesbury by redesignating 2 Electrical and Wireless School.

Dragon Rapide R2486; Dominie I R9548; Proctor I P6130, II Z7220, III R7531; Oxford I BG239.

Disbanded 1st January 1943 at Yatesbury to become 2 Radio School.

3 SIGNALS SCHOOL
Formed 26th August 1940 at Compton Bassett by redesignating 3 Electrical and Wireless School.

No aircraft allocated

Disbanded 1st January 1943 at Compton Bassett to become 3 Radio School.

3 SIGNALS SCHOOL (INDIA)
Formed 19th August 1943 at Hakimpet, India.

Blenheim IV Z7437.

Disbanded 14th May 1944 at Gujrat, India, and absorbed by 10 School of Air Force Technical Training, Hakimpet.

4 SIGNALS SCHOOL
Formed 27th August 1941 at Madley.

Dominie I X7442; Proctor I R7497, II Z7210, III HM296; Magister N5413.

Disbanded 1st January 1943 at Madley to become 4 Radio School.

SIGNALS SQUADRON
Formed 4th January 1942 at Kabrit, Egypt, by redesignating an element of 109 Squadron.

Wellington IC Z8944.

Disbanded by 1st March 1942 at Kabrit to become 162 Squadron.

SINGAPORE OPERATIONAL TRAINING FLIGHT
Formed November 1972 at Chivenor.

Hunter F.74A 523; T.75B 504.

Disbanded 1st July 1973 at Chivenor.

SOUTH AFRICAN AIR OBSERVATION POST FLIGHT
Formed 14th January 1945 at Bari, Italy.

No aircraft known.

Disbanded 29th January 1945 at Bari to become 42 Air Observation Post Flight, South African Air Force.

SOUTHAMPTON UNIVERSITY AIR SQUADRON
Formed 15th February 1941 at Southampton.

Nil (2.41–4.46)	Moth BK841; Moth Minor W7973.
FLP (4.46–.47)	Tiger Moth II; Oxford I.
RUZ (.47–4.51)	Tiger Moth II NM140 RUZ-A.
Nil (4.51–)	Chipmunk T.10 WD391 14; Bulldog T.1 XX551
3.	
Also used	Oxford II BM689; Harvard IIB KF910.

Current 1st April 1998 at Boscombe Down.

SOUTHEAST ASIA COMMUNICATION SQUADRON – see Headquarters Air Command Southeast Asia (Communication) Squadron

SOUTHEAST ASIA COMMUNICATION UNIT – see Air Command Southeast Asia Communication Unit

SOUTHEAST ASIA (INTERNAL AIR SERVICE) SQUADRON – see Air Command Southeast Asia (Internal Air Service) Squadron

SOUTHEASTERN AREA COMMUNICATION FLIGHT
Formed May 1919 at Northolt by redesignating the Northolt Flight.

Avro 504K.

Disbanded 1st April 1920 at Northolt to become the Inland Area Communication Flight.

SOUTHEASTERN AREA FLYING INSTRUCTORS SCHOOL
Formed 1st July 1918 at Shoreham.

Bristol Scout C 1266; Pup N6199; Bristol M.1C C5017; S.E.5a F9097; Camel E9968; Avro 504A D1618, Avro 504K.

Disbanded 31st March 1919 at Shoreham.

SOUTHERN COMMUNICATION SQUADRON, later STRIKE COMMAND COMMUNICATION SQUADRON
Formed 1st August 1963 at Bovingdon by redesignating the Bomber/Fighter/Coastal Commands Communication Squadron. Redesignated the Strike Command Communication Squadron from 1st January 1969.

Anson XIX VL349, T.21 VV958; Devon C.1 VP952, C.2 VP968; Pembroke C.1 WV733, C(PR).1 XF798; Basset C.1 XS784.

Disbanded 3rd February 1969 at Northolt to become 207 Squadron.

SOUTHERN RHODESIA COMMUNICATION FLIGHT
Existed at Belvedere 1943.

Rapide; Leopard Moth; Hornet Moth.

Fate unknown.

SOUTHERN RHODESIAN AIR FORCE
Initially the Air Section of the Permanent Staff Corps from 1934. Began training from November 1935 with civilian Tiger Moths provided by the de Havilland Aircraft Company (Rhodesia) Ltd. Separated 1st April 1939 from the parent territorial organisation to become the Rhodesian Air Unit. Redesignated the Southern Rhodesian Air Force from 19th September 1939. Disbanded 28th June 1940 to become the Rhodesian Air Training Group, RAF.

See: Southern Rhodesia Communication Flight 1 Squadron, Southern Rhodesian Air Force.

SOUTHWESTERN AREA FLYING INSTRUCTORS SCHOOL
Formed 1st July 1918 at Fort Grange, Gosport, by redesignating 1 School of Special Flying.

Avro 504J D7610.

Disbanded 26th February 1919 at Gosport.

'SPARROW' AMBULANCE FLIGHT
Formed July 1944 at Down Ampney within the administrative control of 271 Squadron.

'Sparrow I' K6994 U.

Disbanded April 1945 at Down Ampney.

SPECIAL COMMUNICATION FLIGHT – see Middle East Air Force Special Communication Flight

SPECIAL COMMUNICATION SQUADRON
Formed 1st January 1951 at Kabrit, Egypt.

Dakota IV KJ882; Valetta C.1 VW824, C.2 VX571; Anson XIX VP528; Proctor IV MX454.

Disbanded 1st September 1952 at Fayid, Egypt, to become the Middle East Air Force Special Communication Flight.

SPECIAL DUTIES (RADIO) DEVELOPMENT UNIT
Formed 21st March 1944 at West Raynham.

Anson I; Mosquito.

Disbanded 18th April 1944 at Foulsham to become the Bomber Support Development Unit.

SPECIAL DUTIES FLIGHT, BAGINTON
Formed by mid-1941 at Baginton.

Tomahawk I AH797.

Disbanded (date unknown) at Baginton.

SPECIAL DUTIES FLIGHT, SCULTHORPE
Formed early 1952 at Sculthorpe. Flights made by RAF crews penetrated Soviet airspace on 17th/18th April and 12th/13th December 1952 to gather target data for the planned V-Bomber Force.

RB-45C Tornado.

Disbanded December 1952 at Sculthorpe.

SPECIAL DUTY CATALINA FLIGHT – see 240 Squadron

SPECIAL DUTY FLIGHT, BOSCOMBE DOWN – see Special Duty Flight, Old Sarum/Netheravon/Boscombe Down

SPECIAL DUTY FLIGHT, CHRISTCHURCH – see Special Duty Flight St Athan, Martlesham Heath and Christchurch.

SPECIAL DUTY FLIGHT, INVERGORDON
Formed March/April 1940 at Invergordon.

Short S.30 V3137.

Disbanded May 1940 at Invergordon following the loss of the unit's aircraft at Bodo, Norway.

SPECIAL DUTY FLIGHT, MALTA
Formed December 1941 at Luqa, Malta, by redesignating an element of 221 Squadron.

Wellington VIII HX391.

Existed to a least June 1942 at Luqa.

SPECIAL DUTY FLIGHT, MARTLESHAM HEATH – see Special Duty Flight, St Athan, Martlesham Heath and Christchurch

SPECIAL DUTY FLIGHT, NETHERAVON – see Special Duty Flight, Old Sarum/Netheravon/Boscombe Down

SPECIAL DUTY FLIGHT, NORTHOLT
Formed 28th May 1942 at Northolt.

Defiant II AA418.

Disbanded 1st October 1942 at Northolt to become 515 Squadron.

SPECIAL DUTY FLIGHT, OLD SARUM/NETHERAVON/BOSCOMBE DOWN
Formed by 1926 at Old Sarum for a series of trials by the experimental establishment at Porton. The Flight relocated to Netheravon from September 1928 and to Boscombe Down by May 1930.

F.2B F4745; Horsley II J8606: Junkers F13 J7232; Fox IA J9025; Whitley K4587; Hind K6717.

There is a suggestion the Flight continued to exist under several titles until 1946 when its duties were passed to 'D' Squadron, Aeroplane and Armament Experimental Establishment.

SPECIAL DUTY FLIGHT, ROYAL FLYING CORPS
Formed April 1917 at Vert Galand, France.

B.E.2e; B.E.12a; Pup B2188; F.E.2b C9797.

Disbanded 9th July 1918 at Fauquembergues, France, to become 'I' Flight.

SPECIAL DUTY FLIGHT, ST ATHAN – see Special Duty Flight St Athan, Martlesham Heath and Christchurch

SPECIAL DUTY FLIGHT, ST ATHAN, MARTLESHAM HEATH AND CHRISTCHURCH
Formed 14th November 1939 at St Athan by redesignating the Station Flight, Perth. Headquarters and 'B' Flight moved to Christchurch on 1st May 1940. 'A' Flight lodged at Martlesham Heath until 20th November 1940 and was then replaced by Radio Servicing Sections.

Heyford K4030; Avro 504N AX874; Rota I K4239; Cierva C-30A AP507; Hind K6717; Audax K7421; Harrow I K6963, II K7020; Overstrand K8176; Swordfish I K8349; Battle K9230; Hurricane I L1562; Walrus L2265; Wellington I L4213, IC R1099, VIII Z8702; Mentor L4379; Lysander I L4691, IIIA V9651; Defiant I L6950, II AA420; Beaufort I X8937; Whitley I K7202, V Z6763; Vega Gull; Hudson I N7244; V AM714; Blenheim I L6624, IV P4830; Magister R1951; Havoc I (Pandora) BD122, I (LAM) DG554; Boston I AE461; Beaufighter R2059; I R2066; Anson I R3433; Tiger Moth II T6367; Spitfire I X4933; Minimoa BGA338; Scott Viking II BGA415; Hurricane IIA Z2320; Fox Moth X9305; Bu 131B DR626.

Disbanded 10th November 1941 at Christchurch to become the Telecommunications Flying Unit.

SPECIAL EXPERIMENTAL FLIGHT
Formed 16th May 1918 at Gosport.

B.E.2e C4537; D.H.9 D1764; F.2B D2607; Avro 504K E3800; F.2B D2607.

Existed until at least April 1919 at Gosport.

SPECIAL FLIGHT, ROYAL AIRCRAFT ESTABLISHMENT – see 'S' Flight, Royal Aircraft Establishment

SPECIAL INSTALLATION UNIT
Formed 13th October 1942 at Defford.

Swordfish I L2739; Mitchell II FV915; Firefly I DT933; Lancaster I RF147, III LM365, VII NX618; Anson I NK868; Mosquito XIII HK363, XVII HK236, PR.34 RG229, B.35 TA652; Lincoln I RE250.

Disbanded October 1946 at Defford.

SPECIAL INSTRUCTION FLIGHT
Formed by January 1920 at Almaza, Egypt.

F.2B H1470; Avro 504K E1773; D.H.9 H5629; Snipe E6515.

Existed to at least December 1920 at Almaza and was probably absorbed by 4 Flying Training School.

SPECIAL OPERATIONS (LIBERATOR) FLIGHT
Formed 13th November 1942 at LG.09 (Bir Koraiyim), Egypt, by redesignating an element of 108 Squadron.

Liberator II AL530 Z.

Disbanded 13th March 1943 at Gambut, Libya, to become 148 Squadron.

SPECIAL PROJECTILE FLIGHT, ROYAL AIRCRAFT ESTABLISHMENT – see 'S' Flight, Royal Aircraft Establishment

SPECIAL PERFORMANCE FLIGHT, ABOUKIR
Formed May 1942 at Aboukir, Egypt.

Spitfire VC BP985, HF.VI BS106.

Disbanded October 1942 at Aboukir.

SPECIAL SERVICE FLIGHT, NORTHOLT
Formed 5th September 1942 at Northolt by redesignating the High Altitude Flight.

Spitfire VI BR318, VII BS142, IX BS273.

Disbanded January 1943 at North Weald and absorbed by 124 Squadron.

SPECIAL SURVEY FLIGHT
Formed 5th November 1939 at Seclin, France, as a detachment of 2 Camouflage Unit.

Spitfire PR.III N3071; Hudson; Lockheed 12A G-AFTL.

Disbanded 11th January 1940 at Seclin and absorbed by 2 Camouflage Unit.

SPECIAL TRANSPORT FLIGHT
Formed 1st June 1947 at Kabrit, Egypt.

Dakota IV KJ981.

Disbanded 31st March 1949 at Kabrit and absorbed by the Mediterranean and Middle East Communication Squadron.

SPECIAL TRANSPORT SQUADRON
Formed 1st December 1949 at Kabrit, Egypt.

Dakota III KN377; Anson XIX VP525; Valetta C.1 VX572.

Disbanded 3rd February 1950 at Kabrit to become the Special Communication Squadron.

SPECIALISED LOW ATTACK INSTRUCTORS SCHOOL
Formed 7th December 1942 within 59 Operational Training Unit at Milfield.

Hurricane IV KZ322 S; Master III DL695.

Disbanded 26th January 1944 at Milfield and merged with 59 Operational Training Unit to become the Fighter Leaders School.

SPECIALISED LOW ATTACK INSTRUCTORS SCHOOL (INDIA)
Formed 5th November 1943 at Ranchi, India.

Harvard IIB FE887; Hurricane IIC LD412 F, IID HW725, IV KZ558, XIIA PJ732 B; Beaufort I DW921; Spitfire VC LZ885; Beaufighter X NE527; Auster III MZ103.

Disbanded April 1945 at Ranchi to become the Ground Attack Training Unit.

SPOTTER FLIGHT, KAI TAK
Formed by October 1939 at Kai Tak, Hong Kong, by redesignating an element of the Station Flight, Kai Tak.

Walrus I L2259.

Disbanded (date unknown) at Kai Tak.

SPOTTER FLIGHT, SELETAR
Formed 1st October 1939 at Seletar, Singapore, within 4 Anti-Aircraft Co-operation Unit.

Audax K7316; Swordfish I P4027.

Disbanded 1st November 1939 at Seletar.

(SPOTTER) TRAINING FLIGHT – see Royal Air Force, Leuchars, later Royal Air Force Training Base, Leuchars

1 SQUADRON, RFC, later 1 SQUADRON, RAF
Formed 13th April 1912 at Farnborough by redesignating 1 (Airship) Company, Air Battalion, Royal Engineers.

Beta II; Delta; Eta; Gamma; Zeta.

Disbanded 1st May 1914 at Farnborough to become the Airship Detachment, Royal Flying Corps.

Reformed 1st May 1914 at Brooklands. Became 1 Squadron, RAF from 1st April 1918 whilst at Ste-Marie-Cappel, France.

Longhorn 307; Vickers Boxkite 639; Tabloid 326; Martinsyde S.1 748; Avro 504 753; B.E.8 2130; Caudron G.3 1885; Bristol Scout C 1603; Elephant 7486; Morane L 1849; Morane LA 5080; Morane I A199; Morane BB 5160; Morane N 5069; Morane P A6629; Nieuport 16; Nieuport 17; Nieuport 20 A154; Nieuport 23 B1624; Nieuport 24; Nieuport 27 B6768; S.E.5 A8904; S.E.5a C1114 N; Avro 504K F8748.

Reduced to cadre from 20th January 1920 at London Colney.

Re-established 21st January 1920 at Risalpur, India, as 'B' Squadron. Redesignated 1 Squadron from 1st April 1920.

Snipe IA E8249 3; Salamander F6607; Nighthawk J6925.

Disbanded 1st November 1926 at Hinaidi, Iraq.

Reformed 1st February 1927 at Tangmere.

Nil (2.27–11.38)	*Siskin IIIA J8640, IIIDC J7000; Fury I K2881 E; Hurricane I L1677.*
NA (11.38–9.39)	*Hurricane I L1694 NA-F.*
JX (9.39)	*Hurricane I P3169 JX-T.*
Nil (9.39–6.40)	*Hurricane I N2382.*
JX (6.40–4.51)	*Hurricane I P3169 JX-T, IIA Z2464, IIB BE150 JX-F, IIC Z3455 JX-T, X AG216 JX-O; Typhoon IB R8752 JX-L; Spitfire VC AA920, LF.IXB MK997 JX-F, F.21 LA217 JX-G; Meteor F.3 EE421 JX-A, F.4 VT284 JX-L, F.8 VZ438 JX-E; Harvard IIB KF333 JX-L; Oxford II LX132 JX-N.*
Nil (4.51–6.53)	*Meteor T.7 WG938, F.8 WF642 T; Hunter F.5 WN974 H.*
Also used	*Hawfinch J8776; Moth K1900; Hornet J9682; Master I N9006; Magister P2498; Tiger Moth II T6309; Auster I LB369; Vampire T.11 XD550.*

Disbanded 1st July 1958 at Tangmere.

Reformed 2nd July 1958 at Stradishall by renumbering 263 Squadron.

Hunter F.6 XF383 F, FGA.9 XK139 X, T.7 XL601; Harrier GR.1

XV749 A, GR.1A XW923 23, GR.3 XV754 07, Harrier T.4 XW934 12, T.4A XZ145 14, GR.5 ZD402 04, GR.7 ZD470 01, T.10.

Current 1st April 1998 at Wittering.

1 SQUADRON, SOUTHERN RHODESIAN AIR FORCE
Formed 19th September 1939 at Nairobi, Kenya, by merging 'A' and 'B' Flights of the Rhodesian Air Unit.

Audax K7546; Hart; Hardy; Rapide.

Disbanded 22nd April 1940 at Nairobi to become 237 Squadron, RAF.

2 SQUADRON, RFC, later 2 SQUADRON, RAF
Formed 13th May 1912 at Farnborough by redesignating 2 (Aeroplane) Company, Air Battalion, Royal Engineers. Became 2 Squadron, RAF from 1st April 1914 whilst at Hesdigneul, France.

B.E.1 201; B.E.2 205, B.E.2a 347, B.E.2b 492, B.E.2c 1807, B.E.2d 5741, B.E.2e A1819; B.E.3 203; B.E.4 204; Breguet.G.3 211; Breguet L.2 213; Henry Farman Biplane 208; Blériot XI 219; Longhorn 223; Sopwith RG 243; Henry Farman F.20 244; R.E.5 380; R.E.1 608; Bristol Scout C 1602; Bristol Scout D 5327; Gunbus 1621; Shorthorn 1846; F.K.8 B5782 N.

Disbanded 20th January 1920 at Weston-on-the-Green.

Reformed 1st February 1920 at Oranmore, Ireland, by renumbering 105 Squadron.

Nil (2.20–11.38)	*F.2B F4354; Atlas I J9952; Audax I K2028; Hector I K9741; Lysander I L4694.*

Harrier GR.5s of No 1 Squadron.

KO (11.38–5.41)	Lysander I L4705 KO-X, II L4815 KO-N, III T1532 KO-D.
XV (5.41– .43)	Lysander III T1631 XV-H, IIIA V9328; Tomahawk I AH857, IIA AH942 XV-S, IIB AK144; Mustang I AG623 XV-W.
Nil (.43–9.46)	Mustang I AL995 S, IA FD530, II FR922, III FB242.
OI (9.46–4.51)	Spitfire XIV RM878 OI-C, XI PL793, XIX PM555 OI-K.
B (4.51– .55)	Meteor FR.9 VZ603 B-A, PR.10 WB155 B-A.
Nil (.55–3.71)	Meteor FR.9 WX968 H, PR.10 WB154; Swift FR.5 WN124 S; Hunter FR.10 XF422 H.
Also used	Avro 504K C5946; D.H.9A E731; Venture I J7278; Tutor K3409; Moth Minor W6459; Oxford I V3398; Proctor III HM320; Harvard IIB KF216.

Disbanded 31st March 1971 at Gutersloh, Germany.

Reformed 1st December 1970 at Bruggen, Germany.

Phantom FGR.2 XV402 E.

Disbanded 30th September 1976 at Bruggen.

Reformed 1st October 1976 at Laarbruch, Germany.

Jaguar GR.1 XZ113 30, GR.1A XZ103 23, T.2 XX843 33, T.2A XX834 37; Tornado GR.1 ZA370 A, GR.1A ZD996 I, GR.1T ZA551 X.

Current 1st April 1998 at Marham.

3 SQUADRON, RFC, later 3 SQUADRON, RAF

Formed 13th May 1912 at Larkhill by redesignating an element of No 2 (Aeroplane) Company, Air Battalion, Royal Engineers. Became 3 Squadron, RAF from 1st April 1918 whilst at Valheureux, France.

B.E.2 205, B.E.2a 267; B.E.3 203; B.E.4 204; Blériot XXI 251; Deperdussin Monoplane 252; Nieuport Monoplane 253; Bristol-Prier Monoplane 256; Bristol-Prier 2-seat Monoplane 261; Bristol-Coanda Monoplane 262; Flanders F.4 265; Longhorn 266; Henry Farman F.20 268; Blériot XI 271; Martin-Handasyde Monoplane 278; Grahame-White VII 283; Nieuport IV.G 254; Avro 502 285; Avro Es 288; Sopwith RG 300; Bristol Boxkite 408; Blériot Parasol 606; S.E.2a 609; Tabloid 611; Bristol Scout B 648; Sopwith TB.8 916; Morane L 1829; Morane LA 5120; Morane BB 5137; Morane N; Morane P A268; Nieuport 23 A6781; Avro 504A A1979; Camel B6234 A.

Reduced to cadre from 27th October 1919 at Uxbridge.

Re-established 22nd March 1920 at Bangalore, India, as 'A' Squadron. Redesignated 3 Squadron from 1st April 1920.

Snipe H4883, Snipe DC E6531.

Disbanded 30th September 1921 at Ambala, India.

Reformed 1st October 1921 at Leuchars from the Mobile Flight of 205 Squadron.

D.H.9A H3518; Avro 504K H2479; Walrus N9534.

Disbanded 1st April 1923 at Leuchars to become 420, 421 and 422 (Fleet Spotter) Flights, FAA.

Reformed 1st April 1924 at Manston.

Nil (4.24–11.38)	Avro 504N E9411; Snipe E6342; Woodcock II J7725; Gamecock I J8417; Grebe IIIDC J7527; Siskin IIIDC J9196; Bulldog II J9571, IIA K1633, Bulldog Trainer K3177; Gladiator I K6145.
OP (11.38–9.39)	Gladiator I K7958 OP-Q; Hurricane I L1937 OP-T.
QO (9.39–5.44)	Hurricane I L1937 QO-T, IIB AM293 QO-H, IIC Z3068 QO-F; Typhoon IB EK371 QO-N; Tempest V JN733 QO-A.
JF (5.44– .46)	Tempest V SN168 JF-T.
J5 (.46–4.51)	Tempest V SN339 J5-P; Vampire F.1 VF279 J5-T, FB.5 VV472 J5-J.
A (4.51–5.53)	Vampire FB.5 VV476 A-P.
Nil (5.53–6.57)	Sabre F.2 XB531 B, F.4 XB640 P; Hunter F.4 XF968 R.
Also used	Tomtit J9779; Auster III MT408; Anson XI NK993.

Disbanded 15th June 1957 at Geilenkirchen, Germany.

Reformed 21st January 1959 at Geilenkirchen by renumbering 96 Squadron.

Javelin T.3, FAW.4 XA750 A.

Disbanded 4th January 1961 at Geilenkirchen, Germany.

Reformed 4th January 1961 at Geilenkirchen, Germany, by renumbering 59 Squadron.

Canberra B(I).8 XH204 A, T.4 WH846.

Disbanded 31st December 1971 at Laarbruch, Germany.

Reformed 1st January 1972 at Wildenrath, Germany.

| Nil (1.72–8.86) | Harrier GR.1A XW916 07. |
| A (8.86–) | Harrier GR.3 XZ987 AX, T.4 XZ145 AT, T.4A ZB603 AZ, GR.5 ZD329 AI, GR.7 ZG503 AG, T.10. |

Current 1st April 1998 at Laarbruch, Germany.

4 SQUADRON, RFC, later 4 SQUADRON, RAF

Formed 16th September 1912 at Farnborough from 2 Flight of 2 Squadron. Became 4 Squadron, RAF from 1st April 1918 whilst at Chocques, France.

Nil (9.12–1.39)	B.E.1 201; Breguet L.2 202; Cody V Biplane 304; Longhorn 302; B.E.4 303; Caudron G.2 308; Grahame-White Boxkite 309; Breguet G.3 211; Breguet G.2 312; B.E.2a 314; Sopwith RG 315; B.E.2c 321; Blériot XI 323; Henry Farman F.20 330; R.E.5 334; Grahame-White VIIc 354; R.E.1 362; Tabloid 362; Dunne D.8 366; Shorthorn 371; Avro 500 376; B.E.8 377; B.E.2e 383; Avro 504 390; B.E.2b 396; Morane G 587; Bristol G.B.75 610; Bristol Scout B 648; Bristol Scout C 1603; B.E.2d; Voisin LA 1856; Caudron G.3 1900; Martinsyde S.1 2449; Bristol Scout D 4666; R.E.8 C2411; F.2B J6713 A4; Woodcock J7727; Atlas I J9544; Avro 504K H2316; Audax K1997; Hector K8106.
TV (1.39–5.39)	Lysander II L4741 TV-N.
FY (5.39–9.39)	Lysander II L4753 FY-W.
Nil (9.39–8.45)	Battle N2957; Lysander II P1712, III T1690, IIIA V9449; Master I T8489; Magister T9821; Moth Minor AW151; Tiger Moth II R5215; Proctor I P6178; Dominie I R9562; D.H.89A Z7263; Tomahawk I AH791, IIB AK101; Mustang I AP255 P; Mosquito XVI MM313 T; Spitfire XI PA852 E; XIII P7505; Typhoon FR.IB EK440; PR.1B EK429.
Also used	Hyena J7780; Ajax J8803; Auster III NX534.

Disbanded 31st August 1945 at B.118 (Celle), Germany, to become the High Level Photographic Reconnaissance Flight of 2 Squadron.

Reformed 1st September 1945 at Volkel, Germany, by renumbering 605 Squadron.

NC (8.45– .47)	Mosquito VI SZ980 NC-K.
UP (.47–4.51)	Mosquito VI PZ165 UP-E; Vampire FB.5 WA120 UP-A.
Nil (4.51–3.52)	Vampire FB.5 VZ119, FB.9 WL493.
B (3.52– .54)	Sabre F.4 XB775 B-M.
Nil (.54–1.61)	Sabre F.4 XB773 C; Hunter F.4 WV266 T.
Also used	Oxford I PH289; Vampire T.11 WZ447.

Disbanded 30th December 1960 at Jever, Germany.

Reformed 30th December 1960 at Gutersloh, Germany, by renumbering 79 Squadron.

Swift FR.5 WK293 N; Hunter F.4 XE668 X, F.6 XJ638 D, FR.10 XE625 F; FGA.9 XG252 W.

Disbanded 30th May 1970 at Gutersloh.

Reformed 1st June 1970 at Wildenrath, Germany. Earlier, a UK Echelon of 4 Squadron had formed on 1st September 1969 at West Raynham from an element of 54 Squadron with Hunter FGA.9 and

Hawker Hurricane Mk IICs of No 3 Squadron in 1941.

later Harrier GR.1. This element was absorbed into the parent unit in Germany on 30th September 1970.

| Nil (6.70–9.90) | Harrier GR.1 XV808 L, GR.3 XV738 B, GR.3A XV797 H, T.4 XZ146 Y, T.4A ZB600 R. |
| C (9.90–   ) | Harrier GR.5A ZD430 CL, GR.7 ZG531 CN, T.10. |

Current 1st April 1998 at Laarbruch, Germany.

4A SQUADRON, RFC
Formed January 1918 at Chocques, France, by redesignating 'A' Flight of 4 Squadron to operate with the Portuguese Corps.

R.E.8 A3751.

Disbanded March 1918 at Chocques and absorbed by 4 Squadron.

5 SQUADRON, RFC, later 5 SQUADRON, RAF
Formed 26th July 1913 at Farnborough from an element of 3 Squadron, RFC. Became 5 Squadron, RAF from 1st April 1918 whilst at Acq, France.

B.E.1 201; Deperdussin Monoplane 280; Avro Es 289; Sopwith RG 319; Shorthorn 342; Grahame-White VIIc 354; Longhorn 355; Henry Farman F.20 351; R.E.5 361; R.E.1 362; R.E.8 365; Dunne D.8 366; Blériot XI 374; Avro 500 376; Tabloid 381; B.E.2a 383, B.E.2b 396; B.E.8 391; Avro 504 637; S.E.2 609; Bristol Scout B 644; Martinsyde S.1 749; Bristol Scout C 1603; Gunbus 1616; B.E.2c 1784; Henry Farman F.27 1806; Voisin LA 1868; Caudron G.3 1887; D.H.2 5917; F.E.8 7457; B.E.2d 5742, B.E.2f 2557; B.E.2g A2786; D.H.9 D2891; F.2B C1039.

Disbanded 20th January 1920 at Bicester.

Reformed 1st February 1920 at Quetta, India, by renumbering 48 Squadron.

Nil (2.20–9.39)	F.2B E2421 C; Wapiti I DC J9082; IIA J9509 C; Fairey IIIF S1139 2.
QN	Allocated for the period April to September 1939 but no evidence of use.
OQ (9.39–2.41)	Wapiti IIA K1309; Hart K2129 OQ-P.
Nil (2.41–3.46)	Audax K7315; Hawk AX799; Mohawk IV BS730; Hurricane IID HW878 Y, IIC LD860; Thunderbolt I FL749.
OQ (3.46–8.47)	Tempest II PR559 OQ-R.
Also used	Siskin III J7176; Ajax J8802; Lysander II P9177; Harvard IIB FE687.

Disbanded 1st August 1947 at Mauripur, India.

Reformed 11th February 1949 at Pembrey by renumbering 595 Squadron.

| 7B (2.49–8.51) | Harvard IIB KF920 7B-R; Martinet I EM697 7B-Z; Spitfire LF.XVI SL600 7B-E; Oxford II NJ296; Beaufighter X RD577 7B-P; Vampire F.3 VT815. |

Disbanded 1st August 1951 at Llandow.

Reformed 1st March 1952 at Wunstorf, Germany.

| B | Vampire FB.5 WG843 B-C, FB.9 WR142; Venom FB.1 WE329 B-X, Venom FB.4 WR470. |
| Also used | Vampire T.11 WZ447. |

Disbanded 11th October 1957 at Wunstorf.

Reformed 21st January 1959 at Laarbruch, Germany, by renumbering 68 Squadron.

Nil (1.59–8.86)	Meteor NF.11 WD623 S; Javelin T.3, FAW.5 XA664 P, FAW.9 XH905 E; Lightning F.1 XM164 Z, F.1A XM169 X.
A (8.86–12.87)	Lightning F.3 XP764 AR, F.3A XP693, T.5 XS459 AW, F.6(I) XR754, F.6 XS899 AA,
Also used	Hunter T.7A WV318.

Disbanded 31st December 1987 at Binbrook.

Reformed 1st January 1988 at Coningsby.

| C | Tornado F.3 ZE760 CF, F.3T ZH555 CV. |

Current 1st April 1998 at Coningsby.

6 SQUADRON, RFC, later 6 SQUADRON, RAF
Formed 31st January 1914 at South Farnborough. Became 6 Squadron, RAF from 1st April 1918 whilst at Le Crotoy, France.

Nil (1.14–11.38)	Longhorn 322; Shorthorn 343; Henry Farman F.20 351; R.E.1 608; R.E.5 631; B.E.8 636; F.B.6 704; Henry Farman Biplane 653; B.E.2a 241; Blériot XI 323; Martinsyde S.1 1601; B.E.2c 718; F.E.2a 5642; Bristol Scout C 5311; Elephant 4735; Farman F.56 9173; B.E.2d 5767, B.E.2e 6241, B.E.2f, B.E.2g; R.E.8 A4316; D.H.4 N6930; Avro 504N F2580; F.2B JR6785; Fairey IIIF J9654; Gordon K2722; Hart K4471; Hardy K4054.
ZD (11.38–5.39)	Hardy K4308 ZD-C.
XE	Allocated for the period May to September 1939 but no evidence of use.
Nil (5.39–9.39)	Hardy K4059; Gauntlet I K4101, II K5292.
JV (9.39–7.43)	Hardy K4070; Gauntlet I K4101, II K5331; Lysander I L4709, II L6887 JV-P; Gladiator II N5851; Blenheim IV P4863; Hurricane I V7777, IIC HL832, IID BP188 JV-Z.
Nil (7.43–1.46)	Hurricane IV KZ553 B.
JV (1.46–10.49)	Hurricane IV KZ609 JV-S; Spitfire IX PT470 JV-C; Tempest VI NX187 JV-X.
Nil (10.49-1.69)	Vampire FB.5 VV555 Z, FB.9 WG889; Venom FB.1 WK477 Z, FB.4 WR382; Canberra B.2 WK109, T.4 WH637, B.6 WJ778 K, B.15 WH956, B.16 WJ771.
Also used	Magister R1941; Harvard III EZ357; Vampire T.11 WZ591.

Disbanded 13th January 1969 at Akrotiri, Cyprus.

Reformed 7th May 1969 at Coningsby.

Phantom FGR.2 XT908 P.

Disbanded 30th September 1974 at Coningsby.

Reformed 1st October 1974 at Lossiemouth having commenced training from 1st July 1974 as 6 Squadron (Designate).

| Nil (10.74–8.86) | Jaguar GR.1 XX731 E, T.2 XX139 C. |
| E (8.86–   ) | Jaguar GR.1 XX732 ED, GR.1A XX741 EJ, GR.1B, T.2 XX144 ET, T.2A XX836 ER. |

Current 1st April 1998 at Coltishall.

7 SQUADRON, RFC, later 7 SQUADRON, RAF
Formed 1st May 1914 at Farnborough.

Longhorn; B.E.8; Tabloid 394.

Disbanded 8th August 1914 at Farnborough.

Reformed 29th September 1914 at Farnborough. Became 7 Squadron, RAF from 1st April 1918 whilst at Proven, Belgium.

Henry Farman F.20; Morane H; Blériot XI; Avro Type E 491; Vickers F.B.6 704; Vickers F.B.5; R.E.5 674; Voisin LA; Bristol Scout C 1606; Bristol Scout D 4676; B.E.2c 2750; Morane LA; B.E.2d, B.E.2e A2800, B.E.2f, B.E.2g; R.E.8 E1207.

Disbanded 31st December 1919 at Farnborough.

Reformed 1st June 1923 at Bircham Newton from 'D' Flight of 100 Squadron. Merged with 76 Squadron to become 5 Group Pool from 14th September 1939.

Nil (6.23–11.38)	Vimy IV J7240; Virginia II J6857 C, III J6992, IV J7275, V J7418, VI J7706, VII J8329 B, IX J8908 F, X J7131; Heyford II K4865, III K6873; Wellesley K7716; Whitley II K7247.
LT (11.38–9.39)	Whitley II K7253 LT-L; III K8965; Anson I N5013; Hampden I L4170.
Nil (9.39–4.40)	Anson I N5015; Hampden I P1260.
Also used	Avro 504K D92; D.H.9A J7038.

Disbanded 4th April 1940 at Upper Heyford and merged with 76 Squadron to become 16 Operational Training Unit.

Reformed 30th April 1940 at Finningley.

Hampden I.

Disbanded 20th May 1940 at Finningley.

Reformed 1st August 1940 at Leeming.

MG (8.40–4.51)   Stirling I N3641 MG-D, III EF406; Lancaster I
                   NG229 MG-S; III EE200 MG-A; VI JB675
                   MG-O; I/FE PA414 MG-G; Lincoln II RE347.
XU (6.43– .45)   ('C' Flight) Lancaster I; Lancaster III.
Nil (4.51– 1.56)   Lincoln II SX988.

Disbanded 1st January 1956 at Upwood.

Reformed 1st November 1956 at Honington.

Valiant B(PR).1 WP217, B.1 WZ368, B(PR)K.1 WZ389.

Disbanded 30th September 1962 at Wittering.

Reformed 1st May 1970 at St Mawgan.

Canberra B.2 WJ611, T.4 WJ566, T.11 WJ975, TT.18 WK124, T.19
XA536 L.

Disbanded 5th January 1982 at St Mawgan.

Reformed 1st September 1982 at Odiham.

E   Chinook HC.1 ZA705 EZ, HC.2 ZA681, HC.2A;
                   Gazelle HT.3 ZB627.

Current 1st April 1998 at Odiham.

7 SQUADRON CONVERSION FLIGHT
Formed 16th January 1942 at Oakington.

MG   Stirling I N6032.

Disbanded 7th October 1942 at Oakington and merged with 101,
149 and 218 Squadron Conversion Flights to become 1657 Heavy
Conversion Unit.

8 SQUADRON, RFC, later 8 SQUADRON, RAF
Formed 1st January 1915 at Brooklands. Became 8 Squadron, RAF
from 1st April 1918 whilst at Vert Galand, France.

B.E.2a 336, B.E.2b 492, B.E.2c 1711; Bristol Scout B 648, Bristol
Scout C 1610; B.E.8 740; B.E.2d 6252, B.E.2e 2555; F.K.8 B4190;
F.2A A3325; F.2B D7901.

Disbanded 20th January 1920 at Duxford.

Reformed 18th October 1920 at Helwan, Egypt.

Nil (10.20–4.39)   D.H.9A H3510 L; Nighthawk JR6925; Fairey
                   IIIF J9055 P, Fairey IIIF Floatplane J9158 N;
                   Vincent K4127.
YO (4.39–9.39)   Vincent K4739 YO-W; Blenheim IV L1529.
HV (9.39– .40)   Vincent K4712 HV-L; Blenheim I L6655 HV-Y.
Nil (.40–5.45)   Blenheim I L8433; Maryland I 102 (Free French
                   detachment); Swordfish I L2846; Blenheim IV
                   Z6149, V BA874 A; Hudson IIIA FH285, VI
                   FK625; Wellington X MF455, XIII JA271 A.
Also used   Moth K1212; Tiger Moth I K4253; Traveler I
                   FL656.

Disbanded 1st May 1945 at Khormaksar, Aden.

Reformed 15th May 1945 at Jessore, India, by renumbering 200
Squadron.

Liberator VI KH331 G.

Disbanded 15th November 1945 at Minneriya, Ceylon.

Reformed 1st September 1946 at Khormaksar, Aden, by
renumbering 114 Squadron.

Mosquito VI TE702; Tempest VI NX131 A; Brigand B.1 RH812;
Buckmaster B.1 RP209; Anson XIX VL305; Harvard TT.IIB KF945;

A D.H.9A of No 8 Squadron flying over Iraq in 1926.

193

Auster VI VF525; Vampire FB.9 WL607 B, T.11 WZ560; Venom FB.1 WR337 C, FB.4 WR548 F; Meteor T.7 WA627, FR.9 WX978 G; Hunter T.7 XL565 Y, FGA.9 XG237 T, FR.10 XF460 X.

Disbanded 21st December 1967 at Muharraq, Bahrain.

Reformed 1st January 1972 at Kinloss.

Shackleton T.2 WL787 87, AEW.2 WL747 47; Sentry AEW.1 ZH101.

Current 1st April 1998 at Waddington.

9 SQUADRON, RFC, later 9 SQUADRON, RAF
Formed 8th December 1914 at St Omer, France, by redesignating the Wireless Flight.

B.E.2a 368; Longhorn; Blériot XI 1825; Shorthorn 1841; B.E.2b 484, B.E.2c; Blériot Parasol 577.

Disbanded 22nd March 1915 at St Omer and absorbed by 2, 5, 6 and 15 Squadrons.

Reformed 1st April 1915 at Brooklands. Became 9 Squadron, RAF from 1st April 1918 whilst at Proven, Belgium.

B.E.2; Blériot XI; Longhorn; Avro 504 772; Martinsyde S.1; B.E.2c 5441; R.E.5 688; R.E.7 2351; Bristol Scout C 5297; B.E.2d 5817, B.E.2e 6750; R.E.8 A4366 21; F.2B E9602.

Disbanded 31st December 1919 at Castle Bromwich.

Reformed 1st April 1924 at Upavon.

Nil (4.24–2.39)	Vimy F9152; Virginia IV J7274, V J7425, VI J7560, VII J7706 F, IX J7711 Y, X J7719 Y; Heyford III K5192.
KA (2.39–9.39)	Wellington I L4274 KA-K.
WS (9.39–4.51)	Wellington I L4268, IA L7787 WS-L, IC T2564 WS-X, III X3332 WS-O; Manchester I L7386; Lancaster I ME387/G WS-O, III ED481 WS-N, VII NX784 WS-X; Lincoln II RF477 WS-H; Oxford I BG273 WS-Z.
Nil (4.51–7.61)	Lincoln II SX954; Canberra B.2 WE111, B.6 WH961, B.15 WH982.
Also used	Avro 504K H2968; Handley Page H.P.38 J9130; Vickers 150 J9131.

Disbanded 13th July 1961 at Coningsby.

Reformed 1st March 1962 at Coningsby.

Vulcan B.2 XL385.

Disbanded 1st May 1982 at Waddington.

Reformed 1st June 1982 at Honington

Nil (6.82–8.86)	Tornado GR.1 ZA593 H, GR.1(T) ZA359 U.
A (8.86–)	Tornado GR.1 ZE116 AL.

Current 1st April 1998 at Bruggen, Germany.

9 SQUADRON CONVERSION FLIGHT
Formed 8th August 1942 at Waddington.

WS	Manchester I L7484 WS-D; Lancaster I W4122 WS-U.

Disbanded 9th November 1942 at Waddington and merged with 44 and 49 Squadron Conversion Flights to become 1661 Heavy Conversion Unit

10 SQUADRON, RFC, later 10 SQUADRON, RAF
Formed 1st January 1915 at Farnborough from an element of 1 Reserve Aeroplane Squadron. Became 10 Squadron, RAF from 1st April 1918 whilst at Abeele, Belgium.

Longhorn; Shorthorn; Blériot XI; Martinsyde S.1; B.E.2c 4325; Bristol Scout C 5295; B.E.12; B.E.2d 6253, B.E.2e 7153, B.E.2f 2541, B.E.2g 7194; Nieuport 12 9205; F.K.8 B5757 11; R.E.8 D6737; F.2B E2426.

Disbanded 31st December 1919 at Croydon.

Reformed 3rd January 1928 at Upper Heyford.

Nil (1.28–11.38)	Hyderabad J7742 C; Hinaidi I J9301, II K1914 K; Virginia X J8907 A; Heyford IA K4023 K, III K5194; Whitley I K7186.
PB (11.38–9.39)	Whitley I K7194 PB-E, IV K9020 PB-L.

ZA (9.39–8.45)	Whitley IV K9028 ZA-P, V T4265 ZA-J; Halifax I L9569, II BB324 ZA-X, III MZ902 ZA-R.
Nil (8.45– .46)	Dakota III FZ681, IV KN318 G.
Also used	Handley Page H.P.39 J9130; Vickers 150 J9131; Wapiti IIA J9612.

Disbanded 15th December 1947 at Mauripur, India.

Reformed 4th October 1948 at Oakington by renumbering 238 Squadron.

ZA	Dakota IV KN360 ZA-M.

Disbanded 20th February 1950 at Oakington.

Reformed 15th January 1953 at Scampton.

Canberra B.2 WH666.

Disbanded 15th January 1957 at Honington.

Reformed 15th April 1958 at Cottesmore.

Victor B.1 XA924; B.1A XH615.

Disbanded 1st March 1964 at Cottesmore.

Reformed 1st July 1966 at Fairford.

VC10 C.1 XR809 809, C.1K XV103.

Current 1st April 1998 at Brize Norton.

10 SQUADRON CONVERSION FLIGHT
Formed 17th February 1942 at Leeming.

ZA	Halifax I L9524, II R9376.

Disbanded 7th October 1942 at Riccall and merged with 76 and 78 Squadron Conversion Flights to become 1658 Heavy Conversion Unit.

11 SQUADRON, RFC, later 11 SQUADRON, RAF, later 11 (SHADOW) SQUADRON, RAF
Formed 14th February 1915 at Netheravon by redesignating an element of 7 Squadron. Became 11 Squadron, RAF from 1st April 1918 whilst at Fienvillers, France.

Henry Farman F.20; Vickers F.B.4 649; Gunbus 5455; Vickers F.B.9 7665; Bristol Scout C 5313; D.H.2 5918; Nieuport 16 A126; Nieuport 17 A200; Nieuport 24 B3591; Vickers E.S.1 7756; F.E.2b 7023; F.2B A7174 F.

Disbanded 31st December 1919 at Scopwick.

Reformed 15th January 1923 at Andover by redesignating the Air Pilotage School.

Nil (1.23–7.39)	D.H.9A J7044; Fawn I J7182, II J7205, III J7770; Horsley I J7996, II J8000; Wapiti I J9093, I DC J9082, IIA K1308; Hart K3921.
OY	Allocated for the period April to September 1939 but no evidence of use.
YH (7.39–)	Blenheim I L8520 YH-N.
Nil (–2.48)	Blenheim I L1434, IV T2166; Hurricane IIC LB796 B, IV LB776, XIIA PJ745; Spitfire XIV MV363 N.
Also used	F.2B B8914; Avro 504K E9381; Berkeley J7403; Handcross J7498; Yeovil J7509; Harvard IIB KF118.

Disbanded 23rd February 1948 at Miho, Japan.

Reformed 15th September 1948 at Wahn, Germany, by renumbering 107 Squadron.

OM (10.48–8.50)	Mosquito VI RS639 OM-F.
EX (8.50–4.51)	Mosquito VI SZ984 EX-C; Vampire FB.5 VV634 EX-B.
L (4.51–8.55)	Vampire FB.5 VX474 L-A, FB.9 WR144; Venom FB.1 WE283 L-H.
Nil (8.55-11.57)	Venom FB.4 WR500.
Also used	Vampire T.11 WZ447.

Disbanded 16th November 1957 at Wunstorf, Germany.

Reformed 21st January 1959 at Geilenkirchen, Germany, by renumbering 256 Squadron.

Meteor NF.11 WM253 C; Javelin T.3, FAW.4 XA756 C, FAW.5 XA650 C, FAW.9 XH753 Z.

Disbanded 11th January 1966 at Geilenkirchen.

Reformed 1st January 1966 at Leuchars as 11 (Shadow) Squadron, being 228 Operational Conversion Unit.

Javelin T.3, FAW.9; Canberra T.11.

Disbanded 23rd December 1966 at Leuchars.

Reformed 3rd April 1967 at Leuchars.

Nil (4.67–8.86)	*Lightning F.1 XM147, F.3 XR720 M, F.6 XR765 C.*
B (8.86–4.88)	*Lightning F.3A XR752 BH, F.6 XS901 BJ, T.5 XS458 BT.*

Disbanded 29th April 1988 at Leeming.

Reformed 30th June 1988 at Leeming, having commenced training from May 1988 as 11 Squadron (Designate).

D	*Tornado F.3 ZE789 DD.*

Current 1st April 1998 at Leeming.

12 SQUADRON, RFC, later 12 SQUADRON, RAF
Formed 14th February 1915 at Netheravon by redesignating an element of 1 Squadron. Became 12 Squadron, RAF from 1st April 1918 whilst at Soncamp, France.

Avro 504 760, Avro 504D 794; B.E.2c 2079; Martinsyde S.1 710; B.E.2b 484; Voisin LA 5066; R.E.7 2235; R.E.5 2458; Morane G 587; Bristol Scout C 1606; Morane LA; F.E.2b 6330; Morane BB; B.E.2d 6229; B.E.2e A2738; R.E.8 B7715; F.2B D8095 B5.

Disbanded 27th July 1922 at Bickendorf, Germany.

Reformed 1st April 1923 at Northolt.

Nil (4.23–9.39)	*Avro 504K D8811; D.H.9A J6964; Fawn I J7183, II J7185, IV J7980; Fox I J7943, I DC J7941, IA J7945; Hart K1421; Hind K5550; Battle K7667.*
QE	*Allocated for the period April to September 1939 but no evidence of use.*
PH (9.39–4.51)	*Battle L4952 PH-X; Wellington II W4366 PH-R, III X3988 PH-X; Lancaster I W4366 PH-R, III ED993 PH-J; Lincoln II RA679 PH-N.*
GZ (11.42–7.46)	*('C' Flight) Lancaster I W4922 GZ-A, III DV158 GZ-A2.*
Nil (4.51–7.61)	*Lincoln II SX979; Canberra B.2 WK107, B.6 WH951.*
Also used	*Antelope J9183.*

Disbanded 13th July 1961 at Coningsby.

Reformed 1st July 1962 at Coningsby.

Vulcan B.2 XM597.

Disbanded 31st December 1967 at Cottesmore.

Reformed 1st October 1969 at Honington.

Nil (10.69–8.85)	*Buccaneer S.2 XN977, S.2A XV155, S.2B XW527; Hunter F.6 XF383, T.7 XL573 F, T.7A WV318.*
F (8.85–4.96)	*Buccaneer S.2B XV864 KF; Hunter T.7B XL568 ZF, T.8B XF995 XF; Tornado GR.1 ZA474 FF, GR.1B, GR.1T ZA409 FQ.*

Current 1st April 1998 at Lossiemouth.

13 SQUADRON, RFC, later 13 SQUADRON, RAF
Formed 10th January 1915 at Fort Grange, Gosport, by redesignating an element of 8 Squadron. Became 13 Squadron, RAF from 1st April 1918 whilst at Le Hameau, France.

B.E.2c 4510; Bristol Scout D 8988; B.E.2d 5848, B.E.2e A1841; R.E.8 B5070.

Disbanded 31st December 1919 at Sedgeford.

Reformed 1st April 1924 at Kenley by redesignating the Signals Co-operation Flight.

Nil (4.24–1.39)	*F.2B H1623; Atlas I J9980, I DC K1525; Audax K2015; Hector I K8107; Lysander II L4757.*

AN (1.39–9.39)	*Lysander II L4761 AN-B.*
OO (9.39–11.42)	*Lysander I R2626, II L4772 OO-L, III T1582 OO-B, IIIA V9283 OO-D; Blenheim IV Z6084 OO-F.*
Nil (11.42–4.46)	*Blenheim V EH322 H; Ventura V FP553 D; Baltimore IV FA570 G, V FW369 C; Boston IV BZ568 O, V BZ596 N.*
Also used	*Avro 504N J8563; Battle L4996; Proctor I P6320; Tiger Moth II N6744; Moth Minor X5133; Magister T9707.*

Disbanded 19th April 1946 at Hassani, Greece.

Reformed 1st September 1946 at Ein Shemar, Palestine, by renumbering 680 Squadron.

Mosquito PR.34 PF649 H, III TW114 J; Meteor PR.10 WB174 N; Canberra T.4 WJ872, PR.7 WH801, PR.9 XH171.

Disbanded 5th January 1982 at Wyton.

Reformed 1st January 1990 at Honington.

Tornado GR.1, GR.1A ZG707 B, GR.1T ZA357 T.

Current 1st April 1998 at Marham.

14 SQUADRON, RFC, later 14 SQUADRON, RAF
Formed 3rd February 1915 at Shoreham by redesignating an element of 3 Reserve Aeroplane Squadron. Became 14 Squadron, RAF from 1st April 1918 whilst at Junction Station, Palestine.

Longhorn; B.E.2c 4395; Caudron G.3; Shorthorn; B.E.2e A1801; Martinsyde S.1 710; Martinsyde G.100 7474; D.H.1a 4607; B.E.12a A566; D.H.2 A4779; Bristol Scout C 4688; Bristol Scout D 7032; Vickers F.B.19 A5234; R.E.8 B6604; Nieuport 17.

Disbanded 4th February 1919 at Tangmere.

Reformed 1st February 1920 at Ramleh, Palestine, by renumbering 111 Squadron.

Nil (2.20–4.39)	*Bristol F.2B J6589; D.H.9A J7251; Fairey IIIF J9793 R; Gordon I K3993 L; Wellesley I L2697 U.*
BF (4.39–9.39)	*Wellesley I L2654 BF-F.*
Nil (9.39–9.44)	*Wellesley I K7763; Blenheim IV Z7970 P; Baltimore I AG694, II AG744; Marauder I FK130, IA FK367 J, III HD468.*
CX (9.44–6.45)	*Wellington XIV NB909 CX-K.*
Also used	*Avro 504K H7541; Grebe II J7571.*

Disbanded 25th May 1945 at Chivenor.

Reformed 25th May 1945 at Banff by renumbering 143 Squadron.

Mosquito VI HR436 J.

Disbanded 31st March 1946 at B.72 (Cambrai/Epinoy), France.

Reformed 1st April 1946 at Wahn, Germany, by renumbering 128 Squadron.

CX (4.46–2.51)	*Mosquito XVI PF544 CX-F, B.35 TA694 CX-S.*
Nil (2.51–5.53)	*Vampire FB.5 VX976 X, FB.9 WL493.*
B (5.53–6.55)	*Venom FB.1 WK413 B-Z.*
Nil (6.55–12.62)	*Hunter F.4 WT749 P, F.6 XK138 Y.*
Also used	*Oxford II W6573.*

Disbanded 17th December 1962 at Gutersloh, Germany.

Reformed 17th December 1962 at Wildenrath, Germany, by renumbering 88 Squadron.

Canberra B(I).8 WT336, T.4 WT486.

Disbanded 30th June 1970 at Wildenrath.

Reformed 1st July 1970 at Bruggen, Germany.

Phantom FGR.2 XV464 464.

Disbanded 30th November 1975 at Bruggen.

Reformed 1st December 1975 at Bruggen, Germany, having commenced training from 1st May as 14 Squadron (Designate).

A ( )	*Jaguar GR.1 XX748 AA, T.2 XX833 AY, T.2A XX845 AZ.*
B ( )	*Jaguar GR.1 XZ370 BN.*

Disbanded 1st November 1985 at Bruggen.

Reformed 1st November 1985 at Bruggen, Germany, having commenced training from 1st July 1985 as 14 Squadron (Designate).

B   *Tornado GR.1 ZD842 BZ.*

Current 1st April 1998 at Bruggen, Germany.

15 SQUADRON, RFC, later 15 SQUADRON, RAF, later 15 (RESERVE) SQUADRON, RAF
Formed 1st March 1915 at Farnborough by redesignating an element of 1 Reserve Aeroplane Squadron. Became 15 Squadron, RAF from 1st April 1918 whilst at Fienvillers, France.

Henry Farman F.20; Longhorn; Shorthorn; Avro 504; Blériot XI; B.E.2c 2578; Morane H; Morane L; B.E.2d 6733, B.E.2e A3161, B.E.2f, B.E.2g; Bristol Scout C 4669; F.E.2b 5202; R.E.8 B2276 13.

Disbanded 31st December 1919 at Fowlmere.

Reformed 20th March 1924 at Martlesham Heath within the Aeroplane and Armament Experimental Establishment.

Trials aircraft   *Ferret N192; Vireo N211; Bison N9599; Aldershot I J6853; Heron J6989; Pixie II J7323; Fawn II J7224; Bugle J7260; Venture I J7282; Chamois J7295; Handcross J7500; Virginia IX J7558, X J7275; Gamecock I J7891; F.2B J7643; Hyderabad J7748; D.H.9A J7854; Horsley I J7987, II J8007; Harrier J8325; Fox I J8427; Wapiti J8495; Siskin IIIA J8627; Gloster SS.18 J9125; Atlas J9129; Handley Page H.P.38 J9130; Vickers 150 J9131; Gosport J9175; Antelope J9183; Sidestrand II J9186; Wizard J9252; Bulldog II J9480; Westland F.29/27 J9565; Vickers 161 J9566; D.H.77 J9771; Fox IIM J9834.*

Disbanded 31st May 1934 to become the Armament Testing Squadron, Aeroplane and Armament Experimental Establishment.

Reformed 1st June 1934 at Abingdon.

Nil (6.34–11.38)	*Hart K2967; Hind K5421; Battle K9227.*
EF (11.38–9.39)	*Battle K9233 EF-J.*
LS (9.39–4.51)	*Battle P2177 LS-Y; Blenheim IV R3777 LS-Y; Wellington I L4343, IA N2871, IC T2806 LS-N; Stirling I N3658 LS-E, III BF476 LS-P; Lancaster I LL806 LS-J, III LM490 LS-L, I/Special PD129 LS-R; Lincoln II RF370 LS-A; Washington B.1 WF499 LS-B.*
DJ (.43– .43)	*('C' Flight) Lancaster I NG489 DJ-M.*
Nil (4.51–4.57)	*Washington B.1 WF499 B; Canberra B.2 WK107.*

Disbanded 15th April 1957 at Honington.

Reformed 1st September 1958 at Cottesmore.

Victor B.1 XA925, B.1A XH616, B(PR).1 XA935.

Disbanded 1st October 1964 at Cottesmore.

Reformed 1st October 1970 at Honington.

Buccaneer S.2B XX888; Hunter T.7A WV318.

Disbanded 1st July 1983 at Laarbruch, Germany, and absorbed by 16 Squadron.

Reformed 1st September 1983 at Laarbruch, Germany, having commenced training from 1st July 1983 as 15 Squadron (Designate).

Nil ( )	*Tornado GR.1T ZA544 F.*
E ( )	*Tornado GR.1 ZA455 EJ, GR.1T ZA409 EW.*
D ( )	*Tornado F.3 ZE792 DG.*

Disbanded 18th December 1991 at Laarbruch.

Reformed 1st April 1992 at Honington as 15 (Reserve) Squadron, being the Tornado Weapons Conversion Unit, by renumbering 45 (Reserve) Squadron.

T   *Tornado GR.1 ZA563 TC, GR.1T ZA595 TV.*

Current 1st April 1998 at Lossiemouth.

15 SQUADRON CONVERSION FLIGHT
Formed 26th January 1942 at Alconbury.

LS   *Stirling I N6044.*

Disbanded 4th October 1942 at Waterbeach and absorbed with 214 Squadron Conversion Flight into 1651 Heavy Conversion Flight.

16 SQUADRON, RFC, later 16 SQUADRON, RAF, later 16 (RESERVE) SQUADRON, RAF
Formed 10th February 1915 at St Omer, France, by merging elements of 2, 5 and 6 Squadrons. Became 16 Squadron RAF from 1st April 1918 whilst at Camblain-L'Abbe, France.

R.E.5 745; Gunbus 1618; Blériot XI 1828; Martinsyde S.1; Voisin LA 1877; Shorthorn 5019; B.E.2c 2748, B.E.2d 5810; Bristol Scout C 4670; Bristol Scout D 5302; F.E.2a 5643, F.E.2b 5202; B.E.2e A1820, B.E.2f 6818, B.E.2g A2492; R.E.8 B5010 17; F.K.8 B5837.

Disbanded 31st December 1919 at Fowlmere.

Reformed 1st April 1924 at Old Sarum by redesignating the Co-operation Squadron of the School of Army Co-operation.

Nil (4.24–11.38)	*F.2B F4519; Atlas K1037; Audax K3700; Lysander I L4685, II L4794.*
KJ (11.38–5.39)	*Lysander I L4689 KJ-V, II L4805 KJ-D.*
EE (5.39–9.39)	*Lysander II L4795.*
UG (9.39–5.42)	*Lysander II P1720 UG-L; Gladiator II N2306 UG-R; Lysander III R9107, IIIA V9489.*
Nil (5.42–10.45)	*Lysander IIIA V9292; Tomahawk I AH746, IIA AH934; Mustang I AM102 Y; Spitfire XI PL970 E, IX MK915, XIX PS835.*
Also used	*Tutor K3249; Battle P6572; Tiger Moth II R4958; Proctor I P6256; Master I T8405, Master III W8880; Oxford I R6027; Moth Minor X5120; Auster IV MT284; Mosquito VI NT152.*

Disbanded 19th September 1945 at B.78 (Eindhoven), Holland, the Flights having been absorbed by 2, 26 and 268 Squadrons two days earlier.

Reformed 19th September 1945 at Celle, Germany, by renumbering 268 Squadron.

Spitfire XIV NH864, XIX PS834; Auster IV MT284.

Disbanded 1st April 1946 at Celle.

Reformed 1st April 1946 at Fassberg, Germany, by renumbering 56 Squadron.

EG (4.46– .54)	*Tempest V SN345 FG-K, Tempest II 2 PR776 EG-P; Vampire FB.5 VV656 EG-Z.*
L (.54– .55)	*Venom FB.1 WE431 L-P.*
Nil (.55–6.57)	*Venom FB.1 WK399 F.*
Also used	*Harvard IIB KF401; Vampire T.11 WZ515.*

Disbanded 1st June 1957 at Celle, Germany.

Reformed 1st March 1958 at Laarbruch, Germany.

Canberra PR.3 WF927, B(I).8 XM268 A, T.4 WJ880.

Disbanded 6th June 1972 at Laarbruch.

Reformed 8th January 1973 at Laarbruch, Germany, having commenced training from 1st October 1972 as 16 Squadron (Designate).

Buccaneer S.2B XW538 S; Hunter T.7 XL600 83, T.7A WV318.

Disbanded 29th February 1984 at Laarbruch.

Reformed 1st March 1984 at Laarbruch, Germany, having commenced training on 1st January as 16 Squadron (Designate).

F   *Tornado GR.1 ZA470 FL, GR.1(T) ZA412 FZ.*

Disbanded 11th September 1991 at Laarbruch.

Reformed 11th September 1991 at Lossiemouth as 16 (Reserve) Squadron, being the Jaguar Operational Conversion Unit, by redesignating 226 Operational Conversion Unit.

Jaguar GR.1 XX741, GR.1A XZ108 A, T.2 XX846 A, T.2A XX832 Z.

Current 1st April 1998 at Lossiemouth.

17 SQUADRON, RFC, later 17 SQUADRON, RAF
Formed 1st February 1915 at Fort Grange, Gosport. Became 17 Squadron, RAF from 1st April 1918 whilst at Lahana, Macedonia.

Martinsyde S.1 710; B.E.2c 4124, B.E.2e A3084; D.H.1a 4612;

D.H.2 A2586; Bristol Scout C 5321; Nieuport 17 (on loan from French); B.E.12 6601, B.E.12a A4007; Spad S.VII A8806; Avro 504C 1476; F.K.3a 6200; Bristol M.1C C4913; S.E.5a B613; F.K.8 B3337; D.H.9 C6299; Camel E5172.

Disbanded 14th November 1919 at San Stephano, Turkey.

Reformed 1st April 1924 at Hawkinge.

Nil (4.24–11.38)	Snipe E6544, DC E6478; Woodcock II J8311; Gamecock I J8405; Siskin IIIA J8880, IIIDC J9200; Bulldog IIA K2153, Bulldog Trainer K3177; Gauntlet II K5267.
UV (11.38–9.39)	Gauntlet II K7821 UV-T; Hurricane I L1609 UV-D.
YB (9.39–2.48)	Hurricane I N2359 YB-J, IIA Z2799 YB-P, IIB BE171 YB-B, IIC KZ448; Spitfire VIII LV643, XIVE RN152 YB-E.
Also used	Avro 504K F8770, Avro 504N J750; Hart K3004, Hart Special K4424; Nimrod K2823; Audax K1999; Battle Trainer P6732; Magister P6353; Tiger Moth II R5020; Harvard IIB FE615.

Disbanded 23rd February 1948 at Miho, Japan.

Reformed 11th February 1949 at Chivenor by renumbering 691 Squadron.

UT	Oxford I MP368 UT-Z, II NM408 UT-W; Spitfire XVI TB758 UT-X; Martinet I JN513; Harvard IIB FX222 UT-M; Beaufighter X RD771 UT-7.

Disbanded 13th March 1951 at Chivenor.

Reformed 1st June 1956 at Wahn, Germany.

Canberra T.4 WT487, PR.7 WT525 R.

Disbanded 12th December 1969 at Wildenrath, Germany.

Reformed 16th October 1970 at Bruggen, Germany.

Phantom FGR.2 XV475 D.

Disbanded 30th January 1976 at Bruggen.

Reformed 1st February 1976 at Bruggen, Germany, having commenced training from 1st September 1975 as 17 Squadron (Designate).

B	Jaguar GR.1 XX744 BA, T.2 XX844 BY.

Disbanded 1st March 1985 at Bruggen.

Reformed 1st March 1985 at Bruggen, Germany, having commenced training from 6th January 1985 as 17 Squadron (Designate).

C	Tornado GR.1 ZD788 CB, GR.1A ZA406, GR.1T ZD742 CY.

Current 1st April 1998 at Bruggen.

18 SQUADRON, RFC, later 18 (BURMA) SQUADRON, RAF
Formed 11th May 1915 at Northolt by redesignating an element of 4 Reserve Aeroplane Squadron. Became 18 Squadron, RAF from 1st April 1918 whilst at Treizennes, France.

Henry Farman F.20 558; Shorthorn 533; Avro 504 775; Martinsyde S.1 2827; Martinsyde G.100 7279; B.E.2c 1791; Morane G 591; Caudron G.2 5252; S.E.4a 5610; D.H.2 5916; Gunbus 2883; F.E.2b A5443; D.H.4 A7712 5; D.H.9A E8521 D.

Disbanded 31st December 1919 at Weston-on-the-Green.

Reformed 20th October 1931 at Upper Heyford.

Nil (10.31–5.39)	Moth K1855; Hart K2452; Hind K5474.
GU (5.39–9.39)	Blenheim I L1177 GU-K.
WV (9.39–10.42)	Blenheim I L6693, IV V5386 WV-R, V BA820 WV-R.
Nil (10.42–3.46)	Blenheim V BB181 R; Douglas A-20C 43-33227 M, Boston III (Turbinlite) Z2280 P, IIIA BZ361 Z, IV BZ498 S, V BZ638 T.
Also used	Gladiator II N2300; Magister P6444; Harvard IIB FT374.

Disbanded 31st March 1946 at Hassani, Greece.

Reformed 1st September 1946 at Ein Shemar, Palestine, by renumbering 621 Squadron.

Lancaster GR.3 SW288 G.

Disbanded 15th September 1946 at Ein Shemar to become 'B' Flight of 38 Squadron.

Reformed 15th March 1947 at Butterworth, Malaya, by redesignating 1300 (Meteorological) Flight.

Mosquito VI TE595.

Disbanded 15th November 1947 at Butterworth.

Reformed 8th December 1947 at Netheravon.

Dakota IV KN367 V.

Disbanded 20th February 1950 at Oakington.

Reformed 1st August 1953 at Scampton.

Canberra B.2 WJ733.

Disbanded 1st February 1958 at Upwood.

Reformed 17th December 1958 at Finningley from 'C' Flight of 199 Squadron.

Valiant B.1 WZ372.

Disbanded 31st March 1963 at Finningley.

Reformed 27th January 1964 at Odiham by redesignating the Wessex Intensive Flying Trials Unit.

B	Wessex HC.2 XR504 BF.

Disbanded 30th November 1980 at Gutersloh, Germany.

Reformed 4th August 1981 at Odiham.

B (8.81–)	Chinook HC.1 ZD981 BD.
E ( )	Chinook HC.1 ZA705 EZ.
B ( )	Chinook HC.1 ZA674 BA, HC.2 ZA714; Puma HC.1 XW218 BW; Gazelle HT.3.

Current 1st April 1998 at Laarbruch, Germany.

19 SQUADRON, RFC, later 19 SQUADRON, RAF, later 19 (RESERVE) SQUADRON, RAF
Formed 1st September 1915 at Castle Bromwich by redesignating an element of 5 Reserve Aeroplane Squadron. Became 19 Squadron, RAF from 1st April 1918 whilst at Savy, France.

Shorthorn; Avro 504; Caudron G.3; B.E.2c 2493, B.E.2d 5869, B.E.2e 7212; R.E.7 2361; Bristol Scout; Martinsyde S.1; F.E.2b; R.E.5; B.E.12 6579; Spad S.VII B1537; Dolphin E4514 E.

Disbanded 31st December 1919 at Ternhill.

Reformed 1st April 1923 at Duxford, the sole Flight being attached to 2 Flying Training School.

Nil (4.23–10.38)	Snipe E7599, Snipe DC F2430; Avro 504K F8760; Grebe II J7417, IIDC J7585, IIIDC J7524; Siskin IIIA J8888, IIIDC J9197; Gamecock J8035; Bulldog IIA K2155, Bulldog Trainer K3181; Gauntlet I K4086, II K5292; Spitfire I K9797.
WZ (10.38–9.39)	Spitfire I K9798 WZ-L.
QV (9.39–11.41)	Spitfire I P9386 QV-K, IB X4159, IIA P7423 QV-Y.
Nil (11.41–1.44)	Spitfire VB BM117, VC AR517, IX MA750.
QV (1.44–4.51)	Mustang III FB113 QV-H, IV KH655 QV-R, IVA KM200 QV-P; Spitfire XVIE SL690 QV-A, F.21 LA272; Hornet F.1 PX250 QV-G, F.3 PX293 QV-A.
Nil (4.51–12.76)	Meteor F.4 EE598, T.7 WA672, F.8 WH304 L; Hunter F.6 XE583 D, T.7 XL601; Lightning F.2 XN727 A, F.2A XN781 B, T.4 XM988 T.
Also used	Auster III MZ231, V MT360; Mosquito III VP351.

Disbanded 31st December 1976 at Gutersloh, Germany.

Reformed 1st January 1977 at Wildenrath, Germany having commenced training from 1st October 1976 as 19 Squadron (Designate).

Phantom FGR.2 XV422 J.

Disbanded 9th January 1992 at Wildenrath.

Reformed 23rd September 1992 at Chivenor as 19 (Reserve) Squadron by renumbering 63 (Reserve) Squadron, being an element of 7 Flying Training School. The nameplate was then transferred to the Central Flying School Squadron within 4 Flying Training School from 1st October 1994.

Hawk T.1 XX174, T.1A XX217.

Current 1st April 1998 at Valley.

20 SQUADRON, RFC, later 20 SQUADRON, RAF, later 20 (RESERVE) SQUADRON, RAF

Formed 1st September 1915 at Netheravon from an element of 7 Reserve Aeroplane Squadron. Became 20 Squadron, RAF from 1st April 1918 whilst at Ste-Marie-Cappel, France.

Nil (9.15–9.39)	*B.E.2b 709, B.E.2c 1691; B.E.8a 2150; Blériot Parasol 2862; Blériot XI 4661; Bristol Scout C 5293; F.K.2 5328; Martinsyde S.1 5449; Curtiss JN-3 5636; F.E.2b 6336, F.E.2a 5642; F.E.2d A6480; R.E.7 2299; F.2B H1508 P; Wapiti I DC J9083; IIA J9386 M; Audax K1277.*
PM	*Allocated for the period April to September 1939 but no evidence of use.*
HN (9.39–3.43)	*Audax K4859 HN-E; Blenheim I L8404; Lysander I P1678, II N1251 HN-X; Hurricane IIB KX229 HN-H.*
Nil (3.43– .45)	*Hurricane IIB AP857, IIC BN699, IID KX229 H, IV LD447; Spitfire VIII MD377, XIV MV329 X.*
HN (.45–6.46)	*Tempest F.2 PR602 HN-D.*
Also used	*Harvard IIB FE766.*

Disbanded 1st August 1947 at June 1946 at Mauripur, India.

Reformed 11th February 1949 at Llanbedr by renumbering 631 Squadron.

TH	*Martinet I HN884 TH-K; Harvard IIB KF561 TH-Z; Oxford I PH467; Beaufighter TT.X RD546 TH-N; Spitfire XVI TE448 TH-E; Vampire F.1 TG447 TH-M, F.3 VT866.*

Disbanded 16th September 1951 at Valley.

Reformed 14th June 1952 at Jever, Germany.

L (7.52– .54)	*Vampire FB.9 WR177 L-G, FB.5 VZ229 L-N.*
Nil (10.53–12.60)	*Sabre F.4 XB752 Y; Hunter F.4 WV411 D, F.6 XJ684 B, T.7 XL619.*
Also used	*Vampire T.11 WZ476.*

Disbanded 30th December 1960 at Gutersloh, Germany.

Reformed 1st September 1961 at Tengah, Singapore.

Hunter FGA.9 XG265 K; Pioneer CC.1 XL666.

Disbanded 13th February 1970 at Tengah.

Reformed 1st December 1970 at Wildenrath, Germany.

Harrier GR.1 XV779 Q, GR.1A XV783, GR.3 XZ135 P.

Disbanded 1st March 1977 at Wildenrath.

Reformed 1st March 1977 at Bruggen, Germany.

C (3.77–6.84)	*Jaguar GR.1 XX747 CH.*

Disbanded 30th June 1984 at Bruggen.

Reformed 30th June 1984 at Laarbruch, Germany, having commenced training from 1st April 1984 as 20 Squadron (Designate).

G	*Tornado GR.1 ZA461 GA, GR.1T ZA411 GY.*

Disbanded 1st September 1992 at Laarbruch, Germany.

Reformed 1st September 1992 at Wittering as 20 (Reserve) Squadron, being the Harrier Operational Conversion Unit, by redesignating 233 Operational Conversion Unit.

Harrier GR.5 ZD345 J, GR.7 ZG859 P, T.4 ZB602 R, T.4A ZD990 Q, T.10 ZH665 S.

Current 1st April 1998 at Wittering.

21 SQUADRON, RFC, later 21 SQUADRON, RAF

Formed 23rd July 1915 at Netheravon by redesignating an element of 8 Reserve Aeroplane Squadron. Became 21 Squadron, RAF from 1st April 1918 whilst at La Lovie, Belgium.

R.E.7 2377; Bristol Scout; B.E.2c 1702; B.E.2e; Martinsyde G.100; B.E.12 6573 4; R.E.8 A4351 B.

Disbanded 1st October 1919 at Fowlmere.

Reformed 3rd December 1935 at Bircham Newton by redesignating an element of 82 Squadron.

Nil (12.35–4.39)	*Hind K5377; Blenheim I L1350.*
JP (4.39–9.39)	*Blenheim I L1359 JP-J.*
YH (9.39–3.42)	*Blenheim I L1366, IV V6240 YH-B.*

Disbanded 14th March 1942 at Luqa, Malta.

Reformed 14th March 1942 at Bodney.

YH	*Blenheim IV V5638; Ventura I AE687 YH-P, II AE910 YH-Y; Mosquito VI HR359 YH-N.*
Also used	*Mitchell II FV904; Mosquito III VA925, IV DZ344.*

Disbanded 7th November 1947 at Gutersloh, Germany.

Reformed 21st September 1953 at Scampton.

Canberra B.2 WH729.

Disbanded 30th June 1957 at Waddington.

Reformed 1st October 1958 at Upwood by renumbering 542 Squadron.

Canberra B.2 WH701, B.6 WH949.

Disbanded 15th January 1959 at Upwood.

Reformed 1st May 1959 at Benson.

Twin Pioneer CC.1 XM960 C; Dakota IV; Andover CC.2 XS791.

Disbanded 9th September 1967 at Khormaksar, Aden.

Reformed 3rd February 1969 at Andover by redesignating the Western Communications Squadron.

Devon C.1 VP956, C.2 VP976; Pembroke C.1 XK885; Whirlwind HAR.10 XP330.

Disbanded 31st January 1976 at Andover.

22 SQUADRON, RFC, later 22 SQUADRON, RAF

Formed 1st September 1916 at Fort Grange, Gosport, by redesignating an element of 13 Squadron. Became 22 Squadron, RAF from 1st April 1918 whilst at Vert Galand, France.

Shorthorn 2944; B.E.2a 240, B.E.2c 2053; Blériot XI 4654; Caudron G.2 5258; B.E.8a 2133; Curtiss JN-3 6117; Martinsyde S.1 5442; Bristol Scout C 5294; Avro 504A 2890; F.E.2b A5216; F.2B C4810 N.

Disbanded 31st December 1919 at Croydon.

Reformed 24th July 1923 at Martlesham Heath within the Aeroplane and Armament Experimental Establishment.

(Trials Aircraft)	*Heron J6989; Bugle II J7266; Berkley J7403; Handcross J7498; Yeovil I J7508; Woodcock II J7974; Fokker F.VIIA J7986; Horsley J7511, II J8006; Fox I J8427, V J9154; Witch J8596; Coral J8673; Hawfinch J8776; Aries J9037; Gosport J9175; Antelope J9183; Canberra J9184; Sidestrand J9186; Wizard J9252; Atlas I J9516; Westland F.29/27 J9565; Vickers 161 J9566; Victoria V J9766; Gloster T.C.33 J98332; Siskin III J6998, IIIA J9880.*

Disbanded 1st May 1934 to become the Performance Testing Squadron, Aeroplane and Armament Experimental Establishment.

Reformed 1st May 1934 at Donibristle.

Nil (5.34–4.39)	*Vildebeest I S1709, III K4160.*
VR (4.39–9.39)	*Vildebeest III K4596 VR-H.*
OA (9.39–11.44)	*Vildebeest III K4187 OA-Y; Beaufort I L4450 OA-F, II W6537 OA-F; Maryland I AR704; Beaufighter X NE718 OA-F.*
Nil (11.44-9.45)	*Beaufighter X NE604 A.*

Disbanded 30th September 1945 at Gannavaram, India.

Reformed 1st May 1946 at Seletar, Singapore, by renumbering 89 Squadron.

Mosquito VI; Anson XIX TX186.

Disbanded 15th August 1946 at Seletar.

Reformed 15th February 1955 at Thorney Island.

Sycamore HC.14; Whirlwind HAR.2 XJ763 L, HAR.10 XP354; Wessex HAR.2 XR518, HC.2 XR588; Sea King HAR.3, HAR.3A ZH542.

Current 1st April 1998 at Chivenor with detached Flights at Wattisham and Valley.

23 SQUADRON, RFC, later 23 SQUADRON, RAF

Formed 1st September 1915 at Fort Grange, Gosport, by redesignating an element of 14 Squadron. Became 23 Squadron, RAF from 1st April 1918 whilst at Bertangles, France.

Blériot XI 574; Caudron G.2 5270; Shorthorn 2947; Avro 504A 4024; Martinsyde S.1 4251; B.E.2c 2048; F.E.2b 5215; Elephant 7281; Curtiss JN-3 7310; Spad 7 B3479 M; Spad 13 B6842; Dolphin E4729 P.

Disbanded 31st December 1919 at Waddington.

Reformed 1st July 1925 at Henlow.

Nil (7.25–9.38)	Snipe E6615, Snipe DC F2408; Grebe II J7581 M, IIIDC J7526; Siskin IIIDC J9193; Gamecock I J8041; Bulldog IIA K1673; Hart K1852; Demon K5694.
MS (9.38–9.39)	Demon K5698 MS-G; Blenheim I L1466 MS-N.
YP (9.39–5.45)	Blenheim I L8617 YP-X, Blenheim IV P4844; Beaufighter I R2077; Havoc I BD121 YP-F; Boston III AL459; Mosquito II DD687 YP-E, VI HJ737 YP-R, NF.30 NT326.
Also used	Avro 504N J8499; Hawfinch J8776; Magister P2506; Cygnet II ES915; Owlet DP240.

Disbanded 25th September 1945 at Little Snoring.

Reformed 1st September 1946 at Wittering by renumbering 219 Squadron.

YP (9.46–4.51)	Mosquito NF.30 RL145 YP-C, NF.36 RL193 YP-B.
Nil (4.51–10.75)	Vampire NF.10 WP248 B, T.11 WZ468; Venom NF.2 WR779 G, NF.3 WX843 P; Javelin T.3, FAW.4 XA737, FAW.7 XH960 N; FAW.9 XH890 M; Lightning F.1 XM144 X, F.1A XM169 W, F.3 XP706 R, T.4 XM973 Z, T.5 XS417 Z, F.6 XS938 E.
Also used	Oxford II X7237; Mosquito III HJ852; Meteor T.7 WF812.

Disbanded 31st October 1975 at Leuchars.

Reformed 1st December 1975 at Coningsby having commenced training from 8th October 1975 as 23 Squadron (Designate).

Phantom FGR.2 XV402 A.

Disbanded 30th March 1983 at Wattisham.

Reformed 30th March 1983 at Port Stanley, Falkland Islands, by redesignating an element of 29 Squadron.

Phantom FGR.2 XV464 U.

Disbanded 1st November 1988 at Mount Pleasant, Falkland Islands, to become 1435 Flight.

Reformed 1st November 1988 at Leeming.

| E | Tornado F.3 XE907 EE. |

Disbanded 26th February 1994 at Leeming.

Reformed 1st April 1996 at Waddington by redesignating the Sentry Training Squadron and incorporating the Sentry Operational Conversion Unit.

Sentry AEW.1.

Current 1st April 1998 at Waddington.

24 SQUADRON, RFC, later 24 SQUADRON, RAF

Formed 1st September 1915 at Hounslow by redesignating an element of 17 Squadron. Became 24 Squadron, RAF from 1st April 1918 whilst at Conteville, France.

Gloster Gamecocks of No 23 Squadron at RAF Kenley in 1927.

Curtiss JN-4; Caudron G.3; Avro 504; B.E.2c; Blériot XI; Bristol Scout; Longhorn; Shorthorn; FB.5 2341; D.H.2 A2549; D.H.5 A9435 E; S.E.5a B891 7.

Disbanded 1st February 1920 at Uxbridge.

Reformed 1st February 1920 at Kenley by redesignating the Air Council Inspection Squadron.

Nil (2.20–)	D.H.10 E5459; Vimy F9152; F.2B J6681; D.H.4A F5764; D.H.9A J7310; Avro 504K E3075, Avro 504N J8758; Fairey IIIF J9799; Wapiti I J9096; Tomtit J9772; Moth J9105; Gordon K1745; Tutor K3359; Bulldog IIA K2209; Hart K3747; D.H. 89M K4472; Hind K6706; Audax K7383; Bristol 142 K7557; Tiger Moth BB802; I K2576, II N9444; Wellington I L4263, IA P2522, IC T2567; Mentor L4396; Botha L6128; Nighthawk L6846; Magister L8212; Hudson I N7253, II T9375, III T9429, IIIA FH460, IV AE636, VI AM850, VI FK482; Vega Gull III P1754; Petrel P5638; Proctor I P6179, II Z7211; Hertfordshire R2510; Lysander I R2622, IIIA V9597; Hendy Heck 3 R9138; Dominie I R9549; Dragon Rapide V4724; Electra W9106; Spitfire I 4326, IIA P7759, VA P7920; Fox Moth X9304; Envoy X9370; Phoenix 2 X9393; Dragon X9395; Puss Moth X9439; Reliant X9596; Whitley V Z9134; Flamingo AE444; Ventura II AJ456; Mohawk III AR633, IV AR680; Cleveland AS468; Hornet Moth AV972; Express AX795; Cygnet 2 DG566; Whitney Straight DP237; Warferry ES947; SM.73P OO-AGX; DC-3 OO-AUI; Ensign G-ADST; Skymaster I EW999; Dakota I FD789, III FL559, IV KN489; Fokker F.XXII HM159; Lockheed 12A LA619; Oxford I MP350, II P8833; Goose I MV993; Stampe SV.4B MX457; York VVIP.I MW100, VIP.I MW101, I MW267; Lancastrian C.2 VM701; Hastings C.1 TG523, C.2 WJ327, C(VIP).4 WJ325; Valetta C.2 VX576; Hercules C.1 XV215, C.1K, C.3.
ZK	Allocated for the period April to September 1939.
ZK (4.41– .43)	Gladiator K5200 ZK; Proctor I P5993 ZK; Wellington I N2990 ZK-9; Dakota I FD772 ZK-Y, III KK133 ZK-A.
NQ (.43– .46)	Wellington I N2990 NQ-9; Dakota I FD797 NQ-A, IV KP251 NQ-K.
Autogiro Unit	A civilian 'Autogiro Unit' attached to the Squadron became a service unit on 20th May 1940 and moved to join the Special Duty Flight, Martlesham to form part of a calibration unit within 60 Group.
Air Ambulance Unit	The unit operated within the Squadron between July 1940 and 1945.
School of Air Pilotage	The School operated as a Flight within 24 Squadron between 26th October 1931 and April 1932.

Current 1st April 1998 at Lyneham.

25 SQUADRON, RFC, later 25 SQUADRON, RAF
Formed 25th September 1915 at Montrose by redesignating an element of 6 Reserve Aeroplane Squadron. Became 25 Squadron, RAF from 1st April 1918 whilst at Ruisseauville, France.

Shorthorn; Caudron G.3; Curtiss JN-3 7310; Martinsyde S.1; Avro 504; B.E.2c; F.B.5; F.E.2b 6346; Morane L 5056; F.E.2c, F.E.2d A784; D.H.4 A7442 B; D.H.9A E9705.

Disbanded 31st January 1920 at Scopwick.

Reformed 26th April 1920 at Hawkinge.

Nil (2.20–12.38)	Snipe F2485; Grebe II J7392, Grebe IIIDC J7520; Avro 504K F8794; Horsley I J7995; Siskin IIIA J9325, IIIDC J9218; Fury I K1945, II

	K7277; Gordon I K2729; Hart Trainer K3158; Demon K2905; Gladiator I K6147.
RX (12.38–9.39)	Blenheim I L1437 RX-P.
ZK (9.39–4.51)	Blenheim I L1437 ZK-P, IV N6239; Whirlwind I P6966; Beaufighter IF R2157; Havoc I; Mosquito II HJ713, VI PZ200 ZK-A, XVII HK243/G ZK-Z, T.29 KA280 ZK-Z, NF.30 MT471 ZK-C, NF.36 RL204 ZK-Y.
Nil (4.51–6.58)	Vampire FB.5 VV685, NF.10 WP234 B; Meteor T.7 WF816 Y, NF.12 WS699 S, NF.14 WS723 T.
Also used	Lysander II N1291; Anson I N5183; Mosquito III HJ862.

Disbanded 1st July 1958 at Tangmere.

Reformed 2nd July 1958 at Waterbeach by renumbering 153 Squadron.

Meteor NF.12 WS613 A, NF.14 WS725 G; Javelin T.3, FAW.7 XH909 E, FAW.8 XJ122 E, FAW.9 XH884 C.

Disbanded 31st December 1962 at Leuchars.

Reformed 1st October 1963 at North Coates.

Bloodhound II.

Disbanded 2nd July 1989 at Wyton.

Reformed 1st January 1990 at Leeming.

F	Tornado F.3 ZE808 FA.

Current 1st April 1998 at Leeming.

26 SQUADRON, RFC, later 26 SQUADRON, RAF
Formed 8th October 1915 at Netheravon by redesignating an element of the South African Flying Unit. Redesignated 26 Squadron, RAF from 1st April 1918 whilst in transit to the United Kingdom from Cape Town, South Africa.

B.E.2c 4591; Henry Farman F.27 7753; B.E.2e A3074.

Disbanded 8th July 1918 at Blandford.

Reformed 11th October 1927 at Catterick.

Nil (10.27–2.39)	Atlas I K1004; Audax K3074; Hector K9738.
HL (2.39–9.39)	Hector K9732; Lysander II L4774.
RM (9.39 .44)	Lysander II L4788 RM, III T1429 RM H; Tomahawk I AH791 RM-E, IIA AH896 RM-Y, IIB AK125; Mustang I AG367 RM-Z.
XC (.44–4.46)	Mustang I AG361 XC-Y; Hurricane IIC LF363; Spitfire VB W3423, IX PL985 XC-W, XIV NH925 XC-B.
Also used	Avro 504N J8992; Battle L5051; Anson I L7912; Master I T8849; Dragon Rapide X9386; Proctor I P6320, III Z7206; Oxford II X7292; Moth Minor X9298; Leopard Moth BD146; Tiger Moth II EM903; Puss Moth DR755; Fi 156 VM489; Auster IV MS941, V MT360.

Disbanded 1st April 1946 at B.158 (Lübeck), Germany.

Reformed 1st April 1946 at Wunstorf, Germany, by renumbering 41 Squadron.

XC (4.46–4.51)	Tempest V EJ672, II MW416 XC-D; Vampire FB.5 VV451 XC-F.
J (4.15–11.53)	Vampire FB.5 WA178 J-T, Vampire FB.9 WR157.
Nil (11.53–9.57)	Sabre F.4 XB577 V; Hunter F.4 WT769 B.
Also used	Harvard IIB KF661; Vampire T.11 WZ498.

Disbanded 10th September 1957 at Oldenburg, Germany.

Reformed 7th June 1958 at Ahlhorn, Germany

Hunter F.6 XE535 F.

Disbanded 30th December 1960 at Gutersloh.

Reformed 1st June 1962 at Odiham.

Belvedere HC.1 XG468 A.

Disbanded 30th November 1965 at Khormaksar, Aden, and the aircraft were shipped to Seletar, Singapore, for 66 Squadron.

Reformed 3rd February 1969 at Wyton by redesignating the Training Command Communication Squadron.

Basset CC.1 XS775; Devon C.2 VP968.

Disbanded 1st April 1976 at Wyton.

27 SQUADRON, RFC, later 27 SQUADRON, RAF, later 27 (RESERVE) SQUADRON, RAF

Formed 5th November 1915 at Hounslow Heath by redesignating an element of 24 Squadron. Became 27 Squadron, RAF from 1st April 1918 whilst at Ruisseauville, France.

Elephant 7507 2; D.H.4 B2077; D.H.9 C1316.

Disbanded 22nd January 1920 at Shotwick.

Reformed 1st April 1920 at Mianwali, India, by renumbering 99 Squadron. The Squadron acted as a Flying Training School at Risalpur from 1st October 1939 until 21st October 1940 before reverting to operational status from 10th February 1941.

Nil (4.20–2.42)	*D.H.9A J7057 K; Wapiti IIA K1283 C; Hart K2085; Tiger Moth II T1778; Blenheim I L8507.*
MY	*Allocated for the period April to September 1939 but no evidence of use.*
PT (9.39–2.42)	*Wapiti V J9754 PT-F; Blenheim I L6667 PT-D.*
Also used	*Ajax J8803.*

Dispersed February 1942 at Parabumilih, Sumatra.

Reformed 19th September 1942 at Amarda Road, India.

Beaufighter VI T5208 X; Mosquito II DZ695 V; Beaufighter X NE809 F; Mosquito VI HJ811 J. Also used Harvard IIB FS698.

Disbanded 1st February 1946 at Mingaladon, Burma.

Reformed 1st November 1947 at Abingdon from an element of 46 Squadron.

Dakota IV KK129.

Disbanded 10th November 1950 at Netheravon.

Reformed 15th June 1953 at Scampton.

Canberra B.2 WJ619.

Disbanded 31st December 1956 at Waddington.

Reformed 1st April 1961 at Scampton.

Vulcan B.2 XM594.

Disbanded 29th March 1972 at Scampton.

Reformed 1st November 1973 at Scampton.

Vulcan B.2 XJ823; Vulcan SR.2 XH534.

Disbanded 31st March 1982 at Scampton.

Reformed 12th August 1983 at Marham having commenced training from 1st May 1983 as 27 Squadron (Designate).

Nil (8.83–)	*Tornado GR.1 ZA549 14, GR.1(T) ZA585 05.*
J ( )	*Tornado GR.1 ZA542 JA.*

Disbanded 1st October 1993 at Marham.

Reformed 1st October 1993 at Odiham as 27 (Reserve) Squadron, being the Chinook Operational Conversion Unit, by redesignating 240 Operational Conversion Unit.

Puma HC.1 XW225; HC.2 ZA681.

Current 1st April 1997 at Odiham.

28 SQUADRON RFC, later 28 SQUADRON, RAF

Formed 7th November 1915 at Fort Grange, Gosport, by redesignating an element of 22 Squadron. Became 28 Squadron, RAF from 1st April 1918 whilst at Grossa, Italy.

B.E.2a; Avro 504; B.E.2c 1688; Henry Farman F.20; F.E.2b 5222; D.H.2; Pup; D.H.5; Bristol Scout; Avro 504K H2278; Camel B6345 F.

An element detached to become 'B' Flight, 3 Training Depot Station on 5th September 1917.

Disbanded 20th January 1920 at Eastleigh.

Reformed 1st April 1920 at Ambala, India, by renumbering 114 Squadron.

Nil (2.20–4.39)	*F.2B H1541; Wapiti IIA K1272 S; Audax K5563 F.*
US (4.39–9.39)	*Audax K4849 US-L.*
BF (9.39–12.42)	*Audax K4853 BF-J; Lysander I P1686, II N1273 BF-J.*
Nil (12.42–4.51)	*Hurricane IIB BG975, IIC KZ353 G, IV LD165; Spitfire VIII MT961, XI EN679, XIV TZ117 E, XVIII TP377 Y; Vampire FB.5 WA255, FB.9 WP990 A; Venom FB.1 WR299 A, FB.4 WR540 E; Hunter T.7 WV383, FGA.9 XE535 C.*
Also used	*Hart K2460; Harvard IIB KF369; Auster III NJ963, T.7 WE557; Vampire T.11 XE957.*

Disbanded 2nd January 1967 at Kai Tak, Hong Kong.

Reformed 1st March 1968 at Kai Tak, Hong Kong, by redesignating an element of 103 Squadron.

Whirlwind HAR.10 XP358 S; Wessex HC.2 XT605 E.

Disbanded 3rd June 1997 at Kai Tak.

29 SQUADRON, RFC, later 29 SQUADRON, RAF

Formed 7th November 1915 at Fort Grange, Gosport, by redesignating an element of 23 Squadron. Became 29 Squadron, RAF from 1st April 1918 whilst at La Lovie, Belgium.

Shorthorn 369; Avro 504A 4768; Caudron G.2 5252; B.E.2b 2886, B.E.2c 2065; D.H.2 A2614 5; F.E.8 6383; Nieuport 10 3176; Nieuport 16 A131; Nieuport 17 B1515; Nieuport 23 A6781; Nieuport 24; Nieuport 27; S.E.5a F899 C.

Disbanded 31st December 1919 at Spitalgate.

Reformed 1st April 1923 at Duxford.

Nil (4.23–12.38)	*Snipe E6595; Grebe II J7292, IIDC J7585, III DC J7520; Siskin IIIA J8946, IIIDC J9194; Bulldog II J9587, IIA K2211; Demon K2845.*
YB (12.38–9.39)	*Blenheim I L8372 YB-L.*
RO (9.39–4.51)	*Blenheim I L1375 RO-J, IV P4835; Beaufighter IF R2196 RO-F, VI EL172; Mosquito VI HX824, XII HK129 RO-G, XIII HK522 RO-L, FB.26 KA119, NF.30 NT417 RO-E, NF.36 RK959 RO-X, III VA893 RO-Q.*
Nil (4.51–12.74)	*Mosquito NF.30; Meteor NF.11 WD598 T, NF.12 WS593, Meteor T.7 WL422 X; Javelin T.3, FAW.6 XA825 K, FAW.9 XH848 L; Lightning F.3 XP705 L, T.5 XV328 Z.*
Also used	*Moth K1209; Atlas AC K1593; Audax K5136; Battle L5779; Magister P2467; Oxford II V3819.*

Disbanded 31st December 1974 at Wattisham.

Reformed 1st January 1975 at Coningsby, having commenced training from 1st October 1974 as 29 Squadron (Designate).

Phantom FGR.2 XV442 F.

Disbanded 30th March 1987 at Coningsby.

Reformed 1st April 1987 at Coningsby.

B	*Tornado F.3 ZE207 BL, F.3T ZH553 BY.*

Current 1st April 1998 at Coningsby. Scheduled to disband 30th October 1998.

30 SQUADRON RFC, later 30 SQUADRON, RAF

Formed 24th March 1915 at Moascar, Egypt, by redesignating the RFC Detached Flight Moascar. Redesignated 30 Squadron, RAF from 1st April 1918 whilst at Qubba, Mesopotamia.

Nil (10.14–4.39)	*Longhorn 712; Shorthorn 5909; B.E.2c 4564; Caudron G.3; Martinsyde S.1 4243; Short 184 8043; Voisin LA 8506; Henry Farman F.27 3901; Elephant 7467; Bristol Scout D 7033; B.E.2e A3079; Spad 7 A8806; R.E.8 A4357; Vickers FB.19; D.H.4 A7621; S.E.5a; D.H.9A E776 A; Wapiti I J9078, IIA K1389; Hardy K4058; Blenheim I K7097 P.*
DP (4.39–9.39)	*Blenheim I L4917 DP-G.*
VT (9.39–6.41)	*Blenheim I K7107 VT-B.*
RS (6.41–4.47)	*Hurricane I Z4419 RS-C, IIB BG916, IIC JS447*

A D.H.2 of 29 Squadron RFC in 1916.

RS-Z; Thunderbolt I HD151 RS-R, II KL183
RS-R; Tempest F.2 PR583 RS-G.

Disbanded 1st December 1946 at Agra, India.

Reformed 1st November 1947 at Abingdon by redesignating an element of 238 Squadron.

| JN (4.47–4.51) | Dakota IV KN360 JN-K; Valetta C.1 VL277 JN-H, C.2 VX576 JN-C. |
| Nil (4.51–9.67) | Valetta C.1 VW849, C.2 VX577; Beverley C.1 XM111 D. |

Disbanded 6th September 1967 at Muharraq, Bahrain.

Reformed 1st May 1968 at Fairford.

Hercules C.1 XV210, C.1K, C.3.

Current 1st April 1998 at Lyneham.

31 SQUADRON, RFC, later 31 SQUADRON, RAF
Formed 11th October 1915 at South Farnborough by redesignating an element of 1 Reserve Aeroplane Squadron. Became 31 Squadron, RAF from 1st April 1918 whilst at Risalpur, India.

Nil (10.15–4.39)	B.E.2c 4143; Henry Farman F.20 445; B.E.2e B4472; F.K.8 C3588; F.2B F4320 D; Handley Page V/1500 J1936; Wapiti IIA K1302; Valentia K2340 A.
ZA (4.39–9.39)	Wapiti IIA J9744 K; Valentia JR8231 ZA-Y.
Nil (9.39–9.46)	Valentia K4634 B; Atalanta DG454; DC-2 DG476 Y; DC-3 LR232 E; Dakota I FD787 D, III FL543 J, IV KJ918 Q; Lockheed 12A V4732; Hudson VI FK477; Harvard IIB FT102.

Disbanded 30th September 1946 at Kemajoran, Java.

Reformed 1st November 1946 at Mauripur, India, by renumbering 77 Squadron.

Dakota IV KP272.

Disbanded 15th December 1947 at Mauripur.

Reformed 19th July 1948 at Hendon by redesignating the Metropolitan Communication Squadron.

CB (7.48–3.55)	Anson XII PH817 CB-W, XIX VM351 CB-N; Devon C.1 VP965 CB-G; Chipmunk T.10 WZ864 CB-J.
VS (7.48– .51)	Proctor III DX198 VS-D, IV RM189 VS-F.
Also used	Spitfire XVI SL721, XIX PM659.

Disbanded 1st March 1955 at Hendon to become the Metropolitan Communication Squadron.

Reformed 1st March 1955 at Laarbruch, Germany.

Canberra PR.7 WH773, T.4 WH843.

Disbanded 31st March 1971 at Laarbruch.

Reformed 20th July 1971 at Bruggen, Germany.

Phantom FGR.2 XV415.

Disbanded 30th June 1976 at Bruggen.

Reformed 30th June 1976 at Bruggen, Germany, having commenced training from 1st January 1976 as 31 Squadron (Designate).

| D | Jaguar GR.1 XX825 DA; T.2 XX150 DZ. |

Disbanded 1st November 1984 at Bruggen.

Reformed 1st November 1984 at Bruggen, Germany, having commenced training from 1st September 1984 as 31 Squadron (Designate).

| D | Tornado GR.1 ZD710 DC; GR.1T ZD711 DY. |

Current 1st April 1998 at Bruggen.

32 SQUADRON, RFC, later 32 SQUADRON and 32 (THE ROYAL) SQUADRON, RAF

Formed 12th January 1916 at Netheravon by redesignating an element of 21 Squadron. Became 32 Squadron, RAF from 1st April 1918 whilst at Beauvois, France.

Henry Farman F.20; Vickers F.B.5 5127; Vickers E.S.1; D.H.2 6015; D.H.5 A9258 B2; S.E.5a B166 A.

Disbanded 31st December 1919 at Croydon.

Reformed 1st April 1923 at Kenley.

Nil (4.23– 10.39)	Snipe E6268 2; Avro 504K E9372; Grebe II J7599, IIIDC J7526; Gamecock I J8420; Siskin IIIA J9338, IIIDC J9210; Bulldog IIA K1657, Bulldog Trainer K3179; Gauntlet II K5321.
KT (10.38–9.39)	Gauntlet II K5330 KT-P; Hurricane I L1659.
GZ (9.39–11.42)	Hurricane I P3144 GZ-B, X P5203, IIB AP530, IIC HL859 GZ-F.
Nil (12.42–7.44)	Hurricane IIC KX146; Spitfire VC LZ813, IX JL226 G; VIII JF404 M.
GZ (7.44–5.49)	Spitfire VC JK337, IX NH495 GZ-M, XVIII TP448 GZ-?.
Nil (5.49–1.51)	Vampire F.3 VV198 F, FB.5 VZ234 S, FB.9 WL583 T; Venom FB.1 WR276 G; Canberra B.2 WH875, B.15 WH970.
Also used	Gloster F.20/27 J9125; Avian III J9182; Harvard IIB KF391; Vampire T.11 XE985.

Disbanded 3rd February 1969 at Akrotiri, Cyprus.

Reformed 3rd February 1969 at Northolt by redesignating the Metropolitan Communication Squadron. Redesignated 32 (The Royal) Squadron from 1st April 1995 upon absorbing The Queens Flight.

Basset CC.1 XS772; Sycamore HC.14 XL918; Pembroke C.1 WV703; Andover C.1 XS697, CC.2 XS792; Whirlwind HC.10 XJ763, HCC.12 XR488; HS.125 CC.1 XW788, CC.2 XX508, CC.3 ZE396; Gazelle HT.3 ZB629; HCC.4 XW852; Wessex HCC.4; BAe 146 CC.2 ZE701; Twin Squirrel ZJ139.

Current 1st April 1998 at Northolt.

33 SQUADRON, RFC, later 33 SQUADRON, RAF

Formed 12th January 1916 at Filton by redesignating an element of 20 Squadron. Became 33 Squadron, RAF from 1st April 1918 whilst at Gainsborough.

B.E.2c 2665; B.E.12 6661; Bristol Scout D 5571; B.E.2e A8707; B.E.12a A6317; F.E.2b A5659, F.E.2d B1885; F.2B C4698; Avro 504K E3033.

Disbanded 13th June 1919 at Kirton-in-Lindsey.

Reformed 1st March 1929 at Netheravon.

Nil (3.29–9.38)	Horsley I J7993, II J8605; Hart Trainer J9937; Gladiator I K8048.
SO (9.38–5.39)	Gladiator I K8055 SO-H.
TN (5.39–9.39)	Gladiator I L7620, II L8007.
NW (9.39–5.41)	Gladiator I K7954, II N5752 NW-C; Gauntlet II K5316; Sea Gladiator N5535; Hurricane I V7419 NW.
Nil (5.41–4.44)	Hurricane I P2646, IIB BE131, IIC BE407; Spitfire VB ER773, VC ES128.
5R (4.44-4.51)	Spitfire IX BS239 5R-E; Tempest V EJ886 5R-N; Spitfire XVI NH423; Tempest II PR533 5R-V; Hornet F.3 WB871 5R-P, F.4 WF972 5R-T.
Nil (4.51–3.55)	Hornet F.3 WB870, F.4 WF972.
Also used	D.H.9A DC J8471; Magister P2397; Auster III NJ927; Anson XI NK993; Harvard IIB KF413; Mosquito III RR308.

Disbanded 31st March 1955 at Butterworth, Malaya.

Reformed 15th October 1955 at Driffield.

Venom NF.2 WR785 D.

Disbanded 3rd June 1957 at Driffield.

Reformed 30th September 1957 at Leeming by renumbering 264 Squadron.

Meteor NF.12 WS604 U, NF.14 WS810 S; Javelin FAW.7 XH758 R,

FAW.9 XH879 W. Also used Meteor T.7 WA659 Y, F.8 WK941; Vampire T.11 WZ567.

Disbanded 17th November 1962 at Middleton St George.

Reformed 1st March 1965 at Butterworth, Malaya.

Bloodhound II.

Disbanded 30th January 1970 at Butterworth.

Reformed 14th June 1971 at Odiham.

C	Puma HC.1 XW212 CJ.

Current 1st April 1998 at Benson.

34 SQUADRON, RFC, later 34 SQUADRON, RAF

Formed 12th January 1916 at Castle Bromwich by redesignating an element of 19 Squadron. Became 34 Squadron, RAF from 1st April 1918 whilst at Villaveria, Italy.

Caudron G.3; B.E.2c 4583, B.E.2e 7096, B.E.2f, B.E.2g; R.E.8 B6530; F.2B C4674.

Disbanded 25th October 1919 at Old Sarum.

Reformed 3rd December 1935 at Bircham Newton by redesignating an element of 18 Squadron.

Nil (1.36–9.38)	Hind K4642: Blenheim I L1252 H.
LB (4.39–8.39)	Blenheim I L1252 LB-H.
EG (9.39)	Blenheim I.
Nil (9.39–2.42)	Blenheim I L6606 F, IV V5499.

Disbanded 20th February 1942 at Kalidjati, Java, and absorbed by 84 Squadron.

Reformed 1st April 1942 at Chakrata and Karachi, India.

Nil (4.42–3.45)	Blenheim IV Z6333, V BA616; Hurricane IIC LE795 P; IV LB999; Thunderbolt II HD105.
EG (3.45–10.45)	Thunderbolt II KJ356 EG-U.

Disbanded 15th October 1945 at Zayatkwin, Burma.

Reformed 1st August 1946 at Palam, India, by renumbering 681 Squadron.

Spitfire XIX PM542 F.

Disbanded 1st August 1947 at Palam.

Reformed 11th February 1949 at Horsham St Faith by renumbering 695 Squadron.

8Q (2.49–3.52)	Martinet I PX126; Spitfire XVI TE450 8Q-R; Beaufighter TT.X RD544 8Q-G; Harvard IIB KF405 8Q-6; Oxford I PH418 8Q-L.
6J (2.49–7.51)	Oxford I PH467 6J-E.

Disbanded 20th July 1951 at Horsham St Faith.

Reformed 1st August 1954 at Tangmere.

Meteor T.7 WL422, F.8 WL175 B; Hunter F.5 WP133 L; Vampire T.11 WZ424.

Disbanded 15th January 1958 at Tangmere.

Reformed 1st October 1960 at Seletar, Singapore, by redesignating the Beverley Flight of 48 Squadron.

Beverley C.1 XM104 P.

Disbanded 31st December 1967 at Seletar.

35 SQUADRON, RFC, later 35 (MADRAS PRESIDENCY) SQUADRON, RAF

Formed 1st February 1916 at Thetford by redesignating an element of 9 Reserve Squadron. Became 35 Squadron, RAF from 1st April 1918 whilst at Abbeville, France.

B.E.2c 2664; F.E.2b 6941; Vickers F.B.5; D.H.2; Henry Farman F.20; F.K.3 A8117; F.K.8 B3313; F.2B C4849.

Disbanded 26th June 1919 at Netheravon.

Reformed 1st March 1929 at Bircham Newton. Merged with 52, 63 and 207 Squadrons to become 1 Group Pool from 14th September 1939. Re-established as an independent entity from 1st February 1940.

Nil (3.29–4.39)	D.H.9A J8127, D.H.9A DC J8482 2; Fairey IIIF

K1161; Gordon K2626; Wellesley K8530 G; Battle K7709 35-O.

| WT (4.39–9.39) | Battle K9471 WT-M; Anson I N5265. |
| Nil (9.39–4.40) | Battle K9473; Anson I N4997; Blenheim IV N6174. |

Disbanded 8th April 1940 at Upwood and merged with 90 Squadron to become 17 Operational Training Unit.

Reformed 7th November 1940 at Boscombe Down.

| TL | Halifax I L9490 TL-L, II R9441 TL-S, III HX321 TL-K; Lancaster I RF183 TL-H, III LM346 TL-Q; Lincoln II SX983 TL-S |

Disbanded 23rd February 1950 at Mildenhall to become the Washington Conversion Unit.

Reformed 1st September 1951 at Marham by redesignating an element of the Washington Conversion Unit.

| FB (9.50–4.51) | Washington B.1 WF572 FB-N. |
| Nil (4.51–9.61) | Washington B.1 WF572 N; Canberra B.2 WK133. |

Disbanded 11th September 1961 at Upwood.

Reformed 1st December 1962 at Coningsby.

Vulcan B.2 XL321.

Disbanded 1st March 1982 at Scampton.

35 SQUADRON CONVERSION FLIGHT
Formed February 1942 at Linton-on-Ouse.

| TL | Halifax I L9575, II R9425. |

Disbanded 7th October 1942 at Rufforth and absorbed together with 158 Squadron Conversion Flight into 1652 Heavy Conversion Unit.

36 SQUADRON, RFC, later 36 SQUADRON, RAF
Formed 1st February 1916 at Cramlington by redesignating the Home Defence Flight, Cramlington. Became 36 Squadron, RAF from 1st April 1918 whilst at Newcastle.

B.E.2c 2738; Bristol Scout; B.E.12; B.E.2e; F.E.2b A6442, F.E.2d; Pup C235; F.2B C4896.

Disbanded 13th June 1919 at Usworth.

Reformed 9th October 1928 at Donibristle by redesignating the Coast Defence Torpedo Training Flight.

Nil (10.28–4.39)	Horsley I J7991, II J8001; Vildebeest II K2940, III K4173.
VU (4.39–9.39)	Vildebeest III K4599 VU-J.
Nil (9.39–3.42)	Vildebeest III K4170.

Dispersed 9th March 1942 at Tasikmalaja, Java.

Reformed 22nd October 1942 at Tanjore, India.

| Nil (10.42–9.44) | Wellington IC HE120 F, VIII HX679 V, X HF533 G, XI MP625 Y, XII MP650 Y, XIII MP704 A. |
| RW (10.44–6.45) | Wellington XIV NB912 RW-A. |

Disbanded 4th June 1945 at Benbecula.

Reformed 1st October 1946 at Thorney Island by renumbering 248 Squadron.

Mosquito VI RS610, III VP343; Buckmaster I VA361.

Disbanded 15th October 1947 at Thorney Island.

Reformed 1st July 1953 at Topcliffe.

| T (7.53–4.56) | Neptune MR.1 WX548 T-E. |
| 36 (4.56–2.57) | Neptune MR.1 WX556 36-H. |

Disbanded 28th February 1957 at Topcliffe.

Reformed 1st September 1958 at Colerne by renumbering 511 Squadron.

Hastings C.1 TG510, C.2 WJ328; Hercules C.1 XV220.

Disbanded 3rd November 1975 at Lyneham.

37 SQUADRON, RFC, later 37 SQUADRON, RAF
Formed 15th April 1916 at Norwich by redesignating an element of 9 Reserve Squadron.

No aircraft allocated.

Disbanded 20th May 1916 at Orfordness and merged with the Experimental Flight, Upavon to become the Experimental Armament Squadron within the Experimental Station, Orfordness.

Reformed 15th September 1916 at Woodford Green by redesignating an element of 39 Squadron. Became 37 Squadron, RAF from 1st April 1918 whilst at Woodham Mortimer.

B.E.2d 5778; B.E.12 A6317; B.E.2e 7237; B.E.12a; 1½ Strutter A8251; Pup A651; R.E.7 2232; B.E.12b; S.E.5a; Camel E5141 6; Snipe F2390.

Disbanded 1st July 1919 at Biggin Hill to become 39 Squadron.

Reformed 26th April 1937 at Feltwell from 'B' Flight of 214 Squadron.

37 (4.37–4.39)	Harrow I K6947, II K7001 37-S.
FJ (4.39–9.39)	Harrow I K6959 FJ-B, II K7031 FJ-O; Wellington I L4352.
LF (9.39–3.46)	Wellington I L4352, IA L7779 LF-P, IC T2822 LF-D, II Z8417, III DF686, VIII HF916, X HF614 LF-S; Liberator VI KH407 LF-J.

Disbanded 31st March 1946 at Shallufa, Egypt.

Reformed 15th April 1946 at Fayid, Egypt, by renumbering 214 Squadron.

Lancaster III RF298 T, VII NX792.

Disbanded 1st April 1947 at Shallufa, Egypt.

Reformed 14th September 1947 at Ein Shemar, Palestine, by redesignating an element of 38 Squadron.

Lancaster III RF308 F; Shackleton MR.2 WL800 X.

Disbanded 7th September 1967 at Khormaksar, Aden.

38 SQUADRON, RFC, later 38 SQUADRON, RAF, later 38 (SHADOW) SQUADRON, RAF, later 38 (RESERVE) SQUADRON, RAF
Formed 1st April 1916 at Thetford by redesignating an element of 12 Reserve Squadron.

No aircraft known.

Disbanded 22nd May 1916 at Thetford to become 25 Reserve Squadron.

Reformed 14th July 1916 at Castle Bromwich by redesignating an element of 54 Squadron. Became 38 Squadron, Royal Air Force from 1st April 1918 whilst at Melton Mowbray.

B.E.12 6159; B.E.2b, B.E.2b 6297; F.E.2b B422, F.E.2d A6493.

Disbanded 4th July 1918 at Hawkinge.

Reformed 16th September 1935 at Mildenhall from 'B' Flight of 99 Squadron.

Nil (9.35–12.38)	Heyford I K3493, IA K4041, III K6863; Hendon K5087 E.
NH (12.38–9.39)	Wellington I L4391 NH-A.
HD (9.39– .42)	Wellington I L4307, IA N2953 HD-R, IC P9249 HD-T.
Nil (.42–6.46)	Wellington IC W5624 J, II Z8360 E, VIII LB177 S, X HZ308 A, XI HZ394 S, XIII HZ881 F, XIV NC771 C; Warwick I BV436 X, II HG414.
RL (6.46– .49)	Lancaster III RE120 RL-X.
Nil (.49–3.67)	Lancaster III SW374 Z; Shackleton MR.2 WL798 X.
Also used	Tutor K3276; Magister P2378.

Disbanded 31st March 1967 at Hal Far, Malta.

Reformed 1st July 1970 at St Mawgan as 38 (Shadow) Squadron within 236 Operational Conversion Unit. Redesignated 38 (Reserve) Squadron from 1991.

Nimrod MR.2.

Disbanded 30th September 1992 at St Mawgan to become 42

(Reserve) Squadron, being the Nimrod Operational Conversion Unit.

39 SQUADRON, RFC, later 39 SQUADRON, RAF, later 39 (1 PHOTOGRAPHIC RECONNAISSANCE UNIT) SQUADRON

Formed 15th April 1916 at Hounslow by redesignating an element of 19 Reserve Aeroplane Squadron. Became 39 Squadron, RAF from 1st April 1918 whilst at North Weald.

B.E.2c 4112; Bristol Scout; B.E.12 6493, B.E.12a A6326; F.E.2b 7004; B.E.2e B4453; Nieuport 20; F.K.8 B237; S.E.5; Camel; F.2B B1350.

Disbanded 16th November 1918 during deployment to Bavichove, Belgium, from North Weald.

Reformed 1st July 1919 at Biggin Hill by redesignating 37 Squadron.

Nil (7.18–9.39)	*D.H.9A J7819 5, D.H.9A DC J8471; Fairey IIIF K1699; Wapiti I DC J9083, IIA J9481 9; Hart K2119 9; Audax K4862; Blenheim I L1498.*
SF	*Allocated for the period April to September 1939 but no evidence of use.*
XZ (9.39–12.40)	*Blenheim I L8543 XZ.*
Nil (12.40–9.46)	*Blenheim I L8385; Maryland I AR749; Martin 167F AX690; Beaufort I DE122 D, II AW290 S; Beaufighter X NE362 J; Marauder III HD607 F; Mosquito VI TE662, III VT610, FB.26 KA407.*
Also used	*Avro 504K H2522; Hind K6826; Magister P2401; Ju 87B HK827.*

Disbanded 8th September 1946 at Khartoum, Sudan.

Reformed 1st April 1948 at Khartoum, Sudan.

Tempest VI.6 NX247.

Disbanded 28th February 1949 at Khartoum.

Reformed 1st March 1949 at Fayid, Egypt.

Mosquito NF.36 RK976 F; Meteor NF.13 WM327 E, Meteor T.7 WL431.

Disbanded 30th June 1958 at Luqa, Malta.

Reformed 1st July 1958 at Luqa, Malta, by renumbering 69 Squadron.

Canberra PR.3 WE173 S, PR.9 XH170 E.

Disbanded 1st June 1982 at Wyton to become 1 Photographic Reconnaissance Unit.

Reformed 1st July 1992 at Wyton as 39 (1 Photographic Reconnaissance Unit) Squadron by redesignating 1 Photographic Reconnaissance Unit.

A	*Canberra T.4 WT480 BC, PR.7 WT509 BR, PR.9 XH168 AB.*

Current 1st April 1998 at Marham.

40 SQUADRON, RFC, later 40 SQUADRON, RAF

Formed 26th February 1916 at Fort Grange, Gosport, by redesignating an element of 23 Squadron. Became 40 Squadron, RAF from 1st April 1918 whilst at Bruay, France.

B.E.2c; Avro 504; F.E.8 7624 6; Nieuport 17 B1551 K; Nieuport 23 A6781; S.E.5 A8913, S.E.5a D3540 K.

Disbanded 4th July 1919 at Tangmere.

Reformed 1st April 1931 at Upper Heyford.

Nil (4.31–10.39)	*Gordon I K2625; Hart (Special) K4420; Hind L7176; Battle K9236.*
OX (10.38–9.39)	*Battle K9308 OX-S.*
BL (9.39–2.42)	*Battle K9360; Blenheim IV L9402 BL-U; Wellington IC R1464 BL-L, II W5454.*
Also used	*Blenheim I L1110.*

Disbanded 14th February 1942 at Luqa, Malta. The UK element at Alconbury became 156 Squadron.

Reformed 1st May 1942 at Abu Sueir, Egypt, by redesignating the Middle East detachment of 40 Squadron.

Wellington IC AD651 BL-S, III HF794 BL-W, X HF525 BL-R; Liberator VI KK313 BL-F; Lancaster VII NX683 BL-G.

Disbanded 1st April 1947 at Shallufa, Egypt.

Reformed 1st December 1947 at Abingdon.

Nil (12.47–6.49)	*York C.1 MW206.*
LE (6.49–3.50)	*York C.1 MW309 LE-H.*

Disbanded 15th March 1950 at Bassingbourn.

Reformed 28th October 1953 at Coningsby.

Canberra B.2 WJ605.

Disbanded 1st February 1957 at Upwood.

41 SQUADRON, RFC, later 41 SQUADRON, RAF

Formed 15th April 1916 at Fort Rowner, Gosport, by redesignating an element of 28 Squadron.

No aircraft known.

Disbanded 22nd May 1916 at Fort Rowner, Gosport, to become 27 Reserve Squadron.

Reformed 14th July 1916 at Fort Rowner, Gosport, by redesignating an element of 27 Reserve Squadron. Became 41 Squadron, RAF from 1st April 1918 whilst at Alquines, France.

Vickers F.B.5; D.H.2; F.E.8 7616 2; D.H.5 A9474 F; S.E.5a F5547 Y.

Disbanded 31st December 1919 at Croydon.

Reformed 1st April 1923 at Northolt.

Nil (4.23–1.39)	*Snipe E6316; Siskin III J7173 R, IIIA J8657 O, IIIDC J9203; Bulldog II J9571, IIA K2184 K; Demon K3773; Fury II K7266.*
PN (1.39–9.39)	*Spitfire I K9843.*
EB (9.39–4.46)	*Spitfire I X4178 EB-K, IIA P7666 EB-Z, VA W3185, VB BL248 EB-R, XII EN605 EB-R, XIV.*
Also used	*Dingo J7006; Hawfinch J8776; Gipsy Moth J9927; Avro 504K E3460, Avro 504N K1040; Tiger Moth II T6304; Auster IV MS951; Fw 190F-8 EB.*

Disbanded 1st April 1946 at B.116 (Wunstorf), Germany, to become 26 Squadron.

Reformed 1st April 1946 at Dalcross by renumbering 122 Squadron.

EB (4.46–2.51)	*Spitfire F.21 LA210 EB-X; Oxford I PG944; Harvard IIB KF128; Hornet F.1 PX242 EB-X, F.3 PX294 EB-E.*
Nil (2.51–1.58)	*Meteor F.4 VZ415, Meteor T.7 WF848, F.8 WE867 S; Hunter F.5 WP187 R.*
Also used	*Mosquito III VA927; Vampire T.11 WZ589.*

Disbanded 31st January 1958 at Biggin Hill.

Reformed 1st February 1958 at Coltishall by renumbering 141 Squadron.

Javelin T.3; FAW.4 XA758 S, FAW.5 XA707 A, FAW.8 XJ129 A.

Disbanded 31st December 1963 at Wattisham.

Reformed 1st September 1965 at West Raynham.

Bloodhound 2.

Disbanded 1st July 1970 at West Raynham.

Reformed 1st April 1972 at Coningsby.

Phantom FGR.2 XV493 F.

Disbanded 31st March 1977 at Coningsby.

Reformed 1st April 1977 at Coltishall having commenced training from 1st October 1976 as 41 Squadron (Designate).

Nil	*Jaguar GR.1 XZ363 A, GR.1A XZ107 H, T.2 XX842 T, T.2A XX846 Y.*
G	*Jaguar GR.1 XX748 GK, GR.1A XX970 GH, T.2A.*

Current 1st April 1998 at Coltishall.

42 SQUADRON, RFC, later 42 SQUADRON, later 42 (RESERVE) SQUADRON, RAF

Formed 26th February 1916 at Netheravon by redesignating an

element of 19 Squadron. Became 42 Squadron, RAF from 1st April 1918 whilst at Chocques, France.

B.E.2d 5856, B.E.2e 7073; R.E.8 B2256.

Disbanded 26th June 1919 at Netheravon.

Reformed 14th December 1936 at Donibristle by redesignating 2 Coastal Defence Development Flight, Coastal Defence Development Unit.

Nil (12.36–9.39)	*Vildebeest I K2810, III K4607, IV K6412.*
QD	*Allocated for the period April to September 1939 but no evidence of use.*
AW (9.39–6.42)	*Vildebeest III K6397, IV K6411 AW-D; Beaufort I L4488 AW-F, II AW286 AW-M.*
Nil (6.42–.43)	*Blenheim V BA200 M.*
AW (.43–6.45)	*Blenheim V BA455 AW-X; Hurricane IIC LE623 AW-S, IV KZ244 AW-C, XIIA PJ745.*
Also used	*Anson I N5053.*

Disbanded 30th June 1945 at Dalbumgarh, India.

Reformed 1st July 1945 at Meiktila, Burma, by redesignating 146 Squadron.

AW	*Thunderbolt II KL315 AW-F.*
Also used	*Harvard IIB FE600.*

Disbanded 30th December 1945 at Meiktila.

Reformed 1st October 1946 at Thorney Island by renumbering 254 Squadron.

QM	*Beaufighter X RD578 QM-D.*
Also used	*Harvard IIB KF108.*

Disbanded 15th October 1947 at Thorney Island.

Reformed 28th June 1952 at St Eval.

A (6.52–.56)	*Shackleton MR.1 VP293 A-F, MR.1A WG511 A-A, MR.2 WL743 A-F.*
42 (.56–.68)	*Shackleton MR.2 WL757 42-B, MR.3 XF701 42-B.*
Nil (.68–9.92)	*Shackleton MR.3 WR978; Nimrod MR.1 XV226, MR.2 XV233.*
Also used	*Oxford II W6611; Varsity T.1 WF330.*

Disbanded 30th September 1992 at St Mawgan.

Reformed 1st October 1992 at Kinloss as 42 (Reserve) Squadron, being the Nimrod Operational Conversion Unit, by renumbering 38 (Reserve) Squadron.

Nimrod MR.2 XV226.

Current 1st April 1998 at Kinloss.

43 SQUADRON, RFC, later 43 (CHINA BRITISH) SQUADRON, RAF
Formed 15th April 1916 at Stirling by redesignating an element of 18 Reserve Squadron. Became 43 Squadron, RAF from 1st April 1918 whilst at Avesnes-le-Comte, France.

F.K.3; B.E.2c; Avro 504; Bristol Scout D 7044; 1½ Strutter A8337 A4; Camel D1785 Z; Snipe E8064 F.

Disbanded 31st December 1919 at Spitalgate.

Reformed 1st July 1925 at Henlow.

Nil (7.23–11.38)	*Snipe E8165; Gamecock I J7905; Siskin IIIA J9341 U, IIIDC J9201; Fury K1928.*
NQ (11.38–9.39)	*Hurricane I L1847 NQ-J.*
FT (9.39–5.47)	*Hurricane I P3386 FT-Y, IIA Z2325 FT-N, IIB Z3316 FT-E, IIC HV407 FT-S; Spitfire VC BR288 FT-F, VB ES246 FT-W, VIII MT776 FT-H, IXC JL351 FT-F.*
Also used	*Avro 504K H3105, Avro 504N J8498; Hart Trainer K3157; Harvard III EZ357.*

Disbanded 16th May 1947 at Treviso, Italy.

Reformed 11th February 1949 at Tangmere by renumbering 266 Squadron.

SW (2.49–4.51)	*Meteor F.4 RA425 SW-P, F.8 VZ513 SW-Y.*
Nil (4.51–10.67)	*Meteor F.8 WH466 R; Hunter F.1 WT641 T, F.4 WT719, F.6 XF456 A, T.7 XL613, FGA.9 XJ684 D.*

Also used	*Meteor T.7 VW456 X; Oxford I PG969.*

Disbanded 7th November 1967 at Khormaksar, Aden.

Reformed 1st September 1969 at Leuchars by redesignating the Phantom Conversion Flight.

Nil (9.69–)	*Phantom FG.1 XT860 L.*
A ( )	*Phantom FG.1 XT860 AL.*
G ( )	*Tornado F.3 ZE962 GB, F.3T ZH554 GJ.*

Current 1st April 1998 at Leuchars.

44 SQUADRON, RFC, later 44 (RHODESIA) SQUADRON, RAF
Formed 15th April 1916 at Catterick by redesignating an element of 6 Reserve Squadron.

No aircraft known.

Disbanded 22nd May 1916 at Turnhouse to become 26 Reserve Squadron.

Reformed 24th July 1917 at Hainault Farm by redesignating an element of 39 Squadron. Became 44 Squadron, RAF from 1st April 1918 whilst at Hainault Farm.

1½ Strutter A8778 1; Camel B5402 2.

Disbanded 31st December 1919 at North Weald.

Reformed 8th March 1937 at Wyton.

Nil (3.37–10.38)	*Hind K5401; Blenheim I K7134.*
JW (10.38–9.39)	*Blenheim I L1267 JW-Q; Anson I N9680; Hampden I L4085 JW-A.*
KM (9.39–1.51)	*Hampden I AE202 KM-K; Manchester I L7453; Lancaster I R5508 KM-B, III PB251/G KM-O, I/Spec PD128; Lincoln II RF423 KM-K.*
Nil (1.51–7.57)	*Washington B.1 WF510; Canberra B.2 WH857.*
Also used	*Oxford II EB994.*

Disbanded 15th July 1957 at Honington.

Reformed 10th August 1960 at Waddington by redesignating an element of 83 Squadron.

Vulcan B.1 XA901, B.1A XH476, B.2 XL319.

Disbanded 21st December 1982 at Waddington.

44 SQUADRON CONVERSION FLIGHT
Formed 16th January 1942 at Waddington.

KM	*Manchester I L7430; Lancaster I R5540.*

Disbanded 9th November 1942 at Waddington and merged with 9 and 49 Squadron Conversion Flights to become 1661 Heavy Conversion Unit.

44 SQUADRON HAVOC FLIGHT
Formed 29th December 1940 at Waddington to carry out experimental night fighter defence tactics.

Havoc I BB891.

Disbanded 15th February 1941 at Waddington.

45 SQUADRON, RFC, later 45 SQUADRON, RAF, later 45 (SHADOW) SQUADRON, RAF, later 45 (RESERVE) SQUADRON, RAF
Formed 1st March 1916 at Fort Grange, Gosport, by redesignating an element of 22 Squadron. Became 45 Squadron, RAF from 1st April 1918 whilst at Grossa, Italy.

Avro 504; Martinsyde S.1; B.E.2c; Bristol Scout; F.E.2b; Henry Farman F.20; 1½ Strutter B2583; Nieuport 10; Nieuport 12; Nieuport 20 A6740; Camel B2321 S; Snipe E8081.

Disbanded 31st December 1919 at Eastleigh.

Reformed 1st April 1921 at Helwan, Egypt.

D.H.9A J7832 1; Vimy J7443; Vimy Ambulance J7143; Vernon I J6869, II J7134, III Ambulance J6904; Victoria III J7927.

Disbanded 17th January 1927 at Hinaidi, Iraq, and absorbed by 47 Squadron.

Reformed 25th April 1927 at Heliopolis, Egypt.

Nil (4.29–4.39)	*D.H.9A J7093 2; Fairey IIIF J9655 7; Gordon K2745; Vincent K4682; Wellesley K7774.*

DD (4.39–9.39)	Wellesley K7782 DD-M; Blenheim I L6663.
OB (9.39–5.55)	Wellesley K7782; Vildebeest IV K8087; Blenheim I L6663, IV T1823; Vengeance I AN841, IA EZ879 OB-L, II AN656 OB-H; Mosquito VI RF964 OB-Z; Beaufighter X RD858 OB-V; Brigand B.1 VS859 OB-V, MET.3 VS821; Buckmaster T.1 RP198 OB-Z; Hornet F.3 WB911 OB-B, FB.4 WF973.
Nil (5.55–1.70)	Vampire FB.9 WL555; Venom FB.1 WR312 D; Canberra B.2 WJ632, T.4 WD963, B.15 WJ766, B.16 WT370.
Also used	Harvard IIB KF141; Mosquito III RR290; Vampire T.11 WZ610.

Disbanded 18th February 1970 at Tengah, Malaya.

Reformed 1st August 1972 at West Raynham.

Hunter FGA.9 XG130 61.

Disbanded 26th July 1976 at Wittering.

Reformed 1st January 1984 at Honington as 45 (Shadow) Squadron, being the Tornado Weapons Conversion Unit.

Tornado GR.1 ZA393; GR.1(T) ZA594.

Disbanded 31st March 1992 at Lossiemouth to become 15 (Reserve) Squadron.

Reformed 1st July 1992 at Finningley as 45 (Reserve) Squadron by redesignating the Multi-engine Training Squadron of 6 Flying Training School.

Jetstream T.1 XX482 J.

Current 1st April 1998 at Cranwell as the Multi-engine Training Squadron of 3 Flying Training School.

46 SQUADRON, RFC, later 46 (UGANDA) SQUADRON, RAF
Formed 19th April 1916 at Brooklands by redesignating an element of 2 Reserve Squadron. Became 46 Squadron, RAF from 1st April 1918 whilst at Filescamp Farm, France.

B.E.2c 5773, B.E.2e 7060; Nieuport 12 A3274; Nieuport 20; 1½ Strutter A882; Pup B1719 4; Camel D6603.

Disbanded 31st December 1919 at Rendcomb.

Reformed 3rd September 1936 at Kenley from 'B' Flight of 17 Squadron.

Nil (9.36–4.39)	Gauntlet II K7794; Hurricane I L1802.
RJ (4.39–9.39)	Gauntlet II; Hurricane I L1853.
PO (9.39–6.41)	Hurricane I V7360 PO-B.
Nil (6.41–12.44)	Beaufighter I V8317 C, VI ND175 Y, X JM383 X; Mosquito VI HJ671.
XK (1.45–2.50)	Stirling IV LK555, V PJ971 XK-S; Dakota IV KN241 XK-K.

Disbanded 20th February 1950 at Oakington.

Reformed 15th August 1954 at Odiham.

Meteor T.7 VW452 Z, NF.11 WM260, NF.12 WS611 N, NF.14 WS846 R; Javelin FAW.1 XA621 F, FAW.2 XA776 N, T.3.

Disbanded 30th June 1961 at Waterbeach.

Reformed 1st December 1966 at Abingdon.

Andover C.1 XS603.

Disbanded 31st August 1975 at Thorney Island.

47 SQUADRON, RFC, later 47 SQUADRON, RAF
Formed 1st March 1916 at Beverley. Became 47 Squadron, RAF from 1st April 1918 whilst at Yanesh, Macedonia.

B.E.12 6602; B.E.2c 2720; Avro 504A 7737; F.K.3 6226; Bristol Scout D 5570; D.H.2 A4772; F.B.19 A5226; B.E.2e A8691; S.E.5a B692; Bristol M1C C4909; F.K.8 B3590; D.H.9 C6236, D.H.9A F1086.

Disbanded 20th October 1919 at Beketovka, Russia, to become 11, 12 and 13 Squadrons, Russian 7th Division and to be replaced by the Royal Air Force Training Mission, South Russia.

Reformed 1st February 1920 at Helwan, Egypt, by renumbering 206 Squadron.

Nil (2.20–9.39)	D.H.9 D602 T, D.H.9A JR7107 B; Dolphin J174; Fairey IIIF Floatplane J9802, IVM J9138; Gordon I K2704, Gordon I Floatplane JR9161; Vincent K6362; Wellesley I K8531.
EW	Allocated for the period April to September 1939 but no evidence of use.
KU (9.39–9.42)	Gordon I K2764; Vincent K6364; Wellesley I L2675 KU-O.
Nil (9.42–2.45)	Wellesley I K8528; Beaufort I DE118 S; Beaufighter X NE502 H; Mosquito VI HR523 Z.
KU (2,45–3.46)	Mosquito VI TE650 KU-Y

Disbanded 21st March 1946 at Butterworth, Malaya.

Reformed 1st September 1946 at Qastina, Palestine, by renumbering 644 Squadron.

Halifax VII NA379, IX RT923 H; Hastings C.1 TG524 L, C.2 WD479 K; Beverley C.1 XB285 J.

Disbanded 31st October 1967 at Abingdon.

Reformed 25th February 1968 at Fairford.

Hercules C.1 XV201, C.3 XV302.

Current 1st April 1998 at Lyneham.

48 SQUADRON, RFC, later 48 SQUADRON, RAF
Formed 15th April 1916 at Netheravon by redesignating an element of 7 Reserve Squadron. Became 48 Squadron, RAF from 1st April 1918 whilst at Conteville, France.

B.E.12 6562; F.2A A3340, F.2B C814 12.

Disbanded 1st April 1920 at Quetta, India, to become 5 Squadron.

Reformed 25th November 1935 at Bicester from 'C' Flight of 101 Squadron.

Nil (11.35–9.39)	Fairey IIIF J9162; Cloud K4302; Anson I K6156 C.
ZW	Allocated for the period April to September 1939 but no evidence of use.
OY (9.39–12.42)	Anson I R3318 OY-A; Beaufort I L9821 OY-K; Hudson III V9105 OY-Y, IIIA FH237, V AM546 OY-G.
Nil (12.42–2.44)	Hudson VI FK410 Y; Beaufighter II.
I2 (2.44–1.46)	Dakota III KG394 I2-AM, IV KN413 I2-WH.

Disbanded 15th January 1946 at Patenga, Malaya.

Reformed 15th February 1946 at Kallang, Singapore, by renumbering 215 Squadron.

Dakota IV KP211; Valetta C.1 VX528 Z; Hastings C.1 TG516 GPL, C.2 WD481 GPA; Beverley C.1 XB262 W.

Disbanded 1st April 1967 at Changi, Singapore.

Reformed 2nd October 1967 at Changi, Singapore.

Hercules C.1 XV201.

Disbanded 9th January 1976 at Lyneham.

49 SQUADRON, RFC, later 49 SQUADRON, RAF
Formed 15th April 1915 at Dover by redesignating an element of 13 Reserve Squadron. Became 49 Squadron, RAF from 1st April 1918 whilst at Petite Synthe, France.

B.E.2c 2505; Avro 504; R.E.7; Elephant A4001; D.H.4 A7694 6; D.H.9 C6114 M.

Disbanded 18th July 1919 at Bickendorf, Germany.

Reformed 10th February 1936 at Bircham Newton from 'C' Flight of 18 Squadron.

Nil (2.36–4.39)	Hind K6800; Hampden I L4040.
XU (4.39–9.39)	Hampden I L4039 UX-D.
EA (9.39–4.51)	Hampden I X2900 EA-S; Manchester L7453 EA-T; Lancaster I RA531 EA-S, III DV238 EA-D; Lincoln II RE229 EA-J.
Nil (4.51–8.55)	Lincoln II SX923.
Also used	Hornet Moth BK830.

Disbanded 1st August 1955 at Upwood.

Reformed 1st May 1956 at Wittering.

Valiant B.1 WZ366, B(PR).1 WZ378.

Disbanded 1st May 1965 at Marham.

49 SQUADRON CONVERSION FLIGHT
Formed 16th May 1942 at Scampton.

EA	*Manchester I L7296 EA-Y; Lancaster I R5842.*

Disbanded 9th November 1942 at Scampton and merged with 9 and 44 Squadron Conversion Flights to become 1661 Heavy Conversion Unit.

50 SQUADRON, RFC, later 50 SQUADRON, RAF
Formed 15th May 1916 at Swingate Down by redesignating an element of 20 Reserve Squadron. Became 50 Squadron RAF from 1st April 1918 whilst at Bekesbourne.

B.E.2c 2711; B.E.12 6185; Vickers ES.1 7759; B.E.12a A6308, B.E.12b C9992; B.E.2e B4511; Bristol M.1B A5139; R.E.8 A3840; F.B.19 A2992; F.K.8 B229; Pup B1711; S.E.5a D5995; Camel B7445.

Disbanded 13th June 1919 at Bekesbourne.

Reformed 3rd May 1937 at Waddington.

Nil (5.37–12.38)	*Hind K6737.*
QX (12.38–9.39)	*Hampden I L4076 QX-D.*
VN (9.39–1.51)	*Hampden I P2094 VN-Z; Manchester I L7301; Lancaster I R5689 VN-N, III ME382 VN-A; Lincoln II RE377 VN-D.*
Also used	*Anson I N9829; Magister T9676; Tiger Moth II T6243.*

Disbanded 31st January 1951 at Waddington.

Reformed 15th August 1952 at Binbrook.

Canberra B.2 WJ641.

Disbanded 1st October 1959 at Upwood.

Reformed 1st August 1961 at Waddington by redesignating an element of 617 Squadron.

Vulcan B.1 XH497, B.1A XH500, B.2 XL426, B.2(K) XM571.

Disbanded 31st March 1984 at Waddington.

50 SQUADRON CONVERSION FLIGHT
Formed 16th May 1942 at Skellingthorpe.

VN	*Manchester I R5796; Lancaster I R5843.*

Disbanded 2nd August 1942 at Wigsley and absorbed with 83 Squadron Conversion Flight into 1654 Heavy Conversion Unit.

51 SQUADRON, RFC, later 51 SQUADRON, RAF
Formed 15th May 1916 at Norwich by redesignating an element of 9 Reserve Squadron. Became 51 Squadron RAF from 1st April 1918 whilst at Marham.

B.E.2c 4575, B.E.2d 6256; B.E.12 6161; F.E.2b B417, F.E.2d A6531; B.E.2e A1882; Elephant A4002 8; Amiens C8658; B.E.12b; Avro 504K A9785; Camel.

Disbanded 13th June 1919 at Suttons Farm.

Reformed 15th March 1937 at Driffield from 'B' Flight of 58 Squadron.

Nil (3.37–8.38)	*Virginia X K2666; Anson I K6277 T; Whitley II K7225, III K8941.*
UT (8.38–9.39)	*Whitley II K7228 UT-T, III K8980 UT-E.*
MH (9.39–5.45)	*Whitley III K9008 MH-J, IV K9043 MH-G, V Z9141 MH-J; Halifax II HR951 MH-X, III MZ465 MH-Y.*
LK (–1.44)	*('C' Flight) Halifax II JD266 LK-C.*
C6 (1.44–5.45)	*('C' Flight) Halifax II LK843 C6-F.*
TB (5.45–12.49)	*Stirling V PK115 TB-X; York C.1 MW287 TB-Z.*
MH (12.49–10.50)	*York C.1 MW331 MH-H.*
Also used	*Hudson III AE509.*

Disbanded 30th October 1950 at Bassingbourn.

Reformed 21st August 1958 at Watton by renumbering 192 Squadron.

Varsity T.1 WJ911; Canberra B.2 WJ640, T.4 WJ877, B.6 WJ768,

B.6(BS) WT305, Comet C.2(R) XK655; Hastings C.1 TG507; Nimrod R.1 XW665 65.

Current 1st April 1998 at Waddington.

52 SQUADRON, RFC, later 52 SQUADRON, RAF
Formed 15th May 1916 at Hounslow Heath by redesignating an element of 39 Squadron. Became 52 Squadron, RAF from 1st April 1918 whilst at Abbeville, France.

B.E.2c 2556; B.E.12; R.E.8 A4417 15; B.E.2e 7209, B.E.2f, B.E.2g; 1½ Strutter 7942.

Disbanded 23rd October 1919 at Lopcombe Corner.

Reformed 18th January 1937 at Abingdon by from 'B' Flight of 15 Squadron. Merged with 35, 63 and 207 Squadrons to become 1 Group Pool from 14th September 1939.

52 (1.37–4.39)	*Hind K5411; Battle K7602 52-B.*
MB (4.39–9.39)	*Battle K7602 MB-B; Anson I N5028 MB-X.*
ZE (9.39–4.40)	*Battle L5203; Anson I N5034.*

Disbanded 6th April 1940 at Benson and merged with 63 Squadron to become 12 Operational Training Unit.

Reformed 1st July 1941 at Habbaniya, Iraq.

Audax K7504; Blenheim IV Z9544 X; Baltimore III AG861, IIIA FA367, IV FA571, V FW348.

Disbanded 31st March 1944 at Gibraltar.

Reformed 1st July 1944 at Dum-Dum, India, from 'C' and 'D' Flights of 353 Squadron.

Dakota III FL555, IV KN547 P; Liberator VI KN745; Tiger Moth II DG456; Expeditor; Harvard IIB; Valetta C.1 VX509.

Disbanded 25th April 1966 at Butterworth, Malaya.

Reformed 1st December 1966 at Abingdon.

Andover C.1 XS607.

Disbanded 31st December 1969 at Changi, Singapore.

53 SQUADRON, RFC, later 53 SQUADRON, RAF
Formed 15th May 1916 at Catterick by redesignating an element of 14 Reserve Squadron. Became 53 Squadron, RAF from 1st April 1918 whilst at Boisdinghem, France.

F.K.3; Avro 504; B.E.12; B.E.2e A3162, B.E.2g; R.E.8 A4632.

Disbanded 25th October 1919 at Old Sarum.

Reformed 28th June 1937 at Farnborough.

Nil (6.37–1.39)	*Hector I K8147; Valentia K2344; Blenheim IV L4837.*
TE (1.39–9.39)	*Blenheim IV L4837 TE-G.*
PZ (9.39–2.43)	*Blenheim IV Z5765 PZ-A; Hudson III V9096 PZ-P, IIIA FH271, V AM727 PZ-D, VI FK479.*
Nil (2.43–6.44)	*Whitley VII LA813; Liberator III FK225, V BZ793 H, VI EV899 W.*
FH (6.44–2.46)	*Liberator VI KN748 FH-J, VIII KH222 FH-H.*

Disbanded 28th February 1946 at Gransden Lodge.

Reformed 28th February 1946 at Upwood by renumbering 102 Squadron.

Liberator VI KH200, VIII KN720; Oxford I BF972.

Disbanded 15th June 1946 at Upwood.

Reformed 1st December 1946 at Netheravon by renumbering 187 Squadron.

PU	*Dakota IV KN590 PU-H; Horsa II RZ180.*

Disbanded 31st July 1949 at Waterbeach.

Reformed 1st August 1949 at Topcliffe by redesignating elements of 47 and 297 Squadrons.

Hastings C.1 TG536 GAU; C.2 WD491 GAF; Beverley C.1 XH116 Y.

Disbanded 30th June 1963 at Abingdon and absorbed by 47 Squadron.

Reformed 1st January 1966 at Fairford.

Belfast C.1 XR362.

Disbanded 14th September 1976 at Brize Norton.

54 SQUADRON, RFC, later 54 SQUADRON, RAF
Formed 15th May 1916 at Castle Bromwich by redesignating an element of 5 Reserve Squadron. Became 54 Squadron, RAF from 1st April 1918 whilst at Conteville, France.

B.E.2c; B.E.12; Avro 504; Pup A648 13; Camel B7320 P.

Disbanded 25th October 1919 at Yatesbury.

Reformed 15th January 1930 at Hornchurch.

Nil (1.30–4.39)	Siskin IIIDC J7156; Bulldog IIA K1605, Bulldog Trainer K3178; Gauntlet II K5302; Gladiator I K8015.
DL (4.39–9.39)	Spitfire I K9883 DL-T.
KL (9.39–6.42)	Spitfire I R6708 KL-S, IIA P7354, VA R7279 KL-S, VB AA761, IIB P8697.
Nil (9.42–4.44)	Spitfire VC A58-203.
DL (4.44–10.45)	Spitfire VIII A58-360 DL-R.

Disbanded 31st October 1945 at Melbourne, Australia.

Reformed 15th November 1945 at Chilbolton by renumbering 183 Squadron.

HF (11.45–4.48)	Tempest II MW774 HF-X; Vampire F.1 TG298 HF-F.
Nil (4.48–4.74)	Vampire F.3 VT864 H, FB.5 VZ115; Meteor F.8 WK673, T.7 VZ638 X; Hunter F.1 WW641 B, F.4 WV281 M, F.6 XE645 P, T.7 XL596, FGA.9 XF517 V; Phantom FGR.2 XV475 O.
Also used	Vampire T.11 XE955.

Disbanded 22nd April 1974 at Coningsby.

Reformed 23 April 1974 at Lossiemouth having commenced training from 28th March 1974 as 54 Squadron (Designate).

G	Jaguar GR.1 XZ355 GA, GR.1A XZ377 GC, GR.1B, T.2 XX829 GT, T.2A XX146 GS, T.2B.

Current 1st April 1998 at Coltishall.

55 SQUADRON, RFC, later 55 SQUADRON, RAF, later 55 (RESERVE) SQUADRON, RAF
Formed 27th April 1918 at Castle Bromwich by redesignating elements of 34 Squadron and 5 Reserve Squadron. Became 55 Squadron, RAF from 1st April 1918 whilst at Tantonville, France.

B.E.2c; F.K.3; Avro 504; D.H.4 A2159.

Disbanded 22nd January 1920 at Shotwick.

Reformed 1st February 1920 at Suez, Egypt, by renumbering 142 Squadron.

Nil (2.20–11.46)	D.H.9, D.H.9A J7013 B3; Wapiti II J9240, IIA K1124 B3; Vincent I K6330; Blenheim I L4819, IV T2426 J; Baltimore I AG725, II AG763 X, III AH111 B, IIIA FA333 S, IV FA625 X, V FW291 X; Boston IV BZ564 Y, V BZ588 S; Mosquito FB.26 KA309.

Gloster Meteor F.3s of No 56 Squadron taken on 22nd May 1946.

GM   *Allocated for the period April to September 1939 but no evidence of use.*
Also used   *Nighthawk J6925; Lysander II P1739.*

Disbanded 1st December 1946 at Hassani, Greece.

Reformed 1st September 1960 at Honington.

Victor B.1A XH591, B(K).1 XA930, B(K).1A XH589, K.1 XA926, K.1A XH589, K.2 XH671. Also used Anson XIX TX196.

Disbanded 15th October 1993 at Marham.

Reformed 15th October 1993 at Brize Norton as 55 (Reserve) Squadron, being the VC-10 Operational Conversion Unit, by redesignating 241 Operational Conversion Unit.

VC-10 C.1, C.1K, K.2, K.3.

Disbanded 31st March 1996 at Brize Norton to become the Aircrew and Groundcrew Training Squadron.

Reformed 1st November 1996 at Cranwell as 55 (Reserve) Squadron, being the Dominie T.1 Squadron within 3 Flying Training School.

Dominie T.1.

Current 1st April 1998 at Cranwell.

55 SQUADRON TRAINING FLIGHT – see Air Depot Hinaidi Training Flight

56 SQUADRON, RFC, later 56 (PUNJAB) SQUADRON, RAF, later 56 (RESERVE) SQUADRON, RAF
Formed 8th June 1916 at Fort Rowner by redesignating an element of 28 Squadron, RFC. Became 56 Squadron, RAF from 1st April 1918 whilst at Valheureux, France.

Curtiss JN-3 7310; S.E.5 A8913 B2, S.E.5a B4863 C.

Disbanded 22nd January 1920 at Bircham Newton.

Reformed 1st February 1920 at Aboukir, Egypt, by renumbering 80 Squadron.

Snipe E7522.

Disbanded 23rd September 1922 at Aboukir.

Reformed 1st November 1922 at Hawkinge.

Nil (11.22–9.38)	*Avro 504K E3759, Avro 504N J8994; Snipe F2472, Snipe DC E6484; Grebe II J7417, IIDC J7585, IIIDC J7522; Siskin IIIA J8832, IIIDC J9192; Bulldog IIA K2216, Bulldog Trainer K3181; Gauntlet II K5296; Gladiator I K7988.*
LR (9.38–9.39)	*Hurricane I L1986 LR-Q.*
US (9.39–4.46)	*Hurricane I N2712 US-M, IIB Z2767 US-W; Typhoon IA R7588 US-X, IB DN317 US-C; Spitfire VB AB274, IX MK572 US-B; Tempest V NV974 US-K.*
Also used	*Magister P6354; Tiger Moth II T7241; Blenheim IV Z5866; Auster III NX536; V MT360.*

Disbanded 1st April 1946 at Fassberg, Germany, to become 16 Squadron.

Reformed 1st April 1946 at Bentwaters by renumbering 124 Squadron.

ON (4.46– .47)	*Meteor F.3 EE271 ON-H.*
US (.47–12.50)	*Meteor F.3 EE271 US-H, F.4 VT191 US-Q, T.7 WA670 US-A.*
Nil (12.50–6.76)	*Meteor F.8 WF643 J, T.7 WA629; Vampire T.11 WZ515; Swift F.1 WK207 N, F.2 WK245 H; Hunter F.5 WP116 W, F.6 XG157 H, T.7 XL609; Lightning F.1A XM172 S, F.3 XR725 Y, T.4 XM989 Z, T.5 XS417 Z, F.6 XS897 E.*

Disbanded 28th June 1976 at Wattisham.

Reformed 29th June 1976 at Coningsby having commenced training from 31st March 1976 as 56 Squadron (Designate).

Nil ( )	*Phantom FGR.2 XT914 Z.*
B ( )	*Phantom FGR.2 XV420 BT.*

Disbanded 1st July 1992 at Coningsby.

Reformed 1st July 1992 at Coningsby as 56 (Reserve) Squadron,

being the Tornado F.3 Operational Conversion Unit, by renumbering 65 (Reserve) Squadron.

A	*Tornado F.3 ZG770 AP, F.3T ZH557 AB.*

Current 1st April 1998 at Coningsby.

57 SQUADRON, RFC, later 57 SQUADRON, RAF, later 57 (RESERVE) SQUADRON, RAF
Formed 8th June 1916 at Copmanthorpe ('A' Flight) and Tadcaster ('B' and 'C' Flights) by redesignating an element of 33 Squadron. Became 57 Squadron, RAF from 1st April 1918 whilst at Le Quesnoy, France.

Avro 504A; B.E.2c; F.E.2d A22; D.H.4 H5290; D.H.9A J579 V.

Disbanded 31st December 1919 at South Carlton.

Reformed 20th October 1931 at Netheravon.

Nil (10.31–11.38)	*Hart K2435; Hind K6713; Blenheim I L1148.*
EQ (11.38–9.39)	*Blenheim I L1148 EQ-J.*
Nil (9.39–6.40)	*Blenheim I L8597, IV R3832.*
DX (6.40–11.45)	*Wellington I L4343, IA P9209, IC T2721 DX-S, II W5434 DX-Y, III X3658 DX-P; Lancaster I RA530 DX-Y, III ND503 DX-E; Lincoln II RF386 DX-Y.*
QT (.44 –11.45)	*('C' Flight) Lancaster I, III.*
Also used	*Manchester I L7386; Tiger Moth II T5429.*

Disbanded 25th November 1945 at East Kirby.

Reformed 26th November 1945 at Elsham Wolds by renumbering 103 Squadron.

DX 911.45–4.51)	*Lincoln II RE374 DX-H; Washington B.1 WF555 DX-H.*
Nil (4.51–12.57)	*Washington B.1 WF556; Canberra B.2 WJ977.*
Also used	*Anson XIX TX196.*

Disbanded 9th December 1957 at Coningsby.

Reformed 1st January 1959 at Honington.

Victor B.1 XH616, B.1A XH649, B(K).1A XH616, B(K).2 XH671.

Disbanded 30th June 1986 at Marham.

Reformed 1st July 1992 at Lyneham as 57 (Reserve) Squadron, being the Hercules Operational Training Unit, by redesignating 242 Operational Conversion Unit. Components of the Squadron, the Hercules Conversion Flight and the Hercules Training Flight, merged in 1966 to become the Hercules Conversion and Training Flight. Scheduled to become the C-130J Training Flight.

Hercules C.1, C.1K, C.3 – drawn from Lyneham Transport Wing.

Current 1st April 1998 at Lyneham.

58 SQUADRON, RFC, later 58 SQUADRON, RAF
Formed 8th June 1916 at Cramlington by redesignating an element of 36 Squadron. Became 58 Squadron, RAF from 1st April 1918 whilst at Auchel, France.

B.E.2c, B.E.2e; F.E.2b C9811; F.K.3 A9972; Handley Page O/400 B8811 A2; Vimy F3184.

Disbanded 1st February 1920 at Heliopolis, Egypt, to become 70 Squadron.

Reformed 1st April 1924 at Worthy Down.

Nil (4.24–11.38)	*Vimy IV J7441; Victoria III J7921; Virginia III J6992, V J7421, IX J7131 Q, X J6993 W; Anson I K6272; Whitley I K7209, II K7258; Heyford III K4041.*
BW (11.38–9.39)	*Heyford III K4041; Whitley II K7256, III K8964 BW-R.*
GE (9.39–4.43)	*Whitley III K9000 GE-J, V Z6469 GE-L, VII Z9374 GE-E.*
BY (4.43–5.45)	*Halifax II JP328 BY-H, III PN183 RG364 BY-V.*
Also used	*Avro 504K E9428; Bugle I J7235; Valentia K3162 N.*

Disbanded 25th May 1945 at Stornoway.

Reformed 1st October 1946 at Benson by renumbering 540 Squadron.

OT (10.46–10.51)	*Mosquito PR.34 PF668 OT-Y, III VT589 OT-Z;*

Anson XI NL183, XIX VL357 OT-P; Lincoln B.2 SX991 OT-C.

Nil (4.51–9.70)   Mosquito PR.35 TK656; Anson XIX VP514; Canberra PR.3 WE148, PR.7 WJ819, PR.9 XH168.

Disbanded 30th September 1970 at Wyton.

Reformed 1st August 1973 at Wittering by redesignating an element of 45 Squadron.

Hunter T.7 XF310 T, FGA.9 XJ694 94.

Disbanded 4th June 1976 at Wittering.

59 SQUADRON, RFC, later 59 SQUADRON, RAF
Formed 21st June 1916 at Narborough by redesignating an element of 35 Squadron. Became 59 Squadron, RAF from 1st April 1918 whilst at Fienvillers, France.

R.E.8 C2270; F.2B D2660.

Disbanded 4th August 1918 at Duren, Germany.

Reformed 28th June 1937 at Old Sarum.

Nil (6.37–9.38)	Hector K9698.
PJ (9.38–9.39)	Hector K9690 PJ-B; Blenheim IV L8791 PJ-Y.
TR (9.39–10.42)	Blenheim IV L8793 TR-M; Hudson III V9099, IIIA FH260 TR-X, V AM789 TR-C, VI EW904 TR-S; Liberator II AL507, III FL933 TR-S.
Nil (10.42–8.43)	Liberator III FL933 S; Fortress I AN519, II FA704 R, IIA FK209 J.
1 (8.43–7.44)	Liberator V BZ764 1-J.
WE (7.44–10.45)	Liberator V FL988 WE-R, VIII KH414 WE-B.
BY (10.45–10.50)	Liberator VI KG936 BY-J.
Also used	Anson I N9611; Mentor I L4405.

Disbanded 15th June 1946 at Waterbeach.

Reformed 1st December 1947 at Abingdon.

BY	York C.1 PE108 BY-E.

Disbanded 30th October 1950 at Bassingbourn.

Reformed 1st September 1956 at Gutersloh, Germany, by renumbering elements of the recently disbanded 102 Squadron.

Canberra B.2 WJ613, B(I).8 XK952, T.4 WH843.

Disbanded 4th January 1961 at Geilenkirchen, Germany, to become 3 Squadron.

60 SQUADRON, RFC, later 60 SQUADRON, RAF, later 60 (RESERVE) SQUADRON, RAF
Formed 15th May 1916 at Gosport as 60 Squadron RFC by redesignating an element of 1 Reserve Squadron. Became 60 Squadron, RAF from 1st April 1918 whilst at Fienvillers, France.

Morane G 482; Morane H; Morane I A198; Morane LA 5140; Morane N A122; Morane V A207; Morane BB 5167; Nieuport 16 A133; Spad 7 A253; Nieuport 17 A200 6A; Nieuport 23 B1575 B1; S.E.5 A8913, S.E.5a B533 A.

Disbanded 22nd January 1920 at Bircham Newton.

Reformed 1st April 1920 at Lahore by renumbering 97 Squadron.

Nil (4.20–4.39)	D.H.10A E5453 H; D.H.9A J7030 P; Fairey IIIF S1140 1; Wapiti I DC J9082, IIA J9717 S.
AD (4.39–9.39)	Blenheim I L4911 AD-H.
MU (9.39–2.42)	Blenheim I L8609 MU-X, IV T2291 MU-A.
Nil (2.42–8.43)	Buffalo I AN190; Blenheim IV Z7706.
MU (8.43–10.46)	Hurricane IIC HW788 MU-T; Thunderbolt II KL859 MU-T.
Nil (10.46–11.50)	Spitfire XVIII NH850 Z; Vampire FB.5 WA243, FB.9 WG882 D; Venom FB.1 WR372 E, FB.4 WR533 D; Meteor NF.14 WS810 F; Javelin T.3, FAW.9 XH841 D.
Also used	Hart K2128; Harvard IIB KF107; Spitfire VIII MT600; Vampire T.11 WZ611.

Disbanded 1st May 1968 at Tengah, Malaya.

Reformed 3rd February 1969 at Wildenrath, Germany, by redesignating the Royal Air Force Germany Communication Squadron.

Devon C.1 WB535; Heron CC.4 XR391; Pembroke C(PR).1 XL929; Andover C.1 XS597, CC.2 XS793.

Disbanded 1st April 1992 at Wildenrath and absorbed by 32 Squadron.

Reformed 1st July 1992 at Benson.

Wessex HC.2 XS674 R.

Disbanded 26th March 1997 at Benson.

Reformed 1st April 1997 at Shawbury as 60 (Reserve) Squadron, being the Defence Helicopter Flying School (RAF Element).

Squirrel HT.1 ZJ259 59; Griffin HT.1.

Current 1st April 1998 at Shawbury.

61 SQUADRON, RFC, later 61 SQUADRON, RAF
Formed 5th July 1916 at Wye by redesignating an element of 20 Reserve Squadron.

No aircraft known.

Disbanded 24th August 1916 at Wye and absorbed by 63 Squadron.

Reformed 24th July 1917 at Rochford by redesignating an element of 37 Squadron, RFC. Became 61 Squadron, RAF from 1st April 1918 whilst at Rochford.

Pup A6249; S.E.5a C8711; Camel; Vickers F.B.12c.

Disbanded 13th June 1919 at Rochford.

Reformed 8th March 1937 at Hemswell.

Nil (3.37–3.39)	Audax K7430; Anson K6306 P; Blenheim I K7160 U.
LS (3.39–9.39)	Hampden I L4114 LS-P.
QR (9.39–4.51)	Hampden I P4339 QR-H; Manchester I L7389 QR-J; Lancaster I DV294 QR-K, III ED860 QR-N, II DS604 QR-W; Lincoln II RF463 QR-P.
Nil (4.51–3.58)	Lincoln II SX979; Canberra B.2 WJ752.

Disbanded 31st March 1958 at Upwood.

61 SQUADRON CONVERSION FLIGHT
Formed 27th March 1942 at Woolfox Lodge.

QR	Manchester I L7286; Lancaster I R5853.

Disbanded 16th October 1942 at Swinderby and merged with 97, 106 and 207 Squadron Conversion Flights to become 1660 Heavy Conversion Unit.

62 SQUADRON, RFC, later 62 SQUADRON, RAF
Formed 28th July 1916 at Filton merging elements of 7 Reserve Squadron and 42 Squadron. Became 62 Squadron, RAF from 1st April 1918 whilst at Planques, France.

B.E.2c, B.E.2d, B.E.2e; R.E.7; Avro 504A; F.2B C4630 J.

Disbanded 31st July 1919 at Spich, Germany.

Reformed 3rd May 1937 at Abingdon from 'B' Flight of 40 Squadron.

Nil (5.37–11.38)	Hind K6773; Blenheim I L1108.
JO (11.38–9.39)	Blenheim I L1258 JO-E.
Nil (9.39–2.42)	Blenheim I L1101; Hudson III.

Dispersed 16th February 1942 at Semplak, Java, and absorbed by 1 Squadron, RAAF.

Reformed 30th April 1942 at Dum-Dum, India, by renumbering 139 Squadron.

Hudson III AE540, IIIA FH290 P; Dakota III FD915 L, IV KJ948.

Disbanded 15th March 1946 at Mingaladon, Burma.

Reformed 1st September 1946 at Palam, India, by renumbering 76 Squadron.

Dakota IV KP257.

Disbanded 10th August 1947 at Mauripur, India.

Reformed 8th December 1947 at Manston.

Dakota IV KN276.

Supermarine Spitfire Mk IAs of No 65 Squadron in early 1939.

Disbanded 1st June 1949 at Waterbeach.

Reformed 1st February 1960 at Woolfox Lodge.

Bloodhound I.

Disbanded 30th September 1964 at Woolfox Lodge.

63 SQUADRON, RFC, later 63 SQUADRON, RAF, later 63 (SHADOW) SQUADRON, RAF, later 63 (RESERVE) SQUADRON, RAF

Formed 5th July 1916 at Stirling by merging elements of 43 and 61 Squadrons. Became 63 Squadron, RAF from 1st April 1918 whilst at Samarra, Mesopotamia.

D.H.4; B.E.12; B.E.2c 2846, B.E.2e; Avro 504; F.K.3; R.E.8 A4346; Bristol Scout; Spad S.VII; Elephant; Bristol M.1C; S.E.5a.

Disbanded 17th February 1920 at Baghdad, Iraq, and absorbed by 30 Squadron.

Reformed 15th February 1937 at Andover from 'B' Flight of 12 Squadron. Merged with 35, 52 and 207 Squadrons to become 1 Group Pool from 14th September 1939.

63 (2.37–11.38)	*Hind; Audax K7465; Battle K7650 63-M.*
NE (11.38–5.39)	*Battle K9423 NE-G.*
ON (5.39–9.39)	*Battle L4958 ON-R; Anson I N5035.*

Disbanded 8th April 1940 at Benson and merged with 52 Squadron to become 12 Operational Training Unit.

Reformed 15th June 1942 at Gatwick from an element of 239 Squadron.

Mustang I AG498 P, IA FD546; Hurricane IIC LF330; Spitfire VB BM577 V. Also used Tutor K3396; Master III W8996; Tiger Moth II T7408.

Disbanded 1st February 1945 at North Weald.

Reformed 1st September 1946 at Middle Wallop by renumbering 164 Squadron.

UB (9.46–4.51)	*Spitfire XVI SL689 UB-A; Meteor F.3 EE425 UB-G, F.4 VT280 UB-K.*
Nil (4.51–10.58)	*Meteor T.7 VZ641 Z, F.8 WK720 D; Hunter F.6 XE647 E.*
Also used	*Vampire T.11 WZ421.*

Disbanded 30th October 1958 at Waterbeach.

Reformed 1st June 1963 at Chivenor as 63 (Shadow) Squadron within 229 Operational Conversion Unit, the Tactical Weapons Unit from 2nd September 1974, 2 Tactical Weapons Unit from 1st April 1981 and 7 Flying Training School from 1st April 1992. Redesignated 63 (Reserve) Squadron from 1991.

Hunter (FCS, CFE); Hunter (229 OCU); Hunter, Hawk (TWU); Hawk (2 TWU).

Disbanded 23rd September 1992 at Chivenor to become 19 (Reserve) Squadron.

64 SQUADRON, RFC, later 64 SQUADRON, later 64 (SHADOW) SQUADRON, RAF

Formed 31st August 1916 at Sedgeford by redesignating an element of 45 Squadron. Became 64 Squadron, RAF from 1st April 1918 whilst at Le Hameau, France.

Henry Farman F.20; B.E.2c; F.E.2b A5455; Avro 504; Pup B1839; D.H.5 A9507 E; S.E.5a D6900.

Disbanded 31st December 1919 at Narborough.

Reformed 1st March 1936 at Heliopolis, Egypt by redesignating elements of 6 and 208 Squadrons.

Nil (3.36–2.39)	*Demon K4519; Blenheim I L1469.*
XQ (2.39–9.39)	*Blenheim I L1472 XQ-L.*
SH (9.39–4.51)	*Blenheim I L1474 SH-N, IV P4850; Spitfire I X4770 SH-K, IIA P7747 SH-K, VA W3123, VB W3947 SH-X, IX BS315 SH-K, VB W3320 SH-L, VC AR515; Mustang III FX957 SH-A; Hornet F.1 PX241 SH-N, F.3 PX385 SH-Z; Mosquito III VT593 SH, T.29 KA120.*

Nil (4.51–6.67)	Meteor F.8 WE920 A, NF.12 WS614 J, NF.14 WS733 Z; Javelin T.3, FAW.7 XH788 D, FAW.9 XH842 J.
Also used	Magister P2499; Tiger Moth II DE615; Auster III MZ221.

Disbanded 16th June 1967 at Tengah, Singapore.

Reformed 1st July 1970 at Coningsby as 64 (Shadow) Squadron within 228 Operational Conversion Unit.

Phantom FGR.2.

Disbanded 31st March 1991 at Leuchars.

65 SQUADRON, RFC, later 65 SQUADRON, RAF, later 65 (SHADOW) SQUADRON, RAF, later 65 (RESERVE) SQUADRON, RAF
Formed 1st August 1916 at Wyton by redesignating an element of 46 Squadron. Became 65 Squadron, RAF from 1st April 1918 whilst at Conteville, France.

Various aircraft including Camel F5242 Z; Salamander E5429.

Disbanded 25th October 1919 at Yatesbury.

Reformed 1st August 1934 at Hornchurch.

Nil (8.36–10.38)	Demon K3788; Gauntlet II K5339; Gladiator I K7939.
FZ (10.38–9.39)	Gladiator I K8040; Spitfire I K9906 FZ-L.
YT (9.39–4.51)	Spitfire I L1091 YT-P, IIA P7665 YT-L, VB AA737 YT-K, IX BR141 YT-N; Mustang III FZ193, IV KH642, IVA KM140 YT-E; Spitfire XVI TD134 YT-W; Hornet F.1 PX226 YT-S, F.3 PX346 YT-E; Mosquito III VT609 YT-J.
Nil (12.50–3.61)	Meteor F.8 WL116 O; Hunter F.6 XF507 A, T.7 XL623.
Also used	Magister T9833; Tiger Moth II T7471.

Disbanded 31st March 1961 at Duxford.

Reformed 1st January 1964 at Seletar, Singapore.

Bloodhound II.

Disbanded 30th March 1970 at Seletar.

Reformed 4th May 1971 at Coltishall as 65 (Shadow) Squadron, being the Lightning F.1A and T.3 element of 226 Operational Conversion Unit.

Lightning F.1A, T.3.

Disbanded 30th September 1974 at Coltishall.

Reformed 31st December 1986 at Coningsby as 65 (Shadow) Squadron within 229 Operational Conversion Unit.

Tornado.

Disbanded 1st July 1992 at Coningsby to become 56 (Reserve) Squadron.

66 SQUADRON, RFC, later 66 SQUADRON, RAF
Formed 30th June 1916 at Filton by redesignating an element of 19 Squadron. Became 66 Squadron, RAF from 1st April 1918 whilst at San Pietro-in-Gu, Italy.

B.E.2b, B.E.2c, B.E.2d; B.E.12; Avro 504K; Pup A634 D; Camel D9588 O.

Disbanded 25th October 1919 at Leighterton.

Reformed 20th July 1936 at Duxford from 'C' Flight of 19 Squadron.

Nil (7.36–4.39)	Gauntlet II K7847; Spitfire I K9808.
RB (4.39–9.39)	Spitfire I K9805 RB-R.
LZ (9.39–4.45)	Spitfire I X4321 LZ-F, IIA P7493 LZ-F, VB EP710 LZ-B, VC EE661 LZ-R, VI BS437, IX MK362 LZ-P, XVI TB884.
Also used	Magister P2503; Tiger Moth II T6195.

Disbanded 30th April 1945 at B.106 (Twente), Netherlands.

Reformed 1st September 1946 at Duxford by renumbering 165 Squadron.

HI (9.46–10.49)	Spitfire XVI; Meteor F.3 EE270 HI-H, F.4 RA481 HI-E.
LZ (10.49– .51)	Meteor F.4 VZ415 LZ-J.

Nil (4.51–9.60)	Meteor F.8 WF665 E; Sabre F.4 XB795 F; Hunter F.4 XE681 J, F.6 XJ687 H, T.7 XL605.
Also used	Harvard IIB KF627; Vampire T.11 WZ420.

Disbanded 30th September 1960 at Acklington.

Reformed 15th September 1961 at Odiham by redesignating the Belvedere Trials Unit.

Belvedere HC.1 XG476 F.

Disbanded 17th March 1969 at Seletar, Singapore.

67 SQUADRON, RFC, later 67 SQUADRON, RAF
Formed 12th September 1916 at Heliopolis, Egypt, by redesignating 1st Squadron, Australian Flying Corps.

B.E.2c, B.E.2e 6826; Avro 504K; Elephant A3955; Bristol Scout; B.E.12a A6328; R.E.8 A4405; F.2B A7188.

Disbanded 6th February 1918 at Julis, France, to become 1st Squadron, Australian Flying Corps.

QT	Allocated for the period April to September 1939.

Reformed 12th March 1941 at Kallang, Singapore.

RD	Buffalo I W8243 RD-B; Hurricane IIC BN476.

Dispersed 27th March 1942 at Akyab, India.

Reformed June 1942 at Alipore, India.

RD	Hurricane IIC BP756; Spitfire VIII JG193 RD-S.
Also used	Harvard IIB FE707.

Disbanded 31st July 1945 at Akyab Main, India.

Reformed 1st September 1950 at Gutersloh, Germany.

Vampire FB.5 WA139; Sabre F.4 XB586 X; Hunter F.4 XE689 W. Also used Vampire T.11 XE956.

Disbanded 31st May 1957 at Bruggen, Germany.

68 SQUADRON, RFC, later 68 SQUADRON, RAF
Formed 30th January 1917 at Harlaxton.

D.H.5 A9449 1; S.E.5a C9539 V.

Disbanded 19th January 1918 at Baizieux, France, to become 2 Squadron, Australian Flying Corps.

YA	Allocated for the period April to September 1939.

Reformed 7th January 1941 at Catterick.

WM	Blenheim I X7583 WM-E, IV Z5722 WM-Z; Beaufighter I X7583 WM-F, VI V8592 WM-L; Mosquito XVII HK250 WM-Z, XIX TA389, NF.30 NT317 WM-J.
Also used	Anson I L7912; Oxford II P8982; Spitfire VB W3168; Mosquito III HJ980.

Disbanded 20th April 1945 at Church Fenton.

Reformed 1st January 1952 at Wahn, Germany.

Meteor NF.11 WD651 T.

Disbanded 21st January 1959 at Laarbruch, Germany, to become 5 Squadron.

69 SQUADRON, RFC, later 69 SQUADRON, RAF
Formed 28th December 1916 at South Carlton by redesignating 3rd Squadron, Australian Flying Corps.

RE.8 H7042 J; F.2B C917.

Disbanded 19th January 1918 at Bailleul, France, to become 3 Squadron, Australian Flying Corps.

MJ	Allocated for the period April to September 1939.

Reformed 10th January 1941 at Luqa, Malta, by redesignating 431 (General Reconnaissance) Flight.

Maryland I AR711; Hurricane I V7101, IIA Z3173; Beaufort I W6506; Blenheim IV V6183; Beaufighter I V8222 N; Spitfire IV BP908; Mosquito I W4063; Wellington VIII HX605 L, XIII NC555;

Baltimore I AG709 Q, II AG755 B, III AH152 P, IIIA FA147, IV FA465 B, V FW374 L.

Disbanded 7th August 1945 at B.78 (Eindhoven), Netherlands.

Reformed 7th August 1945 at Cambrai-Epinoy, France by renumbering 613 Squadron.

WI   *Mosquito VI RS611 WI-R.*

Disbanded 31st March 1946 at Cambrai-Epinoy.

Reformed 1st April 1946 at Wahn, Germany, by renumbering 180 Squadron.

Mosquito XVI PF612; Oxford II W6569.

Disbanded 7th November 1947 at Wahn.

Reformed 1st October 1954 at Gutersloh, Germany.

Canberra PR.3 WE144, T.4 WH861.

Disbanded 1st July 1958 at Laarbruch, Germany, to become 39 Squadron.

70 SQUADRON, RFC, later 70 SQUADRON, RAF
Formed 22nd April 1916 at Farnborough. Became 70 Squadron RAF from 1st April 1918 whilst at Fienvillers, France.

1½ Strutter A1514; Pup A626; Vickers ES.1 7757; Vickers FB.19 A5174; Camel B7320 P; Dolphin C8043 Y; Snipe E8057 14.

Disbanded 22nd January 1920 at Spitalgate.

Reformed 1st February 1920 at Heliopolis, Egypt, by renumbering 58 Squadron.

Nil (2.20–11.38)	*Handley Page 0/400 C9719 H; Vimy F3184 T, Vimy Ambulance J6904; Vernon I J6864, II J6886, III J7540; Victoria III J7935 M, IIIA J8061, V K1310; Valentia K3168 K.*
DU (11.38–9.39)	*Valentia K3599 DU-C.*
Nil (9.39–3.46)	*Valentia K2795; Wellington IC Z9023 X, III HF750 L, X NA720 J, VIII HX650, XIII MF267; Liberator VI KK315 C.*
Also used	*Gordon K2609; Magister R1947.*

Disbanded 31st March 1946 at Shallufa, Egypt.

Reformed 15th April 1946 at Fayid, Egypt, by renumbering 178 Squadron.

Lancaster I/FE NX726.

Disbanded 1st April 1947 at Shallufa, Egypt.

Reformed 1st May 1948 at Kabrit, Egypt, by renumbering 215 Squadron.

Dakota IV KP263; Valetta C.1 VW810 MORKK, C.2 VX577; Hastings C.1 TG533, C.2 WD489, C(VIP).4 WJ324; Pembroke C.1 WV730; Argosy C.1 XR107; Hercules C.1, C.3 XV305.

Current 1st April 1998 at Lyneham.

71 SQUADRON, RFC, later 71 (EAGLE) SQUADRON, RAF
Formed 27th March 1917 at Castle Bromwich.

Various aircraft including Camel B7406 W; Snipe E8100 E.

Disbanded 19th January 1918 at Bruay, France, to become 4th Squadron, Australian Flying Corps.

EL	*Allocated for the period April to September 1939.*

Reformed 19th September 1940 at Church Fenton.

Nil (9.40–11.40)	*Buffalo I AS414.*
XR (11.40–9.42)	*Hurricane I P3884 XR-A, X P5171, IIA Z2463 XR-X; Spitfire IIA P7308 XR-D, VB EN783.*
Also used	*Magister P2459; Tiger Moth II DE746.*

Disbanded 29th September 1942 at Debden to become 334th Fighter Squadron, USAAF.

Reformed 16th September 1950 at Gutersloh, Germany.

L (9.50–10.53)	*Vampire FB.5 WA163 L-G.*
Nil (10.53–4.57)	*Sabre F.4 XB710 J; Hunter F.4 XF313 G.*
Also used	*Meteor T.7 WH117; Vampire T.11 WZ585.*

Disbanded 31st May 1957 at Bruggen, Germany.

72 SQUADRON, RFC, later 72 (BASUTOLAND) SQUADRON, RAF
Formed 2nd July 1917 at Upavon by redesignating an element of 'A' Flight of the Central Flying School. Became 72 Squadron, RAF from 1st April 1918 whilst at Baghdad, Mesopotamia.

Avro 504; Pup; D.H.4; Bristol M.1C; S.E.5a; Spad 7 A8806; Elephant.

Disbanded 22nd September 1919 in the United Kingdom.

Reformed 22nd February 1937 at Tangmere by redesignating an element of 1 Squadron.

Nil (2.37–10.38)	*Gladiator I K7978.*
RN (10.38–4.39)	*Gladiator I K7981 RN-D.*
SD (4.39–9.39)	*Spitfire I K9932 SD-N.*
RN (9.39–12.46)	*Spitfire I X4488 RN-C; Gladiator I K8027, II N5645; Spitfire IIA P7895 RN-N, VB BM256 RN-F, VC JG746 RN-E, IX EN250 RN-J, LF.IX PL453 RN-X.*
Also used	*Bf 109G.*

Disbanded 30th December 1946 at Tissano, Yugoslavia.

Reformed 1st February 1947 at Odiham by renumbering 130 Squadron.

FG (1.47–4.51)	*Vampire F.1 TG293 FG-A, F.3 VT821 FG-A.*
Nil (4.51–6.61)	*Vampire FB.5 VZ272 D; Meteor F.4 VW267 I, T.7 WA672, F.8 VZ525 N, NF.12 WS609 B, NF.14 WS724 P; Javelin T.3, FAW.4 XA737 K, FAW.5 XA667 P.*

Disbanded 30th June 1961 at Leconfield.

Reformed 15th November 1961 at Odiham.

Nil (11.61– .70)	*Sycamore HR.14 XG502; Belvedere HC.1 XG464 F; Wessex HC.2 XS678 K.*
A ( )	*Wessex HC.2 XS678 AK.*
E ( )	*Chinook HC.1 ZA713 EN; Puma HC.1.*

Current 1st April 1997 at Aldergrove.

73 SQUADRON, RFC, later 73 SQUADRON, RAF
Formed 1st July 1917 at Upavon by redesignating an element of 'B' Flight of the Central Flying School. Became 73 Squadron, RAF from 1st April 1918 whilst at Beauvois, France.

Camel D8164; Pup A7317; Salamander E5429.

Disbanded 2nd July 1919 at Yatesbury.

Reformed 15th March 1937 at Mildenhall.

Nil (3.37–10.38)	*Fury II K8257; Gladiator I K7963; Hurricane I L1580.*
HV (10.38–9.39)	*Hurricane I L1578 HV-A.*
Nil (9.39–6.40)	*Hurricane I N2358 Z.*
TP (6.40–11.40)	*Hurricane I P2579 TP-J.*
Nil (11.40–5.53)	*Hurricane I V6677, IIB BD930 R; Tomahawk IIB AM464; Hurricane IIC BP177 L; Spitfire VC JK991 E, IX MA630 C, VIII JF560, F.22 PK611 B; Vampire F.3 VV204 E, FB.5 VX476 B, FB.9 WG868; Venom FB.1 WR314 W, FB.4 WR541; Canberra B.2 WD989, B.15 WJ762.*
Also used	*Harvard IIB KF946; Vampire T.11 WZ495.*

Disbanded 17th March 1969 at Akrotiri, Cyprus.

74 SQUADRON, RFC, later 74 SQUADRON, RAF, later 74 (RESERVE) SQUADRON, RAF
Formed 1st July 1917 at Northolt by redesignating an element of 2 Training Squadron. Became 74 Squadron, RAF from 1st April 1918 whilst at St Omer, France.

Pup B7492; Camel B7789; Avro 504 C4474; S.E.5a D276 A.

Disbanded 3rd July 1919 at Lopcombe Corner.

Reformed 1st September 1935 at Hornchurch as the Demon Flight. To Hal Far, Malta, arriving on 11th September and only referred to as 74 Squadron from 14th November.

Nil (9.35–2.39)	*Demon K2905; Gauntlet II K7816.*
JH (2.39–9.39)	*Spitfire I K9931 JH-B.*
ZP (9.39–4.42)	*Spitfire I P9492 ZP-S, IIA P7370 ZP-A, VB AB134.*

Nil (12.42–4.44)	*Hurricane IIA Z4944, IIC HV660; Spitfire VC JL312, IX MA256 K.*
4D (4.44–4.51)	*Spitfire IX PT999 4D-T, XVI TB675 4D-V; Meteor F.3 EE341 4D-G, F.4 VT192 4D-K, T.7 VW430 4D-X, F.8 WA879 4D-C.*
Nil (4.51–9.71)	*Meteor F.8 WF710 J; Hunter F.4 WT764 J, F.6 XE591 G, T.7 XL568 X; Lightning F.1 XM135 R, F.3 XP704 H, T.4 XM974, T.5 XS416 T, F.6 XS920 L.*
Also used	*Auster III MZ221.*

Disbanded 1st September 1971 at Tengah, Malaya.

Reformed 19th October 1984 at Wattisham.

Phantom F-4J ZE350 T, FGR.2 XV401 1.

A Phantom Training Flight operated within the Squadron between 1st February and 31st December 1991.

Disbanded 1st October 1992 at Wattisham.

Reformed 1st October 1992 at Valley as 74 (Reserve) Squadron, being 3 Squadron within 4 Flying Training School.

T	*Hawk T.1 XX165 TM, T.1A XX190 TA.*

Current 1st April 1998 at Valley.

75 SQUADRON, RFC, later 75 SQUADRON, RAF
Formed 1st October 1916 at Tadcaster by redesignating an element of 33 Squadron. Became 75 Squadron, RAF from 1st April 1918 whilst at Elmswell.

B.E.2c; B.E.12 A6325; B.E.2e A8701; F.E.2b; B.E.12b C3094; Avro 504K D9355.

Disbanded 13th June 1919 at North Weald.

Reformed 15th March 1937 at Driffield from 'B' Flight of 215 Squadron.

Nil (3.37–10.38)	*Virginia X K2672; Anson I K6300; Harrow I K6948, II K6995.*
FO (10.38–9.39)	*Harrow I K6954 FO-E, II K6992 FO-X; Wellington I L4371 FO-Q.*
Nil (9.39–4.40)	*Wellington I L4371; Anson I N5017.*

Disbanded 4th April 1940 at Harwell and merged with 148 Squadron to become 15 Operational Training Unit.

Reformed 4th April 1940 at Feltwell by redesignating the New Zealand Flight.

AA (4.40–10.45)	*Wellington I L4322, IA P9206 AA-A, IC R1177 AA-F, II Z8429, III X3751 AA-P; Stirling I BF437 AA-L, III EF408 AA-P; Lancaster I NG113 AA-D, III LM740 AA-B; Lincoln II RF389 AA-A.*
JN (2.43–10.45)	*('C' Flight) Stirling I, III EF163 JN-L; Lancaster I HK544 JN-F, III ND801 JN-X.*

Disbanded 15th October 1945 at Spilsby and authority passed to the Royal New Zealand Air Force.

76 SQUADRON, RFC, later 76 SQUADRON, RAF
Formed 15th September 1916 at Cramlington by redesignating an element of 36 Squadron. Became 76 Squadron, RAF from 1st April 1918 whilst at Ripon.

B.E.2c 2665; B.E.12 A6317; D.H.6 A9571; B.E.2e B4506; B.E.12 6478, B.E.12a A590; R.E.8; B.E.12b C3142; F.2B; Avro 504K E1722.

Disbanded 13th June 1919 at Tadcaster.

Reformed 12th April 1937 at Finningley from 'B' Flight of 7 Squadron. Merged with 7 Squadron to become 5 Group Pool from 14th September 1939.

Nil (4.37–10.38)	*Wellesley K7744.*
NM (10.38–4.39)	*Wellesley K7748 NM-H.*
Nil (5.39–4.40)	*Hampden I P1267; Anson I N5032.*

Disbanded 8th April 1940 at Upper Heyford and merged with 7 Squadron to form 16 Operational Training Unit.

Reformed 30th April 1940 at West Raynham.

No aircraft allocated.

Disbanded 20th May 1940 at West Raynham.

Reformed 1st May 1941 at Linton-on-Ouse from 'C' Flight of 35 Squadron.

MP	*Halifax I L9530 MP-L, II W1006 MP-K, V DK201 MP-P, III NA543 MP-S, VI RG556 MP-D, VII TW794 MP-A; Dakota III FZ688, IV KN559 MP-S.*

Disbanded 1st September 1946 at Palam, India, to become 62 Squadron.

Reformed 9th December 1953 at Wittering.

Canberra B.2 WH914, T.4 WD954, B.6 WJ757.

Disbanded 30th December 1960 at Upwood.

76 SQUADRON CONVERSION FLIGHT
Formed 5th February 1942 at Middleton St George.

MP	*Halifax I L9577, II R9365.*

Disbanded 7th October 1942 at Riccall and merged with 10 and 78 Squadron Conversion Flights to become 1658 Heavy Conversion Unit.

77 SQUADRON, RFC, later 77 SQUADRON, RAF
Formed 1st October 1916 at Thetford by redesignating an element of 51 Squadron. Became 77 Squadron RAF from 1st April 1918 whilst at Turnhouse.

B.E.2c; B.E.12; D.H.6; B.E.2d H8256, B.E.2e B4507; R.E.8; B.E.12b; Avro 504K E3273.

Disbanded 13th June 1919 at Penston.

Reformed 14th June 1937 at Finningley from 'B' Flight of 102 Squadron.

Nil (6.37–11.38)	*Audax K7454; Wellesley K8525.*
ZL (11.38–9.39)	*Whitley III K8977 ZL-P.*
KN (9.39–11.46)	*Whitley III K9015 KN-R, V N1355 KN-X; Halifax II DT666 KN-F, V LK999 KN-O, III NA233 KN-S, VI RG500 KN-G; Dakota IV KK150 KN-C.*
TB (.43–5.45)	*('C' Flight) Halifax V; III; VI NP860.*

Disbanded 1st November 1946 at Mauripur, India, to become 31 Squadron.

Reformed 1st December 1946 at Broadwell by renumbering 271 Squadron.

YS	*Dakota IV KJ866 YS-X.*

Disbanded 1st June 1949 at Waterbeach.

Reformed 1st September 1958 at Feltwell.

Thor.

Disbanded 10th July 1963 at Feltwell.

78 SQUADRON, RFC, later 78 SQUADRON, RAF
Formed 1st November 1916 at Newhaven. Became 78 Squadron, RAF from 1st April 1918 whilst at Suttons Farm.

B.E.2c; B.E.12 A6320; B.E.2e; B.E.12a A595; S.E.5; 1½ Strutter A6906 5; F.E.2d; F.E.9 A4819; B.E.12b; Camel B9287; Dolphin C3862; Snipe E7580.

Disbanded 31st December 1919 at Suttons Farm.

Reformed 1st November 1936 at Boscombe Down from 'B' Flight of 10 Squadron.

Nil (11.36–11.38)	*Heyford II K4870, III K5198; Whitley I K7205.*
YY (11.38–9.39)	*Whitley I K7201 YY-G, IV K9052.*
EY (9.39–4.50)	*Whitley IV K9049, V Z6625 EY-L; Halifax II W1245 EY-B, III MZ414 EY-G, VI PP210, VII TW775; Dakota I FD817, IV KP274 EY-P.*
Nil (4.50-9.54)	*Valetta C.1 VW812, T.3 WJ481.*

Disbanded 30th September 1954 at Fayid, Egypt.

Reformed 15th April 1956 at Khormaksar, Aden.

Pioneer CC.1 XL554; Pembroke C.1 WV705; Twin Pioneer CC.1 XL994 Z; Wessex HC.2 XR527 E.

Disbanded 21st December 1971 at Sharjah, Trucial States.

Reformed 1st May 1986 at Mount Pleasant, Falkland Islands, by merging 1310 and 1564 (Tactical Support) Flights.

Nil (6.86–)	Chinook HC.1 ZA680 T.
S (6.86–)	Chinook HC.1, HC.2 ZA710; Sea King HAR.3 ZA105 S.

Current 1st April 1998 at Mount Pleasant.

78 SQUADRON CONVERSION FLIGHT
Formed 220th January 1942 at Croft.

EY	Halifax I L9563; II L9621.

79 SQUADRON, RFC, later 78 (MADRAS PRESIDENCY) SQUADRON, RAF, later 79 (SHADOW) SQUADRON, RAF, later 79 (RESERVE) SQUADRON, RAF
Formed 1st August 1917 at Gosport by redesignating an element of 27 Training Squadron. Became 79 Squadron, RAF from 1st April 1918 whilst at Beauvois, France.

Dolphin C3944 N.

Disbanded 15th July 1919 at Bickendorf, Germany.

Reformed 22nd March 1937 at Biggin Hill from 'B' Flight of 32 Squadron.

Nil (3.37–11.38)	Gauntlet II K7881.
AL (11.38–9.39)	Gauntlet II K7880 AL-B; Hurricane I L1716 AL-D.
NV (9.39–3.42)	Hurricane I L1698 NV-M, X P5177, IIB Z3156 NV-F.
Nil (6.42–.43)	Hurricane IIC BN681 X.
NV (.43–12.45)	Hurricane IIC LE297 NV-L, XIIC JS465 NV-D; Thunderbolt II KL281 NV-L.
Also used	Hurricane IIA DG613.

Disbanded 30th December 1945 at Meiktila, Burma.

Reformed 15th November 1951 at Gutersloh, Germany.

T (11.51–.56)	Meteor T.7 WG987 T-Z, FR.9 WB121 T-H.
Nil (.56–1.61)	Swift FR.5 WK315 P; Hunter FR.10 XE621.
Also used	Vampire T.11 WZ498.

Disbanded 30th December 1960 at Gutersloh, Germany, to become 4 Squadron.

Reformed 1st January 1967 at Chivenor as 79 (Shadow) Squadron within 229 Operational Conversion Unit and subsequently the Tactical Weapons Unit from September 1974 and 1 Tactical Weapons Unit from July 1978. Redesignated 79 (Reserve) Squadron from 1991.

Hunter (229 OCU); Hunter, Jet Provost (TWU), Hunter, Hawk T.1 XX222, T.1A XX221 (1 TWU).

Disbanded August 1992 at Brawdy.

80 SQUADRON, RFC, later 80 SQUADRON, RAF
Formed 1st August 1917 at Thetford by redesignating an element of 36 Training Squadron. Became 80 Squadron, RAF from 1st April 1918 whilst at Belleville Farm, France.

Camel C67 R; Snipe.

Disbanded 1st February 1920 at Aboukir, Egypt, to become 56 Squadron.

Reformed 8th March 1937 at Kenley from 'B' Flight of 17 Squadron.

Nil (3.47–10.38)	Gauntlet II K5360; Gladiator I K7893.
GK (10.38–5.39)	Gladiator I K7914.
OD (5.39–.40)	Gladiator I K7900 OD-S.
GK (.40–6.40)	Gladiator I K7914.
YK (6.40–1.41)	Gladiator I K8011 YK-S, II N5823; Hurricane I P2544 YK-T.
Nil (1.41–4.43)	Hurricane I Z4163, IIC BN126.
EY (4.43–4.44)	Spitfire VC BP966 EY-H.
W2 (4.44–.52)	Spitfire IX EN172 W2-P; Tempest V JN868 W2-N; Spitfire F.24 PK682 W2-N; Hornet F.3 WB879 W2-B.
Nil (.52–5.55)	Hornet F.3 WB871; F.4 WF977 B.
Also used	Blenheim IV Z9585; Tiger Moth II DE132;

A Hawker Hind day bomber of No 83 Squadron based at Turnhouse between 1936 and 1938.

Harvard IIB KF306; Auster IV MS962, V
MT360; Mosquito III RR270; Bf 109F EY.

Disbanded 1st May 1955 at Kai Tak, Hong Kong.

Reformed 1st August 1955 at Laarbruch, Germany, by renumbering
214 Squadron.

Canberra T.4 WH842, PR.7 WT524. Also used Vampire T.11.

Disbanded 30th September 1969 at Bruggen.

81 SQUADRON, RFC, later 81 SQUADRON, RAF
Formed 7th January 1917 at Gosport by redesignating an element
of 1 Reserve Squadron. Became 81 Squadron, RAF from 1st April
1918 whilst at Scampton.

Various aircraft including 1½ Strutter; Spad 7; Camel B7301.

An element detached and became 'C' Flight, 4 Training Depot
Station on 19th September 1917.

Disbanded 4th July 1918 at Scampton and merged with 11 and 60
Training Squadrons to become 34 Training Depot Station.

Reformed 25th November 1918 at Upper Heyford, also being
allocated the title 1 Squadron, Canadian Air Force.

*Dolphin E4864; S.E.5a E5755. Also used Pup B4158; Avro 504K
E4207; Snipe E8213; Fokker D.VII 6823/18; F.2B E4336.*

Disbanded 28th January 1920 at Shoreham.

WK	*Allocated for the period April to September 1939.*

Reformed 27th November 1939 at Mont Jois, France, by
redesignating the Air Component Field Force Communication
Squadron. An Operational Reserve Flight, equipped with
Blenheims, was an element of the Squadron.

*Hart K3961; Tiger Moth I K4250, II N9125; Cierva C.40 L7590;
Magister L8233; Lysander II P9107.*

Disbanded 15th June 1940 at Andover.

Reformed 29th July 1941 at Debden by redesignating an element of
'A' Flight of 504 Squadron.

Hurricane IIB Z5227 FL-53.

Departed 28th November 1941 from Vaenga, USSR.

Reassembled 6th December 1941 at Turnhouse.

FL	*Spitfire VA P7532, VB BM158 FL-Y, VC JK322 FL-4, IX EN191 FL-Y, VIII JF668 FL-J.*
Also used	*Hurricane IIC LB735; Harvard IIB FE774.*

Disbanded 10th June 1945 at Amarda Road, India.

Reformed 10th June 1945 at Bobbili, India, by renumbering 123
Squadron.

FL	*Thunderbolt II HD185 FL-D.*

Disbanded 30th June 1946 at Kemajoran, Java.

Reformed 1st September 1946 at Seletar, Malaya, by renumbering
684 Squadron.

*Mosquito III RR306, PR.34 RG255 P; Spitfire XVIII TP407 D, XIX
PM574; Anson XIX; Meteor PR.10 VS987; Pembroke C.(PR).1
XF797; Canberra T.4 WH706, PR.7 WH795.*

Disbanded 16th January 1970 at Tengah, Malaya.

82 SQUADRON, RFC, later 82 SQUADRON, RAF
Formed 7th January 1917 at Doncaster by redesignating an
element of 15 Reserve Squadron. Became 82 Squadron, RAF from
1st April 1918 whilst at Agenvilliers, France.

*B.E.2c 4546; Avro 504A A5937; B.E.2e A1844; R.E.7 2401; R.E.8
A3641; F.K.8 F7411.*

An element detached to become 'A' Flight, 6 Training Depot Station
on 12th October 1917.

Disbanded 4th July 1919 at Tangmere.

Reformed 14th June 1937 at Andover from 'B' Flight of 142
Squadron.

Nil (6.37–11.38)	*Hind K6825; Blenheim I L1118.*

OZ (11.38–9.39)	*Blenheim I L1132 OZ-J, IV P4828.*
UX (9.39–3.46)	*Blenheim IV T2162 UX-Y; Vengeance I AN957 UX-Y, IA EZ896 UX-D, II AN703 UX-X, III FB966 UX-X; Mosquito VI HR400 UX-L.*
Also used	*Harvard IIB FE373; Piper Cub Cruiser MA922.*

Disbanded 15th March 1946 at St Thomas Mount, India.

Reformed 1st October 1946 at Benson from the Lancaster Flight of
541 Squadron.

*Lancaster PR.I TW904 E; Anson XI NL228; Spitfire XIX PM612;
Dakota IV KN650 L; Canberra PR.3 WE173, PR.7 WH800.*

Disbanded 1st September 1956 at Wyton.

Reformed 22nd July 1959 at Shepherd's Grove.

Thor.

Disbanded 10th July 1963 at Shepherd's Grove.

83 SQUADRON, RFC, later 83 SQUADRON, RAF
Formed 7th January 1917 at Montrose by redesignating an element
of 18 Reserve Squadron. Became 83 Squadron, RAF from 1st April
1918 whilst at Auchel, France.

Shorthorn; R.E.8; F.E.2b E7082, F.E.2d B1887.

An element detached to become 'B' Flight, 6 Training Depot Station
on 12th October 1917.

Disbanded 31st December 1919 at Croydon.

Reformed 4th August 1936 at Turnhouse.

Nil (8.36–11.38)	*Hind K6638.*
QQ (11.38–9.39)	*Hampden I L4094 QQ-K.*
OL (9.39–4.51)	*Hampden I L4050 OL-L; Manchester I L7385 OL-C; Lancaster I W4905 OL-S, III NE165 OL-Y, VI ND418; Lincoln II RE358 OL-F.*
AS and GB	*Lincoln II aircraft drawn from 83, 97 and 100 Squadrons were coded AS (e.g. RF467 AS-B) for an official visit to Chile in October 1946, but just before the visit commenced they were recoded GB (e.g. RF463 GB-A, RF467 GB-B and RF468 GB-C).*
Nil (4.51–1.56)	*Lincoln II SX975.*
Also used	*Anson I N9909.*

Disbanded 1st January 1956 at Hemswell to become 'Antler'
Squadron.

Reformed 21st May 1957 at Waddington.

Vulcan B.1 XA905, B.2 XJ782.

Disbanded 31st August 1969 at Waddington.

83 SQUADRON CONVERSION FLIGHT
Formed 11th April 1942 at Scampton.

OL	*Manchester I L7280; Lancaster I R5852.*

Disbanded 7th October 1942 at Wigsley and absorbed together with
50 Squadron Conversion Flight into 1654 Heavy Conversion Unit.

84 SQUADRON, RFC, later 84 SQUADRON, RAF
Formed 7th January 1917 at Beaulieu by redesignating an element
of 16 Reserve Squadron. Became 84 Squadron, RAF from 1st April
1918 whilst at Conteville, France.

*B.E.12a, B.E.12; B.E.2c; Nieuport 12 A5200; Curtiss JN-4; Avro
504; 1½ Strutter; S.E.5a H710 P.*

Disbanded 30th January 1920 at Kenley.

Reformed 13th August 1920 at Baghdad West, Iraq.

Nil (8.20–9.39)	*D.H.9A E803; Wapiti I J9079, II J9240, IIA K1405; Vincent K4120; Blenheim I L1380.*
UR	*Allocated for the period April to September 1939.*
VA (9.39–3.41)	*Blenheim I L1381 VA-G.*
Nil (3.41–3.42)	*Blenheim IV T2249 X.*
Also used	*Avro 504K E3483; Audax K5239.*

Dispersed 1st March 1942 at Kalidjati, Java, and withdrawn to India.

Reformed 18th March 1942 at Drigh Road, India.

Nil (3.43–1.45)   Blenheim IV Z9577; Vengeance I AN956 U, II AN700 X, III FD105 U.
PY (1.45–12.46)   Mosquito VI RF699 PY-W.
Nil (12.46–2.53)   Beaufighter X RD801; Brigand B.1 RH776 K; Harvard IIB KF103.

Disbanded 20th February 1953 at Tengah, Malaya.

Reformed 20th February 1953 at Fayid, Egypt, by renumbering 204 Squadron.

Valetta C.1 VW140.

Disbanded 31st December 1956 at Nicosia, Cyprus.

Reformed 31st December 1956 at Khormaksar, Aden, by redesignating the Aden Protectorate Communication and Support Squadron.

Valetta C.1 VW803, C.2 VX579, T.3 WJ481; Sycamore HR.14; Pembroke C.1 WV733; Beverley C.1 XM107 S; Andover C.1 XS645 E.

Disbanded 1st October 1971 at Muharraq, Bahrain.

Reformed 17th January 1972 at Akrotiri, Cyprus, by merging 1563 Flight and an element of 230 Squadron.

Whirlwind HAR.10 XK970 P; Wessex HC.2 XR522, HU.5 XS485, HC.5C XT463.

Current 1st April 1998 at Akrotiri, Cyprus.

85 SQUADRON, RFC, later 85 SQUADRON, RAF
Formed 1st August 1917 at Upavon from 'C' Flight of the Central Flying School. Became 85 Squadron, RAF from 1st April 1918 whilst at Hounslow.

Various aircraft including S.E.5a F8953 V.

Disbanded 3rd July 1919 at Lopcombe Corner.

Reformed 1st June 1938 at Debden from 'A' Flight of 87 Squadron.

Nil (6.38–9.38)   Gladiator K7969; Hurricane I L1651.
NO (9.38–9.39)   Hurricane I L1833 NO-J.
VY (9.39–4.51)   Hurricane I P3854 VY-Q, X P5171; Defiant I N3434; Boston II AH438; Havoc I BJ472 VY-R, II AH523 VY-Z; Mosquito II DD714, III HJ864, IV DZ385, VI NS998, XII HK120 VY-P, XIII HK374, XVII HK245 VY-X, T.29 KA117, NF.30 MV546 VY-P, NF.36 RL174 VY-L.
Nil (4.51–11.58)   Meteor T.7 WL378 W, NF.11 WD615 A, NF.12 WS608 Z, NF.14 WS737 J.
Also used   Master I N7577; Magister P2510; Oxford I T1372, II X7233; Cygnet I ES914; Auster VI TJ324; Tiger Moth II DF211.

Disbanded 30th November 1958 at Church Fenton.

Reformed 30th November 1958 at Stradishall by renumbering 89 Squadron.

Javelin FAW.2 XA774 J, FAW.6 XH702 X, FAW.8 XJ122 E.

Disbanded 31st March 1963 at West Raynham.

Reformed 1st April 1963 at West Raynham by redesignating the Fighter Command Target Facilities Squadron of the Central Fighter Establishment.

Meteor F.8 WK914 Y; Canberra B.2 WE113, PR.3 WE135, T.4 WJ861, T.11 WJ975, T.19 WH904.

Disbanded 19th December 1975 at West Raynham and absorbed by 100 Squadron.

Reformed 19th December 1975 at West Raynham.

Bloodhound II.

Disbanded 31st July 1991 at West Raynham.

86 SQUADRON, RFC, later 86 SQUADRON, RAF
Formed 1st September 1917 at Shoreham by redesignating an element of 3 Training Squadron. Became 86 Squadron, RAF from 1st April 1918 whilst at Northolt.

Various aircraft including Dolphin C3969.

Disbanded 4th July 1918 at Northolt and absorbed by 30 Training Depot Station.

DE   Allocated for the period April to September 1939.

Reformed 6th December 1940 at Gosport.

BX (12.40–8.42)   Blenheim IV V5646 BX-N; Beaufort I L9854 BX-K, II AW361 BX-T.
Nil (8.42–10.43)   Liberator III FK226 G, V BZ870 S.
XQ (10.43–4.46)   Liberator VI KH420 XQ-L, VIII KH291 XQ-Y.
Also used   Oxford I R5974, II X7194.

Disbanded 25th April 1946 at Oakington.

87 SQUADRON, RFC, later 87 (UNITED PROVINCES) SQUADRON, RAF
Formed 1st September 1917 at Upavon by redesignating an element of 'D' Flight, Central Flying School. Became 87 Squadron, RAF from 1st April 1918 whilst at Hounslow.

Avro 504K; Pup; S.E.5a D305; Dolphin C4159 C; Hannoveraner CL.III C13103.

Disbanded 24th June 1919 at Ternhill.

Reformed 15th March 1937 at Tangmere from an element of 54 Squadron.

Nil (3.37–10.38)   Fury II K8271; Gladiator I K7979.
PD (10.38–9.39)   Hurricane L1646.
LK (9.39–12.46)   Hurricane I P2798 LK-A, IIA DR361, IIC Z3779 LK-Y; Spitfire VB EP790, VC JG866 LK-J, VIII JF356, IX NH346 LK-M.

Disbanded 30th December 1946 at Zeltweg, Austria.

Reformed 1st January 1952 at Wahn, Germany.

B (1.52–.54)   Meteor T.7 WH204, NF.11 WD684 B-W.
Nil (.54–1.61)   Meteor NF.11 WD658 A; Javelin FAW.1 XA565 K, FAW.4 XA761, FAW.5 XA645.

Disbanded 3rd January 1961 at Bruggen, Germany.

88 SQUADRON, RFC, later 88 (HONG KONG) SQUADRON, RAF
Formed 24th July 1917 at Gosport by redesignating an element of 1 Training Squadron. Became 88 Squadron, RAF from 1st April 1918 whilst at Harling Road.

F.2B E2610 4.

Disbanded 10th August 1919 at Nivelles, Belgium.

Reformed 7th June 1937 at Waddington by redesignating an element of 110 Squadron.

Nil (6.37–4.39)   Hind K6843; Battle K7630.
HY (4.39–9.39)   Battle K9249.
RH (9.39–4.45)   Battle L5558 RH-J; Blenheim I L1344; Havoc I AW400; Boston III Z2216 RH-A, III (Turbinlite) W8393, IIIA BZ389 RH-E, IV BZ455 RH-S.
Also used   Cygnet II ES914.

Disbanded 6th April 1945 at B.50 (Vitry-en-Artois), France.

Reformed 1st September 1946 at Kai Tak, Hong Kong, by redesignating 1430 (Flying Boat Transport) Flight.

Sunderland V NJ176 F.

Disbanded 1st October 1954 at Seletar, Singapore.

Reformed 15th January 1956 at Wildenrath, Germany.

Canberra B(I).8 WT335, T.4 WH842.

Disbanded 17th December 1962 at Wildenrath to become 14 Squadron.

89 SQUADRON, RFC, later 89 SQUADRON, RAF
Formed 24th July 1917 at Catterick by redesignating an element of 6 Training Squadron. Became 89 Squadron, RAF from 1st April 1918 whilst at Harling Road.

Pup B5955; S.E.5a.

Disbanded 29th July 1918 at Upper Heyford.

LG   Allocated for the period April to September 1939.

Reformed 25th September 1941 at Colerne.

Beaufighter IF X7719 J, VIF X7886 Y; Mosquito VI HX940, XIX TA178; Harvard IIB FE617; Walrus II.

Disbanded 1st May 1946 at Seletar, Singapore, to become 22 Squadron.

Reformed 15th December 1955 at Stradishall.

Venom NF.3 WX930 Q; Meteor T.7 WL459; Javelin FAW.2 XA774 J, FAW.6 XH696 H.

Disbanded 30th November 1958 at Stradishall to become 85 Squadron.

90 SQUADRON, RFC, later 90 SQUADRON, RAF
Formed 8th October 1917 at Shawbury by redesignating an element of 10 Training Squadron. Became 90 Squadron, RAF from 1st April 1918 whilst at Shotwick.

Various aircraft including Dolphin.

Disbanded 29th July 1918 at Brockworth.

Reformed 14th August 1918 at Buckminster by redesignating an element of 38 Squadron.

F.E.2b; Avro 504K.

Disbanded 13th June 1919 at Buckminster.

Reformed 15th March 1937 at Bicester from 'A' Flight of 101 Squadron. Merged with 104 and 108 Squadrons to become 2 Group Pool from 14th September 1939. Re-established as an independent entity from 19th September 1939.

Nil (3.37–10.38)	Hind K6740; Blenheim I K7054 F.
TW (10.38–9.39)	Blenheim I L1283 TW-H, IV L4879 TW-B.
Nil (9.39–4.40)	Blenheim I L1350, IV L4873; Anson I N5085.

Disbanded 8th April 1940 at Upwood and merged with 35 Squadron to become 17 Operational Training Unit.

Reformed 3rd May 1941 at Watton.

WP	Fortress I AN530 WP-F.

Disbanded 10th February 1942 at Polebrook and absorbed by 1653 Heavy Conversion Unit.

Reformed 7th November 1942 at Bottesford.

WP (1.42–9.50)	Stirling I BF414 WP-F, III EE901 WP-U; Lancaster I HK613 WP-Y, III NE149/G WP-A; Lincoln II RF447 WP-P.
XY (3.43–10.44)	('C' Flight) Stirling III EF183 XY-T; Lancaster I NF987 XY-R.

Disbanded 1st September 1950 at Wyton.

Reformed 4th October 1950 at Marham.

WP (10.50–4.51)	Washington B.1 WF502 WP-O.
Nil (4.51–5.56)	Washington B.1 WF491; Canberra B.2 WJ995.

Disbanded 1st May 1956 at Marham.

Reformed 1st January 1957 at Honington.

Valiant B(PR).1 WP223, B(PR)K.1 WZ393.

Disbanded 1st March 1965 at Honington.

91 SQUADRON, RFC, later 91 (NIGERIA) SQUADRON, RAF
Formed 1st September 1917 at Spitalgate by redesignating an element of 11 Training Squadron. Became 91 Squadron, RAF from 1st April 1918 whilst at Tangmere.

B.E.2e; R.E.8; Dolphin J9.

Disbanded 3rd July 1918 at Lopcombe Corner.

HQ	Allocated for the period April to September 1939.

Reformed 9th January 1941 at Hawkinge by redesignating 421 (Reconnaissance) Flight.

DL	Spitfire IIA P8194 DL-M, VB AD548 DL-X, VC AA976 DL-W, XII EN615, XIV RB180 DL-E, IXB NH356; F.21 LA223 DL-Y; Meteor F.3 EE409 DL-F.
Also used	Auster III NX530.

Disbanded 31st January 1947 at Acklington to become 92 Squadron.

92 SQUADRON, RFC, later 92 (EAST INDIA) SQUADRON, RAF, later 92 (RESERVE) SQUADRON, RAF
Formed 1st September 1917 at London Colney by redesignating an element of 56 Training Squadron. Became 92 Squadron, RAF from 1st April 1918 whilst at Tangmere.

Spad S.VII; Pup; Avro 504K; S.E.5a E4024.

Disbanded 7th August 1919 at Eil, Germany.

GR	Allocated for the period April to September 1939.

Reformed 10th October 1939 at Tangmere from an element of 601 Squadron.

GR (10.39–5.40)	Blenheim I L6726 GR-E; Spitfire I N3265 GR-E.
QJ (5.40–12.46)	Spitfire I N3249 QJ-P, VA W3120, VB AD577 QJ-Z, VC BR466, IX EN446, VIII JF502 QJ-4.

Disbanded 30th December 1946 at Zeltweg, Austria.

Reformed 31st January 1947 at Acklington by renumbering 91 Squadron.

DL (1.47–9.50)	Meteor F.3 EE332 DL-E, F.4 RA489 DL-M, T.7 VZ637 DL-Y.
8L (9.50–4.51)	Meteor T.7 WA763 8L-G, F.8 WA763 8L-G.
Nil (4.51–3.77)	Meteor T.7 WH223, F.8 VZ546 C; Sabre F.4 XD710 B; Hunter F.4 XF324 D, F.6 XG186 J, T.7 XL605 T; Lightning F.2 XN727 A, T.4 XM995 T.
Also used	Vampire T.11 XE934.

Disbanded 31st March 1977 at Gutersloh, Germany.

Reformed 1st April 1977 at Wildenrath, Germany, having commenced training from 1st January 1977 as 92 Squadron (Designate).

Phantom FGR.2 XV465 Z.

Disbanded 1st July 1991 at Wildenrath.

Reformed 23rd September 1992 at Chivenor as 92 (Reserve) Squadron, being an element of 7 Flying Training School, by redesignating 151 (Reserve) Squadron.

Hawk T.1 XX167 T.1A XX332 F.

Disbanded 1st October 1994 at Chivenor.

93 SQUADRON, RFC, later 93 SQUADRON, RAF
Formed 23rd September 1917 at Croydon by redesignating an element of 40 Training Squadron. Became 93 Squadron, RAF from 1st April 1918 whilst at Tangmere.

Various aircraft.

Disbanded 17th August 1918 at Tangmere.

Reformed 14th October 1918 at Port Meadow.

Dolphin proposed.

Disbanded 21st November 1918 at Port Meadow.

RN	Allocated for the period April to September 1939.

Reformed 7th December 1940 at Middle Wallop by redesignating 420 ('Pandora') Flight.

HN	Harrow II K7020; Havoc I BB892 HN-G; Wellington IA P9233, IC T2906.
Also used	Battle K7698; Monospar Tricycle N1531; Tiger Moth II R5028.

Disbanded 18th November 1941 at Middle Wallop to become 1458 (Fighter) Flight.

Reformed 1st June 1942 at Andreas.

HN	Spitfire VB BM514 HN-B, VC JL219 HN-X, IX RR193.
Also used	Magister L8054; Bf 108; Junkers W 34.

Disbanded 5th September 1945 at Klagenfurt, Austria.

Reformed 1st January 1946 at Lavariano, Italy, by renumbering 237 Squadron.

Mustang IVA KH798.

Disbanded 30th December 1946 at Treviso, Italy.

Reformed 15th November 1950 at Celle, Germany.

Vampire FB.5 WA109 A, FB.9 WR142; Sabre F.4 XB768 Q; Hunter F.4 XE685 B, F.6 XJ717 Z.

Disbanded 30th December 1960 at Jever, Germany.

94 SQUADRON, RFC, later 94 SQUADRON, RAF
Formed 30th July 1917 at Gosport by redesignating an element of 55 Training Squadron. Became 94 Squadron, RAF from 1st April 1918 whilst at Harling Road.

F.K.8; Pup; Camel; S.E.5a H678 E.

Disbanded 30th June 1919 at Tadcaster.

Reformed 26th March 1939 at Khormaksar, Aden.

Nil (3.39–9.39)	*Gladiator I K7899, II N2290.*
ZG	*Allocated for the period April to September 1939, but not used.*
GO (9.39–4.45)	*Gladiator I L7616 GO-D, Gladiator II N5780; Hurricane I Z4229, IIA Z4945, IIB BP397 GO-J; Hurricane IIC KZ144 GO-N; Spitfire VB EP576, VC JK435 GO-D, IX MH977 GO-B.*
FZ (2.42–5.42)	*Kittyhawk I AK739 FZ-R.*

Disbanded 20th April 1945 at Sedes, France.

Reformed 1st December 1950 at Celle, Germany.

A (12.50– .55)	*Vampire FB.5 WA123 A-R; Venom FB.1 WR293 A-C.*
Nil (.55–9.57	*Venom FB.1 WK432, FB.4 WR425.*

Disbanded 14th September 1957 at Celle.

Reformed 1st October 1960 at Misson.

Bloodhound 1.

Disbanded 30th June 1963 at Misson.

95 SQUADRON, RFC, later 95 SQUADRON, RAF
Formed 8th October 1917 at Ternhill by redesignating an element of 43 Training Squadron. Became 95 Squadron, RAF from 1st April 1918 whilst at Shotwick.

Various training aircraft including Pup C202. Camel then Dolphin proposed but none delivered.

Disbanded 4th July 1918 at Shotwick.

Reformed 1st October 1918 at Kenley by merging elements of 21, 28, 30 and 51 Training Depot Stations.

Dolphin proposed but none delivered.

Disbanded 20th November 1918 at Kenley.

PX	*Allocated for the period April to September 1939.*

Reformed 16th January 1941 at Pembroke Dock from an element of 210 Squadron.

SE (1.41–8.42)	*Sunderland I T9040 SE-E; Hurricane I Z4257.*
Nil (8.42–6.45)	*Sunderland III DV973 P.*

Disbanded 30th June 1945 at Bathurst, Gambia.

96 SQUADRON, RFC, later 96 SQUADRON, RAF
Formed 8th October 1917 at South Carlton by redesignating an element of 45 Training Depot Station. Became 96 Squadron, RAF from 1st April 1918 whilst at Shotwick.

Various aircraft including Pup C331; B.E.2c.

Disbanded 4th July 1918 at Shotwick and absorbed by 51 Training Depot Station.

Reformed 28th September 1918 at Wyton by merging elements of 2, 32, 38 and 46 Training Depot Stations.

Salamander.

Disbanded 9th December 1918 at Wyton.

SJ	*Allocated for the period April to September 1939.*

Reformed 16th December 1940 at Cranage by redesignating 422 (Fighter Interception) Flight.

ZJ	*Hurricane I P3712 ZJ-J, IIC Z3919; Defiant I T4052 ZJ-H, II AA583 ZJ-J; Beaufighter I T3307, II T3415 ZJ-M, VI V8520 ZJ-B; Mosquito III HJ864 ZJ-M, XII HK177, XIII HK379 ZJ-F.*
Also used	*Battle R7409; Blenheim I L8671, IV V5522; Oxford I T1380, II N4765.*

Disbanded 12th December 1944 at Odiham.

Reformed 21st December 1944 at Leconfield.

6H	*Halifax III MZ464 6H-Q; Dakota III FD891, IV KN467 6H-X; Expeditor II KN107.*

Disbanded 1st June 1946 at Kai Tak, Hong Kong, to become 110 Squadron.

Reformed 17th November 1952 at Ahlhorn, Germany.

L (10.52– .55)	*Meteor NF.11 WD622 L-N.*
Nil (.55–1.59)	*Meteor T.7 WL472, NF.11 WD794 H.*

Disbanded 21st January 1959 at Geilenkirchen, Germany, to become 3 Squadron.

97 SQUADRON, RFC, later 97 (STRAITS SETTLEMENTS) SQUADRON, RAF
Formed 1st December 1917 at Waddington by redesignating an element of 51 Training Squadron. Became 97 Squadron, RAF from 1st April 1918 whilst at Netheravon.

Shorthorn; D.H.4; D.H.9 C2158; Handley Page O/400 D8311; Amiens III E5438.

Disbanded 1st April 1920 at Risalpur, India, to become 60 Squadron.

Reformed 16th September 1935 at Catfoss from 'B' Flight of 10 Squadron. Merged with 166 Squadron to become 4 Group Pool from 14th September 1939.

Nil (9.35–4.39)	*Heyford I K3499, II K4868, III K5189; Anson I N5008; Whitley II K7221.*
MR (4.39–9.39)	*Anson I N5011; Whitley II K7234, III K9013.*
OF (9.39–4.40)	*Anson I N5007; Whitley II K7229 OF-A, III K9011.*

Disbanded 8th April 1940 at Abingdon and merged with 166 Squadron to become 10 Operational Training Unit.

Reformed 30th April 1940 at Driffield.

Whitley proposed.

Disbanded 20th May 1940 at Driffield.

Reformed 25th February 1941 at Waddington from an element of 207 Squadron.

OF (2.41–4.51)	*Manchester I L7453 OF-X; Hampden I AE301; Lancaster I R5607 OF-X, III JA846 OF-B; Lincoln II RF516 OF-L.*
ZT	*Allocated to 'C' Flight but no evidence of use.*
AS and GB	*Lincoln II aircraft drawn from 83, 97 and 100 Squadrons were coded AS (e.g. RF467 AS-B) for an official visit to Chile in October 1946, but just before the visit commenced they were recoded GB (e.g. RF463 GB-A, RF467 GB-B and RF468 GB-C).*
Nil (4.51–1.56)	*Lincoln II WD143.*

Disbanded 1st January 1956 at Hemswell to become the 'Arrow' Squadron.

Reformed 1st December 1958 at Hemswell.

Thor.

Disbanded 24th May 1963 at Hemswell.

Reformed 25th May 1963 at Watton by renumbering 151 Squadron.

Canberra B.2 WJ616, T.4 WH839; Varsity T.1 WL687 Y; Hastings C.2 WJ338.

Disbanded 2nd January 1967 at Watton.

97 SQUADRON CONVERSION FLIGHT
Formed January 1942 at Coningsby.

OF	Manchester I L7467; Lancaster I R5895.

Disbanded 16th October 1942 at Swinderby and merged with 61 and 106 Squadron Conversion Flights to become 1660 Heavy Conversion Unit.

98 SQUADRON, RFC, later 98 SQUADRON, RAF
Formed 15th August 1917 at Harlaxton by redesignating an element of 44 Training Squadron. Became 98 Squadron, RAF from 1st April 1918 whilst at St Omer, France.

B.E.2c, B.E.2e; F.K.8; Avro 504K; D.H.4 N5977; D.H.9 D7224 H.

Disbanded 24th July 1919 at Shotwick.

Reformed 17th February 1936 at Abingdon from 'C' Flight of 15 Squadron.

Nil (2.36–4.39)	Hind K6717; Battle K9216.
OE (4.39–)	Battle K9209.
QF (–9.39)	Battle L5442 QF.
Nil (9.39–7.41)	Battle K9452; Anson I R3375; Hurricane IIA Z4049.
Also used	Battle Trainer P6755; Tiger Moth II T7106.

Disbanded 15th July 1941 at Kaldadarnes, Iceland, the Hurricane element having become 1423 (Fighter) Flight.

Reformed 12th September 1942 at West Raynham.

VO (9.42–2.51)	Mitchell II FV914 VO-A, III KJ666 VO-A; Mosquito XVI MM185 VO-E, B.35 TJ120 VO-Z.
L (2.51–4.55)	Vampire FB.5 WE834 L-L; Venom FB.1 WK412 L-Z.
Nil (4.55–7.57)	Hunter F.4 WW649 E.
Also used	Oxford II N4830; Mosquito III TV966; Vampire T.11 WZ514.

Disbanded 25th July 1957 at Jever, Germany.

Reformed 1st August 1959 at Driffield.

Thor.

Disbanded 18th April 1963 at Driffield.

Reformed 19th April 1963 at Tangmere by renumbering 245 Squadron.

Canberra B.2 WE122 J, T.4 WT488, B.15 WD948, E.15 WH964 4.

Disbanded 27th February 1976 at Cottesmore.

99 SQUADRON, RFC, later 99 SQUADRON, RAF
Formed 15th August 1917 at Yatesbury by redesignating an element of 13 Training Squadron. Became 99 Squadron, RAF from 1st April 1918 whilst at Ford Farm.

D.H.4 A7624; D.H.9 D3264, D.H.9A E8561.

Disbanded 1st April 1920 at Mianwali, India, to become 27 Squadron.

Reformed 1st April 1924 at Netheravon.

Nil (4.24–4.39)	Vimy IV J7238; Aldershot J6943, III J6954 8; Hyderabad J7750 T; Hinaidi K1074 T; Heyford I K3497, IA K4039, II K4877, III K5196; Wellington I L4217.
VF (4.39–9.39)	Wellington I L4217 VF-M, IA L7783.
LN (9.39–2.42)	Wellington I L4232, IA N3005, IC R1176 LN-B, II W5436 LN-Y.
Nil (6.42–11.45)	Wellington IC DV875, III HZ180, X HZ950 Z; Liberator VI EW115 S.
Also used	Handley Page 38 J9130; Hornet Moth LV763.

Disbanded 15th November 1945 in the Cocos Islands.

Reformed 17th November 1947 at Lyneham.

York C.1 PE103 AO; Hastings C.1 TG551 GAN, C.2 WD475 GAQ; Britannia C.1 XL636, C.2 XN404.

Disbanded 7th January 1976 at Brize Norton.

100 SQUADRON, RFC, later 100 SQUADRON, RAF
Formed 11th February 1917 at Hingham by redesignating an element of 51 Squadron. Became 100 Squadron, RAF from 1st April 1918 whilst at Ochey, France.

Nil (2.17–4.39)	F.E.2b A852, F.E.2c; B.E.2c, B.E.2d 5844, B.E.2e A3059; Handley Page 0/400 D8302; F.2B H1567; D.H.9A J7074 2; Avro 504K H5173 5; Vimy F9151; Fawn II J7209 3, III J7771 4; Horsley I J7988, II S1238 2; Vildebeest I K2815, II K2931, III K6372.
RA (4.39–9.39)	Vildebeest II K2932, III K6384 RA-T.
Nil (9.39–2.42)	Vildebeest II K2934, III K6385; Blenheim I L6598; Beaufort I.

Disbanded 8th February 1942 at Kemajoran, Java, and absorbed by 36 Squadron.

Reformed 14th December 1942 at Waltham.

HW (12.42–4.51)	Lancaster I ED749 HW-J, III EE181 HW-A2; Lincoln II SX942 HW-L.
AS and GB	Lincoln II aircraft drawn from 83, 97 and 100 Squadrons were coded AS (e.g. RF467 AS-B) for an official visit to Chile in October 1946, but just before the visit commenced they were recoded GB (e.g. RF463 GB-A, RF467 GB-B and RF468 GB-C).
Nil (4.51–9.59)	Lincoln II SX989; Canberra B.2 WH914, B.6 WH945, PR.7 WJ824.

Disbanded 31st August 1959 at Wittering.

Reformed 1st May 1962 at Wittering.

Victor B.2R XL160.

Disbanded 30th September 1968 at Wittering.

Reformed 1st February 1972 at West Raynham.

C	Canberra B(I).8 WT347, B.2 WP515 CD, T.4 WE188, PR.7 WT519 CH, T.11 WJ975, E.15 WH983 CP, TT.18 WJ682 CU, T.19 WJ610; Hawk T.1 XX164 CN, T.1A XX312 CF.

Current 1st April 1998 at Leeming.

101 SQUADRON, RFC, later 101 SQUADRON, RAF
Formed 12th July 1917 at Farnborough. Became 101 Squadron, RAF from 1st April 1919 whilst at Haute Vissée, France.

F.E.2b A5522, F.E.2d; B.E.12, B.E.12a; Pup B2188.

Disbanded 31st December 1919 at Eastleigh.

Reformed 21st March 1928 at Bircham Newton.

Nil (3.28– .35)	Sidestrand II J9187 E.
101 (.35–8.38)	Sidestrand III J9769 101-G; Overstrand K4561 101-U.
Nil (6.38–4.39)	Blenheim I L1118.
LU (4.39–9.39)	Blenheim I L1229, IV N6165 LU.
SR (9.39–4.51)	Blenheim IV P6906 SR-K; Wellington IC R3295 SR-P, III Z1625 SR-H; Lancaster I W4319 SR-N, III JA715 SR-M2; Lincoln II RA689 SR-J; Oxford I NM331 SR-J.
MW	Allocated to 'C' Flight from May 1942, although there is no evidence of use.
Nil (4.51–2.57)	Lincoln II RF499; Canberra B.2 WD938, B.6 WJ756.
Also used	Tutor K3396; Tiger Moth I K4279.

Disbanded 1st February 1957 at Binbrook.

Reformed 15th October 1957 at Finningley.

Vulcan B.1 XA910, B.1A XH482, B.2 XM602.

Disbanded 4th August 1982 at Waddington.

Reformed 1st May 1984 at Brize Norton.

VC-10 K.2 ZA140 A, K.3 ZA150 J, K.4 ZD242 P.

Current 1st April 1998 at Brize Norton.

101 SQUADRON CONVERSION FLIGHT
Formed 6th May 1942 at Oakington.

SR   *Stirling I N6032.*

Disbanded 7th October 1942 at Oakington and merged with 7, 149 and 218 Squadron Conversion Flights to become 1657 Heavy Conversion Unit.

102 SQUADRON, RFC, later 102 (CEYLON) SQUADRON, RAF
Formed 9th August 1917 at Hingham. Became 102 Squadron, RAF from 1st April 1918 whilst at Le Hameau, France.

F.E.2b B486, F.E.2d B1872.

Disbanded 3rd July 1919 at Lympne.

Reformed 1st October 1935 at Worthy Down from 'B' Flight of 7 Squadron.

Nil (10.35–4.39)	*Heyford II K4870 K, III K5188; Whitley III K8948.*
TQ (4.39–9.39)	*Whitley III K8957 TQ-S.*
DY (9.39–5.45)	*Whitley III K8976 DY-E, V T4261 DY-S; Halifax I L9532, II DT800 DY-P, III LW159 DY-P, VI RG505.*
EF (5.45–2.46)	*Liberator III FL992, V FL970, VI EV880 EF-T, VIII KN742.*
Also used	*Anson I R9808.*

Disbanded 28th February 1946 at Upwood to become 53 Squadron.

Reformed 20th October 1954 at Gutersloh, Germany.

Canberra B.2 WK113.

Disbanded 20th August 1956 at Gutersloh, elements becoming 59 Squadron.

Reformed 1st August 1959 at Full Sutton.

Thor.

Disbanded 27th April 1963 at Full Sutton.

102 SQUADRON CONVERSION FLIGHT
Formed 20th January 1942 at Dalton.

DY   *Halifax I L9510, II R9429.*

Disbanded 31st October 1942 at Pocklington and absorbed by 1658 Heavy Conversion Unit.

103 SQUADRON, RFC, later 103 SQUADRON, RAF
Formed 1st September 1917 at Beaulieu by redesignating an element of 16 Training Squadron. Became 103 Squadron, RAF from 1st April 1918 whilst at Old Sarum.

Various aircraft including D.H.9 D3046.

Disbanded 1st October 1919 at Shotwick.

Reformed 10th August 1936 at Andover.

Nil (8.36–4.39)	*Hind K5522; Battle K9261.*
GV (4.39–9.39)	*Battle K9261 GV-A.*
PM (9.39–11.45)	*Battle P2307 PM-K; Wellington IA N2997, IC Z1140 PM-X; Halifax II BB223 PM-B; Lancaster I W4828 PM-G, III JB278 PM-L.*
Also used	*Battle Trainer P6759; Magister T9675.*

Disbanded 25th November 1945 at Elsham Wolds to become 57 Squadron.

Reformed 30th November 1954 at Gutersloh, Germany.

Canberra B.2 WH916.

Disbanded 1st August 1956 at Gutersloh.

Reformed 1st August 1959 at Nicosia, Cyprus, by renumbering 284 Squadron.

Sycamore HR.14 XG517.

Disbanded 31st July 1963 at Nicosia to become 1563 and 1564 (Helicopter) Flights.

Reformed 1st August 1963 at Seletar, Singapore, from 'B' Flight of 110 Squadron.

Whirlwind HAR.10 XP362 R; Wessex HC.2 XS675 C.

Disbanded 1st August 1975 at Tengah, Singapore.

103 SQUADRON CONVERSION FLIGHT
Formed 2nd May 1942 at Elsham Wolds.

PM   *Halifax II R9390.*

Disbanded 10th October 1942 at Elsham Wolds and merged with 460 Squadron Conversion Flight to become 1656 Heavy Conversion Unit.

104 SQUADRON, RFC, later 104 SQUADRON, RAF
Formed 1st September 1917 at Wyton by redesignating an element of 20 Training Squadron. Became 104 Squadron, RAF from 1st April 1918 whilst at Andover.

Various aircraft including D.H.9 D2917; D.H.10.

Disbanded 30th June 1919 at Crail.

Reformed 7th January 1936 at Abingdon from 'C' Flight of 40 Squadron. Merged with 90 and 108 Squadrons to become 2 Group Pool from 14th September 1939.

Nil (1.36–9.39)	*Hind K5514 C; Blenheim I L1181; Anson I N5169.*
PO	*Allocated for the period April to September 1939.*
EP (9.39–4.40)	*Blenheim IV L8795 EP-B.*

Disbanded 6th April 1940 at Bicester and merged with 108 Squadron to become 13 Operational Training Unit.

Reformed 7th March 1941 at Driffield.

EP	*Wellington II Z8345 EP-S, X LN334; Liberator VI KL372 EP-C; Lancaster VII NX736 EP-P.*
Also used	*Lysander II N1224.*

Disbanded 1st April 1947 at Shallufa, Egypt.

Reformed 15th March 1955 at Gutersloh, Germany.

Canberra B.2 WH640.

Disbanded 1st August 1956 at Gutersloh.

Reformed 22nd July 1959 at Ludford Magna.

Thor.

Disbanded 24th May 1963 at Ludford Magna.

105 SQUADRON, RFC, later 105 SQUADRON, RAF
Formed 23rd September 1917 at Waddington by redesignating an element of 51 Training Squadron. Became 105 Squadron, RAF from 1st April 1918 whilst at Andover.

D.H.6; B.E.2b, B.E.2d; D.H.9; R.E.8; F.2B F4380.

Disbanded 1st February 1920 at Oranmore, Ireland, to become 2 Squadron.

Reformed 12th April 1937 at Upper Heyford from 'B' Flight of 18 Squadron.

Nil (4.37–)	*Audax K5590.*
105 (–10.38)	*Battle K7578 105-F.*
MT (10.38)	*Battle K7685 MT.*
Nil (10.38–9.39)	*Battle K9196.*
GB (9.39–1.46)	*Battle K9191 GB-W; Blenheim I L6812, IV L8788 GB-N; Mosquito IV DZ467 GB-P, IX LR508 GB-F, XVI ML956 GB-M.*
Also used	*Magister L5927; Anson I N5023; Tiger Moth II R5192; Master I T8288; Oxford I V4044, II ED109.*

Disbanded 1st February 1946 at Upwood.

Reformed 21st February 1962 at Benson.

Argosy C.1 XP412.

Disbanded 1st February 1968 at Muharraq, Bahrain.

106 SQUADRON, RFC, later 106 SQUADRON, RAF
Formed 23rd September 1917 at Spitalgate by redesignating an

element of 49 Training Squadron. Became 106 Squadron, RAF from 1st April 1918 whilst at Andover.

R.E.8 E57; F.2B F4373.

Disbanded 8th October 1919 at Fermoy, Ireland.

Reformed 1st June 1938 at Abingdon from 'A' Flight of 15 Squadron.

Nil (6.38–5.39)	*Hind K5413; Battle K7679.*
XS (5.39–9.39)	*Anson I N5166 XS-K; Hampden I L4182.*
ZN (9.39–2.46)	*Anson I N9909; Hampden I P1320 ZN-B; Manchester I L7417 ZN-V; Lancaster I R5677 ZN-B, III ND333 ZN-S.*

Disbanded 18th February 1946 at Metheringham.

Reformed 22nd July 1959 at Bardney.

Thor.

Disbanded 24th May 1963 at Bardney.

106 SQUADRON CONVERSION FLIGHT – see also 106 Conversion Flight
Formed 6th May 1942 at Coningsby.

Lancaster I W4778 .

Disbanded 16th October 1942 at Swinderby and merged with 61, 97 and 207 Squadron Conversion Flights to become 1660 Heavy Conversion Unit.

107 SQUADRON, RFC, later 107 SQUADRON, RAF
Formed 8th October 1917 at Catterick by redesignating an element of 46 Training Squadron. Became 107 Squadron, RAF from 1st April 1918 whilst at Lake Down.

D.H.9 D7341.

Disbanded 13th August 1919 at Hounslow.

Reformed 10th August 1936 at Andover.

107 (8.36–10.38)	*Hind K4653; Blenheim I L1288.*
BZ (10.38–9.39)	*Blenheim I L1298 BZ-A, IV N6180.*
OM (9.39–10.48)	*Blenheim I L1162, IV R3816 OM-J; Havoc I AE464; Boston III Z2252 OM-M, IIIA BZ226 OM-O; Mosquito VI LR264 OM-H.*
Also used	*Oxford I T1390, II T1080; Mosquito III HJ973.*

Disbanded 15th September 1948 at Wahn, Germany, to become 11 Squadron.

Reformed 22nd July 1959 at Tuddenham from 'C' Flight of 77 Squadron.

Thor.

Disbanded 10th July 1963 at Tuddenham.

108 SQUADRON, RFC, later 108 SQUADRON, RAF
Formed 1st November 1917 at Montrose by redesignating an element of 52 Training Squadron. Became 108 Squadron, RAF from 1st April 1918 whilst at Lake Down.

D.H.9 D613.

Disbanded 3rd July 1919 at Lympne.

Reformed 4th January 1937 at Upper Heyford from 'B' Flight of 57 Squadron. Merged with 90 and 104 Squadrons to become 2 Group Pool from 14th September 1939.

108 (1.37–10.38)	*Hind K6671; Blenheim I L1202 108-J.*
MF (10.38–4.39)	*Blenheim I L1217 MF-F; Anson I N5158.*
LD (9.39–4.40)	*Anson I N5158; Blenheim I L1269 LD-U, IV L9212.*

Disbanded 6th April 1940 at Bicester and merged with 104 Squadron to become 13 Operational Training Unit.

Reformed 1st August 1941 at Kabrit, Egypt.

Wellington IC Z1044 L, II Z8436; Liberator II AL566 P.

Disbanded 25th December 1942 at LG.237 (Jebil Hamsi), Egypt.

Reformed 10th March 1943 at Shandur, Egypt, from a Flight of 89 Squadron.

Beaufighter I V8691 P, VI ND181 Y; Mosquito XII HK127, XIII MM471 S; Magister P2399.

Disbanded 28th March 1945 at Lecce, Italy.

109 SQUADRON, RFC, later 109 SQUADRON, RAF
Formed 1st November 1917 at South Carlton by redesignating an element of 61 Training Squadron. Became 109 Squadron, RAF from 1st April 1918 whilst at Lake Down.

D.H.9 D5802.

Disbanded 19th August 1918 at Lake Down.

EH	*Allocated for the period April to September 1939.*

Reformed 10th December 1940 at Boscombe Down by redesignating the Wireless Intelligence Development Unit.

HS	*Anson I R9812 HS-G; Whitley V P5053; Wellington IC T2968 HS-S, VI DR481/G, VIA DR485/G; Lancaster I R5485; Mosquito IV DK333 HS-F, IX LR498 HS-O, XVI MM222 HS-X.*
Also used	*Tiger Moth II T6766; Leopard Moth AX858.*

Disbanded 30th April 1945 at Little Staughton.

Reformed 1st October 1945 at Woodhall Spa by renumbering 627 Squadron.

HS	*Mosquito III RR313, XVI RV299 HS-J, B.25 KB490, B.35 VR795 HS-B; Canberra B.2 WJ714, B.6 WJ771.*

Disbanded 1st February 1957 at Binbrook.

110 SQUADRON, RFC, later 110 (HYDERABAD) SQUADRON, RAF
Formed 1st November 1917 at Rendcomb by redesignating an element of 38 Training Squadron. Became 110 Squadron, RAF from 1st April 1918 whilst at Sedgeford.

B.E.2d, B.E.2e B4550; R.E.8; D.H.6; Elephant A6293; F.K.8 C8636; D.H.9 D3117; D.H.9A F1000.

Disbanded 27th August 1919 at Marquise, France.

Reformed 18th May 1937 at Waddington.

Nil (5.37–10.38)	*Hind K6809; Blenheim I K7145.*
AY (10.38–9.39)	*Blenheim I L1304 AY-Y, IV N6198 AY-B.*
VE (9.39–3.42)	*Blenheim IV R3741 VE-A.*
Nil (10.42–11.44)	*Vengeance I AN985 D, IA EZ900 Z, II AN683 D, III FB996, IV FD255; Mosquito VI RF586 C.*

Disbanded 7th April 1946 at Labuan, Borneo.

Reformed 1st June 1946 at Kai Tak, Hong Kong, by renumbering 96 Squadron.

Dakota IV KJ989 N; Valetta C.1 WJ497 U.

Disbanded 31st December 1957 at Changi, Singapore.

Reformed 3rd June 1959 at Kuala Lumpur, Malaya, by merging 155 and 194 Squadrons.

Whirlwind HAR.4 XJ410; Sycamore HR.14 XL822; Whirlwind HAR.10 XR479.

Disbanded 15th February 1971 at Changi, Malaya.

111 SQUADRON, RFC, later 111 SQUADRON, RAF
Formed 1st August 1917 at Deir-el-Ballah, Palestine, by redesignating an element of 14 Squadron. Became 111 Squadron, RAF from 1st April 1918 whilst at Ramleh, Palestine.

B.E.2e A3066; Bristol M.1B A5142; D.H.2; Vickers F.B.19 A5234 4; S.E.5a B139; Nieuport 17 B3597; Nieuport 23; Nieuport 24 B3592 S; F.2B A7194.

Disbanded 1st February 1920 at Ramleh, Palestine, to become 14 Squadron.

Reformed 1st October 1923 at Duxford.

Nil (10.23–4.39)	*Snipe F2441 S; Grebe IIIDC J7524; Siskin III J7152, IIIA J8974, IIIDC J9198; Bulldog IIA K1627; Gauntlet II K5264; Hurricane I L1548.*

TM (4.39–9.39)	Hurricane I L1564 TM-P.
JU (9.39–5.47)	Hurricane I L1973 JU-L, X P5187; Spitfire I N3058, IIA P7288, VB EP166 JU-N, VC EF697 JU-J, IXC EN517 JU-X.
Also used	Avro 504K E3146, Avro 504N J8996; Magister P2509.

Disbanded 16th May 1947 at Treviso, Italy.

Reformed 2nd December 1953 at North Weald.

Meteor F.4 RA368, T.7 WA612 S, F.8 WK693 T; Vampire T.11 XD550; Hunter F.4 WW651 F, F.6 XG129 F, T.7 XL610 Z; Lightning F.1 XM140 R, F.1A XM192 K, F.2 XN788, F.3 XP695 L, T.4 XM992 Z, T.5 XS421 T, F.6 XR747 X.

Disbanded 30th September 1974 at Wattisham.

Reformed 1st October 1974 at Coningsby having commenced training at Coningsby on 1st July 1974 as 111 Squadron (Designate).

Nil ( )	Phantom FGR.2 XV437 F, FG.1 XT873 A.
B ( )	Phantom FG.1 XT863 BG.
H ( )	Tornado F.3 ZE831 HJ.

Current 1st April 1998 at Leuchars.

112 SQUADRON, RFC, later 112 SQUADRON, RAF
Formed 25th July 1917 at Detling from 'B' Flight of 50 Squadron. Became 112 Squadron, RAF from 1st April 1918 whilst at Throwley.

Pup B1772; Camel D6473; Snipe E6643; Avro 504J C4378.

Disbanded 13th June 1919 at Throwley.

Reformed 16th May 1939 aboard HMS *Argus* at Portsmouth.

XO (5.39–9.39)	Gladiator I K7893 XO-S.
Nil (9.39– .40)	Gladiator I K8019; Gauntlet II K5318.
RT (.40–6.41)	Gladiator I K6134 RT-S, II N5918.
GA (6.41–12.46)	Tomahawk IIB AN337 GA-F; Kittyhawk I AK772 GA-Y, III FR315 GA-C; Mustang III HB830 GA-H, IVA KM127 GA-X.
Also used	Hind K6824; Gordon K2719; Magister P2396; Ca 100 GA-2; Ju 87 GA-S.

Disbanded 30th December 1946 at Treviso, Italy.

Reformed 12th May 1951 at Fassberg, Germany.

T (5.51–7.53)	Vampire FB.5 VZ240 T-P.
A (7.53–1.54)	Vampire FB.5 WA372 A-H.
Nil (1.54–5.57)	Meteor T.7 WF782 Z; Sabre F.4 XB978 N; Hunter F.4 XF293 N.

Disbanded 31st May 1957 at Bruggen, Germany.

Reformed 1st August 1960 at Church Fenton.

Bloodhound I.

Disbanded 31st March 1964 at Breighton.

Reformed 2nd November 1964 at Woodhall Spa.

Bloodhound II.

Disbanded 1st July 1975 at Paramali, Cyprus.

113 SQUADRON, RFC, later 113 SQUADRON, RAF
Formed 1st August 1917 at Ismailia, Egypt. Became 113 Squadron, RAF from 1st April 1918 whilst at Sarona, Palestine.

B.E.2e A3095; R.E.8 A4408; Nieuport 17; Nieuport 23; Nieuport 24.

Disbanded 1st February 1920 at Ismailia, Egypt, to become 208 Squadron.

Reformed 18th May 1937 at Upper Heyford.

Nil (5.37–4.39)	Hind K6734.
BT (4.39–9.39)	Hind K6734; Blenheim I L1527.
Nil (9.39– .40)	Blenheim I L1528.
AD (.40–9.43)	Blenheim I L4911 AD-H, IV V6012 AD-P, V BA916.
Nil (9.43–4.45)	Hurricane IIB HW881 X, IIC LA101.
AD (4.45–10.45)	Thunderbolt I HD173 AD-N, II KL221 AD-X.
Also used	Lysander II P1739; Magister P2393.

Disbanded 15th October 1945 at Zayatkwin, Burma.

Reformed 1st September 1946 at Aqir, Palestine, by renumbering 620 Squadron.

Halifax VII PP370, IX RT883 Y; Dakota IV KK204.

Disbanded 1st April 1947 at Aqir.

Reformed 1st May 1947 at Fairford.

Dakota IV KN475.

Disbanded 1st September 1948 at Fairford.

Reformed 22nd July 1959 at Mepal.

Thor.

Disbanded 10th July 1963 at Mepal.

114 SQUADRON, later 114 (HONG KONG) SQUADRON
Formed 22nd September 1917 at Lahore, India, from two Flights of 31 Squadron. Became 114 Squadron, RAF from 1st April 1918 whilst at Lahore, India.

B.E.2c 4143, B.E.2e; Henry Farman F.27; Dolphin C3862; F.2B H1509.

Disbanded 1st April 1920 at Lahore to become 28 Squadron.

Reformed 1st December 1936 at Wyton.

Nil (12.36–3.37)	Hind K5400; Audax K7409.
114 (3.37–4.39)	Blenheim I K7041 114-K.
FD (4.39–9.39)	Blenheim I L1206 FD-H, IV N6155 FD-F.
RT (9.39–11.42)	Blenheim I L1329, IV R3837 RT-T.
Nil (12.42–11.45)	Blenheim V EH322; Douglas A-20C 42-33205 T; Boston III W8329 P, IIIA BZ373 P, IV BZ552, V BZ589; Mitchell II FL178.
RT (11.45–9.46)	Mosquito VI TE659 RT-B, III RR296 RT-N.

Disbanded 1st September 1946 at Khormaksar, Aden, to become 8 Squadron.

Reformed 1st August 1947 at Kabrit, Egypt.

Dakota IV KN331; Valetta C.1 VW157 A.

Disbanded 31st December 1957 at Nicosia, Cyprus.

Reformed 20th November 1958 at Hullavington.

Chipmunk T.10 WP897 F.

Disbanded 14th March 1959 at Nicosia, Cyprus.

Reformed 13th April 1959 at Colerne.

Hastings C.1 TG524, C.2 WD481.

Disbanded 30th September 1961 at Colerne.

Reformed 1st October 1961 at Benson.

Argosy C.1 XN847.

Disbanded 31st October 1971 at Benson.

115 SQUADRON, RFC, later 115 SQUADRON, RAF
Formed 1st December 1917 at Catterick. Became 115 Squadron, RAF from 1st April 1918 whilst at Catterick.

Handley Page 0/400 D4577; F.E.2b A5761.

Disbanded 18th October 1919 at Ford Junction.

Reformed 15th June 1937 at Marham from 'B' Flight of 38 Squadron.

115 (6.37–4.39)	Hendon (loaned by 38 Squadron); Harrow I K6962 215-M, II K7019.
BK (4.39–9.39)	Harrow I K6944, II K7015; Wellington I L4221 BK-U.
KO (9.39–3.50)	Wellington I L4295, IA N2990 KO-P, IC P9297 KO-F, II W5459 KO-Q, III BJ756 KO-Q; Lancaster II DS777 KO-C, I HK555 KO-F, III ND754 KO-F; Lincoln II SX953 KO-H.
A4 (11.43–10.44)	('C' Flight) Lancaster II LL622 A4-F, I HK566 A4-F, III ND800 A4-C.
IL (11.44–8.45)	Lancaster I HK798 IL-L, III NG332 IL-D.
Also used	Stirling I BF416.

Disbanded 1st March 1950 at Mildenhall.

Reformed 13th June 1950 at Marham.

| KO (6.50–4.51) | Washington B.1 WF443 KO-D. |
| Nil (4.51–6.57) | Washington B.1 WF446; Canberra B.2 WJ752. |

Disbanded 1st June 1957 at Marham.

Reformed 21st August 1958 at Watton by renumbering 116 Squadron.

Varsity T.1 WF424 F; Valetta C.1 VX542; Argosy E.1 XR137; Andover C.1 XS640, E.1 XS605, E.3 XS605; E.3A XS639.

Disbanded 1st October 1993 at Benson.

116 SQUADRON, RFC, later 116 SQUADRON, RAF
Formed 1st December 1917 at Andover. Became 116 Squadron, RAF from 1st April 1918 whilst at Netheravon.

Handley Page 0/400 C9745.

Disbanded 20th November 1918 at Feltham.

| ZD | Allocated for the period April to September 1939. |

Reformed 17th February 1941 at Hatfield by redesignating 1 Anti-Aircraft Calibration Flight.

| II | Lysander I R2583, II N1247, III T1430 II-O, IIIA V9619 II-R; Scion Junior AV974; Hurricane I V7112 II-F, X AG205; Spitfire VA R6720; Phoenix II X9338; Tiger Moth II T7471; Hornet Moth X9310; Oxford I N4606, II N6417; Anson I N5145, XII PH625. |

Disbanded 26th May 1945 at Hornchurch.

Reformed 1st August 1952 at Watton by redesignating 'N' Calibration Squadron of the Central Signals Establishment.

Lincoln II WD124 46; Anson XIX VM332 27; Hastings C.1 TG560; Varsity T.1 WL622 R.

Disbanded 21st August 1958 at Watton to become 115 Squadron.

117 SQUADRON, RFC, later 117 SQUADRON, RAF
Formed 1st January 1918 at Waddington. Became 117 Squadron, RAF from 1st April 1918 whilst at Waddington.

D.H.9 C1176 F.

Disbanded 6th October 1918 at Gormanston and absorbed by 141 Squadron.

| EX | Allocated for the period April to September 1939. |

Reformed 30th April 1941 at Khartoum, Sudan, from 'C' Flight of 216 Squadron.

| Nil (4.41–7.42) | Bombay I L5826 P; Wellesley I K7767; Savoia-Marchetti SM.79K AX702 N; Caproni Ca 148 I-GOGG; Proctor I P6128; Gladiator I K6143, II N5756; D.H.86B HK829; Lodestar II EW994; Lockheed 14 AX681; Lockheed 18 AX687; Sentinel I KJ401; Dakota I FD768, III FD937, IV KN326 F; Auster III NJ987. |
| LD (7.42–9.43) | Hudson VI FK390 LD-H. |

Disbanded 17th December 1945 at Hmawbi, Burma.

118 SQUADRON, RFC, later 118 SQUADRON, RAF
Formed 1st January 1918 at Catterick. Became 118 Squadron, RAF from 1st April 1918 whilst at Catterick.

Handley Page 0/400 proposed – used various aircraft including F.E.2b.

Disbanded 7th September 1918 at Bicester.

| RE | Allocated for the period April to September 1939. |

Reformed 20th February 1941 at Filton.

| NK | Spitfire I X4412, IIA P8088 NK-K, VA R6809, VB EN966 NK-D, IXC ML247 NK-N, LF.VB BL718, VII MB763; Mustang III KH515 KN-X, IVA KM236. |
| Also used | Magister P6353; Auster I LB285; Tiger Moth I NM146, II R5028. |

Disbanded 10th March 1946 at Horsham St Faith.

Reformed 10th May 1951 at Fassberg, Germany.

A (4.51–3.55)	Vampire FB.5 WA293 A-C; Venom FB.1 WE388 A-M.
Nil (3.55–7.57)	Hunter F.4 WW657 G.
Also used	Vampire T.11 WZ517.

Disbanded 22nd August 1957 at Jever, Germany.

Reformed 12th May 1960 at Aldergrove by redesignating the Sycamore Flight of 228 Squadron.

Sycamore HR.14 XG544.

Disbanded 31st August 1962 at Aldergrove.

119 SQUADRON, RFC, later 119 SQUADRON, RAF
Formed 1st January 1918 at Andover. Became 119 Squadron, RAF from 1st April 1918 whilst at Duxford.

D.H.9 D5611.

Disbanded 6th December 1918 at Wyton.

| OM | Allocated for the period April to September 1939. |

Reformed 13th March 1941 at Bowmore by redesignating 'G' Flight.

Short S.23M 'C' Class AX659 W; Short S.26M 'G' Class X8274; Catalina I W8419 U.

Disbanded 6th December 1941 at Pembroke Dock.

Reformed 14th April 1942 at Lough Erne.

Catalina IIIA FP528; Sunderland II W6002 R, III JM676 H.

Disbanded 17th April 1943 at Pembroke Dock.

Reformed 19th July 1944 at Manston from the Albacore Flight of 415 Squadron.

| NH | Albacore I X9281 NH-K; Swordfish I L2739, III NF410 NH-F. |
| Also used | Anson I LT188. |

Disbanded 22nd May 1945 at Bircham Newton.

120 SQUADRON, RFC, later 120 SQUADRON, RAF
Formed 1st January 1918 at Cramlington. Became 120 Squadron, RAF from 1st April 1918 whilst at Cramlington.

D.H.9 D1177; Amiens III F1869 (on loan).

Disbanded 21st October 1919 at Lympne.

| MX | Allocated for the period April to September 1939. |

Reformed 2nd June 1941 at Nutts Corner.

OH (6.41–12.41)	Liberator I AM926 OH-F, II AL520 OH-N.
Nil (12.41–7.44)	Liberator III FK228 M, V BZ910 F.
OH (7.44–6.45)	Liberator VIII KH265 OH-X.
Also used	Blenheim IV Z6029; Hornet Moth W5749.

Disbanded 4th June 1945 at Ballykelly.

Reformed 1st October 1946 at St Eval by renumbering 160 Squadron.

BS (10.46–3.51)	Liberator VIII KL533/G BS-G; Lancaster III RF289 BS-G.
A (3.51–4.56)	Shackleton GR.1 VP261 A-J, MR.1A WG511 A-J, MR.2 WR955 A-H.
120 (4.56–)	Shackleton MR.2 WR956 120-A, MR.3 WR990 120-F; Nimrod MR.1, MR.2P XV243.
Also used	Oxford I V3190.

Current 1st April 1998 at Kinloss.

121 SQUADRON, RFC, later 121 (EAGLE) SQUADRON, RAF
Formed 1st January 1918 at Narborough. Became 121 Squadron, RAF from 1st April 1918 whilst at Narborough.

D.H.9 proposed – used various aircraft including F.K.3; R.E.8; D.H.6 A9738.

Disbanded 17th August 1918 at Filton.

JY	Allocated for the period April to September 1939.

Reformed 5th May 1941 at Kirton-in-Lindsey.

AV	Hurricane I P3097, IIB Z3669 AV-D; Spitfire IIA P8133, VB BM590 AV-R.
Also used	Magister T9832; Tiger Moth II DE262.

Disbanded 29th September 1942 at Debden to become 335th Fighter Squadron, 4th Fighter Group, USAAC.

122 SQUADRON, RFC, later 122 (BOMBAY) SQUADRON, RAF
Formed 1st January 1918 at Sedgeford. Became 122 Squadron, RAF from 1st April 1918 whilst at Sedgeford.

D.H.9 proposed – used various aircraft.

Disbanded 17th August 1918 at Sedgeford.

Reformed 29th October 1918 at Upper Heyford by merging elements of 9, 10, 11 and 15 Training Depot Stations.

No aircraft allocated.

Disbanded 20th November 1918 at Upper Heyford.

WM (4.39–9.39)	Allocated for the period April to September 1939.

Reformed 5th May 1941 at Turnhouse.

MT	Spitfire I N3236, IIA P8377, IIB P8257, VB BM352 MT-Z, IXC BS546 MT-J, LF.VB W3407 MT-R; Mustang III FB213, IV KH644, IVA KH678; Spitfire IX TE233, F.21 LA194.
Also used	Magister N3835; Tiger Moth II N6728; Auster I LB373, III MZ227; Harvard IIB FX224.

Disbanded 1st April 1946 at Dalcross to become 41 Squadron.

123 SQUADRON, RFC, later 123 (EAST INDIA) SQUADRON, RAF
Formed 1st February 1918 at Waddington. Became 123 Squadron, RAF from 1st April whilst at Duxford.

D.H.9 proposed – used various aircraft.

Disbanded 17th August 1918 at Duxford.

Reformed 20th November 1918 at Upper Heyford, also being allocated the title 2 Squadron, Canadian Air Force.

D.H.9A E732.

Disbanded 5th February 1920 at Shoreham.

ZE	Allocated for the period April to September 1939.

Reformed 10th May 1941 at Turnhouse.

XE (5.41–4.42)	Spitfire I R7122 XE-E, IIA P8437 XE-K, VB BL474.
Nil (10.42– .45)	Gladiator II N5857; Hurricane IIC JS418 C; Spitfire VC JK446; Thunderbolt I HD106, II KJ241.
XE (.45–6.45)	Thunderbolt II KJ260 XE-S.
Also used	Magister L8209

Disbanded 10th June 1945 at Baigachi, India, to become 81 Squadron.

124 SQUADRON, RFC, later 124 (BARODA) SQUADRON, RAF
Formed 1st February 1918 at Old Sarum. Became 124 Squadron, RAF from 1st April 1918 whilst at Fowlmere.

D.H.9 proposed – used various aircraft.

Disbanded 17th August 1918 at Fowlmere.

A de Havilland Mosquito Mk XVI of No 128 Squadron being loaded with a 4,000 lb HE 'Cookie'. This aircraft went missing over Hanover on 5th February 1945.

| PK | Allocated for the period April to September 1939. |

Reformed 10th May 1941 at Castletown.

| ON | Spitfire I X4108, IIA P8527, VA W3136, VB AB152 ON-T, VI BR579 ON-H, VII MB820 ON-E, IX RK908 ON-G, XVI SM515 ON-C; Meteor F.3 EE400 ON-H. |
| Also used | Magister P6344; Tiger Moth II T8252; Oxford II X7292; Auster I LB328. |

Disbanded 1st April 1946 at Bentwaters to become 56 Squadron.

125 SQUADRON, RFC, later 125 (NEWFOUNDLAND) SQUADRON, RAF
Formed 1st February 1918 at Old Sarum. Became 125 Squadron, RAF from 1st April 1918 whilst at Fowlmere.

D.H.9 proposed – used various aircraft.

Disbanded 17th August 1918 at Old Sarum.

| FN | Allocated for the period April to September 1939. |

Reformed 16th June 1941 at Colerne.

| VA | Defiant I V1132 VA-M, II AA437; Beaufighter II R2451 VA-H, VI V8750 VA-Z; Mosquito XVII HK310 VA-J, NF.30 NT435 VA-S. |
| Also used | Magister P6465; Blenheim I L8656; Oxford II N4851; Mosquito III HJ867. |

Disbanded 20th November 1945 at Church Fenton to become 264 Squadron.

Reformed 31st March 1955 at Stradishall

Meteor T.7 VW425, NF.11 WD614 F; Venom NF.3 WX913 F; Vampire T.11 XD602.

Disbanded 10th May 1957 at Stradishall.

126 SQUADRON, RFC, later 126 SQUADRON, RAF
Formed 1st February 1918 at Old Sarum. Became 126 Squadron, RAF from 1st April 1918 whilst at Fowlmere.

D.H.9 proposed – used various aircraft.

Disbanded 17th August 1918 at Fowlmere.

| UN | Allocated for the period April to September 1939. |

Reformed 28th June 1941 at Takali, Malta, from an element of 46 Squadron.

Nil (6.41–6.42)	Hurricane IIA BV173, IIB Z5118; Spitfire VB W3207; VC AR551 X.
V (6.42–12.42)	Spitfire VB EP332 V-A.
MK (12.42–6.43)	Spitfire VC BR471 MK-P, VIII JF352.
Nil (6.43–4.44)	Spitfire VC MA900 E, IX EN146 X.
5J (4.44–4.46)	Spitfire IXB MK211 5J-Y; Mustang III KH546 5J-Y, IV KM649 5J-J, IVA KM332; Spitfire XVI RW384.
Also used	Auster I LB325; Tiger Moth I NL929.

Disbanded 10th March 1946 at Hethel.

127 SQUADRON, RFC, later 127 SQUADRON, RAF, later 127 (SHADOW) SQUADRON, RAF
Formed 1st February 1918 at Catterick. Became 127 Squadron, RAF from 1st April 1918 whilst at Catterick.

D.H.9 proposed – used various aircraft.

Disbanded 4th July 1918 at Catterick and absorbed by 49 Training Depot Station.

| HF | Allocated for the period April to September 1939. |

Reformed 29th June 1941 at Habbaniya, Iraq, from 'F' Flight of 4 Flying Training School.

Gladiator I K7907, II N5857; Hurricane I P3731.

Disbanded 12th July 1941 at Habbaniya to become 261 Squadron.

Reformed 26th August 1941 at Kasfareet, Egypt, by redesignating an element of 249 Squadron.

Nil (2.42–6.42)	Hurricane I Z4233, IIB Z5388.
EJ (6.42–1.43)	Hurricane IIB BP332 EJ-R, IIC KX102 EJ-U.
Nil (1.43–4.44)	Hurricane IIC KZ113; Spitfire VB AB321, VC MA285.
9N (4.44–4.45)	Spitfire HF.IX NH583, LF.IX RK859, XVI RR257 9N-Y.
Also used	Auster III MZ168; Tiger Moth I NM146.

Disbanded 30th April 1945 at B.106 (Twente), Netherlands.

Reformed 1st November 1957 at Chivenor as 127 (Shadow) Squadron within 229 Operational Conversion Unit.

Hunter.

Disbanded 1st November 1958 at Chivenor to become 234 (Shadow) Squadron.

128 SQUADRON, RFC, later 128 SQUADRON, RAF
Formed 1st February 1918 at Thetford. Became 128 Squadron, RAF from 1st April 1918 whilst at Thetford.

D.H.9 proposed – used various aircraft.

Disbanded 4th July 1918 at Thetford.

| DQ | Allocated for the period April to September 1939. |

Reformed 7th October 1941 at Hastings, Sierra Leone, from the Hurricane Flight of 95 Squadron.

| WG | Hurricane I Z4484 WG-A, IIB BD776 WG-F, IIE BE688 WG-H. |

Disbanded 8th March 1943 at Hastings, Sierra Leone.

Reformed 15th September 1944 at Wyton.

| M5 | Mosquito B.20 KB199 M5-A, B.25 KB449 M5-V, XVI RV319 M5-B. |
| Also used | Mustang IVA KM148. |

Disbanded 31st March 1946 at Wahn, Germany, to become 14 Squadron.

129 SQUADRON, RFC, later 129 (MYSORE) SQUADRON, RAF
Formed 1st March 1918 at Duxford. Became 129 Squadron, RAF from 1st April 1918 whilst at Duxford.

D.H.9 proposed – used various aircraft.

Disbanded 4th July 1918 at Duxford.

| SS | Allocated for the period April to September 1939. |

Reformed 16th June 1941 at Leconfield.

| DV | Spitfire I X4427, IIA P7853, VB AA721, VC EE602 DV-V, VI BR577, IX MH377 DV-B; Mustang I AG595, III FX941 DV-X; Spitfire IX RR185 DV-Q. |
| Also used | Magister P6401; Tiger Moth II T7182; Auster III NK126. |

Disbanded 1st September 1946 at Church Fenton to become 257 Squadron.

130 SQUADRON, RFC, later 130 (PUNJAB) SQUADRON, RAF
Formed 1st March 1918 at Wyton. Became 130 Squadron, RAF from 1st April 1918 whilst at Hucknall.

D.H.9 proposed – used various aircraft.

Disbanded 4th July 1918 at Hucknall.

| TX | Allocated for the period April to September 1939. |

Reformed 16th June 1941 at Portreath.

| PJ | Spitfire IIA P7319, VA X4172, VB BL712 PJ-X, VC AR614 PJ-E. |
| Also used | Magister N3823. |

Disbanded 13th February 1944 at Scorton.

Reformed 5th April 1944 at Lympne by renumbering 186 Squadron.

| AP | Spitfire VB AR511, XIV RM619 AP-D, IXB TE215 AP-A; Vampire F.1 TG352 AP-W. |
| Also used | Tiger Moth I NL929, II R4906; Auster IV MS951. |

Disbanded 31st January 1947 at Odiham to become 72 Squadron.

Reformed 1st August 1953 at Bruggen, Germany.

Sabre F.4 XB949 Z; Hunter F.4 XF294 B. Also used Vampire T.11 XD441.

Disbanded 31st May 1957 at Bruggen.

Reformed 1st December 1959 at Polebrook.

Thor.

Disbanded 23rd August 1963 at Polebrook.

131 SQUADRON, RFC, later 131 (COUNTY OF KENT) SQUADRON, RAF, later 131 (SHADOW) SQUADRON, RAF
Formed 15th March 1918 at Shawbury. Became 131 Squadron, RAF from 1st April 1918 whilst at Shawbury.

D.H.9 proposed – used various aircraft including F.E.2b; D.H.4 C7864.

Disbanded 17th August 1918 at Shawbury.

| RK | Allocated for the period April to September 1939. |

Reformed 30th June 1941 at Ouston.

| NX | Spitfire I X4033, IIA P8180, VB BM420 NX-A, VC EE767, IX MA834 NX-A, VII MD120, VIII JG178. |
| Also used | Magister N3790; Tiger Moth II T6110. |

Disbanded 10th June 1945 at Dalbumgarh, India.

Reformed 10th June 1945 at Ulunderpet, India, by renumbering 134 Squadron.

| NX | Thunderbolt II HD223. |

Disbanded 31st December 1945 at Kuala Lumpur, Malaya.

Reformed 1st October 1958 at Chivenor as 131 (Shadow) Squadron within 229 Operational Conversion Unit.

Hunter.

Disbanded 1st November 1958 at Chivenor to become 145 (Shadow) Squadron.

132 SQUADRON, RFC, later 132 (CITY OF BOMBAY) SQUADRON, RAF
Formed 1st March 1918 at Ternhill. Became 132 Squadron, RAF from 1st April 1918 whilst at Ternhill.

Handley Page O/400 proposed – used various aircraft including Shorthorn F2230.

Disbanded 23rd December 1918 at Castle Bromwich.

| TD | Allocated for the period April to September 1939. |

Reformed 7th July 1941 at Peterhead.

| FF | Spitfire I R7215 FF-E, IIA P8591, VB BM648 FF-R, VC EE683, LF.VB EN922 FF-U, IXB MK810 FF-N, IXE NH575 FF-F, VIII JG323, XIV RN133 FF-B. |
| Also used | Magister P2443; Tiger Moth II T6313. |

Disbanded 15th April 1946 at Kai Tak, Hong Kong.

133 SQUADRON, RFC, later 133 (EAGLE) SQUADRON, RAF
Formed 1st March 1918 at Ternhill. Became 133 Squadron, RAF from 1st April 1918 whilst at Ternhill.

Handley Page O/400 proposed – used various aircraft including F.E.2b.

Disbanded 4th July 1918 at Ternhill.

| YR | Allocated for the period April to September 1939. |

Reformed 31st July 1941 at Coltishall.

| MD | Hurricane I N2669, IIB Z3781 MD-U; Spitfire I N3292, IIA P8191 MD-G, VA P9397, VB BL995 MD-G, IX BS272 MD-B. |
| Also used | Magister L8083. |

Disbanded 29th September 1942 at Great Sampford to become 336th Fighter Squadron, 4th Fighter Group, United States Army Air Corps.

134 SQUADRON, RFC, later 134 SQUADRON, RAF
Formed 1st March 1918 at Ternhill. Became 133 Squadron, RAF from 1st April 1918 whilst at Ternhill.

Handley Page O/400 proposed – used various aircraft.

Disbanded 4th July 1918 at Ternhill.

| AA | Allocated for the period April to September 1939. |

Reformed 28th July 1941 at Leconfield by redesignating an element of 17 Squadron.

| G Prefix | Hurricane IIA Z5253 GA-25. |

Withdrawn 16th November 1941 to the United Kingdom from Vaenga, Russia, and reassembled at Catterick on 7th December 1941.

Nil (12.41–11.43)	Spitfire IIA P7563, VA X4173, VB AB275 B, VC JK118; Hurricane IIB BD704, IIC BP442 X.
GQ (11.43–7.45)	Hurricane IIC PJ779 GQ-U; Thunderbolt I HB992 GQ-H, II KL339 GQ-B.
Also used	Magister L8083; Oxford II AB644.

Disbanded 10th June 1945 at Kyaukpyu, India, to become 131 Squadron.

135 SQUADRON, RFC, later 135 SQUADRON, RAF
Formed 1st April 1918 at Hucknall. Became 133 Squadron, RAF from 1st April 1918 whilst at Hucknall.

D.H.9 proposed – used various aircraft.

Disbanded 4th July 1918 at Hucknall.

| GO | Allocated for the period April to September 1939. |

Reformed 15th August 1941 at Baginton.

| WK | Hurricane I Z5649 WK-C, IIA DG623, IIB BG994 WK-D, IIC LB618 WK-P, IV LB851; Thunderbolt I HB975 WK-L. |
| Also used | Harvard IIB FE720. |

Disbanded 10th June 1945 at Chakulia, Burma (air echelon) and Akyab, Burma (groundcrew) to become 615 Squadron.

136 SQUADRON, RFC, later 136 SQUADRON, RAF
Formed 1st April 1918 at Lake Down. Became 133 Squadron, RAF from 1st April 1918 whilst at Lake Down.

D.H.9 proposed – used various aircraft.

Disbanded 4th July 1918 at Lake Down.

| XY | Allocated for the period April to September 1939. |

Reformed 20th August 1941 at Kirton-in-Lindsey.

Nil (8.41– .44)	Hurricane IIB BN167, IIA Z2389, IIC LD395.
HM (.44–5.46)	Spitfire VIII MT966 HM-U, XIV RN193 HM-A.
Also used	Spitfire VB AB192; Magister I L8226

Disbanded 8th May 1946 at Bombay, India, to become 152 Squadron.

137 SQUADRON, RFC, later 137 SQUADRON, RAF, later 137 (SHADOW) SQUADRON, RAF
Formed 1st April 1918 at Shawbury. Became 133 Squadron, RAF from 1st April 1918 whilst at Shawbury.

D.H.9 proposed – used various aircraft.

Disbanded 4th July 1918 at Shawbury.

| TS | Allocated for the period April to September 1939. |

Reformed 20th February 1941 at Charmy Down.

SF	Whirlwind I P7119 SF-W; Hurricane IV KW198; Typhoon IB JR261 SF-Z.
Also used	Magister I T9908; Tiger Moth II DE510; Auster IV MS951.

Disbanded 26th August 1945 at Warmwell to become 174 Squadron.

Reformed June 1957 at Leeming as 137 (Shadow) Squadron within 228 Operational Conversion Unit.

Javelin.

Disbanded September 1961 at Leeming.

138 SQUADRON
Formed 30th September 1918 at Chingford by merging elements of 1, 5, 36 and 45 Training Depot Stations.

F.2B D8084 S.

Disbanded 1st February 1919 at Chingford.

WO	Allocated for the period April to September 1939.

Reformed 25th August 1941 at Newmarket by redesignating 1419 (Special Duties) Flight.

NF (8.41–3.45)	Lysander I R2626, III T1770; Whitley V Z9146 NF-P; Liberator III BZ858; Halifax II JD172 NF-S, V LK743 NF-J; Stirling IV LK125 NF-S.
AC (3.45–4.47)	Lancaster I PA193 AC-D.
NF (4.47–9.50)	Lancaster I NN781 NF-N; Lincoln II SX951 NF-Z.
Also used	Oxford II N6422; Mosquito III TV966.

Disbanded 1st September 1950 at Wyton.

Reformed 1st January 1955 at Gaydon.

Valiant B(PR).1 WZ384, B(PR)K.1 WZ389, B(K)1 WZ400.

Disbanded 1st April 1962 at Wittering.

139 SQUADRON
Formed 3rd July 1918 at Villaverla, Italy, from 'Z' Flight of 34 Squadron.

F.2B E2285 A; Camel B6313.

Disbanded 7th March 1919 at Blandford.

Reformed 3rd September 1936 at Wyton.

Nil (9.36–4.39)	Hind K5371; Blenheim I K7078 J.
SY (4.39–9.39)	Blenheim I K7064 SY-H, IV N6215 SY-M.
XD (9.39–3.42)	Blenheim I L6796, IV N6218 XD-G; Hudson III AE564.

Disbanded 30th April 1942 at Dum-Dum, India, to become 62 Squadron.

Reformed 8th June 1942 at Horsham St Faith.

XD (6.42– .51)	Blenheim V AZ947; Mosquito IV DZ421 XD-G, IX LR475 XD-W, III HJ855, XVI MM146 XD-H, B.20 KB191 XD-L, B.25 KB390 XD-B, B.35 VP185 XD-N.
Nil (.51–12.59)	Mosquito B.35 TA645; Canberra B.2 WH651, B.6 WJ778.
Also used	Oxford I V4044, II AB722.

Disbanded 31st December 1959 at Binbrook.

Reformed 1st February 1962 at Wittering.

Victor B.2 XL190.

Disbanded 31st December 1968 at Wittering.

140 SQUADRON
RM	Allocated for the period April to September 1939.

Formed 17th September 1941 at Benson by redesignating 1416 (Reconnaissance) Flight.

ZW (8.41–2.42)	Blenheim IV R3825 ZW-L; Spitfire IV R7139 ZW-C, VII R7116 ZW-C.

Nil (2.42–11.45)	Spitfire I X4010, PR.V X4784, PR.IV P9505, PR.VII R6910, PR.XI MB947; Ventura I AE779; Mosquito IX MM249, XVI NS777.
Also used	Wellington IC T2564; Lysander III R9105; Master I N7923; Oxford II R6231; Proctor III Z7208; Vigilant IA BZ108; Mosquito II DD626, III HJ877.

Disbanded 20th September 1945 at Fersfield.

141 SQUADRON, RFC, later 141 SQUADRON, RAF
Formed 1st January 1918 at Rochford from 'A' Flight of 61 Squadron. Became 141 Squadron, RAF from 1st April 1918 whilst at Biggin Hill.

Dolphin C3942; B.E.12 C3195, B.E.12b; Pup; Vickers F.B.26 B1484; B.E.2e B723; F.2B C4631.

Disbanded 1st February 1920 at Baldonnel and absorbed by 100 Squadron.

UD	Allocated for the period April to September 1939.

Reformed 4th October 1939 at Turnhouse.

Nil (10.39–4.40)	Gladiator I K7921; Blenheim I K7059; Battle L5406.
TW (4.40–9.45)	Defiant I L7009 TW-H, II AA405; Beaufighter I X7847 TW-N, II V8253 TW-T, VI V8673 TW-K; Mosquito II DD717 TW-M, VI HR203 TW-C, NF.36 NT500 TW-K.
Also used	Tiger Moth II N6932; Magister P2384; Harvard I P5868; Oxford II N4829.

Disbanded 7th September 1945 at Little Snoring.

Reformed 17th June 1946 at Wittering.

TW (6.46–4.51)	Mosquito III RR307 TW-Y, NF.36 RL145 TW-E.
Nil (4.51–1.68)	Meteor F.4 RA454, NF.11 WM164 Y, T.7 WG936; Venom NF.2 WL827, NF.3 WX928 K; Javelin FAW.4 XA759 759.
Also used	Vampire T.11 XD444.

Disbanded 1st February 1958 at Coltishall to become 41 Squadron.

Reformed 1st April 1959 at Dunholme Lodge.

Bloodhound I.

Disbanded 31st March 1964 at Dunholme Lodge.

142 SQUADRON, RFC, later 142 SQUADRON, RAF
Formed 2nd February 1818 at Ismailia, Egypt. Became 142 Squadron, RAF from 1st April 1918 whilst at Julis, Palestine.

B.E.12 A6328; Elephant A4000; R.E.8 B7710; B.E.2e A3066; F.K.8 C3617; D.H.9 D573.

Disbanded 1st February 1920 at Suez, Egypt, to become 55 Squadron.

Reformed 1st June 1934 at Netheravon.

Nil (6.34–4.39)	Hart K2462; Hind K6655; Battle K7688.
KB (4.39–9.39)	Battle K9321 KB-M.
QT (9.39–10.44)	Battle K9204 QT-G; Wellington II W5455 QT-X, IV Z1338 QT-S, III DF642 QT-J, X LN700 QT-R.

Disbanded 5th October 1944 at Regina, Italy.

Reformed 25th October 1944 at Gransden Lodge.

4H	Mosquito B.25 KB444 4H-B, B.35 TH980.

Disbanded 28th September 1945 at Gransden Lodge.

Reformed 1st February 1959 at Eastleigh, Kenya.

Venom FB.4 WR400. Also used Vampire T.11 XE991.

Disbanded 1st April 1959 at Eastleigh to become 208 Squadron.

Reformed 22nd July 1959 at Coleby Grange.

Thor.

Disbanded 24th May 1963 at Coleby Grange.

143 SQUADRON, RFC, later 143 SQUADRON, RAF

Formed 1st February 1918 at Throwley by redesignating an element of 112 Squadron. Became 143 Squadron, RAF from 1st April 1918 whilst at Detling.

F.K.8 B229; S.E.5a C1802 2; Camel F2175; Snipe E6843.

Disbanded 31st October 1919 at Detling.

TK	*Allocated for the period April to September 1939.*

Reformed 15th June 1941 at Aldergrove from an element of 252 Squadron.

HO (6.41–8.43)	*Beaufighter I T4757 HO-R; Blenheim I L1102, IV N3603 HO-B; Beaufort I L9966; Beaufighter II V8159 HO-V, XI JL890 HO-X.*
2 (8.43–7.44)	*Beaufighter XI, X.*
HO (7.44–10.44)	*Beaufighter X JM279 HO-Y.*
NE (10.44–5.45)	*Beaufighter X LX808 NE-K; Mosquito II DZ700, VI HR373 NE-N.*
Also used	*Mosquito III LR581.*

Disbanded 25th May 1945 at Banff to become 14 Squadron.

144 SQUADRON, RFC, later 144 SQUADRON, RAF

Formed 20th March 1918 at Port Said, Egypt. Became 141 Squadron, RAF from 1st April 1918 whilst at Port Said.

B.E.2e B3683; B.E.12 A6347; Elephant A1600; R.E.8 B6681; D.H.6 C7615; D.H.9 D3100 3.

Disbanded 4th February 1919 at Ford Junction.

Reformed 11th January 1937 at Bicester from 'B' Flight, 101 Squadron.

Nil (1.37–4.39)	*Overstrand K4564; Anson I K6269; Audax K8312; Blenheim K7079.*
NV (4.39–9.39)	*Blenheim I L1324 NV-J; Hampden I L4132 NV-G*
PL (9.39–5.45)	*Hampden I P2080 PL-M; Beaufighter VI JL654 PL-H, X LZ216 PL-N.*
Also used	*Anson I N5080; Blenheim IV V5430; Beaufighter I T3350.*

Disbanded 25th May 1945 at Dallachy.

Reformed 1st December 1959 at North Luffenham.

Thor.

Disbanded 23rd August 1963 at North Luffenham.

145 SQUADRON, RAF, later 145 (SHADOW) SQUADRON

Formed 15th May 1918 at Aboukir, Egypt.

S.E.5a C1767.

Disbanded 6th September 1919 at Suez, Egypt.

SO	*Allocated for the period April to September 1939.*

Reformed 10th October 1939 at Croydon.

SO (10.39–2.42)	*Blenheim I K7159 SO-N; Hurricane I V7422 SO-P; Spitfire I X4337, IIA P7605 SO-N, IIB P8326, VA P8438.*
ZX (4.42–8.45)	*Spitfire VB ER848, VC ES315, IX MT928 ZX-M, VIII LV729 ZX-M.*
Also used	*SM.79 ZX.*

Note   See also the Polish Fighting Team.

Disbanded 19th August 1945 at Treviso, Italy.

Reformed 1st March 1952 at Celle, Germany.

B (3.52–4.54)	*Vampire FB.5 VZ866 B-E.*
Nil (4.54–10.57)	*Venom FB.1 WK408.*
Also used	*Vampire T.11 WZ559.*

Disbanded 15th October 1957 at Celle.

Reformed 1st November 1958 at Chivenor as 145 (Shadow) Squadron within 229 Operational Conversion Unit by redesignating 131 (Shadow) Squadron.

Hunter.

Disbanded 1st June 1963 at Chivenor to become 63 (Shadow) Squadron.

146 SQUADRON, RAF

YZ	*Allocated for the period April to September 1939.*

Formed 15th October 1941 at Risalpur, India, from 'B' Flight of 5 Squadron.

Audax K7316; Buffalo I W8246; Hurricane IIB HL802 J, IIC LB617; Thunderbolt I HD110 L, II KL190 D.

Disbanded 1st July 1945 at Meiktila, Burma, to become 42 Squadron.

147 SQUADRON, RAF

RT	*Allocated for the period April to September 1939.*

Formed administratively 17th October 1941 at Fayid, Egypt, as a transport unit with the intention of equipping the unit with Bombay aircraft from 216 Squadron. With a change in the planned role, the groundcrew supported the operations of 159 and 160 Squadrons while awaiting delivery of their own Liberator bombers.

Wellington II Z8520.

Disbanded 15th February 1943 at Shandur, Egypt, and absorbed by 178 Squadron.

Reformed 1st September 1944 at Croydon.

5F	*Allocated but no evidence of use.*
Nil	*Dakota III KG808, IV KN268; Oxford II W6509; Anson XII PH767, XIX TX238; Proctor III R7567.*

Disbanded 15th September 1946 at Croydon.

Reformed 1st February 1953 at Abingdon by redesignating 1 (Long-Range) Ferry Unit.

Ferried Sabres from Canada to the United Kingdom and Germany, Vampires (FB.9 WR197) and Venoms (WE385) to the Middle and Far East and Swifts and Hunters to Germany.

Disbanded 15th September 1958 at Benson and merged with 167 Squadron to become absorbed by the Ferry Squadron.

148 SQUADRON, RFC, later 148 SQUADRON, RAF

Formed 10th February 1918 at Andover. Became 148 Squadron, RAF from 1st April 1918 whilst at Ford Junction.

F.E.2b D9117.

Disbanded 4th July 1919 at Tangmere.

Reformed 7th June 1937 at Scampton by redesignating an element of 9 Squadron.

Nil (6.37–4.39)	*Audax K7432; Wellesley I L2642; Heyford III K6905; Wellington I L4280; Anson I N5188.*
BS (4.39–9.39)	*Wellington I L4304 BS-Z; Anson I N5188.*
Nil (9.39–4.40)	*Wellington I L4267; Anson I N5188.*

Disbanded 8th April 1940 at Harwell and merged with 75 Squadron to become 15 Operational Training Unit.

Reformed 30th April 1940 at Stradishall.

Wellington IC.

Disbanded 20th May 1940 at Stradishall.

Reformed 1st December 1940 at Luqa, Malta, by redesignating the Wellington Flight, Malta.

Wellington IC HE107 C, II Z8371 A.

Disbanded 31st December 1942 at LG.167 (Bir el Baheira 2), Libya.

Reformed 14th March 1943 at Gambut, Libya, by redesignating the Special Operations (Liberator) Flight.

FS (3.43–1.46)	*Liberator II AL510 FS-W; Halifax II JN896 FS-L, V EB154 J; Lysander IIIA T1750 FS-B; Liberator VI KL545 FS-Z; Halifax A.7 PN244.*

Disbanded 15th January 1946 at Gianaclis, Egypt.

Reformed 4th November 1946 at Upwood.

AU (11.46–4.51)   *Lancaster I TW668 AU-T; Lincoln II SX987*
        AU-Y.
Nil (4.51–7.55)   *Lincoln II SX988.*

Disbanded 1st July 1955 at Upwood.

Reformed 1st July 1956 at Marham.

Valiant B(K).1 XD817, B.1 WZ363, B(PR).1 WZ384, B(PR)K.1 WZ395.

Disbanded 1st May 1965 at Marham.

149 SQUADRON, RFC, later 149 (EAST INDIA) SQUADRON, RAF
Formed 1st March 1918 at Ford Junction. Became 149 Squadron, RAF from 1st April 1918 whilst at Ford Junction.

F.E.2b C9799, F.E.2d A6439.

Disbanded 1st August 1919 at Tallaght, Ireland.

Reformed 12th April 1937 at Mildenhall from 'B' Flight of 99 Squadron.

Nil (4.37–1.39)   *Heyford I K3494, IA K4025, II K4877, III K5199.*
LY (1.39–9.39)   *Wellington I L4272 LY-G.*
OJ (9.39–3.50)   *Wellington I L4272 OJ-C, IA P9218 OJ-O, IC*
        N2783 OJ-W, II W5399 OJ-Q; Stirling I W7461
        OJ-N, III EF412 OJ-F; Lancaster I NG361
        OJ-E, III PB509 OJ-C, I/FE PA410 OJ-X;
        Lincoln B.2 SX982 OJ-W.
TK (4.43–6.45)   *('C' Flight) Stirling III BF570 TK-H; Lancaster I*
        PP686 TK-J.
Also used   *Magister P6462.*

Disbanded 1st March 1950 at Mildenhall.

Reformed 9th August 1950 at Marham.

OJ (8.50–4.51)   *Washington B.1 WF492 OJ-U.*
Nil (4.51–8.56)   *Washington B.1 WF494; Canberra B.2 WJ612,*
        T.4 WJ868.

Disbanded 31st August 1956 at Gutersloh, Germany.

149 SQUADRON CONVERSION FLIGHT
Formed 21st January 1942 at Mildenhall.

OJ   *Stirling I N6122.*

Disbanded 7th October 1942 at Lakenheath and merged with 7, 101 and 218 Squadron Conversion Flights to become 1657 Heavy Conversion Unit.

150 SQUADRON, RAF
Formed 1st April 1918 at Kirec, Macedonia, by merging the 'A' Flights of 17 and 47 Squadrons.

Bristol M.1C C4912; S.E.5a B28; Camel C1599; B.E.12a; B.E.2e; F.K.8.

Disbanded 18th September 1919 at San Stephano, Turkey.

Reformed 8th August 1938 at Boscombe Down.

Nil (8.38–10.38)   *Battle K7667.*
DG (10.38–9.39)   *Battle K9483 DG-O.*
JN (9.39–10.44)   *Battle L4947 JN-C; Wellington IA N2998, IC*
        R1042 JN-A, III X3743 JN-D, X HF482 JN-A.
Also used   *Tiger Moth X9318; Liberator II AL506.*

Disbanded 5th October 1944 at Regina, Italy.

Reformed 1st November 1944 at Fiskerton from 'C' Flight of 550 Squadron.

IQ   *Lancaster I NG333 IQ-X, III JB613 IQ-Y.*

Disbanded 7th November 1945 at Hemswell.

Reformed 1st August 1959 at Carnaby.

Thor.

Disbanded 9th April 1963 at Carnaby.

151 SQUADRON, later 151 (SHADOW) SQUADRON, later 151 (RESERVE) SQUADRON, RAF
Formed 12th June 1918 at Hainault Farm by merging elements of 44, 78 and 112 Squadrons.

Camel B2458 R.

Disbanded 10th September 1919 at Gullane.

Reformed 4th August 1936 at North Weald from 'B' Flight of 56 Squadron.

Nil (8.36–9.38)   *Gauntlet II K5288.*
TV (9.38–12.38)   *Gauntlet II K5276.*
GG (12.38–9.39)   *Hurricane I L1768 GG-K.*
DZ (9.39–10.46)   *Hurricane I P3650 DZ-H; X P5182, Defiant I*
        N1790 DZ-P; Hurricane IIC Z3224; Defiant II
        AA436 DZ-V; Mosquito II HJ655 DZ-V, XII
        HK183 DZ-W, XIII MM437 DZ-F, VI PZ201,
        T.29 KA138, NF.30 MM800 DZ-V.
Also used   *Magister I P2495; Spitfire VB AB167; Anson I*
        N5183; Oxford I P9027, II P8918; Mosquito III
        HJ970.

Disbanded 10th October 1946 at Weston Zoyland.

Reformed 15th September 1951 at Leuchars.

Vampire NF.10 WM675 R; Meteor T.7 VW457 X, F.8 VZ508, NF.11 WD623 S; Venom NF.3 WX805 S; Javelin T.3, FAW.5 XA710 Y. Also used Vampire T.11 XE925.

Disbanded 19th September 1961 at Leuchars.

Reformed 1st January 1962 at Watton by redesignating the Signals Development Squadron.

Lincoln II WD132 C; Hastings C.2 WJ338; Varsity T.1 WF376; Canberra B.2 WH642, T.4 WH839.

Disbanded 25th May 1963 at Watton to become 97 Squadron.
Reformed 1st September 1981 at Chivenor as 151 (Shadow) Squadron within 2 Tactical Weapons Unit.

Hawk T.1.

Disbanded 1st April 1992 at Chivenor.

Reformed 1st April 1992 at Chivenor as 151 (Reserve) Squadron within 7 Flying Training School.

Hawk T.1, T.1A.

Disbanded 23rd September 1992 at Chivenor to become 92 (Reserve) Squadron.

152 (HYDERABAD) SQUADRON, RAF
Formed 1st October 1918 at Rochford.

Camel F1891.

Disbanded 30th June 1919 at Gullane.

YJ   *Allocated for the period April to September*
        1939.

Reformed 2nd October 1939 at Acklington.

UM   *Gladiator II N5640 UM-M; Spitfire I X4550*
        UM-W, IIA P8204, VB EN788, VC LZ807
        UM-V, IX MA454 UM-V, VIII MT946 UM-N, XIV
        RM908 UM-G.
Also used   *Tutor K3344; Hart K6482; Gladiator I K7972;*
        Magister R1916; Harvard I P5868, IIB FE488;
        Tiger Moth II DE446; Harvard IIB FE488;
        Wellington VIII HX532.

Disbanded 10th March 1946 at Tengah, Singapore.

Reformed 8th May 1946 while in transit to Worli, India, by renumbering 136 Squadron.

UM   *Spitfire VIII MT606; Tempest F.2 PR747 UM-L.*

Disbanded 15th January 1947 at Risalpur, India.

Reformed 30th June 1954 at Wattisham.

Meteor NF.12 WS606 E, NF.14 WS749 N, T.7 WL422.

Disbanded 31st July 1958 at Stradishall.

Reformed 1st October 1958 at Muharraq, Bahrain, by redesignating 1417 (Communications) Flight.

Pembroke C.1 WV743 J; Twin Pioneer CC.1 XM285 M.

Disbanded 15th November 1967 at Muharraq.

153 SQUADRON, RAF
Formed 4th November 1918 at Hainault Farm.

Camel.

Disbanded 13th June 1919 at Hainault Farm.

XZ	*Allocated for the period April to September 1939.*

Reformed 24th October 1941 at Ballyhalbert from 'A' Flight of 256 Squadron.

TB (10.41–12.42)	*Defiant I N3381; Beaufighter I X7774 TB-V, VI V8895 TB-F.*
Nil (12.42–9.44)	*Beaufighter VI KW150 E; Hurricane IIC LB677; Spitfire VC LZ976, IX MK950.*
Also used	*Magister L5949; Blenheim I L8515; Oxford II V3719.*

Disbanded 5th September 1944 at Reghaia, Algeria.

Reformed 7th October 1944 at Kirmington by redesignating an element of 166 Squadron.

P4	*Lancaster I NG335 P4-V, III LM754 P4-E.*
Also used	*Magister L8208.*

Disbanded 28th September 1945 at Scampton.

Reformed 28th February 1955 at West Malling.

Meteor T.7 WA615 Z, NF.12 WS613 J, NF.14 WS729 A.

Disbanded 2nd July 1958 at Waterbeach to become 25 Squadron.

154 SQUADRON, RAF, later 154 (MOTOR INDUSTRIES) SQUADRON, RAF
Formed 7th August 1918 at Chingford by merging elements of 33, 37, 39 and 44 Training Depot Stations.

F.2B proposed but no aircraft allocated.

Disbanded 11th September 1918 at Chingford.

KD	*Allocated for the period April to September 1939.*

Reformed 17th November 1941 at Fowlmere.

HT (11.41–11.42)	*Spitfire IIA P8700 HT-X, IIB, VB W3373.*
Nil (11.42–6.43)	*Spitfire VC ES187 C.*
HT (6.43–10.44)	*Spitfire VC ER676 HT-E, IX MA580 H I-S, VIII LV659.*
Also used	*Magister L8164; Harvard II AJ841.*

Disbanded 29th October 1944 at Gragnano, Italy.

Reformed 5th November 1944 at Biggin Hill.

HG	*Spitfire VII MD168 HG-X; Mustang IV KH641, IVA KH680.*

Disbanded 19th March 1945 at Hunsdon.

155 SQUADRON
Formed 14th September 1918 at Chingford by merging elements of 1, 26, 55 and 57 Training Depot Stations.

Avro 504J; D.H.9A E8553 N.

Disbanded 7th December 1918 at Chingford.

FL	*Allocated for the period April to September 1939.*

Reformed 1st April 1942 at Peshawar, India.

Nil (4.42–1.44)	*Mohawk IV BS798 B.*
DG (1.44–8.46)	*Mohawk IV BJ545 DG-C; Spitfire VIII MD220 DG-V.*
Also used	*Hurricane IIB BN898; Harlow PC-5A DR423; Harvard IIB FE422.*

Disbanded 31st August 1946 at Medan, Sumatra.

Reformed 1st September 1954 at Kuala Lumpur, Malaya.

Whirlwind HAR.4 XD188 J.

Disbanded 3rd June 1959 at Seletar and merged with 194 Squadron to become 110 Squadron.

156 SQUADRON
Formed 12th October 1918 at Wyton by merging elements of 27, 35, 52 and 53 Training Depot Stations.

D.H.9A.

Disbanded 20th November 1918 at Wyton and absorbed by 123 Squadron.

TB	*Allocated for the period April to September 1939.*

Reformed 14th February 1942 at Alconbury by redesignating the United Kingdom element of 40 Squadron.

GT	*Wellington IC, III X3697 GT-S; Lancaster I, III EE108 GT-Z, I/Spec PD119.*
YG	*Allocated to 'C' Flight but no evidence of use.*

Disbanded 25th September 1945 at Wyton.

157 SQUADRON
Formed 14th July 1918 at Upper Heyford by merging elements of 3, 43, 56 Training Depot Stations and the Central Flying School.

Salamander.

Disbanded 1st February 1919 at Upper Heyford.

VW	*Allocated for the period April to September 1939.*

Reformed 15th December 1941 at Debden.

RS	*Mosquito II DZ260 RS-B, VI, XVII HK350, XIX MM650 RS-J, NF.30 MV551 RS-W.*
Also used	*Beaufighter II R2454; Mosquito III HJ852; Oxford II P8918; Magister I P2444.*

Disbanded 16th August 1945 at Swannington.

158 SQUADRON
Formed 4th September 1918 at Upper Heyford by merging elements of the Central Flying School and 42, 50 and 53 Training Depot Stations.

Various aircraft.

Disbanded 20th November 1918 at Upper Heyford.

HT	*Allocated for the period April to September 1939.*

Reformed 14th February 1942 at Driffield by redesignating an element of 104 Squadron.

Nil (2.42–4.42)	*Wellington II Z8523 K.*
NP (4.42–6.45)	*Wellington II W5562 NP-Z; Halifax II JN884 NP-F, III LV907 NP-F, VI PP167 NP-S; Stirling V PJ957.*

Disbanded 28th December 1945 at Stradishall.

158 SQUADRON CONVERSION FLIGHT
Formed 6th May 1942 at Linton-on-Ouse.

NP	*Halifax II BB203 NP-Z.*

Disbanded 1st November 1942 at Rufforth and absorbed together with 35 Squadron Conversion Flight by 1652 Heavy Conversion Unit.

159 SQUADRON

NS	*Allocated for the period April to September 1939.*

Formed 2nd January 1942 at Molesworth.

Liberator II AL565 F, III BZ922 S, VI KG843 H, VIII KL662. Also used Harvard IIB FE432.

Between 21st July 1944 and 15th May 1945 a 'Special Flight', formally 160 Special Flight, operated within 159 Squadron using Liberator V BZ938 W and Liberator VI KH170 until absorbed by 1341 (Special Duties) Flight.

Disbanded 1st June 1946 at Salbani, India.

160 SQUADRON

JJ	*Allocated for the period April to September 1939.*

Formed 16th January 1942 at Thurleigh.

Nil (1.42–12.44)	Liberator II AL565 C, III FL945 H, V BZ886 R, VI EV889 H, VIII KG849 A.
BS (12.44–10.46)	Liberator V BZ862 BS-J, VIII KL480 BS-F; Lancaster GR.3 RE158 BS-B.
Also used	Tiger Moth DP265.

Disbanded 1st October 1946 at Leuchars to become 120 Squadron.

161 SQUADRON

AX	Allocated for the period April to September 1939.

Formed 15th February 1942 at Newmarket by merging the King's Flight and an element of 138 Squadron.

MA (2.42–6.45)	Lysander I R2626, III R9106, IIIA V9822 MA-E; Whitley V Z9224 MA-P; Wellington I L7772, IA P2521 MA-P; Albemarle I P1390 MA-L; Hudson I N7221 MA-P, III T9463 MA-L, IIIA FK803 MA-N; Ventura II AE881; Havoc I AW399 MA-S; Halifax II W1012, V DG286 MA-X; Stirling IV LK209 MA-T.
JR (4.44–11.44)	Lysander IIIA V9723 JR-H.
Also used	Oxford II V3677.

Disbanded 2nd June 1945 at Tempsford.

162 SQUADRON

KY	Allocated for the period April to September 1939.

Formed by 1st March 1942 at Kabrit, Egypt, by redesignating the Signals Squadron.

Wellington IC Z9034 Z; Blenheim IV V5508 B, V BA491 L; Baltimore I AG696, II AG805, III AG853 F, IV FA421, V FW429; Wellington DW.I L7771, DW.II HX682 R, X HF733 L; Mosquito VI HJ671. Also used Argus II FZ754.

Disbanded 25th September 1944 at Idku, Egypt.

Reformed 16th December 1944 at Bourn.

CR	Mosquito III HJ993, B.25 KB415 CR-C, B.20 KB189 CR-B.

Disbanded 14th July 1946 at Blackbushe.

163 SQUADRON

NK	Allocated for the period April to September 1939.

Formed 10th July 1942 at Suez, Egypt.

Hudson IIIA FH279, VI FK411.

Disbanded 16th June 1943 at Asmara, Eritrea.

Reformed 25th January 1945 at Wyton.

Mosquito B.25 KB464 T, XVI RV310.

Disbanded 10th August 1945 at Wyton.

164 (ARGENTINE BRITISH) SQUADRON

OO	Allocated for the period April to September 1939.

Formed 6th April 1942 at Peterhead.

FJ (4.42–5.45)	Spitfire VA X4421, VB W3569 FJ-S; Hurricane IID KX171, IV KX413 FJ-M; Typhoon IB EK379 FJ-J.
UB (5.45–8,46)	Spitfire IXE TB567, XVIE TE202 UB-B.
Also used	Magister N3801; Tiger Moth II T6313; Auster III MZ228.

Disbanded 31st August 1946 at Middle Wallop to become 63 Squadron.

165 (CEYLON) SQUADRON

YP	Allocated for the period April to September 1939.

Reformed 6th April 1942 at Ayr.

SK	Spitfire I R6623, VA X4021 SK-S, VB BM271

SK-E, VC EE643 SK-R, IXB ML175 SK-P; Mustang III KH517 SK-T.

Also used	Magister L8209; Tiger Moth I NM121, II T7364; Harvard IIB KF627; Auster I LB325.

Disbanded 1st September 1946 at Duxford to become 66 Squadron.

166 SQUADRON

Formed 13th June 1918 at Bircham Newton.

F.E.2b; Handley Page V/1500 E8273.

Disbanded 31st May 1919 at Bircham Newton.

Reformed 1st November 1936 at Boscombe Down from 'B' Flight of 97 Squadron. Merged with 97 Squadron to become 4 Group Pool from 15th September 1939.

Nil (11.36–6.39)	Heyford III K6862.
GB	Allocated for the period April to June 1939 but no evidence of use.
AS (6.39–4.40)	Whitley I K7184 AS-A, III K8942.

Disbanded 6th April 1940 at Abingdon and merged with 97 Squadron to become 10 Operational Training Unit.

Reformed 27th January 1943 at Kirmington by merging elements of 142 and 150 Squadrons.

AS	Wellington III X3334 AS-W, X HZ314 AS-P; Lancaster I ED731 AS-T2, III ND623/G AS-F.

Disbanded 18th November 1945 at Kirmington.

167 SQUADRON

Formed 18th November 1918 at Bircham Newton.

Handley Page V/1500.

Disbanded 21st May 1919 at Bircham Newton.

WJ	Allocated for the period April to September 1939.

Reformed 6th April 1942 at Scorton.

VL	Spitfire VA R6759, VB AB259.
Also used	Tiger Moth II DL626.

Disbanded 12th June 1943 at Woodvale to become 322 Squadron.

Reformed 1st October 1944 at Holmsley South.

Warwick I BV255, III HG280 X; Dakota III FZ696, IV KK136; Proctor III LZ568; Oxford I NM650; Anson XII PH672.

Disbanded 1st February 1946 at Blackbushe.

Reformed 1st February 1953 at Abingdon by redesignating 3 (Long-Range) Ferry Unit.

QO	Valetta C.1 WD168 QO-P; Meteor T.7 WL346 QO-G; Harvard IIB KF604 QO-N.

Disbanded 15th September 1958 at Benson and merged with 147 Squadron to become absorbed by the Ferry Squadron.

168 SQUADRON

XF	Allocated for the period April to September 1939.

Formed 15th June 1942 at Snailwell by redesignating an element of 268 Squadron.

EK (6.42–7.42)	Tomahawk IIB AK118 EK-A.
OE (7.42–11.42)	Tomahawk I AX900, IIA AH950, IIB BK853 OE-P.
Nil (11.42–10.44)	Mustang I AM112, IA FD444.
QC (10.44–2.45)	Typhoon IB JP677 QC-P.
Also used	Master I N7482, II AZ777; Tiger Moth II T7086; Auster III MZ163.

Disbanded 26th February 1945 at B.78 (Eindhoven), Netherlands.

169 SQUADRON

JQ	Allocated for the period April to September 1939.

Formed 15th June 1942 at Twinwood Farm by redesignating an element of 613 Squadron.

Tomahawk I AH780, IIB AK118; Mustang I AG620. Also used Magister N3788; Master III W8830.

Disbanded 30th September 1943 at Middle Wallop.

Reformed 1st October 1943 at Ayr.

| VI | Beaufighter I R2091; Mosquito II HJ917 VI-N, III HJ870, IV DZ608, VI NS997/G VI-C, XIX MM644 VI-U. |
| Also used | Tiger Moth II EM817; Oxford I T1394, II BM774. |

Disbanded 10th August 1945 at Great Massingham.

170 SQUADRON

| HS | Allocated for the period April to September 1939. |

Formed 15th June 1942 at Weston Zoyland.

BN (6.42–2.43)	Mustang I AG447.
Nil (2.43–1.44)	Mustang I AG391, IA FD543, X AL963.
Also used	Master III W8629; Tiger Moth II DE510; Anson I EF805.

Disbanded 15th January 1944 at Sawbridgeworth.

Reformed 15th October 1944 at Kelstern from 'C' Flight of 625 Squadron.

| TC | Lancaster I NG349 TC-A2, III RF199 TC-J2. |

Disbanded 15th November 1945 at Hemswell.

171 SQUADRON

| RS | Allocated for the period April to September 1939. |

Formed 15th June 1942 at Gatwick.

Tomahawk I AH800, IIA AH895, IIB AK148; Mustang I AM184. Also used Proctor I P6320, Tiger Moth II T7779; Master III W8518.

Disbanded 31st December 1942 at Hartford Bridge, providing a nucleus to form 430 Squadron.

Reformed 7th September 1944 at North Creake from 'C' Flight of 199 Squadron.

| 6Y | Stirling III LJ617 8Y-F; Halifax IIIA NA694 6Y-H. |

Disbanded 27th July 1945 at North Creake.

172 SQUADRON

| LF | Allocated for the period April to September 1939. |

Formed 4th April 1942 at Chivenor by redesignating 1417 (Leigh Light) Flight.

Nil (4.42–8.43)	Wellington VIII HX396 J, XII MP590 Z, XIII JA264.
1 (8.43–7.44)	Wellington XII HF113 1-E, XIII NB809, XIV HF285 1-R.
OG (7.44–6.45)	Wellington XIII NB870 OG-L, XIV MF451 OG-J.

Disbanded 4th June 1945 at Limavady.

173 SQUADRON

| TV | Allocated for the period April to September 1939. |

Formed 9th July 1942 at Heliopolis, Egypt, by redesignating an element of 267 Squadron.

Audax K7512; Hart Trainer K6421; Proctor I P6117, IA P6166; Lysander II P9051; Magister R1882; Beaufighter VI V8344; Boston III Z2162; Blenheim IV Z9584; Anson I LT666; Gull Six AX698; Lockheed 10A AX700 T; Argus II FS507, III KK506; Lodestar II EW986; Junkers 52/3M HK919; Savoia S.79K AX702; Fi 156 'NM'; Moth Major HK839; Rapide HK864; Scion Senior HK868.

Disbanded 29th February 1944 at Heliopolis to become the Middle East Communication Squadron.

Reformed 1st February 1953 at Hawarden by redesignating 4 (Home) Ferry Unit.

Anson XII PH813, XIX VM325 17; Varsity T.1 WJ919; Venom NF.3 WX924.

Disbanded 2nd September 1957 at Hawarden.

174 (MAURITIUS) SQUADRON

| RO | Allocated for the period April to September 1939. |

Formed 3rd March 1942 at Manston by redesignating an element of 607 Squadron.

| XP | Hurricane IIB BE421 XP-G, IIE BE404; Typhoon IB JP671 XP-R. |
| Also used | Magister P6466; Spitfire VB W3513; Tiger Moth II DE612. |

Disbanded 10th April 1945 at B.100 (Goch), Germany.

Reformed 26th August 1945 at B.158 (Lübeck), Germany by renumbering 137 Squadron.

| XP | Typhoon IB RB303 XP-K. |

Disbanded 7th September 1945 at Lübeck.

Reformed 7th September 1945 at Warmwell by renumbering 274 Squadron.

| XP | Tempest V SN179. |

Disbanded 20th April 1946 at B.152 (Fassberg), Germany.

| Also used | Tiger Moth II DE612; Auster III MZ234. |

175 SQUADRON

| GL | Allocated for the period April to September 1939. |

Formed 3rd March 1942 at Warmwell.

| HH | Hurricane IIB BE478 HH-S, IIE BE404; Typhoon IB JP394 HH-E. |
| Also used | Magister T9753; Tiger Moth II T6126; Auster III NJ967, V MT360. |

Disbanded 30th September 1945 at B.164 (Schleswig), Germany.

176 SQUADRON

| AS | Allocated for the period April to September 1939. |

Formed 15th January 1943 at Dum-Dum, India, by redesignating an element of 89 Squadron.

Beaufighter I X7843 R, VI MM916 J; Hurricane IIC KX754; Mosquito XIX TA230 N. Also used Blenheim IV Z9733, V BA715; Harvard IIB FH113.

Disbanded 1st June 1944 at Baigachi, India.

177 SQUADRON

| QF | Allocated for the period April to September 1939. |

Formed 11th January 1943 at Amarda Road, India.

Beaufighter VIC JL628, X LZ118 H, XI JM243.

Disbanded 1st July 1945 at Hathazari, India.

178 SQUADRON

| UL | Allocated for the period April to September 1939. |

Formed 15th January 1943 at Shandur, Egypt, by merging elements of 147, 159 and 160 Squadrons.

Liberator II AL580 T; Halifax II BB385 Q; Liberator III BZ932 Y, VI KH100 V, VIII KH235; Lancaster III SW359 J.

Disbanded 15th January 1946 at Fayid, Egypt, to become 70 Squadron.

179 SQUADRON

| RH | Allocated for the period April to September 1939. |

Formed 1st September 1942 at Skitten by redesignating an element of 172 Squadron.

| Nil (9.42–11.44) | Wellington VIII LA976 R, XIV HF140 X. |
| OZ (11.44–9.46) | Warwick V PN722 OZ-N; Lancaster ASR.3 RE115 OZ-T. |

During February 1946 the Squadron was divided into 179X Squadron, converting to Lancasters, and 179Y Squadron, remaining operational with Warwicks. By May 1946 the Warwicks were withdrawn and on the 1st June 179Y Squadron was renumbered 210 Squadron and 179X Squadron reverted to 179 Squadron.

Disbanded 30th September 1946 at St Eval.

180 SQUADRON

DR	Allocated for the period April to September 1939.

Formed 11th September 1942 at West Raynham.

EV	Mitchell II FL677 EV-N, III KJ684 EV-J; Mosquito XVI PF448 EV-C.
Also used	Oxford II T1254; Mosquito III HJ983.

Disbanded 31st March 1946 at Wahn, Germany, to become 69 Squadron.

181 SQUADRON

WB	Allocated for the period April to September 1939.

Formed 25th August 1942 at Duxford.

EL	Hurricane I V6845, X AG280; Typhoon IA R7589, IB JR317 EL-J.
Also used	Tiger Moth II T6371; Auster III MZ197.

Disbanded 30th September 1945 at B.164 (Schleswig), Germany.

182 SQUADRON

JT	Allocated for the period April to September 1939.

Formed 25th August 1942 at Martlesham Heath.

XM	Hurricane X AG232 XM-P; Typhoon IA R7624 XM-D, IB JR220 XM-X.
Also used	Tiger Moth II DE530; Fw 190 XM-?

Disbanded 30th September 1945 at B.164 (Schleswig), Germany.

183 (GOLD COAST) SQUADRON

LN	Allocated for the period April to September 1939.

Formed 1st November 1942 at Church Fenton.

HF	Hurricane I R2680; Typhoon IA R7649, IB JR128 HF-L; Spitfire IX; Tempest II MW755 HF-N; Spitfire XVI SM230.
Also used	Tiger Moth II T6126; Auster I LB328.

Disbanded 15th November 1945 at Chilbolton to become 54 Squadron.

184 SQUADRON

JM	Allocated for the period April to September 1939.

Formed 1st December 1942 at Colerne.

BR	Hurricane IID KX142, IV KX884 BR-T; Spitfire VB; Typhoon IB JR337 BR-Z.
Also used	Tiger Moth II T7241; Auster III MZ164.

Disbanded 29th August 1945 at B.160 (Kastrup), Germany.

185 SQUADRON

Formed 21st October 1918 at East Fortune by merging elements of 31, 33 and 49 Training Depot Stations.

Cuckoo I N7152, II N6997.

Disbanded 14th April 1919 at East Fortune.

Reformed 1st March 1938 at Abingdon from 'B' Flight of 40 Squadron.

Nil (3.38–4.39)	Hind K5426; Battle K7664.
ZM (4.39–9.39)	Battle K7650; Hampden I L4194 ZM-B.
GL (9.39–4.40)	Hampden I P1274; Hereford I L6007; Anson I N5110.

Disbanded 8th April 1940 at Cottesmore to become an element of 14 Operational Training Unit.

Reformed 8th April 1940 at Cottesmore.

Hampden I.

Disbanded 17th May 1940 at Cottesmore.

Reformed 12th May 1941 at Hal Far, Malta, by merging elements of 261 Squadron and 1430 (Army Co-operation) Flight.

Nil (5.41–5.42)	Hurricane I, IIA Z4942 Y, IIB BG770 D, IIC BE583 T.
GL (5.42–8.45)	Spitfire VB AB264, VC BR321 GL-T, IX RR192 GL-A, VIII JF342 GL-3.
Also used	Bf 109G

Disbanded 14th August 1945 at Campoformido, Italy.

Reformed 15th September 1951 at Hal Far, Malta.

Vampire FB.5 WA377, FB.9 WG926.

Disbanded 1st May 1953 at Habbaniya, Iraq.

186 (DEVELOPMENT) SQUADRON, later 186 SQUADRON

Formed 31st December 1918 aboard HMS *Argus* as 186 (Development) Squadron by merging the Development Squadron, Gosport and an element of 185 Squadron.

Cuckoo I N6927.

Disbanded 1st February 1920 at Gosport to become 210 Squadron.

MR	Allocated for the period April to September 1939.

Reformed 27th April 1943 at Drem.

AP	Hurricane IV KZ398; Typhoon IB JR324; Spitfire VB AR511.
Also used	Tiger Moth II DE570.

Disbanded 5th April 1944 at Lympne to become 130 Squadron.

Reformed 1st October 1944 at Tuddenham from 'C' Flight of 90 Squadron.

XY (1.44–7.45)	Lancaster I NG146 XY-E, III JB475 XY-X.
AP (–7.45)	('C' Flight) Lancaster I RA570 AP-K, III PB483 AP-X.
Also used	Oxford I P8911.

Disbanded 17th July 1945 at Stradishall.

186 (NIGHT) TRAINING SQUADRON – see Reserve Aeroplane Squadrons, later Reserve Squadrons, later Training Squadrons

187 SQUADRON

GP	Allocated for the period April to September 1939.

Formed 1st February 1945 at Merryfield from the Halifax Development Flight of 246 Squadron that continued to operate within the Squadron until 3rd April 1945.

PU	Halifax III MZ416; Dakota III FZ628, IV KK193 PU-H.
OFT	Allocated call sign but no evidence of use.

Disbanded 1st December 1946 at Netheravon to become 53 Squadron.

Reformed 1st February 1953 at Aston Down by redesignating 2 (Home) Ferry Unit.

Oxford I V4281; Anson XII PH545, XIX VM387 A; Venom FB.1 WE479; Meteor FR.9 WX967; Varsity T.1 WJ909.

Disbanded 2nd September 1957 at Aston Down.

187 (NIGHT) TRAINING SQUADRON – see Reserve Aeroplane Squadrons, later Reserve Squadrons, later Training Squadrons

188 SQUADRON

Squadron not formed although the code XD was allocated for the period April to September 1939.

188 (NIGHT) TRAINING SQUADRON – see Reserve Aeroplane Squadrons, later Reserve Squadrons, later Training Squadrons

189 SQUADRON

LM   Allocated for the period April to September 1939.

Formed 15th October 1944 at Bardney.

CA   Lancaster I NG226 CA-J, III ME444 CA-F.

Disbanded 20th November 1945 at Metheringham.

189 (NIGHT) TRAINING SQUADRON – see Reserve Aeroplane Squadrons, later Reserve Squadrons, later Training Squadrons

190 SQUADRON

JB   Allocated for the period April to September 1939.

Formed 1st March 1943 at Sullom Voe by redesignating an element of 210 Squadron.

Catalina IB FP102 L, IVA JX222 W.

Disbanded 31st December 1943 at Sullom Voe to become 210 Squadron.

Reformed 5th January 1944 at Leicester East.

GS (1.44–12.45)   Stirling IV; Halifax III NA135 GS-T, VII NA452 GS-Q.
L9 (1.44–12.45)   Stirling IV LJ818 L9-X; Halifax III NA139 L9-J, VII PN286 L9-D.
Also used   Stirling III EF298.

Disbanded 21st January 1946 at Great Dunmow to become 295 Squadron.

190 (DEPOT) SQUADRON, later 190 (NIGHT) TRAINING SQUADRON – see Reserve Aeroplane Squadrons, later Reserve Squadrons, later Training Squadrons

191 SQUADRON

EV   Allocated for the period April to September 1939.

Formed 17th May 1943 at Korangi Creek, Karachi, India.

Catalina IB FP307 V, IVB JX374 Z.

Disbanded 15th June 1945 at Koggala, Ceylon

191 (DEPOT) SQUADRON, later 191 (NIGHT) TRAINING SQUADRON – see Reserve Aeroplane Squadrons, later Reserve Squadrons, later Training Squadrons

192 SQUADRON

QS   Allocated for the period April to September 1939.

Formed 4th January 1943 at Gransden Lodge by redesignating 1474 (Wireless Investigation) Flight.

DT   Wellington IC N2772 DT-E, III X3566, X HE498 DT-S; Mosquito IV DZ410 DT-K, XVI NS797 DT-N; Halifax II DT737, V DK244 DT-Q, III MZ817 DT-Q.
Also used   Lightning 44-23156; Tiger Moth II T6906.

Disbanded 22nd August 1945 at Foulsham.

Reformed 15th July 1951 at Watton by redesignating the Calibration Squadron of the Central Signals Establishment.

Lincoln B.2 SX980 54; Washington B.1 WZ966 55; Canberra B.2 WJ640, B.6 WJ775; Varsity T.1 WJ940.

Disbanded 21st August 1958 at Watton to become 51 Squadron.

192 (DEPOT) SQUADRON, later 192 (NIGHT) TRAINING SQUADRON – see Reserve Aeroplane Squadrons, later Reserve Squadrons, later Training Squadrons

193 (FELLOWSHIP OF THE BELLOWS) SQUADRON

RQ   Allocated for the period April to September 1939.

Formed 18th December 1942 at Harrowbeer.

DP   Hurricane I AG205, IIC, Typhoon IB PD500 DP-S.
Also used   Tiger Moth II DE943; Auster III MZ136.

Disbanded 31st August 1945 at Hildesheim, Germany.

193 TRAINING SQUADRON – see Reserve Aeroplane Squadrons, later Reserve Squadrons, later Training Squadrons

194 SQUADRON

FW   Allocated for the period April to September 1939.

Formed 13th October 1942 at Lahore, India.

Hudson IIIA FH431, VI FK584 W; Dakota I FD812 K, III FD894 F, IV KJ888 H; DC-3 LR234; Sentinel I KJ398, II KJ457.

Disbanded 15th February 1946 at Mingaladon, India.

Reformed 2nd February 1953 Sembawang, Singapore, by redesignating the Far East Casualty Evacuation Flight.

Dragonfly HC.2 WF315, HC.4 WT846; Sycamore HR.14 XJ381 P.

Disbanded 3rd June 1959 at Kuala Lumpur, Malaya, and merged with 155 Squadron to become 110 Squadron.

194 TRAINING SQUADRON – see Reserve Aeroplane Squadrons, later Reserve Squadrons, later Training Squadrons

195 SQUADRON

NP   Allocated for the period April to September 1939.

Formed 15th November 1942 at Duxford.

JE   Hurricane IIE BE489; Typhoon IB DN389 JE-F.

Disbanded 15th February 1944 at Fairlop.

Reformed 1st October 1944 at Witchford from 'C' Flight of 115 Squadron.

A4 (10.44–8.45)   Lancaster I NN740 A4-F, III LM743 A4-R.
JE (11.44–8.45)   ('C' Flight) Lancaster I HK701 JE-B, III JB475 JE-G.

Disbanded 14th August 1945 at Wrattling Common.

195 TRAINING SQUADRON – see Reserve Aeroplane Squadrons, later Reserve Squadrons, later Training Squadrons

196 SQUADRON

KG   Allocated for the period April to September 1939.

Formed 7th November 1942 at Driffield.

ZO (11.42–3.46)   Wellington X HE163 ZO-U; Stirling III EE975 ZO-G, IV EF292 ZO-C, V PK144 ZO-F.
7T (5.43–3.46)   Wellington X HE398 7T-J; Stirling III, IV EF429 7T-P, V PJ912 7T-L.
Also used   Oxford I PH118.

Disbanded 16th March 1946 at Shepherd's Grove.

196 TRAINING SQUADRON – see Reserve Aeroplane Squadrons, later Reserve Squadrons, later Training Squadrons

197 SQUADRON

AG   Allocated for the period April to September 1939.

Formed 21st November 1942 at Turnhouse.

OV   Typhoon IA R7706 OV-L, IB JP504 OV-Z.
Also used   Tiger Moth II DE564; Auster III MZ249.

Disbanded 31st August 1945 at Hildesheim, Germany.

197 TRAINING SQUADRON – see Reserve Aeroplane Squadrons later Reserve Squadrons later Training Squadrons

198 SQUADRON

PU   Allocated for the period April to September 1939.

Reformed 7th December 1942 at Digby.

TP   Hurricane I P3265; Typhoon IA R7653, IB
                    JP963 TP-T.
Also used   Tiger Moth II T7271; Auster III NX528.

Disbanded 15th September 1945 at B.116 (Wunstorf), Germany.

198 (DEPOT) SQUADRON, later 198 (NIGHT) TRAINING SQUADRON – see Reserve Aeroplane Squadrons, later Reserve Squadrons, later Training Squadrons

199 SQUADRON
DO   Allocated for the period April to September
                    1939.

Reformed 7th November 1942 at Blyton.

EX   Wellington III BK150 EX-S, X HE634 EX-S;
                    Stirling III EF192 EX-J; Halifax III PN374 EX-N.

Disbanded 29th July 1945 at North Creake.

Reformed 15th July 1951 at Watton.

Lincoln B.2 WD131; Mosquito III VA928, NF.36 RK958; Canberra B.2 WJ616; Valiant B.1 WP212.

Disbanded 17th December 1958 at Honington to become 18 Squadron.

199 (DEPOT) SQUADRON, later 199 (NIGHT) TRAINING SQUADRON – see Reserve Aeroplane Squadrons, later Reserve Squadrons, later Training Squadrons

200 SQUADRON
UE   Allocated for the period April to September
                    1939.

Reformed 25th May 1941 at Bircham Newton by redesignating an element of 206 Squadron.

Maryland I AR715; Hudson IV AE615 X, III V9157 N, IIIA FH236, VI FK639 H1; Liberator III BZ900, V BZ884 N, VI KH331/G W. Also used Harvard IIB FE609.

Disbanded 15th May 1945 at Jessore, India, to become 8 Squadron.

200 (DEPOT) SQUADRON, later 200 (NIGHT) TRAINING SQUADRON – see Reserve Aeroplane Squadrons, later Reserve Squadrons, later Training Squadrons

201 SQUADRON
Originally formed 17th October 1914 at Fort Grange, Gosport, as 1 (Naval) Squadron, RNAS becoming 1 Wing, RNAS from June 1915. On 1st March 1916 'A' Squadron of 1 Wing, RNAS was detached and from 3rd July 1916 was known as the 'Detached Squadron'. The unit reverted to 1 (Naval) Squadron, RNAS from 3rd December 1916. Became 201 Squadron, RAF from 1st April 1918 whilst at Fienvillers, France.

Camel E5227 F; Snipe E8102.

Disbanded 31st December 1919 at Eastleigh.

Reformed 1st January 1929 at Calshot by redesignating 480 (Coastal Reconnaissance) Flight.

Nil (1.29–4.39)   Southampton I S1125, II S1058; London I
                    K5262 Z, II K5911 G.
VQ (4.49–9.39)   London II L7042 VQ-W.
ZM (9.39–8.43)   London II K5257 ZM-Y; Sunderland I P9606
                    ZM-R, II T9087 ZM-O, III ML743 ZM-A.
Nil (8.43–7.44)   Sunderland II T9087, III EJ137 T.
NS (7.44–4.51)   Sunderland III ML759, V RN304 NS-L; Sea
                    Otter I JM815; Bv 222C-012 VP501.
A (4.51–2.57)   Sunderland VB889 A-D.

Disbanded 28th February 1957 at Pembroke Dock.

Reformed 1st October 1958 at St Mawgan by renumbering 220 Squadron.

201 (10.58– .66)   Shackleton MR.3 WR977 201-L.
Nil (.66–   )   Shackleton MR.3 WR977 O; Nimrod MR.1
                    XV240, MR.2P XV241.

Current 1st April 1998 at Kinloss.

202 SQUADRON
Originally formed 17th October 1914 at Eastchurch as 2 (Naval) Squadron, RNAS. During June 1915 it was redesignated as 2 Wing, RNAS and on 2nd August moved to France, only to be withdrawn some 10 days later to Dover to prepare for service in the Aegean. 2 (Naval) Squadron, RNAS reformed 5th November 1915 at St Pol, France from 'B' Flight of 1 Wing, RNAS. Became 202 Squadron, RAF from 1st April 1918 whilst at Bergues, France.

D.H.4 D8407 S; D.H.9 B7630.

Disbanded 22nd January 1920 at Spitalgate.

Reformed 9th April 1920 at Alexandria, Egypt, by redesignating an element of 267 Squadron.

Short 184.

Disbanded 16th May 1921 at Alexandria.

Reformed 1st January 1929 at Kalafrana, Malta, by redesignating 481 (Coastal Reconnaissance) Flight.

Nil (1.29–9.39)   Fairey IIID N9777 3, IIIF S1386 5;
                    Southampton II S1228, IV S1648; Scapa
                    K4196 6; London II K5911.
JU   Allocated for the period April to September
                    1939 but no evidence of use.
TQ (9.39–8.43)   London II K6932 TQ-B; Swordfish I Floatplane
                    K8354 TQ-D; Catalina I W8410 TQ-A;
                    Sunderland I N9050, II W6002 TQ-R, III W4024
                    TQ-N.
AX (5.41–8.43)   Sunderland III DV958 AX-T; Catalina I AH562
                    AX-J.
Nil (8.43–7.44)   Catalina IB FP122 C, IVA JX269 S.
TJ (7.44–6.45)   Catalina IVA JX242 TJ-P.

Disbanded 4th June 1945 at Castle Archdale.

Reformed 1st October 1946 at Aldergrove by renumbering 518 Squadron.

Y3 (10.46–4.51)   Halifax VI RG843 Y3-O, IX RT923; Oxford I
                    PG969, II V3729 Y3-Q; Anson XI NL245 Y3-Y,
                    XII PH713 Y3-Y; Hastings MET.1 TG567 Y3-G.
A (4.51– .56)   Halifax VI ST809 A-V; Hastings MET.1 TG567
                    A-G.
Nil (.56–7.64)   Hastings MET.1 TG624 A.

Disbanded 28th August 1964 at Aldergrove.

Reformed 29th August 1964 at Leconfield by renumbering 228 Squadron.

Whirlwind HAR.10 XJ437; Sea King HAR.3 XZ599 S. Also used Chipmunk T.10 WZ846.

Current 1st April 1998 at Boulmer with detached Flights at Lossiemouth and Leconfield.

203 SQUADRON, later 203 (RESERVE) SQUADRON
Originally formed 5th November 1916 at St Pol, France, as 3 (Naval) Squadron, RNAS by redesignating 'C' Squadron, 1 Wing, RNAS. Became 203 Squadron, RAF from 1st April 1918 whilst at Treizennes, France.

Camel B7162.

Disbanded 21st January 1920 at Scopwick.

Reformed 1st March 1920 at Leuchars.

Camel N7355; Nightjar H8536; Avro 504K H2391.

Disbanded 1st April 1923 at Leuchars to become 401 and 402 (Fleet Fighter) Flights.

Reformed 1st January 1929 at Cattewater by redesignating 482 (Coastal Reconnaissance) Flight.

Nil (1.29–4.39)   Southampton II S1229 A; Rangoon K2134;
                    Singapore III K4577.
PP (4.39–9.39)   Singapore III K4584 PP-C.
NT (9.39–3.40)   Singapore III K6912 NT-D.
Nil (3.40–2.45)   Blenheim I L1480, IV Z6157 A, V BA529;
                    Hudson III T9397; Maryland I AR725, II AH402
                    A; Baltimore I AG732 E, II AG833 Y, III AG917
                    G, IIIA FA353 K, IV FA507 R; Wellington XIII
                    JA444 B; Liberator VI KG909 J.

CJ (2.45–4.51)	Liberator VIII KL471 CJ-G; Lancaster III SW337 CJ-A.
B (4.51– .56)	Lancaster III RE206 B-B; Neptune MR.1 WX521 B-L.
203 (.56–9.56)	Neptune MR.1 WX520 203-M.

Disbanded 1st September 1956 at Topcliffe.

Reformed 1st November 1958 at Ballykelly by renumbering 240 Squadron.

203 (11.56– .66)	Shackleton MR.1A WB860; MR.2 WL753 203-G; MR.3 WR974 203-F.
Nil (.66–12.77)	Shackleton MR.3 WR977 B; Nimrod MR.1 XV232.

Disbanded 31st December 1977 at Luqa, Malta.

Reformed 16th October 1996 at St Mawgan as 203 (Reserve) Squadron, being the Sea King Operational Conversion Unit.

Sea King HAR.3, HAR.3A.

Current 1st April 1998 at St Mawgan.

204 SQUADRON
Originally formed 31st December 1916 at Coudekerque, France, as 4 (Naval) Squadron, RNAS from an element of 5 Wing, RNAS. Became 204 Squadron, RAF from 1st April 1918 whilst at Bray Dunes, France.

Camel B3879; Dolphin C3786.

Disbanded 31st December 1919 at Waddington.

Reformed 1st February 1929 at Cattewater.

Nil (2.29–4.39)	Southampton II N9901 4, IV S1648; Scapa K4191; London II K5263.
RF (4.39–9.39)	London II K5911 RF-G; Sunderland I L5802 RF-F.
KG (9.39– .43)	Sunderland I L5798 KG-B, II W6012, III DD833 KG-M.
Nil (.43–6.45)	Sunderland III JM710 X, V ML872 B.
Also used	Catalina IB FP104, IIA VA720.

Disbanded 30th June 1945 at Jui, Sierra Leone.

Reformed 1st August 1947 at Kabrit, Egypt.

Dakota IV KJ934; Valetta C.1 VW165 D.

Disbanded 20th February 1952 at Fayid, Egypt, to become 84 Squadron.

Reformed 1st January 1954 at Ballykelly.

T (1.54– .56)	Shackleton MR.2 WL740 T-X.
204 (.56–4.71)	Shackleton MR.1A WB860 204-L, MR.2 WG555 204-N.

Disbanded 1st April 1971 at Ballykelly.

Reformed 1st April 1971 at Honington by redesignating the Majunga Detachment Support Unit.

Shackleton MR.2 WL748 R; Varsity T.1 WF330.

Disbanded 28th April 1972 at Honington.

205 SQUADRON
Originally formed 31st December 1916 at Coudekerque, France, as 5 (Naval) Squadron, RNAS. Became 205 Squadron, RAF from 1st April 918 whilst at Bois-de-Roche, France.

D.H.4 A7915; D.H.9A F1008 G.

Disbanded 22nd January 1920 at Scopwick.

Reformed 15th April 1920 at Leuchars.

Camel N8191; Panther N7509; Snipe E6525.

Disbanded 1st April 1923 at Leuchars to become 440, 441 and 442 Flights.

Reformed 8th January 1929 at Seletar, Singapore, by redesignating the Far East Flight.

Nil (1.29–4.40)	Southampton I S1043, II S1249; Singapore III K3592.
KM (4.39–9.39)	Allocated for the period 1938 to September 1939.

FV (4.40–3.42)	Singapore III K6918 FV-L; Catalina I W8413 FV-X.

Disbanded 31st March 1942 at Freemantle, Australia.

Reformed 23rd July 1942 at Koggala, Ceylon.

Nil (7.42– 5.59)	Catalina IB FP241 K, IVB JX586 Q; Sunderland V RN288 S.
205 (5.58– .66)	Shackleton GR.1A VP267 205-L, MR.2 WR954 205-F.
Nil (.66–10.71)	Shackleton MR.2 WR954 C.
Also used	Valetta C.1 VX522.

Disbanded 31st October 1971 at Changi, Singapore.

206 SQUADRON
Originally formed 1st November 1916 at Dover (Guston Road) as 6 (Naval) Squadron, RNAS from the Walmer Defence Flight, RNAS. Became 206 Squadron, RAF from 1st April 1918 whilst at Ste-Marie-Cappel, France.

D.H.4 N6390; D.H.9 C6236.

Disbanded 1st February 1920 at Helwan, Egypt, to become 47 Squadron.

Reformed 15th June 1936 at Manston from 'C' Flight of 48 Squadron.

206 (6.36–4.39)	Anson I K6167 206-C.
WD (4.39–9.39)	Anson I K6167 WD-C.
VX (9.39–7.43)	Anson I K6187 VX-E; Hudson I P5143 VX-F, II T9383 VX-Q, III T9431 VX-B, V AM711 VX-U; Fortress I AN520 VX-X, IIA FK213 VX-C.
Nil (7.43–10.43)	Fortress II FA702 P, IIA FL457 F.
1 (10.43–3.44)	Fortress II FA696 1-Y, IIA FL460 1-H.
PQ (10.43–4.46)	Liberator VI BZ984 PQ-S, VIII KK335 PQ-L.
Also used	Blenheim IV Z5735; Oxford II V3837; Boston III W8268.

Disbanded 25th April 1946 at Oakington.

Reformed 17th November 1947 at Lyneham.

York I MW262.

Disbanded 31st August 1949 at Lyneham.

Reformed 1st December 1949 at Waterbeach.

Dakota IV KN701.

Disbanded 20th February 1950 at Waterbeach.

Reformed 27th September 1952 at St Eval.

B (9.52– .56)	Shackleton MR.1A WB832 B-W, MR.2 WG558 B-Y.
206 (.56– .66)	Shackleton MR.1A WG529 206-F, MR.3 XF701 206-E.
Nil (.66–)	Shackleton MR.2 XF701 T; Nimrod MR.1 XV238, Nimrod MR.2P XV228.
Also used	Anson T.21 VV260.

Current 1st April 1998 at Kinloss.

207 SQUADRON
Originally formed 1st November 1916 at Petite Synthe, France, as 7 (Naval) Squadron, RNAS. Became 207 Squadron, RAF from 1st April 1918 whilst at Coudekerque, France.

Handley Page O/100 1459; Handley Page 0/400 B8811 A2; B.E.12 C3180.

Disbanded 20th January 1920 at Uxbridge.

Reformed 1st February 1920 at Bircham Newton by redesignating an element of 274 Squadron. Merged with 35, 52 and 63 Squadrons to become 1 Group Pool from 14th September 1939. Re-established as an independent entity from 9th December 1939.

Nil (2.20–4.38)	D.H.9A E8805 C4, D.H.9A DC J8471; Fairey IIIF J9057 C1; Gordon I J9073 B3; Vincent K4709; Wellesley I K7764.
207 (4.38–4.39)	Battle K9200 207-Z.
NJ (4.39–9.39)	Battle K9200 NJ-Z; Anson I N5111.
Nil (9.39–4.40)	Battle L5277; Anson I N5111.

Disbanded 19th April 1940 at Benson and absorbed by 12 Operational Training Unit.

Reformed 1st November 1940 at Waddington.

| EM | Manchester I L7419 EM-H; Hampden I AE186 EM-A; Lancaster I ED600 EM-P, III; Lincoln II RE400 EM-E. |

Disbanded 1st March 1950 at Mildenhall.

Reformed 4th June 1951 at Marham.

Washington B.1 WF568 W; Canberra B.2 WK102.

Disbanded 27th March 1956 at Marham.

Reformed 1st April 1956 at Marham.

Valiant B(PR).1 WP219, BK.1 WZ400, B(PR)K.1 WZ403.

Disbanded 1st May 1965 at Marham.

Reformed 3rd February 1969 at Northolt by redesignating the Strike Command Communication Squadron.

Devon C.1 VP967, C.2 VP971; Pembroke C.1 WV746, C(PR).1 XF798; Bassett XS777.

Disbanded 30th June 1984 at Northolt.

207 SQUADRON CONVERSION FLIGHT
Formed 16th January 1942 at Bottesford.

| EM | Manchester I L7294; Lancaster I L7530. |

Disbanded 20th October 1942 at Swinderby and merged with 61, 97, and 106 Squadron Conversion Flights to become 1660 Heavy Conversion Unit.

208 SQUADRON, later 208 (RESERVE) SQUADRON
Originally formed 25th October 1916 at St Pol, France as 8 (Naval) Squadron, RNAS by redesignating elements of 1, 4 and 5 Wings, RNAS. Became 208 Squadron, RAF from 1st April 1918 whilst at Teteghem, France.

Camel N6342; Snipe E6175 S.

Disbanded 7th November 1919 at Netheravon.

Reformed 1st February 1920 at Ismailia, Egypt, by renumbering 113 Squadron.

Nil (2.20–4.39)	R.E.8 B5058; F.2B F4791; Nighthawk J6925; Atlas AC KR1573, Atlas Trainer K1472; Audax K3107; Demon K4515; Lysander I L4718.
GA (4.39–9.39)	Lysander I L4711 GA-B.
Nil (9.39–3.44)	Lysander I L4728 B, II L4783; Hurricane I N2611, X P5173, IIB BP604; Tomahawk IIB AN420; Spitfire VC EE741.
RG (3.44–.49)	Hurricane IIAÊZ4967 RG-Y; Spitfire VC EE861 RG-G, VIII JF572 RG-Y, IX MH772 RG-R, XVIII TP385 RG-F.
Nil (.49–12.58)	Spitfire FR.18 TP453 Y; Meteor FR.9 VZ578 R, T.7 VW432; Hunter F.6 XF441 P.
Also used	Avro 504K F8763; Hart Special K3145; Gordon I K2745; Caproni Ca 101 HK859; Harvard IIB KF350; III EX971.

Disbanded 31st March 1959 at Nicosia, Cyprus.

Reformed 1st April 1959 at Eastleigh, Kenya, by renumbering 142 Squadron.

Venom FB.4 WR433 F; Vampire T.11 WZ424; Hunter T.7 XL566 Z, FGA.9 XJ632 K.

Disbanded 10th September 1971 at Muharraq, Bahrain.

Reformed 1st July 1974 at Honington.

| S | Buccaneer S.2A XT278, S.2B XV332 RS. |
| C | Hunter F.6A XG152, T.7 XL616 CA, T.8C XE665. |

Disbanded 31st March 1994 at Lossiemouth.

Reformed 1st April 1994 at Valley as 208 (Reserve) Squadron, being an element of 4 Flying Training School, by redesignating 234 (Reserve) Squadron.

Hawk T.1 XX225, T.1A.

Current 1st April 1998 at Valley.

209 SQUADRON
Originally formed 1st February 1917 at St Pol, France, as 9 (Naval) Squadron, RNAS by redesignating an element of 8 (Naval) Squadron, RNAS. Became 209 Squadron on 1st April 1918 at Clairmarais, France.

Camel H7000 C; A.E.3 B8783.

Disbanded 24th June 1919 at Scopwick.

Reformed 15th January 1930 at Mount Batten.

Nil (1.20–.39)	Iris III S1264, V S1263; Saro A.7; Southampton II S1042, IV S1648; Perth K3581; London K3560; Stranraer K7290; Short R.24/31 K3574; Singapore III K6921 Z.
FK	Allocated for the period April to September 1939 but no evidence of use.
WQ (9.39–3.42)	Stranraer K7290 WQ-N; Lerwick I L7257 WQ-F; Catalina I AH545 WQ-Z, IIA VA703 WQ-M.
Nil (3.42–6.45)	Catalina I Z2142 T, IB FP107 S, IIA VA727 P; Sunderland V PP103 U.
WQ (6.45–4.51)	Sunderland V VB884 WQ-X.
Nil (4.51–2.55)	Sunderland V VB888.
Also used	Swordfish I L2778; Harvard IIB KF126.

Disbanded 1st January 1955 at Seletar, Singapore, and absorbed by 205 Squadron.

Reformed 1st November 1958 at Kuala Lumpur, Malaya, by renumbering 267 Squadron.

Auster VI WJ365; Pioneer CC.1 XL700 Z; Dakota IV KJ810; Pembroke C.1 WV737, C(PR).1 XF798; Twin Pioneer CC.1 XL997 H; CC.2 XN321.

Disbanded 31st December 1968 at Seletar, Singapore.

210 SQUADRON
Originally formed 1st February 1917 at St Pol, France, as 10 (Naval) Squadron, RNAS. Became 210 Squadron from 1st April 1918 at Treizennes.

Camel B7153 X.

Disbanded 24th June 1919 at Scopwick.

Reformed 1st February 1920 at Gosport by renumbering 186 (Development) Squadron.

Cuckoo I N8011.

Disbanded 1st April 1923 at Gosport to become 460 and 461 Flights.

Reformed 1st March 1931 at Felixstowe.

Nil (3.31–5.39)	Southampton I N9899, II S1042; Singapore II N246, III K3594; Rangoon K2809; London K3560; Stranraer K3973; Sunderland I L2165 B.
VG (5.39–9.39)	Sunderland I L5799 VG-D.
DA (9.39–12.43)	Sunderland I L5798 DA-A; Consolidated 28-5 P9630, Catalina I AH531 DA-A, IB FP102, IIA VA729 DA-P, IIIA FP536.

Disbanded 31st December 1943 at Hamworthy.

Reformed 1st January 1944 at Sullom Voe by renumbering 190 Squadron.

Catalina IB FP267, IVA JV931, IVB JX604.

Disbanded 4th June 1945 at Sullom Voe.

Reformed 1st June 1946 at St Eval by renumbering 179Y Squadron.

OZ (4.46–.51)	Lancaster GR.3 RE115 OZ-T.
L (.51–.56)	Lancaster GR.3 SW368 L-Z; Neptune MR.1 WX526 L-X.
210 (.56–1.57)	Neptune MR.1 WX525 210-Y.

Disbanded 31st January 1957 at Topcliffe.

Gloster Gauntlet Mk IIs of No 213 Squadron at RAF display rehearsals in 1937.

Reformed 1st December 1958 at Ballykelly by renumbering 269 Squadron.

210   *Shackleton MR.2 WL793 210-S.*

Disbanded 31st October 1970 at Ballykelly.

Reformed 1st November 1970 at Sharjah, Oman, by redesignating the resident 210 Squadron detachment.

210   *Shackleton MR.2, T.2 WL739.*

Disbanded 15th November 1971 at Sharjah.

211 SQUADRON
Originally formed 8th March 1917 at Dunkerque, France, as 11 (Naval) Squadron, RNAS. Disbanded 27th August 1917 at Hondschoote, France, only to reformed 10th March 1918 at Petite Synthe, France. Became 211 Squadron, RAF from 1st April 1918 whilst at Petite Synthe, France.

D.H.4 B9499; D.H.9 D1733 C.

Disbanded 24th June 1916 at Wyton.

Reformed 24th June 1937 at Mildenhall.

Nil (6.37–9.39)   *Audax K2011; Hind K6842; Blenheim I L6660.*
LJ   *Allocated for the period April to September 1939 but no evidence of use.*
UQ (9.39–2.42)   *Blenheim I L6670 UQ-R, IV L4825.*

Disbanded 19th February 1942 at Kalidjati, Java, and absorbed by 84 Squadron.

Reformed 14th August 1943 at Phaphamau, India.

Wellington VIII LA996; Beaufighter X LZ157 M; Mosquito VI RF751 B.

Disbanded 15th March 1945 at Don Muang, Thailand.

212 SQUADRON
Formed 20th August 1918 at Great Yarmouth. Parented 485 and 486 (Fighter) and 490, 557 and 558 (Light Bomber) flights for varying periods.

D.H.4 A8038; D.H.9 D5793, D.H.9A F959; Camel B3950.

Disbanded 9th February 1920 at Dover (Swingate Down).

QB   *Allocated for the period April to September 1939.*

Reformed 10th February 1940 at Meaux, France, by redesignating an element of 2 Camouflage Unit.

Blenheim IV; Hudson I; Spitfire PR.III N3116, PR.IC P9396.

Disbanded 18th June 1940 at Heston and absorbed by the Photographic Development Unit.

Reformed 22nd October 1942 at Korangi Creek, India.

Catalina I AH550, IB FP231 K, IIA VA716, IVB JX341 H.

Disbanded 1st July 1945 at Red Hills Lake, India, to become 240 Squadron.

213 SQUADRON

Originally formed 15th January 1918 at St Pol, France, as 13 (Naval) Squadron, RNAS by redesignating the St Pol Defence Squadron. Became 213 Squadron, RAF from 1st April 1918 whilst at Bergues, France.

Camel F3944 6; Avro 504K F9782.

Disbanded 31st December 1919 at Scopwick.

Reformed 8th March 1937 at Northolt from 'C' Flight of 111 Squadron.

Nil (3.37–4.39)	Gauntlet II K7806; Hurricane I L1771.
AK (4.39–1.50)	Hurricane I L1790 AK-K, X P5198, IIB BN271, IIC HV609 AK-S; Spitfire VC JG781, IX MJ835 AK-B; Mustang III FB342 AK-X, IVA KH751 AK-E; Tempest VI NX260 AK-Z; Harvard III EX814 AK-K.
Nil (1.50–9.54)	Vampire FB.5 VV633 C, FB.9 WX207 F.
Also used	Magister P6348; Ju 87D-1 S7+LL; Vampire T.11 WZ552.

Disbanded 30th September 1954 at Deversoir, Egypt.

Reformed 1st September at Ahlhorn, Germany.

Canberra T.4 WH841; B(I)6 WT311.

Disbanded 31st December 1969 at Bruggen, Germany.

214 (FEDERATED MALAY STATES) SQUADRON

Originally formed 9th December 1917 at Coudekerque, France, by redesignating 7A (Naval) Squadron, RNAS as 14 (Naval) Squadron, RNAS. Became 214 Squadron, RAF from 1st April 1918 whilst at Coudekerque, France.

Handley Page O/100 3128; Handley Page O/400 C9643 P.

Disbanded 1st February 1920 at Abu Sueir, Egypt, and absorbed by 216 Squadron.

Reformed 16th September 1935 at Boscombe Down by redesignating 'B' Flight of 9 Squadron.

Nil (10.35–1.37)	Virginia X K2664.
214 (1.37–4.39)	Harrow II K6993 214-L.
UX (4.39–9.39)	Harrow II K6989 UX-H; Wellington I L4344 UX-M.
BU (9.39–7.45)	Wellington I L4327, IA N2903 BU-E, IC N2778 BU-R, II W5452 BU-U; Stirling I BK599 BU-R, III EF445/G BU-K; Fortress I AN537, II HB765, III KJ101 BU-H, IIIA SR389 BU-P.
Also used	Tiger Moth BD142.

Disbanded 27th July 1945 at Oulton.

Reformed 27th July 1945 at Amendola, Italy, by renumbering 614 Squadron.

Liberator VIII KG955; Lancaster I PA386 QN-Y.

Disbanded 15th April 1946 at Fayid, Egypt, to become 37 Squadron.

Reformed 5th November 1946 at Upwood.

QN (11.46–4.51)	Lancaster I TW882 QY-V; Lincoln II RE296 QN-BW.
PX	Possibly allocated to 'C' Flight.
Nil (4.51–12.54)	Lincoln II SX958.

Disbanded 30th December 1954 at Upwood.

Reformed 15th June 1955 at Laarbruch, Germany.

Canberra PR.7 WH779.

Disbanded 1st August 1955 at Laarbruch to become 80 Squadron.

Reformed 21st January 1956 at Marham.

Valiant B.1 WP211; B(PR).1 WP223; BK.1 XD812.

Disbanded 1st March 1965 at Marham.

Reformed 1st July 1966 at Marham.

Victor BK.1 XA928; K.1A XH588.

Disbanded 28th January 1977 at Marham.

214 SQUADRON CONVERSION FLIGHT

Formed 10th April 1942 at Waterbeach.

BU	Stirling I N6125.

Disbanded 1st October 1942 at Waterbeach and absorbed by 1651 Heavy Conversion Unit.

215 SQUADRON

Originally formed 10th March 1918 at Coudekerque, France, as 15 (Naval) Squadron, RNAS by merging elements of 7 and 14 (Naval) Squadrons, RNAS. Became 215 Squadron, RAF from 1st April 1918 whilst at Coudekerque, France.

Handley Page O/100 3128; Handley Page O/400 C9714.

Disbanded 18th October 1919 at Ford Junction.

Reformed 1st October 1935 at Worthy Down by redesignating 'C' Flight of 58 Squadron.

Nil (10.35–4.39)	Virginia X K2339; Anson I K6291; Harrow I K6965, II K6971.
BH (4.39–9.39)	Harrow II K7014 BH-L; Wellington I L4388 BH-B.
LG (9.39–4.40)	Harrow II K7031; Wellington I L4387 LG-L, IA N2912 LG-G; Anson I N5030.

Disbanded 8th April 1940 at Bassingbourn to become 11 Operational Training Unit.

Reformed 8th April 1940 at Honington.

Wellington IA.

Disbanded 22nd May 1940 at Bassingbourn and absorbed by 11 Operational Training Unit.

Reformed 9th December 1941 at Newmarket.

Wellington IC HF900 T, X LN268 H; Liberator VI EW284 Q; Dakota I FD780, III KG795 T, IV KN242 J.

Disbanded 15th February 1946 at Kallang, Singapore, to become 48 Squadron.

Reformed 1st August 1947 at Kabrit, Egypt.

Dakota IV KN684 Z.

Disbanded 1st May 1948 at Kabrit to become 70 Squadron.

Reformed 30th April 1954 at Dishforth.

Pioneer CC.1 XL555.

Disbanded 1st September 1958 at Dishforth to become 230 Squadron.

Reformed 1st May 1963 at Benson.

Argosy C.1 XP445.

Disbanded 31st December 1968 at Changi, Singapore.

216 SQUADRON

Originally formed 8th January 1918 at Ochey, France, as 16 Squadron, RNAS by redesignating 'A' Squadron, RNAS. Became 216 Squadron, RAF from 1st April 1918 whilst at Villesneux, France.

Nil (4.18–4.39)	D.H.10 F1868; Handley Page O/100 3127 R; Handley Page O/400 C9643 P; Vimy IV J7451; Victoria III J8231 L, IIIA J8061, IV J7921, V JR8062 J, VI JR8062; Vernon II J6890; Valentia I K3604 W.
VT (4.39–9.39)	Valentia I K3612 VT-D.
SH (9.39–9.41)	Valentia I K3612 SH-F; Bombay I L5820 SH-F.
Nil (9.41–6.75)	Bombay I L5832 R; D.H.86 HK831; Hudson VI FK384 Q; Ventura V FP657; Dakota I FD817, III FL524 M, IV KN689 HA; Valetta C.1 VW189; Comet C.2 XK698, T.2 XK669, C.4 XR395.

Disbanded 30th June 1975 at Lyneham.

Reformed 1st July 1979 at Honington.

Buccaneer S.2B XX900; Hunter T.7 XL609, T.7A XL568.

Disbanded 4th August 1980 at Lossiemouth and absorbed by 12 Squadron.

Reformed 1st November 1984 at Brize Norton.

C   TriStar C.1 ZD952 CE, K.1, KC.1 ZD952, C.2, C.2A.

Current 1st April 1998 at Brize Norton.

217 SQUADRON
Originally formed 14th January 1918 at Dunkerque, France, as 17 (Naval) Squadron, RNAS. Became 217 Squadron, RAF from 1st April 1918 whilst at Bergues, France.

D.H.4 A7935 E.

Disbanded 19th October 1919 at Driffield.

Reformed 15th March 1937 at Boscombe Down.

217 (3.37–4.39)	Anson I K8784 217-N.
YQ (4.39–9.39)	Anson I K8769 YQ-J.
MW (9.39–4.42)	Anson I K6285 MW-F; Beaufort I AW250 MW-Z.
Nil (8.42–9.45)	Hudson III AE555 K, IIIA FH349 S, VI FK441 D; Beaufort I DW888 C; Beaufighter X RD722.
Also used	Blenheim IV Z6030; Tiger Moth II N6842.

Disbanded 30th September 1945 at Gannavaram, India.

Reformed 14th January 1952 at St Eval.

A (1.52–.56)	Neptune MR.1 WX504 A-H.
217 (.56–3.57)	Neptune MR.1 WX511 217-F.

Disbanded 31st March 1957 at Kinloss.

Reformed 1st February 1958 at St Mawgan by redesignating 1360 (Helicopter) Flight.

Whirlwind HAR.4 XD164.

Disbanded 13th November 1959 at St Mawgan.

218 (GOLD COAST) SQUADRON
Formed 24th April 1918 at Dover (Guston Road).

D.H.4 N6390; D.H.9 D5654.

Disbanded 24th June 1919 at Hucknall.

Reformed 16th March 1936 at Upper Heyford by redesignating 'C' Flight of 57 Squadron.

Nil (3.36–2.38)	Hart K6633.
218 (1.38–4.39)	Battle K7660 218-L.
SV (4.39–9.39)	Battle K9252.
HA (9.39–8.45)	Battle K9353 HA-J; Blenheim IV R3666 HA-J; Wellington I L4293, IA P9207, IC R1339 HA-J, II W5448 HA-Z; Stirling I N3714 HA-J, III BK700 HA-W; Lancaster I PD256 HA-J, III PB291 HA-O.
XH (–8.45)	('C' Flight) Lancaster I, III ME545 XH-L.
Also used	Magister P2383; Tiger Moth W6418.

Disbanded 10th August 1945 at Chedburgh.

Reformed 1st December 1959 at Harrington.

Thor.

Disbanded 23rd August 1963 at Harrington.

218 SQUADRON CONVERSION FLIGHT
Formed January 1942 at Marham.

HA	Stirling I N6104.

Disbanded 7th October 1942 at Stradishall and merged with 7, 101 and 149 Squadron Conversion Flights to become 1657 Heavy Conversion Unit.

219 (MYSORE) SQUADRON, later 219 (SHADOW) SQUADRON
Formed 22nd July 1918 at Manston. Parented 406 and 442 (Seaplane), 470 (Fighter) and 555 and 556 (Light Bomber) Flights for varying periods.

RAF C.E.1 N98; Hamble Baby N1962; Sopwith Baby N1019; Short 184 N1264; D.H.9 C1327; Camel F3918 D; Fairey IIIB N2245.

Disbanded 7th February 1920 at both Manston and Westgate.

AM	Allocated for the period April to September 1939.

Reformed 4th October 1939 at Catterick.

FK	Blenheim I L8685 FK-N; Beaufighter I R2070 FK-Y, II R2375, VI V8613 FK-P; Mosquito XII HK128, XIII HK467, XVII HK315 FK-N, T.29 KA120, NF.30 MM813 FK-H, III TV970 FK-V.
Also used	Tutor K3249; Master I N8062; Proctor I P6252; Magister P2375; Oxford I R6015, II BM774; Mosquito III LR519; Auster III MT450.

Disbanded 1st September 1946 at Wittering to become 23 Squadron.

Reformed 1st March 1951 at Kabrit, Egypt.

Mosquito NF.36 RK983; Meteor NF.13 WM312.

Disbanded 1st September 1954 at Kabrit.

Reformed 5th September 1955 at Driffield.

Venom NF.2 WL867 E; Vampire T.11 XD604.

Disbanded 31st July 1957 at Driffield.

Reformed March 1957 at West Raynham as 219 (Shadow) Squadron, being the All Weather Fighter Combat School within the Central Fighter Establishment.

Javelin.

Disbanded December 1962 at West Raynham.

220 SQUADRON, later 220 (SHADOW) SQUADRON
Formed 1st April 1918 at Imbros, Aegean, by redesignating 'C' Squadron, 2 Wing, RNAS. The 220 Squadron numberplate was adopted from September 1919 when 475, 476 and 477 Coastal Patrol Flights were absorbed into the Squadron.

D.H.4 B9477; D.H.9 C6205; Camel D1970.

Disbanded 21st May 1919 at Mudros, Aegean.

Reformed 17th August 1936 at Bircham Newton by redesignating an element of 206 Squadron.

220 (8.36–4.39)	Anson I K6188 220-H.
HU (4.39–6.39)	Anson I K6224 HU-T.
PK (6.39–9.39)	Anson I K6207 PK-M.
NR (9.39–8.43)	Anson I K8818 NR-W; Hudson I N7232 NR-T, II T9369, III V9105, V AM815 NR-D; Fortress I AN530 NR-F.
MB (11.41–1.42)	Used by aircraft on detachment in the Middle East – Fortress I AN518 MB-B.
Nil (7.42–8.43)	Fortress IIA FK186 S.
2 (8.43–7.44)	Fortress IIA FK200 2-B.
Nil (7.44–12.44)	Fortress IIA FL462 W, III HB791 T.
ZZ (12.44–6.45)	Liberator II AL554, III LV342, V BZ743, VI KN703 ZZ-K, VIII KH222 ZZ-J.
8D (6.45–5.46)	Liberator VI KH348 8D-E.
Also used	Blenheim IV T1809.

Disbanded 25th May 1946 at Waterbeach.

Reformed 24th September 1951 at Kinloss.

T (9.51–.56)	Shackleton MR.1 VP257 T-P, MR.1A WB821 T-L, MR.2 WL737 T-K.
220 (.56–10.58)	Shackleton MR.1A WB821 220-L, MR.3 WR979 220-N.
Also used	Anson T.21 VV969.

Disbanded 1st October 1958 at St Mawgan to become 201 Squadron.

Reformed 22nd July 1959 at North Pickenham.

Thor.

Disbanded 10th July 1963 at North Pickenham.

Reformed July 1965 at Kinloss as 220 (Shadow) Squadron, being the Maritime Operational Training Unit and subsequently 236 Operational Conversion Unit at St Mawgan from July 1970.

Shackleton.

Disbanded December 1967 at St Mawgan.

221 SQUADRON
Formed 1st April 1918 at Stavros, Aegean, by redesignating 'D' Squadron, 2 Wing, RNAS. The 221 Squadron numberplate was

adopted from September 1919 when 552, 553 and 554 Coastal Patrol Flights were absorbed into the Squadron.

D.H.4; D.H.9, D.H.9A E8765.

Disbanded 15th October 1918 at Mudros, Aegean, and absorbed by 222 Squadron.

Reformed 18th December 1918 at Mudros, Aegean.

D.H.9A F1094 G.

Disbanded 1st September 1919 at Petrovsk Kaskar, Russia.

VB	Allocated for the period April to September 1939.

Reformed 21st November 1940 at Bircham Newton.

DF (11.40–1.42)	Wellington I R2700, IA N2910, IC W5672, II Z8512, VIII W5655 DF-F.
Nil (1.42–8.45)	Wellington VIII HX487 Y, XI HZ395 M, XII HF119, XIII JA412 S, XIV MP795.
Also used	Gordon K2743; Anson I L9157.

Disbanded 21st August 1945 at Idku, Egypt.

222 (NATAL) SQUADRON
Formed 1st April 1918 at Thásos, Aegean, by merging 'A' and 'Z' Squadrons, 2 Wing, RNAS. The 222 Squadron numberplate was officially adopted from September 1919 when 478, 479 and 480 (Fighter) Flights formed within the Squadron.

1½ Strutter B2582; D.H.4; Camel B7211; D.H.9 D2844.

Disbanded 27th February 1919 at Mudros, Aegean.

UP	Allocated for the period April to September 1939.

Reformed 4th October 1939 at Duxford.

ZD (10.39– .53)	Blenheim I L6638 ZD-A, IV N6147; Spitfire I X4546 ZD-C, IIA P7909 ZD-P, VB AB140 ZD-F, IXB MH765 ZD-X; Tempest V SN188 ZD-A; Meteor F.3 EE450 ZD-K, F.4 VT331 ZD-Y, T.7 VZ633 ZD-Z, F.8 WA814 ZD-N.
Nil (.53–11.57)	Meteor F.8 WA925 P, T.7 WL480; Hunter F.1 WT637 G, F.4 WW650 R.
Also used	Master I N7570; Magister L5953; Oxford II W6635; Tiger Moth II DE509; Auster I LB291, III MZ230.

Disbanded 1st November 1957 at Leuchars.

Reformed 1st May 1960 at Woodhall Spa.

Bloodhound 1.

Disbanded 30th June 1964 at Woodhall Spa.

223 SQUADRON
Formed 1st April 1918 at Mitylene, Greece, by redesignating 'B' Squadron, 2 Wing, RNAS. The 223 Squadron numberplate was officially adopted from September 1919 when 559, 560 and 561 (Light Bomber) Flights formed within the Squadron.

Short 320 N1306; Camel; D.H.4; D.H.9.

Disbanded 16th May 1919 at Mudros, Aegean.

Reformed 15th December 1936 at Nairobi, Kenya, by redesignating an element of 45 Squadron.

Nil (12.36–7.39)	Vincent I K4708; Wellesley I L2685.
QR	Allocated for the period April to September 1939 but no evidence of use.
OA (7.39–5.41)	Wellesley I L2668 AO-B.
Nil (5.41–8.44)	Maryland I AH333; Martin 167F AX692; Baltimore I AG732, II AG777, III AH139, IIIA FA261 J, IV FA403 C, V FW322.
Also used	Hart K4917; Fiat G12.

Disbanded 12th August 1944 at Pescara, Italy, to become 30 Squadron, SAAF.

Reformed 23rd August 1944 at Oulton.

6G	Liberator IV TS528 6G-O; Fortress II SR383 6G-X, III KJ109 6G-F.
Also used	Magister T9742.

Disbanded 29th July 1945 at Oulton.

Reformed 1st December 1959 at Folkingham.

Thor.

Disbanded 23rd August 1963 at Folkingham.

224 SQUADRON
Formed 1st April 1918 at Alimini, Italy, by redesignating elements of 6 Wing, RNAS. 496, 497 and 498 (Light Bomber) Flights formed within the Squadron from September 1918.

D.H.4 B9484; D.H.9 D2794.

Disbanded 15th April 1919 at Pizzone, Italy.

Reformed 1st February 1937 at Manston by redesignating 'C' Flight of 48 Squadron.

224 (1.37–4.39)	Anson I K8818 224-W.
PW	Allocated for the period April to September 1939 but no evidence of use.
Nil (4.39–9.39)	Anson I; Hudson I N7216.
QX (9.39–9.42)	Hudson I N7315 QX-Y, II T9376, III V9092 QX-A, V AM563 QX-X.
Nil (9.42– .44)	Liberator II AL507 Z, III FK230 J, V FL937 H.
XB (.44–11.47)	Liberator V FL228 XB-Y, VI KH751 XB-G, VIII KN753 XB-L; Lancaster GR.3 RE175 XB-P.
Also used	Tiger Moth II N9211; Blenheim IV V5454; Oxford I T1381, II X7282; Fortress IIA FK205; Martinet JN552.

Disbanded 10th November 1947 at St Eval.

Reformed 1st March 1948 at Aldergrove.

XB (5.48– .51)	Halifax VI RG836 XB-J.
B (.51–10.66)	Halifax VI ST804 B-K; Shackleton MR.1 VP287 B-B, MR.1A WB846 B-P, MR.2 WG558 B-R.
Also used	Oxford II V3677; Anson XIX VM386.

Disbanded 31st October 1966 at Gibraltar.

225 SQUADRON
Formed 1st April 1918 at Alimini, Italy, by redesignating an element of 6 Wing, RNAS. 481, 482 and 483 (Fighter) Flights formed within the Squadron in September 1918.

1½ Strutter; Baby N1989; Camel B5683.

Disbanded 18th December 1918 at Pizzone, Italy.

LX	Allocated for the period April to September 1939.

Reformed 9th October 1939 at Odiham by redesignating 614A Squadron ('B' Flight, 614 Squadron).

LX (10.39–4.42)	Battle L5035; Lysander II N1294 LX-T, III R9122 LX-L, IIIA V9293.
WU (4.42–7.42)	Lysander IIIA V9595 WU-F.
Nil (1.42–2.43)	Hurricane I P3112 J, IIC BN360, IIB BG951; Mustang I AG458, P-51 41-137428.
WU (2.43–1.47)	Spitfire VC EF724 WU-X, IX MJ993.
Also used	Master I T8405; Magister T9820; Blenheim IV R3871; Tomahawk IIB AK147; Airacobra I AH651; Proctor I P6317; Dominie I X7336; Argus II FZ736; Auster III NJ959.

Disbanded 30th December 1946 at Campoformido, Italy.

Reformed 1st January 1960 at Andover by redesignating the Joint Experimental Helicopter Unit.

Sycamore HR.14 XG523 L; Whirlwind HAR.2 XJ764 B, HAR.4 XD165 K, HAR.10 XP362 U.

Disbanded 1st November 1965 at Kuching, Malaya.

226 SQUADRON
Formed 1st April 1918 at Pizzone, Italy, by redesignating the Bombing School, Pizzone. 472, 473 and 474 (Fighter) Flights formed within the Squadron in September 1918.

D.H.4 B2148; D.H.9 D2906; Camel F6302.

Disbanded 18th December 1918 at Taranto, Italy.

Reformed 15th March 1937 at Upper Heyford by redesignating 'B' Flight of 57 Squadron.

226 (3.37–4.39)	*Audax K7403; Battle K7597 226-D.*
KP (4.39–9.39)	*Battle K7624 KP-B.*
MQ (9.39–9.45)	*Battle K9182 MQ-J; Blenheim I K7063, IV Z7493 MQ-Y; Havoc I AE464; Boston II AH459, III AL677 MQ-P, III (Turbinlite) W8393; Mitchell II FV905 MQ-S, III KJ613 MQ-S.*
Also used	*Oxford I DF431, II AB696; Mosquito III HJ983.*

Disbanded 20th September 1945 at B.77 (Gilze-Rijen), Netherlands.

Reformed 1st August 1959 at Catfoss.

Thor.

Disbanded 9th March 1963 at Catfoss.

227 SQUADRON
Formed 18th April 1918 at Pizzone, Italy, by redesignating an element of 6 Wing, RNAS. 499, 550 and 551 (Light Bomber) Flights were formed administratively within the Squadron in September 1918.

Caproni Ca.4 N528; D.H.4; D.H.9; Camel C133.

Disbanded 9th December 1918 at Pizzone, Italy.

BU	*Allocated for the period April to September 1939.*

Reformed 1st July 1942 at Aqir, Palestine, by redesignating an element of 10 Squadron.

Halifax II W1151.

Disbanded 7th September 1942 at Aqir to become 462 Squadron.

Reformed 20th August 1942 at Luqa, Malta, by redesignating an element of 248 Squadron.

Beaufighter IC T4666 Y, VI EL270 N, X LX864 O, XI JM233 W.

Disbanded 12th August 1944 at Biferno, Italy, to become 19 Squadron, SAAF.

Reformed 7th October 1944 at Bardney by merging 'A' Flight of 9 Squadron and 'B' Flight of 619 Squadron.

9J	*Lancaster I NN778 9J-H; III.*

Disbanded 5th September 1945 at Bardney.

228 SQUADRON
Formed 20th August 1918 at Great Yarmouth.Parented 324, 325 and 326 (Flying Boat) Flights for varying periods.

Baby N2071; Felixstowe F.2A N4518; Curtiss H.8 8662.

Disbanded 30th June 1919 at North Killingholme.

Reformed 15th December 1936 at Pembroke Dock.

Nil (12.36–4.39)	*Scapa I K7306 Z; London I K5258; Singapore III K6913; Stranraer I K7293 S.*
TO (4.39–5.39)	*Stranraer I K7297 TO-W; Sunderland I N9020 TO-W.*
BH (5.39–9.39)	*Sunderland I N6135 BH-U.*
DQ (9.39–8.43)	*Sunderland I P9600 DQ-T, II T9112 DQ-N, III W4017 DQ-T.*
Nil (8.43–7.44)	*Sunderland III DV977 J.*
UE (7.44–6.45)	*Sunderland III ML770 UE-P, V RN283.*

Disbanded 4th June 1945 at Pembroke Dock.

Reformed 1st June 1946 at St Eval by redesignating 224Y Squadron.

Liberator VIII KK328.

Disbanded 30th September 1946 at St Eval.

Reformed 1st July 1954 at St Eval by redesignating an element of 206 Squadron.

L (7.54– .56)	*Shackleton MR.2 WR960 L-P.*
228 (.56–5.59)	*Shackleton MR.2 WR961 228-Y.*

Disbanded 6th March 1959 at St Mawgan.

Reformed 1st September 1959 at Leconfield by redesignating 275 Squadron.

Sycamore HR.14 XJ919; Whirlwind HAR.4 XD165, HAR.10 XP403. Also used Chipmunk T.10 WZ846.

Disbanded 28th August 1964 at Coltishall to become 202 Squadron.

229 SQUADRON, later 229 (SHADOW) SQUADRON
Formed 20th August 1918 at Great Yarmouth. Parented 428, 429, 454 and 455 (Seaplane) Flights for varying periods.

Baby N2117; Short 184 N2901; Fairey IIIC.

Disbanded 31st December 1919 at Killingholme.

DB	*Allocated for the period April to September 1939.*

Reformed 4th October 1939 at Digby.

RE (10.39–5.41)	*Blenheim I L6737 RE; Hurricane I P3039 RE-D, X P5207.*
HB (5.41–4.42)	*Hurricane I W9326, IIA Z4940, IIB BM964, IIC BN182.*

Disbanded 29th April 1942 at Hal Far, Malta.

Reformed 3rd August 1942 at Takali, Malta by redesignating the air component of 603 Squadron.

X (8.42–1.44)	*Spitfire VC EF638 X-N.*
HB (1.44–4.44)	*Spitfire VC JK521 HB-X.*
9R (4.44–1.45)	*Spitfire IX MH907 9R-Z, XVI SM390 9R-H.*
Also used	*Magister R1976; Tiger Moth II DF182.*

Disbanded 10th January 1945 at Coltishall to become 603 Squadron.

Reformed June 1955 at Chivenor as 229 (Shadow) Squadron within 229 Operational Conversion Unit.

Hunter.

Disbanded November 1957 at Chivenor.

230 SQUADRON
Formed 20th August 1918 at Felixstowe. Parented 327, 328 (Flying Boat) and 487 (Fighter) Flights for varying periods.

Curtiss H.8 8661; Curtiss H.16 N4060; Felixstowe F.2A N4298 AM; F.5 N4838; Camel F3128; Short 184; Fairey IIIB, Fairey IIIC.

Disbanded 1st April 1923 at Calshot to become 480 (Coastal Reconnaissance) Flight.

Reformed 1st December 1934 at Pembroke Dock.

Nil (12.34–9.39)	*Singapore III K4578 X; Sunderland I L2164 Z.*
FV	*Allocated for the period April to September 1939 but not used.*
NM (9.39–1.43)	*Sunderland I T9071 NM-N, II W3987 NM-X, III W4021 NM-W; Dornier Do22 311; Latecoere 298B HB2-5.*
DX (.42–12.42)	*Sunderland I L5806, III W3987;*
Nil (1.43–4.46)	*Sunderland III EJ143 S, V PP158 T.*
4X (4.46–4.51)	*Sunderland V VB887 4X-X; Sea Otter I JM805 4X-Q.*
B (4.51– .56)	*Sunderland V SZ563 B-R.*
230 (.56–2.57)	*Sunderland V SZ582.*

Disbanded 28th February 1957 at Pembroke Dock.

Reformed 1st September 1958 at Dishforth by renumbering 215 Squadron.

Pioneer CC.1 XL702 Y; Twin Pioneer CC.1 XM961 M, CC.2 XP295; Whirlwind HAR.10 XK970 K.

Disbanded 3rd December 1971 at Wittering.

Reformed 1st January 1972 at Odiham having commenced training from 1st October 1971 as 230 Squadron (Designate).

D	*Puma HC.1 XW218 DT.*

Disbanded May 1992 at Gutersloh, Germany, and absorbed by 18 Squadron

Reformed May 1992 at Aldergrove.

Puma HC.1 ZA934 FC.

Current 1st April 1998 at Aldergrove.

231 SQUADRON
Formed 20th August 1918 at Felixstowe. Parented 329 and 330 (Flying Boat) Flights.

Felixstowe F.2A.

Disbanded 7th July 1919 at Felixstowe.

KR	Allocated for the period April to September 1939.

Reformed 1st July 1940 at Aldergrove by redesignating 416 (Army Co-operation) Flight.

VM (7.40–4.43)	Lysander I P1673, II P9075 VM-Z, III R9066 VM-B, IIIA V9408; Tomahawk I AH754, IIA AH947, IIB AK166.
Nil (4.43–1.44)	Mustang I AG513.
Also used	Mentor L4424; Battle K7565, Battle Trainer P6681; Tiger Moth II N9127; Hurricane I P2578; Beaufighter I T3248; Master III DL828.

Disbanded 15th January 1944 at Redhill.

Reformed 7th September 1944 at Dorval, Canada.

Liberator I AM929, II AM259, III FK240, V BZ715; Dakota III FL528, IV KN673; Hudson III FK582, IIIA FK770, VI FK540; Coronado I JX486; Liberator IX JT983; Spartan Executive KD102; Lancaster III RF261; Lancastrian C.2 VL972.

Disbanded 15th January 1946 at Bermuda, the United Kingdom Lancastrian Flight based at Full Sutton becoming 1699 Heavy Conversion Unit.

232 SQUADRON
Formed 20th August 1918 at Felixstowe. Parented 333, 334 and 335 (Flying Boat) Flights for varying periods.

Felixstowe F.2A N4541; F.5 N4041.

Disbanded 5th January 1919 at Felixstowe to become 4 (Communication) Squadron.

XN	Allocated for the period April to September 1939.

Reformed 17th July 1940 at Sumburgh by redesignating 'B' Flight of 3 Squadron.

EF (7.40–7.41)	Hurricane I W9919.
Nil (8.41–2.42)	Hurricane IIB BM903.

Disbanded 25th February 1942 at Tjilitjan, Java, and absorbed by 242 Squadron.

Reformed 19th April 1942 at Atcham.

EF	Spitfire VB EN845 EF-Y, IX LZ950 EF-F, VC ER542.

Disbanded 31st October 1944 at Gragnano, Italy.

Reformed 15th November 1944 at Stoney Cross.

Wellington XVI DV617; Liberator VII EW625, IX JT985; Skymaster I KL984; Lancastrian C.2 VM734; Magister T9818; Auster III NJ864.

Disbanded 15th August 1946 at Poona, India.

233 SQUADRON
Formed 31st August 1918 at Dover (Harbour and Guston Road). Parented 407 (Seaplane), 471 (Fighter) and 491 (Light Bomber) Flights for varying periods.

1½ Strutter 9378; Dolphin C3785; Camel F3956; D.H.9 D597; Short 184 N2939; D.H.4 D8400; Avro 504A D1631.

Disbanded 15th May 1919 at Dover.

Reformed 18th May 1937 at Upper Heyford.

Nil (5.37 –4.39)	Anson I K8830.
EY (4.39–9.39)	Anson I K6282 EY-S; Hudson I N7239.
ZS (9.39–7.42)	Anson I K8815 ZS-O; Hudson I T9284 ZS-J; Blenheim I L8719, IV P4830; Hudson III V9129 ZS-Z, IIIA FK750, V AM555 ZS-N.
Nil (7.42–2.44)	Hudson III T9451 X, IIIA FH424 H.

5T (3.44–12.48)	Anson X NK446; Dakota IV KN258 5T-UJ.
Also used	Oxford I L4663, II N4734.

Disbanded 15th December 1945 at Tulihal, India, and absorbed by 215 Squadron.

Reformed 1st September 1960 at Khormaksar, Aden, by redesignating the Valetta Flight of 84 Squadron.

Valetta C.1 VW195, C.2 VX576.

Disbanded 31st January 1964 at Khormaksar.

234 (MADRAS PRESIDENCY) SQUADRON, later 234 (SHADOW) SQUADRON, later 234 (RESERVE) SQUADRON
Formed 20th August 1918 at Tresco. Parented 350, 351, 352 and 353 (Flying Boat) Flights for varying periods.

Short 184 N2955; Curtiss H.12; Curtiss 12B N4341; Felixstowe F3 N4241.

Disbanded 15th May 1919 at Tresco.

AZ	Allocated for the period April to September 1939.

Reformed 30th September 1939 at Leconfield.

Nil (9.39–5.40)	Battle N2102; Gauntlet II (on loan from 616 Squadron); Tomahawk I AH813, IIA AH886; Blenheim I L1403; Hurricane I P2910.
AZ (5.40–8.45)	Spitfire I N3277 AZ-H, IIA P7296 AZ-P, VB AR364 AZ-W, VC EE720, VI BS146; Mustang III FB184 AZ-R, IV KH649, IVA KM305.
FX (8.45–9.46)	Spitfire IX TD310 FX-C; Meteor F.3 EE254 FX-J.
Also used	Tutor K3305; Magister N3860; Tiger Moth II T7104; Auster I LB312.

Disbanded 1st September 1946 at Boxted to become 266 Squadron.

Reformed 1st August 1952 at Oldenburg, Germany.

W (8.52–1.54)	Vampire FB.5 VV230 W-F, FB.9 WR242 W-B.
Nil (11.53–7.57)	Sabre F.4 XB727 Y; Hunter F.4 XF943 A, F.6 XG204 B.

Disbanded 15th July 1957 at Geilenkirchen, Germany.

Reformed 1st November 1958 at Chivenor as 234 (Shadow) Squadron within 229 Operational Conversion Unit by redesignating 127 (Shadow) Squadron.

Hunter.

Disbanded 2nd September 1974 at Chivenor.

Reformed 2nd September 1974 at Chivenor within the Tactical Weapons Unit. (Redesignated 1 Tactical Weapons Unit from 31st July 1978.)

Hunter; Hawk.

Disbanded 31st August 1992 at Brawdy.

Reformed 1st November 1992 at Valley as 234 (Reserve) Squadron being 2 Squadron, 4 Flying Training School.

D	Hawk T.1 XX161 DQ, T.1A XX191 DT.

Disbanded 1st April 1994 at Valley to become 208 (Reserve) Squadron.

235 SQUADRON
Formed August 1918 at Newlyn. Parented 424 and 425 (Seaplane) Flights.

Short 184 N2960.

Disbanded 22nd February 1919 at Newlyn.

SU	Allocated for the period April to September 1939.

Reformed 30th October 1939 at Manston.

LA (10.39–9.42)	Battle L5008; Blenheim I K7136, Blenheim IV L9324 LA-P; Beaufighter I R2269 LA-A.
Nil (9.42–7.44)	Beaufighter VI X7925 G, X LX944 401, XI JM117.
LA (6.44–7.45)	Mosquito VI HR287 LA-Y.

Also used	Oxford I R6084; Beaufighter II T3150; Magister R1833; Mosquito III HJ977.

Disbanded 10th July 1945 at Banff.

236 SQUADRON
Formed 20th August 1918 at Mullion. Parented 493 (Light Bomber) and 515 and 516 (Special Duty) Flights.

D.H.6 C7547; D.H.9 B7662.

Disbanded 31st May 1919 at Mullion.

FA	Allocated for the period April to September 1939.

Reformed 30th October 1939 at Stradishall.

FA (10.39– .41)	Blenheim I L6815 FA-G, IV T1942 FA-J; Beaufighter I T4724 FA-A.
ND (.41–8.43)	Blenheim IV V5432 ND-A; Beaufighter I T4827 ND-N, VI X8060 ND-E.
Nil (8.43–7.44)	Beaufighter VI JL824 Y, X NE193 H.
MB (7.44–5.45)	Beaufighter X NV171 MB-Y.
Also used	Magister R1816.

Disbanded 25th May 1945 at North Coates.

237 (RHODESIA) SQUADRON
Formed 20th August 1918 at Cattewater. Parented 420 and 421 (Seaplane) Flights.

Short 184 N2913.

Disbanded 15th May 1919 at Cattewater.

MH	Allocated for the period April to September 1939.

Reformed 22nd April 1940 at Nairobi, Kenya, by redesignating 1 Squadron, Southern Rhodesian Air Force.

Audax K7540; Hardy K4313; Hart SR103; Lysander I L4676, II N1206; Gladiator II N5820; Hurricane I Z4767, IIC BP384; Spitfire VB ER925, VC JL236, IX PT412; CR.42.

Disbanded 1st January 1946 at Lavariano, Italy, to become 93 Squadron.

238 SQUADRON
Formed 20th August 1918 at Cattewater. Parented 347, 348, and 349 (Flying Boat) Flights for varying periods.

Curtiss H.16; Short 184; Felixstowe F.2A N4460; F.3 N4419.

Disbanded 20th March 1922 at Cattewater.

TR	Allocated for the period April to September 1939.

Reformed 16th May 1940 at Tangmere.

VK (5.40–5.41)	Spitfire I R6604; Hurricane I P3462 VK-G.
Nil (6.41– .42)	Hurricane I T9531, IIA Z4953, IIB BD866 F, IIC HK846 X.
KC (.42–10.44)	Hurricane IIC; Spitfire VB EP953 KC-G, VC MA331 KC-F, VIII MT777 KC-F, IXC MH529 KC-T.
Also used	Master I N7720; Magister T9683.

Disbanded 26th October 1944 at Gragnano, Italy.

Reformed 1st December 1944 at Merryfield.

FM	Dakota II TJ170, III FZ671 FM-R, IV KP227 FM-J.

Disbanded 27th December 1945 at Parafield, Australia.

Reformed 1st December 1946 at Abingdon by renumbering 525 Squadron.

WF	Dakota III KG391 WF-G, IV KN497 WF-C.

Disbanded 4th October 1948 at Abingdon to become 10 Squadron.

239 SQUADRON
Formed August 1918 at Torquay. Parented 418 (Seaplane) Flight.

Short 184 N2962.

Disbanded 31st May 1919 at Torquay.

XB	Allocated for the period April to September 1939.

Reformed 18th September 1940 at Hatfield by redesignating elements of 16 and 225 Squadrons.

HB (9.40–9.43)	Battle L5025 HB-J; Lysander II L6850 HB-H, IIIA V9519; Tomahawk I AH793 HB-Z, IIA AH890, IIB AK128; Kittyhawk II FS415; Hurricane I P2949 HB-S, X AG119, IIC BN966 HB-X; Mustang I AG356 HB-V.
Nil (9.43–1.45)	Beaufighter I R2146; Mosquito II DZ270, VI PZ170.
HB (1.45–7.45)	Mosquito VI PZ226 HB-B, NF.30 NT362 HB-S.
Also used	Magister T9708; Tiger Moth II T7468; Master I T8568; Hind K5371; Spitfire VB W3168; Oxford II V3833.

Disbanded 1st July 1945 at West Raynham.

240 SQUADRON
Formed 20th August 1918 at Calshot. Parented 345, 346 and 410 (Seaplane) Flights.

Campania N2395; Short 184; Short 320 N1707; Felixstowe F.2A N4286; Curtiss H.12B N4334.

Disbanded 15th May 1919 at Calshot.

Reformed 30th March 1937 at Calshot by redesignating 'C' Flight of the Seaplane Training Squadron. A Special Duty Flight operated within the Squadron from October 1944.

Nil (3.37–4.39)	Scapa I K4195; Singapore III K8566.
SH (4.39–9.39)	Singapore III K8566; London II K5257; Lerwick I L7250.
BN (9.39–6.42)	London II K5258 BN-H; Lerwick I L7250; Stranraer I K7293 BN-Z; Consolidated 28-5 P9630; Catalina I W8405 BN-F, II AM264 BN-X.
Nil (6.42–7.45)	Catalina I AH536, IB FP225 P, II AM269, IIA VA718 K, IVB JX303 X.

Disbanded 1st July 1945 at Red Hills Lake, India.

Reformed 1st July 1945 at Red Hills Lake, India, by redesignating elements of 212 Squadron and the Special Duty Catalina Flight of the former 240 Squadron. The Special Duty Flight disbanded on 15th November 1945.

Catalina IB FP165, IVB JX341; Sunderland V PP131 J.

Disbanded 21st March 1946 at Koggala, Ceylon.

Reformed 1st May 1952 at Aldergrove by redesignating an element of 120 Squadron.

L (5.52– .56)	Shackleton MR.1 WG507 L-E, MR.1A WB860 L-C.
240 (.56–11.58)	Shackleton MR.1A WG507 201-E, MR.2 WL738.
Also used	Oxford I N4775.

Disbanded 1st November 1958 at Ballykelly to become 203 Squadron.

Reformed 1st August 1959 at Breighton.

Thor.

Disbanded 8th January 1963 at Breighton.

241 SQUADRON
Formed 20th August 1918 at Portland. Parented 416 and 417 (Seaplane) and 513 (Special Duty) Flights for varying periods.

D.H.6 C6513; Campania N2363; Short 184 N1259; Wright Seaplane 9841.

Disbanded 18th June 1919 at Portland.

EZ	Allocated for the period April to September 1939.

Reformed 25th September 1940 at Longman by merging 'A' Flight of 4 Squadron and 'A' Flight of 614 Squadron.

RZ (9.40–10.42)	Tiger Moth II N6550; Battle K9199; Lysander I P1699, II N1204, III T1563, IIIA V9707 RZ-P; Master III DL644; Tomahawk I AH757, IIA

	AH947, IIB AK138 RZ-L; Mustang I AG512 RZ-A.
Nil (11.42–)	Hurricane IIB BW885, IIC HW556 K; Spitfire VB ER723.
RZ (.44–8.45)	Spitfire IX MA425 RZ-R, VIII JF659.

Disbanded 14th August 1945 at Treviso, Italy.

242 (CANADIAN) SQUADRON
Formed 20th August 1918 at Newhaven. Parented 408, 409 (Seaplane) and 514 (Special Duty) Flights for varying periods.

Short 184 N2833; D.H.6 C6891; Fairey IIIB N2234; Campania N2380.

Disbanded 15th May 1919 at Newhaven.

| YD | Allocated for the period April to September 1939. |

Reformed 30th October 1939 at Church Fenton.

Nil (10.39–2.40)	Battle L5133; Blenheim I L1521; Hurricane I N2320.
LE (2.40–12.41)	Hurricane I V7467 LE-D, IIA Z2513 LE-A, IIB Z3075, IIC BE872.
Also used	Magister N3952; Harvard I P5865; Master I N7566; Tiger Moth II N6932.

The Squadron left the United Kingdom in November 1941 for the Far East. The air echelon was diverted to Takali, Malta, only to be disbanded and absorbed on 17th March 1942 by 126 Squadron. The ground echelon continued to the Far East, absorbed elements of 232 and 605 Squadrons during February 1942 at Tjilitjan, then disbanded and dispersed on 10th March 1942 at Tasikmalaja, Java.

Reformed 10th April 1942 at Turnhouse.

| LE | Spitfire VA W3118, VB BL729 LE-V, VC JK260 LE-K, IX JL180 LE-E. |

Disbanded 4th November 1944 at Gragnano, Italy.

Reformed 15th November 1944 at Stoney Cross.

| KY (11.44– .48) | Wellington XVI R1521; Stirling V PK157 KY-MW, III LK148, IV LJ669; York I MW328 KY-A. |
| Nil (.48–5.50) | York I MW236; Hastings C.1 TG537 A. |

Disbanded 1st May 1950 at Lyneham.

Reformed 1st October 1959 at Marham.

Bloodhound I.

Disbanded 30th September 1964 at Marham.

243 SQUADRON
Formed 20th August 1918 at Cherbourg, France. Parented 414 and 415 (Seaplane) Flights.

Short 184 N2805; Wright Seaplane 9858.

Disbanded 15th March 1919 at Cherbourg.

| NX | Allocated for the period April to September 1939. |

Reformed 11th March 1941 at Kallang, Singapore.

Buffalo I W8147.

Disbanded 30th January 1942 at Kallang.

Reformed 1st June 1942 at Ouston.

| SN | Spitfire VB AD319 SN-E, VC JK666 SN-V, IX EN148 SN-E. |
| Also used | Magister L8095; Argus II FS512. |

Disbanded 31st October 1944 at Gragnano, Italy.

Reformed 15th December 1944 at Morecambe and embarked immediately for Canada. Began ferry training at Dorval on 7th December, then moved to Australia where the Squadron became operational on 26th February 1945 at Camden.

Dakota IV KK146; Anson XII PH599.

Disbanded 15th April 1945 at Camden, Australia.

244 SQUADRON
Formed 25th July 1918 at Bangor. Parented 521, 522 and 530 (Special Duty) Flights for varying periods.

D.H.6 B3021.

Disbanded 22nd January 1919 at Bangor.

| VM | Allocated for the period April to September 1939. |

Reformed 1st November 1940 at Shaibah, Iraq, by redesignating 'S' Squadron.

Vincent K6363 H; Oxford I L4667; Blenheim IV Z7629 L, V BA163 C; Wellington XIII JA406 G; Argus I FK320.

Disbanded 1st May 1945 at Masirah, Muscat and Oman.

245 (NORTHERN RHODESIA) SQUADRON
Formed August 1918 at Fishguard. Parented 426 and 427 (Seaplane) Flights.

Short 184 N9032.

Disbanded 10th May 1919 at Fishguard.

| DX | Allocated for the period April to September 1939. |

Reformed 30th October 1939 at Leconfield.

Nil (10.39–3.40)	Blenheim I L6797; Battle L5031.
DX (3.40–6.41)	Hurricane I P3762 DX-E.
MR (6.41–8.45)	Hurricane IIB AM315, IIC BE516 MR-W, IIA BV169; Typhoon IB JP660 MR-S.
Also used	Tutor K3407; Spitfire I X4244, VB W3441; Tiger Moth II DE482; Auster III NX500.

Disbanded 10th August at B.164 (Schleswig), Germany.

Reformed 10th August 1945 at Colerne by redesignating 504 Squadron.

MR (8.45– .51)	Meteor F.3 EE286 MR-Q, F.4 RA414 MR-H, T.7 VW484 MR-T, F.8 WA836 MR-E.
Nil (.51–7.57)	Meteor T.7 WA725 L, F.8 WF740 K; Hunter F.4 XE687 G.
Also used	Tiger Moth II T5978; Vampire T.11 WZ469.

Disbanded 30th June 1957 at Stradishall.

Reformed 21st August 1958 at Watton by redesignating 527 Squadron.

Canberra B.2 WJ611, T.4 WT488.

Disbanded 19th April 1963 at Tangmere to become 98 Squadron.

246 SQUADRON
Formed August 1918 at Seaton Carew. Parented 402, 403, 451, 452 (Seaplane) and 495 (Light Bomber) Flights for varying periods.

Short 320 N1703; Baby N2064; Short 184 N2640; F.E.2b A6535; Kangaroo B9983.

Disbanded 15th March 1918 at Seaton Carew.

| MP | Allocated for the period April to September 1939. |

Reformed 5th August 1942 at Bowmore.

Sunderland II W6066 F, III DV978 E.

Disbanded 30th April 1943 at Bowmore.

Reformed 11th October 1944 at Lyneham by redesignating the Liberator Flight of 511 Squadron.

Nil (10.44–7.45)	Liberator VII EW631; Halifax III NA683; Liberator III FK219, VI KH169; Skymaster I KL986.
VU (12.44–10.46)	York VVIP I MW100; VIP I MW101; I MW174 VU-D.
Also used	Proctor III LZ751; Oxford I NM525.

See also The VVIP Flight and the Halifax Development Flight.

Disbanded 16th October 1946 at Holmsley South to become 511 Squadron.

247 (CHINA BRITISH) SQUADRON

Formed 20th August 1918 at Felixstowe. Parented 336 and 337 (Flying Boat) Flights.

Felixstowe F.2A, F.3.

Disbanded 22nd January 1919 at Felixstowe.

HP	*Allocated for the period April to September 1939.*

Reformed 1st August 1940 at Roborough by redesignating the Fighter Flight, Sumburgh.

HP (8.40– .42)	*Gladiator II N2308 HP-B; Hurricane I W9270 HP-Y, X AM275, IIA Z2682 HP-R, IIB Z3662 HP-E.*
ZY (.42–12.49)	*Hurricane IIC BD936 ZY-S; Typhoon IB DN252 ZY-N; Tempest F.2 MW756 ZY-B; Vampire I TG311 ZY-O, F.3 VF334 ZY-S.*
Nil (12.49–5.51)	*Vampire FB.5 VZ222 Z; Meteor T.7 VZ634, F.8 WH468 S; Hunter F.4 WT795 A, F.6 XE581 T.*
Also used	*Tiger Moth II DE877; Harvard IIB KF691; Auster I LB299, V MT365.*

Disbanded 31st December 1957 at Odiham.

Reformed 1st July 1960 at Carnaby.

Bloodhound I.

Disbanded 31st December 1963 at Carnaby.

248 SQUADRON

Formed August 1918 at Hornsea Mere. Parented 404, 405, and 453 (Seaplane) Flights for varying periods.

Short 184 N2922; Baby N2099.

Disbanded 10th March 1919 at Hornsea Mere.

QK	*Allocated for the period April to September 1939.*

Reformed 30th October 1939 at Hendon.

WR (10.39–10.43)	*Blenheim I L1336 WR-E, IV N6239 WR-K; Beaufighter IC T4843 WR-X, VIC EL304 WR-C, X JM331 WR-X.*
DM (10.43–)	*Beaufighter X JM348 DM-Q; Mosquito VI HR632 DM-Q, XVIII MM425 DM-L.*
Nil (–10.46)	*Mosquito XVIII NT224 E.*
Also used	*Hurricane I N2557; Magister R1835; Tiger Moth II T5631; Mosquito III HJ897.*

Disbanded 1st October 1946 at Thorney Island to become 36 Squadron.

249 (GOLD COAST) SQUADRON

Formed 18th August 1918 at Dundee. Parented 400 and 401 (Flying Boat) and 419 and 450 (Seaplane) Flights for varying periods.

Baby N1432; Short 184 N2641.

Disbanded 8th October 1919 at Dundee.

VY	*Allocated for the period April to September 1939.*

Reformed 16th May 1940 at Church Fenton.

GN (5.40–5.41)	*Spitfire I P9507; Hurricane I P3154 GN-H.*
Nil (5.41–3.42)	*Hurricane I Z4502, IIA Z2410, IIB Z2893, IIC Z3081.*
T (3.42–6.43)	*Spitfire VB EP712 T-M, Spitfire VC BR111 T-M.*
GN (6.43–9.44)	*Spitfire VB EP828 GN-O, VC ES306 GN-T, VIII JF953, IX LZ810 GN-P.*
Nil (9.44–8.45)	*Mustang III KH549, IVA KH757.*
Also used	*Hurricane X P5206; Magister L8237; Master I N7749; Harvard IIA EX126.*

Disbanded 16th August 1945 at Brindisi, Italy.

Reformed 23rd October 1945 at Eastleigh, Kenya, by redesignating 500 Squadron.

GN (10.45–3.50)	*Baltimore V FW367 GN-P; Mosquito FB.26 KA417 GN-C; Tempest VI NX170 GN-K.*

Nil (2.50–2.69)	*Vampire FB.5 VV536 B, FB.9 WL612 V; Venom FB.1 WR319 Y, FB.4 WR438 W.*
Also used	*Harvard III EX814; Mosquito III RR309; Vampire T.11 XE991.*

Disbanded 15th October 1957 at Eastleigh.

Reformed 15th October 1957 at Akrotiri, Cyprus, having commenced training from 6th August 1957 at Coningsby as 249 Squadron (Designate).

Canberra B.2 WJ564, B.6 WT370, B.15 WH956, B.16 WJ774.

Disbanded 24th February 1969 at Akrotiri.

250 (SUDAN) SQUADRON

Formed 18th May 1918 at Padstow. Parented 494 (Light Bomber) and 500, 501, 502 and 503 (Special Duty) Flights for varying periods.

D.H.6 C5206; D.H.9 D2963.

Disbanded 31st May 1919 at Padstow.

YE	*Allocated for the period April to September 1939.*

Reformed 1st April 1941 at Aqir, Palestine, by redesignating 'K' Flight.

LD	*Tomahawk IIB AK498 LD-C; Hurricane I V7822, IIC BN122; Kittyhawk I AK919 LD-B, III FR243 LD-R, IV FX616 LD-S; Mustang III FB334.*

Disbanded 30th December 1946 at Treviso, Italy.

251 SQUADRON

Formed 31st May 1918 at Hornsea. Parented 504, 505, 506 and 510 (Special Duty) Flights for varying periods.

Pup B2218; D.H.6 F3393; D.H.9.

Disbanded 30th June 1919 at Hornsea.

FF	*Allocated for the period April to September 1939.*

Reformed 1st August 1944 at Reykjavik, Iceland, by redesignating 1407 (Meteorological) Flight.

AD	*Ventura I AE779; Hudson III V8988 AD-Z, IIIA FK743 AD L; Anson I LT199 AD 4; Fortress II FA712 AD-C, IIA FK210 AD-W, III HB792 AD-D; Warwick I HG174 AD-R.*
Also used	*Mosquito VI LR384.*

Disbanded 30th October 1945 at Reykjavik.

252 SQUADRON

Formed 25th May 1918 at Tynemouth. Parented 495 (Light Bomber) and 507, 508, 509 and 510 (Special Duty) Flights for varying periods.

Short 320 N1705; Baby N2098; D.H.6 B3075; Kangaroo B9971.

Disbanded 30th June 1919 at Killingholme.

GW	*Allocated for the period April to September 1939.*

Reformed 21st November 1940 at Bircham Newton.

PN (11.40–5.41)	*Blenheim I K7087; Beaufighter I R2153 PN-B.*
BT (5.41–11.42)	*Beaufighter I T4767 BT-T.*
Nil (11.42–12.46)	*Beaufighter VI X8073, X NE319 J.*

Disbanded 1st December 1946 at Araxos, Greece.

253 (HYDERABAD) SQUADRON

Formed 7th June 1918 at Bembridge. Parented 412 and 413 (Seaplane) and 511, 512 and 513 (Special Duty) Flights for varying periods.

Baby N1333; Short 184 N9003; Campania N2378; D.H.6 C6578.

Disbanded 31st May 1919 at Bembridge.

TL	*Allocated for the period April to September 1939.*

Reformed 30th October 1939 at Manston.

SW	Battle L5110; Hurricane I L1660 SW-F, X P5179 SW-B, IIB Z3171 SW-P, IIA Z2389, IIC Z3261; Spitfire VC JK868 SW-K, IX PV124, VIII JF899 SW-K, XI.
Also used	Magister R1834; Master I N7567.

Disbanded 16th May 1947 at Treviso, Italy.

Reformed 18th April 1955 at Waterbeach.

Venom NF.2 WR808 H; Vampire T.11 WZ418.

Disbanded 2nd September 1957 at Waterbeach.

254 SQUADRON
Formed May 1918 at Prawle Point. Parented 492 (Light Bomber) and 515, 516, 517 and 518 (Special Duty) Flights for varying periods.

D.H.6 C5203; D.H.9 B7666; Avro 504K D186.

Disbanded 22nd February 1919 at Prawle Point.

HJ	Allocated for the period April to September 1939.

Reformed 30th October 1939 at Stradishall.

QY (10.39–7.42)	Blenheim I K7065, IV T2128 QY-J.
Nil (7.42–10.43)	Beaufighter VIC JL833 O, X JM211 V.
QM (10.43–10.46)	Beaufighter VIC JL828 QM-Q, X RD467 QM-J; Mosquito XVIII PZ468 QM-D.

Disbanded 1st October 1946 at Thorney Island to become 42 Squadron.

Reformed 1st December 1959 at Melton Mowbray.

Thor.

Disbanded 23rd August 1963 at Melton Mowbray.

255 SQUADRON
Formed 25th July 1918 at Pembroke. Parented 519, 520, 521, 522, 523 and 524 (Special Duty) Flights for various periods.

D.H.6 C9415; Camel D9542.

Disbanded 14th January 1919 at Pembroke.

BY	Allocated for the period April to September 1939.

Reformed 23rd November 1940 at Kirton-in-Lindsey.

YD	Defiant I N3312 YD-T; Hurricane I V7304; Beaufighter II R2402 YD-G, VI X8002 YD-G; Mosquito XIX TA437 YD-S, NF.30 NT246.
Also used	Master III W8455; Mosquito III LR585.

Disbanded 30th April 1946 at Gianaclis, Egypt.

256 SQUADRON
Formed June 1918 at Seahouses. Parented 495 (Light Bomber) and 525, 526, 527 and 528 (Special Duty) Flights for various periods.

D.H.6 C7336; Kangaroo B9982.

Disbanded 30th June 1919 at Killingholme.

SZ	Allocated for the period April to September 1939.

Reformed 23rd November 1940 at Catterick.

JT	Defiant I N3445 JT-F; Hurricane I V7010 JT-C, IIB; Defiant II AA417; Beaufighter I X7845 JT-G, VI V8501 JT-R; Mosquito XII HK124 JT-T, XIII MM583 JT-D; Spitfire VIII JF591, IX MA638; Hurricane IIC; Mosquito IX LR461, VI RF680 S, XVI MM335, XIX.
Also used	Oxford II X7129; Mosquito III HJ877, IV DZ357.

Disbanded 12th September 1946 at Nicosia, Cyprus.

Reformed 17th November 1952 at Ahlhorn, Germany.

T (11.52–)	Meteor NF.11 WD645 T-H.
Nil (–1.59)	Meteor NF.11 WD585 B.

Disbanded 21st January 1959 at Geilenkirchen, Germany, to become 11 Squadron.

257 (BURMA) SQUADRON
Formed 18th August 1918 at Dundee. Parented 318 and 319 (Flying Boat) Flights.

Curtiss H.16 N4069; Felixstowe F.2A N4432; Felixstowe F.3 N4235.

Disbanded 30th June 1919 at Dundee.

DT	Allocated for the period April to September 1939.

Reformed 16th May 1940 at Hendon.

ML (5.40–6.40)	Spitfire I N3039; Hurricane I L2101 ML-K.
DT (6.40–5.41)	Hurricane I V6555 DT-A, X P5186, IIC.
FM (5.41–3.45)	Hurricane IIC BN668, IIB Z5050 FM-T, IIA Z2808, X AG277; Spitfire VB BL446; Typhoon IB EJ926 FM-L.
Also used	Tiger Moth II DE355; Master I N7700, III DL577; Auster III MZ231.

Disbanded 5th March 1945 at B.89 (Mill), Netherlands.

Reformed 1st September 1946 at Church Fenton by renumbering 129 Squadron.

A6 (9.46– .51)	Meteor F.3 EE353 A6-E, F.4 VT320 A6-P, F.8 WA880 A6-S.
Nil (.51–3.57)	Meteor F.8 WK943 N, T.7 VW428; Hunter F.2 WN947 W, F.5 WP119 Q.
Also used	Vampire T.11 WZ459.

Disbanded 31st March 1957 at Wattisham.

Reformed 1st July 1960 at Warboys.

Bloodhound I.

Disbanded 31st December 1963 at Warboys.

258 SQUADRON
Formed 25th July 1918 at Luce Bay. Paretned 523, 524 and 529 (Special Duty) Flights for varying periods.

D.H.6 C9452; Fairey IIIA N2850.

Disbanded 5th March 1919 at Luce Bay.

FH	Allocated for the period April to September 1939.

Reformed 22nd November 1940 at Leconfield.

Hurricane I P2857, X P5196, IIA Z2589; Magister N3880; Tiger Moth N6944.

Disbanded 23rd February 1942 at Tjilitjan, Java, and absorbed by 232, 242 and 605 Squadrons.

Reformed 1st March 1942 at Ratmalana, Ceylon, by redesignating 'K' Squadron.

Nil (3.42–8.44)	Hurricane I Z4783, IIB BD881, IIC HV412.
ZT (8.44–12.45)	Thunderbolt I HB991 ZT-X, II HD244 ZT-Z.
Also used	Harvard IIB FE776.

Disbanded 31st December 1945 at Kuala Lumpur, Malaya.

259 SQUADRON
Authorised to form on 20th August 1918 at Felixstowe with Felixstowe F.2A as parent to 342, 343 and 344 (Flying Boat) Flights. A nucleus of 342 (Flying Boat) Flight probably existed on paper before authorisation was withdrawn on 13th September 1919.

VP	Allocated for the period April to September 1939.

Reformed 16th February 1943 at Kipevu, Kenya.

Catalina IB FP133 F; Sunderland V NJ259.

Disbanded 1st May 1945 at Dar es Salaam, Tanganyika.

260 SQUADRON
Formed August 1918 at Westward Ho! Parented 502 and 503 (Special Duty) Flights.

D.H.6 C2087; D.H.9.

Disbanded 22nd February 1919 at Westward Ho!

OB	Allocated for the period April to September 1939.

Reformed 22nd November 1940 at Castletown.

Nil (11.40–2.42)	*Hurricane I W9228 J, IIA Z4953, X P5196.*
HS (2.42–8.45)	*Kittyhawk I ET974 HS-V, IIA FL305 HS-B, III FR829 HS-X; Mustang III HB951, IVA KH854.*
Also used	*Magister T9817; Tomahawk IIB AK181; He 111H HS-?; Fiat G50.*

Disbanded 19th August 1945 at Laveriano, Italy.

261 SQUADRON
Authorised to form on 20th August 1918 at Felixstowe F.2A as parent to 339, 340 and 341 (Flying Boat) Flights. 339 and 341 (Flying Boat) Flights probably existed on paper before authorisation was withdrawn on 13th September 1919.

WY	*Allocated for the period April to September 1939.*

Reformed 2nd August 1940 at Luqa, Malta, by merging 418 (Fighter) Flight and the Fighter Flight, Malta.

Sea Gladiator N5519 R; Hurricane I P3731 J.

Disbanded 12th May 1941 at Takali, Malta, and merged with 1430 (Army Co-operation) Flight to become 185 Squadron.

Reformed 12th July 1941 at Habbaniya, Iraq, by renumbering 127 Squadron.

Nil (7.41–6.44)	*Gladiator I K7928; Hurricane I Z4029, IIA Z4961, IIB AP930 P, IIC BN701 K.*
FJ (6.44–9.45)	*Thunderbolt I HB968 FJ-A, II KL849 FJ-G.*
Also used	*Harvard IIB KF109.*

Disbanded 25th September 1945 at Tanjore, India.

262 SQUADRON
QY	*Allocated for the period April to September 1939.*

Formed 29th September 1942 at 104 PRDU, Hednesford, during embarkation for South Africa.

Catalina IB FP226 J, IVB JX347 D2.

Disbanded 15th February 1945 at Congella, South Africa, to become 35 Squadron, South African Air Force.

263 (FELLOWSHIP OF THE BELLOWS) SQUADRON
Formed 27th September 1918 at Otranto, Italy. Parented 359 (Flying Boat) and 435, 436 and 441 (Seaplane) Flights for various periods.

Baby N2090; Short 184 N1783; Short 320 N1384; Felixstowe F.3; Curtiss H.12B N4330.

Disbanded 16th May 1919 at Taranto, Italy.

SK	*Allocated for the period April to September 1939.*

Reformed 2nd October 1939 at Filton.

HE	*Gladiator I K6145, II N5633 HE-K; Hurricane I P2857, X P5194; Whirlwind I P6969 HE-V; Typhoon IB MN407 HE-Y.*
Also used	*Blenheim I L1123; Magister L8280; Oxford II R6401; Proctor III LZ559.*

Disbanded 30th August 1945 at R.16 (Hildesheim), Germany.

Reformed 30th August 1945 at Lübeck, Germany, by renumbering 616 Squadron.

HE (8.45–5.50)	*Meteor F.3 EE248 HE-C, F.4 EE460 HE-H, T.7 VW489 HE-Z.*
Nil (5.50–7.58)	*Meteor T.7 VW489 Z, F.8 WA920 F; Hunter F.2 WN921 S, F.5 WP108 T, F.6 XE626 P.*

Disbanded 2nd July 1958 at Stradishall to become 1 Squadron.

Reformed 1st June 1959 at Watton.

Bloodhound I.

Disbanded 30th June 1963 at Watton.

264 SQUADRON
Formed 27th September 1918 at Suda Bay, Crete. Parented 439 and 440 Flights (Seaplane).

Short 184 N1651.

Disbanded 1st March 1919 at Suda Bay.

WA	*Allocated for the period April to September 1939.*

Reformed 30th October 1939 at Sutton Bridge.

KV	*Allocated but no evidence of use.*
Nil (10.39–3.40)	*Defiant I L6958.*
PS (3.40–8.45)	*Defiant I N3313 PS-P, II AA404; Mosquito II DD724 PS-G, VI HX834, XII HK166, XIII MM467 PS-S.*
Also used	*Henley L3267; Battle N2159; Master I N7568; Blenheim IV P6911; Oxford I R6024, II P8994.*

Disbanded 25th August 1845 at B.106 (Twente), Netherlands.

Reformed 20th November 1945 at Church Fenton by renumbering 125 Squadron.

VA (11.45–5.47)	*Mosquito NF.30 NT440, NF.36 RL146 VA-J.*
PS (5.47–2.52)	*Mosquito III TW113, NF.36 RL250 PS-H.*
Nil (2.52–9.57)	*Meteor T.7 WH243, NF.11 WD647 S, NF.12 WS675 S, NF.14 WS756 G.*

Disbanded 30th September 1957 at Leeming to become 33 Squadron.

Reformed 1st December 1958 at North Coates.

Bloodhound I.

Disbanded 30th November 1962 at North Coates.

265 SQUADRON
Planned formation from August 1918 at Gibraltar, incorporating the 364, 365 and 366 (Flying Boat) Flights, cancelled.

KU	*Allocated for the period April to September 1939.*

Reformed 11th March 1943 at Kipevu, Kenya.

Catalina I AH548, IB FP311 O.

Disbanded 1st May 1945 at Diego Suarez, Madagascar.

266 (RHODESIA) SQUADRON
Formed 27th September 1918 at Mudros, Aegean. Parented 437 and 438 (Seaplane) Flights for varying periods.

Short 184 N1823; Short 320; Felixstowe F.3 N4360.

Disbanded 1st September 1919 at Petrovsk Port, Russia.

UO	*Allocated for the period April to September 1939.*

Reformed 30th October 1939 at Sutton Bridge.

Nil (10.39–1.40)	*Battle L5365.*
UO (1.40–7.42)	*Battle L5034; Spitfire I N3178 UO-K, IIA P8167 UO-N, VB W3834 UO-P; Typhoon IA R7641 UO-A.*
ZH (7.42–7.45)	*Typhoon IA R7645 ZH-B, IB R8937 ZH-L.*
Also used	*Master I N7685; Henley III L3320; Tiger Moth II DE513; Auster III NJ971.*

Disbanded 6th August 1945 at Hildesheim, Germany.

Reformed 1st September 1946 at Boxted by renumbering 234 Squadron.

FX	*Meteor F.3 EE254 FX-J, F.4 VT238 FX-R.*

Disbanded 11th February 1949 at Tangmere to become 43 Squadron.

Reformed 14th July 1952 at Wunstorf, Germany.

L (7.52– .53)	*Vampire FB.5 VZ262 L-T, FB.9 WR152.*
A (.53– .55)	*Venom FB.1 WE330 A-S.*
Nil (.55–11.57)	*Venom FB.1 WE330, FB.4 WR464 A.*
Also used	*Vampire T.11 XD449.*

Disbanded 16th November 1957 at Wunstorf.

Reformed 1st December 1959 at Rattlesden.

Bloodhound I.

Disbanded 30th June 1964 at Rattlesden.

267 SQUADRON
Formed 27th September 1918 at Kalafrana, Malta. Parented 360, 361, 362 and 363 (Flying Boat) Flights.

Felixstowe F.2A N4092, F.3 N4370; Fairey IIID N9494.

Disbanded 1st August 1923 at Kalafrana to become 481 Flight.

AO	Allocated for the period April to September 1939.

Reformed 20th August 1940 at Heliopolis, Egypt, by redesignating the Communication Unit, Heliopolis.

Nil (8.40–6.46)	Valentia K1313; Audax K3124; Gladiator I K7963, II N5825; Blenheim I L6672; Gull Six AX698; Lysander I L4677, II R1994; Anson I L7976; Hudson I P5163; Proctor I P6116; Magister R1953; Tomahawk IIB AK375; Simoun AX676; Lockheed 10A AX701; Lockheed 14 AX681; Lockheed 18 AX723; DC-2 AX755; Lodestar I EW977, II EW990 B; Dakota I FD774, III FD857 S, IV KN686 U; Percival Q-6 HK838; Moth Major HK839; BF 109F.
KW (.42– .43)	Hudson VI EW961 KW-H; Bf 110D KW.

Disbanded 21st July 1946 at Mingaladon, Burma.

Reformed 15th February 1954 at Kuala Lumpur, Malaya.

Pioneer CC.1 XE514; Devon WB530; Pembroke C.1 WV701, C(PR).1 XF798; Dakota III KP277: Auster VI WJ407, T.7 WE540; Harvard IIB KF126.

Disbanded 1st November 1958 at Kuala Lumpur to become 209 Squadron.

Reformed 1st November 1962 at Benson.

Argosy C.1 XR105.

Disbanded 30th June 1970 at Benson.

268 SQUADRON
Formed August 1918 at Kalafrana, Malta. Parented 433 and 434 (Seaplane) Flights.

Baby N2132; Short 184 N2810; Short 320 N1302; Felixstowe F.3 N4317.

Disbanded 11th October 1919 at Kalafrana.

JN	Allocated for the period April to September 1939.

Reformed 30th September 1940 at Bury St Edmunds by merging 'B' Flight of 2 Squadron and 'B' Flight of 26 Squadron.

NM (9.40–8.42)	Lysander II R1997 NM-L, III T1736, IIIA V9381; Tomahawk I AH775 NM-P, IIA AH897, IIB AK122.
Nil (8.42–10.45)	Mustang I AG413, IA FD535 X, II FR930; Typhoon FR.IB JP371, PR.1B EJ905; Spitfire XIV MV351, XIX PM577.
Also used	Battle N2084; Magister P2437; Tiger Moth II T7408; Moth Minor AV977; Master III DL642; Auster III MZ107, IV MT165.

Disbanded 19th September 1945 at B.118 (Celle), Germany, to become 16 Squadron.

Reformed 19th September 1945 at Cambrai/Epinoy, France, by renumbering 487 Squadron.

EG	Mosquito VI LR385.
Also used	Mosquito III HJ854; Oxford I R6027.

Disbanded 31st March 1946 at Cambrai/Epinoy.

269 SQUADRON
Formed 6th October 1918 at Port Said, Egypt. Parented 431 and 432 (Seaplane) Flights. It seems probable the latter existed only as an administrative entity.

Short 184 N2791; Baby N2132; Felixstowe F.3 N4360; D.H.9 E8997; B.E.2e 6802.

Disbanded 15th November 1919 at Alexandria, Egypt, and absorbed by 267 Squadron.

Reformed 7th December 1936 at Bircham Newton from 'C' Flight of 220 Squadron.

269 (12.36–4.39)	Anson I K6240 269-A.
KL (4.39–9.39)	Anson I K6259 KL-G.
UA (9.39–1.44)	Anson I K6244 UA-J; Hudson I N7376 UA-W, II T9374 UA-W, III T9465 UA-N.
Nil (1.44–3.46)	Hudson IIIA FK737 C, V AM583; Walrus I W2713; Spitfire VB EP175 J; Martinet I NR488.
HK (10.44–3.46)	Warwick I BV356 HK-E; VI HG171; Spitfire VB EP175 HK-J.
Also used	Blenheim I L1229; Oxford I N4775; Tiger Moth II T5878.

Disbanded 10th March 1946 at Lagens, Azores.

Reformed 1st January 1952 at Gibraltar by redesignating an element of 224 Squadron.

B (3.52– .56)	Shackleton GR.1 VP266 B-A, MR.1A WB820 B-S, MR.2 WL748 B-K.
Nil (.56–12.58)	Shackleton MR.1A WB851, MR.2 WL748.

Disbanded 1st December 1958 at Ballykelly to become 210 Squadron.

Reformed 22nd July 1959 at Caistor.

Thor.

Disbanded 24th May 1963 at Caistor.

270 SQUADRON
Formed April 1918 at Alexandria, Egypt.

Sopwith Baby N2131; D.H.9; Short 184 N9076; Felixstowe F3 N4318.

Disbanded 15th September 1919 at Alexandria and absorbed by 269 Squadron.

Reformed 12th November 1942 at Jui, Sierra Leone.

Catalina IB FP152 A; Sunderland III ML849 K.

Disbanded 30th June 1945 at Apapa, Nigeria.

271 SQUADRON
Formed 27th September 1918 at Taranto, Italy. Parented 357, 358, and 367 (Flying Boats) Flights.

Felixstowe F.3 N4317; Baby N1981.

Disbanded 9th December 1918 at Taranto.

ZJ	Allocated for the period April to September 1939.

Reformed 1st May 1940 at Doncaster by redesignating the Civil Aircraft Flight, National Air Communications.

BJ (5.40–1.44)	Harrow I K6937 BJ-C, II K6983 BJ-L; Trimotor X5000; Bombay I L5851; Handley Page H.P.42W G-AAUC; Savoia-Marchetti SM.73P OO-AGS; Whitney Straight BD168; Albatross AX904 BJ-W; Dominie I X7378; Hudson III T9424, V AM816; Dakota III FD904.
YS (1.44–12.46)	Dominie I X7351 YS-A; Dakota III FZ668 YS-J, IV KN625 YS-A.
L7 (1.44–12.46)	Dakota III FZ552, IV KN276.
Also used	Whitley V Z6804; Albemarle GT.I P1407; Oxford I T1256, II V3675; Dragon Rapide W6425; Tiger Moth II T6310; Horsa I HS101; Proctor III LZ696.

See also Sparrow Ambulance Flight.

Disbanded 1st December 1946 at Broadwell to become 77 Squadron.

272 SQUADRON
Formed 25th July 1918 at Machrihanish. Parented 531, 532 and 533 (Special Duty) Flights.

D.H.6 B2961.

Disbanded 5th March 1919 at Machrihanish.

SM	Allocated for the period April to September 1939.

Reformed 18th November 1940 at Aldergrove by merging elements of 235 and 236 Squadrons.

XK (11.40–5.41)	Blenheim IV V5754 XK-A.
Nil (5.41–4.45)	Blenheim IV N3526; Beaufighter IC T3316 M, VI JL646 L, XI JM229 K, X NV270 E.
TJ	Possibly allocated in United Kingdom and later in North Africa.
Also used	Wellington VIII Z8705.

Disbanded 30th April 1945 at Gragnano, Italy.

273 SQUADRON
Formed 30th July 1918 at Burgh Castle. Parented 470, 485 and 486 (Fighter) and 534 (Light Bomber) Flights for various periods.

D.H.4 A8033; D.H.9 D1053; Camel C68.

Disbanded 5th July 1919 at Great Yarmouth.

Reformed 1st August 1939 at China Bay, Ceylon.

HH (8.39–9.39)	Vildebeest III K4156; Seal K4781.
Nil (9.39–3.44)	Vildebeest III K4156; Seal K4781; Swordfish I K8402; Fulmar II X8568; Hurricane I W9296, IIA Z4952 K, IIB BG854 B, IIC LB854 S.
MS (3.44–1.46)	Spitfire VIII MT793 MS-S, Spitfire XIV RN218 MS-F.
Also used	Anson I AX233.

Disbanded 31st January 1946 at Tan San Nhut, French Indo China.

274 SQUADRON
Formed 15th June 1919 at Bircham Newton by redesignating an element of 5 (Communication) Squadron.

Handley Page V/1500 E8293.

Disbanded 20th January 1920 at Bircham Newton to become 207 Squadron.

MU	Allocated for the period April to September 1939.

Reformed 19th August 1940 at Amiriya, Egypt, by merging elements of 33, 80 and 112 Squadrons.

NH	Allocated but no evidence of use.
YK (8.40–9.40)	Morane-Saulnier 406; Potez 63; Gladiator II N5829; Hurricane I P2544 YK-T.
Nil (9.40–4.44)	Gladiator II N5810; Hurricane I Z4064, X P5176, IIB Z5387 O, IIC HL925 O, IIE BE490; Spitfire VC JK942 F.
JJ (4.44–9.45)	Spitfire IX BS474 JJ-N; Tempest V NV947 JJ-S.
Also used	Hart Trainer K5813; Tomahawk IIB AK470.

Disbanded 7th September 1945 at Warmwell to become 174 Squadron.

275 SQUADRON
WS	Allocated for the period April to September 1939.

Formed 15th October 1941 at Valley.

PV	Lysander I L4695, IIIA V9737; Walrus I L2207 PV-Z, II HD925 PV-S; Defiant I N3423; Anson I EG492 PV-F; Spitfire VB BL294.
Also used	Hawk Major BD180; Tiger Moth DE312.

Disbanded 15th February 1945 at Harrowbeer.

Reformed 1st March 1953 at Linton-on-Ouse.

Sycamore HR.13 XD197 A, HR.14 XG506 F; Hiller HTE-2 XB514; Anson T.21 TX193; Whirlwind HAR.4 XJ761.

Disbanded 1st September 1959 at Leconfield to become 228 Squadron.

276 SQUADRON
QM	Allocated for the period April to September 1939.

Formed 21st October 1941 at Harrowbeer by merging the Air Sea Rescue Flights Pembrey/Fairwood Common and Warmwell.

AQ	Lysander III T1696 AQ-H; Walrus I W3026

AQ-N, II X9573 AQ-A; Defiant I T4051 AQ-N; Spitfire IIA P8131 AQ-C, VB EN841; Anson I EG505 AQ; Warwick I HF938, VI HG208.

Also used	Tiger Moth II DE475.

Disbanded 14th November 1945 at Dunsfold.

277 SQUADRON
TP	Allocated for the period April to September 1939.

Formed 22nd December 1941 at Stapleford Tawney by merging the Air Sea Rescue Flights Hawkinge, Martlesham Heath, Shoreham and Shoreham/Friston/Shoreham.

BA	Lysander I P1684, IIIA V9431 BA-S; Walrus I W3097, II HD867 BA-F; Defiant I T3948; Spitfire IIA P8179 BA-T, VB AD366 BA-Z; Sea Otter I JM796; Warwick I BV527, VI HG208.
Also used	Tiger Moth II T7963; Oxford II BM844.

Disbanded 15th February 1945 at Hawkinge.

278 SQUADRON
RY	Allocated for the period April to September 1939.

Formed 1st October 1941 at Matlaske by redesignating the Air Sea Rescue Flight, Matlaske.

MY	Lysander IIIA V9541; Walrus I L2268 MY-A, II HD920 MY-B; Anson I LT592 MY; Spitfire I R6965 MY-P; Spitfire VB AD562 MY-V; Warwick I HF967; Sea Otter I JM885 MY-U.
Also used	Tiger Moth I NM121, II N5448; Master III W8509.

Disbanded 15th October 1945 at Thorney Island.

279 SQUADRON
AU	Allocated for the period April to September 1939.

Formed 16th November 1941 at Bircham Newton.

OS (11.41–11.44)	Hudson I T9284, III V9158 OS-T, V AM700, VI FK402.
RL (11.44–3.46)	Warwick VI HG214 RL-H; Hurricane IIC LD843; Sea Otter I JM861; Lancaster III RF310 RL-G.
Also used	Albemarle GT.I P1409.

Disbanded 10th March 1946 at Beccles, the detached Flight at Pegu, Burma, being absorbed by 1348 (Air Sea Rescue) Flight.

280 SQUADRON
FX	Allocated for the period April to September 1939.

Formed 12th December 1941 at Thorney Island.

YF (2.42–8.43)	Anson I DG922 YF-P.
3 (8.43–7.44)	Anson I AX636; Warwick I BV333 3-F.
MF (7.44–6.46)	Warwick I HG211 MF-X, VI HF984; Sea Otter I JM949.
Also used	Wellington I L4270, IA P2527.

Disbanded 21st June 1946 at Thornaby.

281 SQUADRON
SR	Allocated for the period April to September 1939.

Formed 29th March 1942 at Ouston.

FA	Defiant I N1613; Walrus I R6546; Anson I EG467 FA-F; Hawk Major BD180.

Disbanded 22nd November 1943 at Thornaby and absorbed by 282 Squadron.

Reformed 22nd November 1943 at Thornaby.

FA	Warwick I HF963, VI HG172 FA-L; Sea Otter I JM808; Wellington XIII MF302.

Disbanded 24th October 1945 at Ballykelly.

282 SQUADRON

VA	*Allocated for the period April to September 1939.*

Formed 1st January 1943 at Castletown.

B4	*Walrus I W3084; Anson I DJ617; Hawk Major BD180.*

Disbanded 12th January 1944 at Castletown and absorbed by 278 Squadron.

Reformed 1st February 1944 at Davidstow Moor from an element of 269 Squadron.

B4	*Warwick I HF978 B4-H, VI HG135; Walrus I L2306 B4-Q, II X9571; Sea Otter I JM745 B4-T.*

Disbanded 9th July 1945 at St Eval.

283 SQUADRON

JV	*Allocated for the period April to September 1939.*

Formed 11th February 1943 at Hussein Day, Algiers, Algeria.

Walrus I X9471, II Z1809; Warwick I BV451 B; Oxford I V4098.

Disbanded 31st March 1946 at Hal Far, Malta.

284 SQUADRON

BE	*Allocated for the period April to September 1939.*

Formed 7th May 1943 at Gravesend.

Walrus I W2757; Warwick I BV460 L; Hurricane IIC HW249; Magister R1974.

Disbanded 21st September 1945 at Pomigliano, Italy.

Reformed 15th October 1956 at Nicosia, Cyprus.

Sycamore HR.14 XF269 6; Whirlwind HAR.2 XJ766.

Disbanded 1st August 1959 at Nicosia to become 103 Squadron.

285 SQUADRON

GH	*Allocated for the period April to September 1939.*

Formed 1st December 1941 at Wrexham by redesignating 9 Group Anti-Aircraft Co-operation Flight.

VG	*Lysander I L4737, II P9100, IIIA V9484; Blenheim IV Z5878; Hudson III V9038; Oxford I HN845 VG-A; Defiant TT.I AA353 VG-Z; Tiger Moth II R5238; Martinet I MS507; Beaufighter I R2076; Hurricane IIC LF600, IV LE508; Mustang I AP168.*

Disbanded 26th June 1945 at Weston Zoyland.

286 SQUADRON

QL	*Allocated for the period April to September 1939.*

Formed 17th November 1941 at Filton by redesignating 10 Group Anti-Aircraft Co-operation Flight.

NW	*Lysander II N1249, IIIA V9490; Master II W9077, III W8837; Hurricane I P2754, IIC PG488, IV KX829; Defiant I AA628 NW-A; Mustang I AG386; Hudson III V9155; Tiger Moth II T7024; Oxford I HN138 NW-F; Martinet I MS509.*

Disbanded 16th May 1945 at Weston Zoyland.

287 SQUADRON

YV	*Allocated for the period April to September 1939.*

Formed 19th November 1941 at Croydon by redesignating 11 Group Anti-Aircraft Co-operation Flight.

KZ	*Lysander II L4768, IIIA V9540; Blenheim IV Z5985; Hurricane I P2754, X P5172, IV LD974; Hudson III V9160; Defiant I N1659 KZ-G, Tiger Moth II T7686; Master III W8509; Oxford I*

HN164 KZ-D; Martinet I JN673 KZ-A; Beaufighter I X7626, II V8159 KZ-F; Spitfire VB W3249, IX NH547; Tempest V JN764 KZ-R.

Disbanded 15th June 1946 at West Malling.

288 SQUADRON

VV	*Allocated for the period April to September 1939.*

Formed 18th November 1941 at Digby by redesignating 12 Group Anti-Aircraft Co-operation Flight.

RP	*Lysander II P1733, IIIA V9549; Blenheim IV V5492; Hurricane I T9532, X P5179; Hudson III V9253; Defiant I T4069; Master I T8607, III W8894; Tiger Moth II T7416; Oxford I HN706 RP-H, II P1814; Beaufighter I R2137; Hurricane IV KZ405 RP-J; Spitfire I X4180, VA N3124, VB BM271 RP-C, XVI TB744 RP-Z; Vengeance IV HB528 RP-J; Martinet I EM413.*

Disbanded 15th June 1946 at East Moor.

Reformed 16th March 1963 at Middle Wallop.

Balliol T.2 WG216 L; Chipmunk T.10 WP913; Anson T.21 VV324.

Disbanded 30th September 1957 at Middle Wallop.

289 SQUADRON

TT	*Allocated for the period April to September 1939.*

Formed 17th November 1941 at Kirknewton by redesignating 13 Group Anti-Aircraft Co-operation Flight.

YE	*Lysander II P9104, III P9111, IIIA V9319; Blenheim I L1253, IV N6141; Hudson II AE505, III V9158; Master III W8732; Tiger Moth II N9386; Hurricane I N2558, IIC LF580 YE-W, IV LF106; Oxford I X6801 YE-E; Defiant I DR868; Martinet I JN670 YE-12; Vengeance IV HB359 YE-A.*

Disbanded 26th June 1945 at Andover.

290 SQUADRON

FT	*Allocated for the period April to September 1939.*

Formed 1st December 1943 at Newtownards by merging 1480 (Anti-Aircraft Co-operation) and 1617 (Target Towing) Flights and an element of 289 Squadron.

X6	*Oxford I L4579, II X7251; Tiger Moth II DE165; Hurricane IV KZ190; Martinet I EM522 X6-D; Spitfire VB W3641 X6-H.*

Disbanded 27th October 1945 at B 83 (Knocke-le-Zout), Belgium.

291 SQUADRON

MM	Allocated for the period April to September 1939.

Formed 1st December 1943 at Hutton Cranswick by merging 1613, 1629 and 1634 (Anti-Aircraft Co-operation) Flights.

Henley III L3258; Martinet I MS731 B; Vengeance IV HB442; Hurricane IIC LF623, IV LE923; Master II DL130.

Disbanded 26th June 1945 at Hutton Cranswick.

292 SQUADRON

UZ	*Allocated for the period April to September 1939.*

Formed 1st February 1944 at Jessore, India.

Walrus II HD807; Blenheim IV Z9720; Warwick I HF970 Q; Sea Otter I JM758; Liberator VI KH269.

Disbanded 15th June 1945 at Agartala, India, having, between April and May 1945, created 1, 2, 3, 4, and 5 Air Sea Rescue Flights (Far East) that in turn became 1346, 1347, 1348, 1349 and 1350 (Air Sea Rescue) flights.

293 SQUADRON

XJ	Allocated for the period April to September 1939.

Formed 28th November 1943 at Blida, Algeria, by merging elements of 283 and 284 Squadrons.

ZE	Wellington II W5453; Warwick I BV234 ZE-L; Walrus I X9474 ZE-S, II Z1777; Hurricane IIC LB599; Harvard IIB KF912.

Disbanded 5th April 1946 at Pomigliano, Italy.

294 SQUADRON

AF	Allocated for the period April to September 1939.

Formed 24th September 1943 at Berka, Libya, by redesignating the Sea Rescue Flight.

Walrus I W3050 G, II X9584 C; Anson I L9165; Wellington IC LB126, XI MP616, XIII ME941 U; Warwick I BV482.

Disbanded 8th April 1946 at Basra, Iraq.

295 SQUADRON

HX	Allocated for the period April to September 1939.

Formed 3rd August 1942 at Netheravon from an element of 296 Squadron.

Nil (8.42–2.43)	Whitley V EB289 N; Halifax V EB139 NN.
8Z (11.43–1.46)	('A' Flight) Albemarle GT.I P1379 8Z-M, GT.II V1740 8Z-A; Stirling IV LK439 8Z-S.
8E (2.44–1.46)	('B' Flight) Stirling IV LJ652 8E-X.
Also used	Hart K5819; Horsa I DP816; Albemarle ST.II V1747; Anson I R3429; Oxford I R5960.

Disbanded 21st January 1946 at Rivenhall.

Reformed 21st January 1946 at Tarrant Rushton by renumbering 190 Squadron.

Halifax VII NA343.

Disbanded 1st April 1946 at Tarrant Rushton to become 297 Squadron.

Reformed 10th September 1947 at Fairford.

Halifax IX RT903.

Disbanded 1st November 1948 at Fairford.

296 SQUADRON

KZ	Allocated for the period April to September 1939.

Formed 25th January 1942 at Ringway by redesignating the Glider Exercise Unit.

Hector I K9727; Hart Trainer K6467; Hind I L7185; Hotspur I BT564, II HH240; Whitley V BD415 C.

Disbanded 3rd June 1942 at Hurn to become 296A and 296B Squadrons.

Reformed 12th August 1942 at Hurn by renumbering 296A Squadron.

XH (8.42–11.43)	Whitley V BD493 XH-J.
9W (10.43–1.46)	Albemarle ST.II V1699 9W-H; Halifax V LL330 9W-N, III NA613 9W-J.
7C (3.44–1.46)	Halifax III NA129 7C-M.

Also used by 296, 296A and 296B Squadrons were Lysander IIIA V9722; Albemarle GT.I P1405, GT.I/I P1373, ST.I P1501; Horsa I DP311.

Disbanded 23rd January 1946 at Earls Colne.

296A SQUADRON

Formed 3rd June 1942 at Hurn by redesignating an element of 296 Squadron.

Whitley V – see footnote to 296 Squadron.

Disbanded 12th August 1942 at Hurn to become 296 Squadron.

296B SQUADRON

Formed 3rd June 1942 at Netheravon by redesignating an element of 296 Squadron.

Whitley V – see footnote to 296 Squadron.

Disbanded 12th August 1942 at Netheravon to become the Glider Pilot Exercise Unit.

297 SQUADRON

GS	Allocated for the period April to September 1939.

Formed 22nd January 1942 at Netheravon by redesignating the Parachute Exercise Squadron.

Nil (1.42–7.43)	Whitley V BD672 S; Albemarle I P1409 E.
P5 (7.43– .45)	Albemarle I/II P1471 P5-N, V V1823 P5-S; Halifax III LK848 P5-K, V LL277 P5-B.
L5 (4.44– .46)	Albemarle I P1399 L5-A, I/II P1471 L5-A; Halifax III NA104 L5-V, VII NA401 L5-L.
Also used	Horsa I DP817; Hamilcar I NX861; Tiger Moth II DE303.

Disbanded 1st April 1946 at Earls Colne.

Reformed 1st April 1946 at Tarrant Rushton by renumbering 295 Squadron.

Halifax VII PN286, IX RT762 Z; Hastings C.1 TG603 X.

Disbanded 15th November 1950 at Topcliffe.

298 SQUADRON

QH	Allocated for the period April to September 1939.

Formed 24th August 1942 at Thruxton by redesignating an element of 297 Squadron.

Whitley V EB337.

Disbanded 19th October 1942 at Thruxton.

Reformed 4th November 1943 at Tarrant Rushton from 'A' Flight of 295 Squadron.

Nil (11.43–5.44)	Halifax V DK198 RR.
8A (5.44–8.45)	Halifax V LK988 8A-C, III MZ972 8A-N, VII NA347 8A-J.
8T (5.44–8.45)	Halifax V LL273 8T-Y, III MZ966 8T-K, VII NA344 8T-Q.
Nil (8.45–12.46)	Halifax VII PN292 O.
Also used	Anson I N4871; Oxford II T1102; Moth Minor BK831.

Disbanded 21st December 1946 at Mauripur, India.

299 SQUADRON

AT	Allocated for the period April to September 1939.

Formed 4th November 1943 at Stoney Cross from 'C' Flight of 297 Squadron.

Nil (11.43–1.44)	Ventura I AE733 A, II AE853.
5G (1.44–2.46)	Stirling IV LK241 5G-K.
X9 (1.44–2.46)	Stirling IV LJ812 X9-Z.
Also used	Oxford II R6352.

Disbanded 15th February 1946 at Shepherd's Grove.

300 (MASOVIAN) SQUADRON

ZN	Allocated for the period April to September 1939.

Formed 1st July 1940 at Bramcote.

BH	Battle N2241 BH-G; Wellington IA L7789 P9228, IC R1617 BH-S, IV Z1266 BH-J, III BK516 BH-K, X HF598 BH-E; Lancaster I DV278 BH-A, III JA922 BH-J.
Also used	Anson I R9579.

Disbanded 2nd January 1947 at Faldingworth.

301 (POMERANIAN) SQUADRON

MW	Allocated for the period April to September 1939.

Formed 22nd July 1940 at Bramcote.

GR	Battle L5555 GR-H; Wellington IA P9214, IC R1349 GR-N, IV Z1253 GR-B.
Also used	Anson I R9580; Magister V1089; Tiger Moth II T6304.

Disbanded 7th April 1943 at Hemswell.

Reformed 7th November 1944 at Brindisi, Italy, by redesignating 1586 (Polish Special Duties) Flight.

GR	Halifax II JP231 GR-A, V LL118 GR-C; Liberator VI KG994 GR-R; Warwick I BV250, III HG226 GR-D; Halifax VIII PP324 GR-V.

Disbanded 18th December 1946 at Chedburgh.

301 SQUADRON SPECIAL DUTIES FLIGHT
Formed July 1943 at Tempsford by redesignating the Polish Flight of 138 Squadron.

Halifax V.

Disbanded 4th November 1943 at Derna, Libya, to become 1586 (Special Duties) Flight.

302 (POZNAN) SQUADRON
EG	Allocated for the period April to September 1939.

Formed 13th July 1940 at Leconfield.

Nil (7.40–10.41)	Hurricane I V6570 Q, IIA Z2814 K, IIB Z3982 S.
WX (10.42–1.45)	Spitfire IIA P7610, VB W3953 WX-E, VC EE642, IXC MA843 WX-F, IXE MK177.
QH (1.45–12.46)	Spitfire XVIE TB745 QH-B.
Also used	Battle Trainer P6687; Master I N7890; Magister L8359; Tiger Moth II T6109; Auster III MZ220.

Disbanded 18th December 1946 at Hethel.

303 (WARSAW KOSCISCO) SQUADRON
NN	Allocated for the period April to September 1939.

Formed 22nd July 1940 at Northolt.

RF (8.40–4.45)	Hurricane I P3120 RF-D, X P5180; Spitfire I X4344 RF-R, IIA P7989 RF-U, VB AR376 RF-B, IXC EN172 RF-J, LF.VB BM407 RF-Z; Mustang I AG416, IV KH669 RF-P.
PD (4.45–12.46)	Mustang IVA KM186 PD-A.
Also used	Anson I N5268; Battle Trainer R7399; Magister P6365; Tiger Moth II N6749; Auster I LB277; Martinet I HP136.

Disbanded 11th December 1946 at Hethel.

304 (SILESIAN) SQUADRON
UB	Allocated for the period April to September 1939.

Formed 22nd August 1940 at Bramcote.

NZ (8.40–5.42)	Battle N2233, Battle Trainer P6723 NZ-Y; Wellington IA N2899, IC DV441 NZ-Q.
Nil (5.42–8.43)	Wellington X HZ258 S, XIII HZ551, XIV HF388.
2 (8.43–7.44)	Wellington XIV HF419 2-D.
QD (7.44–12.46)	Wellington XIV HF388 QD-K; Warwick I BV248, III HG340 QD-M; Halifax VIII PP270 QD-G.
Also used	Botha L6114; Anson I R9705; Magister L5993; Oxford II R6353; Tiger Moth II T5631.

Disbanded 18th December 1946 at Chedburgh.

305 (ZIEMIA WIELKOPSKA) SQUADRON
BV	Allocated for the period April to September 1939.

Formed 29th August 1940 at Bramcote.

SM	Battle L5050; Wellington I L4262, IA P2531, IC R1214 SM-N, II Z8343 SM-S, IV Z1272 SM-N, X HF492; Mitchell II FV913; Mosquito VI PZ454 SM-G.
Also used	Battle Trainer P6685; Magister L5996; Oxford II V3515; Mosquito III LR518.

Disbanded 6th January 1947 at Faldingworth.

306 (TORUN) SQUADRON
HK	Allocated for the period April to September 1939.

Formed 29th August 1940 at Church Fenton.

UZ	Hurricane I V7118 UZ-V, IIA Z2964, IIB Z2923; Spitfire IIB P8342 UZ-N, VA R6770, VB AB364 UZ-A; IXC BS200; Mustang I AG416, III FZ196 UZ-D.
Also used	Battle Trainer R7410; Master I N8007; Tiger Moth II T7733; Auster III MZ180; Harvard IIB KF943.

Disbanded 6th January 1947 at Coltishall.

307 (LWOW) SQUADRON
VK	Allocated for the period April to September 1939.

Formed 5th September 1940 at Kirton-in-Lindsey.

EW	Defiant I N1671 EW-D; Beaufighter II R2447 EW-D, VI X8108; Mosquito II DZ741 EW-E, VI HX860, XII HK141 EW-P, XIII HK531, NF.30 NT565 EW-A.
Also used	Battle Trainer R7411, Master I N8009; Magister I L5915; Blenheim I L8438; Oxford I L4553, II V3590; Spitfire VB W3262; Mosquito III HJ853.

Disbanded 2nd January 1947 at Horsham St Faith.

308 (KRAKOW) SQUADRON
BM	Allocated for the period April to September 1939.

Formed 5th September 1940 at Squires Gate.

ZF	Hurricane I V6858; Spitfire I X4471, Spitfire IIA P8022 ZF-L, VB AR292 ZF-F, VC EE660, IX MA299 ZF-P, XVI TD242 ZF-E.
Also used	Battle Trainer R7399; Master I N8010, II AZ817; Magister I L5916; Tiger Moth II DE734; Auster III MT404.

Disbanded 18th December 1946 at Hethel.

309 (ZIEMA CZERWIENSKA) SQUADRON
XV	Allocated for the period April to September 1939.

Formed 7th October 1940 at Abbotsinch.

AR (10.40–11.41)	Battle L5252, Battle Trainer P6733; Lysander III T1521.
ZR (11.41– .43)	Lysander IIIA V9375 ZR-F.
Nil (.43–4.44)	Lysander IIIA V9315; Mustang I AM119 H.
WC (4.44–1.47)	Mustang I AM221 WC-A; Hurricane IIC LF363 WC-F, IV LE749; Mustang III FX908 WC-K.
Also used	Spitfire VB AA858; Master III W8929; Proctor I P6240; Tiger Moth X5108; Harvard IIB KF426; Auster I LB286.

Disbanded 6th January 1947 at Coltishall.

310 (CZECHOSLOVAK) SQUADRON
UG	Allocated for the period April to September 1939.

Formed 10th July 1940 at Duxford

NN	Hurricane I V6797 NN-R, IIA Z2693, IIB Z3325; Spitfire IIA P8472, VB AD462 NN-Y, VC AR610 NN-A, VI BS472, IX MH908 NN-F.
Also used	Battle L5351, Battle Trainer P6725; Magister R1912; Tiger Moth I NL978, II R5028; Auster I LB323, III MZ216.

Disbanded 15th February 1946 at Prague, Czechoslovakia, and transferred to Czech control.

311 (CZECHOSLOVAK) SQUADRON
HD	Allocated for the period April to September 1939.

Formed 29th July 1940 at Honington.

KX (7.40–4.42)	Anson I K6296; Wellington I L4332, IA L7788 KX-E, IC Z1111 KX-N.
Nil (4.42–.45)	Wellington IC R1600 T; Liberator V BZ872 E.
PP (.45–2.46)	Liberator V BZ789 PP-B, VI EV943 PP-F.
Also used	Lysander IIIA V9445; Oxford I R6163.

Disbanded 15th February 1946 at Prague, Czechoslovakia, and transferred to Czech control.

312 (CZECHOSLOVAK) SQUADRON

| KW | Allocated for the period April to September 1939. |

Formed 29th August 1940 at Duxford.

| DU (8.40–2.46) | Hurricane I L1926 DU-J, IIB AP518; Spitfire IIA P8081, VB BM322 DU-S, VC AR501, LF.IXB MH474 DU-F, HF.IX MJ225. |
| Also used | Battle Trainer R7409; Master I N8008; Magister V1028; Tiger Moth AX783, II T8254; Auster I LB315, III MZ221. |

Disbanded 15th February 1946 at Prague, Czechoslovakia, and transferred to Czech control.

313 (CZECHOSLOVAK) SQUADRON

| LH | Allocated for the period April to September 1939. |

Formed 10th May 1941 at Catterick.

| RY | Spitfire I R6898 RY-L, IIA P8193, VB BL525, VC AR520, VI BS146, VII MB763, IX ML261 RY-P. |
| Also used | Magister L5968; Auster III MZ168; Tiger Moth AX783, I NM118, II T6195. |

Disbanded 15th February 1946 at Prague, Czechoslovakia, and transferred to Czech control.

314 SQUADRON

Squadron not formed although the code UY was allocated for the period April to September 1939.

315 (DEBLIN) SQUADRON

| OG | Allocated for the period April to September 1939. |

Formed 8th January 1941 at Acklington.

| PK | Hurricane I V7656 PK-M; Spitfire IIA P7434, IIB P8582, VA W3113, VB EP285 PK-B, IX EN172 PK-K; Mustang III FB179 PK-C, IVA KM469. |
| Also used | Magister T9808; Tiger Moth II T5369; Oxford II T1061; Auster I LB341, III NJ969. |

Disbanded 14th January 1947 at Coltishall.

316 (WARSAW) SQUADRON

| NL | Allocated for the period April to September 1939. |

Formed 12th February 1941 at Pembrey.

| SZ | Hurricane I V6991 SZ-F, IIA Z2792, IIB Z5080; Spitfire IIA P7893, VB AD562 SZ-S, IX BS463, LF.VB AA931 SZ-A; Mustang III FX903 SZ-R, IV KH642. |
| Also used | Battle Trainer R7410; Magister L5932; Tiger Moth II DE526; Auster I LB321, III MZ107. |

Disbanded 11th December 1946 at Hethel.

317 (WILNO) SQUADRON

| WU | Allocated for the period April to September 1939. |

Formed 19th February 1941 at Acklington.

| JH | Hurricane I V7339 JH-X, X P5209, IIA Z2390, IIB Z3975; Spitfire VB AD295 JH-C, IX ML192 JH-P, XVI TE206 JH-A. |
| Also used | Battle Trainer R7399; Magister L8267; Oxford II W6585; Tiger Moth II DE138; Auster III MZ213. |

Disbanded 18th December 1946 at Ahlhorn, Germany.

318 (DANZIG-GDANSK) SQUADRON

| XP | Allocated for the period April to September 1939. |

Formed 20th March 1943 at Detling.

Nil (3.43–11.44)	Hurricane I N2647, IIA DG625, IIB BN270; Spitfire VB EP777, VC EE810.
LW (11.44–8.46)	Spitfire IX PT676 LW-T.
Also used	Bf109-G10 LW; Magister R1943; Argus II FS657; Auster III MZ165; Anson X NK433.

Disbanded 12th December 1946 at Coltishall.

319 SQUADRON

Squadron not formed although the code VE was allocated for the period April to September 1939.

320 (DUTCH) SQUADRON

| SP | Allocated for the period April to September 1939. |

Formed 1st June 1940 at Pembroke Dock.

TD (6.40–10.40)	Fokker T-VIIIW AV958; Fokker C-XIVW.
NO (10.40–8.45)	Anson I W1672 NO-R; Hudson I N7396 NO-V, II T9380 NO-H, III V8983 NO-F, V AM939 NO-E, VI FK458 NO-S; Mitchell II FV970 NO-K, III KJ587 NO-F.
Also used	Koolhoven FK.43 MX459; Short S.20 G-ADHJ; Oxford I R6085, II AP479.

Disbanded 2nd August 1945 at B.110 (Achmer), Germany, and transferred to Dutch control.

321 (DUTCH) SQUADRON

| JS | Allocated for the period April to September 1939. |

Formed 1st June 1940 at Pembroke Dock.

Anson I N9535.

Disbanded 18th January 1941 at Carew Cheriton and absorbed by 320 Squadron.

Reformed 15th August 1942 at China Bay, Ceylon.

Catalina II Y-83 RR, III Y-85 TT; Liberator III FL912, VI KH296 J; Catalina VA Y-86 UU, IVB Y-91 G; Harvard IIB FT201.

Disbanded 8th December 1945 at Kemajoran, Java, and transferred to Dutch control.

322 (DUTCH) SQUADRON

| ZQ | Allocated for the period April to September 1939. |

Formed 12th June 1943 at Woodvale by renumbering 167 Squadron.

VL (6.43–10.44)	Spitfire VB AA976 VL-B, XIV NH699 VL-R, IXB MK320 VL-F.
3W (10.44–10.45)	Spitfire IXB MJ964 3W-V, XVIE TD137 3W-V.
Also used	Tiger Moth II DE484; Auster III MZ230.

Disbanded 7th October 1945 at B.116 (Wunstorf), Germany.

323 SQUADRON

Squadron not formed although the code GN was allocated for the period April to September 1939.

324 SQUADRON

Squadron not formed although the code PQ was allocated for the period April to September 1939.

325 SQUADRON

Squadron not formed although the code EA was allocated for the period April to September 1939.

326 (NICE) SQUADRON

| QU | Allocated for the period April to September 1939. |

Formed 1st December 1943 at Ajaccio, Italy, by redesignating 2/7 'Nice' Escadrille, French Air Force.

91   *Spitfire VC MH594, IX MH717.*

Disbanded November 1945 at Grossachsenheim, Germany, and transferred to French control.

327 (CORSE) SQUADRON
LP   *Allocated for the period April to September 1939.*

Formed 1st December 1943 at Ajaccio, Corsica, by redesignating 1/3 Escadrille, French Air Force.

7E   *Spitfire VC JL231, IX MA466, VIII JF749.*

Disbanded November 1945 at Sersheim, Germany, and transferred to French control.

328 (PROVENCE) SQUADRON
MN   *Allocated for the period April to September 1939.*

Formed 1st December 1943 at Reghaia, Algeria, by redesignating 1/7 Escadrille, French Air Force.

S8   *Spitfire VC JK326, IX NH306, VIII JF296.*

Disbanded November 1945 at Grossachsenheim, Germany, and transferred to French control.

329 (CICOGNES) SQUADRON
OA   *Allocated for the period April to September 1939.*

Formed 3rd January 1944 at Ayr.

5A   *Spitfire VB AA846, VC MH595 5A-B, IX PL379 5A-F, XVI TB497 5A-T.*
Also used   *Tiger Moth II N6619; Auster I LB298, III MZ221.*

Disbanded 17th November 1945 at Exeter and transferred to French control.

330 (NORWEGIAN) SQUADRON
KE   *Allocated for the period April to September 1939.*

Formed 25th April 1941 at Reykjavik, Iceland.

Nil (4.41–5.41)   *Northrop N3P-B 17.*
GS (5.41–3.43)   *Northrop N3P-B 16 GS-B; Catalina IIIA FP533 GS-L.*
Nil (3.43–.44)   *Catalina I W8424, IIIA FP528 W; Sunderland II T9112, III DD843 S.*
WH (.44–11.45)   *Sunderland III NJ181 WH-Z, V ML814 WH-A.*
Also used   *Anson XI NL225.*

Disbanded 21st November 1945 at Sola, Norway, and transferred to Norwegian control.

331 (NORWEGIAN) SQUADRON
LD   *Allocated for the period April to September 1939.*

Formed 21st July 1941 at Catterick.

FN   *Hurricane I R4076, IIB BD762 FN-S; Spitfire I P9440, IIA P8646 FN-K, VB BL403 FN-N, IX MA476 FN-F.*
Also used   *Magister P2389; Tiger Moth II EM838; Auster III MZ212.*

Disbanded 21st November 1945 at Gardermoen, Norway, and transferred to Norwegian control.

332 (NORWEGIAN) SQUADRON
WW   *Allocated for the period April to September 1939.*

Formed 15th January 1942 at Catterick.

HG (1.42–2.42)   *Spitfire VA.*
AH (2.42–9.45)   *Spitfire I L1031 AH-S, VA X4238 AH-L, VB BL339, IX BS249 AH-R.*
Also used   *Magister L8083; Tiger Moth II DE574; Auster III NX530; Fi 156.*

Disbanded 21st September 1945 at Vaernes, Norway, and transferred to Norwegian control.

333 (NORWEGIAN) SQUADRON
VN   *Allocated for the period April to September 1939.*

Formed 5th May 1943 at Woodhaven ('A' Flight) and Leuchars ('B' Flight) by redesignating 1477 (Norwegian) Flight.

Nil (5.43–9.44)   *Catalina I W8424 B, IB FP183 D; Mosquito II DZ754 F, VI HP864 H; Catalina IVA JV933.*
KK (9.44–11.45)   *Mosquito VI HP864 KK-H, XVI PF463; Catalina IB W8424 KK-B, IVA JX265 KK-B.*
Also used   *Oxford II T1101; Mosquito III HJ977.*

Disbanded 21st November 1945 at Fornebu, Norway, and transferred to Norwegian control.

334 (NORWEGIAN) SQUADRON
BJ   *Allocated for the period April to September 1939.*

Formed 26th May 1945 at Banff from 'B' Flight of 333 Squadron.

VB   *Allocated, but no evidence of use.*
Nil   *Mosquito VI RF769.*
Also used   *Tiger Moth II T7237.*

Disbanded 21st November 1945 at Gardermoen, Norway, and transferred to Norwegian control.

335 (GREEK) SQUADRON
XT   *Allocated for the period April to September 1939.*

Formed 10th October 1941 at Aqir, Palestine.

FG   *Hurricane I Z4574, IIA DG636, IIB Z4007 FG-S, IIC KX954; Spitfire VB ER524, VC JG956.*
Also used   *Harvard II AJ805.*

Disbanded 31st July 1946 at Sedes, Greece, and transferred to Greek control.

336 (GREEK) SQUADRON
ZP   *Allocated for the period April to September 1939.*

Formed 25th February 1943 at LG.219 (Matariyah), Egypt.

Hurricane IIC HV505; Spitfire VB ER194 N, VC JK374, IX. Also used Harvard IIB KF968.

Disbanded 31st July 1946 at Sedes, Greece, and transferred to Greek control.

337 SQUADRON
Squadron not formed although the code OK was allocated for the period April to September 1939.

338 SQUADRON
Squadron not formed although the code ML was allocated for the period April to September 1939.

339 SQUADRON
Squadron not formed although the code KN was allocated for the period April to September 1939.

340 (ILE DE FRANCE) SQUADRON
YK   *Allocated for the period April to September 1939.*

Formed 7th November 1941 at Turnhouse by redesignating Groupe 'Ile de France'.

GW   *Spitfire IIA P7915 GW-J, VB W3705 GW-X, LF.VB AD508 GW-F, IXB MJ518 GW-W, LF.XVI TB347 GW-T.*
Also used   *Tiger Moth II T6195; Auster III MZ221; Anson XI NL223.*

Disbanded 27th November 1945 at R.58 (Friedrichshafen), Germany, and transferred to French control.

341 (ALSACE) SQUADRON
PL   *Allocated for the period April to September 1939.*

Formed 18th January 1943 at Turnhouse by redesignating Groupe 'Alsace'.

NL	Spitfire VB AB241, IXB PL256 NL-T, LF.XVI TB519 NL-L.
Also used	Tiger Moth II DE844; Auster III MZ218.

Disbanded 27th November 1945 at R.58 (Friedrichshafen), Germany, and transferred to French control.

342 (LORRAINE) SQUADRON

LK	Allocated for the period April to September 1939.

Formed 1st April 1943 at West Raynham from personnel of the Lorraine Squadron. The titles Escadrilles 'Metz' and 'Nancy' were given to 'A' and 'B' Flights.

OA	Havoc I AE464; Boston II AH462, III Z2236, IIIA BZ314 OA-S, IV BZ443 OA-B; Mitchell II FW181 OA-W, III KJ729 OA-S.
Also used	Spitfire IIA P7434, PR.V P9328; Oxford II N4760.

Disbanded 2nd December 1945 at B.77 (Gilze-Rijen), Netherlands, and transferred to French control.

343 (FREE FRENCH) SQUADRON

ND	Allocated for the period April to September 1939.

Formed 29th November 1943 at Dakar, French West Africa, by redesignating Flotille 7E of the French Navy.

Sunderland III JM704 B.

Disbanded 27th November 1945 at Dakar, French West Africa, and transferred to French control.

344 (FREE FRENCH) SQUADRON

GT	Allocated for the period April to September 1939.

Formed 29th November 1943 at Dakar, French West Africa, by redesignating Flotille 1E of the French Navy.

Wellington XI MP698, XIII MP709.

Disbanded 27th November 1945 at Dakar, French West Africa, and transferred to French control.

345 (BERRY) SQUADRON

AQ	Allocated for the period April to September 1939.

Formed 30th January 1944 at Ayr.

2Y (2.44–9.44)	Spitfire VB AD227 2Y-L, IX PT913 2Y-Y.
Nil (9.44–11.45)	Spitfire IX RK906, XVI TB867.
Also used	Tiger Moth II T6316; Auster III MZ221.

Disbanded 27th November 1945 at R.58 (Friedrichshafen), Germany, and transferred to French control.

346 (GUYENNE) SQUADRON

XL	Allocated for the period April to September 1939.

Formed 15th May 1944 at Elvington.

H7	Halifax V LL227 H7-K, III NA546 H7-G, VI RG592 H7-P.

Disbanded 15th November 1945 at Bordeaux-Merignac, France, and transferred to French control.

347 (TUNISIE) SQUADRON

BB	Allocated for the period April to September 1939.

Formed 20th June 1944 at Elvington.

L8	Halifax V LL237 L8-G, III LL573 L8-B, VI PP165 L8-P.

Disbanded 15th November 1945 at Bordeaux-Merignac, France, and transferred to French control.

348 SQUADRON

Squadron not formed although the code FR was allocated for the period April to September 1939.

349 (BELGIAN) SQUADRON

OS	Allocated for the period April to September 1939.

Formed 9th January 1943 at Ikeja, Nigeria.

GE	Tomahawk I AH859, IIA AH972 GE-H, IIB AK103; Kittyhawk II FS401.
Also used	Harvard IIA EX498.

Disbanded 3rd May 1943 at Ikeja, Nigeria.

Reformed 5th June 1943 at Wittering.

GE	Spitfire VA P7986, VB W3373 GE-X, VC EE660 GE-Z, IX MJ879 GE-G; Tempest V NV919; Spitfire XVIE TE191 GE-G.
Also used	Tiger Moth I NL992, II EM966; Auster III MZ226.

Disbanded 24th October 1946 at Beauvechain, Belgium, and transferred to Belgian control.

350 (BELGIAN) SQUADRON

YM	Allocated for the period April to September 1939.

Formed 12th November 1944 at Valley by redesignating the Belgian Flight of 131 Squadron.

MN	Spitfire IIA P8200 MN-T, VA R6809, VB BM176 MN-F, VC EE766 MN-C, IX MK192 MN-Z, XIV RB154 MN-K, LF.XVI TD325 MN-A.
Also used	Tiger Moth I NL929, II T6313; Magister T9804; Auster IV MS951.

Disbanded 24th October 1946 at Beauvechain, Belgium, and transferred to Belgian control.

351 (YUGOSLAV) SQUADRON

Formed 1st July 1944 at Benina, Libya.

Hurricane IIC KZ449, IV LF507.

Disbanded 15th June 1845 at Prkos, Yugoslavia, and transferred to Yugoslav control.

352 (YUGOSLAV) SQUADRON

Formed 22nd April 1944 at Benina, Libya.

Hurricane IIC LD208; Spitfire VC JG948 J.

Disbanded 15th June 1945 at Prkos, Yugoslavia, and transferred to Yugoslav control.

353 SQUADRON

Formed 1st June 1942 at Dum-Dum, India, by redesignating elements of 62 Squadron and 103 (Coast Defence) Flight, Indian Air Force.

Hudson IIIA FH444 H, VI FK493; Dakota I FD787, III FZ643, IV KK117; Anson X NK352; Warwick III HG243; Expeditor I HB193, II KJ551.
Also used Audax K4845; Blenheim I L4918.

Disbanded 1st October 1946 at Palam, India.

354 SQUADRON

Formed 10th May 1943 at Drigh Road, India.

Liberator V BZ888 S, III FL912 K, VI EV834 Z.

Disbanded 18th May 1945 at Cuttack, India.

355 SQUADRON

Formed 18th August 1943 at Salbani, India.

EG	Possibly allocated.
Nil	Hudson III V9067; Liberator III BZ955 F, VI EW245 D, VIII KN764 F; Harvard IIB FE685.

Disbanded 1st June 1946 at Salbani, India.

356 SQUADRON
Formed 15th January 1944 at Salbani, India.

Liberator VI KL611 W. Also used Tiger Moth II NL765.

Disbanded 15th November 1945 in the Cocos Islands.

357 SQUADRON
Formed 1st February 1944 at Digri, India, by redesignating 1576 (Special Duties) Flight.

Hudson III AM949 A; Catalina IB FP134; Liberator III BZ923 W, VI KH391 Y; Dakota III KG490, IV KJ926 M; Sentinel I KJ379; Lysander III T1688, IIIA V9889 F; Harvard IIB FS794; Auster IV MT351.

Disbanded 7th November 1945 at Mingaladon, Burma, 'C' Flight being absorbed by the Air Headquarters Burma Communication Squadron.

358 SQUADRON
Formed 8th November 1944 at Kolar, India, by redesignating an element of 1673 Heavy Conversion Unit.

TA (11.44–12.44)	Wellington X LN613 TA-L.
Nil (12.44–11.45)	Liberator VI KG977 L.

Disbanded 21st November 1945 at Bishnarpur, India.

360 SQUADRON
Formed 23rd September 1966 at Watton by redesignating the Joint Trials and Training Squadron.

Nil (9.66–)	Canberra T.4 WT488 Y, T.17 WJ981 S.
E (–10.94)	Canberra T.4 WT480, PR.7, T.17 WJ630 ED, T.17A WJ607 EB, TT.18 WJ636 E.

Disbanded 31st October 1994 at Wyton.

361 SQUADRON
Formed 2nd January 1967 at Watton.

Canberra T.17 proposed but no aircraft allocated.

Disbanded 14th July 1967 at Watton and absorbed by 360 Squadron.

400 (CANADIAN) SQUADRON
Formed 1st March 1941 at Odiham by renumbering 110 Squadron RCAF, which had arrived in the United Kingdom on 25th February 1940.

Nil (3.41–4.41)	Lysander III R9001, IIIA V9373.
SP (4.41–12.43)	Tomahawk I AH848 SP-Y, IIA AH895 SP-B, IIB AK124 SP-S; Mustang I AG660 SP-W.
Nil (12.43–8.45)	Mosquito III HJ993, XVI MM356; Spitfire XI PM156, XIII AD556.
Also used	Battle I L5083; Tiger Moth II T6193; Oxford II R6354; Master III W8963; Typhoon IB JR207; Auster I LB322.

Disbanded 7th August 1945 at B.156 (Lüneburg), Germany.

401 (RAM) SQUADRON
Formed 1st March 1941 at Digby by renumbering 1 Squadron, RCAF which had arrived in the United Kingdom on 25th February 1940.

YO (3.41–5.45)	Hurricane I P3872 YO-V, IIB Z3658 YO-N; Spitfire IIA P8191, VB BL829 YO-C, IXB BR982 YO-I.
Nil (5.45–7.45)	Spitfire XIV RM785 T, XVI TE208.
Also used	Magister L8210; Harvard I P5866; Tiger Moth II T7963; Auster III MZ236; Fw 190 YO.

Disbanded 23rd June 1945 at B.152 (Fassberg), Germany.

402 (WINNIPEG BEAR) SQUADRON
Formed 1st March 1941 at Digby by renumbering 2 Squadron, RCAF which had formed on 11th March 1940 at Digby from elements of 110 and 112 Squadrons, RCAF.

AE	Hurricane I V6787, IIA Z2426, IIB BE477 AE-S; Spitfire VB BM272 AE-D, VC EE686, IXB BS428 AE-U, XIV RM804, XVIE TD265.
Also used	Auster III MZ181, IV MS951.

Disbanded 1st July 1945 at B.152 (Fassberg), Germany.

403 (WOLF) SQUADRON
Formed 19th February 1941 at Baginton.

KH	Tomahawk I AH758, IIA AH896 KH-H; Spitfire I R6611 KH-N, IIA P7756 KH-U, VA W3109, VB BL707 KH-C, IXB MJ480 KH-R, XVI TB340.
Also used	Magister L6919; Tiger Moth II T7402; Auster III MZ181.

Disbanded 30th January 1945 at B.154 (Reinsehlen), Germany.

404 (BUFFALO) SQUADRON
Formed 15th April 1941 at Thorney Island.

EE (4.41–8.43)	Blenheim I K7120, IV N3525 EE-H; Beaufighter IIF V8157 EE-P, X JM124 EE-S.
2 (8.43–7.44)	Beaufighter X LZ314 2-P.
EO (7.44–5.45)	Beaufighter X NV427 EO-L; Mosquito VI RF842 EO-C.

Disbanded 25th May 1945 at Banff.

405 (VANCOUVER) SQUADRON
Formed 23rd April 1941 at Driffield.

LQ	Wellington II Z8344 LQ-F; Halifax II W7710 LQ-R; Lancaster I ME445 LQ-U, III PB288 LQ-O, X KB700 LQ-Q.
Also used	Spitfire VB AA966; Tiger Moth II EM812.

Disbanded 5th September 1945 at Greenwood, Canada.

405 SQUADRON CONVERSION FLIGHT
Formed 2nd May 1942 at Pocklington.

LQ	Halifax II R9368.

Disbanded 7th October 1942 at Topcliffe and merged with 408 Squadron Conversion Flight to become 1659 Heavy Conversion Unit.

406 (LYNX) SQUADRON
Formed 16th May 1941 at Acklington.

HU	Blenheim IV V5386; Beaufighter I R2094, II R2473, V R2274, VI KV981 HU-Z; Mosquito XII HK180 HU-A, NF.30 NT433 HU-P.
Also used	Magister P2469; Oxford I NM542, II V3642.

Disbanded 1st September 1945 at Predannack.

407 (DEMON) SQUADRON
Formed 8th May 1941 at Thorney Island.

RR (5.41–8.43)	Blenheim IV Z5882; Hudson I P5116 RR-D, III V9102 RR-X, IIIA FH346, V AM597 RR-F, VI EW921.
1 (8.43–1.44)	Wellington XI MP534 1-E, XII HF115 1-P, XIV HF148 1-P.
2 (1.44–7.44)	Wellington XIV NB856 2-X.
Nil (7.44–6.45)	Wellington XIV MP754 H, XVII MP520.

Disbanded 4th June 1945 at Chivenor.

408 (GOOSE) SQUADRON
Formed 15th June 1941 at Lindholme.

EQ	Hampden I P1166 EQ-K; Halifax V DG233, II DT676 EQ-B; Lancaster II DS704 EQ-W; Halifax III MZ421 EQ-N, VII NP742 EQ-U; Lancaster X KB877 EQ-S.
Also used	Manchester I L7401.

Disbanded 5th September 1945 at Greenwood, Canada.

408 SQUADRON CONVERSION FLIGHT
Formed 16th May 1942 at Syerston.

EQ	No aircraft known.

Disbanded 19th June 1942 at Syerston.

Reformed 20th September 1942 at Leeming.

EQ	Halifax I L9532, Halifax II R9363.

Disbanded 7th October 1942 at Leeming and merged with 405 Squadron Conversion Flight to become 1659 Heavy Conversion Unit.

409 (NIGHTHAWK) SQUADRON
Formed 16th June 1940 at Digby.

KP	Defiant I T3937; Beaufighter II R2479, VI MM865 KP-D; Mosquito XIII MM573 KP-P, XVI MM286.
Also used	Blenheim I L1301; Magister I R1819; Oxford I X6797, II R6395; Master III W8598; Tomahawk IIB AK225; Mosquito III LR540, VI TA489; Auster III NJ975.

Disbanded 1st July 1945 at B.106 (Twente), Netherlands.

410 (COUGAR) SQUADRON
Formed 30th June 1941 at Ayr.

RA	Defiant I V1110 RA-H; Beaufighter I R2244, II T3152; Mosquito II DZ757 RA-Q, VI HJ827, XII HK223, XIII HK500 RA-I, NF.30 MT485 RA-F.
Also used	Blenheim I L8549, IV Z5880; Magister T9874; Oxford I R6024, II T1254; Mosquito III HJ867.

Disbanded 9th June 1945 at B.77 (Gilze-Rijen), Netherlands.

411 (GRIZZLY BEAR) SQUADRON
Formed 16th June 1941 at Digby.

DB	Spitfire IA R7162, IIA P7679, VB AA839 DB-E, IXB MH850, IXE PL320, XVIE TB759, XIV RM873 DB-R.
Also used	Magister L8270; Tiger Moth II EM812; Auster III MT408; Ju 88H-1 DB.

Disbanded 15th March 1946 at B.174 (Utersen), Germany.

412 (FALCON) SQUADRON
Formed 30th June 1941 at Digby.

VZ	Spitfire I P9519, IIA P8250 VZ-F, VB BL259, IXB MJ393 VZ-Z, IXE MJ452 VZ-L, XVIE SM414, XIV RM651.
Also used	Tiger Moth II T5494; Auster III NJ961; Ju 87D-5 VZ-?.

Disbanded 15th March 1946 at B.174 (Utersen), Germany.

413 (TUSKER) SQUADRON
Formed 30th June 1941 at Stranraer.

QL (7.41–1.42)	Catalina I AH549 QL-F.
Nil (1.42–2.45)	Catalina IB FP282, IVB JX333 F.
Also used	Short S.23M AX660.

Disbanded 23rd February 1945 at Bournemouth.

414 (IMPERIAL) SQUADRON
Formed 12th August 1941 at Croydon.

RU (8.41– .43)	Lysander III R9112, IIIA V9445 RU-X; Tomahawk I AH852, IIA AH935 RU-Z, IIB AK185 RU-V; Mustang I AG543 RU-E.
Nil (.43–8.45)	Mustang I AM248 L; Spitfire IX MJ553 G, XIV NH808.
Also used	Tutor K4804; Battle I L5419; Magister L8235; Oxford I T1190; Tiger Moth II T8180; Master I T8620; Cub Coupe BV180; Auster I LB328.

Disbanded 7th August 1945 at B.156 (Luneberg Heath), Germany.

415 (SWORDFISH) SQUADRON
Formed 20th August 1941 at Thorney Island.

GX (8.41–10.43)	Beaufort I N1102 GX-S; Blenheim IV Z5740; Hampden I AT229 GX-O.
NH (10.43–7.44)	Wellington XIII MF639 NH-H; Albacore I L7173 NH-C1.
6U (7.44–5.45)	Halifax III MZ586 6U-Y, VII PN237 6U-T.
Also used	Oxford II BM835; Spitfire IV BP922.

Disbanded 15th May 1945 at East Moor.

416 (CITY OF OSHAWA) SQUADRON
Formed 22nd November 1941 at Peterhead.

DN	Spitfire IIA P7673, VB EN950 DN-P, IX NH188 DN-S, XVI SM397 DN-V, XIV NH692.
Also used	Magister P6408; Tiger Moth II T8180: Oxford II BM835.

Disbanded 15th March 1946 at B.174 (Utersen), Germany.

417 (CITY OF WINDSOR) SQUADRON
Formed 27th November 1941 at Charmy Down.

AN	Spitfire IIA P8570 AN-R, VB AD319 AN-U; Hurricane IIB BH131, IIC BP541; Spitfire VB ER531 AN-N, VIII JF627 AN-M, IX MJ818 AN-V.
Also used	Magister L8277; Macchi MC 202 AN.

Disbanded 1st July 1945 at Treviso, Italy.

418 (CITY OF EDMONTON) SQUADRON
Formed 15th November 1941 at Debden.

TH	Boston III AL475 TH-T; Mosquito II DZ747 TH-A, III HJ870, IV DZ441, VI HR195 TH-P.
Also used	Wellington I L4343; Magister L8338; Tiger Moth II T6258; Oxford I LB537, II BM774; Dominie I X7331; Cygnet DG566.

Disbanded 7th September 1945 at B.80 (Volkel), Netherlands.

419 (MOOSE) SQUADRON
Formed 15th December 1941 at Mildenhall.

VR	Whitley V Z6473; Wellington I L4356, IC Z1083 VR-O, III X3723 VR-H; Halifax II JB900 VR-E; Lancaster X KB732 VR-X.

Disbanded 5th September 1945 at Yarmouth, Canada.

420 (SNOWY OWL) SQUADRON
Formed 19th December 1941 at Waddington.

PT	Hampden I AD869 PT-L; Wellington III Z1724 PT-C, X HE640 PT-E; Halifax III LW380 PT-B, VII LW200; Lancaster X KB923 PT-N.

Disbanded 5th September 1945 at Debert, Canada.

420 SQUADRON CONVERSION FLIGHT
Formed 16th May 1942 at Waddington.

PT	Manchester I L7402.

Disbanded 19th June 1942 at Waddington.

421 (RED INDIAN) SQUADRON
Formed 6th April 1942 at Digby.

AU	Spitfire IIA P7505, VA P7498, VB BM575, IXB MK121 AU-Y, XVIE TD126.
Also used	Magister L5949; Tiger Moth II T5494; Auster III MZ184.

Disbanded 23rd July 1945 at B.174 (Utersen), Germany.

422 (CANADIAN) SQUADRON
Formed 2nd April 1942 at Lough Erne.

Nil (4.42–8.43)	Lerwick I L7260 P; Catalina IB FP105 B; Sunderland III JM679.
2 (8.43–7.44)	Sunderland III ML778 2-S.
DG (7.44–9.45)	Sunderland III ML884 DG-Z; Liberator VIII KN719.

Disbanded 4th September 1945 at Bassingbourn.

423 (CANADIAN) SQUADRON
Formed 18th May 1942 at Oban.

AB (5.42–8.43)	Sunderland II W6000 AB-A, III W6068 AB-N.
3 (8.43–7.44)	Sunderland III EK583 3-J.
YI (7.44–8.45)	Sunderland III ML825 YI-D.
Nil (8.45–9.45)	Liberator VIII KN743.

Disbanded 4th September 1945 at Bassingbourn.

424 (TIGER) SQUADRON
Formed 15th October 1942 at Topcliffe.

QB	Wellington III DF613 QB-X, X LN438 QB-A; Halifax III LW119 QB-O; Lancaster I NG347 QB-P.

Disbanded 15th October 1945 at Skipton-on-Swale.

425 (ALOUETTE) SQUADRON
Formed 25th June 1942 at Dishforth.

KW	Wellington III X3803 KW-H, X HZ355 KW-D; Halifax III MZ954 KW-M; Lancaster X KB934 KW-I.
Also used	Proctor III HM299.

Disbanded 5th September 1945 at Debert, Canada.

426 (THUNDERBIRD) SQUADRON
Formed 15th October 1942 at Dishforth.

OW	Wellington III Z1599 OW-M, X HE905 OW-V; Lancaster II DS689 OW-S; Halifax III LK871 OW-K, VII NP683 OW-M2; Liberator VI KK255 OW-Q, VIII KH179.
Also used	Oxford II V3667; Proctor III HM311.

Disbanded 31st December 1945 at Tempsford.

427 (LION) SQUADRON
Formed 7th November 1942 at Croft.

ZL	Wellington III BK364 ZL-K, X HE906; Halifax V EB246 ZL-S, III NR196 ZL-K; Lancaster I PA271 ZL-W, III ME498 ZL-K.
Also used	Oxford I DF471.

Disbanded 31st May 1946 at Leeming.

428 (GHOST) SQUADRON
Formed 7th November 1942 at Dalton.

NA	Wellington III BK156 NA-Q, X HE239 NA-Y; Halifax V EB275 NA-C, II HX183 NA-E; Lancaster X KB899 NA-V.

Disbanded 5th September 1945 at Yarmouth, Canada.

429 (BISON) SQUADRON
Formed 7th November 1942 at East Moor.

Nil (11.42–8.43)	Wellington III DF622, X HZ303.
AL (8.43–5.46)	Halifax II JD325 AL-F, V LK993 AL-J, III MZ318 AL-F; Lancaster I NG345 AL-V, III ME536 AL-Q.

Disbanded 31st May 1946 at Leeming.

430 (CITY OF SUNBURY) SQUADRON
Formed 1st January 1943 at Hartford Bridge by redesignating an element of 171 Squadron.

Nil (1.43–12.44)	Tomahawk I AH782, IIA AH910, IIB AK189; Mustang I AP253 A.
G9 (12.44–8.45)	Spitfire XIV RM874 G9-L.
Also used	Tiger Moth II T7779; Master III DL767; Auster I LB322, III MZ140.

Disbanded 7th August 1945 at B.156 (Luneberg Heath), Germany.

431 (IROQUOIS) SQUADRON
Formed 13th November 1942 at Burn.

SE	Wellington III HE202 SE-Z; Halifax V LL150 SE-N, III MZ600 SE-N; Lancaster X KB837 SE-X.

Disbanded 5th September 1945 at Dartmouth, Canada.

432 (LEASIDE) SQUADRON
Formed 1st May 1943 at Skipton-on-Swale.

QO	Wellington X HZ518 QO-A; Lancaster II DS848 QO-R; Halifax III LK754 QO-Z, VII NP721 QO-X.

Disbanded 15th May 1945 at East Moor.

433 (PORCUPINE) SQUADRON
Formed 25th September 1943 at Skipton-on-Swale.

BM	Halifax III MZ883 BM-S; Lancaster I RA512 BM-S.

Disbanded 15th October 1945 at Skipton-on-Swale.

434 (BLUENOSE) SQUADRON
Formed 15th June 1943 at Tholthorpe.

WL	Halifax V LL179 WL-K, III NR118 WL-S; Lancaster X KB873 WL-G.
Also used	Tiger Moth AX783.

Disbanded 5th September 1945 at Dartmouth, Canada.

435 (CHINTHE) SQUADRON
Formed 1st November at Gujrat, India.

	Dakota III KG486 H, IV KN511 Z.

Disbanded 31st March 1946 at Down Ampney.

436 (ELEPHANT) SQUADRON
Formed 20th August 1944 at Gujrat, India.

U6	Allocated but no evidence of use.
Nil	Dakota III KG635 P, IV KP224 L.
Also used	Oxford II W6589.

Disbanded 22nd June 1946 at Odiham.

437 (CANADIAN) SQUADRON
Formed 1st September 1944 at Blakehill Farm.

Z2	Dakota III FZ639 Z2-NS, IV KN278 Z2-OL; Anson X NK700 Z2-NW, XI NL199 Z2-NY.

Disbanded 15th June 1946 at Odiham.

438 (WILD CAT) SQUADRON
Formed 10th November 1943 at Digby by renumbering 118 Squadron, RCAF.

F3	Hurricane IV LD973 F3-O; Typhoon IB RB391 F3-Y.
Also used	Auster I LB322, III NX494.

Disbanded 26th August 1945 at B.166 (Flensburg), Germany.

439 (SABRE-TOOTHED TIGER) SQUADRON
Formed 1st January 1944 at Wellingore by renumbering 123 Squadron, RCAF.

5V	Hurricane IV LD570 5V-Z; Typhoon IB RB441 5V-Z.
Also used	Auster III NX494.

Disbanded 26th August 1945 at B.166 (Flensburg), Germany.

440 (CITY OF OTTAWA) SQUADRON
Formed 8th February 1944 at Ayr by renumbering 111 Squadron, RCAF.

I8	Hurricane IV; Typhoon IB RB389 I8-P.
Also used	Auster III MZ142, V MT367.

Disbanded 26th August 1945 at B.166 (Flensburg), Germany.

441 (SILVER FOX) SQUADRON
Formed 8th February 1944 at Digby by renumbering 125 Squadron, RCAF

9G	Spitfire VB EP661, VC EE722, IX MK465 9G-F; Mustang III FB184, IV KH499.
Also used	Auster I LB327, III MZ189; Tiger Moth II T7352.

Disbanded 7th August 1944 at Molesworth.

442 (CARIBOU) SQUADRON
Formed 8th February 1944 at Digby by renumbering 14 Squadron, RCAF.

Y2	Spitfire VB AR550, IXB MK181 Y2-X, IXE PL330 Y2-K; Mustang IV KH641, IVA KH694 Y2-P.

Also used   Auster I LB291, III MZ165.

Disbanded 7th August 1945 at Molesworth.

443 (HORNET) SQUADRON
Formed 8th February 1944 at Digby by renumbering 127 Squadron, RCAF.

2I	Spitfire VC EE617, IXB MK367, XVI TD191 2I-P, XIV NH779.
Also used	Auster III MZ194.

Disbanded 15th March 1946 at B.174 (Utersen), Germany.

450 (AUSTRALIAN) SQUADRON
Formed 16th February 1941 at Williamstown, Australia. Moved to Egypt, assembling on 12th May 1941 at Abu Sueir.

PD (5.41–12.41)	Hurricane I Z4567, IIA Z4953.
OK (12.41–8.45)	Kittyhawk I AL217 OK-P, IA ET918 OK-V, II FS484, III FR787, IV FX515 OK-K; Mustang III FB299.
Also used	Magister P2449; Argus II FS514 S.

Disbanded 20th August 1945 at Lavariano, Italy.

451 (AUSTRALIAN) SQUADRON
Formed 25th February 1941 at Bankstown, Australia, then moved to Egypt, assembling on 12th May 1941 at Aboukir.

Nil (7.41–.43)	Hurricane I Z4603, PR.I Z4231, IIC HL807.
BQ (.43–11.44)	Spitfire VC EE740 BQ-V, IX MH324 BQ-E.
NI (11.44–1.46)	Spitfire IX MJ833 NI-Z, XVI SM465 NI-X, XIV NH895 NI-K.
Also used	Lysander II P9052; Auster I LB375; Spitfire VIII MT546.

Disbanded 21st January 1946 at B.116 (Wunstorf), Germany.

452 (AUSTRALIAN) SQUADRON
Formed 8th April 1941 at Kirton-in-Lindsey.

UD (4.41–6.42)	Spitfire I X4651, IIA P7524, VA W3118, VB AB966.
QY (9.42–12.44)	Spitfire VC BR537 QY-A, VIII A58-516 QY-T.

Transferred June 1944 at Sattler, Australia, to 80 Wing, RAAF.
Disbanded 17th November 1945 at Tarakan, Indonesia.

453 (AUSTRALIAN) SQUADRON
Formed 13th May 1941 at Bankstown, Australia.

TD	Buffalo II W8209 TD-B.

Disbanded 15th March 1942 at Adelaide, Australia.

Reformed 9th June 1942 at Drem.

FU	Spitfire VB AA936 FU-B, IXB MK366 FU-K, IXE NH189 FU-Z, XVI SM184 FU-D.
Also used	Tiger Moth II DE430; Auster I LB378.

Disbanded 21st January 1946 at B.116 (Wunstorf), Germany.

454 (AUSTRALIAN) SQUADRON
Formed 23rd May 1941 at Williamstown, Australia.

No aircraft allocated.

Disbanded 11th July 1941 at Williamstown and absorbed by 458 Squadron.

Reformed 2nd April 1942 at Blackpool, moving to the Middle East to become the servicing echelon of 76/454 Squadron. Established 30th September 1942 at Aqir, Palestine.

Blenheim IV R3901, V BA400; Baltimore III AH129 B, IIIA FA129, IV FA409, V FW853 J. Also used Spitfire IV BP884.

Disbanded 20th August 1945 at Villa Orba, Italy.

455 (AUSTRALIAN) SQUADRON
Formed 6th June 1941 at Swinderby and joined on 1st September by the Australian echelon which had formed at Williamstown, Australia, on 30th June 1941.

UB (6.41–8.43)	Hampden I AE135 UB-C; Beaufighter X LZ407 UB-F.
2 (8.43–7.44)	Beaufighter X NE775 2-X.

UB (7.44–5.45)	Beaufighter X RD332 UB-C.
Also used	Proctor III R7537; Oxford II R6347.

Disbanded 25th May 1945 at Dallachy.

456 (AUSTRALIAN) SQUADRON
Formed 30th June 1941 at Valley.

PZ (6.41–11.41)	Defiant I N3477 PZ-V.
RX (11.41–6.45)	Beaufighter II T3370 RX-Z, VI X8138 RX-Z; Mosquito II DZ299 RX-D, VI HJ817, XVII HK286 RX-A, NF.30 NT241 RX-W.
Also used	Blenheim I L4907; Magister P2464; Oxford I X6802, II P6806; Mosquito III HJ852.

Disbanded 15th June 1945 at Bradwell Bay.

457 (AUSTRALIAN) SQUADRON
Formed 16th June 1941 at Baginton.

BP (6.41–6.42)	Spitfire I X4817 BP-C, IIA P7696, VB BM181.
ZP (8.42–12.44)	Spitfire VC BR542 ZP-Z, VIII A58-466 ZP-H.
Also used	Magister L8054; Tiger Moth II N9326; Ryan STM S-54.

Transferred July 1944 at Sattler, Australia, to 80 Wing, RAAF.
Disbanded 7th November 1945 at Labuan, Borneo.

458 (AUSTRALIAN) SQUADRON
Formed 10th July 1941 at Williamstown, Australia, then moved to the United Kingdom, assembling on 25th August 1941 at Holme-on-Spalding Moor.

Nil (8.41–3.42)	Wellington IV Z1182.
MD (10.42–4.43)	Wellington IC HX606 MD-P, VIII BB457.
Nil (4.43–6.45)	Wellington IC HE124 R, VIII LA979 X, XI MP566, XII MP584 P, XIII MP713, XIV HF400 M.

Disbanded 8th June 1945 at Gibraltar.

459 (AUSTRALIAN) SQUADRON
Formed 10th February 1942 at LG.39 (Burgh El Arab), Egypt.

GK (2.42–.43)	Hudson III V9027 GK-H, IIIA FH302 GK-C.
Nil (.43–4.45)	Hudson IIIA FH428 R, V AM853 J; VI EW971 P; Ventura I FN997, V FP604 H; Baltimore IV FA421 E, V FW485 G.

Disbanded 10th April 1945 at Chivenor.

460 (AUSTRALIAN) SQUADRON
Formed 15th November 1941 at Molesworth from 'C' Flight of 458 Squadron.

UV (11.41–5.43)	Wellington IV Z1486 UV-H; Halifax II W7781 UV-F; Lancaster I R5685, III ED421 UV-U.
AR (5.43–10.45)	Lancaster I ME649 AR-J, III ND521 AR-F2.
Also used	Manchester I L7464; Wellington IC R1695; Master I T8411.

Disbanded 10th October 1945 at East Kirby.

460 SQUADRON CONVERSION FLIGHT
Formed 22nd May 1942 at Breighton.

UV	Halifax II R9390; Lancaster I W4263.

Disbanded 10th November 1942 at Breighton and merged with 103 Squadron Conversion Flight to become 1656 Heavy Conversion Unit.

461 (AUSTRALIAN) SQUADRON
Formed 25th April 1942 at Mount Batten by redesignating an element of 10 Squadron, RAAF.

UT (4.42–8.43)	Sunderland I L5802, II T9085 UT-A, III DV960 UT-H.
Nil (8.43–7.44)	Sunderland II W6050, III EJ154.
UT (7.44–6.45)	Sunderland III ML827 UT-C, V RN282 UT-N.

Disbanded 4th June 1945 at Pembroke Dock.

462 (AUSTRALIAN) SQUADRON
Formed 7th September 1942 at Fayid, Egypt, by merging elements of 10, 76, 227 and 462 Squadrons.

Z5   *Halifax II W7755 Z5-A.*

Disbanded 15th February 1944 en route to Celone, Egypt, to become 614 Squadron.

Reformed 12th August 1944 at Driffield.

Z5   *Halifax III PN168 Z5-T.*

Disbanded 24th September 1945 at Foulsham.

463 (AUSTRALIAN) SQUADRON
Formed 25th November 1943 at Waddington from 'C' Flight of 467 Squadron.

PO (11.43–12.43)   *Lancaster I LL847 PO-D, III ED606 PO-X.*
JO (12.43–9.45)   *Lancaster I DV374 JO-B, III ED949 JO-A.*

Disbanded 25th September 1945 at Skellingthorpe.

464 (AUSTRALIAN) SQUADRON
Formed 15th August 1942 at Feltwell.

SB   *Ventura I AE819, II AJ174 SB-F; Mosquito VI HX912 SB-F.*
Also used   *Mosquito III HJ969; Oxford II V3588.*

Disbanded 25th September 1945 at B.58 (Melsbroek), Belgium.

466 (AUSTRALIAN) SQUADRON
Formed 15th October 1942 at Driffield.

HD   *Wellington III BK435, X HE410 HD-T; Halifax II*

DT559 HD-J, III NP968 HD-B, VI RG494 HD-R; Liberator V FL970, VIII KN734.

Disbanded 26th October 1945 at Bassingbourn.

467 (AUSTRALIAN) SQUADRON
Formed 7th November 1942 at Scampton.

PO   *Lancaster I DV372 PO-F, III ED606 PO-X.*

Disbanded 30th September 1945 at Metheringham.

485 (NEW ZEALAND) SQUADRON
Formed 1st March 1941 at Driffield.

OU   *Spitfire I X4253, IIA P7974, VB AB918 OU-Y, IXB MK245 OU-S, IXE PT525; Tempest V NV682; Typhoon IB EK135.*
Also used   *Magister T9947; Tiger Moth II DE446; Auster III NX537.*

Disbanded 26th August 1945 at B.105 (Drope), Germany.

486 (NEW ZEALAND) SQUADRON
Formed 3rd March 1942 at Kirton-in-Lindsey.

SA   *Hurricane IIA DG621, IIB BD728; Typhoon IB R8704 SA-S; Tempest V SN146 SA-K.*
Also used   *Tiger Moth II DE417; Auster IV MS951; Bu 181.*

Disbanded 7th September 1945 at B.158 (Lübeck), Germany.

487 (NEW ZEALAND) SQUADRON
Formed 15th August 1942 at Feltwell.

An Avro Lancaster Mk I of No 463 (Australian) Squadron is seen here bombing-up. This aircraft collided with a Hurricane during a fighter affiliation exercise at night and crashed near Metheringham on 11th March 1945.

EG	Ventura I AE797 EG-P, II AJ200 EG-G; Mosquito VI HR242 EG-P.
Also used	Oxford I R6027, II X7240; Mosquito III HJ967.

Disbanded 19th September 1945 at A.75 (Cambrai-Epinoy), France to become 268 Squadron.

488 (NEW ZEALAND) SQUADRON
Formed September 1941 at Rongatai, New Zealand.

NF	Wirraway; Buffalo I W8198 NF-U; Hurricane IIB BE632.

Disbanded 2nd March 1942 at Freemantle, Australia, to become 14 Squadron, RNZAF.

Reformed 25th June 1942 at Church Fenton.

ME	Beaufighter II T3410, VI X8027 ME-W; Mosquito XII HK227, XIII MM466 ME-R, NF.30 NT260 ME-F.
Also used	Blenheim I L1371; Magister P2461; Beaufighter I T3307; Oxford I R6015, II W6585; Tiger Moth II T7973; Mosquito III HJ864; Auster III MT450.

Disbanded 25th April 1945 at B.77 (Gilze-Rijen), Netherlands.

489 (NEW ZEALAND) SQUADRON
Formed 12th August 1941 at Leuchars.

Nil (8.41–3.42)	Beaufort I N1089 P; Blenheim IV.
XA (3.42–6.43)	Blenheim IV P4835 XA-H; Hampden I AN120 XA-L.
Nil (6.43–7.44)	Hampden I AD929 L; Beaufighter X LZ435 A.
P6 (7.44–8.45)	Beaufighter X NE210 P6-X; Mosquito VI RF880.
Also used	Blenheim I L1102; Oxford II R6347; Mosquito III RR307.

Disbanded 1st August 1945 at Banff.

490 (NEW ZEALAND) SQUADRON
Formed 28th March 1943 at Jui, Sierra Leone.

Catalina IB FP112 M; Sunderland III ML850 B.

Disbanded 30th June 1945 at Jui.

500 (COUNTY OF KENT) SQUADRON
Formed 16th March 1931 at Manston.

Nil (3.41–4.39)	Virginia X J7566 B; Hart K3816; Hind K6700.
SQ (4.39–9.39)	Anson I N5225 SQ-M.
MK (9.39–11.42)	Anson I N9907 MK-S; Blenheim IV Z6161 MK-T; Hudson III V9094 MK-W.
Nil (11.42–7.44)	Hudson III AE568, V AM732 L; Ventura I FN976, V JS944; Hudson VI FK706 P.
Also used	Tutor K3422.

Disbanded 11th July 1944 at La Senia, Algeria, the aircraft being absorbed by 27 Squadron, SAAF.

Reformed 13th July 1944 at La Senia, Algeria.

Baltimore IV FA517 A, V FW786.

Disbanded 23rd October 1945 at Eastleigh to become 249 Squadron.

Reformed 10th May 1946 at West Malling.

RAA (5.45–.50)	Mosquito III VA882 RAA-A, XIX TA352 RAA-D, NF.30 NT606 RAA-H; Harvard IIB FX432 RAA-R; Meteor F.3 EE352 RAA-A, F.4 EE469 RAA-G, T.7 VZ639 RAA-L.
S7 (.50–.51)	Meteor F.3 EE447 S7-K, F.4 VT169 S7-F, T.7 WF775 S7-Y; Harvard IIB KF718 S7-S.
Nil (.51–3.57)	Meteor F.4 VT288 J, T.7 WH224 Z, F.8 WK655 M; Vampire T.11 WZ469; Harvard IIB KF718 S.

Disbanded 10th March 1957 at West Malling.

501 (COUNTY OF GLOUCESTER) SQUADRON
Formed 14th June 1929 at Filton.

Nil (6.29–4.39)	D.H.9A DC J8491; Wapiti IIA K1373; Wallace I K3564, II K6044; Hart K3891; Hind K5551; Hurricane I L1869.

ZH (4.39–9.39)	Hurricane I L1866 ZH-B.
SD (4.39–4.45)	Hurricane I P3059 SD-N, X P5193; Spitfire I X4165, IA X4990 SD-M, IIA P7563, VB AR448 SD-H, VCBR168 SD-A, IX MJ311 SD-Z; Tempest V EJ605 SD-P.
Also used	Avro 504N J9701 2; Tutor K4819; Battle N2089; Tiger Moth I K4272, II R5252; Magister T9747; Master III W8837; Auster I LB335.

Disbanded 20th April 1945 at Hunsdon.

Reformed 10th May 1946 at Filton.

RAB (5.46–.49)	Spitfire XVIE SL669 RAB-K; Harvard IIB FX420 RAB-C; Vampire F.1 TG419 RAB-P.
SD (.49–.51)	Harvard IIB KF670 SD-A; Vampire F.1 TG419 SD-P; Meteor T.7 WA594 SD-G.
Nil (.51–2.57)	Vampire FB.5 WA303 D, FB.9 WR180; Meteor T.7 VW457 B.

Disbanded 10th March 1957 at Filton.

502 (ULSTER) SQUADRON
Formed 15th May 1925 at Aldergrove.

Nil (5.25–4.39)	Vimy IV J7239; Hyderabad J7742 2; Virginia X K2324; Wallace II K6017; Hind K6763; Anson I N5213.
KQ (4.39–9.39)	Anson I N5234.
YG (9.39–2.43)	Anson I N9918 YG-B; Botha L6231; Whitley V T4168 YG-E, VII Z9124 YG-T.
Nil (2.43–6.44)	Halifax II HR693 O.
V9 (6.44–5.45)	Halifax II JP328 V9-H, III RG369 V9-R.
Also used	Avro 504K D6330, Avro 504N E9352; Tutor K3399; Albemarle I P1436.

Disbanded 25th May 1945 at Stornoway.

Reformed 10th May 1946 at Aldergrove.

RAC (5.46–.49)	Mosquito B.25 KB565 RAC, III RR306, NF.30 MV524 RAC; Oxford II V3398 RAC-Z; Spitfire F.22 PK567 RAC-J; Harvard IIB FX249 RAC-R.
V9 (.49–.53)	Spitfire F.22 PK605 V9-T; Harvard IIB KF707 V9-Q; Vampire FB.5 WG831 V9-H; Meteor T.7 WF824 V9-N.
Nil (.53–3.57)	Vampire FB.5 WA393 C, FB.9 WR128 A; Harvard IIB KF707 V; Meteor T.7 VZ637 P.

Disbanded 10th March 1957 at Aldergrove.

503 (COUNTY OF LINCOLN) SQUADRON
Formed 5th October 1926 at Waddington.

Avro 504K J736; Fawn I J7183, II J6991 1, III J7769, IV J7981; Hyderabad J7752; Hinaidi K1912; Tutor K3340; Wallace II K6042; Hart K3025; Hind K6838.

Disbanded 1st November 1938 at Doncaster to become 616 Squadron.

VJ	Allocated for the period April to September 1939.

504 (COUNTY OF NOTTINGHAM) SQUADRON
Formed 26th March 1928 at Hucknall.

Nil (3.28–4.39)	Horsley I J8019, II S1237; Wallace I K4019, II K6047; Hind K6720.
AW (4.39–9.39)	Hurricane I L1950.
TM (9.39–8.45)	Hurricane I L1931 TM-O, X P5201, IIB Z5082; Spitfire IIA P7358, IIB P8576, VB BL388, VC EE621 TM-R, VI BR189, IX PL256 TM-L; Meteor F.3 EE286 TM-L.
Also used	Avro 504K H2995; Avro 504N J9684 N; Moth K1848; Hart Trainer K3155; Tutor K3246; Master I N7569; Tiger Moth I NL992, II R5028; Magister L5913.

Disbanded 10th August 1945 at Colerne to become 245 Squadron.

Reformed 10th May 1946 at Syerston.

RAD (5.46–.49)	Mosquito NF.30 NT562 RAD-M, III HJ972 RAD-M; Spitfire F.22 PK495 RAD-A; Harvard IIB KF925 RAD-Z; Meteor F.4 VW274 RAD-F, T.7 WA610 RAD-M.

TM (.49– .52)	Harvard IIB KF925 TM-Z; Meteor F.4 VZZ406 TM-EF.
Nil (.52–2.57)	Meteor T.7 WF845, F.8 WH282 K.

Disbanded 10th March 1957 at Wymeswold.

505 SQUADRON
Squadron not formed although the code YF was allocated for the period April to September 1939.

506 SQUADRON
Squadron not formed although the code FS was allocated for the period April to September 1939.

507 SQUADRON
Squadron not formed although the code GX was allocated for the period April to September 1939.

508 SQUADRON
Squadron not formed although the code DY was allocated for the period April to September 1939.

509 SQUADRON
Squadron not formed although the code BQ was allocated for the period April to September 1939.

510 SQUADRON
RG	Allocated for the period April to September 1939.

Formed 15th October 1942 at Hendon from 'A' Flight of 24 Squadron.

Nil	Lysander I R2634; Reliant X9596; Hornet Moth X9321; Puss Moth X9402; Oxford I L4635, II V3854; Spitfire I R7199; Tiger Moth BB802, I K4276, II N9444; Proctor I P6179, III R7569, IV MX451; Vega Gull X9368; Mohawk III AR633; Percival Q-6 X9407; Moth MX463; Hart K2452; Stampe S.V.4B MX457; Anson I EG229; Koolhoven FK-43 MX459; Cygnet HM495; Dominie I X7327.
RG	The Transport Command Meteorological Flight, using the code RG Spitfires I including X4587 RG-B, operated within the Squadron.

Disbanded 8th April 1944 at Hendon to become the Metropolitan Communication Squadron.

511 SQUADRON
SN	Allocated for the period April to September 1939.

Formed 10th October 1942 at Lyneham by redesignating 1425 (Communication) Flight.

BC	Allocated but not used.
Nil (1.42–10.46)	Liberator I AM922, II AL547; Albemarle I/I P1372, I/II P1475, I/III P1510; Halifax II; Dakota III FD869; Liberator VI BZ965, VII EW616; York I MW128; Lancastrian II VM701.

Disbanded 7th October 1946 at Lyneham.

Reformed 16th October 1946 at Lyneham by renumbering 246 Squadron.

York I MW258 MOYCX; Hastings C.1 TG553 MOGAK, C.2 WJ333 MOGAY.

Disbanded 1st September 1958 at Colerne to become 36 Squadron.

Reformed 15th December 1959 at Lyneham.

Britannia C.1 XL638, C.2 XN404.

Disbanded 7th January 1976 at Brize Norton.

512 SQUADRON
UQ	Allocated for the period April to September 1939.

Formed 18th June 1943 at Hendon from an element of 24 Squadron.

HC	Dakota I FD789, III FZ696 HC-AQ, IV KN523 HC-EW; Oxford I NM244, II R6345; Anson X NK533.

Disbanded 14th March 1946 at Bari, Italy.

513 SQUADRON
RZ	Allocated for the period April to September 1939.

Formed 15th September 1943 at Witchford by redesignating a Flight of 218 Squadron.

CS	Stirling III EF465.

Disbanded 21st November 1943 at Witchford.

514 SQUADRON
OV	Allocated for the period April to September 1939.

Formed 1st September 1943 at Foulsham.

JI (9.43–8.45)	Lancaster II LL728 JI-B, I NG121 JI-H, III ME380 JI-E.
A2 (12.43–8.45)	('C' Flight) Lancaster II LL680 A2-H, I NG142 A2-H, III ME425 A2-L.

Disbanded 22nd August 1945 at Waterbeach.

515 SQUADRON
YW Allocated for the period April to September 1939.

Formed 1st October 1942 at Northolt by redesignating the Special Duty Flight, Northolt.

Nil (10.42–2.44)	Defiant II AA542 N; Beaufighter I R2146, II V8191 N.
3P (2.44–6.45)	Mosquito II DD666, VI RS566 3P-F.
Also used	Oxford I N4582, II T1106; Magister L5983; Blenheim V BA168.

Disbanded 10th June 1945 at Little Snoring.

516 SQUADRON
PF Allocated for the period April to September 1939.

Formed 28th April 1943 at Dundonald by redesignating 1441 (Combined Operations Development) Flight.

Tiger Moth II N6789; Lysander II P9105, IIIA V9494; Blenheim IV Z5879; Master II DM203; Mustang I AM181, IA FD549; Anson I N9537; Hurricane IIC LF428.

Disbanded 2nd December 1944 at Dundonald.

517 SQUADRON
SW	Allocated for the period April to September 1939.

Formed 7th August 1943 at St Eval by redesignating 1404 (Meteorological) Flight.

Hudson III V9123; Hampden I AD724; B-17F (detached from 379th Bombardment Squadron, USAAF); Halifax II R9486, V LL220 F, III NA247; Oxford I T1402, II X7194; Proctor III Z7218.

Disbanded 21st June 1946 at Chivenor.

518 SQUADRON
FM	Allocated for the period April to September 1939.

Formed 6th July 1943 at Stornoway.

Nil (7.43–6.44)	Halifax II R9486, V DG304 H.
Y3 (6.44–10.46)	Halifax V LK688 Y3-H, III RG390 Y3-A1; Spitfire VII MD181; Hurricane IIC PG469 Y3-K; Halifax VI RG780 Y3-M.
Also used	Oxford I PG969.

Disbanded 1st October 1946 at Aldergrove to become 202 Squadron.

519 SQUADRON
BP	Allocated for the period April to September 1939.

Formed 7th August 1943 at Wick by redesignating 1406 (Meteorological) Flight.

Z9	Hampden I X3122 Z9-G; Spitfire VI BR307 Z9-X, VII MD141 Z9-T; Hudson III V9118 Z9-R, IIIA FK743 Z9-C; Ventura I AE779, V FP583 Z9-L; Fortress IIA FK213 Z9-G; Halifax III MZ390 Z9-K; Oxford I NM353 Z9-P, II X7238.

Disbanded 31st May 1946 at Leuchars.

520 SQUADRON

JL	Allocated for the period April to September 1939.

Formed 20th September 1943 at Gibraltar by redesignating 1403 (Meteorological) Flight.

2M	Hudson III FH357; Gladiator II N5630; Halifax V LL518 2M-K; Spitfire VB EP412; Hurricane IIC PZ858; Martinet I NR313; Halifax III PN190; Warwick VI HG122.

Disbanded 25th April 1946 at Gibraltar.

521 SQUADRON
Formed 22nd July 1942 at Bircham Newton by redesignating 1401 (Meteorological) Flight.

Blenheim IV T2001; Gladiator II N2307; Spitfire IV BP928, VA P1355, VI R6905; Mosquito IV DK329; Hudson III T9404; Albemarle I/I P1373; Master I T8617.

Disbanded 22nd March 1943 at Bircham Newton to become 1401 and 1409 (Meteorological) Flights.

Reformed 1st September 1943 at Docking.

5O	Gladiator I K7972, II N5902; Hampden I L4204; Hudson IIIA FH380; Ventura I FN984, V JT894 W; Hurricane IIC PZ806; Fortress II FA710, IIA FL450, III HB786; Halifax VI RG787; Master II DL414; Tiger Moth II N6751; Oxford II T1402.

Disbanded 31st March 1946 at Chivenor.

524 SQUADRON
Formed 20th October 1943 at Oban.

Mariner I JX100 A.

Disbanded 7th December 1943 at Oban.

Reformed 7th April 1944 at Davidstow Moor.

7R	Wellington XIII MF335 7R-H; Warwick II HG348.

Disbanded 25th May 1945 at Langham.

525 SQUADRON
Formed 1st September 1943 at Weston Zoyland.

8P	Allocated but not used.
Nil (9.43– .46)	Warwick I BV249; III HG224; Dakota III FL562, IV KN432.
WF (.46–12.46)	Dakota III KG391 WF-G, IV KN417 WF-G.
Also used	Oxford I NM534, II P8923; Proctor III HM350.

Disbanded 1st December 1946 at Abingdon to become 238 Squadron.

526 SQUADRON
Formed 15th June 1943 at Longman by merging 70 and 71 Wing Calibration Flights.

MD	Blenheim I L1363, IV T2001 MD-B; Hornet Moth W9388 MD-R; Oxford II X7200 MD-N; Dominie I R5934 MD-X.

Disbanded 1st May 1945 at Longman and absorbed by 527 Squadron.

527 SQUADRON
Formed 15th June 1943 at Castle Camps by merging 74 and 75 Wing Calibration Flights.

WN	Blenheim IV R3615 WN-Y; Hurricane I P2992 WN-P, X AG146, IIB BP737; Hornet Moth

W9391; Spitfire VB AA915 WN-Y; Oxford I LX122 WN-P; Dominie I HG721.

Disbanded 15th April 1946 at Watton.

Reformed 1st August 1952 at Wyton by redesignating 'R' Squadron of the Central Signals Establishment.

Mosquito B.35 TA708; Oxford I PH131; Anson XIX VL312 25; Lincoln B.2 SX950 R; Meteor NF.11 WM184, NF.14 WS797; Varsity T.1 WL678; Canberra B.2 WK144, PR.7 WH780.

Disbanded 21st August 1958 at Watton to become 245 Squadron.

528 SQUADRON
Formed 15th June 1943 at Filton.

Blenheim IV T2219; Hornet Moth W5772.

Disbanded 1st September 1944 at Digby and absorbed by 527 Squadron.

529 SQUADRON
Formed 15th June 1943 at Halton by redesignating 1448 (Radar Calibration) Flight.

KX	Rota I K4233 KX-F, II L7594; Cierva C.30A AP507 KX-P; C.40A P9639; Hornet Moth W5754 KX-W; Oxford I T1210, II X7238; Hoverfly I KK993 KX-R; Tiger Moth II T6264.

Disbanded 20th October 1945 at Henley.

530 SQUADRON
Formed 8th September 1942 at Hunsdon by redesignating 1451 (Turbinlite) Flight.

Havoc I (Turbinlite) BD111; Boston II (Turbinlite) AH453, III (Turbinlite) AL469; Hurricane IIB JS300, IIC BE580; Magister L8092.

Disbanded 25th January 1943 at Hunsdon.

531 SQUADRON
Formed 8th September 1942 at West Malling by redesignating 1452 (Turbinlite) Flight.

Boston III (Turbinlite) W8257; Hurricane IIC HL658 L; Tiger Moth II T7466.

Disbanded 25th January 1943 at West Malling.

532 SQUADRON
Formed 8th September 1942 at Wittering by redesignating 1453 (Turbinlite) Flight.

Havoc I (Turbinlite) BJ467; Boston I AE470, III (Turbinlite) AL774; Hurricane IIC BD946.

Disbanded 25th January 1943 at Hibaldstow.

533 SQUADRON
Formed 8th September 1942 at Charmy Down by redesignating 1454 (Turbinlite) Flight.

Havoc I AW408, I (Turbinlite) BB898; Boston II (Turbinlite) AH436, III (Turbinlite) W8255; Hurricane IIB BW962, IIC Z3775; Magister R1912; Tiger Moth II T6110.

Disbanded 25th January 1943 at Charmy Down.

534 SQUADRON
Formed 2nd September 1942 at Tangmere by redesignating 1455 (Turbinlite) Flight.

Havoc I (Turbinlite) BD110; Boston I AE465, II (Turbinlite) AH434, III (Turbinlite) AL470; Hurricane IIB AM289, IIC BP760; Magister R1835; Tiger Moth II T7458.

Disbanded 25th January 1943 at Tangmere.

535 SQUADRON
Formed 2nd September 1942 at High Ercall by redesignating 1456 (Turbinlite) Flight.

Havoc I AW410, I (Turbinlite) AW411; Boston II (Turbinlite) AH450; III (Turbinlite) W8393; Hurricane IIB BW924; Magister L8059.

Disbanded 25th January 1943 at High Ercall.

536 SQUADRON
Formed 8th September 1942 at Predannack by redesignating 1457 (Turbinlite) Flight.

Havoc I BT464; Boston II (Turbinlite) AH447, III (Turbinlite) W8274; Hurricane IIC HL862; Magister L8340; Tiger Moth II T6195.

Disbanded 25th January 1943 at Fairwood Common.

537 SQUADRON
Formed 8th September 1942 at Middle Wallop by redesignating 1458 (Turbinlite) Flight.

Havoc I (Turbinlite) AW407; Boston II (Turbinlite) AH472, III (Turbinlite) W8275; Hurricane IIC HL584; Magister L5939; Tiger Moth II R5028.

Disbanded 25th January 1943 at Middle Wallop.

538 SQUADRON
Formed 2nd September 1942 at Hibaldstow by redesignating 1459 (Turbinlite) Flight.

Havoc I (Turbinlite) AW400; Boston II (Turbinlite) AH452, III (Turbinlite) AL760; Hurricane IIC HL570; Magister L8054; Tiger Moth II N6749.

Disbanded 25th January 1943 at Hibaldstow.

539 SQUADRON
Formed 2nd September 1942 at Acklington by redesignating 1460 (Turbinlite) Flight.

Havoc I (Turbinlite) BJ499; Boston I AE471, II (Turbinlite) AH460, III (Turbinlite) W8306; Hurricane IIB AM282, IIC HL603; Magister L8288; Tiger Moth II DE138.

Disbanded 25th January at Acklington.

540 SQUADRON
Formed 19th October 1942 at Leuchars by redesignating 'H' and 'L' Flights of 1 Photographic Reconnaissance Unit.

Nil (10.42–10.46)	Spitfire IV BS362; Mosquito II DD615, IV DZ592, VI RS502 Y, VIII DZ424, IX LR422 O, XVI MM397 W, PR.32 NS589.
DH (11.45–9.46)	Mosquito PR.34 PF679 DH-A.
Also used	Anson XI NL183.

Disbanded 1st October 1946 at Benson to become 58 Squadron.

Reformed 1st December 1947 at Benson from the Mosquito element of 58 Squadron.

DH (12.47–.51)	Mosquito PR.34 PF662 DH-T.
Nil (.51–3.56)	Mosquito PR.34 PF674; PR.34A PF680; Canberra B.2 WD990, PR.3 WE141, PR.7 WJ815 G.
Also used	Oxford II BG543.

Disbanded 31st March 1956 at Wyton.

541 SQUADRON
Formed 19th October 1942 at Benson by redesignating 'B' and 'F' Flights of 1 Photographic Reconnaissance Unit.

Nil (10.42–12.46)	Spitfire IV BP922, X MD199, XI PL775 A; Mustang III FX855; Mosquito IX LR412; Spitfire XIX RM637; Meteor F.3 EE411; Lancaster PR.1 TW884 B.
ES (10.45–12.46)	Spitfire XIX PM612 ES-C.
Also used	Master II DM375; Anson XI NL228.

Disbanded 1st October 1946 at Benson, the Lancaster Flight becoming 82 Squadron.

Reformed 1st November 1947 at Benson.

WY (11.47–.51)	Spitfire XIX PS887 WY-B; Harvard IIB KF464 WY; Meteor PR.10 VS973 WY-A.
A (.51–.54)	Meteor PR.10 VS975 A-N.
Nil (.54–9.57)	Meteor PR.10 WH573.

Disbanded 7th September 1957 at Laarbruch, Germany.

542 SQUADRON
Formed 19th October 1942 at Benson by redesignating 'A' and 'E' Flights of 1 Photographic Reconnaissance Unit.

Spitfire IV AA791, X MD198, XI PA941 H, XIII BM447; XIX PS888; Typhoon IB MN315; Oxford II AB303; Master II DM345.

Disbanded 27th August 1945 at Benson.

Reformed 15th May 1954 at Wyton.

Canberra PR.7 WH795.

Disbanded 1st October 1955 at Wyton.

Reformed 1st November 1955 at Wyton by redesignating 1323 (Canberra) Flight.

Canberra B.2 WJ573, B.6 WH946.

Disbanded 1st October 1958 at Upwood to become 21 Squadron.

543 SQUADRON
Formed 19th October 1942 at Benson from an element of 1 Photographic Reconnaissance Unit.

Spitfire IV BP888, V X4786, XI EN424, XIII AD556; Anson I DJ182.

Disbanded 18th October 1943 at Benson, 'A' Flight being absorbed by 541 Squadron.

Reformed 1st April 1955 at Gaydon.

Valiant B(PR).1 WP221, B(PR)K.1 WZ399; Victor B.2(SR) XL230.

Disbanded 24th May 1974 at Wyton.

544 SQUADRON
Formed 19th October 1942 at Benson from an element of 1 Photographic Reconnaissance Unit.

Oxford II AS705; Anson I DJ182, XI NL229; Maryland I AR744; Wellington IV Z1417; Spitfire IV BR666; Mosquito IV DZ600, VI PZ345, IX LR478, XVI NS502 M, PR.34 RG195.

Disbanded 13th October 1945 at Benson.

547 SQUADRON
Formed 22nd October 1942 at Holmsley South.

Nil (10.42–8.43)	Wellington VIII LB122, XI HZ404, XIII HZ577; Liberator V BZ797 M.
2V (8.43–6.45)	Liberator V FL937 2V-H, VI BZ995 2V-N, VIII KK327 2V-M.
Also used	Oxford I T1194.

Disbanded 4th June 1946 at Leuchars.

548 SQUADRON
Formed 15th December 1943 at Lawntown, Australia.

Nil (12.43–4.44)	Tiger Moth II A17-614; Wirraway,
TS (4.44–10.45)	Spitfire VIII A58-482 TS-M.

Disbanded 31st October 1945 at Melbourne, Australia.

549 SQUADRON
Formed 15th December 1943 at Lawntown, Australia.

ZF	Spitfire VIII A58-379 ZF-Z.

Disbanded 31st October 1945 at Melbourne, Australia.

550 SQUADRON
Formed 25th November 1943 at Grimsby from 'C' Flight of 100 Squadron.

BQ	Lancaster I NG133 BQ-F2, III ED905 BQ-F.

Disbanded 1st November 1945 at North Killingholme.

551 SQUADRON – see Advanced Training Squadrons

552 SQUADRON – see Advanced Training Squadrons

553 SQUADRON – see Advanced Training Squadrons

554 SQUADRON – see Advanced Training Squadrons

555 SQUADRON – see Advanced Training Squadrons

556 SQUADRON – see Advanced Training Squadrons

557 SQUADRON – see Advanced Training Squadrons

558 SQUADRON – see Advanced Training Squadrons

559 SQUADRON – see Advanced Training Squadrons

560 SQUADRON – see Advanced Training Squadrons

561 SQUADRON – see Advanced Training Squadrons

562 SQUADRON – see Advanced Training Squadrons

563 SQUADRON – see Advanced Training Squadrons

564 SQUADRON – see Advanced Training Squadrons

565 SQUADRON – see Advanced Training Squadrons

567 SQUADRON
Formed 1st December 1943 at Detling by redesignating 1624 (Anti-Aircraft Co-operation) Flight.

I4	Hurricane I V7075 I4-J, X P5194, IIC LF584 I4-X; Martinet I MS528 I4-B; Oxford I V4262 I4-N; Spitfire VC AR518, XVI SM243 I4-G; Vengeance IV HB364 I4-Q.

Disbanded 15th June 1946 at West Malling.

569 SQUADRON
Formed administratively on 10th January 1944 to operate within 46 Group.

No aircraft allotted.

Disbanded 1st March 1944.

570 SQUADRON
Formed 15th November 1943 at Hurn.

Nil (11.43–5.44)	Albemarle GT.I P1441 XX, ST.I V1627 KK; Oxford I T1065.
E7 (5.44–1.46)	Albemarle ST.V V1816 E7-Z; Stirling IV EF306 E7-Y.
V8 (11.43–1.46)	Albemarle I P1371 V8-O, ST.I P1653 V8-I, ST.II V1617 V8-S; Stirling IV LK150 V8-H.

Disbanded 28th December 1946 at Rivenhall.

571 SQUADRON
Formed 5th April 1944 at Downham Market.

8K	Mosquito IX LR498, XVI RV362 8K-C.

Disbanded 20th September 1945 at Warboys.

575 SQUADRON
Formed 1st February 1944 at Hendon by redesignating an element of 512 Squadron.

I9	Dakota II FZ698 I9-RW, IV KN431 I9-F; Oxford II W6632; Anson I NK674 I9-M, X NK534 I9-J, XII PH547.

Disbanded 15th August 1946 at Kabrit, Egypt.

576 SQUADRON
Formed 25th November 1943 at Elsham Wolds from 'C' Flight of 103 Squadron.

UL	Lancaster I W4245 UL-S2, III PD235 UL-N.

Disbanded 19th September 1945 at Fiskerton.

577 SQUADRON
Formed 1st December 1943 at Castle Bromwich by merging elements of 6, 7 and 8 Anti-Aircraft Co-operation Units.

3Y	Oxford I V3151 3Y-N, II P1814; Hurricane IIC PG606, IV KZ325; Beaufighter I R2199, X RD713 3Y-R; Spitfire VB BM569 3Y-F, XVI SM511 3Y-J; Vengeance IV HB428.
Also used	Voyager X5324; Tiger Moth II DE879.

Disbanded 15th June 1946 at Castle Bromwich.

578 SQUADRON
Formed 14th January 1944 at Snaith from 'C' Flight of 51 Squadron.

LK	Halifax III LW473 LK-P; Mosquito XVI PF481.

Disbanded 15th April 1945 at Burn.

582 SQUADRON
Formed 1st April 1944 at Little Staughton by merging 'C' Flights of 7 and 156 Squadrons.

6O	Lancaster I NG443, III JA673 6O-L, VI ND418.

Disbanded 10th September 1945 at Little Staughton.

587 SQUADRON
Formed 1st December 1943 at Weston Zoyland by merging 1600 and 1601 (Target Towing) Flights and 1625 (Anti-Aircraft Co-operation) Flight.

M4	Henley III L3267; Master II W9077; Oxford I R6335, II HN168; Hurricane IIC PG488, IV LE395; Martinet I EM412; Harvard I P5866, IIB FS770 M4-S; Mustang I AG449; Vengeance IV HB456; Spitfire XVI TB304 M4-V; Tiger Moth II T7024.

Disbanded 15th June 1946 at Tangmere.

595 SQUADRON
Formed 1st December 1943 at Aberporth by merging 1607, 1608 and 1609 (Target Towing) Flights.

7B	Henley III L3252; Hurricane I P2887, IV KW792; Tiger Moth II T5625; Martinet I NR663 7B-M; Oxford I PH318 7B-T; Voyager X1050; Proctor III Z7220; Mustang I AG357; Spitfire VB BM581 7B-R, IX ML247 7B-F, XII MB804 7B-N, XVI TE300 7B-G; Vampire F.1 VF310; Harvard IIB KF920 7B-R.

Disbanded 11th February 1949 at Pembrey to become 5 Squadron.

597 SQUADRON
Formed administratively 10th January 1944 to operate within 46 Group.

No aircraft allocated.

Disbanded 1st March 1944.

598 SQUADRON
Formed 1st December 1943 at Peterhead by merging 1479 and 1632 (Anti-Aircraft Co-operation) Flights and an element of 289 Squadron.

Oxford I T1024; Lysander II N1210, IIIA V9818; Martinet I EM516; Hurricane IIC LF530; IV LE653; Tiger Moth II T7449.

Disbanded 30th April 1945 at Bircham Newton.

600 (CITY OF LONDON) SQUADRON
Formed 14th October 1925 at Northolt.

Nil (10.25–1.39)	Avro 504K F9720, Avro 504N J8502 2; D.H.9A J8223 C, D.H.9 DC J8472; Wapiti I J9093, IIA K1330; Hart K2473, Hart Trainer K3147; Demon K2847.
MV (1.39–9.39)	Blenheim I L1401 MV.
BQ (9.39–8.43)	Blenheim I L8698 BQ-M, IV P4846 BQ-W; Beaufighter I R2256 BQ-F, II R2279, VI X7887 BQ-K.
6 (8.43–7.44)	Beaufighter VI V8388 6-Y.

| Nil (7.44–8.45) | Beaufighter VI ND172 B; Mosquito XIX TA123 H. |
| Also used | Moth K1214; Tutor K1240; Battle L5032; Magister L8285; Oxford II AS875. |

Disbanded 21st August 1945 at Aviano, Italy.

Reformed 10th May 1946 at Biggin Hill.

RAG (5.46– .49)	Spitfire XIV TZ141 RAG-E, F.21 LA253 RAG-K, F.22 PK392 RAG-U; Harvard IIB KF310 RAG-C.
LJ (.49–4.51)	Harvard IIB KF310 LJ-C; Meteor F.4 VZ429 LJ-Q.
Nil (4.51–3.57)	Harvard IIB KF310 C; Meteor F.4 VW256, T.7 WA628 S, F.8 WH261 Z.

Disbanded 10th March 1957 at Biggin Hill.

601 (COUNTY OF LONDON) SQUADRON
Formed 14th October 1925 at Northolt.

Nil (10.25–1.39)	Avro 504N J8504; D.H.9A J8108, D.H.9A DC J8476; Wapiti I J9101, II J9239, IIA K1341, VI K2238; Hart K2966, Hart Trainer K3154; Demon K2842; Gauntlet II K5311.
YN (1.39–9.39)	Gauntlet II K7888 YN-J; Blenheim I L6680 YN-A.
UF (9.39–4.42)	Blenheim I L8701; Hurricane I L2034 UF-L, X P5208, IIB Z3356 UF-O; Airacobra I AH602 UF-W; Spitfire VA X4172, VB EP455 UF-Y.
1 and 3 (4.42)	Delivery of the Squadron's Spitfires to Malta during April 1942 aboard the USS Wasp resulted in the aircraft carrying the codes '1' and '3' followed by the individual aircraft letter, e.g. Spitfire V BR344 3-M.
UF (4.42–8.45)	Spitfire VC BR113 UF-R, VIII JF447 UF-I, IX MK724 UF-S; Seafire IIC LR640.
Also used	Moth K1852; Tutor K3237; Audax K2025; Magister P6377; Blenheim IV P4831; Baltimore III AG866; Argus II FZ826; Ju 87D UF; Me 110A 2N+HT.

Disbanded 14th August 1945 at Treviso, Italy.

Reformed 10th May 1946 at Hendon.

RAH (5.46– .49)	Spitfire XVI RW394 RAH-W; Harvard IIB FX399 RAH-V.
HT (.49–4.51)	Spitfire XVI SL725 HT-Y; Harvard IIB KF402 HT-Y; Vampire F.1 VF327 HT-A.
Nil (4.51–3.57)	Harvard IIB KF402 Y; Vampire F.1 VF338 E; Meteor F.8 WK783 J, T.7 WA620 P.

Disbanded 10th March 1957 at North Weald.

602 (CITY OF GLASGOW) SQUADRON
Formed 12th September 1925 at Renfrew.

Nil (9.25–1.39)	D.H.9A J7020; Avro 504N K1982; Fawn I J7182, II J7188, III J7770; Wapiti I J9094, IIA J9862; Hart K3044; Hind K5507; Gauntlet II K5301.
LO (1.39–5.39)	Gauntlet II K7879 LO-K.
ZT (5.39–9.39)	Spitfire I K9967 ZT-O.
LO (9.39–5.45)	Spitfire I X4386 LO-G, IIA P8574, VA P7692, VB AA910 LO-A, VC EE687, VI X4173, IXB MJ132 LO-S, IXE PL213, XVI SM350 LO-A.
Also used	Tutor K3305; Harvard I P5867; Magister N3918; Tiger Moth II DE558; Auster I LB349.

Disbanded 15th May 1945 at Coltishall.

Reformed 10th May 1946 at Abbotsinch.

RAI (5.46– .49)	Spitfire XIV TX985 RAI-B, F.21 LA315 RAI-K, F.22 PK369 RAI-B; Harvard IIB KF584 RAI-X.
LO (.49– .53)	Spitfire F.21 LA269 LO-H, F.22 PK578 LO-A; Harvard IIB KF584 LO-X; Vampire F.3 VF335, FB.5 WA453 LO-A; Meteor T.7 WF773 LO-W.
Nil (.53–1.57)	Vampire FB.5 WA453, FB.9 WR261; Meteor T.7 WL480 X.
Also used	Vampire T.11 XD550.

Disbanded 10th March 1957 at Abbotsinch.

603 (CITY OF EDINBURGH) SQUADRON
Formed 14th October 1925 at Turnhouse.

Nil (10.25–4.39)	D.H.9A J8129, D.H.9A DC J8472; Avro 504K E3333, Avro 504N K1822; Wapiti IIA K1144; Hart K3045; Hind K5498; Gladiator I K7927.
RL (4.39–9.39)	Gladiator I K9724 RL; Spitfire I L1070 RL.
XT (9.39–4.42)	Gladiator I K7921; Spitfire I L1067 XT-D, IIA P7597, VA W3113 XT-O, VB W3632.
2 (4.42)	Delivery of the Squadron's Spitfires to Malta during April 1942 aboard the USS Wasp resulted in the aircraft carrying the code '2' followed by the individual aircraft letter.
X (4.42–8.42)	Spitfire VC.
Also used	Moth K1901; Tutor K3454.

Disbanded 3rd August 1942 at Takali, Malta. The air echelon became 229 Squadron whilst the ground element became a servicing unit.

Reformed 27th March 1943 at Misurata West, Libya.

Beaufighter I X7761 H, VI JL626, X LX949 Z.

Disbanded 26th December 1944 en route to the United Kingdom from Port Said, Egypt.

Reformed 10th January 1945 at Coltishall by renumbering 229 Squadron.

XT (1.45–8.45)	Spitfire XVI SM357.
RAJ (6.45– .49)	Spitfire LF.XVI TE477 RAJ-D, F.22 PK504 RAJ-P; Harvard IIB KF449 RAJ-B.
XT (.49–4.51)	Spitfire F.22 PK504 XT-P; Harvard IIB KF699 XT-A.
Nil (4.51–2.57)	Vampire FB.5 WA440 N, FB.9 WL518; Meteor T.7 WF828.
Also used	Auster I LB299.

Disbanded 10th March 1957 at Turnhouse.

604 (COUNTY OF MIDDLESEX) SQUADRON
Formed 17th March 1930 at Hendon.

Nil (3.30–1.39)	D.H.9A DC J8472; Avro 504K H3015, Avro 504N K1043; Wapiti I J9095, IIA K1336; Hart K3893; Demon K4528; Blenheim I L6615.
WQ (1.39–9.39)	Blenheim I L6615 WQ-G.
NG (9.39–4.45)	Blenheim I L8673 NG-H; Gladiator I K8033; Beaufighter I T4638 NG-F, VI MM856 NG-C; Mosquito XII HK181 NG-J, XIII MM528 NG-H.
Also used	Moth K1103; Tutor K3449; Tiger Moth I K4250; Magister L8093; Oxford I T1065, II X7251.

Disbanded 18th April 1945 at B.51 (Lille/Vendeville), France.

Reformed 10th May 1946 at Hendon.

RAK (7.46– .49)	Spitfire XVI SL615 RAK-Y; Harvard IIB FT342 RAK-Z.
NG (.49–4.51)	Spitfire LF.XVI TE189 NG-H; Vampire F.3 VT829 NG-A.
Nil (4.51–2.57)	Vampire F.3 VT816 F; Meteor F.8 WH419 E, T.7 WA620.

Disbanded 10th March 1957 at North Weald.

605 (COUNTY OF WARWICK) SQUADRON
Formed 5th October 1926 at Castle Bromwich.

Nil (10.26–4.39)	Avro 504K E3068, Avro 504N H3017; D.H.9A J7814, D.H.9A DC J8480; Wapiti I J9094, IIA K1147; Hart K2439; Hind K5431.
HE (4.39–9.39)	Gladiator I K7946 HE-R, II N5586 HE-K; Hurricane I N2349 HE-V.
Nil (9.39–3.42)	Gladiator I K7585, II N2305; Hurricane I P3022, IIA Z2351, IIB BD742, IIC BD855.
Also used	Moth K1216; Tutor K3309; Magister L5941; Beaufighter I R2123.

The Squadron embarked on HMS Argus on 1st November 1941 for the Far East. The majority of the pilots were diverted to Hal Far, Malta, and remained until the Squadron disbanded on 17th March 1942. The remaining pilots operated with 242/232 Squadron until 28th February 1942 when they were absorbed into 242 Squadron at Tjilijan, Java.

Reconstituted 7th January 1942 at Hal Far, Malta.

UP   *Hurricane IIB BG753 UP-V.*

Disbanded 17th March 1943 at Hal Far and absorbed by 185 Squadron.

Reformed 7th June 1942 at Ford.

UP	*Havoc I BB895; Boston III AL871 UP-D; Mosquito II DZ657 UP-F, IV DZ441, VI HJ778 UP-A.*
Also used	*Owlet DP240; Oxford I P1895; Magister P6349; Tiger Moth II DE510.*

Disbanded 31st August 1945 at B.80 (Volkel), Netherlands, to become 4 Squadron.

Reformed 10th May 1946 at Honiley.

RAL (5.46– .49)	*Mosquito III, XIX TA351, NF.30 MM790 RAL; Vampire F.1 TG348 RAL-P.*
NR (.49–4.51)	*Vampire F.1 TG374 NR-K, FB.5 VZ336 NR-L; Harvard IIB KF160 NR-D.*
Nil (4.51–3.57)	*Vampire FB.5 WA360 H; Meteor T.7 WA682.*

Disbanded 10th March 1957 at Honiley.

606 SQUADRON
The Squadron never formed although the code BG was allocated for the period April to September 1939.

607 (COUNTY OF DURHAM) SQUADRON
Formed 17th March 1930 at Usworth.

Nil (3.30–3.39)	*Wapiti IIA K1139; Demon K2906; Gladiator I K7992.*
LW (3.39–9.39)	*Gladiator I K6137.*
AF (9.39–5.45)	*Gladiator I K6147; Hurricane I P2617, IIB HL880 AF-B, IIE BE401, IIC HV652; Spitfire VC LZ975, VIII JF809 AF-N.*
Also used	*Avro 504N K1806; Hart K2437; Tutor K3344; Magister P2504; Blenheim IV R3777; Harvard IIB FE593.*

Disbanded 19th August 1945 at Mingaladon, Burma.

Reformed 10th May 1946 at Ouston.

RAN (6.46– .49)	*Spitfire XIV TZ116 RAN-D, F.22 PK384 RAN-F; Harvard IIB KF373 RAN-A.*
LA (.49–4.51)	*Spitfire F.22 PK384 LA-F; Harvard IIB KF193 LA-C.*
Nil (4.51–3.57)	*Vampire FB.5 VZ861 J, FB.9 WR266 B; Meteor T.7 WH225 N.*

Disbanded 10th March 1957 at Ouston.

608 (NORTH RIDING) SQUADRON
Formed 17th March 1930 at Thornaby.

Nil (3.30–10.38)	*Wapiti IIA K1154; Demon K2844.*
PG (10.38–9.39)	*Demon K8209; Anson I N5361 PG-J.*
UL (9.39– .42)	*Anson I N5207 UL-P; Botha I L6239 UL-Z; Blenheim I L4822, IV V5682 UL-B; Hudson V AM642 UL-R.*
Nil (.42–7.44)	*Hudson V AM571 A, VI FK444 P, III T9403, IIIA FK801 J.*
Also used	*Avro 504N K1243; Moth K1833; Hart K3052; Tutor K3397.*

Disbanded 22nd July 1944 at Pomigliano, Italy.

Reformed 1st August 1944 at Downham Market.

6T	*Mosquito B.20 KB358 6T-L, B.25 KB438 6T-F, XVI RV360 6T-F.*

Disbanded 24th August 1945 at Downham Market.

Reformed 10th May 1946 at Thornaby.

RAO (5.46– .49)	*Mosquito NF.30 NT373 RAO-A, III VP351 RAO-P; Oxford I NM409 RAO-M; Spitfire F.22 PK325 RAO-F; Harvard IIB FT457 RAO-N.*
6T (.49–4.51)	*Spitfire F.22 PK340 6T-3; Harvard IIB FT457 6T-N; Vampire F.1 TG377, F.3 VF319 6T-E; Meteor T.7 WA672 6T-H; Oxford I NM409 6T-M.*

Nil (4.51–3.57)	*Vampire F.3 VV206 J, FB.5 VV609 E, FB.9 WX211 G; Meteor T.7 WH223 P.*
Also used	*Tiger Moth II DE565; Vampire T.11 XD550.*

Disbanded 10th March 1957 at Thornaby.

609 (WEST RIDING) SQUADRON
Formed 10th February 1936 at Yeadon.

Nil (2.36–9.39)	*Hart K3053; Hind K6848; Spitfire I L1058.*
BL	*Allocated for the period April to September 1939 but no evidence of use.*
PR (9.39–9.45)	*Spitfire I R6915 PR-U, IIA P7540, VB AA766 PR-J; Typhoon IA R7581, IB JP851 PR-Q.*
Also used	*Tutor K3053; Tiger Moth II DE254; Auster III MT393.*

Disbanded 15th September 1945 at B.116 (Wunstorf), Germany.

Reformed 10th May 1946 at Church Fenton.

RAP (5.46– .49)	*Mosquito XIX TA341, NF.30 NT422 RAP-D, III VA883 RAP-U; Oxford I MP449 RAP-Y; Spitfire XVI TB294 RAP-N; Harvard IIB KF645 RAP-X.*
PR (.49–4.51)	*Spitfire XVIE TB294 PR-N; Harvard IIB KF374 PR-B.*
Nil (4.51–3.57)	*Meteor F.4 VW261, F.8 WA873 H, T.7 WA672 P.*

Disbanded 10th March 1957 at Church Fenton.

610 (COUNTY OF CHESTER) SQUADRON
Formed 10th February 1936 at Hendon.

Nil (2.36–9.39)	*Hart K2424, Hart Trainer K5895; Hind K5400; Hurricane I L2121.*
JE	*Allocated for the period April to September 1939 but no evidence of use.*
DW (9.39–3.45)	*Hurricane I N2620; Spitfire I R6806 DW-N, IIA P7284, VB BL731 DW-J, VC EE745 DW-Y, XIV NH719 DW-R.*
Also used	*Avro 504N K1989; Tutor K3311; Battle N2107; Defiant I L7000; Master I N7570; Magister N3804; Tiger Moth II EM909; Auster IV MS951.*

Disbanded 3rd March 1945 at Warmwell.

Reformed 10th May 1946 at Hooton Park.

RAQ (5.46– .49)	*Spitfire XIV SM876, F.22 PK511 RAQ-N; Harvard IIB FT282 RAQ-Y.*
DW (.49–4.51)	*Spitfire F.22 PK568 DW-E; Harvard IIB FX410 DW-X.*
Nil (4.51-3.57)	*Meteor F.4 VT183, T.7 WA776 S, F.8 WH505 A.*

Disbanded 10th March 1957 at Hooton Park.

611 (WEST LANCASHIRE) SQUADRON
Formed 10th February 1936 at Hendon.

Nil (2.36–5.39)	*Hart K2966; Hind K5390.*
GZ (5.39–9.39)	*Spitfire I L1036 GZ-N.*
FY (9.39–8.45)	*Spitfire I L1038 FY-P, IIA P7774, VB BL636, LF.VB AR605, IX LZ951; Mustang IV KM132 FY-S, IVA KH675.*
Also used	*Tutor K3429; Battle N2101; Magister P2501; Tiger Moth II T8254; Auster III NJ771.*

Disbanded 15th August 1945 at Peterhead.

Reformed 10th May 1946 at Speke.

RAR (5.46– .49)	*Spitfire XIV RM924 RAR-K, F.22 PK520 RAR-M; Harvard IIB KF640 RAR-X.*
FY (.49–4.51)	*Spitfire F.22 PK650 FY-J; Harvard IIB KF640 FY-X.*
Nil (4.51–3.57)	*Meteor F.4 VW278 G, T.7 WA718 X, F.8 WH503 F.*

Disbanded 10th March 1957 at Hooton Park.

612 (COUNTY OF ABERDEEN) SQUADRON
Formed 1st June 1937 at Dyce.

Nil (6.37–7.39)	*Hector K8100; Hart Trainer K3753.*
DJ (7.39–9.39)	*Hector K8101; Anson I N5272 DJ-D.*

WL (9.39–8.43)	Anson I N5272 WL-F; Whitley V Z6475 WL-D, VII Z6961 WL-W; Wellington VIII HX575 WL-Z, X HE927.
Nil (8.43–7.44)	Wellington XII MP628 F, XIV HF190 J.
8W (7.44–7.45)	Wellington XIII NC420 8W-O, XIV ND130 8W-D.
Also used	Tutor K6106; Magister P6400.

Disbanded 9th July 1945 at Langham.

Reformed 10th May 1946 at Dyce.

RAS (5.46– .49)	Spitfire XIV RM901 RAS-F, XVI TE385 RAS-N; Harvard IIB FX283 RAS-S.
8W (.49–4.51)	Spitfire XVI TE400 8W-M; Harvard IIB FS881 8W-X; Vampire FB.5 VZ863 8W-K; Meteor T.7 WF837 8W-M.
Nil (4.51-3.57)	Harvard IIB KF475; Anson XII PH647 P; Vampire FB.5 WA402 A.

Disbanded 10th March 1957 at Dyce.

613 (CITY OF MANCHESTER) SQUADRON
Formed 1st March 1939 at Ringway.

ZR (3.39–6.42)	Hind K5406; Hector K8116 ZR-X; Lysander I R2578, II P1724 ZR-L, IIIA V9373 ZR-P; Tomahawk I BK853, IIA AH905, IIB AK105.
SY (6.42–8.45)	Mustang I AG520 SY-L; Mosquito VI LR366 SY-L.
Also used	Tutor K3412; Magister L8056; Vega Gull P5988; Master II AZ106; Oxford I T1390, II R6350; Proctor I P6174; Moth Minor X5116; Tiger Moth II DE507; Mosquito III HJ981.

Disbanded 7th August 1945 at A.75 (Cambrai-Epinoy), France, to become 69 Squadron.

Reformed 10th May 1946 at Ringway.

RAT (5.46– .49)	Spitfire XIV MV247 RAT-A, F.22 PK563 RAT-Z; Harvard IIB FT409 RAT-1; Vampire F.1 TG389 RAT-G.
Q3 (.49–4.51)	Spitfire F.22 PK543 Q3-F; Harvard IIB FX219 Q3-3; Vampire FB.5 VV616 Q3-K; Meteor T.7 WF778 Q3-5.
Nil (4.51–3.57)	Vampire FB.5 WA107, FB.9 WR257; Meteor T.7 WF778 S.

Disbanded 10th March 1957 at Ringway.

614 (COUNTY OF GLAMORGAN) SQUADRON
Formed 1st June 1937 at Pengam Moors.

Nil (6.37–4.39)	Hind K5478; Hector K9727.
YX (4.39– .40)	Hector K9727 YX; Lysander II P1677, III T1461, IIIA V9588.
LJ (.40–8.42)	Lysander III R9124 LJ-P; Blenheim I L1454 LJ-F, IV V5808 LJ-H.
Nil (8.42–2.44)	Blenheim V BA825 J.
Also used	Tutor K3360; Battle K9434; Magister R1834; Tiger Moth T8261; Moth Minor BK839.

Disbanded 25th January 1944 at Bo Rizzo, Italy.

Reformed 15th March 1944 en route to Celone, Italy, by renumbering 462 Squadron.

Halifax II JP275 N; Liberator VIII KH375; Mosquito IX LR442.

Disbanded 27th July 1945 at Amendola, Italy, to become 214 Squadron.

Reformed 10th May 1946 at Llandow.

RAU (5.46– .49)	Spitfire XVI TE120 RAU-B, F.22 PK320 RAU-I; Harvard IIB KF149 RAU-2; Meteor T.7 WA687 RAU-W.
7A (.49– .50)	Spitfire F.22 PK604 7A-E; Meteor T.7 VZ636 7A-V.
Nil (.50–3.57)	Vampire F.3 VT860 T, FB.5 WE837 D, FB.9 WR253 F; Meteor T.7 WG991 S.

Disbanded 10th March 1957 at Llandow.

614A SQUADRON
Formed 3rd October 1939 at Odiham from 'B' Flight of 614 Squadron.

LJ	Lysander.
LX	Lysander.
Note	614 Squadron aircraft carried the code LJ and those allocated to 225 Squadron used the code LX. Confusion has arisen because it was thought the code LX was also used by 614 Squadron, where in fact at least five aircraft transferred to 614A Squadron had used both codes during October 1939.

Disbanded 9th October 1939 at Odiham to become 225 Squadron.

615 (COUNTY OF SURREY) SQUADRON
Formed 1st June 1937 at Kenley.

Nil (6.37–11.38)	Audax K7381; Hector K7984.
RR (11.38–9.39)	Gauntlet II K7854 RR-K; Gladiator II N5581 RR-C.
KW (9.39–6.45)	Gladiator I K7938 KW-T, II N2304 KW-R; Hurricane I R4194 KW-P, X P5201, IIA Z2354 KW-I, IIB Z5054, IIC Z3070; Spitfire VC JL108, VIII MD324 KW-R.
Also used	Harvard I P5865; Magister N3906; Tiger Moth DG491.

Disbanded 10th June 1945 at Cuttack, India.

Reformed 10th June 1945 at Akyab, Burma, by renumbering 135 Squadron.

| KW | Thunderbolt II KL856 KW-D. |

Disbanded 25th September 1945 at Vizagapatam, India.

Reformed 10th May July 1946 at Biggin Hill.

RAV (7.46– .49)	Spitfire XIV SM829 RAV-U, F.21 LA192 RAV-C, F.22 PK569 RAV-S; Harvard IIB KF200 RAV-X.
V6 (.49–4.51)	Spitfire F.22 PK392 V6-H; Meteor F.4 VT102 V6-S; Harvard IIB FX205 V6-Y.
Nil (4.51–3.57)	Meteor F.4 VZ428 J, T.7 WF858 W, F.8 WH253 F.
Also used	Chipmunk T.10 WB703.

Disbanded 10th March 1957 at Biggin Hill.

616 (SOUTH YORKSHIRE) SQUADRON
Formed 1st November 1938 at Doncaster by renumbering 503 Squadron.

Nil (11.38–4.39)	Hind K6727; Gauntlet II K5364; Battle N2031; Hurricane I L2101.
QJ (4.39–7.41)	Battle N2031; Spitfire I X4330 QJ-G, IIA P7753 QJ-X.
YQ (7.41–8.45)	Spitfire IIB P8447, VA W3185, VB W3560, VI BS111 YQ-P, VII MB768 YQ-X, IX MJ107 YQ-B; Meteor F.1 EE219 YQ-D, F.3 EE243 YQ-F.
Also used	Tutor K3340; Oxford I P9022, II X7292; Magister L8151; Tiger Moth II DE481.

Disbanded 30th August 1945 at B.158 (Lübeck), Germany, to become 263 Squadron.

Reformed 10th May 1946 at Finningley.

RAW (7.46– .49)	Mosquito III LR518, NF.30 NT423 RAW-J; Oxford I NM749 RAW-3; Harvard IIB KF997 RAW-C; Meteor F.3 EE307 RAW-O.
YQ (.49–4.51)	Meteor F.3 EE393 YQ-J, F.4 RA429 YQ-H; Harvard IIB KF997 YQ-C.
Nil (4.51–3.57)	Meteor F.4 VZ413, T.7 VZ640, F.8 WH474 K.
Also used	Tiger Moth I NM121.

Disbanded 10th March 1957 at Worksop.

617 SQUADRON
| MZ | Allocated for the period April to September 1939. |

Formed 24th March 1943 at Scampton by redesignating 'X' Squadron.

AJ (3.43–6.43)	Lancaster III (Special) ED909/G AJ-P.
KC (6.43–4.51)	Lancaster I ED763 KC-Z, III JA894 KC-T, VII NX783 KC-G; Lincoln II RF531 KC-Z.
YZ (.45– .45)	Lancaster I (Special) PD114 YZ-B.
Nil (4.51–12.55)	Lincoln II SX958; Canberra B.2 WH706, B.6 WH946.
Also used	Mustang III HB837; Mosquito VI NT202; Tiger Moth II T6306.

Disbanded 15th December 1955 at Binbrook.

Reformed 1st May 1958 at Scampton.

Vulcan B.1 XH483, B.2 XL318.

Disbanded 31st December 1981 at Scampton.

Reformed 1st January 1983 at Marham.

| Nil (1.83–   ) | Tornado GR.1 ZA608 Z, GR.1(T) ZA601 M. |
| AJ (   ) | Tornado GR.1A ZA458 AJ-A, GR.1B, GR.1T ZA411 AJ-S. |

Current 1st April 1998 at Lossiemouth.

618 SQUADRON
| BN | Allocated for the period April to September 1939. |

Formed 26th March 1943 at Skitten by merging elements of 105 and 139 Squadrons.

Mosquito IV DZ520/G A; Beaufighter II R2401; Mosquito VI PZ280, XVI NS572, XVIII MM425; Barracuda II LS704; Anson I LT188.

Disbanded 21st July 1945 at Narromine, Australia.

619 SQUADRON
| KV | Allocated for the period April to September 1939. |

Formed 18th April 1943 at Woodhall Spa by from an element of 97 Squadron.

| PG | Lancaster I PD441 PG-B, III LM737 PG-A. |
| Also used | Oxford I V4042, II V3522. |

Disbanded 18th July 1945 at Skellingthorpe.

620 SQUADRON
| TF | Allocated for the period April to September 1939. |

Formed 17th June 1943 at Chedburgh from 'C' Flight of 214 Squadron.

QS (6.43–9.46)	Stirling III EF197 QS-Z, IV LJ566 QS-L; Halifax VII PP365 QS-H.
D4 (3.44–9.46)	Stirling IV LJ566 D4-Y; Halifax VII NA458 D4-A.
Also used	Stirling I W7465; Halifax III MZ682, IX RT769; Dakota III KG344, IV KJ939; Horsa I LH403.

Disbanded 1st September 1946 at Aqir, Palestine, to become 113 Squadron.

621 SQUADRON
| ER | Allocated for the period April to September 1939. |

Formed 12th September 1943 at Port Reitz, Kenya.

Wellington XIII JA107 E, XIV NC772 A; Warwick V LM840 Z; Lancaster III RF323 C.

A Tornado GR.1B of No 617 Squadron based at Lossiemouth.

Disbanded 1st September 1946 at Ein Shemar, Palestine, to become 18 Squadron.

622 SQUADRON

UF	Allocated for the period April to September 1939.

Formed 10th August 1943 at Mildenhall from 'C' Fight of 15 Squadron.

GI	Stirling III EF123 GI-A; Lancaster I HK615 GI-Z, III NE146/G GI-F.
Also used	Spitfire VB BL957.

Disbanded 15th August 1945 at Mildenhall.

Reformed 1st November 1950 at Blackbushe.

Valetta C.1 VW141; Chipmunk T.10 WD302.

Disbanded 30th September 1953 at Blackbushe.

623 SQUADRON

ON	Allocated for the period April to September 1939.

Formed 10th August 1943 at Downham Market by redesignating an element of 218 Squadron.

IC	Stirling III LK387 IC-P.

Disbanded 6th December 1943 at Downham Market.

624 SQUADRON

KK	Allocated for the period April to September 1939.

Formed 22nd September 1943 at Blida, Algeria, by redesignating and element of 1575 (Special Duties) Flight.

Ventura II AE948; Halifax II JP205 K, V EB154 A; Stirling IV LK184 Y.

Disbanded 5th September 1944 at Blida, Algeria.

Reformed 28th December 1944 at Grottaglie, Italy.

Walrus I W2797, II Z1756.

Disbanded 30th November 1945 at Littorio, Italy.

625 SQUADRON

NU	Allocated for the period April to September 1939.

Formed 1st October 1943 at Kelstern from 'C' Flight of 100 Squadron.

CF	Lancaster I ME780 CF-A, III DV194 CF-F.

Disbanded 7th October 1945 at Scampton.

626 SQUADRON

SG	Allocated for the period April to September 1939.

Formed 7th November 1943 at Wickenby from 'C' Flight of 12 Squadron.

UM	Lancaster I NF907 UM-K2, III LM362 UM-A2.

Disbanded 14th October 1945 at Wickenby.

627 SQUADRON

WX	Allocated for the period April to September 1939.

Formed 12th November 1943 at Oakington by redesignating an element of 139 Squadron.

AZ	Mosquito IV DZ462 AZ-N, IX ML906, Mosquito XVI ML935 AZ-A, B.20 KB267 AZ-E, B.25 KB533 AZ-N.

Disbanded 30th September 1945 at Woodhall Spa to become 109 Squadron.

628 SQUADRON

ES	Allocated for the period April to September 1939.

Formed 21st March 1944 at Red Hills Lake, Madras, India, from 'B' Flight of 357 Squadron.

Catalina IB FP225 T, IVB JX347 V.

Disbanded 1st October 1944 at Red Hills Lake.

629 SQUADRON

The Squadron never formed although the code LQ was allocated for the period April to September 1939.

630 SQUADRON

BO	Allocated for the period April to September 1939.

Formed 15th November 1943 at East Kirby from 'B' Flight of 57 Squadron.

LE	Lancaster I ME796 LE-S, III ME312/G LE-A.

Disbanded 18th July 1945 at East Kirby.

631 SQUADRON

XX	Allocated for the period April to September 1939.

Formed 1st December 1943 at Towyn by merging 1605 (Target Towing) and 1628 (Anti-Aircraft Co-operation) Flights.

6D	Henley III L3337; Tiger Moth II R4750; Hurricane IIC LF580, IV LE507; Vengeance IV HB333; Martinet I HN884 6D-K; Spitfire VB AA930 6D-H, XVI TE328 6D-Z; Vampire F.1 TG447; Harvard IIB KF627.

Disbanded 11th February 1949 at Llanbedr to become 20 Squadron.

632 SQUADRON

The Squadron never formed although the code LO was allocated for the period April to September 1939.

635 SQUADRON

NB	Allocated for the period April to September 1939.

Formed 20th March 1944 at Downham Market from 'B' Flight of 35 Squadron.

F2	Lancaster II DS682, III PB979 F2-F, VI ND673 F2-V.

Disbanded 1st September 1945 at Downham Market.

636 SQUADRON

The Squadron never formed although the code VZ was allocated for the period April to September 1939.

637 SQUADRON

The Squadron never formed although the code UK was allocated for the period April to September 1939.

638 SQUADRON

The Squadron never formed although the code PZ was allocated for the period April to September 1939.

639 SQUADRON

KX	Allocated for the period April to September 1939.

Formed 1st December 1943 at Cleave by merging 1602, 1603 and 1604 (Target Towing) Flights.

Henley III L3247; Hurricane IV LD976; Martinet I EM576; Tiger Moth II T8192.

Disbanded 30th April 1945 at Cleave.

640 SQUADRON

XA	Allocated for the period April to September 1939.

Formed 7th January 1944 at Leconfield from 'C' Flight of 158 Squadron.

C8   *Halifax III MZ856 C8-S, VI RG604 C8-Z.*

Disbanded 7th May 1945 at Leconfield.

641 SQUADRON
The Squadron never formed although the code EU was allocated for the period April to September 1939.

642 SQUADRON
The Squadron never formed although the code MQ was allocated for the period April to September 1939.

643 SQUADRON
The Squadron never formed although the code QZ was allocated for the period April to September 1939.

644 SQUADRON
FE   *Allocated for the period April to September 1939.*

Formed 23rd February 1944 at Tarrant Rushton by redesignating an element of 298 Squadron.

2P (2.44 –9.46)	*Halifax V LL345 2P-F, III MZ975 2P-U, VII NA348 2P-J.*
9U (2.44–9.46)	*Halifax V LL328 9U-Y, III NA662 9U-Z, VII PN306 9U-K.*
Also used	*Horsa II RZ776.*

Disbanded 1st September 1946 at Qastina, Palestine, to become 47 Squadron.

645 SQUADRON
The Squadron never formed although the code KF was allocated for the period April to September 1939.

646 SQUADRON
The Squadron never formed although the code YG was allocated for the period April to September 1939.

647 SQUADRON
The Squadron never formed although the code ZS was allocated for the period April to September 1939.

648 SQUADRON
The Squadron never formed although the code YT was allocated for the period April to September 1939.

649 SQUADRON
The Squadron never formed although the code HA was allocated for the period April to September 1939.

650 SQUADRON
MA   *Allocated for the period April to September 1939.*

Formed 1st December 1943 at Cark by merging 1614 (Target Towing) Flight and 'D' Flight of 289 Squadron.

T7	*Martinet I HP175 T7-M; Hurricane IV LE396; Tiger Moth I NL991, II N6728.*

Disbanded 26th June 1945 at Bodorgan.

651 SQUADRON
Formed 1st August 1941 at Old Sarum by redesignating 'D' Flight. Incorporated 1907, 1908, 1909 and 1910 Flights. See individual Flights for details.

Nil (8.41– .44)	*Tiger Moth II DE710; Taylorcraft Plus C ES957; Taylorcraft Plus D X7534; Cub Coupe BT441; Voyager X5324; Vigilant IA BZ100; Auster I LB278, III NJ917, IV MT306.*
MA (.44–. 45)	*(HQ Flight) Auster IV.*
MB (.44– .45)	*('A' Flight) Auster IV.*
MC (.44– .45)	*('B' Flight) Auster IV.*
MD (.44– .45)	*('C' Flight) Auster IV.*
Nil (.45–11.55)	*Auster V RT566, VI TW580.*

Disbanded 1st November 1955 at Ismailia, Egypt.

Reformed 1st November 1955 at Middle Wallop by renumbering 657 Squadron. Incorporated 1903, 1906 and 1913 Flights. See individual Flights for details.

Sycamore HC.11 WT923; Auster VI WJ370, T.7 WE593; Chipmunk T.10 WG486.

Transferred 1st September 1957 at Middle Wallop to the Army to become 3, 6 and 13 Flights, Army Air Corps.

652 SQUADRON
Formed 1st May 1942 at Old Sarum.

Nil (5.42– .45)	*Tiger Moth II DE268; Taylorcraft Plus C HH985; Anson I N9536; Auster I LB327, III MZ133, IV MT104; Fi 156 VM897.*
XM (.45–)	*Auster V RT484, VI VF486 XM-P.*
Nil (–9.57)	*Auster VI VF559, T.7 WE569, AOP.9 WZ721; Chipmunk T.10 WB716.*

Transferred 1st September 1957 at Detmold, Germany, to the Army to become 1, 4, 5 and 9 Flights, Army Air Corps.

653 SQUADRON
Formed 20th June 1942 at Old Sarum.

Tiger Moth I K4260, II N6581; Taylorcraft Plus C HH982; Auster I LB266, III MZ182, IV MT131, V MT367.

Disbanded 15th September 1945 at Hoya, Germany.

654 SQUADRON
Formed 15th July 1942 at Old Sarum. Incorporated 1906 and 1907 Flights. See individual Flights for details.

Nil (7.42– .44)	*Tiger Moth II DE635; Taylorcraft Plus D HH982; Auster I LB314, III NJ973, IV MT287, V NJ745.*
QA (.44–5 .45)	*(HQ Flight) Auster IV, Auster V.*
QB (.44–5 .45)	*('A' Flight) Auster IV, Auster V.*
QC (.44–5 .45)	*('B' Flight) Auster IV, Auster V.*
QD (.44–5 .45)	*('C' Flight) Auster IV, Auster V.*
Nil (5.45–6.47)	*Auster V.*

Disbanded 24th June 1947 at Campoformido, Italy.

655 SQUADRON
Formed 30th November 1942 at Old Sarum.

Nil (11.42– .44)	*Tiger Moth II T6963; Auster I LB290, III MZ170.*
PA (.44–8.45)	*(HQ Flight) Auster IV, V.*
PB (.44–8.45)	*('A' Flight) Auster IV, V.*
PC (.44–8.45)	*('B' Flight) Auster IV, V.*
PD (.44–8.45)	*('C' Flight) Auster IV, V.*
Also used	*Auster IV MT244.*

Disbanded 31st August 1945 at Ronchi, Italy.

656 SQUADRON
Formed 31st December 1942 at Westley.

Tiger Moth II T6799; Auster I LB370, III MZ196, IV MT239, V NJ739.

Disbanded 15th January 1947 at Kuala Lumpur, Malaya, to become 1914 (Air Observation Post) Flight.

Reformed 29th June 1948 at Sembawang, Malaya, by redesignating 1914 (Air Observation Post) Flight.

Auster V TJ215, AOP.6 TW641, T.7 WE557, AOP.9 WZ665.

Transferred 1st September 1957 at Kuala Lumpur to the Army to become 2, 7, 11 and 14 Flights, Army Air Corps.

657 SQUADRON
Formed 31st January 1943 at Ouston. Incorporated 1900, 1901, 1903 1906, 1912 and 1913 Flights at various times. See individual Flights for details.

Nil (1.43– .45)	*Tiger Moth II T5364; Auster I LB283, III MZ228, IV MT185.*
TS (.45–1.47)	*Auster V TJ672 TS-D2, VI VF661, T.7 WE598; Hoverfly II KN840 TS-L; Sycamore HC.11 WT924; Chipmunk T.10 WK549.*

Disbanded 1st November 1955 at Middle Wallop to become 651 Squadron.

658 SQUADRON
Formed 30th April 1943 at Old Sarum.

Tiger Moth II T7416; Auster III NX534, IV MT134, V MT363.

Disbanded 15th October 1946 at Hakimpet, India.

659 SQUADRON
Formed 30th April 1943 at Firbeck.

Tiger Moth II T6859; Auster III NK113, IV MT171, V RT470.

Disbanded 14th August 1947 at Lahore, India.

660 SQUADRON
Formed 31st July 1943 at Old Sarum.

Nil (7.43–8.45)   *Auster III NX500, IV MS976, V TJ352.*
BG (8.45–4.46)   *Auster IV MT115 BG-G, V RT480.*

Disbanded 31st May 1946 at Kiel/Holtenau, Germany.

661 SQUADRON
Formed 31st August 1943 at Old Sarum.

Nil (8.43–8.44)   *Tiger Moth II DE319; Auster III MZ237.*
OE (8.44–.45)   *Auster III MZ228, IV MT127.*
Nil (.45–10.45)   *Auster IV MT122, V NJ695.*

Disbanded 31st October 1945 at Ghent, Belgium.

Reformed 1st May 1949 at Kenley, incorporating 1957, 1958, 1959, 1960 and 1961 Flights.

See individual Flights for details.

Disbanded 10th March 1957 at Kenley.

662 SQUADRON
Formed 30th September 1943 at Old Sarum.

Tiger Moth II DE480; Auster III MZ179, IV MT190, V NJ725.

Disbanded 15th December 1945 at B.58 (Melsbroek), Belgium.

Reformed 1st February 1949 at Colerne, incorporating 1956, 1962 and 1963 Flights.

See individual Flights for details.

Disbanded 10th March 1957 at Colerne.

663 SQUADRON
Formed 14th August 1944 at San Basilio, Italy.

Auster III MZ117, Auster IV MT300, V RT461.

Disbanded 29th October 1946 en route to the United Kingdom.

Reformed 1st July 1949 at Hooton Park comprising 1951, 1952, 1953, 1954 and 1955 Flights.

See individual Flights for details.

Disbanded 10th March 1957 at Hooton Park.

664 SQUADRON
Formed 9th December 1944 at Andover.

AW   *Auster IV MT107, V RT515.*

Disbanded 31st May 1946 at Rostrup, Germany.

Reformed 1st September 1949 at Hucknall comprising 1964, 1965, 1969 and 1970 Flights.

See individual Flights for details.
Also used   *Chipmunk T.10 WD299.*

Disbanded 10th March 1957 at Hucknall.

665 SQUADRON
Formed 22nd January 1945 at Andover.

Auster V TJ202.

Disbanded 10th July 1945 at Appeldorn, Holland.

666 SQUADRON
Formed 5th March 1945 at Andover.

Auster V TW462.

Disbanded 30th September 1945 at Appeldorn, Holland.

Reformed 1st May 1949 at Perth comprising 1966, 1967 and 1968 Flights.

See individual Flights for details

Disbanded 10th March 1957 at Perth.

667 SQUADRON
Formed 1st December 1943 at Gosport by merging 1622 and 1631 (Anti-Aircraft Co-operation) Flights.

U4   *Defiant TT.I N3431 U4-J; Hurricane I N2344; Barracuda II BV725; Oxford I HN168, II P8981: Vengeance IV HB529 U4-E; Spitfire XVI TE283 U4-Y; Tiger Moth II T6549.*

Disbanded 20th December 1945 at Gosport.

668 SQUADRON
Formed 16th November 1944 at Calcutta, India.

Tiger Moth II EM750; Hadrian.

Disbanded 10th November 1945 at Fatehjang, India.

669 SQUADRON
Formed 16th November 1944 at Bikram, India.

No aircraft allocated.

Disbanded 31st December 1944 at Bikram, India, to become 671 Squadron.

Reformed 1st January 1945 at Basal, India.

Tiger Moth I NL947; II EM859; Hadrian II FR588.

Disbanded 10th November 1945 at Fatehjang, India.

670 SQUADRON
Formed 30th December 1944 at Fatehjang, India.

Tiger Moth II EM948; Hadrian II KH902.

Disbanded 1st July 1946 at Chaklala, India.

671 SQUADRON
Formed 1st January 1945 at Bikram, India, by redesignating 669 Squadron.

Tiger Moth I NL968, II EM855; Hadrian.

Disbanded 25th October 1945 at Kargi Road, India.

672 SQUADRON
Formed 21st January 1945 at Bikram, India.

Tiger Moth I NL948, II DG485; Hadrian II FR678; Harvard IIB FE703.

Disbanded 1st July 1946 at Chaklala, India.

673 SQUADRON
Formed 27th January 1945 at Bikram, India.

Tiger Moth II; Hadrian II FR736; Auster III NJ803.

Disbanded 25th October 1945 at Kargi Road, India.

679 SQUADRON
Formed 1st December 1943 at Ipswich by merging 1616 (Target Towing) and 1627 (Anti-Aircraft Co-operation) Flights.

3M   *Henley III L3286; Lysander II R2639; Martinet I EM413 3M-S; Hurricane IV KZ708 3M-H; Barracuda II DR154; Vengeance IV FD315; Tiger Moth II DE164.*

Disbanded 26th June 1945 at Ipswich.

680 SQUADRON
Formed 1st February 1943 at LG219, Western Desert, by redesignating 2 Photographic Reconnaissance Unit.

Spitfire IV BR427, VI BS133; Electra AX701; Hurricane X AG153; IIB Z5132, IIC HV295; Spitfire XI EN412; Baltimore IIIA FA372, V FW525; Mosquito IX LR444, XVI MM297 W, PR.34 RG316; Argus II FS658.

Disbanded 1st September 1946 at Ein Shemar, Palestine, to become 13 Squadron.

681 SQUADRON

Formed 25th January 1943 at Dum-Dum, India, by redesignating 3 Photographic Reconnaissance Unit.

B-25 Mitchell MA956; Hurricane IIB AP891 N; Spitfire IV BP935 Y; Mosquito II DZ697 J, IX LR440 V; Spitfire XI PL781 F, XIX PS918 Z; Oxford II AB316.

Disbanded 1st August 1946 at Palam, India, to become 34 Squadron.

682 SQUADRON

Formed 1st February 1943 at Maison Blanche, Algeria, by redesignating 4 Photographic Reconnaissance Unit.

Spitfire IV BR421, XI PL864; Mosquito IV DZ549, VI HJ672 A; Spitfire XIX RM645 I.

Disbanded 14th September 1945 at San Severo, Italy.

683 SQUADRON

Formed 8th February 1943 at Luqa, Malta, from 'B' Flight of 69 Squadron.

Spitfire IV BS496, XI MB772; Mosquito III RR283, VI HJ672 A, XVI NS514; Spitfire XIX RM626.

Disbanded 21st September 1945 at San Severo, Italy.

Reformed 1st August 1950 at Fayid, Egypt.

Lancaster PR.1 RA626 S; Valetta C.1 VX498.

Disbanded 30th November 1953 at Habbaniya, Iraq.

684 SQUADRON

Formed 29th September 1943 at Dum-Dum, India, by redesignating an element of 681 Squadron.

B-25 Mitchell MA956 E; Mosquito VI HJ760 Y, IX LR481 M, XVI NS497 J, PR.34 RG249 U; Beaufighter VI EL364, X RD746 B; Spitfire XIX PM510; Harvard IIB FE476.

Disbanded 1st September 1946 at Seletar, Malaya, to become 81 Squadron.

691 SQUADRON

Formed 1st December 1943 at Roborough by redesignating 1623 (Anti-Aircraft Co-operation) Flight.

5S	*Hurricane I P2575; Defiant I I.III N1728 5S-G; Oxford I PH456 5S-O; Barracuda II DR190; Hurricane IIC LF638; Vengeance IV FD193 5S-R; Martinet I PW981 5S-J; Spitfire VB BL258, XVI TB759 5S-A; Harvard IIB FX222; Tiger Moth II T8192.*

Disbanded 11th February 1949 at Chivenor to become 17 Squadron.

692 SQUADRON

Formed 1st January 1944 at Graveley.

P3	*Mosquito IV DZ637 P3-C, XVI PF392 P3-R.*

Disbanded 20th September 1945 at Gransden Lodge.

695 SQUADRON

Formed 1st December 1943 at Bircham Newton by merging 1611 and 1612 (Target Towing) Flights.

4M	*Henley III L3259; Martinet I PX126 4M-B; Hurricane IV LD567; Spitfire VB AR378; Tiger Moth II N6540; Vengeance IV HB478 4M-W; Spitfire XVI SM254 4M-U; Oxford I PH458 4M-C; Harvard IIB KF331 4M-Q; Beaufighter X RD778 4M-B.*

Disbanded 11th February 1949 at Horsham St Faith to become 34 Squadron.

1435 SQUADRON

Formed 2nd August 1942 at Luqa, Malta, by redesignating 1435 (Fighter) Flight.

V	*Spitfire IV BR662, VB EP436 V-S, VC JK376 V-H, VIII JF419, IX JL252 V-M.*

Also used   *Bf 109G AX*

Disbanded 9th May 1945 at Gragnano, Italy.

800 SQUADRON, FAA

Formed 3rd April 1933 at Netheravon by merging 402 and 404 (Fleet Fighter) Flights, FAA.

Nimrod I S1619 206, II K3654; Osprey I K2779 208, IV K5744; Skua II L2876; Roc I L3061.

Officially taken over by the Admiralty on 24th May 1939 at Worthy Down.

801 SQUADRON, FAA

Formed 3rd April 1933 at Netheravon by redesignating 401 (Fleet Fighter) Flight, FAA.

Flycatcher N9938 512; Nimrod I K2826 521, II K4620 136; Osprey I K2779, III K3623 235, IV K5757; Tutor K3222; Sea Gladiator N5502 135; Skua II L2927.

Disbanded 24th May 1939 at Donibristle to become 769 Squadron.

802 SQUADRON, FAA

Formed 3rd April 1933 aboard HMS *Glorious* by merging 408 and 409 (Fleet Fighter) Flights, FAA.

Nimrod I S1579 571, II K3656; Osprey I K2783, III K3643 549, III Seaplane K3644 590.

Officially taken over by the Admiralty on 24th May 1939 at Dekheila, Egypt.

803 SQUADRON, FAA

Formed 3rd April 1933 at Netheravon by redesignating 405 (Fleet Fighter) Flight, FAA.

Osprey I K2782 288.

Disbanded 1st April 1937 at Colombo, Ceylon.

Reformed 21st November 1938 at Worthy Down from 'B' Flight, 800 Squadron, FAA.

Osprey I K2780; Nimrod I K2838, II; Skua II L2875; Roc I L3063.

Officially taken over by the Admiralty on 24th May 1939 aboard HMS *Ark Royal*.

810 SQUADRON, FAA

Formed 3rd April 1933 at Gosport by merging 463 and 464 (Fleet Torpedo) Flights, FAA.

Dart N9823 02; Ripon S1662 08; Baffin K4073 03; Shark II K8486 531; Swordfish I K8841 534.

Officially taken over by the Admiralty on 24th May 1939 aboard HMS *Ark Royal*.

811 SQUADRON, FAA

Formed 3rd April 1933 at Gosport by merging 465 and 466 (Fleet Torpedo) Flights, FAA.

Ripon II S1563 15; Baffin S1266 614; Tutor K3339; Swordfish I K8440 609.

Disbanded 24th May 1939 at Donibristle and merged with 822 Squadron, FAA to become 767 Squadron, FAA.

812 SQUADRON, FAA

Formed 3rd April 1933 aboard HMS *Glorious* by merging 461 and 462 (Fleet Torpedo) Flights, FAA.

Ripon II S1364 61, IIA S1424 72, IIC K2884; Baffin K3548 71; Swordfish I K5950 63.

Officially taken over by the Admiralty on 24th May 1939 at Hal Far, Malta.

813 SQUADRON, FAA

Formed 18th January 1937 at Gosport.

Swordfish I K8396 587.

Officially taken over by the Admiralty on 24th May 1939 aboard HMS *Eagle*.

814 SQUADRON, FAA
Formed 1st December 1938 at Southampton.

Swordfish I L9775 705.

Officially taken over by the Admiralty on 24th May 1939 at Southampton.

820 SQUADRON, FAA
Formed 3rd April 1933 at Gosport by merging 450 and half of 445 (Fleet Spotter Reconnaissance) Flights, FAA.

Fairey IIIF S1546 741; Seal K3521; Shark I K4350, II K8455 659; Baffin S1553 45; Swordfish I K8860 658.

Officially taken over by the Admiralty on 24th May 1939 aboard HMS *Ark Royal*.

821 SQUADRON, FAA
Formed 3rd April 1933 at Gosport by merging 446 and half of 445 (Fleet Spotter Reconnaissance) Flights, FAA.

Fairey IIIF S1189 726; Seal K4208 730; Shark II K5619 682; Swordfish I L2723 679.

Officially taken over by the Admiralty on 24th May 1939 at Evanton.

822 SQUADRON, FAA
Formed 3rd April 1933 at Netheravon by merging 442 and 449 (Fleet Torpedo Reconnaissance) Flights, FAA.

Fairey IIIF S1785 705; Seal K3481 912; Shark II K5667 902; Swordfish I K6009 912.

Disbanded 24th May 1939 at Donibristle and merged with 811 Squadron, FAA to become 767 Squadron, FAA.

823 SQUADRON, FAA
Formed 3rd April 1933 aboard HMS *Glorious* by merging 441 and 448 Fleet (Spotter Reconnaissance) Flights, FAA.

Fairey IIIF S1346 831; Seal K3519 804; Swordfish I K5967 812.

Officially taken over by the Admiralty on 24th May 1939 at Hal Far, Malta.

824 SQUADRON, FAA
Formed 3rd April 1933 at Gosport by redesignating 464 (Fleet Torpedo) Flight, FAA.

Fairey IIIF S1476 871.

Disbanded 8th October 1934 aboard HMS *Eagle* to become 825 Squadron, FAA.

Reformed 8th October 1935 at Upavon.

Seal K4216 873; Swordfish I K8386 945.

Officially taken over by the Admiralty on 24th May 1939 aboard HMS *Eagle*.

825 SQUADRON, FAA
Formed 8th October 1935 aboard HMS *Eagle* by renumbering 824 Squadron, FAA.

Fairey IIIF S1258 838; Swordfish I K8869 889.

Officially taken over by the Admiralty on 24th May 1939 at Dekheila, Egypt.

SQUADRON CONVERSION FLIGHTS – see Conversion Flights

STAFF NAVIGATORS SCHOOL (MIDDLE EAST)
Formed 15th July 1944 at Gianaclis, Egypt.

Ventura V JS898; Wellington XIII JA539.

Disbanded 30th November 1945 at Ein Shemer, Palestine.

STAFF PILOT TRAINING UNIT
Formed 17th March 1942 at Cark.

Anson I N9645 73; Lysander III T1563; Master I N8047, II AZ695, III W8964.

Disbanded 14th November 1942 at Cark.

Reformed 12th March 1943 at Cark.

Anson I EF933 A3; Magister L8213; Tiger Moth II DE661; Martinet I HN865.

Disbanded 31st December 1945 at Cark.

STANDARDS SQUADRON – see Central Flying School

STANDARDS WING – see Central Flying School

STATION AND TARGET TOWING FLIGHT, SELETAR
Formed 1st June 1951 at Seletar, Singapore, by merging the Towed Target Flight, Seletar and the Station Flight, Seletar.

Beaufighter X; Hornet F.3; Valetta C.1; Harvard IIB; Anson XIX.

Disbanded 1st May 1953 at Seletar to become the Base and Target Towing Flight, Royal Air Force Maintenance Base (Far East), Seletar.

STATION FLIGHTS
Code letters were allocated to Station Flights in September 1945. Only a few of the codes were ever taken up and displayed.

Abingdon	T5	
Acaster Malbis	3T	
Acklington	7I	– Oxford; Martinet TT.I.
Aldergrove	7X	
Ballykelly	8U	
Banff	P6	
Bardney	7U	
Benson	5I	– Anson XI NL183 5I-M, XII PH654 5I-D.
Bentwaters	YB	
Binbrook	CG	
Blackbushe	N9	
Bramcote	TQ	
Brawdy	2H	
Breighton	JQ	
Broadwell	GX	
Buckeburg	N9	
Carew Cheriton	TCE	
	TCW	
Castle Camps	W5	
Celle	WL	– Vampire FB.5 WA195 WL.
Chedburgh	VW	
Chilbolton	IW	
Chivenor	5H	
Colerne	RQ	
Coningsby	KI	
Cosford	TCO	– Anson I EG190 TCO; Tiger Moth II NL760.
Cottesmore	6V	
Cranwell	TCN	– Proctor III HM302 TCN-B.
	FKS	– Proctor IV NP298 FKS-B; Oxford I HN839 FKS-A; Tiger Moth II EM749 FKS-A.
Dallachy	Y5	
Desborough	IE	
Doncaster	SP	
Down Ampney	YO	
Dunsfold	IY	
Duxford	GJ	
Dyce	TU	
Earls Colne	RG	
East Kirby	HV	
Elsham Wolds	LM	
Elvington	EE	
Exeter	VP	
Faldingworth	UN	
Feltwell	LC	
Filton	RR	
Finningley	JV	
Fiskerton	MC	
Foulsham	2N	
Full Sutton	HP	
Gibraltar	5D	
Glatton	MX	
Gransden Lodge	HL	
Graveley	WZ	
Great Dunmow	AN	– Oxford I PH117 AN-P.
Grimsetter	JD	

Halton	Nil	– Oxford I T1250; Auster V MT361; Dominie I HG731.
	THA	– Anson X NK932 THA-B, XII NL171 THA-A, XIX VM314 THA-C; Proctor III BV651 THA-F, IV LA589 THA-J; Tiger Moth II T6984 THA-L.
Hemswell	W3	
Hendon	RU	
Hethel	D6	
Holme-on-Spalding-Moor	BI	
Holmsley South	CC	
Hornchurch	THO	
Horsham St Faith	GD	– Oxford I PH486.
Kemble	DI	
Kenley	FC	
Kirmington	QP	
Kirton-in-Lindsey	VE	
Leeming	WD	
Lindholme	VF	– Oxford T1343 VF-A.
Linton-on-Ouse	MS	– Mosquito III TW117 MS-A; Hornet PX384 MS-K.
Little Staughton	CL	
Llanbedr	DS	
Locking	TLO	– Proctor I P6243 TLO-A; IV LZ804 TLO-A.
Lossiemouth	YU	
Ludford Magna	CY	
Lyneham	N7	
Manorbier	NA	
Manston	FR	
Marston Moor	P2	– Oxford T1103 P2.
Melbourne	T6	
Melton Mowbray	4L	
Mepal	LH	
Merryfield	O8	– Anson AX648 O8-5.
Methwold	SX	
Metheringham	YJ	
Mildenhall	FT	
Moreton-in-Marsh	WR	
Mowbray	4L	
Netheravon	YA	
North Killingholme	GQ	
North Luffenham	AJ	
Northolt	7G	
Oakington	DC	
Odiham	EC	– Proctor III LZ559 EC; Harvard IIB FS761 EC.
Pembroke Dock	6Q	
Pershore	GC	
Perth		– see the Wireless Development Unit and Special Duty Flight St Athan, Martlesham Heath and Christchurch.
Pocklington	K5	
Portreath	4T	
Predannack	LF	
Prestwick	SC	
Rivenhall	FW	
St Athan	TSA	– Proctor III HM351 TSA-A.
St Eval	2A	– Oxford II ED268 2A-C; Martinet I EM439 2A-J.
Sandtoft	OC	
Scampton	1C	– Oxford I LX431 1C-E; Anson XIX VM393 1C-G.
	YF	– Lancaster I ED909 YF-B; Tiger Moth BB790 YF-Z.
Shepherd's Grove	H9	
Silverstone	PI	
Skellingthorpe	G4	
Snaith	4W	
Spilsby	B6	
Stoney Cross	X2	
Stornoway	WT	
Stradishall	9F	– Oxford I PG968.
Sturgate	OS	
Sumburgh	VV	– Mosquito VI RS598 VV-Z.
Swanton Morley	QI	

Swinderby	CH	
Syerston	IA	
Tain	K9	
Talbenny	U2	
Tarrant Rushton	KS	
Tempsford	6B	
Thornaby	RJ	
Tibenham	C5	
Topcliffe	CP	
Tuddenham	CV	
Turnhouse	SU	– Sea Otter JM843 SU-E.
Upper Heyford	IV	– Anson NK954 IV-E; Oxford I NM798 IV.
Upwood	CS	– Oxford II LX527 CS.
Valley	IN	
Waddington	B7	
Warboys	E2	
Waterbeach	N8	
Westcott	E9	
West Malling	4K	– Oxford T1214 4K; Mosquito III VA893 4K; Meteor F.4 VT185.
Wick	FO	
Wickenby	E4	
Wing	G8	
Woodbridge	A9	
Woodhall Spa	B8	
Wrattling Common	3O	
Wymeswold	K8	
Wyton	B3	

STRAITS SETTLEMENTS VOLUNTEER AIR FORCE

Formed 25th March 1936 at Seletar, Singapore, with detached Flights at Penang, Kuala Lumpur and Ipoh.

Tutor K3462; Osprey K3915; Hart K4770; Audax K5143 3.

Disbanded August 1940 at Seletar to become the Malayan Volunteer Air Force.

STRATEGIC RECONNAISSANCE UNIT

No records for the Unit have been found. It is possible that, while 223 Squadron acted as a twin-engine bomber Operational Training Unit with Marylands at Shandur, Egypt, between May 1941 and January 1942, the title referred to the Squadron's operational reconnaissance Flight which operated between November 1941 to at least January 1942 from Fuka, El Gubbi, Timimi, Sidi Azeiz and LG 121.

Maryland I BS761, II AH342; Baltimore I AG697; II AG759.

STRIKE/ATTACK OPERATIONAL EVALUATION UNIT

Formed 5th October 1987 at Boscombe Down. Became an element of the Air Warfare Centre from April 1995.

Harrier T.4 XW267 SP, T.4A XW267 SA, GR.5 ZD328, GR.7 ZG501 E, T.10; Jaguar GR.1B XX748 GK, T.2A XX833 N, T.2B, GR.3; Tornado GR.1 ZD716 O, GR.1A ZG706 E, GR.1B ZA446 E.

Current 1st April 1998 at Boscombe Down.

STRIKE COMMAND AIR TO AIR MISSILE ESTABLISHMENT

Formed 1st May 1968 at Valley by redesignating the Fighter Command Missile Practice Camp.

Chipmunk T.10 WB586.

Disbanded (date unknown) at Valley.

STRIKE COMMAND BOMBING SCHOOL

Formed 1st May 1968 at Lindholme by redesignating the Bomber Command Bombing School.

Varsity T.1 WJ916 T; Hastings C.1A TG536; T.5 TG511.

Disbanded 1st January 1974 at Scampton and absorbed by 230 Operational Conversion Unit.

STRIKE COMMAND COMMUNICATION SQUADRON – see Southern Communication Squadron, later Strike Command Communication Squadron

STRIKE COMMAND DEVELOPMENT UNIT – see Bomber Command Development Unit, later Strike Command Development Unit

SUPERNUMERARY CAMEL FLIGHT – see 487 (Fighter) Flight

SUPREME COMMANDER'S HEADQUARTERS (AIR) COMMUNICATION SQUADRON
Formed 15th August 1947 at Palam, India, by redesignating the Air Headquarters India Communication Squadron.

Dakota III KG507, IV KK163; York I MW102.

Disbanded 17th December 1947 at Palam to become the Royal Air Force Communication Flight.

SUPREME HEADQUARTERS ALLIED EXPEDITIONARY FORCE (RAF) COMMUNICATION SQUADRON
Formed 15th October 1944 at Heston by redesignating the Allied Expeditionary Air Force Communication Squadron.

Vega Gull P5988; Oxford II W6592; Spitfire VB BM514; Mosquito II DZ271; Ventura I FN964; Proctor III HM320; Dominie I NF856; Dakota II TJ170; IV KJ994; Anson I MH181, X NK532, XI NK992, XII PH702; Auster IV MT340, V RT490.

Disbanded 31st July 1945 at Detmold, Germany.

SURVIVAL AND RESCUE TRAINING UNIT
Formed 23rd July 1945 at Calshot by redesignating the School of Air Sea Rescue.

7K   Sea Otter I JM770.

Disbanded 11th April 1949 at Thorney Island.

SWANSEA UNIVERSITY AIR SQUADRON
Formed 15th February 1941 at Swansea.

Nil (2.41–4.46)	*Aircraft provided by 2 Elementary Flying Training School.*
FLN (4.46–7.46)	*Tiger Moth II NM148.*

Disbanded 6th July 1946 at Fairwood Common.

SWIFTER FLIGHT
Probably formed late 1959 at Farnborough under the auspices of the Royal Aircraft Establishment for low altitude high-speed hot weather trials at El Adem, in Libya to investigate the effect of turbulence on airframes.

Canberra B.2 WF890.

Disbanded July 1960.

'T' SQUADRON, EGYPT
Formed by 17th March 1919 at Aboukir, Egypt, by merging the remaining elements of 22 and 23 Training Squadrons.

Avro 504K.

Disbanded June 1919 at Almaza, Egypt.

TACTICAL AIR FORCE (BURMA) COMMUNICATION SQUADRON, later 3RD TACTICAL AIR FORCE COMMUNICATION SQUADRON
Formed 1st December 1943 at Comilla, India, by redesignating the Air Headquarters Bengal Communication Unit. Redesignated 3rd Tactical Air Force Communication Squadron from 28th December 1943.

Dominie I X7408; Lockheed 10A AX700; Sentinel II KJ420; Tiger Moth I NL970, II EM851; Harvard IIB FE415; Dakota I FD803, III FD822, IV KK111; Expeditor I HB158; Thunderbolt II KJ284; Hurricane IIC LB547; Proctor III LZ644; Fox Moth MA954; Anson I MG714; Warwick III HG255; Wellington X HZ422, XIII HZ954; Lockheed 12A LV762.

Disbanded 4th December 1944 at Comilla to become the Royal Air Force Bengal/Burma Communication Squadron.

2ND TACTICAL AIR FORCE COMMUNICATION FLIGHT, later 2ND TACTICAL COMMUNICATION SQUADRON, later 2ND TACTICAL AIR FORCE COMMUNICATION WING, later 2ND TACTICAL AIR FORCE COMMUNICATION SQUADRON, later 2ND ALLIED TACTICAL AIR FORCE COMMUNICATION SQUADRON
Formed 1st June 1943 at White Waltham by redesignating the Army Co-operation Command Communication Flight. Redesignated the 2nd Tactical Air Force Communication Squadron from 1st April 1944 and the 2nd Tactical Air Force Communication Wing from 31st March 1945.

Hurricane I N2325, IIC MW360; Magister T9812; Spitfire VB BL725, VC EE745, IX NH158, XVI TE193; Proctor I P6244, II Z7205, III R7571, IV RM189; Master III DL980; Auster I LB299, III MZ122, IV MS937, V RT493; Hudson I N7208; Oxford II N6373; Tiger Moth II R5041; Vigilant I HL429, IA BZ104; Typhoon IB DN432; Storch VH752; Dakota I FD799, III KG736, IV KN645; Anson X NK530, XI NK986; Messenger RG333, I RH368; Mosquito XVI NS560, B.35 TK609; Tempest V SN217.

Disbanded 15th July 1945 at Buckeburg, Germany, to become the British Air Forces of Occupation Communication Squadron.

Reformed 1st September 1951 at Buckeburg, Germany, as the 2nd Tactical Air Force Communication Squadron by redesignating the British Air Forces of Occupation Communication Squadron. Redesignated 2nd Allied Tactical Air Force Communication Squadron from February 1952.

C (9.51– .52)	*Anson XII PH558 C-E, T.20 VS561, T.21 WB459; Tiger Moth II N6635; Prentice T.1 VR271; Valetta C.1 VX573 C-A.*
Nil (.52–1.59)	*Anson T.20 VS561; Vampire FB.5 WA454, T.11 XE945; Valetta C.1 VW162, C.2 VX573; Devon C.1 VP957; Pembroke C.1 WV705, C(PR).1 XF799; Meteor T.7 WG999, FR.9 WH537, PR.10 WH570, NF.14 WS840.*

Disbanded 1st January 1959 at Wildenrath to become the Royal Air Force Germany Communication Squadron.

2ND TACTICAL AIR FORCE AIR SEA RESCUE UNIT
Formed February 1955 at Sylt, Germany.

Sycamore HR.14.

Disbanded September 1961 at Sylt.

2ND TACTICAL COMMUNICATION SQUADRON – see 2nd Tactical Air Force Communication Flight, later 2nd Tactical Air Force Communication Squadron, later 2nd Tactical Air Force Communication Wing, later 2nd Tactical Air Force Communication Squadron, later 2nd Allied Tactical Air Force Communication Squadron

2ND TACTICAL AIR FORCE COMMUNICATION WING – see 2nd Tactical Air Force Communication Flight, later 2nd Tactical Air Force Communication Squadron, later 2nd Tactical Air Force Communication Wing, later 2nd Tactical Air Force Communication Squadron, later 2nd Allied Tactical Air Force Communication Squadron

2ND TACTICAL AIR FORCE DEVELOPMENT UNIT
Formed 23rd February 1953 at Ahlhorn, Germany.

Canberra B.2 WH700.

Disbanded 19th October 1953 at Wyton to become 1323 (Canberra) Flight.

2ND TACTICAL AIR FORCE INSTRUMENT TRAINING FLIGHT
Formed 1st September 1951 at Gutersloh by redesignating the British Air Forces of Occupation Instrument Training Flight.

Meteor T.7; Vampire T.11.

Disbanded 16th March 1954 at Gutersloh.

2ND TACTICAL AIR FORCE SABRE CONVERSION FLIGHT
Formed 10th March 1953 at Wildenrath, Germany.

Sabre F.4 XB542.

Disbanded 5th June 1954 at Wildenrath.

2ND TACTICAL AIR FORCE SUPPORT UNIT
Formed 15th January 1954 at Buckeburg, Germany.

Vampire FB.9 WL493.

Disbanded 31st May 1954 at Buckeburg.

**3RD TACTICAL AIR FORCE COMMUNICATION SQUADRON –
see Tactical Air Force (Burma) Communication Squadron, later
3rd Tactical Air Force Communication Squadron**

TACTICAL AND WEAPON DEVELOPMENT UNIT (INDIA)
Formed 25th May 1945 at Amarda Road, India, by merging the
Ground Attack Training Unit and the Advanced Flying Training Unit.

*Liberator VI KG853; Mustang IVA KM147; Thunderbolt II KJ167;
Beaufighter X NE459; Hurricane IIC JS445; Seafire III NN228;
Spitfire XIV RM886.*

Disbanded 30th November 1945 at Ranchi, India.

1 TACTICAL EXERCISE UNIT
Formed 1st January 1944 at Tealing by redesignating 1 Combat
Training Wing.

GF	*Allocated but no evidence of use.*
Nil	*Hurricane I P3605, IIA Z2643, IIB BE651, IV LE134; Spitfire I N3122, IIA P7310, VA W3168, VB AR342, VC AR501; Mustang III FB375; Master I T8500, II AZ309; Magister L8148; Martinet I NR297; Dominie I X7342.*

Disbanded 31st July 1944 at Tealing.

2 TACTICAL EXERCISE UNIT
Formed 15th October 1943 at Grangemouth by redesignating 2
Combat Training Wing.

PQ	*Allocated but no evidence of use.*
XB	*Allocated but no evidence of use.*
Nil	*Hurricane I N2604, IV KZ683, X P5196; Spitfire I R7144, IIA P7427, VB AB241, VC AR552; Master I T8564; III DL615; Martinet I HP511.*

Disbanded 25th June 1944 at Grangemouth.

3 TACTICAL EXERCISE UNIT
Formed February 1944 at Poulton.

Hurricane I V7207; Mustang III FB127.

Disbanded 26th March 1944 at Poulton and absorbed by 41
Operational Training Unit.

Reformed 21st March 1944 at Annan by redesignating 4 Tactical
Exercise Unit.

UW (3.44–12.44)	*(1 Squadron) Typhoon IB MN513 UW-N.*
ZX (3.44–12.44)	*(1 Squadron)*
EH (3.44–12.44)	*(2 Squadron) Typhoon IB EK413 EH-V.*
PA (3.44–12.44)	*(2 Squadron) Hurricane IIA Z2752 PA-A, IV LE834 PA-N; Typhoon IB JR186 PA-H; Dragon Rapide W6425 PA-Z.*
Also used	*Master III W8460; Auster I LB312; Mustang III SR414; Martinet I JN307; Oxford I BG234.*

Disbanded 18th December 1944 at Aston Down to become 55
Operational Training Unit;

4 TACTICAL EXERCISE UNIT
Formed 26th January 1944 at Annan by redesignating 55
Operational Training Unit.

*Master II AZ777, III W8652; Hurricane I N2471, IIA DG621, X
P5187; Dragon Rapide W6425.*

Disbanded 21st March 1944 at Annan to become 3 Tactical
Exercise Unit.

TACTICAL WEAPONS UNIT, later 1 TACTICAL WEAPONS UNIT
Formed 2nd September 1974 at Brawdy by redesignating 229
Operational Conversion Unit. Redesignated 1 Tactical Weapons
Unit from 31st July 1978.

*Meteor F.4 VZ467, T.7 WA669 02, F.8 VZ467 01; Hunter F.6
XG194, F.6A XE627 10, T.7 XL593 82, FGA.9 XF419 C; Jet
Provost T.4 XP547 03; Hawk T.1 XX301, T.1A XX315.*

Disbanded 31st August 1992 at Brawdy and absorbed by 7 Flying
Training School.

**1 TACTICAL WEAPONS UNIT – see Tactical Weapons Unit,
later 1 Tactical Weapons Unit**

2 TACTICAL WEAPONS UNIT
Formed 31st July 1978 at Lossiemouth by redesignating an element
of the Tactical Weapons Unit, Brawdy.

*Hunter F.6 XK151, F.6A XF516 E, T.7 XF310 01, FGA.9 XJ688 B;
Jet Provost T.4 XP547 03; Hawk T.1 XX230 230.*

Disbanded 1st April 1981 at Lossiemouth.

Reformed 1st April 1981 at Chivenor by redesignating an element of
1 Tactical Weapons Unit.

Hawk T.1 XX329 C.

Disbanded 1st April 1992 at Chivenor to become 7 Flying Training
School.

TANKER TRAINING FLIGHT
Formed 1st July 1965 at Marham by redesignating the Victor
element of 232 Operational Conversion Unit.

*Victor B.1 XA940, B.1A XH592, K.1A XH647; Chipmunk T.10
WP833.*

Disbanded 13th October 1969 at Marham to become the Victor
Training Unit.

TARGET DEVELOPMENT FLIGHT
Formed (date unknown) at Oakley.

Master III DL843; Martinet I HP216; Vengeance IV FD368.

Disbanded 26th January 1944 at Oakley.

TARGET FACILITIES FLIGHT, BINBROOK
Formed 1st February 1966 at Binbrook within the Fighter Command
Trials Unit. Became an independent unit from 30th June 1967 when
the parent unit disbanded. Parented by 5 Squadron from 1970 until
September 1972, then reverted to being an independent unit.

Lightning F.1 XM137 Y, F.1A XM181 181, F.3 XP741 DD.

Disbanded 31st December 1973 at Binbrook.

TARGET FACILITIES FLIGHT, LEUCHARS
Formed 1st April 1966 at Leuchars. Parented by 23 Squadron from
March 1972.

Lightning F.1 XM135 135, F.1A XM173 173, F.1B XM182.

Disbanded 31st December 1973 at Leuchars and absorbed by 23
Squadron.

TARGET FACILITIES FLIGHT, WATTISHAM
Formed 1st April 1966 at Wattisham.

Lightning F.1A XM144 B; Chipmunk T.10 WK622.

Disbanded 31st December 1973 at Wattisham.

1 TARGET TOWING FLIGHT
Formed (date unknown) at Ismailia, Egypt.

Blenheim

Disbanded 18th June 1942 at Ismailia to become the Air Defence
Co-operation Unit.

1 TARGET TOWING FLIGHT (INDIA)
Formed 1st April 1947 at Drigh Road, India, by redesignating 'A'
Flight, 22 Anti-Aircraft Co-operation Unit.

Vengeance IV FD343; Harvard IIB FS944.

Disbanded 1st August 1947 at Drigh Road and transferred to the
Indian Air Force.

2 TARGET TOWING FLIGHT (INDIA)
Formed administratively 1st April 1947 at Poona, India, by
redesignating 'B' Flight, 22 Anti-Aircraft Co-operation Unit.

No aircraft allocated.

Disbanded 15th April 1947 at Poona.

TARGET TOWING FLIGHT, NICOSIA
Formed (date unknown) at Nicosia.

Beaufighter TT.10 RD548.

Disbanded 1st January 1950 at Nicosia and merged with the Target Towing Flight, Shallufa to become the Middle East Air Force Target Towing Unit.

TARGET TOWING FLIGHT, SHALLUFA
Formed (date unknown) at Shallufa, Egypt.

Beaufighter TT.10 SR916.

Disbanded 1st January 1950 at Shallufa and merged with the Target Towing Flight, Nicosia to become the Middle East Air Force Target Towing Unit.

TARGET TOWING SECTION, SHALLUFA
Formed 1st August 1953 at Shallufa, Egypt.

Beaufighter X RD860.

Disbanded August 1954 at Shallufa.

TECHNICAL TRAINING COMMAND COMMUNICATION FLIGHT
Formed 27th May 1940 at White Waltham by redesignating an element of the Training Command Communication Flight.

Nil (7.44–4.46)	Hurricane I N2329; Tiger Moth II N6456; Spitfire II P7681, IX NH343; Proctor III R7563; Dominie I X7483; Moth Minor W6460; Master II W9075, III DM176; Hornet Moth AW118; Leopard Moth AX865; Wellington III X3952; Auster I LB366.
TWY (4.46–4.51)	Proctor III R7566 TWY-H, IV RM226 TWY-F; Auster V NJ637 TWY-J; Dominie II RL961 TWY-G; Messenger I RH424 TWY-O; Anson I EG604 TWY-B, XII PH595 TWY-B, XIX VP515 TWY-C.
Nil (4.51–4.64)	Oxford I PH374; Proctor IV RM226; Anson XII PH595 D, XIX VM361 A, T.21 VV973 C; Chipmunk T.10 WG320; Devon C.1 VP976; Prentice T.1 VR247.

Disbanded 1st April 1964 at Wyton.

TELECOMMUNICATIONS FLYING UNIT
The Telecommunications Research Establishment formed 1st August 1941 at Worth Matravers by merging the Fighter Experimental Establishment, Middle Wallop (which became the Development Section) and the Blind Landing Detachment of the Royal Aircraft Establishment, Farnborough.

Formed 10th November 1941 at Hurn (as the Research Section, Telecommunications Flying Unit) by redesignating the Special Duty Flight, Christchurch.

The listing below also includes aircraft allocated to the Telecommunications Research Establishment.

(Airspeed) Oxford I V4204, II N6417; Envoy DG663; Horsa I LJ210. (Armstrong Whitworth) Whitley V P4949; Albemarle I P1364, ST.I P1438. (Avro) Anson I EG323, XII PH642, XIX VL300; Lancaster I ED350, II DS628, III JB705, VII NX618, X KB805; Lincoln I RE229, II RF533; Athena T.2 VW891; Tudor 7 VX199. (Boeing) 247D DZ203; Fortress 42-5793, III KJ116. (Boulton Paul) Defiant I AA321, II AA407. (Bristol) Blenheim I L1257, IV P4846; Beaufort I L4457; Beaufighter I R2195, II R2347, VI EL167, X KW290; Brigand B.1 RH798; Freighter VR380. (Consolidated) Liberator II AL507, III BZ857, V FL987, VI BZ963, VIII KG848. (de Havilland) Tiger Moth II T6367; Hornet Moth W5780; Dominie I NR698; Mosquito II DZ301, III HJ859, IV DZ345, VI RF760, IX ML898, XII HJ946, XIII HK369, XVI NS673, XVII HK195, XIX TA193, NF.30 NT540, NF.38 VT676; Hornet F.1 PX222; Vampire F.3 VT858, FB.5 VV446; Devon C.1 VP980. (Douglas) Havoc I BB903; Boston II AH438; Dakota III FZ564. (English Electric) Canberra VN828, B.2 WD929. (Fairey) Battle N2124; Swordfish I K8424; Fulmar II BP793; Barracuda. (General Aircraft) Hamilcar X LA728. (Gloster) Gladiator K5200; Meteor F.3 EE350, F.4 VT342, T.7 VW470, F.8 WH284, NF.11 WD586, NF.14 WS731. (Grumman) Wildcat IV FN212. (Handley

Page) Halifax II R9490, VI RG815, VII LW196; Hastings C.1 TG503. (Hawker) Hurricane I P3641, IIA Z2795, IIC BN878; Typhoon IB MN254; Tempest II MW741, V NX124. (Lockheed) Hudson I T9339, IV AE610, V AM714, VI EW909; Ventura I FN956. (Miles) Magister N5414. (North American) Mitchell II FW141, III KJ599. (Percival) Vega Gull X9455; Proctor III HM338. (Short) Stirling I R9249, III LJ541. (Sikorsky) Hoverfly I KK993. (Supermarine) Spitfire I X4845, VB BM315, IX ML379, F.21 LA326. (Taylorcraft) Auster I LB379, IV MS965. (Vickers) Wellington IC N2761, II W5451, III X3454, IV Z1322, VIII Z8705, X RP589, XI MP516, XII MP505, XIII NB781, XIV PF864, XVIII PG255; Warwick I BV346, III HG218, V LM777, VI HF983; Valetta C.1 VX561. (Vultee) Vengeance IV FD242. (Westland) Lysander III T1439.

Disbanded 1st November 1955 at Defford to become the Radar Research Flying Unit.

TEMPERATURE AND HUMIDITY FLIGHT (THUM FLIGHT)
Formed 1st May 1951 at Hooton Park.

Spitfire XIX PS915, F.24 VN315; Mosquito TT.35 TA641; Meteor F.8 VZ508.

Disbanded 1st January 1958 at Woodvale and absorbed by and operated within 5 Civilian Anti-Aircraft Co-operation Unit until 1st May 1959 at Woodvale.

TEMPORARY 'A' FLIGHT – see 485 (Fighter) Flight

TEMPORARY AIR OBSERVERS SCHOOL
Formed 7th June 1938 at Leconfield.

Heyford II K4868.

Disbanded 16th December 1938 at Leconfield.

TEMPORARY 'D' FLIGHT – see 534 (Light Bomber) Flight

TEMPORARY ARMAMENT TRAINING CAMP, ALDERGROVE
Formed 2nd March 1936 at Aldergrove.

Wallace I K5072.

Disbanded 6th October 1936 at Aldergrove to become 2 Armament Training Camp.

TEMPORARY ARMAMENT TRAINING CAMP, FLIMSTONE DOWN
Formed 15th May 1939 at Flimstone Down.

No aircraft known.

Disbanded by August 1939 at Flimstone Down.

TEMPORARY ARMAMENT TRAINING CAMP, LEUCHARS
Formed 29th March 1935 at Leuchars.

Gordon J9062; Wapiti IIA.

Disbanded 1st April 1938 at Leuchars to become the Temporary Armament Training Station, Leuchars.

TEMPORARY ARMAMENT TRAINING CAMP, NORTH COATES FITTIES
Formed 6th October 1936 at North Coates Fitties.

Gordon K2691.

Disbanded 1st April 1938 at North Coates Fitties to become the Temporary Armament Training Station, North Coates Fitties.

TEMPORARY ARMAMENT TRAINING STATION, LEUCHARS
Formed 1st April 1938 at Leuchars by redesignating the Temporary Armament Training Camp, Leuchars.

Gordon J9062; Henley L3325.

Disbanded 3rd September 1939 at Evanton and absorbed by 8 Air Observers School.

TEMPORARY ARMAMENT TRAINING STATION, NORTH COATES FITTIES
Formed 1st April 1938 at North Coates by redesignating the Temporary Armament Training Camp, North Coates Fitties.

Gordon K2691.

Disbanded 15th August 1938 at North Coates.

TEMPORARY 'C' FLIGHT – see 486 (Fighter) Flight

TEMPORARY 'D' FLIGHT (1) – see 490 (Light Bomber) Flight

TEMPORARY 'D' FLIGHT (2) – see 534 (Light Bomber) Flight

TEST AND EVALUATION ESTABLISHMENT
Formed 1st April 1992 by redesignating the Royal Aircraft Establishment with facilities at Llanbedr and West Freugh.

Meteor D.16 WH453; Canberra TT.18 WH734; Devon C.2 XA880; Sea Vixen D.3 XP924; Hawk T.1 XX160; Jetstream T.2 XX475.

Current at 1st April 1998.

TEST PILOTS TRAINING FLIGHT, later TEST PILOTS SCHOOL
Formed 25th June 1943 at Boscombe Down. Redesignated the Test Pilots School from 15th January 1944.

Hurricane I L2006, IIA Z2399, IIC LD264; Spitfire; Master II DM345, III W8537; Oxford I AS504; Beaufort II AW343; Mosquito; Mitchell; Wellington; Lancaster; Halifax I L9520, II R9436.

Disbanded 18th July 1944 at Boscombe Down to become the Empire Test Pilots School.

TEST PILOTS SCHOOL – see Test Pilots Training Flight, later Test Pilots School

TESTING FLIGHT, later TESTING SQUADRON
Formed 18 July 1916 at Upavon by redesignating an element of the Central Flying School. Redesignated the Testing Squadron by 25th September 1916.

Handley Page O/100 3138; Baby N5; Triplane N5430; D.H.4 A7446; Camel B6289.

Disbanded 16th October 1917 at Martlesham Heath to become the Aeroplane Experimental Station.

THUM FLIGHT – see Temperature and Humidity Flight

TONGUE DEFENCE FLIGHT – see 470 (Fighter) Flight

TORNADO F.3 OPERATIONAL EVALUATION UNIT
Formed 1st April 1987 at Coningsby.

Tornado F.3 ZE756.

Current 1st April 1998 at Coningsby.

TORNADO OPERATIONAL EVALUATION UNIT
Formed 1st September 1983 at Boscombe Down.

Tornado GR.1 ZA376 E, GR.1(T) ZA614; F.3 ZE862.

Current 5th October 1987 at Boscombe Down and absorbed by the Strike Attack Operational Evaluation Unit.

TORNADO WEAPONS CONVERSION UNIT
Formed 8th January 1982 at Honington. Designated 45 (Shadow) Squadron from 1st January 1984.

Tornado GR.1 ZA393, GR.1(T) ZA594.

Disbanded 1st April 1992 at Lossiemouth to become 15 (Reserve) Squadron.

TORPEDO AEROPLANE SCHOOL
Formed 3rd July 1918 at East Fortune.

Shirl N111; Short 184; Cuckoo N74.

Disbanded 14th August 1918 at East Fortune and merged with 1 Torpedo Training Squadron to become 201 Training Depot Station.

TORPEDO BOMBING SCHOOL
Formed 15th April 1942 at Shallufa, Egypt.

Wellington IC.

Disbanded 15th August 1942 at Shallufa to become 5 Middle East Training School.

TORPEDO DEVELOPMENT FLIGHT
Formed by 1925 at Gosport.

Avro 504K H3059; Horsley I J8006, II S1236; Vildebeest S1712; Shark II K4881; Swordfish I K5998.

Disbanded November 1938 to become the Torpedo Development Section (comprising a Torpedo Training Unit, a Torpedo Development Unit and a Torpedo Instructional Section) which in turn became the Torpedo Development Unit from 22nd June 1939.

TORPEDO DEVELOPMENT SECTION – see Torpedo Development Unit

TORPEDO DEVELOPMENT UNIT
Formed 22nd June 1939 at Gosport by redesignating the Torpedo Development Unit of the Torpedo Development Section within the Royal Air Force Station, Gosport.

Vildebeest III K2821, IV K6408; Shark III K8991; Swordfish I L2831; Whitley V N1370; Hampden I L4037, TB.I P1282; Hereford I L6029; Botha I L6347 M; Beaufort I L9833 C; Manchester I L7276; Albemarle I/I P1376; Wellington IC AD646; Lancaster DG595, II DS606; Spitfire VII R7211; Mitchell II FV904; Beaufighter VI X8065, X LZ411; Firebrand II DK374.

Disbanded 15th September 1943 at Gosport and merged with the Torpedo Experimental Establishment to become the Aircraft Torpedo Development Unit.

TORPEDO EXPERIMENTAL FLIGHT – see Royal Air Force Base, Gosport

1 TORPEDO REFRESHER SCHOOL
Formed 3rd February 1943 at Tain by redesignating an element of the Coastal Command Development Unit.

No aircraft known.

Disbanded 28th January 1944 at Tain.

2 TORPEDO REFRESHER SCHOOL
Formed 3rd February 1943 at Leuchars by redesignating an element of the Coastal Command Development Unit.

No aircraft known.

Formation of the unit was abandoned on 9th April 1943.

TORPEDO TRAINING FLIGHT (1) – see Royal Air Force Base, Gosport

TORPEDO TRAINING FLIGHT (2)
Formed 15th January 1934 at Donibristle.

Vildebeest I.

Disbanded 1st May 1934 at Donibristle and absorbed by 22 Squadron.

TORPEDO TRAINING SCHOOL
Formed 30th April 1919 at East Fortune by redesignating 201 Training Depot Station.

Cuckoo.

Disbanded 1st February 1920 at East Fortune.

1 TORPEDO TRAINING SQUADRON
Formed 19th July 1918 at Leuchars by redesignating an element of 208 (Temporary) Training Depot Station.

Cuckoo N7001; F.2B B8937; Shirl N111.

Disbanded 14th August 1918 at Leuchars, and merged with the Torpedo Training School to become 201 Training Depot Station.

TORPEDO TRAINING UNIT, later 1 TORPEDO TRAINING UNIT
Formed by February 1936 at Gosport by redesignating 'A' Torpedo Training Flight of RAF Base Gosport Training Squadron. Redesignated 1 Torpedo Training Unit from 1st January 1943 at Turnberry.

Nil (2.36–5.44)	*Shark II K8471, III K8901; Swordfish I K5974; Botha I L6110; Hampden I P1198; Beaufort I N1001 47; Lysander I L4695; Tiger Moth II*

N9241; Oxford I NM347, II N4732; Moth Minor X5122; Wellington VIII LB237, XI HZ246; Beaufighter X JL951.

TU ( )   Beaufort I – temporary use for the film Coastal Command.

Disbanded 22nd May 1944 at Turnberry and absorbed by 5 Operational Training Unit.

Reformed 1st August 1945 at Turnberry as 1 Torpedo Training Unit.

9K   Beaufighter X RD485 9K-K; Oxford I PG972 9K-A.

Disbanded 10th December 1947 at Thorney Island.

1 TORPEDO TRAINING UNIT – see Torpedo Training Unit, later 1 Torpedo Training Unit

2 TORPEDO TRAINING UNIT
Formed 19th December 1942 at Castle Kennedy.

Lysander I L4695; Tiger Moth II N9213; Beaufort I DX115 37; Oxford II ED191; Beaufighter VI EL289.

Disbanded 29th September 1943 at Castle Kennedy and absorbed by 1 Torpedo Training Unit.

TOWED TARGET FLIGHT, BENTWATERS
Formed January 1945 at Bentwaters.

Martinet I EM549.

Disbanded October 1945 at Bentwaters.

TOWED TARGET FLIGHT, CHANGI
Formed 23rd August 1962 at Changi, Singapore by redesignating an element of the Base and Target Towing Flight, Royal Air Force Maintenance Base (Far East).

Meteor T.7 WH218, F(TT).8 WA880, TT.20 WD606.

Disbanded 1st May 1964 at Changi to become 1574 Flight.

TOWED TARGET FLIGHT, GIBRALTAR
Formed May 1953 at Gibraltar.

Mosquito TT.35 TK610; Meteor F(TT).8 WE970.

Disbanded November 1958 at Gibraltar.

TOWED TARGET FLIGHT, HELWAN
Formed by July 1940 at Helwan, Egypt.

Gordon I K2647.

Disbanded (date unknown) at Helwan.

TOWED TARGET FLIGHT, ISMAILIA
Formed by 1935 at Ismailia, Egypt.

Gordon K2698.

Disbanded 20th September 1935 at Ismailia.

TOWED TARGET FLIGHT, KHARTOUM
Formed 20th September 1935 at Khartoum by redesignating an element of the Towed Target Flight, Ismailia.

Gordon.

Disbanded (date unknown) at Khartoum.

TOWED TARGET FLIGHT, ST EVAL
Formed September 1953 at St Eval.

Martinet I MS513; Mosquito TT.35 TJ151.

Disbanded September 1955 at St Eval.

TOWED TARGET FLIGHT, SCHLESWIGLAND
Formed March 1953 at Schleswigland, Germany.

Mosquito III, TT.35 RS712.

Disbanded 1st May 1958 at Schleswigland.

TOWED TARGET FLIGHT, SELETAR
Formed 15th April 1951 at Seletar, Singapore.

Beaufighter TT.10 RD854; Meteor F(TT).8 WH398; TT.20 WM230.

Disbanded 1st June 1951 at Seletar and absorbed by the Far East Air Force Training Squadron, only to be merged from 1st July 1951 with the Station Flight, Seletar to become the Station and Target Towing Flight, Seletar.

TOWED TARGET FLIGHT, SUTTON BRIDGE
Formed by January 1940 at Sutton Bridge.

Henley L3335.

Disbanded 2nd April 1940 and absorbed by the Station Flight, Sutton Bridge.

TOWED TARGET FLIGHT, TANGMERE
Formed 8th June 1950 at Tangmere.

Martinet I EM555.

Disbanded January 1951 at Tangmere.

TOWED TARGET FLIGHT, TRINCOMALEE
Probably not formed. Seal aircraft shipped from the United Kingdom during June 1939 for the Flight were taken on charge by 273 Squadron on 1st August 1939 at China Bay, Ceylon.

1 TOWED TARGET FLIGHT
Formed 1939 at Ismailia, Egypt.

Gordon; Fulmar; Blenheim; Maryland.

Disbanded 18th June 1942 at Ismailia, Egypt, to become the Air Defence Co-operation Flight.

TRAINING COMMAND COMMUNICATION FLIGHT
Formed by October 1939 at Ternhill.

Harrow II K6990; Mentor L4411; Anson I N4972; Vega Gull W6464.

Disbanded 27th May 1940 at White Waltham and divided to become the Technical Training Command and Flying Training Command Communication Flights.

TRAINING COMMAND PRACTICE FLIGHT
Formed by April 1931 at Manston.

Moth K1225; Atlas K1560; Tiger Moth I K4245; Wallace II K8053.

Disbanded October 1937 at Manston.

Reformed by January 1940 at Woodley.

Harvard I N7120; Master I N7412.

Disbanded 27th May 1940 at Woodley.

TRAINING COMMANDS COMMUNICATION SQUADRON
Formed 1st January 1967 at Topcliffe by redesignating the Northern Communication Squadron.

Bassett C.1; Devon C.2 VP974.

Disbanded 3rd February 1969 at Wyton to become 26 Squadron.

1 TRAINING DEPOT STATION
Formed 30th July 1917 at Stamford by merging elements of 4, 26 and 39 Training Squadrons which became 'A', 'B' and 'C' Flights respectively.

Curtiss JN-3 7310; Curtiss JN-4A B1945; B.E.2c 9988, B.E.2e C7055; F.E.2b; F.K.8 D5075; Avro 504K D7195; D.H.4 B2056; D.H.6 C4281; D.H.9 B9378; Camel C8330; R.E.8 D1549; Pup D4075; F.2B.

An element detached on 14th September 1918, merged with elements from 26, 55 and 57 Training Depot Stations, to become 155 Squadron. A further element detached on 30th September 1918, merged with elements from 5, 36 and 45 Training Depot Stations, to become 138 Squadron.

Disbanded 14th March 1919 at Stamford.

2 TRAINING DEPOT STATION
Formed 15th August 1917 at Lake Down by merging elements of 35, 19 and 9 Training Squadron which became 'A', 'B' and 'C' Flights respectively.

Shorthorn C3499; B.E.2c, B.E.2e B4510; D.H.4 A7629; R.E.8 B8877; D.H.6 C3506; Handley Page O/100 1456.

Disbanded 5th January 1918 at Stonehenge to become 1 School of Aerial Navigation and Bomb Dropping.

Reformed 15th April 1918 at West Fenton (later renamed Gullane).

Bristol Scout D 5598; Pup D4027; Camel E1447; S.E.5a E3932; Avro 504A A527, Avro 504J B3103; F.2B C4658.

Disbanded 21st November 1919 at Gullane.

3 TRAINING DEPOT STATION
Formed 5th September 1917 at Lopcombe Corner by merging elements of 54 and 62 Training Squadrons and 28 Squadron which became 'A', 'C' and 'B' Flights respectively.

B.E.2b, B.E.2e A1361; D.H.5 A9526; D.H.6 A9621; Pup B5967; Avro 504J B3103, Avro 504K D5948; Camel F9628.

Disbanded 15th May 1919 at Lopcombe Corner to become 3 Training Squadron.

4 TRAINING DEPOT STATION
Formed 1st September 1917 at Ternhill by merging elements of 34 and 31 Training Squadrons and 81 Squadron, which became 'A', 'B' and 'C' Flights respectively.

F.K.8; Spad 7; B1622; Avro 504A B3278, Avro 504J D168, Avro 504K D7059; Pup D4158; Dolphin E4505 V; Camel C8; F.2B E2313; D.H.10 F352.

Disbanded 14th March 1919 at Shotwick to become 4 Training Squadron.

5 TRAINING DEPOT STATION
Formed 24th September 1917 at Easton-on-the-Hill by merging elements of 41, 48 and 68 Training Squadrons, which became 'A', 'B' and 'C' Flights respectively.

R.E.8 A4500; Camel B6433; D.H.6 C7677; D.H.9 D527; B.E.2e F9567; F.2B E2166; Avro 504K E2166.

An element detached on 30th September 1918 and joined elements from 1, 36 and 45 Training Depot Stations to become 138 Squadron.

Disbanded 14th March 1919 at Easton-on-the-Hill to become 5 Training Squadron.

6 TRAINING DEPOT STATION
Formed 12th October 1917 at Boscombe Down by merging elements of 82 and 83 Squadrons and 59 Training Squadron which became 'A', 'B' and 'C' Flights respectively.

B.E.12 6161; Camel B2515; Pup B6148; D.H.4 B5521; D.H.6 B2746; D.H.9 C6061; B.E.2e C6904; Avro 504J B8819, Avro 504K E3323; F.K.8 C8614.

Disbanded 15th May 1919 at Boscombe Down.

7 TRAINING DEPOT STATION
Formed 1st November 1917 at Feltwell by merging elements of 18, 63 and 28 Training Squadrons which became 'A', 'B' and 'C' Flights respectively.

Pup C9990; B.E.2e C9987; Camel B7308; Avro 504 B8819, 504A B4341; S.E.5a; D.H.4; D.H.6 C7666; D.H.9 E6888.

Disbanded 22nd April 1919 at Feltwell.

8 TRAINING DEPOT STATION
Formed 1st April 1918 at Netheravon.

B.E.12e A1391; Shorthorn B4700; F.E.2b A6537; D.H.4; D.H.6 A9690; Avro 504A, Avro 504J; Camel C106; R.E.8; Handley Page O/100 3133; Handley Page O/400 C9736.

Disbanded 15th May 1919 at Netheravon to become 8 Training Squadron.

9 TRAINING DEPOT STATION
Formed 15th March 1918 at Shawbury.

B.E.12e A1391; R.E.7 2399; D.H.4; D.H.6; D.H.9 D5599; R.E.8 D1511; Avro 504K D8979.

An element detached on 29th October 1918 and joined elements from 10, 11 and 15 Training Depot Stations to become 122 Squadron.

Disbanded 25th April 1919 at Shawbury.

10 TRAINING DEPOT STATION
Formed 15th April 1918 at Harling Road.

Camel B7359 P, Camel (2 seat) B7289; D.H.4 A7667; B.E.2e C7160; D.H.6 C6633; R.E.8 D1555; D.H.9 D1738; Buzzard D4352; D.H.9A E9709; Dolphin E4774; Avro 504K D8910.

An element detached on 29th October 1918 and joined elements from 9, 11 and 15 Training Depot Stations to become 122 Squadron.

Disbanded 14th March 1920 at Harling Road to become 10 Training Squadron.

11 TRAINING DEPOT STATION
Formed 1st April 1918 at Old Sarum.

D.H.4 A7827; Pup B5327; D.H.6 C6559; B.E.2e C6943; Dolphin C8096; D.H.9 D2901; Avro 504K D9359.

An element detached on 29th October 1918 and joined elements from 9, 10 and 15 Training Depot Stations to become 122 Squadron.

Disbanded July 1919 at Beaulieu to become 11 Training Squadron.

12 TRAINING DEPOT STATION
Formed 1st April 1918 at Netheravon.

R.E.8 4758; Handley Page O/400; D.H.6 C7354; F.E.2b D9130; Avro 504K.

Disbanded 15th May 1919 at Netheravon.

13 TRAINING DEPOT STATION
Formed 1st April 1918 at Ternhill.

D.H.6 B3027; Handley Page O/400 C9637; F.E.2b D9132; Avro 504K D4535.

Disbanded 14th March 1920 at Ternhill to become 13 Training Squadaron.

14 TRAINING DEPOT STATION
Formed 6th June 1918 at Lake Down.

B.E.12 A590; B.E.2e A3140; D.H.4 C6829; D.H.9 D7308; Avro 504K D8801.

Disbanded June 1919 at Lake Down to become 14 Training Squadron.

15 TRAINING DEPOT STATION
Formed 1st April 1918 at Hucknall.

D.H.6 B2606; D.H.9 D1292; Avro 504K E4256.

An element detached on 29th October 1918 and joined elements from 9, 10 and 11 Training Depot Stations to become 122 Squadron.

Disbanded 14th March 1919 at Hucknall to become 15 Training Squadron.

16 TRAINING DEPOT STATION
Formed 21st July 1918 at Amriya, Egypt, by redesignating 194 Training Squadron.

D.H.6 C2033; B.E.2c B6182, B.E.2d F9571, B.E.2e A8688; R.E.8 D1520; D.H.9 D2926; F.K.8 D5038; Camel D6533; F.2B E2294; Avro 504K E3426.

Disbanded August 1920 at Heliopolis, Egypt.

17 TRAINING DEPOT STATION
Formed 21st July 1918 at Abu Sueir, Egypt, by redesignating 57 Training Squadron.

D.H.6 C6516; B.E.2e B3681; D.H.9 D3144; F.K.8 D5122; R.E.8 E1165; F.2B E2293.

Disbanded 25th July 1919 at El Rimal, Egypt.

18 TRAINING DEPOT STATION

Formed 21st July 1918 at Abbassia, Egypt, by redesignating 21 Training Squadron.

B.E.2e A1306; B.E.12 C3141; D.H.6 C5540; D.H.9 D2926; F.K.8 D5053

Disbanded 22nd July 1919 at El Rimal, Egypt.

19 TRAINING DEPOT STATION

Formed 21st July 1918 at El Rimal, Egypt, by redesignating 195 Training Squadron.

Bristol Scout C 5321; Camel C1596; Pup B6047; Nieuport 23 B1654; F.K.8 F4249; Avro 504J, Avro 504K E3602; F.2B B1147.

Disbanded 25th July 1919 at El Rimal.

20 TRAINING DEPOT STATION

Formed 21st July 1918 at Amriya, Egypt, by redesignating 193 Training Squadron.

D.H.6 C7625; Avro 504K E1636; Pup D4084; R.E.8 D1520; S.E.5 E1011.

Disbanded 22nd July 1919 at El Rimal, Egypt.

21 TRAINING DEPOT STATION

Formed 15th July 1918 at Driffield by merging 3 and 27 Training Squadrons.

Spad S.7 A9152; S.E.5a C5433 A; Pup 9152; Avro 504K D130; D.H.6 B2970; F.2B C902.

Disbanded 1st July 1919 at Driffield to become 21 Training Sqaudaron.

22 TRAINING DEPOT STATION

Formed 1st August 1918 at Gormanston by merging 26 and 69 Training Squadrons.

D.H.9 D1360; Avro 504K D5916; R.E.8 E259.

Disbanded 13th June 1919 at Gormanston.

23 TRAINING DEPOT STATION

Formed 1st September 1918 at Baldonnel by merging 31 and 51 Training Squadrons.

D.H.9 D9868; Avro 504J C5980.

Disbanded February 1919 at Baldonnel.

24 TRAINING DEPOT STATION

Formed 15th August 1918 at Collinstown by merging 24 and 59 Training Squadrons.

D.H.9; Avro 504K D5992; Camel F4021; S.E.5a F573.

Disbanded 13th June 1919 at Collinstown.

25 TRAINING DEPOT STATION

Formed 1st September 1918 at Cookstown (later renamed Tallaght) by redesignating 9 Training Squadron.

Avro 504K; D.H.9 D1171.

Disbanded 1919 at Cookstown.

26 TRAINING DEPOT STATION

Formed 15th July 1918 at Edzell by merging 36 and 74 Training Squadrons.

Avro 504K B4352; R.E.8 C2278; D.H.6 B2645; Camel C6757; S.E.5a E5888.

An element detached on 14th September 1918 and joined elements from 1, 55 and 57 Training Depot Stations to become 155 Squadron.

Disbanded 25th April 1919 at Edzell.

27 TRAINING DEPOT STATION

Formed 15th July 1918 at Crail by merging 50 and 64 Training Squadrons.

R.E.8; F.E.2b; Avro 504A B3259, 504K D5911; Camel B5739.

Disbanded 31st March 1919 at Crail.

28 TRAINING DEPOT STATION

Formed 27th July 1918 at Weston-on-the-Green by merging 61 and 70 Training Squadrons.

Camel C68; Avro 504J; Avro 504K D2023; Salamander.

Disbanded March 1919 at Weston-on-the-Green.

29 TRAINING DEPOT STATION

Formed 27th July 1918 at Beaulieu by merging 1 and 73 Training Squadrons.

Avro 504J C5759; Pup D4176; Dolphin D5339; Camel F9635.

Disbanded 28th March 1919 at Beaulieu.

30 TRAINING DEPOT STATION

Formed 15th July 1918 at Northolt by merging 2 and 4 Training Squadrons.

1½ Strutter A1067; Camel B6433; Longhorn B8815; Pup C280; S.E.5a F9568; Avro 504K D25; Dolphin D5261; Snipe E8338.

Disbanded 1st July 1919 at Northolt to become 30 Training Sqadron.

31 TRAINING DEPOT STATION

Formed 1st September 1918 at Fowlmere by redesignating 5 Training Squadron.

B.E.2e B4429; Avro 504K D5725; D.H.4 A7948; D.H.9 D3032.

Disbanded 14th March 1919 at Fowlmere to become 31 Training Squadron.

32 TRAINING DEPOT STATION

Formed 15th July 1918 at Montrose by merging 6 and 18 Training Squadrons.

S.E.5a B135; Pup C235; Camel B7177; Avro 504A B4350, Avro 504J, Avro 504K.

An element detached on 7th August 1918, joining elements from 37, 39 and 44 Training Depot Stations to become 154 Squadron.

Disbanded 30th May 1919 at Montrose.

33 TRAINING DEPOT STATION

Formed 15th August 1918 at Witney by merging 7 and 8 Training Squadrons.

Avro 504K E4338; F.2B C4879.

Disbanded September 1919 at Witney to become 33 Training Squadron.

34 TRAINING DEPOT STATION

Formed 15th July 1918 at Scampton by merging 11 and 60 Training Squadrons and 81 Squadron.

Pup D4128; Camel (2 seat) B3801; Dolphin C8024; Avro 504J, Avro 504K F2188; Bristol Scout D.

Disbanded 5th March 1919 at Scampton and absorbed by 46 Training Depot Station.

35 TRAINING DEPOT STATION

15th July 1918 at Thetford by merging 12 and 25 Training Squadrons.

R.E.8 A3479; D.H.4; D.H.6 A9611; D.H.9 D1117; Avro 504K D2038.

Disbanded 31st May 1919 at Duxford.

36 TRAINING DEPOT STATION

Formed 15th July 1918 at Yatesbury by merging 13 and 66 Training Squadrons.

B.E.12 6142; R.E.8 A4510; Camel (2 seat) B7323; S.E.5a B7799; B.E.2e C6938; D.H.6 C7713; Avro 504K D8912; F.2B E2221.

An element detached on 30th September 1918, joining elements from 1, 5 and 45 Training Depot Stations to become 138 Squadron.

Disbanded 15th September 1919 at Yatesbury.

37 TRAINING DEPOT STATION
Formed 15th July 1918 at Yatesbury by merging 16 and 17 Training Squadrons.

B.E.12a A587; Pup B2164; B.E.2c/e B6162; R.E.8 C2677; D.H.6 C7666; F.2B D2222; Avro 504K F2287.

An element detached on 7th August 1918, joining elements from 33, 39 and 44 Training Depot Stations to become 154 Squadron.

Disbanded 15th May 1919 at Yatesbury to become 36 Training Squadron.

38 TRAINING DEPOT STATION
Formed 15th July 1918 at Tadcaster by merging 14 and 68 Training Squadrons.

Pup B4181; S.E.5a D6009; Avro 504A, Avro 504J, Avro 504K H2293.

Disbanded August 1919 at Tadcaster to become 38 Training Squadron.

39 TRAINING DEPOT STATION
Formed 15th August 1918 at Spitalgate by merging 15 and 37 Training Squadrons.

F.K.3; B.E.2e A4437; Avro 504K; Camel B3801; F.K.8 B9548; F.2B E1911.

An element detached on 7th August 1918, joining elements from 33, 37 and 44 Training Depot Stations to become 154 Squadron.

Disbanded 14th March 1919 at Spitalgate to become 39 Training Squadron.

40 TRAINING DEPOT STATION
Formed 15th August 1918 at Harlaxton by merging 20 and 53 Training Squadrons.

R.E.8 A3543; Camel B7397, Camel (2 seat) B7806; F.K.8 B9608; D.H.6 C9434; Avro 504K.

Disbanded 8th May 1919 at Harlaxton.

41 TRAINING DEPOT STATION
Formed 15th July 1918 at London Colney by redesignating 56 Training Squadron.

S.E.5a C8808; Snipe E7998; Avro 504J/K D4507.

Disbanded October 1919 at London Colney to become 41 Training Squadron.

42 TRAINING DEPOT STATION
Formed 15th July 1918 at Hounslow by merging 28 and 62 Training Squadrons.

Camel H8253; Snipe E8271; Bristol M.1C C4965; Avro 504K D4433.

Disbanded July 1919 at Hounslow.

43 TRAINING DEPOT STATION
Formed 15th July 1918 at Chattis Hill by merging 34 and 43 Training Squadrons.

Avro 504K F9633; Pup; Camel F9631, Camel (2 seat) H8259.

Disbanded 15th May 1919 at Chattis Hill.

44 TRAINING DEPOT STATION, later 44 TRAINING SCHOOL
Formed 15th August 1918 at Oxford by merging 35 and 71 Training Squadrons.

F.2B A7238; Pup B6128; Avro 504K E4336.

An element detached on 7th August 1918, joining elements from 33, 37, and 39 Training Depot Stations to become 154 Squadron.

Disbanded August 1919 at Bicester to become 44 Training Squadron.

45 TRAINING DEPOT STATION
Formed 15th August 1918 at Rendcomb by redesignating 38 Training Squadron.

B.E.2e B6151; F.2B C903; Avro 504J, Avro 504K E3457.

An element detached on 30th September 1918, joined elements from 1, 5, and 36 Training Depot Stations to become 138 Squadron.

Disbanded June 1919 at Rendcomb to become 45 Training Squadron.

46 TRAINING DEPOT STATION
Formed 27th July 1918 at South Carlton by merging 39 and 45 Training Squadrons.

D.H.6 B3054; Pup C258; Dolphin D3594; Avro 504K D4538; Camel E7152.

Disbanded 1st July 1919 at South Carlton to become 46 Training Squadron.

47 TRAINING DEPOT STATION
Formed 15th July 1918 at Doncaster by merging 41 and 49 Training Squadrons.

Pup B4136; Shorthorn B8793; Avro 504K D1978; S.E.5a D8436; Camel F6491.

Disbanded 13th February 1919 at Doncaster.

48 TRAINING DEPOT STATION
Formed 4th July 1918 at Waddington by merging 47 and 48 Training Squadrons.

R.E.8 D1567; Avro 504K E3648.

Disbanded 14th March 1919 at Waddington and merged with 44 Training Squadron to become 48 Training Squadron.

49 TRAINING DEPOT STATION
Formed 15th July 1918 at Catterick by merging 46 and 52 Training Squadrons.

D.H.4; D.H.6 B2701; D.H.9 B4040; R.E.8 B4040; F.K.8 D4964; Avro 504K E2959.

Disbanded 10th March 1919 at Catterick.

50 TRAINING DEPOT STATION
Formed 15th July 1918 at Eastbourne by merging 54 Training Squadron and 206 Training Depot Station.

F.K.8 B279; Bristol M.1C; F.2B C903; Avro 504J D7756, Avro 504K D2069; Camel E9978 F, Camel DC B2438; D.H.6 B2760; D.H.9A.

Disbanded 24th October 1919 at Manston.

51 TRAINING DEPOT STATION
Formed 15th July 1918 at Shotwick by merging 55 and 67 Training Squadrons.

Pup B7516; D.H.6 C241; B.E.2e C7157; S.E.5a D6960; Camel E7297; Dolphin; Avro 504K E9293.

Disbanded 14th March 1919 at Shotwick to become 51 Training Squadron.

52 TRAINING DEPOT STATION
Formed 15th July 1918 at Cramlington by redesignating 75 Training Squadron.

Handley Page O/100 3118; D.H.4; D.H.6 B2683; R.E.8 C2394; D.H.9 D1224; Avro 504K F2270.

Disbanded September 1919 at Cramlington to become 52 Training Squadron.

53 TRAINING DEPOT STATION
Formed 15th July 1918 at Dover (St Margarets) by redesignating 65 Training Squadron.

Avro 504A B3265; D.H.9 D3118; Camel F4189.

Disbanded 15th October 1918 at Dover (Swingate) to become the School for Marine Operational Pilots.

54 TRAINING DEPOT STATION
Formed 20th July 1918 at Fairlop by redesignating 207 Training Depot Station.

Pup C1515; Avro 504K D7660; D.H.9 D1218; Camel F2104.

Disbanded 10th July 1919 at Fairlop.

55 TRAINING DEPOT STATION
Formed 14th July 1918 at Manston by redesignating 203 Training Depot Station.

B.E.2e B4529; D.H.4 B9480; D.H.6 B2773; D.H.9 D472; Avro 504J D4361, Avro 504K D8851; S.E.5a E3951.

An element detached on 14th September 1918, joined elements from 1, 26 and 57 Training Depot Stations to become 155 Squadron.

Disbanded 14th March 1919 at Narborough to become 55 Training Squadron.

56 TRAINING DEPOT STATION
Formed 27th July 1918 at Cranwell by redesignating 201 Training Depot Station.

Spad A8803; Baby N1321; Pup C326; D.H.9 D2001; Avro 504J D7730, Avro 504K D8910; Snipe E7416; Camel F4204.

Disbanded 13th March 1919 at Cranwell.

57 TRAINING DEPOT STATION
Formed 27th July 1918 at Cranwell by redesignating 202 Training Depot Station.

B.E.2c 9473; D.H.4 B9479; D.H.6 B2783; D.H.9 C1244; Avro 504K D8910; Camel F4212; Baby N1996.

An element detached on 14th September 1918, joining elements from 1, 26 and 55 Training Depot Stations to become 155 Squadron.

Disbanded 13th March 1919 at Cranwell to become the Cadet College, Cranwell.

58 TRAINING DEPOT STATION
Formed 8th July 1918 at Cranwell by redesignating 213 Training Depot Station.

B.E.2e A1328; D.H.6 B2787; Handley Page O/100 9446; Handley Page O/400 D4582; F.E.2b D9152; Avro 504K E2929.

Disbanded 13th March 1919 at Cranwell.

59 TRAINING DEPOT STATION
Formed 8th July 1918 at Portholme Meadow by redesignating 211 Training Depot Station.

F.2B C903; B.E.2e C7183; D.H.9 H4231.

Disbanded 14th March 1920 at Scopwick to become 59 Training Squadron.

60 TRAINING DEPOT STATION
Formed 1st December 1918 at Aboukir, Egypt, by merging 22 and 23 Training Squadrons.

Pup D4048; Avro 504J D5486; Camel H760.

Disbanded 22nd July 1919 at Aboukir.

61 TRAINING DEPOT STATION
Formed 15th December 1918 at Tangmere by redesignating 40 Training Squadron.

Avro 504J E4336; F.2B C4793; Camel F6422.

Disbanded 20th June 1919 at Tangmere to become 61 Training Squadron.

201 TRAINING DEPOT STATION
Formed 1st April 1918 at Cranwell by redesignating part of the RNAS Training Establishment.

R.E.7 2260; Camel B7240; Baby N1996; Scout D N5406; Avro 504G N5806; Pup B2203; Avro 504J D7596.

Disbanded 27th July 1918 at Cranwell to become 56 Training Depot Station.

Reformed 14th August 1918 at East Fortune by merging 1 Torpedo Training Squadron and the Torpedo Aeroplane School.

F.2B B8942; Cuckoo N6930.

Disbanded 30th April 1919 at East Fortune to become the Torpedo Training School.

202 TRAINING DEPOT STATION
Formed 1st April 1918 at Cranwell by redesignating part of the RNAS Training Establishment, Cranwell.

B.E.2c 2737, B.E.2e 6259; Handley Page O/400 B9449; D.H.4 B9479; D.H.6 C2128; D.H.9 D2787; R.E.8 D4720.

Disbanded 27th July 1918 at Cranwell to become 57 Training Depot Station.

203 TRAINING DEPOT STATION
Formed 1st April 1918 at Manston by redesignating the RNAS D.H.4 School.

Avro 504G N5807, B.E.2c 9966, B.E.2e B3729; D.H.4 N6412; D.H.6 A9628; D.H.9 D1058; R.E.8 A3744.

Disbanded 15th July 1918 at Manston to become 55 Training Depot Station.

204 TRAINING DEPOT STATION
Formed 1st April 1918 at Eastchurch by redesignating the Naval Flying School, Eastchurch.

B.E.2c 9954; Avro 504A 2921, Avro 504J D7708, Avro 504K D8797; D.H.5; Pup N6169; Camel F9579, Camel (2-seater) B5713; 1½ Strutter N5220; Triplane N5460; Shorthorn N6317; Snipe E8171; D.H.4 A7817; D.H.6 C7767; D.H.9 C6280.

Disbanded March 1919 at Eastchurch.

205 TRAINING DEPOT STATION
Formed 1st April 1918 at Vendôme, France, by redesignating the Royal Naval Air Service Training Establishment, Vendôme.

Curtiss J.N.4 3438; Caudron G.3 N3050; Pup B1820; Camel B2488; Bristol Scout C 3060; Bristol Scout D N5411; Avro 504B 9828, Avro 504J D7512, Avro 504K E1625; D.H.6 C7653.

Disbanded 3rd November 1919 at Vendôme.

206 TRAINING DEPOT STATION
Formed 1st April 1918 at Eastbourne by redesignating the Naval Flying School, Eastbourne.

Pup B1821; Camel B5717; Avro 504A D1602, Avro 504B N6663, Avro 504J E4332.

Disbanded 15th July 1918 at Eastbourne and merged with 54 Training Squadron to become 50 Training Depot Station.

207 TRAINING DEPOT STATION
Formed 1st April 1918 at Chingford by redesignating the Naval Flying School, Chingford.

B.E.2c 9987; Avro 504A B3278, Avro 504B 9826; Nieuport 17 N5875; Bristol Scout D N5397; Avro 504K D7636; R.E.8 E32; 1½ Strutter N5172; Triplane N6303; Camel F9548; D.H.6 A9598; Pup B6086.

Disbanded 20th July 1918 at Chingford to become 54 Training Depot Station.

208 (TEMPORARY) TRAINING DEPOT STATION
Formed June 1918 at East Fortune as the Fleet and Torpedo Pilot Finishing School.

Pup D4034; Camel B7177; Bristol M.1C C4964; 1½ Strutter N5612; Beardmore W.B.III N6688.

Disbanded 19th July 1918 at Leuchars, one element becoming 1 Torpedo Training Squadron and the other the Grand Fleet School of Aerial Fighting and Gunnery.

209 (SEAPLANE) TRAINING DEPOT STATION
Formed 1st April 1918 at Lee-on-Solent by redesignating 'B' Flight, Lee-on-Solent.

Short 184 8068; Short 827 8230; FBA Type B 9617; Sage 4 N116.

Disbanded 15th May 1919 at Lee-on-Solent and merged with 210 Training Depot Station to become the Royal Air Force and Naval Co-operation School.

210 TRAINING DEPOT STATION
Formed by 18th June 1918 at Calshot.

Felixstowe F.2A N4534 G; Short 827 8561; Sage 4 N117; N.T.2B N2578; FBA Type B N2710; Short 184 N9039.

Disbanded 15th May 1919 at Calshot and merged with 209 (Seaplane) Training Depot Station to become the Royal Air Force and Naval Co-operation School.

211 TRAINING DEPOT STATION
Formed 1st April 1918 at Portholme Meadow.

B.E.2e A1287; D.H.6 B2792.

Disbanded July 1918 at Portholme Meadow to become 59 Training Depot Station.

212 TRAINING DEPOT STATION
Formed May 1918 at Vendôme, France.

Caudron G.3 N3051; Caudron G.4 3298; Curtiss J.N.4 8805; Bristol Scout D N5411; Avro 504J D7513, Avro 504K E1624.

Disbanded 3rd November 1919 at Vendôme.

213 TRAINING DEPOT STATION
Formed 17th June 1918 at Cranwell.

Handley Page O/400 B9449.

Disbanded 27th July 1918 at Cranwell to become 58 Training Depot Station.

TRAINING FLIGHT, HALTON
Formed by 28th July 1934 at Halton.

Tutor K3352.

Disbanded mid-1939 at Halton.

2 (TRAINING) FLIGHT, KENYA AUXILIARY AIR UNIT
Formed 6th September 1939 at Nairobi, Kenya.

Moth Major; Gipsy Moth K22; Swallow K21; Tiger Moth K27.

Disbanded 21st August 1940 at Eastleigh to become the Elementary Flying Training School (Kenya).

TRAINING SCHOOLS – see Training Depot Stations, later Training Schools

TRAINING SQUADRON, SYLT
Formed 17th July 1946 at Sylt, Germany, by merging 24 and 25 Armament Practice Camps.

Martinet I MS724 K; Tempest TT.5 SN209.

Disbanded February 1948 at Sylt and probably absorbed by the Armament Practice Station, Lübeck.

TRAINING SQUADRONS – see Reserve Aeroplane Squadrons, later Reserve Squadrons, later Training Squadrons

TRAINING UNIT AND RESERVE POOL
Formed 21st September 1940 at Ismailia by redesignating the Reinforcement and Reserve Pool.

Hardy K4314; Hind K5552; Wellesley K7789; Gauntlet II K7852; Blenheim I L8392; Magister I R1885; Hurricane I N2674.

Disbanded 10th December 1940 at Ismailia to become 70 Operational Training Unit.

1 (TRAINING) WIRELESS SCHOOL
Formed 8th November 1917 at Farnborough by redesignating 1 Wireless School.

B.E.2c 9966; F.2b C4696; F.K.3; F.K.8.

Disbanded 23rd December 1919 at Flowerdown to become the Electrical and Wireless School.

TRANSPORT COMMAND AIRCREW EXAMINING UNIT
Formed 1st November 1945 at Melbourne by redesignating the Aircrew Testing and Grading Unit.

Oxford I; Anson XII; Dakota III KG558; Lancastrian C.2 VM734; York I MW238 (on loan).

Disbanded 7th August 1946 at Bramcote to become the Transport Command Examining Unit.

TRANSPORT COMMAND AIR SUPPORT FLIGHT
Formed 1st February 1953 at Abingdon.

Hastings C.1 TG579, C.2 WD487; Valetta C.1 VX484; Chipmunk T.10 WB673.

Disbanded 14th September 1954 at Abingdon to become 1312 (Transport Support) Flight.

TRANSPORT COMMAND COMMUNICATION FLIGHT, later TRANSPORT COMMAND COMMUNICATION SQUADRON
Formed 8th April 1944 at Hendon being 'C' Flight, the (Transport Command Communication Flight) within the Metropolitan Communication Squadron. Became an independent entity on moving to Upavon during May 1966. Later redesignated the Transport Command Communication Squadron.

Proctor IV NP355; Dominie I NR803; Anson XII PH783, XIX TX172 B/MOALB, T.21 WD413; Devon C.1 VP963; C.2 VP968; Balliol T.2 WN161; Pembroke C.1 WV746; Sycamore HR.14 XG502; Basset CC.1 XS773.

Disbanded 1st April 1964 at Upavon and absorbed by the Western Communication Squadron.

TRANSPORT COMMAND DEVELOPMENT FLIGHT
Formed 14th October 1951 at Abingdon by redesignating the Air Transport Development Flight.

Anson XIX TX184; Hastings C.1A TG582, C.2 WD493; Devon C.1 VP962; Valetta C.1 VW199.

Disbanded 8th February 1957 at Benson.

TRANSPORT COMMAND DEVELOPMENT UNIT
Formed 31st August 1945 at Netheravon by redesignating the Air Transport Tactical Development Unit.

Stirling III LK114, V PJ958; Horsa II RN325; Hadrian II KK793; Hamilcar I NX868, X TK735; Mosquito B.25 KA944; Halifax VII PN259, VIII PP217, IX RT814; Hoverfly I KL110, II KN837; Liberator VI KG915; Dakota III FZ650, IV KN661; Proctor III HM427; York I MW168; Lancaster I RA510, III PB532; Lancastrian C.2 VM702; Buckingham II KV365; Oxford I HM811; Anson I NK178 A, XII PH528, XIX PH845 K; Tiger Moth II T7086; Auster V TJ198; Hastings C.1 TG568, C.2 WD493; Valetta C.1 VL274.

Disbanded 28th February 1950 at Abingdon to become the Air Transport Development Flight.

TRANSPORT COMMAND EXAMINING STAFF
Formed 23rd June 1964 at Benson by redesignating the Transport Command Examining Unit.

No aircraft allocated.

Disbanded 1st August 1967 at Benson to become the Air Support Examining Unit.

TRANSPORT COMMAND EXAMINING UNIT
Formed 7th August 1946 at Bramcote by redesignating the Transport Command Aircrew Examining Unit.

Anson XII PH718, XIX PH815; Dakota III KG558, IV KN452; York I MW204; Lancastrian II VM734; Hastings C.1 TG515; Valetta C.1 VL273.

Disbanded 23rd June 1964 at Benson to become the Transport Command Examining Staff.

TRANSPORT COMMAND METEOROLOGICAL FLIGHT – see 510 Squadron

TRANSPORT SUPPORT PRACTICE CAMP
Formed 1st April 1947 at Netheravon.

Horsa II.

Disbanded 5th January 1948 at Netheravon.

TRANSPORT SUPPORT PRACTICE CAMP (BAFO)
Formed 19th April 1948 at Schleswigland, Germany.

Horsa II; Hamilcar I; Oxford; Tiger Moth II.

Disbanded 1st November 1948 at Schleswigland.

TRANSPORT SUPPORT TRAINING UNIT
Formed 23rd May 1944 at Chaklala, India.

Proctor III LZ660; Harvard IIB FT101; Hurricane IIB HW566, IIC KZ569; Vengeance II; Dakota III FL557, IV; Hadrian II FR583; Liberator VI KH309; Tiger Moth I NL946, II NL807.

Disbanded 11th April 1945 at Gujrat, India, to become 1334 (Transport Support) Conversion Unit.

TRANSPORT TRAINING FLIGHT
Formed 15th June 1942 at Nanyuki, Kenya. Known also as the British Airways Training Unit.

Lodestar I EW981.

Disbanded 28th June 1942 at Nanyuki and absorbed by 70 Operational Training Unit.

TRI-NATIONAL TORNADO TRAINING ESTABLISHMENT
Formed 29th January 1981 at Cottesmore.

B   Tornado GR.1 ZA540 B-12, GR.1(T) ZA323
             B-14.

Current 1st April 1998 at Cottesmore. Scheduled to disband 31st March 1999.

TRIPARTITE SQUADRON – see Kestrel (P.1127) Evaluation Squadron

TROPICAL EXPERIMENTAL UNIT
Formed 1st April 1947 at Khartoum, Sudan, under the auspices of the Aeroplane and Armament Experimental Establishment. Transferred to Castel Benito (Idris from July 1952), Libya, from 1st July 1955.

Lincoln; York I MW112; Tempest VI; Vampire F.3 VG703; Hermes 4 G-ALDA; Balliol T.2 VW898; Sea Venom FAW.21 WM575, FAW.53 WZ894; Gannet AS.4 WN372; Valiant B.1 WP205; Canberra B(I).6 WT326; Auster AOP.9 WZ677; Beverley C.1 XB262; Whirlwind HAR.4 XD164; Hunter; Scout AH.1 XP165.

Disbanded 1st January 1960 at Idris, Libya, to become the Overseas Experimental Unit.

TURNHOUSE COMMUNICATION SQUADRON
Formed 1st October 1952 at Turnhouse by redesignating 66 Group Communication Flight.

Auster VI TJ348; Anson XII PH805, T.20 VS523.

Disbanded 28th February 1958 at Turnhouse.

TWIN PIONEER CONVERSION UNIT
Formed 1st January 1963 at Odiham by redesignating the Twin Pioneer element of 230 Squadron.

Twin Pioneer CC.1 XM285.

Disbanded 5th August 1964 at Odiham to become the Short-Range Conversion Unit.

TYPE FLIGHT – see Central Flying School

TYPE SQUADRON – see Central Flying School

TORPEDO DEVELOPMENT SECTION – see Royal Air Force Base, Gosport Training Squadron

TORPEDO EXPERIMENTAL FLIGHT – see Royal Air Force Base, Gosport Training Squadron

UNIVERSITIES OF GLASGOW AND STRATHCLYDE AIR SQUADRON – see Glasgow University Air Squadron later, Universities of Glasgow and Strathclyde Air Squadron

UNIVERSITY OF BIRMINGHAM AIR SQUADRON – see Birmingham University Air Squadron, later University of Birmingham Air Squadron

UNIVERSITY OF LIVERPOOL AIR SQUADRON – see Liverpool University Air Squadron, later University of Liverpool Air Squadron

UNIVERSITY OF LONDON AIR SQUADRON, later LONDON UNIVERSITY AIR SQUADRON, later UNIVERSITY OF LONDON AIR SQUADRON
Formed 30th September 1935 at the Imperial College of Science and Technology, London, as the London University Air Squadron.

Atlas K2538 X; Tutor K4828; Hart K4959 Y; Audax K5594; Tiger Moth I K4254.

Disbanded 5th September 1939 at Northolt.

Reformed 3rd April 1941 at the Imperial Institute, London. Redesignated the London University Air Squadron from 1946. Reverted to University of London Air Squadron from 1st December 1949.

Nil (4.41–4.46)	*Gipsy Moth DG659; Tiger Moth BB802; Tiger Moth II provided by 3 and 22 Elementary Flying Training Schools.*
FLO (10.46– .49)	*No aircraft known.*
RUL (.49–4.51)	*Tiger Moth I NL985, II DE248 RUL-G; Chipmunk T.10 WB611 RUL-H.*
Nil (4.51–)	*Chipmunk T.10 WP861 D; Oxford II VB861; Prentice T.1 VS651; Harvard IIB KF565 Y; Provost T.1 XF913; Bulldog T.1 XX695 10.*
Also used	*Tiger Moth I NL985;*

Current 1st April 1998 at Benson.

UNIVERSITY OF WALES AIR SQUADRON
Formed 26th August 1963 at St Athan.

Chipmunk T.10 WP804 D; Bulldog T.1 XX628 04.

Current 1st April 1998 at St Athan.

'V' FLIGHT
Formed 25th August 1939 at Ambala, India, by redesignating an element of 60 Squadron.

Blenheim I.

Disbanded 15th December 1940 at Juhu, India.

Reformed February 1941 at Juhu by redesignating an element of 20 Squadron.

Blenheim I; Audax.

Disbanded (date and location unknown).

VANGUARD FLIGHT – see Fighter Command Vanguard Flight

VC-10 OPERATIONAL CONVERSION UNIT – see 55 Squadron, RFC, later 55 Squadron, RAF, later 55 (Reserve) Squadron

'VERSAILLES' FLIGHT – see Groupe 'Ile de France'

VICTOR (B.2) TRAINING FLIGHT
Formed 1st April 1962 at Cottesmore by redesignating 'C' Squadron, 232 Operational Conversion Unit.

Victor B.2 XL188.

Disbanded 6th February 1970 at Wittering and merged with the Victor Training Unit to become 232 Operational Conversion Unit.

VICTOR (B.2) TRIALS UNIT
Formed September 1961 at Cottesmore.

Victor B.2 XL165.

Disbanded 1st February 1962 at Cottesmore to become 'C' Flight, 232 Operational Conversion Unit.

VICTOR FLIGHT
Formed 24th May 1974 at Wyton by redesignating an element of the disbanding 543 Squadron.

Victor SR.2 XH674.

Disbanded 30th May 1975 at Wyton.

VINTAGE PAIR FLIGHT – see Central Flying School

VISTRE FLIGHT
Formed 1st August 1946 at Erlestoke Camp to support the RAF Wing of the Visual Inter-Service Training and Research Establishment.

Dakota IV KN356; Anson I MH231; X NK507; XII PH639 B; Auster V RT483, VI VF550.

Disbanded 15th January 1952 at Old Sarum to become the Joint Concealment Centre (Royal Air Force Element).

VISUAL INTER-SERVICE TRAINING AND RESEARCH ESTABLISHMENT – see VISTRE Flight

VOICE FLIGHT
Formed 15th February 1954 at Kuala Lumpur, Malaya, within 267 Squadron. The Squadron disbanded 1st November 1958 at Kuala Lumpur to become 209 Squadron and the Voice Flight was transferred to the new nameplate.

Dakota IV KP277; Auster VI TW538.

Disbanded 2nd November 1959 at Bayan Lepas Airport, Penang.

VOLUNTEER GLIDING SCHOOLS – see Gliding Schools

VULCAN DISPLAY FLIGHT
Formed (date unknown) within 55 Squadron.

Vulcan B.2MRR XH558.

Disbanded 21st September 1992 at Waddington.

VVIP FLIGHT
Formed December 1944 at Northolt as a detached element of 246 Squadron.

York I LV633; Skymaster I KL980.

Disbanded November 1945 at Northolt.

'W' FLIGHT
Formed 9th February 1940 at Drigh Road, India, by redesignating 'H' Flight.

Blenheim I.

Disbanded 15th December 1940 at Drigh Road.

WALES UNIVERSITY AIR SQUADRON – see University of Wales Air Squadron

WARWICK TRAINING UNIT
Formed 28th June 1943 at Docking.

| FI | Wellington IC R3215; Warwick I BV287 FI-V. |

Disbanded 13th October 1943 at Bircham Newton to become the Air Sea Rescue Training Unit.

WASHINGTON CONVERSION UNIT
Formed 23rd February 1950 at Marham as the B-29 Training Squadron by redesignating elements of 35 Squadron. Redesignated the Washington Conversion Unit from 1st July 1950.

| FB | Washington B.1 WF434 FB-K; Oxford I NM510. |

Disbanded 27th March 1953 at Marham.

WELLINGTON FLIGHT, LUQA – see Wellington Flight, Malta

WELLINGTON FLIGHT, MALTA
Formed October 1940 by merging elements of 49 and 75 Squadrons (at Mildenhall) and 38 and 115 Squadrons (at Marham) operating from Luqa, Malta, from 9th November 1940.

Wellington IC T2877.

Disbanded 1st December 1940 at Luqa to become 148 Squadron.

WESSEX BOMBING AREA COMMUNICATION FLIGHT
Formed by 28th May 1926 at Andover.

D.H.9A J7794.

Disbanded 28th March 1927 at Andover and merged with the Royal

Air Force Staff College Flight to become the Andover Communication Flight.

WESSEX TRAINING FLIGHT
Formed 3rd November 1980 at Benson by redesignating an element of 240 Operational Conversion Unit.

| B | Wessex HC.2 XS676 BV. |

Disbanded 30th April 1982 at Benson.

WESSEX INTENSIVE FLYING TRIALS UNIT
Formed 1st July 1963 at Odiham.

Wessex HC.2 XR502

Disbanded 27th January 1964 at Odiham to become 18 Squadron.

WEST AFRICA COMMAND COMMUNICATION SQUADRON – see West Africa Communication Squadron, later West Africa Command Communication Squadron, later West Africa Communication Squadron

WEST AFRICA COMMUNICATION SQUADRON, later WEST AFRICA COMMAND COMMUNICATION SQUADRON, later WEST AFRICA COMMUNICATION SQUADRON
Formed 31st May 1944 at Waterloo, Sierra Leone. Redesignated the West Africa Command Communication Squadron from July 1945.

Anson I NK902, XII PH678; Lysander III R9022; Dominie I NR700; Argus III KK393; Tiger Moth II EM989; Harvard IIA EX498; Dakota III KG528, IV KJ836.

Disbanded 1st November 1945 at Accra, Gold Coast, and merged with 1314 (Transport) Flight to become the West Africa Transport and Communication Squadron.

Reformed 1st October 1946 at Takoradi, Gold Coast, by redesignating the West Africa Transport and Communication Squadron.

Anson XII PH678; Dakota IV KJ837; Dominie I NR700.

Disbanded 25th September 1947 at Takoradi.

WEST AFRICA TRANSPORT AND COMMUNICATION SQUADRON
Formed 1st November 1945 at Accra, Gold Coast, by merging the West Africa Command Communication Squadron and 1314 (Transport) Flight.

Dakota III KG739, IV KJ836; Dominie I NR700; Anson XII PH679.

Disbanded 1st October 1946 at Takoradi, Gold Coast, to become the West Africa Communication Squadron.

WESTERN COMMUNICATION SQUADRON
Formed 1st April 1964 at Andover by merging the Maintenance Command Communication and Ferry Squadron and the Training Command Communication Squadron.

Anson XIX TX160; Devon C.1 VP952; Pembroke C.1 WV733, C(PR).1 XF796; Basset C.1 XS766.

Disbanded 3rd February 1969 at Andover to become 21 Squadron.

WESTERN DESERT COMMUNICATION FLIGHT – see Communication Flight, Air Headquarters Western Desert

WESTERN UNION EXAMINING SQUADRON
Formed 1st January 1950 at Brize Norton.

Martinet I JN274; Anson XIX TX256 T; Harvard IIB.

Disbanded 31st October 1951 at Little Rissington only to be reformed the next day as a French unit at Villacoublay, France, with attached Royal Air Force personnel. Records cease 31st March 1952 at Villacoublay.

70 WING CALIBRATION FLIGHT
Formed 16th February 1941 at Longman by redesignating 1 Radio Servicing Section Calibration Flight.

Blenheim IV L4867; Hornet Moth W9391; Oxford II X7238; Tiger Moth II T6765.

Disbanded 15th June 1943 at Longman and merged with 71 Wing Calibration Flight to become 526 Squadron.

71 WING CALIBRATION FLIGHT
Formed 16th February 1941 at Dyce by redesignating 2 Radio Servicing Section Calibration Flight.

Blenheim IV T1925; Mentor L4406; Hornet Moth W5781; Tiger Moth II T6766.

Disbanded 15th June 1943 at Dyce and merged with 70 Wing Calibration Flight to become 526 Squadron.

72 WING CALIBRATION FLIGHT
Formed 16th February 1941 at Usworth by redesignating 3 Radio Servicing Section Calibration Flight.

Hornet Moth W5775; Blenheim IV Z6101; Tiger Moth II T5563; Oxford II X7200.

Disbanded 15th June 1943 at Usworth and absorbed by 526 Squadron.

73 WING CALIBRATION FLIGHT
Formed 16th February 1941 at Church Fenton by redesignating 4 Radio Servicing Section Calibration Flight.

Blenheim IV Z6101; Hornet Moth W5778; Tiger Moth II T7613.

Disbanded 30th October 1942 and absorbed by 77 Wing Calibration Flight.

74 WING CALIBRATION FLIGHT
Formed 16th February 1941 at Duxford by redesignating 5 Radio Servicing Section Calibration Flight.

LW   Blenheim IV T2140; Cierva C.30 BV999; Cierva C.30A DR622; Pitcairn PA.39 BW834; Hornet Moth W6422; Tiger Moth II T6768; Hurricane X AG146.

Disbanded 15th June 1943 at Duxford and merged with 75 Wing Calibration Flight to become 527 Squadron.

75 WING CALIBRATION FLIGHT
Formed 16th February 1941 at Biggin Hill by redesignating 6 Radio Servicing Section Calibration Flight.

LW   Blenheim IV N3598 LW-K; Cierva C.40A P9639; Demon K5702; Hornet Moth W5773 LW; Tiger Moth II T6166.

Disbanded 15th June 1943 at Biggin Hill and merged with 74 Wing Calibration Flight to become 527 Squadron.

76 WING CALIBRATION FLIGHT
Formed 16th February 1941 at Filton by redesignating 7 Radio Servicing Section Calibration Flight.

QL (2.41–1.42)   Blenheim IV T2219 QL-N.
LW (1.42–6.43)   Blenheim IV T2219 LW-N.
Also used   Hornet Moth W5747; Tiger Moth II T6863.

Disbanded 15th June 1943 at Filton.

77 WING CALIBRATION FLIGHT
Formed 16th February 1941 at Speke by redesignating 8 Radio Servicing Section Calibration Flight.

Hornet Moth W5747; Blenheim IV Z6168; Dragon Rapide X9457; Tiger Moth II T6862.

Disbanded 6th November 1943 at Speke to become 1 Calibration Flight.

78 WING CALIBRATION FLIGHT
Formed 25th May 1941 at Filton.

Blenheim IV T2219; Hornet Moth AW118.

Disbanded 15th June 1943 at Harrowbeer to become 528 Squadron.

79 WING CALIBRATION FLIGHT
Formed October 1941 at Long Kesh.

Blenheim IV T2004; Dragon Rapide X9457; Hornet Moth W5749; Tiger Moth II T6863.

Disbanded 30th October 1942 at Speke and absorbed by 77 Wing Calibration Flight.

110 WING CALIBRATION FLIGHT
Formed 1st March 1940 at Ringway.

Battle L5211; Leopard Moth X9380; Magister L8061; Proctor III R7567; Vega Gull X9349; Dragonfly X9337; Percival Q-6 X9336; Scion X9364; Monospar X9330; Dragon Rapide X9386; Aldon AW167; Gull Six AX866.

Disbanded 5th May 1941 at Filton.

85 WING COMMUNICATION SQUADRON, later 85 WING COMMUNICATION FLIGHT – see 85 Group Communication Squadron, later 85 Wing Communication Squadron, later 85 Wing Communication Flight, later 85 Group Communication Flight

87 WING COMMUNICATION FLIGHT – see 87 Group Communication Flight, later 87 Wing Communication Flight

WINTER EXPERIMENTAL AND TRAINING FLIGHT, later WINTER RESEARCH ESTABLISHMENT, later WINTERISATION EXPERIMENTAL ESTABLISHMENT
Formed (date unknown) by the Royal Canadian Air Force at Gimli, Manitoba. Redesignated the Winter Research Establishment from 2nd October 1945 on moving to Edmonton, Alberta. Later became the Winterisation Experimental Establishment and finally 1 Winterisation Experimental Flight. A Royal Air Force Section used the facilities until 17th October 1949 when the Aircraft and Armament Experimental Establishment assumed responsibility for trials.

Halifax VI RG814; Lancaster III EE182, X FM148; Lincoln I RE258; Spitfire XIV TZ138; Tempest VI NV999; Meteor F.3 EE361; F.4 RA421; Tempest VI NV999; Spitfire F.24 VN332; Prentice T.1 VR189; Lincoln B.2 SX924; Bristol 170 WJ320; Mk.31 Freighter WH575; Valetta C.1 VL266; Hastings C.1 TG506; Balliol T.2 VR597.

Disbanded 11th November 1951 at Edmonton to become the Canadian Experimental Proving Establishment.

WINTERISATION EXPERIMENTAL ESTABLISHMENT – see Winter Experimental and Training Flight, later Winter Research Establishment, later Winterisation Experimental Establishment

WINTER RESEARCH ESTABLISHMENT – see Winter Experimental and Training Flight, later Winter Research Establishment, later Winterisation Experimental Establishment

WIRELESS AND OBSERVERS SCHOOL, BROOKLANDS
Formed 24th October 1916 at Brooklands by redesignating the Wireless School.

B.E.2c 1794; R.E.7 2402; B.E.2e A1300; R.E.8 A3672.

Disbanded 7th November 1917 at Hursley Park to become the Artillery and Infantry Co-operation School.

WIRELESS AND OBSERVERS SCHOOL, EGYPT
Formed 1919 at Heliopolis, Egypt, by probably redesignating the Wireless School, Egypt.

No aircraft, if any, known.

Disbanded 1919 at Heliopolis.

WIRELESS DEVELOPMENT UNIT
Formed 19th September 1939 at Perth by redesignating the Royal Air Force Detachment, Perth (or the Radio Direction Finding Co-operation Flight).

Blenheim I, IV; Battle; Whitley; Wellington I L4343 (214 Squadron); Hampden I L4191 (185 Squadron); Swordfish I K8881 (on loan); Walrus I L2265; Skua I L2900; Hudson I N7244 (233 Squadron).

Disbanded 24th October 1939 at Perth to become the Station Flight, Perth.

WIRELESS DIRECTION FINDING FLIGHT
Formed by September 1937 at Martlesham Heath.

Anson; Heyford K6902.

Disbanded April 1938 at Martlesham Heath to become the Experimental Co-operation Unit.

WIRELESS EXPERIMENTAL ESTABLISHMENT, later WIRELESS TELEGRAPHY ESTABLISHMENT
Formed 14th December 1917 at Biggin Hill by redesignating the Wireless Testing Park. Redesignated the Wireless Telegraphy Establishment from 2nd April 1918.

1½ Strutter A5252; Vampire I B1484; B.E.2e B6198; Camel C1614 3; S.E.5a B607 1; F.2A, F.2B A7107 6; D.H.4 N6428; D.H.9 B7651; Handley Page O/100 B9450; Handley Page O/400 C3491; Bristol M.1C C4908; Dolphin C3912; F.K.8 C8529; Snipe E8027; Pup D4097 1; Avro 504K D9297.

Disbanded 1st November 1919 at Biggin Hill to become the Instrument Design Establishment.

WIRELESS FLIGHT
Formed September 1914 at Fere-en-Tardenois, France.

B.E.2a 336; Longhorn 1830.

Disbanded 8th December 1914 at St Omer, France, to become 9 Squadron.

WIRELESS INTELLIGENCE DEVELOPMENT UNIT
Formed 14th October 1940 at Boscombe Down by redesignating the Blind Approach Training and Development Unit.

Anson I N9945; Wellington IC T2552.

Disbanded 10th December 1940 at Boscombe Down to become 109 Squadron.

WIRELESS SCHOOL, BROOKLANDS
Formed by April 1916 at Brooklands.

Shorthorn 515; R.E.7 2329; B.E.2c 5441; B.E.2d 6747.

Disbanded 24th October 1916 at Brooklands to become the Wireless and Observers School, Brooklands.

WIRELESS SCHOOL, EGYPT
Formed by early 1918 in Egypt.

B.E.2c.

Disbanded 1919 at Heliopolis to probably become the Wireless and Observers School.

2 WIRELESS SCHOOL
Formed 8th November 1917 at Penshurst.

D.H.6 B3010 10; B.E.2e 7237; Avro 504K E3488; Camel C8312; Snipe E6164.

Disbanded 23rd March 1919 at Penshurst.

WIRELESS TELEGRAPHY ESTABLISHMENT – see Wireless Experimental Establishment, later Wireless Telegraphy Establishment

WIRELESS TELEPHONY SCHOOL
Formed 2nd April 1918 at Biggin Hill.

F.K.8 B4049; R.E.8; B.E.2c, B.E.2d, B.E.2e A1299; F.2B B1291; Elephant A6275; Bristol M.1C; Pup; Camel B5234, C1614; 1½ Strutter A5252.

Disbanded 1st September at Beaulieu.

WIRELESS TESTING PARK
Formed 21st October 1916 at Joyce Green by redesignating an element of the Wireless and Observers School.

1½ Strutter A2409; F.K.8 B4049; R.E.7; B.E.2e B719.

Disbanded 14th December 1917 at Biggin Hill to become the Wireless Experimental Establishment.

WOLVERHAMPTON UNIVERSITY AIR SQUADRON
Planned formation cancelled, although the code FLS was allocated.

WOMEN'S FERRY PILOTS POOL – see Air Transport Auxiliary

'X' (CANADIAN) RESERVE SQUADRON
Formed 27th February 1917 at Long Branch, Canada. Began flying training the next day and became the nucleus for 78, 79, 80, 81 and 82 (Canadian) Reserve Squadrons. Moved to Camp Rathbun on 1st May 1917.

Curtiss JN-4.

Disbanded July 1917 at Mohawk, Canada, when the Reserve Squadrons were established.

'X' FLIGHT, RFC, later 'X' FLIGHT, RAF
Formed 3rd November 1917 at Aqaba, Egypt, as the Detached Flight, 14 Squadron. Redesignated the Special Duty Flight then 'X' Flight, RFC on 18th and 24th November 1917 respectively. Redesignated 'X' Flight, RAF from 1st April 1918.

D.H.2 A4779; B.E.2e; B.E.12 A6323; F.2B A7184; Nieuport 17 B1566.

Disbanded 19th October 1918 at Aqaba.

'X' FLIGHT
Formed May 1940 at Haifa, Palestine.

Gladiator I K7899.

Disbanded June 1940 at Haifa.

Reformed 6th June 1941 at Habbaniya, Iraq, from 'A' Squadron of the Habbaniya Air Defence Wing.

Gladiator I K6140, II N5777.

Disbanded 30th June 1941 at Habbaniya.

Reformed 16th July 1942 at Abadan, Iraq.

Gladiator I K7928, II N5780.

Disbanded 30th October 1942 at Abadan.

'X' SQUADRON
Formed 18th March 1943 at Scampton.

Lancaster.

Disbanded 24th March 1943 at Scampton to become 617 Squadron.

'X' SQUADRON, EGYPT
Formed by 17th March 1919 at Amriya, Egypt, by redesignating an element of 16 Training Depot Station.

B.E.12; R.E.8; D.H.6; F.2B.

Disbanded June 1919 at Almaza, Egypt.

'Y' FLIGHT
Formed 25th August 1939 at Ambala, India, by redesignating an element of 60 Squadron.

Blenheim I L1530.

Disbanded by December 1940 at St Thomas Mount, India.

Reformed February 1941 at St Thomas Mount by redesignating an element of 20 Squadron.

Audax.

Disbanded (date and location unknown).

'Y' (CANADIAN) RESERVE SQUADRON
Formed March 1917 at Long Branch, Canada, as the nucleus for 83, 84, 85, 86, 87, 88, 89, 90 and 91 (Canadian) Reserve Squadrons. Moved to Armour Heights on 6th July 1917.

Curtiss JN-4 C184 A.

Disbanded 6th July 1917 at Armour Heights and absorbed by 91 (Canadian) Reserve Squadron.

'Y' SQUADRON, EGYPT
Formed 17th March 1919 at Heliopolis, Egypt, by redesignating an element of 5 Fighting School. Moved to Wasta 20th March 1919, then to Beni-Suef, Assintby and Almaza.

F.2B; D.H.9; R.E.8; Nieuport; S.E.5a.

Disbanded 21st July 1919 at Assiut, Egypt.

'Y' SQUADRON, IRAQ
Formed late 1940 at Habbaniya. A possible reference to a detachment of 216 or 244 Squadrons.

No aircraft known.

Ceased to exist late 1940 at Habbaniya.

YATESBURY UNIVERSITY AIR SQUADRON
Planned formation cancelled, although the code FLU was allocated.

YATESBURY WIRELESS FLIGHT
Formed 14th May 1940 at Yatesbury by redesignating the D.H.89A Flight of 2 Electrical and Wireless School.

D.H.89A P9588.

Disbanded 26th August 1940 at Yatesbury and absorbed by 2 Signals School.

YORKSHIRE UNIVERSITIES AIR SQUADRON
Formed 15th March 1969 at Church Fenton by merging the Hull and Leeds University Air Squadrons.

Chipmunk T.10 WK638 F; Bulldog T.1 XX643 F.

Current at 1st April 1998 at Church Fenton.

YUGOSLAV HOLDING UNIT – see Yugoslav Training Flight, later Yugoslav Holding Unit

YUGOSLAV TRAINING FLIGHT, later YUGOSLAV HOLDING UNIT
Formed 25th February 1944 at Benina, Libya. Redesignated as the Yugoslav Holding Unit from 1st May 1944.

Harvard IIB FT152; Hurricane IIC.

Disbanded 31st July 1945 at Benina.

YUGOSLAV TRAINING FLIGHT, ROYAL AIR FORCE ELEMENT
Formed February 1945 at Bari, Italy.

Tiger Moth I NL983; II NL834; Harvard IIB KF283; Argus II FS513.

Disbanded 17th August 1945 at Zemunik, Yugoslavia.

'Z' FLIGHT
Formed March 1918 at Istrana, Italy, by redesignating an element of 34 Squadron.

F.2B B1212.

Disbanded 3rd July 1918 at Villaverla, Italy, to become 139 Squadron.

Reformed 30th November 1919 at Taganrog, Russia.

R.E.8; F.2B.

Existed until January 1920 at Rostov, Russia.

Reformed 28th August 1939 at Ambala, India, by redesignating an element of 60 Squadron.

Blenheim I L1532.

Disbanded December 1940 at Dum-Dum, India.

'Z' SQUADRON, AEGEAN
Formed 1st April 1918 at Thásos, Aegean, by redesignating 'Z' Squadron of 2 Wing, RNAS.

No aircraft known.

Disbanded 18th September 1918 at Mudros, Aegean, and merged with 'A' Squadron to become 222 Squadron.

'Z' SQUADRON, EGYPT
Formed 17th March 1919 at Heliopolis, Egypt, by redesignating an element of 5 Fighting School.

Avro 504; B.E.2e A3081; F.K.3 B9563; F.K.8; D.H.9 D3144; R.E.8 C5054.

Disbanded July 1919 at Heliopolis.

'Z' UNIT, BRITISH SOMALILAND
Departed 13th November 1919 from the United Kingdom aboard HMS *Ark Royal* for Berbera, British Somaliland. Operations, as an element of 'Z' Force, commenced from 21st January 1920 from Eil dur Elan.

D.H.9 H5551, D.H.9 Ambulance D3117 6.

The Unit ceased operations on 9th February 1920, withdrew to Berbera on 18th February and was disbanded during April 1920 at Suez, Egypt.

Appendix 1

Unit Identification Codes

The following alphabetical list of unit identification codes includes confirmed allocations, confirmed allocations with no evidence of use and probable use based upon available information.

A   3 Squadron, 5 Squadron, 9 Squadron, 14 Squadron, 39 Squadron, 42 Squadron, 43 Squadron, 56 Squadron, 72 Squadron, 94 Squadron, 112 Squadron, 118 Squadron, 120 Squadron, 201 Squadron, 202 Squadron, 217 Squadron, 266 Squadron, 541 Squadron, 111 Operational Training Unit, 229 Operational Conversion Unit, 1 Photographic Reconnaissance Unit, Royal Air Force College Flying Training School, 4 Flying Training School, 14 (Advanced) Flying Training School, 19 Flying Training School

AA   75 Squadron, 134 Squadron

AB   423 Squadron, 1557 (Radio Aids Training) Flight

AC   138 Squadron

AD   60 Squadron, 113 Squadron, 251 Squadron

AE   402 Squadron, 1409 (Long Range Meteorological) Flight,

AF   294 Squadron, 607 Squadron, Air Fighting Development Establishment, Air Fighting Development Unit

AG   197 Squadron

AH   332 Squadron

AI   20 Operational Training Unit

AJ   617 Squadron, Station Flight North Luffenham

AK   213 Squadron, 1657 Conversion Unit

AL   79 Squadron, 429 Squadron

AM   219 Squadron, 14 Operational Training Unit

AN   13 Squadron, 417 Squadron, Station Flight Great Dunmow

AO   267 Squadron

AP   130 Squadron, 186 Squadron

AQ   276 Squadron, 345 Squadron

AR   309 Squadron, 460 Squadron

AS   83 Squadron, 97 Squadron, 100 Squadron, 166 Squadron, 176 Squadron

AT   299 Squadron, 13 Operational Training Unit, 60 Operational Training Unit

AU   148 Squadron, 279 Squadron, 421 Squadron

AV   121 Squadron

AW   42 Squadron, 504 Squadron, 664 Squadron

AX   161 Squadron, 202 Squadron

AY   110 Squadron, 17 Operational Training Unit

AZ   234 Squadron, 627 Squadron

A2   514 Squadron

A3   1653 Conversion Unit, 230 Operational Conversion Unit

A4   115 Squadron, 195 Squadron

A5   3 Lancaster Finishing School

A6   257 Squadron

A9   Station Flight Woodbridge

B   2 Squadron, 4 Squadron, 5 Squadron, 11 Squadron, 14 Squadron, 17 Squadron, 18 Squadron, 29 Squadron, 56 Squadron, 87 Squadron, 111 Squadron, 145 Squadron, 203 Squadron, 206 Squadron, 269 Squadron, 5 (Pilot) Advanced Flying Unit, 224 Squadron, 230 Squadron, 269 Squadron, Canberra Standardisation and Training Flight, 231 Operational Conversion Unit, 240 Operational Conversion Unit, 4 Flying Training School, 19 Flying Training School, Air Training Squadron, Helicopter Operational Conversion Flight, Royal Air Force College Flying Training School, Wessex Training Flight, Tri-National Tornado Training Establishment

BA   277 Squadron

BB   347 Squadron, 27 Operational Training Unit, 226 Operational Conversion Unit

BC   511 Squadron, Photographic Reconnaissance Development Unit

BD   43 Operational Training Unit, 227 Operational Conversion Unit, Air Observation Post School, Light Aeroplane School

BE   284 Squadron, 8 Operational Training Unit

BF   14 Squadron, 28 Squadron, 54 Operational Training Unit

BG   606 Squadron, 660 Squadron

BH   215 Squadron, 228 Squadron, 300 Squadron

BI   Station Flight Holme-on-Spalding Moor

BJ   271 Squadron, 334 Squadron

BK   115 Squadron, Southern Sector Communication Flight

BL   40 Squadron, 609 Squadron, 1656 Conversion Unit

BM   308 Squadron, 433 Squadron

BN   170 Squadron, 240 Squadron, 618 Squadron, 1401 Flight

BO   630 Squadron

BP   457 Squadron, 519 Squadron

BQ   451 Squadron, 509 Squadron, 550 Squadron, 600 Squadron

BR   184 Squadron

BS   120 Squadron, 148 Squadron, 160 Squadron, 1651 Conversion Unit

BT   113 Squadron, 252 Squadron, 30 Operational Training Unit

BTU   Bombing Trials Unit

BU   214 Squadron, 214 Squadron Conversion Flight, 227 Squadron

BV   305 Squadron

BW   58 Squadron

BX   86 Squadron

BY   58 Squadron, 59 Squadron, 255 Squadron, 23 Operational Training Unit

BZ   107 Squadron, 82 Operational Training Unit

B3   Station Flight Wyton

B4   282 Squadron

B6   Station Flight Spilsby

B7   Station Flight Waddington

B8   Station Flight Woodhall Spa

B9   1562 Flight

C   4 Squadron, 5 Squadron, 17 Squadron, 20 Squadron, 33 Squadron, 100 Squadron, 208 Squadron, 216 Squadron, 1563 Flight, 228 Operational Conversion Unit, 236 Operational Conversion Unit, 237 Operational Conversion Unit, 240 Operational Conversion Unit, 111 Operational Training Unit, Air Training Squadron, Royal Air Force College Flying Training School, 19 Flying Training School, 2nd Tactical Air Force Communication Squadron

CA   189 Squadron

CB   31 Squadron, Metropolitan Communication Squadron

CC   Station Flight Holmsley South

CE   5 Lancaster Finishing School

CF   625 Squadron

CG   Station Flight Binbrook

CH   Station Flight Swinderby

CJ   203 Squadron

CL   Station Flight Little Staughton

CM   107 Operational Training Unit, 1333 Conversion Unit, 42 Group Communication Flight

CO   84 Operational Training Unit

CP   Station Flight Topcliffe

CR   162 Squadron

CS   513 Squadron, Station Flight Upwood

CV   Station Flight Tuddenham

CX   14 Squadron

CY   Station Flight Ludford Magna

CZ   84 Operational Training Unit

C2   Bomber Command Instructors School

C5   Station Flight Tibenham

C6   51 Squadron

C8   640 Squadron

D   11 Squadron, 15 Squadron, 31 Squadron, 230 Squadron, 234 Squadron, Lightning Training Flight, 235 Operational Conversion Unit, Royal Air Force College Flying Training School, 4 Flying Training School, 7 Flying Training School, 14 (Advanced) Flying Training School, 19 Flying Training School

DA   210 Squadron, 273 Maintenance Unit

DB   229 Squadron, 411 Squadron

DC   Station Flight Oakington

DD   45 Squadron, 22 Operational Training Unit

DE	86 Squadron, 61 Operational Training Unit
DF	221 Squadron, Central Bomber Establishment
DG	150 Squadron, 155 Squadron, 422 Squadron
DH	540 Squadron, 1664 Conversion Unit
DI	Station Flight Kemble
DJ	15 Squadron, 612 Squadron
DK	32 Operational Training Unit
DL	54 Squadron, 91 Squadron, 92 Squadron, 421 Flight
DM	248 Squadron
DN	416 Squadron
DO	199 Squadron
DP	30 Squadron, 193 Squadron, 1416 Flight
DQ	128 Squadron, 228 Squadron, 1402 Flight
DR	180 Squadron, 1555 Flight, 1697 Flight
DS	Station Flight Llanbedr
DT	192 Squadron, 257 Squadron
DU	70 Squadron, 312 Squadron
DV	129 Squadron
DW	610 Squadron
DX	57 Squadron, 230 Squadron, 245 Squadron
DY	102 Squadron, 102 Squadron Conversion Flight, 508 Squadron
DZ	151 Squadron
D2	1606 Flight
D4	620 Squadron
D6	Station Flight Hethal
D8	5 Ferry Pool, 22 Maintenance Unit
E	6 Squadron, 7 Squadron, 15 Squadron, 18 Squadron, 23 Squadron, 72 Squadron, 360 Squadron, 5 (Pilots) Advanced Flying Unit, Royal Air Force College Flying Training School, 19 Flying Training School
EA	49 Squadron, 49 Squadron Conversion Flight, 325 Squadron, Central Fighter Establishment
EB	41 Squadron
EC	Station Flight Odiham
ED	21 Operational Training Unit
EE	16 Squadron, 404 Squadron, Station Flight Elvington
EF	15 Squadron, 102 Squadron, 232 Squadron, 36 Operational Training Unit
EG	16 Squadron, 34 Squadron, 268 Squadron, 302 Squadron, 355 Squadron, 487 Squadron
EH	109 Squadron, 3 Tactical Exercise Unit, 55 Operational Training Unit
EJ	127 Squadron, Coastal Command Flying Instructors School, Coastal Command Instructors School
EK	168 Squadron, 1656 Conversion Unit
EL	71 Squadron, 181 Squadron, 10 Operational Training Unit
EM	207 Squadron, 207 Squadron Conversion Flight
EN	27 Operational Training Unit
EO	404 Squadron, 15 Operational Training Unit
EP	104 Squadron, 84 Group Communication Flight
EQ	57 Squadron, 408 Squadron, 408 Squadron Conversion Flight
ER	621 Squadron, 1552 Flight
ES	541 Squadron, 628 Squadron, 229 Operational Conversion Unit
EU	641 Squadron, 26 Operational Training Unit
EV	191 Squadron, 180 Squadron
EW	47 Squadron, 307 Squadron
EX	6 Squadron, 11 Squadron, 117 Squadron, 199 Squadron
EY	78 Squadron, 78 Squadron Conversion Flight, 80 Squadron, 233 Squadron
EZ	241 Squadron, 1380 Conversion Unit, 81 Operational Training Unit
E2	Station Flight Warboys
E4	Station Flight Wickenby
E7	570 Squadron
E9	Station Flight Westcott
F	12 Squadron, 16 Squadron, 25 Squadron, Air/Sea Warfare Development Unit, 6 Flying Training School, 111 Operational Training Unit, 240 Operational Conversion Unit, 4 Flying Training School, 19 Flying Training School
FA	236 Squadron, 281 Squadron
FAA	19 Flying Training School, Royal Air Force College Flying Training School
FAB	19 Flying Training School, Royal Air Force College Flying Training School
FAC	19 Flying Training School, Royal Air Force College Flying Training School

FAD	19 Flying Training School, Royal Air Force College Flying Training School
FAE	19 Flying Training School, Royal Air Force College Flying Training School
FAF	19 Flying Training School, Royal Air Force College Flying Training School
FAG	19 Flying Training School, Royal Air Force College Flying Training School
FAI	20 Flying Training School, 20 Service Flying Training School, Flying Training School, 2 Flying Training School
FAJ	20 Flying Training School, 20 Service Flying Training School, 2 Flying Training School
FAK	20 Flying Training School, 20 Service Flying Training School, 2 Flying Training School
FAL	20 Flying Training School, 20 Service Flying Training School, 2 Flying Training School
FAM	20 Flying Training School, 20 Service Flying Training School, 2 Flying Training School
FAN	21 Flying Training School
FAO	21 Flying Training School
FAP	21 Flying Training School
FAQ	21 Flying Training School
FAS	16 (Polish) Flying Training School
FAT	16 (Polish) Flying Training School
FAU	16 (Polish) Flying Training School
FAV	16 (Polish) Flying Training School
FAW	16 (Polish) Flying Training School
FAX	16 (Polish) Flying Training School
FAY	16 (Polish) Flying Training School
FB	35 Squadron, 24 Operational Training Unit, Washington Conversion Unit
FBA	7 Service Flying Training School, 7 Flying Training School
FBB	7 Service Flying Training School, 7 Flying Training School
FBC	7 Service Flying Training School, 7 Flying Training School
FBD	7 Service Flying Training School, 7 Flying Training School
FBE	7 Service Flying Training School, 7 Flying Training School
FBG	6 Service Flying Training School, 6 Flying Training School
FBH	6 Service Flying Training School, 6 Flying Training School
FBI	6 Service Flying Training School, 6 Flying Training School
FBJ	6 Service Flying Training School, 6 Flying Training School
FBK	6 Service Flying Training School, 6 Flying Training School
FBL	6 Service Flying Training School, 6 Flying Training School
FBM	6 Service Flying Training School, 6 Flying Training School
FBN	6 Service Flying Training School, 6 Flying Training School
FBP	3 Service Flying Training School, 3 Flying Training School
FBQ	3 Service Flying Training School, 3 Flying Training School
FBR	3 Service Flying Training School, 3 Flying Training School
FBS	3 Service Flying Training School, 3 Flying Training School
FBT	3 Service Flying Training School, 3 Flying Training School
FBU	3 Service Flying Training School, 3 Flying Training School
FBV	3 Service Flying Training School, 3 Flying Training School
FBW	3 Service Flying Training School, 3 Flying Training School
FBX	3 Service Flying Training School, 3 Flying Training School
FC	Station Flight Kenley
FCA	17 Service Flying Training School, 17 Flying Training School, 1 Flying Training School
FCB	17 Service Flying Training School, 17 Flying Training School, 1 Flying Training School
FCC	17 Service Flying Training School, 17 Flying Training School, 1 Flying Training School
FCD	17 Service Flying Training School, 17 Flying Training School, 1 Flying Training School
FCE	17 Service Flying Training School, 17 Flying Training School, 1 Flying Training School
FCF	17 Service Flying Training School, 17 Flying Training School, 1 Flying Training School
FCG	17 Service Flying Training School, 17 Flying Training School, 1 Flying Training School
FCI	22 Service Flying Training School, 22 Flying Training School
FCJ	22 Service Flying Training School, 22 Flying Training School
FCK	22 Service Flying Training School, 22 Flying Training School
FCL	22 Service Flying Training School, 22 Flying Training School
FCM	22 Service Flying Training School, 22 Flying Training School
FCT	Empire Central Flying School, Empire Flying School, Royal Air Force Flying College
FCU	Empire Central Flying School, Empire Flying School, Royal Air Force Flying College
FCV	Empire Central Flying School, Empire Flying School, Royal Air Force Flying College

FCW	Empire Central Flying School, Empire Flying School, Royal Air Force Flying College		FGA	Empire Air Armament School, Royal Air Force Flying College
FCX	Empire Central Flying School, Empire Flying School, Royal Air Force Flying College		FGB	Empire Air Armament School, Royal Air Force Flying College
FD	114 Squadron, 1659 Conversion Unit		FGC	Empire Air Armament School, Royal Air Force Flying College
FDA	21 (Pilot) Advanced Flying Unit, 21 (Pilot Refresher Flying School, 1 (Pilot) Refresher Flying Unit		FGE	Empire Air Navigation School, Central Navigation School, Central Navigation and Control School
FDB	21 (Pilot) Advanced Flying Unit, 21 (Pilot Refresher Flying School, 1 (Pilot) Refresher Flying Unit		FGF	Empire Air Navigation School, Central Navigation School, Central Navigation and Control School
FDC	21 (Pilot) Advanced Flying Unit, 21 (Pilot Refresher Flying School, 1 (Pilot) Refresher Flying Unit		FGG	Empire Air Navigation School, Central Navigation School, Central Navigation and Control School
FDD	21 (Pilot) Advanced Flying Unit, 21 (Pilot Refresher Flying School, 1 (Pilot) Refresher Flying Unit		FGI	Aeroplane and Armament Experimental Establishment
FDE	21 (Pilot) Advanced Flying Unit, 21 (Pilot Refresher Flying School, 1 (Pilot) Refresher Flying Unit		FGJ	Aeroplane and Armament Experimental Establishment
FDF	21 (Pilot) Advanced Flying Unit, 21 (Pilot Refresher Flying School, 1 (Pilot) Refresher Flying Unit		FGK	Aeroplane and Armament Experimental Establishment
FDG	21 (Pilot) Advanced Flying Unit, 21 (Pilot Refresher Flying School, 1 (Pilot) Refresher Flying Unit		FGL	Aeroplane and Armament Experimental Establishment
			FGM	Aeroplane and Armament Experimental Establishment
FDI	Central Flying School		FGN	Aeroplane and Armament Experimental Establishment
FDJ	Central Flying School		FGP	Empire Test Pilots School
FDK	Central Flying School		FGQ	Empire Test Pilots School
FDL	Central Flying School		FGR	Empire Test Pilots School
FDM	Central Flying School		FGT	Airborne Forces Experimental Establishment
FDN	Central Flying School		FGU	Airborne Forces Experimental Establishment
FDO	Central Flying School		FGV	Airborne Forces Experimental Establishment
FDQ	10 Flying Instructors School, 8 Elementary Flying Training School		FGW	Airborne Forces Experimental Establishment
FDR	10 Flying Instructors School, 8 Elementary Flying Training School		FGX	Airborne Forces Experimental Establishment
FDS	10 Flying Instructors School, 8 Elementary Flying Training School		FH	53 Squadron, 258 Squadron, 15 Operational Training Unit
			FHA	1 Elementary Flying Training School
FDT	10 Flying Instructors School, 8 Elementary Flying Training School		FHB	1 Elementary Flying Training School
			FHC	1 Elementary Flying Training School
FDU	Beam Approach School		FHE	2 Elementary Flying Training School
FDV	Beam Approach School		FHF	2 Elementary Flying Training School
FDW	Beam Approach School, Central Flying School		FHG	2 Elementary Flying Training School
FDX	Beam Approach School		FHI	3 Elementary Flying Training School
FDY	Airfield Controllers School, School of Flying Control, School of Air Traffic Control		FHJ	3 Elementary Flying Training School
			FHK	3 Elementary Flying Training School
FE	644 Squadron, 56 Operational Training Unit		FHM	4 Elementary Flying Training School
FEA	1 Glider Training School		FHN	4 Elementary Flying Training School
FEB	1 Glider Training School		FHO	4 Elementary Flying Training School
FEC	1 Glider Training School		FHQ	6 Elementary Flying Training School
FED	1 Glider Training School		FHR	6 Elementary Flying Training School
FEE	1 Glider Training School		FHS	6 Elementary Flying Training School
FEG	3 Glider Training School		FHT	6 Elementary Flying Training School
FEH	3 Glider Training School		FHV	7 Elementary Flying Training School
FEI	3 Glider Training School		FHW	7 Elementary Flying Training School
FEJ	3 Glider Training School		FHX	7 Elementary Flying Training School
FEK	3 Glider Training School		FHY	7 Elementary Flying Training School
FEL	3 Glider Training School		FI	1686 Flight, 83 Operational Training Unit, Warwick Training Unit
FEM	3 Glider Training School			
FEN	3 Glider Training School		FIA	11 Elementary Flying Training School
FEP	21 Heavy Glider Conversion Unit		FIB	11 Elementary Flying Training School
FEQ	21 Heavy Glider Conversion Unit		FIC	11 Elementary Flying Training School
FER	21 Heavy Glider Conversion Unit		FID	11 Elementary Flying Training School
FES	21 Heavy Glider Conversion Unit		FIJ	15 Elementary Flying Training School
FET	21 Heavy Glider Conversion Unit		FIK	15 Elementary Flying Training School
FF	132 Squadron, 251 Squadron		FIL	15 Elementary Flying Training School
FFA	10 Air Gunnery School		FIN	16 Elementary Flying Training School
FFB	10 Air Gunnery School		FIO	16 Elementary Flying Training School
FFC	10 Air Gunnery School		FIP	16 Elementary Flying Training School
FFD	10 Air Gunnery School		FIR	17 Elementary Flying Training School
FFE	11 Air Gunnery School		FIS	17 Elementary Flying Training School
FFF	11 Air Gunnery School		FIT	17 Elementary Flying Training School
FFG	11 Air Gunnery School		FIV	21 Elementary Flying Training School
FFI	5 Air Navigation School, 1 Air Navigation School		FIW	21 Elementary Flying Training School
FFJ	5 Air Navigation School, 1 Air Navigation School		FIX	21 Elementary Flying Training School
FFK	5 Air Navigation School, 1 Air Navigation School		FIY	21 Elementary Flying Training School
FFM	7 Air Navigation School, 2 Air Navigation School		FJ	37 Squadron, 164 Squadron, 261 Squadron
FFN	7 Air Navigation School, 2 Air Navigation School		FJA	22 Elementary Flying Training School
FFO	7 Air Navigation School, 2 Air Navigation School		FJB	22 Elementary Flying Training School
FFP	7 Air Navigation School, 2 Air Navigation School		FJC	22 Elementary Flying Training School
FFR	10 Air Navigation School		FJD	22 Elementary Flying Training School
FFS	10 Air Navigation School		FJF	24 Elementary Flying Training School
FFT	10 Air Navigation School		FJG	24 Elementary Flying Training School
FFU	10 Air Navigation School		FJH	24 Elementary Flying Training School
FG	72 Squadron, 335 Squadron		FJJ	28 Elementary Flying Training School
			FJK	28 Elementary Flying Training School
			FJL	28 Elementary Flying Training School
			FJN	29 Elementary Flying Training School
			FJO	29 Elementary Flying Training School
			FJP	29 Elementary Flying Training School
			FJQ	29 Elementary Flying Training School
			FJR	Central Gunnery School

FJS	Central Gunnery School
FJT	Central Gunnery School
FJU	Central Gunnery School
FJV	Central Gunnery School
FJW	Central Gunnery School
FJX	Central Gunnery School
FK	209 Squadron, 219 Squadron
FKA	1511 Beam Approach Training Flight
FKB	1511 Beam Approach Training Flight
FKD	1537 Beam Approach Training Flight
FKF	1547 Beam Approach Training Flight
FKN	Flying Training Command Communication Flight
FKO	21 Group Communication Flight
FKP	23 Group Communication Flight
FKQ	25 Group Communication Flight
FKR	54 Group Communication Flight
FKS	Station Flight Cranwell
FL	81 Squadron, 155 Squadron
FLA	Cambridge University Air Squadron
FLB	Aberdeen University Air Squadron
FLC	Edinburgh University Air Squadron
FLD	Glasgow University Air Squadron
FLE	Queens University Air Squadron
FLF	St Andrews University Air Squadron
FLG	Liverpool University Air Squadron
FLH	Manchester University Air Squadron
FLI	Leeds University Air Squadron
FLJ	Durham University Air Squadron
FLK	Birmingham University Air Squadron
FLL	Nottingham University Air Squadron
FLM	Bristol University Air Squadron
FLN	Swansea University Air Squadron
FLO	London University Air Squadron, University of London Air Squadron
FLP	Southampton University Air Squadron
FLQ	Oxford University Air Squadron
FLR	Perth University Air Squadron
FLS	Wolverhampton University Air Squadron
FLT	Derby University Air Squadron
FLU	Yatesbury University Air Squadron
FLV	Cambridge University Air Squadron
FM	238 Squadron, 257 Squadron, 518 Squadron
FMA	201 Advanced Flying School
FMB	201 Advanced Flying School
FMC	201 Advanced Flying School
FME	202 Advanced Flying School
FMF	202 Advanced Flying School
FMG	202 Advanced Flying School
FMI	203 Advanced Flying School
FMJ	203 Advanced Flying School
FMK	203 Advanced Flying School
FMO	204 Advanced Flying School
FN	125 Squadron, 331 Squadron
FO	75 Squadron, 1665 Conversion Unit, Station Flight Wick
FP	1683 Flight
FQ	12 Operational Training Unit
FR	348 Squadron, Station Flight Manston
FS	148 Squadron, 506 Squadron
FT	43 Squadron, 290 Squadron, Station Flight Mildenhall
FU	453 Squadron
FV	205 Squadron, 230 Squadron, 13 Operational Training Unit
FW	194 Squadron, Station Flight Rivenhall
FX	234 Squadron, 266 Squadron, 280 Squadron
FY	4 Squadron, 611 Squadron, 34 Operational Training Unit
FZ	65 Squadron, 94 Squadron, 23 Operational Training Unit
F1	'F' Flight 1 Anti-Aircraft Co-operation Unit
F2	635 Squadron
F3	438 Squadron
G	20 Squadron, 43 Squadron, 54 Squadron, Joint Anti-Submarine School Flight, 2 Flying Training School, 4 Flying Training School, 5 Flying Training School, 6 Flying Training School, 19 Flying Training School
GA	112 Squadron, 208 Squadron, 16 Operational Training Unit
GB	83 Squadron, 97 Squadron, 100 Squadron, 105 Squadron, 166 Squadron
GC	Station Flight Pershore
GD	Station Flight Horsham St Faith
GE	58 Squadron, 349 Squadron
GF	1 Tactical Exercise Unit, 56 Operational Training Unit

GG	151 Squadron, 1667 Conversion Unit
GH	285 Squadron
GI	622 Squadron
GJ	Station Flight Duxford
GK	80 Squadron, 459 Squadron, 52 Operational Training Unit
GL	175 Squadron, 185 Squadron, 1529 Flight, 14 Operational Training Unit
GM	55 Squadron
GN	249 Squadron, 323 Squadron, Central Bomber Establishment
GO	94 Squadron, 135 Squadron, Central Fighter Establishment
GP	187 Squadron, 1661 Conversion Unit
GQ	134 Squadron, Station Flight North Killingholme
GR	92 Squadron, 301 Squadron, 1586 Flight
GS	190 Squadron, 297 Squadron, 330 Squadron, 83 Operational Training Unit
GT	156 Squadron, 344 Squadron
GU	18 Squadron
GV	103 Squadron, 1652 Conversion Unit
GW	252 Squadron, 340 Squadron
GX	415 Squadron, 507 Squadron, Station Flight Broadwell
GY	109 (Transport) Operational Training Unit, 1383 Conversion Unit
GZ	12 Squadron, 32 Squadron, 611 Squadron
G2	19 Group Communication Flight
G4	Station Flight Skellingthorpe
G7	Bomber Command Film Unit
G8	Station Flight Wing
G9	430 Squadron
H	111 Squadron, School of Maritime Reconnaissance, 1340 Flight, 5 (Pilots) Advanced Flying Unit, 4 Flying Training School, 19 Flying Training School
HA	218 Squadron, 218 Squadron Conversion Flight, 649 Squadron
HB	229 Squadron, 239 Squadron
HC	512 Squadron
HD	38 Squadron, 311 Squadron, 466 Squadron
HE	263 Squadron, 605 Squadron
HF	54 Squadron, 127 Squadron, 183 Squadron
HG	154 Squadron, 332 Squadron
HH	175 Squadron, 273 Squadron
HI	66 Squadron, 63 Operational Training Unit
HJ	254 Squadron
HK	269 Squadron, 306 Squadron, Fighter Leaders School
HL	26 Squadron, Station Flight Gransden Lodge
HM	136 Squadron, 1677 Flight
HN	20 Squadron, 93 Squadron
HO	143 Squadron
HP	247 Squadron, Gunnery Research Unit, Station Flight Full Sutton
HQ	91 Squadron, 56 Operational Training Unit
HR	North-East Sector Communication Flight
HS	109 Squadron, 170 Squadron, 260 Squadron
HT	154 Squadron, 158 Squadron, 601 Squadron
HU	220 Squadron, 406 Squadron
HV	8 Squadron, 73 Squadron, Station Flight East Kirby
HW	100 Squadron
HX	295 Squadron, 61 Operational Training Unit, 203 Advanced Flying School, 226 Operational Conversion Unit
HY	88 Squadron
HZ	44 Group Communication Flight
H3	111 Operational Training Unit
H4	1653 Conversion Unit
H7	346 Squadron
H9	Station Flight Shepherds Grove
I	Central Flying School
IA	Station Flight Syerston
IB	Glider Pick-up Training Flight, 43 Group Communication Flight
IC	623 Squadron
IF	84 Operational Training Unit
II	116 Squadron, 59 Operational Training Unit
IK	Bomber Command Instructors School
IL	115 Squadron
IN	Station Flight Valley
IP	Bomber Command Instructors School
IQ	150 Squadron
IV	Station Flight Upper Heyford
IW	Station Flight Chilbolton

IY	Station Flight Dunsfold
I2	48 Squadron
I4	567 Squadron
I5	1381 Conversion Unit, 105 Operational Training Unit
I6	32 Maintenance Unit
I8	440 Squadron
I9	575 Squadron
J	26 Squadron, 27 Squadron, 111 Operational Training Unit, Royal Air Force College Flying Training School
JA	1652 Conversion Unit
JB	190 Squadron, 1380 Conversion Unit, 81 Operational Training Unit
JC	11 Group Communication Flight
JD	Station Flight Grimsetter
JE	195 Squadron, 610 Squadron
JF	3 Squadron, 1654 Conversion Unit
JG	17 Operational Training Unit
JH	74 Squadron, 317 Squadron
JI	514 Squadron
JJ	160 Squadron, 274 Squadron
JL	520 Squadron, 10 Operational Training Unit
JM	184 Squadron, 20 Operational Training Unit
JN	30 Squadron, 75 Squadron, 150 Squadron, 268 Squadron
JO	62 Squadron, 463 Squadron
JP	21 Squadron, 12 Operational Training Unit
JQ	169 Squadron, Station Flight Breighton, 2 Anti-Aircraft Co-operation Unit
JR	161 Squadron
JS	321 Squadron, 16 Operational Training Unit
JT	182 Squadron, 256 Squadron
JU	111 Squadron, 202 Squadron
JV	6 Squadron, 283 Squadron, Station Flight Finningley
JW	44 Squadron, Central Fighter Establishment
JX	1 Squadron
JY	121 Squadron
JZ	57 Operational Training Unit
J5	3 Squadron
J6	1521 Flight
J7	8 Maintenance Unit
J8	24 Maintenance Unit
J9	1668 Conversion Unit
K	Central Flying School, 1 Flying Training School
KA	9 Squadron, 1685 Flight
KB	142 Squadron, 1661 Conversion Unit
KC	238 Squadron, 617 Squadron
KD	154 Squadron, 30 Operational Training Unit, 226 Operational Conversion Unit
KE	330 Squadron, Merchant Ship Flying Unit
KF	645 Squadron, 1662 Conversion Unit
KG	196 Squadron, 204 Squadron, 1380 Conversion Unit, 81 Operational Training Unit
KH	403 Squadron, 11 Operational Training Unit
KI	Station Flight Coningsby
KJ	16 Squadron, 11 Operational Training Unit
KK	333 Squadron, 624 Squadron, 15 Operational Training Unit
KL	54 Squadron, 269 Squadron
KM	44 Squadron, 44 Squadron Conversion Flight, 205 Squadron
KN	77 Squadron, 339 Squadron
KO	2 Squadron, 115 Squadron
KP	226 Squadron, 409 Squadron
KQ	502 Squadron, 13 Operational Training Unit
KR	231 Squadron, 1667 Conversion Unit, 61 Operational Training Unit, 226 Operational Conversion Unit
KS	Station Flight Tarrant Rushton
KT	32 Squadron
KU	47 Squadron, 265 Squadron, 53 Operational Training Unit
KV	264 Squadron, 619 Squadron
KW	267 Squadron, 312 Squadron, 425 Squadron, 615 Squadron
KX	311 Squadron, 529 Squadron, 639 Squadron, 1448 Flight
KY	242 Squadron, 162 Squadron
KZ	287 Squadron, 296 Squadron
K1	'K' Flight, 1 Anti-Aircraft Co-operation Unit
K2	2 Group Communication Flight
K5	Station Flight Pocklington
K7	6 Operational Training Unit, 236 Operational Conversion Unit
K8	Station Flight Wymeswold
K9	Station Flight Tain
L	11 Squadron, 16 Squadron, 20 Squadron, 71 Squadron, 96 Squadron, 98 Squadron, 210 Squadron, 228 Squadron, 240 Squadron, 266 Squadron, 111 Operational Training Unit, Central Flying School
LA	235 Squadron, 607 Squadron
LB	34 Squadron, 28 Operational Training Unit
LC	Station Flight Feltwell
LD	108 Squadron, 117 Squadron, 250 Squadron, 331 Squadron
LE	40 Squadron, 242 Squadron, 630 Squadron
LF	37 Squadron, 172 Squadron, Station Flight Predannack
LG	89 Squadron, 215 Squadron, 13 Group Communication Flight
LH	313 Squadron, Station Flight Mepal
LJ	211 Squadron, 600 Squadron, 614 Squadron, 614A Squadron
LK	51 Squadron, 87 Squadron, 342 Squadron, 578 Squadron
LL	1513 Flight
LM	189 Squadron, Station Flight Elsham Wolds
LN	99 Squadron, 183 Squadron, 83 Group Communication Flight
LO	602 Squadron, 632 Squadron
LP	327 Squadron, 237 Operational Conversion Unit
LQ	405 Squadron, 405 Squadron Conversion Flight, 629 Squadron
LR	56 Squadron, 1667 Conversion Unit, 31 Operational Training Unit
LS	15 Squadron, 15 Squadron Conversion Flight, 61 Squadron
LT	7 Squadron, 22 Operational Training Unit
LU	101 Squadron, Merchant Ship Flying Unit
LV	57 Operational Training Unit
LW	318 Squadron, 607 Squadron, 74 Wing Calibration Flight, 75 Wing Calibration Flight, 76 Wing Calibration Flight
LX	225 Squadron, 614A Squadron, 54 Operational Training Unit
LY	149 Squadron, Photographic Reconnaissance Unit, 1 Photographic Reconnaissance Unit
LZ	66 Squadron
L-Z	421 Flight
L4	27 Maintenance Unit
L5	297 Squadron
L6	1669 Conversion Unit
L7	271 Squadron
L8	347 Squadron
L9	190 Squadron
M	111 Operational Training Unit, 202 Advanced Flying School, 205 Advanced Flying School, 206 Advanced Flying School, 215 Advanced Flying School, Central Flying School, 102 Flying Refresher School, 1 Flying Training School, 3 Flying Training School, 6 Flying Training School, 7 Flying Training School, 22 Flying Training School, 9 Advanced Flying Training School, 9 Flying Training School, 10 Advanced Flying Training School, 22 Service Flying Training School
MA	161 Squadron, 650 Squadron, 651 Squadron
MB	651 Squadron, 52 Squadron, 220 Squadron, 236 Squadron
MC	651 Squadron, Station Flight Fiskerton
MD	651 Squadron, 133 Squadron, 458 Squadron, 526 Squadron
ME	488 Squadron
MF	108 Squadron, 280 Squadron, Fighter Leaders School, Central Fighter Establishment, 59 Operational Training Unit
MG	7 Squadron, 7 Squadron Conversion Flight
MH	51 Squadron, 237 Squadron
MJ	69 Squadron, 1680 Flight
MK	126 Squadron, 500 Squadron, 20 Operational Training Unit
ML	257 Squadron, 338 Squadron, 12 Operational Training Unit
MM	291 Squadron
MN	328 Squadron, 350 Squadron
MOTU	Maritime Operational Training Unit
MP	76 Squadron, 76 Squadron Conversion Flight, 246 Squadron
MQ	226 Squadron, 642 Squadron
MR	97 Squadron, 186 Squadron, 245 Squadron
MS	23 Squadron, 273 Squadron, Station Flight Linton-on-Ouse, Hornet Conversion Flight
MT	105 Squadron, 122 Squadron
MU	60 Squadron, 274 Squadron
MV	600 Squadron, 53 Operational Training Unit
MW	101 Squadron, 217 Squadron, 301 Squadron, 5 Coastal Patrol Flight, 1641 Flight
MX	120 Squadron, 1653 Conversion Unit, Station Flight Glatton
MY	27 Squadron, 278 Squadron
MZ	617 Squadron, 83 Operational Training Unit
M1	'M' Flight, 1 Anti-Aircraft Co-operation Unit
M2	33 Maintenance Unit

M4	587 Squadron	OT	58 Squadron
M5	128 Squadron	OU	485 Squadron
M6	83 Group Communication Flight	OV	197 Squadron, 514 Squadron
M7	41 Group Communication Flight	OW	426 Squadron
M8	4 Group Communication Flight	OX	40 Squadron, 22 Operational Training Unit
M9	1653 Conversion Unit	OY	11 Squadron, 48 Squadron, 13 Operational Training Unit
N	Flying Refresher School, 101 Flying Refresher School, 6 Flying Training School, 7 Flying Training School, 22 Flying Training School, 111 Operational Training Unit, 202 Advanced Flying School, 215 Advanced Flying School, 2 Basic Air Navigation School, Central Flying School, Royal Air Force College Flying Training School, 1 Flying Training School, 2 Flying Training School, 3 Flying Training School, 14 (Advanced) Flying Training School, 22 Service Flying Training School Flying Training School	OZ	82 Squadron, 179 Squadron, 210 Squadron
		O3	Bomber Command Development Unit
		O5	Bomber Support Development Unit
		O8	Station Flight Merryfield
		P	202 Advanced Flying School, 207 Advanced Flying School, 1 Flying Training School, 2 Flying Training School, 3 Flying Training School, 6 Flying Training School, 7 Flying Training School, 9 (Advanced) Flying Training School, 9 Flying Training School, 10 (Advanced) Flying Training School, 22 Flying Training School, 22 Service Flying Training School, 207 Flying Training School
NA	1 Squadron, 428 Squadron, Station Flight Manorbier		
NB	635 Squadron, Fighter Command Communication Flight/Squadron Training School		
NC	4 Squadron	PA	655 Squadron, 3 Tactical Exercise Unit, 55 Operational Training Unit
ND	236 Squadron, 343 Squadron, 1666 Conversion Unit		
NE	63 Squadron, 143 Squadron	PB	10 Squadron, 655 Squadron, 1684 Flight, 26 Operational Training Unit
NF	138 Squadron, 488 Squadron		
NG	604 Squadron	PC	655 Squadron
NH	38 Squadron, 119 Squadron, 274 Squadron, 415 Squadron	PD	87 Squadron, 303 Squadron, 450 Squadron, 655 Squadron
NI	451 Squadron	PE	1662 Conversion Unit
NJ	207 Squadron, Merchant Ship Flying Unit	PF	516 Squadron, 43 Operational Training Unit, 51 Operational Training Unit, 227 Operational Conversion Unit, Air Observation Post School
NK	118 Squadron, 163 Squadron, 31 General Reconnaissance School		
NL	316 Squadron, 341 Squadron	PG	608 Squadron, 619 Squadron
NM	76 Squadron, 230 Squadron, 268 Squadron	PH	12 Squadron
NN	310 Squadron, 303 Squadron	PI	Station Flight Silverstone
NO	85 Squadron, 320 Squadron	PJ	59 Squadron, 130 Squadron
NP	158 Squadron, 158 Squadron Conversion Flight, 195 Squadron	PK	124 Squadron, 220 Squadron, 315 Squadron
		PL	144 Squadron, 341 Squadron
NQ	24 Squadron, 43 Squadron	PM	20 Squadron, 103 Squadron, 103 Squadron Conversion Flight
NR	220 Squadron, 605 Squadron		
NS	159 Squadron, 201 Squadron, 52 Operational Training Unit	PN	41 Squadron, 252 Squadron, 1552 Flight
NT	203 Squadron, 29 Operational Training Unit	PO	46 Squadron, 104 Squadron, 463 Squadron, 467 Squadron
NU	625 Squadron, 1382 Conversion Unit, 240 Operational Conversion Unit, 242 Operational Conversion Unit	PP	203 Squadron, 311 Squadron, 25 Operational Training Unit
		PQ	206 Squadron, 324 Squadron, 2 Tactical Exercise Unit, 58 Operational Training Unit
NV	144 Squadron, 79 Squadron		
NW	33 Squadron, 286 Squadron	PR	407 Squadron, 609 Squadron
NX	131 Squadron, 243 Squadron, Central Fighter Establishment	PS	264 Squadron
NY	1665 Conversion Unit	PT	27 Squadron, 420 Squadron, 420 Squadron Conversion Flight
NZ	304 Squadron		
N7	Station Flight Lyneham	PU	53 Squadron, 187 Squadron, 198 Squadron
N8	Station Flight Waterbeach	PV	275 Squadron
N9	Station Flight Blackbushe, Station Flight Buckeburg	PW	224 Squadron, 57 Operational Training Unit
O	202 Advanced Flying School, 203 Advanced Flying School, 205 Advanced Flying School, Central Flying School, Flying Refresher School, 101 Flying Refresher School, 2 Flying Training School, 3 Flying Training School, 6 Flying Training School, 7 Flying Training School, 8 Flying Training School, 9 (Advanced) Flying Training School, 9 Flying Training School, 22 Flying Training School, 22 Service Flying Training School	PX	95 Squadron, 214 Squadron
		PY	84 Squadron, 1527 Flight
		PZ	53 Squadron, 456 Squadron, 638 Squadron
		P2	Station Flight Marston Moor
		P3	692 Squadron
		P4	153 Squadron
		P5	297 Squadron
		P6	489 Squadron, Station Flight, Banff
OA	22 Squadron, 223 Squadron, 329 Squadron, 342 Squadron	P8	87 Group Communication Flight, 87 Wing Communication Flight
OB	45 Squadron, 260 Squadron, 53 Operational Training Unit		
OC	Station Flight Sandtoft	P9	58 Operational Training Unit, Air/Sea Warfare Development Unit
OD	80 Squadron, 6 Operational Training Unit, 56 Operational Training Unit		
		Q	Central Flying School, 2 Flying Training School, 3 Flying Training School, 7 Flying Training School, 14 (Advanced) Flying Training School
OE	98 Squadron, 168 Squadron, 661 Squadron		
OF	97 Squadron, 97 Squadron Conversion Flight		
OG	172 Squadron, 315 Squadron, 1332 Conversion Unit, 1665 Conversion Unit	QA	654 Squadron
		QB	212 Squadron, 424 Squadron, 654 Squadron
OH	120 Squadron	QC	168 Squadron, 654 Squadron
OI	2 Squadron	QD	654 Squadron, 42 Squadron, 304 Squadron
OJ	149 Squadron, 149 Squadron Conversion Flight	QE	12 Squadron, Central Fighter Establishment
OK	337 Squadron, 450 Squadron, 3 School of General Reconnaissance	QF	98 Squadron, 177 Squadron, 1323 Flight, Navigation Training Unit
OL	83 Squadron, 83 Squadron Conversion Flight	QG	53 Operational Training Unit
OM	11 Squadron, 107 Squadron, 119 Squadron	QH	298 Squadron, 302 Squadron
ON	56 Squadron, 63 Squadron, 124 Squadron, 623 Squadron	QI	Station Flight Swanton Morley
OO	13 Squadron, 164 Squadron, 1663 Conversion Unit	QJ	92 Squadron, 616 Squadron, British Air Forces of Occupation Communication Squadron
OP	3 Squadron, 11 Operational Training Unit, 32 Operational Training Unit		
		QK	248 Squadron, 3 Armament Practice Station
OQ	5 Squadron, Fighter Leaders School, 52 Operational Training Unit	QL	286 Squadron, 413 Squadron, 76 Wing Calibration Flight
		QM	42 Squadron, 254 Squadron, 276 Squadron
OR	Bomb Ballistic Unit	QN	5 Squadron, 214 Squadron, 28 Operational Training Unit
OS	279 Squadron, 349 Squadron, Station Flight Sturgate	QO	3 Squadron, 167 Squadron, 432 Squadron

QP	Station Flight Kirmington
QQ	83 Squadron, 1651 Conversion Unit
QR	61 Squadron, 61 Squadron Conversion Flight, 223 Squadron
QS	192 Squadron, 620 Squadron
QT	57 Squadron, 67 Squadron, 142 Squadron
QU	326 Squadron, Royal Air Force Northern Ireland Communication Flight, Headquarters Royal Air Force Northern Ireland Communication Flight
QV	19 Squadron
QW	1516 Flight
QX	50 Squadron, 224 Squadron, Coastal Command Communication Flight
QY	254 Squadron, 262 Squadron, 452 Squadron, 1666 Conversion Unit
QZ	643 Squadron, 4 Operational Training Unit
Q3	613 Squadron
Q6	1384 Conversion Unit
Q7	29 Maintenance Unit
R	205 Advanced Flying School, Central Flying School, 2 Flying Training School, 3 Flying Training School, 22 Flying Training School, 22 Service Flying Training School,
RA	100 Squadron, 410 Squadron
RAA	500 Squadron
RAB	501 Squadron
RAC	502 Squadron
RAD	504 Squadron
RAG	600 Squadron
RAH	601 Squadron
RAI	602 Squadron
RAJ	603 Squadron
RAK	604 Squadron
RAL	605 Squadron
RAN	607 Squadron
RAO	608 Squadron
RAP	609 Squadron
RAQ	610 Squadron
RAR	611 Squadron
RAS	612 Squadron
RAT	613 Squadron
RAU	614 Squadron
RAV	615 Squadron
RAW	616 Squadron
RB	66 Squadron
RC	5 Lancaster Finishing School
RCA	Reserve Command Communication Squadron
RCB	12 Reserve Flying School
RCC	13 Reserve Flying School
RCD	12 Reserve Flying School, 15 Reserve Flying School
RCE	61 Group Communication Flight
RCF	62 Group Communication Flight
RCG	63 Group Communication Flight
RCH	64 Group Communication Flight
RCI	66 Group Communication Flight
RCJ	17 Reserve Flying School
RCK	3 Reserve Flying School
RCL	14 Reserve Flying School
RCM	1 Reserve Flying School
RCN	4 Reserve Flying School
RCO	6 Reserve Flying School
RCP	7 Reserve Flying School
RCQ	8 Reserve Flying School
RCR	11 Reserve Flying School
RCS	16 Reserve Flying School
RCT	18 Reserve Flying School
RCU	22 Reserve Flying School
RCV	24 Reserve Flying School
RCW	25 Reserve Flying School
RCX	2 Reserve Flying School
RCY	5 Reserve Flying School
RCZ	9 Reserve Flying School
RD	67 Squadron
RE	118 Squadron, 229 Squadron, Central Fighter Establishment
RF	204 Squadron, 303 Squadron, 1510 Flight
RG	208 Squadron, 510 Squadron, 1472 Flight, Station Flight Earls Colne
RH	88 Squadron, 179 Squadron
RJ	46 Squadron, Station Flight Thornaby
RK	131 Squadron
RL	38 Squadron, 279 Squadron, 603 Squadron

RM	26 Squadron, 140 Squadron
RN	72 Squadron, 93 Squadron
RO	29 Squadron, 174 Squadron, 32 Operational Training Unit
ROA	661 Squadron, 1957 Flight, 1958 Flight, 1959 Flight, 1960 Flight, 1961 Flight
ROB	662 Squadron, 1956 Flight, 1962 Flight, 1963 Flight
ROC	663 Squadron, 1951 Flight, 1952 Flight, 1953 Flight, 1954 Flight, 1955 Flight
ROD	664 Squadron, 1964 Flight, 1965 Flight, 1969 Flight, 1970 Flight
ROG	666 Squadron, 1966 Flight, 1967 Flight, 1968 Flight
RP	288 Squadron
RQ	193 Squadron, Station Flight Colerne
RR	407 Squadron, 615 Squadron, Station Flight Filton
RS	30 Squadron, 157 Squadron, 171 Squadron, 229 Operational Conversion Unit
RSA	23 Reserve Flying School
RSB	10 Reserve Flying School
RT	112 Squadron, 114 Squadron, 147 Squadron
RUA	Aberdeen University Air Squadron
RUB	Birmingham University Air Squadron
RUC	Cambridge University Air Squadron
RUD	Durham University Air Squadron
RUE	Edinburgh University Air Squadron
RUG	Glasgow University Air Squadron
RUL	London University Air Squadron, University of London Air Squadron
RUM	Manchester University Air Squadron
RUN	Nottingham University Air Squadron
RUO	Oxford University Air Squadron
RUQ	Queens University Air Squadron
RUS	St Andrews University Air Squadron
RUY	Leeds University Air Squadron
RUZ	Southampton University Air Squadron
RV	1659 Conversion Unit
RU	414 Squadron, Station Flight Hendon
RW	36 Squadron
RX	25 Squadron, 456 Squadron
RY	278 Squadron, 313 Squadron
RZ	241 Squadron, 513 Squadron
R1	'R' Flight, 1 Anti-Aircraft Co-operation Unit
R2	Pilotless Aircraft Unit
R4	18 Armament Practice Camp, 1 Armament Practice Station
R8	274 Maintenance Unit
S	78 Squadron, 208 Squadron, 207 Advanced Flying School, 1564 Flight, Central Flying School, Royal Air Force Technical College, 3 Flying Training School, 8 Flying Training School, 8 (Advanced) Flying Training School
SA	486 Squadron
SB	464 Squadron
SC	Station Flight Prestwick
SD	72 Squadron, 501 Squadron
SE	95 Squadron, 431 Squadron
SF	39 Squadron, 137 Squadron
SG	626 Squadron
SH	64 Squadron, 216 Squadron, 240 Squadron
SJ	96 Squadron, 21 Operational Training Unit
SK	165 Squadron, 263 Squadron
SL	13 Operational Training Unit
SM	272 Squadron, 305 Squadron
SN	243 Squadron, 511 Squadron, 230 Operational Conversion Unit
SO	33 Squadron, 145 Squadron
SP	320 Squadron, 400 Squadron, Station Flight Doncaster
SQ	500 Squadron
SR	101 Squadron, 101 Squadron Conversion Flight, 281 Squadron
SS	129 Squadron, 1552 Flight
ST	228 Operational Conversion Unit, 54 Operational Training Unit
SU	235 Squadron, Station Flight Turnhouse
SV	218 Squadron, 1663 Conversion Unit
SW	43 Squadron, 253 Squadron, 517 Squadron, 1678 Conversion Unit, 1678 Flight
SX	1 Coast Artillery Co-operation Unit/Flight, Station Flight Methwold
SY	139 Squadron, 613 Squadron
SZ	256 Squadron, 316 Squadron

S6	41 Group Communication Flight, Maintenance Command Communication Flight
S7	500 Squadron
S8	328 Squadron
S9	16 Group Communication Flight
T	15 Squadron, 36 Squadron, 74 Squadron, 79 Squadron, 112 Squadron, 204 Squadron, 220 Squadron, 249 Squadron, 256 Squadron, 1 Coastal Patrol Flight, 1417 Flight, 3 Flying Training School, 14 Advanced Flying Training School
TA	358 Squadron, 4 Operational Training Unit, 235 Operational Conversion Unit
TAL	Communication Flight Aldermaston
TB	51 Squadron, 77 Squadron, 153 Squadron, 156 Squadron
TBR	Royal Air Force Staff College Flight
TC	170 Squadron
TCA	1 Radio School
TCE	Station Flight Carew Cheriton
TCN	Station Flight Cranwell
TCO	Station Flight Cosford
TCR	1 Radio School
TCW	Station Flight Carew Cheriton
TD	132 Squadron, 320 Squadron, 453 Squadron, 82 Operational Training Unit
TDE	Empire Radio School, Royal Air Force Technical College
TE	53 Squadron, 1401 Flight, Station Flight Desborough
TF	620 Squadron, 29 Operational Training Unit
TFA	School of Photography
TH	20 Squadron, 418 Squadron
THA	Station Flight Halton
THE	Parachute Test Unit
THI	Aeroplane and Armament Experimental Establishment
THL	24 Group Communication Flight
THO	Station Flight Hornchurch
TIH	1 Royal Air Force Film Production Unit
TJ	202 Squadron, 272 Squadron, 52 Operational Training Unit
TK	143 Squadron, 149 Squadron
TL	35 Squadron, 35 Squadron Conversion Flight, 253 Squadron
TLO	Station Flight Locking
TM	111 Squadron, 504 Squadron
TMA	4 Radio School
TMD	4 Radio School
TME	4 Radio School
TML	4 Radio School
TN	33 Squadron, 30 Operational Training Unit
TO	228 Squadron, 61 Operational Training Unit, 203 Advanced Flying School, 226 Operational Conversion Unit, 228 Operational Conversion Unit
TOC	Officers Advanced Training School,
TP	73 Squadron, 198 Squadron, 277 Squadron
TR	59 Squadron, 238 Squadron
TQ	102 Squadron, 202 Squadron, Station Flight Bramcote
TS	137 Squadron, 548 Squadron, 657 Squadron, 1900 Flight, 1901 Flight
TSA	Station Flight St Athan
TSI	Royal Air Force (Belgian) Training School
TSM	4 Radio School
TSN	Royal Air Force (Belgian) Training School
TSO	27 Group Communication Flight
TT	289 Squadron, 1658 Conversion Unit
TTE	22 Group Communication Flight
TU	Station Flight Dyce, 1 Torpedo Training Unit
TV	4 Squadron, 151 Squadron, 173 Squadron, 1660 Conversion Unit
TW	90 Squadron, 141 Squadron
TWM	School of Photography
TWY	Technical Training Command Communication Flight
TX	130 Squadron, 11 Operational Training Unit
TY	24 Operational Training Unit
T2	46 Maintenance Unit
T5	Station Flight Abingdon
T6	Station Flight Melbourne
T7	650 Squadron
U	8 Flying Training School, 8 (Advanced) Flying Training School, 22 Flying Training School, 22 Service Flying Training School
UA	269 Squadron
UB	63 Squadron, 164 Squadron, 304 Squadron, 455 Squadron
UD	141 Squadron, 452 Squadron
UE	200 Squadron, 228 Squadron

UF	601 Squadron, 622 Squadron, 24 Operational Training Unit
UG	16 Squadron, 310 Squadron, 1654 Conversion Unit
UH	1682 Flight, 21 Operational Training Unit
UJ	27 Operational Training Unit
UK	637 Squadron
UL	178 Squadron, 576 Squadron, 608 Squadron
UM	152 Squadron, 626 Squadron
UN	126 Squadron, Station Flight Faldingworth
UO	266 Squadron, 19 Operational Training Unit
UP	4 Squadron, 222 Squadron, 605 Squadron
UQ	211 Squadron, 512 Squadron, 1508 Flight
UR	84 Squadron, 13 Operational Training Unit
US	28 Squadron, 56 Squadron
UT	17 Squadron, 51 Squadron, 461 Squadron
UU	61 Operational Training Unit, 226 Operational Conversion Unit
UV	17 Squadron, 460 Squadron, 460 Squadron Conversion Flight
UW	3 Tactical Exercise Unit, 55 Operational Training Unit
UX	82 Squadron, 214 Squadron, 1476 Flight, Central Fighter Establishment
UY	314 Squadron, 10 Operational Training Unit
UZ	292 Squadron, 306 Squadron
U2	Station Flight Talbenny
U3	Radio Warfare Establishment
U4	667 Squadron
U5	3 Ferry Pool, 51 Maintenance Unit
U6	436 Squadron
U7	1697 Flight
V	126 Squadron, 1435 Flight, 1435 Squadron
VA	84 Squadron, 125 Squadron, 264 Squadron, 282 Squadron
VB	221 Squadron, 334 Squadron, 14 Operational Training Unit
VD	Central Gunnery School
VE	110 Squadron, 319 Squadron, Station Flight Kirton-in-Lindsey
VF	99 Squadron, Station Flight Lindholme
VG	210 Squadron, 285 Squadron
VI	169 Squadron
VJ	503 Squadron
VK	238 Squadron, 307 Squadron, 85 Group Communication Flight
VL	167 Squadron, 322 Squadron
VM	231 Squadron, 244 Squadron, 1561 Flight
VN	50 Squadron, 50 Squadron Conversion Flight, 333 Squadron
VO	98 Squadron
VP	259 Squadron, Station Flight Exeter
VQ	201 Squadron, 18 Operational Training Unit
VR	22 Squadron, 419 Squadron
VS	31 Squadron, Metropolitan Communication Squadron
VT	30 Squadron, 216 Squadron, 1556 Flight
VU	36 Squadron, 246 Squadron
VV	288 Squadron, Station Flight Sumburgh
VW	157 Squadron, Station Flight Chedburgh
VX	206 Squadron
VY	85 Squadron, 249 Squadron
VZ	412 Squadron, 636 Squadron
V4	6 Maintenance Unit
V6	615 Squadron, Radio Warfare Establishment
V7	Central Signals Establishment
V8	570 Squadron
V9	502 Squadron
W	234 Squadron, 205 Advanced Flying School, 3 Air Navigation School, Central Flying School, 4 Flying Training School, 5 Flying Training School, 8 Flying Training School, 8 (Advanced) Flying Training School
WA	264 Squadron
WB	181 Squadron, Bomber Command Instructors School, Bomber Command Instrument Rating and Examining Flight
WC	309 Squadron
WD	206 Squadron, Station Flight Leeming
WE	59 Squadron, 23 Operational Training Unit
WF	238 Squadron, 525 Squadron
WG	128 Squadron, 26 Operational Training Unit
WH	330 Squadron, Armament Practice Station Acklington
WI	69 Squadron
WJ	167 Squadron, 17 Operational Training Unit
WK	81 Squadron, 135 Squadron, 1310 Flight, 1316 Flight
WL	434 Squadron, 612 Squadron, Station Flight Celle
WM	68 Squadron, 122 Squadron

WN	527 Squadron
WO	138 Squadron
WP	90 Squadron
WQ	209 Squadron, 604 Squadron, 12 Group Communication Flight
WR	248 Squadron, Station Flight Moreton-in-the-Marsh
WS	9 Squadron, 9 Squadron Conversion Flight, 275 Squadron
WT	35 Squadron, Station Flight Stornoway
WU	225 Squadron, 317 Squadron
WV	18 Squadron
WW	332 Squadron
WX	302 Squadron, 627 Squadron
WY	541 Squadron, 261 Squadron, 28 Operational Training Unit
WZ	19 Squadron, Station Flight Graveley
W2	80 Squadron
W3	Station Flight Hemswell
W4	Glider Pick-up Training Flight
W5	Station Flight, Castle Camps
W6	18 Maintenance Unit
X	229 Squadron, 603 Squadron, 203 Advanced Flying School, 205 Advanced Flying School, 3 Air Navigation School, Central Flying School, 2 Flying Training School, 4 Flying Training School, 5 Flying Training School, 6 Flying Training School, 8 Flying Training School, 8 (Advanced) Flying Training School
XA	489 Squadron, 640 Squadron, Essex Sector Communication Flight
XB	224 Squadron, 239 Squadron, 2 Tactical Exercise Unit
XC	26 Squadron
XD	139 Squadron, 188 Squadron, 13 Operational Training Unit
XE	6 Squadron, Central Bomber Establishment
XF	168 Squadron, 19 Operational Training Unit
XG	16 Operational Training Unit
XH	218 Squadron, 296 Squadron
XJ	293 Squadron, 13 Operational Training Unit
XK	46 Squadron, 272 Squadron
XL	346 Squadron, 1335 Conversion Unit, 20 Operational Training Unit, 226 Operational Conversion Unit
XM	182 Squadron, 652 Squadron, 1902 Flight, 1903 Flight, 1904 Flight, 1905 Flight, 1908 Flight, 1909 Flight
XN	232 Squadron, 22 Operational Training Unit
XO	112 Squadron, 57 Operational Training Unit
XP	174 Squadron, 318 Squadron
XQ	64 Squadron, 86 Squadron
XR	71 Squadron, 2 Group Communication Flight
XS	106 Squadron
XT	335 Squadron, 603 Squadron, 1657 Conversion Unit
XU	7 Squadron, 49 Squadron
XV	2 Squadron, 309 Squadron
XW	18 Operational Training Unit
XX	631 Squadron
XY	90 Squadron, 136 Squadron, 186 Squadron, 203 Advanced Flying School
XZ	39 Squadron, 153 Squadron
X2	Station Flight Stoney Cross
X3	111 Operational Training Unit
X6	290 Squadron
X8	6 Group Communication Flight
X9	299 Squadron
Y	205 Advanced Flying School, 206 Advanced Flying School, 1 Flying Training School, 22 Flying Training School, 22 Service Flying Training School
YA	68 Squadron, Station Flight Netheravon
YB	17 Squadron, 29 Squadron, Station Flight Bentwaters
YD	242 Squadron, 255 Squadron
YE	250 Squadron, 289 Squadron
YF	280 Squadron, 505 Squadron, Station Flight Scampton
YG	156 Squadron, 502 Squadron, 646 Squadron
YH	21 Squadron, 11 Squadron
YI	423 Squadron
YJ	152 Squadron, Station Flight Metheringham
YK	80 Squadron, 274 Squadron, 340 Squadron
YL	27 Operational Training Unit
YM	350 Squadron, 1528 Flight, 1529 Flight
YN	601 Squadron
YO	8 Squadron, 401 Squadron, Station Flight Down Ampney
YP	23 Squadron, 165 Squadron
YQ	217 Squadron, 616 Squadron
YR	133 Squadron, 20 Operational Training Unit
YS	77 Squadron, 271 Squadron
YT	65 Squadron, 648 Squadron
YU	Station Flight Lossiemouth
YV	287 Squadron, 48 Group Communication Flight
YW	515 Squadron, 1660 Conversion Unit, 230 Operational Conversion Unit
YX	614 Squadron, 54 Operational Training Unit
YY	78 Squadron, 1332 Conversion Unit, 241 Operational Conversion Unit
YZ	146 Squadron, 617 Squadron, 1651 Conversion Unit
Y2	442 Squadron
Y3	202 Squadron, 518 Squadron
Y5	Station Flight Dallachy
Z	205 Advanced Flying School, 3 Air Navigation School, 229 Operational Conversion Unit, 5 Flying Training School
ZA	10 Squadron, 10 Squadron Conversion Flight, 31 Squadron, Metropolitan Communication Squadron
ZB	1658 Conversion Unit
ZD	6 Squadron, 116 Squadron, 222 Squadron
ZE	52 Squadron, 123 Squadron, 293 Squadron, Central Fighter Establishment
ZF	308 Squadron, 549 Squadron
ZG	94 Squadron, 322 Squadron, 10 Operational Training Unit
ZH	266 Squadron, 501 Squadron
ZJ	96 Squadron, 271 Squadron
ZK	24 Squadron, 25 Squadron
ZL	77 Squadron, 427 Squadron
ZM	185 Squadron, 201 Squadron
ZN	106 Squadron, 300 Squadron
ZO	196 Squadron
ZP	74 Squadron, 336 Squadron, 457 Squadron, 1473 Flight, 25 Operational Training Unit
ZQ	322 Squadron, Bomber Command Instructors School, Fighter Interception Unit, Central Fighter Establishment
ZR	309 Squadron, 613 Squadron, 2 Operational Training Unit, 107 Operational Training Unit, 1333 Conversion Unit
ZS	233 Squadron, 647 Squadron, 1336 Conversion Unit
ZT	97 Squadron, 258 Squadron, 602 Squadron, 20 Operational Training Unit
ZU	1664 Conversion Unit
ZV	19 Operational Training Unit
ZW	48 Squadron, 140 Squadron, 1359 Flight
ZX	145 Squadron, Polish Fighting Team, 3 Tactical Exercise Unit, 55 Operational Training Unit
ZY	247 Squadron
ZZ	220 Squadron
Z2	437 Squadron
Z4	10 Maintenance Unit
Z5	462 Squadron
Z8	45 Maintenance Unit
Z9	519 Squadron
1	59 Squadron, 172 Squadron, 206 Squadron, 407 Squadron, 601 Squadron, 3 School of General Reconnaissance, 1 Radio School
1C	Station Flight Scampton
2	143 Squadron, 220 Squadron, 304 Squadron, 404 Squadron, 407 Squadron, 422 Squadron, 455 Squadron, 603 Squadron, 3 School of General Reconnaissance, 2 Radio School
2A	Station Flight St Eval
2B	272 Maintenance Unit
2H	Station Flight Brawdy
2I	443 Squadron
2K	1668 Conversion Unit
2L	9 Maintenance Unit
2M	520 Squadron
2N	Station Flight Foulsham
2O	84 Group Communication Flight
2P	644 Squadron
2Q	88 Group Communication Squadron
2V	547 Squadron, 18 Group Communication Flight
2W	3 School of General Reconnaissance
2X	85 Operational Training Unit
2Y	345 Squadron
3	280 Squadron, 423 Squadron, 601 Squadron, 3 School of General Reconnaissance
3B	23 Maintenance Unit
3C	1 Lancaster Finishing School
3D	4 Ferry Pool, 48 Maintenance Unit
3E	100 Group Communication Flight

3F	British Air Forces of Occupation Communication Wing	7R	524 Squadron
3G	111 Operational Training Unit	7S	83 Group Support Unit
3H	80 Operational Training Unit	7T	196 Squadron
3J	13 Maintenance Unit	7U	Station Flight Bardney
3K	1695 Flight	7X	Station Flight Aldergrove
3L	Fighter Command Control and Reporting School	7Z	1381 Conversion Unit
3M	679 Squadron, 48 Group Communication Flight	8A	298 Squadron
3O	Station Flight Wrattling Common	8B	1508 Flight
3P	515 Squadron	8C	12 Maintenance Unit
3S	3 Group Communication Flight	8D	220 Squadron
3T	Station Flight Acaster Malbis	8E	295 Squadron
3V	1 Group Communication Flight	8F	105 Operational Training Unit, 1381 Conversion Unit
3W	322 Squadron	8H	8 Group Communication Flight
3X	38 Maintenance Unit	8I	2 Armament Practice Station, Armament Practice Station Acklington
3Y	577 Squadron		
4	3 School of General Reconnaissance, 4 Radio School	8K	571 Squadron
4A	2 Group Communication Flight	8L	92 Squadron
4B	5 Group Communication Flight	8P	525 Squadron
4D	74 Squadron	8Q	34 Squadron
4E	1687 Flight	8T	298 Squadron
4H	142 Squadron	8U	Station Flight Ballykelly
4J	5 Maintenance Unit	8V	6 Operational Training Unit, 60 Operational Training Unit
4K	Station Flight West Malling	8W	612 Squadron
4L	Station Flight Mowbray	8Y	15 Maintenance Unit
4M	695 Squadron	8Z	295 Squadron
4Q	59 Operational Training Unit, Coastal Command Fighter Affiliation Training Unit	9C	82 Operational Training Unit
		9E	British Air Forces of Occupation Communication Squadron
4S	Central Signals Establishment	9F	Station Flight Stradishall
4T	Station Flight Portreath	9G	441 Squadron
4U	30 Maintenance Unit	9I	326 Squadron
4W	Station Flight Snaith	9J	227 Squadron
4X	230 Squadron, 1692 Flight	9K	1 Torpedo Training Unit
4Z	1699 Flight, 1699 Conversion Unit, Bomber Command Communication Squadron	9M	1690 Flight
		9N	127 Squadron
5	3 School of General Reconnaissance, School of Air Sea Rescue, 5 Middle East Training School, 10 Radio School	9O	44 Maintenance Unit
		9P	85 Operational Training Unit
		9R	229 Squadron
5A	329 Squadron	9T	Signals Flying Unit
5D	Station Flight Gibraltar	9U	644 Squadron
5F	147 Squadron	9W	296 Squadron
5G	299 Squadron	9X	2 Ferry Pool, 1689 Flight
5H	Station Flight Chivenor	9Y	20 Maintenance Unit, 132 Operational Training Unit
5I	Station Flight Benson	09	9 Group Target Towing Flight
5J	126 Squadron	10	10 Group Target Towing Flight
5K	39 Maintenance Unit	11	11 Group Target Towing Flight
5N	38 Group Communication Flight	12	12 Group Target Towing Flight
5O	521 Squadron	13	13 Group Target Towing Flight
5R	33 Squadron	26	26 Anti-Aircraft Co-operation Unit
5S	691 Squadron		
5T	233 Squadron		
5V	439 Squadron		

TRANSPORT COMMAND 'O' SERIES RADIO CALL SIGNS

The 'O' series of Transport Command radio call signs was introduced by the Spring of 1944. All codes began with the letter 'O', the second letter identified the type of aircraft, the third letter indicated the parent unit and the last letter being assigned to an individual aircraft. The code letters were, as time passed, often displayed in abbreviated form.

6	600 Squadron, 11 Radio School	OAA	24 Squadron
6B	Station Flight Tempsford	OAP	Air Dispatch Letter Service Squadron
6C	Photographic Reconnaissance Development Unit	ODA	24 Squadron
6D	631 Squadron	ODC	238 Squadron, 436 Squadron
6F	1669 Conversion Unit	ODE	62 Squadron
6G	223 Squadron	ODF	147 Squadron
6H	96 Squadron, 1688 Flight	ODJ	78 Squadron
6J	34 Squadron	ODK	512 Squadron, 241 Squadron
6O	582 Squadron	ODM	436 Squadron
6Q	Station Flight Pembroke Dock	ODN	271 Squadron
6R	41 Operational Training Unit	ODO	437 Squadron
6T	608 Squadron	ODP	216 Squadron
6U	415 Squadron	ODR	48 Squadron
6V	Station Flight Cottesmore	ODS	575 Squadron
6Y	171 Squadron	ODT	53 Squadron
6Z	19 Maintenance Unit	ODU	77 Squadron, 31 Squadron
7	12 Radio School	ODV	10 Squadron
7A	614 Squadron	ODW	52 Squadron
7B	5 Squadron, 595 Squadron	ODY	1333 (Transport) Conversion Unit
7C	296 Squadron	ODZ	British Overseas Airways Corporation
7D	57 Maintenance Unit	OFA	10 Squadron, 437 Squadron
7E	327 Squadron		
7G	Station Flight Northolt		
7H	84 Group Communication Flight		
7I	Station Flight Acklington		
7K	Survival and Rescue Training Unit		
7L	59 Operational Training Unit		
7M	1 Parachute Training School		
7N	Signals Flying Unit		

OFB	77 Squadron, 271 Squadron	MOBC	242 Operational Conversion Unit
OFD	575 Squadron	MOBM	84 Squadron
OFG	46 Squadron	MODA	24 Squadron, 1 Parachute and Glider Training School
OFN	575 Squadron	MODB	53 Squadron
OFR	238 Squadron	MODC	24 Squadron, 27 Squadron, 62 Squadron
OFT	187 Squadron	MODD	238 Squadron
OFU	233 Squadron	MODF	30 Squadron, Airwork
OFV	271 Squadron	MODG	Queens Flight
OFZ	British Overseas Airways Corporation	MODW	Silver City
OHC	1665 Heavy Conversion Unit	MOFA	18 Squadron
OHD	301 Squadron	MOFB	77 Squadron
OHL	113 Squadron	MOFC	Unknown (possibly 62 Squadron)
OKD	24 Squadron	MOFG	46 Squadron, 114 Squadron
OKZ	British Overseas Airways Corporation	MOGA	53 Squadron, 99 Squadron
OLB	246 Squadron	MOGB	47 Squadron
OLL	111 Operational Training Unit	MOGC	242 Operational Conversion Unit
OLM	206 Squadron	MOGH	70 Squadron
OLN	466 Squadron	MOGP	48 Squadron
OLP	426 Squadron	MOGX	Unknown (possibly an Abingdon Wing Squadron)
OLW	86 Squadron	MOGZ	24 Squadron
OLX	220 Squadron	MOHA	297 Squadron
OLZ	British Overseas Airways Corporation	MOHC	295 Squadron, 113 Squadron
OQZ	British Overseas Airways Corporation	MOHD	47 Squadron
ORJ	51 Squadron	MOJA	99 Squadron
ORK	242 Squadron	MOKD	24 Squadron
ORL	46 Squadron	MOLG	Queens Flight
ORO	158 Squadron	MONY	Metropolitan Communication Squadron
ORP	196 Squadron, 299 Squadron	MOPT	2nd Tactical Air Force Communication Squadron
ORS	299 Squadron	MORC	242 Operational Conversion Unit
ORT	1588 (Heavy Freight) Flight	MORG	30 Squadron
OSD	232 Squadron	MORK	Unknown
OSK	233 Squadron	MORM	84 Squadron
OXG	163 Squadron	MORT	2nd Tactical Air Force Communication Squadron
OYA	511 Squadron	MOSC	30 Squadron
OYB	246 Squadron	MOTA	216 Squadron
OYC	511 Squadron	MOVF	622 Squadron, Airwork
OYD	24 Squadron	MOWA	40 Squadron
OYF	242 Squadron	MOWB	59 Squadron
OYZ	1384 Conversion Unit	MOYA	51 Squadron
OZZ	British Overseas Airways Corporation	MOYB	59 Squadron
		MOYC	511 Squadron
		MOYD	24 Squadron, 59 Squadron
		MOYF	242 Squadron
		MOYG	206 Squadron
		MOYX	242 Squadron
		MOYU	Supreme Commander's Headquarters (Air) Communication Squadron

TRANSPORT COMMAND 'MO' SERIES RADIO CALL SIGNS

From 1945 an additional prefix, the letter M, was added and unit radio call signs were reallocated.

MOAY	31 Squadron
MOAZ	Colerne Communication Squadron

Appendix 2

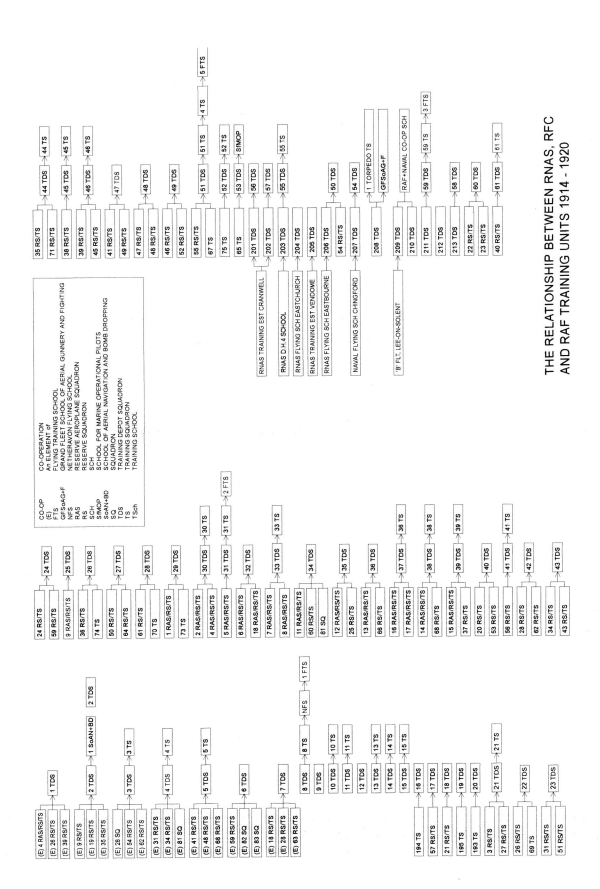

THE RELATIONSHIP BETWEEN RNAS, RFC
AND RAF TRAINING UNITS 1914 - 1920

Appendix 3

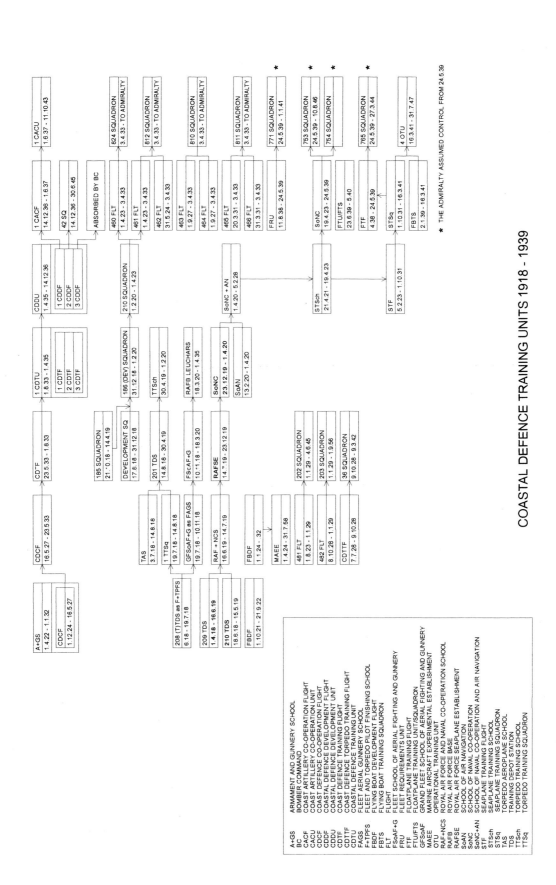

COASTAL DEFENCE TRAINING UNITS 1918 - 1939

★ THE ADMIRALTY ASSUMED CONTROL FROM 24.5.39

A+GS	ARMAMENT AND GUNNERY SCHOOL
BC	BOMBER COMMAND
CACF	COAST ARTILLERY CO-OPERATION FLIGHT
CACU	COAST ARTILLERY CO-OPERATION UNIT
CDCF	COAST DEFENCE CO-OPERATION FLIGHT
CDDF	COASTAL DEFENCE DEVELOPMENT FLIGHT
CDDU	COASTAL DEFENCE DEVELOPMENT UNIT
CDTF	COAST DEFENCE TRAINING FLIGHT
CDTTF	COAST DEFENCE TORPEDO TRAINING FLIGHT
CDTU	COASTAL DEFENCE TRAINING UNIT
FAGS	FLEET AERIAL GUNNERY SCHOOL
F+TPFS	FLEET AND TORPEDO PILOT FINISHING SCHOOL
FBDF	FLYING BOAT DEVELOPMENT FLIGHT
FBTS	FLYING BOAT TRAINING SQUADRON
FLT	FLIGHT
FSoAF+G	FLEET SCHOOL OF AERIAL FIGHTING AND GUNNERY
FRU	FLEET REQUIREMENTS UNIT
FTF	FLOATPLANE TRAINING FLIGHT
FTU/FTS	FLOATPLANE TRAINING UNIT/SQUADRON
GFSoAF	GRAND FLEET SCHOOL OF AERIAL FIGHTING AND GUNNERY
MAEE	MARINE AIRCRAFT EXPERIMENTAL ESTABLISHMENT
OTU	OPERATIONAL TRAINING UNIT
RAF+NCS	ROYAL AIR FORCE AND NAVAL CO-OPERATION SCHOOL
RAFB	ROYAL AIR FORCE BASE
RAFSE	ROYAL AIR FORCE SEAPLANE ESTABLISHMENT
SoAN	SCHOOL OF AIR NAVIGATION
SoNC	SCHOOL OF NAVAL CO-OPERATION
SoNC+AN	SCHOOL OF NAVAL CO-OPERATION AND AIR NAVIGATION
STF	SEAPLANE TRAINING FLIGHT
STSch	SEAPLANE TRAINING SCHOOL
STSq	SEAPLANE TRAINING SQUADRON
TDS	TORPEDO AEROPLANE SCHOOL
TAS	TRAINING DEPOT STATION
TTSch	TORPEDO TRAINING SCHOOL
TTSq	TORPEDO TRAINING SQUADRON

Appendices 4 and 5

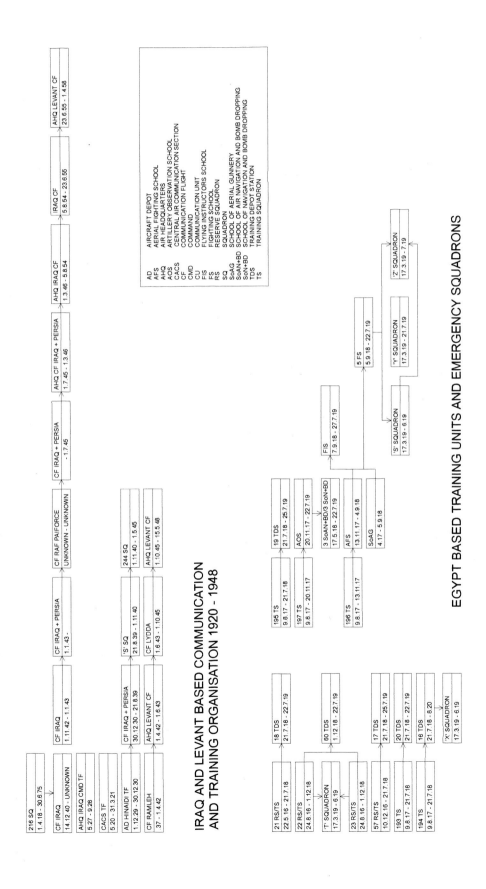

216 SQ
1.4.18 - 30.6.75

CF IRAQ
14.12.40 - UNKNOWN

AHQ IRAQ CMD TF
5.27 - 9.28

CACS TF
5.20 - 31.3.21

AD HINAIDI TF
1.12.29 - 30.12.30

CF RAMLEH
37 - 1.4.42

CF IRAQ + PERSIA
1.11.42 - 1.1.43

CF IRAQ
1.1.43 -

CF RAF PAIFORCE
UNKNOWN - UNKNOWN

CF IRAQ + PERSIA
- 1.7.45

AHQ CF IRAQ + PERSIA
1.7.45 - 1.3.46

AHQ IRAQ CF
1.3.46 - 5.8.54

IRAQ CF
5.8.54 - 23.6.55

AHQ LEVANT CF
23.6.55 - 1.4.58

CF IRAQ + PERSIA
30.12.30 - 21.8.39

'S' SQ
21.8.39 - 1.11.40

244 SQ
1.11.40 - 1.5.45

AHQ LEVANT CF
1.4.42 - 1.6.43

CF LYDDA
1.6.43 - 1.10.45

AHQ LEVANT CF
1.10.45 - 15.5.48

IRAQ AND LEVANT BASED COMMUNICATION AND TRAINING ORGANISATION 1920 - 1948

AD   AIRCRAFT DEPOT
AFS   AERIAL FIGHTING SCHOOL
AHQ   AIR HEADQUARTERS
AOS   ARTILLERY OBSERVATION SCHOOL
CACS   CENTRAL AIR COMMUNICATION SECTION
CF   COMMUNICATION FLIGHT
CMD   COMMAND
CU   COMMUNICATION UNIT
FIS   FLYING INSTRUCTORS SCHOOL
FS   FIGHTING SCHOOL
RS   RESERVE SQUADRON
SQ   SQUADRON
SoAG   SCHOOL OF AERIAL GUNNERY
SoAN+BD SCHOOL OF AIR NAVIGATION AND BOMB DROPPING
SoN+BD SCHOOL OF NAVIGATION AND BOMB DROPPING
TDS   TRAINING DEPOT STATION
TS   TRAINING SQUADRON

195 TS
9.8.17 - 21.7.18

197 TS
9.8.17 - 20.11.17

196 TS
9.8.17 - 13.11.17

19 TDS
21.7.18 - 25.7.19

AOS
20.11.17 - 22.7.19

3 SoAN+BD/3 SoN+BD
17.5.18 - 22.7.19

AFS
13.11.17 - 4.9.18

SoAG
4.17 - 5.9.18

FIS
7.9.18 - 27.7.19

5 FS
5.9.18 - 22.7.19

'S' SQUADRON
17.3.19 - 6.19

'Y' SQUADRON
17.3.19 - 21.7.19

'Z' SQUADRON
17.3.19 - 7.19

21 RS/TS
22.5.16 - 21.7.18

22 RS/TS
24.8.16 - 1.12.18

'T' SQUADRON
17.3.19 - 6.19

23 RS/TS
24.8.16 - 1.12.18

57 RS/TS
10.12.16 - 21.7.18

193 TS
9.8.17 - 21.7.18

194 TS
9.8.17 - 21.7.18

'X' SQUADRON
17.3.19 - 6.19

18 TDS
21.7.18 - 22.7.19

60 TDS
1.12.18 - 22.7.19

17 TDS
21.7.18 - 25.7.19

20 TDS
21.7.18 - 22.7.19

16 TDS
21.7.18 - 8.20

EGYPT BASED TRAINING UNITS AND EMERGENCY SQUADRONS

307

Appendix 6

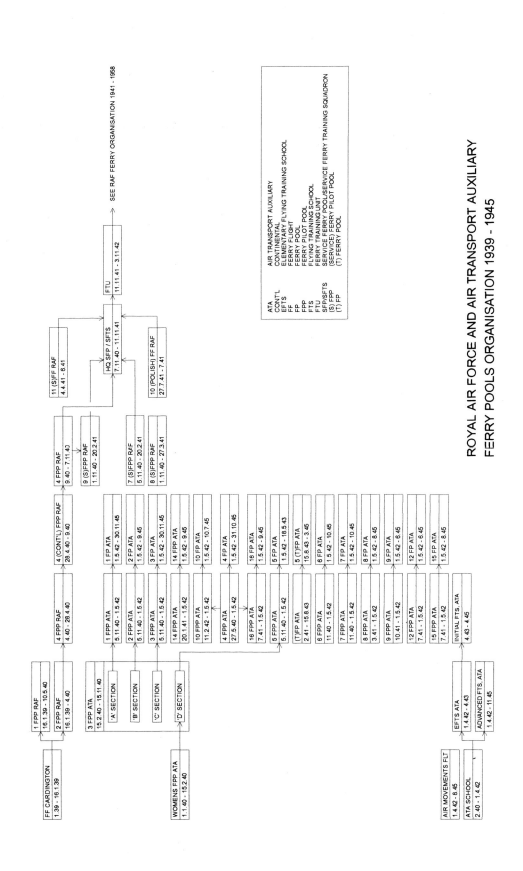

ROYAL AIR FORCE AND AIR TRANSPORT AUXILIARY
FERRY POOLS ORGANISATION 1939 - 1945

Appendix 7

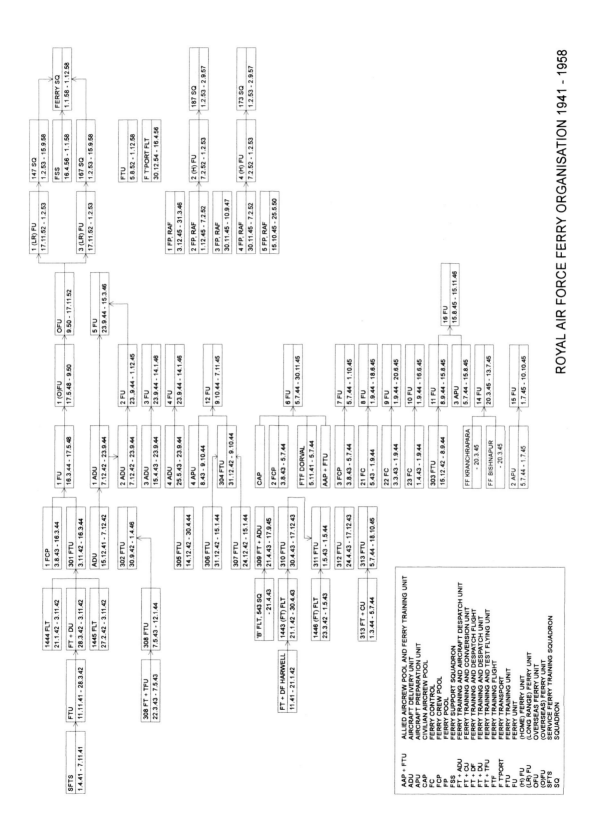

ROYAL AIR FORCE FERRY ORGANISATION 1941 - 1958

AAP + FTU	ALLIED AIRCREW POOL AND FERRY TRAINING UNIT
ADU	AIRCRAFT DELIVERY UNIT
APU	AIRCRAFT PREPARATION UNIT
CAP	CIVILIAN AIRCREW POOL
FC	FERRY CONTROL
FCP	FERRY CREW POOL
FP	FERRY POOL
FSS	FERRY SUPPORT SQUADRON
FT + ADU	FERRY TRAINING AND AIRCRAFT DESPATCH UNIT
FT + CU	FERRY TRAINING AND CONVERSION UNIT
FT + DF	FERRY TRAINING AND DESPATCH FLIGHT
FT + DU	FERRY TRAINING AND DESPATCH UNIT
FT + TFU	FERRY TRAINING AND TEST FLYING UNIT
FTF	FERRY TRAINING FLIGHT
F TPORT	FERRY TRANSPORT
FTU	FERRY TRAINING UNIT
FU	FERRY UNIT
(H) FU	(HOME) FERRY UNIT
(LR) FU	(LONG RANGE) FERRY UNIT
OFU	OVERSEAS FERRY UNIT
(O)FU	(OVERSEAS) FERRY UNIT
SFTS	SERVICE FERRY TRAINING SQUADRON
SQ	SQUADRON

Appendix 8

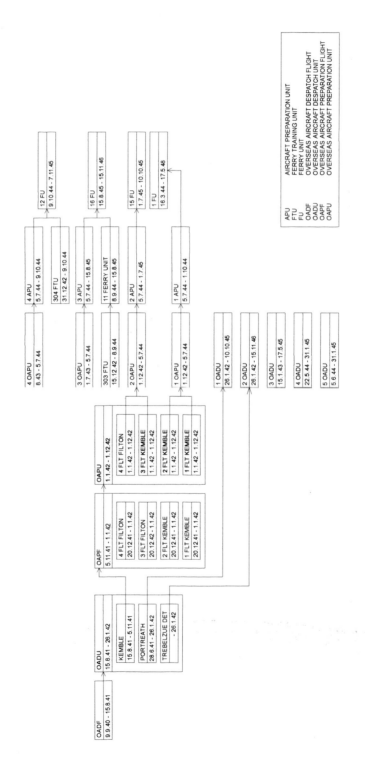

UK BASED OVERSEAS AIRCRAFT DELIVERY AND PREPARATION ORGANISATION

Appendices 9, 10 and 11

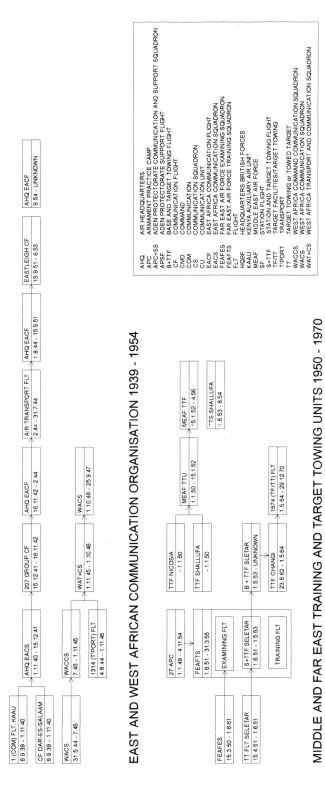

EAST AND WEST AFRICAN COMMUNICATION ORGANISATION 1939 - 1954

MIDDLE AND FAR EAST TRAINING AND TARGET TOWING UNITS 1950 - 1970

ADEN BASED COMMUNICATION ORGANISATION 1940 - 1971

Appendix 12

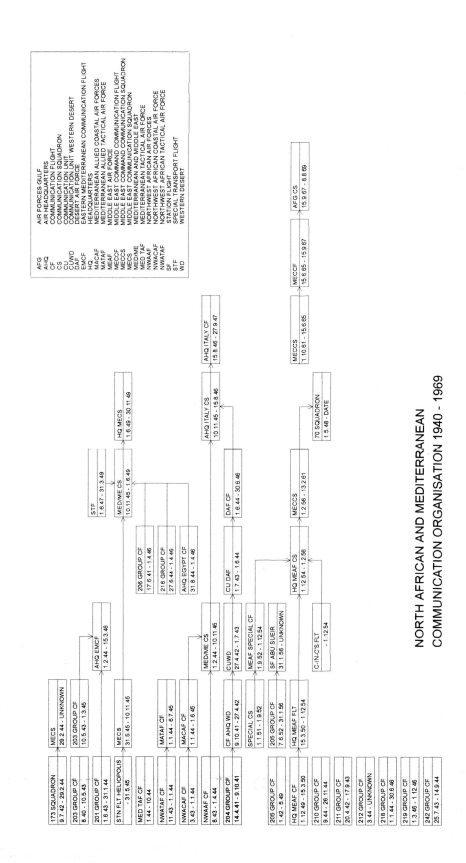

NORTH AFRICAN AND MEDITERRANEAN
COMMUNICATION ORGANISATION 1940 - 1969

Appendix 13

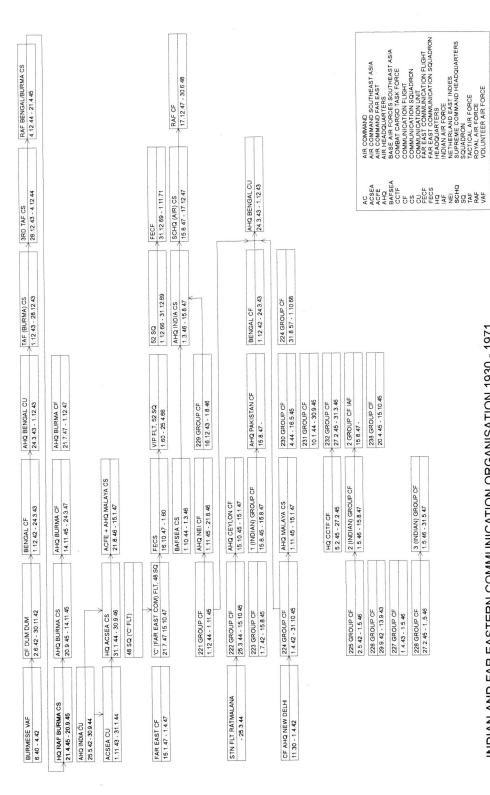

INDIAN AND FAR EASTERN COMMUNICATION ORGANISATION 1930 - 1971

Appendix 14

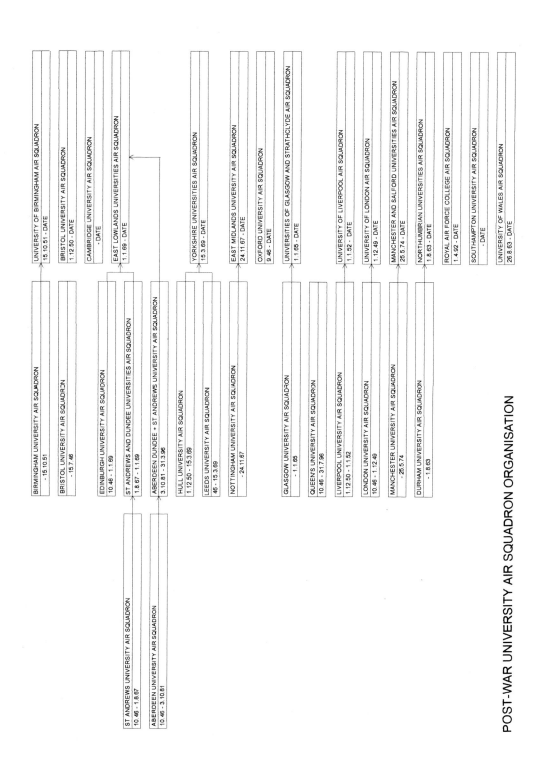

ST ANDREWS UNIVERSITY AIR SQUADRON
10.46 - 1.8.67

ABERDEEN UNIVERSITY AIR SQUADRON
10.46 - 3.10.81

BIRMINGHAM UNIVERSITY AIR SQUADRON
- 15.10.51

UNIVERSITY OF BIRMINGHAM AIR SQUADRON
15.10.51 - DATE

BRISTOL UNIVERSITY AIR SQUADRON
- 15.7.46

BRISTOL UNIVERSITY AIR SQUADRON
1.12.50 - DATE

EDINBURGH UNIVERSITY AIR SQUADRON
10.46 - 1.1.69

CAMBRIDGE UNIVERSITY AIR SQUADRON
- DATE

ST ANDREWS AND DUNDEE UNIVERSITIES AIR SQUADRON
1.8.67 - 1.1.69

EAST LOWLANDS UNIVERSITIES AIR SQUADRON
1.1.69 - DATE

ABERDEEN DUNDEE + ST ANDREWS UNIVERSITY AIR SQUADRON
3.10.81 - 31.3.96

HULL UNIVERSITY AIR SQUADRON
1.12.50 - 15.3.69

YORKSHIRE UNIVERSITIES AIR SQUADRON
15.3.69 - DATE

LEEDS UNIVERSITY AIR SQUADRON
46 - 15.3.69

NOTTINGHAM UNIVERSITY AIR SQUADRON
- 24.11.67

EAST MIDLANDS UNIVERSITY AIR SQUADRON
24.11.67 - DATE

OXFORD UNIVERSITY AIR SQUADRON
9.46 - DATE

GLASGOW UNIVERSITY AIR SQUADRON
- 1.1.65

UNIVERSITIES OF GLASGOW AND STRATHCLYDE AIR SQUADRON
1.1.65 - DATE

QUEEN'S UNIVERSITY AIR SQUADRON
10.46 - 31.7.96

LIVERPOOL UNIVERSITY AIR SQUADRON
1.12.50 - 1.1.52

UNIVERSITY OF LIVERPOOL AIR SQUADRON
1.1.52 - DATE

LONDON UNIVERSITY AIR SQUADRON
10.46 - 1.12.49

UNIVERSITY OF LONDON AIR SQUADRON
1.12.49 - DATE

MANCHESTER UNIVERSITY AIR SQUADRON
- 25.5.74

MANCHESTER AND SALFORD UNIVERSITIES AIR SQUADRON
25.5.74 - DATE

DURHAM UNIVERSITY AIR SQUADRON
- 1.8.63

NORTHUMBRIAN UNIVERSITIES AIR SQUADRON
1.8.63 - DATE

ROYAL AIR FORCE COLLEGE AIR SQUADRON
1.4.92 - DATE

SOUTHAMPTON UNIVERSITY AIR SQUADRON
- DATE

UNIVERSITY OF WALES AIR SQUADRON
26.8.63 - DATE

POST-WAR UNIVERSITY AIR SQUADRON ORGANISATION

Appendix 15

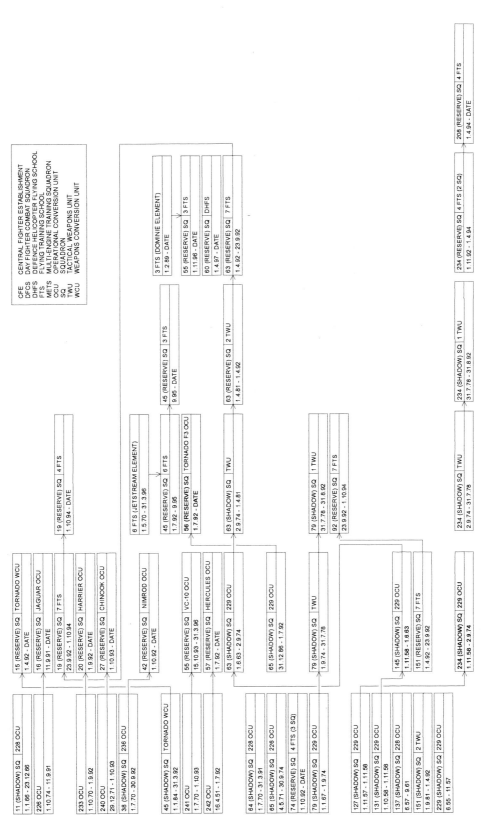

THE RELATIONSHIP BETWEEN SHADOW/RESERVE SQUADRONS AND PARENT UNITS

Appendix 16

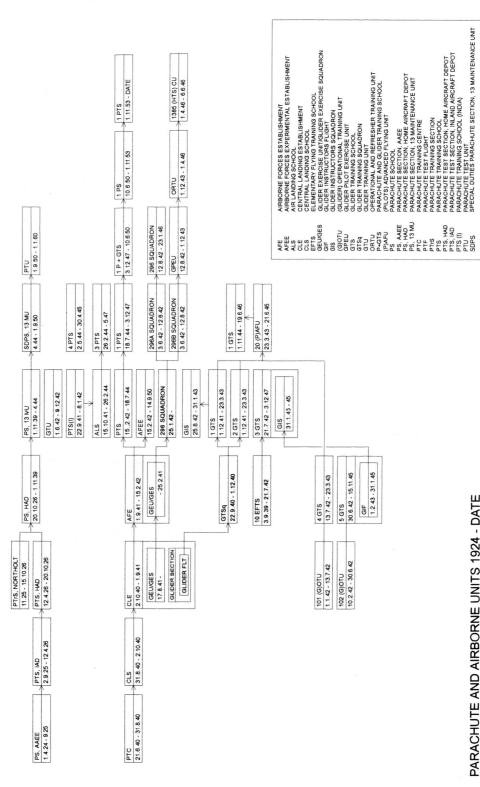

PARACHUTE AND AIRBORNE UNITS 1924 - DATE

AFE	AIRBORNE FORCES ESTABLISHMENT
AFEE	AIRBORNE FORCES EXPERIMENTAL ESTABLISHMENT
ALS	AIR LANDING SCHOOL
CLE	CENTRAL LANDING ESTABLISHMENT
CLS	CENTRAL LANDING SCHOOL
EFTS	ELEMENTARY FLYING TRAINING SCHOOL
GEU/GES	GLIDER EXERCISE UNIT/GLIDER EXERCISE SQUADRON
GIF	GLIDER INSTRUCTORS FLIGHT
GIS	GLIDER INSTRUCTORS SQUADRON
(G)OTU	(GLIDER) OPERATIONAL TRAINING UNIT
GPEU	GLIDER PILOT EXERCISE UNIT
GTS	GLIDER TRAINING SCHOOL
GTSq	GLIDER TRAINING SQUADRON
GTU	GLIDER TRAINING UNIT
ORTU	OPERATIONAL AND REFRESHER TRAINING UNIT
P-GTS	PARACHUTE AND GLIDER TRAINING SCHOOL
(P)AFU	(PILOTS) ADVANCED FLYING UNIT
PS	PARACHUTE SCHOOL
PS, AAEE	PARACHUTE SECTION, AAEE
PS, HAD	PARACHUTE SECTION, HOME AIRCRAFT DEPOT
PS, 13 MU	PARACHUTE SECTION, 13 MAINTENANCE UNIT
PTC	PARACHUTE TRAINING CENTRE
PTF	PARACHUTE TEST FLIGHT
PTrS	PARACHUTE TRAINING SECTION
PTS	PARACHUTE TRAINING SCHOOL
PTS, HAD	PARACHUTE TEST SECTION, HOME AIRCRAFT DEPOT
PTS, IAD	PARACHUTE TEST SECTION, INLAND AIRCRAFT DEPOT
PTS (I)	PARACHUTE TRAINING SCHOOL (INDIA)
PTU	PARACHUTE TEST UNIT
SDPS	SPECIAL DUTIES PARACHUTE SECTION, 13 MAINTENANCE UNIT